The Blackwell Companion to
Contemporary Islamic Thought

Blackwell Companions to Religion

The Blackwell Companions to Religion series presents a collection of the most recent scholarship and knowledge about world religions. Each volume draws together newly-commissioned essays by distinguished authors in the field, and is presented in a style which is accessible to under-graduate students, as well as scholars and the interested general reader. These volumes approach the subject in a creative and forward-thinking style, providing a forum in which leading scholars in the field can make their views and research available to a wider audience.

Published

The Blackwell Companion to Judaism
Edited by Jacob Neusner and Alan J. Avery-Peck

The Blackwell Companion to Sociology of Religion
Edited by Richard K. Fenn

The Blackwell Companion to the Hebrew Bible
Edited by Leo G. Perdue

The Blackwell Companion to Postmodern Theology
Edited by Graham Ward

The Blackwell Companion to Hinduism
Edited by Gavin Flood

The Blackwell Companion to Political Theology
Edited by Peter Scott and William T. Cavanaugh

The Blackwell Companion to Protestantism
Edited by Alister E. McGrath and Darren C. Marks

The Blackwell Companion to Modern Theology
Edited by Gareth Jones

The Blackwell Companion to Christian Ethics
Edited by Stanley Hauerwas and Samuel Wells

The Blackwell Companion to Religious Ethics
Edited by William Schweiker

The Blackwell Companion to Christian Spirituality
Edited by Arthur Holder

The Blackwell Companion to the Study of Religion
Edited by Robert A. Segal

The Blackwell Companion to the Qur'ān
Edited by Andrew Rippin

The Blackwell Companion to Contemporary Islamic Thought
Edited by Ibrahim M. Abu-Rabi'

Forthcoming

The Blackwell Companion to the Bible and Culture
Edited by John F. A. Sawyer

The Blackwell Companion to Eastern Christianity
Edited by Ken Parry

The Blackwell Companion to Catholicism
Edited by James J. Buckley, Frederick Christian Bauerschmidt and Trent Pomplun

The Blackwell Companion to Contemporary Islamic Thought

Edited by

Ibrahim M. Abu-Rabi'

Blackwell
Publishing

BLACKWELL PUBLISHING
350 Main Street, Malden, MA 02148-5020, USA
9600 Garsington Road, Oxford OX4 2DQ, UK
550 Swanston Street, Carlton, Victoria 3053, Australia

First published 2006 by Blackwell Publishing Ltd

1   2006

Library of Congress Cataloging-in-Publication Data

The Blackwell companion to contemporary Islamic thought / edited by Ibrahim M. Abu-Rabi'.
    p.   cm.—(Blackwell companions to religion)
    Includes bibliographical references and index.
    ISBN-13: 978-1-4051-2174-3 (hardcover : alk. paper)
    ISBN-10: 1-4051-2174-2 (hardcover. : alk. paper)
    1. Islam—21st century.   2. Religious awakening—Islam.   I. Abu-Rabi', Ibrahim M.
    II. Series.
    BP161.3.B56   2006
    297.209′05—dc22

                                                                                                2005026433

A catalogue record for this title is available from the British Library.

Set in 10 on 12.5 pt Photina
by SNP Best-set Typesetter Ltd., Hong Kong
Printed and bound in Singapore
by C.O.S. Printers Pte Ltd

The publisher's policy is to use permanent paper from mills that operate a sustainable forestry
policy, and which has been manufactured from pulp processed using acid-free and elementary
chlorine-free practices. Furthermore, the publisher ensures that the text paper and cover board
used have met acceptable environmental accreditation standards.

For further information on
Blackwell Publishing, visit our website:
www.blackwellpublishing.com

Contents

Notes on Contributors   ix

Editor's Introduction: Contemporary Islamic Thought: One or Many?   1
Ibrahim M. Abu-Rabi'

Part I   Trends and Issues in Contemporary Islamic Thought   21

1   Contemporary Turkish Thought   23
    Şahin Filiz and Tahir Uluç

2   Transformation of Islamic Thought in Turkey Since the 1950s   39
    Ahmet Yildiz

3   Bediuzzaman Said Nursi's Approach to Religious Renewal and its
    Impact on Aspects of Contemporary Turkish Society   55
    Şükran Vahide

4   Islamic Thought in Contemporary India: The Impact of Mawlana
    Wahiduddin Khan's Al-Risāla Movement   75
    Irfan A. Omar

5   Sayyed Abul Hasan 'Ali Nadwi and Contemporary Islamic
    Thought in India   88
    Yoginder Sikand

6   Madrasah in South Asia   105
    Jamal Malik

7   75 Years of Higher Religious Education in Modern Turkey   122
    Mehmet Pacaci and Yasin Aktay

8   Hassan Turabi and the Limits of Modern Islamic Reformism   145
    Abdelwahab El-Affendi

9   An Overview of al-Sadiq al-Mahdi's Islamic Discourse   161
    Hassan Ahmed Ibrahim

10 Islamic Thought in Contemporary Pakistan: The Legacy of 'Allāma
    Mawdūdī   175
    Abdul Rashid Moten

11 The Futuristic Thought of Ustaz Ashaari Muhammad of Malaysia   195
    Ahmad Fauzi Abdul Hamid

12 Religion, Society, and Culture in Malik Bennabi's Thought   213
    Mohamed El-Tahir El-Mesawi

13 Hassan Hanafi on Salafism and Secularism   257
    Yudian Wahyudi

14 Towards a New Historical Discourse in Islam   271
    Ali Mabrook

Part II   Secularism, Modernity, and Globalization in Contemporary Islamic Thought   283

15 The Second Coming of the Theocratic Age? Islamic Discourse after
    Modernity and Postmodernity   285
    Aslam Farouk-Alli

16 Europe Against Islam: Islam in Europe   302
    Talal Asad

17 *Ummah* and Empire: Global Formations after Nation   313
    Mucahit Bilici

18 Between Slumber and Awakening   328
    Erol Güngör (Translated by Şahin Filiz and Tahir Uluç)

19 Islam and Secularism   338
    Asghar Ali Engineer

20 A "Democratic-Conservative" Government by Pious People:
    The Justice and Development Party in Turkey   345
    Metin Heper

21 Secularism and Democracy in Contemporary India: An Islamic
    Perspective   362
    Syed Shahabuddin

Part III   The Question of *Jihād* and Terrorism in Contemporary Islamic Thought   375

22 Islam, Terrorism, and Western Misapprehensions   377
    Muhammad Fathi Osman

23 Indonesian Responses to September 11, 2001   387
    Muhammad Sirozi

24 The World Situation After September 11, 2001   408
    Khursid Ahmad

Part IV   Islamism, Sufism, and Pluralism in Contemporary
Islamic Thought   423

25 *Sirāt al-mustaqīm* – One or Many? Religious Pluralism among Muslim
    Intellectuals in Iran   425
    Ashk Dahlén

26 Contemporary Islamic Movements in Southeast Asia: Challenges and
    Opportunities   449
    Ahmad F. Yousif

27 Transformation of Political Islam in Post-Suharto Indonesia   466
    Mun'im A. Sirry

28 The Pilgrimage to Tembayat: Tradition and Revival in Islamic Mysticism
    in Contemporary Indonesia   482
    Nelly Van Doorn-Harder and Kees De Jong

Part V   Justice, Dependency, and International Relations in
Contemporary Islamic Thought   507

29 Hindu Fundamentalism in Contemporary India: A Muslim Perspective   509
    Zafarul-Islam Khan

30 Political Discourse of the Organization of the Islamic Conference   527
    Abdullah al-Ahsan

31 Culture of Mistrust: A Sociological Analysis of Iranian Political Culture   544
    Mehrdad Mashayekhi

32 What Do We Mean By Islamic Futures?   562
    Ziauddin Sardar

33 Islam and the Science of Economics   587
    Syed Farid Alatas

Part VI   Women in Contemporary Islamic Thought   607

34 Muslim Feminist Debates on the Question of Headscarf in
    Contemporary Turkey   609
    Ayşe Kadıoğlu

35 "Islamic Feminism": Negotiating Patriarchy and Modernity in Iran   624
    Nayereh Tohidi

36   An Islamic Critique of Patriarchy: Mawlana Sayyed Kalbe Sadiq's
     Approach to Gender Relations   644
     Yoginder Sikand

Index   657

Notes on Contributors

Ibrahim M. Abu-Rabi' is Professor of Islamic Studies and Christian–Muslim Relations at Hartford Seminary and editor of *The Muslim World*. He has authored *Intellectual Origins of Islamic Resurgence in the Modern Arab World* (State University of New York Press) and *Contemporary Arab Thought: Studies in Post-1967 Arab Intellectual History* (Pluto Press), and edited several books.

Ahmad Fauzi Abdul Hamid is Senior Lecturer in Politics at the School of Distance Education, Universiti Sains Malaysia, Penang, Malaysia. He writes on the politics of Islam in Malaysia and has contributed articles to many leading journals such as *Kajian Malaysia, Indonesia and the Malay World, The Islamic Quarterly, Islamic Culture, Islamic Studies, Asian Studies Review, Global Change, Peace & Security*, and *Islam and the Modern Age*.

Khursid Ahmad is a leading Muslim scholar and thinker of the Jamaat-e-Islami in Pakistan. He directs the Institute of Policy Studies in Islamabad, Pakistan and is the head of the Islamic Foundation in Leicestershire, England.

Abdullah al-Ahsan is Professor of History and Civilization at International Islamic University Malaysia. Two of his major books are *OIC: Introduction to an Islamic Political Institution* (1988) and *Ummah or Nation: Identity Crisis in Contemporary Muslim Society* (1992). He is currently working on *Muslim Society: From Crisis to Catastrophe*.

Yasin Aktay teaches at Seljuk University in Konya, Turkey. He is a leading scholar in Islamic social and political thought in modern Turkey.

Syed Farid Alatas is Associate Professor of Sociology at the National University of Singapore. He is the author of *Democracy and Authoritarianism: The Rise of the Post-Colonial State in Indonesia and Malaysia* (Macmillan, 1997). He is currently working on a book on Muslim ideologies and utopias.

Talal Asad is Professor of Anthropology at the Ph.D. Program of CUNY Graduate Center in New York. He is interested in the phenomenon of religion (and secularism) as an integral part of modernity, and especially in the religious revival in the Middle East. Connected with this is his interest in the links between religious and secular notions of pain and cruelty, and therefore with the modern discourse of human rights. His long-term research concerns the transformation of religious law (sharī'ah) in nineteenth- and twentieth-century Egypt with special reference to arguments about what constitutes secular and progressive reform. He has published several books in the above areas, especially *Formations of the Secular* (Stanford University Press); and *Genealogies of Religion* (Johns Hopkins University Press).

Mucahit Bilici is a Ph.D. candidate in sociology at the University of Michigan, Ann Arbor. He has written several critical articles on Islamic thought in contemporary Turkey and the interplay between nationalism and religion in Muslim societies.

Ashk Dahlén is lecturer of Iranian Languages and Islamic Studies at Uppsala University, Sweden. He is the author of *Islamic Law, Epistemology and Modernity. Legal Epistemology in Contemporary Iran* and has published several articles on Persian literature, Sufism, and Islamic thought. He is a member of the Iranian Academy of Philosophy.

Abdelwahab El-Affendi is a Senior Research Fellow at the Centre for the Study of Democracy, University of Westminster and coordinator of the Centre's Project on Democracy in the Muslim World. Educated at the Universities of Khartoum, Wales, and Reading, he is author of *Turabi's Revolution: Islam and Power in Sudan* (1991), *Who Needs an Islamic State?* (1991), *Revolution and Political Reform in Sudan* (1995), *Rethinking Islam and Modernity* (2001), and *For a State of Peace: Conflict and the Future of Democracy in Sudan* (2002). He has contributed to many leading journals, including *African Affairs*, *Encounter*, *Journal of International Affairs*, *Futures*, *Muslim World*, and the *International Journal of Middle Eastern Studies*, and to such works as *The Routledge Encyclopedia of Philosophy* (1998), *Social Science and Conflict Analysis* (1993), *Islam and Justice* (1997), *Islam and Secularism in the Middle East* (2000), *Islamic Thought in the Twentieth Century* (2003), and *Understanding Democratic Politics* (2003). Dr. El-Affendi is a member of the Consultative Council of the Arab Human Rights Organisation in the UK, and a trustee of the International Forum for Islamic Dialogue. Dr. El-Affendi also contributes regular columns to *Al-Quds al-Arabi* (London) and the *Daily Star* (Beirut).

Mohamed El-Tahir El-Mesawi is Assistant Professor at the Kulliyyah of Islamic Revealed Knowledge and Human Sciences, International Islamic University Malaysia. His academic and intellectual interests include Islamic legal theory, modern and contemporary Islamic thought and religion, and modernity studies. His publications include, among others, *A Muslim Theory of Human Society*, *The Qur'anic Phenomenon*, *The Question of Ideas in the Muslim World*, and *On the Origins of Human Society*.

Asghar Ali Engineer is a prolific Indian author on Islamic subjects. He directs the Center for the Study of Society and Secularism in Mumbai, India.

Aslam Farouk-Alli teaches Arabic and Islamic Studies at the University of Cape Town, South Africa. He is the editor of the *Annual Review of Islam in South Africa* (ARISA), associate editor of the *Journal for Islamic Studies* (JIS), and managing editor of the *Journal* *for the Study of Religion* (JSR). His main research interest is contemporary Islamic thought.

Şahin Filiz is Professor of Islamic Philosophy and Turkish-Islamic Thought at Divinity School of Seljuk University in Konya, Turkey. He writes on traditional and contemporary Islamic philosophy.

Metin Heper is Professor of Political Science at Bilkent University in Ankara, Turkey, and a founding and Council member of the Turkish Academy of Sciences. He is author of *The State Tradition in Turkey, Historical Dictionary of Turkey, Ismet İnönü: The Making of a Turkish Statesman,* and *The State and the Kurds in Turkey: The Question of Assimilation* (forthcoming). Professor Heper's edited or co-edited books include *Islam and Politics in the Middle East, Turkey and the West: Changing Political and Cultural Identities, Politics in the Third Turkish Republic, Strong State and Economic Interest Groups: The Post-1980 Turkish Experience, Political Parties and Democracy in Turkey, The State and Public Bureaucracies: A Comparative Perspective,* and *Institutions and Democratic Statecraft.*

Hassan Ahmed Ibrahim is Professor of History, International Islamic University Malaysia. His research interests include the history and politics of the Middle East, Sub-Saharan Africa, and Islamic revivalism.

Ayşe Kadioğlu is Associate Professor of Political Science in Sabanci University, Istanbul, Turkey. She is the author of *Cumhuriyet Iradesi, Demokrasi Muhakemesi* (*Republican Will, Democratic Reason*), 1998, Metis, Istanbul.

Zafarul-Islam Khan studied in India, Egypt, and the UK where he obtained a Ph.D. from Manchester University. He is director of the Institute of Islamic and Arab Studies, New Delhi since 1988, and editor of *Muslim and Arab Perspectives* since 1993 and *The Milli Gazette* since 2000. He is author and translator of over 40 books in Arabic, English, and Urdu including *Hijrah in Islam* (Delhi, 1996) and *Palestine Documents* (New Delhi, 1998). He has organized as well as attended dozens of conferences and seminars in India and abroad. He frequently appears as a commentator on Islamic and South Asian issues on radio and TV channels including Aljazeera and BBC Arabic.

Ali Mabrook obtained his Ph.D. in philosophy from Cairo University, where he taught for many years. He is currently Visiting Professor of Islamic Studies in the Department of Religious Studies, University of Cape Town, South Africa.

Jamal Malik is Professor of Religious Studies and Muslim Religious and Cultural History at the University of Erfurt. He is author of *The Colonialization of Islam* (New Delhi: Manohar and Lahore: Vanguard, 1996, 2nd edition 1998), *Islamische Gelehrtenkultur in Nordindien* (Leiden: E.J. Brill, 1997), and edited volumes *Perspectives of Mutual Encounters in South Asian History 1760–1860* (Leiden: E.J. Brill, 2000), *Muslims in Europe. From the Margin to the Centre* (Münster: LIT, 2004), and *Religious Pluralism in South Asia and Europe* (New Delhi: Oxford University Press, 2004).

Mehrdad Mashayekhi teaches at the Department of Sociology and Anthropology at Georgetown University in Washington, DC. He writes on contemporary Iran.

Abdul Rashid Moten is Head and Professor of Political Science at the International Islamic University Malaysia. He has been teaching at university level for about 35 years in various countries. He has published 10 books and contributed about 80 articles to internationally refereed journals on Islam and the Muslim world. He is also editor of the *Journal of Intellectual Discourse*.

Irfan A. Omar is Assistant Professor of Islamic Studies at Marquette University. He is co-editor (with Bradford E. Hinze) of *Heirs of Abraham: The Future of Jewish, Christian, and Muslim Relations* (Orbis, 2005). He served as guest editor for the special issue of *Islam and Christian–Muslim Relations* (Birmingham, UK), entitled, "Islam in Dialogue," 15/1 (January 2004), and is currently an associate editor of the *Journal of Ecumenical Studies*.

Muhammad Fathi Osman is a leading scholar in contemporary Islamic thought. He directs the Institute for the Study of Islam in the Contemporary World in Los Angeles, CA.

Mehmet Pacaci is Associate Professor of Islamic Studies at the Divinity School in Ankara, Turkey.

Ziauddin Sardar, writer, broadcaster and cultural critic, is regarded as one of the leading public intellectuals in Britain, featuring recently among *Prospect's* Top 100. He is the author of the classic studies *The Future of Muslim Civilisation* (1979, 1987) and *Islamic Futures: The Shape of Ideas to Come* (1985). The most recent of his over 40 books include *Postmodernism and the Other* (1998), *The A to Z of Postmodern Life* (2002), *Islam, Postmodernism and Other Futures: A Ziauddin Sardar Reader* (2003), his autobiography *Desperately Seeking Paradise: Journeys of a Sceptical Muslim* (2004), and the co-authored international best-sellers, *Why Do People Hate America?* (2002) and *American Dream, Global Nightmare* (2004). A Visiting Professor of Postcolonial Studies, Department of Arts Policy and Management, the City University, London, Professor Sardar is the editor of *Futures*, a monthly journal of policy, planning, and futures studies and co-editor of *Third Text*, a critical journal of visual art and culture. He is a regular contributor to the *New Statesman* magazine and has a regular presence on radio and television in the UK.

Syed Shahabuddin is a former Ambassador of India, former Member of Parliament and former editor of *Muslim India*. He is currently President of All-India Muslim Majlis-e-Mushawarat. He writes regularly on contemporary issues, both national and international.

Yoginder Sikand is a reader in the Department of Islamic Studies at the Hamdard University, New Delhi, India. He is the author of *The Origins and Development of the Tablighi Jama'at*, and *Muslims in India Since 1947*.

Muhammad Sirozi is Associate Professor of Islamic Education at Program Pascasarjana IAIN Raden Fatah in Palembang, Indonesia.

Mun'im A. Sirry is a Ph.D. student in the Religious Studies program at Arizona State University, USA. He has written the following: *Resisting Religious Militancy* (Jakarta:

Airlangga, 2003), *Islamic Dilemma, Democratic Dilemma* (Jakarta: Gugus Press, 2002), *A History of Islamic Law: An Introduction* (Surabaya: Risalah Gusti, 1996).

Nayereh Tohidi is Associate Professor of Women's Studies and Sociology at California State University, Northridge and a Research Associate at the Center for Near Eastern Studies of UCLA. She has written extensively on gender and social change, women and modernization, democracy and Islamism in the Middle East and Central Eurasia, especially Iran and post-Soviet Azerbaijan. Her latest publications include: *Globalization, Gender and Religion: The Politics of Women's Rights in Catholic and Muslim Contexts* (Palgrave, 2001); *Women in Muslim Societies: Diversity within Unity* (Lynne Rienner, 1998); and "Women, Building Civil Society, and Democratization in Post-Soviet Azerbaijan," in *Post-Soviet Women Encountering Transition* (Woodrow Wilson Center Press and the John Hopkins University Press, 2004).

Nelly van Doorn-Harder is Associate Professor of Islam and World Religions at Valparaiso University. Her areas of study are Islam in Southeast Asia, Muslim–Christian relations and Christianity in the Middle East. She is the author of *Women Shaping Islam: Reading the Qur'an in Indonesia* (University of Illinois Press, 2006) and has written several books on the Copts of Egypt.

Yudian Wahyudi is Assistant Professor of Islamic Legal Philosophy (*Falsafat al-Tashri' al-Islami*) at the Sunan Kalijaga State Islamic University (Yogyakarta, Indonesia), and received his Ph.D. from McGill University in 2002 with the dissertation "The Slogan 'Back to the Qur'an and the Sunna': A Comparative Study of the Responses of Hasan Hanafi, Muhammad 'Abid al-Jabiri and Nurcholish Madjid." During his residency as a visiting scholar at the Islamic Legal Studies Program, Law School, Harvard University (2002–4), he wrote what he considers to be the second and third volumes of his dissertation: "The Problem of Psychologism in Qur'anic Legal Hermeneutics" and "Shari'a and State in Egypt, Morocco and Indonesia," respectively.

Şükran Vahide is a freelance writer and translator. She has written extensively on Said Nursi, and has translated a large part of his collected works into English. Her published works include *The Author of the Risale-i Nur, Bediuzzaman Said Nursi* (1992); and *Islam in Modern Turkey: An Intellectual Biography of Bediuzzaman Said Nursi* (2005).

Tahir Uluç is research assistant at Selçuk University Divinity School in Konya, Turkey. He has translated several books and articles from Arabic into Turkish. In addition, he is fellow of the Turkish Academy of Sciences.

Ahmet Yildiz works at the Atatürk Library in Ankara, Turkey. He has written several articles on Islam and politics in contemporary Turkey.

Ahmad F. Yousif is Associate Professor at the Institute of Islamic Studies, University of Brunei. Previously, Dr. Yousif taught at the International Islamic University Malaysia and the Department of Religious Studies, University of Ottawa (Canada), where he obtained both his M.A and Ph.D. degrees.

EDITOR'S INTRODUCTION
Contemporary Islamic Thought: One or Many?

Ibrahim M. Abu-Rabi'

The progress of opinion is fluid and indefinite; it does not easily lend itself to any system of dates and clear-cut chronological divisions.
D.C. Somervell, *English Thought in the Nineteenth Century* (London: Methuen & Co., 1929), 1.

Modernization has taken place throughout the world through a series of social, political, and cultural movements that, unlike movements of change and rebellion in many other historical situations, have tended to combine orientations of protest and those of center-formation and institution-building. It has fostered the establishment of a universal civilization in which different societies have served one another as mutual reference points . . . The continuous spread of these assumptions throughout the world in a variety of guises – liberal, national, or socialist movements and ideologies – has greatly undermined the basis of legitimation found in historical or "traditional" societies.
S.N. Eisenstadt, "Post-Traditional Societies and the Continuity and Reconstruction of Tradition," *Daedalus: Journal of the American Academy of Arts and Sciences*, Winter 1973, 6.

The Renaissance breaks with medieval thought. Modern thought distinguishes itself from that of the medieval period by renouncing the dominant metaphysical preoccupation. The importance of partial truths is systematically valorized, while the pursuit of absolute knowledge is left to amateurs.
Samir Amin, *Eurocentrism* (New York: Monthly Review Press, 1989), 79.

Enlightenment thought . . . embraced the idea of progress, and actively sought that break with history and tradition which modernity espouses. It was, above all, a secular movement that sought the demystification and desacralization of knowledge and social organization in order to liberate human beings from their chains.

David Harvey, *The Condition of Postmodernity: An Enquiry into the Origins of Cultural Change* (Oxford: Blackwell, 1989), 12–13.

In his seminal 1946 essay entitled "Politics and the English Language," George Orwell bemoans the decline of English prose after World War Two, and points out that what is troublesome about some major English writing is *lack of precision, sheer incompetence, and vagueness*. This insight into the political language of England in the 1940s is, more or less, applicable to a good number of Western writings on Islam and the Muslim world, especially the journalistic type of writing. Our journalistic prose has often confused such terms as: (i) Islam; (ii) the Muslim world; (iii) Islamic history; and (iv) Islamic revivalism or fundamentalism.

The concept "contemporary Islamic thought" reflects a wide variety of intellectual currents dominating the contemporary Muslim world since roughly the end of World War Two, the rise of the nation-state and the beginning of the decolonization process. It is possible to delineate four major intellectual movements dominating contemporary Muslim intellectual life: (i) nationalism; (ii) Islamism; (iii) Westernization; and (iv) state ideology. Far from being monolithic, each of the preceding categories contains a diverse number of positions on national, religious, political, social, and economic issues and problems.[1]

Because of the complexity of the contemporary Muslim world and the nature of the political dynamics that have given rise to the nation-state in this world, it is impossible to talk of one homogenous Islamic intellectual history. In order to begin to analyze the different intellectual forces and modalities of the contemporary Muslim world, it is imperative to highlight the different intellectual histories of this world. Although there are some major commonalities between the several intellectual histories that make up contemporary Islamic thought, each intellectual history has responded to a unique set of circumstances and criteria that have in turn defined it over the past several decades. For example, the Partition of India and the subsequent creation of the modern nation-states of India and Pakistan in 1947 define, to a large extent, the contemporary intellectual history of Islam in South Asia. In the same vein, the emergence of the nation-state in Indonesia after centuries of Dutch colonialism defines the intellectual experience of the Muslims in that country.

It is only in the preceding sense that one can discern multiple intellectual histories in the contemporary Muslim world. These multiple intellectual histories reflect the complex cultural and economic transformations taking place in the Muslim world since the nineteenth century, to say the least, that is to say, since the advent of Western capitalism into many a Muslim country. As such, multiple intellectual histories have registered the cultural, religious, and intellectual responses to this encounter and documented the rise of new social classes, new blocs of power, and new intellectual forces in almost every Muslim country. This has been the more poignant since the official end of colonialism in the 1950s and 1960s.

In the political area, many journalists and political scientists have written the general outlines, at least, of the political history of the modern Muslim world. In a more specialized way, due to academic division of labor, a number of scholars have written the social and political histories of each Muslim country. However, writing the intellectual histories of the modern and contemporary Muslim world has been a formidable task indeed. To carry this out requires a team of scholars who are versed in several Islamic and Western languages and who are familiar with the social, economic, and intellectual histories of the modern and contemporary Muslim world. The collection of articles in *The Blackwell Companion to Contemporary Islamic Thought* is intended to fill a major lacuna in this area and alert us to the various currents of thought dominant in the contemporary Muslim world and their articulation of the questions and challenges facing it. In addition, this collection of articles helps us formulate comprehensive perspectives on the current movements of thought in Muslim societies.

Speaking of multiple Islamic intellectual histories reflects the following criteria: one is the diversity of intellectual trends in each intellectual history; second is the host of issues and problems each intellectual history tackles; and third is the starting point of each intellectual history. For example, as mentioned above, contemporary Islamic intellectual history in South Asia is more or less predicated on the Partition of India and Pakistan in 1947 and the intellectual, moral, and political questions and burden generated by such Partition. In the case of Indonesia, contemporary Indonesian intellectual history begins more or less after the independence of the country in 1945 and as a response to the great problems facing the country since independence. In the same vein, Arab intellectual history in both the Middle East and North Africa begins with the onset of the decolonization process of the 1950s and 1960s and the construction of the nation-state in different parts of the Arab world. Contemporary Turkish thought, on the other hand, owes its existence to the Kemalist experiment and the foundation of the modern Turkish Republic in 1923. In the latter case, it is quite impossible to address all the Turkish trends of thought emerging in the post-Republic phase without coming to grips with the intellectual genesis of Kemalism and its aversion to religion, that is, Islam in its private and public pronouncements and practices.[2]

So far, we have discerned four broad currents of thought in the contemporary Muslim world and ascertained that each current is deeply diverse, extremely complex, and is the product of various vital political, philosophical, religious, social, and historical conditions and formations. In other words, although some intellectual historians, such as the American Lovejoy,[3] argue that intellectual history is an autonomous field of knowledge, it is autonomous to the extent that it reflects the social and intellectual forces of each country. And it is a basic fact that these forces have been in constant interplay with one another.

Several worldviews constitute a people's intellectual history and as such, intellectual history is necessarily multidisciplinarian by nature. It cuts across different fields of specialization, especially philosophy, theology, history, politics, and political economics. It is also guided by different philosophical and ideological positions. As it is clear in the various essays included in this *Companion*, ideology is at the heart of intellectual history. In other words, even a careful reading of any particular worldview constituting intellectual history will not render a purely objective picture of that trend. *Intellectual history is ideological by nature.* Being ideological, one must read the constituent elements of intellectual history against their social, economic, and political backgrounds and contexts. What this means is that, "Intellectual history cannot claim to be the true or only history . . . It exists only in connection with, and in relation to, the surrounding political, economic, and social forces. The investigation of subjects of intellectual history leads beyond the purely intellectual world, and intellectual history per se does not exist."[4]

Because of the different worldviews they represent, intellectual historians do not work on the assumption of a shared specific method. This justifies the notion that intellectual history lacks one governing problematic. In effect, contemporary Islamic intellectual histories, far from being reduced to one problematic, are distinguished at the core by a variety of conceptual approaches and questions with varying degrees of intensity and interrelationship.

One may summarize these problematics as both internal and external. On the internal side, modern and contemporary Muslim intelligentsia have wrestled with the meaning of Muslim identity and tradition and their relevance to the contemporary concerns of the Muslim world. For example, Muslim women have begun to examine the position of the primary sources of Islam, that is to say, the Qur'an and hadith, on women and the relevance of these primary sources to the current realities of the Muslim world. The debate on women and Islam is most poignant in such countries as Iran, Turkey, Malaysia, Egypt, and Pakistan. On the external side, Muslim intellectuals have been wrestling with the big questions of modernity and globalization, their impact on Muslim societies, and the relationship between the Muslim world and the advanced capitalist West. All of these debates have something to say about the nature of the state, i.e., the ruling system, in the Muslim world. In other words, part of the story of multiple intellectual histories in the Muslim world revolves around the meaning of "the state" in contemporary Muslim intellectual discourse and the political elite's influence on contemporary Muslim societies. One might add that the intellectual history of "the state" in the modern and contemporary Muslim world is yet to be written. In other words, the intellectual history of the political elite in the contemporary Muslim world must be written in order to reflect the ideological positions of this elite over a period of time and its position on national as well as foreign issues.

In reading the articles of this *Companion*, it is imperative to form a general sense of the elite in contemporary Muslim societies. By and large, one can differentiate four different types of elite in the Muslim world: (i) political elite; (ii) business elite; (iii) military elite; and (iv) intellectual elite. One must pay special attention to the connection between the political and intellectual elite in the contemporary Muslim world. Although it is quite difficult to summarize this relationship in a few sentences, it suffices to say that the political elite of many Muslim countries does not hail from the educated classes and that power and wealth have been used by the ruling power elite to acquire knowledge or acquire men of knowledge who can be useful in maintaining the political and social status quo. To a large extent, the power elite has also put to use some religious intelligentsia in order to promote the status quo in the eyes of the masses. This is true in almost every Muslim country. However, that is not to say that all religious intelligentsia have been subservient to the state. A good number of them have opposed the authority of the political elite and their international allies.[5]

The Blackwell Companion to Contemporary Islamic Thought wrestles with the works of those Muslim intellectuals who represent a variety of social and intellectual positions, and in that sense the various articles in this *Companion* will help us appreciate the core ideas discussed by some of the main intellectuals in the contemporary Muslim world. Some of these intellectuals belong to well-established religious classes in Muslim societies. They transmit a complex Islamic tradition in a highly dynamic age. Others have only recently risen to the fore. This is true, for example, with Ustaz Ashaari of Malaysia, whose grassroots organization has been banned by the government due to its challenge of the state's official religious discourse. (See Ahmad Fauzi Abdul Hamid's article on Ustaz Ashaari in this *Companion*.) The same can be said about the case of Fethullah Gülen of Turkey, living in exile in the United States since 2000, for his movement represents a great challenge to the authority of the Turkish state.[6] Gülen is a popular religious intellectual who has established and led the most powerful social and religious Islamic movement in contemporary Turkey, a movement that has been seen by some as posing a great danger to the Kemalist foundations of the Turkish Republic. Gülen was educated in the religious tradition current in East Turkey after the foundation of modern Turkey. His interpretation of the religious idiom has made him an attractive figure to a good number of religious intelligentsia in contemporary Turkey.

It is important to bear in mind that being an intellectual in the contemporary Muslim world is a difficult undertaking, indeed. The intellectuals, by and large, have been active in the anti-colonialist struggle and have had a vision about the construction of the nation-state after independence. However, a good number of contemporary Islamic intellectuals feel betrayed by the political elite of their countries. Some have actively tried to change the status quo, as in the case of religious leaders in Iran, while others, as in the case of the intellectuals of the Justice Party in Turkey, have opted to democratize their societies without attempting to change the Kemalist foundations of the state. A third type of Muslim intelligentsia and professional has opted to migrate to the West to seek their personal fortunes as an exit from their own dilemmas. The migration of intellectuals to Europe and North America has been a saga of the Third World since the dawn of imperialism. The rise of the United States to world prominence exacerbated the "brain drain" from the heart of the Muslim world. Therefore, it is erroneous to identify Muslim intellectual histories with just the intellectual forces present in the Muslim world. Many Muslim intellectuals in the West try every day to articulate a new identity that is in consonance with their social and political realities in the West.

The relationship of the intellectuals with the masses is very complex in contemporary Muslim societies. Religious intellectuals, by and large, have kept in touch with the masses. However, a good number of religious intellectuals have adopted the official side of the government line and represented the elite in their dealings with the masses. It is important to be guided, though not limited, by Antonio Gramsci's ideas on the meaning of intellectual and power, culture and politics, exile and creativity, civil society and religion. The distinction made by Gramsci between ecclesiastical and organic intellectuals might be helpful in dispelling some ambiguity about the role of the intellectual in contemporary Arab society. What prevents us from postulating that the most organic intellectual in the Muslim world of late has been the ecclesiastical activist, he or she who speaks the language of the masses and identifies with their suffering and predicament?

On the whole, contemporary Islamic intellectual histories have dealt with the following questions and challenges. First is the issue of decolonization and political independence. Most Muslim countries have gained their independence from European colonialism only in the past several decades. Has political independence translated into a healthy process of modernization or economic development without any major objection from the Center? Second, in the decolonization process, all sorts of nationalist, secular and religious forces participated in order to rid their societies of European hegemony and exploitation. There was a measure of balance in the fight against the colonial structure. What happens to this balance after independence? How do some forces highjack political decisions after independence? Third, the Muslim world has experienced a tremendous demographic explosion since independence. What have been the ramifications of such an explosion on the infrastructure of modern Muslim societies and what happens to the population born after independence? Fourth, as a result of the lack of development in the countryside, the rural poor migrate to the cities or even overseas, as in the case of many people from North Africa. What is the fate of the new urban poor and the relationship between this phenomenon and religion or religious activism in contemporary Muslim societies? Fifth, there is the big question of the emerging political elite in Muslim societies after independence and the role of the military in politics and the shape of civil society. All of these are major questions that await answers. It is not farfetched to argue that liberal democracy is not a reality in most, if not all, Muslim countries. Why has this been the case? Is this due solely to internal factors? Furthermore, the political elite in the Muslim world has put religion, that is to say, Islam, to its use. It has not shown a tendency to free religion from the patronage of the state, and as a result, a good number of the religious intelligentsia have taken the side of the state against the poor. The religious intelligentsia has been effectively co-opted. Sixth, one must raise questions about the social origins of the ruling elite in contemporary Muslim countries. What class interests do they represent? What is their connection to world capitalism? Are they interested in democratizing their societies? Seventh, what happens to the Islamist movements after independence? The major ones were established during the colonial era and fought colonialism as vehemently as did the nationalist and secular forces. What is their fate in Southeast Asia, South Asia, the Middle East, and North Africa? Eighth, what is the role of intellectuals in the Muslim world after independence? This is a huge question with many possible answers. By and large, because of the prevailing political conditions in the Muslim world and the rule of either a military or tribal dictatorship, the intelligentsia has become disenchanted with the political structure and some resorted to silence or migration. The process of the "brain drain" is a direct result of actions on the part of the ruling elite in the contemporary Muslim world to accommodate their intelligentsia and secure a free environment for academic research and intellectual freedom, where the intelligentsia can thrive and help the intelligentsia of the *ancien regime* transcend their predicaments and problems. Ninth, oil is a major commodity in the modern world-system. This has created a unique situation in the Gulf states, where a number of underdeveloped countries with meager populations are protected by capitalist interests and are developed overnight in order to meet the demands of the capitalist market. Are the Gulf states modernized? In other words, are they part of the historical project of modernity? Do they lack modernism? Do they have modernization? Tenth is the question of Palestine. Is this the never-fading issue? What has been its impact on the Muslim world? Is it true that Western and American support of Israel and the lack of support for Palestinian rights have solidified the anti-American forces in the Muslim world? Or are these forces angry with America and the West because of what they endured under colonialism and neo-colonialism? Eleventh, one notices after independence the virtual lack of knowledge that Muslim countries have about each other. Educated people in Cairo, Istanbul, Karachi, and Jakarta know more about the West than they do about other Muslim countries. This phenomenon of the colonial past is still a problem today. How is it possible to develop inter-Islamic consciousness in an age of increasing specialization and in an age controlled by the Center? Furthermore, it is important to note that the educated people of the non-Arab Muslim world (i.e., Pakistan, Malaysia, and Indonesia) know more about the Arab world than vice versa. Of course, much of this is due to the impact of Islam on these societies. This brings us to a whole host of questions about the lack of economic and political coordination in the Muslim world and its weak position *vis-à-vis* the world capitalist system. Twelfth is the status of religious sciences in the modern and contemporary Muslim world. There is no doubt that since its inception, the Islamic religious phenomenon contributed to the urbanization and modernization of the Muslim world. Islam is based on a sacred text, on literality. The Muslim world in the early modern period built a comprehensive system of madaris in order to impart Islamic teachings to the youth. In addition, Islamic civilization developed more or less an intact Islamic urban and literary cultural and religious system. However, all of this collapsed with the advent of colonialism in the Muslim world in the eighteenth and nineteenth centuries.

The Nineteenth-Century Background of Contemporary Islamic Thought

In documenting the salient features of modern and contemporary Islamic intellectual histories, let us first focus our attention on the primary concerns of the Muslim intelligentsia at the end of the nineteenth and the beginning of the twentieth centuries. Only in this way can we understand the problematics of contemporary Islamic thought. As a reaction to the penetration of Western capitalist modernity into all aspects of Muslim societies from the Arab world to Southeast Asia, a significant number of Muslim intellectuals began to write down the general outlines of a new intellectual project that is often referred to as "Islamic modernism." In the Arab world, Iran and the late Ottoman period[7] was represented by such luminaries as Jamāl al-Dīn al-Afghānī, Muḥammad 'Abduh, Muḥammad Rashīd Riḍa, Bediuzzaman Said Nursi (in his early phase), and a host of other religious scholars and thinkers who were intent on finding a rapprochement between their grand Islamic tradition and the scientific and philosophical achievements of capitalist modernity. In South Asia, the project of Islamic modernism was represented by such thinkers and activists as Sayyid Ahmad Khan, Amir Ali, Mawlana Abu al-Kalam Azad, and others.[8] In Southeast Asia, most notably in Indonesia, the project of Islamic modernism was represented by the Muhammadiyyah organization and its founder, Muhammad Dahlan.[9]

The major features of classical Islamic modernism were as follows: (i) the revival of rational elements in the Islamic tradition; (ii) finding Islamic solutions to the challenges of the West; (iii) embracing the philosophical and scientific features of modernity; (iv) constructing new academic and religious institutions to meet the challenges of modernity; (v) the revival of Kalam science; and (vi) the revival of Islamic languages and focus on foreign languages. Islamic modernism can be said to be composed of two major features at the beginning of the twentieth century: (i) on the one hand, it was deeply conscious of foreign occupation and its intellectual and educational design aimed at eradicating foreign control. This was the case with the Muhammadiyyah; (ii) on the other hand, it saw the salvation of Muslims as being united with the foreign presence, as can be seen in the movement represented by Khan in India at the end of the nineteenth century. However, the logical outcome of both sides of Islamic modernism was to lay down the blueprint for an independent homeland for Muslims in the Middle East, Southeast Asia, and South Asia.

Along with the rise of nationalism in different parts of the Muslim world in the latter part of the nineteenth and early twentieth centuries, Islamic modernism paved the way for the foundation of the nation-state in the modern Muslim world. In Indonesia, for example, Islamic modernism combined with nationalism and the rise of other Islamist parties to power led directly to the creation of modern Indonesia. The same combination of factors can be seen in the case of Pakistan.

Independence, national struggle, and the creation of modern institutions have been the landmark of contemporary Islamic thought. In the case of the Muslims of South Asia, the Partition of India and Pakistan has been a watershed in both contemporary Islamic intellectual and Indian intellectual histories. It is quite impossible to understand the huge issues besetting contemporary Islamic thought in South Asia without understanding this pivotal historical event and its intellectual, religious, social, political, and economic consequences and realities.

The Meaning of Salafiyyah in Modern and Contemporary Islamic Thought

In general, the Salafiyyah refers to a diverse number of religious and intellectual forces in the modern and contemporary Muslim world that have taken their inspiration from the primary sources of Islam and that opt to live their contemporary lives in a way that is resonant with the ideals of the past and demands of the present. One can divide the Salafiyyah movement into three forms: pre-colonial, colonial, and post-colonial. The best example of the pre-colonial is the Wahabiyyah, which has had a marked impact on modern and contemporary Islamic thought since its inception at the end of the eighteenth century in Arabia. One may consider the Wahabiyyah a great revolutionary movement in its initial thrust, since it relied on a comprehensive ideology of radical social and political change. It intended to purify society of superstition and negative social practices. The second is the colonial Salafiyyah. In the Arab world, it is represented by such scholars as 'Abd al-Qādir al-Jazā'irī, Aḥmad al-Mahdī, al-Sanūsī, Ḥassan al-ʿAṭṭār, al-Saffār, Jamāl al-Dīn al-Afghānī, Muḥammad ʿAbduh, and Rashīd Riḍa. The third is the post-colonial Salafiyyah represented by such religious scholars and activists as Mawlana Mawdūdī, ʿAbd al-Qādir ʿAwdah, Yūsuf al-Sibāʿī, ʿAllāl al-Fāsī, Sayyid Quṭb, and Muḥammad Quṭb. One must not forget the several militant Salafi movements, such as the *jihād* and Jamaʿah al-Islamiyyah in Egypt. Unlike the major Salafi trends, these movements seek to establish the Islamic polity through a military take-over of the state.

Many Salafi thinkers, especially from the Ahmad Khan school of thought in South Asia, sought accommodation with Westernization, as mentioned above. The Alighrah movement spearheaded by Khan in the nineteenth century produced generations of Muslim intellectuals in South Asia that sought accommodation between Islamic tradition and Western modernity. By and large, this movement was not critical of colonialism and Westernization. It is only in the twentieth century that some Salafi thinkers, especially those belonging to Islamic revivalist movements, began to contemplate the disastrous implications of capitalist culture and philosophy for Islamic metaphysics and ethics. Such revivalist thinkers as Khurshid Ahmad, Sayyid Quṭb, Muḥammad Bāqir al-Ṣadr, Muḥammad Ḥussain Faḍlallah, and Rāshid Ghannoushi have been critical of Western colonialism and its implications for the Muslim world. Because of its aggressive nature, capitalist modernity forced Salafi thinkers to seriously consider capitalist modes of production and their impact on modern Muslim societies.

One can consider Islamism as a natural outgrowth of the nineteenth-century Salafiyyah, especially in its ʿAbduh and Afghānī formulations. Islamism can be summarized both as an indigenous response to triumphant imperialism and the deep sense of political, religious, and intellectual malaise enveloping Arab society in the interwar period, especially after the abolition of the Ottoman caliphate in 1923. Being a response to the penetration of the modernity of imperialism in the different corners of the Arab world has always defined Islamist identity as intricately linked to that of the West. In a sense, this aggressive modernity has forced Islamism to be an avid observer of things Western, and has led it to present a comprehensive critique of the Western worldview and strategies in the Muslim world. This important dimension characterizes the thought of such people as Ḥassan Banna, Sayyid Quṭb, Muḥammad Faḍlallah, and many others. Although critical of imperialist modernity, both nineteenth-century Salafiyyah and interwar Salafiyyah adopted one key idea of Western modernity: the notion of reform and progress. However, one must draw an important distinction between the notion of progress as espoused by modernity and that as understood by the Islamic Salafiyyah. The Salafiyyah espousal of progress is not at all divorced from its appreciation of the centrality of the Islamic intellectual tradition and its modern intellectual positions.

In the Arab world, for example, and especially before 1967, the Salafiyyah was on the defensive while Arab nationalism was on the offensive. The 1967 defeat drastically changed this: it weakened and even paralyzed nationalism and forced it to revert to Islamic themes in its public pronouncements. In the words of the Egyptian thinker Ghali Shukri, the Salafiyyah "mushroomed" after the 1967 defeat. This happened in such countries as Syria, Egypt, and Jordan. A similar phenomenon took place in Iraq, especially after the second Gulf War.

After considering this historical sketch of the religious permutations of Salafiyyah, one must remember that the Salafiyyah movement in the Middle East was responding to a different set of circumstances than that in the Gulf states, especially the Wahabiyyah Salafiyyah in Saudi Arabia. In several Gulf states and most notably in Saudi Arabia, the Salafiyyah was intimately wed to the state to the extent that only an astute observer could distinguish the subtle difference between the state and the Wahabiyyah. The state claimed adherence to Islamic identity and the modernization of society. While the Salafiyyah in such countries as Syria and Egypt was on the defensive in the pre- and even post-1967 era, this was not the case in the Gulf states. The tribal Gulf state needed the Salafiyyah in order to boost its imported modernization programs in the 1960s and the 1980s and it needed it once again to attack Iraq in the second Gulf War. Furthermore, one may argue that the official Salafiyyah in most countries in the Gulf took the side of the state against Iraq after its occupation of Kuwait.

It is important to note that the Salafiyyah included a number of distinguished Shi'ite thinkers in the Arab world, most notably Muḥammad Bāqir al-Ṣadr of Iraq and Muḥammad Ḥussain Faḍlallah of Lebanon. These two thinkers, in particular, have had a major impact not just on Shi'ite youth but on Sunnite youth as well. In addition, one must not forget the major impact of the 1979 Iranian revolution on Arab consciousness in general and the Salafi outlook in particular.

The success of the Iranian revolution was seen as the concrete embodiment of genuine Islam in an Islamic society. A number of Salafi thinkers began to publicize the ideas of such figures as Ali Shari'ati and Imam Khomeini. Iran's contemporary intellectual history has been deeply influenced by the Khomeini revolution of 1979; the debates within Iran since that time are important. In treating the Salafi trend with its complex components in contemporary Arab thought, it is important to invoke the famous distinction drawn by Maxime Rodinson between "Official Islam" and "Popular Islam." To begin with, this is more than an academic sociological distinction about the nature of religion in contemporary Arab society. "Official Islam" represents the position of the state on religion and its various mechanisms, both subtle and concrete, to define a manageable relationship between the two. The constitution of almost every Arab state proclaims that Islam is the official religion of the country and that the *sharī'ah* is the main source of legislation. Besides raising questions about non-Muslims in Arab societies where the *sharī'ah* is the main source of legislation, this official position raises the fundamental question about the religious elite who enjoy the support of the state. This religious elite, dispersed as it is in different corners of the country, gains the official patronage of the state through the creation of a ministry for endowment and religious affairs, whose function becomes to keep those rebellious young preachers who may not heed the call of official reason in check.

Liberalism, Nationalism, and Marxism in the Muslim World

Besides Salafiyyah in its bewildering varieties, liberalism has had a real presence in the Muslim world since the nineteenth century. It is beyond the scope of this *Companion* to deal with liberal, nationalist, and Marxist trends of thought in the Muslim world in any comprehensive manner. However, the reader must bear in mind that these tendencies have coexisted with the Islamic trend of thought, have influenced and been influenced by it. It suffices to mention that liberalism in Western thought refers to a mode of thought that reflected the economic and cultural aspirations of the nascent bourgeoisie. In its different economic and political activities, liberalism prides itself on the notions of liberty and democracy. As a complex bourgeois movement, liberalism sought to achieve a number of things: philosophically, it sought to introduce a radical break between metaphysics and rationalism or between faith and reason. Liberalism no longer considered metaphysics to be the queen of sciences; an unfettered exercise of thought was considered the new criterion for progress. To be sure, the progress of science in the nineteenth century gave liberalism an edge over all religious philosophies. Economically, liberalism sought to achieve the unobstructed movement of goods. *Laissez-faire* capitalism was its natural expression in the eighteenth and nineteenth centuries. Socially, liberalism was for constituting a new social and work ethic that was not defined by either religion or tradition, or where religious philosophies occupy a marginal position. Educationally, liberalism preaches a new type of liberal education that rejects the control of religious reason and institutions.

Modernization and Religious Revivalism

Although we can date the beginning of contemporary Islamic thought to roughly the 1950s, its seeds were planted in the nineteenth and at the beginning of the twentieth centuries. The Muslim world's response to the challenges of colonization was multifaceted; it sought to revive or reconstruct the religious, social, political, and economic institutions of the modern Muslim world. On the whole, *three different movements channeled this response: modernization, nationalism, and religious revivalism.*

The European challenge to the Ottoman Empire in the nineteenth century helped awaken the central authority from its slumber and encouraged it to launch an ambitious program of modernization called the Tanzimat, which began in the early part of the nineteenth century. The Empire responded by adopting Tanzimat, a wholesale modernization of Ottoman society from the top down. Ottoman political and military elite were aware of the necessity of taking drastic "modernization measures" if they wished to keep the Empire afloat. Most leading Ottoman bureaucrats and intelligentsia, including the religious intelligentsia, were firmly behind modernization. The *ulama* supported modernization in the hopes that "the welfare of the *ummah*" would be safeguarded.[10] Although the different nineteenth-century Ottoman sultans put their weight behind the Tanzimat, the process did not prevent the collapse of the Empire by the end of World War One. However, before the Empire folded, a new breed of secular Ottoman intelligentsia arose, and a small part of that intelligentsia saw the salvation of the state in adopting Westernization. They saw this as the only solution to the backwardness of the state. The discourse of this community of people centered on a new understanding of nationalism, secularism, and progress.

Therefore, in the case of Turkey, contemporary intellectual history begins with the construction of the ideological foundations of Kemalism in the 1920s. Atatürk was a charismatic figure who desired the modernization of his country and people along European lines. One must situate the rise of different trends of thought in Turkey in the context of Kemalism and its impact on Islamic and leftist currents of thought. To a large extent, Islamic intellectual history in contemporary Turkey has been a response to the challenge of Kemalism to religious identity. One can discern four major trends of Islamic thought in contemporary Turkey: the first is the pacifist, represented by the thought of Bediuzzaman Said Nursi, a leading theologian of world renown who wrote the *Magnum Opus Risaleh Nur*, and who founded a community known as the Nur community.[11] The second is an educational Islamic movement represented by the theologian Fethullah Gülen, mentioned above. The third is the Islamic activist represented by the Refah party and the fourth is an activist moderate Islamic movement that works within the Kemalist system and that currently holds power in Turkey. (See Metin Heper's article in this *Companion.*) In addition to these representations of Islam, there is a host of Sufi brotherhoods that are still active in Turkey nowadays.

As mentioned above, nationalism represents the second tier of nineteenth-century Muslim response to the predicament of the Muslim world and Western challenges. Nationalism, in Anderson's celebrated phrase, "is an imagined political community – and imagined as both inherently limited and sovereign."[12] Nationalism is a limited imagining of the nation, much more limited, let us say, than Christendom or the Muslim *ummah*. Nationalism did not have to defend a stagnant past, although very often it resorted to inventing its own past in order to give a certain measure of authenticity to its actions. The nationalist movement in the Muslim world led the nation in a struggle against colonialism, which paved the way to creating several nation-states in the Muslim world. As a matter of course, nationalist leaders of the Muslim world did not use religious themes in their speeches or slogans. Such personalities as Ahmed Sukarno in Indonesia, Kemal Atatürk in Turkey, Muhammad 'Ali Jinnah in Pakistan, and Jamal 'Abd al-Nasser in Egypt represent this trend. Being highly charismatic, these founding figures fought for the political independence of their nations from the West while being at the same time envious of Western scientific and political achievements. Although they fought political domination by the West, they opted to model their societies according to the Western philosophy of life. It is interesting to examine the conditions in which Third World nationalisms arose. Much literature has appeared on the social or philosophical origins of European nationalism, but very little addresses the origins in the Muslim world. Overall, nationalism in the Muslim world fought very hard to liberate itself from imperialism in two important domains: the spiritual and the institutional. On the spiritual level, as Partha Chatterjee ably shows, nationalism seeks to ensure its sovereignty on the personality of the nation, its past, and cultural identity. On the institutional level, it seeks to establish its nationalist state by learning from Western science and institution building.[13]

The rise of nationalism in India is particularly interesting. Most of the Indian intelligentsia of the nineteenth century, regardless of their religious affiliation, were united on an ambitious nationalist program of ridding the country of British domination.[14] Any cursory reading of the career of the Indian Congress from the latter part of the nineteenth century until the 1947 Partition will undoubtedly reflect this preoccupation. However, under pressure from the British and because of certain religious and economic conditions, some Indian Muslims began to contemplate a separate state from the Muslims of India, which became Pakistan after Partition.

However, one must examine the genesis of nationalism in India from the prism of intellectual history. Modern Islamic intellectual history in India begins roughly after the failure of the Indian Mutiny against the British in 1857, which signaled the breakdown of the Mughal Empire and the onset of a new age for both Muslims and Hindus in India. Between 1857 and the end of World War One, several religious and intellectual tendencies developed among the Muslims of India competing for the formulation and definition of Islamic identity there. The following major movements arose: (i) the Alighrah movement, which was represented by Sir Ahmad Khan and his colleagues, and which advocated political and cultural openness to the English and their methods of teaching; (ii) the al-Khilafat movement, which aimed at preserving the Ottoman Empire; and (iii) the Muslim League. The al-Khilafat movement was Pan-Islamic in orientation and anti-British. In addition to these organized religious and intellectual bodies in Muslim India, there were a host of traditional educational institutions such as the Dar al-Ulum, established in Deoband at the end of the nineteenth century. The Dar al-Ulum is still committed to its original vision of disseminating traditional Islamic education in South Asia and creating bridges between the traditional religious elite and the masses. One of its most brilliant representatives is Sayyed Abul Hasan 'Ali Nadwi (See Yoginder Sikand's article on Mawlana Nadwi in this *Companion*.)[15]

Since Partition, there has been some confusion about the true identity of Pakistan. Was Pakistan created for the Muslims of India or was it created as an Islamic state?[16] The careers of the founders of Pakistan and the movement behind the establishment of the country have reflected this uncertainty.[17] What is certain is that only a portion of Indian Muslims were interested in migrating to Pakistan after Partition, and initially, the Jamaat-e-Islami, founded by Abu al-'Ala al-Mawdūdī in 1941, stood against Partition on the grounds that the future Islamic state would be limited to Pakistan only.[18] The Pakistani movement was spearheaded by the Muslim "salariat class" of North India, a class that was "the product of the colonial transformation of Indian social structure in the nineteenth century and . . . comprised those who had received an education that would equip them for employment in the expanding colonial state apparatus as scribes and functionaries."[19] This class did not represent the interests of the majority of the Muslim peasants in rural India or those of the Muslims in south India. This explains why the majority of Muslims in the south and in the rural areas did not migrate to Pakistan after Partition. However, the creation of Pakistan did not solve the problems of Muslims in India. In 1971, Pakistan lost East Pakistan, and Bangladesh was established in the name of Bengali nationalism.

It is clear that the Partition left a deep mark on both Muslims and Hindus in South Asia. It signaled the failure of unitary Indian nationalism to establish one independent state after the termination of British colonial authority in India. However, both India and Pakistan opted to create a secular and not a religious system after independence. It is within this secular system in each country that one has to locate the debates around the big issues in each country, such as the creation of a religious state. This has been the more pertinent in the case of the Jamaat-e-Islami after the migration of its founder to Pakistan in 1948. Mawdūdī never opted for Pakistan and he was one of the opponents of the Pakistan resolution in 1942. In other words, he did not see eye to eye with the Muslim League, which was fighting valiantly for the creation of a state for the Muslims of India. Mawdūdī did not initially opt for Pakistan since his Islamist vision of constructing an Islamic state all over India would have been greatly diminished. And diminished it was by the time that Mawdūdī and the top leadership of the Jamaat-e-Islami chose to migrate to Pakistan. (See Abdul Rashid Moten's article in this *Companion.*)

It is within the parameters of the nation-state of both India and Pakistan that one must discuss Islamic intellectual history and its evolution to the present. Whereas the bulk of Islamic intellectual history in Pakistan has revolved around the Islamicity of the state and the necessity of constructing an Islamic political and economic system to be compatible with modernity, the bulk of Islamic intellectual history in India has revolved around the preservation of the secular and democratic foundations of the modern Indian nation-state. Muslims as a minority in India, albeit a major minority of around 15 percent of the population, have by and large eschewed the Islamic pretensions of Pakistan, remained loyal to the indivisibility of India, and constructed their intellectual debates around the best ways and means to construct an Islamic identity in a secular environment. That is to say that even the most Islamist of movements in India, the remnant of the Jamaat-e-Islami, has been fighting to preserve the secular identity of the Indian state and against the Hinduization of the state. This is remarkable in view of the fact that the intellectual and political agenda of the Jamaat-e-Islami in Pakistan has been for the Islamization of the state.

Since the creation of Pakistan, the Jamaat-e-Islami and other Islamist movements in the country have failed to establish an Islamist political system, which defines to a large extent the intellectual debates of Islamists in Pakistan. There is no doubt that the intellectual leaders of the Jamaat, such as the founder Mawdūdī, Khurshid Ahmad, and others, have remained faithful to the vision of creating an Islamist system in the country. Opposed to that has been the nationalist and secularist vision of the founders of Pakistan, which has been kept intact by the army in the country.

The third major response to the challenge of European colonization was Islamic revivalism. At the outset, it is crucial to differentiate among four major groups or classes of revivalism in the modern Muslim world: (i) pre-colonial; (ii) colonial; (iii) post-colonial; and (iv) post-nation-state. The Wahabiyyah of Saudi Arabia is a pre-colonial Islamic movement, which was created in reaction to internal Muslim decadence and sought to revive Islamic practices in light of a strict adherence to Islamic law and theology. To do so, the charismatic figure Muhammad ibn 'Abd al-Wahab allied himself with the Saudi family, which led to the creation of the modern Saudi state.

Examples of the second form of colonial Islamic revivalism are the Muhammadiyyah and Nahdatu ul-Ulama organizations in Indonesia, both established in the first half of the twentieth century.[20] We can also add the Muslim Brotherhood of Egypt and the Jamaat-e-Islami of India. These were mass-oriented social and religious movements committed to ambitious programs such as the reform of Islamic education or the control of political authority in preparation for implementing the *sharī'ah* in the larger Islamic society.

The onset of the nation-state in the Muslim world in the middle of the twentieth century and the supervision of the religious institution by the state, coupled with the failure of the nation-state on many fronts, resulted in the emergence of post-colonial forms of Islamic revivalism, which reflected extremist interpretations of religion and resorted to violence to achieve their objectives. The Egyptian *jihād* of the 1970s and 80s is a case in point.

The Taliban stands to be one of the major Islamist movements arising in response to the disintegration of the nation-state in Afghanistan. The Taliban emerged in response to the failure of the secular nation-state to build a new civil society and also to the failure of the urban Islamist movement in Afghanistan to arrest the further disintegration of the state, especially in the wake of the withdrawal of Soviet forces in the late 1980s.[21] The Taliban movement arose in the context of the severe chaos taking place in the country in the 1990s, especially after the "Americans had turned their backs on the ruins of Afghanistan."[22]

It is clear that the most significant post-nation-state Islamist movements, that is, the Egyptian *jihād*, the bin Laden movement, which must be examined against the wider context of Saudi Arabia in the 1970s and 80s, and the Taliban, appeared at major historical junctures in contemporary Islamic history, precisely when secularism and the nation-state became exhausted, and when new possibilities of establishing a novel Islamist order seemed to arise.

The Question of Islam and Modernity

As various essays in this *Companion* show, modernity is the key to the main debates taking place in the Muslim world since the nineteenth century. Generally speaking, there are two ways to approach the question of "Islam and modernity." A host of Muslim theologians argue that Muslim tradition holds the answers to the many dilemmas that modernity has produced in the Muslim world. The most representative thinker of this trend, Seyyed Hossein Nasr, argues that "To conclude, a conscious and intellectual defense must be made of the Islamic tradition. Moreover, a thorough intellectual criticism must be made of the modern world and its shortcomings. Muslims cannot hope to follow the same path as the West without reaching the same impasse or an even a worse one, because of the rapidity of the tempo of change today. The Muslim intelligentsia must face all these changes mentioned here, and many others, with confidence in themselves. They must cease to live in the state of a psychological and cultural sense of inferiority."[23] Here, it is not clear what exactly Islamic tradition is and whether or not the contemporary Muslim intelligentsia is expected to bypass modernity or coexist with it. The former is most likely the position of the author. However, Nasr does not tell us *how* to bypass a modernity that has permeated the entire Muslim world in the past 200 years.

The second approach to dealing with "Islam and modernity" is to delve into the impact of modernity on actual Muslim countries, political, ideological, and social movements, states, power elite, and social formations in general. This is a more plausible approach than the former. In this approach, one must wrestle with a number of significant questions and not just Muslim tradition, per se. Because of the triumph of modernity and the colonization of a significant portion of the Muslim world in the seventeenth, eighteenth, and nineteenth centuries, it is quite impossible to speak of two separate paths of evolution, development, or change. The fate of the Muslim world has been entwined with that of the West for at least the past two centuries. (See Ziauddin Sardar's article in this *Companion*.)

The modern world-system and in principle, capitalism, has been the most potent result of modernity. Its impact on the world's economic and social structures has been without parallel. Therefore, the task of the Muslim intelligentsia must not be confined to developing Islamic paradigms or theories about Muslim tradition; neither should it be confined to the Islamization of knowledge. This is not feasible in the modern world where modernist capitalism has engendered profound changes in modern and contemporary Muslim societies, changes that cannot be understood by using "traditional Islamic paradigms or epistemes." In this case, I take issue with Ziauddin Sardar's contention that "The task before Muslim intelligentsia, then, is to develop, using the epistemology of Islam, alternative paradigms of knowledge for both natural and social sciences and to conceive and mold disciplines most relevant to the needs of contemporary Muslim societies. Only when distinctive Islamic paradigms and associated bodies of knowledge have evolved can Muslim scholars contemplate achieving synthesis on an appropriate footing with knowledge created by Western civilization."[24]

To put it bluntly, the Arab and the Muslim worlds cannot boast an Arab or Muslim civilization at present. The political and economic elite in the Arab or Muslim worlds, regardless of their culture, are true participants in the civilization of capitalism. True, there is an Arab or Muslim culture, but it is currently dominated by the larger capitalist civilization. We cannot compare a normative civilization (Islamic worldview) to a concrete and historically present civilization; that is, the global capitalist civilization. That is to say that it is impossible to fathom modern global identity outside the rubric of capitalism. We cannot view religious identity outside the domination of the capitalist system. Capitalists (proponents of a capitalist civilization) can be found all over the world, including the Muslim world, and class conflict still defines social relations. Furthermore, the Muslim world, unlike Europe, has failed to develop its capitalist system in the modern period and has thus become dependent on the world capitalist system, which has been pioneered by the West. The Muslim world has *culture*, but lacks its own distinctive *civilization*. Some articles in *The Blackwell Companion to Contemporary Islamic Thought* struggle with the concept of 'Islamic civilization' and reflect the ambivalence of some contemporary Muslim intellectuals about the revival of Islamic civilization under the current global conditions.

It is clear that capitalist civilization is dominant worldwide, although it has crystallized in various cultural and social forms depending on the country in which it flourishes. The capitalist system is strongest in North America, Europe, and Japan, with North America taking the leading role in world economic and scientific affairs. Here one must draw a distinction between globalization and Americanization, or between globalization and hegemony. Globalization is an objective socio-historical and economic process that began in the sixteenth century from the remnants of the feudal system. It has gone through major transformations ever since then. On the other hand,

Americanization or American hegemony is the product of the leading scientific and economic role the United States has played in the present world capitalist system. (See Mucahit Bilici's article in this *Companion*.) Britain was the dominant capitalist power in the nineteenth century and the first half of the twentieth. Therefore, globalization and American hegemony are not necessarily synonymous. At this point in time, however, the United States is the sole leading power, but it is unlikely that it will play this role forever.

Why is it important to come to grips with contemporary globalization? Since the nineteenth century, the Arab and Muslim worlds have been hard pressed to find solutions to their dependency on the capitalist West. Although the Muslim world has witnessed several political movements, most notably nationalism (which attempted to put an end to the structural and economic dependency of the Muslim world on the West), no viable solution has been found. The crisis of the social system in the Muslim world has resulted from the international division of labor under capitalism and the current hegemony of the United States. By and large, the political elite in the Muslim world either benefit from this division of labor or are unable to alter it to their advantage.

Has globalization been advantageous to the political elite in maintaining their authority? Has globalization weakened the contemporary state in the Muslim world? I think that globalization has often aided the political elite in the Muslim world in spreading their version of "false consciousness" by means of the mass media and given them the technological means to exercise full hegemony over society. Capitalism in the Muslim world, although concentrated in few hands, is deeply entrenched. It is part of the global capitalist system. As such, it competes with other capitalist groups or formations in the pursuit of unlimited wealth and power, when possible. Domestically, Arab capitalism assumes a relentless pursuit of power in order to protect its economic interests while constantly pursuing greater wealth. Instead of working for the progress of its society, capitalism in the Arab world seeks only the preservation of its hegemony and the expansion of its control. This expansion takes the form of a meager investment in religious institutions in order to exploit the religious feelings of the masses for its materialist ends.

One may say that modernity is an historical project with around 500 years of history. Since the inception of modernity, the world has gone through unparalleled major epistemological, industrial, scientific, economic, political, and military transformations that have affected every corner of the world. One can locate significant markers or paths in the historical march of modernity: the European discovery of the New World; the Protestant Reformation; the Industrial revolution; the Enlightenment and its idea of progress; secularism; colonialism; nationalism; the creation of the nation-states, etc.

The Enlightenment was the seed bed of modernity in the seventeenth and nineteenth centuries. David Harvey is correct when he says that, "Enlightenment thought embraced the idea of progress, and actively sought that break with history and tradition which modernity espouses. It was, above all, a secular movement that sought the mystification and desacralization of knowledge and social organization in order to liberate human beings from their chains."[25]

Most scholars of Islamic studies in the West follow, more or less, a Eurocentric approach by considering modernity to be a positive and somewhat monolithic process since its inception. Those in the field have been enamored of the philosophical formulations of such scholars as Jürgen Habermas, Richard Rorty, Vattimo, and others, who do not for a moment consider the polarization created by modernity between one world and another, between one's civilization and another's backwardness. There has not yet been a critical appraisal of this phenomenon in the field of Islamic studies. Fazlur Rahman wrote the most significant book on Islam and modernity from an Islamic perspective.[26] To date, few scholars have followed in his footsteps. The field is still waiting for a major reflection on the problematic of modernity and Muslim responses to it or interaction with it. I hope that the various articles in *The Blackwell Companion to Contemporary Islamic Thought* will help us formulate the right questions about the state of modernity and religion in the contemporary Muslim world.

Finally, most of the trends discussed by the authors in this *Companion* discuss the public manifestations of Islam and some present what they consider to be an Islamic perspective on the current situation. It is quite important to understand the position of Islam in the contemporary nation-state in the Muslim world and in the larger context of the dominance of capitalism in contemporary Muslim societies. There is no doubt that both State and Islamism have exploited religion to advance and/or protect certain political and economic interests. One may argue that in many Muslim countries, the political elite have failed to offer a coherent nationalist program or ideology to rid their societies of economic dependence and political stagnation since independence. In some Muslim countries, authoritarianism seems to be the mode of political practice. Democracy has not been deeply anchored in contemporary Arab and Muslim societies. Because of widespread social, economic, and demographic changes taking place in the past five decades, religion has gained more public prominence than ever before. In the ensuing social and economic dislocation experienced by a significant number of people, religion has offered hope and solace.

Notes

1. See my *Contemporary Arab Thought: Studies in Post-1967 Arab Intellectual History* (London: Pluto Press, 2004), especially chapters 1 and 2.
2. See P. Kinross, *Atatürk: The Rebirth of a Nation* (London: Phoenix Giant, 1995).
3. See O. Lovejoy, *Essays in the History of Ideas* (New York: George Braziller, 1955).
4. F. Gilbert, "Intellectual History: Its Aims and Methods," *Daedalus*, 100(1), 1971, 94.
5. Compare the current political elite in the Muslim world to what American sociologist C. Wright Mills had to say about the American elite in the 1950s: "By the middle of the twentieth century, the American elite have become an entirely different breed of men from those who could on any reasonable grounds be considered a cultural elite, or even for that matter cultivated men of responsibility. Knowledge and power are not truly united inside the ruling circles; and when men of knowledge do come to a point of contact with the circles of powerful men, they come not as peers but as hired men. The elite of power, wealth, and celebrity do not even have a passing acquaintance with the elite of culture, knowledge and

sensibility; they are not in touch with them although the fringes of the two worlds some-times overlap in the world of the celebrity." C. Wright Mills, *The Power Elite* (New York: Oxford University Press, 1957), 351.

6. See Bayram Balci, *Missionaires de l'Islam en Asie centrale: Les ecoles turques de Fethullah Gülen* (Paris: Maisonneuve and Larose, 2003), and John Esposito and Hakan Yavuz (eds.), *Turkish Islam and Secular State: The Gülen Movement* (Syracuse: Syracuse University Press, 2003).

7. See M. Sait Ozervarli, "Kalam in the late 19th and 20th Centuries," *The Muslim World*, 89(1), 1999, 91–102.

8. See Aziz Ahmad, *Islamic Modernism in India and Pakistan, 1857–1964* (London: Oxford University Press, 1967), and Mushirul Hasan, *Islam in the Subcontinent: Muslims in a Plural Society* (New Delhi: Manohar, 2002).

9. See George Kahin, *Revolution and Nationalism in Modern Indonesia* (Cornell: Cornell University Press, 1952).

10. "Leading ulema not only sanctioned and supported the innovations initiated by the Sultans and their military and civil advisors, both Ottoman and European. Some of them also played a major role in conceiving, suggesting, and planning reforms on European lines." Uriel Heyd, "The Ottoman Ulema and Westernization in the Time of Selim III and Mahmud II." In Albert Hourani, Philip Khoury and Mary Wilson (eds.), *The Modern Middle East: A Reader* (Berkeley: University of California Press, 1993), 30.

11. See Ibrahim M. Abu-Rabi' (ed.), *Islam at the Crossroads: On the Life and Thought of Bediuzza-man Said Nursi* (Albany: State University of New York Press, 2003).

12. Benedict Anderson, *Imagined Communities* (London: Verso, 1991), 6.

13. Chatterjee argues that "anticolonial nationalism creates its own domain of sovereignty within the colonial society well before it begins its political battle with the imperial power. It does this by dividing the world of social institutions and practices into two domains – the material and the spiritual. The material is the domain of the 'outside,' of the economy and state-craft, of science and technology, a world where the West had proved its superiority and the East had succumbed. In this domain, then, Western superiority had to be acknowl-edged and its accomplishments carefully studied and replicated. The spiritual, on the other hand, is an 'inner' domain bearing the 'essential' marks of cultural identity. The greater one's success in imitating Western skills in the material domain, therefore, the greater the need to preserve the distinctness of one's spiritual culture. This formula is, I think, a fun-damental feature of anticolonial nationalisms in Asia and Africa." Partha Chatterjee, *The Nation and its Fragments: Colonial and Postcolonial Histories in the Partha Chatterjee Omnibus* (New Delhi: Oxford University Press, 1999), 6.

14. Some leading Muslim thinkers, notably Sayyid Ahmad Khan, were pro-British. According to M.J. Akbar, "This disciple of the British [Ahmad Khan] became hero to the elite of a com-munity which had lost its pride and confidence after a century of stagnation; whose leaders had degenerated from emperors to caricatures; whose poetry had collapsed from philoso-phy to self-deprecation or lament; whose vision was so debilitated that when asked to sur-render self-respect in return for bread, it happily did so. For a pat on the back and a knighthood, Sayyid Ahmad Khan happily denounced the bravery of those numerous Muslims who fought the British in the wars of 1857. Inevitably, he could not resist becom-ing a bit of a caricature himself, wearing English clothes after his knighthood in 1888 and acquiring a knife and fork for his table. But he still did his writing still sitting on the floor." M.J. Akbar, *Nehru: The Making of India* (London: Viking, 1988), 16–17.

15. "Deoband was a centre of conservative Islam where young men of religious turn of mind were trained in theology, Islamic history and other old-fashioned disciplines. Western

learning was taboo, for it was one of the fundamental beliefs of the school that any truck with the infidel was tantamount to a compromise with heresy." A.K. Aziz, *The Making of Pakistan: A Study in Nationalism* (Lahore: Sang-E Meel Publications, 2002), 178.

16. This question is at the heart of many studies of modern Pakistan. See Akbar Ahmed, *Jinnah, Pakistan and Islamic Identity: The Search for Saladin* (London: Routledge, 1997); Tariq Ali, *Can Pakistan Survive? The Death of a State* (London: Penguin, 1983), and Lawrence Ziring, *Pakistan in the Twentieth Century: A Political History* (Karachi: Oxford University Press, 1997).

17. See Jean-Luc Racine, "Pakistan: Quel islam pour quelle nation? *Le Monde Diplomatique*, December 2001, 12–13.

18. Mushirul Hasan, *Legacy of a Divided Nation: India's Muslims since Independence* (Boulder: Westview Press, 1997), 69.

19. Hamza Alavi, "Pakistan and Islam: Ethnicity and Ideology," in Fred Halliday and Hamza Alavi (eds.), *State and Ideology in the Middle East and Pakistan* (New York: Monthly Review Press, 1998), 68.

20. On the Muhammadiyyah, consult the major study by Deliar Noer, *The Modernist Muslim Movement in Indonesia, 1909–1942* (Kuala Lumpur: Oxford University Press, 1978); see also George Kahin, *Nationalism and Revolution in Indonesia* (Ithaca: Cornell University Press, 1952) and Robert Hefner, *Civil Society: Muslims and Democratization in Indonesia* (Princeton: Princeton University Press, 2000).

21. See M. Hassan Kakar, *Afghanistan: The Soviet Invasion and the Afghan Response, 1979–1982* (Berkeley: University of California Press, 1995).

22. John K. Cooley, *Unholy Wars: Afghanistan, America and International Terrorism* (London: Pluto Press, 2000), 7.

23. Seyyed Hossein Nasr, *Islam and the Plight of Modern Man* (London, 1975), 148.

24. Ziauddin Sardar, *Islamic Futures: The Shape of Ideas to Come* (London: Mansell, 1985), 104.

25. David Harvey, *The Condition of Postmodernity: An Enquiry into the Origins of Cultural Change* (Oxford: Blackwell, 1989), 12–13.

26. Fazlur Rahman, *Islam and Modernity: Transformation of an Intellectual Tradition* (Chicago: University of Chicago Press, 1982).

PART I

Trends and Issues in Contemporary Islamic Thought

1 Contemporary Turkish Thought   23
   Şahin Filiz and Tahir Uluç
2 Transformation of Islamic Thought in Turkey Since the 1950s   39
   Ahmet Yildiz
3 Bediuzzaman Said Nursi's Approach to Religious Renewal and its
   Impact on Aspects of Contemporary Turkish Society   55
   Şükran Vahide
4 Islamic Thought in Contemporary India: The Impact of Mawlana
   Wahiduddin Khan's Al-Risāla Movement   75
   Irfan A. Omar
5 Sayyed Abul Hasan 'Ali Nadwi and Contemporary Islamic
   Thought in India   88
   Yoginder Sikand
6 Madrasah in South Asia   105
   Jamal Malik
7 75 Years of Higher Religious Education in Modern Turkey   122
   Mehmet Pacaci and Yasin Aktay
8 Hassan Turabi and the Limits of Modern Islamic Reformism   145
   Abdelwahab El-Affendi
9 An Overview of al-Sadiq al-Mahdi's Islamic Discourse   161
   Hassan Ahmed Ibrahim
10 Islamic Thought in Contemporary Pakistan: The Legacy of
   'Allāma Mawdūdī   175
   Abdul Rashid Moten
11 The Futuristic Thought of Ustaz Ashaari Muhammad of Malaysia   195
   Ahmad Fauzi Abdul Hamid
12 Religion, Society, and Culture in Malik Bennabi's Thought   213
   Mohamed El-Tahir El-Mesawi
13 Hassan Hanafi on Salafism and Secularism   257
   Yudian Wahyudi
14 Towards a New Historical Discourse in Islam   271
   Ali Mabrook

CHAPTER 1

Contemporary Turkish Thought

Şahin Filiz and Tahir Uluç

The objective of this chapter is to critically evaluate contemporary Turkish thought from a historical and sociological perspective and shed new light on its evolution from the beginning of the Republic to the present time. The foundation of the Republic of Turkey in 1923 was a watershed in modern Turkish history leading to the emergence of a new nation-state and a contemporary Turkish thought, which will be analyzed in this chapter.

This new Turkish nation-state inherited massive problems from the Ottoman Empire. From the beginning, this nation-state has grappled with two major issues. The first issue has been that of constructing a new Turkish identity different from that of the Ottoman state. The second issue has been that of importing and internalizing Western values *en masse*. These values have been expressed and manifested in such concepts as nationalism, secularization, and modernization of the country. In the view of the founders of the Republic, Turkey was not merely a piece of land, but also a nation in the modern sense. In other words, the construction of the new nation was seen as the "re-building of a non-existent past," rather than a departure from the tradition of the East or Islam.

To appreciate the critical transformation of intellectual life in contemporary Turkey from that of the late Ottoman period to the contemporary period, a brief analysis of the intellectual developments in the late Ottoman period will be useful. One may delineate three major trends of thought at the time. These are: (i) a Pan-Islamic Ottoman trend of thought that stood for the modernization of the state; (ii) a nationalist trend of thought that emphasized the Turkish nation at the expense of the other nationalist/ethnic components of the Empire; and (iii) a Westernized trend of thought that took Westernization as the only model for the Ottoman state to follow. Very often, the difference between category (i) and (ii) gets blurred.

The third category, Westernized trend in Ottoman thought, was represented by such luminaries as Abdullah Cevdet, Celal Nuri, and Kılıçzade Hakkı, who attempted to build a Turkish version of the Enlightenment. However, these thinkers failed to construct solid philosophical foundations for any Turkish Enlightenment due to their narrow interpretations of European Enlightenment. Nevertheless, a small but influential number of pre-World War One Ottoman thinkers were in agreement on the notion that Islamic tradition was no longer compatible with the conditions of modernity. Kemal Atatürk took the lead in the political realm to apply a strict separation between the religious and public spheres, thus greatly boosting the Westernized trend in Ottoman thought. Atatürk's main goal was to "modernize" Islam, so to say, as a means of creating a new identity for the Turkish nation.[1]

The foundation of the Turkish Republic in 1923 officially set in motion Kemalism as the ideology *par excellence* of the new Turkish nation. Islamic ideology had played a leading role in the Ottoman Empire but it failed to compete with the rising ideology of Kemalism in the 1920s and 1930s. "Religion was relying upon institutions that had political implications inconsistent with the basic principles of the new state; those institutions could no longer stand, even inharmoniously, side by side the secularized sector . . . A secular conception of national unity negated both the traditional and the 'modernist' view of a state associated with or based upon religion. This negation was symbolized by the abolition of the sultanate, soon followed by the abolition of the caliphate, and the establishment of a republican form of government based upon the sovereignty of the people constituting a nation."[2] The decade of the 1940s witnessed a significant impact on the life of Turkey due to certain external and internal factors. The external factors were the rise of fascism in Europe and the entry of the United States in World War Two on the side of the Allies, which enabled Kemalist Turkey to play the card of democracy and secularism. The internal factors can be seen with Kemalism trying to institutionalize its ideology by building schools and other institutions. One can locate the current predominant school of contemporary Turkish historiography and theoretical thought in this period.

During this time a number of influential intellectuals supported the notions of democracy and secularism and the number of academic and intellectual periodicals rose rapidly. Of interest in this regard have been such leading periodicals as *İnsan* (*Human Being*), *Yeni Adam* (*New Man*), and *Yurt ve Dünya* (*Home and the World*). Of the many Turkish intellectuals, such thinkers as Fuad Köprülü, Hilmi Ziya Ülken, and Niyazi Berkes, who was from Cyprus but was trained in Turkey, are noteworthy.

With the coming of Adnan Menderes to power in 1950, a radical shift in Turkish politics took place. Menderes encouraged a multi-party system and thus opened the way for new political and intellectual forces to emerge on the Turkish intellectual scene in the 1950s and 1960s. Further accelerating change was the speedy industrialization of the country after the foundation of the Republic, which produced new social classes that had been thitherto non-existent. This was to be seen especially with the new Turkish bourgeoisie that had social, political, and economic aspirations that were somewhat different from those of the bureaucrats who had ruled Turkey until then.

The rise of new social classes in Turkey coincided with the onset of the Cold War. In this new world situation, Turkey found itself in the Western camp taking an active role in the fight against communism and other radical ideologies. On the intellectual scene, the journal *Forum* played an active role in opposing communist ideology and in calling for a closer cooperation between Turkey and the West.

To a certain extent, the Cold War had a dramatic impact on Turkish intellectual life. Those intellectuals who identified themselves with the state and Kemalism supported the official line on the Cold War. Others, mainly on the left, opposed the Cold War although they were not adverse to Kemalism, especially in its official stand on a strict separation between state and religion.

One of the main consequences of the social, political, and economic transformations of Turkish society in the decades following the foundation of the Republic was the rise of Islamism in Turkey in the 1960s. This political Islamism has owed its rise to other Islamist movements in the Muslim world, as well. Turkish Islamists relied a great deal on the intellectual contributions of the main thinkers of Mawdūdī's Jamaat-e-Islami in Pakistan and India and the Muslim Brothers in Egypt. A great number of books were translated from both Urdu and Arabic, and Islam was presented as an alternative to all political models including in particular democracy. The rise of Islamism in Turkey was therefore not a reflection of the indigenous cultural dynamics of Turkish society, and that, for the most part, Turkish Islamism rejected Kemalism out of hand.

In addition to the increase of Islamism in Turkey in the 1960s, a new form of social Islam was on the rise in that decade. Turkey at that time was a developing economy and society and was modernizing rapidly. This rapid development led to the migration of a large number of people from the countryside to the major urban areas, such as Ankara, Istanbul, and Izmir. The new migrants from the countryside carried with them their own "flexible" notions of Islam that one may term "folk Islam." This "folk Islam" venerated saints and certain forms of hierarchies. This form of Islam has its own heroes and institutions, which played a significant role in the assimilation of the Turkish peasantry into the cultural and religious life of the big cities in Turkey. The decade of the 1970s was a focal one in the adaptation of the peasantry to city life. "Much of post Second World War Turkish political history seems to hinge on the dilemma facing the Westernising secularist elite: either to have free elections, and thereby to hand over electoral victory to parties willing to play up to the religiosity of the countryside and small towns, or to uphold the Kemalist heritage, but only at the cost of overruling the popular vote. It seemed that they could have democracy, or secularism, but not both . . ."[3]

Turkish political culture was badly shaken by the military coup that took place in 1980. This coup shook the confidence of the Turkish intelligentsia in the state. Some intellectuals argued that the main aim of the coup was to perpetuate the control of the tiny Turkish elite over the people and the economy of the country. The coup made it difficult for Turkish intellectuals to take an active role in politics. In addition, the coup made it possible for a large number of intellectuals, from the left and the religionist circles, to subject Kemalism to severe criticism. Kemalism was seen as a symbol of economic and political dominance by the few against the many. One of the consequences of the coup was the creation of a new synthesis in Turkish politics, which can be referred to as Islamism and nationalism. This new synthesis and trend of thought was defined by thinkers such as Erol Güngör.

A General Contour of Turkish Intelligentsia

Two major characteristics are common to all the post-republic Turkish intellectuals.[4] The first characteristic is that they were overwhelmed by the economic, political, and military power of the West. So the West and their stand toward the West was their major element in defining their identity. Second, these intellectuals took on the same mission, which was to save the country. Of course, this does not mean they were agreed on all the matters always. An example has been the term *aydın* (enlightened person), which was coined in the 1950s by Turkish leftist thinkers to distinguish themselves from Islamist and Ottomanist thinkers, who by and large have preserved the Ottoman word "*münevver*" to connect themselves to the past.

One needs to keep in mind the fact that the coups have had a defining impact on Turkish intellectual life. This is all the more true with the 1980 takeover for it led to a drastic rise in the number of "civil thinkers." In fact, this rise was the very consequence of the ban from governmental posts, which was imposed upon the thinkers and intellectuals by the authority of martial law.[5]

With the rise of a post-modernist discourse, the above new intellectual class came to place a great emphasis upon the native Turkish culture. But we should call attention to the lack of their depth in the political and intellectual backdrop of this new trend. So modern Turkish intellectualism failed to produce its own indigenous stance in the case of the Turkish post-modernist trend, but rather blindly reiterated the slogans.[6] In addition to the emergence of the post-modernist discourse, there was a multitude of factors that had a strong impact on Turkish intellectual life. In this context, I would like to mention Turgut Özal's coming to power in Turkey and Gorbachev's adoption of the policy of *Perestroika* in the Soviet Union along with the demise of the communist bloc. As a result of the political and economic changes in Turkey's northern neighbor, the polarization between the right and left, secularist and anti-secularist gave way to a polarization between statist thinkers and the supporters of civil society. The statist discourse is represented by a host of nationalist-conservative thinkers such as Dündar Taşer, Mümtaz Turhan, Erol Güngör, and Orhan Türkdoğan, along with some leftist intellectuals such as Attila İlhan and Baykan Sezer. The flank of civil society supporters is largely made of Islamist-conservative and leftist thinkers.

Attention should be drawn to the fact that the major difference between the above two trends lies in their stance with respect to Western values. While the former group has serious misgivings about the notion of civil society and modernism being identified with Westernism, the latter views Westernism as the only way to achieve democratic rights. The term "conservative Westernism," which was recently minted by Tayyip Erdoğan, leader of the Justice and Development Party, to define their position *vis-à-vis* the West well exemplifies the rapprochement between the Islamists and Westernism. In the final analysis, we should come to realize that Islamism in the context of Turkey has replaced the component of Turkish nationalism in relation to the Turkish Westernization or modernization.

Intellectual Identity Crisis

The National Struggle, which led to the creation of the modern Turkish Republic in 1923, no doubt made a considerable contribution to the development of the new Turkish identity. We need to bear in mind the fact that this identity is made up of Ottoman, Muslim, and Turkish components. Nevertheless, in the early years of the

Republic, the endeavors to build a nation in the modern sense by excluding the Ottoman and Islamic components – for which Halk Evleri (Public Houses) were set up in place of Türk Ocakları (Turkish Associations) – ended in failure. In addition, insistence upon this mode of an identity-building process led the society to identity crises and broke the single Turkish identity into three pieces as "Ottoman, Turk, and Islam." Therefore the components of Islam and Ottoman culture, which soon intermingled, have been very often in clash with Turkish nationalism. One can easily see the reflections of such a polarization between Turkism and Islamism-Ottomanism in such writings as *The Development of Secularism in Turkey* (1964) and *Türkiye'de Çağdaş Düşünce Tarihi* (*History of Modern Thought in Turkey*, 1966) by Niyazi Berkes.

Toward the 1980s, we see rapprochement between Islamism and Turkish nationalism. The harmonization of Islamism with Turkish nationalism was developed and advocated by Aydınlar Ocağı (The Association of Intelligentsia). Later Turgut Özal, the founder of the Motherland Party, further cultivated this discourse by incorporating it into his famous quadruple of liberalism, leftism, nationalism, and Islamism. In addition to Özal's Motherland Party, the National Salvation Party and the Nationalist Movement Party also harbored the same ideology. But, while the former placed greater emphasis upon Islam, the latter laid greater stress upon Turkish nationalism.

Thanks to the adoption of a multi-party system in the 1950s, Islam gained a huge power in the Turkish political realm. In this political course, while the rightist political parties envisioned the ways to hunt for votes from the countryside, the traditionalist section of society came to face a deep identity crisis as a result of the large-scale migrations. In this context, it should be noted that Sufi orders came once again to gain influence in the political and economic realm in the early 1970s.

In addition to the political ramifications of the domestic migrations a host of momentous developments in the economic field took place as well. Having until then been the carrier and representative of traditional Islam, the tradesmen adopted temporalism and subjectivism, which are central to modernity, and thereby played a leading role in the instrumentalization of Islam. The attempts of economic legitimizations on the religious bases in Turkish society secularized the religious communities and contributed to the rise of the consumerist culture seen in capitalism.[7]

As regards the leftist-Westernized trend of thought in Turkey, the social conditions of the 1960s, which favored academic studies of economics and politics as two leading disciplines, gave vigor to the Kadro movement. In this environment, the notions of Socialist revolution and freedom were first enunciated by Hikmet Kıvılcımlı (d. 1971) in his *Tarih Öncesi-Tarih-Devrim-Sosyalizm* (*Pre-History-History–Revolution–Socialism*). In his *Devrim Üzerine* (*On Revolution*), Doğan Avcıoğlu (d. 1983) holds that a revolution is a social fight. As a leftist thinker, Mehmet Ali Aybar (d. 1995) attempted to make a synthesis between Kemalism-socialism and democracy in his *Bağımsızlık, Demokrasi, Sosyalizm* (*Independence, Democracy, and Socialism*). Though the synthesis seems to have been broken from Kemalism by such followers of the *Yön* movement as Mihri Belli (b. 1916) and Doğu Perinçek (b. 1942), these figures have never failed to join the broken-off intellectual faction in face of the threats of *irtica* (reactionism).

This movement relied heavily on the statist ideology in maintaining a revolutionary outlook. It tried to reconcile statist and Kemalist ideologies with socialism. The *Yön* movement, which arose in the years in which the Third-World ideology reached its peak, drove the Turkish intelligentsia into a premature ambition for seizing Turkish political power. Furthermore, it adopted an ideology of using force to change the system. However, it neither developed a program nor succeeded in its ambition of coming to power in the early 1970s.

Turkish intelligentsia could not make good use of the 10 years between 1961 and 1971 due to their obsession with Cold War ideology and they swerved to populism. The democratic and liberal settings that wiped out the dichotomy of masses versus intelligentsia led to a filling of the vacuum, on the part of the left flank, which emerged after the downfall of the "bureaucrat" intellectual class. The *Yön* movement and Turkish Labor Party fostered leftist ideology on the base of Anglo-American empiricism, rather than Marxism.[8]

Referred to as "Leftist Islam," the movement tried to interpret Islam in harmony with secularism and Turkish nationalism. Osman Nuri Çerman in his *Modern Türkiye İçin Dinde Reform* (*Religious Reform for Modern Turkey*) and Cemil Sena in his *Hazreti Muhammed'in Felsefesi* (*The Prophet Muhammad's Philosophy*) called for worship in the native language, undressing Islam from Arab cloth and, in turn, Turkicizing and rendering Islam compatible with a moral and scientific attitude approved by Kemalism. Sabahattin Eyyüboğlu (d. 1978) and Macit Gökberk (d. 1993) furthered this discourse to an extent that it overlapped with the Turkish humanism of heterodox-Alawi character.

The left flank failed to follow a steady line in its quest for identity because most of the leftist thinkers did not bestow due consideration upon what they forfeited. Due to the collapse of the leftist ideology, the Marxist and socialist thinkers suffered a great loss of public credibility. As a consequence, they were forced to redefine themselves with a new identity. Undoubtedly, the growing popular culture contributed largely to this endeavor. Until then, the intellectual class had been composed of a relatively narrow and homogeneous family. Their primary role was to introduce science, education, and culture to the masses. The present-day tableau is quite different: because the masses now have a wider access to higher education, the number of individuals who could join the intellectual class radically increased. Hence, the once culturally leading position of the small and privileged groups of intellectuals who centered around a few universities disappeared.

The identity crisis revealed itself through the journals of growing number and varying contents in the 1980s. The post-1980 journals addressed the social problems in a way radically different from such journals as *Kadro* and *Yön*. Journals of post-1980 such as *2000'e Doğru* (*Toward the Millennium*), *Nokta* (*Point*), *Yeni Gündem* (*The New Agenda*), *Gergedan* (*Hippopotamus*), and *Argos* shifted attention to the millennium, rather than clinging to the past. Coinciding with the late 1990s, the Islamist journals forsook the "confrontation with the regime." Due to its theoretical shallowness, Islamic radicalism has lost ground in front of the globalized liberalism in Turkey; the proponents of this movement have put aside their former strict attitudes in exchange for the blessings of capitalism and political power.

By and large, the above journals focused on the foreign thinkers unknown to the Turkish people in the 1980s. In an attempt to gain more exposure for the country with the outside world, they advocated a global economy at the possible expense of the Turkish national culture. As for the Islamist journals, they concentrated their attentions on the outside Islamist movements through translations.

Populism was another symptom of the identity crisis of the Turkish intelligentsia. The intellectuals of Turkey began writing about their lives. Local affairs, society, and paparazzo news occupied the headlines. This is clear evidence of a departure from meaningful discussion of national values to the "global culture." The tension between the modern and post-modern came to the surface. The notion of coexistence superseded such dichotomies as secularist versus anti-secularist and left versus right in the 1980s and 1990s. Two leading pre-1980 thinkers, Attila İlhan and İdris Küçükömer, overturned the definitions of reactionary versus progressive. After this short investigation into Turkish intellectual life, we can proceed to describe some prominent intellectuals and their views in brief.

Leftist Thinkers

Hasan Ali Yücel (1897–1961)

Hasan Ali Yücel involved a large variety of tendencies such as revolutionism, Turkish nationalism, Kemalism and Mawlawī-Sufi ideals in his thought. He supervised the project of Turkish and Islamic encyclopedias between the years 1938 and 1946, during which he was minister of education. He ensured translation of a number of Western classics into Turkish. Yücel is seen as one of the pivotal figures of the Turkish Renaissance. To him, Atatürk dismantled the rule of despotism.[9]

Pertev Naili Boratav (1916–98)

Boratav made a huge contribution to the socialization of the Kemalist ideology. In addition, he set down an inventory of Turkish folklore. Boratav believed that the way Westerners interpreted the word "Orient" reflects the Western colonial point of view, which sees the East as colonized countries. To the West, the East was stuck somewhere in one or another of several development phases. The East is charged with supplying raw material for the West.

Niyazi Berkes (1908–88)

The journal *Yön* did play an important role in the change of Niyazi Berkes' mindset. The influence he exerted on the Turkish intelligentsia was quite limited mainly because he eschewed the daily affairs of politics. Yet Berkes made a tremendous contribution to Kemalist ideology by cultivating a new school, which deserves to be called "Berkesism." Though he brought a slight novelty to the economic doctrine of the *Yön* movement, Berkes broadened and developed Kemalism as far as to carve out a pan-Kemalist *Weltan-*

schauung. The works of Berkes had a deep impact on the post-1960 studies of sociology and politics.

Halide Edip Adıvar (1882–64)

Adıvar is known for her novels, political activities, and academic pursuits. She established a close friendship with famous Turkish nationalists such as Ziya Gökalp and Yusuf Akçura, and worked in Türk Ocakları (Turkish Associations). In her early novels, which are of an emotional character, she mainly dealt with the psychological problems of educated women in a context of love and marital relationships. In her late writings, she moved from the individual toward the social. *Yeni Turan (The New Turan,* 1912) in which she elaborated on the ideology of Turkish nationalism is seen as the work of a transition stage.

Kemal Tahir (1910–73)

For a long while, Tahir remained at the core of intellectual debates with his thesis of society and history, which forms the major theme of his novels. His stress on the Turkish culture *vis-à-vis* the Western was embraced by Baykan Sezer. Tahir holds that Turkish society is dissimilar to the West for its line of development is fundamentally different. Unlike its Western counterparts, the Ottoman society is a non-class society. Thus, Turkish novelty should reflect its own social reality. In his first village novel, *Sağırdere (The Deaf Creek,* 1955) and *Körduman (The Blind Smoke,* 1954) which is a continuation of *Sağırdere,* he elaborates on Turkish villagers' problems, village economy, and values without detaching them from their historical context. This differs from the approach, to the village, of the authors of the Village Institute background. His position is also diametrically opposed to Yaşar Kemal's in his *İnce Memed (Thin Memed).*

To put in the words of Fethi Naci, "He used the tools of social sciences, rather than the tools of expression specific to the literature."[10] *Devlet Ana (The Mother State,* 1967), in which he made expression of his views as to the Asian Type of Production (ATP), sparked hot debates. To him, the gravest mistake the Ottoman governing elite made was the attempt to Westernize the country, which was embarked on with the abolishment of the Janissary troops. Nevertheless, the ATP (Marx's view was introduced into the Turkish socialist discourse in the 1960s) is the shortest way – without having need of capitalization or feudalization – to achieve modern socialism. The Republic's Westernization project was a grave mistake as was that of the Ottoman. Tahir asserts that all the reforms Atatürk realized since the foundation of the Republic are such slight and toy-like reforms that they cannot be reckoned as upper structures in a hierarchy. The abrogation of the sultanate is not valid because it was not voted by the Turkish Parliament. If we were now to have the caliphate, millions of Muslims would follow us. Tahir asserts that Kemalism is evidently a backward ideology. The notion of the pure

Turkish language is a straightforward treachery to the homeland.[11] He sees the social-ist movement in Turkey as an agent of the Westernization.

İsmail Hakkı Baltacıoğlu (1886–1978)

İsmail Hakkı represents the profile of the Turkish intellectual who came from the lower class and took a Western style of education. He acted as a link connecting the Ottoman Empire to the Republic, the Second *Meshrutiyet* to Kemalism. He always kept his ideo-logical allegiance to Ziya Gökalp in sociology and education, and remained near to Atatürk and İsmet İnönü. Acting as an executer of the Union and Progress policies in the field of education, Baltacıoğlu had edited the journal *Yeni Adam* until the 1960s, which involved nationalist, traditionalist, secular, statist, and revolutionist views. Like Gökalp, he wanted to see the people who live in the Republic of Turkey "embrace the Turkish identity and evolve from being subjects to modern citizens." As he espoused the Turkicization of the religion, he can be classified in the conservative-nationalist category including such figures as Peyami Safa, Mümtaz Turhan, and Şekip Tunç. In this respect, he might be regarded as a link connecting the "progressive" discourse, viz., the revolutionist Kemalists, to the conservative, that is, the nationalist-conservative groups. The above five tendencies of the journal *Yeni Adam* demonstrate that Kemalism has a socialist character. İsmail Hakkı provided a deep insight into the way the conser-vative group wants to view Atatürk.

Doğan Avcıoğlu (1926–83)

After İsmail Hakkı, the ideology of Kemalist socialism was maintained by Avcıoğlu. He contributed to the stipulation of the 1961 Constitution once he was elected from the Republican People's Party to the constitutional parliament. He played an active role within post-1960 Turkish politics through the journal *Yön*. He published the journal together with Mümtaz Soysal and Cemal Reşit Eyüboğlu until 1967. In his writ-ings he defended "Kemalist socialism." He stressed maintaining the Kemalist revolu-tions in the infrastructure and went against Pan-Turkism. He says, "Turkey would be able to defeat reactionaries with the army's helping hand." As a socialist thinker, he did not fail to identify the nationalist-conservative discourse with reactionism though he has a strong nationalist vein. Not only did Kemalism's illegitimate marriage with social-ism produce such a view that blames the nationalism of racism, and Islam of reac-tionarism, it also justified its intellectual support, on the basis of lack of thought freedom, to the terrorist acts perpetrated by the separatist, micro-ethnic and micro-sectarian groups of Marxist–Leninist character in the 1990s. Because of the left, Kemalism was turned into the official ideology and the state both came into clash with its unwavering supporters, viz., the nationalist-conservative groups, and became vul-nerable to leftist Kemalism, which came to act as a champion of the separatist move-ments. The direction that leftist Kemalism swerved in the 1990s was in opposition to the national culture and religious values. Nevertheless, on the eve of the millennium, the Turkish left found the Islamists by its side in the fight against the common enemy, i.e., the "nation state and national culture."

Tarık Zafer Tunaya (1916–91)

Taking part in the commission which laid down the 1961 Constitution, Tunaya claims that Western civilization is the leading civilization, and it should be considered as a universal achievement of humanity. So the ultimate aim of the Turkish revolution should be to join the Western civilization. To his mind, this has been necessitated by the depressing conditions; it is not because of admiration of the West, nor is it a fantasy. Turks have been a civilized society since pre-Islamic times. Thus, they would never lose their identity within the Western civilization. In contrast to Third-World nationalism, the Kemalist mode of nationalism champions Westernization, and aims at achieving a level of competing with the powerful Western countries.[12]

Şerif Mardin (1926–)

Mardin's post-1960 writings mainly focused on a critique of Marxism. He positioned himself at the center in the early 1960s, but in the late 1960s and the early 1970s, he participated in the opposition flank. His conclusive works are ones that he wrote in the 1960s. His writings of the 1980s were filled with the shortcomings of the modernist and conservative intelligentsia prior to him.

Şerif Mardin is known as the Max Weber of Turkish sociology. He believes that the modernization of the Republic period is indicative of the departure from the past and the beginning of a new era. The Kemalist project is the "first Turkish modernity project". In this regard, Kemalism is both a project of transformation and a sweeping social design. In Kemalism, political rationalization is prior to and definitive for economy and culture.

Because Turkish modernization looked on the masses as an "object" of transformation, it produced a conflicting relationship between the center and the periphery. The modernization history of Turkey is at the same time the history of pushing Islam off the *ummah* structure. As popular Islam was affected by Kemalism, believes Mardin, the relationship growing between Kemalism and popular Islam based on Orthodox-Sunni Islam would confront a serious problem of validity.[13]

Baykan Sezer (1939–)

Baykan Sezer is one of those who first realized that the sociology being set up "from the West, for the West and because of the West" did not meet the needs of Turkish society.

He asserts that it is not possible to understand the present Turkish society without investigation into the Ottoman. Because the historical continuity is indispensable, a departure from the past would not help to understand the West. The most serious mistake the Turkish left has done is to turn a blind eye on the splendor of the Turkish-Ottoman history. Thus, in a good number of points, he followed in the footsteps of Kemal Tahir. In opposition to Kıray, he thinks that sociology is not an experimental discipline, but rather a method of addressing the society as a flowing reality.

To him, it would be odd to edify any Turkish sociology ignoring the Turkish-Ottoman history. He takes exception to those who mention Turkish society within the category of the underdeveloped societies on the basis that the Ottoman society was marked by feudalism.

Sezer attempts to interpret Turkish society and Turkish history in reference to two major incidents, which demonstrate that the stages of Turkish history do not conform to the Western scheme. (i) The Turkicization of Anatolia: This means that Turks left their homeland but were able to maintain their identity. (ii) The Ottoman's adoption of Westernization: He believes that Westernization begs attention, and it is impossible to become Westernized without participation in the colonialist world order. Though Turkey has become Westernized, it failed to achieve the desire. The import sociology precluded us from understanding ourselves.[14]

The return to the Turkish-Ottoman culture and the indigenous Turkish sociology demonstrates that the Gökalpian synthesis of "Turkicization, Islamization, and modernization" has survived until now. Nonetheless, trivial political interests and popular culture have since the 1990s overshadowed this synthesis and emasculated Turkish theoretical thought.

Rightist Thinkers

Ziya Gökalp (1876–1924)

Although the period in which Ziya Gökalp lived is outside the scope of the present study, we are forced to touch briefly on his views for two reasons. First, Gökalp has had a lasting impact on both the right and left intellectual trends. So it would be impossible to understand the post-Republican thought in general, and the rightist worldview in particular, without taking into consideration his views. Second, though he inspired both the rightist and leftist intelligentsia, his synthesis most resonated through the rightist thinkers.

The rightist intellectuals took up his ideas to the extent that the leftist thinkers, who were enchanted by the spell of the rising micro-ethnic and micro-sectarian trends in the 1990s, came to renounce Gökalp's revolutionist and groundbreaking views of which they once made use. The left flank relinquished to the right the sheer rightist Gökalp, whose revolutionist and innovative aspects were left to oblivion by the right. While he was clothed in a "nationalist-conservative" guise and presented as an enthusiastic defender of the traditional structure inherited from Sunnism and the Ottoman, his revolutionist and innovative aspects were brushed aside.[15]

Fuad Köprülü (1890–1966)

Being the founder of a school in Turkish historiography, Köprülü contributed largely to the studies of the Turkish literary history. By doing so, he became the first Turkish scholar and politician among the nationalist flank to stand up and break the Orientalist sway on Turkology studies. Köprülü's studies on Turkish history were continued by his students, among whom are Abdülkadir İnan, Faruk Sümer, Abdülbaki Gölpınarlı, Pertev Naili Boratav, Osman Turan, Mustafa Akdağ, and Halil İnalcık. He was deeply influenced by Gökalp's nationalist ideas. He combined the Turkist ideology with modern historiography and laid down the foundation for studies in the field of heterodox Islam.

Mümtaz Turhan (1908–69)

Gökalp influenced Turhan in developing his thoughts and incorporating the intelligentsia and masses into the Turkish national unity, making good use of science and technology in the fostering of social institutions. To him, national culture is fundamental to be a nation. What he understands from Westernization is used to enrich the national culture. Turkish nationalism arose as a historical response to the imperial desires of the West and the separatist demands in the shadow of the Ottoman Empire's fall. Turhan has much in common with Berkes in terms of influencing a number of Turkish intellectuals.

Hilmi Ziya Ülken (1901–74)

Ülken is mentioned along the same lines as Mardin and Baykan Sezer, who are known for descriptive and analytic methodology. He influenced modernist intellectuals in the early years, and conservative intellectuals in the late years of his career (1940–50). He criticized both Orientalists and Eastern scholars. The mistake of the Easterners is to render all subjects the matter of faith and thereby deviate from the essence of Islam.

In the view of Ülken, Turks' conversion to Islam did not bring about a serious conflict for Turkish identity. This is because the pagan beliefs failed to produce a holistic worldview, rather than the close similarity between the pre-Islamic Turkish beliefs and Islam. Nevertheless, when the Turks were faced with the foreign model, i.e. the West, they experienced their first trauma because of the huge gap between the new model and the Muslim tradition. Ülken was opposed to Gökalp's views as he found artificial the distinction Gökalp made between civilization and culture. He likens Gökalp's distinction to that which was made between substance and form in scholastic minds. To him, one cannot imagine a cultural spirit without technology. Knowledge does not compromise its holistic and interconnected nature. Western technology cannot be separated from its civilization.[16]

Erol Güngör (d. 1983)

The following remarks of Güngör on secularism reflect the growing inclination of the Turkish right to the nationalist-conservative discourse and, in turn, its abandonment of the Gökalpian statism, which infringes in the religious sphere:

> The Republic of Turkey is a secular state. The hegemony of the clergymen or the sway of religious considerations over the state cannot be approved of. However, some politicians intervene in religious affairs and, some intellectuals want the state to meddle even in the way of worshipping. These interventionist secularists sometimes succeeded to have the opportunity to use the state power against the religion. If Turkey would be tardy to adopt the democratic system, it would be quite possible to change the way, language and time of worshipping. Those who are most crazy for the reformation in religion would never worship even once though all kinds of reforms were put into effect. You would say, "One can be interested in religious affairs though one does not personally have a faith." To be interested in religious affairs is quite different from intervention in the affairs of a pious person.[17]

The Present Situation of Turkish Intellectual Life

Modern Turkish thought is replete with diverse profiles of intellectuals who have striven to shape Turkish political power. Islamist, Westernist, and nationalist thinkers have all desired political power and control of the state apparatus. Of the above trends, Islamism might be considered to be an offshoot of the Kadro movement's tendency to manipulate political power.

The spread of Islamism in the 1960s gave vigor to the vulgarization inaugurated by the uncontrolled flow of migration from the rural areas to the big cities. The exaltation of peasantry led the emigrants living in the suburbs to hold faster to the custom which they "brought with themselves from their villages." In the following years, we see an inclination to urbanization. The urban culture sacrificed the national culture, instead of the vulgar one, for the sake of getting rid of peasantry and continuing the Westernization project, but it failed to achieve these aims; in addition, this process instigated the creation of subcultures. The intellectuals' loss of confidence in the state, caused by the 1980 military coup, led both to the departure from Kemalism and weakened the sense of loyalty to the state.

As emphasized by Meeker, the rise of Islamist discourse in the 1970s and 1980s was a response to the identity crisis resulting from the passage from *Gesellschaft* to *Gemeinschaft*. He points out that "... the Muslim intellectuals make their appearance in the wake of a period of ideological exhaustion precisely because Islam is perceived as an alternative to the conflicting constructions of modernity. But when they speak of Islam, they do not have in mind the traditional beliefs and practices of the Turkish *Gemeinschaft*; rather, they envision an Islam that was never perfectly realized in Turkey, one that is based on divine revelation and orthodox practice, not on past customary practices in the Ottoman or any other Islamic Empire."[18] Islamism in Turkey seems to be critical of the Westernist modernization project. In the 1980s, Islamism "came as a response to the crisis of dependent modernization in Turkey. In the 1980s, a large marginalized and dispossessed segment in the metropolitan centers joined the petite bourgeoisie of provincial towns in support of Islamist politics."[19] So the supporters of the Islamist movement included "the large university student population, especially upwardly mobile youths who must compete with the established urban middle and upper-middle classes; members of the unskilled young urban sub-proletariat whose number has increased with the migrations and a higher level of unemployment; and some from the state-employed petit bourgeoisie, proletarianized by falling real wages and high inflation, particularly since the early 1990s."[20]

Having until then been divided into five groups – Islamist, Turkist, Westernist, Kemalist, and socialist – Turkish intellectuals gradually evolved into two groups as secularist versus anti-secularist and then statist versus pro-civil society. Such a transformation demonstrates that these apparently various intellectual typologies and political-intellectual identities are basically similar and interpenetrative categories.

The "statist" intellectualism of today is composed of conservative-nationalist thinkers. Some religious communities and Sufi brotherhoods are included in this category as well. But the most important section of this group is those who call themselves "the supporters of civil society"; though the supporters of civil society are diametrically opposed to each other, they become united in the common stress in their micro-ethnic and micro-sectarian aspirations.

In the wake of the political failure of the leftists, a secular version of a Westernization argument has been converted by the Islamists, who are nowadays on the rise in politics, into a "conservative Westernization," and then into a Westernization process to be adopted fully. The intellectuals who have been in a clash with the nation have taken the place of the intellectuals who have been in a clash with the state. So nothing important has changed.

Political concerns and practices outweigh intellectual concerns. Turkish political life has impeded the progress of Turkish intellectual life. But the military coups seem to have mitigated the severity of the hindering politics, which has no intellectual tradition.

There are several reasons for this:

1. Although the age of empires passed a long time ago, the Ottoman Empire, which had been suffering successive defeats and territorial losses since 1683, collapsed far later than it should have done. This late downfall of the Empire delayed the formation of the Turkish nation-state.
2. The young Republic grappled with the problems of the post-modern age before it had completed the phase of nation-state required by the modern age.
3. For daily and populist concerns, Turkish intellectuality undermined successively Kemalism, statist tradition, leftist discourse, religious values, and finally national culture.
4. In the pre-1980 period, Westernization and modernization had been characterized by the leftist discourse. Today Westernization has its "religion." To

run against the former was reckoned as opposition to Kemalism. To go against the latter may now be considered as opposition to the ideal of civil society or even to Islam. This is so therefore that to discuss the disadvantages of participation in the European Union (EU) is now put on a par with indifference to the cause of women's head covering.

Turkish nationalism, Westernism, and Islamism can be seen as three major lines of post-1950 Turkish thought. There has been a strong interaction between those ideologies, and so there emerged a number of auxiliary currents such as Kemalism, liberalism, and conservatism, all of which can be viewed as the conglomeration of the above major lines. One ought to note that though the former three ideologies seem to be divergent from and opposed to each other, they are, in fact, complementary to one other in that they are concerned about the well-being of the country as a whole.

At the beginning of the Republic, Turkish nationalism and Westernism were the two fundamental components of the state ideology, but the 1980s witnessed rapprochement between Westernism and Islamism, and Turkish nationalism left its place to Islamism. Since then, the Westernization project has continued but with the substitution of Islamism for Turkish nationalism. At present, it seems to be Turkey's long-term bid for joining the EU that holds together Islamists and Westernists ever more strongly. While the Westernists thereby aim to integrate with the European civilization, the Islamists envisage an expanded freedom in religious practices. Moreover, the current conflict over the EU can be seen as a reflection and continuation of the tension between the center and the periphery, which goes back to the foundation of the Republic.

Notes

1. Himmet Hülür and Anzavur Demirpolat, "Aydın Kimliği, Seçkincilik ve Süreklilik (Intellectual Identity, Elitism, and Continuation)," *Selçuk Üniversitesi Sosyal Bilimler Enstitüsü Dergisi*, 5, 1999, 380–2.
2. Niyazi Berkes, *The Development of Secularism in Turkey* (Montreal: McGill University Press, 1964), 481, 510.
3. Ernest Gellner, *Muslim Society* (Cambridge: Cambridge University Press, 1985), 59–60.
4. Contemporary Arab intellectualism suffered quite similar problems. For further information see, Ibrahim Abu-Rabi', *Contemporary Arab Thought. Studies in Post-1967 Arab Intellectual History* (London: Pluto Press, 2004), 1–39.
5. See Ali Akay, "Aydınlar Üzerine Bir Bakış (A Glance at the Intellectuals)," in *Türk Aydını ve Kimlik Sorunu* (Istanbul: Bağlam Publications, 1985), 423–36.
6. See Himmet Hülür, "Toplumsal Bilim Söyleminde Yerellik (Localism in the Discourse of Social Science)," *Selçuk İletişim*, 1/3, 2000, 114.
7. Anzavur Demirpolat, "Türkiye'de İslami İktisat Ahlakının Yükselişi, Rasyonalite ve Kapitalizm: Konya Örneği (The Rise of Islamic Ethic of Economy in Turkey, Rationality and Capitalism: The Case of Konya)," *Selçuk İletişim*, 2/4, 2003, 200.
8. Yavuz G. Yıldız, Türk Aydını ve İktidar Sorunu, 373.
9. Hasan Ali Yücel, *Hürriyet Gene Hürriyet* (*Freedom Again Freedom*), (Ankara: İş Bankası Publications, 1954), II/368–71.

10. *Cumhuriyet Ansiklopedisi* (*The Republic Encyclopedia*), (Istanbul: YKY Publications, 2003), III/328.

11. Kemal Tahir, *Notlar* (*The Notes*), (Istanbul: Bağlam Yayınları, 1992), 56–274.

12. Tarık Zafer Tunaya, *Devrim Hareketleri İçinde Atatürk ve Atatürkçülük* (*Atatürk and Atatürkism within the Revolutionist Movements*), (Istanbul: Baha Press, 1964), 6, 120, 122.

13. See E. Fuat Keyman, "Şerif Mardin Toplumsal Kuramı ve Türk Modernitesini Anlamak (To Understand Şerif Mardin's Social Theory and Turkish Modernity)," *Doğu-Batı*, 4/16, 2001, 9–29.

14. See Baykan Sezer, "Türk Sosyologları ve Eserleri (Turkish Sociologists and Their Writings)," *Sosyoloji Dergisi*, 3/1(1989), 4; Baykan Sezer, *Sosyolojinin Ana Başlıkları* (*The Main Headings of Sociology*), (Istanbul: İstanbul Üniversitesi Edebiyat Fakültesi Publications, 1985), 50–65; Baykan Sezer, *Sosyolojide Yöntem Tartışmaları* (*Methodological Debates in Sociology*), (Istanbul: Sümer Press, 1993), 15–200.

15. For further information, see Ziya Gökalp, *Türkçülüğün Esasları* (*The Main Principles of Turkism*), (Istanbul: İnkılap ve Aka Press, 1978), 90–4; Ziya Gökalp, *Türkleşmek, İslamlaşmak, Muasırlaşmak* (*Turkicization, Islamization, Modernization*), (Istanbul: İnkılap ve Aka Press, 1976), 10–20.

16. Taşkın Takış, "Değerler Levhasının Tersine Çevrilişi: Hilmi Ziya Ülken (The Overturn of Plate of the Values: Hilmi Ziya Ülken)," *Doğu-Batı Dergisi*, 3/12, 2000, 96, 100–9.

17. Erol Güngör, *Sosyal Meseleler ve Aydınlar (Social Problems and Intellectuals)*, (Istanbul: Ötüken Press, 1993), 123.

18. Michael E. Meeker, "The New Muslim Intellectual in the Republic of Turkey," in Richard Tapper, ed., *Islam in Modern Turkey. Religion, Politics and Literature in a Secular State*, (London: I.B. Tauris, 1991), 216–17.

19. Haldun Gulalp, "The Crisis of Westernization in Turkey: Islamism versus Nationalism," *Innovation: The European Journal of Social Sciences*, 8/2, 1995.

20. Nilufer Narli, "The Rise of the Islamist Movement in Turkey," *Middle East Review of International Affairs*, 3/3, 1999, 42.

CHAPTER 2

Transformation of Islamic Thought in Turkey Since the 1950s

Ahmet Yildiz

Introduction

Islamic thought as a concept does not signify Islam as a religion *per se*, it rather denotes the totality of intellectual, cultural, and political products by the Muslim elite, namely *ulama* and intelligentsia. The relationship between the Islamist movement and Islamic thought is that Islam for the first time put its stamp on a certain scheme of political action. Islam in this way has been interpreted as a project of political liberation formed under the instigation of Western political, economic, and cultural power. Hence, from its beginning, Islamism has been equally religious and political. As a political project, it aimed at the restoration of the state power both domestically and internationally through the incorporation of Western science and technology. As a religious project, it reinterpreted Islam, which was the source of the state's legitimacy, so as to Islamize the Western concepts of progress and development. Despite its emphasis on the return to the original sources, the Islamic movement could not achieve the religious renewal (*tajdīd*) in conclusive terms, and its religious emphasis has been replaced by a convenient political pragmatism. In this respect, Islamic thought and Islamic movement correspond to the same thing. Islamism involves ideas and speculations as well as activism. While Islamic movement reveals the activism of Islamism, Islamic thought denotes the intellectual watercourse of that activism. Therefore, they are in close transivity and can be merged under the same rubric as Islamism.[1]

Islamic thought in a sense can be seen as "literal/textual Islam." Being textual-based partly involves the literature created by the historical *ulama*, but essentially, it exposes the Qur'an, the books of the tradition, codified sources of *fiqh* and general Islamic literature. The Western references can be added to this list as well. In this respect, the range of Muslim thinkers has a wide variety that cannot be limited to the class of *ulama*. It includes intellectuals, engineers, writers, journalists, and professional politicians, in short, both intellectuals and intelligentsia with its traditional and modern strands.

In this chapter, I will discuss the articulation and differentiation of Islamic thought in Turkey in relation to such ideas as nationalism, conservatism, democracy, liberalism, socialism, and Kemalism, in particular, during the multi-party era in Turkey with special emphasis on the period of its diversification and politicization (1970s to 1990s). This period will receive special emphasis because Islamic thought for the first time in the Republican history became a self-confident, legitimate, and to an important extent, legal partner in the deliberative public space, however delimited its boundaries may be.

It is difficult to delimit the boundaries of Islamic thought compared to other currents of thought because, while the definition of Islamism in the social and political litera-ture could be highly expandable, those who feel themselves as Islamists are very few. It is important to distinguish between Islam and Islamism in that the former cannot be represented by any person, group, or corporate body while the latter is a locus of multiple representation.

The delimitation of the Islamic discourse is required also by the problem of dual legitimacy that this concept embodies. The prevailing understanding of secularism in Turkey equates Islamic thought with reactionarism and sees it as contradictory to the principle of laicity, which has led to the ban on its legal existence. Due to the problem of social as well as political legitimacy over Islamic thought, Muslim thinkers and movements have adopted an indirect language. Accordingly, demands motivated by Islamic sentiments have been expressed around such idioms as human rights, justice, democracy, freedom of religion and conscience, loyalty to the national religious char-acter of Turkish nation, patriotism, and moral and familial values.

The legitimacy problem of Islamic thought arises not only due to the restrictions imposed by the militant secularist Republican establishment but also to the reserva-tions of Muslim thinkers themselves. However it is defined, there is no shared definition of Islamism by all Islamists. Hence, the appellation "Islamism" has been generally used by outsiders. Those known as Islamists prefer to call themselves plainly Muslim. There-fore, in a country populated in a great majority by Muslims, the question of how to dif-ferentiate Islamism assumes importance. S. Sayyid's definition seems to be promising in this regard. According to Sayyid, Islamism is a project in which one as a Muslim posi-tions his relations from within the historical formation and traditions of Islam and renders this for himself as a reference map. Hence, an Islamist is one who acts in accor-dance with a utopia defined by a language that emanates from the texts deemed to be Islamic in their various forms.[2]

The evolution of Islamic thought in Turkey can be thought of in two ways. The first way is a subject-based approach and it argues that Islamism does not denote a fact that emerged and ceased to exist in a historical context. It puts Muslim *ulama*, intellectuals, and intelligentsia as the primary agents and makes a periodization by drawing upon the religious, cultural, and political perceptions of these three agents. Taking into consideration the new risks and opportunities associated with the intellectual, socio-economic, and political environment in which the perceptions of these agents were shaped, there are three periods in terms of the evolution of Islamic thought in Turkey: (i) the period of Islamic thought (1908–50); (ii) the period of the Islamic move-ment (1950–90s); (iii) the period of "pure" Islamic thought which Islam, no longer being considered as a position of power, has been taken to mean an alternative

Weltanschauung on intellectual and ethical grounds in view of the idea of "Western civilization" (post 2000).

The second way of periodizing the evolution of Islamic thought in Turkey is context-based. Bringing together these two approaches, in this study, I will make use of both constructivist and contextualist approaches. I will focus on the intellectual and political background that nourished Muslim thinkers, the sources that illuminated them, their intellectual and activist profiles, as well as the concepts they used, the issues they problemitized and the discussions they triggered.

This chapter will deal with the evolution of Islamic thought in Turkey over five periods, but will combine the first and second ones.[3]

1. The period of accommodation (1870s–1924): This period is characterized by a defensive modernization in order to "save" the Ottoman-Islamic state and preserve Islamic culture.
2. The period of withdrawal (1924–50): This period is marked by withdrawal from public space to the world of inner self against the authoritarian modernization.
3. The period of articulation with modernist rightism (1950s–70).
4. The period of confrontation and challenge (1970s–97): A period in which the Islamic movement as a distinct and independent movement of thought gained a new momentum after the 1979 Iranian Revolution and challenged the supremacy of the Western model in intellectual, moral, and power terms by trying to capture the state and use it as a tool for Islamizing the society.
5. The period of reflexivity and self-critique (post 1997). After the so-called "post-modern coup" of February 28, 1997, Islamic intellectual and urban-dominated discourse entered a new phase of self-questioning by positioning itself willingly to an individual-based Islamic perspective without forgetting the idea of Muslim community, and tried to formulate Islam more in moral and social terms rather than giving primacy to the political, and refrained from open confrontation with the still militant secular state.

Periods 1 and 2. "Accommodation and Withdrawal": Late Ottoman and Early Republican Islamic Thought

Islamism as a movement of thought emerged in the last quarter of the nineteenth century. It sprang from the notion of salvaging the state. Its prescription for salvation was the Islamization of "society" by restoration of state and education. Among the main concepts that Islamists advanced were renewal (*tajdīd*), revival (*iḥyā'*), and reform (*iṣlāḥ*). The determining parameters of the Islamist thought in the late Ottoman period embodied a state-centric perspective, Cartesian thinking, conception of a mechanical universe, the idea of progress, the grasp of modern/Western science as a savior, the sublimation of technological achievements, and as a necessary corollary of all these, the ideal of a heaven on earth.

The embodiment of this line of thinking involved the propositions such as the following: the Muslim world is in a state of disarray and humiliation in military, economic, and political terms. The underlying reasons for this are the intellectual, ethical and spiritual backwardness and decadence. The guilty for these sins is not Islam but tradition, the established institutions, and wrong and mischievous historical understandings and practices due to foreign influences. Interestingly, the regime of sultanate was considered to be among the most important causes of this unacceptable state of decay.

Drawing upon these propositions, Islamist thought of the late Ottoman period offered a return to the Qur'an and the Sunnah by reviving the path of the righteous predecessors (*selef-i salihin*). Essentially, Islamic thought in this period had two pillars: the first pillar prioritized the return to the fundamentals of Islam (Salafism), and the second one grasped Islam in rationalist terms (modernism). The opening of the gate of jurisprudence (*ijtihād*) was considered to be the basic instrument of finding solutions from within the religion to the newly emerged problems. The activation of the spirit of *jihād* as a setback against the Western imperialist expansion was another basic suggestion.[4]

The distinction between real Islam, historical Islam, and ideal Islam, the acceptance of Western supremacy and Muslim backwardness, attributing the roots of Western material progress to Islam, perception of scientific knowledge as value-free and accordingly, the interpretation of the Qur'an in the light of scientific developments, and the Islamization of Western political institutions such as parliament, elections, and popular consent by drawing Islamic parallels to them were the qualifying features of Islamist thought. This eclecticism tried to reconcile Islam and modernity and led to the adoption of a thoroughly apologetic mood and thinking. Therefore, we can say that the contours of Islamic thought in the late Ottoman period, among the leading figures of which were Said Halim Pasha, Mehmet Akif (the writer of the Turkish national anthem), Eşref Edip Fergan, Muhammed Hamdi Yazır and Bediuzzaman Said Nursi,[5] have been shaped in reactive terms marked by the heavy impact of the Ottoman confrontation with the "victorious West." This gave Islamic thought a historical rather than a purely essentialist character.

After the establishment of the Republic, Islamism implied an incomplete struggle of emancipation and became an umbrella for a new struggle of emancipation against the self-colonization Turkey experienced under the Kemalist model. The residuals of the Islamism of the late Ottoman period continued as a well-established spring in Turkish Islamic thought during the Republican period in terms of its main problem of saving the state. Due to this state-centric tendency, Islamic thought in Turkey always hosted Turkish nationalism as a strong component and never assumed an anti-Western/modern character, as some might argue.[6]

The triumph of Western nationalism as the hegemonic ideology in the Republican period pushed Islam out of the public realm. Unlike Ottoman Islamism, the early Republican Islam became a popular "underground" movement rather than a state-led one. The introduction of the printing press and newspapers had not changed the Ottoman literate class, which was under the supervision of the state in its production of thought into intelligentsia, a group that is normally relatively independent in its thinking and intellectual productions. Because both the state and Islamists had the same ideals, this state of affairs did not constitute a problem in the evolution of Turkish Islamic thought. In the Republican period, however, the interpretation of Islam was under the control of the state and assumed an authoritarian character. Both the Directorate of Religious Affairs and the higher institutes of Islam contributed to the supervision of the religion by the state rather than the creation of independent Islamic thinking, which may feed the Muslim community in an organic fashion.

During the single-party period (1924–46), the tradition of Islamic thought experienced a radical interruption. Only when the transition to multi-party democracy took place, could Islamic thought take a fresh breath and begin openly to question the absolutes of the Kemalist Westernism. The single-party period of militant state secularism can be considered a period of interregnum (*fetret*) in terms of the production of Islamic thought. Islamism in this period was not a legitimate partner in formulating public policies. Rather, it was portrayed as the main enemy of the state and the source of backwardness, called in official militant secularism as *irtica* (reactionarism). During the setting up of the new Republican regime, Islamism was in opposition to the ruling ideology that continued to express its "outrage" towards militantly anti-Islamic state policies. When Turkey decided to join the "democratic camp" formed after World War Two, there was a deeply felt confrontation between Islamism and Kemalist states. This change determined the contours of the political game in the following periods.

Period 3. The Rebirth of Islamic Thought as a Rightist-Nationalist Movement (1950–1970)

With the transition to multi-party politics, the Republican People's Party (RPP), then in power, began to react to the societal opposition from the Democrat Party (DP) that adopted a political language reinforced by religion, and hence tried to soften its stance *vis-à-vis* Islam. This state of affairs created a relatively tolerant atmosphere for the recovery of religious thought. The DP authored such symbolic revolutionary acts as the Arabic call to prayer (*azan*) and compulsory religion classes in schools. Yet the DP was deeply committed to the secularist understanding of the Republic and therefore had no intention of creating a political order based on solely religious credentials. The DP was tolerant towards individuals, and to a certain extent, societal Islam, but heavily against political Islam. It allowed for a liberalized social milieu for Islam as a living space without sacrificing Kemalism, however.[7]

The political opposition gained its visibility in this period thanks to its emphasis on the RPP's repressive policies over religious life and maintained its existence via appeal to religious motives. Nonetheless, the realm of state was under the strict control of the Kemalist ruling elite, and it was this elite that had the monopoly of the final say over the political game. The Muslim masses began to rediscover politics in this relatively "free" period and made its reappearance from the terrain that it had been forcefully imprisoned. Islamic demands were basically centered around the expectation to live according to Islam in the private realm. Accordingly, for the religious groups that emerged under the title of *cemaat*, the most crucial issue was the capability to have access to religious education and the study of the Qur'an, the traditions of the Prophet, *ilm* u hal (catechism), and Nursi's *Risale*. Gradually the demands of these groups began to encompass the social realm in the form of having access to public religious education, Qur'an courses and the increasing number of schools for preachers and prayer leaders (İmam-Hatip Okulları).

The basic feature of Islam in the 1950s is nationalist conservatism.[8] Its political discourse reflects a sense of victimization by Kemalist policies of self-colonization. Until the beginning of the 1970s, Islamic thought and activism were led by such figures as Bediuzzaman Said Nursi, Süleyman Hilmi Tunahan, Necip Fazıl Kısakürek, and Hüseyin Hilmi Işık. The common denominator of all was the importance attached to a religious understanding of the world based on national and spiritual values.

The background of Islamic thought in this period was shaped not by the legacy of late Ottoman Islamic thought but by an updated idea of revising the Republican revolution, which would characterize the political Islam of the 1980s. Deployed within a nation-state framework, this revisionism could easily be translated to a form of religious nationalism because Islamism has evolved as a liberationist/salvationist ideology. Conservative thought and political discourse, which formed the backbone of all rightist discourses and policies including Islamism, offered an alternative national identity based on religious identity. This led the national identity to assume a religious coloring while reinforcing the allegiance of religious groups to the national state.[9] This in turn made centrist right, ultra-nationalism, and religious conservatism allies for a certain period of time.

During the 1960s, Islamic thought discovered the Muslim thought at large via the intensive efforts of translation from such leading Islamist figures as Mawdūdī in Pakistan and Sayyid Quṭb in Egypt. Thanks to gaining access to "global" currents of Islamic thought, Turkish Islamic thought became more universally oriented despite its inward-oriented nationalist-local leanings. Democracy was imported into the Islamic vocabulary in this decade following the new, relatively pluralist and open public sphere partly created by the 1960 constitution. Democracy was politically instrumental in opposing single-party rule and therefore had an additional legitimacy in the Turkish Islamic thought from the 1960s on. One of the most conservative and radically Islamist periodicals republished in the 1950s was Eşref Edip's *Sebilürreşad*. Yet "democracy" and "freedom" were its two principal references. This conception of democracy reflected an instrumentality structured around the idea of democracy as a channel suitable for incorporating the will of the religious masses into the public sphere. Unlike the Muslim countries with a colonial past, Islamic discourse in Turkey has always had a democratic reference.

Period 4. Diversification and Over-politicization of Islamic Thought (1970s–1990s)

The 1970s witnessed the crystallization of a distinct Islamic identity differentiated from the leftist and rightist varieties under the impact of an *ummah*-based perspective triggered by the translated Islamic literature and catalyzed by the Kurdish Islamists. This was not so much an intellectual as it was a political differentiation. The Islamic movements in Egypt, Pakistan, and later, Iran and the works of Ḥassan Banna, Sayyid Quṭb, Mawdūdī, and Ali Shariati were particularly influential in shaping Turkish Islamic thought towards a more universal conception of Islam, and thus the understanding that Islam is not something limited to personal life but also has public claims, took root in the Turkish form of Islamism.

Towards the end of the 1970s, the Islamization of state institutions and the idea of the Muslim world as the horizon of Turkish Islamism, translated into politics in the motto of the "Muslim common market" by the National Salvation Party (NSP). The ideology of the NSP (National Outlook) was based on the equation of nation and religion. With Islam becoming a public actor, the NSP played an important role in shifting Islamism from a nationalist-conservative creed towards a transnational perspective. This Muslim world-oriented perspective which perceived the Western world as alien at the least and as enemy at the most had an effect on religious groups in later years as well. The so-called Islamic Revolution in Iran carried this understanding further. This transnational conception of Islamic *ummah* gained further momentum with the end of the Cold War in the hands of religious groups.

With the decline of the line that grasped Islam first and foremost as a political reference, the transnational Turkish Muslim mind adopted a global imagination that made possible the interaction with Western values and institutions, namely basic rights and liberties, economic and political liberalization, democratization and civil initiatives with simultaneous rupture from traditional understanding. One may say that the waves of globalization deeply affected Muslim thought in Turkey.

The 1980s witnessed internal differentiation among Muslim groups, and their legal and intellectual legitimacy in partaking in public debates. In this respect, the post-1980 period is a most dynamic, vivid and intellectually colorful period. The parameters of the public debate were set by such concepts as civil society, liberalism, human rights, and participatory democracy. The focus of this debate was the criticism of the official ideology, the recognition of other and peaceful coexistence, to which the notion of a democratically constructed societal contract was basic. It was claimed that the state-civil society pattern of relation in Turkey lacked legitimacy in that its constitution was not the outcome of a societal contract but rather reflected an authoritarian, "from above" imposition. The idea of a plural society based on multiplicity of law and the so-called Medina document were the models advanced by some Muslim intellectuals.

The intellectual efforts led by a renowned Muslim intellectual Ali Bulaç to develop an Islamic conception of a plural society based on different groupings of law were the overt manifestation of the postmodern wave. The construction of such Western ideals as pluralism, rule of law, and fundamental rights and liberties under an Islamic guise via reconstruction of historical Islamic institutions and practices expressed the Islamization of the values of "the positive West." As Muslim intellectuals began to comprehend better the different modalities of modernity and epistemological paradigms, the image of the West gained a more positive recognition.

This was the moment of intersection between postmodernism and Islamism, common to both of which was the criticism of the prevailing Western mode of modernity.[10] Unlike the intellectual representatives of traditional Muslim groups, independent Muslim intellectuals completely divorced themselves from nationalist rightism and gained inspiration from more universal sources. The arrival of post-modernism in Turkey before globalization provided the opportunity to critique the modernist mono- poly over the public sphere. The fact that Muslim intellectuals had a legitimate say in the public sphere did not mean that they all espoused the same theses and took the same positions. As a matter of fact, they had radically contrasting strands. For example, the works of İsmet Özel, a leading Muslim intellectual and poet, suggested rejection of modern science, and especially, technology towards the end of the 1970s on the grounds that it caused alienation in the Muslim conscious. Ironically, Özel was a pro- ponent of Islamic political hegemony and therefore was a strong supporter of the parties of the National Outlook movement, which were heavily developmentalist in technological terms.

The post-modernist impact on the Turkish Muslim intellect in political terms, however, can be seen in two early figures: Ali Bulaç and Bahri Zengin. The post- modernist and pluralist model of Ali Bulaç was introduced with reference to the con- tract made by the Muslim Prophet and the Jews of Medina after Hijrah. The first part of this contract regulated the relations between the Ansar and Muhajiroun. The second part involved the relations between Muslims and Jews in Medina and set a treaty of non- aggression between them, while making them ally with each other against the attacks of third parties. Muslims, though in the minority, were the founding party and the Muslim Prophet was appointed as the arbitrator. The intention was to show that Islamic historical experience was not alien to the notion of pluralism, which would imply that Islam cannot claim to be an intrinsically authoritarian theocracy. It was possible to develop an Islamic political model based on civil liberties and recognition of basic human rights.[11]

The reinterpretation of the Medina Treaty so as to secure a firm ground for an Islamic pluralist and participatory model of politics was in fact an obvious example of the post-modern perspective. The end of the positivist myth of modern science as the only form of truth, the loss of faith in the notion of linear progress, the failure of Marxism, the awkward need for social cohesion deepened by the so-called wild capi- talism of Turgut Özal's neo-liberal policies and Kemalist militancy of modernism all made the notion of "Adil Düzen" (Just Order) advanced by the Welfare Party very popular and paved the way for the politics of multi-culturalism and identity. This also made possible the reconstruction of traditional patterns of communal life. The carriers of this line of thought were followed by masses uprooted from villages and towns, and hence newcomers to the cities. They were socialized in the secular institu- tions and had no classical Islamic education. Their references were mainly Western rather than Islamic. The use of Western intellectual tools to critique the West became a common practice.

The model of the Medina Treaty as a search for a pluralistic society represents the culmination of Turkish Islamic thought in the 1980s and 1990s. The conception of society as a project through an Islamic content wrapped in Western political discourse points to an unresolved dilemma in Turkish Muslim thought. A second element in this public debate was a project based on the conception of multiple-law polity. Led by such adherents of the National Outlook as Bahri Zengin and Abdurrahman Dilipak, this project was in a sense an adaptation of the early Islamic practice or rather the Ottoman millet system. The objective in such social prescriptions was to carve out pockets of social space for Muslims in Turkey so that they live according to their religious affiliation based on consent and pluralism.[12]

The same leitmotif was sustained through the Welfare Party's motto of "Just Order". This political campaign was aimed at the rehabilitation of the Turkish political system based on the welfare state model instead of a radical transformation. All three projects – the model of Medina, a multi-law polity, and Just Order – were sympathetic imitations of a plural conception of polity justified by reference to certain Islamic practices. But they all missed a principal point that in modern times there is individual existence which in no way can be reduced to or absorbed into any communal affiliation, and that modern society by definition is characterized by cross-cutting identifications which makes the assumption of an homogeneous, non-conflictual communal existence nearly impossible.

Apart from Muslim intellectuals, the expression of Islamic thought at the level of religious groups involving sufi and non-sufi groupings delineated a more pragmatic approach and basically tried to create and protect a proper environment in order to make most use of "opportunity spaces," which would enable them to carve a strong foothold for peaceful existence.[13] Their understanding is in line with a secular democracy that recognizes Islam as a legitimate and peaceful element and allows Muslim groups to teach, propagate, and live in accordance with their faith. For these groups Islam is first personal, second social, and last political. Therefore, politicization of Islam is not a must and does not have any precedence over personal and societal levels. This line of thinking urges dialogue between faiths and civilizations traditionally conceived to be antagonistic. Most of these groups, the most prominent of them being the Gülen movement of Nurcu splinter,[14] therefore do not have any ideological reservation towards Turkey's accession to the European Union. This opportunistic approach has a cost as well: the internal secularization. Such groups suffer from a group-based oligarchy crystallized around the leader cult, which relegates individuality to non-importance.

The last brand of Islamic thought is represented by highly marginal yet vocally influential radical factions. One of their leading figures is Ercümend Özkan. He calls for overthrow of the established regime, by any means necessary. This reactionary rejectionism is a modern form of Hariji–Salafi comprehension and it has no historical mainstream Islamic basis. This radical and dogmatic posture not only rejects the established political regime, but also targets Muslim groups who prefer to maintain good relations with society at large. Despite its vocality, this line of Islamic thought in present-day Turkey has lost all its credibility and therefore is no longer an actor worthy of consideration here.

The major actors in the emergence of a distinct Islamic political identity are parties of the National Outlook movement led by Necmettin Erbakan, an overt manifestation of intransitivity between Islamism and nationalism. National Outlook is a generic term expressing the specific tradition that has produced various political parties with religiously informed political agendas in Turkey. Erbakan considered parties of the National Outlook, especially the National Salvation Party (NSP) and the Welfare Party (WP), as the political extension of the Turkish-led "global Muslim community" (ummah).[15] Those parties represent an endeavor for reconciliation of traditional Islam and modernism at the political level. In this regard, the WP's understanding of religion is based not on a "fundamentalist" reading of Islamic history but on pragmatic discourse of an epic, heroic past. The articulation of that heritage with modernism confined to scientific and technological developments and in this context the belief that the religion is the leitmotif of "development and progress", a Muslim version of the Weberian idea, was the schematic framework on which the WP's discourse of religion was established.

The intellectual sources and material connections of Erbakan and his friends molded their minds into an interesting synthesis of traditional Sunni-based Islamic culture and Sufi worldview embedded in a developmentalist discourse. The heroic conception of history by the National Outlook, the adoration of the glorious past, and the expression of the road leading to the solution for the present-day problems through an heroic imagination of the past under the motto of "a great Turkey once again," are evident reflections of a growth-oriented developmentalist perspective structured around a territorially grounded Islamic nationalism. The National Outlook vigorously advance the idea that the dependent and powerless position of the Muslim world at large and Turkey in particular was associated with the dominance of global Western imperialism, which makes anti-Westernism an integral part of that discourse.

The main question of the National Outlook is a continuation of the intellectual agenda of the nineteenth-century Islamists with the predicament "Islam versus the West." The dilemma was to find an explanation for the rising fortune of the West in view of the continuously declining power of the Ottoman Empire, or more properly the Muslim world. The Islamic *Weltanschauung* was imperative to meet the overall Western challenge. What Necmettin Erbakan called "Millî Görüş" (the National Outlook) was nothing but this according to him. Islam and nation were conflated in the double meaning of *millî* in Turkish i.e. religious or national, the implication of which was determined by the intent of the user.

The ideological core of the National Outlook is a combination of a traditionalist discourse and a "modern," defensive, positivist conception of the so-called Western science and technology. This science and technology is readily welcomed through its naturalization by reference to its Islamic roots. The Turkish nation is believed to have undergone a deep moral degeneration due to the emulation of the Western way of life, which was also responsible for the breakdown of the Ottoman "eternal" order. Therefore, regaining the historical grandeur depends on both material and spiritual development.

With its populist and pragmatic politics, National Outlook has become an eclectic ideological program with its articulation in the 1990s of "Just Order" discourse. Drawing upon such Islamic injunctions as social solidarity and absence of interest (*riba*), the Just Order appeal was a critic of capitalism at macro level. Like other propositions of the National Outlook, it was based on the interpretation of Islam as preached by Erbakan and his close associates, yet not justified on the basis of Islam. Taking their legitimacy from Islam and their legality from the established political regime, the parties of the National Outlook, in that capacity, have given birth to a double discourse producing irresolvable inner contradictions. Yet, what is claimed is that its core formulation is capable of providing what Turkey needs, independent of time and place, and thus it is not amenable to change in accordance with changing circumstances, because the National Outlook does have axiomatic certitude. The categorical rejection of ideological change is closely related with the connection, even identification, of the National Outlook with Islam itself. Ironically enough, the impact of the post-modernist political wave on the Muslims did not result in a change in the political posture of the National Outlook. It preserved its classical "axiomatic" purity against such political contagion by perpetuating a positivist conception of development based on Islamic nationalism, the main bastions of which were material as well as spiritual growth, heavy industry and in particular the national defense industry. In the last analysis, one can readily suggest that the National Outlook was not intended for clearing the account of Islam with modernity; rather it was a political movement whose main motto could probably be that "it is we who can create a better modernity."[16]

After the mid-1980s, the public visibility of Islam drastically increased. While its social manifestations remained local, intellectually it became more universal, i.e. more interested in the problems of the Muslim communities as a whole. This distinction corresponds to a socially more traditional and intellectually more literate Islamism. This widening angle between social and intellectual spaces became a graphic feature of Islamism in these years. In this respect, political Islamism is a movement of forming and protecting the balance between the social and intellectual with a view to reinforce religion. Therefore, the Islamization policies pursued by the state in this decade, the transfer of the important figures of Turkish nationalism to Islamism following a period of questioning the meaning of such concepts as state and nation, and the increasing primacy of the Kurdish question were functional in the universalization tendency of Islamism. Yet, in the last analysis, nationalism continues to be the final determinant in Turkish Islamism.

Period 4. Post-1997: Reflexivity and Questioning the "Self" and "Other"

In the late 1990s, political demands were preceded by civil and societal ones. The early years of the 1990s, however, were the years that Islamists realized the importance of politics and political participation. This realization was accompanied by a questioning process as to where the state stands in the route to establish an "Islamic state." The nature and function of the link between the realization of Islamic ideals and the modern state as the principal instrument of those ideals were brought to the intellectual agenda.

In February 28, 1997 a military coup took place in Turkey. Kemalist military forced the then Prime Minister Erbakan to resign together with other members of the cabinet. The official Islamization policies imposed by the military after the 1980 coup had enhanced the Islamic social movements and contributed to the formation of demands for the political public space to be regulated Islamically. In the process, Islamic movements reached the capacity to create an alternative public space and gained an immense power of political mobilization. In the 1994 local general elections, an openly Islamist party, the Welfare Party, for the first time in the Republican history won over its secular rivals and became the first such party to be elected. In the 1995 national elections, it again registered a great victory and became the major partner of the following coalition government. This was the beginning of a naked confrontation between Islamism and the civil–military Kemalist secularist establishment. The soft coup that occurred in the form of a declaration of the National Security Council under the heavy pressure of the military wing instructed the ruling coalition headed by the leader of the Islamist Welfare Party, Necmettin Erbakan, to implement 18 directives that represented a counter move against Islamization policies initiated by the military after the 1980 coup. These directives epitomized a crude positivist intellect to reengineer the whole social and political realms and viewed the political Islam as the number one enemy of public order. The coup of February created a crisis of self-confidence for the Islamist movements, relegated the Islamic visibility once again towards the private realm, and led to a reflexive thinking among Muslim intellectuals as well as movements with a view of political empathy founded upon the notion of defining first the Islamic self and then its other accordingly.

In this asymmetrical confrontation between Islamism and the Kemalist establishment, Islamism was left alone by its traditional allies, i.e. nationalist and conservative groups. The iron curtain used for containing Islamism turned out to be very tough. Despite this, Islamism neither intellectually nor ideologically wanted voluntarily to concede to the so-called "laicist" dictat. February 28 became a touchstone that revealed the conjunctural nature of the relation between Islamism and rightist conservatism. Rightist conservatism divorced itself thoroughly from Islamism in order not to be identified with it and hence to have a separate life of its own, a position that politically proved to be very costly. Ironically, this divorce, unlike the prior pattern of relation that gave rightism a superior hand *vis-à-vis* Islamism, produced a new conservatism characterized by Islamic dominance represented by the Justice and Development Party (Adalet ve Kalkınma Partisi) known in Turkish as the AKP, which became the ruling party after the November 3, 2002 elections.

The AKP is a party that rejects political Islamism as its ideological backbone yet is inspired by it, especially in its understanding of morality, which found its manifestation in the appellation that the party elite saw as appropriate for their ideological program: "conservative democracy".[17] Inspired by Özal's policies of free market and political liberalism, the AKP severed its ties with political Islamism and defined a new role for Islam that narrowed its political manifestations. In order to widen the spaces of public liberties that shackle the larger Islamic interests, the AKP showed great enthusiasm and diplomatic effort in securing Turkey's accession to the European Union, a unique political determinant that is capable of pushing for change in the military structured Turkish polity. Thus the AKP, in its all features, is a concise expression of "rationalized" Islam in the political framework set by the coup of February that gives prime importance to ascribing to religion a non-political role.

During the post-February 28 process, Islamists clearly learned the hard lesson that democracy as the frame of a political game is not something to play with. On the contrary, it is vital if Islamists are to have a proper legitimate place in the public realm in their confrontation with the secularist establishment. In this way, we may expect traditional Islamism to interact with modernity within a deliberative plane on the one hand, and differentiation and individualization among Muslim groups on the other. All this may lead Islamists to adopt democratic politics as a *sine qua non*, and not just a bastion for pragmatic, self-centered bargaining. Naturally, the internalization of democracy by Islamists on theoretical as well as practical grounds is necessary but

not sufficient for the emergence of a democratic landscape in Turkey. The democratization of the general political context, particularly the rejection of the militarist understanding of laicism, is also a must.

The securitization of everything that carries an Islamic overtone after 9/11 and the
grasp of Islam and Muslims in exclusively real politics terms increased the cohesion
around the idea of *ummah* among religious Muslims and further deepened the feeling
of victimization by "the West" that led to a universal mood of resistance against forced
Westernization along political lines. All this has contributed to the local Islamic groups'
will to leave aside their parochial glasses and become partners of a universal anti-
Western mobilization. This repoliticization brought about by globalization may cause
the narrowing of the intellectual space in the Muslim plane.[18]

By Way of Conclusion

Islamic thought in the late Ottoman and early Republican years until the 1950s has
some principal differences from the strands of Islamic thought that prevailed during
the post-1950 multi-party politics through the 1990s. While pre-1950 Islamism was
a state-centered reform movement, the latter had a positioning distant from, even
against the state. The former placed relatively more emphasis on an intellectual plane
vis-à-vis the political one. The latter as a movement on the political periphery/opposi-
tion had a stronger socioeconomic and political component but a relatively weak intellectual aspect. It was believed that a strong intellectual formation would come into
existence after the attainment of political power. The leadership profile of the former
was composed of *ulama*, intellectual *ulama* or an elitist group who had undergone a traditional or modern education and therefore its connection with the historical scientific
and intellectual legacy of Islam was quite strong. The leadership profile of the latter, on
the other hand, was composed of intellectuals and intelligentsia involving engineers,
lawyers, writers, journalists, and professional politicians with a Western-style education. Therefore, its link with the historical legacy of Islam has been very weak. While
the former adopted a fundamentalist/Salafi attitude towards tradition, it preserved its
ties despite its embrace of what is modern. The latter carried this reaction to the edge
and condemned, in some occasions, tradition, as exemplified in the 1990s by Yaşar Nuri
Öztürk, a modernist theologian and charismatic preacher, under the motto of "the
Qur'anic Islam."

We can trace the history of Islamism in the Muslim lands including Turkey back
more than a century, but the intellectual dimension of this movement is relatively
recent. Islamic thought and movements carrying out a struggle for power under a distinct perspective of man and society with their own references that distance them from
other political movements became independent and distinct only after the end of
1960s. Until that time, Islamism remained in a defensive and apologetic position
against the instigation of Western modernism, and therefore sought alliance with
rightist, modernist political movements especially in the case of Turkey. The most
important reason for this is that Islamic thought rejected all kinds of leftist suggestions
on the implicit assumption that leftism is nothing more than mere atheism. During the

period that can be called pre-Islamism (1920s to 1970s), communism in Turkey represented the core content of secularism. Therefore, we cannot see a serious product of Islamic thought in this period, with the exception of Said Nursi's writings, *Risale-i Nur*, which reintroduced a core Islamic worldview in a militantly anti-Islamic *milieu* where Muslim masses were in desperate need of basic Islamic idioms. Pre-Islamism embodied the reaction and a survival strategy for the religious elite. Against the Kemalist modernization project, which removed religion as a frame of reference, they sought protection in exchange for anti-communism. In this way pre-Islamism could cling to a point of compromise between Kemalism and rightist modernism.

The post-1970s witnessed the emergence of Islamism as a distinct political identity and its divorce from other "kin" currents of thought and movements. Islamic thought emerged as a powerful self-reflection of national problems with an increasing tendency to widen its horizons on a transnational plane. With the ideological vacuum created by the sweep of the socialist left in the 1980s, Islamic thought gained precedence over other currents of thought and became one of the main channels for manifesting the Kurdish grievances. On practical grounds, it contributed to the emergence of a sociopolitical context that carried the Welfare Party (WP) into power and became influential in the determination of the idioms of its political discourse.

The mispoliticization of Islam during the 1990s, however, was an important element in the dethroning of the WP from power and the following regime of cleansing Islam from the public sphere. These anti-Islamic policies came to a halt with the 2002 national elections. The Justice and Development Party with its Islamically sensitive political liberalism came to power and a new era began that reflected a novel experience for Islam–democracy reconciliation.

In the new millennium, an Islamic understanding of putting the individual at the center and attaching importance to pluralism has come to the fore. The increasing urbanization of Turkey, the expansion of horizon brought about by globalization, the self-confidence inspired by postmodern perspectives that put an end to the conception holding the Western modernity as the only grand narrative of the truth, has radically influenced the Islamist way of reading the secular and sacred. According to Bulaç, individual preferences, new Islamic formations that are more voluntaristic and less organically moved, an open public space and a consciousness that has a religious perspective on life as a product of the Islamization process from below, are the leading features of this period. And they decrease the emphasis on political centralism and state-centric salvationist mood. Though there is a change with millennium Islamism, this does not mean a radical rupture from the preceding patterns of Islamism.[19]

The focus of Turkish Islamism is not the establishment of a social and political order regulated by Islamic principles, but an Islamism aimed at the creation of conditions that would make the daily and institutional practice of Islam possible through forcing the state and other forces into negotiation and a more just and equal distribution of resources in Turkey. In this sense, solidarity with other Muslim countries and groups has not been given prime importance though it incorporated such themes as Islamic unity, religious brotherhood, commonality of being oppressed by capitalism, and Zionism into its political discourse. Therefore the leitmotif of the *ummah* is not a constituent of Islamic thinking and discourse.[20] The Marxist-turned Islamist poet and thinker İsmet Özel's strong emphasis on Turkishness, despite his claim of equality between Turkishness and Islam, is a symbolically important indication of this inward-oriented, nationalistic consciousness that impedes any internalized transnational Islamic horizon in the form of essential allegiance to the *ummah*.

There are two crucial questions in the evolution of Turkish Islamic thought during the Republican period. The first is the relation of Islamism with the Republican ideology, Kemalism, and the second, representations of Islamism. The first question allows us to better understand the evolution of Islamic thought in Turkey and the infiltration of Western ideas of democracy, secularism, and modernity into Islamic discourse and their instrumentalization. The second question may help us to comprehend the standing of Muslim intellectuals. Actors of Islamic thinking consist not only of intellectuals but also of a variety of intelligentsia including bureaucrats, preachers, doctors, engineers, and teachers, which yield to the emergence of miscellaneous representations of Islam that is essentially non-academic. This state of affairs has partly changed during the 1990s with the contributions of academics advancing an interpretation based on a literate understanding and hermeneutics approach. This contribution, however, is focused on the internal transformation of religious thought rather than its relation to the public space. The various representations of Islamism around Islamic brotherhoods, foundations, associations, journals, and magazines are aggregated and articulated by Muslim intellectuals. This mediation is crucial in transmitting Islamic thinking, values and practices into wider society in the form of meaningful and intellectually acceptable translations. Separate from all Islamic representations in organic terms, Turkish Muslim intellectuals are in a position to explicate the dilemmas of the Islamic thought by going back and forth between the social and the intellectual.[21]

The transformation of "Islamic intellectual" into "Muslim intellectual" in the post-millennium period is an evident indication of the pluralization in Islamic identity marked by a "civic" Islamic consciousness. Islam as a religion and Islamism as dynamic/historical interpretations of Islam will continue their evolution. In present-day Turkey, Islamic thinking has a fractured and differentiated nature. It embodies a widening spectrum of discussion spaces. Therefore, we cannot mention "Islamic thought or identity" in singular terms. What we have arguably is a plurality of Islamic thinking and identity.

Notes

1. Ahmet Aksu, "Türkiye'de İslami Hareketin Gelişim Süreci," *Dünya ve İslam*, 3, 1990, 101–3.
2. Cited by Yasin Aktay, "Sunuş," in *Modern Türkiye'de Siyasi Düşünce: İslamcılık*, vol. 6 (Istanbul: İletişim, 2004), 18.
3. In this periodization, I have drawn upon Ferhat Kentel's description of the history of Islamic thought in Turkey. See Ferhat Kentel, "1990'ların İslami Düşünce Dergileri ve Yeni Müslüman Entelektüeller," in *Modern Türkiye'de Siyasi Düşünce: İslamcılık*, vol. 6 (Istanbul: İletişim, 2004), 722–3.
4. İsmail Kara, *Türkiye'de İslamcılık Düşüncesi, Metinler/Kişiler I*, 3rd edn. (Istanbul: Kitabevi, 1997), 15–66.

5. Nursi in his later writings during the early Republican period overtly criticizes his stance in the period concerned and states that his basic mistake was to take the propositions of the modern science as value free and absolutely true, and hence judging the Qur'anic injunctions accordingly. See Bediuzzaman Said Nursi, *Mektubat* (Istanbul: Yeni Asya Neşriyat, 1994), 426–7. For Nursi's thought, one of best sources is Şerif Mardin, *Religion and Social Change in Modern Turkey: The Case of Bediüzzaman Said Nursi* (Albany: State University of New York Press, 1989).

6. Nuray Mert, "Türkiye İslamcılığına Tarihsel Bir Bakış," in *Modern Türkiye'de Siyasi Düşünce/İslamcılık*, vol. 6 (Istanbul: İletişim Yayınları, 2004), 412–13.

7. Doğan Duman, *Demokrasi Sürecinde Türkiye'de İslamcılık* (Izmir: Dokuz Eylül Yayıncılık, 1997), 34–46,

8. Tanıl Bora, *Türk Sağının Üç Hal: Milliyetçilik, Muhafazakarlık, İslamcılık* (Istanbul: Birikim, 1998).

9. Mert, "Türkiye İslamcılığına Tarihsel Bir Bakış," 414.

10. Mücahit Bilici, "Küreselleşme ve Postmodernizmin İslamcılık Üzerindeki Etkileri," in *Modern Türkiye'de Siyasi Düşünce/İslamcılık*, vol. 6 (Istanbul: İletişim Yayınları, 2004), 799–803.

11. For Bulaç's views, see Ali Bulaç, "Birarada Yaşamanın Mümkün Projesi: Medine Vesikası," *Bilgi ve Hikmet*, 5, 1994; see also Ali Bulaç, *Din, Devlet ve Demokrasi* (Istanbul: Zaman Kitap, 2001).

12. This project was used as a pretext by the Turkish Constitutional Court in 1998 when it took the decision to close down the then party of the National Outlook movement, the Welfare Party.

13. For a competent evaluation of the evolution of Islamic *cemaats* in Turkey in terms of the perspective of "opportunity spaces" see Hakan Yavuz, *Islamic Political Identity in Turkey* (New York: Oxford University Press, 2003).

14. For the Gülen movement, see M. Hakan Yavuz and John L. Esposito (eds.), *Turkish Islam and the Secular State: The Gulen Movement* (New York: Syracuse University Pres, 2003).

15. For the National Outlook movement see Necmettin Erbakan, *Milli Görüş* (*National Outlook*) (Istanbul: Dergah Yayınları, 1975).

16. For the articulation of politics in Islamist terms as understood by the National Outlook perspective, see Ahmet Yıldız, "Politico-Religious Discourse of Political Islam in Turkey: The Parties of National Outlook," *Muslim World*, 93/2, 2003, 187–210.

17. Yalçın Akdoğan, *Muhafazakar Demokrasi* (Ankara: AK Parti Yayınları, 2003).

18. Ahmet Çiğdem, "İslamcılık ve Türkiye Üzerine Bazı Notlar," in *Modern Türkiye'de Siyasi Düşünce: İslamcılık*, 27. See also his *Taşra Epiği: Türk İdeolojileri ve İslamcılık* (Istanbul: Birikim Yayınları, 2001), 127–43.

19. Ali Bulaç, "İslamın Üç Siyaset Tarzı veya İslamcılığın Üç Nesli," in *Modern Türkiye'de Siyasi Düşünce: İslamcılık*, 49–50.

20. Çiğdem, "İslamcılık ve Türkiye Üzerine Bazı Notlar," 26–7.

21. Ibid.

CHAPTER 3

Bediuzzaman Said Nursi's Approach to Religious Renewal and its Impact on Aspects of Contemporary Turkish Society

Şükran Vahide

Bediuzzaman Said Nursi (1877–1960) was distinguished from other religious leaders in the Islamic world in recent times by his seeking to reverse its decline *vis-à-vis* the West not through political struggle or the establishment of the Islamic state or other means, but through the revitalization of faith or belief (*imān*). He identified the gravest danger to "the edifice of Islam" as coming from the decay of its intellectual underpinning, which had been weakened over the centuries by currents of alien thought and was then facing renewed threats in the form of materialist philosophy and modernity, which he expressed in terms of "philosophy"[1] and "modern civilization." The greatest danger these posed was to the faith of the mass of believers. Hence in Nursi's view, the restatement of the basic tenets of the Islamic religion, and "the renewing and strengthening of belief" through new methods, were of paramount importance and took precedence over every other form of struggle aimed at reconstruction.

To reorient believers towards their Maker and instill in them a Qur'anic worldview in the way Nursi envisaged would also render them capable of coping with the intellectual and ethical challenges of the rapid secularization and Westernization that took place in Turkey following the founding of the Republic in 1923. Such building of morally strong believers would lead inevitably to the strengthening and consolidation of society, which he felt was threatened with dissolution due to the displacement of Islam. Although Nursi's writings, known collectively as the *Risale-i Nur*, uncompromisingly expound the fundamentals of belief while refuting the bases of materialist philosophy, the method of serving religion that he developed has, since 1950, for the most part been implemented successfully within Turkey's secular system. The *Risale-i Nur* has continued to be popular among succeeding generations, despite the changes wrought by the ongoing secularization process, just as it was taken up enthusiastically in the early years of the Republic by sections of the Anatolian populace raised in Ottoman times. With its many bifurcations and offshoots, the movement that grew up around the *Risale-i Nur* (the Nur community or movement) continues to be one of the largest religious movements in Turkey, making it a significant social and political force within the country.[2] It is also active in a number of other countries worldwide.

This chapter will examine two areas of Nursi's thought that are directed towards religious renewal and that have had an impact on various aspects of Turkish society. These are firstly his ideas related to the revitalization of belief and moral renewal; and secondly, his ideas concerning the character and functions of the Nur movement, and its mode of struggle in a secular society. The two areas are interrelated. The latter will include discussion of Nursi's attitude towards political struggle in the cause of religion, as well as throwing light on his understanding of secularism.

It will assist in explaining the impact and continued relevance of Nursi's thought if we look briefly at his aims and endeavors in the early period of his life during the final decades of the Ottoman Empire. For although he himself divided his life into two distinct periods, which he called the Old and New Said, and there were fundamental changes in his stand towards a number of matters, this early period has a direct bearing on the matters discussed in this chapter, particularly in respect of his stated goals in life and his acquaintance with the currents of European thought that became progressively influential in Turkey.

From his earliest youth, Bediuzzaman Said Nursi[3] was possessed with the desire to restore Islam to its rightful position as "master of the sciences" and fount of knowledge, for it was the source of "true" civilization and human progress. To this end he dedicated himself to the reform and updating of madrasah education in his native eastern Anatolia, and of the disciplines taught therein. His particular concern was firstly with *'ilm al-kalām* (theology), as the main means of intellectual defense against the attacks of rationalistic skepticism, and secondly, with *tafsīr* (Qur'anic exegesis), as the means of explicating Islam's principal beliefs. Nursi's conventional education was minimal, but through his own exertions he obtained a firm grounding in both the traditional madrasah sciences, and, uniquely among members of the learned profession in the East at that time, in the modern physical and mathematical sciences. Fundamental to his projects for the restructuring of education was the reintroduction of the latter and their combined teaching with the religious sciences:

> The religious sciences are the light of the conscience; the sciences of civilization are the light of the intellect. The truth is made manifest through the combining of the two. The students' aspirations will take flight with those two wings. When they are separated, it gives rise to bigotry in the one, and wiliness and skepticism in the other.[4]

Prompted by explicit outside threats, around the turn of the century Nursi took the decision to focus his attention on the Qur'an itself. We are told that all the sciences he had learnt became "steps to understanding it." However, according to his own account, the pressing social and political questions of the day diverted him, and it was only later that he addressed himself to it seriously.

Nursi became involved in the struggle for constitutional government, and for three or four years after the Constitutional Revolution of 1908 worked for its acceptance, especially among his fellow-countrymen of the Eastern Provinces. During these years, which he spent partly in Istanbul publicizing the problems of the East and trying to win support for his projects, he witnessed at first hand the debates that raged around current issues.[5] The initially few, but active, proponents of materialism and positivism contributed to the debate. Nursi did not take part in these polemics, but in his works of the period he replied to some of the materialists' assertions, in order to dispel the doubts they had raised about aspects of the Qur'an and matters of belief. He thus became closely acquainted both with the liberal ideas of constitutionalism, some of which he himself adopted, and with positivism and other philosophical currents whose advocates in Turkey were challenging Islam in the name of science.

Following World War One and Ottoman defeat, Nursi suffered a spiritual crisis, and after a period of inner turmoil, emerged as the New Said. The upshot of this inner struggle or quest for "a way to the essence of reality" was that he took the Qur'an with its message of pure divine unity (*tawhīd*) as his "sole guide," and attempted to divest himself of the influences of "philosophy" and science. These had "plunged him into materiality" and provided him with no answers to the fundamental questions he had been driven to ask by war, death, and the transitoriness of things.

Nursi supported the independence struggle and was invited to Ankara by the national government. He eventually arrived there from Istanbul sometime around the time of the Turkish victory in October 1922, and was offered various religious posts in the Eastern Provinces by Mustafa Kemal, who wanted to profit from his influence. Nursi, however, refused them, for he perceived that his hopes for the country's future were at odds with the new leaders' plans for its Westernization and secularization. It had been his intention to assist in remaking Turkey as a center of Islamic civilization. He concluded that political opposition would serve no positive ends, so renouncing political involvement of all kinds, he returned to Van where he retired into solitude. It was from there that in March 1925, following the Shaikh Said Revolt, he was rounded up together with many of the region's tribal and religious leaders, and thousands of its people, and sent into exile in western Anatolia. Contrary to the government's accusations, he had advised against the revolt. Regarded as a potential threat by the government, he was held for the next 25 years in what was nominally exile, but was often little better than house arrest. He served three terms of imprisonment along with numbers of his students. It was under these constraining conditions that Nursi wrote the *Risale-i Nur*, in which he sought to explicate the basic teachings of the Qur'an in such a way as to refute the basic assumptions of positivist philosophy, one of the ideological bases of the new state. It will be useful before examining how Nursi tackled these problems, to mention a few facts about the series of reforms that were enacted after the founding of the Republic.

It was Mustafa Kemal's avowed aim "to achieve an unconditional transformation to Western civilization,"[6] and to build a modern nation-state out of what remained of the Ottoman Empire. Such a project required the rapid modernization, Westernization, and therefore secularization of Turkey. The process had begun with the modernizing governmental reorganization known as the Tanzimat (1839–76); its military, legal, bureaucratic, and educational reforms, together with subsequent measures, had to a great extent reduced the areas of Islamic jurisdiction, in effect secularizing the state. Yet despite these reforms, apart from the official classes who were involved with the reformed institutions in some capacity, the character, culture, and identity of the Muslim population remained largely unaffected. After taking the momentous steps of abolishing first the sultanate (November 1, 1922) and then the caliphate (March 3, 1924), therefore, most of the rapid succession of reforms enacted by Mustafa Kemal were directed at social and cultural institutions, which would effectively remove all outward signs of Islam, and strike at the root of popular culture.[7] In addition, a radically reformed "national" education system, the function of which was to inculcate "universal, humanist, secular, positivist" principles,[8] was also to educate the people in the six principles of Kemalism.[9] Of these latter principles, which were made both the program of the party founded by Mustafa Kemal, the Republican People's Party (RPP), and the ideological basis of the state, nationalism and secularism were the most stringently enforced. The intention was to eliminate all existing religious identities, and create a uniform secular, nationalist identity.

The Revitalization of Belief and Moral Renewal

This section will describe the method Nursi developed to prove the essential teachings of the Qur'an in the face of the projected replacement of Islam, not only as a system of government but also as a religion and way of life, by Western systems and philosophies. It forms the basis of his extensive writings, the purpose of which was to renew and revivify the people's faith, and was undoubtedly one of the chief reasons for their impact, both in the early years of the Republic and subsequently.

Said Nursi was an Islamic scholar and teacher who in his writings propounded orthodox Sunni doctrines related to all the principal tenets of belief, on occasion citing arguments refuting Mu'tazilite and Predestinationist (Jabriyyah) tendencies and other deviations from "the middle way." In this sense, his thought is not original; his main contribution, which may be seen as innovative, was, besides his making his goal the revitalization of the faith of ordinary believers, the method he developed to do this. Arguably, in his early works there is a discernible influence of modernist trends, especially in his emphasis on science and rationalism. The distinguishing mark of the New Said was the primacy he gave to revelation over reason,[10] and his endeavors to prove the Qur'an's "miraculousness" (i'jāz) and self-sufficiency as a source of knowledge and of the principles and precepts of human life. In fact, he admits that as the Old Said he tried to fight the materialist philosophers with their own weapons, which probably refers to his attempt to develop a rationalist method, but that this was unsuccessful.[11] So as the New Said he strove to develop a method or system of thought inspired directly by Revelation, that is, a purely Qur'anic method. And this he claimed to have achieved with the *Risale-i Nur*. It comprises several elements.

The chief elements of Nursi's new method occurred to him during his transition into the New Said, and are based on observation of and reflective thought (*tefekkür*) on the beings and processes of the natural world in the manner of the Qur'an. The key concept here is what Nursi called "*manâ-yı ḥarfî*" (lit. the significative meaning [of things]), a term he borrowed from Arabic grammar[12] by which he meant considering or "reading" things for the meanings they express and "on account of their Maker;" in other words, the Qur'anic viewpoint or way of looking at things. This is in contradistinction to materialistic science and philosophy, which look on beings as signifying only themselves (*manâ-yı ismî* – the nominal meaning [of things]). For example, he writes:

According to the Qur'anic view, all the beings in the universe are letters, expressing through their significative meaning, the meaning of another. That is, they make known the names and attributes of that Other. Soulless philosophy for the most part looks in accordance with the nominal meaning and deviates into the bog of nature.[13]

As a methodological device, the significative (*ḥarfî*) viewpoint is supported by, or functions through, "deductive argumentation in the form of proofs."[14] Beings are seen as evidence for their Maker's attributes and are pondered over in such a manner as to deduce proofs of them. Using argumentation of this sort, Nursi offers numerous proofs of the Creator's existence and unity, and for the resurrection of the dead and other "pillars of belief," as well as for many other cosmic truths. Likening the universe to a book, he emphasizes the mutually interpretative relationship between it and the Qur'an; that is, he demonstrates how, by both expressing the same truths, the one interprets and expounds the other.[15] Furthermore, by "reading" the beings in the world around us in this way, he is at the same time seeking to point out the invalidity of the basic postulates of naturalism, positivism, and other materialistic philosophies: the concepts of nature, causation, chance, and coincidence. With this approach, Nursi is also intending to clarify confusions caused by these concepts. For instance, in his *Treatise on Nature*, he says: ". . . [T]here are certain phrases that are commonly used and imply unbelief. The believers also use them, but without realizing their implications." He then lists three such phrases: "Causes create this." "It forms itself (spontaneous generation)." And "It is natural. Nature . . . creates it," and through nine "impossibilities," proceeds first to demonstrate their logical absurdity, and then to prove the necessity and truth of divine unity.[16] Part of the "First Impossibility" of the third phrase is as follows:

If the art and creativity, which are discerning and wise, to be seen in beings, and particularly in animate beings, are not attributed to the pen of determining and power of the Pre-Eternal Sun and instead are ascribed to nature and force, which are blind, deaf, and unthinking, it becomes necessary that nature should either have machines and printing-presses for their creation, or include in everything the power and wisdom to create and administer the universe. The reason for this is as follows:

The sun's manifestations and reflection appear in all fragments of glass and droplets on the face of the earth. If those miniature, reflected imaginary suns are not ascribed to the sun in the sky, it has to be accepted that an actual sun exists (lit. has external existence) in every tiny fragment of glass smaller than a match-head . . . In exactly the same way, if beings and animate creatures are not attributed directly to the manifestation of the Pre-Eternal Sun's names, one has to accept that present in each being, especially if it is animate, are a nature, a force, or quite simply a god, possessing infinite power and will, knowledge and wisdom. Such an idea is absurd . . .[17]

Nursi expanded and elaborated his method when he started to write the *Risale-i Nur* in exile. Allegorical comparisons are a device he came to make extensive use of, an example of which is given in the quote above. He said they were inspired by the comparisons of the Qur'an and are an aspect of its miraculousness since, like "telescopes" and "stairs," they are a means of bringing close and reaching distant, lofty truths. They thus induce certainty, causing "the intellect, as well as the imagination and fancy, and the soul and caprice . . . to submit."[18] Nursi often uses such comparisons to illustrate the superiority in various fields of the Qur'an, belief and guidance, over "philosophy" and misguidance.

It may be noted at this point that because of the function Nursi foresaw the *Risale-i Nur* fulfilling in the particular conditions of the twentieth century, he endeavored to bring together in complementary fashion different disciplines and types of knowledge. His objective was to revivify belief through developing new teaching methods, where existing forms were inadequate or had been abolished. As a popular didactic work, therefore, the *Risale-i Nur* performs the function primarily of *tafsīr* (Qur'anic exegesis or explication), and of such other traditional madrasah sciences as logic, *'aqā'id* (doctrine), *uṣūl al-dīn* (the principles of religion), and *kalam* (theology). Nursi himself emphasized its primary function, perhaps because of its original, unfamiliar form and style.[19] He also called it "a work of *kalam*,"[20] and has been credited with carrying out a genuine renewal (*tajdīd*) in this field.[21] He looked on the work as being in the madrasah tradition, yet, since, as he frequently stressed and is noted in the next section, it addresses the human inner faculties (the heart) in addition to the intellect, it is probably fair to say that he intended it to perform also what he perceived to be the essential functions of Sufism.[22] Nevertheless, he denied any connection with Sufism, although he was frequently accused by the government of founding a new *tarikat* (Sufi order). The orders had been declared illegal in 1925 and their activities banned. Nursi was not opposed to Sufism, but stated that he considered it inappropriate for modern times since it was ill-equipped to respond to the attacks of science and materialism. Some writers have found elements of his style and method to be reminiscent of Sufi works.[23]

A further significant matter is Nursi's incorporating modern scientific knowledge in his expositions of the Qur'an's verses. This had been one of the main features of his projected reformulation of the madrasah sciences in his youth (as had been the bringing together of the three main educational traditions represented by the learned profession, Sufism, and modern secular education), but it was as the New Said with his discovery of the Qur'anic method based on the significative (*ḥarfī*) viewpoint that he may be said to have achieved it. He concluded that when considered from the significative viewpoint, "the physical sciences become knowledge of God."[24] What this amounts to is that Nursi utilizes scientific facts when describing the processes of the natural world to prove "the truths of belief." For example,

It is as if each particle were aware of every single task . . . for it hears and obeys every dominical command that courses through the air. It aids all animals to breathe and to live, all plants to pollinate and grow, and cultivates all the matters necessary for their survival. It directs and administers the clouds, makes possible the voyaging of sailing ships, and enables sounds to be conveyed, particularly by means of wireless, telephone, telegraph and radio, as well as numerous other functions.

Now these atoms, each composed of two such simple materials as hydrogen and oxygen and each resembling the other, exist in hundreds of thousands of different fashions all over the globe; I conclude therefore that they are being employed and set to work in the utmost orderliness by a hand of wisdom.[25]

There are numerous such examples in the *Risale-i Nur*. It could be added that very often the imagery Nursi uses to depict the universe is distinctly Newtonian or mechanistic in that he likens it to "a machine," or "factory," or "clock," made up of component parts. His interpretation is, however, strictly Qur'anic, as mentioned. Nursi's main purpose here was most probably educative, and, by updating Qur'anic exegesis by authentic methods, to demonstrate how science might be used to prove the truths of religion rather than to confute them. Furthermore, he intended to rebuff the imputed clash and conflict between religion and science that had caused so much confusion and was intended to discredit Islam. In this connection, it should be pointed out that in distinction to post-Enlightenment Western thought, which is epistemologically "compartmentalized" and based on the fundamental differentiation and dichotomy between mind and matter, body and soul, science and religion, and so on, Nursi tried to establish an "epistemological wholeness" and organic relations between the various categories of knowledge, revealed and scientific, and art, ethics, and belief,[26] and within man himself with his many faculties. This is consistent with the Qur'an and its insistent teaching of divine unity. The fundamental epistemological dissimilarity between the Qur'an and "philosophy" is also the basis of the dissimilarity between the harmonious interrelation of man, society, civilization and the cosmos as taught by the Qur'an on the one hand, and the conflict underlying all man's relations as taught by "philosophy" on the other, that Nursi was at pains to illustrate with his many comparisons between the two.

Belief and man

Nursi's treatment of belief or faith (*imān*) is one of the most original and effective aspects of the *Risale-i Nur*, and his persuasive analyses are certainly one of the main reasons for the work's impact on successive generations. In this brief discussion, it will be useful to consider it in tandem with his treatment of man; that is, the human being.

Nursi's intention with the above-mentioned method was to gain for people a dynamic, living faith that he calls "belief by investigation" (*imān-ı tahkikî*). This form of belief, which is a conscious affirmation and verification, is the opposite of "belief by imitation," which can be easily dispelled by doubts. Belief by investigation may be attained through reasoning reflective thought on the divine works and names, and rises in degree and strength to the number of the names and cosmic truths that are thus comprehended. According to Nursi, "it contains degrees to the number of the manifestations of the divine names," and may "reach the degree at which the whole universe may be read as though it were a Qur'an."[27] Such belief is thus closely linked to the sort of knowledge (*'ilm*) he terms "the sciences of belief (*'ulum-u imaniye*)." The vital property of such knowledge is its being "the light and sustenance for man's many subtle inner faculties:" "after entering 'the stomach' of the mind, the matters of belief that come with [such] knowledge are absorbed by the spirit, heart, inner heart, soul, and other subtle faculties; each receives its share according to its degree."[28]

Belief in God and its necessary corollaries, knowledge of God and worship, are, according to Nursi, the purpose of man's being "sent to this world." They are also his innate or primordial duty. So too, belief in God is "the highest aim of creation and its most important result."[29] By virtue of these complementary facts, it is only through belief that human beings can find happiness and fulfillment. This constitutes one of the main themes of the *Risale-i Nur*, which Nursi elaborates with numerous allegories, comparisons, and arguments. It is also an area in which he points out the paradoxes and failures of "philosophy" and "misguided science," which, although their stated aim is the conquest of human happiness, have rather brought humanity pain and suffering, since they have sought it in worldly pleasures and through their false principles and viewpoint. With these comparisons, which disclose both the reality and the causes of "the misguided's" circumstances, Nursi is aiming to deter "the sensible among them" by demonstrating that "in misguidance is a sort of hell in this world, and in belief, a sort of paradise." It was to this analytical, psychological approach that Nursi ascribed the *Risale-i Nur*'s spread, despite all the hostile propaganda and efforts to prevent it.[30]

Nursi's whole system of thought hinges on his understanding of the human "I" or ego, and on the concepts of the significative meaning of things and the nominal meaning, which have been described. The "I" is one aspect of the Trust assumed by man,[31] which he can truly carry out only when he ascribes to the "I" a significative meaning. That is to say, when a person's "I" understands that it is "mirror-like" and that its power, knowledge, ownership, and other attributes are merely apparent, and are imaginary "tiny units of measurement" for understanding the Creator's true knowledge, power, and ownership – that "[the 'I'] is a measure that makes known the absolute, all-encompassing and limitless attributes of the Necessary Being," then the person will see the universe as it is in reality and "the duties it is performing." He will abandon his imaginary ownership and ascribe all power to the True Owner. He thus purifies his soul, and truly carries out the Trust. Conversely, "if the 'I' views itself solely in the light of its nominal and apparent meaning, if it believes that it owns itself and its attributes, then it betrays the Trust." For as it ascribes power to itself, so it will ascribe power to causes in the outside world and fail to see the universe for what it is; it will associate partners with God on a grand scale.[32]

Nursi's approach to ethics and moral renewal

Moral renewal was a question to which Nursi attached the greatest importance, both in the early period of his life,[33] and as the New Said after the foundation of the Republic. However, in that he treats ethics as a dimension of his cosmology or of the cosmic system, in this second period his approach differs considerably. He does discuss ethical and moral questions in a variety of other contexts, but essentially his approach is to present moral precepts and values as a part of the whole (holistic) Qur'anic order or system.[34] The precepts of "justice, frugality, and cleanliness" may be taken as an example.

To show how basic these three qualities are to human life, Nursi points out how they are manifested in the cosmos as universal laws and govern all beings. Briefly, the wisdom (hikmet) apparent throughout the universe "turns on economy and lack of waste," commanding man to be frugal. And the justice and balance in all things enjoin justice on him. While the constant cleansing "cleans and beautifies all the beings in the universe. So long as man . . . does not interfere, there is no true uncleanliness or ugliness in anything." In this way Nursi points out how closely connected these Qur'anic injunctions and Islamic principles are with the universe, and that it would be as impossible to uproot them as it would be to change the universe's form.[35] That is to say, he convincingly shows that if one acts contrarily to them, one does so in defiance of the whole universe.

Thanks and gratitude to Almighty God are another example. In a short piece entitled *On Thanks*,[36] Nursi cites some of the many Qur'anic verses enjoining thanks, and demonstrates how both the Qur'an and the Qur'an of the universe "show thanks to be the most important result of creation."

Conscious thanks and praise for the innumerable bounties dispersed through the universe are also the chief of man's three primordial "duties." These bounties he receives and experiences on multiple expanding levels, from that of the physical senses to that of belief, which extends beyond the sphere of contingency.[37]

Another universal principle or law that Nursi explains, this time to berate the idle and urge the lazy to work, is that of the pleasure to be found in exertion and work. He illustrates his point persuasively with a series of delightful examples from the animal, vegetable, and mineral realms.[38]

Nursi's vision of the cosmos also connects man to all beings, revealing the existential brotherhood and love between him and all things.[39]

Many of the moral qualities that Nursi wishes to impress on his readers, he explains within the framework of his comparisons between the ways of revelation and philosophy, contrasting them with their opposites. At the base of these is the concept of *ubûdiyet*, which may be translated as worshipful servitude or service of Almighty God, and is the worshipful attitude that a believer adopts when he internalizes the Qur'anic (*harfî*) viewpoint.[40] Ethics are of course an inseparable part of religion, or even the same thing,[41] and proceed directly from belief. Thus, in other contexts Nursi links desirable qualities with a particular tenet of belief. For example, he enjoins "contentment and resignation" on himself when suffering his unjust imprisonment since it was divinely determined (*kader*), and to meet it with "endless thanks and patience" since it was also necessitated by divine wisdom and mercy, and even to magnanimously forgive the officials responsible.[42]

The moral quality Nursi emphasizes above all others, however, is sincerity (*ihlas*). As the quality he most wanted to inculcate in his students, it is discussed in the following section.

The Main Features of the Nur Movement, and its Mode of Struggle in a Secular Society

In this section, an attempt will be made to outline Nursi's ideas concerning the functions, character, and mode of service of the Nur community, and to indicate the areas of Turkish life – religious, social, cultural, ethical, and political – on which they have had most impact. A number of studies have been published on developments associated with the movement subsequent to Nursi's death in 1960, and its impact on political and other matters.[43] Here, discussion will be limited to the movement's main features and to its activities during his lifetime.

A striking feature of the community that grew up around Nursi's writings was its focussing on these writings rather than on their author, despite his powerful charisma. This marked a shift from the traditional focus on the shaikh or religious leader that was notable among the Sufi orders. It has been said that the Nur community pioneered this transition,[44] which, with improvements in education and communications, was in time adopted by the orders,[45] and by Islamic groups generally. This aspect of the Nur movement thus paved the way for the expansion, revitalization, and diversification of the Islamic movement in Turkey in the final decades of the twentieth century.[46]

As a mode of religious struggle, text-orientation was to an extent forced on Nursi. For both the surveillance under which he was kept in his places of exile, and the constraints legal and otherwise on numbers of people forgathering, particularly for any activity that could be construed as religious, precluded his teaching personally or acting as a religious guide in the traditional sense. However, this looking to the text for guidance was also his choice. For he always modestly insisted that he was a mere student of the *Risale-i Nur* like his students; that is, the Nur students. One reason for this was his wish not to obscure "the sacredness of the Qur'an" reflected in his writings, and so negate their effectiveness.[47] Another was the question of "sincerity," which is discussed below.

Moreover, the movement itself grew up around the *Risale-i Nur*; the *Risale* was its *raison d'être*. It was composed of students dedicated to the writing out and dissemination of the *Risale* in the extremely adverse conditions of the early years of the Republic, whom Nursi strove to bind into a cohesive community. Notwithstanding both the economic hardships, and the persecution suffered by the Nur students, punctuated by terms of mass imprisonment, their numbers increased as they spread Nursi's writings. Women and children were no less keen to participate in this joint effort to spread "the lights of the Qur'an," despite the practical difficulties involved – the overall literacy rate in Turkey in 1928 was only around 8 percent.[48] In the course of time, the underground campaign to disseminate the *Risale-i Nur* undoubtedly had the secondary effects not only in keeping alive the Arabic script after it was banned at the end of 1928, but also in raising the literacy and cultural levels of large numbers of people.

Central to Nursi's conception of how service of the Qur'an and belief may be carried out effectively in contemporary society is the notion of the collective personality (*şahs-ı mânevî*).[49] According to Nursi, the modern age is the age of the community or social collectivity, and the collectivity gives rise to a spirit or collective personality through which it can function much more productively than if represented by an individual, no matter how powerful.[50] Individual persons would most likely be defeated in the face of "the aggressive collective personality of misguidance." Thus, one of Nursi's main endeavors was to impress on his students the importance of such a collective personality and to inculcate in them the moral qualities necessary for its formation. The chief of these was sincerity, the greatest strength of the *Risale-i Nur*'s way,[51] and its basis. It necessitated renouncing the ego so as "to transform the 'I' into 'we'; that is, to give up egotism and to work on account of the *Risale*'s collective personality." For ". . . To have a large pool, the ice-blocks of the ego and personality have to be cast into the pool and melted."[52] This required that they should seek nothing but God's pleasure in their actions, practice self-abnegation before their brothers, and participate in their communal struggle with resolute, unwavering devotion.

A letter instructing the students in other qualities Nursi deemed vital, namely *taqwa*, variously translated as fear of God, God-consciousness, or piety, and good works (*amel-i salih*) states clearly the function he foresaw them, as students of the *Risale-i Nur*, fulfilling in society. This, by their "avoiding sins and what is forbidden" (*taqwa*) and "acting within the bounds of what is commanded and in the way of winning God's pleasure (good works)," was to resist and repair the [moral] corruption caused by the "shaking" of the rules and precepts of Islam.[53] This function he frequently mentions in his writings and court defenses, but usually without defining precisely what it entails. The letter here is useful in that it links the *Risale-i Nur*'s "repairing" function to another area of Turkish life on which Nursi had an impact: his revival of the traditional emphasis on "personalistic" social relations and related ethics, and his seeking to reform society through the reform of the individual.[54] In contrast to the modernist view of society in which individual persons are merely components or "lifeless atoms" subject to the mechanistic functioning of fixed laws, and subordinate to the entities of state and society, Nursi, following the Qur'an, situates persons at the center of social relations; he puts them in the traditional categories of father, mother, children, the aged, the youth, the sick, and so on, and treats them in terms of ethics. An example is the above-mentioned letter:

> Respect and compassion, the most important principles in administering social life, have been badly shaken. In some places it has had grievous consequences, concerning aged parents. . . . [W]herever the *Risale-i Nur* encounters this fearsome destruction, it offers resistance and repairs the damage.[55]

That is to say, Nursi intended through the *Risale-i Nur*'s proofs of "the truths of belief" to strengthen traditional Qur'anic values and institutions, so as to combat the disintegrative forces unleashed by modernization, and repair their harm. For, indeed, a specific purpose of the new educational system, and the other secularizing reforms, and the whole drift of cultural Westernization, was "the liberation of the individual from the collective constraints of the Muslim community," and "to replace (the) personalistic ties . . . by a set of rules that tried to obviate control . . . ,"[56] and to substitute Islamic ethics with positivistic ones.

Nursi's great fear, especially with the rise of communism, was that the rejection of Islamic behavioral norms would lead to a moral decline and slide into anarchy, because, he argued, "Muslims do not resemble others; if they abandon their religion and divest themselves of their Islamic character, they fall into absolute misguidance, becoming anarchists, so that they can no longer be governed." In consequence, although the Nur students' primary duty was "to save belief and teach the people about 'belief by investigation,'" their second duty was "to save this nation and country from the danger of anarchy."[57] Nursi frequently emphasized this function of the *Risale-i Nur*, also making it one of his main lines of defense in the court cases brought against him. He pointed out that by strengthening the five principles of "respect, compassion, refraining from what is prohibited (*ḥarām*), security, and the giving up of lawlessness and obedience to authority," the Nur students were preserving public order and saving social life from anarchy.[58] He therefore impressed on the authorities that they should realize "the country and nation's" need for the *Risale-i Nur*, rather than trying to suppress it.[59]

Religious repression continued in Turkey until the coming to power of the Democrat Party (DP) in the elections of May 1950, although with the beginnings of the multiparty system[60] after the end of the World War Two, the government made some concessions to the people's religious needs. The Soviet Union's domination over eastern Europe, and its belligerent demands over the Istanbul Straits, probably with a view to extending communist influence over the Middle East, helped to push Turkey into joining the Western alliance, now led by the United States.

Nursi's continuing struggle has to be seen against the backdrop of increasingly severe treatment, culminating in 20 months' imprisonment in Afyon in 1948–9. The Nur community took shape as events unfolded, its members being molded and tempered by their lengthy ordeal. Nursi was the main defendant in three major trials, in connection with which he was imprisoned together with varying numbers of his students, a result of which a fair proportion of his writings with effect from 1935, consist of his defense speeches, and petitions and letters to judicial and other authorities. At every trial virtually the same charges were brought against him, although he was acquitted by Denizli Court: founding a secret political organization, founding a Sufi order, engaging in activities that "might" disturb public order, exploiting religion for political ends,[61] and so on. The onus was on Nursi to prove the falsity of the charges. It should not be understood from this, however, that Nursi tailored his method of service under force of circumstance to fit the charges – although undoubtedly he conducted his defenses very skillfully. As the next section will show, it was his view that such a method was necessitated by the adoption of the secularist principle. Moreover, the harsh and completely unjustified treatment the Nur students received may be seen as serving to forge them into a disciplined, self-sacrificing, and seasoned community capable of pursuing their goals in unfavorable conditions of all kinds.

Positive action and jihād of the word

Nursi defined their struggle in terms of positive action and *jihād* of the word (*jihād-ı mânevî*), by which he meant a non-physical or moral *jihād*. In a passage interpreting the verse, "Let there be no compulsion in religion," (2:265), he argues that given the circumstances of the day, *jihād* should take this form:

> By [the matters of] religion being separated from [those of] this world on that date, freedom of conscience, which is opposed to force and compulsion in religion, and to religious struggle and armed *jihād* for religion, [was accepted as] a fundamental rule and political principle by governments, and [this] state [also] became a secular republic. In view of this, [*jihād*] will be a non-physical religious *jihād* with the sword of 'belief by investigation' (*imān-ı tahkikî*). . . . a great hero in the contest of this *jihād* of the word . . . is the *Risale-i Nur* . . . for its immaterial sword has solved hundreds of the mysteries of religion, leaving no need for physical swords. . . .
>
> . . . It is due to this mighty mystery that the *Risale-i Nur* students do not interfere in the politics and political movements of the world and their material struggles, nor attach importance to them, nor condescend to [any involvement with] them. . . . They feel not anger at their enemies, but pity and compassion. They try to reform them, in the hope that they will be saved.[62]

As is seen from this, Nursi's interpretation of secularism was at variance with the official version, which, inspired by French thought, sought the eventual elimination of religion since it held it to be the chief obstacle to progress, or at least its complete domination by the state. He therefore always denied the persistent accusations that he had contravened the principle of secularism. He argued that "freedom of conscience governs everywhere in this age of freedom,"[63] and that accordingly, since "secularism means being impartial, . . . the government should not interfere with the religiously-minded and pious, the same as it does not interfere with the irreligious and dissipated."[64]

According to this line of argument, it was perfectly licit for the Nur community to pursue its endeavors to strengthen and save religious belief through the *Risale-i Nur*. Nursi asserted also that at the present time there is a vast difference between internal *jihād* (within the realm of Islam – *İslam dairesinde*) and external *jihād*. Force may only be used against outside aggression.[65] Nevertheless, given the potentially volatile situation and the facts that he and his students were in a defensive and vulnerable position *vis-à-vis* the authorities and subject to constant provocation by their agents, he constantly stressed their "duty" of preserving public order and security, and insisted that they directed all their energies to their *jihād* of the word and always acted positively, disregarding worldly currents and avoiding any actions that might lead to strife. Avoidance of direct involvement in political and social matters has thus become one of the most distinctive characteristics of the Nur movement. Nursi offered numerous reasons for his insistence on this question. The main ones are as follows.

Firstly was "the sacredness" of the Nur students' service, and its importance, alluded to in the passage quoted above. According to Nursi, their striving to win eternal life for themselves and others was incomparably more important than the misguided's efforts to secure fleeting worldly life, so they should evince no curiosity about worldly affairs. Moreover, preoccupation with peripheral, political matters causes a person to neglect his essential duties and to waste his life on trivia,[67] as well as causing heedlessness and damaging belief and spiritual life.[68]

Also, because of the partisan nature of politics, a person who becomes involved with them cannot preserve his sincerity; the likelihood is that he will sacrifice everything for his political ideals. "Whereas the truths of belief and sacred service of the *Risale-i Nur* may not be made the tool of anything . . . and have no aim and purpose but God's pleasure."[69] Political involvement may thus lead to the degradation, exploitation, and betrayal of the Qur'an's truths.[70]

Nursi says too that having been exposed to the misguidance of science, what the people of Islam now most need is to be shown "the light of the Qur'an," so their hearts can be healed and their belief saved. If confronted by "the club of politics," it either scares them off or causes them to waver and doubt, and even to disbelieve. They have to be shown the light and be guided to it.[71] Moreover, there are people open to the truth in all political currents, so the one presenting them should remain impartial.

The reason Nursi cites most often for his opposition to political involvement is that it may lead to the harming of innocents, which is contrary to the "compassion, truth, right, and conscience" of the *Risale-i Nur*, and to justice. He often explains this in connection with the verse, "No bearer of burdens can bear the burden of another,"(Qur'an, 6:164, etc.) interpreting it as, "no one is answerable for another's error or crime, even a relative's." The brother, family, or children of a criminal cannot be held responsible for him and made to suffer due to partisanship, as is often the case.[72] He reckoned that it was because the 500,000 Nur students had complied with this principle that the forces working to disturb public order had failed to do so, while they had succeeded in other countries.[73]

Finally, Nursi was anxious that the Nur students should act in a conciliatory manner towards believers, including heretics and even Christians, so that "nothing should happen in social and political life that might prevent the spread of the *Risale-i Nur* in the Islamic world."[74]

For a more complete picture, however, the above reasons should be seen in tandem with the expansion of the Nur students' activities after the coming to power of the DP and its partial relaxation of strict secularist policies of the single-party era.

Expansion in the 1950s

The Democrat Party era (1950–60) marked a watershed for Nursi and the Nur students in that it provided the opportunity for him both to train a new generation of young students, and after the *Risale-i Nur* was finally cleared by Afyon Court in 1956 to establish the guidelines for its greatly expanded publication, and to found the system for the "*dershanes*" (Nur study centers), all of which were key elements in the formation of the now swiftly growing Nur movement and its future activities.

These last 10 years of Nursi's life are sometimes differentiated from the New Said period and called the Third Said period. According to some sources, the name refers to the expansion of the movement's activities,[75] while according to others, it refers to an expansion of Nursi's own activities,[76] for on the coming to power of Menderes and the DP, he gave them his enthusiastic support and, with the aim of "making politics serve religion," concerned himself to an extent with political developments.

Arguably, this was not much of a departure from his earlier practice. During his trials in Denizli (1943–4) and Afyon (1948–9) and the years between he had sent numerous petitions and letters putting his case to departments of government and the judiciary. Similarly, he had sent letters of advice such as the one (ca. 1946) to Hilmi Uran, the ex-Minister of the Interior and then General Secretary of the RPP, warning that the Turkish nation could resist the communist threat only by relying on the Qur'an.[77] With the Democrats, he extended this practice: he sent a few chosen students to Ankara to further their case, and from time to time wrote letters of encouragement or advice to Menderes and other members of the government. The most significant of these explain what Nursi called "fundamental Qur'anic laws;" that is, fundamental revelational principles the application of which would remedy economic, social, and political ills that had arisen from the introduction of principles of "human" origin; that is, principles originating in Western philosophy.[78]

In this connection, it may be recalled that Nursi had been an ardent supporter of constitutional government at the beginning of the century. Now that Turkey had a government that was sympathetic to Islam and intended (or so he hoped) to govern in accordance with principles congruent with "Islamic" government, Nursi equated it with the constitutional government of that time. During the 1950s he republished for his younger students some of his works – those cited here are newspaper articles – of the former period, but substituted the word "constitutionalism" with "republicanism:" "Republicanism consists of justice, mutual consultation, and restriction of power to the law."[79] In another, the original title of which was "Long live the illustrious *sharī'ah*!" which he changed to "Long live the fundamental laws of the Qur'an!", he equated constitutionalism with "republicanism and democracy (*cumhuriyet ve demokrat*)."[80]

From this it is understood that in the tradition of Namık Kemal, and following him virtually all the Ottoman intellectuals and *ulama* of the day,[81] Nursi accepted as "Islamic," representative government in a Muslim society when based on such principles as justice, consultation, and the law. He therefore urged the Democrat government to adopt and apply the above-mentioned principles.

Again during this period, Nursi both sought ways of disseminating the *Risale-i Nur* in the Islamic world, to strengthen "the brotherhood of belief," and he encouraged Menderes to heal the breach with it and re-establish ties. In this connection, he supported Turkey's joining the Baghdad Pact in 1956, writing Menderes and the President, Celal Bayar, a letter of congratulation.[82]

These are all questions that were influential on the future course of the Nur movement. Another, interfaith dialogue and cooperation, was pioneered by Nursi in the 1950s, and has subsequently been advanced by some branches of the Nur movement.

With the change in the configuration of world powers after the Second World War, Nursi modified his attitude towards the West and looked positively on it in so far as it upheld Christian values. So too, within the framework of adherence to revelational principles, he advocated cooperation between Muslims and Christians in combating aggressive atheism.[83] He himself initiated dialogue with Christian leaders by, in 1950, having one of his works sent to the Pope in Rome, and, in 1953, personally visiting the Greek Orthodox patriarch in Istanbul, Patriarch Athenagoras. Underlying these moves was Nursi's urgent wish to bring about reconciliation on all levels in order to establish universal peace.

The Nur community's positive action and efforts to strengthen society in the face of "the immaterial destruction" of irreligion, and its support for the Democrat Party, won the government's confidence. As one historian has noted, by acknowledging its support, the Democrats implicitly legitimized the movement.[84] It was a great victory for Nursi, vindicating his method and rewarding his 30 years of patient, silent struggle. Although the Nur students were still subject to police raids and had to act with caution, they were free to publish the Risale-i Nur. For the first time, its volumes were printed in the Roman alphabet on modern presses. The movement was not suppressed, and Nur study centers (dershanes) were opened all over the country. In Diyarbakır and the East there were around 200 in operation, with "four or five" for women in the town itself.[85] Nursi also encouraged the Nur students to turn their houses into "home madrasah," allotting time to communal readings of the Risale, the distinctive feature and central activity of the Nur movement. The movement grew in influence,[86] especially as the government's popularity waned in the second half of the 1950s, its vote in the 1957 elections allegedly being a decisive factor in the Democrats' victory.[87] In the decades following Nursi's death, its influence further increased as it grew in strength and numbers.[88]

Conclusion

Bediuzzaman Said Nursi's endeavors in the field of religious renewal were directed towards the revivification of faith in the fundamental "pillars of belief." For in his view, it was through the strengthening and reconstruction of these foundations, "the refuge" of the mass of believers, that Islam could best withstand the onslaughts of modernity and overwhelming currents of materialist thought of Western origin. When faced with their particular manifestation in Turkey, he expounded in the Risale-i Nur a comprehensive system of thought which was inspired by the Qur'an and which sought to situate "the truths of belief" within a coherent picture of the cosmos that was informed by modern science and would provide a "modern" God-centered alternative to the positivist vision. Nursi's main objection to materialist philosophy was that, because of – in his view – its false principles and denial of the metaphysical, it was detrimental both to the individual and to society. In his writings, therefore, he attempted to bring together and combine different disciplines so as to prove the essentials of religion in a way that would both afford intellectual certainty, and satisfy spiritual needs and man's inner faculties. The revival of Qur'anic values and ethics thus effected would strengthen the bonds of society. In this way he sought to compensate for the failures and deficiencies of the modernizing project and to mend its harms.[89]

Nursi's belief in the self-sufficiency of the Qur'an obliged him at the outset to turn down offers of posts in the new government and to not allow himself to be co-opted into its cadres.[90] This was the main reason for the years of persecution he suffered. His conception of religious struggle in terms of jihād of the word and positive action, however, transformed the disadvantages into advantages and made possible the eventual successes of the Nur movement in carrying out religious renewal in a secular society.

Notes

1. The term philosophy is used in the *Risale-i Nur* to denote aspects of Western civilization: "European philosophy and human science . . . are the spirit of [modern] civilization." See Bediuzzaman Said Nursi, *The Words* (Istanbul: Sözler Publications, 2002), 423. It is often used to mean natural philosophy, naturalism, or a materialist interpretation of science, or may refer to modernity with its science and technology. It represents the dominance of reason and rejection of revelation.
2. See Hakan Yavuz, *Islamic Political Identity in Turkey* (Oxford: Oxford University Press, 2003).
3. For Nursi's life, see relevant sections in Şükran Vahide, *Islam in Modern Turkey: An Intellectual Biography of Bediuzzaman Said Nursi* (Albany: SUNY Press, 2005).
4. Bediuzzaman Said Nursi, *Münâzarat* (Istanbul: Sözler Yayınevi, 1977), 72.
5. See Niyazi Berkes, *The Development of Secularism in Turkey* (New York: Routledge, 1998), 347ff; S. Hayri Bolay, *Türkiye'de Ruhçu ve Maddeci Görüşün Mücadelesi* (Ankara: Akçağ, 1995).
6. Berkes, *Development of Secularism*, 464.
7. See Erik J. Zürcher, *Turkey: A Modern History* (London: I.B. Tauris, 2001), 200–1.
8. See Sina Akşin (ed.), *Türkiye Tarihi* (Istanbul: Cem Yayınevi, 1989), iv, 471–4.
9. For the six principles, see Şerif Mardin, "Religion and Secularism in Turkey," in Hourani *et al.* (eds.), *The Modern Middle East* (London: I.B. Tauris, 1993), 365; Dietrich Jung with Wolfgango Piccoli, *Turkey at the Crossroads: Ottoman Legacies and a Greater Middle East* (London: Zed Books, 2001), 75–8.
10. Nursi stated that "the doors of *ijtihād*" were open, but that in the "stormy" conditions of the times (1929) when denial is rife and Islam is under attack by "the customs of Europe and legions of innovations," they should be kept fast shut." See, *Words*, 495.
11. Bediuzzaman Said Nursi, *Letters 1928–1932*. Eng. trans. Şükran Vahide (Istanbul: Sözler Publications, 2001), 516.
12. Bediuzzaman Said Nursi, *Barla Lahikası* (Istanbul: Envar Neşriyat, 1994), 348; Farid al-Ansari, "The Theory of Ethics in Bediuzzaman Said Nursi's Works," in *Sixth International Symposium: Globalization, Ethics and Bediuzzaman Said Nursi's Risale-i Nur* (Istanbul: Sözler Publications, 2004), 292.
13. Bediüzzaman Said Nursi, *The Flashes Collection*. Eng. trans. Şükran Vahide (Istanbul: Sözler Publications, 2000), 156.
14. Bediüzzaman Said Nursi, *Mesnevi-i Nuriye*. Turk. trans. Abdülkadir Badıllı (Istanbul: 1998), 236.
15. See, for example, Bediuzzaman Said Nursi, *The Rays Collection*. Eng. trans. Şükran Vahide (Istanbul: Sözler Publications, 2002), 163; Nursi, *Words*, 145, 251.
16. See, Nursi, *Flashes*, 232–54.
17. Nursi, *Flashes*, 238–9.
18. Nursi, *Letters*, 443–4.
19. See, for example, Nursi, *Letters*, 434, 437; *Rays*, 90, 399, 512–13; Nursi, *Kastamonu Lahikası* (Istanbul: Envar Neşriyat, 1994), 48.
20. See Nursi, *Barla Lahikası*, 162; *Kastamonu Lahikası*, 172; Nursi, *Emirdağ Lahikası* (Istanbul: Envar Neşriyat, 1992), i, 90.

21. See Muhsin 'Abdulhamid, *Modern Asrın Kelam Alimi, Bediüzzaman Said Nursi*. Turk. trans. Veli Sırım (Istanbul: Nesil, 1998), 63ff. See also Hamid Algar, "The Centennial Renewer: Bediuzzaman Said Nursi and the Tradition of *Tajdid*," *Journal of Islamic Studies* 12/3, 2001, 291–311.

22. In several places in the *Risale-i Nur* Nursi quotes Shaikh Ahmad Sirhindi, "the hero and sun of the Naqshbandi Order," as saying, "The final point of all the Sufi ways is the clarification and unfolding of the truths of belief" (*Letters*, 40) and, "The unfolding in clarity of a single truth of belief is preferable to a thousand miraculous deeds and mystical visions" (*Rays*, 188) Nursi also stated that the *Risale-i Nur* contained "the essence of all the twelve great *tarikats*." See, *Emirdağ Lahikası*, ii, 54. Moreover, he confessed that among his "masters" were al-Ghazali and Jalal al-Din Rumi, Sirhindi, and 'Abd al-Qadir Gilani. The latter two were instrumental in his finding his path during his transformation into the New Said and were influential on him in various ways, but not in Sufism. Sufism, perhaps, should not be confused with "spirituality."

23. See, for instance, Algar, "The Centennial Renewer," 306; Hamid Algar, "Sufism and *Tarikat* in the Life and Work of Bediuzzaman Said Nursi," *Journal of the History of Sufism*, 3, 2001, 217; Şerif Mardin, *Religion and Social Change in Modern Turkey: The Case of Bediuzzaman Said Nursi* (Albany: SUNY Press, 1989), 176. For Nursi's own comparisons between the methods of the *Risale-i Nur* and both *'ilm al-kalam* and Sufism, See, *Letters*, 388–9.

24. Nursi, *Mesnevî*. Tr. Badıllı, 86.

25. Nursi, *Rays*, 133.

26. See Mehmet S. Aydın, "The Problem of Theodicy in the *Risale-i Nur*," *Islam at the Crossroads: On the Life and Thoughts of Bediuzzaman Said Nursi* (New York: SUNY Press, 2003), 219, 222–3.

27. Bediuzzaman Said Nursi, *The Key to Belief* (Istanbul: Sözler Publications, 1998), 104–5.

28. Nursi, *Letters*, 389.

29. Nursi, *Letters*, 265.

30. Nursi, *Rays*, 639–40.

31. See Qur'an, 33:72.

32. Nursi, *Words*, 558–60.

33. See, Bediuzzaman Said Nursi, *The Damascus Sermon* (Istanbul: Sözler Publications, 1996), 25–58.

34. A number of writers have referred to this aspect of Nursi's thought. See Mardin, *Religion and Social Change*, 224; al-Ansari, "The Theory of Ethics," 282–4.

35. Nursi, *Flashes*, 402.

36. Nursi, *Letters*, 428–32.

37. Nursi, *Flashes*, 456–7.

38. Nursi, *Flashes*, 169–73.

39. Nursi, *Flashes*, 324; Nursi, *Letters*, 342.

40. See, Nursi, *Words*, 562.

41. See al-Azzawi, "The Ethical System in Said Nursi's Works," *Sixth International Symposium: Globalization, Ethics, and Bediuzzaman Said Nursi's Risale-i Nur*, 247, quoted from Taha 'Abdel Rahman.

42. Nursi, *Flashes*, 329.

43. Yavuz, *Islamic Political Identity*, Chapters 7, 8; Hakan Yavuz, "Print-Based Discourse and Modernity: The Nur Movement," *Third International Symposium on Bediuzzaman Said Nursi 1995* (Istanbul: Sözler Publications, 1997), ii, 324–50; M. Hakan Yavuz, "*Nur* Study Circles (*Dershanes*) and the Formation of New Religious Consciousness in Turkey," in Ibrahim Abu-Rabi' (ed.), *Islam at the Crossroads*, 297–316; Metin Karabaşoğlu, "Text and Community:

An Analysis of the *Risale-i Nur* Movement," in Ibrahim Abu-Rabi' (ed.), *Islam at the Crossroads*, 263–96.

44. Yavuz, "Print-Based Discourse," 327–8.
45. See Mardin, *Religion and Social Change*, 230; Yavuz, *Islamic Political Identity*, 130.
46. For detailed discussion, see Yavuz, *Islamic Political Identity*, 103–31.
47. Nursi, *Letters*, 377.
48. Feroz Ahmed, *The Making of Modern Turkey* (London: Routledge, 2002), 82.
49. The concept of the collective or corporate body was introduced into Ottoman thought by Namık Kemal, who took it from Rousseau. See Şerif Mardin, *The Genesis of Young Ottoman Thought* (Syracuse: Syracuse University Press, 2000), 333–4. There is no conception of, or provision for, corporate bodies in the *sharī'ah*. See, Bernard Lewis, *The Emergence of Modern Turkey* (London: Oxford University Press, 1968), 393. Nursi adopted the idea in his youth along with others of Namık Kemal, but in the later period assigned it novel functions.
50. See Bediuzzaman Said Nursi, *Mesnevî-i Nuriye*. Turk. Trans. Abdülmecid Nursi (Istanbul: Envar Neşriyat, 1994), 102.
51. Nursi, *Kastamonu Lahikası*, 149.
52. Nursi, *Kastamonu Lahikası*, 143.
53. Nursi, *Kastamonu Lahikası*, 148–9; Nursi, *A Guide for Youth* (Istanbul: Sözler Publications, 1991), 79–81.
54. Mardin offers illuminating discussion of these latter matters in *Religion and Social Change*, 10–13, 165–71.
55. Nursi, *A Guide for Youth*, 81. For further examples, see, Nursi, *Words*, 674–6; *Rays*, 203–5, 242–7; *Letters*, 492–7.
56. Mardin, "Religion and Secularism," 368–73.
57. Nursi, *Emirdağ Lahikası*, i, 21.
58. See Nursi, *Kastamonu Lahikası*, 137, 241; *Rays*, 372.
59. Nursi, *Kastamonu Lahikası*, 241; *Emirdağ Lahikası*, i, 78.
60. The DP was officially registered January 7, 1946. See, Zürcher, *Turkey*, 221ff.
61. See, for example, Nursi, *Emirdağ Lahikası*, i, 28; ii, 127–8.
62. Nursi, *Rays*, 290.
63. Nursi, *Letters*, 503.
64. Nursi, *Rays*, 386, 305. See also, Bediuzzaman Said Nursi, *Tarihçe-i Hayatı* (Istanbul: Envar Neşriyat, 1996), 219, 231.
65. Nursi, *Emirdağ Lahikası*, ii, 242.
66. Nursi, *Emirdağ Lahikası*, i, 43–4; *Rays*, 384.
67. Nursi, *Rays*, 223–4.
68. Nursi, *Emirdağ Lahikası*, i, 56–8.
69. Nursi, *Emirdağ Lahikası*, i, 38–9.
70. Nursi, *Rays*, 372; *Kastamonu Lahikası*, 117–18, 146.
71. See Nursi, *Flashes*, 143–4; *Letters*, 68–70.
72. See Nursi, *Emirdağ Lahikası*, i, 39; ii, 241; *Rays*, 372.
73. Nursi, *Emirdağ Lahikası*, ii, 77.
74. Nursi, *Kastamonu Lahikası*, 247.
75. Nursi, *Tarihçe*, 612.
76. Necmeddin Şahiner, *Bilinmeyen Taraflarıyla Bediüzzaman Said Nursi* (Istanbul: Nesil, 2004), 383.
77. Nursi, *Emirdağ Lahikası*, i, 217–20.
78. For discussion of these ethical principles, see, Vahide, *Islam in Modern Turkey*, 317–18, 327–9.

79. Nursi, *Damascus Sermon*, 78.
80. Bediuzzaman Said Nursi, *Divan-ı Harb-i Örfî* (Istanbul: Sözler Yayınevi, 1975), 53.
81. İsmail Kara, *İslamcıların Siyasî Görüşleri I: Hilafet ve Meşrutiyet* (Istanbul: Dergah Yayınları, 2001), 50, 97ff.
82. Nursi, *Emirdağ Lahikası*, ii, 222–5.
83. See Nursi, *Flashes*, 203–4 ff, 8; Şükran Vahide, "An Outline of Bediuzzaman Said Nursi's Views on Christianity and the West," in Ian Markham and İbrahim Özdemir (eds.), *Globalization, Ethics and Islam* (Basingstoke: Ashgate Publishing, 2005), 115–16.
84. Zürcher, *Turkey*, 245.
85. Nursi, *Emirdağ Lahikası*, ii, 231.
86. Binnaz Toprak, "The Religious Right," in Hourani *et al.* (eds.), *The Modern Middle East*, 638.
87. Vahide, *Islam in Modern Turkey*, 330.
88. Zürcher, *Turkey*, 201.
89. Şerif Mardin has noted aspects of these. See Mardin, "Reflections on Said Nursi's Life and Thought," in Ibrahim Abu-Rabi' (ed.), *Islam at the Crossroads*, 46; Mardin, *Religion and Social Change*, 25.
90. The great majority of the *ulama* were absorbed into the state system. See Hugh Poulton, *Top Hat, Grey Wolf, and Crescent* (London: Hurst, 1997), 99–100.

CHAPTER 4

Islamic Thought in Contemporary India: The Impact of Mawlana Wahiduddin Khan's Al-Risāla Movement

Irfan A. Omar

Introduction

Born in 1925 in Badharia, Azamgarh in north India, Mawlana Wahiduddin Khan turned 80 on January 1, 2005. If we calculate his age according to the *Hijri* calendar, as he himself prefers, he passed his eightieth year more than two years ago. Mawlana Khan lost his parents at an early age and was brought up under the supervision of his paternal uncle, Sufi Hamid Khan. He studied at Madrasatul Islah in Sarai Mir where he graduated in 1944.

Mawlana Khan has had a rather challenging and, by all standards of scholarly rigor, a productive and stimulating life. He is still vigorously engaged in community as well as scholarly activities and travels often to international peace conferences, attends inter-religious meetings, and addresses gatherings of Muslims and non-Muslims all over India and abroad. His writings continue to fill the pages of the monthly journal *Al-Risāla* (published since 1976 in Urdu and in English since 1984) and many other publications. One thing he does not do is "preach," in mosques that is. Because of his stature as a scholar and community leader, he is often invited to give the *khuṭba*, a sermon that precedes Muslim congregation prayers on Fridays. However, he never accepts such invitations because, as he related to this author, he is not a preacher type.

His long gray hair, flowing beard, and the white traditional Indian outfit, on top of which he wears a rather worn-out grayish white overcoat most times of the year, reveal his Sufistic sympathies. His profile is sometimes reminiscent of Rabindranath Tagore, which may be significant if we consider Mawlana Khan's public image as a modern-day Muslim "guru" in the eyes of an increasing number of Hindus. His is a rather monastic look. But there is no monasticism in Islam, as Mawlana Khan would say, and so his appearance is perhaps a reflection of his simple taste and pietistic posture.

The "Nationalist" Mawlana

Mawlana Wahiduddin Khan is a leading scholar of Islamic thought among Indian Muslims today. In fact, he has been called one of India's "foremost Islamic scholars" and a "nationalist Mawlana."[1] Mawlana Khan was presented with one of the highest national awards in India, the "Padma Bhushan," in January 2000. He is also the recipient of many other community and peace activist awards from various national and international organizations. In 2002, he was invited to Zug, Switzerland by the Nuclear Disarmament Forum to receive the "Demiurgus Peace International Award," which is given annually in recognition for one's "achievements in the field of strengthening peace among nations."[2]

Wahiduddin Khan combines knowledge of the traditional religious sciences ('ulūm al-dīn) with the cultural, sociopolitical, and ethical discourse of his times. He is an avid reader and keeps himself updated on current events. He often draws on his knowledge of contemporary events to highlight the moral plight of our times. His familiarity with the foundational literature on science and religion, ethics, and political discourse informs his own writings in Islamic moral theology. Widely traveled, he shows exceptional knowledge of and interest in Western as well as modern ethical concerns. His writings display an eagerness to apply the lessons learned from his explorations to critical issues facing Muslim societies both in India and elsewhere.

Mawlana Khan has authored well over a hundred works, many of which have been translated from Urdu into Arabic, English, and Hindi. He has published numerous articles in newspapers and journals and has given countless interviews to such prominent national and international media outlets as *The Times of India*, *The Indian Express*, *Newsweek*, the BBC, the All India Radio, and many others. As mentioned above, his writings fill the pages of the *Al-Risāla* Urdu monthly of which he has been the editor-in-chief since its inception in 1976. As founder-president of "The Islamic Center" established in 1970, Mawlana Khan has presided over a kind of Islamic movement that is fundamentally different from all other movements in contemporary Muslim history. Known as the "Al-Risāla movement," and which Mawlana Khan often calls "mission," it has gradually influenced and shaped Muslim thinking over the last 40 years, a measure of which can be found in the changing attitudes of the Indian Muslim leadership in the late 1990s.[3]

Muslim religious and political leadership for the most part ignored Wahiduddin Khan in the early phase of his mission and dubbed him varyingly as "anti-Muslim," a "Libyan agent," and, more recently, the "Hindu agent." They felt that his conciliatory and self-critical tone was not apropos of Islam's dignified past status in India. In their view the solution to Muslims' problems was to be found in taking a hard-line approach and invoking the law to curb Hindu right-wing attacks on Islam and Muslims. Khan, on the other hand, advocated a dialogical approach and he himself initiated direct talks with several Hindu leaders and right wing groups. By the late 1990s most of the Muslim leaders had effectively come to realize that their confrontational approach had basically emboldened the forces of Hindu militant extremism and caused a sharp increase in the number of problems faced by Muslims. Thus, somewhat cognizant of the social forces at work, they presently have become less confrontational, less law invoking, and more conciliatory towards Hindus.

What distinguishes Wahiduddin Khan from scores of other *ulama* in the Muslim world in general and in India in particular is his very *idea* of Islam.[4] He sees Islam as a personal struggle for faith in God and sincere reaching out to God in pursuit of a life of piety. Simply put, he is emphatically opposed to any political understanding of Islam. To him, political struggles of Muslims around the world cannot and must not be promoted on the basis of Islamic teachings. Islamic lifestyle and culture are decisively separate from any worldly matters that engage Muslims. This does not necessarily imply a dichotomized view of being Muslim in a world that is increasingly secular. It simply disallows the construction of an artificial connection between Islam's religious calling and Muslims' worldly challenges. Khan does not denounce politics as such, but he argues that politics is a matter of choice whereas Islam is not. One may or may not take up a political cause such as a separatist movement organized in Kashmir but one must not confuse such causes with Islam.[5] His critics have argued that taking up causes in defense of the community is integral to Islam and therefore must be regarded as an activity which is part of one's faith. Mawlana Khan could not agree more. However, he argues that political separatism, which is blindly pursued without reflection on either the alternate solutions to the problems, whatever they may be, or the consequences of separatist struggles where the very freedom and stability of society they are trying to secure are threatened and eroded are not and cannot be reconciled with the teachings of the Qur'an and hadith.

Islam and the Other

Wahiduddin Khan's perception of the world does not include the "other." He is critical of the generally dichotomized view of some Muslim leaders who interpret Islam as an ideology pitted against other, in their view, deviant ideologies, that is, the worldview which sees "us" vs. "them" without regard for the complications that such a worldview may pose in the real world. In fact, the ideologizing of Islam has reached a point where in some Muslim groups the process of identifying "us" is limited to those who subscribe to the narrow interpretations of that group. Thus rhetorically, "us" for such groups may rhetorically mean all Muslims, but in reality it includes only those who agree with the authoritative voice that speaks on behalf of the group while claiming to speak on behalf of the whole of Islam itself.

Khan deconstructs this ideological worldview presented in the name of the faith. He understands "Islam" – an individual's *quiet* surrender to the will of God – as primarily a personal relationship between the believer and God. This understanding of Islam, he argues, emanates from the Qur'an and was lived out by Prophet Muhammad as evidenced through a careful study of his *sīrah*.

The Al-Risāla movement today represents a growing number of Muslims, many of whom come from the intellectual and managerial classes. The movement has many followers who work independently and are not dues-paying members; the organization has no structure except the implicit recognition of Mawlana Khan's spiritual leadership. Those who agree with his way of explaining Islam support the movement by continuing to follow his writings by subscribing to the journal *Al-Risāla*. Through his continuous efforts, Mawlana Khan aims to transform attitudes by infusing what he calls a "moral spirit" in the practice of Islam, particularly in regard to relations with the so-called "other." Thus the Al-Risāla movement is primarily a movement for moral reform. Today Khan's following includes not only Muslims, but also Hindus and people from other faiths whose participation has added a whole new layer of complexity to this unique Islamic movement, and has also confirmed his own belief that the moral campaign alone is the heart and soul of Islamic revivalism.

Islam and Politics

Mawlana Khan's understanding of Islamic revival is quite different from the political revivalists of the nineteenth and twentieth centuries in many Muslim lands who sought to instill the masses with nationalistic and/or Islamic sentiments against the then colonial masters. In this regard, Khan's view is diametrically opposed to all contemporary violent manifestations of revivalism in the name of Islam. He argues that Islamic movements that seek to carry out their struggles in militant terms, variously known as "terrorists" and "*jihādis*," are doing a disservice to Islam and Muslims.

Khan's idea of Islamic revival is the very antithesis of the many political struggles (with their potential for the eruption of violence) launched in the name of Islam in recent decades in various parts of the Muslim world. In fact, Khan is opposed to any politicization of religion as well as to involving religion in political struggles. Simply put, he thinks it is a good idea to separate religion and politics, a notion resisted by many other Muslim intellectuals. Given the nature of complexities around this notion, there is no easy solution to this debate and the Muslim discourse today contains arguments on both sides of this great divide.

Wahiduddin Khan, like Abul Kalam Azad (d. 1958), also argues for a temporal separation of religious and political action. Based again on the prophetic example, he justifies such a separation for the sake of the end result.[6] The establishment of an Islamic state is nowhere required either in the Qur'an or in the Sunnah of the Prophet Muhammad. The prophets came to "warn" humankind of the impending danger if they failed to heed the will of God. By confusing a political agenda with our spiritual goals we not only misunderstand *dīn* or faith as enunciated in the Qur'an, we also endanger our social causes by being labeled as divisive and sectarian in an increasingly pluralistic world. To Khan, politicization of religion is known to create problems for the Muslim community's development; hence it is against the spirit of Islam. For him, the separation between religious and political spheres is meant to maintain religious freedom while continuing dialogue on matters of the world where Muslims and non-Muslims can find a common ground in the spirit of cooperation and national interest.

Thus, while the task of many Muslim organizations is to mobilize Muslims to promote Muslim political action (this includes the nonviolent as well as potentially violent groups), Khan's mission, by contrast, strives for an intellectual and ethical revival which will conform Muslim behavior to what Khan calls the faith and practice of the Prophet Muhammad and his companions. In fact the bulk of the short narratives filling the pages of *Al-Risāla* and some of his other works draw on stories of the ṣahāba (companions of the Prophet) in order to highlight the moral and its possible applications to contemporary situations.

Key Objectives of the Al-Risāla Movement

As far as one can glean from the collective writings of Mawlana Khan, the Al-Risāla movement seems to be emphasizing two main principles.

A. Muslims need to exercise greater self-criticism and not be ashamed of the past mistakes of their forebears. They must not be bound to history and should not insist on glorifying it, especially since it is known to contain many less than glorious moments. Muslims should engage in *ijtihād* and rethink and articulate anew the core message of Islam in light of modern challenges and its applications. This amounts to a reform from within.[7] The key components of this rethinking are nonviolence and reconciliation.

1. *Self-criticism as a means to reform from within*
    Mawlana Khan has often placed greater responsibility upon Muslims for the ills in their midst. For example, throughout the 1980s he argued that communal riots, which were mostly anti-Muslim riots and pogroms, happened because Muslims provoked Hindu extremist groups by their confrontational posture against the Hindus. This provocation may not have warranted whole-scale destruction of Muslims' lives and property, but in Khan's view it was sufficient to constitute favorable conditions in which violence could take place. Furthermore, it is common knowledge that when Muslims are in the minority they would naturally stand to lose in any such conflict. Therefore it is the Muslims who will always have a greater responsibility to ensure such conditions do not arise wherein their communal and financial interests may become targets. In other words, Khan consistently puts forth the argument that conflict takes place because of the willingness and presence of two or more opponents. Furthermore, he places blame for inflamed circumstances, which often result in violence, squarely on Muslim leadership, both religious as well as political. If Muslims could learn to be patient, to resist temptations to react unkindly, and to practice tolerance even when provoked, then conflict could certainly be avoided. Thus Khan advocates an extreme form of pacifism. To many Muslims this is a harsh verdict coming from a Muslim scholar.

2. *Nonviolence and reconciliation as central to Islam in the twenty-first century*
    Being a traditional scholar, Mawlana Khan cites the Qur'an to justify his
    approach of reconciliation. In the tradition of Azad, Khan argues for a model
    of *cooperation* with other communities and *participation* in the process of
    nation building, rather than the model of *conflict* and *impasse* some Muslim
    leaders, both in the 1940s and since independence, seem to have encouraged.
    In his writings, he often cites the episode of *Ḥudaybiyah*, which occurred in
    early Islam during the time of the Prophet. It involved the peaceful resolu-
    tion of a potential conflict and possible confrontation between the Muslims
    of Medina and the Quraysh of Mecca over the issue of pilgrimage to the
    Ka'bah. This event has sometimes been characterized as the cornerstone of
    Muslim success in the early stages of Islamic expansion even though it was
    seemingly a humiliating defeat for Muslims. Not only does Khan imbue this
    thesis of reconciliation with an imperative tone, he also argues that this is
    the only possible Islamic behavior in the present scheme of things in India
    and elsewhere. Violence, he says, "is against the spirit of the age" and there-
    fore Muslims must part with it even if there is enough justification for it. The
    path to peace and the establishment of an Islamic society must originate from
    a *Ḥudaybiyah*-style, diplomatic, non-confrontational, non-aggressive, and
    ultimately non-political approach.

B. Muslims must engage in dialogue with others (with an intention to invite
    them to learn about Islam) because of the present realities of Indian polity.
    Muslims thus need to re-orient themselves to living in a pluralistic and multi-
    cultural ethos. They must develop inter-cultural, inter-religious, and inter-
    ethnic relations in order to cooperate on issues such as providing greater
    access to education and inculcating moral values. Khan believes that this
    form of activism, which to him is utterly Islamic, would attract others to
    Islam and hence allow Muslims to carry out one of their core Islamic duties
    of calling people to Islam, or da'wah.

1. *Dialogue with the "other"*
    Wahiduddin Khan is a rare person in the sense that in his capacity as an *'ālim*
    (religious scholar) he has shown a way for Muslims to engage in dialogue
    with members of other faiths. He has made particularly great inroads in
    establishing conversations between Muslims and Hindus on a host of issues.
    In his effort to win over the Hindu right-wing groups, he has participated in
    their meetings to show what he calls "true" Islam – an Islam which does not
    "otherize" or seek to alienate and an Islam which calls for peace, not revenge
    and retaliation. To some extent these efforts to bring the extremists among
    Hindus closer to accepting Muslims as fellow Indians (as opposed to how they
    are otherwise viewed as "foreigners") have been productive. Khan has won
    respect among many such Hindus maintaining an interesting "alliance."
    However, some real fruit of this interesting relation building with extremist
    Hindu elements has been the effect on other moderate and eclectic Hindus.
    Many other Hindus have begun to pay greater attention to Islam and often

have greater sympathies with Muslims while being critical of the extremist elements within their own religion.

In Mawlana Khan's view, it is imperative that Muslims seek direct talks with their Hindu neighbors and try to build bridges with them instead of creating an environment of hostility by regarding them as the "other."[8] In past conflicts, Muslims often invoked the law and relied on help from the government to resolve the conflicts. Khan believes that Muslims should try harder to resolve their differences directly with their Hindu opponents.

Thus, in Khan's view, dialogue can benefit all communities by facilitating cooperation on common issues across the board, but such a dialogue is also open to missionary activity. Hence all communities would have the right to "present" their religious teachings to others without engaging in proselytization as such.

2. *Engaged Islam*

Khan emphasizes the need for Muslims to become part of the national "mainstream" and contribute to the nation as a whole. Khan's primary impetus comes from the teachings of the Qur'an and the hadith. Muslims' main goal should be to become an exemplary moral community that lives out the principles of Islam by following the teachings of the Qur'an and the Sunnah of the Prophet Muhammad. At the same time they have a responsibility to the nation of which they are a part. Thus they must not neglect their public duties as citizens of India without relinquishing their religious objectives and requirements. In his view these two are perfectly reconcilable from a Qur'anic perspective. While the Islamic notion of a *sharī'ah*-based state is valid, it is not an absolute requirement for living out Islam faithfully.[9] The vision of many Islamic movements in recent history and even in present-day India is based on the design of an Islamic state where in their view by applying the Islamic law in its totality Muslims will be able to live out their faith in ideal terms. This is a fantastic thesis from Mawlana Khan's perspective not only because the goal of establishing an Islamic state remains implausible for various reasons, once established, but also it is not certain that a viable manifestation of Islamic law can be agreed upon by all participants of such a state. Furthermore, a significant portion of *sharī'ah* (some would say the most vital part of it) is already applied by Muslims in their daily lives without having to establish an Islamic state. Thus it seems foolish to risk current Muslim resources on an objective which by all accounts falls short in the dividends it *might* yield in a distant future.

Mawlana Khan argues that as minorities Muslims can find copious ways to live out their religious and spiritual responsibilities. At the same time they must engage with other religious communities in contributing to the demands of their specific sociocultural ethos. As citizens of a secular nation, they must accept the pluralistic ethics in relation to worldly matters while their religious and cultural principles are safeguarded within a secular system that provides for complete freedom of religious practice and propagation. Sectarian struggles should be put aside and not be confused with religious struggles.

Islam and Secularism

Many Muslim leaders today are attempting to show that secularism is not necessarily bad for religion but rather is a workable solution to inter-religious friction. In particular the Muslim religious leadership, notably in Indonesia, has been speaking of a reconstruction of the traditionalist discourse that seeks to align Islam with modern geo-political realities. Mawlana Khan can be counted among the few who have championed this trend in the Indian subcontinent. He speaks of the need for *ijtihād* (providing fresh insights in legal matters based on a re-examination of the sources of Islamic law) for a systematic adaptation of Muslim life and thought to the changing times. One of the challenges for Muslims is to learn to engage within the realm of secularism and religious pluralism as a means to peace and inter-religious harmony.

Muslim minorities in many countries have supported secularism in order to maintain a level of religious and cultural freedom in many countries. But in India this has not been the case; Muslims have rather been suspicious of secularism, afraid that, as a minority, they would lose their cultural and religious heritage to the overwhelming influence of the majority (Hindu) culture and religion. The Indian *ulama* especially have not been in favor of the secularization of Muslims and hence did not elaborate on it. Therefore individuals like Wahiduddin Khan are pioneers among the *ulama* class in openly "theologizing" about such notions as secularism and relating it directly to the fundamental ways of being a Muslim.

In the early years of independent India, the term secularism was almost always wrongly translated into Urdu as "*ghayr mazhabi*" (irreligious) and wrongly equated with "*la diniyat*" (atheism).[10] Since Urdu was the main language of communication for the Muslim masses, gradually there emerged a general feeling of disgust with secularism since Muslims believe that their religion "restrains them from accepting the autonomy of worldly life which is the basis of secularism."[11] Ziya-ul Hasan Faruqi, one of the early Muslim intellectuals associated with the Jamia Millia Islamia and an associate of such secular Muslim intellectuals as Zakir Hussain, Abid Hussain, and Mohammad Mujeeb, wrote extensively in an effort to convince the Muslim masses that secularism in India is not synonymous with atheism. Neither does it mean rejection of religious values:

> It is a secularism based on democratic traditions and liberal thought and is not only tolerant toward religion but grants to all full freedom of religious faith and practice. [Furthermore Muslims must] also realize that in a country like India it is only this brand of secularism which can provide safeguards for their cultural and religious freedom and can give strength to their status as a religious minority.[12]

While it is true that the "idea of the secular state involves a theological question . . . ," in practice the history of Islam reveals that, except for the first few years, the Islamic state had always maintained a mundane and secular status. Whereas tension existed between the ḥukkām (political authorities) and the ulama (religious authorities), the latter generally supported the secular arrangement of the state for a variety of reasons; an important one being that "a stable political system, whatever its nature, was better than a state of anarchy."[13]

Citing Sa'id Ahmad Akbarabadi, an influential Indian 'ālim, Faruqi reminds us that there are two aspects of Islam – dīn and sharī'ah, "while dīn is immutable, the sharī'ah has been constantly changing." Further, the changes (or reform) in the sharī'ah are essential in order to keep it current with the times. These changes, however, are limited to those things on which the injunctions of the Qur'an are not explicit, for example, polygamy, which may be "controlled, or abolished" as per the necessity of the times.[14]

But there is a danger in holding such views, especially when it comes to dealing with Muslims who are still very religious (read, "traditional") in their outlook and do not accept change and innovation very easily. As Mushir-ul Haq also notes, for change to take place in these old traditions, religious sanction is a must. Without the blessing of the ulama, secularism would not be accepted by Muslims since they have been made to view it as an innovation (bida').[15]

Mawlana Wahiduddin Khan argues that secularism as practiced in India is not anti-Islamic since there are no arguments against it in the Islamic legal tradition. An important principle of fiqh (jurisprudence) is that "everything is lawful unless it is declared unlawful" (al-aṣl fi al-ashyā' al-ibaḥah). Since there is no clear regulation concerning secularism, it should not be rejected prima facie.[16] Instead it should be examined in light of the needs and demands of the community. Muslims have a choice to either accept or reject it on the basis of rational arguments. Like the secular Muslim leaders discussed above, Khan believes that secularism does not hinder either the growth or the sustenance of the Muslim way of life in India.[17]

Mawlana Khan argues that when we are concerned with matters of belief, worship, and the hereafter, we must adhere to the letter of the Qur'an. But where worldly matters are concerned, we are permitted to accept commonly held views insofar as they do not contradict or negate the former.[18] Mawlana Khan often draws from the prophetic example to establish his point, claiming that Prophet Muhammad is known to have followed pre-existent regulations in matters of the world. The Prophet respected established international customs and regulations as binding unless they were seen as an impediment in practicing his faith. Therefore one can and must respect international laws and even adapt useful practices insofar as they do not prevent one from following one's religious beliefs. Wahiduddin Khan not only approves of secularism but he also deems it necessary to separate religious matters from political aspirations for the sake of the growth of Muslim societies around the world.[19]

Mawlana Wahiduddin Khan is perhaps one of the most significant voices from among the ranks of the ulama in India to support the idea of secularism, not just as it is implemented in India but universally. Mawlana Khan says, echoing Akbarabadi, that secular India is neither dār al-ḥarb nor dār al-Islām; instead it is dār al-da'wah, a land full of opportunities for the Islamic mission. Secularism has many beneficial aspects for Muslims, which they did not have in the past. It allows for freedom of speech and propagation of one's faith to others. This to him is fundamentally significant because Muslims' main task in this world is to engage in da'wah, or to be more precise, 'amr bil-

ma'rūf, nahi 'an al-munkar, promoting the good and forbidding what is evil.[20] Thus, secularism is not only beneficial to the Islamic cause, but it also mirrors Islam's own vision of a pluralist society.[21] Secularism is one form of a social system promoting diversity and allowing each component of a diverse society to operate and grow *interactively* (as manifest in national aspects) as well as *independently* (as manifest in religious aspects) at the same time.[22]

For Khan secularism and pluralism are indicators of good health in any society and allow for growth of all religions as they compete with each other in "good works" – for the noblest of all in the eyes of God is the one striving most earnestly in the direction of what is righteous.[23] The Qur'anic focus is on interaction rather than just a verbal exchange of ideas; hence Khan's emphasis on engaging other communities in dialogue as well as on Muslim participation in the national mainstream culture of India.[24]

The Impact and the Current Focus

Even though Khan primarily wrote on the general issues of Islamic life and ethics as well as Islam's interrelationship with the modern age, he has also been writing on the life and struggles of Indian Muslims. From the beginning of the movement, his main focus has been reform among Indian Muslims with respect both to how they view Islam as a faith and how they live out that faith as a minority group in the midst of others with differing historical perspectives. One major element of Khan's thought has been his passionate call for the rebuilding of mainstream Indian culture. He projects a bright future for Muslims in India if and only if they become a giving people contributing to the national growth, politics, economy, culture, and to society as a whole. Muslims should become unreservedly involved in nation building; they should become part of the mainstream. By remaining in their limited spheres of activity, and railing about their personal problems without regard for those of others, they are viewed as sectarian at best. In addition, an antagonistic response from the Hindu right wing has been increasing due to reactionary Muslim politics. Therefore a different strategy is needed to counter the anti-Muslim trends, removing those conditions that allow the Hindu extremist groups to portray Muslims as alienated from their nationalistic ethos.

As a self-imposed rule, Mawlana Khan did not speak of politics and of politicians until very recently. He argued for a long time that he was apolitical, that he was not affiliated with or in favor of any party or political group. But analysis of his writings from the last few years reveals a slight shift in his posture; he projects for himself a wider role, which is infused with a nationalistic tone. He is no longer apolitical and has begun to assume a role of a political commentator but with an orientation toward social harmony. For example, the special issue of *Al-Risāla* Urdu (July 1999) is entitled "*Ta'mīr-i Hind*" (*Building India*), in which Khan deals with issues of nation building and social and religious harmony, particularly critiquing select political and religious leaders. In his previous writings he had refrained from such open critique of his contemporaries, especially political leaders.

Recently another shift in his movement may be noticed. This is regarding his interactions with non-Muslims who have come to understand him, as he would agree, better than Muslims do. Many of these individuals, mostly Indians, and all professionals working in various fields such as journalism, finance, etc., have engaged him for guidance and "counseling" and in the case of some, for conversion to Islam.[25] This is a new dimension of his mission and leadership, which is still unfolding and needs careful study.

For the past two years he has been holding bimonthly sessions called the "spiritual class," in which a dedicated group attentively engages him in conversation on matters of faith. Almost all of these individuals have had little or no interest in Islam prior to their coming into contact with Mawlana Khan. Some of them come from Hindu backgrounds and now reportedly are practicing Muslims. By coming into contact with Mawlana Khan, they say, their lives have changed for the better. A small loyal group among them have taken to accompanying Mawlana Khan on his travels in India and abroad, hence the title of one of his recent articles, "Class on Wheels."[26]

Conclusion

Wahiduddin Khan does not project himself as a reformer. He outlines the nature of his mission in his pioneering book, *Fikr-e-Islāmī* as *ijtihād*. In his view, reform (*islāh*) implies the existence of a faulty ideal requiring reform. Islam, as for many earlier revivalists who have attempted *tajdīd* (renewal), still consists of those very ideals that existed at the time of the Prophet Muhammad. There are no changes required insofar as Islam is concerned. It is Muslims who have forgotten how to reinterpret and reapply Islam in every age according to the needs and circumstances of the time. Thus his task is to provide this reinterpretation of Islam for today's Muslims and those non-Muslims who are willing to collaborate on building and maintaining a multi-cultural ethos.

He argues that what is lacking in the Indian Muslim community at large is a coherent vision of the reapplication (by way of *ijtihād*) of the Islamic ideals. These ideals in Khan's interpretation are pluralism, tolerance of differences, utilizing peaceful means to activism and becoming progressive within the scope of the teachings of Islam.[27]

Even though Mawlana Khan remains a controversial figure in India because of his critique of contemporary *ulama* and due to his innovative interpretation of Muslim history, his view of Islam and the role of Muslims in the twenty-first century is increasingly making sense even to those who did not previously agree with him. Thus it may be said that the future holds positive prospects for the principles enunciated by Mawlana Khan. Once he is no longer living, successive generations will encounter these principles and rationale without any subjective bias against the man.

Notes

1. John F. Burns, "Gandhi's Ashes Rest, but Not His Message," *The New York Times*, January 31, 1997. In Indian and international media coverage he has been identified variously as a chief spokesperson for the Muslims of India; a "liberal" Muslim scholar; and even a Sufi.
2. *Al-Risāla* Urdu, August 2003.

3.   Mawlana Khan has been assisted in his mission by two of his children, the younger of his two sons, Dr. Saniyasnain Khan, and his daughter, Dr. Farida Khanam, both of whom are accomplished scholars and have established themselves as authors/editors. They have worked closely with Mawlana Khan since the beginning of his mission, managing the logistics of the mission and also doing translation work and public relations. Farida Khanam is primarily responsible for translating Mawlana Khan's works into English. Dr. Zafarul Islam Khan, the elder son, is also a noted scholar of Islam and Muslim intellectual traditions and history. He is not particularly associated with the Al-Risāla movement and for the most part disagrees with his father's approach to Muslim reform in India. Mawlana Wahiduddin Khan, interview by author, New Delhi, January 21, 1998.

4.   Wahiduddin Khan was formerly a member of the Jamaat-e-Islami (founded in 1941) of Mawlana Abu'l 'Ala Mawdūdī (d. 1979). He worked with the Jamaat for 15 years before resigning due to ideological differences. For more on the nature of these differences, see Mawlana Wahiduddin Khan, *Tā'bīr kī ghalatī*, second edn. (New Delhi: Maktaba Al-Risāla, 1987 [1963]), 19.

5.   Mawlana Wahiduddin Khan, interview by author, New Delhi, January 6, 2004.

6.   This refers to a hadith reported in Bukhari and Muslim regarding the issue of what to do about a selfish ruler where the Prophet is quoted as saying, "give them [the rulers] their due and ask God your due." Mawlana Wahiduddin Khan, *Fikr-e-Islāmī* (New Delhi: Al-Risāla Books, 1996), 160.

7.   Mawlana Khan does not think Islam needs reform but rather Muslims' understanding of Islam needs to be corrected. See his *Fikr-e-Islāmī*.

8.   Wahiduddin Khan, "Hindu–Muslim Dialogue," *Al-Risāla* English, November–December, 1994, 15.

9.   Christian W. Troll, "Sharing Islamically in the Pluralistic Nation-State of India. The Views of Some Contemporary Indian Muslim Leaders and Thinkers," in *Christian-Muslim Encounters*, Yvonne Y. Haddad and Wadi' Z. Haddad (eds.), (Gainesville: University of Florida Press, 1995), 245–62.

10.   Ziya-ul Hasan Faruqi, "Indian Muslims and the Ideology of the Secular State," in *South Asian Politics and Religion*, D. Smith (ed.), (Princeton: Princeton University Press, 1966), 140. See also Abid Husain, *The Destiny of Indian Muslims* (Lahore: Qadira Book Traders, 1983).

11.   Mushir-ul Haq, *Islam in Secular India* (Simla: Indian Institute of Advanced Study, 1972), 1.

12.   Faruqi, "Indian Muslims and the Ideology of the Secular State," 149.

13.   Ibid., 139–42. Coulson argued similarly that in Islamic history there had been a convenient separation of religious and political spheres even though ideologically it never found much support. See Noel James Coulson, *A History of Islamic Law* (Edinburgh: Edinburgh University Press, 1964).

14.   Faruqi, "Indian Muslims and the Ideology of the Secular State," 148. See also Sa'id Ahmad Akbarabadi, "Hindustan ki shar'i haithiyat (India's Status in Light of *Sharī'ah*)," *Burhan*, July–September, 1966, 190–7.

15.   Haq, *Islam in Secular India*, 86.

16.   Mawlana Wahiduddin Khan, *Din-i kamil* (New Delhi: Maktaba al-Risāla, 1992), 365.

17.   For more on this issue, see Irfan A. Omar, "Islam and the Other: The Ideal Vision of Mawlana Wahiduddin Khan," *Journal of Ecumenical Studies*, 36/3–4, 1999, 423–38.

18.   *Al-Risāla* Urdu, September 1998, 23.

19.   Khan, *Din-i kamil*, 366.

20.   Referring, among others, to the verses 3:104 and 110 of the Qur'an.

21.   Mawlana Wahiduddin Khan, interview by author, New Delhi, India, January 21, 1998.

22. Mawlana Wahiduddin Khan, "A Return to Secularism," interview in *Asiaweek*, January 13, 1993; and also his "The Future of Secularism," *The Hindustan Times*, April 25, 1996.

23. The Qur'an says: "And each one has a goal toward which he turns; so race one another in good works . . ." 2:148a; see also 49:13, 4:1, in *The Meaning of the Glorious Koran*, trans. M. M. Pickthall (New York: New American Library, 1953).

24. Irfan A. Omar, "Indian Muslims and the Search for Communal Harmony: Some Notes on Mawlana Wahiduddin Khan," *Studies in Contemporary Islam*, 2/1, 2000, 60–6.

25. In a recent interview with the author (January 6, 2004), he acknowledged a shift in his attention towards non-Muslims or the new Muslims who regularly come to him for general discussions and learning about Islam.

26. See *Al-Risāla* Urdu, November 2004, which published accounts by some of these close disciples relating their transformation experience in their own words.

27. Mawlana Wahiduddin Khan, "Co-Existence of Religions in India," *The Times of India*, August 19, 1993.

CHAPTER 5

Sayyed Abul Hasan 'Ali Nadwi and Contemporary Islamic Thought in India

Yoginder Sikand

Faced with the ominous rise of Hindu fascism and an increasingly Hinduized state, the Muslims of India struggle to preserve their separate identity, which they see as under grave threat. Post-Partition Indian Muslim scholars have been particularly concerned with reinforcing the faith and identity of their fellow religionists, while at the same time asserting the need for Muslims to critically engage with the wider society to protect and promote their interests. The balance that they have sought to maintain between commitment to Islam and to the notion of the universal Muslim *ummah*, on the one hand, and to the Indian state on the other, has not been free from tension. In the fascist Hindutva imagination, the Indian Muslims are continuously reviled as Pakistani "fifth columnists," as "enemies of the nation," and so on, and their patriotism is said to be suspect. The Muslim as the menacing "other" occupies a central place in Hindutva discourse, and this has been used to legitimize large-scale anti-Muslim violence. Matters have been made more complicated with the activities of anti-Indian and anti-Hindu Islamist groups in Kashmir and in neighboring Pakistan, thus further reinforcing widespread anti-Muslim prejudices in India and thereby strengthening the Hindu right.

The late Sayyed Abul Hasan 'Ali Nadwi (d. 1999), more popularly known as 'Ali Miyan, was one of the leading Indian *ulama* of modern times, recognized in Muslim circles worldwide for his scholarship and his dedication to the cause of Islamic revival. This chapter provides an introduction to his life and works and a broad overview of his writings. It focuses, in particular, on Nadwi's own vision for Islam in contemporary India, striving to reconcile the Islamic commitment of the Muslims of the country with their status as citizens of a nominally secular state and as members of a multi-religious society.

Early Life

Abul Hasan 'Ali Nadwi was born in 1913 at Takiya Kalan, also known as Daira-i Shah 'Alimullah, a village near the town of Rai Bareilly, in the present-day Indian state of Uttar Pradesh. His family, which claimed descent from the Prophet Muhammad, had produced numerous illustrious scholars and Sufis. Among the several leading Islamic scholars and activists that the family had produced, and in whom Nadwi took great pride, was Sayyed Ahmad Barelwi, the charismatic eighteenth-century leader who had launched a failed *jihād* against the Sikhs in the Punjab.[1]

As a child, Nadwi was sent to the village mosque school, where he studied the Qur'an and learnt Arabic and Urdu. His father, Sayyed 'Abdul Hai Hasani, an accomplished Islamic scholar in his own right[2] and the rector of the famous Nadwat ul-'Ulama madrasah[3] in Lucknow for many years, died when he was nine, and he was brought up by his mother, a pious woman who had memorized the entire Qur'an by heart. A particularly important influence on him at this stage was his elder brother, Sayyed 'Abdul 'Ala, who later assumed the post of director of the Nadwat ul-'Ulama. From his brother Nadwi learnt Arabic and studied books on the life of the Prophet. By this time he had developed a deep commitment to the cause of Islam. This was accompanied by a growing antagonism to the West, which he began to see as responsible for much of the misery of the Muslims the world over. As one of his biographers notes, he was now fired by a "hatred of the West," not of individual Westerners as such but of "Western oppression."[4] This was to have a lasting impact on his subsequent life and in his championing of Islam as an alternative to Western "decadence."

In order to train as an *'ālim* he was sent to the Nadwat ul-'Ulama for higher Islamic studies. Established in 1898, the Nadwat saw itself as a leading center for the training of reformist *ulama*. He also traveled to Lahore, where he studied the Qur'an for a while under Mawlana Ahmad 'Ali (d.1962). In 1931, he went to Azamgarh to study with the noted Islamic scholar, Sayyed Sulamian Nadwi at the Dar ul-Musannifin, established by the renowned Mawlana Shibli Nu'mani (d.1914). The next year he went to Deoband, where he studied Qur'anic commentaries under the noted Deobandi *'ālim*, Mawlana Sayyed Hussain Ahmad Madani. Alongside his study of the Qur'an and Islamic law, he began taking an interest in Sufism as well, being enrolled into various Sufi orders.[5]

A major turning point in Nadwi's life came in 1934, when he was appointed to teach Arabic and Qur'anic commentary at the Nadwat ul-'Ulama. The Nadwat was to remain central to his life thereafter, just as he was to remain central to the life of the madrasah, turning it into a widely recognized center for Islamic research.[6] He continued teaching at the madrasah even after he was appointed its rector in 1961 after the death of his brother, a post that he occupied till his own death.

It was at the Nadwat that Nadwi's great skills as a writer and orator were able to develop and flourish. He is credited with having written almost 180 books, mostly in Arabic and some in Urdu. Many of these books have since been translated into various other languages. Nadwi's particular interest lay in Islamic movements, and his first full-length study was on the *jihād* movement of his ancestor Sayyed Ahmad Shahid, begun in 1936 and completed three years later. Another of his major literary achievements was his five-volume *Tarikh-i Da'wat-o-'Azimat*, a history of revivalist movements among Muslims in India. Nadwi wrote extensively on the poet-philosopher Iqbal and his quest for a normative Islamic social order and polity, on the life and works of Mawlana Muhammad Ilyas, the founder of the Tablighi Jamaat, on the contributions of Muslims and Islam to world culture, and a series of books on Islam in the contemporary Arab world, where he had traveled widely, stressing the glory of the Arab contribution to Islam and human progress, calling upon them to go back to their Islamic roots, while at the same time bitterly castigating dictatorial Arab regimes for their secularism, their cultural and political enslavement to the West and their often brutal suppression of Islamist movements. He was also critical of such ideologies as nationalism, communism, and pan-Arabism, which he saw as having taken the place of Islam as the guiding light of the Arabs and as having caused their downfall. Having traveled extensively in the United States and Europe, Nadwi also penned several books and tracts on contemporary Western civilization, condemning it for what he regarded as its crass materialism, for what he saw as its immorality and godlessness, but at the same time insisting that Muslims should not hesitate to benefit from its scientific achievements.

Nadwi's writings were concerned to present Islam as a comprehensive worldview. As such, therefore, he echoed the argument of the Islamists that an Islamic state was essential for the laws of *sharī'ah* to be implemented in their entirety. However, he was, at the same time, a realist, aware that this was out of the realm of human possibility in the contemporary Indian context. He argued that an Islamic political order could be established in India only in some remotely distant future. Rather than struggling directly for it in the present, he believed that the Indian Muslims should focus their energies on missionary efforts and trying to build what he saw as a truly Islamic society, on the basis of which alone could an ideal Islamic political order come into being.[7]

Besides his voluminous scholarly output, Nadwi was occupied with several Indian as well as international Islamic organizations. In recognition of his outstanding contribution to Islamic studies and to the cause of Islam, he was awarded the Shah Faisal Award in 1980. In addition to serving as the rector of the Nadwat ul-'Ulama, he was the head of the Dini Ta'limi Council (The Religious Education Council), Uttar Pradesh, member of the Standing Committee of the Dar ul-Musannifin, Azamgarh, member of the Consultative Committee of the Dar ul-'Ulum madrasah, Deoband, chairman of the Oxford Centre of Islamic Studies, director of the Foundation for Studies and Research, Luxembourg, member of the Organizing Committee of the Islamic Center, Geneva, member of the Board of Directors of the Rabita al-Adab al-Islami al-'Alami (The World Committee for Islamic Literature), Amman, member of the Standing Committee of the Rabita al-'Alami al-Islami (The World Muslim League), Mecca, member of the Consultative Committee of the Jami'a al-Islamiya (Islamic University), Medina, as well as visiting professor at the universities of Damascus, Medina, and Marrakesh. His involvement with these organizations and institutions enabled him to travel widely, both in India as well as abroad, which, in turn, exercised a major influence on his own writings as well as his work among the Muslims of India, to which we now turn.

Muslims as a Minority: Between Faith and Citizenship

Nadwi's views on Muslims living as a minority in India and how this predicament could be reconciled with an understanding of Islam as going beyond personal piety to embrace collective affairs as well as the polity, must be seen in the context of his understanding of the historical role of Islam in India. Nadwi portrays a romantically ideal picture of much of the history of the Muslim presence in India. Thus, he says, the first Muslims came to India "supremely unconcerned with worldly aims and ambitions" guided only by "the lofty sentiment of religious service." The message of equality and social justice that the early Sufis preached struck a powerful chord among the people, especially the "low" castes, and scores of them embraced Islam at their hands. For their part, successive Muslim kings of India are said to have been "men of courage and ambition," who "carried the country to glorious heights of progress and prosperity." They considered themselves as "divinely-appointed trustees of God's land and servants of His people." The Muslims who came to India from abroad settled down in the country for good, thus making it their home, unlike, for instance, the British. As such, their contributions to Indian culture have been immense. It was under Muslim rule that most of India was unified into one administrative unit and the country was brought into contact with the outside world. Muslims helped develop new styles of architecture, art, dress, language, and literature, as well as promoting trade, agriculture, and industry. More importantly, Islam provided the Indians with the concept of Divine Unity, bitterly critiquing polytheism, priesthood, idolatry, and various superstitious beliefs and practices. Its message of social equality and women's rights, too, had a profound impact, and many Hindu reformist sects owed their inspiration to Islamic influence. In more recent times, Muslims also played a leading role in the struggle against British imperialism and for the cause of Indian freedom.[8]

Because of the great contributions that Muslims have made to Indian history and culture, Nadwi argued, they have as much right to live in India as equal citizens as do people of other faiths. As he put it, "The Muslims are not only citizens of an equal status with anybody in India; they are also among its chief builders and architects, and hold a position second to none among the peoples of the world for selfless service to the motherland."[9] This argument appears to have been directed both at Hindu chauvinists, who insisted that Muslims must either migrate *en masse* to Pakistan or else give up their separate religious identity, and at the Muslim supporters of the "two-nation" theory who did not see any possibility for peaceful coexistence between Hindus and Muslims living in the same country.

Muslim leaders in post-1947 India have had to deal with the question of Pakistan squarely. Lingering mistrust among Hindus about the alleged role of the Muslims who stayed behind in India in the Partition of the country, as well as accusations of Muslims being Pakistani fifth columnists, forced Nadwi to come out strongly in favor of a united India, though his patriotism was not tainted with anti-Pakistan sentiment.[10] Although Nadwi had studied under such protagonists of the Pakistan movement as Mawlana Ashraf 'Ali Thanawi, he was opposed to the demand for the creation of a separate state for the Muslims of India even at the height of the Pakistan movement in the 1940s.[11] In this regard he was influenced by the leading *ulama* of the Deoband seminary with whom he had studied, and who were known for their fierce opposition to the "two-nation" theory, which Nadwi considered to be a "folly."[12] Opposed to the demand for Partition, principally because he felt that only in a united India would Muslims be able to carry on with their religious duty of missionary work, Nadwi insisted that Muslims could live along with others in a common homeland in peace and harmony and yet remain true to their religious commitments.[13]

Distancing himself from the Muslim League, Nadwi moved closer to other Muslim organizations. In 1940, he came under the influence of Sayyed Abul 'Ala Mawdūdī, the founder of the Jamaat-e-Islami, a fierce critic of the Muslim communalism of the League, and a passionate advocate of an Islamic state. Impressed with Mawdūdī's "bold rebuttal of the attacks and conspiracy of Western writers, Jews and Christians, against Islam," he joined the Jamaat,[14] being put in charge of its activities in Lucknow. This relationship proved short-lived, however, and he left the Jamaat in 1943.[15] He is said to have been disillusioned by the perception that many members of the Jamaat were going to "extremes" (*ghulu*)[16] in adoring and glorifying Mawdūdī as almost infallible, this being seen as bordering on "personality worship" (*shaksiyat parasti*). At the same time, he felt that many of them believed that they had nothing at all to learn from any other Islamic scholars. He was also concerned with what he saw as a lack of personal piety in Mawdūdī and leading Jamaat activists and with their criticism of other Muslim groups.[17]

It is likely that the Jamaat's own understanding of the Islamic mission in the Indian context, based as it was on the primacy of the political struggle to establish an Islamic state, was also a crucial factor for Nadwi's parting of ways with Mawdūdī. It appears that while Nadwi shared much the same understanding of Islam, as an all-comprehensive way of life, with the Islamic political order a necessary pillar, he differed from the Jamaat on the crucial question of strategy, seeing the Jamaat's approach as unrealistic in the Indian context. This opposition to the Jamaat's approach continued even after 1947, although Nadwi maintained cordial relations with Mawdūdī, and never failed to meet him whenever he visited Pakistan.[18]

Nadwi's differences with the Jamaat come out clearly in his book *'Asr-i Hazir Mai Din Ki Tahfim-o-Tashrih* (*Understanding and Explaining Religion in the Contemporary Age*), penned in 1978, which won him, so he wrote in his introduction to its second edition published in 1980, fierce condemnation from leading members of the Jamaat. Here, Nadwi took Mawdūdī to task for having allegedly misinterpreted central Islamic beliefs in order to suit his own political agenda, presenting Islam, he claimed, as little more than a political program. He accused Mawdūdī of equating the Islamic duty of "estab-lishing religion" (*iqamat-i dīn*) with the setting up of an Islamic state with God as sov-ereign and law maker. At Mawdūdī's hands, he said, "God" (*ilah*), "the sustainer" (*rabb*), "religion" (*dīn*), and "worship" (*'ibadat*) had all been reduced to political concepts, sug-gesting that Islam is simply about political power and that the relationship between God and human beings is only that between an all-powerful king and His subjects. However, Nadwi said, this relationship is also one of "love" and "realization of the Truth," which is far more comprehensive than what Mawdūdī envisaged.[19]

Linked to Nadwi's critique of Mawdūdī for having allegedly reduced Islam to a mere political project was his concern that not only was such an approach a distortion of the actual import of the Qur'an but also that it was impractical in the Indian context. Thus, he argued, Mawdūdī's insistence that to accept the commands of anyone other than God was tantamount to *shirk*, the crime of associating others with God, as this was allegedly akin to "worship," was not in keeping with the teachings of Islam. God, Nadwi wrote, had left several areas of life free for people to decide how they could govern them, within the broad limits set by *sharīʿah*, and guided by a concern for social welfare. Further, Nadwi wrote that Mawdūdī's argument that God had sent prophets to the world to establish an Islamic state was a misreading of the Islamic concept of prophethood. The principal work of the prophets, Nadwi argued, was to preach the worship of the one God and to exhort others to do good deeds. Not all prophets were rulers. In fact, only a few of them were granted that status. Nadwi faulted Mawdūdī for "debasing" the "lofty" Islamic understanding of worship to mean simply "training" people as willing subjects of the Islamic state. In Mawdūdī's understanding of Islam, he wrote, prayer and remembrance of God are seen as simply the means to an end, the establishment of an Islamic state, whereas, Nadwi argued, the converse is true. The goal of the Islamic state is to ensure worship of God, and not the other way round. If worship can be said to be a means at all, it is a means for securing the "will of God" and "closeness to Him."[20]

If the Islamic state is then simply a means for the "establishment of religion" and not the "total religion" or the "primary objective" of Islam, it opens up the possibility of pursuing the same goals through other means in a context where setting up an Islamic state is not an immediate possibility, as is the case in contemporary India. Nadwi refers to this when he says that the objective of *iqamat-i dīn* needs to be pursued along with *hikmat-i dīn* ("wisdom of the faith"), using constructive, as opposed to destructive, means. Eschewing "total opposition" (*kulli mukhalifat*), Muslims striving for the "establishment of the faith" should, he wrote, adopt peaceful means such as "understanding and reform" and "consultation." Muslims should make use of all available legitimate spaces to pursue the cause of the "establishment of religion," propagating their message through literature, public discussions, training volunteers, winning others over with the force of one's own personality, and establishing contacts with governments, exhorting them to abide by *sharīʿah*, seeking to convince them of the superiority of the solutions to worldly problems that Islam is said to provide. It is clear that such spaces are available even in Muslim minority contexts, and Nadwi suggests that Indian Muslims, too, should seek to take advantage of these to pursue the mission of the "establishment of the faith," even in the absence of realistic possibilities for the immediate setting up of an Islamic state.

Although Nadwi agreed with Mawdūdī in arguing for the necessity of an Islamic state, he insisted that "wisdom" demanded that the strategies for attaining the goal be formulated in accordance with existing social conditions. Thus, he noted, it was not necessary for a political party to directly launch a movement for the cause, especially if the odds were heavily weighed against it. A more realistic approach would be, he said, to "prepare people's minds" for Islamic government through a "silent revolution." Although these remarks seem to have been directed at Islamist groups working in

Muslim majority countries, Nadwi clearly saw this pragmatic approach as the only feasible way to carry on with the mission of "establishing the faith" in the Indian context.
To Nadwi's multifarious missionary efforts in post-1947 India, all of which were
directed towards this one overarching goal, we now turn.

Muslims in Post-1947 India

With the Partition of India in 1947, Indian Muslim leaders were forced to come to terms
with the grave threats with which the community was now confronted. Even the
Jamaat-e-Islami was forced to reconsider its strategies on more realistic lines. It abandoned "the rule of God" (*hukumat-i ilahiya*) as its immediate goal, substituting it with
"the establishment of the faith" (*iqamat-i dīn*). It even went so far as to insist that in the
given circumstances it saw democracy and secularism, which Mawdūdī viewed as the
twin evils of Western political thought, as indispensable, for the only alternative would
be Hindu fascism. In the context of anti-Muslim violence and growing Hindu aggression, which he saw as bent on the "cultural genocide" of the Muslims and as aimed at
turning India into "another Spain," Nadwi, too, insisted that Muslims adopt a pragmatic strategy that would enable them to reconcile their commitments to their faith,
on the one hand, and their responsibilities towards their country, on the other.[22]

Clearly, Nadwi seems to have felt, the Islamic imperative of struggling for the "establishment of the faith" need not necessarily take the form of political activism alone.
There were other, perhaps more efficacious, means to the same goal, focussing on the
individual believer, instilling in him a commitment to the faith. Gradually, as the
number of such individuals grew, and others, influenced by the moral virtues that they
witnessed in them, began to take an interest in Islam, if not actually converting to
the faith, an Islamic society could be created, Nadwi believed, on the basis of which an
Islamic political order could emerge. Nadwi was pragmatic enough to realize that
efforts to establish an Islamic state in India without building up an Islamic society that
would encompass a majority of the people of the country was utopian. Hence his insistent appeal to the Muslims to focus their energies on strengthening their commitment
to their faith as well as engaging in missionary work among others.

An indication of this growing pragmatism was Nadwi's wholehearted participation
in the work of the Tablighi Jamaat, which he first came in touch with in 1943. The Tab-
lighis consciously eschewed political activity, refraining from communal controversy
and conflict. With its simple message of faith in God, the Tablighi Jamaat probably suggested itself to Nadwi as the most pragmatic strategy for Muslims in India to adopt.
Nadwi remained deeply appreciative of the Tablighi Jamaat till the end, exhorting the
students and teachers of the Nadwat to take part in its work and even going so far as
to publish a biography of its founder.

Nadwi was equally appreciative of the role of the traditional madrasah in promoting Islamic awareness, seeing the *ulama* as the rightful leaders of the masses in
the absence of Muslim political authority. He clearly saw that in post-1947 India the
centuries-old tradition of Islamic learning as well as the very Islamic identity of the
Muslims were under grave threat, and insisted that one of the principal tasks before

the community was the preservation of Islamic knowledge through the madrasah system. Nadwi played a key role in the setting up of the Dini Ta'limi Council (The Religious Education Council) in 1959, which aimed at providing religious education to Muslim children through a chain of mosque schools. The Council, which Nadwi headed for many years, also sought to combat negative portrayals of Muslims and Islam in textbooks used in government schools.[24]

Political Involvement

Faced as the Muslim community was with problems that demanded a political solution, Nadwi was forced against his will to enter the field of politics.[25] In his autobiography Nadwi wrote that prior to 1964 he had no interest in political affairs, being immersed in his scholarly pursuits. A sudden spurt in violent attacks against Muslims instigated by Hindu chauvinists, as well as the continuing indifference of the government to Muslim problems, led him to turn his attention to politics. At a time when the role of the state had extended into almost every sphere of life, he wrote, the Muslims could not afford to remain aloof from politics. To do so would be tantamount to "collective suicide," for they would not be able to protect their identity and even their lives in the face of the growing threat of Hindu aggression as well as the Hinduization of the state.[26] Accordingly, in 1964 Nadwi, along with other leading Muslim figures, set up the Muslim Majlis-i Mushawarat (The Muslim Consultative Assembly) to chalk out a political strategy for the Muslims. Nadwi saw the Majlis as playing a central role in mobilizing Muslim voters as a powerful political force. The Majlis was intended to create a dialogue with established political parties in order to inform them of the problems of the Muslims, and to promote intercommunal amity in the country.[27] By thereby seeking to integrate the Muslims into the mainstream of political life in India, the Majlis, as Nadwi saw it, was also intended to enable Muslims to prove to others their Qur'anic status of *khair ummat* (the best community). It was only in a climate of peace, Nadwi wrote, that non-Muslims would be willing to listen to the Islamic "invitation."[28]

The setting up of the Majlis was a sign that the Muslims were no longer willing to be treated as a passive vote-bank of the Congress Party. Incensed at the Congress' indifference to Muslim problems, Majlis leaders argued the need for Muslims to seek to enter into alliances with other political parties, promising Muslim votes in return for assurances of protection of Muslim interests. As Nadwi stressed, the Muslims "had not written out a letter of slavery" for any party, arguing that the Congress could no longer take the Muslim vote for granted. Rather, he said, Muslims, acting within the framework of the Indian Constitution, would support political forces that could guarantee protection of their lives, property, and religious freedom.[29] Contrary to Nadwi's expectations, however, the Majlis died a premature death not long after it was born.

Nadwi believed that as a minority, Muslims needed to work along with existing political parties, rather than set up one of their own. The legacy of the Muslim League had left too many scars to allow Nadwi to contemplate the possibility of a separate Muslim party. This did not mean, Nadwi insisted, that Muslims should not organize on their own as a separate bloc, and on that basis seek to create a dialogue with other political forces to protect their own interests. In fact, this is what, in addition to the Majlis, the Muslim Personal Law Board (MPLB) and the Babri Masjid Action Committee, in both of which Nadwi played a leading role, actually intended. The MPLB was set up in 1972, and Nadwi headed it from 1983 till his death. Its purpose was to protect Muslim personal laws from interference by the state and to combat what were seen as "un-Islamic" practices among the Muslims.

In a country where *sharī'ah* was applicable only to the realm of personal affairs, Nadwi saw the threat of tampering with Muslim personal law by the state as tantamount to a "conspiracy" against Islam. Thus, he asserted, "We cannot ever allow anyone to impose on us any other social and cultural system and personal law. We understand this as an invitation to apostasy, and so we must oppose it as we would oppose any invitation to renouncing our faith. This is our right as citizens of this country, and the Indian Constitution not only allows for this but positively supports us in our quest for the preservation of our democratic rights and freedoms."[30] Although Nadwi envisioned *sharī'ah* as all-encompassing, extending even to collective affairs, by thus accepting its jurisdiction being restricted to personal affairs as the basic minimum acceptable to Muslims, he saw the possibility of the Indian Muslims coming to terms, at least for the present and the immediate future, with what, in theory, is a secular polity.

Nadwi saw secularism, understood both as state neutrality towards all religions as well as harmony between followers of different faiths, as indispensable for a plural society like India and for protecting Muslim interests. Even at the height of the Babri mosque controversy, in the early 1990s, when Hindu zealots, targeting a mosque in the town of Ayodhya, which they alleged had been built on the ruins of a temple dedicated to the god-king Ram, unleashed a wave of attacks against Muslims, Nadwi counseled dialogue and restraint, rather than retaliation and conflict. Warning Muslims not to take to the path of violence, he sought to present a solution to the dispute that might satisfy both sides.[31] He met with Hindu religious leaders to help evolve a mutually acceptable solution, believing that the matter should not be left to politicians who had a vested interest in communal conflict.

In the wake of the destruction of the Babri mosque in December 1992, Nadwi reacted by issuing an appeal for calm. He called for the reconstruction of the mosque on its original site, a ban on all organizations preaching communal hatred, and a "storm-like movement" for promoting intercommunal harmony and patriotism. He bitterly criticized the action of some Muslims in Pakistan and Bangladesh who reacted to the destruction of the Babri mosque by attacking Hindu temples there. He condemned this as "a negation of the teachings of Islam," adding that Muslims in these countries should protect their non-Muslim minorities and serve as a "model" for Hindus in India to emulate *vis-à-vis* their own minorities.[32] Appealing to Muslims not to lose heart in the face of mounting attacks and to desist from counter-violence, Nadwi argued that they should respond by seeking to protect their separate communal identity and by engaging in Islamic missionary work, and, in this way, try to "bring India to the right path." They must, he said, turn to God for help, repent of their sins, abide by the commandments of God, and recite the Qur'an regularly, particularly those verses of the holy book that talk about "peace," "security," "victory," and "divine assistance." At this juncture, he pointed out, Muslims must remember that particularly since they are a minority, they should strive for peaceful coexistence with people of other faiths, and work with them for social justice. They must not despair in this hour of trial, but, instead, should steadfastly endure tribulations in the path of God, not hesitating even to sacrifice their lives as martyrs for their faith.[33]

Inter-Religious Dialogue

In the wake of mounting attacks against Muslims, inter-religious dialogue assumed a particular urgency for Nadwi. The need for Muslims to reach out to the wider society first suggested itself to him in the early 1950s in the course of his involvement with the work of the Tablighi Jamaat. While appreciating the work of the movement among the Muslim masses, he felt that it had tended to neglect the role of the *ulama* in the affairs of the country as a whole. The *ulama*, he felt, had a special role to play in promoting awareness among the Muslims of the changing social conditions in the country, in order to make them "ideal citizens" and capable of "obtaining the leadership of the country." As he put it:

> If you make Muslims one hundred per cent mindful of their supererogatory prayers, making them all very pious, but leave them cut off from the wider environment, ignorant of where the country is heading and of how hatred is being stirred up in the country against them, then, leave alone the supererogatory prayers, it will soon become impossible for Muslims to say even their five daily prayers. If you make Muslims strangers in their own land, blind them to social realities and cause them to remain indifferent to the radical changes taking place in the country and the new laws that are being imposed and the new ideas that are ruling people's hearts and minds, then let alone [acquiring] leadership [of the country], it will become difficult for Muslims to even ensure their own existence.[34]

Accordingly, Nadwi began efforts to reach out to non-Muslims, seeking to establish better relations between Muslims and them, this being seen as necessary for missionary work. Such efforts at interaction took various forms. Thus, for instance, Nadwi began taking an interest in the efforts of the Dalits in their struggles against caste oppression, having as early as 1935 met with Dr. Ambedkar, the Dalit leader, inviting him to accept Islam along with his followers.[35] He established close ties with the Bangalore-based English fortnightly *Dalit Voice*, releasing its inaugural issue in 1980. *Dalit Voice* advocated an alliance between all marginalized communities in India, including Dalits, Backward Castes, Tribals, Sikhs, Christians, Buddhists, and Muslims, against "upper" caste Hindu oppression, and Nadwi was an enthusiastic supporter of the cause.[36] In order to reach out to well-meaning non-Muslims, as well as to highlight Muslim problems, Nadwi was instrumental in setting up the English weekly *One Nation Chronicle*, which, after it failed to take off, was replaced by the fortnightly *Nation and the World*. Both names were deliberately chosen to reflect an insistence that Muslims, too, considered themselves part of the Indian "nation," and, therefore, could not afford to be ignored.[37] Nadwi served as head of the trust under whose auspices the journal was published. Sayyed Hamid, editor of the journal, writes that Nadwi saw the journal as promoting among its readers "balance and goodwill" among people of different communities.[38]

Nadwi called for inter-religious dialogue between Muslims and others, particularly Hindus, envisaging this as going beyond mere theological exchange to take the form of joint efforts for building a more harmonious and just society. In his introduction to a survey of Muslim contributions to Indian culture, he wrote that for people of different faiths to peacefully live together, it was necessary that they should understand each other's religion and culture, regarding whatever they found good therein as "precious and worthy of encouragement and preservation."[39] When two civilizations meet, he remarked, there is always a two-way process of interaction between them, each being influenced and molded by the other. Such interaction must not be seen as necessarily negative, because "human existence is based on the noble principle of give and take." In this, he wrote, "lies its strength and glory."

It was because of such exchanges in the past, he commented, that numerous reformers, influenced by Islam, emerged among the Hindus, preaching the unity of God and the oneness of all humankind. On the other hand, as a result of being open to indigenous cultural influences the Muslims of India developed their own "individual national character" that sets them apart from Muslims elsewhere. Not all these influences may be wholesome, Nadwi remarked, pointing to the existence of caste, social discrimination, and extravagant customs among the Indian Muslims as examples of the "baneful" impact of their encounter with Hindu society. However, he noted, by not hesitating to adopt positive features of the surrounding culture with which it had come into contact, Indian Muslim culture had developed "a beauty and richness which is characteristically its own."[41] Overall, he said, Muslims had actually "benefited immensely" from the "ancient cultural heritage" of India. In particular, it had, he wrote, enabled them to successfully meet the onslaught of Western culture, preserving their cultural heritage largely intact, in contrast to Muslims living in "so-called Islamic countries." Further, he added, the depth and profundity of Indian Muslim thought, particularly Sufism, was a result of the interaction of Islam with "social, cultural and intellectual processes native to India."[42] This cultural dialogue had endowed the Muslims with a rootedness in the Indian context so that they "operate not like an alien or a traveler but as a natural, permanent citizen who has built his home in the light of his peculiar needs, circumstances, past traditions and new impulses." Nadwi insisted that it was thus "utterly futile" to expect Muslims to "lead a life of complete immunity from local influences."[43]

While not advocating a form of inter-faith dialogue that might lead Muslims to compromise on their faith, being convinced that Islam was indeed the only perfect religion, Nadwi advocated what could be called a "dialogue of life," appealing for people of different religions to work together for common purposes. He saw the struggle against violence as the single most urgent need of the times, and here Muslims could work together with others to establish a more peaceful and just society. He often spoke out against extremism of all sorts, insisting that what was required was a band of missionaries who could "douse the flames of hatred and enmity." In this way, Hamid writes, Nadwi taught the Indian Muslims how they could "live in a religiously plural society in such a way that their beliefs could remain free from the stain of communal prejudices and conflict," while "living together with others in harmony by respecting each other's religious beliefs." He insisted that rather than being a "barrier" in the path of Islamic missionary work, such a stance was actually a "facilitator".[44]

The *Payam-i Insaniyat* ("The Message of Humanity") was Nadwi's principal vehicle for the promotion of better relations between Muslims and others. The noted Shi'ite leader, Mawlana Kalbe Sadiq, a close associate of Nadwi in the MPLB, writes that the *Payam-i Insaniyat* was Nadwi's "favorite program," which he envisaged as a means to "bring peace to India," through which alone the Muslims could "obtain their true stature."[45] As its name suggests, it was intended to be a forum where people of different faiths could come together on the basis of their common humanity and belief in common values. The Muslims had a special role to play in this regard for, as Nadwi saw it, it was they who had first "gifted the message of humanism, love, tolerance and concern for social welfare to the people of the country."[46] Further, it was the religious duty of the Muslims to do so, for their status as the "best community" in the Qur'an was bestowed upon them precisely because they "enjoin what is good and forbid what is evil."[47] As such, Hamid writes, it was also geared towards bringing Muslims to interact with others for addressing issues and problems of common concern, thus trying to reverse the trend towards "separatism" that had made them "indifferent" to these issues.[48] Nadwi insisted that the Muslim community could no longer "live in its on imaginary world [. . .] cut off from the mainstream of national life." Rather, they needed to join hands with others in building the country,[49] for their lives were "inextricably linked to each other's." The *Payam-i Insaniyat*, as he saw it, pointed to the most appropriate way in which Muslims could play a leading role in building a new India.[50]

The origins of the *Payam-i Insaniyat* go back to the early 1950s, when, in the wake of growing attacks on Muslims by Hindu chauvinist groups, Nadwi began addressing joint Hindu–Muslim public rallies, calling for communal harmony.[51] In the course of his interaction with Hindus he discovered that many of them had doubts about Islam, which, he recognized, not only further widened the distance between Hindus and Muslims but also stood in the way of the spread of Islam. This led him, in 1974, to formally launch the *Payam-i Insaniyat* as an effort to promote better relations between Muslims and people of other faiths. Although Nadwi envisaged it as a popular movement, it failed to take such a form, revolving around himself as a charismatic personality. Because of this, after his death it witnessed a sudden decline. Although it did not have any registered office or members, it later gave birth to more organized bodies such as the Society for Communal Harmony, consisting of a group of Hindu and Muslim intellectuals committed to the cause of communal harmony, and the Forum for Communal Understanding and Synthesis, with broadly the same objectives.[52]

The activities of the *Payam-i Insaniyat* consisted, largely, of organizing public rallies addressed by Nadwi, his deputy Mawlana 'Abdul Karim Parekh of Nagpur, as well as other Muslim and Hindu leaders, and publishing literature in various languages on communal harmony from an Islamic literature penned by Nadwi himself. Nadwi's speeches at *Payam-i Insaniyat* rallies generally focussed on moral values that people of all religions generally hold in common, on communal hatred, violence and oppression of marginalized groups, on growing materialism, immorality and corruption in public life, and on other such issues of concern to Indians irrespective of religion, while at the same time claiming that Islam could offer an ideal antidote to all of these. While calling for closer cooperation between people of different faiths, Nadwi insisted that Muslims must steer clear of any moves towards a "unity of religions" (*wahdat-i adyan*), as that, as he saw it, was a "great strife" (*fitnah*), which could threaten to undermine the notion of Islam's uniqueness and superiority.[53] He, however, maintained that India as a whole as well as each community individually could progress only in a climate of peace. For this people of all communities must learn to live together in harmony despite their differences. Islam, he stressed, actually enjoined upon Muslims the task of building friendly relations with others, rather than alienate them or turn them into enemies. "The prophets," he declared at a *Payam-i Insaniyat* gathering in 1978, "always strove to make sure that the beads of humanity always remained strung in one necklace." On the other hand, he said, "Satan always tries to break the necklace and cause the beads to collide against each other."[54] Inspired by his speeches, Nadwi claimed, some Hindu extremists were provoked to remark that "Muslims are more concerned than us to save this country."[55] The same enthusiastic response does not, however, seem to have been evoked when, in 1978, under Nadwi's instructions, his deputy, Mawlana 'Abdul Karim Parekh, met the head of the Hindu chauvinist Rashtriya Swayamsevak Sangh, and sought to convey the message of the movement to him, in an effort to convince him "how much concern the Muslims have for the country."[56]

Insisting that Islam positively enjoined peace among peoples of different faiths, Nadwi argued that Muslims had a special role to play in the work of the *Payam-i Insaniyat*. Not only was this their religious duty, it was, he said, also indispensable if they were to live in security and able to progress as a minority. He likened the movement to the *half-i fuzul*, a group headed by Muhammad in Mecca before he was appointed as a prophet, and consisting entirely of non-Muslims, mainly pagan Arabs. Just as the *half-i fuzul* aimed at helping the poor and the oppressed, irrespective of religion, and "enjoining the good and forbidding the evil," so, too, Nadwi said, must Muslims in India today work along with people of other communities for spreading "true" religion, peace, love and justice, for Muslims, he insisted, have been appointed by God for that very purpose. Further, it was in the vital interests of the Muslims themselves, he said, to see that India was spared the ravages of violence. At a public gathering at Hyderabad in 1998, Nadwi remarked that the welfare of each community living in the country was dependent on the welfare of all the other communities as well. Each Indian had two homes, his own little hut as well as the large mansion that is India. The interests of the mansion have to be placed before those of the hut, for if there was no peace and prosperity in the former then the inhabitants of the latter could never prosper.[57] "It is but natural," Nadwi noted at another *Payam-i Insaniyat* rally, "that a passenger traveling in a boat would not allow someone else to make a hole in it," for in that case all the passengers would sink together. The only way the Muslims, as a minority, could live with respect in any country was by proving their usefulness to others. They could also, by their actions, show others that Islam had a viable, in fact, the "ideal" solution, to all the problems afflicting the country. In this way, by "saving" India and thereby "winning the love and confidence" of its people, God would "provide an opportunity for Muslims to occupy the leadership of the country."[58]

Nadwi envisaged the *Payam-i Insaniyat* as a means for Muslims to establish friendly relations with people of other religions, so that in this way they could impress them with the teachings of Islam and clear their misunderstandings about the religion. By bringing Muslims and others to work together to solve common problems, the *Payam-i Insaniyat*, Nadwi believed, would provide a means for Muslims to carry on with the Islamic duty of missionary work. Thus, at a speech delivered at a *Payam-i Insaniyat* rally in the aftermath of the bloody riots at Bhiwandi in 1984, in which dozens of Muslims were killed, Nadwi remarked that although the Muslims had been living in the country for well over a thousand years they had failed in their duty of explaining the teachings of their faith to the Hindus and impressing them with the same. Instead of befriending them, Muslims had alienated them, turning them into enemies. The time had now come, he said, that through efforts like that of the *Payam-i Insaniyat*, Muslims must show others what "jewels they hide in their hearts," how deeply inspired they were by their religion to "show love and human concern" for others, and how "useful" they actually were for the country as a whole. Islam, he insisted, was actually a religion of peace, and its true followers had "love, not hatred, for all humanity," for all human beings, irrespective of religion, were God's creatures and, hence, brothers to each other. Muslims, he said, should seek to convince others of this through their actions, and one way to do this was to work along with them for a more peaceful and just Indian society. This, he argued, would be a great service that they could render to both India as well as Islam.[59] Nadwi commented that God had chosen India to be their country, and this being their home they should exhibit "love" for it. Islam, he said, positively encouraged them to have "love for their land," and the best way in which they could express their patriotism was to work against oppression of all kinds, joining hands with others for this cause, while also carrying on with the mission of spreading the message of Islam that God had entrusted them with.[60]

In advocating peace with others, Muslims, Nadwi insisted, would not be betraying their religion. Rather, he pointed out, Islam is clear that human beings, irrespective of religion, race, caste, and class, are "the most precious" of God's creation, and an "expression of Divine mercy." Hence, Muslims should strive for peace and must also raise their voices against all forms of oppression. In this way, they would show others that they are "indispensable" to the country, rather than a burden.[61] But peace, he pointed out, could not be had if one community sought to impose its beliefs or culture on the others. Religious freedom was a must in a religiously plural society, and for this, Nadwi argued, true secularism (*na mazhabiyat*) – state neutrality *vis-à-vis* all religions – and democracy were indispensable, or else nothing could save India from the grave threat of a fascist take-over.[62] His words are proving to be truly prophetic, as recent events so tragically illustrate.

Notes

1. Muhammad Hasan Ansari, *Hazrat Mawlana Sayyed Abul Hasan 'Ali Nadwi: Hayat Aur Karnamey Aur Unke Malfuzat – Ek Ajma'ali Khaka* (Lucknow: Maktaba-i Jami'at ul-Mu'minat, 1999), 18–24.

2. He was the author of the *Nuzhat al-Khawatir*, an eight-volume encyclopedia containing details of over 5000 Indian *ulama*, and the *as-Shaqafat ul-Islamiya fi'l Hind*, a history of Arabic learning in India. He headed the Nadwat ul-'Ulama from 1915 till his death in 1923.

3. Established in 1898, the Nadwat sought to provide a harmonious blend of traditional Islamic and modern education.

4. 'Abdullah Abbas Nadwi, *Mir-i Karavan* (New Delhi: Majlis-i 'Ilmi, 1999), 31–8.

5. Ibid., 26–34.

6. Muhammad Nafis Hasan, *Meri Tamam Sarguzasht: Sayyed Abul Hasan 'Ali Nadwi* (Delhi: 2000), 32.

7. 'Abdullah Abbas Nadwi, op. cit., 48.

8. Sayyed Abul Hasan 'Ali Nadwi, Muslims in India (Lucknow: Academy of Islamic Research and Publications, 1980), 8–21. It is interesting to note that Nadwi here sees Muslims as outsiders who have settled in India, while ignoring the vast majority of Indian Muslims who are actually descendants of indigenous converts. It is remarkable how he echoes the views of anti-Muslim Hindu ideologs.

9. Ibid., 8–21.

10. In his comments on the role of the Muslims in the Indian freedom struggle he writes of the participation of Muslims in the Congress, but consciously ignores their role in the Pakistan movement. He glosses over this by alleging that the Partition was largely a result of communal tendencies within the Congress, the role of Hindus in instigating anti-Muslim violence, social discrimination, "communal suspicion" and the "political immaturity" of the Indians in general (Ibid., 120–1).

11. Sayyed Abul Hasan 'Ali Nadwi, *Karavan-i Zindagi*, vol. 1 (Lucknow: Maktaba al-Islam, 2000), 250.

12. Sayyed Abul Hasan 'Ali Nadwi, *Muslims in India*, op. cit., 121.

13. Hasan, op. cit., 113.

14. 'Abdullah Abbas Nadwi, 61.

15. Rizwan Ahmad Nadwi, "Sayyed Abul Hasan 'Ali Nadwi: Shaksiyat-o-Kirdar," in *Rabita* (Delhi, 2000), 44.

16. Sayyed Abul Hasan 'Ali Nadwi, *Karavan-i Zindagi*, op. cit., 242.

17. Hasan, op. cit., 33.

18. Sayyed Abul Hasan 'Ali Nadwi, *Karavan-i Zindagi*, op. cit., 245.

19. Sayyed Abul Hasan 'Ali Nadwi, *'Asr-i Hazir Mai Din Ki Tahfim-o-Tashrih* (Dar ul-'Arafat, Lucknow, 1980), 20–73.

20. Ibid., 66–98.

21. Ibid., 109–23.

22. Sayyed Abul Hasan 'Ali Nadwi, *Karavan-i Zindagi*, vol. 3 (Lucknow: Maktaba al-Islam, 1998), 82.

23. 'Abdullah Abbas Nadwi, op. cit., 163.

24. Hasan, op. cit., 136.

25. Sayyed Hamid, "Mawlana 'Ali Miyan", in *Rabita* (Delhi, 2000), 53.

26. Hasan, op. cit., 85–6.

27. Hasan, op. cit., 141.

28. Sayyed Abul Hasan 'Ali Nadwi, *Karavan-i Zindagi*, vol. 2 (Lucknow: Maktaba al-Islam, 1998), 102.

29. Ibid., 90–103.

30. Muhammad 'Abdur Rahim Quraishi, "Muslim Personal Law Tehrik Hazrat Mawlana 'Ali Miyan Ke Daur-i Sadarat Mai", in *Rabita* (Delhi, 2000), 112.

31. He suggested that the mosque be taken over by the Archaeological Survey of India as a protected monument. Muslims should be allowed to pray in the mosque, while in the courtyard a "historical and cultural" memorial to Ram could be built and where "historical information" on Ram could be disseminated (Sayyed Abul Hasan 'Ali Nadwi, *Karavan-i Zindagi*, vol. 2, op. cit., 152).

32. Hasan, op. cit., 156-58.

33. Sayyed Abul Hasan Ali Nadwi, *Karavan-i Zindagi*, vol. 5 (Lucknow: Maktaba al-Islam, 1994), 180–6.

34. Quoted in Hasan, op. cit., 35.

35. Ansari, op. cit., 89.

36. Interview with V. T. Rajshekar, editor of *Dalit Voice*, Bangalore, February 1, 2001.

37. In this Nadwi was in agreement with the views of Deobandi scholars like Mawlana Hussain Ahmad Madani on composite nationalism, of the Hindus and Muslims of India being members of a common nation. He, however, made a crucial distinction between patriotism (*watan dosti*) and national chauvinism ("nation worship" or *watan parasti*), asserting that while Islam positively enjoined the former, it was opposed to the latter, seeing it as *shirk* (associating any being with God) and as leading to bloody strife. See, for instance, Sayyed Abul Hasan 'Ali Nadwi, *Calamity of Linguistic and Cultural Chauvinism* (Lucknow: Academy of Islamic Research and Publications, n.d.).

38. Sayyed Hamid, op. cit., 49–50.

39. Sayyed Abul Hasan 'Ali Nadwi, *Muslims in India*, op. cit., 1.

40. Sayyed Abul Hasan 'Ali Nadwi, *Muslims in India*, op. cit., 76.

41. Sayyed Abul Hasan 'Ali Nadwi, *Muslims in India*, op. cit., 68.

42. Sayyed Abul Hasan 'Ali Nadwi, *Muslims in India*, op. cit., 76.

43. Sayyed Abul Hasan 'Ali Nadwi, *Muslims in India*, op. cit., 68.

44. Sayyed Hamid, op. cit., 51.

45. Sayyed Kalbe Sadiq, "Mawlana Sayyed Abul Hasan 'Ali Nadwi: Ek Nazar-i 'Aqidat," in *Rabita* (Delhi, 2000), 47.

46. Sayyed Hamid, op. cit., 51.

47. Sayyed Abul Hasan 'Ali Nadwi, *Reconstruction of Indian Society: What Muslims Can Do* (Lucknow: Academy of Islamic Research and Publications, n.d.), 34.

48. Sayyed Hamid, op. cit., 51.

49. Sayyed Abul Hasan 'Ali Nadwi, *Reconstruction of Indian Society: What Muslims Can Do*, op. cit., 2.

50. Sayyed Abul Hasan 'Ali Nadwi, *Reconstruction of Indian Society: What Muslims Can Do*, op. cit., 15.

51. S. M. Rabey Hasan Nadwi, "The Philosopher of Islam: A Close-Up," in Shariq 'Alavi (ed.), *The Fragrance of the East* (Lucknow: 2000), 23.

52. Hasan, op. cit., 132–3.

53. 'Abdul Karim Parekh (ed.), *Murshid-i Ruhani Musleh-i Ummat Hazrat Mawlana Sayyed Abul Hasan 'Ali Nadwi Urf 'Ali Miyan Sahib Ke Khutut Mufassir-i Quran Hazrat Mawlana 'Abdul Karim Parekh Sahib Ke Nam* (Delhi: Farid Book Depot, 1999), 33.

54. Hasan, op. cit., 123.

55. Muhammad Ayub Nadwi, "Sayyed Abul Hasan 'Ali Nadwi Aur Tehrik-i Payam-i Insaniyat," in *Rabita* (Delhi, 2000), 117. Also, Hasan, op. cit., 125.

56. Parekh, op. cit., 140.

57. Sayyed Abul Hasan 'Ali Nadwi, *Karavan-i Zindagi*, vol. 4 (Lucknow: Maktaba al-Islam, 1999), 55–7.

58. Sayyed Abul Hasan 'Ali Nadwi, *Karavan-i Zindagi*, vol. 2, op. cit., 114–25. Nadwi argued that it was only the Muslims who could save India because Islam alone could provide a solution to the problems of the country. Thus, at an address to the faculty and students of the Dar-ul 'Ulum madrasah at Deoband he asserted that "Muslims have been born for the leadership and custodianship of the entire world. Only Muslims can save this country because they alone have faith in the Unity of God, in human equality, and in a complete system of social justice and in the Hereafter" (*Karavan-i Zindagi*, vol.2, op. cit., 309).

59. Muhammad Ayub Nadwi, op. cit., 118–19.

60. Hasan, op. cit., 132.

61. Hasan, op. cit., 128.

62. Hasan, op. cit., 129–30.

CHAPTER 6

Madrasah in South Asia[1]

Jamal Malik

Considerable criticism has been directed toward traditional Islamic educational institutions, the madrasah (the Arabic word for school), on the basis that they are a breed-
ing ground for terrorism and a training camp for *jihād*, as had already been suggested
by the Pakistani Anti-Terrorism Ordinance 2001, one month before the dreadful
attacks on the World Trade Center and the Pentagon. The powerful perception of the
supposedly unilateral inter-relatedness between religious schools and *jihād*, between
mullah and violence, produced and perpetuated fear in the public mind in the West. As
a result, the relationship between state power and civil rights has been subjected to very
severe restrictions – and without major reactions from the public. This has enabled governments to push through restrictive policies in a way not known before, as was the
case with General Parvez Musharraf's announcement of a crack-down on violent organizations early this year, which seemed to come as a relief to the world.

Efforts in Pakistan and other Muslim countries to integrate madāris (plural of
madrasah) into the national educational systems are not new, but they are currently
seen as a part of the war on terrorism. Even in secular India, the approximately
100,000 madāris – one-quarter of which are teaching different syllabuses with students sometimes more qualified than those from formal universities – have become
subject to scrutiny and suspicion, as was the case in May 2001 under the Home
Minister L.K. Advani.

However, since madāris fulfill the needs of religious education, it seems rather un-
satisfactory and indeed too simplistic to equate madāris with terrorism, as is suggested
in General Parvez Musharraf's historic but moralizing speech of January 12, 2002. In
post-colonial tradition he indulges in a rather sweeping "othering" of the *ulama*, reminiscent of the nineteenth-century topos of the mad mullah. Even if the General ap-
preciates religious schools as excellent welfare and educational organizations, better
even than non-governmental organizations (NGOs) and even if he is aware of the
madrasah's political role, he cannot disguise the fact that he is influenced by the notion

that religious scholars are narrow-minded and propagate hatred. The country's future was to be a non-theocratic but an Islamic welfare state, he postulates.

To understand the speech and the policy of the crack-down, it seems proper to scan the structural, formative, and normative developments in the field of Islamic education in the subcontinent that have been regarded as responsible for the latest scenario.

It is evident that there is a variety of *ulama* institutions, e.g. there are mosques, khanqahs, shrines, maktabs, waqf, and madāris. All of them have a long tradition in South Asia, since they were often sponsored by the ruling classes and notables in qasbahs (garrison posts and local market towns with an Islamic scholarship) and residency towns. Especially religious schools (dīni madāris) were of utmost importance both for the national as well as the cultural integration process. In this regard religious schools may be regarded as a continuation of the Nizamiyya tradition in Baghdad,[2] when it became prominent under the Saljuq wazir in 'Abbasid caliphate, Nizam al-Mulk al-Tusi, in the eleventh century as a means not only for countering the rising Isma'ili da'wah and the spread of Shi'ite "heresies" and of the Mu'tazilah but also for mass education, and to integrate the empire. In this way the foundation stone was laid for the establishment of state-loyal scholarship, which would theologically legitimize the state. Sciences taught at the madāris provided centers of training for theologians and the service elite and, thus, were to become models for quasi-universities in the Islamic world.

And, Islamic law encouraged pluralism, so that a science of disputation ('ilm al-khilāf) was developed, being a part of Islamic legal training. This went so far that a doctrine of mura'āh al-khilāf (concession to disputed doctrine) was demanded from the jurists to accommodate opposite views.[3] Hence, law stood in the forefront of the syllabus, rather than theology, which was an extracurricular activity.[4] In spite of the "science of the classification of the sciences," which had divided the sciences into traditional (naqliyyah) and rational ('aqliyyah), sacred (dīniyyah), and profane (dunyawiyyah), there were "no separate madāris exclusively for religious education . . . Theology became a regular subject in the madrasah curriculum in later periods. . . ."[5] and thus highlighted religious identity, which was to become a major issue in South Asia.

The contemporary increase of madāris in the subcontinent is reminiscent of the precolonial times when the country was dotted with them.[6] When dealing with these institutions, however, state intervention has to be taken into account, since it is the state that has had a major impact on traditional institutions. Thus, in our context, the modern or colonial (state) sector is considered to be the significant other.

I would like to throw some light on the background of these developments, by showing how state policies have been changing traditional education in content and form during the last decades and how autonomous religious institutions have reacted to these policies. I will also discuss the normative changes in religious education, the social and regional background of religious scholars, and the latest trends resulting from state encroachment into these autochthonous institutions. The focus is thus laid on the struggle between reform-Islam as perceived by state authorities and Muslim avant-garde on the one hand, and the targets of change, the Islamic scholars, on the other. A short introductory note on the historical background of reforms in the field of Islamic education will provide the basis for the argument of this presentation, namely that state Islam has produced new – albeit uncontrolled – dynamics among religious scholars.

A Historical Glance

In the Muslim world, the eighteenth century was one of great cultural achievements with reformist ideas and a new approach to life, as can be discerned particularly in the writings of (Sufi-)poets of that time, exemplified in literary salons and the advent of the Urdu language. Parallel to these paradigmatic cultural and scientific changes, the normative patterns also changed, culminating, for instance, in the reform and standardization of education, as developed by, among others, scholars in northern India. Emphasis was placed on the so-called rational sciences with Islamic law, logic, philosophy, syntax and Arabic language, being important subjects. This syllabus – the *dars-e nizami* – called after its founder, Mulla Nizam al-Din (d.1748) from Sihala in northern India, offered a general education designed for the service elite.[7]

The *dars-e nizami* was, to a certain extent, later incorporated by the colonial masters into their institutions, e.g., the madrasah in Calcutta, and it (*dars-e nizami*) was subject to several reforms even before the advent of nation-states on the subcontinent. These reforms go back to the nineteenth century – although there had been a reformist trend headed by the Delhi school and scholars like Shah Wali Ullah (d.1762), who had postulated mystic revaluation and the promotion of what has been called the traditional, transmitted sciences (*manqulat*). This tradition was also part of an inter-regional network, and had a profound emancipating power.[8]

However, in the nineteenth century – in the wake of colonial penetration – with the introduction of new systems of education, the madrasah turned into an institution exclusively for religious learning, while some groups made use of Islamic symbolism to mobilize against colonial power. Other South Asian Muslims tried to change, reform, or conserve it, as a means to counter colonialism, which had threatened to marginalize both traditional scholars and social order, especially after 1857. Various Sunnite schools of thought emerged, such as the Deobandis, the Barelwis, and the Ahl-e Hadith.[9] They appealed to specific social groups and were tied to particular regions, and thereby added to the religious and societal complexity of South Asia. And so law, devotional mysticism, and prophetic tradition determined their different orientations.

Yet another movement, the modernist Aligarh school, tried to anglicize the Muslim educational system, but this was contested by the Council of Religious Scholars (Nadwat al-Ulama), which aimed at an integration of both religious and secular education. Established in 1893, the Nadwat demanded, besides curricular reforms, an alliance of all Muslims.[10] These reforms, however different they may have been, were thought to be achievable only through "modernization." It was in this context that modernity came to be regarded as the opposite of tradition and thus determined the fate of Muslim education, from the nineteenth century onwards. Religious institutions that did not subscribe to this development were marginalized but still provided knowledge to the majority of Muslims. This led to a dramatic societal split and disintegration in Muslim societies. It was only the recent wave of Islamization that has given the madrasah new life, however unwillingly and ambivalently. But before turning to *ulama* institutions in Pakistan let us first give a short overview to the situation in independent India.

As is well known, religious schools are independent in economic terms, financed through donations, *zakat, sadaqat, tabligh*, publications, and *waqf*, etc. In contemporary India there were only three major madāris run totally on government resources: Madrasah 'Aliyah Calcutta, Madrasah 'Aliyah Rampur, and Madrasah Shams al-Huda Patna. We are not so much concerned with these rather courtly institutions, neither will we dwell on Aligarh, Jamia Millia Islamia in Delhi, Jami'ah Nizamiyya in Hayderbad, or the Madrasah Nizamiyya in Lucknow which was established by 'Abd al-Bari Farangi Mahalli in 1905. All these institutions have already been discussed academically from different aspects.

What is more relevant to us is the development and impact of religious schools that are run without major governmental ideological or financial support like the majority of religious schools or those having a transnational significance like the Nadwat al-Ulama.

Religious schools have been the target of reforms also in the twentieth century, when several state madrasah boards came into being, like the one in Bihar established in 1922 which, in 1990, controlled more than 900 madāris with more than 80,000 students in the province, or the Madrasah Education Board Calcutta established shortly before independence.[11] Notwithstanding the macro-political developments following 1947, that had a decisive effect on society, the number of madāris increased after Partition, probably as a manifestation of Muslim fear of the Hindu majority. They might have provided the Muslim minority with a broad institutional framework on the microlevel, like the manifold shrines of holy men.

This increase was followed by several attempts to reorganize the numerous religious schools, not only because "The scope for the intellectual development of Muslim community through these institutions is tremendous," but also because "75 percent of the Muslims, especially in Uttar Pradesh, Bihar and Bengal are literate because of these maktabs and madrasahs."[12] Over a decade ago it was estimated that there were "more than 20,000 maktabs and madrasahs in India," housing several thousand students.[13]

Despite a number of attempts to reorganize the madāris – e.g., the Central Waqf Council in 1965, Deeni Talimi Council in the United Provinces, in West Bengal, Assam and Bihar in 1978 and 1981 – by integrating formal education (mathematics, geography, history, etc.) and setting up a network of religious schools, the institutions seem to have little organizational or academic links on the basis of schools of thought in independent India, except for different state Madrasah Education Boards. Indeed, these boards provide partly finances and degrees recognized by several Indian universities, by al-Azhar in Cairo, and by Medina University of Saudi Arabia.

Even Deoband, the most popular *ulama* institution in the subcontinent, or the Dar al-Ulum in Saharanpur seem to have no umbrella madrasah organization in India. Only the Nadwat al-Ulama, "one of the most outstanding institutions for imparting instruction in the Islamic Sciences . . . (with) one of the finest libraries of the Subcontinent,"[14] presently provides education to about 4000 students, approximately 2000 thereof being boarders. Its well-organized network had more than 60 affiliated religious schools, run by graduates of its seminary in Lucknow, spread all over the country, particularly Bihar, United Provinces, Kerala and Assam, as well as in Pakistan, Nepal and Bangladesh. In 1990 the Nadwat organization could show some 13,250 students and more than 3320 teachers.[15] Therefore, the Nadwat considers itself to be an umbrella organization of Muslim educational institutions. Presupposition to the affiliation is the curriculum taught at the Nadwat, which offers integrated education (modern subjects, English, etc.), as well as missionary activities. The budget of the school in Lucknow amounted to nearly 5 million Indian rupees, mostly from private donations.[16]

Its popularity is due to the activities of its late rector, Sayyed Abul Hasan 'Ali Nadwi (d. 1999), a well-known Muslim thinker, member of the Rabita al-'Alam al-Islami and chairman of different Muslim and Indian societies (All-India Muslim Personal Law Board, Islamic Literature, etc.).[17] While it is true that the Nadwat stands for a secular position, which would support national integration, and in this way has developed a clearly different position from the more politically inclined Jamaat-e-Islami, some of Sayyed Abul Hasan 'Ali Nadwi's statements were not bare of postulates that could have put him in line with Islamists.

Traditionally, madāris also have cultural and political significance. And it is because of their potential as a nucleus for Muslim reform, development and mobilization, that "a special effort (therefore) must be made to get the information to these institutions."[18] However, this would imply state intervention, which again is incompatible with the constitutional immunity of private educational institutions in India. Therefore, the developments and changes in Indian madāris will more or less remain private initiatives. While, after 1947, in independent India these schools were left more or less untouched by the secular state, some attempts have been made recently to modernize the madrasah system, notably under the eighth Five-Year Plan, 1992–97. The objective of the scheme of "Modernization of Madrasah Education", launched in 1993–4 and administered by the Ministry of Human Resource Development, was to encourage these traditional institutions by giving financial assistance to introduce science, mathematics, social studies, Hindi, and English to their curriculum. Only registered voluntary organizations, which have been in existence for three years, were considered for assistance. In the first phase, primary classes of middle and secondary level madāris were to be covered. In the second phase (during the ninth Five-Year Plan), the coverage was extended to institutions providing education equivalent to secondary stage. The performance of the scheme was to be reviewed after three years of its operation. Initially, the recommendations of the Working Group on modernization of madāris had suggested a meager grant of iRs 91.65 crores (916.5 million) for the ninth Five-Year plan (1997–2002). But the amount actually provided was iRs 48 crores (480 million), while the total amount actually released did not exceed iRs 16 crores (160 million). But "to make the Scheme viable an allocation of at least Rs 500 crore should be made for the Scheme in the tenth Five Year Plan."[19] So far, the plan was rejected by major madāris because madrasah education was linked with national security.

In Pakistan, as in most other Muslim countries, the situation was quite different right from the very beginning. Political leaders have always been interested in bringing the madāris into the mainstream national system of education, in order to try to curb their financial and political autonomy.

State Encroachments in a Nation-State

State encroachments in Pakistan became prominent fairly early, with Ayub Khan's nationalization of religious endowments and schools during the 1960s. He had plans to utilize their traditional autonomy for the nation-building process and to attach them to the state-run infrastructure. Connecting traditional Islam to modern political systems seemed to be an adequate measure to motivate the scholars for national ideology. The institutional affiliation of these schools to state machinery was to be paralleled by curricular reforms which, however, aroused a feeling of deficiency among the representatives of religion.[20] They therefore established umbrella organizations for religious schools – just prior to the proclamation of the West Pakistan Waqf Property Ordinance 1961.

The main tasks of these umbrella organizations were to reform and to standardize their educational system, and of course, to counter state authority collectively. But as the *ulama* are no monolithic block, they organized themselves, their adherents, and their centers according to different schools of thought, that is Deobandis, Barelwis, Ahl-e Hadith, the Shi'ites and the Jamaat-e-Islami, a recently founded religio-political party. The Deobandis in Pakistan established the Wifaq al- Madāris al-'Arabiyya in Multan in 1959. In the same year the Barelwis founded the Tanzim al-Madāris al-'Arabiyya in Dera Ghazi Khan/Punjab while the Shi'ites set up the Majlis-e Nazarat-e Shi'a Madāris-e 'Arabiyya in Lahore. The Ahl-e Hadith had already set up the Markaz-e Jam'iyyat Ahl-e Hadith in Lyallpur (today's Faisalabad) in 1955. The Jamaat-e-Islami, on the other hand, started organizing its religious schools under the Rabita al-Madāris al-Islamiyya from Lahore only in 1982.

During Bhutto's time in government Islamic scholars were able to negotiate some concessions, but it was with the advent of so-called Islamization in the late 1970s, that state activities touching on traditional institutions in general and centers of Islamic learning in particular took increasing effect.

In fact, madāris are widespread in South Asia, and they not only play a decisive role in the dissemination of knowledge, but also have a considerable moral impact on local culture. They also have social functions and can be mobilized in political crises for a variety of purposes. Their political significance, both external and internal, is immense. So religious schools have a significant educational, societal and political potential, although most of them had been pushed to the margins of the political process before the beginning of Ziyaul Haq's Islamization policy, when they regained significance, partly as an alternative educational system. So we shall now turn to the changes that occurred in religious education and schools during the recent past, and show the complex interrelatedness of a unifying state policy and religious scholars in a multicultural incremental society.

Islamization of the *Ulama*

As in other Muslim countries, the Islamization policy in Pakistan has resulted in a new dimension of curricular reform and has ushered in a new phase of institutionalization. For the first time the degrees of religious schools were put on a par with those of the formal education system and recognized by the University Grants Commission. To be sure, their formal recognition was connected with certain conditions: instead of the eight-year syllabus taught hitherto, the students were now supposed to be instructed by a modernized syllabus lasting 16 years. This meant that the religious scholars would have to follow the suggestions of the "National Committee on Religious Schools" established in 1979.[21] The report of the Committee suggested making

> concrete and feasible measures for improving and developing Deeni-Madrassahs along sound lines, in terms of physical facilities, curricula and syllabi, staff and equipment etc. etc. so as to bring education and training at such madrassahs in consonance with the requirements of modern age and the basic tenets of Islam . . . to expand higher education and employment opportunities for the students of the madrassahs . . . integrating them with the overall educational system in the country . . .[22]

The committee's demands aimed at an integrationist curriculum, but were ignored by the Deobandi Wifaq and also by the Barelwi Tanzim in their new religious courses while at the same time the *ulama* were able to enlist official recognition by minor modifications, thereby gradually being put in the position of exercising more and more influence on the secular sector. This demonstrates the ability of religious scholars to meet demands for innovation and pragmatism without acting against their own interests. The idea of this reformed Islam ostensibly stood in contrast to the concepts of most of the *ulama*, however. Consequently, these suggestions provoked considerable reaction for some time, but with the insistent pressure of the government and its support – i.e. through *zakat* money, as we shall see – and with the equating of their degrees with those of national universities in 1981/82, the *ulama* became more and more convinced of the potentially positive consequences of this policy for them. They did adapt the curriculum by merely adding subjects from the formal primary education system to their own syllabus, and Arabic instead of English was used on the certificates. Thus, the duration of education was extended from eight to 16 years, but grades one to eight and nine to 16 represented parts of totally separate systems of education: the first was secular, as taught in formal schools, complemented by "Reading the Qur'an" and "Basics of Islam"; the second continued the traditional dars-e nizami. So the *ulama* showed their ability to secure official recognition by implementing these minor changes, and they were gradually able to exercise more and more influence on the government's policy.

Theoretically, these degrees, once recognized, were to open up economic mobility and possibilities of promotion for the graduates. However, as we shall see, there was no consideration of how and where the now officially recognized armies of mullahs would be integrated into the job market. This shortsighted planning soon resulted in considerable problems.

Parallel to these administrative and curricular reform measures, the economic situation of religious schools was changed and, indeed, improved with the assistance of funds disbursed through the central and provincial *zakat* funds set up by the government in 1980: 10 per cent of the alms collected from current accounts through *zakat*-deducting agencies go to religious education if curricular reform and political loyalty are observed. These additional financial resources enhanced the budgets of religious schools considerably, making up as much as one-third of their annual income, and were exclusively at the disposal of the rectors of the religious schools, e.g., the *ulama*. This certainly created new expectations and new patterns of consumption especially in terms of the material conditions of madāris, such as higher salaries, investment for alterations, modernization of school buildings, etc.

Results and Reactions

As a result of these changes, a new dimension of mobility of these scholars and their centers of learning can be discerned. One is tempted to speak of an expanding indigenous infrastructure that in the early 1990s had already had far-reaching consequences: Firstly, the prospect of *zakat* grants resulted in a mushrooming of madāris, mostly in rural areas. In response, the government has introduced various measures to try to stem the tide, but this has only resulted in new problems. *Zakat* funds for these schools were curtailed and registration under the Societies Act 1860 made obligatory. In 1984, the disbursement of *zakat* was limited to those schools that had already been registered for at least four years. Moreover, since 1985, madāris have had to present a Non-Objection Certificate issued by the respective Deputy Commissioner if they want to be eligible for *zakat* funds. Recent policy has been even stricter. Secondly, the number of the graduates of higher religious schools – not to speak of students in religious schools in general – was constantly on the rise, as these institutions now also offer formal primary education with officially recognized degrees. Thirdly, the Islamization policy brought in a new phase of institutionalization among umbrella organizations, so that the number of affiliated schools has increased tremendously (growth rates up to 1000 percent in only seven years, e.g., 1977–86). Fourthly, the data available on religious schools also shed light on their spatial distribution and the social and regional background of their students.

The Deobandis, Barelwis, and Shi'ites recruit their students and graduates from rural and tribal areas which – from the point of view of modernization theories – are infrastructurally and economically not at all or only partly developed and where the parceling of land has produced a few large land-holders and huge masses of small land-holders and peasants as well as landless laborers without jobs. Their regions of origin, however, display a high degree of functioning traditional order and social relations.

The Deobandis prevail in the North West Frontier Province (NWFP) and in Baluchistan, where tribal society exists, in parts of the Punjab and of Sindh. Until the mid-1980s, their graduates for the most part hailed from some districts of the NWFP and especially from Afghanistan. Recently, however, the Deobandis increasingly recruit their scholars from Punjab, which has been a stronghold of the Barelwis. Also, the

Deobandi centers of graduation have shifted in recent times: Karachi has replaced their traditional catchment areas of Peshawar and increasingly draws graduates from foreign countries (however, excluding Afghans) and from Punjab, Sindh, and Baluchistan. Moreover, the available data suggests that in very few cases graduates originate from traditional scholar families. However, here changes have occurred during the last decade: even more students come from families whose heads carry the title of Mawlana (Arabic: "our master"; in this context meaning religious scholar).

The Barelwis, in contrast, continue to find their social basis predominantly in rural areas, mainly in the highly densely populated province of Punjab and parts of Sindh, in areas where the cult of holy men is extremely popular and widely practiced and where a high concentration of land-holdings exists, while tribal areas are hardly targeted for circulating their thought. Again, during the last decade, every third graduate of both schools of thought – Deobandi and Barelwi – has shown a religio-scholarly family tradition. Moreover, in the case of both groups, one may now find an increasing inter-provincial and rural–urban migration from the place of origin to the new centers of graduation.

The Shi'ites, who have also formalized and organized their schools tightly for the first time under the regime of Ziyaul Haq as a result of the latter's Sunnite tendency, have two spatial areas of concentration: in the Northern Areas and in some districts of Punjab dominated by folk Islam, such as the districts of Jhang and Sargodha. A migration to the center of their cult and scholarship in Lahore is also clearly discernible.

The Ahl-e Hadith, in contrast, have their stronghold in what may be called commercial centers and important internal market places in northern Punjab and in Karachi, just analogous to their original social basis in Northern India in the nineteenth century. Apparently, they have no ambitions to expand into other regions, which leaves vacuums in their infrastructure in NWFP and in Sindh and especially in Baluchistan.

The religious schools of the Jamaat-e-Islami, which has started organizing its institutions only very lately, can be found mostly in politically perceptive areas, be they near the Afghan border or in important political centers such as provincial capitals and Islamabad. Its graduates mostly hail from urbanized regions, even though some areas, like the NWFP, show rural background. It should be added, however, that affluent Muslims – also in India – hardly ever send their children to madāris which, thus, care for the poor.

The analysis thus demonstrates that each school of thought has its own reserved area, be it tribal, rural, urban, trade-oriented, or even strategic. The candidates for graduation of the Deobandis, Barelwis, and Shi'ites may be understood above all as representatives of the traditional sector. For that reason, one may find them primarily in areas traditionally structured. As they have some representatives in intermediary social sectors – sectors economically, socially, and normatively lying between modern and traditional systems – they are also settled in zones with a certain degree of official seizure, such as in urban Sindh or other modernized districts, i.e., in northern Punjab. This is true for members of the Ahl-e Hadith and of the Jamaat-e-Islami in particular. Hence, heterogeneity of Islam in Pakistan is traceable in regional patterns.

This distribution of land among different schools of thought corresponds to the socio-economic structure of the respective geographical regions. It naturally involves political power, has promoted the regionalism of Islam, which challenges, rejects and interferes with the enforcement of universalizing normative Islam as is propagated by the avant-garde and the government.

Religious schools do not only have important social, cultic, educational, and economic functions and significance. As can be derived from frequent statements, they are of quite some importance in areas pertaining to internal and external politics as well and therefore cannot be ignored. On the surface, they played a significant role in the so-called holy war of Afghanistan since they recruited and trained some of the holy warriors (mujahidin). The Dar al-Ulum Haqqaniyya near Peshawar, which was the main center of Deobandi scholarship in Pakistan up to the 1980s, is one of many institutions in point. Moreover, in politically sensitive areas in the vicinity of the Afghan border, new religious schools – particularly of the Jamaat-e-Islami – have been established especially for that purpose and they receive appropriate funds for that task from official *zakat* funds.

Internally, religious schools are not to be abandoned either, for they produce the majority of members and leaders of religious-political parties and associations, such as the Barelwi-dominated Jami'at-e Ulama-e Pakistan and the Jami'at-e Ulama-e Islam of the Deobandis. The schools can be mobilized for peculiar ends through financial and political incentives, particularly in periods of crisis, as was the case in the movement of the Pakistan National Alliance against Bhutto in 1977. As the schools and their personnel have direct access to the masses, their pacification is most important for the center. However, all the more astonishing is the connection of *zakat* disbursement to religious institutions with particular circumstances. Conditions like these inevitably led to a stiffening of the positions of some influential politicized religious dignitaries. Out of fear of dependency, they have rejected the acceptance of *zakat* money as political bribery, as in the case of a branch of the Deobandis led by the son of the late Mufti Mahmud, Mawlana Fazl al-Rahman, a current leader of the Majlis-e Muttahida-ye Amal (MMA). In doing so, they referred to a fatwa of the Mufti, who had called the *zakat* system illegal because it came from deductions from interest-bearing accounts. The boycott of the *zakat* system was, however, limited mainly to the politically restless province of Sindh and to a stronghold of the Deobandis. Here they had apparently allied themselves with local nationalists. In order to counter this boycott and to subject the province to the control of the government, Islamabad started to support other loyalist schools, particularly many of the Barelwis, the Jamaat-e-Islami, the Ahl-e Hadith, and some loyalist Deobandis. Again, the Dar al-Ulum Haqqaniyya is one main center of the latter group, with Mawlana Sami ul-Haq heading it. Bearing this tendentious policy in mind, one tends to have the impression that through specific support of the traditional infrastructure of politically convenient *ulama*, a contrast to or bulwark against popular opposition is being established.

The state, for a time, was successful – in cooperation with Islamist groups and a religious elite – in imposing its own Islamically sanctioned measures and thus legally expanding colonial structures such as the economic and educational system. Recently, similar encroachments have been attempted in the field of the judicial system through the Shari'at Bill. At the same time, the number of religious institutions has increased considerably as a result of financial privileges related to Islamization policy. The gov-

ernment did succeed partially in damming up the mushroom-growth of religious institutions by means of a precise new policy, which succeeded at least in part in subduing
parts of the clergy and their centers to its own interests. The shortsighted Islamization
policy has, however, created massive unforeseen but theoretically foreseeable problems.

In the wake of the formalization and reform of religious schools, an increasing trans-
provincial north–south migration from rural to urban areas can be observed, a sign of
the degree of spatial mobility of the young religious scholars. Students from specific
regions then look for schools and teachers who comply with their cultural perceptions
and ethnic affiliations and the search for corresponding institutions that create iden-
tity-giving substructures in an urban environment, which may otherwise be perceived
as alien and even hostile. The migrant scholars-to-be gather in the metropolis and
potentially contribute to conflicts that are often religiously and ethnically motivated.
The fact that the number of religious schools and their students have grown spectac-
ularly in urban, and even more in rural areas, also suggests that it is not only cities that
have become locations of increasing conflict. The hinterland has also been drawn more
and more into the sphere of religiously legitimized battles. Thus, the Islamization policy
has promoted the institutionalization of different groups, on the one hand, but has fostered their politicization and even radicalization, on the other. And since contemporary
regimes are not able or willing to integrate *ulama* in a productive way, their increasing
marginalization and deeper friction within society are the results. The prognosis is not
bright: Following the tremendous increase in numbers of religious scholars and their
centers of learning, a great potential for conflict has arisen, because young theologians
have been pouring into the labor market, especially in urban areas. Tens of thousands
of formally recognized students whose degrees are now equivalent to the MA in
Arabic/Islamiyyat have little prospect of employment. So far, in all reform measures,
corresponding planning for the labor market has been neglected by government functionaries. Employment for these *ulama* is not available, either in the courses offered for
Qur'anic studies in formal schools – courses that should have been a foundation for the
promised Islamization of the country, or in reading circles and mosque schools that
should have improved the poor literacy rate. This lack of planning and the consequent
imbalance between graduates and employment opportunities is mainly the result of the
prejudice of the officials themselves. The American advisor on religious education made
the following criticism: "Reservations were voiced by various officials of the provincial
Departments of Education about recruiting 'Mawlanas' for the schools on the suspicion that they would divide the students on the basis of their own preferences for a particular 'Maktab-i-Fikr'." He hastened to add that "these suspicions, however, were
proved in the field to be ill-founded. Such suspicions should never be allowed to affect
the making of educational policy at any level."[23]

It is only as teachers of Arabic courses, which have been promoted since 1979, that
some young scholars have found some jobs. These courses, however, targeted Pakistanis going to work in the Middle East, and so were motivated primarily by pragmatic
monetary considerations. On a different front, the military, against the background of
the Cold War, has been encouraging the recruitment of religious scholars since 1983
– with foreign aid. In the medium term, this has led to new values and structures in
the army, especially at junior levels of command.

With the official support of religious scholars in the 1980s and even in the 1990s, the political strength of representatives of this section of Islamic traditionalism has increased unmistakably. Thus, the Islamization policy – or better the politics of de-traditionalization – has ultimately forced the politically dominant sector to rethink its own position. The center may be pushed onto the political defensive, a position from which it could extricate itself only by violence, and with increasing alienation from the rest of the society. This danger exists especially when indigenous social and educational structures, such as endowments, alms and religious schools, still existent and mostly functioning, cannot be adequately replaced and thousands of unemployed mullahs who have access to the masses are not successfully integrated. This policy has clearly boomeranged – "The spirits which they conjured up . . ."

The conflicts in the rural hinterland, particularly during recent years, have in fact pointed to a wider, pervasive crisis, the result which state functionaries and their foreign advisors had not taken into account, a policy based on ill-considered and misconceived modernistic perceptions. As a consequence, the bearers and protagonists of various Islamic traditions have taken self-defensive and isolationist, albeit radical positions, a development which is also taking place in other Muslim regions.[24]

Meanwhile, the revolution in raised expectations has pushed many graduates of religious schools into the hands of different players: Their role in the Cold War in Afghanistan, when they were shortsightedly exploited by certain groups and governments, their role in post Cold-War Afghanistan, when once again, they were caught up in power politics supported by different secret services,[25] and now in the post-Taliban era, when some of them have taken sides with terrorist groups.

The Coming of the Mullah

The rhetoric of Islamic symbolism and *jihād* has shown that it can be effectively used as a means of self-defense against foreign encroachments. Consequently, there has been constantly increasing pressure on the state by religious elements. The Council of Islamic Ideology set up in the 1960s, and the Pakistani Federal Ministry of Religious Affairs, should not therefore be blamed for issuing outrageous Islamic proposals.[26] Similarly, the failure to reform the Blasphemy Law in 1994 and 2001,[27] or the madāris in 1995 and 2001, is simply a reflection of the aggressive mood of the *ulama*.

In fact, in May 2000, Islamic parties, who recruit their members from religious schools, were powerful enough to demand several Islamic provisions,[28] some of them met instantly by the government. But in order to increase control over them, the current regime came up with yet another madrasah reform proposal, such as the Pakistan Madrasah Education (Establishment and Affiliation of Model Dini Madāris) Board Ordinance, 2001 (August), and setting up a madrasah regulatory authority under the Madāris Registration Ordinance 2002 in June,[29] but the move came up against strong resistance from those running the madāris. It was said that by the end of 2002 madāris should be overhauled. Given the meager amount allocated for madāris reform by the Executive Committee of the National Economic Council in January 2004 one may again have doubts about the outcome. Only PakRs 5.7 billion (5700 million [Pakistani rupees]) are to be spent on 8000 madāris,[30] eventually leaving each madrasah with not too much amount to maneuver, even if this amount is much larger than the one allocated for the Indian scheme "Modernization of Madrasah Education" noted above.

Having said that, let us briefly return to the speech of January 12, 2002, in order to look at the ongoing battle between the clergy and the state. It is true that General Musharraf called for a peaceful sunnatization of life worlds, referring to Islamic mysticism and prohibiting madrasah students from going for divine force (khuda'i fauj). The reconstruction of tradition ought to serve to raise the madrasah and bring it to a level with the mainstream.[31] The major task seems to be to open up the job market for the graduates. Similarly, mosques should be reformed in order to guarantee a secular and modernized society, otherwise Pakistan will be marginalized – and radicalized. This policy[32] clearly aims at controlling approximately 20,000 madāris with approximately 3 million students, and more than 50,000 mosques – a solid power structure.[33]

The control of the ulama seems to be even more important since there has traditionally been a movement across the borders of Pakistan with Afghanistan, India, and Kashmir. This is especially true of some ethnic groups, who may outnumber their fellow ethnic group in Afghanistan, and are linked by family networks, commercial connections, and religio-political solidarity. Hence, despite the Pakistan government's recent strict policy against foreign students, Afghan students of religious schools have given their promise to continue their Islamic education in Pakistan.

Perspectives

To conclude: The reforms envisaged by the state have produced an imbalance that has resulted in a variety of problems, some of which were temporarily alleviated through jihād in Afghanistan. In the wake of these developments, several different branches of Islamic learning and madāris have emerged. We need to distinguish: firstly, students of religious schools in general, secondly, mujahidin or freedom fighters, thirdly, Taliban, and fourthly, Jihādi groups.

As far as the first category is concerned, they have been subject to several reforms from within and from without, but have played a quietist role. Because of traditional ties with Afghanistan and other neighboring countries and as a result of the use of jihād rhetoric, some students were used as foot soldiers in the Cold War. This is the second group – the mujahidin. In order to keep this group under control and to keep a grip on the region for economic and political purposes, another version was established by interested parties: these were the Taliban. Both the mujahidin and the Taliban are known for their forced recruitment of young children in madāris and refugee camps. As for the fourth category, the Jihādis, some of them can be traced back to groups returning to Pakistan from other battlefields such as Kashmir and Afghanistan, their leaders being middle-class and secular educated men, rather than madrasah students, though madrasah students have also joined the militant and radical groups. There seems little doubt that some of these organizations run private armies, collect compulsory donations, and indulge in militant and terrorist activities. Some of them, such as Lashkar-e Tayyiba and Jaish-e Muhammad, have made a regional conflict, the Kashmir cause, their *raison d'être*. But what is the reason behind their radicalization? Mere hatred, violence, and the obsession for *jihād*? It is true that the struggle for victory over a super-power and their alleged connections to some international networks enhances their feeling of Islamicity, no matter how blurred and intangible that may be. But it is the objective material conditions plus the symbolic power of regional conflicts, such as Palestine and Kashmir, that make up for the explosive mixture, because these conflicts represent the suppression of whole nations.

However international these organizations may be, they have arisen primarily as a result of an internal problem caused by political mismanagement, as we have explained, and they have subsequently been exploited by external powers. In these circumstances it is too easy as well as false to blame the mullahs and Islamic learning alone, let alone using the simplistic and stupid metaphor of the "axis of evil," which seems to ignore the diversity of the situation. This muscle flexing divides the world into goodies and baddies.

The role of external powers in South Asia has been outlined elsewhere, and should be held responsible for these developments as much as the role of the state, a state, that has been constructing and perpetuating a martial climate all over the country. The dramatic flaunting and celebration of military power on national occasions such as Pakistan Day, the propagation of *jihād* in textbooks even in formal schools[34] and daily on television for the cause of Kashmir, etc. are cases in point. This state-promoted violence and hatred from childhood onwards might be part of the painful nation-building process and search for ideology, but it certainly fails to instill tolerance and acceptance of plurality under the students. Instead the tensions unleash the struggle between the haves and have-nots. The alarming increase in kidnapping for ransom in the cities as well as in rural areas, the killing of whole families by senior family members because of lack of material resources are causes of major concern. In this scenario religious schools provide at least space for some kind of education and survival, and what is more important, they use the variety of religious repertory to make sense of the predicaments people are facing in a highly fragmented society. The growing presence and visibility of religious power in the public sphere shows this struggle between the neo-colonial elite – mostly the military that has been ruling in Muslim countries – and religious scholars who have been exploited in different quarters but have constantly been denied their share, very dramatically. In the face of these developments the making of an epitomizing prophet is easy: the ladinist savior, who would lead the campaign against suppression. It should be noted that the basis of this Islamically tuned radicalism still has indeed a very secular basis: social conflict, poverty, suppression. The basis is not Qur'an, but social reality, which is put into an Islamic symbolism only. Formerly violence and terror were legitimized nationally, today use is made of the Islamic repertory, not because this violence is or has become Islamic or religious, but because the political discourse has shifted.

Certainly, the latest crack-down policy can hardly diminish the significance and power of these groups, because they reflect systemic problems. Unless these problems, e.g., material conditions of the common people be improved and regional conflicts be solved, are tackled, these groups will start operating under different names, change their *modus operandi* or shift their operations to elsewhere making use of trans-

Islamic networks. As a popular divine has opined, a reaction was brewing: "This government is paving the way for Islamic revolution by creating hurdles for the Islamic parties." The divine hastened to add, "There may not be instant reaction but they will respond once the dust is settled . . . We are just watching the situation but the silence will not last for long. . . The timing of this announcement by the president [e.g., crackdown] has raised suspicion in the minds of religious people. It is being done under U.S. pressure."[35] And he asked "If they were terrorist groups, then why were they allowed to operate for such a long time?"

The criminalization of the *ulama* therefore seems no option at all. In a country that is heavily under their socio-cultural and religious influence, a dialog of bullets is a dead end. Instead, it is more important to integrate these sections of society properly in order to prevent a cold war before it gets too hot and becomes a war that no one can deal with.

Notes

1. This is an updated version of, "Dynamics among Traditional Religious Scholars and their Institutions in Contemporary Pakistan," in *Madrasa. La Transmission du Savoir dans le Monde Musulman*, Nicole Grandin and Marc Gaborieau (eds.), (Paris: 1997), 168–82; *idem*, "Traditional Islamic Learning and Reform in Pakistan," *International Institute for the Study of Islam in the Modern World – ISIM Newsletter*, 10 (Leiden: 2002), 20–1.
2. See Gary Leiser, "Notes on the Madrasa in Medieval Islamic Society," *The Muslim World*, 76, 1986, 16–23; Dominique Sourdel, "Réflexions sur la diffusion de la madrasa en Orient du XIe au XIIIe siècles," *Revue des Etudes Islamiques*, 44, 1976, 165–84; Janine Sourdel-Thomine, "Locaux d'enseignements et madrasas dans l'islam médiéval," *Revue des Etudes Islamiques*, 44, 1976, 185–97.
3. Muhammad Khalid Masud, "Religious Identity and Mass Education," in *Islam in the Era of Globalization*, Johan Meulaman (ed.), (London: Routledge Curzon, 2000), 233–46, here p. 237.
4. G. Makdisi, *The Rise of Colleges: Institutions of Learning in Islam and the West* (Edinburgh: Edinburgh University Press, 1981).
5. Masud, "Religious Identity," 237.
6. See G.W. Leitner, *History of Indigenous Education in the Punjab since Annexation and in 1882* (New Delhi: 1971, first edition 1883: Languages Department Punjab).
7. For that tradition see Francis Robinson, *The 'Ulama of Farangi Mahall and Islamic Culture in South Asia* (New Delhi: permanent black, 2001).
8. For this context see Jamal Malik, "Muslim Culture and Reform in 18th Century South Asia," *Journal of the Royal Asiatic Society*, 13/2, 2003, 227–43.
9. For these movements and groups, see Barbara D. Metcalf, *Islamic Revival in British India, Deoband 1860–1900* (Princeton: Princeton University Press, 1982).
10. For this movement see Jamal Malik, *Islamische Gelehrtenkultur in Nordindien. Entwicklungsgeschichte und Tendenzen am Beispiel von Lucknow* (Leiden: E.J. Brill, 1997).
11. See Kuldip Kaur, *Madrasa Education in India: A Study of its Past and Present* (Chandigarh: Centre for Rural and Industrial Development, 1990), 225; for madrasah education in India in general see S. Maqbul Ahmad, "*Madrasa* System of Education and Indian Muslim Society," in S.T. Lokhandwalla (ed.) *India and Contemporary Islam* (Simla, 1971), 25–36;

Mohammad Akhlaq Ahmad, *Traditional Education among Muslims; A Study of some Aspects in Modern India* (Delhi: B.R. Publishing Corporation, 1985). Unfortunately, no recent data were available on the contemporary state of *ulama* institutions in Bangladesh. See, however, A.K.M. Ayyub Ali, *History of Traditional Education in Bangladesh (down to A.D. 1980)* (Dhaka: Islamic Foundation Bangladesh, 1983).

12. Kaur, *Madrasa Education*, 254.

13. See Kaur, *Madrasa Education*, 210; see also Anjuman-e Nida-ye Islam (ed.), *Fihrist Madāris-e 'arabiyya diniya* (Kalkutta: Anjuman-e Nida-ye Islam, 1404/1983).

14. See Ziyaud-Din A. Desai, *Centres of Islamic Learning in India* (New Delhi: Ministry of Information and Broadcasting, 1978).

15. This is based on a list provided by the administration staff of the Nadwat in October 1990.

16. *Muslim India*, 111(1993), 125.

17. Compare Jan-Peter Hartung, *Leben und Wirken von Sayyid Abû l-Hasan al-Hasanî an-Nadwî (1913–1999) als Beispiel für religiös politische Netzwerke in Südasien* (Ph.D. Islamic Studies, University of Erfurt, 2003).

18. Cited in *Muslim India*, 127, July 1993, 323.

19. See Hamdard Education Society, *Evaluation Report on Modernization of Madrasa Education (UP)* (New Delhi: 2003); an interesting overview is provided by Amir Ullah Khan, Mohammad Saqib, and Zafar H. Anjum, *To Kill the Mockingbird. Madarsah* (sic!) *System in India: Past, Present, and Future*, http://www.indiachinacentre.org/bazaarchintan/pdfs/madarsas.pdf, consulted 20 Feb. 2004.

20. Cf. Government of Pakistan, *Report of the Committee set up by the Governor of West Pakistan for Recommending Improved Syllabus for the Various Darul Ulooms and Arabic Madrasas in West Pakistan* (Lahore: 1962).

21. See Government of Pakistan, Ministry of Religious Affairs, *Riport qaumi kamiti bara-ye dini madāris Pakistan* (Islamabad: 1979).

22. The report, however, recognized the role of religious schools as transmitters of the cultural heritage and also the students' strong motivation to learn, which was unknown within the formal system where there was much corruption; see Gov. of Pakistan, *Riport qaumi kamiti*, 115f and 8f.

23. Yusuf Talal Ali, *Draft chapter on Islamic Education for inclusion in the Report of the President's Task Force on Education* (Islamabad: 1982, mimeo), 6.

24. For further readings consult Dale F. Eickelman and James Piscatori, *Muslim Politics* (Princeton: Princeton University Press, 1996).

25. Ahmed Rashid, *Taliban: Militant Islam, Oil and Fundamentalism in Central Asia* (New Haven: Yale University Press, 2000).

26. Such as the verdict of *riba* by the Supreme Court Shariat Appellate Bench in 1999, abolition of the old Family Law Ordinance (men can practice polygamy without permission of their first wives, women only may marry with a *wali*), the acceptance of Taliban idol-bashing by the Ministry of Religious Affairs, closure during prayer times, when defaulters are to be punished, no songs and dances on PTV, no women in advertisements, insurance declared un-Islamic, *kalima* on the flag, Friday as weekly holiday, etc.; see Khaled Ahmed, "The Myth of 'Misinterpreted' Islam," *The Friday Times* (Pakistan: January 11–17, 2002).

27. The idea was that instead of filing a blasphemy case with the police, a senior administration official should oversee the procedure.

28. That is (i) Integration of special Islamic provisions of the constitution of 1973 into the Provincial Constitution Order of Oct. 1999. (ii) Keeping separate electoral for Muslims and Non-Muslims for elections at district and commune level. (iii) Implementation of Friday as the holy day. (iv) Anti-Islamic activities of NGOs be banned. (v) Government should guar-

antee not to touch madāris and Jihādi groups. While the first two demands were achieved during the next few months, the rest is still to be negotiated.

29.   See *The Gazette of Pakistan*: Ordinance No. XL of 2001. And, Hukumat-e Pakistan, *Model Dini Madāris*, Wizarat-e Madhhabi Umur, Shubah-ye dini madāris (Islamabad: n.d.). Compare also Hukumat-e Pakistan, *Pehli Salanah Report (August 2001 – September 2002)* (Islamabad: Pakistan Madrasah Education Board, 2002).

30.   Cf. *The News*, "Rs 5.7 b allocated for madāris reforms" (January 8, 2004). This amount is a very small portion in relation to the overall projects worth 185.6 billion.

31.   In working out his message in Urdu language, General Musharraf makes deliberate use of Islamic symbolism and vocabulary (*huquq al-'ibad, shari'at*, etc.), but crucial words from the vocabulary of secular society, such as *tolerance, intellectual difference and debate, freedom of thought*, etc., are used in the English language version.

32.   General Musharraf has reiterated his policy on several occasions (such as January 17, 2002), as when he addressed religious scholars at a two-day National Conference of Ulama and Mashaikh in Islamabad, under the aegis of the Minister for Religious Affairs. Again the General asked the *ulama* to play their role for the benefit of the common man and leave the matter of *jihād* to him. He announced that all party funds would be checked, and in future, no new mosque or madrasah would be opened without prior permission of the government, and no one would be allowed to call for *jihād*.

33.   Interestingly enough, Pakistani stocks rose 2.4 percent following General Musharraf's speech. *The News* (January 15, 2002), p. 11.

34.   "Textbooks and the Jihādi mindset", *DAWN* (February 12, 2002).

35.   *The News* (January 15, 2002), 11.

CHAPTER 7

75 Years of Higher Religious Education in Modern Turkey

Mehmet Pacaci and Yasin Aktay

The modern-day Turkish Republic was built upon the ashes of the old Ottoman Empire. In order to create a completely new and more powerful entity, those who formed the Republic discarded the earlier structure wherein religion was an integral part of the state and adopted instead a secular model. Kazamias summarizes what the founders of Turkey did to create a secular state:

> In 1923 the Ministry of Education took over the administration and control of all religious schools and all their means of support. In the same year, the teaching of religion was proscribed in all state schools. The abolition of the caliphate in 1924 was followed by the closing of all *medreses* and other separate religious schools, by the elimination of the august office of *şeyhülislam*, and by the replacement of the Ministry of Religious Law with a Presidency of Religious Affairs under the prime minister. In 1928, Article 2 of the first Constitution of the Republic of Turkey, which had made Islam the state religion, was amended, providing for disestablishment; and in 1937 the principle of secularism was incorporated in the Constitution. In the meantime, jurisdiction of the courts of the *şeriat* had been taken over by lay, Western-modeled courts, and a Turkish Civil Code, a virtual replica of the Swiss Civil Code, had replaced the orthodox private Mohammedan laws. By 1930, what few secondary schools for religious leaders had survived went out of existence, and by 1933, the foundering Faculty of Theology of Istanbul University was also abolished.[1]

The Turkish Republic has nonetheless inherited much from its Ottoman predecessor, such as the religious tradition of the nation and, quite paradoxically, so-called Westernization and modernization. In spite of the fact that religion has been displaced from the actual structure of the state, contention regarding religious issues has continually persisted throughout the course of the 75-year history of the new state. Religion in education or, more specifically, the issue of religious education has always been an indication of the position of the state *vis-à-vis* the religious culture of the country. In this chapter, we will focus on the development of higher religious education in modern Turkey during its 75 years of existence.

Table 7.1 Curriculum of the Faculty

Courses	Year 1	Year 2	Year 3	Year 4
Glorious Tafser (Tefsir-i Şerif)	3	3	3	3
Hadith and Methodology of Fiqih (Hadis ve Usul-i Fıkıh)	2	2	2	2
Science of Fiqih (İlm-i Fıkıh)	2	2	2	2
Methodology of Fiqih (Usul-i Fıkıh)	2	2	2	–
Science of Theology (İlm-i Kelam)	2	2	2	2
History of Islamic History (Tarih-i Din-i İslam)	2	1	1	1
General History (Tarih-i Umumi)	–	–	–	1
Methodology of Teaching (Usul-i Tedris)	–	–	1	1
Total	13	12	14	12

The idea of a higher religious academy has its roots in the philosophy of the Ottoman era. According to Ülken, one of the first deans of the Faculty of İlahiyat, Ankara, the very notion of a Faculty of İlahiyat appeared at the same time as that of the modern university in Ottoman Turkey. The actualization of the project was effected by Emrullah Efendi, the Minister of Education (*Maarif Nazırı*) at the time.[2] At an independent university, a faculty separate from that of the medrese was convened for the first time. Emrullah Efendi was the mastermind of the theory known as the "Tuba tree" (*Tuba Ağacı*), which is an upside-down tree believed to exist in Paradise according to Muslim tradition. This theory promoted a rational and modern type of education from the highest to the lowest levels.[3] The implementation of that theory resulted in the opening of a university (*Daru'l-Funun*) in 1908.[4] This university included a branch called *Ulum-u Aliye-i Diniyye*, which was later called *Ulum-i Şer'iyye*. This is an early example of what would later become the faculties of İlahiyat, which are branches of higher religious education characterized by their freedom from secular concerns. The curriculum of the faculty was as shown in Table 7.1.

Later, some changes occurred and, for the fourth year, İlm-i Hikmet (Knowledge of Wisdom/Philosophy), Tarih-i Edyan (History of Religions), Siyer-i Nebevi (Life of the Prophet), Kitabiyet-i Arabiyye and Türkiyye (Arabic and Turkish Literature) courses including Usul-i Fıkıh (Methodology of Fiqh) were added to the program.[5] In 1913, a new regulation was imposed upon the university by Emrullah Efendi. The reorganization of the departments (*Şu'be*) was as follows:

- Department of Tafser and Hadith
- Department of Theology
- Department of Philosophy
- Department of Fiqh
- Department of Religious Ethics (Ahlak-ı Şer'iyye) and Life of the Prophet (Siyer)

With these changes, courses such as İlm-i Ahlak-ı Şer'iyye ve Tasavvuf (Science of Religious Ethics and Mysticism), Garb Felsefesi (Western Philosophy), Felsefe ve Tarihi Felsefe (Philosophy and History of Philosophy), and İlm-i Hilaf (Discipline of Contravention) were added to the curriculum.[6]

On September 11, 1919, a new law closed the faculty as a result of opposition to the traditional offerings. The reasoning was that the traditional medrese were sufficiently structured to provide the Turkish people with religious education, and, therefore, there was no need for any other institutions with the same purpose. The medrese, meanwhile, were also experiencing deep transformation in an effort to modernize. According to Ülken, graduates of the medrese began to achieve prominence. Hoca Tahsin Efendi, for instance, taught modern psychology, while İzmirli İsmail Hakkı in *Yeni İlm-i Kelam* compared *kelam* doctrines with Western philosophy. Ali Sedat Bey promoted and taught modern logic and methodology.[7] In fact, a considerable number of *ulama* supported or substantially contributed to modernization reforms in the Ottoman state.[8]

When Western influence expanded to the Ottoman State, contemporary ideas in the field of education emerged. Yet, traditional modes of education persisted alongside new ones. Eventually, this coexistence created a dualism in the structure of the educational system of the state. In this dual composition, the medrese gave a traditional and religiously rooted education, whereas the mekteb provided a Westernized or modern type of education. Kazamias refers to this dualistic nature in his account of the inauguration of the Galatasaray Lise as a mekteb in French style. The supporters of the new establishment were called *Tanzimatcı*. They were known as the defenders of reform in the state and of the Westernization of the institutions and cultural life of the empire. At the other extreme, however, stood the conservatives, who believed in the traditional institutions and were the champions of Islam and religious schooling. They were the so-called *Medreseci*.[9]

This mekteb–medrese dualism continued until the parliament of the new Turkish Republic passed the law of unification of instruction (*Tevhid-i Tadrisat*) on March 3, 1924. This happened only a year after the declaration of the new Turkish State on April 23, 1923. The secular character of the state and the law of unification of instruction had the most profound and permanent influence, not only on education in general, but on religious education in particular. According to this law, education now fell under the authority of the Ministry of Education. With this law, all mektebs and medreses were attached to the Ministry of Education both administratively and financially.

As with any issue related to religion, there was much heated discussion about the concept of secularism in government, which was held as one of the necessary principles of the new Turkish State. Following the establishment of a new faculty, these continuing discussions played themselves out both in parliament and the media. Many were loath to abandon the Muslim traditions of the country. On the one hand, many approved of the secular quality of the state, but on the other, the people's religious demands were not to be denied. This situation was a painful paradox in the minds of modern Turks.

Fierce debate ensued regarding the interpretation and execution of the law by the government of the time. The closing of the medrese by the Ministry of Education gave rise to considerable opposition. The decision to shut down the medrese by Vasıf Bey, the

Minister of Education, was considered by the conservative media as a gravely biased attack against the old institutions. An article in *Sebilurreşad* interpreted the initiative as ruining the families of 16,000 scholars and advocated the reconstruction of the medrese rather than their elimination.[10] The opposition, moreover, regarded the medrese as a primary source for students of higher religious education in Turkey. They argued that without the medrese, the Faculty of İlahiyat would be left without students and become obsolete.[11]

In contrast, an article in *Cumhuriyet* written by Falih Rıfkı described the action as very brave and as the eradication of 16,000 dogmatists in one night.[12] İsmet İnönü gave a speech against the opposition at a Teachers Union meeting in 1925. He referred to the central point of the contention as well as the government's persistence on its revolutionary position regarding religious education and also religion itself:

> We have already known that opinions would be advanced that certain institutions should have been reformed rather than closed by the Unification of Instruction Law and we also have predicted the results of this kind of objection. The Great Assembly, however, already has decided. To accelerate the goals that are to be gradually achieved is to make a revolution. . . . We believe that the initiative has nothing to do with being irreligious. . . . The cleanest and the most authentic form of Islam has been manifested among us . . . You teachers! You will give a national type of education, not a religious and international one. We will witness that the religious training is not an attack against the national and that both types of the educations will be performed in their own modes.[13]

The revolutionary action of the government continued to be disputed in later years. In 1955, Halide Edip Adıvar, one of the few significant females involved in the struggle for Turkish independence, criticized the government's treatment of the medrese. She regarded the medrese as the most important source of students for the Faculty of İlahiyat and believed that the struggle against corrupted forms of Islam would be easier if the way she suggested had been taken. She said:

> It has been a great error to close the medrese which had already taken a modern way. Had the *evkaf* schools been closed first these (medrese) would have carried on religious education and the establishment of Faculty of İlahiyat would have been done on these already settled foundations when we separated the state from the religion. This would have saved us, on the one hand, from Medieval narrow-mindedness, and on the other hand, we would not have approached towards the cliff of the dogmatism (for the satisfaction of our natural religion instincts) through a sect that is based on ignorance and came from abroad; it is also ignorant and irrelevant to the enlightening and eminent principles of Islam.[14]

In fact, every action the government took regarding religious education caused dissatisfaction. In the polemics of the day, definitions both of secularism and religion were demanded and proffered. Defenders of religious tradition emphasized the historic role of religion in creating the nation and suggested definitions of laicism as something not against religion along with the reforms. Their arguments were founded on the premise that religious education was needed to uphold the moral requirements of Turkish society.[15] Ahmet Cevdet, the chief editor of *İkdam*, for instance, defended the necessity of religious education for young generations of the nation. He wrote, "Unless a nation gains a proper religious education it cannot develop a strong country. Then, no other youth throughout the world is so incomplete as Turkish youth and nation." He concluded "Such a youth (as a Turkish one) cannot form a nation. . . ."[16] The same argument was repeated after more than half a century. Bolay argued the necessity of religious education to prevent the disassociation of man from his transcendental source. He emphasized the integrative function of Islam for the citizens of Turkey.[17]

Advocates of laicism have been inclined to see religion as a barrier to modernization and regard the medrese and religion itself as a source of ignorance and dogmatism. They concluded, in accordance with their definition of laicism, that a secular state is not required to give any religious education.[18] Sadrettin Celal Bey, in an article published in *Son Telgraf*, argued that religion had been the primary agent of ignorance and corruption in the country. A secular state, he continued, does not interfere with the religious beliefs of the people. He regarded religion as a personal matter to be kept out of matters of state. He believed that leaving religious education to the family and abolishing state-sponsored religious courses were the necessary consequences of a secular republic.[19]

Mehmet Oğlu İhsan, a teacher, replied to the above-mentioned article by Sadreddin Celal Bey in *Son Telgraf*. He emphasized the use of religious education in the ethical and moral education of the younger generations and stated that religious education was not a barrier to achieving modernization.[20]

By the authority of the fourth article of the law of unification of instruction, the İmam-Hatip schools at the secondary level and Darulfünun Faculty of İlahiyat at the higher level were opened. The opening of the latter was on April 21, 1924. It was projected that the faculty would meet the need for religious instruction and help train specialists in religion, who were also fluent in modern scientific methods. The curriculum of the faculty was designed to promote a modern and active understanding of religion. The eighth article of the regulation (*Talimatname*), which formulated the three-year İlahiyat education, lists the names of the courses as follows:

- Tafsir and History of Tafsir, Hadith and History of Hadith (Tefsir ve Tefsir Tarihi, Hadis ve Hadis Tarihi)
- History of Fiqh (Fıkıh Tarihi)
- Sociology (İctimaiyyat)
- Ethics (Ahlak)
- History of Islamic Religion (Din-i İslam Tarihi)
- Arabic Literature (Arap Edebiyatı)
- Philosophy of Religion (Felsefe-i Din)
- History of Theology (Kelam Tarihi)
- Muslim Philosophers (İslam Feylesofları)
- History of Mysticism (Tasavvuf Tarihi)
- History of Philosophy (Felsefe Tarihi)
- Islamic Esthetics (İslam Bediiyyatı)
- Prevailing Islamic Sects (Hal-i Hazırda İslam Mezhepleri)
- Ethnography of Muslim Nations (Akvam-ı İslamiyye Etnoğrafyası)

- Religious History of Turks (Türk Tarih-i Dinisi)
- History of Religions (Tarih-i Edyan)[21]

According to the regulations, students who wanted to register for the Faculty were required to have graduated from high school and also must have passed an entrance examination in Arabic and Persian. The faculty was allowed to accept students from İmam-Hatip schools as well. In the first year, the faculty received more than 400 ex-students from the higher levels of *Daru'l-Hilafe* and *Medresetu'l-Mutehassisin,* both of which had been closed earlier.[22]

Right after the decision to open the Faculty of İlahiyat, bitter criticism appeared in the media. Again, two groups were prominently featured. This time, both of the groups criticized the government for this initiative. One of them criticized the curriculum of the faculty as religious narrow-mindedness and strictness in education and life in general. The other group directed its criticism toward the inadequacy of the curriculum in giving a real religious education. According to the latter group, this was because basic religious sciences were not sufficiently employed in the curriculum. In an article in *Sebilurreşad*, they stated the curriculum was neither a curriculum of natural science nor that of a Faculty of İlahiyat.[23] A similar criticism on the general character of the curriculum was vocalized in the Parliament as well. Rasih Kaplan, for instance, an MP from Antalya, argued that the faculty taught the history of religions rather than Islam.[24] In fact, the criticism of the laicists that the curriculum promoted religious dogmatism unquestionably fails. Almost every effort of the faculty provides a contemporary and novel approach toward religious matters. Criticism from conservatives who expect a more traditional form of religious education seems more accurate. The content of the issue number 14 published in the fourth year can be given as a sample of the modern approach of the faculty members:

- (Yaltkaya), Mehmed Şerefeddin, "İslam'da İlk Fikri Hareketler ve Dini Mezhepler" (First Thought Movements and Religious Sects in Islam), pp. 1–27
- İzmirli Ismail Hakkı, "İslam'da Felsefe Cereyanlary" (Philosophical Trends in Islam), pp. 28–45.
- (Ayni), Mehmet Ali, "Nefs Kelimesinin Manaları" (The Meanings of the Word "Nefs"), pp. 46–52.
- Halil Halid, "İsmaililer, Ağa Han, Hint Müslümanları" (Ismalites, Agha Khan, and Indian Muslims), pp. 53–60.
- (Baykara) Abdulbaki, "Tevhid Kelimesinin Tarihi Safhaları" (The Historical Stages of the Word "Tawhid"), pp. 61–72.
- (Yorükhan) Yusuf Ziya, "Tahtacılar" (Tahtacis), pp. 73–80, (Er, 1993, 59).

The anxieties and predictions regarding from where the students of the faculty would come unfortunately were realized. It was for no other reason than the lack of students that the faculty was closed in 1933. Since İmam-Hatip schools were not given the status of lycée/high school, their graduates could not register at the faculty. Furthermore, graduates of the faculty were deprived of many rights of graduates of other faculties.[25]

After the closing of a Faculty of Theology in Istanbul, the opening of a new one appeared on the agenda of the Turkish Parliament following the seventh convention of the Republican People's Party (RPP) in the late 1940s. The proposition of opening a second Faculty of Divinity raised the same furor in Parliament and the media that opening the first had seen. Opening a new Faculty of Theology promptly set forward the issue of the secular character of the state once again. The traditionalist wing of the ruling RPP advocated revising the definition of secularism. They argued that secularism was misunderstood and misapplied in Turkey. They claimed that it was understood as bringing up the young without religion and the consequence was immorality. According to traditionalists, religion had a moral purpose with an important role in social life. Despite the fact that Islam was the religion of the majority in the country, it had become inferior *vis-à-vis* other religions. There was, then, a disparity in favor of the non-Islamic minority religions in the country. Religious communities had established their own independent organizations all over the world. But in Turkey, this opportunity was not afforded to Muslims. Hence, they contended, the presidency of Religious Affairs should be independent and equipped to educate Turkish men for religious service. Having recognized religion as having moral value, they maintained that new generations should have a solid religious education.

The secularist and revolutionist members of the party, however, were fearful of the potential impact of religion on the secular character of the state. Once again, they insisted on confining religious matters to the realm of the private. According to the secularist wing of the party, religion could easily be abused in the hands of the corrupt. They appealed to racial and national values by referring to a famous saying by Mustafa Kemal: "The ultimate power of a Turk is immanent in his noble blood." Thus, religion should be regarded as a phenomenon between an individual Turk's conscience and God.[26] The seventh convention, rejecting the traditionalists' considerations, declared strict revolutionism.[27]

The suggestion that was advanced to settle this issue came from the Assembly Group of the RPP itself. This was one of the results of democratization in Turkey. Because of its promise for liberation in religion and religious education, the Democratic Party won 62 seats in the Parliament. This forced the leadership of the RPP to make a serious adjustment in its policy of religion.[28] The party in power also began to realize rapid change in the balance of the vote profile in favor of opposition parties on account of their strong emphasis on religion. The RPP, at that time, had a negative image with regard to religion in the eyes of its constituents. Tunaya[29] counted 24 parties in Turkey, most of which were alike regarding their emphasis on freedom of religious matters. Eventually, the RPP recognized the compelling necessity of reviewing and modifying its policy with respect to religion. Shortly after the seventh congress, it became obvious that the RPP could no longer ignore the demand for more attention to religion. As a result of this transformation, the RPP suggested founding a new Faculty of İlahiyat. Clearly, the RPP regarded itself as the only real protector of the modern Turkish Republic.[30] In late January 1948, deputies İbrahim Arvas and Fatin Gökmen tabled a bill to this effect in Parliament. In February 1948, the council of the RPP approved a report calling for the establishment of a Faculty of İlahiyat as well as some other religious institutions of education. The program and texts for this education were to be prepared by the Presidency of Religious Affairs and eventually they were subject to the approval of the Ministry of Education. The new Nation Party also stated that it favored the establishment of a Faculty of İlahiyat in Istanbul on July 22, 1948. In addition, on May 20, 1948, the RPP suggested to the Ministry of National Education that in order to open courses in İmam and Hatip, secondary school graduates could register after completing military service. Thus, the Ministry of Education opened courses of İmam and Hatip in eight different places within a 10-month period. The goal of these courses was to overcome the shortage of qualified men who could lead prayers and funeral ceremonies. But creating a proper concept of theory as well as a project of higher religious education was still a burdensome issue.[31]

Tahsin Banguoğlu, the Minister of National Education, touched upon the matter of the faculty curriculum in a report. He reflected that the new definitions of secularism, religion, and university might appear for many as deviant from true secularism. Banguoğlu stated that:

> The subjects that will be studied on the Faculty will be religious in majority, like exegesis (*tefsir*), tradition (*hadis*), jurisprudence (*fıkıh*). Besides, such courses from the Faculty of Language, history and geography as well as ethics, psychology, sociology will be taught ... Again the language courses of the Faculty of Literature will be the associate courses. Furthermore history of religions and some other religions comparatively will be learned ... Theology is by itself an autonomous discipline, while the Faculty of Literature is only a faculty of human sciences. In this respect by its foundation we will not repeat the mistake that once was made at the University of Istanbul. The essential core here will be the religious sciences.[32]

The very same mistake articulated by Banguoğlu had been mentioned as well by Baltacıoğlu, an adviser to Atatürk for so-called religious reform, in the same session of the Parliament. Baltacıoğlu commented on the character of the new faculty as follows:

> ... in that Faculty of İlahiyat (in Istanbul) I also had some responsibility. In one sense, we realized that it was a kind of Faculty of sociology. But here, the Islamic sciences will be essential, and the sociological sciences will be secondary. .... After fifty years I have come to the conviction, and I do not refrain from expressing it from this seat, that if a person who acquires all of the disciplines such as ethics, aesthetics and literature doesn't receive religious education to be given by the government, then human personality cannot be complete.[33]

The prevailing optimism was reflected in the media, as well. On January 31, 1948, the influential editor, Cihat Baban, pointed out in *Tasvir* that such a proposal was not a deviation from secular principles and that religion was both an individual and a social matter. He also claimed that if Turkey did not bother to train religious specialists, false convictions would spread among the people. He added to this that Turkey must also harness the might of Islam over and against Soviet pressure. On February 4, 1948, M. Tuncer, writing in an İzmir-based paper *Yeni Asya* opined that the state must train a society of well-informed, patriotic religious vanguards who could teach religion to the people in these difficult times.[34] These sentiments were echoed by Nadir Nadi, editor of

Turkey's semi-official paper, *Cumhuriyet*, when he reiterated the need for religious guides (*Din Rehberleri*) on February 12, 1948. A number of influential scholars and politicians also faced the creation of the Faculty of İlahiyat with a sympathetic welcome and expressed their hopes regarding its ability to provide urgently required modern and enlightened religious leadership. Ahmed Remzi Yüreğir, for instance, expressed his strong belief that the faculty would be "no place for superstition mongers."[35]

In the national Parliament, however, much anxiety continued to be expressed lest the new Faculty of Theology once again helped generate the rigidity and obscurantism of the old medrese. Defending the initiative was the duty of the Minister of National Education Tahsin Banguoğlu. He announced that "it will be worthy of Atatürk's Revolution and will not work in the spirit of the medrese, but will work against regressive trends."[36] He replied that the proposed Faculty of Theology was a natural result of the reform processes set in motion by Atatürk, and said:

> This idea is essentially of a nature that will put to rest our friends' anxieties. We are not of the opinion that the old *medrese* should be revived. School and *medrese*, beginning with the *Tanzimat*, lived side by side for a hundred years and bred people who had two different sorts of mind. This person with a two-fold mentality rolled throughout a whole century with an internal struggle. The Faculty of Divinity that we are about to establish will not work with this manner of thinking . . . In this respect the Faculty of İlahiyat will be established as a scientific body and apart from encouraging regressionist movements it will indeed function as an arm against them to impede them and to annihilate them. The Faculty of Divinity will be a torch of light like other scientific institutions that have been established since the *Tanzimat* and, therefore, the superstitions will escape before this radiance like bats.[37]

The next significant step leading to the creation of the new Faculty of İlahiyat occurred when the Senate of Ankara University decided to examine this project on January 7, 1949. Shortly after that, on January 23, 1949, the program of the new Republican cabinet led by M. Şemseddin Günaltay was declared. Günaltay was a student of religious sciences, a medrese graduate and a distinguished historian. Günaltay pledged to follow Western democratic models and to defend the principles of the Turkish revolution. Freedom of conscience was declared holy in his program.[38]

The issue was finally brought to Parliament by the government following the decision of the Senate of Ankara University to open a Faculty of Divinity. The proposition was made on May 3, 1949, with the following leading incentive: "In order to make the investigation of religious questions according to the possible scientific principles, and also to provide the required conditions for raising men of religion effective in their profession and comprehensive in their thinking, the Senate of Ankara University has decided that a Faculty of Divinity is to be opened in accordance with its Western counterpart . . ."[39]

Meanwhile, Banguoğlu tried to explain the purpose of opening the Faculty of İlahiyat, distinguishing the concept of faculty from that of the medrese. He believed the medrese to be places in which to learn the tenets of Islam, whereas the faculties were "houses of science, they endeavor to make comparison, observation and finally, if possible, explanation."[40]

Table 7.2   Program of the Faculty for 1949–50 academic year[43]

Courses	Hours/week	Lecturer
Arabic	6	Prof. Necati Lugal at the FLHG*
Persian	2	Prof. Necati Lugal at the FLHG
Foreign language (English, French, German)	4	Followed at the Foreign Language Dept. of FLHG
Sociology	2	Mehmet Karasan at FLHG
Logic and Philosophy of Sciences	4	Hamdi Ragıp Atademir at FLHG
Islam and History of Sects	4	Prof. Yusuf Ziya Yörükan
History of Islamic Art	2	Prof Remzi Oğuz Arık
Comparative History of Religion	2	Prof. Hilmi Ziya Budda

* FLHG stands for the Faculty of Language, History and Geography in Ankara University.

Emin Soysal (Maraş), referring to the mektep and medrese dualism that had occurred in the past, defended the opening of the Faculty:

> Was Great Atatürk irreligious? No! He was never an irreligious person. Great Atatürk was a great person who wanted this country to develop and improve along a European way. . . . This country is in need of this institution and verily there is a great need of it.[41]

Thus, the law that authorized the formation of the new faculty took effect on June 10, 1949, and, at the outset, a teaching staff was appointed for a period of up to seven years. This included a dean, eight professors, 15 docents and 29 research assistants The law included an allocation of 43,000 Turkish lire (TL) for the budget of the Faculty of Divinity until the coming fiscal year beginning on March 1, 1950. According to the reports, only 39,865 TL were apparently spent in this first half year.[42]

During the first semester, over 85 students enrolled in the faculty for the four-year program. Out of this number, 80, consisting of 58 male and 22 female students, successfully completed the first semester. In the second semester, 130 new lycée/high school graduates were registered. The Faculty graduated a total of 40 students in 1953, nine of whom were female.[44]

The curriculum of the Faculty of İlahiyat changed drastically in 1972. The four-year program increased to five years. In the first three years, Arabic and foreign language courses were emphasized and the last two years were allocated to specializing in two basic areas. Two departments, accordingly, were established in the faculty, the Tafsir and Hadis Department, and the Theology and Islamic Philosophy Department.

For 10 years, the Faculty of İlahiyat at Ankara remained the single institution for religious higher education, except for the İslam Tetkikleri Enstitüsü, which had been working under the auspices of the University of Istanbul.

Ten years after the establishment of the faculty in Ankara, a higher Islamic institute (*Yüksek İslam Enstitüsü*) opened in Istanbul on November 19, 1959. Several reasons were given for the need for a new higher religious educational institution. Again, İsmail Hakkı Baltacıoğlu made a distinction between the Faculty of İlahiyat in Ankara and the Darulfünun: the latter was to emphasize a kind of sociology of religion and the former to deal with religious issues in order to meet the needs of religious service for the people. Even though the latter was expected of the Faculty of İlahiyat in Ankara, there were still some problems in training specialists to guide believers in religious rituals and practices. As Başgil argued (1985), the Faculty of İlahiyat focused on training philosophers and sociologists of religion. This was the first reason given for opening another higher institution for religious education. Secondly, the number of the İmam-Hatip schools had considerably increased (there were 19 İmam-Hatip schools in the country at that time) and the need for teachers could not be met solely by the graduates of the Faculty in Ankara. Also, at that stage, the Imam-Hatib schools and the faculty were regarded as quite separate establishments and there was no attempt to associate the two. The former was established to foster men of religion like *imams* and *hatibs*, while the latter was more of an intellectual center for a scientific understanding and interpreting Islam for adapting to the needs of the changing world. Hence, it was intended primarily to train teachers for Imam-Hatib schools as well as offer courses of religion at ordinary secondary schools and lycées.[45]

Newly opened higher Islamic institutes grew with the increase in the number of İmam-Hatib schools. In 1971, a new institute appeared in Erzurum called the Faculty of Islamic Sciences. With the initiative of the rector of Atatürk University, the faculty started a five-year program on July 22, 1971, open only to İmam-Hatip school graduates. It suffered from a shortage of academic personnel in the early years. The curriculum of the faculty was similar to that of the other higher religious education of the time. It included some pedagogical courses as well.[46]

Each of the institutes and the Faculty of Islamic Sciences in Erzurum were eventually transferred into the faculties of İlahiyat by the extensive reforms of the Council of Higher Education (CHE) (*Yüksek Öğretim Kurulu*) in 1982. This procedure was a kind of recovery operation for the higher Islamic institutes, since they were suffering from the stagnant character of their curriculum. The curriculum really gave the impression of having been an extension of a secondary religious school. The same courses were repeatedly followed in the course of the four-year education: Arabic, Hadith (Prophetic Tradition), Exegesis, Qur'anic Recitation, Theology (*Kelam ve Akaid*). Hence, one of the reasons that the CHE converted them into faculties was the very appeal of the institutes. Yet, there was another compelling reason for this conversion and it was related to the *coup d'état* in 1980. The reforms of the CHE were considered to be the second attempt at the unification of education. As a matter of fact, seven institutes of higher Islamic knowledge were transformed into faculties of İlahiyat and the same curriculum was applied all over Turkey. The old curriculums of İlahiyat education were reviewed in accordance with the criticisms directed toward them. Thus, in the first year, students were taught Arabic, some introductory learning regarding the Qur'an, and some practical issues on Islam. The emphasis on teaching Arabic was a particularly favorable amendment to the curriculum, even though before the reform, Arabic had been part of the education at the Faculty of İlahiyat in Ankara. Rahman stated that he had given lectures in Arabic in Turkey, and several in the audience discussed matters with him in Arabic. He added that this was unique to the Arab world, except to a limited extent in Indonesia.[47]

The curriculum has been revised many times and is still evolving. On April 23–5, 1981, the Faculty of İlahiyat in Ankara hosted the "First Religious Education Seminar in Turkey." An associate professor, among many other academics, seriously criticized the curriculum and the teaching methods in the faculties of the time. Papers entitled "The Problems of Religious Education in Faculties," "The Shortcomings in Higher Religious Education," and "Religious Education in Higher Islamic Institute and its Problems" discussed the curriculum and teaching methods at length. According to the author of one paper, for instance, to achieve an effective curriculum, it was important to recognize that the prevailing curriculum was replete with obsolete and unimportant courses. After the unification of the higher religious institutions, several meetings were held to discuss the coordination of the faculties and the development of the curriculum. One such meeting was organized by Samsun Ondokuz Mayıs University, entitled "The Symposium of the Instruction of Religious Sciences in Higher Education" (*Yükseköğretimde Din Bilimleri Öğretimi Sempozyumu*) on October 21–3, 1987. In this gathering, Bayraktar Bayraklı, the Professor of Islamic Education at the Faculty of Divinity of Marmara University, delivered a paper that was characteristic in outlining some of the problems of the curriculum of the Faculties of İlahiyat. He criticized the conception of education that relies solely upon the teacher's efforts in the classroom. He also suggested that the definition of "student" should be modified. The curriculum should be altered to provide greater participation of the students. There were, to him, some artificial divisions in the content of the courses. For example, the Qur'an and the exegesis of the Qur'an were given in different courses and in two different languages, one in Arabic and the other in Turkish. He also complained about the excessive number of courses. Bayraklı believed it more important for students to be able to follow the contemporary debate on Islamic and modern issues rather than studying debates that took place among certain schools in early Islam. In 1988, another symposium, entitled the "Symposium of Religious Education and Service," was held in Ankara as a result of a joint initiative of the Presidency of Religious Affairs at Ankara University and the Foundation of Religious Affairs. This symposium dealt with secondary religious education from the perspective of religious services. After a year, another symposium was organized by the Faculty of İlahiyat of Samsun Ondokuz Mayıs University called "Religious Sciences Today and Their Problems" (*Günümüz Din Bilimleri Sempozyumu*, June 27–30, 1989). Sixty-three academics of the nine Faculties of İlahiyat presented their papers on the problems in various areas of higher religious education in Turkey in 10 sessions. The symposia had varying degrees of influence on later modifications of the curriculum, beginning in 1991. For example, many courses required for pedagogical formation were dropped or made optional. The number of Arabic courses was increased. The first year was devoted to Arabic education as a preparatory/preliminary one. Some optional courses were added, such as Contemporary Islamic Movements in the Islamic World, Interrelationships among Today's Religions, Contemporary Movements of Philosophy, The History of the Islamic Countries and their Geography. In 1992, the departmental structure of the faculties was revised as follows:

- The Basic Islamic Sciences Department
- Philosophy and the Religious Sciences Department
- Islamic History and Arts Department

While efforts to increase the quality of education were proceeding, something else happened as well. At present, there are 23 faculties of İlahiyat in Turkey. The increase in number first took place with the conversion of higher Islamic institutes to faculties of İlahiyat. Until the late 1980s, there were only nine faculties. In 1987 Harran University (Şanlıurfa) Faculty of İlahiyat became the tenth faculty. In 1993 Sakarya University, Karadeniz Technical University (Rize), İnönü University (Darende), Dicle University (Diyarbakır), Süleyman Demirel University (Isparta), and Yüzüncü Yıl University (Van); in 1994 Gazi University (Çorum), Fırat University (Elazığ), Cumhuriyet University (Sivas), and Çukurova University (Adana); in 1995 Onsekiz Mart University (Çanakkale); in 1996 Istanbul University; in 1997 Sütçüiman University (Kahramanmaraş) and Osman Gazi University (Eskişehir) added one Faculty of İlahiyat to their campuses. A faculty in Akdeniz University was officially decided to be opened, but this has not as yet happened.[48]

The new Faculty of İlahiyat in Ankara played a significant role in the case of the Faculty of Islamic Sciences. The staff and the deans of the new faculties of İlahiyat were mostly appointed from the Faculty of İlahiyat in Ankara. In 1993, the deans of six of the nine faculties of İlahiyat were graduates of the Faculty of Ankara. Only recently were deans appointed from their original staff. With this development, the new policy of the CHE became effective. To support the newly established universities outside the main big cities, numerous academics were reassigned to them. Since 1982–3, some 30 academic personnel of different levels have left the Faculty and gone to other universities, due to the lack of academic positions allocated in Ankara.

In 1988, initiatives for a new higher religious educational institution were proffered by the President of the Presidency of Religious Affairs, Prof. Dr. Mustafa Said Yazıcıoğlu, who was originally from the Faculty of İlahiyat in Ankara. No sooner was he appointed to the position on June 17, 1987 (he stayed in the position until January 3, 1992) than he realized that the officers of the establishment were themselves poorly educated. He officially wrote to the CHE demanding they open an institute with a higher quality of officers. The CHE agreed to do so and, in fact, they opened a two-year middle level institute between İmam-Hatip school and the Faculty of İlahiyat. It was called the Higher İlahiyat School of Profession (İlahiyat Meslek Yüksek Okulu). In his letter, Professor Yazıcıoğlu remarked that the Presidency had 54,476 officers working in mosques and teaching Qur'anic courses and yet only 2209 of them had received higher religious education. Accordingly, the Executive Board of the CHE decided to establish four Higher İlahiyat Schools of Profession in Ankara, İzmir (Dokuz Eylül University), Istanbul (Marmara University), and Bursa (Uludağ University) on December 29, 1988. It was stipulated that only officers who had graduated from İmam-Hatip schools and had worked for the Presidency for at least two years would be eligible. They were also asked to obtain the required mark from the Central Student Selection Examination. Certain pedagogical courses, such as sociology and psychology of education and general and special teaching methods, measuring and evaluation beside basic religious courses such as Arabic, Tafsir, Hadith and history of religions were included in the curriculum.

In 1989, two İlahiyat faculties in Istanbul and İzmir opened the new program and accepted students. Later, in 1992, Erzurum Atatürk University and Bursa Uludağ University did, as well Van Yüzüncü Yıl University to the far east and Trabzon Technical University to the north registered students in 1994. The program has not yet been opened in Ankara.

Recently, another notable program with a purpose similar to that of the Higher İlahiyat School of Profession has been developed under the auspices of Professor Yazıcıoğlu. In the early 1990s he realized that the Higher İlahiyat School of Professions program would not be sufficient to improve the academic levels of the officers of the Presidency within the short time necessary. In 1998, there were only 1095 students: 589 of this number were female, 506 students were male.[49] Therefore, he suggested developing yet another institute focusing on different aspects of the educational system. According to statistics, officers who had graduated with a higher religious education still made up only 3.76 percent of that population.[50] Yazıcıoğlu's project, however, could not be implemented until 1998. The Executive Board of the CHE made a decision on July 11, 1997 to institute a program called the Pre-BA İlahiyat Program (*İlahiyat Önlisans Programı*). Unfortunately, the process could only begin with another decision by the Board on December 11, 1997. According to the decision, the goal of the program was to elevate the level of the education of the officers who work at the state organizations in the category of religious service who had graduated from İmam-Hatip schools.[51] The fact that Professor Yazıcıoğlu had been a member of the CHE in addition to having been the President of Religious Affairs provided him with an intimate knowledge of the shortcomings of the organization. It was this unique perspective that inspired him to see the progress carried out. In fact, what occurred was that the program of the Faculty of İlahiyat of Ankara University and the Open Education Faculty of Anadolu University worked together. The strictly academic part of the program, such as preparing curriculum, textbooks and television lessons, was accomplished by the Faculty of İlahiyat. Coordination of remote education was conducted by the Open Education Faculty of Anadolu University based in Eskişehir. The textbooks were printed and television lessons prepared according to the curriculum at the Anadolu University. The program officially began in the 1998–9 school year. About 4000 officers of Religious Affairs and graduates of İmam-Hatip schools were accepted, having passed the Student Selection Examination given to graduates of secondary education all over the country. Because the two-year program seeks to provide the opportunity to all officers graduating from İmam-Hatip schools, the required marks for acceptance to the program are kept quite low. The mark was 105 for the 1998 examination. The Faculty of İlahiyat in Ankara has recently instituted another initiative for the betterment of the curriculum. In 1997, Professor Mustafa S. Yazıcıoğlu, dean of the Faculty of İlahiyat of Ankara University, created a committee composed of young academics of the faculty, and put them in charge of developing the curriculum. The goal of the new program was "to train a type of İlahiyat graduate who can depend on the

Qur'an itself as the most basic source of the religion, rightly evaluate the cultural heritage, interpret daily life as well as produce solutions to the problems that are faced." The document they released outlined the basic principles of the program and also stated that it hoped to provide the students with an understanding of the general concepts of culture and history, besides basic knowledge of religious sciences. In the program this committee envisioned two kinds of courses. First are the compulsory courses, which give a basic knowledge of a specialized field. The purpose of the other group of courses, namely the "elective courses," which starts in the fifth semester, is to unify the theoretical and practical goals of the education. For the latter, the courses are designed to meet the needs of an interdisciplinary education for the İlahiyat students and to ensure that the students follow current developments in their chosen field. In this new program, the number of elective courses has been increased as much as possible, and therefore, they have reached up to roughly 40 percent of the overall courses in the last two years. Even though the program was prepared for the İlahiyat in Ankara, the CHE has mandated the program for faculties all over the country.

The committee was also responsible for designing another program called the Primary Education Religious Culture and Moral Knowledge Teacher Program (İlköğretim Din Kültürü ve Ahlak Bilgisi Öğretmenliği). It focussed upon the courses of the İlahiyat field. The pedagogical part of the program became a general program prepared by the CHE for all faculties graduating teacher candidates. To conduct the program, departments were established in the Faculties of İlahiyat. These are in Atatürk (Erzurum), Çukurova (Adana), Dicle (Diyarbakır), Dokuzeylül (İzmir), Erciyes (Kayseri), Istanbul, Marmara (İstanbul), Ondokuz-Mayıs (Samsun), Selçuk (Konya), and Uludağ (Bursa) universities. They were chosen from universities that have a particular expertise in pedagogical courses. Except for Istanbul and Diyarbakır, because of a shortage of staff, the faculties accepted students for the program in the 1998–99 academic year. The graduates of this four-year program will specifically be trained as teachers of religious culture and moral knowledge in the eight-year primary education system.

In 1999, the faculty decreased the number of new students to 2370. Out of this number, 1890 students were part of the regular İlahiyat program and 480 participated in the Religious Culture and Moral Knowledge Teacher program, in accordance with the formation of İlahiyat education.[53] Some in the right-wing media regarded the drop in number as an expression of hostility towards the faculties of İlahiyat. In an informative composition in *Yeni Şafak*, the changes were given under the title "İlahiyatların Fermanı İmzalanmış" (The Execution Edict of İlahiyats has been Signed) (May 13, 1998).

In the 1997–8 academic year, there were 14,320 students in all faculties of İlahiyat throughout Turkey. Of this number 4487 were female students and 9833 were male. The Faculties of İlahiyat accepted 1120 new female and 2098 new male students, totaling 3218 students in the same year. There were 328 female graduates and 1091 male graduates that same year, making a total of 1419 students.[54] The graduates of the faculties have the opportunity to find positions either in the Ministry of Education, as teachers, or at various levels of the presidency of Religious Affairs. This is because

Table 7.3 Four-year İlahiyat education program developed in 1997[52]

First year			
First semester		**Second semester**	
Courses	Credit	Courses	Credit
Arabic	9	Arabic	9
Major Themes of the Qur'an	2	Reciting the Qur'an and Tajwid	2
Islamic History I	2	History of Hadith	2
Foreign Language	4	Foreign Language	4
Turkish I	2	Islamic History II	2
Introduction to Psychology	2	Turkish II	2
Computer	3	Introduction to Sociology	2
Principles of Kemalism and History of Revolution	2	Principles of Kemalism and History of Revolution	2
Fine Arts/Physical Training	0		

Second year			
Third semester		**Fourth semester**	
Courses	Credit	Courses	Credit
Arabic	4	Arabic	4
Reciting the Qur'an and Tajwid	2	Methodology of Tafsir	2
History of Tafsir	2	Hadith	2
Foreign Language	4	Foreign Language	4
Methodology of Hadith	2	History of Theology	2
Islamic History III	2	Reciting the Qur'an and Tajwid	2
History of Ancient Philosophy	2	History of Islamic Philosophy	2
Turco-Islamic Literature	2	History of Isamic Civilisation	2
Psychology of Religion	2	Sociology of Religion	2
Logic	2	History of Turco-Islamic Art	2

Third year			
Fifth semester		**Sixth semester**	
Compulsory courses	Credit	Compulsory courses	Credit
Arabic	2	Arabic	2
Tafsir	2	Methodology of Islamic Law II	2
Study of Qur'an Translations	2	Systematic Theology I	2
Methodology of Islamic Law	2	History of Islamic Sects I	2
Theological Schools	2	History of Religions II	2
Modern Age Philosophy	2	History and Philosophy of Mysticism	2

Table 7.3 *Continued*

<table>
<tr><th colspan="4">Third year</th></tr>
<tr><th colspan="2">Fifth semester</th><th colspan="2">Sixth semester</th></tr>
<tr><th>Compulsory courses</th><th>Credit</th><th>Compulsory courses</th><th>Credit</th></tr>
<tr><td>History of Religions</td><td>2</td><td>Elective Course</td><td>2</td></tr>
<tr><td>Elective Course</td><td>2</td><td>Elective Course</td><td>2</td></tr>
<tr><td>Elective Course</td><td>2</td><td>Elective Course</td><td>2</td></tr>
<tr><td>Elective Course</td><td>2</td><td>Elective Course</td><td>2</td></tr>
<tr><th>Elective courses</th><th>Credit</th><th>Elective courses</th><th>Credit</th></tr>
<tr><td>Hadith Criticism</td><td>2</td><td>Contemporary Comments on Hadith and Sunnah</td><td>7</td></tr>
<tr><td>Reciting the Qur'an</td><td>2</td><td>Philosophy of History.</td><td>2</td></tr>
<tr><td>Semantic of the Qur'an</td><td>2</td><td>History of Science in Islam</td><td>2</td></tr>
<tr><td>Method and Critique of History</td><td>2</td><td>Islamic Arts and Aesthetics</td><td>2</td></tr>
<tr><td>History of Islamic Institutions</td><td>2</td><td>History of Education in Islam</td><td>2</td></tr>
<tr><td>Methodology in Social Sciences</td><td>2</td><td>History of Turkish Thought</td><td>2</td></tr>
<tr><td>Turkish Religious Music</td><td>2</td><td>Turkish Theologians</td><td>2</td></tr>
<tr><td>Persian</td><td>2</td><td>Ottoman Turkish</td><td>2</td></tr>
<tr><td></td><td></td><td>Turkish Religious Music</td><td>2</td></tr>
<tr><td></td><td></td><td>Astronomy and Sciences of Space</td><td>2</td></tr>
<tr><td></td><td></td><td>Persian</td><td>2</td></tr>
<tr><td></td><td></td><td>Modern Biology</td><td>2</td></tr>
<tr><th colspan="4">Fourth year</th></tr>
<tr><th colspan="2">Seventh semester</th><th colspan="2">Eighth semester</th></tr>
<tr><th>Compulsory courses</th><th>Credit</th><th>Compulsory courses</th><th>Credit</th></tr>
<tr><td>Islamic Law I</td><td>2</td><td>Islamic Law</td><td>2</td></tr>
<tr><td>Systematic Theology II</td><td>2</td><td>Religious Oratory</td><td>2</td></tr>
<tr><td>History of Islamic Sects II</td><td>2</td><td>Philosophy of Religion II</td><td>2</td></tr>
<tr><td>Religious Education</td><td>2</td><td>Islamic Philosophy of Ethics</td><td>2</td></tr>
<tr><td>Philosophy of Religion I</td><td>2</td><td>Elective Course</td><td>2</td></tr>
<tr><td>Elective Course</td><td>2</td><td>Elective Course</td><td>2</td></tr>
<tr><td>Elective Course</td><td>2</td><td>Elective Course</td><td>2</td></tr>
<tr><td>Elective Course</td><td>2</td><td>Elective Course</td><td>2</td></tr>
<tr><td>Elective Course</td><td>2</td><td></td><td></td></tr>
<tr><th>Elective courses</th><th>Credit</th><th>Elective courses</th><th>Credit</th></tr>
<tr><td>Contemporary Approaches to the Qur'an</td><td>2</td><td>Qur'anic Judgments and Modern Law</td><td>2</td></tr>
</table>

Table 7.3 *Continued*

Elective courses	Credit	Elective courses	Credit
Comparative Islamic Law	2	Contemporary Trends of Philosophy	2
Religious Trends in Turkey	2	Contemporary Theological Problems	2
Reciting the Qur'an	2	Inter-religious Dialogue	
Contemporary Muslim Thinkers	2	Contemporary Islamic Trends	2
Comparative Folk Beliefs	2	Contemporary Trends in Education	2
Contemporary Mystical Trends	2	History of Turkish Republic	2
Ottoman Turkish	2	Problems of Philosophy of Religion	2
Paleography and Epigraphy	2	Philosophy of Ethics	2
Public Relations			
Texts on Religion and Literature			
Texts on Classical Theology			
Selected Hadith Texts			
Religious Texts in Foreign Language			
Arabic Eloquence			

of their knowledge of Persian as well as Arabic and a Western language. Thus far the graduates of the faculties of İlahiyat can teach special courses at İmam-Hatip lycée (İHL). They have also taught courses of religious culture and moral knowledge at ordinary lycée and secondary schools. Moreover, they have been permitted to give some cultural lessons.

Graduates could also find positions at the Prime Ministry, the Turkish Radio Television organization and at the State Archives because of their knowledge of Ottoman Turkish. The Ministry of National Defense used to recruit a certain number of students as teachers at the military secondary and higher schools or at the moral departments of the Land, Sea and Air forces[55] until the very early 1990s.

Recent changes by the CHE have resulted in three different İlahiyat programs in the above-mentioned faculties. Thus, graduates of the faculties are directed mostly towards positions within the Ministry of Education. On July 11, 1997, the CHE decided to redetermine the work areas of the graduates of the faculties of İlahiyat. The graduates were divided into three categories according to the different programs they had followed. The Primary Education Religious Culture and Moral Knowledge Teacher Program produces teachers for primary schools. Religious Culture and Moral Knowledge teachers for secondary schools are trained in a three-semester MA program, which is only available at the Faculty of İlahiyat in Ankara, and which accept graduates of ordinary four-year

İlahiyat BA programs. Another MA program is instituted for training teachers for the İmam-Hatip lycées in Ankara.

During the course of the 50-year history of the İlahiyat, a tradition gradually took shape. The faculties of İlahiyat, especially the one in Ankara, developed along lines unique to themselves. The Professor of Exegesis, Süleyman Ateş, for instance, engaged in polemics regarding whether the people of Scriptures, Jews and Christians (*Ehl-i Kitab*) would achieve ultimate salvation, that is, Heaven.[56] The Professor of Theology, Mehmed Dağ of Samsun, one of the two translators of Fazlur Rahman's well-known work *Islam* into Turkish wrote an article on the non-necessity of head covering. In İzmir, the Professor of Philosophy of Religion, Mehmed S. Aydın, the co-translator of Mehmed Dağ in the translation of Rahman's book, and the Professor of the History of Islamic Sects, and Etem Ruhi Fığlalı, the author of various books on the contemporary Islamic sects, especially on Shi'ite Islam, are also good examples of such a tradition. Academics from the Faculty of İlahiyat have most recently constituted the editorial board of the journal *Islamic Research* (*İslami Araştırmalar*), which is based in Ankara. For the last 10 years, this journal has been known for its critical view of traditionalism and its rather modernist approach towards religious issues. Some special issues, such as on women in Islam, the history of the Qur'an and on hadith criticism, created something of a furor. The younger generation of the same society is now editing another quarterly named *İslamiyat*, which began in 1998. The chief editor of the journal is Mehmet S. Hatiboğlu, a hadith scholar who is very well known for his critical approach to tradition. Together, these men have created and best represent the new tradition of the Faculty of İlahiyat of Ankara. The tradition is known simply as Islamic modernism.

The Faculty of İlahiyat in Ankara is preparing to celebrate its fiftieth anniversary. With a few exceptions, this is also the fiftieth anniversary of higher religious education in modern Turkey. During the last 50 years, 22 more faculties have been established. The state has increasingly acknowledged the people's need for formal higher religious education over the course of time. Modern Turkey has been pursuing an understanding of Islam as it applies in that country for 75 years. This has resulted in a reconciliation of the Turko-Islamic tradition, which is unique to Turkish heritage, and modern interpretations of Islam. This goal, in fact, has been affirmed at every opportunity. In an article published in the daily *Hürriyet* on the recent changes of the İlahiyat, the program writer[57] wrote glowingly of the citizens' achievement in fulfilling and living the tenets of Islam. He believes that the people's knowledge of Islam in Turkey is the result of thousands of years of history along with customs that have evolved based upon Islam's espousal of tolerance.

Also, the purpose of higher religious education, besides increasing the quality of the graduates who will potentially staff the Ministry of Education and Presidency of Religious Affairs, was articulated as:

> to be able to train our youngsters in Islam and to raise them as the individuals who are aware that they are citizens of a secular, democratic and social law state . . . and also are proud of being citizens of the Turkish Republic as well as the Turkish nation; and that if one hears *ezan* (call for prayer) and if the glorious Turkish flag is flying then we owe this

to great leader Atatürk and his colleagues in the army and in the politics who founded the Republic.

In the following years the initiatives for updating the higher religious education have advanced. Specialists, from all over Turkey, of higher religious education organized another conference and discussed the problems of restructuring and the future of the education at İsparta Süleyman Demirel İlahiyat Faculty in October 2003. A less comprehensive initiative regarding the issues was taken by the quarterly *İslamiyat* in 2004.

The Pre-BA İlahiyat program (*İlahiyat Önlisans Programı*), for instance, attracted many more students from İmam-Hatip schools. The program mostly reached its goal of elevating the level of education of the religious service people. The İmam-Hatip graduates, however, find it difficult to be successful enough to register for any higher education program after a new rule regulating university entrance. The new rule directs İmam-Hatip graduates specifically towards higher religious education, as almost the only option, rather than other fields. Moreover, because of its heavy conditions for secondary school graduates in general (in which İmam-Hatip schools are regarded), the rates of entering university drastically dropped from 192,786 in 1998–99 to 64,534 in 2002–3, for instance. On the other hand, the condition of 105 points from the university entrance examination has been lifted and all İmam-Hatip graduates have had the right to register for the program without taking the examination since 2001. As a result more than 40,000 of İmam-Hatip graduates including the ones already appointed as servicemen in Religious Affairs consisted of about 100,000 students of the Open Education Faculty of Anadolu University in 2002. In the following year 14,000 new students joined. Although theoretically the graduates of the open İlahiyat program can also continue their higher education in full BA programs the opportunity is rarely given because of the quota allocated to higher religious education. In 2004 for instance, only 445 İmam-Hatip graduates could register at 22 İlahiyat faculties. Nonetheless, recently some projects have been suggested to change the two-year program to a four-year full higher religious education like the İlahiyat program. With this new two-year program the graduates of the Pre-BA program will complete their higher religious education in four years, benefiting from internet technology.

The Primary Education Religious Culture and Moral Knowledge Teacher Program has generated more than 250 graduates from the Ankara İlahiyat since its inauguration in 1998. The three-semester MA program to educate both secondary school religious culture and moral knowledge teachers and İmam-Hatip religious course teachers produced about 150 graduates from the Ankara University İlahiyat Faculty in 2003. The fact that the quotas for religious course teachers in primary and secondary schools as well as the İmam-Hatip schools given by the Ministry of Education were very low led to concern among the students of İlahiyat faculties about their future. The Ministry allocated only 100 positions for religious teachers between 2000–4. *That the number needed to be more than 1000 created a positive atmosphere among the students in 2004.* In spite of the difficulties in establishing the teacher education programs, the actual situation promotes specialization in certain areas in order to provide better work opportunities for their graduates. Süleyman Demirel University and Cumhuriyet University İlahiyat faculties have taken the initiative in order to specialize in educating their students from the İlahiyat program for the area of religious service. This initiative, therefore, aims at producing more qualified graduates to work at the presidency of Religious Affairs.

In the last two years the bid to enter the European Union has increasingly affected higher religious education both formally and qualitatively as it influences all aspects of life at different levels in Turkey. Because higher education in general has entered a process of integration with the EU education system the İlahiyat faculties also have been affected. For the time being the process mostly encourages raising the standards of higher education in all aspects to those of the EU within the framework of its higher education developing programs. Therefore an intense effort has been made by the İlahiyat faculties to be accredited by and integrated within the European university system. In this context Ankara University İlahiyat Faculty has already signed a cooperation agreement, both at the level of students and staff members, with Erlangen University in Germany. In the near future the number of such agreements will increase.

Notes

1. Andreas M. Kazamias, *The Education Quest for Modernity in Turkey*, (Chicago: University of Chicago Press, 1966), 185f.
2. See Akşit, Bahattin, "Islamic Education in Turkey. Medrese Reform in Late Ottoman Times and İmam-Hatip Schools in the Republic," in Richard Tapper (ed.), *Islam in Modern Turkey: Religion, Politics and Literature in a Secular State* (London: I.B. Tauris, 1991), 159.
3. Recai Doğan, "II. Meşrutiyet Dönemi Eğitim Hareketlerinde Din Egitim-Ögretimi," *Ankara Üniversitesi İlahiyat Fakultesi Dergisi*, XXXVIII, 1998, 367–98f.
4. Hilmi Ziya Ülken, "İlahiyat Fakiiltesinin Geçirdigi Safhalar," *İlahiyat Fakültesi Albümü, 1949–1960*, 1961, 3.
5. Mustafa Ergün, *II. Meşrutiyet Döneminde Eğitim Hareketleri,1908–1914* (Ankara: Ocak Yayınları, 1996), 260.
6. Ergün, *II. Meşrutiyet*, 259ff.
7. Ülken, İlahiyat, 5.
8. Doğan. II. Meşrutiyet, 1998; see also Kazamias, *The Education Quest*, 71ff.
9. Kazamias, *The Education Quest*, 66.
10. "Ocak Sondürmek De Meziyet İmiş," *Sebilurreşad 9 Teşrinievvel, 1340*, XXIV/620, 1925, 348f.
11. Yahya Afif, "İnhilal Eden İlim Ordusu," *5 Haziran 1340*, XXIV/603, 1924, 69.
12. Falih Rıfkı, 2 Teşrinievvel, 1340, "Bize Atatürkçü Hoca Lazım, Şeriat Uleması Değil!," (*Cumhuriyet*, 1924), 1.
13. İnönü, 1925, 76f.
14. Halide Edip Adıvar, *Türkiye'de Şark,Garp ve Amerikan Tesisleri* (Istanbul: Doğan Kardeş Yayınları, 1955), 104.
15. Ethem Ruhi, 30 Teşrinievvel, 1340 "Ahlak-ı Diniyye Filmi," *Sebilurreşad*, XXIV/623, 1924, 398; Ahmet Cevdet, 11 Kanunievvel, 1340, "Yegane Çare-i Selamet Ahlak-i Diniyyedir," *Sebilurreşad*, XXV/629, 1924, 79; Hasan Hikmet, 1340, 1924, 89ff.
16. Ahmet Cevdet, 27 Eylül, 1340, s. 1

17. Süleyman Hayri Bolay, "Yüksek Öğretimde Din Eğitimi," in *Milli Eğitim ve Din Eğitimi İlmi Seminer Tebliğleri* (Ankara: Aydınlar Ocağı Yayınları, 1981), 177–86.

18. Sadrettin Celal, 6 Agustos 1340, "Terbiyenin Esasları," *Son Telgraf*, 51, 2.

19. Sadrettin Celal, 23 Temmuz, 1340, "Muallimler ve Cumhuriyet," *Son Telgraf*, 37, 3.

20. Mehmet Oğlu İhsan, 26 Temmuz, 1340, "Muallimler ve Cumhuriyet (Sadreddin Bey'e Cevab)," *Son Telgraf*, 40, 1924, 3.

21. İstanbul Darulfununun Şahsiyeti Hükmiyesi Hakkında Kanun, Darulfünun Talimatnamesi, 1932, 6 Burhaneddin Matbaası, Istanbul.

22. W. Frederick Frey, "Education: Turkey," in Robert E. Ward-Dankwart and A. Rustow (eds.), *Political Modernization in Japan and Turkey* (New Jersey: Princeton University Press. 1970), 217.

23. Yahya Afif, 29 Mayıs 1340, "Vebali Müderris Beylerin Boynuna," *Sebilurreşad*, XXIV/602, 1924, 57.

24. Minutes of TBMM, Term II, vol. XVIII, 297.

25. Osman Ergin, *Türkiye Maarif Tarihi* (Istanbul, 1977), 1742; also see Parmaksızoğlu, *Türkiye'de Din Eğitimi* (Ankara: Milli Eğitim Basımevi, 1966), 25.

26. Minutes of the 7th Congress of the RPP (1948), 449–65.

27. Tarık Zafer. Tunaya, *İslamcılık Akımı*. Simavi Yayınları, second edn. (1991), 185.

28. Davut Dursun. *Din Bürokrasisi: Yapısı, Konumu ve Gelişimi.* İşaret Yayınları (Istanbul, 1992), 192.

29. Tunaya, *İslamcılık Akımı*, 179–80.

30. Dursun, 192–3

31. Ibid.

32. Minutes of TBMM, Term VIII, vol. XX, 227–84.

33. Ibid.

34. Howard Reed. "The Faculty of Divinity at Ankara I. II," *Muslim World*, 46, 1956, 305.

35. Reed, 309.

36. Ibid.

37. Ibid.

38. Ibid., 305–6.

39. Münir Koştaş, "Ankara Universitesi Kuruluş ve Tarihçesi," *Ankara Üniversitesi İlahiyat Fakültesi Dergisi*, XXXI, 1989, 8.

40. Minutes of TBMM, Term VIII, vol. XX, 227–84.

41. Ibid.

42. Reed, 309.

43. *İlahiyat Fakültesi Albümü*, 1961, 14.

44. *İlahiyat Fakültesi Albümü, 1949–1960* (Ankara: Türk Tarih Kurumu Basımevi, 1961), 16.

45. Annual of the Istanbul, YİE (Yüksek İslam Enstitiütusü) (Istanbul: Yüksek İslam Enstitütüsü Vakfı Yayınları, 1982).

46. Muhammet Şevki Aydın, Cumhuriyet Döneminde Din Eğitim Öğretmeni Yetiştirme ve İstihdamı (1923–98), an unpublished dissertation (1999), 99f.

47. Fazlur Rahman, *Islam and Modernity: Transformation of an Intellectual Tradition* (Chicago: University of Chicago Press, 1982), 98.

48. Aydın, 119.

49. YÖK (Yüksek Öğretim Kurulu) Yayın ve Dokümantasyon Daire Başkanlığı Tez Veri *Merkezi* (Ankara, 1999).

50. *DİB (Diyanet İşleri Başkanlığı) 1997 Yılı İstatistikleri* (Ankara, 1998).

51. Murat Barkan, *Nasıl Çalışmalıyım? Rehber Kitap* (Eskişehir: Anadolu Üniversitesi Yayınları, 1998), 6.

52. İlahiyat Fakülteleri Öğretmen Yetiştirme ve Lisans Programları (1998), 47–53.
53. Kamuran Zeren, "İlahiyata Kota," *Hürriyet*, May 11, 1998.
54. YÖK (Yüksek Öğretim Kululu) APK Daire Başkanlığı (Ankara, 1999).
55. Koştaş, 1989.
56. Ateş, 1991.
57. Zeren, 1998.

CHAPTER 8

Hassan Turabi and the Limits of Modern Islamic Reformism[1]

Abdelwahab El-Affendi

At one point in the second half of the 1970s Hassan Turabi, no stranger to controversy, suddenly found himself at the center of a fierce and rather unusual storm. Turabi, a former law professor who had been educated at London University and the Sorbonne, had only recently been released from a long period of political detention, being accused of helping to destabilize the regime of the then President Ja'far Numairi (1969–85). The main Islamist party, the Muslim Brotherhood, which Turabi led since 1964, dominated student politics and was active within the trade unions and the opposition National Front (NF). In this capacity, it had engineered, or participated in, a number of civilian and military uprisings against the military regime between 1969 and 1977, when NF leaders struck a deal with the regime.

Following that deal, Turabi was appointed (controversially) to a senior post in the Sudanese Socialist Union, the only legal political party in the country. However, the new controversy in which Turabi found himself embroiled had little to do with politics, not directly anyway. It revolved around the apparently trivial, even grotesque, question of whether, if a fly fell into someone's drink, he/she should immediately throw the beverage away, salvage some of it, or dip the fly completely into the cup and then drink happily.

The latter advice is the one apparently recommended by the Prophet Muhammad, according to a report in the collection of Bukhari, regarded by the majority of Sunni Muslims as the most authentic compilation of prophetic words and deeds (al-Zabidi, 1986). This advice has become the subject of controversy in recent times, given the state of knowledge in medicine today. Some apologists tried to argue the soundness of this advice by adducing help from medical science, and even regarded this as a miracle, in that advanced knowledge, which could only be divine in origin, must have guided the Prophet in making this insightful proposal.

Turabi would have none of this, rejecting this advice outright, a position that was not received kindly by the traditionalist majority. In the exchanges that ensued, Turabi attempted to deploy a whole battery of methodological devices, which, he believed, would enable the reformer to deal with the problems posed by traditional Islamic jurisprudence. First he challenged the common Sunni belief in the veracity of all the reports contained in Bukhari's collection. While the diligence Bukhari displayed in checking and rechecking his sources and scrutinizing the accuracy of their reports is commendable, one cannot ascribe infallibility to Bukhari and other hadith compilers and all their sources. So reports like this one, which appear to contradict reason and the established findings of modern science, may be dismissed as not being authentic.[2]

However, even if the report could be reliably traced to one of the Prophet's companions, the person in question could have been mistaken in what he reported. He may even have had motives or a vested interest in purposefully misreporting the statement or incident in question. Even supposing that a problematic report could be traced to the Prophet himself without any identifiable lapses in the chain of transmission, or possible explanations from the motives and defects of the transmitters, then it could still be challenged. The basis for such a challenge is the distinction between what the Prophet did and said in his capacity as a human being, and what he did and said in his capacity as a Messenger of God. The first could cover a wide range of advice and actions relevant to worldly matters, such as specific acts he had performed as a military leader or in his personal and individual capacity. Not all these acts are normative, unless covered by explicit rules indicating this. There are many instances, in fact, of the Prophet admitting error in such matters.

These remarks appeared to touch what Sunni Islam regard as the core of Islamic doctrine. Reformers since the early centuries of Islam have always called for a return to the "original sources" of the faith. By this they meant the Qur'anic revelation and the practice of the Prophet and his immediate successors, the (four) rightly guided caliphs. The Qur'an as the direct unmediated Word of God was the top of this hierarchy. But the normative authority of the Prophet was no less central, since the distinction between which utterances of his could be classified as Qur'anic verses is ultimately based on his own explicit instructions. The Prophet's companions also play a crucial role in this hierarchy, having faithfully transmitted the Prophetic remarks and contextualized them. In the final analysis, the authoritative hadith compendia, Qur'anic exegeses and jurisprudential works complete this circle, providing as they do the framework for ascertaining which is which. Turabi's challenge to these pillars of doctrine threatened to bring the whole system down.

The Conservative Reaction

It was no surprise, therefore, that his attitude should create unease at first and an outright revolt within the movement later. A small group from within the Muslim Brotherhood's conservative wing led a revolt that kept festering until it crystallized in 1980 in a formal split (El-Affendi, 1991, 85–9; Makki, 1990, 90–2). The loose coalition that led the split was made up of old political rivals of Turabi's and traditionalists and neo-Salafis. Most disliked Turabi's political pragmatism and ideological "flexibility." The Salafis in particular resented his toleration of the dominant Sufi Islam of Sudan.

Politically, most opposed the deal with Numairi, and Turabi's reluctance to join the Egyptian-led International Organization of the Muslim Brotherhood.

While this coalition did not achieve much success in carrying the rank and file with it, it succeeded in putting Turabi on the defensive. He was forced to withdraw or tone down most of his remarks, and adopt a more cautious attitude, trying to steer clear of similar controversies. But the opponents did not let up, and the campaign against Turabi soon moved abroad. In 1980, an Egyptian cleric, who also happened to be a leading figure in the Egyptian Muslim Brotherhood, wrote a letter to the top figure in the *ulama* hierarchy in Saudi Arabia, Shaykh 'Abdul-Azīz Bin-Bāz, complaining that he had been informed of "a man named Dr. Hassan Turabi, who occupies a post of Minister of Religious Affairs or something of that sort, and who propagated very outlandish views." These included: denying that adulterers should be stoned to death, approving the marriage of Muslim women to Jews or Christians, arguing that conversion by a Muslim to Christianity or Judaism is not apostasy, alleging that no set penalty exists in Islamic law for alcohol taking, arguing that the principles of Islamic jurisprudence or the terminology of the science of hadith were not binding on Muslims today; and, finally, seeing no objection to men and women mixing together. On account of these allegations, the correspondent called on Bin-Bāz to do what was necessary to stop the propagation of these "dangerous ideas."[3]

Bin-Bāz duly passed the letter on to Turabi and asked him to answer the allegations, which he did. In a letter to Bin-Bāz, he denied making public any views on the issue of stoning of adulterers, saying that he merely consulted a small circle of people on a view on this matter expounded by the late prominent Egyptian 'ālim, Shaykh Muhammad Abu-Zahra. On the marriage of Muslim women to non-Muslims, Turabi said that he had only made some tentative remarks to American Muslims who were facing problems of women converts whose husbands remained non-Muslim. On the question of apostasy, he denied having made a distinction on account of the religion to which the believer converts, but only discussed some views by recognized Islamic authorities who regarded apostasy to refer only to those waging war against the community. On the issue of the penalty for drinking, Turabi said that his views were put forward in the context of negotiations to reform the laws during the early phase of Numairi's Islamization program, and were meant to win over members of the Law Revision Committee who approved the banning of alcohol, but disagreed about the penalty. On the issue of jurisprudential principles, Turabi argued that the view expressed by him distinguished between principles based on clear Islamic injunctions, and those devised by later jurists, which he did not consider binding. With regard to the segregation of the sexes, he argued that women were not segregated at the time of the Prophet, and that some Muslims today see the segregation of women and their confinement to the home as a substitute for proper religious education.

In concluding his letter, Turabi complained that he had been the target of a politically motivated campaign of vilification by figures from the Egyptian Muslim Brotherhood, which was behind most of these allegations. The problem today, he added, was not the existence of deviant or heretical Islamic views, but the rejection of Islam in its entirety by whole generations of Muslims. The return to Islam must take this into account and accept many compromises in the transitional phase.[4]

Notwithstanding this conciliatory tone, the campaign against Turabi's views continued unabated in conservative circles. In the early 1980s, one critic named ibn Malik (probably a pseudonym) published a booklet entitled *Al-Ṣārim al-Maslūl fi'l-Rad 'Alā al-Turabi Shātim al-Rasūl* (*The Unsheathed Sword, in Reply to Turabi, Abuser of the Prophet*).[5] In the book, the text of the "incriminating" lecture in which Turabi first put forth his views on hadith was published verbatim, with scathing rejoinders to his assorted "heresies." The campaign gained added vehemence following Nimeir's Islamization policies of 1983–5, and the allegations were voiced freely during the democratic interlude of 1986–9. The exchanges became more heated as Turabi's high-profile contributions to the debate on Islamization became the center of much attention in Sudan and beyond.

The Vision Restated

The points of contention are at the heart of the liberal and reformist views of traditional Islam, and were the focus both of liberal critiques of "fundamentalists" who wanted to reassert the traditional vision, and of apologetics, which sought to defend that vision. Turabi in this regard occupied the peculiar position of being the leader of the "fundamentalist" camp and the proponent of relatively "liberal" views within that camp. When he became Attorney General and Minister of Justice again in 1988, Turabi gave the most frank expression of his views in this area, in particular with relation to the issues of the rights of women and non-Muslims in an Islamic state.

Turabi was challenged publicly on these views in a televised debate in June 1988, when it was put to him that his proposals for exempting the predominantly non-Muslim South from the implementation of Islamic law had no basis in *sharī'ah*, which categorically rejected any co-existence with non-Muslims except on unequal terms. He was also questioned on the right of non-Muslims and women to accede to top posts in an Islamic state. His reply was that he saw no objection to either, adding that relations between Muslims and non-Muslims could only be based on agreements acceptable to both sides. Reaching such deals was not against Islamic law, but actually reflected its spirit and it used to be the practice of Muslims since the time of the Prophet. Turabi also rejected the traditional view that Muslims were bound to go to war against non-believers, saying that such a view reflected the dominant international situation in pre-modern times, but is no longer compatible with the present conditions where international law guarantees peace for all.[6]

These views were fiercely attacked by conservatives, as shown by an article published in *Al-Ayyām* daily on June 30, 1988 by a certain Abdalla Fadallah Abdallah, who accused Turabi of defying *sharī'ah* by propagating eccentric views not supported by any credible authority. Turabi's claim that some schools of thought held the view that women could become judges was meant to give the false impression that some of the four major (Sunni) schools of jurisprudence endorsed this ruling, which was not the case. Only isolated figures offered such opinions. Turabi's view that *jihād* was not relevant today contradicts the overwhelming consensus of all major religious authorities. In particular there is no disagreement among Muslim jurists that pagans should be fought without let-up. This applies to adherents of "African creeds" in Sudan, whom Turabi wants to make part of his "Islamic state." Modern and traditional authorities dispute Turabi's views that non-Muslims occupied leading roles in Muslim polities in the past, and writers like Abu'l Ala Maududi did show that non-Muslims have never occupied executive roles in Muslim polities, nor did they participate in electing the caliph. Thus Turabi's claim that non-Muslims have equal rights under Islamic law has no basis whatsoever in *sharī'ah*.

Turabi's submission in late 1988 of new "Islamic laws" to the Constituent Assembly occasioned another attack. Critics argued that the laws which Turabi tabled did not conform to *sharī'ah*, and were based on a secular constitution that provided for equal access to key posts in the state for non-Muslims (Musa, 1988). Turabi bases his views on Qur'anic verses that gave the Prophet the option of not adjudicating in disputes between non-Muslims. But many authorities interpret these verses differently, and hold that they had been abrogated by later provisions in the Qur'an itself. The argument from the model of the Medina state, which Turabi called a "federal state" between Jews and Muslims, is also disingenuous, since the Medina arrangement was more of a defense pact than a state. Jews were never given any right to exercise authority over Muslims as part of that pact (Musa, 1988).

Like his practical proposals, Turabi's methodological proposal for reforming *sharī'ah*, as expounded in his book *Tajdīd al-Fikr al-Islami* (1987), angered many conservatives. In particular his call for "a contemporary interpretation of the Qur'an," which he justified by arguing that "every Qur'anic exegesis in the past had reflected the spirit of its time," was condemned as a sacrilegious quest to subordinate the Qur'an to the exigencies of reality, and not vice versa. This view, and the claim that Islam had never taken its final shape but must evolve with time, was seen by one leading critic as "a call for a new religion, and not a renewal of religion" (Ibrahim, 1995, 49–56). It also contradicted the consensus of Muslim authorities who regard the time of the Prophet as the normative summit to which all Muslims must aspire. Turabi also seeks to distinguish his project, which he terms the "development or modernizing of religion" (*taṭwīr al-dīn*) from the renewal of religion (*tajdīd al-dīn*). The latter referred to the revival of past modes of thinking and behavior, while the former involves the "adapting of religion to new phases of life." This shows clearly his subversive intent, and his determination to make religion adapt to reality rather than reform and correct this reality so that it may conform to religious norms. His express views about the role of women and non-Muslims, and his rejection of many explicit hadith predicting the return of Christ or the rise of the Mahdi are clear indications of how he envisages this "development". If fashion favored more freedoms for women, we are supposed to race in that direction, regardless of what the Qur'an and hadith said, and if it becomes the vogue to allow non-Muslims to lord it over believers, then that is the direction in which we should "develop" our religion. And if the idea of waging war in the cause of Islam had been "left behind by the time" then we should abandon this sacred duty for all time (Ibrahim, 1995, 59–70).

Turabi's attempts to distinguish between the "essence" of religious commitment and eternal religious values on the one hand, and their "particular manifestations" and applications that are changeable with circumstances, on the other are equally reprehensible. It makes it very difficult to distinguish his views from those held by secularists or heretics who teach that forms of religious observance can change with time and circumstance. Turabi even goes a step further, arguing that every region and community "could select a form of worship appropriate to it." He also assails those who call for moderation and cautious adaptation of traditional beliefs to the changing times, and calls for radical and "daring" defiance to tradition, while condemning all those who adhere to the heritage as "rigid" and "timid". He thus wants to cancel all the contributions of past generations and go back directly to the original sources, as if the contributions he condemns were based on anything other than a conscientious and informed reading of those sources (Ibrahim, 1995, 73–4, 79–83).

Any doubt about the damaging and subversive import of Turabi's methodological proposals is dispelled when we see his application of these proposals in practice. His call for women to mix freely with men and occupy top posts in the state contradicts the provisions of *shari'ah*, which does not recommend women to go out to work except in dire need, and under conditions of strict segregation. Turabi justifies his defiance of the consensus of all *ulama* over the centuries by arguing that women's liberation is going to happen anyway (Turabi, 1973), forgetting that what he calls "traditional society" is quite capable of defending itself and winning. The current Islamic resurgence is proof of that, and defeatist calls like Turabi's will not affect the determination of Muslims to live according to the exigencies of their faith, come what may (Ibrahim, 1995, 198–200, 203–4).

The Liberal Reaction

While Turabi stirred up anger within traditionalist ranks, he was not the darling of the liberals either. Except for a brief period in the early 1970s when the Muslim Brotherhood's support for democracy made it acceptable to a wide section of the political spectrum, the movement and its leadership became the target of increasingly acrimonious criticism from most political groups. The hostility became more pronounced as the movement stuck by Numairi during his last few years of extreme unpopularity and supported his controversial Islamization program.

In his assessment of that period, Numairi's former foreign minister, Mansour Khalid, took issue with Turabi and his supporters for trumpeting Numairi's reforms, which were the "incarnation of barbarism and religious fanaticism," as the "dawn of a new Islamic civilization" (Khalid, 1986, 128, 132, 140). Khalid does not disagree with Turabi on the need to transcend traditional Islamic thought and give a totally new expression to Islamic values more appropriate to our time. But he accuses Turabi of not having lived up to the ideals he propagated, and even going back on enlightened stances he held earlier. Turabi had argued in 1968 that the Islamic constitution embodied the rule of law and not of men, and that it abhorred theocracy, rejected dictatorship, and safeguarded individual rights. Again in 1977, Turabi joined a committee set up by Numairi to revise Sudanese laws, which recommended a very cautious approach to amendments, lest precipitate action may cause severe disruption in prevailing norms or lead to chaos. However, no sooner had Numairi announced his precipitate and chaotic reforms in September 1983, than Turabi turned back against all those wise positions and fully backed measures which enhanced dictatorship and made a mockery of justice (Khalid, 1986, 32–6, 237–9).

On the rights of women and non-Muslims, Turabi and his supporters either tried to argue disingenuously that traditional Islamic jurisprudence guaranteed these rights, or insisted that the laws they proposed safeguarded them, neglecting provisions in these same laws which either abrogated or at least diluted these rights. Turabi was the first to realize that the September 1983 laws contravened Article 38 of the 1973 Constitution, which guaranteed equality for all citizens before the law, because he intervened with the Speaker of the People's Assembly (Parliament) in 1984, urging him to pass the constitutional amendments proposed by Numairi to avoid the laws "becoming unconstitutional" (Khalid, 1986, 43).

In their support for Numairi's reforms and his proposed constitutional amendments, the Islamists have displayed serious intellectual and moral shortcomings, failing to distinguish between Islam's eternal values and the historical expression of these values in traditional societies of centuries gone by. While they condemn traditional jurists for their rigidity in interpreting Islam, they have not themselves hesitated to endorse the charade of 1983–5, which took Islamic values and institutions out of their historical context and distorted them beyond recognition. This was most evident in the 1983 Penal Code, which amended only 10 articles out of 450 of its "secular" predecessor. All it did was to introduce the Ḥudūd (Islamic punishments) without even taking care to redefine the crimes to accord with the provisions of traditional Islamic law, thus resulting in applying religiously based punishments to "secular" crimes. Nevertheless, the supporters of those laws trumpeted this collage as an unprecedented legal revolution that marked the end of colonial domination in the legal sphere and heralded the dawn of a new Islamic civilization. Turabi himself was at the forefront of those defending these laws and their excesses. He excused the excessive application of amputation sentences following the institution of "emergency courts" in April 1984 as "an Islamic necessity," but described the setting up of exceptional courts as a bold move which paved the way for Sudan "to offer its original contribution to human civilization after a period in which it had occupied a marginal and dependent position" (Khalid, 1986, 58–76, 110–11, 113, 152–7, 281).

All this is a far cry from Turabi's otherwise valid remark to a conference in Khartoum on September 25, 1984 that "the Prophetic model of Islam, with its texts and legal practices, is an eternal normative standard, which must nevertheless undergo evolution in its concrete expressions in order to realize the same values under different circumstances" (Khalid, 1986, 244). But this is precisely what the reforms of 1983–5 failed to do. What they achieved was quite the opposite: they took Islamic institutions and policies out of their historical context, depriving them in the process of all meaning and significance. The legal and constitutional provisions enacted or proposed then displayed "a horrifying confusion of claimed Islamism, distorted democracy and the legal institution of despotism," stamping Islam in the process with practices that were "the remotest from its spirit of democracy and respect for man" (Khalid, 1986, 248).

Contending that there is an Islamic alternative to democracy, Turabi pointed to some of the practices during the Medina period and the Mahdist state in Sudan as partial applications of this presumed alternative, while expressing some reservations about how Islamic history embodied these practices. However, Turabi and his supporters forget that the modern democratic state is based on the accountability of the ruler, politically through the parliament, and legally through the ability of the judiciary to overrule his decisions in certain circumstances. All these safeguards were not known in the traditional Islamic state during any phase of its history, making violence the only means through which the populace could react against injustice (Khalid, 1986, 259–61).

On the equally pivotal question of human rights, the Islamists, and especially Turabi, painted themselves into a corner. They kept arguing that Islam recognized basic human rights and freedoms long before the West. But when confronted with concrete questions, they were not able to substantiate their claims. When Turabi was quizzed during the 1967 deliberations on the constitution on whether it was possible for a non-Muslim to become the head of state under an Islamic constitution, he wriggled and squirmed for quite a while before answering in the negative. This showed how uneasy he was with his own stance on the matter, and highlights the intellectual and moral predicament of the Islamists who wanted to impose on reality social institutions incompatible with it. The predicament of the modern Islamists is further compounded by their purported rejection of all the achievements of modern civilization, which they condemn as "alien" and "godless," while being quite happy in practice to avail themselves of all these "godless" achievements without any qualms (Khalid, 1986, 267, 287–90).

In sum, Khalid argues, it could be said that both Turabi's theoretical proclamations and practical positions are the antithesis of his claims to a modernizing and enlightened contribution to the revival of Islam. In fact, Turabi embodies in his conduct the "ossification of traditional Islamic jurisprudence" which he decries so much, and reflects the attitude of men who "lived with their minds outside history." The revival of Islam can only become a reality by assimilating all the positive contributions of modern civilization, a task that requires a radical rethinking of Islamic categories similar to what the Catholic Church had attempted to do in Vatican I and II. The Islamists are not qualified to perform this task due to their intellectual failings, which are compounded by moral failings that are not less serious. These have been reflected in their enthusiasm for Numairi's distorted Islamic policy, and the way they supported and promoted dictatorship and barbarism in the name of Islam during that period. When they later tried to distance themselves from that embarrassing position, they did not do so by re-evaluating their earlier stance and criticizing it. Instead, they resorted to historical distortion and intellectual blackmail to silence their critics, and continued to condemn as heretics those who opposed the stance they themselves admit was erroneous (Khalid, 1986, 418–29, 436).

Creeping Secularization?

Turabi's ideas were also criticized from a similar perspective by another Sudanese liberal, who points in similar terms to the gap between Turabi's words and deeds, arguing that Turabi sounds at times more like a social scientist than a religious reformer when he differentiates clearly between the eternal and human aspects of religion. But while acknowledging a clear theoretical distinction between religion as such and its various expressions, in practice, the Islamists are quick to condemn any opponent who contests their particular interpretation of Islam as a heretic and unbeliever (Ali, 1991, 165).

Turabi's calls for the democratization of *ijtihād* and shifting it away from traditional *ulama*, and his advocacy of the widest possible freedom for its practice, also makes him sound quite liberal. It also betrays aspects of the imperceptible secularization of the movement's perceptions and orientations (Ali, 1991, 172–5). Yet these ideas are negated by the Islamists' latent conservatism, revealed in their inability to clearly answer questions such as: how can we distinguish between form and content in religious expression, given that form and content are often one and the same? Or: what would guarantee that the *ijtihād* of the wider community through its elected representatives in parliament would conform to the "eternal" Islamic principles? Here Turabi advocates some form of "supervision" by official authorities, which in fact translates into the institution of a formal religious authority in Islam, something that is contrary to the spirit of the religion, which had not known any formal religious authority in the past, and does not recognize one (Ali, 1991, 172–3).

These contradictions are inherent in the project of Islamist "renewal" itself. As a sociological phenomenon, religious renewal is an attempt to adapt modern transformations to the religious truth as encapsulated in the religious text. This can be achieved in one of two ways: either to adapt the reality and make it conform to the exigencies of the text as traditionally understood, or to attempt to reinterpret the text to make it conform to the new reality. However, the second option, which the Islamists espouse, overlooks the fact that it would appear impossible to achieve a genuinely modernizing project without a break with tradition. The failure of the Islamists to realize this is at the root of their problem. Fundamentalist thought wants to separate the achievements of modernity from its values and philosophical preconditions, such as rationality, freedom, objectivity and the critical outlook. The other problem is that Islamists dream of a renewal of Islamic thought which would precede the renewal and modernization of social and economic relations. They just seek to treat the symptoms of backwardness rather than its real causes (Ali, 1991, 165–7).

At a more practical level, while we find Turabi pretends to reject the anti-democratic prescriptions of Sayyid Quṭb and Abu'l al-Mawdūdī, he nevertheless expresses numerous reservations about democracy. He argues that democracy has, in Sudan, "been spurious and vulnerable to internal failures and external imperialist manipulations." He also tries to distinguish between the Western concept of democracy and the Islamic concept of *shurah* (consultation) in a deliberate attempt to weaken and dilute democracy. Turabi himself admits that Islamic political thought had not provided any significant contributions in the area of democratic government, apart from the insistence on consultation and the supremacy of *sharī'ah*. The democratic credentials of the movement are further compromised by its insistence on equating itself with the community, a motif that is reiterated constantly in its discourse. It was no surprise, therefore, that, when the movement came to power after the coup of 1989, its style of government was extremely anti-democratic. It monopolized power in all fields, adopted a totalitarian stance *vis-à-vis* civil society and committed serious abuses of human rights under various pretexts. In the end, its claims of empowering society and energizing political participation could only retain any significance if we accept their claim that the society and the movement were identical (Ali, 1991, 193–204).

Reform or Reformation?

Ali recommends outright secularism as a remedy to the crisis of revivalism, a proposition seen by another Sudanese liberal (Abdullahi An-Na'im) as a non-starter (Ali, 1991, 8; An-Na'im, 1990, 1–2). An-Na'im also argues that Islamic revivalism in its usual manifestations is not the answer either. The contributions of men like Turabi, who stands out as "an effective spokesman for the contemporary proponents of *sharī'ah*," in fact points to the limits of that type of Islamic reformism, which remains bound by the terms of the tradition. While Turabi spoke frequently of the need for reform and flexibility, he did so mainly in general terms, and was usually evasive when attempts were made to pin him down to specifics. For example he speaks of women's "rightful place in public life," without specifying what this rightful place might be, in particular since he relates it to *sharī'ah*, which we know discriminates against women. The way he addresses the rights of non-Muslims also leaves many gaps and does not seem to consider full citizenship rights for them. Similar vagueness is seen when he claims that, in an Islamic state, the powers of the ruler are subject to *sharī'ah*, neglecting the fact that no agreement was reached among traditional jurists on any definite provisions that would allow this (An-Na'im, 1990: 39–43). It is safe to say, therefore, that the ideas of Turabi do not advance us much beyond traditional Islamic thought. This has meant that Muslims seeking to come to terms with modernity have only one of two options: "either to continue to disregard *sharī'ah* in the public domain, as used to be the case for the majority of modern Muslim states, or to proceed to enforce *sharī'ah* principles regardless of constitutional, international law and human rights objections." The first option An-Na'im finds "objectionable as a matter of principle," as well as being unrealistic given the rising demands for re-Islamization. The second he finds "morally repugnant and politically untenable," in particular since it subjects women and non-Muslims "to many indignities and humiliation" (An-Na'im, 1990, 58–9).

The only solution left is thus to find an "adequate reform methodology" which would enable Muslims to live according to their faith while fully enjoying "the benefits of secularism," which include respect of human rights, constitutional and democratic safeguards and the opportunity to live in peace within the international community. Such a methodology An-Na'im finds in the ideas of his mentor, the late Mahmoud Muhammad Taha (1909–85), who proposed a revolutionary concept of "reverse abrogation," of Qur'anic texts. According to this concept, we have to read the Qur'an "backwards," so to speak. While the Qur'an laid down some basic principles in the early stages of revelation, elaborating on them and supplying detailed rules of conduct later, we have now to try to transcend the historical expressions of these values, including those of the time of the Prophet and his immediate successors, hitherto regarded as highly normative by the whole Muslim community. What needs to be done is to look at the broad principles laid down, mainly, but not exclusively, in the Meccan period (the first part of the Prophet's mission before emigrating to Medina and setting up the Muslim community there), and subordinate specific legal provisions spelt out in the Qur'an or specified by the Prophet (and the rules derived from those subsequently) to these more general principles. The latter are designated as "primary verses," while the more specific are termed "subsidiary verses." In Taha's words, "we consider the rationale beyond the text. If a subsidiary verse, which used to overrule a primary verse in the seventh century, has served its purpose completely and become irrelevant for the new era, the twentieth century, then the time has come for it to be abrogated and for the primary verse to be enacted. In this way, the primary verse has its turn as the operative text in the twentieth century and becomes the basis of the new legislation. This is what the evolution of *sharīʿah* means" (An-Naʿim, 1990, 59–60). (The term "evolution of *sharīʿah*" (*taṭawwur al-sharīʿah*) of course resonates with Turabi's own concept of "development of religion" (*taṭwīr al-dīn*).)

The conclusions of An-Naʿim are as startling as his premises are familiar. The call for the radical reconstruction of *sharīʿah* by "reading backwards" and separating the fundamental principles from their historical expressions is far from uncommon. But the decision to scrap the bulk of the concrete heritage, including much of the Prophet's own sayings and practice, to say nothing of getting rid of a significant portion of the Qur'an was shocking.

But An-Naʿim's proposals met with resistance from secularists who saw irreconcilable contradictions in this "secular founding of a religious state". An-Naʿim, these critics argue, accepts the "benefits of secularism" such as modern constitutionalism, human rights, and international law, in addition to getting rid of the "inconvenient" texts in Qur'an and hadith and rejecting the authority of traditional and modern *ulama*. But he still maintains the sacred foundation of the state, which will reproduce the struggles over who controls this "sacred" authority once more. As a result, we are left with a "confused secular state," which is rejected by secularists because of its religious foundations, and shunned by the Islamists who do not concur on the line of reasoning that led to its establishment. In such a state, religious legitimacy, "if it is not a mere mask confined within determined limits it cannot exceed, will automatically, in virtue of its inner mechanisms, generate endless forms of despotism which would throw away the benefits of secularism with which An-Naʿim is so enamored" (Ahmed, 1996, 66–70).

An-Naʿim's work was subject to a wide range of criticisms, which we cannot cover comprehensively here. But one would like to refer in passing to the comment of Ishtiaq Ahmed that even though An-Naʿim is at pains to label his solution Islamic, it is clear that "the moral weight of constitutionalism and universal human rights weighs heavier with him than loyalty to dogma," thus making his "a rational response of a Muslim rather than the Islamic response of a rational intellectual." This leads Ahmed to wonder why An-Naʿim would not consider secularism as an option which could strengthen Islam in the same way as the Founding Fathers in the United States advocated secularism to protect religion from being corrupted by politics (Ahmed, 1993: 71) (To which An-Na'im's reply was that, if he were to get his way, the rational response of the Muslim intellectual and the Islamic response of the rational intellectual would be one and the same (An-Na'im, 1993, 105–7).)

The Predicament Defined

The rival attempts by Turabi and An-Na'im to find the door out of the confines of tradition, rather than jumping over the wall, or "exploding a bomb" to blow away the front door, as Yalman characterized the approach of Kemal Atatürk and his colleagues in Turkey (Yalman, 1973) seem to have run into similar barriers. Turabi's attempt to radically reappraise the Islamic heritage are of the type some critics may readily dismiss as traditional *islāḥī* (reformist) methodology (Arkoun, 1993). But the strong traditionalist reactions to his critical evaluation of the early generation of Muslims, and his daring to question remarks of the Prophet himself, show the limits beyond which it is difficult to advance. On the question of Qur'anic exegesis, Turabi had moved beyond theory to practice, and is now busy compiling his own interpretation of the Qur'an, with predictably startling "revelations" (Turabi, 1998). But the problem remains: What can give these new readings any authority? Given the violent reaction among the guardians of tradition, why should these modern readings be seen as less arbitrary than their predecessors? And if the ancients have read the Qur'an with the eyes of their time, making numerous concessions to prevailing norms and traditions, how is any other reading going to get beyond its time and the prevailing norms and interests? What makes a particular "modern" reading so privileged, in view of the fact such a reading is, in contrast to the ancients, acutely conscious that it was manipulating the texts to support predetermined views and preconceived prejudices? Every reading of the texts in this context becomes potentially secularizing in that it self-consciously starts from premises derived from without the particular religious view in question.

In contrast to Turabi, An-Na'im's proposals start from the incompatibility of *sharī'ah* with modern norms and end up with a formula that is not so incompatible, a rather suspicious feat of *hocus pocus*. But even here, his formula falls short. On the controversial issue of Islamic punishments, An-Na'im admits that his methodology would not be able to do away with these, since "there are no verses [in the Qur'an] on which one could rely in challenging the very explicit and categorical verses providing for Ḥudūd." His suggestion was, therefore, "to limit their application in practice" (An-Na'im, 1991, 109), a very uncontroversial suggestion that even the present Sudanese government has gone a long way to implement.

The fundamental question which the stances of both Turabi, An-Na'im, and others pose is this: where is the Archimedean point on which one can stand to evaluate the totality of the Islamic heritage from outside it? If, as Arkoun recommends (Arkoun, 1987) and Turabi actually does, one is to stand judge over whether the early generation of Muslims and the following generations were truthful and/or perceptive in understanding the divine message and conveying it, what would be the basis of such a judgment, given that it can only use the material supplied by those generations? The attempt to rewrite Islamic doctrine radically demands an unprecedented charismatic authority. Only prophets and saints could convincingly say to believers: "It is written, but I say unto you . . ."

The proponents of revolutionary views need to carry the masses with them, for they certainly cannot hope to have the support of the doctors of the religion, who are by definition the guardians of the heritage. If Turabi's and An-Na'im's experience is anything to go by, then the problem is that both the traditionalists, who appear to be in the majority, and the secularists, who are the more influential politically, reject these reformist proposals. This would rob the Islamist movements of their most precious asset: their democratizing potential. The modernizing Islamic movements could contribute to democratization and stability in Muslim states if they could carry the traditionalist masses with them in support of a viable modernizing project. But if their programs were to be as unpopular with the masses as those of their modern secularist rivals, as well as alienating the influential modern sectors and non-Muslim constituencies, then such programs must by necessity be anti-democratic.

In the case of Sudan, this is precisely what happened. Turabi's radical reformatory ideas aroused suspicions in the very constituency he was supposed to rely upon: the traditional religious establishment. However, the alliance of the movement with Numairi's authoritarian regime and the support for his crude Islamization policies also alienated the other potential constituency: the Islamic liberals. This made it inevitable that the Islamization program espoused by the movement would have to be implemented in conditions of less-than-perfect democracy, to put it very mildly indeed.

Conclusion

As mentioned above, Turabi's ideas are not only problematic in themselves, but they have faced difficulties during practical implementation when Turabi's party ascended to power under the military regime after June 1989. Turabi was accused, as we have seen, of deviating from some of his earlier prescriptions, especially with regard to democracy and reform. Overall, his experiment in power was a total disaster, not least for him. He has not only lost much of his credibility, but also his grip on power and freedom, as his more powerful supporters turned against him. He was stripped of his powers in an internal "coup" in December 1999 and jailed in February 2001 for over two years. He was released in late 2003 only to be re-arrested in March 2004, accused of plotting a coup.

During his decade in power, Turabi's position on such issues as opposition to multiparty politics and press freedoms have undergone some changes and faced worldwide criticism. Since his fall from power, he has made some revisions to his ideas, but they do not appear to signal a major shift from his earlier stance, since he has as yet failed to engage in meaningful self-criticism. In fact, his "revisions" appear to take more the character of polemics against his opponents than attempts at genuine rethinking. His estranged followers who remain in government, on the other hand, continue to adhere to the overall intellectual framework outlined by him earlier. Their political rupture with him did not signal any shift towards a new radically different approach. If anything, the movement's capacity to generate new ideas has suffered considerably as a result of his departure.

Turabi's contribution to modern Islamic thought and practice on re-Islamization appears to reveal some of the more serious limitations of modern Islamic reformism. At one level, modern Islamist leaders who want to radically rethink Islamic doctrine in defiance of prevalent attitudes appear to rob modern Islamism, at least in the short term, of its democratizing potential. Islamists who want to reformulate doctrine in terms that are unfamiliar to the masses are effectively back in the same boat with their secularist rivals, unless, of course, they are exceptionally charismatic. Hassan Turabi's peculiar predicament stems from the fact that he has antagonized the traditionalists on doctrinal grounds, and the same time alienated the liberal modernizers on political and intellectual grounds. His politics has come to overshadow his otherwise promising reforming ideas. As a politician, he had to engage in many unpopular maneuvers that had more often than not been in direct contradiction with the values he had been propagating. The double handicap of expediency politics and radical reformist ideas inevitably leads to authoritarianism. While the radical reformer places himself above and outside doctrine as the masses see it, the politician wants to push through his program by manipulation and compromise. In both cases, mass support and moral authority are compromised, and coercion becomes indispensable.

The traditionalists do not fare much better in confronting reality. Their insistence on sticking to the traditional message, however impractical that may be, may respond to a tendency in Muslims to prefer to "keep *sharī'ah* intact and inviolable in theory even if that was not possible in practice" (An-Na'im, 1990, 6). This meant that traditionalists would prefer *sharī'ah* to be replaced by secular laws than to be modified and adapted to meet emergent needs and perceptions. And thus traditionalists contribute in their own way to stagnation and secularization.

Yet the anomie resulting from the failure of all these schools of thought has led to stagnation and favored despotism. And despotism is an unstable and a very dangerous affair, not least for the despots themselves. The recent developments in Sudan are a sharp illustration of this. For Turabi, it had been a very expensive lesson learned way too late.

Notes

1. This article was written during a period when I had been a beneficiary of a grant from the United States Institute of Peace. I am grateful to the Institute, and to the then Grant Director David Smock, for the generous support given. Needless to say, the views expressed here are strictly my own.
2. Turabi's views on this matter are scattered in many sources. The author has compiled them from publications and personal interviews with Turabi and associates. See El-Affendi, 1991, ix–xix, 166–180 and Turabi 1984. Cf. Ibrahim, 1995, 13–21.
3. The text of the letter of 'Abdul-Badī' Saqr, dated 24 Dhu al-Qa'ida 1400 AH (October 4, 1980) is reproduced in Ibrahim, 1995, 233–4.

4. Text of letter reproduced in Ibrahim, 1995, 237–42. No date is given for the letter, but Bin-Bāz's letter to him was dated October 26, 1980.
5. The book aptly reproduces the title of a polemical work by Ibn-Taymiyyah.
6. A transcript of the debate was published in *Al-Ayyām* daily on June 19 and 20, 1988, and is also reproduced in Ibrahim, 1995, 208–32.

Bibliography

Ahmed, Atif, "Ma'azaq al-Sharī'a wa Taḥaddiyat al-Taḥdīth" (The Predicament of *Sharī'ah* and the Challenges of Modernization), *Riwāq 'Arabī*, I/4, October 1996.

Ahmed, Ishtiaq, "Abdullahi An-Na'im on Constitutional and Human Rights Issues," in Tore Lindholm and Kari Vogt, eds., *Islamic Law Reform and Human Rights: Challenges and Responses* (Copenhagen: Nordic Human Rights Publications, 1993).

Ali, Haydar Ibrahim, *Azmat al-Islām al-Siyāsī: Al-Jabha al-Islāmiyya al-Qawmiyya Namūdhajan* (*The Crisis of Political Islam: The National Islamic Front as an Example*) (Casa Blanca: Centre for Sudanese Studies, 1991).

An-Na'im, Abdullahi Ahmed, *Towards an Islamic Reformation: Civil Liberties, Human Rights and International Law* (Syracuse: Syracuse University Press, 1990).

— "Towards an Islamic Reformation: Responses and Reflections," in Tore Lindholm and Kari Vogt, eds., *Islamic Law Reform and Human Rights: Challenges and Responses* (Copenhagen: Nordic Human Rights Publications, 1993a).

— "Constitutional Discourse and the Civil War in Sudan," in W.M. Daly and A.A. Sikainga, eds., *Civil War in the Sudan*, (London: British Academic Press, 1993b), 97–116.

Arkoun, Muhammad, *Rethinking Islam Today* (Washington DC: Centre for Contemporary Arab Studies, 1987).

— "The Concept of 'Islamic Reformation'," in Tore Lindholm and Kari Vogt, eds., *Islamic Law Reform and Human Rights: Challenges and Responses* (Copenhagen: Nordic Human Rights Publications, 1993).

Daly, M.W. and Sikainga, A.A. eds., *Civil War in the Sudan* (London: British Academic Press, 1993).

Deng, Francis, *War of Visions: Conflict of Identities in Sudan* (Washington, DC: The Brookings Institution, 1995).

El-Affendi, Abdelwahab, *Turabi's Revolution: Islam and Power in Sudan* (London: Grey Seal Books, 1991).

Gellner, Ernest, *Conditions of Liberty: Civil Society and its Rivals* (London: Hamish Hamilton, 1994).

Ibrahim, Abdul-Fattah Mahjoub M., *Al-Duktor Ḥassan al-Turābī wa Fasād Naẓariyyat Taṭwīr al-Dīn* (Cairo: Bayt al-Hikmah, 1995).

Khalid, Mansour, *al-Fajr al-Kādhib: Numairi wa Taḥrīf al-Sharī'a* (*False Dawn: Numairi and the Distortion of Sharī'ah*) (Cairo: Dar al-Hilal, 1986).

Makki, Hassan, *Al-Ḥaraka al-Islāmiyya fi'l-Sūdān* (Khartoum: IRSS, 1990).

Malik, Abu Abdallah Ahmed ibn, *Al-Ṣārim al-Maslūl fi'l-Rad 'Alā al-Turāii Shātim al-Rasūl*.

Mazrui, Ali, "The Multiple Marginality of Sudan," in Yusuf Fadl Hassan, ed., *Sudan in Africa* (Khartoum: Khartoum University Press, 1971), 240–55.

Musa, Awad al-Karim, "Mashrū' al-Qānūn al-Jinā'ī Mukhālif li'l-Sharī'a" (The Draft Penal Code is Contrary to *Sharī'ah*), *Al-Khartoum*, November 24, 1988.

Sikainga, Ahmad Awad, "Northern Sudanese Political Parties and the Civil War," in W.M. Daly and Ahmed A. Sikainga, eds., *Civil War in the Sudan* (London: British Academic Press, 1993).

Turabi, Hassan Abdallah, "Al-Dīn wa'l-Tajdīd," *Al-Fikr al-Islāmī*, 1/2, September 1984, 13–45.

— *Tajdīd al-Fikr al-Islāmī* (Jeddah: Al-Dār al-Sa'ūdiyya, 1987).

— *Al-Tafsīr al-Tawḥīdī* (*The Unitary Interpretations [of the Qur'an]*) (Khartoum: Hay'at al-A'māl al-Fikriyya, 1998).

Yalman, Nur, "Some Observations on Secularism in Islam: The Cultural Revolution in Turkey," *Daedalus*, 102/1, Winter, 1973.

al-Zabidi, Zaynul-Abidin A.A., *Mukhtaṣar Ṣaḥīih al-Bukhārī* (Beirut: Dar al-Nafa'is, 1986).

CHAPTER 9

An Overview of al-Sadiq al-Mahdi's Islamic Discourse

Hassan Ahmed Ibrahim

Like all other Mahdist movements, the Sudanese Mahdiyyah was about to fade in history after the bloody overthrow in 1898/99 of the radical and isolated religo-political regime that supported it. Nonetheless, Mahdism, or rather Neo-Mahdism, survived under the umbrella of a modern politico-religious party, the Umma Party (founded in 1945), which discarded violence and abandoned religious extremism. The credit of this historic transformation should go, first and foremost, to the architect of Neo-Mahdism, 'Abd al-Rahman al-Mahdi[1] (1885–1959), and, subsequently, to his most favored grandson, al-Sadiq (1936–),[2] whom he had groomed for a future leading role in the party and the country. Al-Sadiq al-Mahdi, the *de facto* leader of the Neo-Mahdism since 1961, had, on his part, tried his utmost to follow in the footsteps of his visionary grandfather. Indeed, al-Sadiq had recently proudly recorded that his "grand-father established a religious organization as a modern and moderate avatar of the Mahdist revolution," and that he "led that group, modernized its organization and democratized its decision making organs,"[3] though, he had elsewhere admitted that he did not acquire much of his mentor's mastery of manipulation which is seemingly important in Sudanese politicking. However, based on the core of al-Sadiq's sizable Islamic discourse, of which some pieces are not in print, this chapter focuses on an interesting aspect of his colorful, but rather controversial, career, namely his input into contemporary Islamic thought, that will be studied under some selected subheadings.

The Mahdist Notion

The concept of the Mahdiyyah, which broadly claims that God will send at the end of time "the" Mahdi (the rightly guided), or, from time to time "a" Mahdi, to end oppression and establish justice, had been strongly opposed by Ibn Khaldun and a modern Azharite scholar, Shaykh Sa'd Muhammad Hassan, who had both cast doubt on its Islamic roots. They maintained that the Mahdiyyah is, at best, a notion that is not firmly substantiated by the Qur'an or the authentic Sunnah (the Prophet's tradition).[4]

While admitting that neither the words Mahdi or Mahdiyyah had been specifically mentioned in the Qur'an, and that none of the hadiths (sayings of the Prophet) recorded in *al-Ṣaḥīhayyn* of Bukhari and Muslim speak of the Mahdiyyah, al-Sadiq al-Mahdi had, nonetheless, maintained, in a number of scholarly works on the issue,[5] that the Mahdiyyah is in essence Islamic.

In the private communication mentioned above, al-Sadiq claimed that the Mahdiyyah had been authenticated in 23 hadiths ascribed to the Prophet and recorded in "three of the six books of true (*ṣaḥīḥ*) prophetic traditions": three in al-Tirmidhi, seven in Ibn Maja, and 13 in Abu Daud's traditions. Muslim religious and political thought, al-Sadiq continues, interpreted those hadiths in terms of 10 schools of thought about Mahdism. Three of them are Shiʻite: (i) "The Twelvers," who claim that the Mahdi is the twelfth *imām* in a specific line of succession from ʻAli ibn Abi Ùalib through his wife Fatima; (ii) "The Seveners," who assert that the Mahdi is the seventh in that line of succession; and (iii) "The Zaydis," who think in terms of "plurality of revolutions," i.e. the Mahdi may be any qualified descendent of Fatima who stands up to injustice. Four other schools are: (iv) Sunnite, i.e. the Expected Mahdi should appear before the end of time; (v) the *imām* expected to restore Islam in each century; (vi) Ibn Kathir's contention that the Mahdi is the twelfth in number of outstanding Muslim leaders starting with the four rightly guided caliphs; and finally (vii) al-Razi's concept of "leaders of the Islamic community who stand up as witnesses to the truth of the Islamic message." Two other schools are: (viii) Sufi, namely that the Mahdi is the *ghawth* – chairman of the occult hierarchy of saints; and (ix) Ibn ʻArabi's concept that the Mahdi is the right hand of the prophetic light (*al-nūr al-Muḥammadī*). The tenth school is al-Farabi's philosophical school, articulated in his book *The Perfect City*, which claimed that the Mahdi is the head of that city.

While referring to these schools of Mahdism, the literature of the Sudanese Mahdiyyah (1881–98), al-Sadiq opined, revealed that his great-grandfather's Mahdiyyah constituted a distinct eleventh school that rejected eschatology and miraculous signs for the appearance of the Mahdi. Moreover, this literature shows that the Sudanese Mahdi had taken his mission by instructions from the Prophet in a Sufi vision, but he knew that the Islamic community would outlive his own life. Al-Sadiq summarized his unique view on the issue of the Mahdiyyah by recording that the Sudanese Mahdi "had divorced Mahdism from eschatological considerations, from end of time signs and from traditional speculations about Mahdism. He tied his message to his own pious credentials, to the urgency of reform, to the function of reviving the Qur'an and Sunnah, and to the supreme authority vested in him by Divine calling to fulfill that function."[6]

Islam and Social Change

Contrary to the prevalent presumption, within and outside the Muslim world, of the "rigidity" of Islam, al-Sadiq al-Mahdi maintained that Islam ordained a dynamic response to social change. The Qur'an cited the experiences of other peoples, expressed interest in their achievements, and took an open attitude toward "the adoption of useful ideas and institutions of foreign origin."[7] Armed with this Qur'anic licence, 'Umar ibn al-Khattab, the second rightly guided caliph, had, for example, confidently copied some Persian experiences such as the land tax called *al-kharāj* and the book-keeping system of the *diwān*, and the early Muslims actively indulged in the acquisition of the then well-known philosophies. This flexibility and universality, which had been largely Muslim during the first phase of Islamic history, had, furthermore, enabled Islam "to reshape the cultures of the civilized world," and introduced Europe to the concepts of "religion based on conscience rather than on establishment," and "faith based on a holy text rather than a holy man."[8]

This flexibility, al-Sadiq continued, is also glaringly reflected in the noticeable freedom, enjoyed by the numerous schools of Muslim law,[9] to interpret the Qur'anic text in a variety of ways to suit their communities and circumstances. To facilitate this process, Muslim jurists had innovatively introduced numerous devices, which had occasionally been employed to justify *fatwas* (Islamic edicts) that may not be explicitly supported by a Qur'anic text. Chief among those devices were *al-ijmā'* (consensus), which allowed "dominant trends in public opinion to influence legislation" and *al-qiyās* (analogy), which permitted "the extension of a rule into further horizons." Others were *al-istihsān* (juristic preference), which made it possible for "rational consideration to override textual ones", *al-istislāh* or *al-maslahah al-mursalah*, which affirmed public interest, and *al-istishāb*, which maintained the possible acceptance of customs and practices that do not contradict the specifically prohibited. Finally was the device of *al-naskh* (abrogation) of one revealed text by a later one.[10]

However, as al-Mahdi had credibly argued, this dynamic and open-minded attitude was gradually marginalized, and, by the end of the twelfth century CE, it was practically eclipsed in favor of the phenomenon widely known as *taqlīd* (blind following or imitation). By then a large sector of the jurists dogmatically declared the end of the thus far actively pursued *ijtihād*, or creative reasoning in the interpretation of the Qur'anic text and prophetic tradition. This meant that succeeding Muslim scholars no longer had any initiative, but had to follow the rulings and principles laid down by their predecessors.

Al-Sadiq tried to understand, not to justify, the phenomenon of *taqlīd*. In his book, *Jadaliyyat al-Aṣl wa al-'Aṣr*,[11] which may be loosely translated as *The Dialectics of Identity and Modernization*, and other scholarly pieces, he critically analyzed the underlying factors for the dominance of *taqlīd*, and articulated its far-reaching repercussions in the world of Islam. His first factor for this "sacredness" to the *ijtihād* of the pioneering scholars may be grouped under the title *'Awāmil ma'rifiyyah I'tiqādiyyah* (knowledge and doctrinal factors). The closure of the door of *ijtihād*, al-Sadiq maintained, was not a political decision, but an outcome of the long-held presumption that the scholarship of the early scholars is not for "discussion", so to speak, because it is "the" knowledge that had been sanctioned by God, and should therefore be strictly followed. The advocates of the *taqlīd* had, furthermore, narrowly understood, or rather misunderstood, the Islamic principle of submission to God's will, which they erroneously took as the total negation of man's role. Another factor for the institution of the system of *taqlīd* was, in al-Sadiq's words, "certain historical circumstances." The early Islamic system of government, which was in essence "a type of participatory populism,"[12] had been replaced, since the time of the Ummayads, by successive authoritative monarchic regimes that terminated freedom of thought and action, and established "a class-based economy" that subordinated the interests of the community to the selfish interests of the rulers and their ilk. While a small activist sector of the frustrated Muslim populace resisted this developing despotism and grave injustice through violent revolutionary uprisings, the majority expressed their abhorrence by "effecting a withdrawal from the existing body politics."[13] They found shelter in the emergent Shi'ite community, and in the quietist shelters provided by the Sufis. Moreover, the would-be four founders of the Sunni schools of law "pursued their activities at an arms-length from governments of their day" in order to protect the *sharī'ah* from the selfish interests of the sultans.

To many of the pious Muslims, the *taqlīd* was also needed to shield the faith against some rational and oriental philosophies that had crept into Muslim land as a result of its interaction with other civilizations. Most dangerous of all was what Sayyid Qutb (executed August 1966) called *al-isti'mār al-fikrī wa'l rūhī*[14] – the Western intellectual and spiritual colonialism, and the concurrent ultra-secular drive of some local politicians and intellectuals, such as Kamal Atatürk, Taha Hussain, and Salama Musa, who had misleadingly insisted that modernization is synonymous[15] with Westernization, and had thus threatened the very identity of Islam and the dignity of the Muslims.

As al-Sadiq al-Mahdi had correctly observed, this radical traditionalist approach had been reflected in the ideologies of many of the *jihād* movements in modern and contemporary times, including his great-grandfather's nineteenth-century Mahdiyyah. They insisted that the adoption of the "historically relevant" political system of the *Khilāfah* (caliphate) is a religious duty, adamantly refused to deal with the West, *Jāhilliyat al-Qarn al-'Ishrīn* (the modern *jāhilliyah*), as Sayyid Qutb called it, or the Satan as later dismissively named by Khomeini and Osama bin Laden.

While understanding the historical factors that triggered the pervasion of the regime of *taqlīd*, al-Sadiq al-Mahdi seems to be convinced that the consequential intellectual stagnation of this system had tarnished the image of the contemporary *tajdīd* wave itself and harmed the interests of the Muslim *ummah* at large. It destroyed its "inner vitality" and "purposefulness," and placed it in a historical limbo cut off between the seventh and twenty-first centuries, thus preparing it "for foreign domination."[16] Al-Sadiq's position against *taqlīd* was specifically articulated in the following statement, "The system of *taqlīd* was instituted with the purpose of protecting the cause of righteousness. It served that cause at the cost of spiritual and intellectual initiative and substituting rigidity for the flexibility of Muslim social teachings."[17]

Al-Mahdi had seen in the dogmatism and, more importantly, *al-intiwā'* (reactionary tendency) of the contemporary Salafi movements an imminent danger to Islam and the Muslims, and had therefore urged them to revise their path. In particular, he cautioned them, Islam does not dictate a specific system of government, be it the caliphate or any other, and that any system may be Islamic as long as it fulfills two sets of conditions: viz. a set of general principles, including popular participation and observance of justice; and the application of Islamic legislation in an enlightened and rational manner.[18] While pinpointing some basic drawbacks of the Western civilization,[19] al-Sadiq had, nonetheless, emphasized that it had achieved great accomplishments that should be appreciated and never belittled. The current mainstream Muslim position that concentrates on these shortcomings is, in al-Mahdi's words, *wahamun sakhīf*[20] (foolish illusion).

Knowing that history is a guide, al-Sadiq al-Mahdi urged his co-religionists to restore the historic flexibility of Islam in their own world. This could be attained without wondering "outside the pale of Islam" as the phenomenon itself is Islamic to the core.[21] When non-Muslim opinion refers to Islamic fundamentalism, al-Sadiq maintained, "it is the system of *taqlīd* that they should have in mind."[22] Al-Sadiq should also be hailed for being a contemporary pioneer, and an active participant, since the 1970s, in calling for a new functional *ijtihād*, which he gave the neo-logism *ijtihād 'asrī*,[23] to address the needs of the modern state. In this position, he was presumably guided by his great grandfather's famous comment on the *ijtihād* of the early scholars, viz. "They are men and we are men, and we should exist ourselves as they did."

It is worth noting here that al-Sadiq had criticized, in varying degrees, all the contemporary experiments that apply to the *sharī'ah*: in Pakistan, Iran, Afghanistan, Nigeria, and in his own country, the Sudan. He dismissed Numairi's 1983 Islamic laws as faulty in essence, formulation, and application particularly because they ignored the essential prerequisites for the establishment of the Islamic state. Far from being Islamic, he considered them as a futile political maneuver to gain popularity for an unpopular regime at the expense of the major Islamic forces in the Sudan. Similarly, he criticized the current Islamization program in the Sudan that has been orchestrated, since 1989, by the extremist National Islamic Front (NIF). The request of its ironically called "salvation" (*inqādh*) regime to vow a *bai'ah* for its leader, 'Umar al-Bashir, its apostation of Muslims who disagreed with it and its *zaka* law had all, in al-Mahdi's opinion, departed from Islamic *dawābit* (conditions). In Iran, al-Sadiq called for the replacement of *wilāyat al-faqīh* (the right of absolute rule by the supreme theologian) by *wilāyat al-jamhūr* (the rule of the people), allowing the *faqīh* to have a symbolic status only. He also criticized the failure of the Iranian regime to accommodate "the other," which led to a cycle of violence. In hindsight, al-Sadiq had criticized the short-cut "surgical operation" that led in 1947 to the creation of Pakistan because it has been harmful to the interests of its Muslim population as well as to the remaining Muslims of India. Al-Sadiq had been particularly outspoken in his criticism of the ultra reactionary program of the former Taliban regime, particularly its dismissal of democracy as un-Islamic. But his position towards the complicated issue of the *sharī'ah* in Nigeria had not significantly gone beyond the general remark to approach it "in a rational, orderly way, and shut away any heated action and reaction." All in all, these so-called Islamic programs have been, in al-Sadiq's view, "associated with a dictatorship, which, short on legitimacy, embraced Islam to dress up its usurpation power."[24] In a number of scholarly Islamic gatherings, al-Mahdi proposed to convene a special conference "to study the lessons of contemporary Islamization, and to make an objective analysis of the experiences and issue a guiding declaration for the whole Muslim community."[25]

However, al-Sadiq al-Mahdi's bold position *vis-à-vis* dogmatism and extremism had not always been undertaken without hazards to his integrity and even risks to his own safety. Suffice it to mention here that Numairi's trial and execution in 1985 of Mahmud

Muhammed Taha,[26] under the guise of apostasy, was meant to be a warning to al-Sadiq that he may be next in the line if he continued his opposition to the regime's alleged Islamic laws of 1983.[27] He was also subjected to intimidation, imprisonment, and exile by the dictatorial and fictitiously "Islamic" regimes of Numairi (1969–85) and 'Umar al-Bashir (since 1989).

Nonetheless, one may occasionally find a difficulty in reconciling some of al-Mahdi's enlightened views with his actual political performance when in power, specifically so on two occasions and on two significant issues. First was the unconstitutional expulsion in November 1965 of the democratically elected members of the communist party from the constituent assembly, and the dissolution of the party itself shortly after al-Mahdi's assumption of the premiership in June 1966. These drastic measures were taken under the pretext of an isolated blasphemous speech by a student of reported communist tendencies, and because, in the then apologetic words of al-Sadiq, "the very existence of the communist party contradicted the belief in the existence of God, Sudan's sovereignty with an international creed [and its call for] class dictatorship."[28] Irrespective of the validity of these charges, the measures taken were incompatible with al-Sadiq's expressed commitment to *al-shūra*, democracy and the democratic process. His latest expression in this connection was given in a statement in August 2003 in which he demanded that the United Nations set up "a Good Governance Watch" that should be "based upon four pillars: participation, accountability, transparency and the Rule of Law."[29] However, that anti-communist drive had seemingly been instrumental in triggering the May 1969 military coup that ousted al-Sadiq from the premiership and suspended the parliamentary system for 16 years.[30]

Secondly, notwithstanding his repeated and unreserved condemnation of Numairi's "Islamic" laws, appropriately known as the "September [1983] laws", al-Mahdi, who had shortly afterwards occupied the premiership, hesitated to scrap (*kans* in his words) these reactionary and opportunist laws forthwith, and satisfied himself with freezing them. However, he defended his position by claiming that the "Islamization program" of his government, which rejected the traditional division of the world into the abode (*dār*) of Islam and that of war, had actually started the mechanism to orderly replace these laws by an alternative Islamic legislation that would safeguard the constitutional rights of the non-Muslims.[31] But this process came to an abrupt end by the NIF *coup d'état* in 1989[32] that had, however, abruptly ended al-Sadiq's second premiership. But many people have difficulty in accepting this argument.

Islam and Human Rights

The Universal Declaration of Human Rights (UDHR) of December 10, 1948 stipulated in article 1 that "all human beings are born free and equal in dignity and rights. They are endowed with reason and conscience and should act towards one another in a spirit of brotherhood."[33] However, with the active support of many Muslim rulers, some Muslim scholars maintained that certain parts of the UDHR, specifically the preamble and five of its articles (4, 5, 16, 18, and 19) contradict Islamic injunctions. Based on their interpretation of the Qur'anic five "verses of the sword,"[34] they argued that Islam prohibited co-existence (*al-muwālāh*) with the non-believers, including the "Peoples of the Book." It furthermore required Muslims to forcefully protect their unique culture and religious identity, which, in their view, had already been fundamentally threatened by a statement in the UDHR preamble, viz. "Whereas it is essential to promote the development of friendly relations between nations."[35] They therefore call upon Muslims to reject the Declaration, or, at least, profoundly dilute it.

In a couple of scholarly works, of which a seminar paper entitled "Islamic Perspectives on the Universal Declaration of Human Rights"[36] is perhaps the most important, al-Sadiq al-Mahdi disagreed with those scholars who, in his words, "lived through historical experiences." Their presumption is superficial, fails to comprehend the overall humanistic message of Islam, and is therefore "beside the point." Their reading of the five verses of the sword "is shallow as these verses prohibit Muslims from initiating hostilities against others, and allow them to only fight to deter aggression." Islam is therefore a peaceful religion that urges its followers to observe "the other," and it calls for cooperative inter-religious and inter-state relations.[37] This accommodative message is spelled out in no fewer than 100 verses dispersed among 48 chapters of the Qur'an. Al-Sadiq dismissed the enthusiastic support of many Muslim rulers to this rejectionist position as "ridiculous and irrelevant." Far from being triggered by any religious considerations, these rulers, and their "apologists" are motivated by their awareness that the UDHR constituted a direct threat to their despotism and the legitimacy of their totalitarian rules.[38]

In his balanced support for the UDHR, al-Sadiq records, "Islam means submission to the Will of God. If the Will of God is the source of pre-destination, then submission to the Will of God negates any human volition. The revealed texts of Islam may be quoted to support both pre-destination and free will. Without free will morality and human endeavor become nonsensical. Free will is itself part of the design of mankind."[39] He further stresses that Islam recognizes human worth vividly and in a more permanent and inalienable manner than other religious and the secularist doctrine as well. Al-Mahdi sees no contradiction between the revelation and reason. On the contrary, "reason is a pre-condition for belief," as the Qur'an does not address those who have not yet developed it because of immaturity or lost it because of insanity.[40]

Those who claim that the UDHR is incompatible with Islam, be it the Muslim rejectionists or human rights activists, cite in support for their case the position of Islam towards slavery[41] and religious freedom and the Islamic canonical punishments known as the *Hudūd*. However, as explained below, al-Sadiq al-Mahdi goes a long way to counter these and other accusations in order to emphasize his conviction that Islam is basically in line with the UDHR.

While admitting that the Qur'an recognizes slavery, and that Muslim societies practiced this inhuman activity, al-Mahdi cautioned from jumping to the erroneous presumption that Islam does not endorse article 4 of the Declaration, viz. "No one shall be held in slavery or servitude, slavery and the slave trade shall be prohibited in all their forms."[42] For the relevant verses in the Qur'an do not describe slavery as a favorable practice, but only regulate an existing institution, and make several regulations for its gradual abolition. It should be remembered that slavery had, by the seventh century, been deeply rooted in all human societies, and its abrupt eradication was bound to ignite great upheavals.[43] Indeed, in al-Mahdi's view, the slavery article of the UDHR receives unqualified support from the Qur'an as clearly demonstrated in the following verse: "O mankind! We created you from a single (pair) of a male and female, and made you into nations and tribes, that ye may know each other (not that ye despise each other). Verily the most honored of you in the sight of Allah is (he who is) the most right-eous of you. And Allah has full knowledge and is well acquainted (with all things)."[44]

There is a consensus among Muslim jurists that the Ḥudūd specifies six canonic pun-ishments, in addition to the retributive canon "an eye for an eye and a tooth for the tooth." These are: (i) death for al-riddah (apostasy); (ii) arm amputation for theft; (iii) cross-amputation, death, or banishment for al-ḥarābah (armed robbery); (iv) stoning to death for adultery and 100 lashes for fornication; (v) 80 lashes for alcohol consump-tion; and (vi) 80 lashes and witness disqualification for sexual allegations that are unsupported by three other witnesses.

However, al-Sadiq al-Mahdi argued that the Ḥudūd should not be taken out of context, but had to be viewed within the philosophy behind them, namely to be in essence a deterrent against crime, and the strict conditions for their application, which requires a welfare state and an Islamic social order which fights crime by spiritual, moral, social, and economic means, and the institution of justice in general.[45] All this permitted a high degree of flexibility. In this respect, al-Sadiq quoted two precedents undertaken by 'Umar ibn al-Khattab, the second rightly guided caliph. In the first, he refused to punish two employees for stealing a camel, and fined their employer because he underpaid them, and in the second he suspended the punishment for theft during a period of famine ('ām al-ramādah). It is on this very ground that al-Mahdi criticized Numairi's so-called "Islamic way" and his September 1983 laws.[46] As for extra-marital intercourse, the required proof is so exacting, four trustworthy witnesses who saw the offenders in action, that it is virtually impossible to establish. To deter unsupported sexual allegations, that could poison the society through character assassination between competitors and foes, Islam had commendably imposed severe punishments on the offenders. It should also be remembered that Islam had provided alternative pun-ishments for these canonic punishments: al-diyah that allows material benefits for the victim or his family, and al-ta'zīr (discretionary punishment), which "in essence means mundane criminal law that measures punishment to crime and evolves with socioeco-nomic conditions."[47] From this discussion, one may suggest that al-Sadiq seems to be of the bold opinion that the Ḥudūd may, even should, be frozen.

Article 18 of the UDHR, which guarantees the absolute right of everyone "to freedom of thought, conscience and of religion," including "freedom to change his reli-gion," and "freedom, either alone or in community with others and in public or private, to manifest his religion in teaching, practice, worship and observance,"[48] provoked a heated debate over the compatibility of the presumed riddah punishment with the current standard human rights. However, al-Sadiq al-Mahdi appears to consider the traditional fatwa of capital punishment to the riddah to be obsolete and Islamically unsubstantiated. Though the Qur'an abhors and condemns change in religious belief, it is silent about any temporal punishment for apostasy. Moreover, the authenticity of the hadiths on which these jurists based their judgment on the issue of the riddah, in al-Mahdi's view, is doubtful. However, while possibly justified in the past as a "political expediency" to guard against treason, this punishment has become politically counter-productive in the modern world where Islam is growing at the expense of other religions. An Islamic degree imposing any kind of punishment for a change of religion could be reciprocated to the detriment of the one-third of the Muslim population living as minorities in non-Islamic countries, including the approximately 12 million living in Europe and the United States.[49]

Notwithstanding this bold view on the *riddah* issue, al-Sadiq al-Mahdi had, to say the least, refrained from openly condemning Numairi's trial and execution of the 76-year-old Mahmud Muhammad Taha, the controversial leader of the vocal and elitist party, the Republican Brothers, on January 18, 1985 under this very same charge. This instigated charges of insincerity and double standards against al-Mahdi from some quarters within and outside the Sudan. But al-Sadiq's lack of enthusiasm for Taha seemed to have been motivated by the latter's preaching, like the Bahais and Qaddianes, of a cult that "went beyond the denunciation of *taqlīd* to the emptying of Islam itself."[50] For he claimed that Islam has two messages, a limited one for the seventh century and a universal message, *al-risālah al-thāniyah*, which embodied the Meccan Qur'anic verses.[51] This queer doctrine had infuriated many Muslims within and outside the Sudan, including the militant Ansar, the power-base of al-Sadiq al-Mahdi. We should also remember that Taha had abused al-Mahdi in some of his publications, including *Hādha Huwa al-Sadiq*! (This is al-Sadiq!).

The biological, physiological, and psychological differences between men and women had been the basis for much discrimination against the latter. Some early, and contemporary, Muslim jurists had decreed inferior status for women, e.g. half status as witness and half a share in inheritance. While not going all the way to suggest total gender equality, al-Sadiq al-Mahdi emphasized that Islam masterminded a gigantic leap for the liberation of women 14 centuries ago, and thus could not possibly preach their degradation. The issue for him, and to other contemporary Muslim thinkers, is "not superiority and inferiority of status", but "a calculus of moral and material of making the family a viable social unit." Hence a woman's "half status" as witness concerns only financial matters on which she is not usually acquainted and therefore less aware. However, if she acquired such an expertise, she would be eligible for full witness status. Similarly half a share in inheritance for a woman is linked with the duty of men as breadwinners to the family. Nonetheless, if circumstances changed and society demanded it, a deceased "may freely dispose with a third of the inheritance."[52]

Al-Sadiq al-Mahdi had also disagreed with the extremists' claim that the *sharī'ah* requires women to be confined to the household, and to have no political rights or the rights to occupy public posts. In his drive to refute this conservative position, al-Sadiq protested that the Qur'an had highly praised the character and good governance of the only woman that it referred to, Balqis, the queen of the Kingdom of Saba'. Besides, it emphasized, in several verses, the equality of all believers, men and women alike, and made them responsible for all their deeds. The Prophet had on some occasions consulted women and took their advice, and many women have been recognized as reliable narrators of the prophetic tradition.

In an open letter, displayed over the Internet, to the *Amīr* of Qatar commending his latest decision to grant women a measure of political rights, al-Sadiq al-Mahdi maintained that the *sharī'ah* confers upon women the rights of election and standing for membership of parliaments. Women have the right to be a witness and the right to elect is a form of being a witness. Membership of legislative bodies is a kind of *wakālah* (representation), which is permissible for Muslim women. Their denial of these, and similar rights, al-Mahdi continued, "would create a contradiction between them and their age" that could, in turn, lead to a serious *fitnah* (dissension) that Muslims are religiously ordained to avoid.[53] However, unlike Fahmi Huwaydi,[54] and a few other Muslim intellectuals, al-Sadiq al-Mahdi does not seem to be in favor of women's occupancy of the position of head of a state, or, at least, he is silent on the issue.

Contrary to the opinion of some jurists, al-Sadiq al-Mahdi argued that marriage is a "voluntary civil contract" not a "religious sacrament," in which the two parties engage freely, hence it may include a provision that gives the wife the right of divorce. As for polygamy, al-Sadiq emphasizes that it is not an Islamic duty, and is limitedly permitted to resolve certain problems, such as differences in the couple's sexuality, and numerical imbalance between men and women in a society. Nonetheless, al-Mahdi revolutionarily maintains that polygamy may be prevented. In fact, perhaps following a *fatwa* of Muhammad 'Abduh, al-Sadiq records, "Since Islam requires equality treatment for the wife concerned, and since it is recognized that such equality is impossible, it is possible to legalize against polygamy without violating Islam." Furthermore, he continues, "if the self-image of women develops in such a way that they cannot tolerate polygamy, as is happening with educated and modernized women, the prevention of polygamy may be in the interest of social stability, a sacred purpose for Islamic injunctions."[55]

Muslim–Muslim Dialog

We have sufficient evidence to contend that al-Sadiq al-Mahdi was a pioneering contemporary politician – a scholar who urged, since the dramatic success in 1979 of the Iranian Islamic revolution, the necessity of a Muslim–Muslim dialog to settle the historic doctrinal and political differences between the Shi'ites and Sunnites. Under the apparent influence of the nineteenth-century's legacy of *ḥakīm al-sharq* (the sage of the East), Jamāl al-Dīn al-Afghānī (1837–97),[57] al-Mahdi maintained that what binds the two sects – one message, one Prophet, and the same Holy Book – is much more fundamental than "the psychological and intellectual barriers" that had been created between them over the long years of bitterness and hostility. In both Sunnite and Shi'ite experiences there are ideas that could bridge this historic gap. Jordan, a Sunnite country, had, for example, consulted Shi'ite schools of Islamic law, like the Ja'fari and the Zaidi, for formulating its civil code of 1976, while numerous Shi'ite scholars, like 'Ali Shari'ati, emphasized the role of the *shuratic* concept of *wilāyat al-Jamhūr* rather than that of *wilāyat al-faqīh*, "thereby coming closer to Sunni conceptions." Though rather lethargic, the dialog conducted in the late 1970s between Sulayman al-Bushra and Sayyid Abdul Husain, then respectively Shaykh of al-Azhar and the head of the Shi'ite *ulama* in Lebanon, could be utilized to stimulate a meaningful dialog between the co-religionists.[58] But this seems to be rather optimistic as the differences between the Sunnites and the Shi'ites were, and still are, so deeply rooted that the chance of success for such a dialog is quite remote. However, al-Mahdi's initiative brought him rebukes and charges of irreligiosity from many Sunni quarters. Interestingly in a *tête-à-tête* debate, in Baghdad sometime in 1987, between the then Sudanese premier Sadiq al-Mahdi and the former Iraqi president Saddam Hussain, the latter had reportedly shouted at his "guest" for supporting *al-Furs al majūs* (the heathen Persians), while al-Sadiq lectured him on the origins and development of Shi'ite thought.[59]

Conclusion

Islamic thought is so rich that it is hard for a contemporary Muslim intellectual to be really original or a trailblazer in the full sense of the word. However, irrespective of this proviso and the brutal, but largely utopian,[60] criticism of al-Sadiq al-Mahdi's local politicking, it is fair to suggest that he has an imprint in the broader, indeed universal, field of contemporary Islamic thought. As a great-grandson of the Sudanese Mahdi, and the leader of the largest and historically militant religious party in the Sudan, one would have expected al-Sadiq to be a fervent advocate of the current rigid and uncompromising Islamic wave. But the above bird's eye view of his diversified Islamic discourse gives us weighty evidence to maintain that he had systematically and consistently opposed this irrelevant and reactionary attitude towards the question of identity, and preached an enlightened one, which is more consistent with the Islamic message. Admittedly, however, occasionally there was no congruity between al-Sadiq the theorist and the politician. But this rare dichotomy, which may have been triggered by the sensitive and sensational issues involved, and the extremely fluid status of Sudanese politics, should not be allowed to belittle the man's significant contribution in the arena of Islamic intellectualism. His apologists had even argued that he could have then delivered on those and other issues, had the electorates given his party a massive mandate to rule the country single-handedly. However, such an "idealist" position may no longer be possible in the increasingly diversified and polarized Sudanese society, and the Neo-Mahdists should be prepared to work and cooperate with the other major political forces to uplift the country from its present tragic abyss. Now that a new peaceful era is seemingly on the horizon, the issues of Islamic entity, identity, and outlook are expected to be hotly debated. It is here that al-Sadiq al-Mahdi's progressive views on Islam and social change would be most relevant and useful.

Notes

1. For a study of the career of 'Abd al-Rahman al-Mahdi, see my book entitled *Sayyid 'Abd al-Rahman al-Mahdi: A Study of Neo-Mahdism in the Sudan 1899–1956* (Brill, Leiden, 2004).
2. Unlike many leaders of traditional Muslim parties and sects, al-Sadiq al-Mahdi is well versed in both Islamic disciplines and modern thought.
3. Al-Sadiq al-Mahdi, "Islam and the West: 11 September 2001–8 February 2002" (an unpublished paper 2002).

4. In his *Muqaddimah*, chapter 52, Ibn Khaldun studied the issue of the Mahdiyyah under the indicative title *Fi Amr al-Fatimi*, while Shaykh Sa'd articulated his position in a book entitled *Al-Mahdiyyah fi al-Islam*.

5. Of al-Sadiq's scholarship on the Mahdiyyah is his book *Yasalunaka 'an al-Mahdiyyah* (Beirut 1965), and a private communication in which he articulated his views on the originality of the Mahdiyyah in Islam.

6. Al-Sadiq al-Mahdi, "My Views on the Mahdiyyah," a personal communication.

7. Al-Sadiq al-Mahdi, "Islam, Society and Change", in John Esposito (ed.), *Voices of Resurgent Islam* (New York 1983), 233.

8. Al-Sadiq al-Mahdi, "Social Change in Islam," an unpublished lecture presented at Sokoto University, Nigeria, on April 25, 1980. In another undated lecture delivered in the Islamic University of Omdurman, Sudan, al-Sadiq detailed his argument of the tremendous impact of the Muslims on Europe, which, in his words, "transported her out of the age of darkness."

9. Early jurists developed several schools of Muslim law of which, in al-Sadiq's view, eight have become famous: Hanafi, Maliki, Ja'fari, Zaidi, Shafi'i, Hanbali, Zahiri, and Ibadi.

10. Al-Sadiq al-Mahdi, "Islam, Society and Change," in Esposito, op. cit., 238.

11. This book, published in Khartoum, June 2001, is based on a paper, with the same title, that al-Mahdi presented in a conference organized by the Egyptian ministry of *al-waqf* (endowment) in Cairo during the period May 31–June 3, 2001.

12. Al-Sadiq al-Mahdi, "Islam, Society and Change," in Esposito, op. cit., 234.

13. Al-Sadiq al-Mahdi, "Islam and Revolution in the Middle East and North Africa", an unpublished paper, 3.

14. Sayyid Qutb, *Dirasat Islamiyyah* (Cairo, 1967), 162, quoted by Ibrahim Abu Rabi', *Intellectual Origins of Islamic Resurgence in the Modern Arab World* (Albany: State University of New York Press, 1996), 133. In chapters 4–6 (pp. 92–219) of this book, Abu Rabi' gives an elaborate assessment of the career and thought of Sayyid Qutb, whom he calls "the master theoretician of Islamic resurgence" at this stage, p. 144.

15. Al-Sadiq al-Mahdi, "*Al-Din wa al-Wuhdah al-Wataniyyah*," a lecture delivered at the Nigerian Institute for International Affairs, Lagos, Nigeria, on June 28, 2001.

16. Al-Sadiq al-Mahdi, "Islam, Society and Change," in Esposito, op. cit., 236.

17. Ibid., 236. In this respect al-Sadiq al-Mahdi quoted Malik bin Nabi's famous statement, "The Muslim world was colonized because it was colonizable."

18. See above, pp. 7–8.

19. In al-Mahdi's view, the two major drawbacks of the Western civilization are its denial of *al-ghayb* (the transcendental or the beyond), and its lack of supreme spiritual and moral values. Al-Sadiq al-Mahdi, *Al-Tatruf al-Dini wa Atharuhu 'ala al-Amn al-Qawmi al-Sudani* (Khartoum, 1986), 11–12.

20. Ibid., 11.

21. See below, pp. 2–3.

22. Al-Sadiq al-Mahdi, "Islam, Society and Change," in Esposito, op. cit., 236.

23. Al-Sadiq al-Mahdi, *Al-Tatruf al-Dini wa Atharuhu 'ala al-Amn al-Qawmi al-Sudani*, 13. This booklet is based on a lecture, under the same title, that al-Sadiq delivered in the High Military Academy, Khartoum, on January 28, 1986.

24. Al-Sadiq al-Mahdi, "Lessons from Modern Islamization Programmes," a lecture delivered at Arewa House, Kaduna, Nigeria, on June 30, 2001, 2, 11.

25. Ibid., 10.

26. Ibid., 12.

27. A letter by Mansur Khalid, a former top aide of Numairi, to *The Times* (London), February 9, 1985, quoted by Gabriel Warburg, *Islam, Sectarianism and Politics in Sudan since the Mahdiyyah* (London, 2003), 164. See also Abdel Salam Sidahmed, *Politics and Islam in Contemporary Sudan* (Richmond, Surrey, 1997), 138.

28. G. Warburg, *Islam, Nationalism and Communism in a Traditional Society: The Case of the Sudan* (London, Franc Cass 1978), 117. Under the interesting sub-heading "democracy for the faithful," Abdel Salam Sidahmed gives an account of these dramatic events and their impact on the future of liberalism in the country (89–94). He records that they had "perhaps signaled the end of the liberalist tendency which appeared in the 1930s, and was significant through the era of the nationalist Movement and the 1950s," Sidahmed, op. cit., 93. However, 'Abd al-Mahmud Abu al-Amin, the secretary general of the Ansar organization and a close aide of al-Sadiq, had recently admitted that the expulsion of the communist MPs and the dissolution of the party was "a grave political mistake," for which he publicly apologized on behalf of the Ansar and the Umma party. For this long interview, see *Al-Bayan* newspaper, July 7, 2004.

29. Al-Sadiq al-Mahdi, "An Inter-religious Council at the United Nations," a statement read at the summit of world leaders, held at Seoul, Korea, August 11–16, 2003.

30. Mahmud Galander, an insider of the May regime, wrote his personal observations on that era in a book entitled *Sanawat al-Numairi* (*The Years of Numairi*), (Cairo, 2005).

31. Interestingly, al-Sadiq al-Mahdi had carefully avoided in all his discourse the usage of the traditional Islamic nomenclature *al-dhimiyyin* (non-Muslims under the protection and rule of Muslims), apparently because of its offensive nature to the susceptibilities of the traditional and Christian citizens in the southern and other parts of the Sudan.

32. Al-Sadiq al-Mahdi, "Lessons from Modern Islamization Programmes," 6.

33. Article 1 of the UDHR that was adopted and proclaimed by the General Assembly, resolution 217A (III) of December 10, 1948.

34. Verses 4, 5, 9, 29, and 36 of chapter 9.

35. The preamble of the UDHR.

36. This is an unpublished 14-page paper that had been presented in a seminar on the Universal Declaration of Human Rights, date and place of the seminar is not specified.

37. Al-Sadiq detailed his position towards the issue of inter-civilizational dialog in a paper, entitled "*Mustaqbal al-'Alaqah bayn al-Hadarah al-Islamiyyah wa al-Hadarat al-Ukhra*," which he presented at the fourteenth conference of the Egyptian Ministry of Endowment, Cairo, May 2002.

38. Ibid., 2 and 12.

39. Ibid., 3.

40. Ibid., 3.

41. Among those who maintained that Islam legitimized slavery is Bernand Lewis in his booklet *Race and Colour in Islam* (New York, 1971).

42. Article 4 of the UDHR.

43. Al-Sadiq al-Mahdi, "Islamic Perspectives on the UDHR," 4.

44. 49:12.

45. Al-Sadiq al-Mahdi discusses these issues in detail in part one of his book *al-'Uqubat al-Shar'iyyah wa Mawqi'iha min al-Nizam al-Islami* (Khartoum, 1984).

46. Al-Sadiq al-Mahdi, "Lessons from Modern Islamization Programmes," 4–5.

47. Al-Sadiq al-Mahdi, "Islam Perspectives on the UDHR," 6.

48. Article 18 of UDHR.

49. Al-Sadiq al-Mahdi, "Islamic Perspectives on the UDHR," 9.

50. Al-Sadiq al-Mahdi, "Islam, Society and Change," in Esposito, op. cit., 236. For more information about Taha's trial and his execution, see Gabriel Warburg, *Islam, Sectarianism and Politics in the Sudan since the Mahdiyyah*, 160–5, and Sidahmed, *Politics and Islam in Contemporary Sudan*, 122–3 and 136–8.
51. Taha articulated this view in two books *Tariq Muhammad* (Khartoum, 1966) and *Al-Risalah al-Thaniyyah min al-Islam* (Khartoum, 1967).
52. Al-Sadiq al-Mahdi discussed the issue of gender equality in a book entitled *Al-Mar'ah wa Huququha fi al-Islam* (2nd edition, Khartoum, 2002).
53. A letter from al-Sadiq al-Mahdi to the Prince of Qatar, displayed over the Internet.
54. Fahmi Huwaydi expressed his support to the right of a woman to be a head of state in an article entitled "*Al-'Adalah wa laysa Dhukurat Wali al-Amr au Unuthatuhu, al-Majallah*," March 29, 1997.
55. Al-Sadiq al-Mahdi, "Islamic Perspectives on the Universal Declaration of Human Rights," 8.
56. Al-Sadiq al-Mahdi praised the Iranian Islamic revolution which represented, in his words, "a genuine uprising against domestic injustice and foreign subservience." Al-Sadiq al-Mahdi, "Lessons from Modern Islamization Programmes," 8. To the fury of many Muslim rulers, he established cordial relations with the Iranian leaders, which qualified him to try, with Ahmed Mukhtar Ambo, an ex-president of Unesco, to find a peaceful resolution to the American hostages' crisis of 1979. Al-Sadiq al-Mahdi, "Islam and the West, 11 September 2001–8 February 2002," 11.
57. In a number of articles, published in *al-'Urwah al-Wuthqa*, al-Afghani urged the then Ottoman Caliph and the Shah of Iran to reconcile the differences between the Sunnite and the Shi'ite, and to form a united Muslim front against European imperialism.
58. Al-Sadiq al-Mahdi, "Islam and Revolution in the Middle East and North Africa," 24. Earlier, on the apparent initiative of Shaykh Hasan al-Bana (d. 1949), an organization, called *Dar al-Taqrib*, was formed in Cairo to reconcile the different Islamic sects. It adopted Shaykh Rashid Rida's (d. 1935) slogan "Let us cooperate on what we have agreed upon, and excuse each other on what we have disagreed on."
59. Personal information from the then Sudanese ambassador in Iraq.
60. This criticism had particularly been launched by the prominent, but diametrically opposite, Sudanese intellectuals Mansur Khalid and Mahdi Amin al-Toum. See, for example, the former's book, *The Government They Deserve: The Role of the Elite in Sudan's Political Evolution* (London, 1990), 423–4, and the latter's message published in *Al-Sharq al-Awsat*, January 14, 1993.

CHAPTER 10

Islamic Thought in Contemporary Pakistan: The Legacy of 'Allāma Mawdūdī

Abdul Rashid Moten

Sayyid Abul A'la Mawdūdī is a name to conjure with in contemporary Muslim thought and movement. He was a source of knowledge and inspiration, and even those who differed with his method and the movement, do not question the value of his contribution. Mawdūdī's appeal and relevance are due primarily to his impact on the historical situation of which he was a part. He reflected and represented the value and importance of Islam, and stimulated and summoned his fellow Muslims to its revivification and implication. The themes he dwelt upon like the importance of state, the legitimacy of political authority, the unbreakable link between faith and deeds, the need for commitment, integrity, and striving for Islamic revival are vital and relevant for all those who have joined the contemporary Islamic movement as well as for those who wish to understand the increasing momentum of the worldwide Muslim re-awakening. In South Asia, where Mawdūdī's ideas took shape, his influence has been more pronounced. His ideas unquestionably dominate Islamic political thinking in the Indo-Pakistani subcontinent. This has become all the more evident as Pakistani secular nationalism has scored one failure after another, and thereby removed itself from the growing surge of Islamic political thought and action. This sociopolitical study enquires about the value and validity of the ideas of Mawlana Mawdūdī and assesses their relevance to contemporary Pakistan and the Muslim world.

Muslim Identity Formation

Sayyid Abul A'la Mawdūdī was born on September 25, 1903 into a respectable family of strong religious traditions at Aurangabad, Deccan, India. Mawdūdī's education was short and unsystematic. He did not attend legendary institutions such as Al-Azhar. In fact, he attained mastery of Islamic sciences outside the regular educational institutions and obtained certificates from three famous teachers of Madrasah Aliyah Arabiyyah Fatehpuri, Delhi. Mawdūdī produced 67 works, some of them monumental in length and depth, and edited two journals. He founded the Jamaat-e-Islami (the Islamic Party) in 1941 and led it until 1972. The Jamaat has embodied his ideology and has played a significant role in the history and politics of Pakistan, India, Bangladesh, Sri Lanka, the south Asian communities of the Persian Gulf, Great Britain, and North America.

Sayyid Mawdūdī started with the assumption that the Muslim world is faced with a profound need to assert its identity. Under the circumstances, as ever, a clear conception of the human being, his purpose, and his destiny become of utmost significance. Interpreting Islam in progressive manner, Mawdūdī provided unambiguous answers to these questions. The human being is the vicegerent of Allah, the Creator, the Ruler, and the Sovereign of the universe. It is his duty, his responsibility, to transform the earth, which is his trust in accordance with the values enshrined in the Qur'an and the Sunnah of the last Prophet of Islam.

This designation of mankind as Allah's vicegerent ennobles and sanctifies man, his life, his activities, and his relationships with fellow human beings. Since all are vicegerents they are all equal, which leaves no scope for injustice and oppression, hatred, and greed. It is then the Muslim's duty to struggle hard for the victory of Islam. The goal being the elevation of one's humanity, the methods used to achieve that goal should, therefore, remain subordinate. Activities aimed at eradicating poverty, exploitation and injustice, and at improving the quality of life should be seen as a means and not an end in itself. Clearly then, such a view of life has tremendous significance for the human being's relationship with his fellow beings, with the environment and with the inanimate objects around him.

The concept of vicegerency has another implication. Being a vicegerent and a trustee, the Muslim is to serve Allah, a being bigger than himself, larger than mankind as a whole. The ultimate object of his loyalty is Allah, a transcendental power, a notion that helps to check human arrogance and to control human ego. It reminds man of his humble station in the totality of the cosmos. Given the fact that power in its various dimensions has always been at the very heart of the great conflicts in history, reminding man of his actual condition is of utmost significance and vital for the creation of a sane, rational society.

The identity of man as a vicegerent and a slave of Allah at one and the same time are embodied in the revolutionary concept of *tawḥīd*, which is the foundation of Mawdūdī's scheme of ideas. Through this concept, he reminded men that the spiritual and the material, this world and the hereafter, constitute a single continuum; that there are two fundamental forms of society in existence, one based upon *tawḥīd* and the other upon *shirk* (the assignments of partners to Allah) – the two being in perpetual conflict; and that man's duty as a vicegerent is to be active, to work for the glory of Islam in obedience to and for the sake of Allah. Mawdūdī's entire life was consumed in communicating this idea and in helping man discover his humanity, which is his spiritual essence.

What Mawdūdī said could have been said by those well versed in Islam – the *ulama*. But they were busy either with "amulets, intonations and prayer beads" and thereby sapping the vigor of the Muslim community or with questions concerning the details of *fiqh* (religious jurisprudence) and distracted the Muslims off the foundations of Islam "until they forget what they were created for and ignored the sublime purposes for which Islam stands."[1] Mawdūdī therefore directed his scathing attack against these traditional figures of authority accusing them of betraying the people and was, in turn, accused by traditional authorities as being the least qualified to provide an interpretation of Islam. The *ulama*'s critique of Mawdūdī was, however, no more than a polemic usually with unsubstantiated accusations.[2]

The problem with the general body of *ulama* was not that they did not understand Islam but that they evinced no recognition that the truth they so clearly saw needed restating in modern times. Their failure was their inability to relate Islam to modernity, to communicate it effectively and to make intelligible or accessible to modern man the inner reality of the faith. Mawdūdī represented this modern trend and carried it vigorously forward. His writings suggest that his primary concern was the modern man. His *magnum opus*, the *Tafhīm al-Qur'an* was written for the consumption of "middle-class educated Muslims" and therefore, using Urdu as his medium of expression, he tried "to render the flawless Arabic of the original into flawless Urdu."[3] Commanding a masterly prose style, Mawdūdī is one of the most widely read Muslim authors of today.

Mawdūdī, unlike the majority of *ulama*, was alive to the problems of modernity as they confront the Muslim world. All his writings bear evidence of his acute awareness of the situation and problems of the present age. On innumerable occasions he cited in support of his arguments, recent researches in the fields of physics, medicine, archeology, economics, and the like. He covered an extremely wide spectrum of subjects, all vindicating the position of Islam by discussing the matter not merely from an ethical and spiritual viewpoint but also from an economic, political and sociological angle appropriate to the subject matter. He clarified for the modern reader aspects of Islamic approach and explained how Islam furnishes man with definite guidance in political, social, economic and cultural matters. His success in explaining the relevance of Islam in modern tines may be debated and analytical depth of his understanding of modern sciences can be faulted but there is no doubt that he was aware of the importance of issues and problems confronting the modern mind. Mawdūdī's appeal has grown in geometric progression largely among those educated strata of society which are supposed to be modernized in the Western sense of the term.

Mawdūdī's basic goal in "Muslim identity formation" was to make Islam the supreme organizing principle in the social and political life of the Muslim *ummah*. The concept upon which he based this was *iqamāt-i dīn*, which literally means "the establishment of religion." According to this idea, all institutions of civil society and the state must be totally subordinated to the authority of divine law as revealed in the Qur'an and practiced by Prophet Muhammad. Islam, which is a universal and comprehensive way of life, is a well-ordered system, a consistent whole with set answers to all problems. Its fundamental postulate is *tawḥīd* and its envisaged scheme of life is known as *sharīʿah* and is established on the bedrock of faith. It is on that foundation that the edifice of moral, social, political, and economic system is created. The ideal Islamic society, to Mawdūdī, consists of people who, through putting their faith in Islam, have liberated themselves from all allegiances except to Allah; such a society would be free and "theo-democratic" and its citizens would be as equal as the teeth of a comb.[4]

Muslims, according to Mawdūdī, belong to the *ummah wasaṭah* (just and balanced community), and, as such, are duty bound to enjoin what is right and forbid what is evil. The Qur'an, he wrote, is not a book of abstract theories and religious enigmas to be unraveled in monasteries and universities; it is a book of movement and agitation revealed to invite the people to the one right way of Allah. Consequently, Islam is the religion of revolutionary struggle and utmost exertion (*jihād*) aimed at shattering the myth of the divinity of demi-gods and promoting the cause of Allah by establishing the Islamic political order. Islam, therefore, is a dynamic force, a worldwide revolutionary movement bent upon transforming the world to be in accord with its tenets and principles to benefit mankind. "*Jihād* is but another name for the attempt to establish the Divine Order; the Qur'an therefore declares it to be a touchstone of belief."[5] In this struggle, there is no room for bystanders, spectators and backsliders, and the venture is so crucial that, neglecting it, "one has no means left to please Allah." To Mawdūdī, *jihād* meant fighting oppression by pen and by involvement in public affairs. Undeterred by time and expediency, he dedicated his life to the cause of Islam. The persisting needling of the government in the renaissance movement he founded and led, and hardships and personal discomfiture he endured on a number of occasions in Pakistani prisons (October 4, 1948–May 28, 1950; March 28, 1953–May 25, 1955; January 6, 1964–October 10, 1964; January 29, 1967–March 16, 1967) and once under the threat of a death sentence by the military tribunal (on May 9, 1953) are perhaps indicative of the significance of the man and his ideas.

Mawdūdī's ideas and writings are nothing new and in that sense he was not an original thinker. He himself disclaimed that he had discovered any new principle or doctrine; he was presenting only what the Qur'an and the Sunnah have taught. He simply reminded his fellow Muslims of the most ancient covenant between the Creator and His creation and of, what is termed in the Qur'an, a "transaction of sale": "Surely, Allah has bought of the believers their persons and their property for this that they shall have a paradise in exchange" (9:111). Mawdūdī did not repudiate the past, he simply renewed it and made it relevant to the present and future. It is in this sense that Mawdūdī emerges as the most systematic thinker of modern Islam. His major contribution, as aptly summarized by Khurshid Ahmad:

> [i]s that he has devoted himself to the socio-politico-cultural aspect of Islam and has discussed those problems which the writers on Islam were avoiding for a long time in recent past. He has tried to meet the new intellectual challenge of the West and has presented Islam in the language of today. In political thought, his main contribution is that he has not only presented the teachings of Islam in a clear, precise, cogent and convincing way but has also interpreted them for our times and has tried to suggest the form which the Islamic tenets can take to crystallise in the world of twentieth century.[6]

Two-Nation Theories

Mawdūdī's political thought was conditioned by the sociopolitical and religious environment in which he lived and operated. The pre-independent Indian environment was dominated by three major political forces: the British Raj, the Indian National Congress, and the All-India Muslim League. While the British rule was steadily weakening in determination and effective powers, the Indian National Congress was concerned with uniting the Indians for independence. The British and the Congress were determined to preserve the unity of India (though for different reasons) while the All-India Muslim League was wedded to the concept of Muslim nationalism, seeking a homeland for the Muslims of the subcontinent. Indeed, the poet-philosopher of Islam, ʾAllamah Muhammad Iqbal (1876–1938), had made, in 1930, a proposal for a separate Muslim homeland. Iqbal had a federated India in mind with a consolidated Muslim state as its constituent unit. Ten years later Muhammad Ali Jinnah (1876–1948), once hailed as the ambassador of Hindu–Muslim Unity, took up Iqbal's notion of a separate Muslim homeland and enunciated what became known as the "two-nation" theory. He talked of Islam and Hinduism as two "different and distinct social orders" whose adherents can never evolve a "common nationality." He added, "Musalmans are a nation according to any definition of a nation, and they must have their homelands, their territory and their state."[7] Accordingly, the Muslim League in its annual session at Lahore adopted on March 23, 1940 a resolution, subsequently known as "the Pakistan Resolution." It called for the creation of independent Muslim states in the Northwestern and Eastern zones of the subcontinent where the Muslims constituted the majority of the population.

Mawdūdī, however, argued that a national government based on secular or Muslim nationalism would not be qualitatively different from the imperial government of India. Nationalism was an alien concept imported by colonialism to break up the unity of the Muslim world. They likewise injected Western currencies, influence, thought, and all sorts of heresies into the Islamic way of life. Being a divisive phenomenon, a nation state cannot be helpful in bringing about the Islamic sociopolitical system. Mawdūdī, therefore, rejected the existence of Muslim nationalism as incompatible with Islam which is universal. His interest was in *iqāmat-i dīn* establishing the Islamic way of life. The methodology for the establishment of Islam's ascendancy, Mawdūdī argued, was not through the nationalist struggle. He argued that a national struggle may produce a nation-state for the Indian Muslims, but definitely not an Islamic state. He also mounted scathing criticism against the Muslim League for having accepted the West's supremacy in the realm of knowledge, culture, and philosophy. Thus, the Jamaat-e-Islami and the All-India Muslim League were advocating solutions to the Muslim problem from two different perspectives: one passionately involved in a national struggle for independence and the establishment of a separate homeland for Muslims, and the other struggling for the domination of pristine Islam as a complete way of life.

Mawdūdī, however, was vehemently opposed to the Congress that tried to mobilize Muslims in the ethos of secular democracy, and to wean them away from the Muslim League on strictly economic issues. The Congress called for Hindu–Muslim unity-based "composite nationalism," which Mawdūdī felt was impossible to achieve. He argued that if the Muslims accept this type of nationalism and join the Congress, they would be annihilated and absorbed into the Hindu majority. "What was uppermost in my mind," wrote Mawdūdī, "was to keep alive in the Muslims a sense of their separate entity and prevent their absorption into a non-Muslim Community."[8] To Mawdūdī,

Muslims constituted a "brotherhood" entrusted with a comprehensive system of life to offer the world. Were they to practice Islam faithfully, the matter of a national homeland would become "absolutely immaterial." He argued for the Muslim community to turn inward and revive the traditions that once brought it power, glory, and prosperity. In his voluminous writings, Mawdūdī argued that if India's Muslims were to survive as a community, they would have to treat Islam as their "way of life," not merely as a system of faith and worship. They must merge their personalities and existences into Islam. They subordinate all their roles to the one role of being Muslims. Mawdūdī's greatest contribution of the time was that he made Muslims cognizant of their identity and raised in them fervor to organize their polity on the principles of Islam. While opposing Muslim nationalism, Mawdūdī was promoting the cause of "two-nation" theory. He even presented "two-nation" theories of his own. He proposed dividing India into two culturally autonomous democratic entities functioning either as a federation or as a loose confederation. The articles he wrote to that effect were collected and published in his three-volume Urdu book, *Musalman awr Mawjudah Siyasi Kashmakash* (*Muslims and the Current Political Crisis*). His writings provided the Muslim League with much needed intellectual ammunition to fight the nationalist movement. Mawdūdī is therefore recognized as an intellectual force behind the two-nation theory and a front against united Indian nationalism. According to I.H. Qureshi, "Mawdūdī's rejoinder was . . . logical, authoritative, polite and devastating. . . . It did not win him too many adherents and followers, but it did serve the purpose of turning sincere and intelligent Muslims away from the Congress who mostly swelled the ranks of the Muslim League as followers of the Quaid-e-Azam."[9] Contrary to the prevailing view, Mawdūdī did not oppose Pakistan. He, however, opposed the Muslim League and its leadership. His concern then was Islam, and the ability of those who sought to represent it. The period between the founding of the Jamaat in 1941 and the advent of Pakistan in 1947 was spent in mobilizing public opinion for the propagation and adoption of an Islamic ideological concept with a view to transforming India into an abode of Islam.

Islam in Pakistan

Following the Partition of India in 1947, Mawdūdī, along with many party leaders, moved to Pakistan and established the headquarters of the Jamaat-e-Islami of Pakistan in Lahore. The multiple reinforcing cleavages, elite incoherence, and tortuous and complicated political maneuverings during the formative phase of Pakistan, perhaps, influenced the Jamaat leaders to become active in Pakistani politics.

The Jamaat, according to Israr Ahmad, adopted the following two-point program:

1. To embark upon a comprehensive movement for the implementation of Islamic ideology in order to convert to Islam the newly established state of Pakistan.
2. To bring about a revolutionary change in the political leadership of the country so that the resources of the state are harnessed in the service of Islam.

Israr Ahmad blames Mawdūdī for restricting the scope of Jamaat's activities by its exclusive concern for the Muslims to the exclusion of non-Muslims and for transforming the Jamaat into a nationalist organization serving the cause of Islam in Pakistan.[10] Mawdūdī's reasons for subscribing to an "Islam in Pakistan" thesis were twofold. First, for an ideology to be useful, it must have an empirical import and make reference to particular cases or examples because it is impossible to build a pattern of life merely in the abstract. Second, for an ideology to attract worldwide attention, it must demonstrate its worth by evolving a happy and successful system of life and must present its theories and fundamental principles in operation. Consequently, Mawdūdī thought it essential to have the Islamic state established in one country first so as to be emulated worldwide later.

The Jamaat started an organized campaign to realize the first of the two objectives. On January 6 and February 19, 1948, Mawdūdī delivered two lectures at the Law College in Lahore in which he demanded the Constituent Assembly of Pakistan to accept the following four demands:

1. That the sovereignty belongs to Allah alone and that the state shall exercise its authority as His agent.
2. That sharīʿah will be the basic law of the land.
3. That the laws in conflict with sharīʿah will gradually be repealed and that no such laws shall be enacted in future.
4. That the state in exercising its powers shall not transgress the limits prescribed by Islam.

The Lahore lectures were followed by a tour of Pakistan in April and May 1948, extensive lobbying with the members of the Constituent Assembly, and a concerted public campaign to press upon the leaders to incorporate the above points into the constitution of Pakistan. On March 7, 1949 the Constituent Assembly passed the Objectives Resolution embodying the four-point demand. With the passage of the Resolution, Pakistan, according to Mawdūdī, in principle took the shape of an Islamic state. It is not the Resolution *per se* but the fact of it being adopted by the government in response to the unanimous demand of the people to lead an Islamic way of life that made it an Islamic state. It would be an exaggeration to credit Mawdūdī and his organization exclusively for the success. However, the organized strength of the Jamaat under Mawdūdī's leadership did play a major role. It may thus be construed as a triumph of Mawdūdī and the Jamaat-e-Islami of Pakistan.

The Resolution, setting forth the ideals and values, acted as a guide for constitution makers in Pakistan in 1956, 1962, 1972, and 1973 in devising an Islamic order for the country. It was incorporated, with minor modifications, in all the constitutions of Pakistan. The Objectives Resolution was made a substantive part of the constitution by President General Ziyaul Haq through a constitutional amendment that was promulgated on March 2, 1985.

The Objectives Resolution did not produce the desired result. Understandably, the institutionalization of Islam in Pakistan would have jeopardized the vested interests of the feudal and capitalist forces as well as that the of civil–military bureaucracy.

The Jamaat consequently intensified its efforts through public meetings, contacting members of parliament, and mobilizing strong public pressure to make Pakistan a truly Islamic republic. Mawdūdī produced several treatises on Islamic political theory, Islamic law and constitution, Islamic judicial and legal structures and the modalities for ushering in the Islamic political system in Pakistan. It is to the credit of Mawdūdī that he introduced Islamic idioms and concepts into the unfolding national political discourse and launched a vigorous campaign for the Islamization of Pakistan. Mawdūdī coined or popularized concepts like "Islamic ideology," "Islamic politics," "Islamic constitution," "*iqāmat-i dīn,*" "*nizam-e-Mustafa,*" and "Islamic way of life." These concepts became key elements of Islamist discourse in Pakistan.

Mawdūdī's intensification of efforts for the Islamic system involved him in intense conflicts with authorities. The dispute took many forms: the 1953 riots against the minority Ahmadi community and the *Report of the Court of Inquiry* which followed, bringing into sharp focus the secularist view in polar opposition to the view of the positive Islamic state, and debate over the constitution of 1956 preceded by the formulation of the basic principles of the Islamic state by 31 *ulama*. This was in response to the challenge thrown by the government to the *ulama* to produce a unanimous statement on the nature of the Islamic constitution. In the conference of the *ulama* gathered to produce an Islamic constitution, Mawdūdī took the lead and laid the basis for the productive cooperative effort. "Mawdūdī read his principles first, and these were supported with some additions by the members of the board."[11] There was also heated debate over the constitution of 1962, which initially erased the word "Islamic" from the country's nomenclature but was reinserted later on to read Islamic Republic of Pakistan. "This was due largely to the advocacy of this idea by Mawdūdī that the constitution was so amended."[12]

Although the constitution of 1956 envisioned the law and administration of the state as "modern even broadly secular," it endorsed the concept of an Islamic state and designated Pakistan as an Islamic Republic. It required the Head of State to be a Muslim, contained the preamble based upon the Objectives Resolution and provided for nullification of law repugnant to the Qur'an and the Sunnah. The constitution of 1962 contained somewhat similar provisions though it considerably watered down the Islamic character of the state. This is largely due to the high-handed method of Ayub Khan's military regime.

The Islamic provisions of these constitutions, undeniably, were merely "high-sounding phrases" having no correspondence with the country's sociopolitical and legal set up. It is, however, difficult to ignore their importance as an index to the relevance of Islam as the framework of the state. They also provided evidence of the success of Mawdūdī and his supporters "in getting Islam acknowledged as the basis of Pakistan's constitution. It is not possible for any government to reverse this decision."[13]

Islam as Ideology

In facing contemporary challenges it is not enough to preach sermons and invite people to adopt high moral standards. Rather, it is necessary to bring about fundamental rupture with conventional norms of life. Mawdūdī argued relentlessly to think within the totality of the Islamic system and recognize its relevance to the contemporary situation. Without moral values as internal to and constitutive of it, the system is bound to aberrate, as it did, and develop an ethic, which run counter to Islam. Consequently, government and political office became an instrument for self-gratification and the brute exercise of power. The present malaise could be corrected only if people are mobilized and a total transformation of society is actualized. This could be done not by borrowing alien ideologies but by the very tradition that other secular ideologies consider as the opium of the masses. But in order to achieve this, Islam has to be presented into the terms of modern reality. Mawdūdī's greatness lay in accomplishing this Herculean task of explaining the real nature of the faith.

Mawdūdī stated unequivocally that Islam is not a religion in the sense commonly understood by Western usage – that is no more than the sum of several beliefs, rituals and sentiments – but rather a system of life that deals with all aspects of man's existence and performance. It is a belief system, a complete way of life, a message and a movement for the establishment of an Islamic order. It is a "revolutionary ideology" consisting of the worship of Allah, belief in the Hereafter, and adherence to the practice of the Holy Prophet. It is comprehensive and total. In addition to its other-worldly dimension, it has a strong this-worldly dimension. Mawdūdī showed righteous discontent and irritation with the partial vision of Islam which predominates the Muslim world. He scorned those who believe that Islam has nothing to do with the cultural, political, economic, legal, judicial and other matters pertaining to this world. The Qur'an teaches not simply "to preach" Islam but "to act upon it, promote it, and actually enforce it."

It is this emphasis on the sociopolitical aspect of the Islamic scheme for human life which distinguishes Mawdūdī from others who looked down upon power, political authority, and action as something beneath them, in itself contemptible and hence to be eschewed. For Mawdūdī, the fusion of religion and politics is the dictate of Islam and cannot be disregarded. The choice between Creator and Caesar simply does not arise. For Islam, there is no Caesar, there is only Allah and His Messenger. The *sharīʿah* incorporates the temporal within the spiritual. There is an added reason for Mawdūdī's emphasis upon politics and authority. While there are ideological orientations and movements in all branches of scholarship and human thought, it is politics that gives ideology its social experience, its practical articulation and meaning. This is hardly surprising since ideology and politics are inextricably intertwined and coterminous such that politics has ideology as its operational framework that gives it its meaning while politics provides a mode by which ideology is translated into practical actions. This gives the ideas their practical relevance in the real world.

According centrality to power and authority in human affairs is also an answer to the problems of inequality and oppression which have dominated all discussions about political and economic structures since the dawn of civilization. To Mawdūdī,

> Whenever corruption is let loose in the world, whatever injustice is done, whenever tyranny or oppression exists, whatever poison flows in the veins of human culture, economic life and politics, whatever misuse of resources and human knowledge for destruction instead of welfare and enlightenment there may be, the reason is bad leadership.[15]

Power and authority are "the decisive factors in human affairs." Just as the train moves in the direction intended by the driver, human civilization travels in the direction determined by those controlling the centers of power. Right, pious leadership ensures good, healthy society. A society in the hands of rebels "drifts towards rebellion against Allah, towards man's exploitation by man and towards moral degeneration and cultural pollution."[15] Human salvation therefore depends upon wresting control of power and authority and placing it in the hands of those who are righteous and committed to following the Divine guidance. Power and authority is desired not for itself but to root out the evils afflicting humanity since, as Mawdūdī said, "Corrupt rule is the root of all evils you find in the world."

Mawdūdī's motive in "politicizing" Islam has been misunderstood and misinterpreted by many and was specifically criticized by "traditional" scholars. Mawdūdī was accused of promoting "*Mawdūdiyāt*," teachings particular only to him, and of encouraging heterodoxy within Islam. Many *ulama* also argued that Mawdūdī had sacrificed the intellectual foundations and the spiritual expressions of the Islamic faith, which had supported individualist tendencies in the past.[16] Far from reducing Islam into a political formula, Mawdūdī sought to sanctify politics by bringing it within the fold of Islam, such that man's political life is always situated within the larger frame of his religious and spiritual life. This is the most reliable defense against the corrupting influence of politics. Muslims have been enjoined by Allah to seek power or to get the support of a ruling authority, Mawdūdī explained:

> so that I may, with the force of the coercive powers of the state, establish virtue, eradicate evil, eliminate surging tide of corruption and vulgarity, set at right the disruption engulfing humanity and administer justice according to your revealed law.[17]

Power thus tamed helps actualize the Islamic system, which is impossible by mere verbal invitation and sermon preaching. It is, therefore, incumbent upon every Muslim to define and apply the relevance of Islam to every single item in human living and create a universal order in which the totality of Islam can be operationalized. Mawdūdī understood and conveyed the very heart of the message of Islam and this is perhaps the reason for his importance and his success in influencing the thinking of Muslim intellectuals all over the world.

Implied in Mawdūdī's urging to action, to plunge into the exuberant task of creating a humane world order is the recognition that there is inherent in the structure of this world a right socioeconomic and political shape, which is profoundly relevant to the quality of life within it, and that the meaning of dynamism lies in the degree to which these have been actualized. Nevertheless, there has been an apparent failure on the part of Muslims to generate an interpretation of Islam that could serve as a workable theory of politics, economics, and society in the present situation. Breaking the impasse of Muslim quietude and creating an acceptable framework constitutes the most formidable challenge to Muslim intellectuals today. Mawdūdī tried hard and produced a lucid blueprint of an Islamic order detailing the constitutional and legal features around the *sharī'ah* of an Islamic state. He is more explicit than most of his contemporaries in his stand for the principles of electiveness of rulers, their accountability to the ruled, their obligation to consult the elected representative of the people, and the right of ordinary citizens to criticize all those in power and authority. It must be pointed out that Mawdūdī did not delve into the technical world of the specialist, but has expounded the essentials of Islamic approach in economics, political, cultural, and other fields of activity. The ultimate social, economic, and political goal of Islam is the establishment of justice and elimination of tyranny and oppression. It aims at individual freedom, social dignity, and universal equity, in short, promoting all that is good and proper and preventing all that is harmful and evil.

Islam and the Economy

Islam is not only organically related to politics but is also integral to the economic structure of the state. Mawdūdī mentioned private property, freedom of enterprise, *laissez-faire* etc., as the basic tenets of modern capitalism and recognized an element of truth in these principles for which he has been called "a Muslim Adam Smith" of Pakistan.[18] He, however, found capitalism carrying these principles to the extreme by undue emphasis on self-interest and profit motive, and by legislating usury (*riba*), which caused widespread suffering and privation. The capitalist economy, he wrote, is dominated by an "inhuman evil," usury. Its trade cycle is in the hands of the usurious bankers, brokers, industrialists, and business magnates; unemployment is acute and there is poverty amidst plenty. The communist system, on the other hand, showed some achievements in the sphere of social welfare and state planning but this was achieved at a great cost in terms of human lives. Communism deprived people of their liberty and denied moral values. Corruption became rampant and a totalitarian regime came to be established, which took recourse in extreme repressive measures. Islam cuts the roots of capitalism but unlike communism preserves man's freedom and his link with God. Islam, in other words, is a golden mean between capitalism and communism.

Within certain limits, Islam accepts private property and makes no distinction between means of production and forces of production nor does it aim at equal distribution of wealth. The materialistic concept of economic equality, Mawdūdī argued, is against nature and any artificial imposition of such equality would inevitably fail. Islam, therefore, calls for just and equitable distribution of wealth in the society. Islam ensures economic justice by providing equality of opportunity, which makes formation of static classes or groups impossible. Along with economic justice, Islam uses two methods which put an end to social imbalance and contradictions. First, it puts some restrictions on the earning and accumulation of wealth. For instance, in the means for the acquisition of wealth it makes a distinction between the permissible and the prohibited and imposes obligatory *zakah*, wealth tax, at varying rates. In addition, Islam gives general command of voluntary spending in the way of God and thus establishes the rights of the state and the entire community over an individual's wealth. Second, Islam guarantees social security for those who are unable to earn a livelihood. It is the duty of an Islamic state to arrange for employment, clothing, education, and the like for all citizens.[19]

In the matter of economy, as in others, Mawdūdī gave priority to the non-economic goals of safeguarding the freedom of the individual and his moral and ethical development. Social justice, equality of opportunity, and cooperation came next in his list of objectives of the Islamic economic system. One lacuna in Mawdūdī's economic thinking is the omission of the role of absentee landlordism in curtailing people's freedom especially in Pakistan. While Mawdūdī realized the menace of monetary *riba* and explained the rationale for its prohibition in Islam, he failed to understand that absentee landlordism is a disguised form of *riba* concerning agricultural land. This omission has resulted in the elimination of the much-needed revolutionary spirit from the Islamic movement in Pakistan. Mawdūdī must have realized this and hence the Jamaat Manifesto for the 1970 elections in Pakistan opened with a categorical statement opposing both landlordism and modern Western capitalism.

In any case, the declared purpose of Islamic economics is to identify and establish an economic order that conforms to Islamic scripture and traditions. Its core positions took shape in the 1940s, and three decades later efforts were made to implement them in many countries. In Pakistan, Malaysia, and elsewhere, governments are now running centralized Islamic redistribution systems known as *zakah*. More than 70 countries have Islamic banks that claim to offer a *riba*-free alternative to conventional banking. Pakistan, Iran, and a few other countries have made every form of interest illegal. They have convinced all banks, including foreign subsidiaries, to adopt, at least formally, Islamic methods of deposit making and loan taking. Attempts are also under way to disseminate religious norms of price setting, bargaining, and wage determination.

Reform and Revolution

Mawdūdī realized that the prevailing iniquitous dehumanizing order cannot be replaced by a humane order unless there is a fundamental change in attitudes and values. Mawdūdī did not think that it is possible or even desirable to bring about societal transformation overnight. Nor did he succumb to the illusion that the road to a new order could be paved merely with pious wishes and good intentions. It is useless to blame the adversary or bewail the times in which one's lot was cast. However heavy the odds, it was the duty of a faithful never to feel helpless. What he should do first is to make a beginning with himself by getting rid of selfishness from his heart. This suggests that change is dependent upon the moral strength of the changing agent. As he puts it boldly

> the human life is governed not by physical laws, but by moral laws . . . the fundamental cause of man's rise and decline and the greatest influence on his destiny is the extent and quality of his moral strength.[20]

To him, the moral being is the human being. Morality is the shield against corruption and temptations to abuse power.

The conviction that the corrupting influence of power can be checked by adhering to moral precepts may seem utopian, unlikely to work in practice. The successful demonstration of "humanity at its best" by some 400 companions of the last Prophet of Islam in running the state of Medina and Mawdūdī's own success in producing a group of people characterized by personal integrity and unquestioned sacrificial vigor for the cause of Islam was enough to suggest that his method could work. In any case, for Mawdūdī this was the only method. The problem of tyranny, exploitation and injustice had to be tackled at the root. The best way, Mawdūdī argued, is to train all those who volunteer for service to Allah before allowing them to undertake *jihād* and establish Allah's rule on earth. Mawdūdī's stress on the salutary effect produced by the morally upright is a pointer to the lack of these qualities in any existing state and a consequent drift toward unparalleled catastrophe.

The social transformation advocated by Mawdūdī presupposed changes in the minds and hearts of men. The French, Nazi, and Russian revolutions have erred in adopting the tools of hatred and violence and in trying to change men by bluntly reacting against status quo and its wholesale destruction. The need is to tackle the problem of change within man, in his thoughts, motives, and behavior pattern. Such changes cannot be produced overnight. They cannot be accelerated or even anticipated beyond a point. In society, as in the human organism, there is a safe rate of change. Voluntary and peaceful changes may be slow, but they may be more enduring. Non-violent participatory change has occurred throughout history. As Erich Fromm points out, "the liberation of the working class from the status of objects of ruthless exploitation to that of the influential economic partners in Western industrialized society is an example of non-violent change."[21] Such changes, however, have been the exception rather than the rule. But it is the exception that Mawdūdī aimed at. The Islamic revolution aiming at total transformation of society is to be brought about piece-meal beginning with the personal reformation of the individual. Mawdūdī, who spent his life battling against social obscurantism, colonial domination, and national prejudice knew that great, lasting changes could not be ordained at will and at short notice.

Violence and Revolution

Thus, Mawdūdī differed profoundly from the tradition that considers violence as a defining characteristic of revolution. His main point of divergence from that tradition lay in his conception of the evolutionary process. He viewed revolution as involving more than the overthrow of a political regime. Revolution is a process of comprehensive and fundamental change in the system, which requires, first and foremost, changing the man himself, his outlook, his motivation and his personality.

Mawdūdī insisted on the evolutionary approach for carrying out social change. He was opposed to all unlawful, unconstitutional, and subversive acts and distrusted political radicalism of any kind. Respect for law and order was indispensable to the civilized society and hence he cautioned the revolutionaries to resist the temptation of resorting to the methods and techniques of "secret movements and bloody revolutions." Mawdūdī did not believe that anything positive could result from disrupting the social order. Furthermore, creating disorder "is against the wish of Allah." Islamic movement is for the cause of Allah and it should be conducted openly and peacefully even at the risk of courting hardship and miseries.

> Whatever I have done, I have always done it openly within the boundaries of law and exist-
> ing constitution, so much that I have never violated even those laws which I have fought
> hard to oppose. I have tried to change them through lawful and constitutional means and
> never adopted the path of violation of the law.[22]

Mawdūdī justified his predilection for a non-violent approach on theoretical as well
as practical grounds. Thus one argument was that it is against the natural order of
things to force change: "We should not overlook the basic law of nature that all stable
and far-reaching changes in the collective life of people come about gradually." From
the practical point of view, if change was to be lasting it had to be carried out slowly;
for "the more sudden a change, the more short-lived it generally turns out to be". A
perusal of the Qur'an and hadith reveals that the last Prophet of Islam had adopted a
gradual but effective approach to translate Islamic ideals into reality. He did admit,
however, that the Prophet Muhammad did resort to force but only to resist persecution,
and yet no more than 1200 people were killed on both sides in the course of all the
wars fought during the Prophet's time. Keeping in view the history of violent revolution in the world, the prophetic revolution deserved to be called a "bloodless revolution." While insisting on the revolutionary approach, Mawdūdī did not rule out the
possibility of resorting to force in exceptional cases. Force was to be used to resist ruthless persecution, which makes the peaceful propagation of Islam impossible. Force is
never used to compel anybody to embrace Islam against his will. Its purpose is only to
establish conditions conducive to free propagation of Islam.

Force also plays a role in creating an Islamic character in the people but it is to be
used only as a last resort. The order of precedence in the Islamic movement would be,
first, to reform people's minds through education and preaching. Second, to build their
character along Islamic lines. Third, to take steps to prepare strong public opinion
which fosters good and suppresses evil. Fourth, to establish such a social, economic,
and political order that facilitates doing good deeds and shuns all evil practices. Should
all these attempts fail, then force is to be used only "as a last resort" and should be used
so openly and mercilessly that it deters all criminal tendencies.

Mawdūdī's evolutionary approach to societal transformation gave priority to a
change in political leadership of the country so that the resources of the state are harnessed in the service of Islam. The revolutionary movement, Mawdūdī contended, has
no choice but to capture state authority, for without it the pious order that Islam envisages can never be established. Additionally, it becomes impossible for the revolutionary
party itself to act upon its own ideals under an alien state system.

> A man who believes in communism cannot order his life on the principles of communism
> while in England or America, for the capitalist state system will bear down on him with all
> its power and it will be quite impossible for him to escape the retribution of the ruling
> authority. Likewise, it is impossible for a Muslim to succeed in his intention of observing
> the Islamic pattern of life under the authority of a non-Islamic system of government.[23]

However, Mawdūdī declared that the capturing of the state power must be accomplished through constitutional means, i.e., elections, since *sharī'ah* forbids resorting to

unconstitutional means for the transformation of the political system. Consequent upon this decision, the Jamaat took part in almost all elections and failed miserably to capture power. Jamaat's participation in electoral politics had an adverse effect on the moral behavior of its members. The Jamaat degenerated from an ideal Islamic revolutionary party into a right-wing political party, along with the adoption of all the practices that may be objectionable from an Islamic point of view but which are perhaps unavoidable for running a purely partisan election campaign. Some of Mawdūdī's followers, especially the student wing of the Jamaat, did resort to violence. This is interpreted as retaliatory measures occasioned by the use of ruffians and hooligans by secular political elite bent upon denying the Islamic forces a space for open political participation and competition. In general, however, the Jamaat and its supporters did not abandon the democratic method temporarily to attain power by violent means. In the 2002 elections, the Jamaat forged an alliance with Islam-based parties and succeeded in forming a government in the North West Frontier Province of Pakistan.

Islam, Modernity, and Tradition

Mawdūdī saw the need for enlightened Muslims if the Islamic revolution was to succeed. Unfortunately, the Muslims were in retreat. "Their minds and souls have passed under the sway of the West. Their thinking is being molded by Western ideas and their intellectual powers are developing in accordance with the principles of Western thought. . . ."[24] This "dangerous situation" has given rise to two extreme reactions: the "static" and the "defeatist". The "static" Muslim literature opposing technology and scientific progress demonstrated the moral failure of the West and asserted the validity of the Muslim heritage as a whole. These were essentially a reaction against Western criticism rather than a confident statement of Islam. Mawdūdī reproached the "static" religious conservatives for rigorous formalism and for their unwillingness "to comprehend the principles and essential features of the new civilization of the West . . . and to fit these new instruments of progress, in keeping with the principles of Islam, into the educational system and social life of the Muslims."[25] The "defeatist" reaction came from the modernist Muslims, the Westernized elite. They acknowledged superiority of Western culture and values and tried to mold Islam along Western lines. Over time, these two postures hardened, the former leading to dogmatism and the latter degenerating into the subordination of Islamic value systems to the abstract values of science and reason. Least concerned about the existing socioeconomic and political realities of the Muslims, they were rendered only marginally relevant to the welfare of the Muslim community and of the whole human race. The education system the modernists have adopted is an alien one and is causing incalculable damage to the Muslim *ummah*. This education system, Mawdūdī lamented, has produced "brown Englishmen," "Anglo-Mohammedans," and "Anglo-Indians."[26] Thus Mawdūdī argued that allowing such an indiscriminate welcome to everything modern was the greatest danger to the *ummah*, since it would subject the entire nation to psychological enfeeblement.

Many Muslim reformers in the past have tried to remedy this sickness. Sir Syed Ahmad Khan (1232–1316 AH/1817–1898 CE) and Muḥammad ʿAbduh (1260–1323 AH/1845–1905 CE), to name just two, have been most famous in this respect. They believed that what the system needed was the addition of Western sciences to our existing curriculum of Islamic disciplines. Their view was based on the assumption that Western sciences were value neutral and that they would not do any harm to Islamic values. President Jamal ʿAbd al-Nasser of Egypt put this idea into practice by changing the very character of al-Azhar, but without any fruitful results in the area of modern sciences and technology. Worse still, the traditional Islamic teachings, desperately in need of reform, remained as sterile as ever. The Westernizing Muslim modernists, even if they meant well in their desire to defend Islam, in effect presented a truncated and deformed Islam.

To Mawdūdī, such educational reforms would prove to be unproductive, even counterproductive. What is needed, according to him, is to reorient the system and to Islamize the knowledge. To Islamize, to Mawdūdī, is "to critically analyze the Western humanities and sciences and to bring them into line with the teachings of Islam."[27] It is a process of critical evaluation and appreciation as against blind imitation, and a process of sifting, filtering and reconstruction as against wholesale rejection of Western thought and destruction. The aim is to critically appreciate and reformulate social sciences within the framework of Islam. It is interesting to note that Mawdūdī's definition of Islamization of knowledge and its characteristics, given in 1936, is similar to that propounded in 1982 by the late Dr. Ismail Raji al-Faruqi (1346–1406 AH/1921–1986 CE) in his epoch-making booklet, *Islamization of Knowledge*. According to al-Faruqi, "to recast knowledge as Islam relates to it is to Islamize it." This means: "to redefine data, to rethink the reasoning and relating of the data, to re-evaluate the conclusions, to re-project the goals and to do so in such a way as to make the disciplines enrich the vision and serve the cause of Islam."[28] As conceived by Mawdūdī, Islamization of Knowledge aims at ameliorating the crisis of the Muslim mind by addressing the problem of the body of Western knowledge and Islamic heritage and legacy. Its aim is to provide to the Muslim *ummah* a vision, and an ideologically oriented sound methodology to confront contemporary challenges and to reclaim its lost glory.

Emphasizing science and reason, Mawdūdī urged critical evaluation and assessment of both the Muslim heritage and Western science. He urged that the Muslim heritage be analyzed against its historical background and if the legacy is found to be inadequate or erring, the terms of the divine status of the Qur'an and the normativeness of the Sunnah and their relevance to the problems of the present should be corrected. Attempts at molding the society along Islamic lines would be all the poorer if it did not take the legacy into account and did not benefit from the insights of the ancestors. Extremes of rejection or wholesale glorification is due either to the inaccessibility of the legacy to the modern mind or of the inability of the traditionally trained scholars to discover and establish the relevance of the heritage to the present-day problems. Mawdūdī's call is to break this impasse to facilitate restructuring the world order. Likewise, Western civilization should be subjected to critical analysis from the standpoint of Islam. Its methodology, foundational principles, historical development, and achievements should be surveyed and analyzed. Thereafter, healthy achievements of

Western civilization in terms of its scientific and technological progress, in so far as they are value-free and are in conformity with Islamic principles, should be appreciated, abstracted and assimilated into the Islamic scheme of life. These ideas enabled Muslim intellectuals like Ismail al-Faruqi and others whose "Islamization of Knowledge" project carried forward some of Mawdūdī's key points.

As conceptualized by Mawdūdī, the process of Islamization of Knowledge must tackle the problem of education. He felt strongly that a genuine revival of the *ummah* is possible only if the education system is revamped and its faults corrected. What is actually required is for the system to be formed anew. To this end, Mawdūdī proposed educational reforms for secondary, higher secondary, and university levels. His emphasis, however, was on the university level for which he spelled out the modality for the implementation of his reforms.

The "model university" envisaged by Mawdūdī found its practical manifestations in the 1980s in many parts of the Muslim world especially in the International Islamic University, Islamabad. It is also manifested by the well-managed International Islamic University in Malaysia (IIUM). Established in 1983, IIUM's philosophy is "the integration of religious knowledge and worldly sciences, together with the vision of Islamization of human knowledge. . . . As such the university is not limited to Islamic theological studies but is a comprehensive professional institution of higher learning in which the teaching of all fields of knowledge is infused with Islamic values and the Islamic philosophy of knowledge."[29] This is a fully residential university open to students from all over the world. The conduct of students and teachers is subject to supervision. They are expected to follow the Islamic way of life. At IIUM, "all professional courses are taught in English, but students are required to reach the level of advanced Arabic proficiency. Students taking the *sharīʿah*, Arabic, and Revealed Knowledge courses must, of course, take them in Arabic, but their minor courses are offered in English."[30] It has a well-established "Research Centre" which promotes research of all kinds and encourages scholars to produce textbooks in all fields from an Islamic perspective. Thus, the IIUM can be considered a custodian of the knowledge that aims at producing ideologically sound Islamic leadership. Indeed, the university proclaims itself to be the "Garden of Knowledge and Virtue."

Conclusion

Mawdūdī's primary concern has been the reinstatement of Islamic values through education, legislation, and reform and this is receiving a good deal of attention all over the Muslim world today. Pakistan, the homeland of Mawdūdī, has sporadically been reasserting Islamic values in all realms of society in accordance with the concept of *nizam-e Mustafa*.

Equally discernible is the new trend in Muslim thinking on economic and legal issues. It should be remembered that Mawdūdī has not only written on economic problems but has also inspired quite a number of writers who are now in the forefront of devising Islamic economic models. The core of the new economic thinking revolves around the issue of usury (*riba*) which, according to Mawdūdī, is completely forbidden in Islam. After a decade of discussions involving the distinction between usury and interest, Muslims are now unanimous in condemning interest as *riba* and have embarked upon experimentation with Islamic banking systems eschewing the use of interest and other kinds of transactions prohibited in Islam. Beginning with the Islamic Development Bank in 1975, some 97 Islamic banks have been established all over the world. Similarly, attempts are underway to modify existing civil, criminal, and personal laws with the help of provisions available in the *sharī'ah*. Mawdūdī's method of returning to core principles in the Qur'an and the Sunnah and reaching a studied opinion as to how the problems confronting the present age should be resolved in their light seems to be more and more acceptable. There are, nevertheless, varying degrees of constitutional espousal of Islamicity as well as differences in the degree to which values enshrined in the Qur'an and the Sunnah have penetrated the interstices of the Muslim social fabric. The basing of legislation on the *sharī'ah* will have no magical effect unless a total transformation of society takes place. This necessitates knowing the righteous path, understanding the present day reality and imposing the one upon the other. This was the mission of Mawdūdī and this is the relevance of his thought for the contemporary situation in the Muslim world.

The ongoing Islamic reassertion is symptomatic of the crises confronting the world. It is an index, as well, of the fact that the malaise is still unresolved. It nevertheless symbolizes initiative, creativity and a sense of beginning. In the current drive to stress Islamic identity, Mawdūdī's works have played a remarkable role. He succeeded in motivating a large part of the alienated Muslims to identification with Islam. He has laid down ideas and directions that can be followed in carrying forward his *jihād*. Mawdūdī intended to stimulate thought and create an intellectual tradition where critical attitude is the norm. Mastery and assessment of the Muslim heritage, critical analysis of the Western civilization from the standpoint of Islam, and establishing the specific relevance of Islam to the world today is the legacy of Mawdūdī and is essential for the balanced growth of a humane world order.

The Jamaat-e-Islami, based on the teachings of Mawdūdī, is a more politically assertive group that tries to reach both lay Muslims and non-Muslims. Mawdūdī spoke of a universal Islamic movement, inculcating Islamic precepts and praxis among Muslims. Implicit in this message is the need to create an Islamic society based on Qur'anic egalitarian ideals wherever Muslims lived. An avowed intention of the Jamaat-e-Islami is to bring about a revolution in the political leadership of society, reorganize political and socioeconomic life along Islamic lines, and finally, to establish an Islamic state. When Pakistan was created, the Jamaat-e-Islami launched a public campaign to seek popular support for the implementation of the *sharī'ah* and demanded an "Islamic Constitution". Mawdūdī pursued his evangelical goals through non-militant means. He advocated the use of constitutional and legal means to pursue the objectives of the movement. He also advocated training camps to imbibe his adherents with Islamic values. Some of his adherents did resort to violent means, which is attributable to the impatience of the secular elite and their resorting to violence in dealing with Islamic forces.

At the time of Mawdūdī's death (September 22, 1979), Pakistan had already made sufficient progress in promoting the Islamic way of life. The conceptual basis of Islam has been partly realized, which no government in future would ignore. This is the major achievement of Pakistan's experiment in promoting an Islamic system. This is the legacy of Sayyid Abul A'la Mawdūdī.

Notes

1.   Abul A'la Mawdūdī, *Jihad fi Sabil Allah* (Lahore: Islamic Publications, 1962).
2.   Abu Athar Afaqi, *Fitna-e-Mawdūdīat per ek aur be lag tabsirah* (Urdu) (Jauharabad: Idara Adbastan, 1976).
3.   Abul A'la Mawdūdī, *Tafhim Al-Qur'an*, Vol. I (Lahore: Idarah Tarjumanul Qur'an, 1978), 6–11. This monumental Urdu *Tafhim* is in six volumes and was written over a period of 30 years from 1942 to its completion in 1972.
4.   The term Mawdūdī used to identify the Islamic state is "theo-democracy" which means "kingdom of Allah" administered not by a priestly class – of which Europe had a bitter experience – but by the entire Muslim population in accordance with the *sharī'ah*.
5.   Sayyid Abul A'la Mawdūdī, *The Islamic Movement: Dynamics of Values, Power and Change*, Khurram Murad (ed.), (Leicester: The Islamic Foundation, 1984), 79.
6.   Abul A'la Mawdūdī, *Islamic Law and Constitution*, Khurshid Ahmad (trans. and ed.), (Lahore: Islamic Publications, 1967), 34–5.
7.   Jamil-ud-Din Ahmad (ed.), *Some Recent Speeches and Writings of Mr. Jinnah* (Lahore: Mohammad Ashraf, 1974), Vol. I, 178, 180.
8.   Sayyid Abul A'la Mawdūdī, *Jamaat-e-Islami ke 29 Sal* (*29 Years of Jamaat-e-Islami*) (Lahore: Jamaat-e-Islami, 1976), 25.
9.   Ishtiaq Husain Qureshi, *Ulama in Politics* (Karachi: Ma'arif Limited, 1974), 339, 351.
10. Israr Ahmad, *Tehrik-e-Jama'at-e-Islami: Ek Tehqiqi Mutala'ah* (*The Jamaat-e-Islami Movement: A Critical Study*) (Lahore: Markazi Anjuman Khuddam al-Qur'an, 1990), 118–21, 123–6.
11. Leonard Binder, *Religion and Politics in Pakistan* (Berkeley: University of California Press, 1963), 216.
12. A.K. Brohi, "Mawlana Abul A'la Mawdūdī: The Man, the Scholar, the Reformer," in Khurshid Ahmad and Safar Ishaq Ansari, eds., *Islamic Perspectives: Studies in Honour of Mawlana Sayyid Abul A'la Mawdūdī* (Leicester: The Islamic Foundation, 1980), 301.
13. S. Zakir Ijaz (trans.), *Selected Speeches and Writings of Mawlana Mawdūdī* (Karachi: International Islamic Publications, 1982), Vol. II, 285–6.
14. Mawdūdī, *The Islamic Movement: Dynamics of Values, Power and Change*, 71.
15. Mawdūdī, *Tafhim Al-Qur'an*, Vol. II, 77.
16. See Muhammad Zakaria, *Fitnah-e-Maududiyat* (Karachi: Kutub Khanah Mazhari, 1976).
17. Mawdūdī, *Let us be Muslims*, Khurram Murad (ed.), (Leicester: The I Islamic Foundation, 1985), 286.
18. Hafeez Malik, "The Spirit of Capitalism and Pakistani Islam," *Contributions to Asian Studies*, 2 (July 1971), 75.
19. See Mawdūdī, *Islam awr jadid Ma'ashi Nazariyat* (*Islam and Modern Economic Systems*) (Delhi: Markazi Maktabah Jamaat-e-Islami Hind, 1969) and *Ma'ashiyat-e-Islam* (*Islamic Economics*) (Lahore: Islamic Publications, 1969).
20. Mawdūdī, *The Islamic Movement: Dynamics of Values, Power and Change*, 94.
21. Erich Fromm, *May Men Prevail* (New York, Doubleday, 1964), 5.
22. *Nawa-e-Waqt*, November 10, 1963 quoted in Maryam Jameelah, *Islam in Theory and Practice* (Lahore: Mohammad Yusuf Khan & Sons, 1978), 334.

23. Abul A'la Mawdūdī, *Jihad in Islam* (Malaysia: International Islamic Federation of Student Organization, 1981), 19.

24. Abul A'la Mawdūdī, *The Sick Nations of the Modern Age* (Lahore: Islamic Publications Ltd., 1966), 10. This work first appeared as an article in the *Tarjuman al-Qur'an*, Lahore, October 1935.

25. Mawdūdī, *The Sick Nations of the Modern Age*, 11.

26. Ibid., 16.

27. Ibid., 17–18.

28. Ismail Raji al Faruqi, *Islamization of Knowledge: General Principles and Work plans* (Virginia: International Institute of Islamic Thought, 1402/1982), 15.

29. M. Kemal Hassan, "International Islamic University at Kuala Lumpur," in John L. Esposito, ed., *The Oxford Encyclopedia of the Modern Islamic World* (New York: Oxford University Press, 1995), 211. M. Kemal Hassan was appointed the Rector of IIUM in 1999.

30. Ibid., 212.

CHAPTER 11

The Futuristic Thought of Ustaz Ashaari Muhammad of Malaysia

Ahmad Fauzi Abdul Hamid

This chapter discusses futuristic aspects in the messianic thought of Ustaz Ashaari Muhammad, who is well known among circles and observers of Southeast Asian Islam as the founder-leader of Darul Arqam, an Islamic movement banned in August 1994 by the Malaysian authorities for allegedly embracing and spreading heterodox teachings. Ustaz Ashaari subscribes to a unique vision of Southeast Asia as the future center of Islamic civilization in the post-modern world. This essentially messianic vision has been procured via a rigorous study of hadith literature and empirical knowledge gained during overseas tours. Ustaz Ashaari's thought becomes particularly important against the background of global messianic expectations as the new millennium meets the early phase of the Islamic century. In addition, Ustaz Ashaari's method of relying on contemporary economic prowess belies the economic backwardness befalling Muslims worldwide and the economic downturn affecting Southeast Asia since 1997.

Ustaz Ashaari strives to realize his vision through his establishment and leadership of movements that exhibit unconventional methods of managing economic and social development. Founded in 1968 as a small religious gathering in Kuala Lumpur, Darul Arqam had developed, by 1994, into a self-styled economic empire commanding huge influence among the national sociopolitical elite. In material terms, its tangible accomplishments were phenomenal, certainly for a movement that professed to operate on a strictly Islamic basis.[1] Until its demise in 1994, Darul Arqam, albeit being Malaysian-based, acquired a heavily transnational orientation, revolving especially around Southeast Asian countries. Convinced that an economically developed Islamic state and society would eventually come about in Southeast Asia, Ustaz Ashaari's followers throughout the region have continually sustained Islamic-oriented businesses and companies under various names, before gradually regrouping them under the aegis of Rufaqa' International Limited in 2002. In Malaysia, continuous retention under the Internal Security Act (ISA) of their leaders, consistent state monitoring, and the closing down of their communal villages have not prevented Ustaz Ashaari's followers from shifting ground towards erecting economically successful urban Islamic communities.

Under the restriction order imposed on him, Ustaz Ashaari cannot move from his designated district of residence, viz. Gombak (1994–2002) and since February 2002, Labuan island, off the Bornean coast of the state of Sabah. He has to remain indoors after 6 p.m., and all visitors have to be screened by the specially allocated security officers. He has to report to the nearest police station once a week. However, out-of-district breaks may be and have been given upon special requests made due to unforeseen circumstances, such as family death and illnesses. Needless to say, such requirements have greatly hampered communication between him and his followers.

In 1997, Ustaz Ashaari registered a private limited company, Rufaqa' Corporation, based in Bandar Country Homes, Rawang, Selangor, without relying on assets and capital from the disbanded Darul Arqam. Beginning with herbal-based health products, Rufaqa' focused upon establishing small and medium enterprises based in "Islamic townships," which refer informally to Rufaqa"s conspicuous string of business premises dominating parts of industrial estates. Within a few years, and despite prevailing economic uncertainty, Rufaqa' quickly expanded to all states in Malaysia. Today, with its multiple business networks operating 40 different types of businesses, Rufaqa"s business enterprises arguably constitute the best among economic initiatives offered by Islamic movements in Malaysia.[2]

Despite stern denials, the state, still seeing Ustaz Ashaari as a threat to national security, has constantly leveled accusations that Rufaqa' was trying to revive Darul Arqam, and in February 2002, banished Ustaz Ashaari and his immediate family to Labuan. In Labuan, business opportunities for Rufaqa' have been blocked by the local authorities, but Rufaqa' has managed to outwit the state by conducting businesses using the licenses of local Chinese businessmen oblivious to Rufaqa"s alleged heterodoxy and willing to cooperate with Rufaqa'. Muslims in Labuan have been persuaded by federal agents to desist from any communication and business links with Rufaqa', but through the non-Muslim business network, Rufaqa' now handles one bakery and five restaurants in Labuan. Having brought with him part of Rufaqa"s physical and human capital, reports have emerged detailing Ustaz Ashaari's "luxurious" lifestyle and rapport with Labuan's grassroots communities.[3]

Ustaz Ashaari has achieved economic success by strenuously maintaining a *taqwa*-based approach to business and development. Literally taken to mean "the fear of God", *taqwa* is stated in the Qur'an as being the source of God's help, through which all of Muslims' triumphs are effected. For example, "If the people of the towns had but believed and *feared Allah*, We should indeed have opened out to them (all kinds of) blessings from heaven and earth. But they rejected (the truth) and we brought them to book for their misdeeds" (Al-A'rāf 7: 96) and "And for *those who fear Allah*, He (ever) prepares a way out, and He provides for him from (sources) he never could expect . . . And for *those who fear Allah*, He will make things easy for them" (At-Talāq 65: 2–4). Rufaqa"s business meetings were seen to focus primarily on the relationship between *taqwa* and "God's bank," by which is meant that through *taqwa*, God will shower bounties on business enterprises undertaken in the name of the struggle for God.

Without going into the doctrinal controversies surrounding the proscription and eventual disbandment of Darul Arqam, the author now wishes to look at traits in the messianic worldview of Ustaz Ashaari Muhammad differentiating his movements not only from contemporary resurgent Muslim trends, but also from previous messianic movements.[4]

Messianism in Sunni Islam

As a subject, the phenomena of messianism and millenarianism have never been short of controversy. At the popular level, they have been associated with the world of celestial happenings, ancient prophecies, and Doomsday cults, which have often ended tragically with mass suicides and other violent aftermaths. These appeared to have multiplied dramatically with the advent of the new millennium, occurring near in time to such heavenly events as the passing of comets Halley in 1986 and Hale-Bopp in March 1997; the conjunction of planets in May 2000, and the closest approach of Mars to the earth in August 2003. Most anthropologists would describe messianic movements as a universal manifestation of social protest, being religions of the oppressed, disappointed, marginalized, and desperate communities. Yearning for a swift crumbling of the present social order, such victims of capitalist-based modernization were prone to pin their utopian hopes for a future golden age on a certain savior, whose miraculous coming and feats may have been foretold, if only vaguely, in medieval texts. Indeed, outbursts of millenarianism may be detected in all major religions and civilizations.[5]

Islamic millenarian expectations have revolved around the figure of Imām al-Mahdi, the messiah whose advent near the end of time has been pronounced by many hadiths, i.e. sayings or actions of the Prophet Muhammad as reported by his companions or wives, and passed through successive Muslim generations until ultimately compiled.[6] In fact, eschatological hadiths relate that, chronologically, the proclamation of al-Mahdi will be followed by specific events, viz. the appearance of the Dajjal, the descent of the Prophet Jesus who will kill the Dajjal, the appearance of the destructive tribes of Gog and Magog, and the rule of al-Mahdi over the world for five or seven or nine years and followed by that of the Prophet Jesus for 40 years, after a series of triumphant wars against the infidels. Ultimate peace will only prevail under the leadership of al-Mahdi and Jesus Christ, when Islam will reign supreme over the world. Following the passing away of al-Mahdi and Jesus Christ, Islam will decline again, until the moment when believers' lives are taken away by God, such that the Great Hour, i.e. the physical destruction of the planet earth, will be experienced only by unbelievers.[7]

In orthodox Sunni Islam, scholars have discussed the subject of al-Mahdi in conjunction with the famous hadith regarding the promised *mujaddid* (reformer), as narrated by Abu Hurayrah and found in the collection of Abu Dawud: "Allah will raise, at the head of each century, such people for this *ummah* as will revive its Religion for it." This explains the fact that Mahdist expectations have been strongest during the beginning of every Islamic century.[8] Mahdism has come to embody not only a theological belief in the coming of a final deliverer towards the end of time, but also a political belief in the destiny of the *ummah* to undergo regeneration under the Mahdist leadership of a centennial *mujaddid*. Hence for instance, the Umayyad caliph Umar Abd al-Aziz (d. 720), conventionally regarded as the *mujaddid* of the first Islamic century, was also referred to in respectable religious circles as al-Mahdi. Hopwood describes the Sunni version of al-Mahdi, *vis-à-vis* the Shi'ite view, as a *"mujaddid* (renewer). . . . who is not necessarily the harbinger of the Last Day but a more humble figure to guide the *ummah* back to the right path."[9]

Discussions revolving around the concept of al-Mahdi in Sunni Islam have exacted most interest from Sufis, who regard al-Mahdi as the last and spiritually greatest saint. Consequently, many Mahdist revivalist movements have had Sufi origins and inclinations. In fact, these movements were at the forefront of anti-colonial uprisings in the peripheral Muslim lands, whose societies had been severely disaffected by Western capitalist intrusion and military domination. While retaining a spiritual orientation, such movements took up many aspects more conventionally identified with modernist reformism, such as flexibility in opening the gates of *ijtihād* (independent reasoning) and an uncompromising rejection of foreign innovations, which had infiltrated traditional Sufi orders. Examples are the Diponegoro revolt in Dutch Java (1825–30), the Sanusiyyah agitations in late nineteenth-century Libya, and the anti-British Mahdist revolt in the Sudan (1881–5).[10]

In short, all messianic movements have up till now been proven in time to be not Mahdist in the scriptural sense. But this does not mean they were not Mahdist in orientation, in the sense of their having derived political inspiration from the apocalyptic belief in al-Mahdi. Therefore, the Mahdist doctrine wields not only theological significance, but is also valuable in generating reformist movements, particularly in times of economic and social discontent when the longing for a golden age becomes pervasive. The very idea that al-Mahdi's coming as a divine promise is assured raises collective social hopes of Muslims and motivates them to work for the betterment of the *ummah*, despite seemingly irreversible setbacks. In this sense, Mahdism encourages activism rather than a passive acceptance of the status quo. Very much a taboo to standard-bearers of official Islam, it has been and can still potentially be a powerful political weapon of Muslim revivalists.

Nonetheless, in the past century, Sunni Islamic movements have evidently discarded Mahdism, deeming it as irrelevant, from their agenda of resurgence. Mahdism has been relegated to the realm of fringe Sufi groups, Shi'ites, and heterodox movements. Contemporary revivalists have raised legitimate concern at the detrimental effects of past bogus claims by Mahdist aspirants,[11] but the existence or even abundance of Mahdist pretenders does not necessarily mean Mahdism constitutes a deviation or represents a liability to Islamic resurgence. This is borne out by the social and economic activism of Darul Arqam and Rufaqa' Corporation in Malaysia.

The Messianism of Ustaz Ashaari Muhammad

On August 5, 1994, the National Fatwa Council (NFC) of Malaysia unanimously ruled that Darul Arqam's teachings had deviated from Islam. Of the 10 charges of theological deviationism directed against Darul Arqam, two broad issues were of primary significance, viz. the theological validity of the *Aurad Muhammadiah*[12] and the nature of Darul Arqam's belief in the messianic advent of al-Mahdi. These issues had consistently been the sources of contention between the official religious authorities and Darul Arqam, as revealed in public statements by representatives of the Islamic Affairs Division of the Prime Minister's Department (BAHEIS: *Bahagian Hal Ehwal Islam Jabatan Perdana Menteri*), and the heated exchanges that took place between both sides in the form of books, booklets and documents on the matter.[13]

Technically, *Aurad Muhammadiah* enjoins the recitation, individually after each daily prayer, of seven verses in the correct order, preceded by the first chapter of the Qur'an. These verses, four and three of which are to be read 10 and 50 times respectively, are together a collection of Qur'anic verses, the *kalimah shahādah* (the attestation of faith: "there is no God but Allah, and Muhammad is the Messenger of Allah") and a *salawāt* (salutation of peace upon the Prophet Muhammad). But controversy arose as to the belief that the *Aurad Muhammadiah* was taught directly by the deceased Prophet Muhammad to its founder, Shaykh Muhammad Abdullah Al-Suhaimi, during a *yaqazah* – direct communication, in a state of consciousness, between two human beings, one or both of whom may have been deceased and therefore present in spiritual and not physical form. Two further allegedly deviant ritual practices of the *Aurad Muhammadiah* are its allegedly longer *kalimah shahadah* and the practice of *tawassul* as contained in its *tahlīl*.[14]

On the issue of messianism, three fundamental points distinguish Ustaz Ashaari's millenarian beliefs from past messianic trends. Firstly, his conditional belief that Shaykh Muhammad Abdullah Al-Suhaimi, whose grave is said to exist in Kelang, Malaysia, is in fact being "kept" alive in the spiritual world by God to prepare for his reappearance as al-Mahdi. Based on the prevailing chaos in the contemporary world and the prediction made by Jalal al-din al-Suyuti (d. 1505) that al-Mahdi would appear around 1407 AH, Ustaz Ashaari believes that al-Mahdi is the anointed savior of the fifteenth Islamic century, and the last in the list of celebrated *mujaddids*.[15] Ustaz Ashaari's postulation that the founder of the *Aurad Muhammadiah* is the most plausible candidate for the Mahdiship is based on arbitrary suggestions made by his grandson Mohd. Taha Suhaimi, upon circumstantial evidence tracing his ancestry to the Prophet Muhammad through his daughter Fatimah, and on physical features and a name which accorded with the description of al-Mahdi in hadiths, as testified by those who met him in his lifetime. One of them, known as Kiyai Mahmud, was said to have personally heard Shaykh Muhammad Abdullah Al-Suhaimi's prognosis that the resurgence of the *Aurad Muhammadiah*, after a brief decline following his occultation, would occur under the leadership of a man named "Ashaari Muhammad."[16]

Ustaz Ashaari's belief in the Mahdiship of Shaykh Muhammad Abdullah al-Suhaimi apparently puts it on a similar terrain with the Twelver Shi'ites, who also believe in the occultation of al-Mahdi prior to his promised reappearance. From the Sunni perspective, no scriptural justification exists to support the theory of al-Mahdi's occultation. In defense, Ustaz Ashaari cites the precedence of the Prophet Jesus and the People of the Cave, both of whom were thought to have died by their contemporaries but who in reality are being kept by God in an unknown world until the moment of their destined re-emergence.[17] Furthermore, al-Mahdi's antithesis, the Dajjal, is also arguably in occultation. This view is based on a lengthy hadith which tells how Tamim al-Dari, a Christian convert to Islam, was stranded during a voyage in a remote island where he met and spoke with a beast shackled in a monastery. The creature claimed to be the Dajjal, as was verified by the Prophet upon hearing Tamim's story. Some Sunni *ulama* and Sufis did share Ustaz Ashaari's view of al-Mahdi's occultation. Supporting evidence for this include a statement from Ibn 'Arabi (d. 1240) and the testimony of Shaykh Hasan al-Iraqi (d. 1525), whose personal encounter with Al-Mahdi was cited by Ustaz Ashaari.[18]

The second distinctive feature of Ustaz Ashaari's messianism relates to his placing unprecedented emphasis on the purported advent of a "youth of Bani Tamim," a mysterious figure who has been described in hadiths as hailing from the East and serving as al-Mahdi's main vizier. Even though the appearance of this assistant of al-Mahdi has been foretold in hadiths, a historical examination of Messianism in Islam reveals a complete lack of attention given to such a figure, whom Ustaz Ashaari believes will establish an Islamic state in the east as the foundation for al-Mahdi's leadership of the Second *ummah*. The advent of al-Mahdi, as a matter of principle, must be preceded by the success of the youth of Bani Tamim, who will eventually hand over political power to al-Mahdi. In other words, the youth of Bani Tamim is the lesser savior whose political triumph will usher in more significant victories at the hands of the principal savior, al-Mahdi. The youth of Bani Tamim's triumph in the East is therefore a necessary condition for the advent of al-Mahdi. Previous claims to the Mahdiship can be categorically repudiated by pointing to their lack of a revivalist predecessor from the tribe of Tamim.[19]

Perhaps due to the vagueness of the identity of the youth of Bani Tamim, whose pedigree and physical characteristics, unlike al-Mahdi's, are scarcely elaborated in hadiths, no messianic truth-seeker or power-seeking pretender has been eager to come forward and claim his rank. Furthermore, unlike al-Mahdi, who is described in hadiths as a caliph who magnanimously distributes money without counting it, the youth of Bani Tamim is not associated with power and wealth he can willfully dispense. In the manner of a tug boat which paves the way for larger vessels, the youth of Bani Tamim merely opens avenues for and introduces al-Mahdi to the *ummah*. His main accomplishment, a state propped up by devoted followers known as the *ikhwān* (brothers), is prepared for al-Mahdi, not for himself. As such, staking a direct claim for the Mahdiship is misguided. Sincere revivalists should instead be healthily aspiring for the coveted position of the youth of Bani Tamim, as urged by Ustaz Ashaari:

> Based on hadiths, we are also informed that the revival of Islam in the East happens in the hands of a man from Bani Tamim (Qurayshy clan) [sic]: the man who will hand over the black banner to Imam Mahdi. This means the struggles of the man of Bani Tamim and of Imam Mahdi are closely related, connected and occur in succession. Perhaps the relationship between the prophets Aaron and Moses provide a fair comparison. I see both the man of Bani Tamim and Imam Mahdi as being concurrent *mujaddids*. [Any member of] the Muslim *ummah* should make the effort to become the man of Bani Tamim as mentioned in hadiths so that the schedule of Allah happens in his hands. There is nothing wrong or extreme in competing to become the anointed man; this is the way it should be. But if we are not capable of accomplishing such high ambitions, we must search for another more able person. When such a person clearly exists, we must follow him and assist his

struggle. There is no need to devise some other method. . . . Please feel welcome to grab
this opportunity. The identity of the *mujaddid* or the man of Bani Tamim has not been fixed.
This means that whosoever has the chance to qualify as the man of Bani Tamim.

Based on his study, Ustaz Ashaari enumerates some characteristics of the youth of Bani
Tamim and the *ikhwān*:

> He is of Arab ancestry, hailing from the Quraishy clan of Bani Tamim. But he has very few
> Arab features as a result of his lineage having been mixed with non-Arabs [via marriage].
> . . . His female followers appear like black crows, while the men wear turbans and green
> robes. The sight of them moving together in groups is awe-inspiring. . . . The black banner
> which he carries in the East also flaps in Khurasan: a country behind a river (*mā warāa un
> nahar*). This means he is the leader of the same movement in the East and in Khurasan.
> . . . The Eastern-born leader will approach a man waiting for him in the country behind
> the river, called al-Harith Harrath. As the outcome of his struggle, the man of Bani Tamim
> obtains the reins of government in one of the countries in the East. It is this ruling power
> that will be handed over to Imam Mahdi.[20]

The third peculiarity of Ustaz Ashaari's messianism is his conviction that Southeast
Asia plays a dominant role in determining the course of Islamic resurgence towards
the end of time. Holding that the Malay–Indonesian world is the "East" referred to in
hadiths and scholarly opinions, Ustaz Ashaari is thereby convinced of a Malaysian
provenance of the youth of Bani Tamim. This belief is founded upon the hypothesis that
many Sunni Arab families emigrated to the Far East to flee from persecution during the
last century or so, such that a possibility arises that inter-marriages between Bani
Tamim emigrants and Malays actually produced Bani Tamim generations with diluted
Arab features. Added to this is circumstantial evidence obtained from personal encounters and dialogues with foreign *ulama* who express the view that the level of Islamic
consciousness among the masses in Malaysia is comparatively higher than anywhere
else in the *ummah*. Logically, if the present constitutes a period near the end of time,
the East mentioned as the provenance of the youth of Bani Tamim has to be one in
which Islam is fertile at grassroots level. Best fitting the picture among Southeast Asian
nation states, Malaysia's pivotal role and the position of Malays as its core ethnic group
in the final resurgence of Islam are practically destined.[21]

Is Ustaz Ashaari claiming the mantle of the youth of Bani Tamim for himself, and
claiming his followers to be the *ikhwān* of the youth of Bani Tamim and thereby of
al-Mahdi? This was arguably insinuated in several statements, and most strongly in
the employment since 1993 of a new personal title, viz. *Abuya Shaykh Imam Ashaari
Muhammad at-Tamimi*; the surname "at-Tamimi" clearly suggesting Bani Tamim
origins. Even if Ustaz Ashaari was suggesting that he is the youth of Bani Tamim who
is destined to lead an Islamic state in the East, no scriptural justification exists to incrim-
inate him theologically. Problems encountered with the authorities relate to the doctrine's political implications, that Ustaz Ashaari is destined to lead Malaysia in the
not too distant future. Yet, inner conviction does not necessarily lead to the adoption
of organizational methods which can readily be transplanted from one structure to
another; in Darul Arqam's case, from a Muslim-oriented movement structure to a

multi-racial state structure. No evidence exists of tangible preparations made by Darul Arqam to wrest power via militant or electoral means. As far as Ustaz Ashaari is concerned, if he is destined to become Malaysia's leader one day, it will be through God's will, triggered by the *taqwa* of his followers.[22]

To Ustaz Ashaari, futuristic hadiths, on which his futuristic thought is based, are to be understood in the aspirational sense. Muslims are encouraged to aspire and exert themselves into realizing the qualities of figures touted to become history makers. It is not impossible that God grants them, due to their *taqwa* and efforts, the particular vocation which is open to Muslims. Even if it was proven in time that they are not the individuals mentioned in the hadiths, both human and systemic reforms effected by them can still be benefited from. But the pursuit of such aspirations has to be realistic. Since al-Mahdi's name and physical characteristics have been specified by hadiths, it is unwise for Muslims lacking those traits to bear Mahdist aspirations. It will be more realistic doctrinally to strive to become the youth of Bani Tamim whose traits and features have been shielded from public knowledge. Or rather, in line with Ustaz Ashaari's interpretations, they have been purposely kept open for aspiring takers to endeavor to achieve the post. An example often quoted by Ustaz Ashaari is the hadith relating the downfall of Byzantine Constantinople to "a good King, a good army and good people," which was only realized at the hands of the Ottoman ruler, Muhammad al-Fatih, popularly known in the West as "Mehmet the Conqueror," in 1453. In the more than 800 years between the conquest and the Prophet Muhammad's death, his Companions and succeeding generations never stopped trying to accomplish God's promise on Constantinople. The most illustrious Companion, who was martyred during his vain attempt to conquer Constantinople, was Abū Ayyūb al-Ansārī, whose fatal expedition was launched during the reign of the first Umayyad caliph, Mu'awiyah Abu Sufyan (d. 680).[23]

Therefore, while Ustaz Ashaari refrains from categorically making exclusive claims for his followers as the "chosen people" of the *ummah*, he does explicitly mention Darul Arqam's endeavor to realize the steps needed to qualify them as the *ikhwān* of the youth of Bani Tamim:

> We in Darul Arqam are striving to realize this promise. After striving for the resurgence in the East, we headed towards Khurasan in great numbers, just as Allah seized the area from the hands of the Communists. Khurasan is the place for the flapping of the black banner from the East where there is a man, al-Harith Harrath, as mentioned in the hadith. We want to be the first to meet him.[24]

Ustaz Ashaari earnestly espouses the theory of the reverse flow of Islamic resurgence: that the ultimate revival of the *ummah* will be generated from the periphery towards the Islamic heartlands of the Middle East. In Ustaz Ashaari's geographical map, the *ikhwān* from Southeast Asia will bring Islam to *asoibs* – followers of al-Mahdi, but lower in rank to the *ikhwān*, in Khurasan – an area interpreted as a long stretch of land encompassing most of Afghanistan and Uzbekistan, parts of Iran and Pakistan, and extending until the region of Yunnan in China. While the numbers of *ikhwān* reach a maximum of 500, *asoibs* may approach thousands in quantity. Not restricted to

Khurasan, *asoibs* may also be found in the East. Hence Southeast Asia and Khurasan function as the pulse and backbone respectively of the Islamic resurgence. The meeting between the youth of Bani Tamim and al-Harith Harrath – al-Mahdi's guide in his mission of returning Islam to Mecca, is regarded as portending an imminent coming of al-Mahdi. The widely publicized trips made by Darul Arqam to Uzbekistan and Yunnan in 1992–3 were part of exploratory expeditions into Khurasan in search of al-Harith Harrath and *asoibs*. In conjunction with the launching of its "Khurasan Operation," Darul Arqam inaugurated its International Center in Islamabad, Pakistan in January 1992. The scenario above has been detailed out:

> From this base, Darul Arqam concocts plans and strategies to explore Khurasan further, especially Uzbekistan, since a lot of hadiths on the period near the end of time are related to Uzbekistan. For instance, the hadiths on the fortunate land of *mā warāa un nahar*, *asoibs*, al-Harith Harrath, and the unfurling of the Black Banner, which signify the near coming of Imam Mahdi. *Mā warāa un nahar* – the land behind the river, according to the *ulama* is situated between Samarqand and Bukhara. More accurately, *mā warāa un nahar* is situated in Termez, a small town at the side of the Amu Darya river [in Uzbekistan]. . . . It is here that *asoibs* are being prepared. According to signs of hadith, *asoibs* in Uzbekistan will combine forces with Islamic strivers from the East especially, and also with Islamic activists from other parts of the world. Then they will move together to Syam [Greater Syria]. From there, they will proceed to Haramayn: the Forbidden Lands of Mecca and Medina. Imam Ashaari at-Tamimi is convinced that if the revival of Islam at the end of time can be portrayed as a human body, the East is the pulse (life) while Khurasan is the backbone. In other words, the East acts as the initiator and leader of the resurgence, and Khurasan becomes its supporter and prime auxiliary. The East–Khurasan combination, or specifically, the joining of forces between *asoibs* from the East under al-Mansur (the man of Bani Tamim) and the chosen *asoib* (leader of *asoibs*) from Khurasan, viz. Al-Harith Harrath. . . . [is] the closest sign of the advent of the supreme leader, Imam Mahdi. With the fall of Russia and the weakening of America, Islam is gradually on the rise. Each step of decline of the infidel system is accompanied by a step of rise of Islam. . . . happening especially in Malaysia. This is exuberating news to be relished by the East, Khurasan and the entire world. Now it is the East's turn to lead the promised revival. This is what Imam Ashaari at-Tamimi and Darul Arqam have been trying to prove.[25]

Needless to say, Ustaz Ashaari does openly aspire to become the youth of Bani Tamim, the precursor of al-Mahdi, and does encourage his followers, and Malay-Muslims in general, to accomplish the dignified status of the *ikhwān*, failing that, *asoibs*. In fact, he has taken action in what he understands would trigger events unleashing God's eschatological schedule which he calls "Allah's schedule for Muslim *ummah*": the title of a bilingual tract published in 1993 in conjunction with Darul Arqam's Silver Jubilee celebrations. The millenarian activity of establishing the youth of Bani Tamim as Malaysia's political leader and al-Mahdi as the leader of the *ummah* has been checked temporarily by the confinement of Ustaz Ashaari and state repression of his followers. As the "head" of the fifteenth Islamic century draws to a close, very little time is left for Ustaz Ashaari to realize his eschatological schedule. By Ustaz

Ashaari's own count, the "head" of a century, during which a *mujaddid* is promised, comprises a period of 25 years.[26]

The Southeast Asian Connection

Darul Arqam's influential presence in neighboring countries in Southeast Asia since embarking on its international era in the 1980s has been well documented.[27] Ustaz Ashaari's protracted sojourn abroad (1988–94) resulted in the expansion of Darul Arqam's influence to Central Asia, the Middle East, and Europe, particularly the United Kingdom and France. Large sections of Darul Arqam publications were increasingly devoted to colorful pieces of coverage of overseas visits by Darul Arqam leaders and their meetings with journalists, intellectuals, government officials, and political leaders from, among others, Thailand, Indonesia, the Philippines, Turkey, Jordan, China, and Uzbekistan. Sizable Darul Arqam communities developed in these countries, but everywhere, in line with Ustaz Ashaari's theory of Malay leadership of the *ummah*, leadership of the overseas bases and settlements remained in the hands of Malays, many of whom were students. Following among the non-Malay local populations was modest.

The heavily transnational orientation in Darul Arqam's map enabled Ustaz Ashaari to elaborate his political principles and global ambitions without restraint, reaching a climax in 1994, and ultimately prompting the Malaysian political establishment to demand his extradition and detention under the ISA. Notwithstanding his extensively transcontinental travels, Southeast Asia's pivotal position in Ustaz Ashaari's geopolitical thought and agenda was irreplaceable. Dividing the world into three zones, viz. the tropical areas such as Southeast Asia, the dry and rough areas such as the Middle East, and the four-season areas such as the West, he analyzed each zone in terms of its peoples' varied attitudes and cultures. Southeast Asians' gentleness, conditioned by the area's mild climate, made them receptive to truth even at a time when the Islamic empires had fallen. Ustaz Ashaari praised President Suharto of Indonesia for his latest tilt towards Islam, and interpreted such changes as indicative of his place in "Allah's Schedule" as the forerunner to *Ratu Adil* (Just Prince), the popular Indonesian equivalent of al-Mahdi.[28]

As a measure of its success in Southeast Asian neighboring countries, the repression of Darul Arqam was lamented by the countries' grassroots population, especially those who had benefited from its investments and social work. Cordial relations were cemented through mixed marriages between Darul Arqam's Malaysian and non-Malaysian nationals. At the national level, only the Brunei government followed the Malaysian government's line of declaring Darul Arqam an illegal entity. In Indonesia and Thailand, Ustaz Ashaari's followers freely continue their business and educational activities. Their publications continue to propagate messianic messages from Ustaz Ashaari, whose version of "Allah's Schedule" remains the central theme in his overseas followers' transnational priorities. The coverage by these foreign-based publications shows that Ustaz Ashaari's political clout and stature overseas is significant. For example, Jakarta-based *Kebenaran* revealed the meeting between Abdurrahman Wahid and Ustaz Ashaari in the latter's home in Bandar Country Homes, Rawang, during which Abdurrahman consulted Ustaz Ashaari on the prudence of his candidacy in the 1999 Indonesian presidential election. It is from Rufaqa' Indonesia, whose economic success has been phenomenal, that books pushing through Ustaz Ashaari's messianic thought are being produced and distributed to Malaysia.[29]

In Labuan, Ustaz Ashaari continues to receive visitors from all walks of life and nationalities. Foreign scholars have included Dr. Abdussalam Harras from Morocco (May 2002), Shaykh Abdul Ghafur from Uzbekistan (October 2002) and Dr. Imaduddin Abdurrahim, an Indonesian modernist (April 2003). The author's examination of notes taken from meetings between Ustaz Ashaari and his business directors reveal that the future roles of Southeast Asia in general and of Malaysia in particular remain important in his messianic thought. For example, among Rufaqa' members, the meeting between Ustaz Ashaari Muhammad and Shaykh Abdul Ghafur in Labuan has been touted as the historic encounter between the youth of Bani Tamim and al-Harith Harrath, signifying al Mahdi's imminence.

Although messianism does not surpass *taqwa* as the priority in Ustaz Ashaari's struggle, it bolsters his followers' conviction, especially when contemporary events are linked to his prognostications. These include predictions of Anwar Ibrahim's entry into the ruling party and government, of the Soviet Union's downfall, of the decline of Khomeini's influence in Iran after 10 years, and of the persistence of the Iraq–US war. Prior to Anwar Ibrahim's shocking dismissal as Deputy Prime Minister in 1998, Ustaz Ashaari had told Anwar that he would fail in his quest to become Prime Minister. As to the recent global scenario, the terrorist threat to the USA's own soil, as exemplified by the deadly attacks on the World Trade Center and Pentagon on September 11, 2001, has been taken to verify Ustaz Ashaari's prediction that "America would be weakened from within." However, Dr. Mahathir's resignation as Prime Minister and replacement by Abdullah Ahmad Badawi in 2003 severely tested Ustaz Ashaari's followers' conviction, as Ustaz Ashaari was known to have held the belief that Ghafar Baba, the once Deputy Prime Minister (1987–93), would eventually become Prime Minister amidst internal political turmoil. [30]

Conclusion

Ustaz Ashaari's thought represents a unique blend of Sufi traditionalism and progressive reformism characteristic of modernist Islamic thought. While devoted to the practice of *Aurad Muhammadiah*, Ustaz Ashaari's Sufism was not a separate discipline to be pursued for innate spiritual values and mystical experiences. Instead, Sufism is the vehicle to transform individual selves towards perfection as members of the *ummah* actively implementing Islam as a comprehensive way of life. Ustaz Ashaari's messianism rejects a complacent attitude towards the future, as had been feared by the modernists, but rather encourages economic activism as a preparation for the better times ahead promised by the advent of a *mujaddid*. Ustaz Ashaari's educational background and doctrinal standpoints are avowedly traditionalist, yet his views and actions in implementing them hardly subscribe to the traditionalist "closing of the door of *ijtihād*" doctrine. If we take two Indonesian organizations, *Muhammadiyyah* and

Nahdlatul Ulama (NU), as extreme and opposing poles in a spectrum of Southeast Asian Islamic thought, Ustaz Ashaari lies somewhere in the middle. He is neither a modernist in the manner of *Muhammadiyyah*, nor a traditionalist in the style of NU. But veering closer towards traditionalism, he is best described as a neo-traditionalist, just as Abdurrahman Wahid of NU has been called a neo-modernist.[31] The cordial, if brief, meeting between Abdurrahman and Ustaz Ashaari in 1999, referred to above, adds substance to the existence of a confluence of ideas in contemporary Southeast Asian Islamic thought. The coming together of traditionalism and modernism may never have been closer than in the most recent times.

Among Malaysian Islamic thinkers, Ustaz Ashaari distinguishes himself as being the most futuristic, in a peculiarly mostly Malaysian-oriented manner. Admittedly, futuristic thought has been part of the cultures of nations which strive to be progressive. It is in the spirit of Islam to be forward-looking, as shown by the Qur'an: "The Romans have been defeated, in a land close by, but they, (even) after (this) defeat of theirs, will soon be victorious. . . ." (Ar Rūm 30: 2–3). This spirit is a far cry from the romanticism that has developed in Muslim reflections on the history of the *ummah*, contributing to its protracted decline. While this fact is accepted by Islamic scholars, hardly any have come forward with a critically futuristic perspective of the course of the *ummah*. Ustaz Ashaari arguably offers such a perspective.

Notwithstanding the political controversy it has aroused, Ustaz Ashaari's futuristic thought should have been valued as an immense intellectual contribution to Islamic thought in general, and to Islamic eschatology in particular. Based on the huge body of eschatological hadiths, Ustaz Ashaari offers fresh interpretations which, in legal matters, would have amounted to the practice of *ijtihād*. Very different from philosophers whose scholarly theories are left to successive generations to interpret and realize, Ustaz Ashaari himself mobilizes people towards the accomplishment of his messianic theories. In doing this, he is able to make sure that the principles of his thought are adhered to without misrepresentation. His followers have been taught to strive for the qualities as mentioned in the hadith: "There will always be a ta'ifah (community) from amongst my *ummah*, that will practice the way of truth, they will not be destroyed by their detractors, until the Day of Judgment."[32] They are utterly convinced that theirs is the path of God. Combined together, futuristic thought and action by convinced devotees become potentially subversive, and find ready enemies within the existing political establishment.

Ironically, since Ustaz Ashaari's prolonged detention, scholars have come forward with ideas similar to Ustaz Ashaari's theory of "Malay leadership of the *ummah*." For example, Hilmy Bakar Almascaty, an Indonesian formerly at Malaysia's International Islamic University (IIUM), came up in 1994 with the book *The Malay Ummah: The New World Power of the Twenty-First Century* (Malay), which asserted the potential of Malay-Muslims and outlined the planning required of them to lead the Islamic resurgence in the coming millennium. Professor Hashim Musa of the University of Malaya, in a *Berita Harian* (April 24, 2001) article, "Malays Should Bear the Duty of Preserving Islamic Civilization" (Malay), argued: "Malay-Muslims, almost half a billion in number, form the largest Muslim group in the East. In the history of Islamic civilization, the center constantly changes, from Arabia to Turkey, North Africa, Spain and Central Asia. Now signs show that the center has begun to shift to the East. Are we, the Malay-Muslims, as the biggest Muslim group in the East, prepared to bear the responsibility and trust in maintaining and contributing towards the rebuilding of an Islamic civilization of global standard in this third millennium?" Similar remarks concluded his paper, "The Empowerment of Malay Civilization as the Basis for Constructing a Malaysian Civilization" (Malay), presented at the Second International Malay Studies Conference in Beijing, China, in October 2002.

Within the *ummah*, the feasibility of Ustaz Ashaari's theory can be deducted from the following recognition of Southeast Asian Muslims by Muhammad Nejatullah Siddiqi, an eminent Saudi Arabian-based economist:

> The Muslims of South East Asia – of Malaysia, Indonesia, and possibly the Muslim minorities in resurgent China – are better equipped to lead the process of regeneration than the rest of the Muslim world. They are uncommitted to any powers. They are unconstrained by promises to keep and debts to repay. Their approach to Islam is simple and elementary – something which besides its disadvantages also keeps them away from the strangulating hold of a scholarship unfit to lead in the modern world. They can learn. Many others can hardly so. And most important of all, they are already on the road to economic prosper-

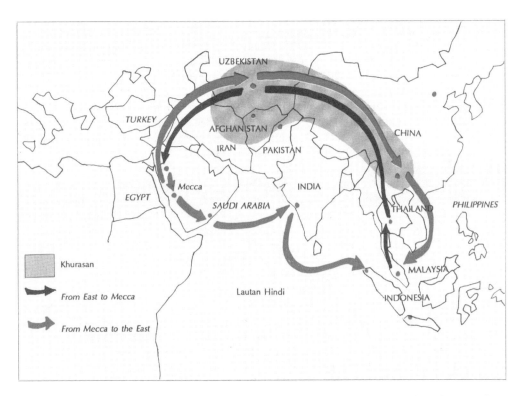

Figure 11.1   The reverse flow of Islamic Revival (Source: Darul Arqam, *25 Years of Darul Arqam: The Struggle of Abuya Syeikh Imam Ashaari Muhammad At Tamimi* (Kuala Lumpur: Penerbitan Abuya, 1993), 176.)

ity, security and strength – something which may elude other Muslim countries for a long time to come.[33]

Appendix

Figure 11.1 describes Ustaz Ashaari Muhammad's theory of the reverse flow of Islamic resurgence. The shaded area is Khurasan. The arrows pointing rightwards were the paths by which Islam reached Malaysia. The arrows pointing leftwards are the routes through which Islam will return to its birthplace, Mecca.

Notes

1. For details on Darul Arqam's material achievements, see Darul Arqam, *25 Years of Darul Arqam: The Struggle of Abuya Syeikh Imam Ashaari Muhammad at Tamimi* (Kuala Lumpur: Penerbitan Abuya, 1993), chapter 13; Muhammad Syukri Salleh, "An Ethical Approach to Development: The Arqam Philosophy and Achievements," *Humanomics*, 10/1, 1994, 25–60; "Allah's Bounty: Al-Arqam sect draws strength from business empire," *Far Eastern Economic Review*, September 1, 1994.
2. Rufaqa' Corporation Sdn. Bhd. (profile), Rawang, n.d.; "Former Al-Arqam redefines itself," *New Sunday Times*, April 30, 2000; "Banned Al-Arqam cult thriving under business umbrella," *Straits Times*, February 9, 2002; Muhammad Syukri Salleh, "The Businesses of Islamic Movements in Malaysia" (Malay), *Pemikir*, 31, 2003, 142–8.
3. Ustaz Ashaari's enforced expulsion to Labuan made headline news in *Berita Harian*, February 7, 2002. On his success in Labuan, see: "Ashaari expands influence in Labuan" (Malay), *Buletin Utama*, April 21–24, 2002; "Residents plead that Asa'ari's placing be revised" (Malay), *Berita Harian*, September 5, 2002; "Al-Arqam followers' lifestyles need to be monitored" (Malay), *Berita Harian*, November 28, 2002; "What is lost by Asyaari's prosperity?" (Malay), http://www.harakahdaily.net/print.php?sid=3510.
4. For related issues, see Ahmad Fauzi Abdul Hamid, "Political Dimensions of Religious Conflict in Malaysia: State Response to an Islamic Movement," *Indonesia and the Malay World* 28/80, 2000, 32–65; Ahmad Fauzi Abdul Hamid, "Sufi Undercurrents in Islamic Revivalism: Traditional, Post-Traditional and Modern Images of Islamic Activism in Malaysia – Part 2," *The Islamic Quarterly* LXV/3, 2001, 177–98; Ahmad Fauzi Abdul Hamid, "Diverse Approaches to Rural Development in Malaysia: The FELDA and Darul Arqam Land Settlement Regimes," *Islamic Culture*, LXXV/2, 2001, 57–92.
5. "Millenarianism" refers to the belief in an awaited utopia on earth founded upon the predicted coming of a messiah. In the Christian context, "millenarianism" refers to the belief in the 1000 years when Christ will reign on earth, as foretold in the Book of Revelation. See Mohamed Yusoff Ismail, "The Mahdist Phenomenon is Universal'" (Malay), *Utusan Malaysia*, July 21, 2000; Justus M. van der Kroef, "The Messiah in Indonesia and Melanesia," *The Scientific Monthly*, 75, 1952, 161–5; Vittorio Lanternari, *The Religions of the Oppressed: A Study of Modern Messianic Cults* (New York: Alfred A.Knopf, 1963); and Ed Dobson and Ed Hindson, "Apocalypse Now? What Fundamentalists Believe About the End of the World," *Policy Review*, 38, 1986, 16–22. For reports on Doomsday cults, see "Inside the Cult of Death," *Time*, April 7, 1997, and "Nostradamus Predicted that the World Would

End this Summer: Why are so Many Japanese Taking him Seriously," *Time*, July 5, 1999.

6. Literally, "al-Mahdi" means "the rightly guided one" and is also referred to as *Al-Mahdi al-Muntazar*, i.e. the Expected Mahdi. See Wilfred Madelung, "Al-Mahdi," in Charles E. Bosworth *et al.*, eds., *The Encyclopaedia of Islam*, vol. V (Leiden: E.J. Brill), 1230–8; and Zeki Saritoprak, "The Mahdi Tradition in Islam: A Social-Cognitive Approach," *Islamic Studies*, 41/4, 2002, 651. For hadiths on al-Mahdi, see Ibn Kathir, *The Signs Before the Day of Judgement* (London: Dar Al Taqwa, 1991), chapter 6; Abdullah ibn As-Siddiq, *Jesus, Al Mahdi and the Anti-Christ* (New York: As-Siddiquyah Publishers, 1985); and Amin Muhammad Jamaluddin, *The Armageddon War and the Advent of the Mahdi* (Malay) (Kuala Lumpur: Pustaka Syuhada, 2001), chapter 3.

7. The Dajjal represents the Islamic version of the Antichrist: the epitome of evil who will tyrannically rule the world for 40 days before being slain by Jesus Christ. Unlike Christians, Muslims have never believed that Jesus was crucified. Instead, he was said to have been raised by God to the heavens at the same time that Judas, Jesus' betrayer, was made to assume Jesus' physical characteristics and ultimately died on the cross. The Dajjal will exert influence over the whole world, causing pandemonium for 40 days, entering every city except Mecca and Medina, tempting the world's population to follow the false religion by performing miracles akin to magic, and leading the Jews into war against al-Mahdi. During this fifth of al-Mahdi's wars, Jesus Christ will descend onto earth, join al-Mahdi in battle and eventually kill the Dajjal. Death of the Dajjal will be the apogee of al-Mahdi's feat. After al-Mahdi's seven wars, Gog and Magog appear. Gog and Magog are two Turkic tribes currently restrained behind a barrier built by Zulqarnain, the popular Islamic equivalent of Alexander the Great. Upon collapse of the barrier, Gog and Magog will disperse, spread corruption, destroy plants, and commit atrocities. God, in response to prayers said by Jesus, kills them by sending a kind of worm in the napes of their necks. For a chronicle of these eschatological events, see As-Siddiq, op. cit., chapter 3; Ibn Kathir, op. cit., 41ff; and Jamaluddin, op. cit., chapter 4, 184–206.

8. Sayyid Abul A'a Maududi, *A Short History of the Revivalist Movement in Islam* (Lahore: Islamic Publications, fifth edition, 1981), 33–4; Yohanan Friedmann, *Prophecy Continuous: Aspects of Ahmadi Religious Thought and its Medieval Background* (Berkeley: University of California Press, 1989), chapter 4.

9. Derek Hopwood, "A Pattern of Revival Movements in Islam?," *Islamic Quarterly*, 15/4, 1971, 151. Beliefs concerning the Expected Mahdi never became an essential part of the Sunni creed, unlike in the Shi'ite sect, whose historiography contains strong arguments and beliefs pertaining to various aspects of al-Mahdi. The subject matter on al-Mahdi is absent from the two most authentic hadith collections of Bukhari (d. 870) and Muslim (d. 875), such that medieval systematic theologians scrupulously avoided discussion on al-Mahdi. See H.A.R. Gibb and J.H. Kramers, *Shorter Encyclopaedia of Islam* (Leiden: E.J. Brill, 1974), 310–11; Maududi, op. cit., 45–51; Madelung, op. cit., 1231, 1235; K.H. Sirajuddin Abbas, *The Sunni Creed* (Malay) (Kota Bharu: Pustaka Aman Press, sixth edition, 1991), 128; Saritoprak, op. cit., 673–4.

10. On Sufi conceptions of al-Mahdi, see Muhammad Labib Ahmad, *Who is Imam Mahdi?* (Malay) (Singapore: Pustaka Nasional, 1980), 29–31; and Saritoprak, op. cit., 659–60. For accounts of anti-colonial movements in peripheral Muslim lands, see Justus M. van der Kroef, "Javanese Messianic Expectations: Their Origin and Cultural Context," *Comparative Studies in Society and History*, 1, 1959, 309; Lanternari, op. cit., 213–14; Edward Mortimer, *Faith and Power: The Politics of Islam* (London: Faber and Faber, 1982), 73–9. On the arbitrary division of Muslim lands into a center and periphery, see Ahmad Fauzi Abdul Hamid,

"Islamic Resurgence: An Overview of Causal Factors, A Review of 'Ummahtic' Linkages,"
IKIM Journal, 9/1, 2001, 30–8.

11. Al-Maududi, op. cit., 43–4, 147–9; Muhammad Labib Ahmad, op. cit., 32–45.

12. *Aurad Muhammadiah* refers to a *tariqah* (Sufi order) founded in Mecca in the early twenti-
eth century by Shaykh Muhammad Abdullah Al-Suhaimi (b. 1259 AH), a scholar of
Javanese-Arabic descent who moved to Singapore and eventually settled down in Kelang,
Malaya. See Mohd Taha Suhaimi, *The History of Syeikh Muhammad Suhaimi's Life* (Malay)
(Singapore: Peripensis, 1990). *Tariqah* involves systematic chanting of *dhikr* (remembrances
of God) as practiced by Sufis: practitioners of *tasawwuf*, i.e. the branch of knowledge in
Islam enjoining the purification of the soul (*tazkiyah al-nafs*) in attaining the true meaning
of God and the self. See Ashaari Muhammad, *Aurad Muhammadiah: The Conviction of Darul
Arqam* (Malay) (Kuala Lumpur: Penerangan Al-Arqam, 1986), 10.

13. BAHEIS, *An Explanation to the book "Aurad Muhammadiah: The Conviction of Darul Arqam"*
(Malay) (Kuala Lumpur, 1986); BAHEIS, *The Deviation of Darul Arqam's Theology* (Malay)
(Kuala Lumpur, 1993); Ashaari Muhammad 1986, op. cit.; Ashaari Muhammad, *Be
Careful in Making Allegations* (Malay), (Kuala Lumpur: Penerangan Al-Arqam, 1989); *Berita
Harian*, July 16, 1994; *The Star*, August 6, 1994.

14. Sufis regard *yaqazah* with the late Prophet Muhammad as a *karamah* (miracle) accorded to
the *awliya'* (saints) (Ashaari Muhammad 1986, op.cit., chapter 6). In the *Aurad Muhammadiah*, the practitioner acknowledges, after the conventional *kalimah shahadah*, the additional figures of the righteous caliphs viz. Abu Bakr (d. 635), Umar (d. 644), Uthman (d.
656), and Ali (d. 661), and of the future al-Mahdi (ibid., chapter 9). *Tawassul* refers to the
practice of invoking intermediaries, usually saints, when making *do'a* (supplication) to God.
The issue of the permissibility of *tawassul* has long been a source of contention between
Islamic traditionalists, who allow it, and Islamic modernists, who forbid it; see Sirajuddin
Abbas, op. cit., 284–301, 316–26. *Tahlil* refers to religious chantings that testify that Allah
is the One and Only God. The *tahlil* of *Aurad Muhammadiah* refers to specific chantings
recited rhythmically in congregation by practitioners of the *Aurad Muhammadiah* on Thursday and Sunday nights, and include the controversial phrases: "O Saints of God, do listen,
help us for the sake of God, do listen" (Ashaari Muhammad 1986, op. cit., 119–27,
143–51).

15. Ashaari Muhammad, *Who is the Mujaddid of the Fifteenth Century?* (Malay) (Kuala Lumpur:
Penerangan Al-Arqam, 1987), 648–54; Ashaari Muhammad, *My Contemplations* (Malay)
(Kuala Lumpur: Penerangan Al-Arqam, 1988), 257.

16. Mohd. Taha Suhaimi, op. cit., 67, Ashaari Muhammad 1986, op. cit., 178; Ashaari
Muhammad 1989, op. cit., 48–9, 84.

17. Ashaari Muhammad 1986, op. cit., 179–80; Ashaari Muhammad 1989, op. cit., 50–1.
The People of the Cave refer to seven unitarian Christian youths who fled from the persecution of the Roman Emperor Decius (reigned 249–51 AD), ending up in a cave in Asia
Minor where they were put to sleep for 309 years. Their story is told in the Qur'an (Al-Kahf
18: 9–26). In a hadith narrated by Ibnu Abbas, the People of the Cave are said to be the
assistants of al-Mahdi, such that they must now be in occultation waiting for the realization of their eschatological role. On the contrasting Twelver Shi'ite view of al-Mahdi's
occultation, see Sirajuddin Abbas, op. cit. 127–8.

18. On Tamim al-Dari's encounter with the Dajjal, see Ibn Kathir, op. cit., 48–51, and David J.
Halperin, "The Ibn Sayyad Traditions and the Legend of Al-Dajjal," *Journal of the American
Oriental Society*, 96, 1976, 223. On Shaykh Hasan al-Iraqi's encounter with al-Mahdi, see
Ashaari Muhammad 1986, op. cit., 171–3; and Madelung, op. cit., 1236–37.

19. Ahmad Fauzi Abdul Hamid, *The Malaysian State of the Youth of Bani Tamim: Secrets of the Glorious Ummah* (Malay) (Kuala Lumpur: Abuku Hebat, 1999), 115; Ashaari Muhammad, *Exploring the Islamic Administrative System* (Malay) (Kuala Lumpur: Penerbitan Hikmah, 1993), 188, 200.

20. The previous two quotations are from Ashaari Muhammad, *Allah's Schedule for the Muslim Ummah* (Kuala Lumpur: Bahagian Pengeluaran Minda Syeikhul Arqam, 1993), 38–40.

21. Ibid., 41–3; Darul Arqam, *Message from the East*, 18–20; Ahmad Fauzi Abdul Hamid, *The Malaysian State of the Youth of Bani Tamim*, 124–6. In support, often quoted is the hadith, "A people will come out of the East who will pave the way for the Mahdi" (Ibn Kathir, op. cit., 22).

22. Ashaari Muhammad, *The Implementation of Hudud Law in Society* (Malay) (Kuala Lumpur: Penerbitan Hikmah, 1992), 88–97; Ahmad Fauzi Abdul Hamid, *The Malaysian State of the Youth of Bani Tamim*, chapter 4.

23. Ashaari Muhammad, *Thoughts to Change Attitudes* (Malay) (Kuala Lumpur: Penerangan Al-Arqam, 1990), 249–55; Ashaari Muhammad, *Allah's Schedule*, 30–1; Ashaari Muhammad, *President Soeharto Follows the Schedule of Allah* (Malay) (Kuala Lumpur: Penerbitan Abuya, 1993), 11–12.

24. Ashaari Muhammad, *Allah's Schedule*, 42–3; cf. Ahmad Fauzi Abdul Hamid, "The Malay-Islamic World in the Thought of Ustaz Ashaari Muhammad," in Abdullah Hassan, ed., *Proceedings of The Second International Malay Studies Conference, Volume 1* (Malay) (Kuala Lumpur: DBP, 2002), 10–12.

25. Darul Arqam, *25 Years of Darul Arqam*, 175–7. Overall, Ustaz Ashaari's theory concurs with the hadith, "Islam will return to its place of origin like a snake returning to its hole," as quoted in Darul Arqam 1992, op. cit., 4.

26. Ashaari Muhammad 1987, op. cit., xiv, 43.

27. Darul Arqam, *Al-Arqam in the International Media* (Malay) (Kuala Lumpur: Penerangan Al-Arqam, 1989). For details on Darul Arqam's expenditure, human capital, and assets in Southeast Asia, see Darul Arqam, *25 Years of Darul Arqam*, 184, 186, 198; and Muhammad Syukri Salleh 1994, op. cit., 36, 44–5, 48–50.

28. Ashaari Muhammad, *Strides of the Struggle* (Malay) (Kuala Lumpur: Jabatan Syeikhul Arqam, 1991), chapter 12; Ashaari Muhammad, *Presiden Soeharto Follows Allah's Schedule*.

29. On the Ustaz Ashaari-Abdurrahman Wahid meeting, see *Kebenaran*, 7/1 (1999), quoting from the magazines *Tempo*, October 24, 1999, and *DR*, 11/XXXI/25, October 1999. For Rufaqa' Indonesia's success stories, see the five-page report in the Jakarta-based magazine, *Gatra*, 2–3/10, December 2003. Two Indonesian books promoting Ustaz Ashaari's thought are Abu Muhammad Atta', *The Youth of Bani Tamim: The Precursor of Imam Al-Mahdi* (Malay-Indonesian) (Jakarta: Penerbit Giliran Timur, 1998) and Abdurrahman R.Effendi and Gina Puspita, *Abuya Syeikh Imam Ashaari Muhammad At Tamimi: Is He the Mujaddid of This Century?* (Malay-Indonesian) (Jakarta: Penerbit Giliran Timur, 2003).

30. Ustaz Ashaari believes that Ghafar Baba has a significant role to play in "Allah's Schedule". See Ahmad Fauzi Abdul Hamid, "Reforming PAS?," *Aliran Monthly* 23/6, 2003, 13. On the USA's weakening from within, see Ahmad Fauzi Abdul Hamid 2002, op. cit., 13. On Ustaz Ashaari's predictions pertaining to Anwar Ibrahim, see Shuib Sulaiman, *PM Dr. Mahathir on the Brink of Downfall* (Malay) (n.p.: Merbok Enterprise, 1994), 40, 70, 84–92; and Zabidi Mohamed, *Tersungkur di Pintu "Syurga": The Untold Truth and Inside Story of Al-Arqam and I.S.A. (Detention Without Trial)* (Kuala Lumpur: Zabidi Publication, 1998), 151.

31.   Greg Barton, "Neo-Modernism: A Vital Synthesis of Traditionalist and Modernist Islamic Thought in Indonesia," *Studia Islamika* 2/3, 1995, 1–75; Greg Barton, "Indonesia's Nurcholish Madjid and Abdurrahman Wahid as Intellectual *ulama*: The Meeting of Islamic Traditionalism and Modernism in neo-Modernist Thought," *Islam and Christian-Muslim Relations* 8/3, 1997, 323–50.

32.   Quoted in Ashaari Muhammad 1987, op. cit., 3; and Ashaari Muhammad, *Allah's Schedule*, 31; cf. Saritoprak, op. cit., 659.

33.   Muhammad Nejatullah Siddiqi, "Towards Regeneration: Shifting Priorities in Islamic Movements," *Encounters: Journal of Inter-Cultural Perspectives* 1/2, 1995, 24.

CHAPTER 12

Religion, Society, and Culture in Malik Bennabi's Thought

Mohamed El-Tahir El-Mesawi

Introduction

This chapter attempts to provide a condensed account of the philosophical and socio-logical thought of the twentieth-century eminent Algerian thinker Malik Bennabi (1905–73). It focuses on his views pertaining to religion, society, and culture. The present chapter consists of three main sections that are prefaced with a short bio-graphical sketch outlining the major stages of Bennabi's life and career.

As will become clear in the pages that follow, Bennabi's works in general and his *The Qur'anic Phenomenon* in particular stand out as one of the most well-informed intellec-tual responses to, and engagement with, modern Western philosophical and scientific thought. A sense of the unity of human history, a critical and profound philosophical bent of mind, and a sharp awareness of the cross-cultural and intellectual currents at work in the West and the Muslim world: these are major traits of his treatment of various theological, moral, social, and cultural issues. These features are consolidated and given full scope by what can be seen as a visionary passion driving toward tran-scending the prevailing thought categories, not through shallow and haughty ideo-logical attitude, but through a conscious and creative intellectual commitment to analysis and systematic theorizing. This, it seems, is what enabled Bennabi to boldly question some of the fundamental intellectual premises of modern Western culture and civilization and to realize some of their grave epistemological and moral consequences, while at the same time appreciating the achievements and the benefits it has brought to mankind.

Malik Bennabi: A Biographical Sketch

Without indulging in any critical considerations as to the insufficiency or non-verifiability of Bennabi's autobiography,[1] there seems to be a general agreement between those who have written about him on the major events and stages of his life and career. In this sketch we shall provide those major events and stages without any elaboration.

- 1905: Born in January in Constantine, Malik Bennabi belonged to a family of established religious tradition. He received his primary Qur'anic and French schooling at the small city of Tébessa (on the Tunisian–Algerian border) where his father worked as an officer in the Islamic judiciary.
- 1921–5: Bennabi completed his secondary studies at the madrasah or Lycée Franco-Arabe of Constantine. During this period he came into contact with the nascent reformist current launched by Shaykh 'Abd al-Hamid ibn Bādis.
- 1925: First attempt to pursue his graduate studies in France, unsuccessful due to lack of financial means.
- 1927: Following many attempts to find a job, Bennabi was finally appointed as assistant officer to the *sharī'ah* court of Aflou in the far western province of Oran.
- 1928: He was transferred to the court of Chelghoum Laid (in the eastern region of the country) from which he resigned following a dispute with a French clerk of the civil court of the small town.
- 1929: Bennabi embarked on an unsuccessful business enterprise.
- 1930: The centenary of French occupation of Algeria. With his father's financial support, Bennabi went to Paris to continue his studies. Following a politically motivated rejection of his application to join the Institut des Langues Orientales de Paris, he joined a polytechnic school from which he graduated as an electrical engineer in 1935.
- 1931: He joined the *Association des Jeunes Chrétiens*, a Christian youth society in search of spirituality and pious conduct. On the platform of this society, he gave his first public talk under the title "Pourquoi somes-nous musulmans?" (Why are we Muslims?) In the same year, he became the vice-president of the Muslim Students Association of North Africa. Under the pressure of difficult financial conditions as a result of unemployment and his family's worsening economic situation, Bennabi made unsuccessful attempts to migrate to the Hejaz, Egypt and Albania.
- 1938: An old friend from Tébessa put him in contact with an association of immigrant Algerian workers at the city of Marseille looking for a person who could conduct literacy tuition for them. Bennabi became the director of the Centre Culturel du Congrès Musulman Algérien founded by the Association. The success of the center attracted the attention of the French authorities, which soon closed it down after a few months of intense activity.
- 1940: Following a call for competitive examination by the Japanese embassy in Paris, Bennabi submitted to the latter a study on Islam and Japan.
- Bennabi's life conditions worsened due to World War Two and the total breakdown of relations between Algeria and France after November 1942. He was compelled to accept a job in Germany. There he managed to write his first and seminal book *Le Phénomène Coranique* (*The Qur'anic Phenomenon*) – the manu-

script was subsequently destroyed during an air raid. Rewritten from memory, the book was first published in 1946 in Algiers.

- After the liberation of France and as a result of a cabal mounted by the mayor of Dreus where he was living, Bennabi and his wife, a French convert to Islam, were put under police custody.
- From 1946 Bennabi started his unbroken career as a writer.
- 1947: He published his only novel *Lebbeik* depicting the spiritual and geographical journey of a poor Algerian pilgrim to Mecca and Medina.
- 1948: Publication of his controversial *Les Conditions de la Renaissance* (*The Conditions of Renaissance*).
- 1949–55: Bennabi committed himself to a sustained contribution to the major Muslim press in Algeria, especially *La République Algérienne* (of the Democratic Union led by Ferhat Abbas) and *Le Jeune Musulman* (of the Ulama Association led by Shaykh Muhammad Bashir al-Ibrahimi).
- 1954: His fourth major book *La Vocation de l'Islam* was published in Paris by the renowned Editions du Seuil.
- 1956: Bennabi was invited to India to present his book *L'Afro-Asiatisme* in which he set out the theoretical and cultural foundations of the non-alignment movement whose first seeds were sown during the Bandung Conference in 1955. He left France illegally and ended up in Cairo where he decided to settle down.
- On September 1, 1956 he requested the political leadership of the Algerian National Liberation Front (FLN) in Cairo to be employed as military male nurse with the fighting units of the National Liberation Army (ALN) inside Algeria so that he could write the internal history of the revolution. He received no reply to his request.
- June 1957: Bennabi published in Arabic, French, and German a booklet under the title *SOS Algeria* in which he denounced the atrocities and genocide committed by the French army against the Algerian people. He then continued to promote the Algerian cause by his own means.
- 1957–62: Bennabi organized a series of informal seminars of ideological edification for Muslim students in Cairo. The publication of the French and Arabic versions of his book *L'Afro-Asiatisme* was made possible thanks to a sponsorship by the Egyptian government. During this period, he traveled regularly to Syria and Lebanon to deliver public talks and meet with intellectuals and thinkers. Besides the translation into Arabic of his earlier books, Bennabi's intellectual activity at this stage resulted in a number of important books, such as *Milād Mujtamaʿ* (*On the Origins of Human Society*), *Fikrat Commonwealth Islāmi* (*The Idea of an Islamic Commonwealth*) and *al-Sirāʿ al-Fikri fi'l-Bilād al-Mustaʿmarah* (*The Ideological Struggle in the Colonized Countries*).
- 1963: After Algeria's independence he returned home where he was assigned by President Ahmad Ben Bella to establish a center for cultural orientation. Weary of the bureaucratic routine that delayed the approval of the project, Bennabi launched from his home a regular intellectual forum where he focused on the issues of culture and civilization.

- 1964: Appointed as Director of Higher Education. Meanwhile he continued his intellectual activity and contributed regularly to the local press, especially the French journal *Révolution Africaine* in which he wrote almost weekly.
- 1968–70: After resigning from his official post, Bennabi devoted himself to seminars and conferences both at home and abroad. During this period, he founded the annual Conference on Islamic Thought that lasted up to the 1980s.
- At this stage of his intellectual career, Bennabi published a number of other important books. They include, among others, his two-volume memoirs, *Le Problème des idées dans le monde musulman*, *al-Muslim Fi 'Alam al-Iqtiāād*, *Perspectives Algeriennes*, *L'Islam et la démocracie*, *l'Oeuvre des Orientalistes*, etc.
- October 31, 1973: After a tour that took him in 1971 and 1972 to a number of places from Makkah to Damascus and Beirut where he delivered talks about "the Muslim's role in the last third of the twentieth century", Bennabi breathed his last in Algiers where he was buried.

Modernity and Beyond

One major feature of the forces that unleashed the phenomenon of modernity was those forces' antagonism to tradition in all its forms. Tradition was mainly identified with religion. This meant that an utterly uncompromising crusade had to be waged against religion and the church – its formal and institutional embodiment – so that modernity's program to *de-traditionalize* society and culture could be implemented. Regardless of the multiple factors that were in play and that finally shaped the historical destiny and cultural character of Europe from the seventeenth to the twentieth century, reason and science emerged as the crowned twins with whom ultimate authority should rest. The reason that was now claiming universality for its principles and dictates was one whose *bêtes noires* – tradition, authority, emotion, example, etc. – had to be confronted and fiercely combated.[2] As for science, it found its model in physics as philosophically conceptualized by Descartes and mathematically formulated by Newton in terms of his clock-like, self-sufficient universe.

Accordingly, beliefs and values could only be sanctioned if they pass the test of reason and science. Reality and truth are only what can be vindicated by the canons of reason and measured by the yardstick of science. This is all well and fine, but it is not the actual problem. Indeed, throughout its age-long experience mankind has always resorted to reason and science, no matter how both reason and science might have been conceived in different civilizations and by different peoples. Humans throughout their long history have done so in order to vindicate their beliefs and values, to understand their position in the world, to comprehend reality and truth, to regulate the affairs of their life, and to deal with nature and the different realms of existence.

What has really characterized reason and science within the context of Western modernity and constituted their problem at the same time, is their reductionist secular and materialistic orientation. Driven by a desire to free values from the parochialism that allegedly surrounded them in so-called pre-modern societies and cultures, the process of rationalization resulted in the deconsecration of values and desacralization of life. Due to a strong drive to demystify and control nature and attain certainty in knowing it, science ended up limiting nature to physical phenomena and equating the latter with the quantifiable that can and must ultimately be subsumed under precise mathematical equations.

Thus, reason, with its universal canons and ontological principles as advocated by early philosophical theorists of modernity such as Descartes, was progressively receding in favor of a conception of human rationality in which it was narrowly identified with science. The narrowing of human rationality and reason was based on "the enormous metaphysical assumption that the reality to which science has access is the whole of reality." This means that human beings "have no other source of knowledge nor any other means of reasoning." A doctrine or ideology of scientism thus emerged whose first victim was universal reason itself. Likewise, human rationality had to be "subordinated to contemporary science whatever it may happen to be saying." It followed from this that philosophy and rationality became "the handmaiden of science rather than its rational underpinning." This, indeed, was a major development of modernity towards reductionism in human knowledge and vision of the world. This reductionism sought to bring "everything down to the level of physical explanation."[3] By reducing rationality from a holistic outlook to a physicalist conception of the world and reality and by making reason a mere instrument of science as patterned after physics, modernity left the door wide open to relativism in the various aspects of thought and life.

Perhaps one of the most devastating outcomes of these developments can be seen in the loss of meaning that has pervaded almost all aspects of human life. Even physical objects, which in the beginning constituted the subject of study for the natural sciences, have been torn asunder and no more constitute an objective reality. This has been further consolidated and given more philosophical grounding by revolutionary developments in the physical and natural sciences. Quantum mechanics, in particular, "deprived matter of the solidity it was thought to possess"[4] and destructively affected "the program of modern philosophy."[5] The subject-matter of scientific knowledge itself was now at stake. Actually, "the very notion of an objective nature of the world independent of our knowledge of it came under attack."[6] Thus, "scientific knowledge is no longer knowledge of things as they are 'out there' in an objective world but only in relation to an observer. In a sense, we see what we expect to see in accordance with our own mental patterns."[7] Under these circumstances, it is only natural to speak about the eclipse and end of reason, to bid farewell to it, or to announce the end of science, and, indeed, to herald the end of everything including modernity itself.[8]

This situation, a logical consequence of modernity's own fundamental premises, has been severely aggravated by post-modern trends. In modernity's project reason was assigned the position of authority and was therefore considered the reference for human thought and life, while science taught us that there was some rationality and hence a certain structure in the world. By contrast, post-modernity has almost done away with all that. As it pulled man out of his traditional worldviews and value systems, modernity promised him alternatives that would be based on reason and enlightened by science. It did not thus deprive him totally of a frame of reference and certain absolutes in which to ground himself and his experience. Post-modernism, on the contrary, is effecting a real dislocation of the human condition and experience. This dislocation is tied up with a number of assumptions about reality that go "far beyond mere relativism." One main feature of post-modernist thought with its new assumptions is that "things and events do not have intrinsic meaning" and that there is "only continuous interpretation of the world."[9] Accordingly, reality, whether natural or social,[10] has always to be invented and reconstructed time and again. Nothing has truth or meaning in itself. Everything is in permanent flux. The only absolute is total "fluidity" and permanent change. For post-modernist thinkers such as Jean François Lyotard, the epistemological mark of "post-modernity is the loss of authoritative conceptual structures to serve as the "foundation" of rational knowledge."[11] Regardless of the various brands of post-modernism that writers have tried to map out, one of them seems to hold sway over the others. It is a kind of post-modernism characterized by absolute relativism according to which "objective truth is intolerable and non-existent." In this brand of post-modernism, "not only is any transcendent center of reality disavowed, but the unrelieved flux that replaces it has no center."[12] As many post-modernist philosophers tell us, humanity is at present experiencing the total collapse of all grand narratives (i.e., religion, philosophical systems, ideologies, etc.), which in the past underpinned and sustained human experience and consciousness.

Thus, if modernity advocated a reductionist, materialist and secular view of the world, post-modernity is advocating a completely fragmented world in which there is no anchoring point for human consciousness and experience. Not only has the object fallen apart, but the subject himself has also vanished. Instead of modernity's subject, who of course implies the existence of an object, invention is being made of "a floating individual with no distinct reference points or parameters."[13]

In the wake of modernity's struggle against tradition and religion, man was left without heart and soul, but at least it was said that reason and its time-honored ally, science, would take care of him. Now post-modernity is cutting up his head and stripping him of his mind. What is then left is a soulless and mindless body that is being pampered by a sweeping culture of consumerism and nihilism. With the post-modern turn of mind, the problem has assumed alarmingly more dangerous dimensions. The evil-guided, power-thirsty, and business-oriented manipulations of genetic engineering are indeed precipitating humanity not only into the unknown, but also into the assuredly destructive.[14] Thus, it is no more a question of increasing dehumanization as René Dubos, for example, long ago complained.[15] The problem now is not that we are facing the end of man in the philosophical and sociological sense that had appeared to Michel Foucault in his archeological critique of modern social sciences.[16] In what seems to be a reconsideration of his thesis on the end of history, Francis Fukuyama has actually warned against what he considers the most significant threat from biotechnology consisting in the possibility of altering human nature and thereby moving the world into a "post-human" stage of history. Thus, we are informed that we are ushering towards man's end in a psychological, biological, and physical sense.[17]

It is, in my opinion, against this intellectual and historical background that Bennabi's severe criticism of Cartesian rationalism and his strong rejection of scientism in his book *The Qur'anic Phenomenon* can better be appreciated. With the foresight of a visionary, he was able to discern to what consequences Descartes' rationalism and the scientism whose philosophical foundations he was laying down could ultimately lead. In criticizing the Cartesian rationalist doctrine, Bennabi's concern was not in fact with Descartes' belief or disbelief, nor was he having any problem with reason and science as such. What was of the utmost concern for Bennabi was the conception of reason and science as utterly antithetical to religion and revelation. His argument in *The Qur'anic Phenomenon* and in other works too is unmistakably informed by a sharp awareness of what may be called modernity's self-negation, which included almost all its major 'isms, including even its most cherished notions of rationalism, humanism, and scientism.[18]

This self-negation can only be seen as a logical consequence of modernity's fundamental inclination towards magnification. In other words, the magnification, for instance, of reason and science led to an absolutizing of the scientific worldview and to a belief in the absolute capability of human reason and power to control nature and history and to answer all the ultimate questions that have never ceased to be of serious concern for the human mind. Understandably, this magnification and absolutizing could only take place with the price of rejecting all supernatural or extra-human authority and negating all transcendent reality. By rejecting divine authority and negating metaphysical reality as expressed in Nietzsche's infamous announcement of the death of God, modernity, to put it in Bennabi's terms, had to fall into a process of deifying other entities, thereby absolutizing other authorities. But once it is realized that those absolutized authorities and deified entities cannot provide the promised panacea, the only alternative is to lose faith in them and to usher in the post-modern age with its absolute fluidity and continuous flux.

Man, Religion and Science in Bennabi's Thought

That is why Bennabi strongly insists that modernity's antagonism towards religion should not be understood merely as a conflict between religion and science or reason. For him, it is question of a conflict between two basically different philosophical systems and visions of the world. It is a conflict "between theism and materialism, between the religion that has God as a basis and that which postulates matter as an absolute."[19] It is, in the final analysis, a battle for the ultimate meaning of life, the nature of man and the origin and destiny of the world, with all that this involves and necessitates at the psychological, sociological, philosophical, and cosmological levels.[20] As mentioned previously, the particular significance of Bennabi's work on the Qur'an can be fully realized in the light of the far-reaching developments that have occurred in that context. It is a self-aware intellectual engagement with the secular premises and materialistic scientistic worldview of modernity.

In developing his argument, Bennabi adopted an interdisciplinary approach, which can be said to be unprecedented in Qur'anic and Islamic studies in general. Insights from various disciplines and branches of knowledge have been intelligently cast together to develop a new method to the study of religion in general and the Qur'an in particular. This approach drew on philosophy, archeology, history, astronomy, sociology, philosophical anthropology, comparative religion, and psychology. Its purpose was to examine religion and prophethood as objective phenomena that transcend all historical contexts and socio-cultural configurations. Bennabi's objective was to overcome the inadequacies and shortcomings of the reductionist and subjectivist theories that have dominated modern studies of religion and religious phenomena across the different disciplines of social science. He starts from a basic observation agreed upon by so many scholars and thinkers of different backgrounds. It concerns the fact that religion "has been the condition for human life in all ages and climes."[21] However, unlike so many modern thinkers, he does not explain this fact away by relying on historicist, subjectivist or positivist interpretations.[22] Instead, he sees in the different manifestations of religion throughout human history, from "the simple dolmen to the most imposing temple," the clearest evidence as to the deep-rootedness of the religious and metaphysical preoccupation in human life and history. Although the presence of religion has been so manifest and permanent that it compelled sociologists to describe man as "a fundamentally religious animal," the real problem, according to Bennabi, does not lie at the level of this factual and true observation, nor can it be resolved by it. It rather lies at a more fundamental plane, that of the interpretation and understanding of the ultimate source and true significance of the religious phenomenon confirmed by such an observation. Thus, the question pertains to whether man is "a religious animal" in an innate way by virtue of an original disposition of his nature, or whether he has acquired this quality due to some initial cultural accident that has reverberated throughout human history.[23]

In dealing with this issue, Bennabi points out that modern Western thought has been misguided by a scientistic and positivist bent of mind that looks at all phenomena in physical terms, while being totally oblivious to the very fundamental principles underlying positive science itself. Driven by a Cartesian reflex, this thought "reduces everything to the earthly level" of existence.[24] In his view, the ideological thrust and passion for scientism and positivism are responsible for the blindness and failure of the dominant modern Western mind in realizing the inconsistencies and inadequacies of the various systems and theories it has evolved for the interpretation of the different phenomena, notably religion. For Bennabi, being inextricably linked to the realm of human thought and consciousness that cannot be understood in mere physical terms, religion can only find its true explanation at another level of reality that does not turn its back on scientific thought or ignore its discoveries, but realizes its limitations in relation to the vast phenomena standing beyond the material and phenomenological world. It is a level of reality where human understanding acknowledges science not as a goddess pitted against religion, but as a humble servant of human progress, while it still conforms to the philosophical and logical requirements of the human mind. It is a question of thought in which the "metaphysical truth transcends but does not exclude the temporal truth."[25]

Accordingly, religion can only be properly understood by linking it to the imperative order of the *willful, conscious,* and *creative* power that has given existence to all things, including man who embodies thinking matter *par excellence.* It is thus not a mere psychic and mental activity of the human being that can simply be reduced to some physical and biological factors. Rather, it is something inscribed in the order of the universe as a law characteristic of the human spirit. In other words, religion springs from the primordial command of the Creator who has endowed the human species with a specific nature distinguishing it from all animal species no matter how close a physical affinity man might have with some of them. It is likewise a cosmic fact and perennial reality that cannot be reduced to a mere cultural category acquired by human beings over history or relative to the early and primitive stages of human socio-cultural development,[26] as evolutionary theories have been relentlessly teaching.

In this connection, it is worth mentioning that this psycho-cosmological view of religion was expressed, albeit sometimes in indecisive terms, by a number of Western philosophers and scholars who seem to have attempted to emancipate themselves from the yoke of materialism and positivism. As a leading figure in psycho-analysis who established his own brand of it (i.e. analytical psychology), Carl Jung's views (often referred to by Bennabi) deserve special attention here. In an attempt to avoid the inaccuracies of the materialist conception of the psyche, Jung developed his famous "theory of archetypes" according to which the proper understanding of religion can be achieved by relating it to a *collective unconscious* that constitutes a *"psychic reality* shared by all humans."[27] In Jung's view, this "collective unconscious contains the whole spiritual heritage of mankind's evolution born anew in the brain structure of the individual."[28] However, despite the importance of this notion of a common and universal "spiritual heritage" of mankind, the renowned scholar fell short of addressing the compelling question as to the origin of the said "universal collective spiritual heritage." On the contrary, he explained it away by simply relating it to the evolution of mankind. A possible explanation of this is that, being philosophically inspired by the Kantian tradition[29] and imbued with the spirit of the dominating positivistic and scientistic mind of his age, Jung eschewed "from any metaphysical or philosophical considerations."[30]

Be that as it may, in considering religion's different expressions (such as totemism, polytheism, and monotheism), Bennabi's aim was to achieve two main objectives. The first objective was to establish the perennial nature of the religious phenomenon as a characteristic of human nature. Hence, man is described as a *religious animal* or *homo religiosus*.[31] The second objective was to establish the veracity of the Qur'anic revelation and authenticity of Muhammad's prophetic call. This objective was pursued through an examination of both the Qur'an and the Prophet's personality within the wider historical context of the monotheistic tradition and prophetic movement, which have characterized three major living religious traditions of the world, i.e., Judaism, Christianity, and Islam. For this, he proposed a method in which both phenomenology and psychological analysis should play a prominent role. Likewise, the particular case of Islam is linked to the religious phenomenon in general, while its messenger is regarded as the final link in the chain of the prophetic movement. Similarly, the Qur'anic revelation is considered as the culmination of the stream of monotheistic thought. On the other hand, a comparative historical and psychological analysis is necessary to grasp the relationship between the prophets (messengers) and their messages and detect the common characteristics determining their personality and behavior.

To address the latter issue, Bennabi looked into the life and career of the Israelite Prophet Jeremiah whose book and historical authenticity have been spared by modern Biblical criticism.[32] In contradistinction with his counterpart, the pseudo-prophet

Hanania, the examination of the specific case of Jeremiah revealed to him the follow-ing features as distinctive characteristics of genuine prophethood.

1. An absolute power eliminating the prophet's personal will and determining his final and permanent behavior with respect to his missionary career.
2. A unique and categorical judgment on the future course of events tran-scending all logic of history reasoned out by ordinary human beings.
3. The comparison between Jeremiah and other Biblical prophets such as Amos and the Second Isaiah revealed a third feature that consists of the similarity and continuity in the manifestation of the previous two features in all prophets.

Equally manifested in the case of Prophet Muhammad, these features, according to Bennabi, can neither be explained as mere subjective traits of the prophet nor as a result of a disturbed mental state and unbalanced personality, as modern critics would have us believe. On the contrary, they indicate the impersonal character and external prove-nance of the prophetic call. This call is such that it imposes itself on the person of the prophet and subdues his will in an absolute way. The prophets' resistance to the prophetic call furnishes further evidence as to the impersonal and external character of prophethood. They all wished and, in practice, positively tried to avoid it altogether. This resistance is a clear indication of the opposition between their free will and the determinism that subordinates their will and subjugates their self.

After establishing the phenomenological characteristics of the prophetic movement, which spans so many centuries of human history since the Patriarch Abraham up to the last Qur'anic revelations vouchsafed unto Muhammad, Bennabi then turned to examining the Qur'an from both a phenomenological and a psychoanalytic perspec-tive. As he puts it, besides its thematic continuity with earlier Scriptures manifested in its essential message to mankind, especially its spiritual and moral teachings grounded on monotheism, the Qur'an itself provides a very important clue underlining its belong-ing to the phenomenon of revelation which intimately accompanied the prophetic movement. Thus, the Qur'an taught Muhammad, its recipient and conveyor, that he was "no innovator among the apostles" (Qur'an, 46: 9). This means that he was not "preaching anything that was not already preached by all God's apostles" before him.[33] In other words, Muhammad was only a link, the last one as proclaimed by the Qur'an itself (Qur'an, 33: 40), in the long chain of prophets unto whom God had vouchsafed his messages. Accordingly, he was, like them, subject to the same laws. Hence, the char-acteristics of prophethood mentioned above were equally manifested in him.

But apart from its phenomenological characteristic as belonging to the phenome-non of revelation and as being the culmination of religious monotheism, there is another important aspect by virtue of which the Qur'an constitutes a phenomenon in itself. Its revelation over almost 23 years makes it more than just an "event" as Bishop Cragg once wrote.[34] If a phenomenon can be defined as an event that repeatedly occurs under the same conditions, then the sequence of the Qur'anic revelations over more than two decades falls clearly under this definition. One aspect of the phenomenologi-cal manifestation of the Qur'an concerns its recipient and carrier, the Prophet himself, while the other concerns the mode of revelation. At the Prophet's level, the Qur'anic revelations were always accompanied by certain psycho-physiological changes that could easily be seen by those present with him. As for the revelations themselves, they occurred according to definite measures and in varying time intervals in such a way that was clearly indifferent to the personal state of the person who was receiving them. In other words, those revelations were taking place irrespective of the Prophet's grief and sufferings or wishes and aspirations.

For Bennabi, these phenomenological characteristics of the Qur'an vividly indicate its impersonality and externality with regard to the Prophet's self. This implies that the ideas and knowledge content of the Qur'an supersede the Prophet's personal knowledge and transcend his consciousness. We might express this point in Cragg's beautiful words. The Qur'an, said the Anglican bishop, "was never a personal ambition, an anticipated dignity, a private honour. Except as a divine mercy, it could not have been."[35] However, an objection can be raised here. Admitting the impersonal and external character of the Qur'an *vis-à-vis* Muhammad's self, there is still room for supposing that it mirrored the knowledge and ideas – religious, literary, historical, and scientific – that were available in his environment and age. To this hypothesis, on which many Western scholars built their studies of Islam and its Prophet, Bennabi has devoted a great deal of analysis that actually runs throughout all the chapters of his book *The Qur'anic Phenomenon*. A psychological and intellectual portrait of the Prophet, before and after the prophetic call, has been carefully drawn to first establish the demarcation line between the Prophet's personal knowledge and ideas, on the one hand, and the content of the Qur'an, on the other. Then, a comparative and historical examination of a wide range of Qur'anic themes has been carried out to demonstrate that the true reality of the source of the Qur'an can only be conceived on a transcendent, metaphysical plane, a *metapsychism*, far above the psychic reality of its recipient and the mentality and knowledge of his milieu and age.

As pointed out earlier, Bennabi's book was a mature and well-thought effort to respond to the intellectual challenges of modern Western scientific thought and engage with its philosophical premises. In fact, it can be seen as an inauguration of a new kind of Islamic theological and philosophical thinking to explore Qur'anic eternal truths and principles in new lights and from wider perspectives than was possible for classical Muslim scholars. Indeed, the approach Bennabi suggested and the methodology he applied in his study of the Qur'an are challenging and worthy of serious consideration by those who seek to open new avenues for the revival of Islamic thought and reconstruction of Muslim society and civilization. His reformulation of the issue of *i'jāz*, or the inimitability and "matchlessness" of the Qur'an, is worthy of special attention. Instead of the linguistic and literary considerations that constituted the main focus of most classical Muslim scholars and many authors in the modern era, he attempted to address the question of *i'jāz* within the wider philosophical and historical context of the religious phenomenon and prophetic movement by examining it in relation to the miracles of both Moses and Jesus and in relation to the themes reflecting the development of human religious consciousness. In doing so, Bennabi wanted to invite his readers to a different reading of human religious history and a different understanding of the human condition that goes far beyond the mere concerns of Muslims. This is because the Qur'an, once again we borrow Cragg's words, "relates to the larger world on the outer side of [Muslim] experience wherever man, either in his religions or his secularity, is found."[36]

Likewise, in developing his analytic and phenomenological approach to the Qur'an, Bennabi's target is not simply the Muslim who is in need of a sound appreciation and understanding of the Qur'an on which his personal faith and conviction should be based. He is also as much concerned about those who want to deal with the Islamic Scripture merely as a subject of academic inquiry. In other words, this approach is deemed to enable the non-Muslim to reach an equally adequate and just appreciation of the Qur'an whose bearing is not restricted to the Muslim who has possessed it by faith and personal experience. Perhaps we can say, using the words of Kenneth Cragg, Bennabi's method in dealing with the Qur'anic phenomenon "will allow the Qur'an to be possessed from without – possessed, that is, not by the propagandist who wishes to decry or the dilettante who wills to sentimentalize – but by the seriously concerned who has at once both yearning and reservation, both attraction and misgiving."[37]

As mentioned above, modernity's positivistic conception of reason and its scientistic ideology have had detrimental consequences for the meaning of reality that have been seriously aggravated by post-modernist thought. In the wake of the unfolding processes of globalization in almost all the spheres of human life, those consequences need not be overemphasized here. Bennabi's reflections and insights can rightly be seen as a consolidation of the efforts by many thinkers and scholars all over the world. Such thinkers and scholars are actually involved in a struggle not only against the reductionist and nihilist trends that have pushed humanity into the abyss of secularization and the post-religious era, but also against the forces that are pushing her onto the precipice of a menacingly post-human age.

Bennabi's *The Qur'anic Phenomenon* was not simply the beginning of his intellectual career as a visionary thinker and writer. When he ended it with the statement that religion "appears to be inscribed in the order of the universe as a law characteristic of the human spirit,"[38] he did not make an empty statement or play on words. In this book, he has in fact laid down the philosophical and methodological foundations of his subsequent works. It can safely be ascertained that those works were, literally speaking, an elaboration and substantiation of the central thesis developed here about man and religion in terms of social and cultural theorizing.[39] In other words, Bennabi's intellectual concern about religion and its place in human existence and life was not confined to the general philosophical level discussed above, as will be made clear in the course of the following pages.

Society and Culture: Towards a New Paradigm

One fundamental question arises whenever we attempt to study and understand scientifically human social life and try to understand the nature of society. Why do human beings associate and form groups and communities? Is it because of a biological necessity inherent in the species? In other words, are human beings driven by their instincts to associate with one another and identify themselves with a certain form of collective life? Is it the inexorable external circumstances that objectively compel them to live in a community? Or, does that reason lie in a subjective will whereby human individuals deliberately choose to live collectively and form a society?[40]

Since very early in human history, it has been observed that man is a social or political (from the word *polis* meaning city) being. Likewise, he has formed different kinds of association, such as the family, the kinship group, the tribe and the nation.[41] However, the statement that "man is a social being or animal" does not, by itself, provide any explanation that would account for the question of how and why humans live collectively. It simply pinpoints a fact. Such a question has been one of the everlasting central issues of human thought over which scholars and thinkers of all ages and cultures have not ceased to ponder and formulate different views and theories. According to some scholars, the reason for man's social character stems from the inherent weakness of his biological structure that makes it beyond each individual's capacity to fulfill his basic needs of food and security on his own. Human beings were therefore compelled to cooperate with each other in order to satisfy those needs, and this gave rise to the social organization of human life.[42] In his now classic work on social psychology, McDougall expressed the view that the inclination of humans to group and communal life has its origin both in their instinctive and their biological make-up.[43] Since it is not our aim to review the literature available on the subject, what has been mentioned would be sufficient to pave the way for our discussion of Bennabi's point of view on the issue at hand.

Bennabi has devoted one of his most important works, *On the Origins of Human Society*,[44] to this question. However, he has not limited his discussion thereof to this book alone. To begin with, he unequivocally states that the natural and instinctual drive of human beings to live together or, to use his own expression, *the group instinct*, is not the real cause or reason for the formation of society. It is simply a means, rather. For him, society is an organism that involves more than the mere aggregate of individuals whose function is to satisfy the natural needs mentioned above. That is to say, society consists of what he considers "constant fundamentals to which it owes its continuity more or less independently of its individual members".[45] To explain the above statement, Bennabi argues that it might happen that under some historical circumstances a society disintegrates and subsequently disappears as an entity and order without, however, this affecting its individual members as such. On the contrary, they would still preserve the natural instinct and disposition to live as a group. In his view, this shows that the instinctive drive is only a factor that contributes in determining, but does not, on its own, determine man's quality as a social being. The fundamentals to which human society owes its existence and continuity consist of the following three things: (i) the historical source of the process of change; (ii) the elements susceptible to be transformed, through that process, from a pre-social to a social state; and (iii) the universal laws and norms governing that process.

To develop his solution to the fundamental question raised above, Bennabi starts by making a basic anthropological classification between different forms of human association. According to that classification, there are two types of human communities or groups: the "ahistorical natural static groups" and the "historical dynamic groups." While the life of the first type has not undergone any serious transformation either in its content or its form, that of the second has undergone a deep and total transformation in terms of its pattern, motives, and content. The first type is not, in Bennabi's view, of real interest to the enterprise of social science, especially sociology, since the human groups belonging to it are not different from some animal species living in conglomerations, in that they are subject to the laws of mere biological and instinctual life. The human groups belonging to this type do not carry out any historical mission (in terms of generating culture and building civilization), except the biological preservation of the species.[46] Therefore, they can be seen as merely representing "ethnographic material" that may be used by creative societies to build civilization.[47] On the contrary, it is the historical type that is of special interest to Bennabi. This is because it represents the dynamic society that has been subject to the laws of social and historical change, thus undergoing profound transformation both in its character and features according to a specific historical finality.

The natural biological and instinctual structure of the human species provides what Bennabi calls "the vital energy" necessary for the society to carry out its collective concerted action and fulfill its function in history. Nevertheless, the process whereby history borrows from nature this "vital energy" is not as simple as it might at first appear. The reason for this can be expounded as follows. If it does not undergo a process of conditioning and adaptation by being subordinated to a specific order inspired by a sublime ideal, this vital energy may destroy society itself. It is the ideal that actually brings about the reorganization and reorientation of the vital energy and transforms it in such a way that it will not simply function for maintaining the survival of the species. Rather, it also functions in compliance with the social functions of the human being as a moral agent in the concerted civilizational action of society. Thus conceiving a complementary relationship between history (= society) and nature (= species), Bennabi admits that it is a natural fact that the human being must drink, eat, procreate, possess, and struggle for the preservation of the species. However, these primordial natural activities, he insists, have to be controlled and oriented in line with the goals conforming to the progress and development of the species. Hence, if we were to consider that human individuals associate and live in communities and groups for the purpose of satisfying their biological and instinctive needs in order to guarantee the survival of their species, this would not make any real difference between mankind and other animal species enjoying certain forms of collective life. Therefore, it is not simply for the preservation of the species that humans associate and form societies, he strongly emphasized. Rather, the reason why human beings conglomerate lies at another level, that of the cultural development and moral advancement of the species. This is, as he emphatically puts it, "the essential truth about human society."[48] In other words, human beings engage in social life as psycho-temporal factors. Likewise, they act not only in terms of their temporality, of their material needs, but also in terms of their psychism, of their spirituality. As he insists, it is here that the complete reality of man lies, "which must be taken into account for seizing it in its totality."[49]

To illustrate this point, he refers to marriage and the formation of the family as an elementary form of social life. If this activity is urged by the mere preservation of the species, free sexual intercourse between the male and female would be sufficient to satisfy that need. It would, on the one hand, accord with the biological laws governing the species and, on the other, increase the number of its individuals. Nevertheless, we find that the conjugal relationship has always taken place, in all societies, according to "a symbolic religious ceremony." Such a ceremony is usually meant to confer a special meaning and significance upon the union of the male and female as a contract that complies not only with the biological needs of the species but also with the moral objectives of society. Looking at this issue from an Islamic point of view, it can be stated that by sanctifying one particular form of sexual relationship, marriage "involves a vow, a public acknowledgement, and therefore cannot be reduced simply to legitimation of the sexual bond." Indeed, marriage constitutes "the act that gives a concrete form to the order of existence and gives sexuality a new significance" by surrounding "the sexual relationship with the maximum publicity."[50] It thus appears clearly that Bennabi understands the concept of progress as the historical vocation of human society in a comprehensive sense encompassing the spiritual, moral, mental, and material levels. Even if "need" is accepted as being the reason underlying the association of human beings into communities and societies, it cannot, in Bennabi's view, account for human society's cultural dynamics and historical development, nor is it enough to explain the phenomenon of the civilization which is characteristic of historical societies. To him, this interpretation of the birth of human society may conform to what he considers as the *amoebic stage* of consciousness in human social and historical evolution.[51]

Now that we turn to the interpretation of the birth of human society based on external factors, the main line of Bennabi's argument concerning the biological instinctual thesis outlined previously needs to be brought into more prominence. Stated in specific terms, his formulation of the relationship between nature and history or species and society has to be retained in mind for it is of great significance for the following discussion, especially as regards the analysis of the constitution and dynamics of society. It has to be acknowledged in this connection that Bennabi has not addressed the question whether or not the origin of human society resides in the external circumstances separately. However, his position in this respect can be inferred from his discussion of the dialectical and historical materialist thesis expounded by Karl Marx and his followers and the challenge–response thesis advocated by Arnold Toynbee.[52]

In Marx's opinion, the relations into which the human beings engage in their social life are determined by the prevailing "material productive forces" and, hence, are "indispensable and independent of their [i.e. humans'] will". As he further argues, "[t]he mode of production of material life conditions the social, political, and intellectual life processes in general. [And] it is not the consciousness of men that determines their being but, on the contrary, their social being that determines their consciousness."[53] Despite the fact that in the previous statement Marx is primarily concerned with the process of social change and the historical forces underlying it, we can deduce his position concerning the issue at hand from another passage in which he satirically criticized a group of eighteenth-century thinkers who had addressed this issue. For him, those thinkers had erred and therefore were worthy of scorn and contempt because they had tried to explain the origin of human social relations by a "so-called universal consent of mankind" or "a conventional origin."[54] As can be seen from these statements, Marx clearly adheres to an objectivist interpretation according to which the external factors stand at the root of the genesis of society and social phenomena.

As for Toynbee's challenge–response thesis, its author has summarized as follows. "Our formula for the growth-progression would be", says Toynbee, "a challenge evoking a successful response generating a fresh challenge evoking another successful response and so on, pending a breakdown; our formula for the disintegration-progression would be a challenge evoking an unsuccessful response, generating another attempt, resulting in another failure and so on, pending dissolution."[55]

To avoid talking in general theoretical terms, Bennabi points out that, under close scrutiny, the previous two interpretations of the rise of society and civilization are unable to account for innumerable cases in history. Taking the rise of Islamic society and civilization as a concrete example testifying to the profound spiritual and socio-historical transformation brought about by Islam, he observes the following. For so many centuries, the pre-Islamic Arabs had lived in the Arabian Peninsula and faced different challenges of natural and historical character. However, history has not recorded any response on their part to those challenges resulting in any transformation of their life. Similarly, when we look at the economic conditions and the forces and relations of economic production, we find that they did not undergo any real change that would make us expect the rise of a new mode of life and a different type of social organization. Yet, with the advent of the Qur'anic revelation and the inculcation of spiritual and moral values it brought, a different type of society and a new civilization came into being that cannot in any way be interpreted in terms of the conceptual categories suggested by Marx and Toynbee. Therefore, a different explanation is needed.

A Spiritual Interpretation of the Genesis of Human Society

Before delving into an exposition of Bennabi's views in this regard, a few words are in order to shed more light on the notion of "historical societies" due to its conceptual importance in his sociological analysis. This can be further illustrated by the observation that the function of the natural static type does not, according to him, transcend the mere preservation of the species through the satisfaction of the basic biological needs of its individuals. Such a function would accord with the biology-instinct based interpretation of human group formation. But since the function of the historical type is not confined to merely securing the survival of the species, this interpretation is not sufficient. Accordingly, the historical type rather consists in consciously transforming the human and natural environment by generating new forms of life and organization through thought and labor. Likewise, he maintains, if it is nature that provides the species, it is history that creates society. Put differently, the purpose of nature is to preserve the existence (and survival) of the species, whereas the purpose of history is to lead the course of evolution towards a higher form of life that we call civilization.

In line with his main thesis according to which social life denotes historical change and the rise of culture and civilization, the meaning Bennabi assigns to the term "historical societies" clearly transcends the racial and geopolitical boundaries to embrace the cultural and spiritual foundations of human association. Thus, his concern is essentially focused on large human entities which enjoy relatively long historical durations, span over relatively vast geographical areas and espouse a certain ideal and set of moral values on the basis of which a specific pattern of conduct and a particular mode of life emerge. This clarification does not, it should be admitted here, flow immediately from the literal level of Bennabi's work. However, it is solidly supported by the fact that nowhere in his books does he speak of small human entities as societies, be that on racial or geopolitical grounds. Whenever such entities are treated in specific contexts, they are rather referred to as peoples such as the Algerian, the Egyptian, or the French people. Accordingly, we would frequently encounter the reference to such large cultural and civilizational entities as the Islamic, the Christian European (or Western), the Chinese (Buddhist and subsequently communist), or the Hindu society. Even when he mentions, for example, the Arab society, it is always qualified as Islamic, either explicitly or tacitly depending on the context.

In his reflection on the origins of human society, Bennabi introduces two important concepts. In his view, the personality of the human individual in historical societies consists of two fundamental identities, which he expresses by the term "equations." On the one hand, there is an inborn natural identity which is the outcome of the act of creation of God Who has fashioned "man in the best conformation" (Qur'an 95: 4) and "conferred dignity upon the children of Adam" (Qur'an, 17: 70). On the basis of this identity, the human being is endowed with all the positive qualities, physical as well as mental and spiritual, corresponding to the functions that this particular creature is meant to perform. The fact that this created identity or dimension of the individual's personality is common to all the human species does not imply, Bennabi cautions, that all the individuals have the *same* "best conformation"[56] in respect of their physical and mental endowments. Rather, it simply means that irrespective of his natural advantages or disadvantages, each human being is endowed with the ability to make the best possible use of his inborn qualities and faculties and of the environment to which he is exposed.[57] The human being's given identity, Bennabi insists, is not subject to any kind of alteration or corruption under whatever circumstances, for it carries the original dignity conferred by God on mankind.[58]

On the other hand, we have an acquired social dimension or identity that is the result of socio-cultural and historical processes. Unlike the first one, this identity varies from one society to another and, within one and the same society, from one generation to another according to the level of cultural and civilizational development. Thus, the personality of the human individual is a complex entity composed of two identities: one that represents his essence and value as a human being created by God in the best conformation, and one that represents his value as a social being molded by society. Only by taking these two identities into consideration can we achieve a sound understanding of the human social reality, he strongly insists.[59]

The question that arises here is the following: how do these two identities relate to the issue at hand, namely the origin of, or the reason underlying, human association and the genesis of society?

Since the birth of society in the sense specified by Bennabi is concomitant with the rise of culture and civilization, its advent is due to a fundamental idea that imparts to a static natural human group "the thrust that drives it onto the stage of history."[60] In other words, the transformation of a human group from a stagnant, pre-civilizational and ahistorical status of life into a social, civilized and historical one, takes place when its members perceive a new meaning for their existence in the universe. This means that the forces lying at the origin of any historical movement of cultural and social change are essentially of a spiritual and psychological nature. This understanding stems from the fact that the inborn natural dimension mentioned above is fashioned in such a manner that man "would look beyond his earthly horizon so as to discover in his own self the genius of earth as well as the sublime and transcendental value of things."[61] Thus it is the mental equipment and spiritual and moral disposition of the human beings that underlie their association in societies in a continuous pursuit of "an ideal of moral perfection towards which civilization has never ceased to move as its ultimate end."[62] Conformably, Bennabi argues, a human group starts moving on the path of civilization as a society when a moral ideal enters the scene. This ideal attaches the individuals to a specific historical finality endowing their lives with meaning and value and orienting their vital energies towards the achievement of certain goals and the actualization of certain values. This brings into strong relief the reason why Bennabi repeatedly insists on considering human social organization as a stage in which human beings transcend "the inferior [needs] and laws inherited from the animal order",[63] that is, the biological and instinctive impulses mankind shared with other animal species.

Thus, Bennabi's sociological thought proceeds from his fundamental thesis according to which man's religiosity is an inborn quality that emanates from human spiritual and mental constitution and conforms to the laws of the cosmic order. Accordingly, he considers that religion lies at the origin of all historical societies and that it has thus been the most inexhaustible source of moral ideals and values for human life. He maintains that the "extraordinary circumstance" to which thinkers and social scientists have always attempted to trace back the birth of human society is neither the mere challenge posed by the environment, nor the means and forces of material production. Nor does it lie in the mere biological-instinctual constitution of the human species. Rather, it is the advent of religion the seeds of which are sown very deep in the life and history of humankind. Religion thus provides the basis for an ethos that is developed and consolidated hand in hand with the social evolution and cultural development of the human group. It also functions as the main catalyst facilitating the essential synthesis of human society and civilization; that is to say, it brings about the bio-historical synthesis of man, soil, and time. Likewise, Bennabi further argues, the spiritual relationship between God and man that is regulated by religion is at the origin of the social relationship linking human beings with one another. By linking the social relations to spiritual religious roots, he perceives human social existence as ontologically grounded in the metaphysical order of things. Such perception derives, in our opinion, from the Qur'anic account of the advent of mankind on earth. According to this account, God had informed the angels that He was "about to establish on earth one who shall inherit it" (Qur'an, 1: 30). This notion of the human species entitled to the "inheritance" of the earth is expressed by such suggestive and all-encompassing terms like *khilāfah* (vicegerency) and *amānah* (trust) (Qur'an, 1: 30; 6: 165; 33: 72). As Ibn Khaldun expressed it, it was "God's desire to settle the world with human beings and leave them as His representatives on earth." For the author of *The Muaqaddimah*, this "is the meaning of civilization" which constitutes the subject-matter of the "new science" he set out to establish.[64]

Likewise, religion, in Bennabi's opinion, is the ultimate source that gives birth to the social relationship in the form of a moral ideal and thus it "naturally inscribes itself in the origin of all human transformations."[65] Furthermore, he contends that while the social and religious relationships represent, from the historical perspective, two concomitant events, they mark, from the "cosmo-genetic" point of view, the advent of one and the same process of social change in which the social relationship stands as the effect of the religious one. In other words, the social relationship linking the individual to society constitutes the temporal manifestation of the spiritual relationship with God. In all accounts, he further argues, human beings organize themselves as a society that generates culture and establishes civilization. In both cases, he remarks, human beings either transcend their worldly life towards a metaphysical "ideal" specified by revelation or they, at least, transcend their present situation towards a future ideal that takes the form of a social project for which successive generations strive. Given its cosmic nature, religion, in Bennabi's view, is the only source that can provide the necessary and most efficient and enduring catalyst that brings about the essential synthesis of human civilization by integrating into a coherent, dynamic whole its primary factors, namely man, soil, and time. It thus imparts to everyone the *will* of civilization through transforming the human being's soul and endowing his/her existence with meaning and direction.[66]

We have already seen that human social organization, for Bennabi, is as a stage in which human beings do not associate with each other according to the mere requirements of nature, but according to some historical finality in terms of which they would produce culture and establish civilization. In his understanding, human social organization is that stage in which the elementary activities and vital energies of the individuals are oriented in such a manner that they would function not simply in conformity with the survival of the species, but also, and more importantly, with its moral advancement and cultural progress, thus transcending the natural level of animal life.

Relating this formulation of the relationship between nature and history (or species and society) to his central thesis that religion is at the origin of human social association once again brings to the fore the fundamental Islamic concepts of *khilāfah* and *amānah* mentioned previously. Being one of the essential concepts constitutive of the Islamic worldview, this idea of mankind being assigned the position of *khilāfah* or vicegerency to God has been formulated by Bennabi in quite a unique fashion. As he puts it, by controlling and orienting his primordial activities in conformity with the advancement of the species, the human being actually participates in the divine scheme of action; and his participation is ultimately governed by his religious obligation and accountability (*taklīf*) in that he is subject to the law of moral progress. This means that the spiritual relationship between God and man creates and determines the social bonds that link every individual with his fellow humans. In other words, human beings' religious obligation and accountability is the determinant factor of the internal structure of the twofold power of the human being that makes the integrated activities of the individual's instincts and vital energy function in accordance with his social and historical vocation as a moral being. Accordingly, religion is at the basis of man's vertical bond with God and his horizontal relationship with fellow human beings.

Accordingly, Bennabi looks at human society within the framework of the Islamic worldview and in terms of the ethical function that human beings are supposed to fulfill in the temporal world. The spiritual forces, which, as we have seen, underlie human social action and historical existence, are, therefore, ethically motivated. As a *homo religiosus* and moral agent, the efficacy of the human being's action in the socio-historical realm is situated, according to Bennabi, between two limits: *wa'id* (warning) and *wa'd* (promise) as expounded by the Qur'an. In his view, warning represents the lowest level beneath which there is no room for any effective effort, while promise constitutes the highest level beyond which all human effort is impossible, for in such a situation the severity of the challenge overpowers the spiritual and moral strength with which man is endowed. Accordingly, human consciousness is placed under the most favorable conditions enabling it to respond to all challenges that are, in the final analysis, spiritual in nature. Within the two limits of warning and promise, he maintains, the spiritual strength of the individual is proportionate to the efficacious effort furnished by society as it acts according to the dictates of a mission, that is to say, according to the requirements of its historical goals.

It is quite obvious that the aforementioned argument concerning the dynamics and efficacy of the spiritual forces underlying human social and historical action is a reformulation of Toynbee's challenge–response thesis. In fact, Bennabi is quite clear regarding the necessity of such a reformulation as the said thesis cannot, in its initial form, lead us to a sound understanding of the origin and finality of the historical movement which gave rise, for example, to the Islamic society.

Constitution of Human Society

To start with, it would be both appropriate and helpful to put Bennabi's sociology in perspective and bring his methodology into focus. Taking the latter point first, it can be said that, stated in general terms, Bennabi's methodology works at two different, yet closely interrelated, levels. While the first level is that of analysis consisting in the dissection of the phenomena at issue into their basic constituents with a view to discovering their structure, the second one is that of synthesis and consists in looking at the phenomena under consideration in the course of their movement and interaction so as to grasp their dynamics.

These are necessary and complementary methodological steps without which any sound and comprehensive understanding of human social phenomena will remain beyond reach. It thus appears that Bennabi's methodological approach to the study of social phenomena aims at integrating the synchronic (or cross-sectional) and diachronic (or sequential) perspectives, with a clear emphasis placed, however, on the latter perspective. As seen earlier, he lays stronger stress on the dynamic aspects of human social existence as an ongoing multidimensional process of socio-historical and cultural change or, to put the same point differently, as a process of becoming.[67] Accordingly, his methodology "is both analytic and constructive".[68] It is in relation to this methodological awareness that Bennabi's early insistence upon the necessity of a "different" or "new sociology" for the Third World in general and the Muslim world in particular can be properly appreciated. The role of such sociology, he believed, should be both a liberating and a constructive one. As he understood it, the liberating dimension of that sociology should, in the main part, be critical. That is, it has to analyze and detect the social pathologies in Muslim lands that represent the burdening legacy of the post-Almohad[69] age of civilizational decadence coupled with the distorting legacy of the colonial era. Thus, in its critical aspect this "new sociology" is perceived in terms of a socio-cultural science whose main task is to purge the Muslim life and environment of the long-seated germs of *colonizability*.[70] Its constructive role should consist of edifying a fundamental culture aimed at the radical transformation of Muslim "social being" and restoring and reconstructing the "social relations network" in the Muslim *ummah*. The ultimate purpose of this new sociology should be to realize anew the essential synthesis of the primary factors of civilization, namely man, soil and time.[71]

Let us now turn to the other point; that is, to put Bennabi's sociology in perspective. When dissected into its primary components, human society is revealed, according to Bennabi, as a compound of three essential categories, or realms, consisting of persons, ideas, and objects.[72] To him, history as the cumulative human social action is basically the outcome of the interplay between these three realms impressed in the space–time continuum. It is thus woven out of the activities and ideas of the human beings as well as of the input and influences of material things and objects. Not operating in isolation from one another, these social categories rather represent what Bennabi calls the *parameters* of the "concerted action" of human society in history. According to him, the pattern of this concerted action is determined by ideological models originating in the *realm of ideas* and applied through means that are derived from the *realm of objects* in order to achieve ends and objectives set up by the *realm of persons*. As indicated by Bennabi, the idea of a concerted action carried out by the three social categories constituting human society necessarily implies the existence of a set of bonds whose function is to link together the components of each one of the three realms as well as the latter to one another such that they become an integrated harmonic whole. Consisting of the totality of the necessary social relations or what he calls the social relations network, this set of bonds constitutes a fourth, yet latent, realm in itself.

Thus, the *social relations network* stands for the structural patterns both within and between the realms of persons, ideas, and objects. In Bennabi's view, it is through such structure that the impact and activities of the three realms of persons, ideas and objects is connected and synthesized. Both in its direction and scope, this synthesis brings about the *transformation* of the features of human life or, to express it more accurately, unleashes the historical movement and development of society. For Bennabi, this relational structure is so vital for the concerted action of human society that the first task a society would undertake at the very moment of its birth would be to establish its social relations network even before its three constituent realms reach maturity and take full shape. Indeed, he strongly argues, any subsequent development of a society after its birth depends fundamentally on that network. This is because human society, for him, is not a mere collection or juxtaposition of persons, ideas, and objects; it is rather the synthesis of these three realms into a coherent and dynamic whole. That is, broadly speaking, the analytic and conceptual framework of Bennabi's sociology. In fact, the greater part of his work can be seen as a reflection on, and elaboration of, two major issues in this framework, namely:

1. How are the above-mentioned realms of persons, ideas, and objects structured, and how do they interact with one another?
2. What are the sociocultural and historical manifestations of that structuring and interaction?

By comprising the social actors, both as individual and collective agents, it is quite obvious that the realm of persons should occupy a more prominent place within the relational structure and network of society. This explains Bennabi's extensive treatment of this realm from a variety of perspectives in an attempt to understand and define both the factors and conditions that contribute to the shaping and determination of human social action. Since a more detailed account of the realm of persons is to be made later in this chapter, it will be both convenient and illuminating now to have an overview of the other two realms.

As we have already seen, in Bennabi's sociological analysis, society is a specific and dynamic form of human collective life and organization that comes into existence as the humans beings espouse a specific ideal and set of moral values. This understanding justifies his giving priority to the realm of ideas over that of objects. However, this does not mean that he overlooks or underestimates the latter realm. On the contrary, he strongly maintains that the realm of objects plays so vital a part that human social existence and action is inconceivable without it. Yet, compared to his extensive analysis of the place of the realms of both persons and ideas in the constitution and dynamics of human society, Bennabi's treatment of the realm of objects is markedly limited. This in fact presents us with a situation that stands in need of clarification lest his stand be erroneously understood.

At the outset, there is a need to elucidate what the realm of objects represents in Bennabi's sociological thought. Upon closer examination of his usage of this term on different occasions, what appears most compatible with his analytic and conceptual framework is that the realm of objects refers to whatever material things (both natural or man-made) are used or may be used by the human beings to sustain their life. It thus concerns all the material aspects of human social life and existence. It can be argued from this that, since the human species is imbedded in the material realm of nature, the human beings would not therefore fail to pursue their material needs and evolve the proper means for their satisfaction as the long and accumulated experience of mankind has shown. Accordingly, his major concern is not to argue for the obvious importance of the realm of objects for human social existence on the biological and material plane. What matters most for him is to examine and comprehend its psycho-sociological and cultural significance and impact within the dynamic relational structure of society throughout the different stages of its development. In other words, he is

more preoccupied both with the analysis and conceptualization of the dialectical relationship and interplay of the realms of persons and objects as it is, or should be, mediated through the realm of ideas. Moreover, Bennabi's sociological and cultural analysis
is unmistakably informed by the Islamic view that nature, from which the realm of
objects is derived either directly or indirectly through different manufacturing
processes, stands in a position of subservience *vis-à-vis* the realm of persons. Hence,
the latter realm is in a position of mastery over the realm of objects specifically by virtue
of a Divine will to appoint mankind as God's vicegerent on earth, as we have already
seen.

Thus, for Bennabi, there is no question of whether or not human beings as members
of a society deal with the realm of material things and phenomena to extract the bounties of nature in order to satisfy their material needs and sustain their existence. This
is something already guaranteed by what he considers the inferior laws of the animal
order.[73] Rather, what needs to be investigated pertains to the psycho-sociological and
cultural conditions under which the realm of persons would interact with, and be
involved in, the realm of objects. It is in the light of these considerations that one can
appreciate Bennabi's view concerning the ultimate or real wealth of human society. As
he puts it, the real wealth of a society does not actually consist of the objects it uses but
rather of the ideas it possesses. Consequently, if for any adversities (e.g. wars, natural
catastrophes) a society is partly or entirely deprived of its realm of objects, the harm
affecting it because of that will not be so devastating. But the disaster will be much
more harmful if such a society at the same time fails to maintain its realm of ideas. By
the same token, when it succeeds in salvaging its ideas, it would actually have saved
everything, since it would be able to reconstruct its realm of objects based on it. As will
be seen in the next pages, Bennabi's analysis and conceptualization of human society
and its dynamics is further deepened and elaborated in his treatment of the question of
culture as one of the main themes of his thought.

Culture and Sociological Analysis[74]

Culture was a central and recurrent theme in Bennabi's thought, for it never ceased to
occupy his mind throughout his intellectual career. There is not one of his works in
which he does not deal with this topic in one way or another, or at least refer to its
importance. Yet, despite the growing interest in Bennabi's works during the last three
decades of the twentieth century, his conceptualization and theorization of culture
have not received sufficient scholarly attention.

Bennabi's aim was not to discover new data or to provide hair-splitting descriptions
of what might constitute culture. He also had no interest in merely reproducing what
Clifford Geerts justly called the "conceptual morass" that had been developed around
the subject of culture, as was the case with most Arab thinkers and academicians who
wrote about it in his time. Bennabi's approach was totally different. He was in search
of what constitutes the essence of culture,[75] that essence which enables us to visualize
it as a mode of living and a program of action, equipping human beings with the skill
of living together meaningfully and in harmony with their environment.

Chronologically speaking, Bennabi first expressed his views on culture in a chapter of his book *Les Conditions de la Renaissance* that was first published in 1948. In this book, he discussed what he called the idea of "cultural orientation" defined as soundness of foundations, harmony and resolution of movement and unity of purpose. In that context, he defined culture as the mode of being and becoming of a people. This mode of being and becoming has an esthetic, ethical, pragmatic, and technical content. Throughout the 1950s and 1960s, these preliminary views were on various occasions subjected to further reflection, elaboration, and deepening until they crystallized in what can be considered a truly Bennabic theory of culture. This theory took its final shape in his book *The Question of Culture*.

A major concern motivating much of Bennabi's thought about culture is the quest for a way out of the impasse in which mankind has been stuck by the desire for power that is overwhelmingly prevalent in modern Western culture. The world, he insists, is in pressing need of an ecumenical humanism that will safeguard the human species from imminent destruction. The notion of humanism has been one of the foremost ideals preached by modern Western civilization. Nevertheless, Bennabi considers that this humanism has been plagued by formalism and shallowness and lacks any solid moral foundation owing to its origins within a culture that derived its roots from the Greco-Roman humanities. Modern Western humanism has found its most resounding formulation in the Universal Declaration of Human Rights. However, Bennabi argued, this humanism has amounted to no more than a mere artistic and literary work, as it is deprived of the metaphysical and transcendent basis of the original dignity invested in the humankind by its Creator.[76]

According to Bennabi, every social reality is in its essence and origin an actualized cultural value that conditions both man's being and environment in a specific manner. It follows from this that the problem of culture in Muslim and Third World countries arises at a very fundamental level relating to the frame of reference according to which any civilizational change and transformation of society should take place. At this level, its function for civilization is similar to the function of blood for living organisms.[77] This means that we need to look at culture as a process of becoming that is inextricably linked to the question of social reconstruction. From this perspective of socio-historical becoming, culture should have, according to Bennabi, a twofold definition that takes into consideration the problems of the present and the aspirations of the future. Accordingly, he argues that culture, far from being merely a simple close entity, has a rather complex and dynamic nature that can be thought of at two important levels. In his own words, "culture is first and foremost a certain *ambience* within which the human being moves; it [thus] nourishes his inspiration and conditions the efficacy of his [social] interactions. It is an atmosphere made up of colors, tunes, customs, shapes, rhythms, and motions which [all] impart to his life an orientation and [provides him with] a particular model that stimulates his imagination, inspires his genius and incites his creative faculties."[78]

Two concepts figuring in the above statement need to be underlined here: *orientation* and *model*. In fact, almost throughout all his works, Bennabi's major concern has been to answer two fundamentally interrelated questions. First, what is the historical voca-tion of the Muslim both at the individual and collective levels, and how can the Muslim world regain its place in the world scene as an active participant in the affairs of humankind? Second, according to what model should the Muslim conduct and activities be patterned in order to fulfill the requirements of that vocation? Bennabi is of the view that culture has an important role to play in this regard. His severe criticism of both reformist and modernist movements in Muslim countries can best be appreciated in this light. In his opinion, those movements were so deficient that they conceived social and civilizational reconstruction as mere accumulation of objects or, at best, a syncretism of disparate elements that are heaped up haphazardly. Thus, they failed to comprehend it as a harmonious and integrated edifice of *things* and *ideas* that hold together in a logical and organic manner and fulfill definite functions for the sake of realizing a specific ideal of life.[79]

Bennabi's conception of culture as "becoming" implies that it has to be understood as a relationship between the individual and society. This relationship involves a process of interaction and mutual commitment between the two poles whereby the conduct of the individual contributes to the shaping of the general mode of life of society and is shaped by it. In this connection, he argues that all the differences pertaining to the definition of culture basically depend on how one understands the nature of this relationship. Thus, if primacy is given to individual actors, emphasis will be placed on the psychological and ideational aspects of culture. If, on the contrary, primacy is given to society as a total entity, emphasis will rather be laid on the objective and structural aspects. To him, both stands are seriously flawed, for it is not a question of mutual exclusion between the two poles of human social life and, hence, between the two dimensions of culture. It is a matter of complementary duality rather than (mutually) exclusive dualism.

Accordingly, the complex and dynamic nature of culture and its embodiment of the reciprocal relationship and mutual commitment between the individual and society require that any attempt at defining it should adopt the methodology used in the study of complex phenomena. This can be done by determining both its subjective psychological and objective sociological components and establishing the necessary links between them within the framework of that mutual commitment in order to formulate a definition of culture in terms of a realizable educational program functional with the task of reconstruction.

As a step in that direction, Bennabi advances the view that culture is "the environment in which the individual psychic being is shaped just as the organic make-up of a person is conditioned by the [natural] physical environment surrounding him."[80] In his opinion, this way of looking at the question of culture allows us to conceive its impact on human society by drawing an analogy between culture and blood. It is a scientific fact that blood consists of the red and white corpuscles (or the erythrocytes and leukocytes) floating in the plasma and maintaining the vitality and equilibrium of the living organism as well as constituting its self-defense mechanism. So too, culture can be conceived as a special kind of plasma that carries the popular ideas of the masses as well as the esoteric and scientific ideas of the elite. These two categories of ideas nourish the society's creative genius and civilizing élan and constitute its self-defense mechanism. As such, culture supplies both the elite and the lay people with unified orientations, common tastes, and shared dispositions.[81]

Furthermore, this conception of culture involves an unconscious dimension since not all the members of a society assimilate culture and become integrated to it through conscious discursive processes, nor do they, at a certain age, consciously choose the way to that integration. Thus, it follows that there is no room for reducing culture to science or even equating it with knowledge in general. Confounding culture and science is, Bennabi insists, pernicious to any proper understanding of the import and function of either of them. Therefore, a clear line of demarcation has to be drawn between the two concepts in order to avoid the grave error of using them interchangeably. As he avers, "culture always generates science, but science does not always generate culture."[82] Hence, culture is more general and encompassing than science.

In his understanding, science tends to be impersonal in the sense that the man of science always stands as a subject observing things with a view to dominating and manipulating them. As he puts it, in science it is a question of the positivist mind "turned to the realm of phenomena." In contrast, culture, being something more comprehensive than science, creates the observer himself and provides him with the mirror for observing those things and phenomena as well as for observing his own self.[83] Thus, while science enables human beings to exert their influence on the realm of material things and phenomena within their reach, culture is their way to achieve harmony between that realm and their inner selves as well as to establish their relations with one another. In other words, culture is the source that provides human beings with the means of self-control and mastery over both nature and the products of their own genius. Put differently, science consists of those procedures and methods by means of which the human intellect applies itself to the realm of things and natural phenomena. By contrast, culture consists of the intersubjective wealth of symbols, values, ideas, traditions, and tastes that allows human beings to regulate and harmonize their relationships and interaction with one another, with their environment and with the universe at large. As such, culture provides the individual, through various psychological processes of assimilation, with the *personal criteria* by means of which he/she judges his/her conduct and action and accommodates them to the society's mode of life.[84]

This point can be expressed differently as follows. While culture embraces the inner dimensions of the human self's relationship with the different levels of existence thus giving primacy to subjectivity and transcendence in human life, science rather tends to concern itself with the external dimensions of things and phenomena of the natural world, including human beings themselves. It thus accords primacy to objectivity and externality in the human relationship with the different realms of existence. Yet, Bennabi is far from the subject–object dichotomy plaguing many a school of thought. His emphasis on the fact that science itself both as theories and procedures cannot be dissociated from the cultural universe within which it takes shape gives warrant to this understanding of his position.

In addition to these clarifications made so as to trace the distinctive lines between culture and science with regard to both the nature and function of each, there is yet another kind of confusion against which Bennabi warns us. This time, we are summoned not to confuse culture with "culture products and by-products." The reason is that any confusion in this regard will dangerously misguide us on both the mechanisms and function of culture in the same way the confusion between industry and the manufactured products will terribly mislead us on the nature of the former. As Bennabi further maintains, human social life is fundamentally dependent upon two inevitably necessary spheres. On the one hand, there is the *biosphere* without which the physical and biological development of the human beings is inconceivable in this world. On the other hand, there is what he calls the *noosphere*[85] that makes the spiritual and mental development of the human species possible. Culture, in the last analysis, is but the manifest expression of this second sphere. One important idea that emerges from the foregoing discussion and that is emphasized throughout Bennabi's works is that culture is the source by means of which the members of a society construct their worldview and establish their relations with reality and with one another.[86]

Not only human beings depend on culture for their social life and historical existence. This too applies to material things and objects; they would remain obsolete, inanimate and valueless outside the framework of culture. To bring this point home, Bennabi invites us to imagine a man-made satellite landing in the midst of a supposedly "culture-less" group or one that has no communication at all with the culture in which the satellite has been produced. Such a device will have no meaning or value for such people except that it is a mass of matter. This is because it will be lacking the language and code by means of which it can convey its specific message. This means that not only does culture provide human beings with the means of communication and exchange with one another, but it also does so with respect to material things and objects, both natural and man-made. Moreover, according to Bennabi, even ideas and concepts are subject to the same inexorable law. This latter point will be examined in more detail later.

Dynamics of Culture and Human Social Action

In accordance with his view about the cultural essence of social reality, Bennabi maintains that whatever substance exists in the one, necessarily exists in the other. "If we analyze a social reality, that is to say, a concrete social activity, we will discern in it, both in its instantaneous state and progressive course, four basic elements which we can express in pedagogic terms as an ethics, an esthetics, a technique and a practical logic."[87] These basic components of social action determine, in his view, the characteristics and orientation of culture in accordance with their interconnectedness within the framework of that action. At any rate, no social action, he declares, can be imagined without certain ethical and social motivations, without (a) definite pattern(s) according to which it takes place, and without fulfilling some aesthetic criteria. All these elements, he carries on, represent *sine qua non* conditions for the efficacy of social action.[88] Thus, if the ethical component determines the ethos of culture and if culture is, as seen above, a specific *ambience*, it is then evident that the esthetic component plays an equally significant role in it. For Bennabi, creativity is inextricably linked to the esthetic sensibility of the social actor, that is to say, the latter's efficacy is also subject to esthetic criteria.

As he further explains, esthetic values contribute to creating a particular human type. Thanks to its esthetic affinities and tastes, this type would endow life with a specific rhythm and gives history a particular orientation. This means that human social action depends, in its motivation, direction, and form, on ethical and esthetic factors. On the other hand, social action cannot yield its results unless it draws upon dynamic factors whose function is to facilitate the material development of human society. In Bennabi's view, it is technique and pragmatic logic that impart dynamism to social action and facilitate the actualization of its ethical and esthetic dimensions. The imperative nature of technique and practical logic is underscored by the fact that the modern experience of mankind has witnessed one of the greatest developments in human social life. That is, the advent of new, indeed unprecedented, scientific and technological forces that have drastically influenced the human condition in terms of greatly controlling and accelerating the course of history.[89] It has to be mentioned here that technique, in Bennabi's usage, seems to refer to science both in its theoretical and applied forms. For him, the role of science or technique is to provide human actors with the means through which they establish their relations with, and deal with, the realm of things and objects.[90]

As for practical logic, its function lies "in conditioning the form, style and rhythm of social action, that is all its dynamic aspects."[91] The difference between technique and practical logic can further be explained in the following way. On the one hand, technique refers to the power by means of which the humans exert their mastery over the material realm. On the other hand, practical logic consists of the "way action is connected with its means and objectives, in order to avoid estimating how easy or difficult things are without depending on criteria derived from the social environment and its potentials." In other words, practical logic means "to attain the utmost benefit from the available means."[92] Likewise, the import of practical logic is to get, from the available means, the maximum results in the minimum span of time. In this respect, Bennabi observes that the root cause of the inefficacy of human social action lies in the absence of the criteria that would link such action to both its means and ends. Practical logic is thus intimately linked with the question of creativeness both at the individual and collective levels of society.[93]

An important aspect of Bennabi's thinking in this respect must be highlighted here. Despite his strong emphasis on the place of technique and practical logic in the shaping of human social action and in the composition and generation of culture, he does not consider these two factors to be the ultimate determinants of the characteristics of a society's culture. In his opinion, it is rather the dialogical relationship between ethics and esthetics that determines in an essential way a culture's characteristics and orientation, depending on whether primacy is given to one or the other factor. Accordingly, he argues that the historical experience of mankind has oscillated between two main types of culture: an ethically centered type and an esthetically oriented one.[94]

When it degenerates, an ethically centered culture, according to Bennabi, would mostly sink into mysticism, escapism, vagueness and mimesis. By contrast, an esthetically centered culture would degenerate into ponderousness, consumerism, materialism and imperialism. Signalizing the wide gap alienating ethics and esthetics from one another in the modern Western culture that has dominated the globe, Bennabi believes that the modern mind is in great need for a cultural revolution in order to realize the genuine synthesis of the beautiful and the real. The problem, he insists, ought to be addressed from a universal perspective. In this connection, he maintains that Islam provides "essential cultural elements just as it provides geopolitical elements of particular importance" for such an enterprise.[95] More important than this, Islam has provided two fundamental principles in order to protect mankind against all forms of physical or spiritual oppression. The first principle consists of putting in the Muslim conscience an essential limit to the *will to power*. Hence, the Qur'an states without any ambiguity: "As for that [happy] life in the hereafter, We grant it [only] to those who do not seek to exalt themselves, nor yet to spread corruption, for the future belongs to the God-conscious" (Qur'an, 28: 83). The second principle consists of announcing and emphasizing the essential dignity of man that transcends all boundaries of color, race, nationality, and belief. Thus, the Qur'an brings to human dignity and value their solid metaphysical foundation, when it says: "Now, indeed, We have conferred dignity on the children of Adam" (Qur'an, 17: 70).[96]

As he has explained, the cultural universe is not a lifeless world. On the contrary, it has "a life and history of its own." It has "a becoming." Its internal dialectic depends upon the interaction of the parameters of social action, namely: "the persons, the objects and the ideas."[97] As seen above, while the category of persons stands for the totality of the members of society, and while that of ideas represents the system of ideas and values espoused by the persons, the category of objects includes both the natural and manufactured objects, that is, the material sources of life.[98] Consequently, social action is exclusively the outcome of the phenomenal interaction between these three categories or realms, and depends, both in form and direction, on the historical relationship linking them together and varying according to the socio-cultural age of society. Looked at from a different perspective, the realms of persons, ideas, and objects constitute the parameters of social action. This is because such action cannot be imagined without the existence of social agents, a material and institutional (i.e. structural) context in which and by means of which such agents would act, and an ideational frame of reference according to which the motivations, purposes and course of action are defined. Pointing out that the human "agential" and the material–structural aspects are the most easily realizable dimensions of social action owing to their concrete and tangible nature, Bennabi notices that the ideational aspect is the least discernible one though no action can actually be accomplished without it. For him, human action has thus to answer two fundamental questions: the "why" and "how," that is, the *motivations* and *operational modalities* determining that action.[99]

From this, Bennabi proceeds to another level in his analysis of human socio-cultural reality. It is a matter of fact that social action is inconceivable without the human actors who carry it out. Hence, it is quite natural that the realm of persons should occupy a central place in the cultural world. However, human beings cannot, Bennabi insists, be efficacious actors in the socio-historical scene susceptible of producing and receiving culture unless they are transformed into an integrated whole or coherent synthesis. Accordingly, the first and foremost condition for the rise of culture is the integration of individuals into a coherent whole. But what is the integrating force that makes human beings efficacious socio-historical agents?

The answer, according to Bennabi, is that this integrating force consists of moral ideals and values. He says, "the role of the moral ideal is precisely to construct the realm of persons without which neither the realm of ideas nor that of objects will have any *raison d'être*."[100] In this connection, he reminds us of the fundamental place and role of religion in human life. As the reader may well recall, Bennabi's view is that moral values are ontologically grounded in the metaphysical order of existence through the spiritual God-man relationship as instituted by religion. In accordance with that argument, he contends that the idea of religion being the source of integrative moral values has been clearly expounded by the Qur'an as in the following Qur'anic verses:

> He it is Who has strengthened you with His succor, and by giving you believing followers (63) whose hearts He has brought together: [for,] if you had expended all that is on earth, you could not have brought their hearts together [by yourself]: but God did bring them together. Verily, He is almighty, wise. (Qur'an, 8: 62–3)

These verses, he observes, underscore the notion of "binding and unifying" signified by the word "religion" in its Latin origins. Thus, he infers, moral ideals and values whose function is to unite human individuals and integrate them into one coherent whole are essentially of a religious nature dawning with Divine revelation. Accordingly, ethics constitute a fundamental component of culture in the absence of which the realm of persons is no more than isolated atoms. As he further explains, the isolated disintegrated human individual is totally unable both to receive and transmit culture, let alone to produce it. In order to appreciate this point, Bennabi invites us to reflect on the actual misfortune of the shipwrecked English sailor whose story inspired Daniel Defoe in his celebrated novel *Robinson Crusoe* as well as the many cases known in anthropological literature as *l'enfant sauvage*, that is the wild infant case.[101]

In addition to its role as a binding force that integrates the members of society, the moral principle determines the historical vocation and orientation of human society by setting up the motivations and ends for human social action. For Bennabi, social action cannot be conceived as a conscious, purposive action unless it draws upon such ethical ends and motivations. The moral factor is both a matter of social and logical necessity. It determines in a great measure the efficacy of human social action. In other words, the efficacy of human societies increases or decreases depending on the strength or weakness of moral principles' impact on them.[102]

As seen previously, esthetic considerations have a prominent place in human social action. Bennabi has formulated their relationship with the ethical considerations as follows. If the ends and motivations of action are determined, as we have just seen, by the moral ideal, its shape and form are to be determined by the esthetic factor, which at once determines another crucial aspect of human social efficacy. In his view, it is the esthetic factor that actually endows ethical and moral values with more acceptability and radiation and thus increases the efficacy of human social conduct and action. As he argues, when deprived of esthetic taste and affinity, the moral action and conduct of the human being may turn into an "arid and repulsive act."[103] Likewise, there is a necessary and fundamental relationship between ethics and esthetics in the fabric of human social action. Ethics plays an important role in terms of setting up the model for human conduct and determining the motivations and ends of social action. Esthetics plays an equally important role by shaping the general lifestyle of society and giving human moral conduct and social action tasteful and acceptable forms and shape. This crucial link between ethics and esthetics is manifestly underlined in the Islamic framework, Bennabi affirms. In both the ways it inculcated moral values and the modes it prescribed for their implementation and actualization, Islam gave special regard to the esthetic aspect. Its aim is to cultivate a sense of finesse and esthetic sensibility that would endow human social life with beauty and attraction.[104] Beauty, he argues, is a major source of inspiration in human life that cannot be dissociated from the sense of what is ethically good and acceptable. It thus affects both the thought and behavior of the members of human society. Like ethics, Bennabi takes the esthetic factor in its broad sense so as to concern every aspect of human life, both at the individual and collective levels.

Clearly, Bennabi's reflection on the role of ethics in human life and society appears to depart from the common view of ethics as simply a set of rules and principles that govern, or should govern, human behavior. His insistence that the moral ideal or principle, as he preferred to call it, determines both the ends and motivations of social action, seems to derive from a broad conception of ethics as ethos. In addition to the rules human conduct has to comply with, this conception includes the values human beings strive to actualize and the goals they struggle to achieve. Thus, Bennabi's analysis leads to the following important conclusion about human social life. The integration of the realm of persons depends in an essential manner on ethics and esthetics as major components of culture. In other words, human social relations are embedded in, and nurtured by, what may be called, in line with his terminology, ethico–esthetic plasma.

The above statement paves the way to the second constituent of the cultural world, namely the realm of ideas. Emphasizing the central place of this realm in human social existence, Bennabi held that there is a *universal canvas* for human social action according to which the latter cannot be brought about. Simultaneously with the visible elements, this universal canvas encompasses an ideational element representing both its motivations and operational modalities. It should be mentioned at the outset of our examination of this realm that Bennabi's concern is not directed to the ontological and epistemological status of ideas. His foremost interest is rather to investigate the life and dynamics of ideas in human social existence, or what he often calls the *career* of ideas in human history.

The function of ideas in human social existence, for him, is not merely figurative or decorative. They rather assume a fundamental role as integrating forces of human society to the course of history. In this respect, he draws our attention to one important aspect. The efficacy of ideas as forces of socio-historical change does not depend solely on their internal consistency, authenticity, or compatibility with reality. Even false and inconsistent ideas can be so efficacious that they may be at the origin of storming events in the history of mankind. Therefore, their relationships within a given cultural world and the prevailing psycho-sociological circumstances are determinant factors in the social efficacy and historical destiny of ideas.

It should be pointed out here that Bennabi does not provide any further detail concerning the notion of "false and inconsistent ideas." Nevertheless, this notion can be understood in light of two examples used in his work. The first example belongs to the domain of science, whereas the second pertains to the realm of ideologies. As he put it, the "idea of the philosopher's stone" played an influential role in the development of scientific thought during the Middle Ages, although it has no scientific genuine value. Only after Lavoisier had made his discoveries in chemistry did such a false idea disappear from the realm of science. The second example concerns Marxism. In Bennabi's view, Marxist ideology suffered serious philosophical inconsistency and some of its basic assumptions are utterly incompatible with the nature of things. He even went as far as considering it a mere internal crisis of modern Western civilization. However, this did not prevent it from being at the origin of great historical events and socio-political revolutions of far-reaching impact in the twentieth century. According to him, this socio-historical efficacy of Marxism has to be understood from a psychological standpoint. In his opinion, Marxism had derived a great deal of its psychological ingredients and dynamism from the fertile ground provided by the very Christian culture against which it revolted. This endowed Marxism with the appeal of a motivating spiritual creed. What is worth noting here is the fact that, as early as the 1960s, Bennabi predicted that the socio-political order based on the Marxist doctrines would, sooner or later, collapse as the "spiritual drive" supporting it fades away![105]

Accordingly, Bennabi theorizes, ideas have their "Archimedean moment," that is to say the historical moment in which they meet with the psycho-sociological and cultural conditions favorable for them to fulfill their function as forces of socio-historical change. This observation explains the fact why some ideas in human history have to "emigrate" from the place (i.e. the socio-cultural context) in which they first appear or "to remain in abeyance" for some generations until they meet with their Archimedean moment or grace. This "emigration" or "expatriation" of ideas as well as their "remaining in abeyance" occur, according to Bennabi, in two stages of the socio-historical evolution of human society. The first is when the human social environment in which such ideas come into being is so dynamic and developed that no psycho-sociological forces are left idle, thus ready to become carriers of those ideas.[106] The second is when such human social environment has reached a state of senility and weariness corresponding to what Bennabi calls "the post-civilization stage." At this stage, society loses the sense of its vocation as well as genuine and creative rapport with the "matrices" of its original cultural world. As a result, it starts disintegrating in such a manner that its psycho-sociological forces become irresponsive to the call of ideas as forces of socio-historical change.[107]

Thus, we are here presented with one of the fundamental laws in the sociology of ideas. By governing the life and dynamics of ideas in human social existence, this law applies not only to "single" scientific or technological ideas, but it also, more importantly, applies to whole ideational and value systems such as religion and ideological systems.[108] In this respect, another closely related aspect in the sociology of ideas is also signalized. According to Bennabi, to enter history as efficacious forces of change, ideas need always to acquire a sense of sacredness and sanctity in order to acquire legitimacy and mobilize the psycho-sociological and cultural forces of human society. Likewise, false ideas, he contends, have always been compelled to wear a mask of authenticity just like a burglar entering a house with a false key. Without this sense of sanctity and sacredness that was attached to the notions of science, progress and civilization, Europe, Bennabi argues, would not have been able to lay down "the foundations for the twentieth-century civilization internally and to establish its domination over the world internationally." Therefore, it can be inferred that a cultural order in its formative stage would "always seek support in sacred values" as a means of establishing its legitimacy in the psychology of the people.[109]

These pertinent remarks on the conditions of the integration of ideas to the course of human history pave the way for the examination of the realm of ideas as one of the parameters of cultural life and social action. According to Bennabi, this realm consists of two principal categories of ideas: *les idées imprimées* and *les idées exprimées*, that is, the *impressed* and the *expressed* ideas. Comparing the realm of ideas to a disk, he maintains that every historical society has its own *disk* whose fundamental *notes* are differently imprinted in the subjectivity of its members. These fundamental notes, or impressed ideas, constitute the centers of polarization for the vital energies and psycho-sociological forces of that society, as we have seen above. The centrality and specific character in human social and cultural existence of this category of ideas is emphasized by the use of such suggestive terms as master ideas (*idées maîtresses*), driving ideas (*idées forces*), driving forces, and archetypes.

It appears from Bennabi's analysis that this category of ideas is limited in number and universal in scope. Due to their place in human society's existence as matrices of its cultural world, these archetypes consist of the core ideas and central values that constitute the fundamental components of the society's worldview. They provide its members with the prism through which they perceive their place in the universe, understand their vocation in history, and establish their relationship with the different realms of existence. Thus, they form the ultimate source of inspiration for the society's cultural genius and intellectual creativity as well as the forces of orientation for its vital and psycho-sociological energies. As indicated by Bennabi, insofar as the members of a society maintain a psychologically genuine and creative rapport with its archetypes, all its activities, including its produced ideas, will be molded accordingly.

Let us, before moving to another level of analysis, make the following clarification regarding Bennabi's use of the term "archetype." Readers who are particularly familiar with Jungian analytic psychology may rightly note unmistakable similarity of terminology between Malik Bennabi and Carl G. Jung. However, a careful examination of the conceptual framework of both thinkers reveals that this apparent similarity does not imply any essential concurrence, neither in the ontological meaning of the concept of "archetypes" nor in their content. However, this does not preclude a great possibility of agreement between them in respect of the function such archetypes are supposed to fulfill in human socio-historical existence.

Thus, Bennabi's archetypes stand for the core ideas and fundamental values around which a society's life revolves. On the other hand, Jung's archetypes are clearly reminiscent of Plato's Forms or Ideas and refer to "the existence of definite forms in the psyche which seem to be present always and everywhere."[110] In his opinion, these forms are the "primordial images" engraved in the collective unconscious of mankind and have an ever-recurrence in the psychic experiences of the individual.[111]

For Bennabi, these archetypes might derive from a Divine revelation such as the Qur'an, or from a humanly constructed system of ideas that have crystallized and acquired an enduring status. They provide human society with a worldview and a framework guiding its movement and anchoring its existence and providing it with a specific direction and orientation.[112] On the contrary, Jung's archetypes originate from the accumulated psychic experience that constitutes the collective unconscious of the human species. Thus containing "the whole spiritual heritage of mankind," Jung's archetypes "act like maps projected by the psyche onto the world, and out of them arise all the most powerful and perennial ideas in art, religion, philosophy and science."[113] Likewise, it is possible to identify Bennabi's archetypes in terms of both time and space, while such a task remains beyond reach as far as Jung's are concerned.

Since our focus in this section is on the problem of culture dynamics in human social existence, we need to bear in mind Bennabi's argument concerning the role of ideas in terms of conditioning and orienting human society's vital energies in accordance with the requirements of moral and cultural development. Besides man, soil, and time, when society comes into existence, its real and permanent wealth consists of its archetypes or impressed ideas on the basis of which it progressively constructs its system or realm of ideas that, in turn, gradually takes root in distinctive cultural plasma. It is the relation patterns of those archetypes with the other components of the cultural world that ultimately determine the characteristic features of a society's civilization and culture in contrast to other societies.

The following question arises in this respect: How are the relations of a society's archetypes historically manifested within its cultural universe?

We saw at the beginning of our inquiry into the realm of ideas, that it comprises, besides the impressed ideas or archetypes of the society's cultural universe, another category, namely the *expressed ideas*. Now assuming that the foundational status of those archetypes would have become clear in light of the preceding discussion, our examination of the expressed ideas is believed to supply an accurate answer to the question raised above. In Bennabi's conceptual framework, the expressed ideas stand for the entire range of theoretical, scientific, technical and operational ideas produced by a society and by means of which it conceptualizes, expresses, projects, and actualizes its archetypes in the course of its historical experience. This point attracts our attention to one important line of distinction between the two categories. While Bennabi considers that the impressed ideas pass down in an "intact" state from one generation to another, he admits that the expressed ideas have to undergo a process of accumulation, adaptation, and modification that would allow each generation to meet the necessities of its respective historical circumstances. This distinction underlines two crucial aspects of the realm of ideas. First, the archetypes or impressed ideas, owing to their universality and limit in number, seem to assume an absolute and transcendental status. Second, the expressed ideas are, on the contrary, bound with the vicissitudes of time and thus subject to the laws of historical growth and change.

The viability, resiliency, and efficacy of the society's expressed ideas depend, in Bennabi's opinion, upon two essential criteria. First, their reflection of, and faithfulness to, its archetypes constitute the authenticity criterion without which such ideas have no roots and relevance in the society's cultural universe. Deriving from a special rapport stamped with "creative tension" that the members of the society would entertain with those archetypes, this authenticity criterion endows the expressed ideas with "a sacred note", thus increasing their socio-historical efficacy. For Bennabi, the "ethical and aesthetic sensitivity," which would grow out of the society's relationship with its archetypes, provides an important clue to the measurement of the incoherence within the realm of ideas as well as of social deterioration in general. In fact, the authenticity criterion can be understood in such a way that the category of expressed ideas may include whatever ideas and concepts that a society "borrows" from other civilizations and incorporates in its own cultural universe and realm of ideas through different processes of adjustment, adaptation, and assimilation.[114]

The second criterion pertains to the ability of the expressed ideas to provide adequate responses and efficient solutions to the theoretical, cognitive, moral, and practical problems confronting society in its historical evolution. It is worth noting, in this connection, that Bennabi's understanding of culture dynamics does not exclude the possibility for a society to borrow and adopt ideas, concepts and solutions originating in a different cultural universe. For him, there is no weaker position, in human socio-cultural affairs, than rejecting enlightenment by the ideas and experiences of others or benefit from their achievements. Nevertheless, he is quite clear regarding the following point. Such "borrowings" and "adoptions," he insists, will be devoid of any value and may even be counterproductive and harmful if they are not submitted to a process of adjustment and adaptation in order to make them concord with the moral and spiritual foundations of the society borrowing them.[115] Put differently, in order that such borrowings contribute positively to the civilizational development of the borrowing society, they must be such that they would enable it to achieve the goals and ends that actually derive from its original archetypes. Likewise, it is assumed that, through such a process of adjustment and adaptation, the "borrowings" can be incorporated in such a way that they would become an integral part of society's expressed ideas, thus echoing its archetypes and reflecting its spirit. This means that an expressed idea, whether internally produced (home-made) or borrowed from another civilization, would have an artificial existence that makes it historically irrelevant; hence it would lack any social significance or function as it is cut off from the moral and spiritual roots of society.

Now that we proceed to examine the realm of objects constituting the third parameter of the cultural world, it should be mentioned that Bennabi did not conceive the role of objects in cultural processes in isolation from that of ideas. To him, both the idea and the object contribute to the production and dissemination of culture in an irrevocably connected manner. This situation raises, he acknowledges, a serious difficulty regarding the objective differentiation between the respective roles of each, especially when we study culture as an ongoing process in which all the culture components are fully integrated in a continuous dynamic movement. However, and in conformity with the central place he ascribes to ideas in human social existence, Bennabi suggests the following analogy to remove this difficulty.

The relationship between the role of the idea and the object in cultural processes can be compared to the relationship, in mechanics, between the "arm and the "wheel" in those apparatuses that transform "translational" motion into a "rotational" one. As is established in mechanics, although the "arm" is the mover, it cannot overstep what is known as the "dead center" without the support of the "wheel" thanks to the energy encompassed by the latter. In his view, this analogy at once underlines the mutual dependency between the idea and the object and brings into prominence the primacy of the former by virtue of its "creative power" (*point mort*). Yet Bennabi observes that neither the idea nor the object is able to generate culture in the absence of what can be called a *sense of transcendence* at the level of the human being. Without such a sense of transcendence the realms of both ideas and objects are, historically and sociologically speaking, devoid of any cultural value and social efficacy. This sense of transcendence, he explains, can be understood in terms of a special bond linking the human being to the idea and the object. As that sense of transcendence fades away, this "bond" breaks down and the human being ultimately loses mastery over both ideas and objects. In such a situation, his/her relationship with them is so superficial and ephemeral that "it neither raises a question nor creates a problem"; hence, with such an ephemeral and superficial relationship, man's creative energies would literally remain idle.[116]

Although the point made here by Bennabi allows for further argument, especially in respect of the philosophical connotations that the idea of "transcendence" might imply, it is beyond the immediate concern of this study to embark on such an argument. However, we should not fail to stress the following point. There seems to be an attempt by Bennabi at overcoming the dichotomous conception of culture displayed in the work of some leading Western social scientists, such as the distinction between "adaptive" and "material" culture made by the American anthropologist William Ogbern and Pitirim Sorokin's typology of "ideational" and "sensate".[117]

From the above exposition, the reader could realize how broad and comprehensive Bennabi's conception of culture is. For him, culture is not simply customs that consist of the acquired patterns of behavior and belief transmitted in a society from one generation to another, as professed by Ruth Benedict.[118] Moreover, he does not look at it as merely a subjective aspect of human life that lies exclusively at the level of individual actors. He also does not see it as something that only concerns the objective side of the human experience by considering it as the product of total entities and overwhelming structures of society. More importantly, Bennabi does not conceive culture as an antithesis to, or negation of, nature. On the contrary, human beings, in his view, are always engaged in a dialogical relationship with two worlds. On the one hand, they are engaged in a continuous dialogue and exchange with the human and ideational realms that contribute to the shaping of their being and personality. On the other hand, they are engaged in another equally important dialogue with nature. The latter conveys its messages to them through "the language of colors, sound, smells, movements, shadow and light, forms and images." Human beings assimilate all these messages in the form of cultural elements that become integrated to their moral existence and fundamental being. According to Bennabi, when these cultural elements provided by nature are absorbed in our psychological and mental being, they grow "in our minds as scientific ideas that are translated into technical models and artistic expressions in the world of fashion and industry." They also might exalt, "thus inspiring the musician with a fascinating composition, the painter a wonderful painting, and the poet a mystical poem."[119] In other words, far from being antithetical to nature, culture is rather regarded by Bennabi as entailing the human involvement in and cooperation with natural phenomena and processes and their reorientation in line with human purposes and concerns.

The Question of Cultural Crisis

In Bennabi's scheme of thought it is the relationship of a society with its archetypes that shapes the phenomenal interplay of its constituent realms of persons, ideas and objects and ultimately determines its fate in history. As a society ceases to have a creative relationship with its original archetypes, it stops generating new efficacious ideas representative of those archetypes and capable of regulating its vital (instinctive) energies and endowing its collective action with meaning and orientation. Then, it naturally and precipitously slides into a state of idolatry and polarization either around the "person" or the "object," that is to say personality cult and *choseisme*. Bennabi explains this situation as follows. When a society reaches the stage of civilization thanks to its archetypes or impressed ideas, cultural equilibrium between the major realms constituting the human society (i.e. persons, ideas and objects) must be preserved if civilization and culture are to grow smoothly and creatively. In his view, a culture crisis starts when incoherence takes place between the society's impressed and expressed ideas. This incoherence is manifested in the fact that the latter category of ideas no longer reflects and represents the former category. Then, the crisis grows and reaches alarming, indeed destructive, scales, as the society's cultural world undergoes an imbalance and breakdown in the relationships of its constitutive elements (i.e. the person, the idea, and the object). This imbalance and breakdown takes the form of what Bennabi calls *despotism* of the person or the thing. This gives rise to the two phenomena of *personification* and *choseisme*. If the equilibrium is not restored and the object or the person continues to supersede the idea, society will ultimately slide into the post-civilization stage. In this connection, Bennabi argues that the present state of the Muslim world is the outcome of its submergence into the post-civilization stage in which it is now facing *choseisme* together with all its psycho-sociological and political consequences.

   For Bennabi, the failure of a society to generate creative efficacious ideas that do not betray the original ideal that had given birth to it, is not a mere intellectual problem that concerns only an elite of scholars and specialists. For as soon as this happens, thus giving way to idolatry and polarization around the person or the object, another type of ideas will come into being as a substitute. These *ersatz* ideas, to use Bennabi's own term, will serve to camouflage the society's general apathy, to nurture atomism in the individuals' thinking, to justify sectarianism and egocentrism among its people, thus paving the way for its decline and *colonizability*.

Put differently, this state of affairs comes about as the society's archetypes or impressed ideas "fade away from the disk of its civilization and its generated, or expressed, ideas, become mere whistling and crackles." This situation marks the society's historical betrayal of its origins, its atomization because of the lack of common motivations, the exhaustion of the moral and aesthetic tension at the level of its individual members, the lifelessness of its cultural world, and the general deterioration and apathy of its social fabric. Thus, Bennabi ascertains, ersatz ideas, whether advocated in the name of authenticity or borrowed from the cultural world of another civilization in the name of modernization, are no more than carriers of a specific genre of viruses that ultimately erode the very moral, cultural, and material foundations of a society. With its archetypes or *impressed ideas* betrayed and its *expressed ideas* dead and turned into virus carriers, society has only to undergo the nemesis of history aggravated by the deadly reaction of the borrowed ideas which have left their roots in the original cultural world from which they were borrowed. According to Bennabi's analysis, over no less than two centuries, the Muslim world has become the scene where "a dead idea attracts, indeed invites, a deadly idea." This is because the post-Almohad Muslim mind has been condemned in such a way that it is unable to discern and absorb "anything except what is futile, absurd and even deadly."[120]

As a consequence of this, the Muslim world at present "undergoes the nemesis of the archetypes of its own cultural universe as well as the terrible revenge of the ideas it has been borrowing from Europe without taking into consideration the conditions that would preserve their social value. This results in the depreciation of both the inherited and acquired ideas, thus generating the most pernicious harm to the moral and material development of the Muslim world."[121] This has resulted, according to Bennabi, from the fact that Muslims have, on the one hand, lost true and creative contact with the archetypes of their original cultural universe and, on the other, failed to establish genuine and fruitful contact with the cultural universe of Europe. Therefore, it is only to be expected that Muslim life now suffers from the effects of the implacable twofold revenge of both the inherited and the borrowed ideas.

In line with his argument that culture constitutes the basis for the reciprocal relationship and interdependence between the individual and society, Malik Bennabi is of the view that culture crisis is in essence a breakdown of that interdependence relationship. Correspondingly, culture crisis manifests itself in two interrelated ways: the ceasing or diminution of society's control over the individual's conduct and breakdown of social constraint, on the one hand, and the failure or inability of the individual to practice criticism and to protest against society, on the other. In both instances, Bennabi insists, a culture crisis comes about whose ultimate outcome is the disintegration of civilization. As he indicates, social phenomena are not stagnant, nor do they take place in an enclosed field. It is rather closely connected to the complex processes of social life in a dialectical manner. It is through such dialectical and interactive interconnectedness that social phenomena grow and perpetuate their consequences. Accordingly, culture crisis as a social phenomenon would grow, together with its consequences, right from the stages where it can be easily remedied up to the stage where no remedy is practically possible. Whatever the failures and setbacks befalling a society might be, they are at bottom the manifest expression of its cultural and civi-lizational crisis at a specific phase of its historical development, Bennabi strongly argues. As culture crisis reaches the point of no return, the only solution to overcome it is "a comprehensive cultural revolution, which is, in fact, a new start in social life." For Bennabi, the reaction to culture crisis is by no means identical. It varies from one society to another and, in the same society, from one historical stage to another, in accordance with the level of civilizational development.[122]

Conclusion

In the preceding pages, our main concern has been to unravel and explicate what can be deemed as the philosophical and theoretical foundations of Bennabi's thought. Our analysis of his views concerning religion, society, and culture has clearly shown to what extent these three major themes of his work are threaded together through a unified and integrated perspective deriving its underpinnings from the unitarian Qur'anic worldview and Islamic universal vision of the human condition. From the methodological point of view, his treatment of those themes was carried out according to an interdisciplinary perspective. Based on this fundamental philosophical framework and consistently with it, Bennabi attempted his treatment of various practical, politi-cal, social, economic, cultural and educational issues that were pressing in his time, whether at the particular level of Muslim countries or at the global level of the world. In fact, Bennabi labored to develop a whole program in which such issues are tackled on various occasions and in numerous articles and speeches that need to be carefully studied in order to bring the components and features of that program into strong relief and assess them in light of his philosophical and theoretical system delineated here. Although we entertain a great desire to embark on such an undertaking, the nature and scope of the present chapter does not allow for it. We only hope that some future opportunity will make this project realizable.

Notes

1. F. Bariun, *Malik Bennabi: His Life and Theory of Civilization* (Kuala Lumpur: Muslim Youth Movement of Malaysia, 1993), 69. In 1965, Bennabi published in French part one of his autobiography *Mémoires d'un témoin du siècle* under the title "L'Enfant" (The Child) in Algiers and this was translated into Arabic by Marwān Qanawāti. Originally written in French, part two was translated by the author and published in 1970 in Beirut under the title "al-Tālib" (The Student). The Arabic translation of both parts has been published in one single volume in Damascus by Dār al-Fikr under the title *Mudhakkirāt Shāhid li'l-Qarn* (*Memoirs of a Witness of the Century*). They cover the period from Bennabi's date of birth until September 1939. Some sources close to his family affirm the existence of a sequel to these two parts and that for one reason or another its publication is being purposely halted!
2. Ernest Gellner, *Reason and Culture* (Oxford: Blackwell, 1992), 55–110.

3. Roger Trigg, *Rationality and Science: Can Science Explain Everything?* (Oxford: Blackwell, 1993), 60 and 81.

4. Charles Le Gai Eaton, *Remembering God: Reflections on Islam* (Chicago: ABC International Group, 2000), 30.

5. Stephen Toulmin, *Cosmopolis: The Hidden Agenda of Modernity* (Chicago: University of Chicago Press, 1990), 147.

6. Lawrence Sklar, *Philosophy of Physics* (Oxford: Oxford University Press, 1995), 7.

7. Eaton, op. cit., 30.

8. See for example, Max Horkheimer, *The Eclipse of Reason* (New York: Continuum, 1974 [1947]); Paul Fayerbend, *Farewell to Reason* (London: Verso, 1987); Vattimo Gianni, *The End of Modernity*, Jon R. Snyder (trans.) (Cambridge: Polity Press, 1988); John Horgan, *The End of Science* (London: Abacus, 1998 [1996]).

9. David Dockery, "The Challenge of Postmodernism", in David Dockery, ed., *The Challege of Postmodernism: An Evangelical Engagement* (Grand Rapids, MI: Baker Books, 1995), 14.

10. I intentionally do not here talk about metaphysical or transcendental reality because it does not constitute part of the scheme of things of modernity and post-modernity.

11. Toulmin, op. cit., 172.

12. Carl F. H. Henry, "Post-modernism: The New Spectre", in David Dockery, op. cit., 38.

13. Pauline Rosenau, *Postmodernism and the Social Sciences* (Princeton: Princeton University Press, 1992), 54.

14. See for example Mae-Wan Ho, *Genetic Engineering: Dream or Nightmare, The Brave World of Bad Science and Big Business* (Penang, Malaysia: TWN, 1998). The author is a British biologist and a fellow of the US National Genetics Foundation.

15. René Dubos, *So Human an Animal* (New York: Charles Scribner's Sons, 1968), 3–9.

16. Michel Foucault, *The Order of Things: An Archeology of the Human Sciences* (London: Routledge, 1992).

17. Francis Fukuyama, *Our Posthuman Future: Consequences of the Biotechnology Revolution* (New York: Farrar, Straus and Giroux, 2002).

18. Lawrence E. Cahoone, *The Dilemma of Modernity* (New York: The State of University of New York Press, 1988), 17.

19. Malik Bennabi, *The Qur'anic Phenomenon: An Essay of a Theory on the Qur'an*, Mohamed El-Tahir El-Mesawi (trans.), (Kuala Lumpur: Islamic Book Trust, 2004), 31. (Unless otherwise indicated, our exposition of Bennabi's views in this section on religion draws mainly on this book.)

20. Mohamed El-Tahir El-Mesawi, *A Muslim Theory of Human Society: An Investigation into the Sociological Thought of Malik Bennabi* (Kuala Lumpur: Thinker's Library, 1998), 11–18.

21. Serge Mascovici: *The Invention of Society* (Cambridge: Polity Press, 1993), 33.

22. For detailed expositions of different theories of religion, see the following works: Bryan S. Turner, *Religion and Social Theory* (London: Sage Publications, 1983); Malcolm B. Hamilton, *The Sociology of Religion* (London: Routledge, 1995); Daniel L. Pals, *Seven Theories of Religion* (Oxford: Oxford University Press, 1996).

23. Malik Bennabi, *On the Origins of Human Society*, Mohamed El-Tahir El-Mesawi (trans.) (Kuala Lumpur: Islamic Book Trust, 2002), 80; *The Qur'anic Phenomenon*, op. cit., 30.

24. M. Bennabi, *The Qur'anic Phenomenon*, 41.

25. M. Bennabi, *L'Afro-Asiatisme: Conclusions sur la Conférence de Bandoeng* (Cairo: Imprimerie Misr S.A.E., 1956), 256.

26. Muhammad Bāqir al-Sadr, *al-Madrasah al-Qur'aniyyah* (Beirut: Dār al-Ta'āruf, 1981), 115–18.

27. Brian Morris, *Anthropological Studies in Religion* (Cambridge: Cambridge University Press, 1987), 168.
28. J. Campell (ed.), *The Portable Jung* (Harmondsworth: Penguin Books, 1971), 45–6.
29. J. J. Clarke, *In Search of Jung* (London: Routledge, 1992), 32.
30. Carl Gustave Jung, *Psychology and Religion* (New Haven: Yale University Press, 1966), 2. Cf. Clarke, op. cit., 35.
31. M. Bennabi, *On the Origins of Human Society*, 80.
32. Edouard Montet, *Histoire de la Bible* (Paris: Payot, 1924), 74.
33. Fakhr al-Dán Muäammad ibn 'Umar al-Rāzá, *al-Tafsár al-Kabár* (Beirut: Dār al-Kutub al-'Ilmiyyah, 1411/1990), vol. 14/28, 7; Nāsir al-Din Abu Sa'ad 'Abd Allāh al-Baydāwá, *Anwār al-Tanzil wa Asrār al-Ta'wil* (Beirut: Dar al-Fikr, 1416/1996), vol. 5, 178.
34. Kenneth Cragg, *The Event of the Qur'an: Islam in its Scripture* (Oxford: Oneworld, 1994 [1971]). Cragg's work is noteworthy in that he tried in it to bring into prominence the phenomenological aspects of the Qur'an. However, his analysis tends to obliterate the concept of *wahy* by trying to explain it in terms of the human genius of the Prophet.
35. Kenneth Cragg, *The Event of the Qur'an*, 38–9.
36. Ibid., 185.
37. Ibid., 186.
38. Bennabi, *The Qur'anic Phenomenon*, 262.
39. El-Mesawi, op. cit., 45–160.
40. Ram Krishna Mukherjee, *Society, Culture and Development* (New Delhi: Sage Publications, 1991), 11–12.
41. Mukherjee, op. cit., 12; Ibn Khaldun: *The Muqaddimah*, Franz Rosenthal (trans.) (London: Routledge & Kegan Paul, 1967), vol. 1, 89; Muhammad al-Tāhir Ibn 'Ashur: *Usul al-Nizām al-Ijtimā'i Fi'l -Islām*, Mohamed El-Tahir El-Mesawi (ed.) (Amman: Dār al-Nafais, 2001), 171.
42. Ibn Khaldun, op. cit., vol. 1, 98–101; Ibn 'Àshur, 171; Mukherjee, 13.
43. William McDougall, *An Introduction to Social Psychology* (New Delhi: Atlantic Publishers and Distributors, 1994).
44. Malik Bennabi, *On the Origins of Human Society: The Social Relations Network*, Mohamed El-Tahir El-Mesawi (trans.) (Kuala Lumpur: Islamic Book Trust, 2002). (Since our exposition of Bennabi's views on society draws mainly on this book, we will refer to it only in the case of direct quotations. Cross-references to his other works will, however, be made whenever relevant.)
45. M. Bennabi, *On the Origins of Human Society*, 9.
46. M. Bennabi, *Ta'ammulāt* (Damascus: Dār al-Fikr, 1991), 157.
47. Piotr Sztompka, *The Sociology of Social Change* (Oxford: Blackwell Publishers, 1993), 146.
48. M. Bennabi, *Ta'ammulāt*, 158.
49. M. Bennabi, *Islam in History and Society*, Asma Rashid (trans.) (Kuala Lumpur: Berita Publishing, 1991), 90.
50. Abdelwahab Bouhdiba, *Sexuality in Islam*, Alan Shridan (trans.) (London: Routledge & Kegan Paul, 1985), 15.
51. M. Bennabi, *Islam in History and Society*, 81.
52. One main reason why Bennabi paid special attention to these two interpretations might be because they had gained quite a wide audience among Arab intellectuals and academicians during the 1950s and 1960s when he was developing his views.
53. Karl Marx, 1859, quoted in Mukherjee, op. cit., 150–1.
54. Karl Marx, *Capital* [1949], vol. 1, 64; quoted in Mukherjee, op. cit., 152.

55. Arnold Toynbee, *Study of History*, quoted by Mazheruddin Siddiqi: *The Qur'anic Concept of History* (Islamabad: Islamic Research Institute, 1984), 197.

56. M. Bennabi, *al-Muslim Fi 'Alam al-Iqtisād* (Damascus: Dār al-Fikr, 1987), 91–2; *Ta'ammulāt*, 135.

57. Muhammad Asad, *The Message of the Qur'an* (Gibraltar: Dar al-Andalus, 1984), 961; Rāzi, op. cit., vol. 11, 13–16; Muhammad al-Tāhir Ibn 'Ashur, *Tafsir al-Tahrir wa al-Tanwir* (Tunis: Maison Souhnoun, 1997), vol. 15, 420–9; Muäammad Hussain Tabtaba'I, *al-Mizān Fi Tafsir al-Qu'ān* (Beirut: Mua'assat al-A'lmi li'l-Maæbu'at, 1991), vol. 13, 152–7, and vol. 20, 365–6.

58. M. Bennabi, *Ta'ammulāt*, 27 and 135.

59. M. Bennabi, *al-Muslim Fi 'Alam al-Iqtisād*, 91.

60. M. Bennabi, *The Question of Ideas in the Muslim World*, Mohamed El-Tahir El-Mesawi (trans.) (Kuala Lumpur: Islamic Book Trust, 2003), 22.

61. M. Bennabi, *Shurut al-Nahdah* (Damascus: Dār al-Fikr, 1987), 24–56.

62. M. Bennabi, *The Qur'anic Phenomenon*, 36.

63. M. Bennabi, *Shurut al-Nahdah*, 80.

64. Ibn Khaldân, op. cit., vol. 1, 91.

65. M. Bennabi, *Islam in History and Society*, 89.

66. M. Bennabi, *Shurut al-Nahdah*, 56 and 65.

67. M. Bennabi, *The Question of Culture*, Abdul Wahid Lu'lu'a (trans.) (Kuala Lumpur: Islamic Book Trust and International Institute of Islamic Thought, 2003), 9–40 and 48.

68. Fawzia Bariun, "Malik Bennabi and the Intellectual Problems of the Muslim Ummah," *The American Journal of Islamic Social Sciences*, 9/3 (1992), 329.

69. Almohad (al-Muwahidun) dynasty, founded by Muhammad ibn Tumart in 1133 CE, ruled over the entire Muslim West (i.e. North Africa and part of Muslim Spain) for more than a century and held a prominent, if not the foremost, rank in the contemporary world. To historians, this was an era that flourished in the field of thought and culture with scholars such as Ibn Tofayl, Ibn Rushd, al-Shātibi. With the death of the fifth Almohad ruler in the year 1293, the first symptoms of decline became noticeable. This dynasty finally ended in the year 1269 with the death of its last ruler, 'Ulā Idris al-Wāthiq. According to Malik Bennabi, the end of the Almohad dynasty marked the end of the second phase of the Islamic civilizational cycle. Thereafter, the Muslim world plunged into what he calls the post-Almohad age that coincides with the phase of decadence and disintegration, thus paving the way for colonizability and its corollary, colonialism.

70. *Colonizability* (Fr. colonisabilité), a term coined by Bennabi to denote the state of a society that is susceptible to be colonized and dominated by others. Accordingly, he considers that colonialism was a consequence, rather than a cause, of the internal conditions and structures of Muslim and Third World societies. For more elaboration on this subject and its relationship with its correlate colonialism, see his book *Shurut al-Nahdah*, 149–60.

71. M. Bennabi, *Shurut al-Nahdah*, 44–51; *Pour Changer l'Algérie* (Algiers: S.E.C., 1990), 9–16.

72. M. Bennabi, *On the Origins of Human Society*, 27; *The Question of Ideas in the Muslim World*, Mohamed El-Tahir El-Mesawi (trans.) (Kuala Lumpur: Islamic Book Trust, 2003), 13–16 and 20–3; *The Question of Culture*, Abdul Wahid Lu'lu'a (trans.) (Kuala Lumpur: Islamic Book Trust, 2003), 21–45.

73. M. Bennabi, *Shurut al-Nahdah*, 80.

74. In the remaining part of this chapter dealing with the issue of culture, our discussion will mainly draw on the following two books of Bennabi: (i) *The Question of Ideas in the Muslim World*; and (ii) *The Question of Culture*. Therefore, only in cases of direct quotation will reference be made to them.

75. Clifford Geerts, *The Interpretation of Cultures* (London: Fontana Press, 1993), 4.
76. M. Bennabi, *L'Afro-Asiatisme*, 293.
77. Ibid., 161 and 165.
78. Ibid., 163–4.
79. M. Bennabi, *L'Afro-Asiatisme*, 87; *Islam in History and Society*, 23–40; *Shurut al-Nahdah*, 44–51.
80. M. Bennabi, *al-Qadayā al-Kubrā* (Damascus: Dār al-Fikr, 1992), 80.
81. M. Bennabi, *L'Afro-Asiatisme*, 166.
82. M. Bennabi, *Pour Changer l'Algérie*, 56–9.
83. M. Bennabi, Ibid., 59–60; *Ta'ammulāt*, 148–9.
84. M. Bennabi, *Pour Changer l'Algérie*, 60; *On the Origins of Human Society*, 115.
85. *The Question of Culture*, 67. It is interesting to point out that this notion of noosphere being the ideational realm for the spiritual and mental development of human beings has constituted a major field of philosophical and sociological investigation by the leading French philosopher Edgar Morin. See volume 4 of his *magnum opus La Méthode* entitled *Les Idées. Leur habitat, leur vie, leur moeurs, leur organisation* (Ideas: Their Habitat, Life, Habits and Organization (Paris: Seuil, 1991).
86. F. Bariun, op. cit., 171.
87. M. Bennabi, *L'Afro-Asiatisme*, 166.
88. M. Bennabi, *al-Qadayā al-Kubrā*, 88.
89. M. Bennabi, *L'Afro-Asiatisme*, 173–4.
90. M. Bennabi, *Ta'ammulāt*, 151.
91. M. Bennabi, *L'Afro-Asiatisme*, 174.
92. M. Bennabi, *The Question of Culture*, 60.
93. M. Bennabi, *Ta'ammulāt*, 151.
94. M. Bennabi, *Ta'ammulāt*, 151–2; *al-Qadayā al-Kubrā*, 85–6.
95. M. Bennabi, *L'Afro-Asiatisme*, 295–7.
96. Ibid., 289–94.
97. M. Bennabi, *The Question of Ideas*, 46.
98. M. Bennabi, *On the Origins of Human Society*, 51–2 and 73; *The Question of Culture*, 42.
99. M. Bennabi, *The Question of Ideas*, 10–11.
100. M. Bennabi, *Ta'ammulāt*, 148.
101. M. Bennabi, *The Question of Ideas*, 11; *The Question of Culture*, 66.
102. M. Bennabi, *Ta'ammulāt*, 148.
103. Ibid., 150–1.
104. Ibid., 149–50.
105. M. Bennabi, *Shurut al-Nahdah*, 60; *al-Muslim Fi 'Alam al-Iqtisād*, 44–5; *The Question of Ideas*, 111–12.
106. M. Bennabi, *On the Origins of Human Society*, 67.
107. M. Bennabi, *al-Muslim Fi 'Alam al-Iqtisād*, 16.
108. M. Bennabi, *On the Origins of Human Society*, 67–8; *The Question of Ideas*, 25–6 and 68–9.
109. M. Bennabi, *The Question of Ideas*, 69.
110. Carl G. Jung, *The Archetypes and the Collective Unconscious* (London: Routledge, 1991), 42.
111. Carl G. Jung, *Psychological Types*, H. G. Baynes (trans.) (London: Routledge, 1989), 442–46; see also Clarke, op. cit., 116–27.
112. M. Bennabi, *The Question of Ideas*, 34.
113. Carl G. Jung, *Complete Works*, vol. 9, 99, cited by Clarke, op. cit., 117.
114. M. Bennabi, *The Question of Ideas*, 43–4.
115. M. Bennabi, *On the Origins of Human Society*, 122–3.

116.   M. Bennabi, *The Question of Culture*, 29–32.
117.   Sztompka, op. cit., 152.
118.   Cahoone, op. cit., 246.
119.   M. Bennabi, *The Question of Culture*, 39–40.
120.   M. Bennabi, *The Question of Ideas*, 102–4.
121.   Ibid., 109–10.
122.   M. Bennabi, *The Question of Culture*, 65.

CHAPTER 13

Hassan Hanafi on Salafism and Secularism

Yudian Wahyudi

This chapter deals with the efforts of the Egyptian philosopher Hassan Hanafi (b. 1935) to bridge the gap between Salafism and secularism, the two principal conflicting ideologies in his homeland, from the perspective of his reform project known as "Heritage and Reform" or "Islamic Left." His first step involves deconstructing the allegedly legitimate Islamic tradition to the effect that the Muslim community would split into 73 groups, all of whom would ultimately find themselves in Hell, with one exception, namely, the Ahl al-Sunnah (People of the Prophet's Tradition). The hadith of "the safe group" is, to begin with, weak by virtue of the fact that it contradicts a sound hadith stating that the Muslim community will not split over *dalalah* (going astray) and another hadith stating that disagreement in the community is a *rahmah* (blessing). The hadith of "the safe group," he insists, was in fact fabricated to condemn the opposition forces of the classical Islamic era (Kharijism, Shi'ism, and Mu'tazilism) while at the same time affirming the claims of the pro-establishment group (Ash'arism). The hadith of "the safe group" is in fact spurious, but many have since used it to promote their interests. It was in reaction to this view that Hanafi decided to try reconciling the various rival groups of his own day, in particular: (i) Al-Ikhwan al-Muslimun (Muslim Brotherhood) – which for him represents the Islamic community (Al-Jama'ah al-Islamiyyah) or the Islamic movement (Al-Harakah al-Islamiyyah) or Islamism in general; (ii) communism (Marxism); (iii) liberalism; and (iv) Nasserism (nationalism and socialism). It is worth noting, however, that to avoid any confusion, the term Salafism in this chapter will always designate the Muslim Brotherhood, whereas secularism stands for liberalism, Nasserism, and Marxism. This is how Hanafi sees the world, and it is this polarization that he sets out to resolve.[1]

The Moment of the Salafi–Secularist Encounter

The opposition of Salafism and secularism, Hanafi reminds his readers, is a false dualism, just as are those of religion and state, religion and science, authenticity and contemporaneity, God and nature, God and man, soul and body, world and afterlife, and man and woman. The West had to face these superficial definitions in its journey to modernity because the more it promoted modernism, the more it found impossible the task of reconciling church and state, religion and reason, faith and science, Aristotle and nature. The West finally opted for the new, while leaving aside the old. The former, in Hanafi's estimation, included reason, science, nature, and man's capability of understanding, analysis and criticism, whereas the old encompassed church, religion, faith, Aristotle, and Ptolemy. The tension became even stronger in the European consciousness because it based its entire system of education on these allegedly contradictory dualisms, and in turn spread them into Africa, Asia and Latin America through colonization and various media. Since the dawn of the Arab Renaissance in the eighteenth century, this enthusiasm for the new has grown in Arab culture. Yet instead of seeking to reconcile the seemingly contradictory sides, many Arab thinkers, Hanafi contends, adopted the logic of "either–or," resulting in a division of the Arab community into two mutually opposing groups. Thus the classical Arab heritage and the invasive new came into conflict following the Western model, especially over secular and scientific trends, as was the case with Shibli Shumayl, Farah Antun, Salama Musa, Ismail Mazhar, Zaki Najib Mahmud, and Fouad Zakariyya.[2]

This split, says Hanafi, took place at the lowest point in Arab culture. Creativity had ceased, while imitation dominated. When confronted by problems, many Arab thinkers preferred quoting classical authorities to undertaking *ijtihād* (creative process) themselves, resulting in the submergence of reality in their classical heritage. By preferring this method to any really fresh solution, these Arab thinkers disappointed many others, who in turn looked to the invasive West for their answers. These two artificial solutions overlapped each other at the expense of actually resolving any problems. Moreover, despite their respective claims, Hanafi argues, neither group contained true *mujtahids* (creative thinkers). The Salafis transmitted from the traditionalists, and the secularists from the modernists. The inevitable tension between Salafism and secularism rose when the Arab national states were weak. And instead of joining forces to strengthen these states, both Salafism and secularism turned their differences into war and bloodshed, as they did in Egypt, Algeria, and Syria, with each wing positioning itself to take over on the demise of these nations. When, however, the states recovered and needed their help, Salafism and secularism renewed their rivalry, as Salafism did with secularism in Nasser's Egypt (1952–70). For their part, the secularists took revenge against the Salafis in Sadat's time (1970–81), whereas under the pretext of promoting Enlightenment against Darkness, Salafism had its revenge on secularism in the third Egyptian Republic (under Mubarak). However, Hanafi criticizes most Arab observers for ignoring the fact that both Salafism and secularism have their negative and positive dimensions, which are intermingled in Arab culture.[3]

The attack on secularism, Hanafi argues, was justified by reference to its perceived negative attributes, which he defines under two headings. First of all, its ancestor was Western material secularism, under the influence of which both capitalism and communism came into being. Atheism in turn followed materialism, leading to rejection of Allah, prophethood, and revelation. In order to find greater acceptance, Hanafi argues, the secularists ought to have looked to Salafism, which promoted the perfect unity of religion and world, soul and body, and God's and man's rights. This unity is clear in the concept of *maqāṣid al- sharī'ah* (aims of Islamic law). Indeed, even Salafis would be surprised at the extent to which Islamic law is secular, given its foundation in human life and reality, and its concern to protect the public interest. Therefore, the word secular (*waḍʿī*) is not a monopoly of the secularists, nor are the words intellect, science, nature, progress, man, rights, duties, and citizens. Second, the secularists, by imitating the West, lost all hope of winning support from the Salafis. The secularists, in the eyes of the Salafis, supported Westernization models, while calling for a disconnection from heritage. Through this, they became the representatives of Western civilization, and were identified with the powers that be. By contrast, Salafism was able to outdo secularism by taking over its traditional role of defending the weak against the powerful, supporting authenticity against Westernization, giving priority to "self" over "other," and defending the self against the dangers that might threaten it, as in the phase of liberation from colonialism. All national freedom movements in Egypt, Morocco, Tunisia, Libya, Egypt, and Lebanon, Hanafi assures us, were self-defensive. Their success was proof that the ancient always lived on in the Arab soul; nevertheless, it does not mean that Salafism was free from weaknesses.[4]

Hanafi criticizes Salafism for being wholly dependent on religious heritage, for relying principally on the religious disciplines, whereas reality required worldly sciences. To solve this problem, he advises the Salafis to learn from the positive aspects of secularism, i.e., by applying the technologically based science to nature in order to understand its laws and solve its mysteries, by which they would truly return to the pristine teachings of Islam, as is their primary claim. Ritualism has always been a second drawback of Salafism. Modern reality demands ideologies, political strategies, national action, and social development plans – all of which, Hanafi notes, can easily be found by the Salafis in secularist principles. Salafism in fact shows itself to be un-Islamic by being conservative, by always giving priority to God's will over man's will and natural laws, by regarding transmission as the foundation of reason, and even by limiting leadership to Qurayshites. Secularism, on the other hand, can be seen as more Islamic for believing in progress as the essence of the cosmos and the law of life, and for holding the principle that "the present is better than the past." Finally, the backward-looking position of the Salafis equated it in the eyes of many with the out-of-date "yellow books," not to mention the antique cultures of shaykh *vis-à-vis* scholar, commoner *vis-à-vis* elite and religious *vis-à-vis* national universities. The Salafis should, Hanafi advises, incorporate the forward-looking ethos of secularism into their backward practice, as the Islamic reform movement attempted following the lead of al-Afghani, or as modern liberal thought has done since al-Tahtawi and Khayr al-Din al-Tunisi. Finally, the Salafis should replace their narrow Qurayshite-oriented leadership with secular openness, which bases its political philosophy on the social contract. In its Western incarnation, secularism had succeeded in transforming people from being subjects of the Church into inhabitants of a society, from slaves into masters of their own fate, or from feudal peasants into free citizens. Hanafi reminds the secularists, however, that it was Islam that started liberating people when slavery was the dominant socio-political system of the Roman and Persian Empires.[5]

Dialoging Method

The conflict between Salafism and secularism, according to Hanafi's diagnosis, has something to do with their respective, logical methods. The Salafis deduce absolute reality from the literal meaning of a text and apply it to a particular fact, whereas, by contrast, the secularists base their analyses on observation, by quantitatively concluding social laws from individual and social experiences. Therefore, the secularists do not share the Salafi belief in truth as *a priori* given, as an *a priori* written text, or as outside history, time and place, certain and not probable, but rather as a truth grounded in reality, to which *a priori* judgment – favored by the Salafis – is not an accurate approach. Their methodological differences in turn resulted in different ways of expression, since the Salafis used the language of rhetoric to argue their case and the secularists that of numbers – the latter of which for Hanafi is more communicative and more convincing. The Salafis arbitrarily transferred the success of early Muslims at using the deductive method to solve their current problems. In principle, deduction, Hanafi asserts, is valid, but in practice it needs additional detail, since truth cannot be deduced solely from *a priori* principles and sources, but also from its particularities. The Salafis should, therefore, regard induction as supporting and perfecting deduction, since the former is the reverse of the latter. The former, in Hanafi's classical Islamic terminology, is *ta'wīl* (verticalization), while the latter is *tanzīl* (horizontalization). The text itself, as the secularists correctly understood, is not a purely absolute source outside time, place, context or human understanding, since it had a socio-historical setting (*asbāb al-nuzūl*). Hanafi also reminds his fellow Salafis that the text was a response to the problems that reality posed, and for which people had tried in vain to find answers. In this context, revelation came to confirm some of these after people had given their best effort to the task.[6] Since text and reality are two sides of the same coin, text without reality (normal in Salafi practice) removes a potential solution, whereas reality without text, favored by the secularists, leaves one trapped in relativism.[7]

The Salafis have strangely misused the vertical method to undermine, avoid, reject and even replace reality (with something else), as Abu al-A'la al-Mawdūdī and Sayyid Qutb did. Despite their either–or logic, however, Islam never sees reality as pure evil, or as false and deceptive, since Islam also makes it a field for the expression of *fiṭra* (human natural disposition). Hanafi offers the last verse of the Qur'an (Q.5: 3) as proof that Islam, in its interaction with Judaism, Christianity, and Hanafism (the religion of Abraham) in the Arabian context, to a great extent improved and perfected reality. The Salafis, Hanafi continues, have selectively taken the text out of its context, resulting in partial and even contradictory understandings. While the text is part of a whole that should be understood in its totality, Salafis have tended to consider Islamic legal texts as the sum total of Islam. The truth, he counters, is that Islamic legal texts, including those on criminal law (*Ḥudūd*), form only a small part of the literature of Islamic rulings. Therefore, the Salafis' definition of Islamic texts as those alone that command and prohibit gives the impression that Islam is a punishment-oriented religion, since the Salafis make no mention of those texts that encourage mercy, love, friendship, good interaction, and communications. Text, Hanafi reminds his fellow Salafis, is language, which needs understanding and interpretation. They should not generalize it, since it is not one single category, but can be classified into real and metaphor, exoteric and interpretable, unequivocal and equivocal, global and detailed, unconditional and conditional. Underlining the reader's role in understanding the Qur'an, classical Muslim thinkers like the Mu'tazilites, philosophers, and Sufis went beyond the Qur'an's literal meaning in order to understand its purpose. The spirit of the text, which they called *faḥwa al-khiṭāb* and *laḥn al-khiṭāb*, is for them more indicative of meaning than the letter of the text that the Salafis defended.[8]

Inductive method, Hanafi reminds his Salafi fellows, can help explain their reality and change their rhetoric and slogans into quantitative truth. On the other hand, numbers, Hanafi reminds his secularist audience, are not immune to mistakes when calculation is less accurate. Statistics, like deduction, are always subject to inaccuracy, since they will never be able to calculate a totality, whereas rough fact does not represent the totality. Similarly, although quantitative analysis should always be supported with qualitative reading, reading itself may mislead, as it can be mistaken and pluralistic. It is also insufficient to hope for description, analysis, understanding, and knowing without providing mechanisms for change and improvement in opposition to the Salafists, who began by orienting the text toward reality almost without interpreting the text or observing the contents of reality, as was the case with the transmission patterns of Islamic propagandists and reformists like Muhammad ibn Abd al-Wahhab. The two methods, both the Salafis and the secularists should know, are different but complementary because deduction is simply the reverse of induction, and vice versa. A unified method, Hanafi stipulates, is a condition for unity of thought, and a way of erasing hostility between the two mutually exclusive groups. Under the guidance of these complementary, and not contradictory, methods, both groups can work towards achieving one and the same goal: the general public interest.[9]

This unity of method, according to Hanafi, had already been realized in classical Arabo–Islamic culture. Islamic legal theory (*uṣūl al-fiqh*), for instance, accomplished this by combining root (*aṣl*) and branch (*far'*), a process he sees as a combination of deduction and induction, verticalization and horizontalization, and text and reality. Given that the root is the known text, i.e., ruling and case – it can only be known through the analysis of text in terms of language, its textually stated cause, and by the occasions of revelation, as well as by the abrogating and abrogated verses. On the other hand, the branch can only be known through experimentation with, observation and analysis of its effective, formative or correlative causes in the external word. Given that the cause is in the root and is known through deduction, the cause in the branch can be known through induction, because the branch takes the cause of the root. That is why Islamic legal philosophers (*uṣūliyyun*) called analogy (*qiyās*) the process of "extending the legal value from the root to the branch due to their similarity in terms of cause." All knowledge, adds Hanafi, needs two principles: permanent elements and changing elements. Muslim legal philosophers disagree over what forms the permanent takes in different genres of text, but the element of change for them is always social reality, which he in turn identifies as colonialism, backwardness, oppression, division, corruption, laziness, identity loss and mass indifference. Faced with these social realities, Salafis and secularists disagree only in terms of the method they would use to solve them. In such a context, Hanafi maintains, methodological pluralism is acceptable because the unity of goal and purpose allows for a pluralism of methods. Since confronting one method with another can, however, lead to national divisions (especially in the case of Egypt), both deduction and induction must be seen to complete each other. Method, he reminds both sides in the conflict, is a means and not an end: disagreement over it should, therefore, lead not to enmity or killing, but to complementary and pluralistic approaches to the same problem, as the Qur'an 5: 48 teaches.[10]

Dialoging Language

The existence of a common language is necessary to solve the Salafi and secularist conflict, as it can help minimize their respective, more extreme expressions. Although both groups use different terminologies, due to their origin in two different discourses separated by a time span of more than a millennium, their meanings are often similar. The Salafis simply miscommunicate their ideas by using traditional words. Instead of modernizing these centuries-old Islamic terms, they employ them as they were originally used in the formative period, and as a result find their audience limited to specialists like *ulamas* and shaykhs in Islamic universities and other institutions. To reach a non-traditional audience, Hanafi advises the Salafis to take the chance of using the secularist vocabulary. It is true that the secularists took their new idioms from modern Western culture, but their meaning does not differ to any significant degree from the classical Islamic terms the Salafis use. The Salafis will be able to see the similarities between their language and that of the Secularist meanings if they contextualize their renewed meanings and, thus, avoid misunderstanding. The Salafis, for example, take for granted the words *imān* (belief) and *kufr* (disbelief) as, respectively, positive and negative – in the process categorically excluding Secularist interpretations of their content. However, this is not really the case, since the meanings of these Islamic terms can turn out to be the opposite: for instance, believing in other than Allah, for example, is rejected, whereas disbelieving in the *ṭāghūt* (tyrant) is respected. In a slightly different sense, words like *shirk* and *tawhīd* can be extended to the sense, in the case of *shirk*, of associating Allah with power, status, property, fame, and the temptations of life – all of which are condemned – while *tawhīd* can mean unifying individuals, society and humanity, which is respected. The secularists, in his point of view, made a great contribution to these newly interpreted goals now in use among the Salafis.[11]

The secularist vocabularies, Hanafi reminds his fellow Salafis, are popular to the extent that they take as their model international language and culture, since they contain modern words pertaining to concepts such as evolution, development, planning, change and reform. However, they are not strange to proponents of modern Islamic reform, which forms a bridge of sorts between Salafism and secularism. Modern Islamic reformists realize, unlike the Salafis, that theologically closed terminologies, like the words *dīn* and *Islam*, cannot simply be accepted without the use of reason, question, or discussion. People usually understand the word *dīn* (religion) in contradistinction to that of *dunya* (world). In this context, they see it as a concept that deals more with the hidden world than the physical one, resulting in a fatal reduction that excludes secularist interpretations. In fact, the word *dīn* in its true Islamic sense, Hanafi reminds his Salafi audience, encompasses the physical world, reality, society, people, public interest and all that the secularists speak about. The Salafis should, therefore, recast their ideas in modern terms as the secularists did in order to communicate their common concerns. Likewise, the word Islam, as it is commonly used, gives the impression that it is solely the religion that the last Prophet brought, due to which fact its followers are called Muslims. The pure traditional usage of this terminology by the Salafis has widened the gap between themselves and the secularists. In fact, the word Islam, for Hanafi, means comprehensive, rational, and natural religion. It is the religion of *bara'at al-aṣliyya* (original innocence in opposition to original sin), the one and the same religion practiced since the time of Adam down to Noah, Abraham, Moses, Jesus, and Muhammad. Since it also encompasses everyone who believes in God and does good deeds, the concept of Islam includes other Eastern religions. The Salafis should, therefore, clarify that by Islam they mean a religion of all human beings, a notion that the secularists, according to Hanafi, have already conceived.[12]

In diametrical contrast to the secularists' worldly orientation, the Salafis use metaphysical terms, which often deal more with the hidden world than with the apparent one, more with the afterlife (*akhira*) than with these worldly matters, more with human beings after death rather than the life before it. The Salafis' excessive discussion of jinn, angels, *ṣirāt* (bridge), *mizān* (scale), and *khawd* (reservoir, lake), and paradise and hell-fire has diverted their attention from societal problems. They seem to live in a different world. It is thus quite natural for the secularists to question the usefulness of discussing such arcane concepts for solving the world crisis. In their own right, the secularists disregarded this wrong-headed discussion and turned their attention instead to talking about immediate and practical matters like injustice, justice, enmity, and struggle, even though all of these – Hanafi reminds his secularist interlocutors – can be found in some of the Salafi vocabularies and their afterlife symbols. It is only that the Salafis cannot bring themselves to express such matters in realistic and practical language, as the secularists do. Were they able to, the Salafis could share their common concerns about such problems as poverty, drought and famine, hunger, oppression, exploitation, hopelessness, marginalization, justice, income distribution, transportation and settlement with the secularists. If only they could recast these public interests, which are the foundation of Islamic legislation, in the worldly terms of the secularists, a major step would be taken towards rapprochement between the two factions.[13]

Another problem is that the Salafis often use legal and imperative terms that require absolute loyalty and application because they see themselves as being in charge of applying Islamic law for their communities. Considering every Islamic ruling as *farḍ* (obligation) and applying *Ḥudūd* as unavoidable, the Salafis have mistakenly transformed their discourse into a means of subjugation and terror against state and society. Nevertheless, these terminologies, Hanafi warns the Salafis, do not ignore human freedom, free choice, and developing nature and its spontaneity. To communicate better their ideals, the Salafis can borrow the secularists' more spontaneous and natural terms, since the secularists, in the true spirit of Islam, use them to express the human desire for liberation. The secularist terminologies recognize human basic needs, but the Salafis should know this. Hanafi insists that they, to a great extent, express the very ideals of *maqāṣid al-sharī'ah*, i.e., preserving life, reason, religion, pride, and property. On the other hand, Islamic law, he reminds his secularist audience, is natural and secular. It even creates some of the legal maxims that serve these purposes just like "emergencies allow every body to do the prohibited," "no obligation beyond human capability" and "avoiding evils is given priority over taking benefits." The Salafis need to borrow the secularists' positive language, which calls people to struggle, *ta'mīr* (emendation, restoration, civilization or prosperity of the country), work, production and investment, and this because they are often the meanings hidden in classical terms like *jihād*, *'amal* (action), *sa'y* (effort), *kadd* (pain, labor, examination), and *ijtihād* (intellectual endeavor). If the Salafis and the secularists are still reluctant to use their mutually exclusive terms, they can, Hanafi suggests, employ a third language, which is Salafi and secular at the same time. This would include such words as *ard* (land), *sha'b* (nation), *qawm* (people), *fi'l wa 'amal* (work and action), *'aql* (reason), *'ilm* (science), and *ṭabī'a wa fiṭra* (nature). These natural vocabularies, Hanafi argues, do not need to be the subject of dialogue because they are already (albeit unwittingly) shared by the Salafis and the secularists.

The Purpose of Dialogue

The Salafi–secularist conflict can be solved if both sides minimize their respective absolute purposes. The Salafis, Hanafi urges, have to shift their discourse from centering on and defending God to man, society, and history-oriented secularist ideals. On the other hand, the secularists should "Salafize" their human-centered concept of religion as not an end in itself as the Salafis claim, but merely a way of ensuring that people remain content while realizing their self-interest. For not only is religion always alive in traditional societies like that of Egypt (a very significant sociological fact that the secularists should not overlook), but it is also capable of materializing the general purposes of Islamic law, which are defined as public interests in the secularist discourse. For this reason the secularists must be willing to share their humanist claims with their Salafi competitors, who in turn should relinquish their arbitrary pretension to be *the* spokesmen of God. This suggestion, in Hanafi's view, entails that the Salafis shift their position from speaking from the center of power (which is God, since they keep insisting that no power is stronger than His), to declaring His rights to be for, and not against, human beings' reality and history. When they stop seeing criticism as posing a threat to God or as an indication of lack of belief, and start considering alternate interpretation as *ijtihād* rather than as blasphemy (which they would arbitrarily punish with the *ḥadd al-riddah* (death sentence)), the Salafis will be able to accommodate the secularists, who consider themselves proponents of international human rights and as citizens. For their part, the secularists, whose starting point is the "real" world, are equally called upon to transfer their stance from defending human rights on their own behalf to defending them in the name of God and sometimes the state. Predictably, they will be attracted to the call to *ijtihād*, which promises to give them one reward if their effort is wrong and two if right, because many of them are Muslim by faith.[15]

The Salafis should, for their part, lift their embargo on dialogue by re-evaluating their absolute dualism. Instead of confronting God with nature, this world with the next

world, life with death, belief with disbelief, as the secularists did when blindly transfer-
ring Western secular concepts to the Arab world in the eighteenth century, the Salafis
should return to Islamic duality by integrating both positive and negative into undivided elements of existence, as the secularists did in their practical usage of one-
dimensional discourse, which involved using terms like constitution, society, citizen,
moral, and politics. Another drawback of the Salafis, in his view, can be seen in
their assumption of the "good" side in their unfair dualist vision of the world. This
unilateral claim naturally places the secularists on the "bad" side. Marginalized in
this way, the secularists would, of course, feel alienated. To ease tensions, the Salafis
should no longer defend this paradigm and at the same time should redefine the
secularist status from being the Salafis' chief target to being an equal partner in
dialogue. This, Hanafi says, means bringing their theological perspective down to earth
by taking a case-by-case approach. They ought to start taking man as man without
dividing him into soul *vis-à-vis* body, reality as it is without dividing it into right and
wrong, and behavior as it is without dividing it into lawful and unlawful. If the Salafis
adopt this stance, they will be able to abandon their dominant pyramidal worldview,
which contrasts the top with the bottom or the best with the worst. The abolition of
their hierarchical vision of the universe, which divides society into such diametrical
opposites as the ruling *vis-à-vis* the ruled and master *vis-à-vis* slave, will draw the
secularists to their side, since these latter reject the pyramidal worldview and place
all phenomena at the same level of analysis in terms of religion, society, politics, and
constitution.[16]

On the other hand, Hanafi urges the secularists to rethink their purpose in the
context of the Arab classical heritage in order to appease the Salafis, since human
beings have always been at the center of the Arab-Islamic tradition. The Salafis should
have been able to satisfy their secularist counterparts by stressing the principle of
Islamic theology that Allah not only expresses Himself in human language, but also
identifies Himself with their attributes like knowledge, power, life, hearing, sight,
speech, and will – the implication being that Allah highly respects human beings. The
only difference – and here he asks his Salafi audience not to misunderstand him – is
that these attributes are absolutely applied to the Divine Essence, but made relative to
human beings in order that He may be intelligible to them. Moreover, all of His 99
attributes, he reassures the secularists, are general human ideals on justice, mercy,
glory, and generosity and not simply pure theological notions as the Salafis tend to
understand them. The secularists will be further satisfied if they look at the position of
human beings in the concept of *maqāṣid al-sharī'ah*, since in contrast to the Salafis'
literal and God-oriented interpretation, the concept in its classical sense is directed
towards preserving life, intellect, religion, pride and poverty almost entirely through
secular ways. Islamic legal maxims (*'ilm al-qawā'id al-fiqhiyyah*) were even established
to regulate human life as the highest purpose of *sharī'ah*. To strengthen his argument,
Hanafi quotes some of these: "*la ḍarara wala ḍirār* (neither harming nor counter-
harming)," "*'adam jawaz taklīf mala yuṭāq* (not obliging someone to do something
beyond his capability)," "*raf' al-haraj* (the elimination of hardship from Islamic obligations)," "*dar' al-mafasid muqaddam 'ala jalb al-masalih* (avoiding [real] dangers is
given priority over taking [imaginary] benefits)," and "*dar' al-ḥudūd bi al-shubuhāt*

(preventing the application of Islamic criminal law by [invoking] the principle of 'ambiguity')."[17]

Despite their claims, the Salafis, Hanafi admits, tend to ignore their own classical Islamic heritage. For in contrast to the tendency of the Salafis to jump from a fact to literal expressions of the Qur'an and the Sunnah, classical Islamic legal philosophers explained human actions in terms of *sabab* (cause), *sharṭ* (condition), and *mani'* (barrier) in order to judge them fairly. For example, a thief's hand cannot be amputated if he has been forced to steal due to hunger, joblessness or poverty, since the condition for the prescribed *ḥadd* punishment is self-sufficiency, full justice, steady employment and the fulfillment of all basic human needs (by the state), which are conditions rarely present in such cases. The Salafis, moreover, oddly assign priority to *fiqh al-'ibādāt* (ritual affairs) over *fiqh al-mu'āmalāt* (social affairs), even though the latter are more significant than the former, since the end of Islamic law is social law, which is perfectly represented in the horizontal dimension of the *mu'āmalāt*. The secularists would, in Hanafi's eyes, come ideologically closer to the Salafis if the latter were to change their focus from *'ibādāt* to *mu'āmalāt*. On the other hand, the secularists should (in his evaluation) re-analyze their own human discourse, for it is hard for the Salafis to see man in terms of a changing, individual being, a real person with all his faults and virtues, and not as a universal man transcending state, national or ethnic boundaries. The secularists are thus spiritually obliged to adjust their Sophist Pythagorean slogan "man is the measure of everything" to the more Egyptian or Arab perspective, since in its original existence secularism gave rise to nihilism – acceptance of which by the Salafis would be tantamount to abandoning their very foundation of Islam. The secularists not only need to jettison the slogan, which contributed to colonialism and even World War Two, but also correct their own dry understanding of man, by incorporating Sufi humanism into it. The theories of Perfect Man and Human Love, within which Divine Love manifests itself, have the potential to bridge secularist–Salafi tensions. Divinity without humanism, Hanafi reminds the Salafis, can descend into oppression, but humanism without divinity, he warns the secularists, can get trapped in relativism.[18]

Power Sharing

Power sharing is the most sensitive intersection of the Salafi and secularist conflict in the Egyptian political arena because both are politically oriented movements. They must, for this reason, back away from their respective ideological positions. Instead of simply rejecting existing governments as man-made political systems, the Salafis should first anchor their slogan "Sovereignty Belongs to Allah" in classical Islamic legal theory. Both the Salafis and the classical Islamic legal theorists, Hanafi notes, are in agreement that God rules through His law. They differ only in terms of who will represent Him to execute His law. To bridge this gap between themselves and the secularists, the Salafis are required to adapt to the classical Islamic legal theorists' stance that Allah rules through legitimate representatives (*ahl al-hall wa al-'aqd*). Since leadership according to this interpretation is based on election, contract and oath of allegiance, a Muslim leader is by definition more a representative of the people than of Allah. It will also make it easier for the Salafis to deconstruct their absolute acceptance of Ibn Taymiyya's *fatwa* (legal opinion), if they first understand the Qur'anic verses "Those who do not judge based on what Allah has sent are *kafirūn* (infidel), *fasiqūn* (vicious) and *zalimūn* (injust)" within the holistic framework of the Qur'an, which gives human beings as His vice-regents on earth the right to interpret the Scripture in many different ways. As the product of politically motivated *ijtihād*, Ibn Taymiyya's *fatwa*, which ruled out the legitimacy of the Muslim Tatar government for not grounding its rule on (the literal meaning of) Allah's *sharī'ah*, binds nobody. And since the *fatwa* is nothing more than a relative and contextual moral advice, the Salafis should not arbitrarily impose it on their contemporaries. On the other hand, Hanafi urges the secularists to avoid giving their support to atheistic secularism, but instead incorporate into their slogans words like "Freedom," "Democracy," and "Free Election."[19]

The Salafis and the secularists will, in Hanafi's estimation, be able to put an end to the contradiction between theocracy and democracy, originally inherited from the West, if they open their political will to the above mutual understanding. The secularists should begin sharing the power they have monopolized since the fall of the caliphate in 1924, a political domination that had led the Salafis to coin their slogans "Islam is the solution" or "Islam is the alternative." Since these slogans emerged to replace the failure of Arab secular ideologies like liberalism, Arab nationalism, socialism, and Marxism in modernizing Arab countries, the secularists, Hanafi demands, should accommodate Salafi interests by treating them on an equal footing instead of assassinating their leaders as the liberal and socialist-Nasserist Governments did. What is more, instead of oppressing the Salafi-oriented opposition forces in the name of the law and constitution, the secularist ruling parties should give the opposition the chance to exercise their constitutional rights. The secularists can significantly reduce Salafi resentment if they, as the ruling elite, start filling the gap between the rich and the poor, on the former of which the Salafis usually focused their struggle. The appeal for the secularists was to erase illiteracy, to stabilize prices, to provide settlement, transportation and jobs, and to reduce Egypt's dependence on imports while empowering the domestic economic sector. In short, the secularists can solve Egypt's problems as a developing country only by involving the Salafis as their equal partners.[20]

On the other hand, the Salafis, Hanafi reminds the secularists, wish to use their third slogan "Apply Islamic Law!" as a means of escaping the system that predominates at the moment. The Salafis consider the secularists as jeopardizing people's interests by issuing unfair regulations on labor, salary, settlement, tax, export, import, publication, education, and health. These laws, he reminds the secularists, did in fact contradict each other for being constantly changed in accordance with the desires of the secularist ruling elite, as well interest and pressure groups. Following this unhealthy practice, ordinary people put their interests above the law by adjusting it to their immediate goals. In this context, the slogan "Apply Islamic Law!" was used to materialize, especially as they strongly believed that, unlike the dominant man-made laws, God's laws will do justice and rule out injustice. However, Hanafi disagrees with the Salafi plan of applying *Ḥudūd* (Islamic criminal laws), since Islamic law is an undivided unity, within which the *Ḥudūd* form only a small part. The Salafis thus promote a misguided Islamization by demanding that people fulfill their duties before receiving their rights. This stance, Hanafi assures the secularists, is in diametrical opposition to the priority of Islamic law, which first gives people their rights before demanding their duties. The state should first satisfy the rights of its citizens, which include their natural entitlements to food, clothes, education, health, transportation and settlement. If they, for example, steal after the state has fulfilled all these obligations, it may be possible to apply the specified punishment to him, but only under such circumstances, seeing as the *Ḥudūd* come at the end, and not at the beginning, of the spectrum of duties *vis-à-vis* rights. Therefore, the Salafis need to reverse their priorities by promoting the fulfillment of human basic needs, as the secularists did, in order to show their mercy to people instead of frightening them with threats of harsh punishment.[21]

Both the Salafis and the secularists should finally strengthen and protect their respective national states because improving what has existed, Hanafi argues, is better than destroying and rebuilding it in the name of alternate solutions. The Salafis had, for example, gained power in Sudan, but they were unable to satisfy their own people for lack of socio-economic plans and managerial skills, a failure that the Egyptian Salafis should not repeat. The second characteristic of the state that both the Salafis and the secularists should strengthen and protect is that of economic and political independence, so that it can avoid pawning its national will in the name of bread, corn, aid or in the name of security, military, and political temptation. This state should be able to defend its foundations from within, by accommodating the Salafi strengths, and not from outside, by putting aside the secularist weaknesses. The state should be truly democratic, by allowing Egyptians to freely elect their representatives. To smooth the expression of this actual political power, the secularists will have to share the power with the Salafis by abolishing state-sponsored political parties. The state, Hanafi further stipulates, should be able to undertake dialogue with the existing Egyptian schools of thought and political powers, as it is a manifestation of Egyptian social contract. Since it is based on pluralism, this state will be unifying. In this way, the Salafis are called to express their elected popular power through national *ijmāʿ* (consensus) hand in hand with the secularists. Finally, both the Salafis and the secularists should not forget that their conflicting trends originated in one and the same Egyptian modern school of thought. The Egyptian nationalism, as first manifested in the Orabi Movement of 1882, was Jamāl al-Dīn al-Afghānī's interpretation of Salafism in the Egyptian need for liberation from foreign occupation. Without practicing this united front, both the Salafis and the secularists, Hanafi reasons, will scatter their potential.[22]

Notes

1. Hassan Hanafi, *Al-Daʿwa li al-Ḥiwār* (Cairo: Al-Hayʾa al-Misriyya al-ʿAmma li al-Kitab, 1993), 6–7; *idem, Min al-ʿAqidah ila al-Thawrah* (Cairo: Madbuli, 1988), 393–407; *idem, Dirasat Falsafiyya* (Cairo: The Anglo-Egyptian Bookshop, 1987), 121–2; *idem, Al-Din wa al-Thaqafah wa al-Siyasah* (Cairo: Dar Qibaʾ, 1998), 213; *idem, Al-Din wa al-Thawrah fi Misr 1952–1981* (Cairo: Madbuli, 1988), 6, 6–7; and *idem, Al-Haraka al-Islamiyya fi Misr* (Cairo: Al-Muʾassasah al-Islamiyyah li al-Nashr, 1986), 10–11.

2. Hanafi, *Al-Din wa al-Thaqafah wa al-Siyasah*, 238 and 257–8; *idem*, *Al-Haraka al-Islamiyya fi Misr*, 36; idem, *Al-Da'wa li al-Ḥiwār*, 26 and 69; *idem*, *Qadaya Mu'asira*, 3rd edition (Cairo: Dar al-Fikr al-'Arabi, 1987), 2, 16–17 and 32–3; and *idem*, *Islam in the Modern World* (Cairo: The Anglo-Egyptian Bookshop, 1995), 2, 46.

3. Hanafi, *Al-Din wa al-Thaqafah wa al-Siyasah*, 258–9; *idem*, *Al-Da'wa li al-Ḥiwār*, 46; *idem*, *Humum al-Fikr wa al-Watan al-'Arabi* (Cairo: Dar Qiba', 1998), 2, 180–6; and *idem*, *Qadaya Mu'asira*, 2, 16–17.

4. Hanafi, *Al-Din wa al-Thaqafah wa al-Siyasah*, 259; *idem*, *Al-Haraka al-Islamiyya fi Misr*, 19–23 and 30; idem, *Al-Din wa al-Thawrah fi Misr*, 6, 15–17; *idem*, *Dirasat Falsafiyya*, 52–3; and *idem*, *Al-Da'wa li al-Ḥiwār*, 30–3.

5. Hanafi, *Al-Din wa al-Thaqafah wa al-Siyasah*, 260–1; *idem*, *Dirasat Falsafiyya*, 547–8; *idem*, *Al-Da'wa li al-Ḥiwār*, 9–11 and 33–46; *idem*, *Al-Haraka al-Islamiyya fi Misr*, 19; and *idem*, *Al-Din wa al-Thawrah fi Misr*, 6, 15.

6. It is not surprising that Umar's opinions, Hanafi says, were often justified by revelation, since the Qur'anic method is that question came from reality and revelation answered it. In this way, a number of Qur'anic verses begin with the phrase "They ask you about" alcohol, gambling, and spirit. This is one of the greatnesses of Islamic revelation, which was revealed gradually in order that people read it slowly. Hanafi, *Al-Din wa al-Thaqafah wa al-Siyasah*, 289–90

7. Hanafi, *Al-Din wa al-Thaqafah wa al-Siyasah*, 289–90; *idem*, *Al-Da'wa li al-Ḥiwār*, 9–11; *idem*, *Al-Haraka al-Islamiyya fi Misr*, 19; and *idem*, *Al-Din wa al-Thawrah fi Misr*, 6, 15.

8. Hanafi, *Al-Din wa al-Thaqafah wa al-Siyasah*, 73, 290–1; *idem*, *Al-Haraka al-Islamiyya fi Misr*, 46; *idem*, *Al-Da'wa li al-Ḥiwār*, 9–11; *idem*, *Ḥiwār al-Ajyal* (Cairo: Dar Qiba', 1998), 502; *idem*, *Humum al-Fikr wa al-Watan al-'Arabi* (Dar Qiba', 1998), 1, 17; and *idem*, *Qadaya Mu'asira* (Beirut: Dar al-Tanwir, 1981), 1, 185.

9. Hanafi, *Al-Din wa al-Thaqafah wa al-Siyasah*, 291–2 and 396; *idem*, *Humum al-Fikr wa al-Watan al-'Arabi*, 2, 192–4; *idem*, *Dirasat Falsafiyya*, 147; and *idem*, *Al-Da'wa li al-Ḥiwār*, 9–11.

10. Hanafi, *Al-Din wa al-Thaqafah wa al-Siyasah*, 292–3 and 396; *idem*, *Al-Da'wa li al-Ḥiwār*, 9–11, 13–14, 51 and 112–16; *idem*, *Humum al-Fikr wa al-Watan al-'Arabi*, 2, 173–7; *idem*, *Al-Turath wa al-Tajdid: Mawqifuna min al-Turath al-Qadim*, 4th edition (Cairo: Al-Mu'assa al-Jami'iyya li al-Dirasat wa al-Nashr wa al-Tawzi', 1992), 160 and 172–5; *idem*, *Al-Haraka al-Islamiyya fi Misr*, 13; and *idem*, *Qadaya Mu'asira*, 1, 183.

11. Hanafi, *Al-Din wa al-Thaqafah wa al-Siyasah*, 83 and 294–5; *idem*, *Humum al-Fikr wa al-Watan al-'Arabi*, 2: 196–202; idem, *Al-Turath wa al-Tajdid*, 112–15; *idem*, *Dirasat Falsafiyya*, 27 and 547–8; *idem*, *Al-Da'wa li al-Ḥiwār*, 7–9 and 42; and idem, *Qadaya Mu'asira*, 1, 63.

12. Hanafi, *Al-Din wa al-Thaqafah wa al-Siyasah*, 295–6; *idem*, *Al-Turath wa al-Tajdid*, 116–23; *idem*, *Al-Da'wa li al-Ḥiwār*, 7–9; and *idem*, *Religious Dialogue and Revolution: Essays on Judaism, Christianity & Islam* (Cairo: Anglo Egyptian Bookshop, 1977), 231–7.

13. Hanafi, *Al-Din wa al-Thaqafah wa al-Siyasah*, 297–8; *idem*, *Al-Da'wa li al-Ḥiwār*, 7–9.

14. Hanafi, *Al-Din wa al-Thaqafah wa al-Siyasah*, 298; and *idem*, *Al-Da'wa li al-Ḥiwār*, 7–9.

15. Hanafi, *Al-Din wa al-Thaqafah wa al-Siyasah*, 300–1; *idem*, *Dirasat Falsafiyya*, 21–2, 27 and 149–50; and *idem*, *Al-Da'wa li al-Ḥiwār*, 11–12 and 46.

16. Hanafi, *Al-Din wa al-Thaqafah wa al-Siyasah*, 300–2; and *idem*, *Al-Haraka al-Islamiyya fi Misr*, 36.

17. Hanafi, *Al-Din wa al-Thaqafah wa al-Siyasah*, 298; *idem*, *Al-Da'wa li al-Ḥiwār*, 7–9; and *idem*, *Islam in the Modern World*, 2, 167–8.

18. Hanafi, *Al-Din wa al-Thaqafah wa al-Siyasah*, 304–5; *idem*, *Al-Da'wa li al-Ḥiwār*, 58–9; and *idem*, *Islam in the Modern World*, 2, 167–8.

19. Hanafi, *Al-Din wa al-Thaqafah wa al-Siyasah*, 260–1; idem, *Islam in the Modern World*, 2, 167–8; idem, *Al-Din wa al-Thawrah fi Misr*, 6: 15; idem, *Al-Da'wa li al-Ḥiwār*, 9–11; and idem, *Qadaya Mu'asira*, 1, 183.

20. Hanafi, *Al-Din wa al-Thaqafah wa al-Siyasah*, 83 and 313–14; idem, *Al-Haraka al-Islamiyya fi Misr*, 62–3; idem, *Al-Da'wa li al-Ḥiwār*, 45; idem, *Al-Din wa al-Thawrah fi Misr*, 6: 362–9; and *Islam in the Modern World*, 2: 9–14.

21. Hanafi, *Al-Din wa al-Thaqafah wa al-Siyasah*, 316–18; idem, *Al-Da'wa li al-Ḥiwār*, 46; and idem, *Islam in the Modern World*, 2, 167–8.

22. Hanafi, *Al-Din wa al-Thaqafah wa al-Siyasah*, 241–2 and 316–17; idem, *Al-Haraka al-Islamiyya fi Misr*, 23–4; idem, *Dirasat Falsafiyya*, 76; idem, *Al-Da'wa li al-Ḥiwār*, 64–5 and 689–721; and idem, *Jamal al-Din al-Afghani: Al-Mi'awiyya al-Ula (1897–1997)* (Cairo: Dar Qiba', 1998), 11–19.

CHAPTER 14

Towards a New Historical Discourse in Islam[1]

Ali Mabrook

Perhaps no one will argue that currently the *ummah* (Muslim collective) is being pulverized. There is an intense pressure, seemingly inescapable, and a pervading sense of decline, there are setbacks on every front. Failure appears as the destiny of every reform, and collapse is the end of every awakening. To this extent, all attempts at reform and progress still remain in the sphere of dreams, desires, even illusions, despite almost two centuries of striving and enterprise.

Naturally, many have mobilized to lift this gloom off the shoulders of the *ummah*. Many have engaged – especially after the numerous catastrophes that have befallen the *ummah* – in a process of critique and revision of the thought and theses that have come to be known as the "Arab awakening discourse" (*Khiṭāb al-Nahḍah al-ʿArabi*). Despite the tremendous fertility of this critical movement, it includes a very apparent shortcoming, represented by a reading of the causes of decline of discourse not within the discourse itself, but outside.[2]

An analysis from within the discourse enters into a relationship with the regimes of thought that arise by circumstance, dealing with these as absolute structures outside of time. The result is completely isolated from any historical or civilization contexts produced by them. This implies that its image of these regimes of thought is ahistorical. This is the most important impasse of the discourse – in all its diverse trends. Undoubtedly, this ahistoricity is not the illness of these regimes of thought in as much as it is the illness of the discourse itself. Some point out that the impasse of the discourse lies in its disregard of history and simply surpassing it. And further, that "some of the reasons for the crippling of our contemporary awakening, which we have initiated in the last century, is that we have not as yet discovered historical consciousness."[3] It seems as if a prerequisite for transcending this impasse is for the discourse to crystallize and complete its historical consciousness.

In truth, the ahistoricity of this discourse does not in any way mean the absence of any notion of "history," but rather the absence of history as a framework of human action and progress and a form of human consciousness of the world; or history as a creative process coming forth from forms of existence that are more developed and effective. Therefore, what remains is a conception of history that dominates the discourse and which inculcates "ahistoricity." Naturally, it is a conception of history as a process of failure and decline that cannot be lifted except by leaping from this location to a point outside. Not even the Arab liberalist, reformist, or even secularist, knows how to transcend the collapse of his reality except by leaping to a point outside, which he borrows and transmits from the Other.

In spite of the importance of the awareness of this fact, clinging on to it cannot transcend the impasse within the discourse. For this reason, it remains that this fact is no more than a point of departure for moving towards an awareness of what establishes it. This is because an analysis of the discourse cannot lead to something that is beyond the awareness of its ahistoricity. This awareness of what establishes ahistoricity cannot be accomplished except from outside of the discourse; I mean from outside the Islamic tradition in which this discourse is so deeply rooted. In truth, the presence of the legacy in contemporary Arab discourse goes beyond simply its restoration and employment in numerous trends within contemporary discourse, to the establishment of its underlying deep structure. Therefore, it is necessary to examine how the legacy of the discourse establishes its ahistoricity.

It must be said that there is no absolute absence of history in our classical legacy;[4] it is inherently present, specifically in the Science of Dogma ('Ilm al-'Aqā'id), which is central to the construction of contemporary consciousness. This is confirmed by realizing that the conception of history that regulates the contemporary awakening discourse (Khiṭab al-Nahdah al-Mu'āṣir) is completely rooted in a notion that came to be dominant and hegemonic in the Science of Dogma; what is being referred to in this instance, is the Ash'arite conception of history as a process of failure and decline from an idealistic transcendental moment to regressive moments that follow it. This is a decline that cannot be lifted from within this history, but from outside, since it is impossible except by leaping to that transcendental moment, repeating it, and unifying with it. It therefore seems that there are other conceptions of history that are different and even contradictory, which are contained within the Science of Dogma. The displacement and removal that they have been exposed to – together with the dogmatic systems that they naturally contain – prevented these concepts from impacting upon this consciousness in any way. In this way the effectiveness of the Ash'arite conception of history in shaping and formulating the structure of the awakening discourse is bound to the hegemony of Ash'arism, not only as a system of belief, but also as a collective psychological memory among people, which directs their behavior and determines their systems of value and crystallizes – which is most important – their ways of thinking and their worldviews.

It now seems that the various conceptions of history that are contained in the Science of Dogma were formulated in very close connection with the issue of imamate, (leadership established on the basis of religious dictates). As such, the connection between imamate and history is made manifest.

"Imamate," or politics, involves thinking about various principles and rules that govern a specific social context at a certain moment. As such, the starting point for whoever thinks about imamate is the present, from which he may move towards the past seeking that which may be used to establish the present, fix it, disturb it, or even destroy it.

"History," on the other hand, is a statement about the past[5] that intends to admonish or to make one take heed in most instances, but it seems that all thinking about the past is also thinking about the present. This is because it inevitably seeks either to fix the present or to disturb it. As such, the starting point here is the past, from which the historian departs, to the present, intending either to fix or to disturb.

As such, imamate is thinking in the present, which in most cases considers the past, while history is always thinking in the past with an eye on the present. The future is a dimension that is absent in both "imamate" and "history." In spite of their opposing points of departure, the present seems to be their common objective, either to fix or to disturb. There is no doubt that the link between them is crystallized in their common objective, which means that the one is established by the other and in turn establishes the other as well. History finds in imamate its meaning and foundation, and similarly, imamate finds in history its significance and meaning. If there were historians who wrote on imamate and politics[6] then it should be possible for theologians to write about imamate and history. Because no theologian has written such a book this matter has not been researched by anyone seeking to explore the relationship and the link between the two. This has resulted in the impoverishment of both imamate and history.

The many studies on imamate have not resulted in transcending the few peripheral issues surrounding it, or tracing its development in a specific time period or doctrinal school, going on to consider a more comprehensive significance. There are no studies that have given imamate a specific import that transcends the boundaries that regard it as legislation for guiding the practice of politics, transforming it into a frame for constructing perceptions and crystallizing concepts. History, in most cases, is also engaged simply as practice, in spite of the many studies on it, where all efforts are halted at the point of grasping its principles, tracing its tools, subject-matter, and methods, without going on to consider it as an epistemological and theoretical discourse that includes this practice and directs it. Thus, imamate and history are predominantly dealt with as spheres for political and historiographical practices, and not as epistemological discourses. In spite of the importance of this type of interaction with them, it remains impoverished and limited. Perhaps the link between them is what conveys them from the sphere of practice to the world of discourse. This is because this link exposes the substratum relationship between them,[7] which forces the one to transcend its external surface to reach that which is contained within its depths.

Despite the starting point for both history and imamate being the past and the present, as has been stated earlier, the link between them – paradoxically – is exposed through the future in a fundamental way. In truth, the foundational role played by imamate in history becomes essentially apparent from that which is contained in history concerning perceptions of the future. It becomes apparent that the position of the dissenters around imamate was formulated around appraising the dispute on the imamate of the first four caliphs and the consequences thereof. The Ash'arites in general argued that what had transpired was the best in all aspects. Others, to the contrary (like the Shi'ites), argued that that which would have been the best did not transpire at all. A third group (the Mu'tazilites) went beyond the context of choosing the best outcome in this matter, and looked into what had transpired and was said and done, analyzing and striking a balance, before passing judgment on what was the best in this issue. In contrast, others (like the Shi'ites) argued that that which would have been the best did not transpire at all. A third group (the Mu'tazilites) went beyond the context of choosing the best outcome in this matter, looked into what had transpired and was said and done, and thereafter analyzed and struck a balance before passing judgment on what was best. According to this dispute history appeared to degenerate from the ideal past (already fulfilled) to an unachieved ideal (to be fulfilled in the future). The third position supported neither degeneration nor ascension to an absolute model outside of history but analysis and equilibrium in which history is a realistic course determined by human consciousness and action. This without doubt implies a deep dispute over the "future." Is it degeneration and collapse, or ascension and transcendence, or an open horizon determined by human consciousness and action?

There is as such a shift from politics as a support, or as an antagonist, or as a means of dislodging, to history as the fulfillment of what is best, or as its unfulfillment, or history as analysis and equilibrium. The future, accordingly, is either collapse, ascension, or an open horizon. It is possible to express this relationship with the following diagram:

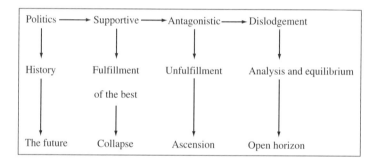

In this way, history emerges out of imamate, and the perception of the future is specified, starting from the link between them. This leads to that which is being alluded to in this study, not that which is explored by imamate or by history, as they are understood currently. It is their link that makes them uncover an internal and implicit content richer than that which they explore on the surface. Therefore, a methodological system that is appropriate for this objective is required, naturally departing from the fact that the nature of the subject determines the system of the methodology and defines it.

The problem of methodology is raised very pointedly for the researcher in the field of Islamic studies. It seems in most cases as if the methodology was formulated within epistemological and civilization contexts different from the specific context of the subject under study. In this instance, "the subject" is generally reduced to merely an arena in which the researcher exhibits his knowledge of the methodology. As such, the subject comes into being only for the sake of the methodology, especially if the methodology – which is the case in many instances – is a part of the embellishments of modernity, under whose influence many are swayed. It must be noted that this "sacrifice" of the subject results in – paradoxically – the fading away of the methodology and its dis-appearance, since the real aim of any methodology is to produce exact knowledge of a certain subject. If the methodology fails in achieving this aim it will be transformed from being a methodology for studying a subject to be itself a subject for study. This means that it loses its essence as a methodology. As such, the dominance of the method-ology over the subject does not only result in the marginalizing of the subject, but also the marginalizing of the quintessence of the methodology. However, this should not lead to the counterpoint dominance of the subject over the methodology, so that the methodology vanishes under the dominance of the subject. This counterpoint domi-nance would lead to the incapacity of the researcher to produce true knowledge of the subject, resulting in boring repetition. This repetition impoverishes the subject and leads to its disappearance, since the subject is unable to unfold everything it encom-passes. It even prevents revealing its truest import in the context of a comprehensive structure that includes it with other subjects. It therefore seems essential to start with the issue of methodology from a point outside the domination of the subject over the methodology, or vice versa.

If it seems that the substance of the relationship between methodology and subject comes from the ability of the methodology to produce true knowledge of the subject, then this should be a ruling principle of the relationship between them, i.e., the ability to produce knowledge that was not possible before. This does not apply to the produc-tion of knowledge of the subject only, but also to the methodology. The relationship between the two is determined, on the one hand, by the ability of the methodology to unlock closed aspects of the subject and to pave the way to expressing what is implicit in it, and on the other hand, by the ability of the subject to respond to the discipline of the methodology and to benefit from it in expressing that which is unsaid. Also, the revealing of the potentialities of the methodology has not been realized before. This could possibly mean that the relationship between the two is determined by the one benefiting from the other in revealing its potentialities and possibilities. Hence, the methodology will not be a set of solid rules that falls upon the subject like a predeter-mined fate, but an open horizon in which the subject develops and unfolds. In this way, the subject also transforms into an open horizon in which the methodology develops and fulfills its potential. This perhaps suggests that the methodology is not a fully formed entity that does not accept any development, but it achieves – according to the nature of the subject, of course – growth and evolution through dialogue and interaction with other methodological systems. Hopefully, raising the question of methodology in this way represents an attempt to transcend a specific problem in Islamic studies, i.e., the alienation of methodology from subject.

Beginning from the principle that it is the subject that determines and specifies the methodology, it is necessary to firstly define the subject and to gain familiarity with it, so that it is thereafter possible to determine the methodology and to specify its elements.

Indeed, "the subject" is a part of the legacy; but why must this legacy be investigated and researched? It seems that – and contemporary Arab thought bears this out – it is impossible to initiate any awakening from a starting point outside of the legacy. This is because in this case (if at all possible, of course) it will be a distorted clone of the other, in which the essence of the subject fades away and disappears. On the other hand, the awakening cannot be effected by ruminating over the legacy and re-consuming it. In this case it will be no more than repetition, in which the essence of awakening disappears. This requires that "the legacy" be made the subject of an epistemological position in which it will be the cornerstone of the awakening, but not by repetition, of course. Hence, if the legacy is "the subject," then the methodology is the "reading" of the legacy.

Reading means striving to produce knowledge of the legacy that goes beyond simply repeating it. From this perspective, all of the atavistic approaches towards the legacy can never be representative of a reading of it because they only repeat the legacy without the slightest impact upon it by the reader/subject. In this case the reader is merely a part of the legacy and is incorporated and encompassed by it (i.e. the reader is negated by the legacy), while the legacy does not represent a part of the reader (i.e. it is not incorporated or encompassed by the reader) and the reader does not dominate over it. Therefore, reading requires a double presence, i.e., of that which is being read (the legacy) and of the reader (the subject). The absence of either does not produce a reading. The presence of that which is being read only produces a repetition not a reading, and the presence of the reader only produces a projection, not a reading. If repetition, then, is the disease of the atavistic reading (if such an expression is permissible), then projection is the disease of the ideological reading through which the legacy simply becomes an arena from which many project their ideological delusions. The ideological reading is any reading that takes its starting point from ideologies outside of the legacy (which are modern ideologies, of course), and then proceeds to formulate an interpretation of the legacy that justifies this ideology and supports, through this interpretation, attempts to impose the ideology upon reality. A plurality of ideologies directed to this type of reading does not result in a plurality of readings, rather it only means that a single reading mechanism diversifies and changes its orientations. As such, there is no difference between the liberal reading of the legacy according to Zaki Najib Mahmud[8] from one perspective, and the historical materialist reading of Hussain Murruwa and Tayyib Tizini[9] from the other. Both readings submit to a single factor in which the legacy seems compelled to speak [in the terms] of the ideology imposed upon it from outside, sometimes through "selection" (Zaki Najib Mahmud), and at other times through "compulsion," which seems in its framing reluctant to speak in the terms of historical materialism.

This exaggeration of the role of the reader at the expense of the reading matter can also be critically applied to the phenomenological reading of the legacy by Hassan Hanafi:[10] "Every reading begins with some awareness, firstly, awareness of what the reader needs, what does he want to read in the text, what he wants the text to say to him; it is the reader who reads the text and who gives it its significance."[11] For Hanafi, the traditional text is simply a framework within which he places his own ideas.[12] In this way, the issue of "legacy and renewal" transforms, in this reading, into a "re-interpretation of the legacy according to the dictates of the time . . . (so that) the legacy is the means and renewal is the objective (*tèlos*)."[13] Or, the legacy is the footnote and renewal is the body of the text suspended upon it. In truth, the legacy is actually not required for itself but for the contemporary needs of the collective subject. However, to give it existence for the sake of this subject requires that it be dominated over, which cannot be achieved except through producing scholarly knowledge with it that does not ignore it being a phenomenon that has an objective existence in some way, with its own specific rules. Perhaps, this production of scholarly knowledge with the legacy cannot be achieved except by tracing it back to its epistemological, historical, and ideological contexts in which it arose and developed. This is what the phenomenological reading is unable to do because it does not know anything other than referring to the intuitive context of the reader.

If it seems that there is another type of epistemological reading of the legacy that has been formulated recently, seeking to transcend the impasse of its ideological reading, ideology again represents an impasse for this epistemological reading itself. This is because this ideology represents a hidden agenda that directs this reading in a way that is no longer submissive to its specific internal logic.[14] In spite of the fact that this reading adopts the mechanisms of epistemological analysis attempting to attain constants and profound systems that regulate the production of knowledge within the legacy as well as productive mechanisms for it, the destiny of this reading and its consequences – for instance, in the work of al-Jabiri[15] – exposes an intensive and hidden presence of an ideology that impairs and disables the possibilities of his reading. The ideology dominating al-Jabiri's reading that is referred to is an ideology of interruption and differentiation between the Mashriq (Arab-East) and the Maghrib (Arab-West), which has resulted in several stereotypes that place the Mu'tazilites together with the Ash'arites under a single epistemological system. A judicious, unbiased analysis uncovers a disparity between the Mu'tazilites and the Ash'arites, not only at the level of ideological bases – but more importantly – at the level of epistemological constants which regulates their knowledge production. It may be noted here as well that Ibn Khaldun was compelled to abandon his affiliation to the discursive Ash'arite epistemological system and to associate with a different epistemological system that represents a complete break with the discursive Ash'arite epistemological system. The truth is that al-Jabiri was compelled to make this amalgamation and separation in submission to the ideology dominating over him. The forced epistemological amalgamation of the Mu'tazilites with the Ash'arite epistemological system represents an attempt to negate any differentiation within the Mashriqi circle. The Mashriqi structure is discursive, gnostic, and illuminist in its essence, meaning that it is empty of any rationalist and critical presence.

Therefore, introducing the Mu'tazilite rationalist and critical sense will undoubtedly shatter the Mashriqi structure. It is thus necessary to reluctantly amalgamate the Mu'tazilites within this structure while ignoring their critical rationalism and emphasizing their discursivity, which is absolutely no different from that of the Ash'arites. The same applies to Ibn Khaldun, where it was necessary to ignore his Ash'arite discursivity, to facilitate his amalgamation with other Andalusian and Maghribi thinkers from a different epistemological system. This is once again a projection produced by the ideology of interruption that occupies al-Jabiri's consciousness, or even subconsciousness. However, it is a hidden and evasive projection this time, which comes from the fact that the concept of interruption represents, in several contexts, a performative epistemological instrument that al-Jabiri turns into an ideology rather than leaving as a concept. This means that ideology is veiled by him in the robe of neutrality and is as such evasive.

In spite of these readings remaining prominent landmarks ruled over by the prevalent epistemological horizon of the time, and by the historical context that regulates them, in a lengthy procession moving towards the renewal of the legacy and the production of scholarly knowledge with it, they seem possessed by various kinds of subjective obstacles that proscribe their effectiveness entirely. It is therefore necessary to be aware of the limits of these readings, seeking to go beyond their subjective obstacles. Any reading that wishes to interconnect with these previous readings must insist upon an epistemological and scholarly approach to the legacy (transcending projection and crude subjectivity) and must be emancipated from any ideological bias, or rather be aware of it and dominate over it, at the very least. The requirement of emancipation from ideological bias or dominating over it seems related to the production of scholarly knowledge with the legacy and is dependent upon it, i.e., the epistemological awareness of the legacy is what emancipates the reader from the authority of prior ideological bias. The ideological bias alludes to a defect in the reader's methodological procedure, or in its application. The declared procedures of any reading are usually expressed very accurately and pointedly, but in practical application during reading they lose their accuracy and pointedness, for many reasons. These could include the nature of the subject being read, or the uncontrollable bias of the reader. It is thus necessary for the reader of the legacy not only to qualify his methodological procedures and instruments, but also to examine the effectiveness of these procedures and instruments after applying them to his reading.

In this study the interaction and dialogue between several methodological systems will dominate over analysis, since this interaction and dialogue seems more capable of producing knowledge that may be regarded to be more precise. Perhaps the most effective methodological system in this instance is the "structuralist system," which aims to capture the deeply imbedded structure of a text, or a group of texts (by a particular author, school, or orientation) and to strive to explain all of the diversions and conversions within it through a single axis that is capable of encompassing all of the shifts within the text in a way that any particular idea in these texts finds its justification and logic within this fixed structure. The value of this methodology is derived from its ability to free the reader from all bias and prejudices, so that he or she may begin by reading and analyzing the text itself seeking to extract the embedded structures within it only through the reading. It may perhaps be said here that the matter rests upon the boundaries of "understanding and explanation" only. In truth, understanding and explanation alone are not able to produce knowledge of texts, and it is therefore necessary to complement this step with interpretation. In this regard, the historical methodology is of value and importance because it examines the extent of historical veracity of the structural constants uncovered through reading, in addition to tracing the contexts of the emergence of structures through it as well, and the way in which it transforms in a particular phase to a system that is specific to mechanisms of development that are separate from the context of history itself. The truth is that this separation from history is realized in history and by virtue of it, not in spite of it. In a word, this methodology represents a move from the "text" to the "world," since the confinement of the reader within the text leads to the production of closed knowledge that is not explainable in any way. The limitations of this knowledge are perhaps derived from the fact that the text is not created in a private space, but is a product conditioned (epistemologically) by various texts prevalent at the time of writing, and (historically) by various problems and inquiries raised by reality. In spite of being conscious of the fact that the historical and epistemological limitations of the text are not direct or vulgar, but rather complex and discreet, this awareness is not reason enough to ignore these limitations and to conceive of the text as separate from them, as it would transform – in this instance – into a fragile structure located in a vacuum. In spite of this, it is necessary to be aware of the fact that it is not possible to reduce the text to these historical and epistemological conditions outside of it since the text naturally strives to transcend these conditions and to flee from them . . . as such, its perennial presence.

Hence, historicity, in this instance, does not mean "looking into historical and social events in juxtaposition and arranging, reporting, and acknowledging them as a specific theoretical phenomenon. . . ". In a subject like theology, for example, some prefer to narrate historical facts as if theology is only a part of general history. So, when the Mu'tazilites are mentioned, the incident between Wasil ibn 'Ata' and al-Hasan al-Basri and the emergence of the Mu'tazilites as a result of the former's withdrawal from the latter's circle is mentioned; when the issue of the creation of the Qur'an is mentioned, the inquisition of Ibn Hanbal in the periods of al-Ma'munn, al-Mu'tasim, and al-Mutawakkil is mentioned;[16] when the Shi'ites are mentioned, the names of the imams and prominent figures are mentioned." History, in this case, seems to be a purely extraneous factor that impoverishes and fragmentizes thought, ignoring any internal mechanisms for development and growth encompassed in it. Historicity would thus refer to the deep, internal determinants of thought without which we are unable to visualize or explain this thought. Regarding the emergence of Mu'tazilism for example, it may be noticed that historicity does not allude to the poor external cause concerning the withdrawal of Wasil from al-Hassan's circle, but rather to the various epistemological and historical considerations prevalent in society and which do not relate to an incident that can be pointed out and referred to, but which have, however, made the emergence of Mu'tazilism necessary. This historicity transcends the event under which Mu'tazilism emerged and extends to its significance and meaning at the time of its appearance.

Holding that it is possible to distinguish between sets of rules and steps (while fully cognisant of its arbitrary nature) the distinction may be expressed in the following manner:

1. Placing every conception, thought, or pre-judgment upon a text, author, or doctrinal school between brackets, thereby initiating reading without any bias and leaving the text to reveal its internal system. As such, there would be no consideration given to Ash'arism as the median between Mu'tazilism and Jabriyyah with regard to the issue of human actions (*khalq al-Af'āl*), and in the same way, no consideration is given to the opinion that emphasizes the extremism of the Mu'tazilites pertaining to issues of theology (*'Ilm al-'Aqā'id*), in addition to other views and pre-judgments that hinder the production of scholarly knowledge of the texts of these doctrinal schools.

2. The reading of a text not as a group of particular ideas in proximity to each other, but rather as a web within which these ideas are woven, so that emphasis is directed to uncovering the comprehensive constant (*Thabitan Kulliyan*) that regulates these particular ideas and explains them, giving them meaning and credibility. Undoubtedly uncovering this constant is the aim and objective of the reading.

3. Focusing upon this constant in the reading implies the minimization of the differences that may be apparent within a group of texts by the same author, or from the same doctrinal school. What is of significance in this case is that there is a comprehensive constant that regulates these texts and is capable of explaining and rendering credible such differences, and not only the similarities between texts.

4. If the text (in theology, naturally) incorporates a comprehensive structure that regulates its specific subject-matter and channels effort to uncover this structure, then the specific subject-matter incorporates structural systems, which in turn verify the comprehensive structure and are verified by it in the process. It is thus possible to speak with regard to the Ash'arite pattern, for example, about a comprehensive structure that regulates the pattern in its entirety, and specific structures pertaining to issues like prophecy (*al-Nubuwwa*), human actions (*Khalqal-Af'āl*), preference (*al-tafḍīl*), and attributes (*al-Ṣifāt*), etc., which are structures that acquire their specificity from the specificity of the particular issues that arise from them. Just as much as it is an examination of the structure of the particular issue by the comprehensive structure of the pattern verifying this particular structure, it verifies the comprehensive structure of the pattern as well. This examination is founded upon the continuous oscillation between the comprehensive and specific structures.

5. In truth, this examination of the structures seems limited because it is confined within its own limits, and as such it is necessary to examine them – in the final step – beyond these limits, that is, in history and reality. Here too, the examination is founded upon the continuous oscillation between these structures and history and reality. Through this continuous oscillation the interaction and integration of their components is confirmed. This oscillation alludes to the fact that it is not only the structure that is explained and confirmed by history, but the structure explains history and bestows upon it discipline and logic.

In this manner the steps of analysis are integrated, verifying the mechanisms of "understanding" and "interpretation," which together, are the aim and final goal of the methodology.

If it is thus apparent that the effectiveness of the reading requires consciousness of the context of that which is being read, then it is equally apparent that in order to perfect this effectiveness, consciousness of the context of the reader is also required. This is because the reader – like that which is being read – does not exist in a vacuum but in a web of prevalent relationships at a specific moment; i.e., he is a reader in history, of history, and for history. As such, he engages in reading possessing certain historical and epistemological limitations that play a role in his understanding and assimilation of the reading matter, and its reshaping. The reader is not a neutral consciousness, or in a state of original purity, but imbedded within problems that limit and frame him, problems of both contemporary Arab thought and reality. The social problems include backwardness, dependency, defeatism, fragmentation, inequality, injustice, etc., while the major theoretical shortcoming of contemporary Arab thought seems to be its incapacity to produce relevant knowledge that is capable of emancipating the current reality from its crisis. These are the problems that limit and frame the context of the reader. Because consciousness of these problems is absolutely essential for the sake of a reading that is more productive and effective, it should be the point of departure for any analysis of the *turath*.

Notes

1. This is the introductory chapter of: 'Ali Mabruk, *'An al-Imama wa al-Siyasah wa al-Khitab al-Tarikhi fi "ilm al-Aqa'id* (Imamate, Politics and Historical Discourse in the Science of Dogma) (Cairo: Markaz al-Qahira li Dirasat Huquq al-Insan, 2002) translated by Aslam Farouk-Alli. The English translation was edited and revised by Shathley Q.
2. In the opinion of some, the decline of the discourse is linked to the context and circumstances for the rise of the bourgeoisie and the Arab elite who were in possession of the reigns of the *Nahdah* in the transformation era of the European bourgeoisie from the liberal stage to the imperialist stage. This imposed upon it a dependent nature, which basically resulted in the accommodation of its own personal interests with those of the dominant European bourgeoisie so that its entire project was dominated by this concern, and no other. The Marxists – who are more radical and accomplished in their critique – adopted this analysis, while the liberal wing continued speaking about the despotic and opportunistic nature of the ruling regimes as a reason for the decline. The arena of discourse, in all cases, seemed to be free of any blame, and only the other remained in the guilty dock.
3. Hassan Hanafi, "Limadha Ghaba Mabhath al-Tarikh fi Turathina al-Qadim," in *Dirasat Islamiyyah* (Cairo: al-Anjla al-Misriyyah, 1981), 416.
4. Perhaps the absence that was mentioned by Hassan Hanafi in the reference before is an absence of history as a progressive process from the Ash'arite legacy, which came to dominate the structure of consciousness. This is an absence that is not contested. The Ash'arite legacy is either bereft of any conception of history, or there are other conceptions of history within the legacy, generally, that have been marginalized or displaced. None of this has been dealt with in Hanafi's research.
5. As was stated by al-Maqrizi: "To report what happened in the world in the past," quoted from Franz Rosenthal, *'Ilm al-Tarikh inda al-Muslimin*, trans., Salih Ahmad al-'Ali (Beirut: Mu'assasat al-Risalah, 1983), 2nd edn., 26.
6. A book with the same title, *al-Imamah wa'l Siyassah*, has been ascribed to the classical scholar, Ibn Qutayba.
7. Even if it were supposed that it is an absolutely external link, it still remains a link between imamate and history as well . . . this is because history has emerged, even in its earliest narrative forms, as one of the requirements of the nascent (Islamic) state, which implies that

it is always stuck to politics. cf. 'Abdallah al-'Arwi, *al-'Arab wa al-Fikr al-Tarikhi* (Beirut: Dar al-Haqiqah, 1973), 2nd edn., 85.

8.   Zaki Najib Mahmud, *Tajdid al-Fikr al-Arabi* (Cairo: Dar al-Shuruq, n.d.).

9.   Hussain Murruwa, *al-Naza 'at al-Madiyyah fi'l Falsafah al-'Arabiyyah al-Islamiyyah* (Beirut: Dar al-Farabi, 1981); Tayyab Tizini, *Min al-Turath ila al-Thawrah* (Beirut: DarIbn Khaldun, 1976), 1st edn., vol. 1.

10.   Hassan Hanafi, *Min al-'Aqidah ila'l Thawrah* (Cairo: Madbuli, n.d.).

11.   Hassan Hanafi, "Qira'at al-Nass," *Dirasat Falsafiyyah* (Cairo: al-Anjlaw al-Misriyyah, 1987), 546.

12.   In his latest writings like *Min al-'Aqidah ila'l Thawrah*, Hanafi adopts the practice of attaching his ideas to the traditional text and expressing these in the body of his own text, thereby relegating the traditional text completely to the footnotes. This is not merely a formality, but an expression of his methodology.

13.   Hassan Hanafi, *al-Turath wa al-Tajdid* (Cairo: al-Anjlaw al-Misriyyah, 1987), 2nd edn. 11.

14.   This does not mean that it is possible for a reading to be free of any ideological presence. This is obviously impossible, because the absence of an ideology is a kind of ideology itself. Therefore, the issue is solely concerned with a reading that does not adopt an ideology as its starting point (because it turns the reading into an abusive, stereotypical activity) and with a reading in which ideology is beyond the control of one's consciousness of it.

15.   Muhammad 'Abid al-Jabiri, *Takwin al-'Aql al-'Arabi* (Beirut: Dar al-Tali'ah, 1984), 1st edn.; *Bunyat al-'Aql al-'Arabi* (Beirut: Markaz Dirasat al-Wihdah al-'Arabiyyah, 1986).

16.   Hasan Hanafi, *al-Turath wa al-Tajdid*.

PART II

Secularism, Modernity, and Globalization in Contemporary Islamic Thought

15 The Second Coming of the Theocratic Age? Islamic Discourse after
    Modernity and Postmodernity   285
    Aslam Farouk-Alli
16 Europe Against Islam: Islam in Europe   302
    Talal Asad
17 *Ummah* and Empire: Global Formations after Nation   313
    Mucahit Bilici
18 Between Slumber and Awakening   328
    Erol Güngör (Translated by Şahin Filiz and Tahir Uluç)
19 Islam and Secularism   338
    Asghar Ali Engineer
20 A "Democratic-Conservative" Government by Pious People:
    The Justice and Development Party in Turkey   345
    Metin Heper
21 Secularism and Democracy in Contemporary India:
    An Islamic Perspective   362
    Syed Shahabuddin

The Second Coming of the Theocratic Age? Islamic Discourse after Modernity and Postmodernity

Aslam Farouk-Alli

No serious scholar of Islam can deny the impact that modernity and postmodernity have had upon contemporary Islamic thought. In this chapter I will outline how current Islamic thought has been impacted upon by these intellectual discourses. I will proceed from the inception of modernity and go on to discuss developments in the postmodern period. In my final analysis I will discuss contemporary Islamic thought and the discontents of modernity and postmodernity. By taking recourse to the work of current-day Islamist thinkers who are responding to the intellectual challenges of modernity and postmodernity, we are able to gauge the deep introspection that these two very important paradigms have effected upon contemporary Islamic discourse. From this perspective then, the impact of modernity and postmodernity upon Islamic discourse can hardly be construed negatively. The secular/Islamist polemic is an essential contributing factor to the emergence of a clearer conception of Islamic identity in current times.

While the issue of identity will not be addressed in significant detail, the critique of modernity and postmodernity that is offered is certainly compelling evidence suggesting the emergence of a far more articulate and clearer Islamic self-image. The task of exploring the conception of an authentic Islamic self-image is beyond the scope of this chapter, but interrogating the philosophical discourses of modernity and postmodernity is an absolutely essential preliminary step that lays the necessary groundwork for such a venture.

Islamic Thought and Modernity

Before considering the relationship between Islamic thought and modernity, it is important to briefly survey the background that gave rise to modernity. This should place us in a position to satisfactorily appreciate the aspirations and disappointments invoked by this important paradigm of thought.

It is generally contended that the roots of modernity as a philosophical discourse can be traced back to the period of the Enlightenment. In the Middle Ages, prior to the Enlightenment, Europe was gripped in the clutches of an intense struggle between science and religion. The discoveries of great figures like Kepler, Copernicus, Gilbert, and Galileo provided a basis on which to challenge traditional religious worldviews concerning the nature of the universe. The price paid for challenging religious cosmological doctrines was very high. Galileo, for example, faced persecution for positing scientific theories that ran contrary to the religious dogma of the Catholic Church. However, the changing tides ensured that the tyrannical rule of the Church did not last much longer.

The Enlightenment marked a decisive epistemological break from the thought paradigm of the Middle Ages. The Christian Church's hegemony over institutions of knowledge and its power to determine the very nature of knowledge was now being challenged. The central role of religious ideas in politics was also brought into question. Within the broader spectrum of world history these changes were as significant as the classical Graeco–Roman outlook (which flourished up to the fourth century AD) and the triumph of Christianity in the Roman Empire. The emergent Christian worldview replaced the Graeco–Roman outlook and proceeded to dominate Europe until the seventeenth century.[1]

With the onset of the eighteenth century modern ideas and arguments that came to the fore shifted the focus of the looking glass. Philosophers now began to openly scrutinize the worldview of the Church. The Enlightenment also became known as the *age of reason* because the philosophy of that time emphasized reason and rationality over the speculative theology of the Church. Rationalism and empiricism were now core elements of epistemology, displacing speculative and theological metaphysics. Concepts like reason, empiricism, science, universalism, progress, individualism, tolerance, freedom, uniformity of human nature, and secularism, resonate throughout this period. These major themes form the very core of philosophical modernity and are still invoked today.

Thus, the Enlightenment removed religion as principle and base of identity and replaced it with reason. Human worth was now measured in terms of ethics and utility rather than creed and piety.[2] In return for a compromise on faith, modernity was able to rekindle the imagination and instill confidence in the ability of the subjective-self. Modernity rewarded humankind's spiritual loss with material gain. The scientific advances made in the last four centuries surpassed the collective efforts of every epoch preceding them. In spite of the material success of the Enlightenment, the philosophy that it had conceived would exact an extremely costly toll on humanity later on in history. The darker side of modernity shadowed a culture of suffering and genocide.

Developments in the Muslim world were by no means as drastic. Foremost, there was no fundamental epistemological shift from a hegemonic religious paradigm to a militantly rationalist one. Science, reason, and religion coexisted in a relatively peaceful relationship. As early as the twelfth century the great philosopher of Islam, Abu Hamid al-Ghazali, advocated the view that the best of sciences were those that combined transmitted (religious) knowledge with rational knowledge and where revelation is accompanied by opinion. In terms of scientific discovery the Dark Ages of Europe were a time of illumination in the Muslim world. Philosophy as well as the natural sciences were pursued with vigor.

Although the advances that were made in the Muslim world in this period served as an important foundation for the European Enlightenment, there was no sharp turn upward toward great breakthroughs. Consequently, the later advances and discoveries in Europe enabled the West to transcend its geographic confines and reverberations were soon felt throughout the world. Famous centers of learning in the Islamic world were surpassed by their Western counterparts. With the onset of modernity history witnessed the emergence of the West as a new world power.

European scientific advances granted the West dominance second to none. Along with material superiority came power, followed by a tremendous thirst for conquest. The military force of the West easily satiated its territorial appetite and in a relatively short period of time two-thirds of the world was colonized. Military colonization was inevitably accompanied by cultural invasion that proved to be far more exacting. The intellectual and cultural heritage of Islam – along with that of other civilizations – was forced into dormancy.

While scholars have argued that the world had been disenchanted – freed from superstitious, mythical beliefs – by Western modernity, one can say with certainty that the West was simultaneously enchanting the rest of the world. By the late eighteenth/early nineteenth century the Ottoman Empire awakened to the changing world realities and embarked upon a systematic and comprehensive program of modernization. The bitter reality was that the newly emerging world was not that of the *ulama*; its languages were French, Italian and English, and its logic, idioms and methods were all equally foreign to Muslims.[3] Such desperate attempts at modernization only served to emphasize the superiority of the West over the Muslim world. Not only did Muslims imitate the West in its methods of governance but it also began imbibing its very philosophy of living.

The fact that Western modernity was a product of a very specific and unique experience is lost to such attempts at imitation. The impact of these imitative attempts is what is still being grappled with today. Islamic thought is now permeated with a philosophy that has entered from without. It may be argued that this is not unique in any way and that no philosophy remains untouched by syncretism. However, the failure or success of such conflations depends entirely on whether any common ground exists between what are indeed very distinct paradigms. Tensions are bound to arise in any endeavor that hopes to mix the unmixable. In spite of these tensions, there are always those who are willing to attempt such a rapprochement. Thus, the relationship between contemporary Islamic discourse and modernity must now be considered so as to gauge the impact of such attempts.

In the nineteenth century the West advocated and firmly believed in the inevitability of progress and the power of human reason. The Western mindset made a clear break with the past and maintained a strong forward-looking orientation. Ideas of God and transcendence slowly became fading memories.

The attraction of modernity invoked varying responses from Muslim intellectuals. The Muslim mindset, in contrast, was strongly attached to a glorious past and could not easily break away from its roots. It still maintained an undeniably atavistic posture.

Upon reflection, one is able to empathize with such a position. For Muslim intellectuals of the early twentieth century Islam still had much to offer in terms of its philosophical orientation and depth. Even though modernity had given the West the upper hand in terms of material progress, this was by no means reason enough to dismiss the Islamic worldview altogether.

This sentiment finds full expression in the thought of Jamāl al-Dīn al-Afghānī. For al-Afghānī, Islam was foremost a belief in the transcendence of God *and* in reason. At a very early stage, al-Afghānī had realized that reason alone was not sufficient for humankind's prosperity. Although he enjoined embracing modernity, he remained weary of the strains it placed upon religion. His disciple Muḥammad 'Abduh followed a similar trajectory. 'Abduh asked how the gap between Islam and modernity could be bridged and answered that Muslims had to accept the need for change based on the principles of Islam. This tradition of engaging modernity was continued by the likes of Hassan al-Banna and Sayyid Quṭb. More recent scholars like the late Muhammad al-Ghazali contended that certain elements of the modern West had to be accepted, but there are certain philosophical standpoints that are unacceptable to Islam.

All the above intellectuals represent an engagement with modernity that is more or less critical. Such expressions were inevitably labeled fundamentalist and enjoyed little credibility among those that strongly upheld and embraced modernity. As will be seen later, in view of the broader scope of social discourse, voices of resurgent Islam were seen as no more than intellectual aberrations by the proponents of modernity who appropriated the dominant Western discourse that still preached the doctrine of modernity with full confidence. This would not continue indefinitely and the rise of postmodernity gave legitimacy to many divergent voices, including that of Islam. However, it is imperative that we consider modernist trends within the Islamic tradition before moving on to discuss postmodernity and the rise of critical alternatives to modernity.

As suggested, many Muslim scholars were willing to embrace modernity far more warmly. In most cases this involved making substantial adjustments to traditionally held views. I will consider the case of one such scholar, Bassam Tibi, in order to represent this position. There are naturally as many opinions on the project of modernity as there are scholars engaged in its study. It would be naive as such to treat the entire spectrum of discourse as homogeneous and static. However, there are certain trends that can be assumed to be representative of a mainstream position. Tibi's discourse consequently emerges as a good general reflection on modernity because he assumes an overtly apologetic posture toward it. He is therefore well placed for the expressed purpose of drawing out the contrast between Islam and modernity.

Tibi has published several works related to Islam and modernity.[4] For him, the European project of modernity is normative in terms of determining what constitutes knowledge. He not only affirms the aims of the Enlightenment project but also regards them as necessary for progress and development. I will outline some of the philosophical implications of modernity and link them to Tibi's thought before going into a detailed exposition of his views. I will thereafter consider criticisms of this position. This should lead us to a general critique of modernity.

For Tibi, modernity is a cultural project that triggered off a man-centered secular worldview and as such an insight into the capability of man to know and to change his social environment autonomously, regardless of supernatural forces such as God's will.[5] On this basis he asserts that modernity, as an epistemology, is a French achievement inspired by René Descartes. This epistemology entrenches the principle of subjectivity, which – in philosophical terms – refers to individual freedom. In its form of self-consciousness, subjectivity determines all aspects of modern culture, in particular, modern knowledge.

Descartes' epistemology impacted profoundly upon the course of knowledge. As Richard Harland explains: "The Cartesian philosophy of the *cogito* proclaimed the private 'I think' as the only possible source for truth and explanation after the external phenomena of the world had all been 'doubted' away."[6] He further asserts that the "I" philosophy tradition of Descartes, Kant, and Husserl is the primary and self-sufficient base upon which knowledge is to be founded – primary and self-sufficient not in the way of objective things, but in the way of an undetermined creative source. As a result, all of these philosophers make a space for individual free will in their philosophies. In this regard, Tibi is careful to point out that this is not an atheistic position. He argues that even Descartes acknowledges that God creates man but that man is able to create knowledge on his own, by his own means.

Therefore modernity, as described by Tibi, results in what Parvez Manzoor has described as a "de-divinised public order." A natural consequence of this development is that ultimate values in such a social structure are political and existential as opposed to religious and trans-existential, which is the normative ideal in Muslim communities.[7] In epistemological terms this represents a shift from metaphysics to positivism. Practically, this is manifested in replacing belief in the presence of absolute knowledge that resides beyond human capacity with the pursuit of partial knowledge that could be gathered and verified through scientific methods. Stated differently, this is a shift from belief in an absolute truth that controlled human life to belief in partial scientific truths that could be used by humans to control nature.[8]

As a result of this shift, an increasing number of social scientists consider metaphysics a fading religious pastime and hold that it should have been driven away from the human mental endeavor a long time ago. Tibi is no different and develops this orientation further, arguing that the only viable approach to Islam in the modern world is the sociological one.

Considering Tibi's emphatic and wholehearted endorsement of modernity, it comes as no surprise that he considers resurgent voices of Islam as being fundamentalist – in the full pejorative sense. He as such asserts that contemporary Muslim fundamentalists contest the secular knowledge based on the cultural project of modernity, as well as the worldview related to it. He bases this on his conception of modernity, which he regards as being composed of an institutional dimension – an idea he borrows from Anthony Giddens – as well as a cultural project, as held by Habermas. For Tibi these two concepts are inextricable. Any society wishing to make a successful transition to a modern social system needs both. The problem is that while the institutional dimension of modernity has been globalized, the cultural project has not, even though this possibility was not dismissed in the early post-colonial period. Later, however, cultural reassertion advocated the rejection of alien knowledge, which meant banishing cultural modernity. Tibi finds it paradoxical that in the case of Islam the adoption of alien instruments, i.e. modern science and technology was endorsed. He as such refers to this phenomenon as "the Islamic dream of semi-modernity," which indicates "Muslim fundamentalist ambivalence *vis-à-vis* modernity and its tendency to split it into two components."[9]

For him the basic dilemma of contemporary Muslims with regard to their attitudes toward modern knowledge is that they simultaneously envisage adopting the instruments of modernity while rejecting its cultural underpinnings. In so doing, Tibi contends that they separate the achievements of modernity from the very knowledge that led to it and first made it possible.

He argues that the essence of cultural modernity is the Cartesian *cogito ergo sum*, i.e. that knowledge of man stems from the doubt out of which certain human knowledge of the objective world grows. For him fundamentalism submits man to Allah's will whereas Cartesianism helps man to recognize himself as *res cogitans* – a thinking subject. In epistemological terms this translates as a shift from a religious worldview to a modern worldview. In rather prejudicial fashion Tibi thus concludes that any project – whether religious, postmodern, or fundamentalist – that questions this worldview results in irrationalism.[10]

Tibi would thus have us believe that the root problem with any alternative worldview lies in its conception of knowledge. Only modern Western knowledge is normative and the expression of any alternative that seeks to embark "on the de-Westernization of knowledge" is simply not epistemologically grounded. This is also the major objection that Tibi raises against Islam.

Islam and all other de-Westernized sciences are not founded on the modernist principle of abstract subjectivity, which is the view that man is able to establish human knowledge of the objective world and to subject these discoveries to the pursuit of satisfying human needs. Tibi argues that Islamized sciences – though not traditional – are subordinated to religious traditions and as such do not permit the reflective posture of the Westernized sciences. By his estimation these attitudes toward modern science and technology do not contribute to the accommodation of modern knowledge that Muslim people urgently need for the development of their societies. He further holds that such attitudes reflect the beginnings of a new counter-scientific trend in Arab culture. His biggest fear is that the politics of the Islamization of knowledge could result in "a new era of flat-earthism."[11]

Tibi further contends that the twentieth century is the age of global confrontation between secular cultural modernity and religious culture. He raises several questions that explicitly indicate his commitment to the secular vision of modernity. He asks why it is that Muslims are unable to share this view; why do they always use the fact of colonial rule to dismiss cultural modernity; and why do they involve the belief in Allah to disregard the ability of man. His explanation for all of this is that Muslim fundamentalist efforts to de-Westernize knowledge seek to reverse the "disenchantment of the world" and thus to subject man to supernatural powers. Tibi's implication is glaringly obvious: any reassertion of Islam runs the risk of taking us back to the Dark Ages.

What is most striking about his entire argument is its complete endorsement of classical modernity. He seems to see very distinct similarities between the European Enlightenment and the current need for Islam to modernize. Just as Europe had freed itself from the shackles of Christianity, so too must the Arab/Muslim world be emancipated from the stifling teachings of Islam. This obviously suggests that he sees fit to parallel the Christian paradigm of the Middle Ages with that of Islam. At the very least, such an extrapolation is glaringly naive.

Critics have pointed out several other problems with Tibi's discourse. These will very briefly be considered before discussing the more general critiques of the modernist project he so passionately endorses. Pieterse points out that Tibi's work presents a rather severe case of dichotomic thinking which caricatures both the West and Islam. He argues that Tibi equates the West with modernity, which in turn is neatly lined up with Cartesianism. In a similar way Islam is homogenized under the heading of "Islamic fundamentalism."[12] Parvez Manzoor's far more fiery response criticizes Tibi for exhausting all his energies only to produce a one-sided indictment of "Muslim fundamentalism" and offering an ill-conceived and ineptly executed apology of modernity. He goes even further, arguing that Tibi's vision of modernism is intellectually dated, philosophically shallow, and ideologically docile.[13] Even though this last criticism seems fully justified, it does not spare the task of responding to the claims that Tibi makes. The fact that Tibi chooses to subject Islam to a modernist critique justifies an exploration of the critiques of modernity. It is thus necessary to consider both the philosophical and ideological critiques raised in response to modernity.

Criticisms of Modernity

By now it should be clear that modernity has been defined in terms of beliefs and values identified with Enlightenment thought, relentless pursuit of progress, and control of nature for the well-being of humanity. These beliefs and values have been conceptualized by way of promises and ideals held to be lofty and true, in the most absolute sense. As such, the failure of these promises and the discontent of these ideals would naturally lead to crisis. The aspirations of the modernist vision of society have been expressed by many contemporary scholars, of which Tibi is just one example. In what follows some of the shortcomings of this vision will be explored. This should lead back to the philosophical underpinnings of modernity, which will then be critiqued. The counter-wave against modernity gave rise to postmodernity, which will be considered hereafter.

The American scholar John Esposito eloquently pronounces that "the world at the dawn of the twenty-first century challenges the 'wisdom' and expectations of the prophets of modernity."[14] Current skepticism toward modernization and development theory challenges the longstanding claim that the development of modern states and societies requires Westernization and secularization. Although Westernization has indeed developed and advanced the bureaucratic mechanisms of modern society, it has not been nearly as successful at eradicating the predicaments of humanity. In this regard Parvez Manzoor contends that the expression "crisis of modernity" needs to be understood in terms of modernity's inability to redeem its promise of delivering a model of perfect historical order. Explaining further, he emphasizes that modern societies are not helpless at facing the inner challenges of governance and economy, which are primary determinants of the human condition in terms of the modernist vision, nor are modern polities vulnerable to any threats by external enemies. Rather, upholders of the modernist vision are perplexed by the realization that their global city is not a city of humanity.[15]

Ali Bulaç, a Turkish Islamist scholar, lends his support to this criticism by focusing on the plight of the environment as well as the individual. He claims that although modernism had promised paradise on earth, it has instead turned the entire planet into a living hell. He goes further, adding that along with pollution of the environment modernism has also succeeded in polluting the soul.[16] While many have equated the Western discourse of modernity with secularism, not much attention has been focused on the above description of modernity as a dual pollutant, which encompasses more than just a philosophy that advocates the separation of Church and state. Abdelwahab Elmessiri is one of the few scholars to have elaborated on this in some detail.

Elmessiri contends that the identity of Western modernity is more in keeping with what he refers to as comprehensive secularism. The separation of Church and state is a worldview that cannot claim any comprehensiveness and he thus refers to it as partial secularism. He argues that such a worldview confines itself to the realm of politics and perhaps economics, but maintains complete silence on absolute or permanent values, be they moral, religious or otherwise. It also does not address itself to ultimate things like the origin of humanity, human destiny, the purpose of life, and other matters.

By contrast, he points out that comprehensive secularism is a completely different outlook that does not merely aim at the separation of Church and state and some aspects of public life; it aims at the separation of all values – religious, moral, or human – not only from the state but also from public and private life and from the world at large.[17] For him, it is in this comprehensive regard that Western modernity and secularism are almost synonymous. In referring to one the other is also tacitly implied. As such, Elmessiri defines Western modernity as the adoption of value-free science as the basis of humanity's world outlook and as a source of values and norms. This outlook reorients the individual to follow value-free laws instead of modifying the world to fit human needs and aspirations. History itself stands witness against and testifies to the disastrous consequences of this worldview. However, in order to manifest this more clearly there has to be a move toward a more holistic reading of history, more specifically, a more holistic reading of the history of secularism itself.

Elmessiri argues that in the Western world the paradigmatic sequence of immanentization (i.e. the shift from a transcendental worldview to a material one), and therefore secularization, modernization, and naturalization, began sometime in the Middle Ages. This occurred when some economic enclaves "freed" themselves from Christian values or concepts such as "fair price." He goes on to explain that only strictly economic criteria now applied to economic activity and success and failure were stripped of any moral or human considerations. He thus asserts that the economic sphere was immanantized, becoming value-free, referring only to itself, its criteria and standards being immanent in it. This development established a pattern that repeated itself in all other spheres of human activity.[18]

Another significant example of this pattern alluded to by Elmessiri is that of the political sphere. He draws our attention to the birth of the theory of the modern state during the Renaissance. The state, in this instance, became value-free, justifying itself by the *raison d'état* rather than seeking legitimacy on a religious or moral basis. As a result the realm of politics freed itself from any values external to it, and was judged by criteria immanent to it. In similar vein, all spheres of human life, including science, were freed from religious and moral values and considerations, becoming self-sufficient, self-regulating, self-transforming, and self-explanatory.

Elmessiri bemoans the fact that this emergent secular worldview was never clearly articulated because the history of secularism was monitored by the Western social sciences in a piecemeal and diachronic fashion. This history was fragmented into various bits, first humanism and/or the Reformation, the Enlightenment, rationalism, and utilitarianism; then the counter-Enlightenment, Romanticism, and Darwinism; then positivism, existentialism, phenomenology; and finally the end of history and postmodernism. This piecemeal approach concealed many of the more appalling aspects of the Western modernist worldview. Elmessiri argues that this resulted in some of the most shameful ideologies of the recent past like racism, imperialism, and Nazism being seen as mere aberrations, having a history of their own, distinct from the history of secularism and modernity. When the Western modernist worldview is approached holistically it becomes apparent that these so-called aberrations are in fact part and parcel of the Western civilizational model.

His central contention is that by grasping this overall unity and articulating it into a comprehensive paradigm – thereby developing a uniform and complex paradigm of secularism – we are able to unmask the relationship between the Enlightenment and deconstruction; between modernization, modernism, and postmodernism; between Nietzcheanism and Hitler, pragmatism and Eichmann; between rationalism, imperialism, and the Holocaust. From the vantage-point of this novel paradigm it becomes much easier to expose the moral and sociopolitical trappings of the modernist vision.

Elmessiri points out that in light of the above it is not plausible to regard oppressive ideologies of the past and the present – like Nazism and Zionism – as exceptional cases because modernist discourse reflects a general pattern of extermination that began in the West from the time of the Renaissance in countries like North America, right up to the present in countries like Vietnam, Chechnya, and Bosnia.[19]

On the basis of this analysis, his contention that there is a direct link between Western civilization and genocide is quite compelling. He supports this position on several grounds. First, he points out that Western civilization is a technological civilization that elevates progress at any price, even to the detriment of humanity. The resultant hardship and suffering, both physically and spiritually, are not of much significance in a culture that supports the principle of the survival of the fittest and ignores traditional values like being charitable to the weak and lending assistance to those in need. By this logic the Nazis were able to legitimate the extermination of the Jews because they were viewed as non-productive or useless. This was admittedly an extreme solution but Elmessiri argues that other Western countries like America and Poland bear a certain degree of culpability because they refused to give asylum to this "useless" ethnic grouping.

A second trend that justifies drawing parallels between genocide and Western culture is that the "solution" to the Jewish problem adopted by the Nazis shares many similarities with solutions adopted by other Western imperialist countries. The genocide of the Red Indians of America is an appropriate example. Elmessiri points out that Nazism and imperialism share the common belief of the superiority of the Arian race.

Finally, he points out that a central trait of Western civilization – and a phenomenon common to both Zionism and Nazism – is the rationality of its procedures and methods and the irrationality of its objectives and goals. He notes that this is a characteristic of Western civilization that has also been discussed in the writings of Max Weber, the famous sociologist. Perhaps the best examples of this antinomy between objective and method are the Nazi death camps and the systematic expulsion of Palestinians from their homeland. In both these cases horrendous atrocities are afflicted upon a target population with the utmost precision and planning.

Distinguished Canadian philosopher Charles Taylor raises similar criticisms of modernity. He identifies three malaises of modernity that challenge blissful human existence. These are individualism, the primacy of instrumental reason, and the loss of freedom resulting from the preceding two. In his words: "The first fear is about what we might call a loss of meaning, the fading of moral horizons. The second concerns the eclipse of ends, in face of rampant instrumental reason. And the third is about a loss of freedom."[20]

Taylor equates individualism with a loss of purpose. Its darker side involves a centering on the self, which both flattens and narrows our lives making them poorer in meaning and less concerned with others or society. These results are manifested in expressions such as "permissive society," "me generation," or the prevalence of narcissism.

He explains the second malaise of modernity – instrumental reason – as a kind of rationality that we draw on when we calculate the most economical application of means to a given end. In this scheme of things maximum efficiency and the best cost–output ratio is the measure of success.

Bringing the two together, he argues that on the political level individualism and instrumental reason have frightening consequences. He points out that giving weight to instrumental reason, in serious moral deliberation, may be highly destructive. Elmessiri has aptly demonstrated this earlier. Taylor thus concludes that any society structured around instrumental reason imposes a great loss of freedom on both individuals and the group because it is not only our social decisions that are shaped by these forces. He rightfully contends that an individual lifestyle is hard to sustain against the grain. In other words, yielding to the pressure of conformity is no less a loss of freedom then submitting to the dictates of instrumental reason.

Although the modernist vision was inspired by the potential of the individual at its inception, history has clearly shown that this has not always been to the advantage of either the individual or society. As has been argued above, humanity – as a collective – has had to suffer the consequences of what has only recently been recognized as a warped vision. Modernity, as a philosophy, did indeed aspire toward moral and sociopolitical uplift and therefore its failure can only be attributed to an inherent weakness in its vision.

Parvez Manzoor, a trenchant critic of modernity, provides an apt and concise summary of the main contentions raised against it and it is worth quoting him at length. In his unique style, Parvez Manzoor points out:

- that the truth claims of Enlightenment reason are based on circular logic;
- that the notion of a sovereign, transcendent and ahistorical subject whose reason is the touchstone of all knowledge is extremely "problematic";
- that the doctrine of progress is "paradoxical";
- that the cult of freedom which renders all "taboos" illegitimate and unnecessary is inimical to the preservation of any kind of moral, and by extension, social and political order;
- that the charter of the modern political community, nay any political community, is always parochial and exclusive;
- that the universality of justice and rights is a metaphysical claim that cannot be redeemed within a sociopolitical context;
- indeed, that the jurisdiction of both reason and meaning extends far beyond the cosmopolis of modernity.[21]

Hindsight sometimes casts harsh glances upon the past and it therefore has to be remembered that time alone can tell whether visions of the future are to meet with success or not. Bearing this in mind, Parvez Manzoor indicates that the delegitimation of modernity is important because it not only opens up a new intellectual space, but also creates a different agenda for a dialogue between modernists and others. Most scholars now reject the claims made by modernity as rather tenuous. This marked the shift, once again, from one paradigm of thought to another. Loss of faith in the project of modernity was accompanied by the onset of postmodernity.

From the Discontents of Modernity to Postmodernity

Seyyed Hossein Nasr, a prominent contemporary Islamic scholar, remarks that until Descartes the various levels of reality that determined human existence were understood in relation to God. Then, with the onset of Cartesian rationalism, individual human existence became the criterion of reality and truth. In the mainstream of Western thought, ontology gave way to epistemology, epistemology to logic, and finally logic was confronted by the antirational "philosophies" so prevalent today.[22]

Abdelwahab Elmessiri is once again helpful in charting out the course that saw the shift from modernity and its discontents to postmodernity.[23] As mentioned earlier, he argues that modernity – and therefore comprehensive secularism – is a form of immanence, implying that rising levels of secularization meant rising levels of immanentization. This naturally leads to the virtual disappearance of God as the transcendental organizing power in the universe:

We can view the whole process of immanentization/modernization/secularization in terms of the death of God discourse. God first became incarnate not in man but in

humanity as a whole, and not temporarily but permanently. This led to the rise of humanism and the solipsistic subject. This humanism became racism when God is incarnate in
one people; it becomes fascism when God is incarnate in the leader. . . . But the process
went on inexorably, and immanentization (secularization/modernization) went deeper.
The center kept on shifting and the incarnations became too many, until we were faced
with multiple centers. Nature itself was fragmented and atomized. Losing its stability,
coherence, and self-referentiality, it could no longer serve as a stable center.[24]

We now have to turn our attention to postmodernism in order to make sense of the
shift from a fixed center – as in the case of modernity – to the rise of multiple centers,
multiple alternatives, and a multiplicity of truths.

The Postmodern Worldview

Many scholars express the view that postmodernity is no more than a continuation or
a further unfolding of modernity. Elmessiri describes postmodernity as a move from
"the solid logocentric stage of modernity to its liquid stage, the stage of materialist
irrationalism and antiheroism and a centerless world."[25] Whereas modernity
had renounced the authority of religion – displacing metaphysics in favor of reason –
postmodernity no longer asserts anything positive or substantive. Postmodern theory
renounces even reason as a foundational theory of norms:

> Modernist consciousness, which progressively shifted its gaze from "reason" to "nature"
> to "history", now proclaims that there exists no Archemedian point, no foundational text,
> that may guide our humanity towards any desirable or conceivable goal. Rather, the admis-
> sion is that reason is unable to overcome the antinomy of norm and history, that the "is"
> of world-history does not lead to any "ought" of the human existence.[26]

So, while postmodernity does indeed proceed on the same continuum as modernity,
it can be more accurately described as "the rejection of modernist ideology in a modern
world."[27] Modernist ideology had previously dictated that reason alone can prevail and
that only through reason can human beings conquer and control nature. At the very
least, modernist ideology sought to cast a firm and absolute foundation that served as
the basis of reality. Postmodernity, by contrast, argues that there are multiple realities
that are not necessarily related.[28] The postmodern condition is one that transcends the
arguments and battles of which view of reality was true to the position that none are
true.[29] This skeptical posture is a true reflection of the fundamental axiomatic principle of postmodernist thought: suspicion and rejection of all "grand narratives."

Postmodernists refer to any legitimating discourse as a "grand narrative" or a "meta-
narrative." Meta-narratives or grand narratives are referred to as such because they
claim to be able to account for, explain, and subordinate all lesser narratives. Religious
ideologies like Islam and Christianity and political ideologies like Marxism are also
examples of grand narratives in that they provide the ethos or worldview according to
which the individual – and ultimately society – fashions his/her very existence.

Reason – as a concept that informs truth and acts as the criterion for determining what constitutes knowledge – is another paradigm example of a grand narrative. It gained ascendancy in the eighteenth century when it was applied to every area of life like religion, morality, politics, and social life. Reason served as the foundational norm that was used to justify everything, just as religion before it.

> [Postmodernism] rejects the pursuit of "grand narratives" and denies the possibility of acquiring comprehensive knowledge through "scientific" methods. For postmodernism, *reason* cannot be a reliable source of knowledge because reason itself is a hegemonic project. Ultimate truth is impossible to attain because everyone has his/her own truth.[30]

It should now be manifestly clear that the postmodern response to the crisis of modernity – the failure of its grand narratives – has been to relativize all truth claims. Whereas modernists sought to find meaning in totality, later scholars pointed out that the only secure thing about modernity is its insecurity; it is in a perpetual state of flux and it is this flux that defines the main nature of postmodernity.[31] Whereas progress had been the distinguishing feature of modernity, nihilism or the loss of any spiritual center is what distinguishes postmodernity. While modernity sought to establish a foundational text – a foundational norm or grand narrative – that legitimated and explained its project, postmodernity vociferously rejected any kind of foundational text. In spite of this rejection, critics have argued that postmodern discourse is in itself nothing more then another grand narrative. It is as such imperative to consider this, as well as other criticisms of postmodernism.

Powell makes the point that the notion that people have stopped believing in grand narratives because such narratives marginalize minorities inadvertently makes the assumption that all people universally believe in justice, which is in itself another grand narrative.[32] Therefore, postmodernism is as guilty as modernism for perpetuating grand narratives. In denying any fixed or stable center, postmodernism entrenches a center-less world in a constant state of flux as the norm or only reality. Such relativism is not arbitrary and in fact engenders a unique philosophy of its own. For example, Elmessiri points out that postmodernism even has its own metaphysics despite its frantic attempt to deny any metaphysical stance.[33] He is of the view that while postmodernism denies transcendence, totality, permanence, and duality, its very denial has shown its true philosophical identity as an expression of the metaphysics of immanence. This is a point that has been alluded to earlier.

While most critics concede that postmodernism has indeed proven to be effective as a critique of modernity, they also point out that it does not constitute an alternative social and political project due to its inherent cynicism and nihilism. However, postmodernist discourse has won favor with almost every marginalized ideology because of its inherent pluralistic nature. While it is not emphatic in endorsing any given position, it is by no means categorical in dismissing any given view either. This has created plenty of space for groups previously rejected by mainstream, hegemonic ideologies like modernity. A pertinent example is the re-emergence of religion and spirituality. The case of Islam will now be stressed to emphasize and explore this rebirth.

From Postmodernism to Islamism

Ibrahim M. Abu-Rabi' contends that the resurgence of religion in both industrial and peasant societies is one of the most significant features of transcending postmodernism.[34] One may even argue that it is a resurgence borne out of the exasperation of treading on shaky ground. While postmodernism is to be fully acknowledged for creating the space that made such a resurgence possible, it has failed dismally – as a philosophy – to provide a firm foundation for an alternative worldview. As a result, people have increasingly begun turning back to religion.

Islamism, or the influence of an Islamic worldview in the sociopolitical sphere, is a specific example of this resurgence. Islamism is viewed as a product of the frustration of the promises of Western modernization and, more specifically, represents a critique of modernism that displays remarkable similarities with postmodernism.[35] These similarities include a rejection of the determinism, rationalism, and positivism of the modernist paradigm.[36] However, there are fundamental differences between Islamism and postmodernism that ultimately make them incompatible. Bulaç explains that Islam is ultimately a "total doctrine" that rejects the universalism and relativism of postmodernism.[37]

In spite of the fundamental differences, it is quite enlightening to explore the fascination that postmodernism holds for Islamists. Mustafa Armagan, another Islamist thinker, is helpful in this regard. He explains that:

> [. . .] postmodernism is attractive to Islamists because: (1) it shows the failures and limitations of modernism; (2) given the exhaustion of modernism, the postmodernist search for alternatives opens up an opportunity for Islam; (3) in their rejection of the secular uniformity of modernism, postmodernists freely borrow from tradition and religion which Islamists advocate; (4) the postmodernist emphasis on diversity and (5) the announcement of the death of "meta-narratives" strengthens the hand of Islam in its struggle against modern "isms" such as socialism, positivism, or Darwinism.[38]

Returning to the critique of postmodernism, Armagan argues that postmodernist "playfulness" results in the rejection of a unitary point of reference for truth and thereby endorses the acceptance of multiple perspectives as equally valid. He therefore holds that this constitutes a second wave of secularization. Explaining further, he argues that in the first phase of secularization, undertaken by modernism, the self recreated the outside world (society, state, nature, art, religion, etc.) by using reason.

> In the current phase of secularization, the self has begun to reflect on the outside world, which the self created through reflection in the first place. Modernists, although secularized, still retained the traditional notion of a distinction between form and essence. For the postmodernists, however, form is everything – style constitutes content and rhetoric makes up reality.[39]

Because of this, he regards postmodernism as a commercial paganism that turns religions into playthings and cannot as such be an ally to Islam. The stage is therefore now set for deep and critical introspection that should produce compelling solutions to the exigencies of everyday life. As is clearly apparent, such solutions are now being sought from Islam's very own unique tradition.

Conclusion

By now it should be quite apparent that Islamic discourse did not readily surrender to the charms of the dominant discourses of modernity and postmodernity. There is no denying that certain scholars made strong cases in favor of modernist or postmodernist orientations, but these attempts only served to enhance the dissent of those who chose to speak in favor of an authentic Islamic alternative, in addition to embellishing their discourse with an added sophistication. What these unfolding developments clearly stress is that the discourses of modernity and postmodernity were by no means compelling enough to prompt a wholesale abandonment of the intellectual project of authentic Islam.

It is in this light that we need to appreciate the rekindling of an authentic Islamic ideal or foundational text as an alternative to modernity and postmodernity. Condemnation of modernity's grand-narrative solutions reaches near climax so it seems odd that Muslims should be arguing for the re-establishment of the foundational text – albeit on their own terms. Added to this is the skeptical voice of postmodernism still cautioning against the adoption of any grand narrative whatsoever.

What is precisely established from the above exposition is that any Second Coming of the theocratic age does not necessarily imply simplistic atavistic posturing by Muslim intellectuals. Now more than ever, Islamic authenticity is being expressed in terms of moral existential imperatives. How one may aptly define Islamic authenticity or determine what the sources of these moral existential imperatives are must be the task of another inquiry. But for now it is enough to assert that Islamic discourse after modernity and postmodernity holds much more promise than unfounded fears of a return to an era of "flat-earthism."

Notes

1. Huston Smith, *Beyond the Post-Modern Mind* (New York: Crossroad, 1982), 5.
2. Isma'il Raji al-Faruqi, "Meta-Religion: Towards a Critical World Theology," *The American Journal of Islamic Social Sciences*, 3/1, 1986, 17.
3. Basheer M. Nafi, *The Rise and Decline of the Arab-Islamic Reform Movement* (London: Crescent Publications Ltd., 2000), 37–8.
4. For a listing of these works, see: Bassam Tibi, "Culture and Knowledge: The Politics of Islamization of Knowledge as a Postmodern Project? The Fundamentalist Claim to De-Westernization," *Theory, Culture & Society*, 12/1, 1995, 24.
5. Ibid., 8.
6. Richard Harland, *Superstructuralism: The Philosophy of Structuralism and Post-Structuralism* (London: Metheun, 1987), 43.

7.   S. Parvez Manzoor, "Historical Order, Rational State, or Moral Community? Islamic Politi-cal Theory and the Challenges of Modernity," in M. M. Abul Fadl, ed., *Proceedings, Twenty First Annual Conference of the Association of Muslim Social Scientists*, (Herndon, Virginia: IIIT, 1993), 415–30.

8.   Haldun Gulap, "Islamism and Postmodernism," *Contention* 4/2, 1995, 62.

9.   Tibi, "Culture and Knowledge," 3.

10.   Ibid., 10

11.   Ibid., 19

12.   J.N. Pieterse, "A Severe Case of Dichotomic Thinking," *Theory, Culture & Society*, 13/4, 1996, 125–6.

13.   S. Parvez Manzoor, "Reason-without-Text confronts Text-without-Reason," *The Muslim News (UK)*, 113, 1998, 6.

14.   John L. Esposito, "Islam and Secularism in the Twenty-First Century," in J.L. Esposito and A. Tamimi, eds., *Islam and Secularism in the Middle East*, (London: C. Hurst & Co. Ltd., 2000), 1.

15.   S. Parvez Manzoor, "Islam and the Crisis of Modernity," http://www.algonet.se/~pmanzoor/, in *Parvez Manzoor's Homepage: Reconciling Transcendence with Existence*, October 21, 2000.

16.   Bulaç's views are cited in: Gulap, "Islamism and Postmodernism," 67.

17.   Abdelwahab Elmessiri, "The Dance of the Pen, the Play of the Sign: A Study in the Rela-tionship between Modernity, Immanence, and Deconstruction," *The American Journal of Islamic Social Sciences*, 14/1, 1997, 2.

18.   Abdelwahab Elmessiri, "Secularism, Immanance and Deconstruction," in J.L. Esposito and A. Tamimi, eds., *Islam and Secularism in the Middle East*, (London: C. Hurst & Co., 2000), 74.

19.   'Abd al-Wahab al-Masiri (Abdelwahab Elmessiri), *al-Sahyuniyyah wa'l Naziyyah wa Nihayat al-Tarikh: Ru'yah Hadariyyah Jadidah* (Cairo: Dar al-Shuruq, 1997), 11.

20.   Charles Taylor, *The Ethics of Authenticity* (Cambridge, MA: Harvard University Press, 1991), 10.

21.   Parvez Manzoor, "Islam and the Crisis of Modernity."

22.   Seyyed Hossein Nasr, *Traditional Islam in the Modern World* (London: Routledge & Kegan Paul, 1987), 100.

23.   Elmessiri, "The Dance of the Pen, The Play of the Sign," 6–9.

24.   Ibid.

25.   Ibid., 8.

26.   S. Parvez Manzoor, "Modernity, Transcendence and Political Theory," *Encounters: Journal of Inter-Cultural Perspectives*, 5/1, 1999.

27.   Gulap, "Islamism and Postmodernism," 61.

28.   Ibrahim Abu-Rabi', "Beyond the Postmodern Mind," *The American Journal of Islamic Social Sciences*, 7/2, 1990, 251.

29.   Smith, *Beyond the Post-Modern Mind*, 233.

30.   Gulap, "Islamism and Postmodernism," 62.

31.   Abu-Rabi', "Beyond the Postmodern Mind," 252.

32.   James N. Powell, *Postmodernism for Beginners* (New York: Writers and Readers Publishing, Inc., 1998), 33.

33.   Elmessiri, "The Dance of the Pen, The Play of the Sign," 10.

34.   Abu-Rabi', "Beyond the Postmodern Mind," 255.

35.   Gulap, "Islamism and Postmodernism," 59.

36. Haldun Gulap, "Globalizing Postmodernism: Islamist and Western Social Theory," *Economy and Society* 26/3, 1997, 429.

37. Cited in: Gulap, "Globalizing Postmodernism," 429.

38. Ibid.

39. Ibid., 430.

CHAPTER 16

Europe Against Islam: Islam in Europe

Talal Asad

I

It is a banal but nonetheless important fact that in liberal democracy the mass media are an indispensable source of information about the contemporary world, information that is necessary to the formation of responsible political opinion. The liberal intelligentsia is supposed to be an integral part of this process – reflecting on, analyzing, and explaining the wider implications of this information. Yet too often it fails in this task, content to support and be supported by the dominant discourse of the media.

For some years now the Western media have been reporting on events of violence whose perpetrators identify themselves as members of religiously inspired movements: in the West Bank and Gaza, Jewish zealots attack and kill Palestinians; in Egypt, Muslim zealots murder policemen, Copts and other civilians; in Algeria, the scale of terror directed by the Islamic Salvation Front at overthrowing the present unconstitutional regime escalates to unmanageable proportions; in India, the Hindu nationalist movement targets Muslims, foments riots, threatens to take over state power, and upper-caste Hindus burn transgressive outcastes alive; in Iran, a despotic Islamic government persecutes religious minorities and homosexuals; in the United States, "pro-life" Catholics and Protestants threaten abortion doctors with death. All of this is part of what one academic has called "the revenge of God" against the secular Enlightenment.[1]

These and similar developments have been endlessly commented on, in the media and in academic publications. Are they all so many symptoms of rejection of modernity? Or are they desperate expressions of modern aspirations that have been too long frustrated? Analyses and explanations abound. But interest in these events in the Western media and among the Western intelligentsia is notably uneven. Thus on the whole "Islam" tends to be regarded as a greater moral and political affront to modernity than other religious traditions. The violent activities of Islamic militants ("fundamentalists") are often identified with the essence of an entire historical tradition. Even when there is no direct violence, Islam appears as the bearer of a frightening tradition that calls insistently for the joining together of politics and religion. It threatens thereby to undermine the very foundation of modern values that are said to be exemplified in Europe and North America.

The uneven focus on events of religious violence lends credibility to the perception that Islam is a major threat to the West. The names of authors who have dealt recently with this topic are legion. But prominent among them is Harvard political scientist Samuel Huntington. In a much-discussed article published in the influential US periodical *Foreign Affairs*, he argues at length that "a central focus of conflict for the immediate future will be between the West and several Islamo-Confucian states."[2] The historian of modern Egypt P.J. Vatikiotis has no difficulty in assuming that Islamic conflict with the West means Islamic hostility to the entire world, since the West is the world: "the present wave of Islamic resurgence," he tells his readers, "is not merely intensely hostile to the rest of the world, but also preaches violent combat against it (or at least against those it considers to be its leaders), including the promotion, sponsoring, and organization of acts of terrorism."[3] The orientalist Bernard Lewis uncovers a frightening international conspiracy. Referring to the governments of Muslim countries, he asserts that "They have built up an elaborate apparatus of international consultation and, on many issues, cooperation: they hold regular high-level conferences, and despite differences of structure, ideology, and policy, they have achieved a significant measure of agreement and common action. In this *the Islamic peoples* are in sharp contrast with those who profess other religions."[4] Jews and Catholics, Lewis would have us believe, have no organizations for international consultation or cooperation!

Certainly such irresponsible views are not universal among Western "experts on Islam." Many have, quite sensibly, rejected the underlying assumption, including John Esposito.[5] In a later number of *Foreign Affairs*, the question is debated by Leon Hadar (who argues effectively that there is no real threat) and Judith Miller (who maintains that there is). However, more important than the arguments and evidence mobilized in this debate – which is being constantly replicated in Western publications and the media – is the fact that regardless of the position taken by individuals in the debate the questions which underlie it remain urgent: "Is the Islamic revival really dangerous? If so, what exactly does it threaten?" Those for whom the answer to the first question is in the affirmative refer sometimes to "Western interests" and sometimes to modern values – and assume an easy connection between the two.

Thus Western public opinion is more alarmed about violent and authoritarian tendencies that appear to be generated by "Islam" than by those attributable to other religions. One may note in passing a vicious circle in which the more the media focus on incidents and developments that can be assigned to "Islam," the more disproportionate the alarm becomes.

But there is another interesting selectivity: Western media are far more interested in threats to literary writers than in the cruelties perpetrated against other human beings.

It should come as no surprise that worldwide publicity is given to the death threats made by Muslim zealots against the British Salman Rushdie, and against the Bangladeshi novelist Nasreen Taslima. (Perhaps it is understandable that Taslima, being a less accomplished author, should find her case less widely publicized than that of

Rushdie. Besides, she writes not in English but in an Asian tongue.) It is, nevertheless, worth reflecting on why far less interest is taken by the Western media in the torture and killing of non-literary individuals by governments (for example, political prisoners in Egypt,[6] Palestinians in Israel,[7] Kashmiris in India[8]). Is it because the Western liberal middle classes regard the lives of literary figures to be more valuable than those of other mere mortals? Or is it, as some claim, because threatening them principles are involved that affect the fundamental constitution of modern liberal society? When, over the last four years, I have pointed out this unevenness of moral concern to my liberal friends, they have often responded by claiming that in attacking authors, the zealots of Islam are attacking freedom of speech, and in seeking to murder critics of religion they are trying to kill the liberties on which modern society itself is built. But if that is thought to be an adequate explanation of the unequal emotional responses to human outrage, one may be led to the following disquieting thought: some of our secular liberals are more easily moved by what they see as *an affront to transcendent sacred principles* (like other religious zealots) than by actual instances of gross cruelty to particular human beings. The "principles" are, so it appears, highly emotive symbols of the personal identity of liberals.

This becomes more evident when we examine the remarkable lack of interest, among most "public intellectuals" in Europe and North America, in the recent case of the Egyptian defense lawyer, Madani. According to an international report, 'Abdel Harith al-Madani, the defense lawyer of certain outlawed groups for whom he was apparently trying to mediate with the government, was arrested and severely tortured to death in police custody.[9] The case of torture and murder (only one of a very large and growing number in Egypt today) has of course been denied by the state authorities, but they nevertheless refuse to allow an independent autopsy. Now one might suppose that public intellectuals in Western countries concerned to defend modern secular liberties would create a public outcry – if not quite as passionate as in the Rushdie case (he was, we will be reminded, A Famous Author) then at least one as loud as the one being heard over Taslima. For not only is this simply the case of a real murder under torture (as opposed to mere death threats). It is also a case where fundamental modern liberties – freedom from torture, and the right to legal representation without intimidation – are directly attacked by a government. Yet this case (and several others) is not even noticed by the literary intelligentsia in the West, nor pursued by those who have access to its media, in its human specificity. This is because – so I would suggest – it cannot be construed as an attack on the sacred symbols defining the collective identity of a literary intelligentsia that regards itself as the guardian of the secular, modern state.

If "Islam" abroad is represented as a threat to secular liberal symbols, then Muslims living in the West must at the very least be regarded with suspicion. Media representations, selectively and ideologically organized, focus on threats at home and threats "out there," and often work in tandem with certain fears of the liberal intelligentsia who see the "Islamic-Arab world" as pushing its foreign religious identity *into* Europe through migration.[10] In this there is a convergence with the opportunistic designs of politicians, as in the recent harassment of the North African immigrants in France authorized by Interior Minister Charles Pasqua. Of course, when such harassment appears to the liberal conscience to go too far, the same press that contributes to the representation of aggressive and intolerant Islam comes forward to defend victimized Muslims.

For example: in a single issue of *The Guardian Weekly* (August 14, 1994) the six items on "Islam" were headlined as follows: "France rounds up Algerian extremists," "Christians in Iran face attack," "Malaysia outlaws Sufis," "Tunisia stifles Islamist threat," "Nasreen fatwa hides Bangladesh paradox," "France stands firm on Algeria." All the items thus heralded alarming news about Muslims, and there was no item about Muslims that wasn't negative. Yet a week later the same paper carried a worried article headed, "Expulsion fever grips France" detailing gross police injustices against Algerian immigrants, and a thoughtful editorial warning that "France is tilting at windmills if it believes that an Algerian army-backed regime can still be saved by cash from the country's creditors, or that it would help to outlaw the Islamic Salvation Front (FIS) throughout Europe and America . . . President Mitterand and his then still socialist government lost their way in Algeria when they decided to back the annulment of the 1992 elections." At the time, however, most of the Western press, whether liberal or not, supported that annulment too.

I should state clearly at this point that in my view Muslims who demand the death or punishment of Taslima or Rushdie cannot under any circumstances be excused, let alone supported. However, I distance myself from aspects of the dominant discourse in which these affairs are being characterized and presented in the media. It is necessary to say this because the public debate in the West is generally articulated in terms of simple alternatives – one either stands unconditionally with Rushdie (and now also Taslima) or one excuses the zealots. I have no hesitation in condemning the death threats, but I also question the Western liberal discourse that informs the public about such matters. In particular I question: (a) its assumption that "religion" is the major threat to the principles of tolerance and democracy; (b) its part in constructing "an Islamic enemy"; (c) its privileging of the fate of literary authors as against other victims of cruelty; (d) its sacralization of the principle of freedom of speech. In brief, I question the assumption that the people who attack these literary authors are part of the larger forces that threaten modernity itself.

II

Is "religion" integral to these disruptive forces? It can hardly be denied that the great acts of human cruelty and destruction in the twentieth century have been carried out by secular governments (Nazi Germany, Stalinist Russia, Mao's China, etc.) not religious ones. In the United States, which is a model of liberal-democratic government and of the constitutional separation of Church and state, we have witnessed until very recently the intolerance of McCarthyism, anti-Semitism, and legal apartheid between whites and blacks; today we have the pervasive miseries of entrenched racism and massive poverty. In Israel, bastion of democracy in the Middle East, systematic racism against Palestinians remains institutionalized. None of these well-known facts entails the superior virtue of "religious" states, of course. I cite them here only to challenge the easy secularist connection between intolerance and "religion." There is more to be feared, I suggest, from some of the trends generated by secular modernity: the sovereignty of the nation-state, non-European countries flooded with weapons manufactured and sold by the West, worldwide pollution and depredation of the natural environment, the development and application of sophisticated technologies of social control, a global economy of unbounded consumption whose movements are poorly understood, etc. I stress that I am not presenting an apocalyptic scenario, nor denouncing "modernity." With all its problems this is the only world we have, and we must try to live in it as best we can. I say merely that in identifying "religion" as the real threat to tolerance and sanity we allow ourselves an easy escape from the massive problems that confront the modern world.

If religion is often thought of as a major danger, "Islam" is often represented as a uniquely intractable instance of active religion in the modern world. In a modern world "religion" has – or at any rate, we believe that it should have – its proper appointed place. Islam, presented as a "religious civilization," is a construct not only of the media but also of intellectual discourse. That is the discourse in which the rich and diverse history of Muslim societies across three continents and one-and-a-half millennia is reduced to the essential principles of a distinctive "religious civilization."

Such essentialist characterizations of "Islamic civilization" are carried out some-times sympathetically and sometimes with hostile intent, but in either case they prompt people to explain the many authoritarian or violent trends in Muslim countries in terms of an essential "Islam." There are several objections to such an explanatory procedure, but I shall confine myself here to the most obvious: No liberal in the West would suggest that the Gush Emunim in Israel represents the essence of Judaism, or that the assassi-nation of abortion doctors in the United States by pro-life activists represents the essence of Christianity. Liberal scholars today would rightly object to the suggestion that the powerful authoritarian campaign throughout India for Hindutva (which some observers have likened to Nazism)[11] expresses the essence of "Hinduism"; yet Western writers continue to identify an essential "authoritarianism" in Muslim countries and attribute it to Islam's monotheistic beliefs.

The Western intellectual discourse on "Islamic civilization" goes back at least to the first half of the nineteenth century, but in our own day scholars (von Grunebaum, Gibb, Watt, Lewis, Crone, and Cook, Geertz, Gellner, and many others) have continued to reproduce it. This discourse is not invariably hostile, but it does make it possible to rep-resent the contemporary Islamic revival as the outcome of civilizational essence react-ing violently in self-defense against the challenge of modernity. I contend that the very ideal of "civilization" – a nineteenth-century invention – is not helpful for thinking con-structively about the cultural and political problems of our time. On the other hand "tradition" – often falsely opposed to "modernity" and "reason" since the Enlighten-ment – is a far more promising concept.

III

Islam is a major tradition in countries where Muslims live. It is not the only tradition, of course, but one that still constitutes a significant part of the lives of most Muslims.

Because Muslim societies are in crisis, Islamic tradition is in crisis too. It has to be defended, argued through, and reconstructed if it is to be viable. I refer here not simply to intellectual traditions, to philosophy, theology, history, etc., which (so we are continually told by critics of Islam) are in a state of decay. I am thinking in the first place of ways of living that are articulated, in diverse conditions, by Islamic tradition. But in order to be viable we should not take it for granted that tradition needs to be remade in the image of liberal Protestant Christianity.

People now are increasingly conscious of living in a single interdependent world, but Muslim societies have always been variously conscious of their dependence on other civilizations, especially on the Hellenic and Persian worlds and on Indian, Chinese, and African societies. Muslim empires in the past (contrary to what has been alleged about Islamic intolerance) were more tolerant of a diversity of religions and cultures than Europe was. Hence, even Europe may have something to learn from that history of comparative tolerance. Western scholars who concede this history sometimes insist that non-Muslims lived under Muslim rule as "second-class citizens." Such expressions seem to me entirely anachronistic because no one in those hierarchical empires was "a citizen," and the mass of Muslim subjects cannot in any meaningful sense be regarded as part of "the ruling class." Besides, Muslim rulers often employed Christians, Jews, and Hindus in positions of power and trust – who therefore had authority over Muslims. In saying this I do not intend to imply that Muslim rulers and populations were never bigoted and never persecuted non-Muslims. The social and moral assumptions around which such empires and kingdoms were constructed are, of course, no longer viable, but they did embody certain principles of toleration that were absent not only in Latin Christendom, but in post-Enlightenment European states too. They did not require everyone (whether Muslim or not) to live according to a single set of "self-evident truths."

What I wish to emphasize here is that the zealotry so characteristic of many Islamic political movements in recent times is a product not of the mainstream historical tradition of Islam. It is the product of *modern* politics and the *modernizing* state. Many academic commentators have pointed to the modern ideologies and organizations characteristic of contemporary Islamists. Such analyses are nearly always conducted to demonstrate the speciousness of the claim to authenticity made by these movements. By asserting that there is a sharp split between "traditional Islam" and "modern developments" these analysts imply that authentic ("traditional") Islamic tradition cannot be genuinely modern.

I believe that these commentators are mistaken in making this sharp opposition. But, more importantly, they rarely go on to ask themselves what their conclusion indicates about modern historiography and the modernizing state. They fail to note that it is the unprecedented ambition of the latter, its project of transforming the totality of society and subjectivity in the direction of continuous productive progress, that creates a space for a correspondingly ambitious Islamist politics. Islamist history had no such space. That space, with its totalitarian potentialities, belongs entirely to Western modernity.

Indeed, there was no such thing as a state *in the modern sense* in Islamic history – or, for that matter in pre-modern European history. There were princes, of course, and dynasties (the modern Arabic word for "state" *dawlah*, is an extension of the classical

Arabic word for "dynasty"), who headed centralized institutions for securing law and order, extracting tax, etc. But there was no *state* in the modern sense of a sovereign structure that stands apart from both governors and governed, which it is the government's duty to maintain, and which articulates, through the territory it controls, the entirety of *society*.

Western orientalists, as well as Muslims who call for the establishment of an Islamic state, have taken for granted that the rise of Islam in the seventh century saw the establishment of a theocratic state in Arabia, one in which religion and politics were indissolubly fused together. For Islamists and orientalists later Muslim history is seen as a falling away from that model, a process in which a separation occurred between religious and political institutions. For Islamists this separation constitutes the betrayal of a sacred ideal that Muslims are required as believers to restore: for orientalists the lingering connection defines a schizophrenic compromise that has always prevented a progressive reform of Islam. (These *political* histories, incidentally, should not be confused with the belief held by pietists that successive generations after the Prophet declined in virtue.)

But contemporary Muslim scholars are beginning to ask whether it is right to represent Islamic history in these terms at all. That representation, it may be argued, is the product of a nineteenth-century European historiography in which the modern categories of "religion" and "state" are used anachronistically. After all, the Prophet Muhammad did not seek divine authority for all his political actions, and it is known that his followers often argued with him without being branded apostates. He had to rely on personal loyalty and on persuasion to keep his followers because he possessed no coercive state institutions. Indeed, it was the Prophet's immediate political successor, Abu Bakr, who first undertook military action against fellow Muslims throughout the Arabian peninsula designed to subordinate them by force to centralized political authority. It was he who introduced the argument that obedience to an Islamic prince was a necessary part of being a Muslim.

However, I stress that even the principle of subordination to an Islamic prince does not constitute an Islamic state in the modern sense. This is a complex historical and theological theme which cannot be pursued here. I touch on it merely in order to question the idea that the indisputable fact of original Islamic theocratic state remains the real cause of contemporary Islamist ambitions.

In my view it is irresponsible to invite readers to regard Islamist politics as an outgrowth of tendencies essential to an *original* politico-religious Islam. The idea that Islam was originally – *and therefore essentially* – a theocratic state is, I argue, a nineteenth-century European one, developed under the influence of evolutionary theories of religion. Of course its European origin does not in itself render it invalid. My reason for mentioning that nineteenth-century origin is simply that if today's Islamic militants have accepted this perspective as their own, this does not make it *essential to Islam*. (It is necessary to add, however, that my argument is not intended to undermine the validity of any kind of "politicized Islam": I claim only that "a religious state" is not essential to the tradition of Islam.)

It also won't do to represent all forms of Islamic revival as merely accidental growths caused by deteriorating economic conditions combined with Western ideologies. People respond to contemporary conditions, they are not passively determined by them. Their traditions and interpretations of history, and therefore their formulation of the problems they face, are part of these conditions.

In fact, Islamic movements of revival predate the impact of Western modernity in Muslim countries. Thus in the eighteenth century (to go back no farther) there were several attempts at social reform and theological renewal in the Muslim world. In general the reforming thinkers took pains to distinguish between the absolute truth of the divine text and the authority of interpretive positions adopted by traditionalists and legal scholars over the centuries. Perhaps the most interesting of these eighteenth-century thinkers was Shah Waliyullah of Delhi, writing at the time of the breakup of the Mughal Empire in India. In Arabia, at the same time, a Najdi reformer Muhammad bin 'Abd al-Wahhab joined forces with the Saud family to establish the political entity that eventually became today's Saudi Arabia. A little later, in the second half of the eighteenth century, Osman dan Fodio developed far reaching educational and political reforms in West Africa on the basis of a carefully argued Islamic position. Like other Muslims of their time, they accepted unquestioningly the divine authority of the Qur'an, and the exemplary status of the Prophet. Yet each produced remarkably distinctive theological and practical solutions to what he perceived as the principal problems of his place and time. The rich and subtle thought of Shah Waliyullah contrasts with the austerity of Ibn 'Abd al-Wahhab, and the latter's rigor with Osman dan Fodio's principled flexibility. These and other Islamic reformers have their intellectual heirs today, Muslims who attempt, with varying resources and in very different conditions, to address the problems of the modern world. They should not be seen, therefore, as simply reacting to Western ideas and conditions.

When analyzing the violence – collective and individual – which we witness in Euro-American countries perceptive analysts point to the conclusion that something is structurally wrong with their political systems as well as with their economies. That conclusion is certainly widespread among most Muslims about their own countries. (It is often wrongly stated by Westerners that Arab-Muslims are allergic to self-criticism. Such statements confuse despotic rulers with the people they rule.)[12] In any society whose inhabitants undergo and acknowledge a wide-ranging social crisis, intense and passionate conflict over principles of renewal are almost inevitable – and thus zealotry finds its place, as European history surely attests. In this respect those who insist on secularism as the solution to all our political ills are no different than the zealots who speak in the name of Islam – or, for that matter, in the name of any other living religious tradition.

IV

The prospectus of the conference held in Leiden in September 1994, entitled "Islam and Politics in the European Community," noted that "some orientalist publications have pointed out the relevance, for the present situation of Muslims in Western Europe, of the division of the world into the 'House of Islam' and the 'House of Unbelief' (or the 'House of War') as it is found in the Islamic legal tradition. Doubt is expressed about the religious permissibility of political loyalty toward a non-Muslim government and about participation in non-Muslim political structures."

This typical piece of anti-Muslim slander makes two unwarranted assumptions: (a) that even if that ancient doctrine has no institutional backing in Europe, most Muslims living there will be guided by it; (b) that Muslims are not open to reinterpretation of that doctrine although Christian Europeans have been able to reinterpret legal doctrines that are very similar.[13] It also ignores the fact that large numbers of colonial Muslims in Africa and Asia have lived as subjects of European governments, and only very rarely has their opposition to those governments invoked that doctrine.

Anyone familiar with European history will not be too surprised at this orientalist attempt to discredit Muslims resident in Europe. There is, after all, a long European tradition of finding reasons for excluding religious minorities from the essential nation. Theological tracts proving that Catholics (in Protestant countries) and Protestants (in Catholic countries) are not to be trusted abound in modern European history. The dismal story of European anti-Semitism is too well known to be rehearsed here. And yet one wonders whether the orientalists who now talk of Muslim minorities with detailed scholarly suspicion have learned anything from that unhappy story of European prejudice against Jews. Can it be that they are now able to displace their previous animus against Jews toward a religious minority that is politically even less powerful – the Muslims in Europe? This would certainly help to explain why most Europeans accept the double standards applied to Muslims and Jews. Certainly, Orthodox Jews could be criticized for most of the things for which pious Muslims in Europe are continually denounced – including patriarchal families, the ritual slaughter of animals, the legal status of women with regard to marriage and divorce, etc. It seems that European intellectuals are afraid to criticize Jews in public, so they redouble their attacks on Muslims.

Muslim residents in Europe should certainly not be confused with states and political movements in the Muslim world – even if there are sometimes connections between them. But in any case, we should not give in too easily to the demands of European nationalists for absolute and exclusive loyalties from their citizens. One can participate in a responsible and committed fashion in political structures without conceding the validity of such demands. As it is, bankers and trade unionists, intellectuals, scientists, and artists, all have personal and professional attachments that transcend the borders of the nation-state. Jews, Catholics, and recent immigrants in a world of increasing migration, all have loyalties that are not exhausted by the constitutional demands of the nation-state. Why should Muslims in Europe be expected to be different?

It is often asked whether Muslim communities can really adjust to Europe. The question is more rarely raised as to whether the institutions and ideologies of Europe can adjust to the modern world of which culturally diverse immigrants are an integral part. Europeans were, after all, ready to change their attitudes to accommodate Jewish communities with an unprecedented respect.

It is only since World War Two that we encounter the frequent use of the term "Judeo-Christian civilization" as an indication of that change. The new idea of Judaism as an integral part of "Christian civilization" – and not merely a prelude to or a tolerated margin of it – has credibility not because of an indisputable "objective" past, but because Euro-Americans now wish to interpret and reconstruct another kind of relevant past for their civilization. (Of course anti-Semitism is not dead in Europe or America. But anyone who aspires to respectability in the liberal democracies of the West cannot afford to be identified publicly as an anti-Semite.) There is no good reason whatever why, as Muslim immigrants become full members of European states and the European Community, Europe's past achievements – for that is what talk about its "civilization" amounts to – should not be reconstructed in richer and more complex ways, in order to accommodate Islamic history. After all, much of the intellectual and social history of medieval Christendom is intimately linked to that of medieval Islam.

So too, one hopes that another kind of history-for-the-present may emerge in countries where Muslims are in a majority – overlapping with that of other societies, and connected to them by a multiplicity of relations, in a fashion quite unlike the one envisaged by Huntington. This does not mean that the differences between Muslims, Christians, and Jews should be synthesized into a lowest common denominator to which all can happily subscribe. Nor does it mean that every identity should become so mobile that – as some postmodernists would have it – no one can be continuously one kind of moral being belonging to a distinctive community. What it does mean is that the members of each tradition should be prepared to engage productively with members of others, challenging and enriching themselves through these encounters.

Too often in post-Enlightenment society "to tolerate" differences simply implies not taking them seriously. This has certainly been the attitude behind religious toleration bequeathed to the modern secular state by the European Enlightenment. But it is no longer adequate to regard "religion" simply as a type of *private belief*. In a political world where everyone is said to have the right to construct himself or herself, "religion" is now also a base *for publicly contested identities*. As such it is at the very center of democratic politics, from which only the most determined anti-democratic power can keep it out.

Can we not break away from the fundamentalist vision of a single authentic (i.e., European) modernity, and help to construct multiple modernities? It remains to be seen how many Europeans will actually be drawn to this option despite the strong sense that most of them still have of their cultural triumph in the world at large.

Notes

1. Giles Kepel, *The Revenge of God: The Resurgence of Islam, Christianity and Judaism in the Modern World* (Cambridge: Polity, 1993).
2. S. Huntington, "The Clash of Civilizations," *Foreign Affairs*, 72/3, 1993, 48.
3. "Islam on the Move? The Will to Power," *Encounter*, November, 1989, 49.
4. B. Lewis, *The Political Language of Islam* (Chicago: 1988), 3; emphasis added.
5. John Esposito, *The Islamic Threat: Myth or Reality?* (New York: Oxford University Press, 1992).
6. See the account of continuing practice of large-scale detention of civilians and torture by the Egyptian security forces as reported in *Human Rights Abuses Mount in 1993: US Policymakers Should Hold President Mubarak Accountable* (New York: Human Rights Watch, Publications, 1993).

7. *See A License to Kill: Israeli Undercover Operations Against "Wanted" and Masked Palestinians* (New York: Human Rights Watch Publications, 1993), which recounts the activities of official Israeli units disguised as Palestinians: especially the killing of Palestinian youths who are neither "wanted" nor carrying firearms, and who are shot when they are posing no immediate danger to the lives of others.

8. Human Rights Watch documents rape, torture, arson, and summary executions of civilians by the Indian security forces in Kashmir. See *The Human Rights Crisis in Kashmir: A Pattern of Impunity* (New York: Human Rights Publications, 1994).

9. *The Lawyers Committee for Human Rights Delegation in Cairo, Egypt May 24–7, 1994 Finds Unanswered Questions in Events Surrounding the Death of Lawyer 'Abdel Harith Madani* (New York: Human Rights Watch Publications, 1994).

10. "In principle, there is scope for growing cooperation between Western Europe, with its stagnant and aging population, and the Maghreb, with its growing and increasingly young one. Within twenty years the combined populations of Morocco, Algeria, and Tunisia could be twice as big as France's: the knocking at Europe's door will grow louder. But 1.5 m North Africans already live in France, and one consequence is that racial tensions run high. What if Western Europe turns in future to new sources of labor, such as fellow Christians from the newly accessible countries of Eastern Europe, rather than to the Muslim south?" "The Arab World: A Survey," *The Economist*, May 12, 1990, 9.

11. Sumit Sarkar, "The Fascism of Sanity Parivar," *Economic and Political Weekly*, January 30, 1993.

12. Whether we like it or not, Islamists are among the strongest critics of their own society. In Egypt, for example, the Islamist newspaper *ash-Sha'b* regularly carries detailed criticisms of economic and political conditions, projects, policies – even Egyptian secularists confess that its record of investigative journalism on such issues is more impressive than that of any other periodical.

13. In the ancient world the legal category *terra nullius* was applied by Romans to land not occupied by them. In medieval Christendom it referred to land not occupied by Christians. In the eighteenth and nineteenth centuries it was land not occupied by European imperial states. Today it simply means land that is not claimed by one sovereign state or another.

CHAPTER 17

Ummah and Empire: Global Formations after Nation

Mucahit Bilici

The ideas and practices of *ummah* and empire predate modernity. Both *ummah* and empire existed long before the eighteenth and nineteenth centuries gave birth to the idea of nation. Today, under the challenge of globalization, the nation-state system is giving way to a new configuration. As space opens for alternative imaginations, both *ummah* and empire are returning, but with a difference. The resurgence of these two entities is not a simple return of their pre-national forms, however. Their contemporary articulations are mediated by the experiences of nation and nation-state. Each, therefore, inherits certain elements from nation, but at the same time represents significant departures from it. Not only are the two concepts different in relation to nation; they are different in relation to one another. Contemporary interactions between empire and *ummah* can be interpreted as a continuation of the confrontation between transnational Islamism and Western imperialism. Yet such an interpretation fails to capture the commonalities of these two post-national formations.

In this chapter I argue that the nascent reconfiguration of power and culture in the global arena leads to a confrontation between a deterritorialized empire and a fluid colony. I develop my argument through a consideration of the following issues: (i) nation and its dissemination; (ii) globalization and deterritorialization; and (iii) post-national formations of *ummah* and empire. I propose answers to such questions as: In what ways are current popular invocations of *ummah*, as articulated by global actors like Osama bin Laden, different from the original conception of *ummah*? How is the current American-led empire different from conventional empires? Where does the real "clash" lie?

Some Preliminary Notes

- **Empire**: Postcolonial theory has popularized the concept of empire and used it in many ways. Among the most recent articulations of the concept is that of Hardt and Negri.[1] Relying on Foucauldian poststructuralist insights, they define "empire" as lacking boundaries and having a global character, while at the same time lacking a specific center. My use of the concept, however, diverges somewhat from theirs. Empire is a power-enforcement machine with a global reach. But while it is largely post-territorial, I believe that it still hinges on a "center." I take the United States to be the center of empire. On a related note, I believe that the guiding principles of the empire are Hobbesian. Formulations of self and group identity vary, but the Hobbesian articulation remains the dominant articulation in Western policy circles. Further justification of this choice lies in the overwhelmingly Hobbesian nature of power relations between Western powers and Muslim geographies.

- **Ummah**: My definition of the concept of *ummah* is based on its articulation in the work of Said Nursi (1877–1960).[2] Why Said Nursi? First, while expressed in contemporary terms, it follows closely to the classical Islamic articulation of the concept. Second, it is the Turkish voice, a distinct and underrepresented viewpoint which deserves amplification in discussions of the contemporary Muslim intellectual landscape.

- **Nation**: The most widely accepted definition is Benedict Anderson's idea of "imagined communities" based on "print capitalism."[3] While I embrace Anderson's definition in general, I am not satisfied with his emphasis on *print*. I believe that nationalism is less about *print* and more about *capitalism*. In other words, Anderson's emphasis does not really highlight the core dynamic that brought about the *aggressive* element in nationalism. In my opinion, only part of the newness of nationalism is attributable to capitalism's print and mass production capabilities. The other part springs from an underlying utilitarianism unleashed by capitalism. The core of nationalism, its spirit, is not print but *self-interest*, which found expression through capitalism at that time. Following in the footsteps of Polanyi, I also embrace the critique of the Marxist approach to the idea of self-interest as a given, natural, and universal category.[4] If print helped build the body of the nation by knitting individuals into a singular body, then the soul of nation flowed from utilitarian *self-interest*.

Social Closure: Self Versus Other

Nation is the form by which the majority of human polities organize themselves today. To understand the nature of nation, one must have a theoretical grasp of the dynamics that operate at the boundary between self and other. "Nation" is a rather recent invention; the history of this divide is very old. And the nation is but one of its historical products. Like nation, individual, religious community, race, class, and ethnicity, are all constituted through particular processes of delineation.[5] In other words, they are historical examples of *classification*, or what Weber calls social closure.[6]

Social closure is a useful conceptual tool for understanding the formation of identities. It refers to the closure of corporal, social, cultural, and economic opportunities to outsiders. For example, the individual is a corporally invested form of social closure.

The works of Freud and Lacan shed a great deal of light on the development of the sense of self or the appropriation of one's own body in early childhood.[7] The "I" comes into being not as an emanation of the individual, but as the result of an encounter with an *other*. In the case of the economically invested social group – the class – the border that separates the bourgeoisie from the working class is control over the means of production and economic interests. This border has been historically challenged and expanded through various struggles of class, gender, and citizenship.[8] The sociologist Rogers Brubaker, for example, conceptualizes "citizenship" as a form of social closure.[9] Race and ethnicity are also forms of social closure, even though they choose different terrains of operation. While the former constitutes itself mostly through biology, the latter tends to inscribe itself on culture. However, none of these forms of social closure are universal. Nor are they essential.

From totemism, tribe, class, and race to modern systems of certification and ethnic groupings, there are many historically specific processes of classification or attempts at social closure. Because the collective social identity always entails some form of communal self-definition, it is invariably founded on the marked opposition between "us" and "other/s."[10] As Comaroff points out, the irreducible fact of identity implies the cultural/political structuring of the physical/social universe on the basis of self and other. It is the opposition between self and other that is primordial, not the content of the distinction.

> [T]he marking of contrasting identities – of the opposition between self and other, we and they – is "primordial" in the same sense that classification is a necessary condition of social existence. But the way in which social classification is realized in specific forms of collective identity, ethnicity no less than any other, is always a matter to be decided by the material and cultural exigencies of history.[11]

Individual, ethnicity, nation, and other social groupings are all social constructions and must be contextualized within time, space, and politics. The next section of this chapter focuses on nation as a dominant yet historical form of social closure.

Man Created *Nation* in His Own Image

> The soldier who falls defending his flag certainly does not believe he has sacrificed himself to a piece of cloth. Such things happen because social thought, with its imperative authority, has a power that individual thought cannot possibly have . . . Hence, there is a realm of nature in which the formula of idealism is almost literally applicable; that is the social realm. There, far more than anywhere else, the idea creates the reality.[12]

Nation is a modern type of community – a community of readers, listeners, and viewers of political power. It is exposure to a single text that produces a community of readers (an audience) as a collectivity of individuals more or less preoccupied with similar things. Community is built and sustained in the consciousness of individuals who are exposed to a common public sphere. Scholars of nationalism such as Deutsch and

Anderson show how nation is made possible by the incorporation of scattered individuals into a single body with the thread of communication.[13] It is the common subjection to a power (generally the state) that gives boundaries to modern political communities. Nation thus relies heavily on the *media* through which individuals are connected and even constituted. In a sense, nation is the arrest (enclosure) of a previously amorphous constellation of individuals by a political authority (state) within a discourse of commonwealth. It is for the most part projected onto a certain *territory*. Nation, however, is not the only form of imagined community. Anderson, for example, refers to other forms of social closure, such as the religious community and the dynastic realm, as precursors of nation. These were communities mediated and thus formed through sacred text/language and political subjection, respectively. According to Craig Calhoun, the institutionalization of a public sphere is at the heart of the project of nation.[14] The convergence of print (and other forms of) media with the mass-productive capacity of capitalism has given rise to an unprecedented form of imagination. As noted earlier, I add a new emphasis to Anderson's definition. For me there are two important conditions under which the imagination of nation became possible: (i) the conquest of the souls of individuals – generally by the instruments of power (in the Foucauldian[15] sense); and (ii) the *economization* of the communal *body politic*. To put it differently, the first condition is consolidation of the communal body and the second is its mobilization within a *utilitarian framework*.

I will further elaborate on the concept of nation with respect to several dimensions. Though not exhaustive, the following dimensions are singled out as of central importance:

1. the *historical background* of nation;
2. its economic foundations, or rather its *utilitarian core*;
3. its *ontological assumptions*.

(1) *Historical background*: The origins of the idea of nation can be traced back to the Enlightenment. The story of nation therefore must touch upon the rise of *humanism* and *utilitarianism*. The Enlightenment idea of the "autonomy" of the individual goes hand in hand with the development of utilitarianism's *self-interested individual*. This story can be deployed in different ways. Any such story must rely in one way or another on the idea of *population*, the rise of *society* as a precondition for the emergence of nation. Nation is basically a grafting of the Enlightenment's individual onto a political collectivity. In other words, nation is constituted upon the premises of *homo economicus*. The domestically harmonious, externally self-interested, and *organic* image of nation corresponds to this initial conception of the individual.

Furthermore, the idea of nation is inextricably linked to the exercise of power in modern society. Because the nation is "a sovereign body politic," the story of nation has to unfold with reference to its two constitutive elements: body and politics, or *population* and *power*. The rise of nation is coterminous with, on the one hand, the transformation of power from sovereign to disciplinary[16] and governmental, and on the other hand, with the object of this power, that is, the population and its evolution. The process that Foucault describes under the rubric of *governmentality* traces the contours of these developments.[17] In the early modern period, depersonalization of power and the penetration of economic thinking into the sphere of politics through the activities of mercantilism constituted important milestones in the crystallization of nation into a sovereign body politic.[18]

(2) The second dimension of nation that requires attention is the extent to which nation is based on "self-interest." The Hobbesian concept of *Leviathan* is an early formulation of the body politic, where a sovereign king and his subjects constitute a contractual political entity that secures the commonwealth.[19] This political body is built out of conflictual atoms of self-interested individuals around an organizing principle of "common utility." The rise of such notions as the *common good* as *obedience to law* and *reasons of state* marks an important moment in the consolidation of the political body as nation.[20] The nation achieves internal homogeneity, that is, the souls of individuals are conquered by the central state power through the disciplinary institutions of sciences, schools, prisons, hospitals, military, and the like. Once the nation reaches internal homogeneity, it begins to act like a utilitarian individual. In the final analysis, nation is a community based on *utilitarian economic* premises.

(3) Finally, the ontological assumptions of nation are also dramatically different from those of earlier forms of social closure or imagined communities such as religious communities and dynastic realms. To begin with, no nation is imagined as coterminous with mankind.[21] Moreover, unlike earlier forms of imagined community, nation perceives itself, first, as *autonomous* and second, as the *center* of the temporal and spatial universe. In other words, the *self* in the nation is neither God nor divine king but the *nation* itself. Nation is the *self*; the *other* is all that remains outside. In the case of nation, the relationship between self and other is deployed as *nation* (self) versus *other nations* (other).

The autonomous and self-centered nation is inserted into an imaginary world shaped by a *scarcity* of objects of desire and competition (e.g., economic/political utilities or power in general). Thomas Malthus, both as the father of the science of population and as the theorist of scarcity, has come to symbolize the origins of this world in which nation finds itself. The assumption of scarcity, which regulates that impersonal sovereign body politic, the nation, sets the stage for a Hobbesian world of nations. Nation becomes a potentially belligerent community.

Arising within the political walls of the nation-state, nation lives by the logic of scarcity and conflictuality. In the next section I highlight how this conflictual nature of nation overflowed its native locus and spread to the rest of the world.

Nation-State and its Dissemination

At the risk of contradicting the literature on Creole nationalism, which contests my assumptions here, I argue, following my earlier definition of nation, that nation-state is primarily a West European invention. It is so to the extent that modern capitalism is European. Given the historical and geographical specificity of nation-state, how did the contemporary world come to be so dominated by this form of political organization? There exists a literature of rationalization. For example, Meyer speaks of a "world society" and a rationalistic culture.[22] I suggest that we employ instead the insights provided by students of organizational sociology. DiMaggio and Powell offer a schema that distinguishes three ways in which isomorphism occurs in the world of economic corporations.[23] They are *coercive*, *mimetic*, and *normative*. Let us look at the spread of the organizational form called nation-state through the lens of these categories. Here are three ways the world might have been made into a world of nation-states:

1. *The coercive way*: Europeans disseminated the nation-state by means of their colonial power over weaker communal entities in places such as Africa and India. Another example of the coercive spread of nation-state is the infliction of the Holocaust, which culminated in the formation of yet another nation-state, Israel. If colonialism was the explosion of the European idea of nation, the Holocaust was its implosion.
2. *The mimetic way*: Nation-state found its way to the rest of the world partly through modernization, as a process that most of the uncolonized societies underwent of their own volition in order to catch up with their Western counterparts. Examples would be Turkey, Iran, and Russia.
3. *The normative way*: Post-colonial nation-building was profoundly shaped by the hegemonic presence of nation-state as the only conceivable/imaginable form of political organization. Post-Second World War state formation in Africa and Asia, and post-communist nation-state building in Central Asia and the former Yugoslavia further populated the remainder of the globe with nation-states.

Globalization, Deterritorialization, and Postnational Formations

The nation-state persisted as the dominant form of political organization around the globe for more than a century. Today, however, this political form is being seriously challenged by the process of globalization.[24] The idea of nation is being called into question both theoretically and practically.

As Appadurai notes, the practical challenge lies in the increasing movement of human beings, money, ideas, and commodities through the borders of nation-states and their increasing inability to control them.[25] Among the most interesting phenomena is the process of *deterritorialization*, which has been referred to as "the cultural condition of globalization."[26] Some have called this emergent configuration in the political geography of the world a *postnational constellation*.[27] Societies and social groups are increasingly escaping the confines of the nation-states. The processes of deterritorialization and increased connectivity have made possible the rise of a "transnational public sphere."[28] By creating new spaces for transnational actors (state or otherwise), globalization has reconfigured the space of imagination for *subnational* and *supranational* actors. Examples include multinational corporations and ethnic groups, as well as terrorist organizations such as al-Qaeda. Unfortunately, literature on Islam in general and terrorism in particular tends to characterize both violent and civil Islamic movements as predominantly anti-global and anti-Western.

It is striking that, contrary to the eurocentric, capital-centric narrative which suggests that the Islamists or Islamic activists are against globalization, the majority of Muslim societies celebrate the eclipse of the oppressive nation-states within which they have long felt themselves imprisoned.[29] In Turkey, for example, the most enthusiastic supporters of the nation's integration with the European Union are Islamic communities and Kurdish ethnic groups. Globalization has in effect reopened the global cultural/political terrain to the participation of all cultures, including that of Muslims. Globalization has triggered and revitalized the idea of *ummah* as a postnational form of imagination for Muslims, particularly for diasporic communities in the metropolitan centers. As noted by Appadurai, "the imagination today is a staging ground for action, and not only escape."[30]

"As the nation-state enters a terminal crisis," says Appadurai, "we can certainly expect that the materials for a postnational imaginary must be around us already." In other words, the theoretical challenge of globalization entails a search for non- or postnational forms of community. It is in this context that the concept of *ummah* attracts theoretical attention.

Ummah: Another Imagined Community

In this discussion I shall draw mainly on the writings of Said Nursi of Turkey. Basically, *ummah* is the community of Muslim believers. The concept refers to the totality of those who submit to the teachings of any prophet. According to Islamic precepts, the Prophet Muhammad is the last prophet and those who follow him are part of what is called a Muslim *ummah*.[31] The processes that connect dispersed individuals are very much similar to those of nation. It is exposure to a single narrative through sacred texts and images that renders otherwise unrelated individuals a community. In this section I will discuss several aspects of the imagined community of *ummah*:

1. its assumptions about *individual human* beings;
2. the place of *political economic thinking* in its imagination;
3. its *ontological assumptions*.

First of all, *ummah* is a community premised upon the belief that there is a God. Human beings are created as part of a larger universe. Human beings are the only segment of creation endowed with the capacity to "misrecognize reality" (in a Lacanian sense).[32] They exercise free will in their recognition of God. A human being is defined not as an economic being (e.g., *homo economicus*) but as a being who strives to maximize religiously defined virtues. In the Muslim imagination, a human being is *not* an *autonomous* entity, nor is he or she the *center* of the universe. A human being is simply a conscious representative of the entire creation. He or she is created as God's vicegerent on earth.[33] The centrality attributed to the human being in Islam is quite different from the centrality of man in humanism. According to Nursi, humans are not only equal as created beings, they are also equally far from being the address of worship – the *center*, in Derrida's sense of the term.[34]

Second, economy is conceived of as only one dimension of human being and it is articulated mainly in terms of subsistence. Muslim societies have a market, but it is an adjunct to society. The impetus that *ummah* as a construct gives to the individual is not primarily political. Just like any form of social closure, *ummah* as a community also engages in a search for well-being. This does not, however, directly and inherently emanate from the idea of *ummah*. The bases upon which *ummah* is built are neither economic nor primarily political. *Ummah* is a body politic but not primarily in political terms. *Ummah* is an imagined community, limited but *not sovereign*.

Third, the ontological assumptions of *ummah* are of fundamental importance to the question of self and other. In the case of *ummah*, the *self* is not the *ummah* itself, but *God* – and more importantly, the *other* is (each and every member of) the *ummah*. In other words, the constitutive divide that gives rise to *ummah* is established vertically between the believer and God. The *primary addressee* of *otherization* through the formation of *ummah* is the *ummah* itself. *Ummah* is a self-othering community. Creation is constituted in contradistinction to God. Human beings (and *ummah*) as part of creation are expected to believe that all that is positive is from God and all that is negative originates from human beings. Furthermore, in structuralist terms the *center* is God; creation is the structure. The relationship between *ummah* and other communities around (and within) it must be understood in connection with these ontological assumptions.

To further illustrate some of the juxtapositions above, we can look into Said Nursi's representation of the two categories. He does not compare them by specifically labeling them as such. Nevertheless, there are sections in his works where he compares the modern Western culture with the Islamic one. He considers the question of nationalism by juxtaposing it to its Islamic alternatives. The following excerpt is an example of such a comparison. Nursi defines the dominant modern culture in the West in contradistinction to what he calls the Qur'anic wisdom.[35] He argues that Western culture,

> accepts *power* as its basis in social life. Its aim is *benefits*. It recognizes *conflict* as its principle for life. Its bond for communities is *nationalism*. And its fruits are "gratifying the appetites of the soul and increasing human needs." However, the mark of power is *aggression*. The mark of benefits – since they are insufficient for every desire – is "jostling and tussling." While the mark of conflict is "strife," the mark of nationalism – since it is to be nourished by devouring others – is "aggression." Thus, it is for these reasons that it [western civilization] has devastated the happiness of mankind.
>
> As for the Qur'anic wisdom, its basis is "truth" instead of power. It takes "virtue and God's pleasure" as its aims in place of benefits. It takes the principle of *reciprocity* as the principle of life in place of the principle of conflict. And it takes the ties of religion, familiarity, and country to be the ties bonding communities. Its aim is to form a barrier against the lusts of the soul, urge the spirit to sublime matters, satisfy the high emotions, and urging man to the human perfections, make him a true human being.[36]

Said Nursi recognizes the idea of community or group identity as something necessary. To the extent that it functions as a nominal category, the idea of nation itself is also seen as natural. What is seen as problematic in the idea of nation is the ontological assumptions of autonomy and utilitarianism which anchor the modern concept of nation. In other words, Nursi sees the division between self and other as inevitable, but he does not consider this division necessarily conflictual. For the elimination of con-flict, however, what is needed, to put it in Hobbesian terms, is an immortal Leviathan (God) whose overarching presence can eliminate the claims for "self"ness within the sphere of creation. In one of his most intricate texts ("Thirtieth Word" in *The Words*), Nursi articulates a theory of human nature and argues that the sense of self is given to human beings as a unit of measure to enable them to understand the attributes of God.[37] Once they have used this tool (the sense of self) human beings should abandon it and along with it all claims to ownership, including corporal ones. This is Nursi's theory of misrecognition. For Nursi, there is room for the sense of *self* but not for *self-ishness*. In a similar vein, there is room for the idea of nation as a nominal category inducing a certain internal solidarity, but not for nationalism. From the ideas of Nursi, one may conclude that *ummah* is not simply a bigger or a deterritorialized nation. For Nursi, the difference between the two is qualitative. The next section will further illu-minate this difference.

Ummah and Nation Compared

Although both are imagined communities, nation and *ummah* rely on totally different ontological assumptions. Unlike the territorial nature of nation, *ummah* is not neces-sarily a territorial community. More important, the process of *otherization* works fun-damentally differently in nation and *ummah*. In the former, *the other* is other social groupings, while in the latter the community itself sees itself as *the other vis-à-vis* God. This initial division shapes the relationship between *ummah* and the other communi-ties it confronts. Unlike nation, which is a utilitarian project, *ummah* is founded upon such non-economic bases (ideals) as virtue and piety. Both communities have almost the same attributes for their "self"s: the self in nation (nation) has the same attributes as the self in *ummah* (God). (Hence, the well-known resemblance between nationalism and religion which gave rise to the discourse of "nationalism as a modern religion.") Connection with the center (self) or membership to the community is enacted in the form of citizenship in the case of nation; in the case of *ummah* it takes the form of worship. The nation seeks homogeneity. The *ummah* aspires to expand, yet does not seek homogeneity. Nation requires compulsory conversion; *ummah* is by definition unable to impose conversion, although it is known historically to have encouraged conversion through social/legal incentives.

Having established this genealogy of the two concepts, I contend that contemporary appropriations of the idea of *ummah* by some Islamist movements or terrorist groups such as al-Qaeda are not, in fact, an alternative to the idea of nation, because the legacy of (anti)colonialism has given rise to a new conception of *ummah*. Now *ummah* is seen by modernized/Westernized Muslim movements as a Muslim nation. In his discussion of contemporary Islam and violence, Bruce Lawrence also refers to Islamist movements of the last century as (Muslim) nationalist movements.[38] Similarly, I would argue that some forms of contemporary "Islamism" are simply anti-colonial nationalisms colored by religion – in this case, "Muslim nationalism." In other words, it is due to the impact of colonialism on Muslim societies in the last century that the concept of *ummah* has been reappropriated and rearticulated into a form of "nation".

The origins of "Muslim nationalism" can be traced back to the anti-colonial Muslim thinkers and activists of the early twentieth century. Pioneering Islamic/Islamist intellectuals such as Sayyid Qutb and Mawdūdī were products of colonized Muslim societies, Egypt and India respectively.[39] In the case of uncolonized Turkish society, the response to colonial harassment took the form of a modernization process. It is within this context that the Muslim nationalist Sultan Abdulhamid II politically mobilized the institution of caliphate, probably for the first time, in order to generate power against British colonialism and domestic nationalistic insurgencies. The multicultural Ottoman Empire as a state of (diverse) people was gradually transformed into a "nation of (this time, *Muslim*) citizens." Abdulhamid's pan-Islamist policy was a "secular" (nationalist) project aimed at the construction of a Muslim nation. This project was accelerated by the Young Turks and finalized by the Kemalists as a homogeneous, secular, Muslim Turkish Republic. This nationalizing, secularizing modernization project took place at the expense of ethnic and religious groups in Anatolia. The massacre of Armenians under the rule of the Young Turks was a reflection *par excellence* of the *nationalization of Muslimness*. Unsurprisingly, secularization and Westernization in the non-Western world almost always means nationalization. In the case of late Ottoman modernization, the convergence of nation and *ummah* – that is to say, the *nationalization of ummah* – combined with other forces to produce conflict and massacres.

Modern nationalistic self-interest on the part of Muslims like Osama bin Laden leads them to depart from traditional Muslim practice which adheres to rules of combat closely resembling the principles of the Geneva Conventions. For many Muslims horrified by both colonial aggression and the terrorism of 9/11, those attacks are yet another instance of the adoption of the language of the colonizer by the colonized.

Confrontation between Empire and *Ummah*

In a discussion of the emergent global order, Manuel Castells distinguishes between *powerless places* and *placeless powers*.[40] This distinction is useful to our discussion. It reflects the new nature of the relationship between power and place. In this new configuration of power, deterritorialization of culture and fluidity of power set in motion the interplay between two asymmetric powers: *empire* and *ummah*.

The nature of the political and cultural configuration emerging after nation has been a subject of wide debate. Among the popular arguments is Huntington's idea of a "clash of civilizations." The choice of "clash of civilizations" rather than, say, "clash of powers" or of states, reveals a particular perception. Here civilization is rooted in the combined deployment of culture and power. While *ummah* (Islam) stands at the culture end of the civilizational continuum, empire (the West or the US) occupies the power end of the spectrum. What makes the confrontation of empire and *ummah* so rich and unique is the fact that, more than ever before, culture has become the main battleground. Analysts like James Woolsey, former director of the Central Intelligence Agency, discuss this new war as World War IV (after the two World Wars and the Cold

War).[41] Despite Huntington's tendency to identify civilizations with religions, this particular conflict is not actually between religions. Rather, it is a conflict between utilitarian civilization and Islam as the only religion/culture that continues to defy it.

It is interesting to note that the transformation of *ummah* at the hands of Islamists draws it closer to the Western concept of nation. Furthermore, while the idea of *ummah* is being replaced in some quarters by a Muslim nationalism, the Western idea of nation is also being rearticulated. The transformation of American power at the hands of neo-conservative ideologs into a post-territorial empire is gradually coming to fruition, although it is being resisted and confronted in many ways.

In more practical terms, the symbolic conflict between neoconservative circles and Osama bin Laden is a conflict between *Hobbesian empire* (post-territorial colonialism) and *Westernized ummah* (Muslim nationalism). Despite its conspicuous character, this conflict is unlikely to remain central. The more profound conflict is between Hobbesian empire and non-Western *ummah*. In this conflict non-Hobbesian Western articulations of global society and non-Western *ummah* have more in common than Hobbesian empire and Westernized *ummah*. The war is not between Islam and the West, but between the imperialistic expansion of a Hobbesian civilization and Islam. In this war, Islam is likely to become a banner to which many other resistant cultures and conceptions of humanity will flock. This ideological polarization is a response to the globalization of the American empire as an economic and military power. In the next – rather speculative – section I will discuss the ways in which this new (American) empire differs from conventional ones.

New (American) Empire

The Washington Post columnist Charles Krauthammer argues (in a speech he delivered at the American Enterprise Institute's annual dinner, where he received the Irving Kristol Award, February 10, 2004) that the American "empire" cannot be defined as an empire because it is different from all other preceding empires, including the Roman and the British. He argues that Americans do not want to stay in the places they occupy. As soon as they invade a place (e.g. Iraq), argues Krauthammer, they immediately look for an "exit strategy." This, in his view, makes American domination non-imperial.

The question, then, is what made American forces "enter" the place to begin with? Why does the empire enter a place from which it immediately seeks an exit strategy? What does it hope to achieve? The difference on which Krauthammer bases his justification of American empire is indeed important. It does not make the American empire a non-empire, but rather a new kind of empire. A quick comparison may be helpful here.

The old colonial empire settles itself and settles others as well. It wants to have control in order to generate power. This is linked to its reliance on territory, raw materials, and other resources. It looks for stability. The new colonial empire, on the contrary, settles (often temporarily) in order to unsettle others. It seeks to open up space (if not necessarily place) to continue its existing control over "others." It is *deterritorial* or rather *post-territorial*. It needs not only resources, but also ideas/culture. It attempts to secure the free and structuring flow of capital.

The new empire operates under new conditions: systemic integration, an increased dominance of finance capital. It relies heavily on the hegemony of ideas and beliefs. It needs ideas to dominate as much as it used to need weapons and economic power in order to establish hegemony. In this shift culture is no longer a secondary element of domination, it becomes the main target of empire. Behind this change lie the increasing importance of "trust," "belief," and other non-material generators of "value."

Empire and "Islam / *Ummah* as a Fluid Colony"

Empire meets resistance to its further expansion and consolidation in the form of ideas and beliefs. Its hegemony is challenged not by economic or military powers but by challenges to its basic operating assumptions (e.g., *homo economicus*, self-interest, consumption). A fascinating aspect of the evolution of this nascent empire is the gradual expansion of its arsenal. For example, today American military aircraft not only drop weapons of mass destruction but also packages of food (as in Afghanistan) or tools of mass persuasion (as in the case of the television stations launched in Iraq). Empire works in a subtle way, converting all cultures and religions in the territories it expands into. The relationship between globalization and expediency of culture is one expression of this trend.[42] Empire, which is the historical culmination of capitalism in the form of a pure hegemonized American political power, has successfully converted and castrated the religions and cultures of Europe and most of Asia. It has been disruptive and subjugative in places like Africa. The collapse of the Soviet Empire has removed a further political shield, exposing already weakened religio-cultural elements, which now seem defenseless. Their revival is interrupted by the triumphant advent of imperial culture itself. China is currently in the throes of a cultural conversion to capitalism, despite its desire to remain politically autonomous. Today, empire has achieved a global reach and the map of its domination overlaps with almost all cultural zones save one: the zone of Islam.

Islam is the only surviving and vibrant "culture" over which empire has yet to achieve dominion. This is strikingly different from a territorial argument. Almost all Muslim territories, which are mostly organized in the form of (authoritarian, at times dictatorial) nation-states, are under conspicuous control of the empire (with the exception of Iran, whose relative autonomy *vis-à-vis* the empire accounts for its infantile democracy). The empire is less interested in territorial control than in non-territorial resources. What, then, is the new *imperial capital* that the empire in question is after?

What empire wants is not democracy. This does not mean, however, that the empire will never want democracy. Indeed, democracy in and of itself is seldom relevant to the demands of empire. What empire wants is global *access*. If that access is to be provided by a collaborating dictator, the imperial desire will take the form of stability. If the dictator (no matter if he was raised up initially by the empire) blocks that access, then the desire will take the form of a need for democracy and hence a "liberation/occupation" of the place.

Once empire consolidates its territorial domination in the form of instant access to all cultural zones and political organizations (states), it is likely to rely on two things. The first is its seductive power in the form of consumer culture and promises of pleasure. The second is criminalization of resistant "culture" and identities. Hence we see a discursive construction of Islam as part of a "cultural clash," Islam as fundamentalism, or the framing of Islam within the language of "war on terrorism."

This war, the spokespeople of the empire declare, has no end and no particular location. Beyond the rhetorical aspect of such formulations lies a serious recognition and thus a description of the new colonial target. The war against this new colonial target might crystallize in the form of territorial occupations, but its scope is never reducible to any place or, for the moment, any time. The enemy is everywhere and nowhere. It is not only deterritorialized but disembodied. It might have been a text, but it no longer requires printed paper. The enemy is an idea. It is fluid.

At the same time that empire achieves global reach, its colony becomes fluid. Empire's desire to "arrest" the last colonial target remains partially successful. The colony is on the run. It may congeal around certain communities or locales, but it retains its ability to hide, to flow. Its fluidity renders state borders and military capabilities obsolete. The enemy is not only outside the state, it is also within. That is what makes (territorial) domination insufficient.

Empire needs to color, objectify, and thus make visible its enemy. It has to rework certain labels and engage in surgical operations to delineate the colony against which it is at war. It comes as no surprise that we see a growing debate about "modernizing Islam," an insistence on the distinction between *good* and *bad* Muslims. The empire feels insecure, for the culture it criminalizes lurks, unoccupiable, behind every territory, language, and culture.

Conclusion

The material and intellectual encounters between empire and *ummah*, the two postnational formations of globalization, are still developing – they defy any conclusive evaluation. The current debates about empire and *ummah* tend to fall within the realm of intellectual speculation. Yet it is clear that in an increasingly interconnected world, old vertical divisions (nation-states) are giving way to horizontally sliced, fluid global entities (*ummah* and empire). The difficulty of situating these new–old formations stems both from their inchoate characters and from the complexity of their interaction. The form of that interaction most visible today is what is popularly known as the "war on terrorism." Their interaction will continue to evolve, shifting from material and military to intellectual, and as it does so we shall need more refined perspectives to catch up with the realities.

Notes

1. Michael Hardt and Antonio Negri, *Empire* (Cambridge, MA: Harvard University Press, 2000).

2. Şukran Vahide, *Bediuzzaman Said Nursi: The Author of Risale-i Nur* (Istanbul: Sozler Publications, 2000) and Ibrahim Abu-Rabi', ed., *Islam at the Crossroads* (Albany, NY: State University of New York Press, 2003).

3. Benedict Anderson, *Imagined Communities: Reflections on the Origin and Spread of Nationalism*, revised edition (London: Verso, 1991).

4. Karl Polanyi, *The Great Transformation* (Boston: Beacon Press, [1957] 2001).

5. Eviatar Zerubavel, *The Fine Line* (New York: Free Press, 1991).

6. Max Weber, *Economy and Society* (Roth and Wittich, eds.) (Berkeley: University of California Press, 1968), 342.

7. Jacques Lacan, *Écrits: A Selection*, trans., Alan Sheridan (New York: W.W. Norton & Co., [1966] 1977).

8. Immanuel Wallerstein, *After Liberalism* (New York: New Press, 1995), 126–44; and Norbert Elias, *Civilizing Process* (Oxford: Blackwell, [1939] 1980).

9. Rogers Brubaker, *Citizenship and Nationhood in France and Germany* (Cambridge, MA: Harvard University Press, 1992), 21.

10. John Comaroff, "Of Totemism and Ethnicity: Consciousness, Practice and the Signs of Inequality," *Ethnos*, 52, 1982, 305.

11. Comaroff, "Of Totemism," 306.

12. Emile Durkheim, *Elementary Forms of Religious Belief*, trans., K.E. Fields (New York: Free Press, 1995), 229.

13. Karl Deutsch, *Nationalism and Social Communication: An Inquiry into the Foundations of Nationality* (Cambridge, MA: MIT Press, 1953); and B. Anderson, *Imagined Communities*.

14. Craig Calhoun, "Nationalism and the Public Sphere," in Jeff Weintraub and Krishan Kumar, eds., *Public and Private in Thought and Practice* (Chicago: University of Chicago Press, 1997), 97.

15. Michel Foucault, *Discipline and Punish: The Birth of the Prison* (New York: Penguin Books, 1975).

16. Foucault, *Discipline and Punish*, 135.

17. Michel Foucault, "Governmentality," in Burchell, Gordon, Miller, eds., *The Foucault Effect* (London: Harvester Wheatsheaf, 1991), 87–104.

18. For an elaboration of the concept of "governmentality" see Mitchell Dean, *Governmentality: Power and Rule in Modern Society* (London: Sage Publications, 1999).

19. Thomas Hobbes, *Leviathan* (Pelican Classics, [1651] 1968).

20. Foucault, "Governmentality," 95.

21. Anderson, *Imagined Communities*, 7.

22. John Meyer, "The Changing Cultural Content of the Nation-State: A World Society Perspective," in G. Steinmetz, ed., *State/Culture: State-Formation after the Cultural Turn*, (Ithaca: Cornell University Press, 1999), 123.

23. P.J. DiMaggio and W.W. Powell, "The Iron Cage Revisited: Institutional Isomorphism and Collective Rationality in Organization Fields," in W.W. Powell and P.J. DiMaggio, eds., *The New Institutionalism in Organizational Analysis* (Chicago: University of Chicago Press, 1991), 63–82.

24. Mike Featherstone, ed., *Global Culture: Nationalism, Globalization and Modernity* (London: Sage, 1990); Roland Robertson, *Globalization: Social Theory and Global Culture* (London: Sage, 1992); John Tomlinson, *Globalization and Culture* (Chicago: University of Chicago Press, 1999).

25. Arjun Appadurai, *Modernity at Large: Cultural Dimensions of Globalization* (Minneapolis: University of Minnesota Press, 1996).

26. Tomlinson, *Globalization and Culture*, 106.

27. Jürgen Habermas, *The Postnational Constellation: Political Essays*, ed., trans., Max Pensky (Cambridge, MA: MIT Press, 2001).

28. Guidry, Kennedy, and Zald, eds., *Globalizations and Social Movements* (Ann Arbor: University of Michigan Press, 2000), 1–20.

29. Ali Bulaç, "Kuresellesme Islami tehdit ediyor mu?" (Does Globalization Threaten Islam?), *Zaman*, July 25, 2001, Istanbul.

30. Appadurai, *Modernity at Large*, 7.

31. al Faruqi, Isma'il Raji, *Al-Tawhid: Its Implications for Thought and Life* (Herndon, VA: International Institute of Islamic Thought, 1982).

32. For Lacan, subject comes into being as a product of *mis*recognition.

33. Qur'an, 2:30

34. Said Nursi, *Mesnevi-i Nuriye* (Istanbul: Sozler Publications, 1990).

35. Said Nursi, *Sozler* (Istanbul: Sozler Publications, 1990).

36. Nursi, *Sozler*, 103.

37. Nursi, *Sozler*, 535.

38. Bruce B. Lawrence, *Shattering the Myth: Islam Beyond Violence* (Princeton, NJ: Princeton University Press, 1998), 23.

39. Lawrence, *Shattering the Myth* and Abu-Rabi' Ibrahim, *Intellectual Origins of Islamic Resurgence in the Arab World* (Albany, NY: State University of New York Press, 1996).

40. Manuel Castells, The Information Age, Volume 1: The Rise of the Network Society (Oxford: Blackwell, 1996), 10.

41. R. James Woolsey, *WW IV: Who We're Fighting – And Why* (Washington DC: The Foundation for the Defense of Democracies, May 2003).

42. George Yudice, *The Expediency of Culture: Uses of Culture in Global Era* (Durham: Duke University Press, 2003), 29.

CHAPTER 18

Between Slumber and Awakening[1]

Erol Güngör
(Translated by Şahin Filiz and Tahir Uluç)

To speak of Islamic revivalism implies that the Muslim world had been dormant until recent times. However, numerous perspectives exist on the Muslim world's dormancy and its present resurgence. In their analysis of the situation, the proponents of resurgence begin with earlier mistakes. They naturally have an understanding of the reasons behind dormancy and are able to discern between dormancy and awakening.

At this stage in history, we (Muslims) are overwhelmed by a number of contradictory ideas, which cannot all be right at the same time. In addition, raising the question of "which view represents the truth?" will lead us to add another view to the present ones. In order to avoid confusion, for there is much of it nowadays, I prefer to shed some light on the subject by focussing on the faulty reasoning behind the present errors. To achieve an accurate conclusion, which problems should we discern and to which points should we pay special attention?

Let us begin with the popular views. Most commonly Muslims think the following about Islamic history: As a system of spiritual and ethical values, Islam flourished and spread during the Prophet's life, and afterwards, the 'Abbasid and Umayyad Empires diluted Islamic ethics by paying more attention to politics and power than Islamic spirituality. Meanwhile, Muslims made considerable progress in the fields of science and the arts and created a civilization, which became a model for other nations. However, in subsequent ages, the Crusades and the Mongol invasions shook the Muslim world from its very foundation. The period of Turkish domination prevented the decline of the Muslim world by preserving its political integrity. However, in the sixteenth century, the Muslim world began to rapidly decline in all fields of knowledge. The beginning of the disintegration of the Ottoman Empire (in the seventeenth and eighteenth centuries) marked the inception of (spiritual and material) slavery in the Muslim world. Since World War Two, the Muslim world has struggled to rid itself of this slavery, and in recent times, having achieved its political independence, the Muslim world has striven to face up to the challenges which come from other world powers.

One may agree with this picture in general terms; it describes the major turning points and eras of Islamic history. In the final analysis, however, the above perspective does not offer any deep analysis or exposition. Nonetheless, if one carefully examines the above popular discourse, one will discover that it sheds some light on the "reasons" behind the decline. According to this perspective, one such reason was the "departure" from Islam. That is to say, if early Muslim rulers had heeded the Islamic injunctions and prohibitions, Muslims would not have incurred such catastrophes. Although Islam preached brotherhood and unity, Muslims fell prey to disunity; although Islam encouraged seeking knowledge, Muslims remained ignorant; although Islam commanded justice, injustice prevailed; and although Islam preached simplicity and contentment, Muslims were inclined to a life of luxury and extravagance.

In view of the above, the age of decline began when Muslims in general and their political elite in particular turned away from Islam. If we were to possess a definite criterion (in fact, such a criterion exists in matters of faith) to decide what adherence to or departure from Islam really means, we could easily verify this thought. For instance, we could decide whether the Ottoman sultans and functionaries preceding Murad IV were less pious than those who came before. Furthermore, we could claim that Bayezid II was more pious than his son, Selim, and Ahmed I more pious than Murad IV. Neither can it be asserted that the Ottoman functionaries who came after Selim III were less pious than their predecessors.

Those who claim that social and political decline stems solely from departure from religion think that religion includes what they consider to be the "factors" of progress. Religious devotion, they explain, includes perfect performance of religious services, the ensuring of justice and piety, as well as the pursuit of technologic developments. Here, I think, an error in logic appears, which is called tautology: to suppose that religious devotion is equal to the production of civil progress and then to accuse the predecessors of departing from Islam is to say, "They declined because they declined."

What people understand about adherence to Islam differs from one age and condition to another. As a result, many of us may argue that the way Islam was understood in the past centuries is incorrect. Likewise, our mode of thinking is closely related to the present problems of the world in which we live. Upcoming generations will probably trace our mistakes to our shortcomings in understanding Islam. Hence, the meaning of the phrase "adherence to Islam" undergoes continual change. But the essentials of Islam never change. Unlike individual interpretations of Islamic texts, the core of Islam remains the same. While religion itself remains the same, human perception of religion is ever changing. Therefore, we should look into external causes of change itself, and not into Islam or human beings. In other words, we must focus on the dynamics that play a significant role in shaping the perception of human beings and in influencing the people of different ages in different ways. That is to say, to assess change, one must come to terms with the factor of generational change rather than of people as human beings.

Looking at the same topic from a different perspective, one can say the following: Let us assume that the main debate concerns the level of adherence to Islamic values, and not the various interpretations of Islamic decrees. Assuming, as I do, that the essence of Islam never changes, how can one explain the fact that human beings are sometimes devoted to religion and other times are not? There are external factors that increase or decrease adherence to religion, and also determine the nature of adherence *per se*. As far as I am concerned, we should focus on these conditions and factors, rather than plunging ourselves into the never-ending disputes as to how one should understand Islam.

One may also argue that the so-called ages of decline did not depart from Islam that radically. On the contrary, the people were deeply committed to Islam because of the need to rely on religion in times of change, which would enhance the status of religion in society. Human beings seek each other's help when they are not able to overcome a crisis or problem facing them. It is more likely that they would appeal to the help of the Supreme Reality more sincerely than ever when, in spite of using all their human powers, they are not able to overcome a problem. For instance, in times of social crisis, people become more pious to keep from losing spirit. Furthermore, they think of disaster as a divine punishment caused by their wickedness and corruption. We witnessed the same situation in the Muslim world in the years following the Mongol invasion. Also, the Muslims sought tranquility in spirituality in the years subsequent to the catastrophes caused by World War One. In fact, such an attitude does not disagree with the essence of Islam. For Islam itself demands Muslims to invoke God alone and ask Him to lighten their burden. Therefore, it is quite natural for Muslims to appeal to God when they need His help.

I do not speak of these matters to prove that religious senses become stronger at difficult times. But my aim is just to demonstrate that people by no means turn away from religion in times of crisis. Having discussed this issue, I can investigate the reason why the Muslim world has been in decline.

One must not conclude from the above discussion that religion has nothing to do with the rise and fall of societies. On the contrary, it is an undoubted fact that Islam has played significant roles in every stage of the formation of Islamic civilization. Some argue that Islamic civilization does not belong to Muslims alone since the books which the Jewish and Assyrian scholars translated into Arabic served as a foundation in two significant fields, that is, science and philosophy. It is a well-known fact that the early Muslims learned astronomy, mathematics, philosophy, and medical sciences from non-Muslims. In addition, these non-Muslims directed the well-known works of translation. However, such works do not detract from the originality of Islamic civilization; neither do the services of non-Muslim translators diminish the roles of Muslim scholars. Although Jews, Christians, and Zoroastrians had been in possession of the works of ancient civilizations, they were not able to create such a civilization. Nor were the nations who could be considered rightful owners of these works able to make any considerable progress. So it was Islam that gave stimulus to the Muslims to benefit from these books before exceeding them.

Another important topic we should discuss is the role that the madrasah (schools for learning traditional Islamic sciences) versus the khanqahs (Sufi lodges) – or what Westerners called "Orthodox Islam versus Sufi Islam" – played in Muslim history. In Turkey, thinkers of the left are agreed that both the madrasah and khanqahs held Muslim countries back. But contemporary Islamists have different views concerning the position of the two institutions in respect to religion itself. A good number of Muslim

intellectuals in Muslim majority countries think that Islamic reformism should be confined to Sunni Islamic faith and its implementation in the present age. They think
that Sufism led Muslims astray from Islam's genuine spirit. "Muslim reformers"
contrasted the Sufi version of Islam with the Sunni faith as it materialized during the
age of the Prophet and his disciples and called for the return to pure Islam without
Sufism.

To start with, I should clarify some terms. It was in the eighth century that the
dichotomy between Sufism and Sunni Islam first arose. With the spread of Sufism, this
conflict became more obvious. As a matter of fact, the term "Sunni Islam" is used as
correspondent to the "Shi'ite Islam." At the beginning, Sufism emerged as a lifestyle
and "the philosophy of life" in daily usage. But because it later produced some beliefs
parallel to this lifestyle, it gained some meanings opposite to, or outside of, the Sunni
Islamic faith. Although Sufism is an Islamic stream in essence, it undoubtedly borrowed
from the Greek and Indian traditions. As Sufism grew out of a simple, individual life
and took the shape of a well-organized movement, some thoughts and groups conflicting with the official Islamic doctrine came to either take refuge in or merge with
Sufism. Especially, in the Abbasid period, the Shi'ite and Batini infiltration into the Sufi
movement brought the Muslim world into chaos. It is widely accepted that one of the
drives of establishing madrasah was to fight these alien beliefs. Also, it was in the
eleventh century that the confusions in the field of faith were exacerbated and that
Ghazālī shouldered the mission of fighting against the heretic beliefs.

In the eleventh and twelfth centuries, Sunni Islam, with the aid of the madrasah,
overcame the chaos of belief. Sufism also came out of this chaos by decontaminating
itself of unorthodox beliefs and taking a character similar to that of Sunni Islam. Now
Sufism, in the forms of Sufi orders and lodges, seems to have assumed a valid shape. It
is interesting that the end of this chaos came at the same time as the achievement of
political stability. Since then, Sufi orders have been adherent to Sunni doctrine in Sunni-
dominated regions. Even the *Bektāshī* order, which is known as the order most opposed
to the Sunni doctrine, relies upon *sharī'ah*. The reason why many orders have adopted
the appellation 'Alawī is to show that their spiritual genealogy goes back to 'Alī b Abī
Ṭālib, rather than that they have adopted a way against Sunni Islam. In brief, in the
years of the Seljuki rise, Sufism came to cleanse itself of the elements that opposed
Sunni Islam doctrine. Since the fourteenth century, scarcely any serious conflict has
appeared between the khanqahs and the madrasah.

The disagreement between Sufism with (Orthodox) Islamic doctrine and the (mainstream) Muslim community originates, not from the fact that it consists of some
elements derived from foreign beliefs, but from the fact that Sufism is relevant and susceptible to arbitrary interpretations. The Sufi movement grew around figures claiming
to have, or be accredited with, extraordinary powers. Sheikhs or spiritual masters
establish an authority over people through their exceptional ability whereby they
obtain knowledge and control the spiritual realm. The madrasah rejects such an
authority. The *ulama* trained in madrasah prefer a rational doctrine over the irrational
claims of the sheikhs. This rational character of the madrasah enables the *ulama* to be
less subjective and to gain a "democratic" character. While the sheikh acts as a spiritual mentor of a certain group of people, the madrasah scholars address all Muslims.

The *ulama*'s authority relies upon *sharī'ah* (Islamic law) itself; their arguments are open to all to verify their truthfulness.

As explained above, the reason why a majority of Muslims have followed the moderate Sunni path, while the Sufi brotherhoods have remained small groups, is that the madrasah system has a rational and democratic character. As opposed to what some claim, it is not the case that those who are ignorant are entrenched in strict beliefs, whereas those with refined minds took up the Sufi path.

Over time, the khanqahs and the madrasah came to a happy compromise. In addition, they have coexisted and become interwoven. The Sunni doctrine recognized Sufi miracles, yet it added that such miracles cannot be considered as (universal) religious proofs. In return, the khanqahs quit all opposition to *sharī'ah*, saying that it would continue to guide souls on the path to gnosis and knowledge, while staying within the borders of *sharī'ah*.

The critics of Sufism assert that, in general, this movement stands for retreat from the world and thus directs Muslims' attention and energy beyond this world. This claim is not totally groundless. One can find many examples to corroborate this claim. Furthermore, it is true that the essence of Sufism is to endeavor to transcend the tangible and physical world. Therefore, those who drove themselves forth as "reformists" opposed the ascetic life of Sufi orders. Instead, they followed a simple and rational way of life as embodied by the Prophet Muhammad, but which did not neglect this world. More significantly, the reformists maintain that Muslims should hold fast to the objective proofs of the *sharī'ah*, instead of the subjective interpretations of the saints. Nevertheless, the intuitive and emotional character of Sufism affected even the anti-Sufi reformists on different levels. We know that the figures who represent the madrasah doctrine outside of Sufism, such as Ibn Taymiyya, Muhammad bin 'Abd al-Wahhab, and Sanūsī, employed the Sufi practices of *dhikr* (invocation) and *murāqabah* (contemplation). Furthermore, among them are ones who applied *kashf* (spiritual unveiling) as a way of acquiring knowledge.

So, there no longer exist two opposite interpretations of Islam. Yet in recent decades, it has become a popular conviction that the Sufi way of life engendered many negative consequences in the past as a result of the fact that Salafi ideas have prevailed among youth who have reformist and fundamentalist tendencies. However, if one carefully examines such groups, one will come to realize that they also espouse the same Sufi elements as did earlier masterminds. It is natural that these young people may sometimes find and consequently become upset with Sufi beliefs and practices that disagree with Islamic principles. However, they should take into account the fact that schismatic groups did not play important roles in the decline of Muslims. Another significant reason for which they take a skeptical stand toward Sufism is that they have discovered nothing in Sufism to satisfy their reformist aspirations. If one intends to actualize a social reform, one should ground the reform in objective principles, which would be accepted by and related to all sections of society. Alas, Sufism does not involve such things. On the contrary, Sufis are the people who primarily focus on their own inward tranquility and individual salvation. No reformist dares to say "Come, come, whoever you have been, even a Zoroastrian or an idolater; even you who have broken your word one thousand times." In order to speak this way, one has to peel from himself his sense of social responsibility. On the other hand, the social reformist says, "Keep being a Muslim and hold fast to the straight path." Although the Sufi words are pleasant, they certainly do not promote a clear sense of social responsibility.

However, just because something does not work in regulating social order, it does not mean that we should discard it. Given the fact that Islam rejects monasticism, Muslims should tolerate the nuances of the path that people have chosen to draw near to God. Likewise, while the reformists support freedom, they oppose blind imitation; they call for free personal effort (*ijtihād*) and getting rid of traditional fetters.

Another significant issue is the position that madrasah have held in the Islamic civilization and thought. Many consider madrasah themselves to be the hotbed of evil. Some others view the corruption of the madrasah as the leading reason for the decline. So what is the real role of the madrasah in the rise and fall of the Islamic civilization?

Typical Turkish intellectuals have tended to hold narrow-minded people responsible for the decline of the madrasah. I think, however, that the madrasah was a significant part of Islamic civilization, but, from the sixteenth century onward, they have been in decline in parallel to the whole structure of Muslim civilization.

Even in modern times, the madrasah can be reckoned as ideal educational institutions with many distinguished features. Leading contemporary educational institutions, such as the famous British universities, have for centuries preserved these features. Many modern Western universities are living examples of such classical madrasah. All these institutes of higher education once gave priority to the learning of theology. In addition, they were an organic part of religious life and religious networks. While these institutions in the West underwent a radical transformation in the course of time, the Islamic madrasah became stagnant and, furthermore, they went backward.

The madrasah followed a system in which the teachers, who were well-versed in various sciences, offered a systematic education for students. This is quite similar to modern universities. Here, the crucial point is that the education was not fixed in strict forms. The course was preferred over the classroom. A student had the right to take whatever class from whichever professor he liked. Furthermore, a student was not forced to complete his education in the madrasah where he had started learning. He could continue his education in another madrasah where he could find a professor who was well-versed in a given science. This created a productive atmosphere of competition both in and between the madrasah. As to the examinations, they were carried out by a committee. The system followed in the promotion and appointment of professors was more similar to that of German and British universities than to present Turkish universities. I will give here no more detail, for it is not my main point.

The main problem lay in the content of the education. The term "scholasticism" was coined to express the belief which once prevailed in European universities that knowledge could be obtained only from the books of past authorities, not by way of experience or observation. Aristotle was one of the authorities at that time. So if his books did not offer a solution to a problem, scholars did not need to search for the solution anywhere else. While Islamic universities offered a rather rational education in the Medieval Ages, European universities were immovably entrenched in scholasticism. In the course of time, the latter laid the foundation for modern sciences, while the former fell into scholasticism and declined.

By the sixteenth century, the Islamic madrasah taught technical science in an experimental way along with traditional Islamic sciences. For example, the Süleymaniye Complex (in Istanbul) included a school of medical sciences that taught mathematics. But after the sixteenth century, the madrasah curricula became stuck in traditional Islamic sciences. I think there is a close relationship between that fact and the decline of the Ottoman Empire. It is very common in the history of Europe that technical sciences were disfavored because their results might contradict the premises of Christian theology being taught. But such a conflict did not exist in our history; thus, we are not able to explain the decline in rational sciences on the bases of any kind of pressure. So how can we explain the decline in the madrasah?

One should search for the answer to this question in the general decline of Islamic civilization, including the Ottoman madrasah. The decline goes back to pre-Ottoman ages. On a different occasion, I have discussed the effects of the Mongol invasion on the Muslim world. Some scholars, and in particular Muslim historians, see the Mongol invasion as the principal reason for the decline. As stated above, shortly after the Mongols scorched Muslim territories, they were assimilated into Islamic civilization. Furthermore, Muslims resumed their activities in the field of science and arts. Nevertheless, one should not miss the point that supports those who postulate about the Mongol invasion, which is that although sciences and arts survived, they shrank and became limited to a few centers in the centuries following the Mongol invasion. In addition, the invasion demoralized the Muslims.

In my view, what primarily confuses the minds is the coincidence of the timing of the decline and the Mongol invasion. However, it does not follow that one necessarily led to the other. Having already lost much of its vigor, the Muslim world collapsed entirely as a result of the Mongol blow. As for the stagnation of the Muslim world, it is a completely different matter and, as a matter of fact, it is no use to elaborate on this question to which no satisfactory answer has been given so far.

The Ottoman madrasah did not lag behind the Muslim world in terms of science. In fact, scientific developments in the European universities began to emerge in the sixteenth century. The reason underlying the Ottoman's indifference to the sciences was probably that no serious developments had occurred in these sciences for centuries. Therefore, it would make no difference whether or not one studied them. However, the rise in the West of a superior civilization was caused by a succession of scientific developments and inventions that invalidated old scientific theories. The Ottomans remained distant from these developments mainly because the material results of these developments appeared very late; in addition, up until this time, the Ottomans had not faced any serious social and political challenges to bother them.

The madrasah is an institution, and like other institutions, it can be maintained only by human beings. In this regard, I would like to discuss the decline of the madrasah in the context of the change which took place in the minds of the madrasah intelligentsia.

One may pose the question, "Why were the madrasah not able to renew themselves while Christian European institutes of education were able to?" As a matter of fact, the history of modern Turkish institutions is very late. That is to say, it is very recently that the madrasah faced a challenging rival that would force them to renew themselves. We know that there were many attempts to reform the madrasah, yet all the efforts ended in failure because of the abolishment of the madrasah. In fact, the madrasah had lost their position and role long before the idea of the reformation arose; no one expected the madrasah to produce solutions for the depressing problems of the country.

The most important consequence of the marginalization and stagnancy of the madrasah is that a long and difficult time passed before a new intellectual class emerged. In fact, this formation has not yet been completed. That is to say, so far, there has not emerged a class of intellectuals who possess a modern education and are as close to our people and culture as were the *ulama* in the past.

Several dates have been identified for the great changes that took place in the European mind. But one can say that these changes roughly fall within the period between the early sixteenth and the late seventeenth centuries. Bronowski refers to this period as the "scientific revolution." Truly, it is in the years between 1500 and 1700 that the great transformation of mentality which underlies modern rational thought and important inventions took place.

As is well known, the Europeans became acquainted with ancient Greek works through the Arabs (the Muslim world) and, consequently, Aristotelian thought dominated the whole of Christian thought. Philosophy, science, and the methodology of sciences were all based on Aristotle. As for astronomy as a science, it was a wholesale adoption of the Greek astronomer Ptolemy's system. All the mechanisms of physics also came from Aristotle. Scholars were engaged in writing commentaries and annotations on the great authorities' words, instead of performing their own systematic observations and experiments. Although some people criticized and found Aristotle's physics and Ptolemy's astronomy imperfect, they nevertheless failed to suggest stronger alternative systems. Therefore, the two systems remained unchanged for centuries. Copernicus abolished Ptolemy's system as well as the Christian cosmology, which was established thereon. Copernicus' books were published in 1543. Following Copernicus, Kepler discovered his famous principles of the movements of planets (1609–19). In the same century, Galileo destroyed Aristotelian physics by measuring exact time and performing his famous experiments on gravity; he opened up a new age by developing the telescope, which had previously been used to entertain people at fairs.

Such scholars as Copernicus, Kepler, and Galileo did not appear by chance at all. On the contrary, they were the most prominent out of a huge troop of scholars. Take for example the British Royal Society and the French College, which were established respectively in 1660 and 1666. Such scholars as Huygens, Boyle, Bacon, Newton, and Halley, who are known even to a student of secondary and high school, all flourished during the same century. One can better realize the extent of progress Europe made when such philosophers as Descartes, Locke, and Hobbes are added to the above scientists.

However, the above-mentioned names did not mean "all Europe." In other words, their influence did not reach all the corners of Europe. In addition, despite the Church's doubts and concerns, these scholarly activities did not break away from Christian thought. Nonetheless, this was the way that the foundation of modern Western civilization was laid, and soon it would bear practical fruits.

At the same time, our madrasah were undergoing a reversion from rational thinking to scholasticism. In Fatih Sultan Mehmed's reign, the Ottomans brought Uluğ Bey's students to Istanbul to do astronomical researches. But in the seventeenth century when the Westerners were realizing ground-breaking developments in astronomy, the last Ottoman observatory was abolished and its function was reduced to timekeeping of ritual prayers. This act had nothing to do with reactionism or religious conservatism. The *Tahāfut* (incoherence) debate which Fatih held between Hocazade and Hatipzade marked the end of philosophical thought in the Ottoman. In the Ottoman madrasah, medical sciences and mathematics were taught until Süleyman the Magnificent. Then the Ottoman madrasah were converted to theology schools offering exclusively Islamic jurisprudence, theology, Qur'anic exegesis, hadiths, Arabic grammar, and rhetoric. There Aristotle's theory of the four elements (soil, air, water, and fire) and Ptolemy's geography and astronomy were still prevailing at that time. The books being written were explanations of earlier works. The debates of the madrasah *ulama* focused on what leads one away from Islam. The *ulama* were so distant from rational thinking that even in the seventeenth century, some *ulama* wrote such absurd things as suggesting that if one were to immerse a thread into fly feces and then plant it, a mint plant would sprout.

The madrasah *ulama* knew very well the sciences which they saw as the only sciences. In fact, we do not know the philology of Western languages as profoundly as the *ulama* knew that of Arabic. Nor are our lawyers as well-versed in Western law as the *ulama* were in Islamic jurisprudence. We can say the same for the fields of logic, Islamic theology and so on. But they believed that these were all the sciences and no one could change them. They thought that knowledge would increase only by way of reading books or by making logical comparisons between books. That is the very point at which Europe passed through its mental transformation, but Turkey seems not to have completed the same transformation.

However, I feel it appropriate to clarify a few points to prevent any misunderstanding. At the time when the "scientific revolution" appeared in Europe, the scientific mentality was not established in a modern sense. It would not be right to put the studies of that age on a par with those of modern universities. For instance, being probably one of the most important scholars among those mentioned, Copernicus aimed at religious-esthetic dimensions in his astronomical pursuits. His primary aim was to show how God created the universe in a simple and splendid harmony, as opposed to Ptolemy's complicated theory. He foresaw that the mentality of his time, and especially the Church, would denounce him due to his new explanation of the universe. But he never foresaw that his discoveries would be taken as a starting point in shaping a new cosmology. As for Kepler, he was an astrologer; so he endeavored to correctly ascertain the orbits of stars just because of his astrological interests.

The second point we need to bear in mind is that the Church is not the only institution opposed to the scientific revolution. The Church's opposition to these inventions was understandable because the discoveries of Copernicus, Galileo, and others disagreed with the teachings of the Old and New Testaments. But ironically enough, most of the objections to the scholars came from the universities. In the age of Galileo and Kepler, the leading scholars of the European universities filled their minds with superstitious and mythological kinds of information. The thinkers and scholars who started the modern age had to exert themselves to wipe out this very mentality. To give an example, I would like to tell an incident narrated by Fontenelle.

According to rumors, all the teeth of a seven-year-old boy fell out in 1593, in Silesia. But there sprang a golden tooth in place of one molar. Horstius, professor of medical sciences in Helmstad University, wrote a book on this tooth and said therein that the tooth was partly miraculous and partly natural. God granted it, he went on, to the boy in order to solace the Christians who suffered from the Turks! In the same year, Rullandus wrote something about this golden tooth to pretend that historians said something concerning this event as well. In conclusion, although many scholars wrote and spoke of this allegedly extraordinary event, none of them said clearly whether the tooth was golden or not. Then it turned out that it was just a golden foil quite skillfully glued on the tooth. The point I want to make here is that they wrote numerous books regarding this event, but the idea of consulting a jeweler came to their minds very late.

It would be unfair to generalize about all the *ulama* by using the above story of the fly feces and the mint. The point is that, in terms of unfamiliarity with biological truths, the *ulama* were not much ahead of those who uttered the nonsensical things regarding the golden tooth. In fact, it was as early as the beginning of the eighteenth century that Copernicus' system was introduced to Turkish readers; in the appendix of Ibrāhīm Müteferrika's *Cihānnümā*, Copernicus' system and the objections of Galileo to Aristotelian physics were elucidated. Yet they died out like cries in desert and had no repercussions.

Note

1. Erol Güngör, *İslam'ın Bugünkü Meseleleri* (*Contemporary Problematics of Islam*), (Istanbul: Ötüken Publications, Sixth Edition, 1989), 26–46.

CHAPTER 19
Islam and Secularism

Asghar Ali Engineer

Is Islam compatible with secularism? This question is quite important in the present context, particularly in the twenty-first century. Both non-Muslims and orthodox Muslims feel that Islam is not compatible with secularism. Fundamentalist Muslims totally reject secularism as anti-Islamic and *ḥarām* (forbidden). Mawlana Mawdūdī, founder of Jamaat-e-Islami, had said, while leaving for Pakistan in 1948, that those who participated in secular politics were raising the flag of revolt against Allah and His Messenger. The Saudi *ulama*, too, denounce secularism as strictly prohibited in Islamic tradition.

The fundamentalist Hindus, on the other hand, say that Muslims support secularism while in minority in any country and oppose it while in majority. But this is not wholly true. Some Muslim countries like Saudi Arabia and others do reject secularism but all Muslim majority countries do not. For example, Indonesia does not reject secularism though 85 percent of its population comprises Muslims. However, by and large, it is true that many Muslim majority countries opt for Islamic state or at least make Islam a state religion.

It is important to note that there is some difference between an Islamic state and Islam being a state religion. In an Islamic state all laws must strictly conform to Islamic *sharī'ah* but if a country declares "Islam as its religion," it means that Islam is preferred to all other religions and it enjoys more privilege than other religions in the country. In 1948 Islam was declared the state religion in Pakistan, but Pakistan did not become an Islamic state until Ziyaul Haq declared it to be an Islamic state in the late 1970s. He then began to enforce *sharī'ah* laws in Pakistan.

Islam is declared to be incompatible with secularism because in a secular state there is no place for divine laws, and secular laws are unacceptable to Islam. Also it is believed that in Islam religion and politics cannot be separated. On these grounds secularism is totally rejected by orthodox Muslims. They also think that secularism is atheistic, and atheism has no place whatsoever in Islam. Islam strongly emphasizes faith in Allah. These are some of the grounds which make orthodox Muslims uneasy with the very word secularism. Islam emphasizes life hereafter and secularism means only those matters which pertain to this world. There is no place for the world hereafter as far as secular philosophy is concerned.

I would examine here whether these assertions are true and whether Islam is really incompatible with secularism. Firstly, one must make a distinction between what is theological and what is historical. The concept that religion and politics cannot be separated is more historical than theological. In fact the Qur'an does not give any concept of the state; it only gives the concept of the society. The Qur'an is concerned with morality rather than polity. An upright conduct, justice, truth, benevolence, compassion, and human dignity are very basic to the Holy Scripture. It repeatedly asserts these values. Thus it clearly means that these values are very fundamental to an Islamic society rather than to a state.

The view that religion cannot be separated from politics in Islam is due to this primary concern with these Islamic values. It was thought by early Islamic *ulama* and jurists that if religion was separated from politics, the rulers would totally neglect these fundamental Islamic values and would behave in a manner which would only satisfy their greed for power. In fact in those days there was no concept of secularism as a philosophy of humanism. The *ulama* were afraid that if religion and politics were separated there would be absolutely no check on the conduct of the rulers. In fact, one does not find clear articulation to this effect (that religion cannot be separated from politics in Islam) in any early Islamic source. This formulation itself is of nineteenth-century origin when colonial powers began to impose secular laws in Islamic countries, i.e. the laws which were not basically derived from *sharī'ah*.

In the early Islamic period there were no other laws than the *sharī'ah* laws. And since there was no such concept of the state in the Qur'an, the Islamic state itself is an historical construct. The structure of the Islamic state evolved over a period of time. The Qur'an and hadith were the primary sources for the new state. It is important to note that before Islam there was no state in Mecca or Medina. There was only a senate of tribal chiefs who took collective decisions and it was tribal chiefs who enforced those decisions in their respective tribal jurisdiction. There were obviously no written laws but only tribal customs and traditions. Any decision had to be taken within the framework of these customs. There was no other source of law.

However, after Islam appeared on the social horizon of Mecca, the scenario began to change. In Medina the Prophet laid the framework of governance through what is known as *Mithaq-e-Madina* (Covenant of Medina). This Covenant also basically respects tribal customs to which adherents of Judaism, Islam, and pre-Islamic idol worshippers belonged. Each tribe, along with the religious tradition it belonged to, was treated as an autonomous unit in the Covenant, which has been described in full detail by Ibn Ishaqe, the first biographer of the Prophet. Thus the Covenant of Medina respected both the tribal as well as religious autonomy of the inhabitants of the town. It can also be said to be the first constitution of the state in making. The Covenant laid down certain principles, which are valid even today in a secular state. When the covenant was drawn up by the Prophet of Islam, *sharī'ah* as a body of law had not evolved. In this important Medinan document what is most important is that the Prophet did not compel the different tribes of Jews and idol worshippers to follow the Islamic law.

A state structure began to evolve only after the death of the Prophet when vast areas of other territories were conquered and new problems began to arise. During the Prophet's time the governance was limited almost to a city. He did not live long after the conquest of Mecca. But after his death the jurisdiction of the state expanded much beyond the frontiers of Arabia. During the Prophet's time people were more concerned with day-to-day problems of marriage, divorce, inheritance etc. on the one hand, and theft, robbery, murder etc. on the other, for which the Qur'an and the Prophet were the only source of guidance. The people asked the Prophet for guidance and followed his pronouncements or the Qur'anic injunctions voluntarily. There was no state machinery to enforce it. There was neither any police force nor any regular military. There was no separate judiciary either. As far as the Prophet was concerned he was a legislator, an enforcer of laws (executive), and also a judge (representing judiciary). He combined all three functions.

Thus it will be seen that there was no regular state structure during the Prophet's own time as he was a unique personality who could combine all these functions for judicious governance, in addition to being a source of law. However, the death of the Prophet created a vacuum and no other person could fill it. Also, as pointed out above, the conquest of other territories created more complex problems. Now there was a need for enforcement of laws as people in far-off places with no commitment to Islam would not follow the laws voluntarily as they did in Medina in the Prophet's time. Thus a police force was needed to enforce the laws. Also, during the Prophet's time people volunteered to fight against enemies of Islam and there was no need for a paid regular army. Now after his death a need was felt for a paid regular army. The border areas had to be guarded constantly. There were no such borders before.

The corpus of *sharī'ah* was being evolved and for new situations guidance could no more be had from the Prophet. One either had to look for verses in the Qur'an or in hadith, which the Prophet's companions remembered, or one had to resort to analogy by keeping analogous situations in mind. That was how the corpus of *sharī'ah* evolved slowly. The primitive Islamic state was democratic in spirit and the caliphs often consulted their colleagues and companions of the Prophet while making any decision so as to conform to the Qur'anic values. Thus the Qur'an and hadith then were the main sources of law. But in secular matters like building up institutions like the army or police or bureaucracy, they did not hesitate to borrow concepts from other sources like Roman or Persian. Thus the second caliph Umar borrowed the concept of *diwān* (i.e. maintaining records of salaries to a paid army and bureaucracy). Similarly the caliphs were called upon to legislate on matters like land ownership, and suspension of certain punishments during times of emergency like famine, etc.

The conquests, internal strife among the Muslims, struggle for power among different tribes, groups and personalities, and many other factors created strong pressures so much so that the institution of caliphate itself did not survive. It was ultimately replaced by monarchy and dynastic rule. This was totally against the spirit of the Qur'an. These changes became inevitable under the fast developing situation. The Islamic jurists had to come to terms with these new developments and to legitimize them somehow. Once the institution of caliphate was replaced by dynastic rule, it could never be restored throughout Islamic history. Monarchy and dynastic rule persisted until Western colonial rule took over.

It was under colonial rule that Muslims began to discover the virtues of democracy and saw in the caliphate a "golden period of Islamic democracy." It is true that during the dynastic rule *shari'ah* could not be ignored and the rulers had to keep the *ulama* in good humor. However, they often found ways to go around and violate the spirit of *shari'ah*. But they never ceased to pay obeisance to it. The situation changed drastically with the onset of colonial rule during the nineteenth century in the Islamic world. Many laws were enforced by the colonial rulers who were secular in origin. The Western countries themselves were once governed by the Church and it was the Church law that was supreme. The reformation changed all that and the struggle against the Church gave rise to the concept of secularism. Thus there was an intense fight between the Church and the ruling princes who desired independence from the hegemony of the Church. The emerging bourgeois class too wanted to be free of the sacred rule and saw immense benefits in the secularization of politics and society. Thus it took more than three centuries in the West for the secularization of society and marginalization of religion and religious institution. When colonial rule was established in Asian and African countries, many of which happened to be Islamic countries, the process of secularization had traversed a great distance in the metropolitan countries.

Thus the the technological supremacy of the colonials posed a great challenge to Islam. The religious leaders and intellectuals in these colonized countries found refuge in the "glory of the past" and some were overwhelmed by the supremacy of the West and began to advocate secular modernization. Many reform movements thus were born in Islamic countries. Jamāl al-Dīn al-Afghānī and Muḥammad 'Abduh of Egypt were among them. Some others, however, totally rejected the secularism of the West and launched intense efforts to revive the past. Revivalist and reformist movements jostled with each other for social and political space. Among those who faced the Western challenge were those who rejected religion altogether and adopted the secular humanism of the West. However, they remained in the minority.

Islamic societies, however, found it more challenging to adopt change and adjust to it smoothly. Many sociologists ascribe this resistance to change inherent to the teachings of Islam. This, however, is not true. No religion including Islam is prone or opposed to change. The causes of resistance to change lie in the society, not in religion. In fact most of the Muslim societies were led by feudal lords and failed to produce a modern bourgeois class. In these societies there was no well-entrenched mercantile or industrial class. It is as much true of Indian Muslims as of other Muslim countries. The Hindus, on the other hand, had a centuries-old merchant class, which smoothly adjusted itself to modern industrial capitalism. Thus those who took to modern industrial capitalism felt the need for secularization and social change. The pressures for change were the result of the changing historical reality for them.

The Muslims, on the other hand, felt no such need for change, as there was no well-entrenched mercantile class to effect a smooth change over to modernity. Also, in most of the Muslim countries, including India, Islam was embraced by weaker and poorer sections of society, for it appealed to them due to its emphasis on equality and justice. Those sections had no felt need for modernization and they remained under the tight grip of traditional *ulama* who were anyway opposed to the process of secularization.

Also, unlike other religions, Muslims had well-developed *shari'ah* law which was unanimously accepted as divine in origin. Most of the religious leaders thus rejected the very concept of secular law as unacceptable. The *ulama*, as pointed out above, had a strong grip over the hearts and minds of the poor and illiterate masses and used the social base to oppose any change. The feudal lords, too, had not much use for secularism and readily struck an alliance with the *ulama* giving them their full support. Thus the ulama strongly resisted any change in *sharī'ah*. Not only that, they would not even admit of any reform. Those like Muḥammad 'Abduh and others who advocated *ijtihād* (creative interpretation of *sharī'ah* in view of modernization and change) were marginalized. Those important socioeconomic factors cannot be ignored while discussing Islam and secularism.

Before we proceed further I would like to throw some light on some inherent limitations of secularism. In the nineteenth century rationalism became a dogma. The rationalists and secularists almost began to worship reason and dismissed religion with contempt. In fact the rationalists have been as contemptuous of religion as the faithful have been of secularism. Both have refused to admit the limitations of their respective positions. One can say that as there are religious fundamentalists so there are rational or secular fundamentalists. These secular fundamentalists have no respect for believers whom they consider as nothing less than "superstitious." Even certain cultural practices are considered as such. Some of them even refuse to admit the emotional richness of life.

There has to be a balance between reason and faith. Faith is as important to human existence as reason. Reason, in fact, is a tool that humans use to achieve their goal. Reason can never become absolute though its usefulness as a tool cannot be minimized. Faith, on the other hand, is not a tool but a belief in higher values. These values are fundamental to a meaningful life on this earth. Reason at best ensures a "successful" life but not a meaningful one. It is faith in values like compassion, justice, equality, non-violence etc. that make human life meaningful. Thus a creative synthesis between reason and faith is absolutely necessary for a successful and meaningful life on this earth. Sacral and secular should not be treated as two poles or antagonistic contradiction. They are, rather, complementary to each other.

The faithful should also bear in mind that faith should not mean blind imitation of past traditions. Faith has to be in values, not in past traditions. As absolute secularism could lead to a life devoid of meaning and responsibility towards fellow human beings so absolute faith could lead to blind surrender to an authority, which leads to highly exploitative practices. One has to guard against such a possibility by employing rationality. In other words while reason should not become arrogant, faith should not become blind.

If understood in this sense there should be no contradiction between reason and faith and between religion and secularism. Islam is also compatible with secularism, seen from this perspective. If secularism is interpreted as an atheistic philosophy, no believer in religion would accept it, let alone a believer in Islam. Islam, as pointed out above, lays strong emphasis on belief in God and unity of God. Muslims believe in the divine revelation of the Qur'an and in Muhammad being a Messenger of Allah. One need not challenge these beliefs in the name of secularism. Secularism should be taken in a political rather than a philosophical sense. Secularism in a political sense creates social and political space for all religious communities.

The nineteenth-century rationalism and modernism are under challenge today. Our period is characterized as a postmodernist period in which religious pluralism rather than rejection of religion is accepted. Postmodernism recognizes the limitations of reason and accepts the validity of religious ethos. We are now in a world that is far removed from the struggle between Church and laypeople. The Church has also accepted the inevitability of secularization of society. It no longer enjoys the hegemonic position it held before the reformation. It has apologized for the persecution of scientists for discovering new scientific truths. It has also accepted the concepts of democracy and human rights. There is, thus, no serious contradiction between Church and secularism.

Islam, it must be noted, has no concept of an organized church. No single religious authority is considered absolute. However, the *ulama* promoted the concept of consensus (*ijmā'*), which is quite democratic. In fact consensus has been considered as one of the sources of Islamic law in Sunni Islam. Also, there is the concept of *ijtihād*, which infuses the spirit of dynamism and movement, though, of late, the *ulama* have refrained from using it for change. However, pressures are building in Islamic societies for using the concept of *ijtihād*. All Islamic societies are in the throes of change and modernization. Islamic laws are no longer a stagnant pool of old traditions. Changes are being effected.

As there is no organized church in Islam the *ulama* are divided on the issues of modernization and change. In Iran there is an intense struggle between the conservatives and the reformists. In Saudi Arabia the process of change is there for anyone to see, although the monarchy is quite cautious and wants to include the orthodox *ulama*. However, social pressures are building in Saudi society in favor of change and modernization. Even in Afghanistan under the Taliban, the regime was more coercive than consensual. In other words, the Taliban enjoyed political and not social hegemony.

Islam admits to freedom of conscience and democratic rights. Islam also officially accepts religious pluralism in as much as it is Qur'anic doctrine to hold other prophets in equal esteem. The Prophet provided equal social and religious space to all religions present in Medina, as pointed out above, through the Covenant of Medina. The leaders of Jami'at al-Ulama in India rejected the concept of two nations and supported composite nationalism on the basis of this Covenant. Religious pluralism and composite nationalism, which are the very spirit of secularism today in India, are not incompatible to Islam. All Islamic leaders of India have accepted Indian secularism. Even the Jamaat-e-Islami has not only accepted Indian democracy and secularism but has also set up a democratic and secular front.

The other characteristic of secular democracy is a respect for human dignity and human rights. The Qur'an expressly upholds both. It is true that some rulers in the Islamic world reject the concept of human rights as Western in origin and not fit for their society, but it is to preserve their own absolute and unchallenged rule rather than upholding the Islamic doctrinal position. It is a cultural and political rather than a religious problem. There are different political systems in different Islamic countries from monarchy to military dictatorship to limited democracy to democracy. But it would be naive to blame Islam for this. One has to look into the political history of the country rather than search for its causes in Islamic doctrines. Islamic doctrines do not nurture any concept of absolutism as perhaps no other religion does. In fact the Qur'an's emphasis is on consultation (*shūra*), and even the Prophet used to consult his companions in secular matters.

It will thus be seen that Islam is not incompatible to secularism if it does not mean rejection of religious faith. Throughout the world today there is increasing emphasis on harmonious coexistence of different religious faiths and Islam had inculcated this spirit from the very beginning of revelation of the Qur'an. The doctrine that religion and politics cannot be separated in Islam is a later historical construct rather than Qur'anic doctrine. It is a human construct rather than a divine revelation. One of the important aspects of modern secularism is, of course, separation of religion from the state. While the state should not interfere in religious autonomy, religious authorities should not poke their noses into affairs of the state. The Indian *ulama* had accepted this position with a good conscience throughout the freedom struggle and it was on this basis that they became allies of the Indian National Congress.

In Muslim majority countries, the state suffers from lack of autonomy. Again, one should not look for causes in religious teachings but in the socio-political history of those countries. These countries have hardly emerged from their feudal past. There is no history in these countries of democratic struggles of the people. Also, most of these countries have very small religious minorities and these minorities have historically accepted the religious hegemony of Islam. It will take quite some time for this position to change as the feudal past has a strong presence in these countries. However, there are strong pressures building and human rights movements are emerging in all these countries. Globalization may not be desirable for many other reasons but it is creating conditions for close interaction among various cultures and political systems. The information revolution also is a tide that cannot be stopped and is making a deep impact on every aspect of life. Muslim countries cannot remain aloof from this and have to become open to new ideas and forces.

CHAPTER 20

A "Democratic-Conservative" Government by Pious People: The Justice and Development Party in Turkey

Metin Heper

The founders of the Turkish Republican party (Republican People's Party (*Cumhuriyet Halk Partisi* – CHP)) (1923) opted for total Westernization. Believing that the guilty party for the demise of the Ottoman Empire (1299–1918) was primarily Islam itself, they initiated a cognitive revolution that aimed at freeing the mind from the "dogmatic thinking that Islam had inculcated in people." Their goal was that of educating new generations of "Turks who would think logically." For this purpose, they closed religious schools, religious courts as well as religious orders, lodges, and shrines. They also set up a Directorate for Religious Affairs. This Directorate, affiliated to the prime ministry, was given the task of appointing all the prayer leaders and preachers of the mosques in the country and monitoring the sermons delivered at those mosques for helping to develop and maintain an enlightened Islam. Still, the latter Islam had to be a source for nothing more than personal ethics. Therefore, among other things, they wished to see a clear separation between religion and the state.

On the whole the Westernization project of the founders of the Republic that included not only an extensive revamping of the educational system but also the borrowing of civil, penal, administrative, and commercial laws intact from Switzerland, Italy, France, and Germany, respectively, was quite successful. People started to departmentalize their lives. On the one hand, they scrupulously practiced their religion; on the other hand, they led quite secular lives.[1] In the multi-party period that started in 1945, people did not vote for a political party only because it was a religiously oriented party; they expected the political party to deliver goods and services. Even when political Islam became widespread in many Muslim countries in the circa post-1979 era, in Turkey the votes of the religiously oriented political parties kept fluctuating; they have not displayed a secular increase.

However, Turkey's *cognitive* revolution was not complemented by a *cultural* revolution. The founders' reform project, known as *Kemalism*, which was derived from the name of the founder himself – Mustafa Kemal Atatürk – could not provide guidelines for everyday behavior and morality. Also, both in the Ottoman Empire and in Republican Turkey one did not come across aristocracy and bourgeoisie that could inculcate on the people their own cultural norms. Under the circumstances, Islam continued to shape several dimensions of the attitudes and values not only of the people but also of the rulers. The 1924 Constitution in Turkey had adopted civic nationalism; those who professed loyalty to the state were to be considered Turk regardless of their religion and language. Still, governments in that country allowed Bosnian immigrants to Turkey because they were Muslims, although they did not speak Turkish, but did not let the *Gagauz* Turks in Romania to immigrate to Turkey because they were Christians, although they spoke Turkish. Also, the people, including the well-educated ones, in conversation and writing continued to use words that had Islamic rather than secular connotations, like *günah* (sinful) instead of *ziyan* (wasteful).

As noted, Turkey made a transition to multi-party politics in 1945. The single-party period that had started in 1923 came to an end in the wake of the 1950 national elections when the Democratic Party (*Demokrat Parti* – DP) defeated the CHP and came to power. However, the CHP, which had been instrumental in launching the Republican reforms, continued to perceive itself as the guardian of those reforms. In contrast, the DP's image of itself was that of the defender of the "national will" as against "the state's will." The former included the people's religious preferences and aspirations, which, given the earlier cognitive revolution, were quite innocent: people basically wanted more mosques and to see their religious orders, lodges, and shrines legalized so that they would be able to live their religion more freely and fully. The Democrats provided funds for more mosques, and they did not make strenuous efforts to prevent the resurfacing of religious orders, lodges, and shrines although under law they were still forbidden. Then and later, the people in Turkey did not long for a return to *sharī'ah*. Opinion polls conducted at the turn of the century have shown that although around 20 percent of the people said they were for such a rule, when further probed it turned out only 10.7 percent of the people were for a man marrying with four wives, 14.0 percent for women receiving lesser percentage of inheritance than men, 13.9 percent for divorce according to Islamic law, and only around one percent for the stoning to death of women who had engaged in adultery.[2]

Yet, the "soft attitude of the DP" toward the Islamic aspirations and preferences of the people was one of the reasons why the military removed the Democrats from power in 1960. The makers of the new (1961) Constitution, many of which were CHP sympathizers, did not want a repeat of the DP phenomenon in Turkey – a political party "diverting from the secularist path" and taking harsh measures against its detractors. They thus introduced proportional representation to prevent majority rule and expanded the scope of the basic rights and liberties so that governments in Turkey could no longer resort to authoritarianism against their critics. The unforeseen consequences of these provisions were the polarization of politics and the inability of the coalition governments to deal with the threat the polarization in question posed for democracy and the socio-economic life in Turkey. The liberal provisions of the 1961 Constitution facilitated the flourishing of ideological politics of the left and the right and their armed clash in the streets. The coalition governments from 1961 until 1964 could not function in a harmonious manner because their members came to have virtually irreconcilable differences. The CHP continued to act as the guardian of the "state's will," and the Justice Party (*Adalet Partisi* – AP) as that of the "national will." An almost exclusive focus on "high politics" lingered on in the 1965–71 period too when the AP was in government and the CHP in opposition. Consequently, those two secular parties could not cooperate and take effective measures against the widely spread political violence.

It was at this juncture that the first religiously oriented political party of the Republican period – the National Order Party (*Milli Nizam Partisi* – MNP) (1970–1) – was formed. The initiative for its establishment came from the then Sheikh of the Nakhsibandi Order, a certain Mehmet Zait Kotku, who thought Turkey was in need of moral development. In his submission, moral development would have given rise to material prosperity and political stability "that the country badly needed." Kotku's project of moral development, which resembled the Protestant ethic, did not have the underpinnings of political Islam – a yearning for a state based on Islam – for Kotku Islam was not the end, but a means for secular ends. Kotku's project aimed at the revitalization of some of the tenets of Islam for bringing about a spiritualist awakening that, it was thought, would lead to spirited endeavors and hard work on the part of the people.

The idea of moral development became an inspiration for the MNP and the four successor parties – the National Salvation Party (*Milli Selamet Partisi* – MSP) (1972–80), the Welfare Party (*Refah Partisi* – RP) (1983–98), the Virtue Party (*Fazilet Partisi* – FP) (1998–9), and the Felicity Party (*Saadet Partisi* – SP) (1999 to the present). The MNP and the MSP adopted the idea of so-called "National View" – the state preparing the ground for both material and moral development, and moral development in turn facilitating the emergence of a national conscience, that is, the flourishing of a will to make determined efforts for the benefit of the community at large. The RP, FP, and the SP targeted a "Just Order" (*Adil Düzen*) – a social order that was both rational and just.

However, whether in government (the MSP was several times a coalition member in the 1973–9 period and the RP was a coalition member in the 1996–7 period) or in opposition, under Necmettin Erbakan – the leader of the MNP, MSP, and RP and the behind-the-scenes leader of the FP and the SP – these parties went beyond merely borrowing themes from Islam and also tried to further Islamize both society and the state. They, for instance, tried to turn Haghia Sofia (the former Byzantine church in Istanbul) from a museum to a mosque, render Friday a weekend day, and prevent the introduction of the compulsory eighth-year secular education. More critically, from time to time, both Erbakan and some other members of these parties talked of Muslims forcefully coming to power, if necessary.

Although Erbakan and his associates could achieve none of these objectives and Erbakan's fiery statements along those lines seemed to have been resorted to in order to appease the radical Islamists both within and without these parties, Erbakan's statements in particular but also the attempts of these political parties to Islamize the society and the state led to their closure by the Constitutional Court (MNP, RP, WP, and VP) or by the military (MSP). Also in a society that had gone through a successful cognitive revolution in the 2002 national elections, the votes of the SP, the last and present religiously oriented political party of this genre, dwindled to less than two percent.

The Justice and Development Party

Identity

The Justice and Development Party (*Adalet ve Kalkınma Partisi* – AKP) is a product of the dissatisfaction of some members of the religiously oriented political parties with the MNP to the SP concerning the discourse and praxis of those parties. It is true that from the MNP to the SP, the religiously oriented political parties in Turkey had gradually become more and more system oriented. Whereas the first of these political parties, the MNP, had perceived an incompatibility between Islam and the secular order, the last in this category of political parties, the SP, demanded only that the state and Islam should not meddle in each other's affairs. Similarly, while the MNP had not allowed women to take part in party activities, female candidates from the SP have been elected to Parliament and some of them even smoked cigarettes and consumed alcohol in public. However, at the same time the MNP–SP line continued to insist on going further than an Islamic version of Protestant ethic; they toyed with the idea of political Islam and they perceived the secular political parties from an "us versus them" perspective. These political parties thus marginalized themselves in the polity and, consequently, they were all closed. The dissatisfied members of the SP, the so-called Innovators (*Yenilikçiler*), led by Recep Tayyip Erdoğan and his closest colleague Abdullah Gül, first tried to capture the leadership in the SP. When they failed (by a rather close margin), they formed the AKP (May 14, 2000). At the November 4, 2002 elections, the AKP obtained 34.6 percent of the votes and thus the majority of seats in Parliament and formed a government all by itself.

While they were still the members of the SP, the Innovators referred to themselves as "Muslim democrats" in an effort to underline their belief in political pluralism and their tolerance for the secularly oriented political parties. Then they extricated themselves from the MNP–SP line altogether and declared that they were not "Muslim democrats," but "conservative democrats" to emphasize the fact that they were reverting to the earlier idea of political morality, stripped of its political Islam dimension. They have considered themselves as pious people whose moral qualities such as industriousness, just behavior, respect for the people, tolerance for rivals, and search for peace and harmony in the community and society would inevitably reflect upon their politics. Yet, they have not thought of Islam as even one of the sources for their policies and programs. As Erdoğan once poignantly put it, they were pious people, but preferred secular politics.[3]

Although what Erdoğan quipped adequately sums up the AKP's political philosophy, it is in order to take it up in greater detail. Some important dimensions of this new approach to politics are the following.[4]

State–religion relation

- Freedom of conscience is of utmost importance. This freedom also involves the freedom of living one's religion in accordance with one's belief. The state should not be able to impose its own dogma upon society.
- The state should be equidistant to all religions and thoughts, making possible their peaceful coexistence.
- The state too should be freed from the clutches of any kind of dogma. Forming a political party in the name of religion, or to even give such an image, is the greatest harm one can render to religion. Religion is a common belief system; nobody has a right to use it for partisan purposes and thus give rise to divisions in society and politics. Also, nobody has a right to try to make others more pious.
- In politics, one may take one's cues from traditional values; one should not, however, transform the latter into an ideology. Reflection in politics of one's personal views and feelings based on religion is only to be expected; however, it does not clash with laicism.

Tradition, order, and freedom

- Freedom and order are not phenomena that negate each other; in fact, one cannot have one without the other. Yet, the freedom to tinker with customs, traditions, norms of morality, and religious life cannot be approved. On the other hand, society is not individualism's coffin but its cradle. Such institutions as the family, school, and civil societal organizations enable the individual to defend his/her rights and freedoms against the state.

Consensus and harmony

- Divisiveness, radicalism, and conflict should be replaced by unity, moderation, and consensus.

Democracy

- It is necessary to attribute special significance to democracy for it (a) prevents the imposition of dogma from above; (b) allows the articulation of different points of view; and (c) makes it possible to take lessons from past mistakes.
- Arbitrary rule that tramples upon collective and individual rights and liberties should be rejected.
- The growth of the state at the expense of the family, school, and other civil societal institutions politicizes the former and limits the scope of individual rights and freedoms. The authority of the state should not do away with individual rights and freedoms.
- Fundamentalism is the greatest threat to democracy because it rejects dialogue. One should accept the fact that s/he may be wrong and others may be right. The most important characteristic of democracy is to have faith in the commonsense of the people.

- The state should withdraw to its primary sphere of responsibility. In its own sphere of responsibility, however, the state should display an effective and dynamic performance. The concentration and monopolization of authority is not an apt strategy, for the reasoning faculties of men have their limits. Thus there is a need not only for the limitation but also for the horizontal distribution of power. Civil society is indispensable for democracy. The state cannot satisfactorily resolve all the issues the country faces.
- It is necessary to keep in mind both the social realities and the requisites of the modern world.

Change
- It is necessary to avoid promoting revolutionary change. Commonsense should substitute both the rationalism and the revolutionary. Rationalism is not rational. Ideals are important; yet, they should be balanced by other equally important considerations.
- It is necessary to avoid being against any kind of change from taking place. Everything that exists today cannot be inappropriate, for they have developed through long centuries of trial and error. Tradition is significant not because it is related to the past, but because it is a carrier of past experience and wisdom. However, a nostalgic approach to tradition should be avoided.

Globalization
- It is necessary to protect the individual against the state and enable him/her to take initiative, render societal groups and organizations politically efficacious actors, provide constitutional protection to the rights and freedoms of minorities, and improve and protect the religious and ethnic groups' freedom of expression and means of representation.
- On the one hand, the difference of identity is one of the fundamental freedoms of the present age; on the other hand, awareness of being a citizen and of common values is also very important.
- Differences constitute richness; at the same time, it is necessary to reconcile and harmonize the differences. Local cultures should be preserved; yet, cultural relativism should not end up in a rejection of universal norms and values.

In the summer of 2003, Abdullah Gül, the AKP government's foreign and deputy prime minister, stated that his party has a philosophical depth and this is what distinguishes that political party from other political parties in Turkey. He pointed out that they successfully reconcile their values and belief systems with modernity. Gül said that they always had a vision of a Muslim and, at the same time, a contemporary country where men and women take part in an egalitarian manner in a transparent government. He concluded his remarks by pointing out that in the last analysis theirs was a civilization project; in his view Turkey could be an inspiration to the other countries in the geography it is situated.[5] In the AKP's First General Congress in September 2003, Erdoğan made similar observations. He pointed out that their congress was the congress of his "sublime nation and that has carried the country to new horizons." He added that Turkey has been forming a close link between its "deep cultural roots and its honorable future." Then, echoing Martin Luther King, Erdoğan concluded his remarks by saying, "I dream of a Turkey which will be the strongest bridge between civilizations."[6]

The AKP's conservative democracy as reflected in the maxims given above indeed aims at a successful reconciliation of past and present, tradition and modern, religion and state, society and state, Islam and democracy, conflict and consensus, order and freedom, morality and rationality, and global and indigenous. Not unlike its immediate predecessor, the AKP disapproves of the meddling of both the state and religion in the affairs of the other. In addition, however, it grants that not only the state but also the religion may have its dogmas, and that in its view both are undesirable. The AKP, therefore, is for a government by pious people who have *moral principles*, but not for a government by Islamists who have *religious dogmas*. The moral principles they have in mind include responsiveness to the religious preferences and aspirations of the people; yet, the AKP view is that while serving the people it cannot give short shrift to the imperatives of the modern world. According to Erdoğan, "the AKP seeks to reconcile people's preferences and aspirations with responsible government."[7]

The AKP sees in democracy a strong guarantee against the imposition of dogmatic thinking both from above (the state) and from below (society) and the possibility of drawing clear lines between the jurisdictions of the state and society. It wishes to clip the wings of the state to some extent, while rendering whatever is left of it efficient and effective. It attributes to the society (family, schools, and civil societal organizations) the task of socializing individuals into a feeling of solidarity with others and enabling them to defend their rights and freedoms against the state. However, the AKP takes a strong stand against fundamentalism that may have its roots in society as well. The AKP's conception of democracy derives from a faith in the commonsense of the people and its own emphasis on harmony and dialogue. Again echoing King, Erdoğan once stated, "I have a dream in which conflict turns into competition, tension into dialogue, and polarization into democratic harmony."[8] Erdoğan talks about "democratic harmony"; he believes in *dynamic consensus*, which is the product of persuasion, not in *static consensus*, which is imposed by one group upon others. The AKP also aims to reconcile the vertical (acting in a responsible, statesmanlike manner) and the horizontal (acting to satisfy the preferences and aspirations of the people) dimensions of democracy. Let us again turn to Erdoğan: "Before the AKP came to power, those who preferred to pursue ideological politics equated politics with radicalism and those who preferred populism lacked an overall vision. The former made politics a prisoner of their prejudices; the latter rendered politics a means of political patronage."[9]

The AKP has a Burkean approach to change. It conceives of rationalism as being not rational because in its view man's reasoning faculties have their limits. The party perceives the revolutionary as utopian and thus not acceptable, because it does not consider man as omnipotent and because the party has respect for the commonsense of the people, which "derives from their accumulated wisdom." Yet the AKP does not have too lofty a conception of tradition; according to the AKP, when necessary the traditional should be replaced by the modern.

The AKP has a balanced approach to globalization, too. The party welcomes differences; yet, it also underlines the necessity of harmonizing those differences. This is what Erdoğan on one occasion offered on this issue: "We do not have in mind an exclusive conception of citizenship. We are citizens of Turkey, not Turkish citizens [if "Turkish" here is taken in a *definitional*, but not in a *nominal* sense]. Yet we should all the time reinforce our awareness of being citizens of Turkey. We should keep in mind that language, religion, and ethnicity are all subaltern values. There is above them the all-embracing concept of constitutional citizenship [being a citizen of Turkey by virtue of having professed loyalty to the Turkish state]."[10] Particularly striking here is the party's emphasis on the protection of the rights of minorities (which in Turkey means the non-Muslim citizens of the country)[11] and not pursuing discriminatory policies toward them. Following the car-bomb attacks on the two synagogues in Istanbul in 2003, Prime Minister Erdoğan had been criticized for not having made a particular reference to the victimized Jewish Turks too when he denounced the attacks. Erdoğan responded to those criticisms by saying, "Why should the prime minister of Turkey make a reference to the specific [that is, ethnic, religious, and sectarian] identities of his/her citizens? All of those who lost their lives are Turkish citizens, irrespective of their religions."[12]

Policies and Praxis

In its first year in office, to what extent has the AKP lived up to its discourse concerning its identity as a conservative-democratic party, which it preferred to "democratic Muslim"? Has the party been engaged in dissimulation (*takiyye*) and successfully concealed its ulterior motive of bringing about a state based on Islam, as the bulk of its secular detractors claimed or has it chosen a path that is quite different from the one its predecessors traversed?

While the AKP sees some societal institutions including religion as sources of individual morality, the party views the (secular) Republican precepts as sources of social and political solidarity. An AKP MP, Ömer Çelik, who is very close to Erdoğan, argued in May 2003 in an Istanbul daily that there is in Turkey a need for an official ideology and his reference was no other than Kemalism. Not unlike Dankwart A. Rustow, Çelik is of the opinion that national unity is an indispensable prerequisite for a viable democracy. Çelik thinks that Kemalism designates "the codes of collective existence", and as such he finds that worldview *sine qua non* of democracy in Turkey.[13] In the same vein, the head of the Education and Training Council of the Ministry of Education, Ziya Selçuk, appointed to that post by the AKP, thinks that in Turkey there are "very few common denominators" except Kemalism.[14] In the fall of 2003, the Ministry of Education was working on a project of how to make students better appreciate Atatürk and his reforms. In this project, they were cooperating with the members of the Secretariat-General of the National Security Council – the mouthpiece of the staunchly secularist Turkish military. Both Çelik and Selçuk were reflecting the views of Prime Minister Erdoğan who in his preface to the book on conservative democracy has noted that there is no conflict between democracy and republicanism and that in fact they would complement each other. Earlier, on May 19, 2003, on the eighty-fourth anniversary of Atatürk's landing in the city of Samsun on the Black Sea coast in northeast Turkey to start the Turkish War of Independence, Erdoğan in that city declared that whatever Atatürk and his associates believed then he and his colleagues too believe in and like them they will also try to take Turkey to enlightened tomorrows.

Needless to point out, The AKP's notion of Kemalism is somewhat different from the Kemalism of the bulk of the secularist elite in Turkey. The AKP leaders criticize the secularist elite for taking Kemalism as "an ideology that calls for the state to dictate how people practice their religion," for instance, through the Presidency of Religious Affairs and through the Constitutional Court and the Council of Higher Education who together regulate the head dress of female students in the universities. The AKP leaders think the state should have more faith in the commonsense of the people. Their interpretation of Kemalism may in fact be closer to how Atatürk and his associates actually perceived republicanism. As already mentioned, the latter had given rise to a cognitive revolution – an effort to enable the people to think rationally – and this project was a great success. So, the AKP asks, why under the circumstances should the elite not have faith in the commonsense of the people in general and in their representatives in Parliament in particular? The AKP thus views the Kemalist "codes of collective existence," "one of the few common denominators" people in Turkey have, as a worldview of *how* to think, and not as an ideology of *what* to think. The AKP was criticized for using the European Union (EU) pretext to hastily democratize the country. Its critiques saw behind such efforts on the part of the AKP "the ulterior motive of making possible 'one man, one vote, once'." Deputy Prime Minister Gül responded to such criticisms in August 2003 by saying that those views in the last analysis falsely assume that Turkey does not deserve a democratic system of government because the Turks are not considered mature enough.

The AKP's faith in the commonsense of the people constitutes the basic premise of their views on democracy. They think because people have commonsense one can reason with them. So, in their opinion, there is no need for authoritarian rules and practices. Even before the rather critical vote on the government resolution on the deployment in southeastern Turkey and the transit passage through that territory of American troops on the eve of and during the recent Iraq war, the AKP leaders did not see a need to arrange for a binding decision in that party's Parliamentary Group. Rather they held "persuasion sessions" with groups of the AKP parliamentarians. In December 2003, the AKP government submitted to Parliament a bill for substantially decentralizing government to render it both "democratic and rational." As has been explained by Erdoğan, the aim is that of "replacing the unaccountable administration that does not pay attention to human rights by an administration based on universalistic and democratic criteria." It is hoped that "an administration that utilizes resources efficiently and effectively and allows people's participation in local administration will bring the state and citizen together and help Turkey to realize its great potential."[15]

In conformity with Erdoğan's statement that the members of the AKP are pious people who prefer to rule the country in a secular manner, the party has not placed Islam and the related issues at the top of their political agenda. Instead, they set as their priorities Turkey becoming a full member of the EU on the one hand and socio-economic problems, in particular unemployment, education, health, and the legal system in that country on the other. The AKP leaders stated that the EU issue and the socio-economic problems were far more important than the turban issue, which will be taken up below. They managed to achieve some major reforms in order to make Turkey's legal system conform to the Copenhagen criteria. Also toward the end of their first year in government the Turkish economy began to display significant improvement. For instance, for the first time in the last 20 years the rate of inflation was below the 30 percent mark.

At the same time the AKP studiously kept Islam away from its policies. One of the occasions during which their resolve on this issue was tested was the General Council Meeting of the religiously oriented Association of Independent Industrialists and Businessmen (*Müstakil Sanayiciler ve İşadamları Derneği* – MÜSİAD) held on April 23, 2003 and attended by Prime Minister Erdoğan and five other ministers. MÜSİAD was against the government's pro-US policy on the eve of and during the recent Iraq war. They displayed on the screen in the conference hall the following three verses from the Qur'an in the hope of influencing the government policy on this matter:

- You who believe! Take not my enemies and yours as friends, offering them (your) love even though they have rejected the truth (Al-Mumtaḥina [She that Is to be Examined], 1).
- When it is said to them: Make no mischief on earth they say, "Why, we only want peace!" (Sūrat al-Baqarah [The Cow], 11).
- Of a surety, they are the ones who make mischief, but realize it not (Sūrat al-Baqarah, 12).[16]

In response to the message that the Association was trying to give him in a subtle manner, Erdoğan made the following points: Turkey was going through a rather delicate period. The government was trying not to lose sight of the broad picture by avoiding being made prisoner of some specific issues. In order to accelerate Turkey's progress toward contemporary civilization there is a need to keep close relations with major countries. As citizens of this country everybody had to have a similar vision; however, not everybody had to think alike on each and every issue. Some might say had they been in government they would have scrapped the agreements Turkey had made with the International Monetary Fund (IMF). But, in the present era, you had to pay attention to the IMF. If you rejected the IMF, the whole world would reject you. After having made these points, Erdoğan and other ministers left the meeting. Two months later, in his preface to Akdoğan's *Muhafazakar Demokrasi* Erdoğan wrote the following: "The AKP is not trying to emulate the past or some other civilization. It is attempting to conduct politics at universal standards although it is doing so in accordance with its own particular viewpoint [read, "political morality"]." In an interview with *The New York Times* (January 8, 2003), Erdoğan stated that: (a) he values the secular premises of the state; (b) the AKP does not have in mind a state based on religion; (c) in any case, an individual can have a religion, a state cannot. On this issue, the AKP's program tersely states that the party views secularism as indispensable for democracy and thus the party categorically disapproves of the exploitation of the sacred for political ends.

Accordingly, the AKP government has not, for instance, tried to remove the ban on the wearing of headscarves by female university students. In fact, this matter was not raised by the AKP during the 2002 election campaign. There was no provision concerning the headscarf in a number of university reform bills prepared by two ministers of education.

However, the secularist continued to be vigilant concerning the issue and has not allowed even a relatively minor violation of the norm. Soon after they had come to power, the Speaker of Parliament, Bülent Arınç, took his turbaned wife along when he went to the airport to see the president and his wife off on a state visit. This created uproar among the bulk of the secularists in the country. On National Sovereignty Day (April 23, 2003), the president and the top military commanders made it known that they were not going to attend the National Sovereignty Day reception at Parliament because Arınç's turbaned wife was going to be there as hostess. Arınç's last-minute statement that his wife was not going to attend the reception did not change their minds. On Republican Day (October 29, 2003), President Ahmet Necdet Sezer invited the AKP parliamentarians, including Prime Minister Erdoğan, but not their wives while he invited everybody else with their partners. The president stated that not only university classrooms but also the presidential palace, meeting halls of Parliament, and the like are public spaces and "in secular Turkey women with headscarves are not allowed to step into those places."

Not unexpectedly, the AKP leaders have not agreed with this view. They have argued that the Turkish constitution stipulates the sanctity of the freedom of conscience. The headscarf is a personal preference of the people, being related to the style of life that people should be free to choose. Zeynep Babacan, wife of Ali Babacan, minister of state responsible for the economy, reacted to the treatment meted out to the wives of the AKP politicians by saying, "The turban I am wearing is not a political symbol. Some may seem bigoted and fanatical, but one should not think that all those who cover themselves are bigoted fanatics."[17] Ahsen Unakıtan, wife of Kemal Unakıtan, minister of finance, tied her turban at the back of her neck as some secular women in Turkey do. Mrs. Unakıtan said: "I started to wear my turban like this when my husband and I went to a reception at the Turkish Embassy in London. I did not want our diplomats to become embarrassed because of my turban. . . . If I tie my turban the way I do now everybody in Turkey will feel relaxed."[18] Mrs. Unakıtan's last words reflect the general attitude of the AKP toward politics; the party values harmony in politics and acts accordingly. As if to complement Mrs. Unakıtan's observations Parliament Speaker Arınç has pointed out that he will never take his wife to an official reception and then said: "In order to prevent tension from arising in the polity, I shall act in that way even if I shall be ashamed of what I shall be doing."[19] The party's view on the turban issue was best described by Mehmet Aydın, minister of state responsible for religious affairs: "We ourselves shall not solve the turban issue; however, [sooner or later] the issue will by itself be resolved."[20] Hilmi Çelik, minister of education, brought clarity to the enigmatic statement of Aydın when he stated: "The turban issue cannot be resolved by law. There is a need for a large scale consensus on it."[21]

In its approach to such other critical issues as education and civil bureaucracy, too, the AKP government has *not* drawn upon Islam; it has instead come up with secular arguments, although the bulk of the secularists have not believed them and again attributed to them ulterior motives. Concerning education in Turkey, the AKP has argued that the Turkish educational system, in particular universities and vocational schools, needed a thorough upgrading. Concerning the universities, Erdoğan and the minister of education have pointed out that they wish to see in Turkey more modern and contemporary universities. They were of the opinion that the universities should not be "ideological and political clubs." Faculty members should be world-known scholars, having received awards from prestigious academic institutions abroad. Universities should have close relations with industry and people. They should have financial autonomy. Among other things they should be able to generate some of their revenues themselves. Finally, there should be more democracy in the institutions of higher learning: some of the powers of the Council of Higher Education should be transferred to the Inter-University Council and, similarly, executive committees and senates at the universities should take over some of the powers of the rectors and deans.

When the ministry of education came up with a new draft law that stipulated that with the law going into effect the terms of the present rectors and deans will be terminated, the bulk of the secular establishment began to strongly and vocally register their opposition to the reform project, arguing that the AKP government was really interested in bringing to key positions at the universities faculty members who had sympathies toward that government. Thereupon the ministry put on its website the draft law and stated that it was expecting evaluations and criticisms of university administrations and other related institutions. The minister visited a number of universities and had discussions with rectors and faculty members. However, the then head of the Council of Higher Education, Kemal Gürüz, who always had strong opinions against the AKP, as well as several rectors, remained adamantly opposed to a higher education reform by the AKP government. Erdoğan changed the minister of education in order to alleviate the tension. The new minister came up with a substantially watered down version of the draft law. That too was not acceptable to the secular establishment. The prime minister invited the rectors to his office and told them that they should work in close cooperation with the ministry and come up with a reform law. At the present writing (October 2005), no progress has been made on this issue.

Concerning vocational schools in Turkey, the AKP government has argued that previous governments had not encouraged vocational school education in Turkey as many other countries had done. They had not paid attention to upgrading the quality of education in those schools and, in fact, had discouraged pupils from attending those schools by making it more difficult for them to continue their education at universities. The government announced that it was thinking of redressing this situation. This policy of the AKP government immediately brought to Turkey's political agenda the prayer leader and preacher schools. These schools had been established to train prayer leaders and preachers; their curriculum was a replica of non-vocational secondary schools plus courses on Islam. However, the graduates of these schools had to obtain marks much higher than the graduates of the non-vocational schools to be able to attend a university.

Not unexpectedly the bulk of the secularists were again greatly disturbed. They pointed out that these schools were producing a far greater number of prayer leaders and preachers than Turkey needed; those who could not obtain a government job would be additional fodder for political Islam. They argued that opening the gates of universities to the graduates of these schools would facilitate the AKP government's efforts to pack the upper echelons of the civil service with their own pro-political Islam supporters.

The minister of education countered these arguments by stating that many parents who send their children to those schools do not want their children to become prayer leaders and preachers. The minister argued that many parents wish their children to have a solid education in their religion or, somewhat short of that, at least become citizens with personal integrity. In the minister's opinion, since Turkey was a democratic country the government had to have respect for parents' preferences. If the people were interested in learning their religion, the prayer leaders and preacher schools were the proper places to do that; "otherwise people may learn superstition and may think it is Islam." With these considerations in mind, the AKP government prepared the necessary amendments to the existing legislation; it was duly approved by the AKP majority in Parliament. However, the president vetoed it. If Parliament had again approved the vetoed law the president could not have vetoed it for a second time. However, the AKP government has not taken any further action on the issue.

Another rather controversial issue during the first year the AKP government was in power was the appointments that government made to the civil service. The bulk of the secularists thought the AKP would have used this as another means of bringing about a state based on Islam by packing the civil service with "Islamists." Consequently, the latter was very critical of almost every appointment made to the higher echelons of the service. Here, too, the AKP government came up with arguments that had little to do with the motives its detractors attributed to it. The government argued that for the dismal failure of the previous government attested by the results of the last elections one could not hold responsible only politicians; bureaucrats were also responsible for the unsuccessful policies pursued by the previous government. The AKP leaders said they had ambitious projects for Turkey, and therefore they needed a new cadre of qualified, dynamic, industrious, and honest bureaucrats who had successful past records and who could work as members of a team. Prime Minister Erdoğan said: "My bureaucrats should be able to understand my policies without my explaining to them those policies in detail. They should even be familiar with my body language."[22] The detractors of the government disclosed "pro-political Islam statements" that some of the appointees had made in the past. In response, Prime Minister Erdoğan said that the bureaucrats his government appointed to the bureaucracy should be appraised, not keeping in mind who they were 15 years ago, but taking into account who they are today.[23] He insisted that the people they have appointed to key posts were well qualified for the responsibilities they were saddled with. He mentioned the new Head of the Treasury, a certain Mesut Pektaş, who had a B.A. from the English-medium Middle East Technical University in Ankara and a M.B.A. from Northwestern University in the USA, and who had earlier served as the secretary-general of the Treasury; he mentioned another appointment to the same agency, a certain İbrahim Çakmak, who had worked for Lehman Brothers for 14 years, and the Director of Lehman Brothers had applauded the decision. At the same time, the prime minister granted that some of the appointments may not have been the most appropriate ones; however, he added that if he found out that an appointment has been with a view to political Islam he would himself terminate that appointment.

As noted in passing above, the AKP government has had egalitarian discourse and praxis concerning the non-Muslim citizens of Turkey and their belief systems. When two synagogues in Istanbul were car-bombed, Erdoğan pointed out that "Those who have committed this crime against our nation and humanity will be summarily caught and will be handed out the appropriate sentences, irrespective of whom they are and what their intentions have been. No ideal, no goal, and no end can justify terror against innocent people."[24] He then visited the Chief Rabbi in Istanbul accompanied by 70 politicians and expressed his deepest condolences. This was the first time a Turkish prime minister had paid a visit to the Chief Rabbi. On Christmas Day (2003), Erdoğan celebrated this sacred day of the Christian citizens of Turkey by declaring, "I share with great happiness the feelings of love, solidarity, and tolerance which are always felt intensely on the anniversary of the birth of the Prophet Christ, and view them as the common values of humanity. I pray to God that this anniversary of the birth of the Prophet Christ would be an occasion for glad tidings for everybody."[25] The AKP government also changed the word "mosque" to "temple" in the Reconstruction Act so that the Germans settled on the Mediterranean coast could build their places of worship there.

To what extent do the AKP parliamentarians and the members of the party organization as a whole agree with the new discourse and praxis of the party leaders delineated above? An opinion poll carried out in August, 2003 on 220 AKP and SP administrators in the local organizations of these two political parties has shown that the AKP administrators are far more secularly oriented than the SP ones. While 60.5 percent of the SP administrators defined themselves as "Islamists," only 13.1 percent of the AKP administrators defined themselves as such. Similarly while only 24.4 percent of the SP administrators agreed with the statement that "Islam should not be used for political purposes," that percentage went up to 67.7 in the case of the AKP administrators. Yet the picture is not so rosy for the AKP leadership. Close to 40 percent of their administrators see themselves as Islamist and more than one-third of them wish to use Islam for political purposes. This is despite the fact that while founding the party the AKP leadership had made every effort to recruit to the party "those who had left behind their old ideologies and who looked ahead."[26] In Parliament, the government's second resolution for allowing the deployment of American troops and their transit passage through southeastern Turkey was defeated by the votes of some AKP parliamentarians. And occasionally, the AKP parliamentarians and even ministers made Islamist and/or Third-Worldist sounding statements. Parliament Speaker Arınç made a diplomatic gaffe when on an official visit to Japan he said, "I hope when the Japanese people see this mosque I am visiting and come to know the people who pray here they would convert to Islam."[27] The minister of public works objected to Turkish contractors joining the reconstruction of Iraq along with contractors from the United States, "a country that brought ruins to Iraq."[28] The AKP leadership has been making strenuous efforts to bring such tendencies into line with their own discourse and praxis. More than once Erdoğan warned the AKP ministers and parliamentarians to act "responsibly." Erdoğan even removed ministers from their posts if they strayed from the party line. As time goes by they have been becoming more and more successful in their efforts along those lines.

Conclusion

The AKP government in Turkey stays away from the Islamic fusion of religion and politics. On the other hand, being pious people they seem to be influenced by the Qur'anic injunction of getting involved in politics and pursuing policies beneficial to the majority. If they perceive such efforts as *jihād*, they seem to take it no more than as "exerting oneself" and as a "holy struggle against evils within *oneself*." They give the impression of being puritanical; however, they are certainly not revolutionaries. They are sympathetic to *taqlīd* (emulation) only *vis-à-vis* Western ideas and practice. They are practicing Muslims without any hostility toward secularism. They do not view *Gharb*, the Arabic word for the West, as the place of darkness and the incomprehensible, thus frightening. They are devout persons but at the same time they are pragmatists. They innovate not in Islamic scriptures, but in politics, economics, and social problems of Turkey. They adopt Western concepts and practices, while trying to adapt them to the indigenous environment. Yet they do not allow the past to interfere with their efforts to grapple with the contemporary realities in a rational manner. The present-day Turkish Islam discussed in this chapter may be considered as a persuasive refutation of the theory of the clash of civilizations. After all, in several Western countries for many people Christianity or Judaism constitute significant dimensions of personal morality while there is a relatively strict separation between religion and the state. The AKP project is not any different from this formula. Whether or not that project may be a successful model for other Muslim realms is, of course, another story.

Notes

1. See, *inter alia*, Selma Ekrem, *Turkey: Old and New* (New York: Scribner and Sons, 1947), 19, 71; Howard Reed, "Revival of Islam in Secular Turkey," *Middle East Journal*, 8, 1954, 267–82.
2. See Ali Çarkoğlu and Binnaz Toprak, *Türkiye'de Din, Toplum ve Siyaset (Religion, Society, and Politics in Turkey)* (Istanbul: Türkiye Ekonomik ve Sosyal Araştırmalar Vakfı (TESEV), 2000), 70–9. Also see Ali Çarkoğlu, "Religiosity, Support for Şeriat, and Evaluations of Secularist Politics in Turkey," *Middle Eastern Politics*, 40, 2004, 111–36.
3. *Hürriyet* (Istanbul daily), November 11, 2002.
4. Unless otherwise indicated on the AKP's conservative democracy, we draw upon Yalçın Akdoğan, *Muhafazakar Demokrasi* (Conservative Democracy) (Ankara: AK Parti, 2003). Akdoğan is a close advisor of Erdoğan. Erdoğan wrote a preface to this book.
5. *Milliyet* (Istanbul daily), August 25, 2003.
6. *Hürriyet*, October 12, 2003.
7. Ibid.
8. *Milliyet*, October 14, 2003.

9. *Hürriyet*, October 12, 2003.
10. *Hürriyet*, June 29, 2003; September 3, 2003.
11. According to the Treaty of Lausanne signed in 1924, following the Turkish War of Independence, only the non-Muslim citizens of Turkey are considered as minorities. They thus have the rights of practicing their own religion and shaping their educational systems in accordance with the needs of their communities.
12. *Sabah* (Istanbul daily), November 19, 2003
13. *Star*, May 8, 2003.
14. *Hürriyet*, September 21, 2003.
15. *Hürriyet*, October 3, 2003.
16. All, Yusuf Ali translations.
17. *Hürriyet*, May 12, 2003. In Turkey, only 15.7 percent of the women wear a turban (*turban*), while 53.4 wear the traditional but non-religious headscarf (*başörtüsü*), and 27.3 neither. Those who put on a veiled dress (*çarşaf*) is no more than 3.4 percent (Çarkoğlu and Toprak, *Türkiye'de Din, Toplum ve Siyaset*, 22).
18. *Hürriyet*, June 1, 2003.
19. *Sabah*, April 25 2003.
20. *Milliyet*, June 6, 2003.
21. *Hürriyet*. June 10, 2003.
22. *Milliyet*, April 19, 2003.
23. *Hürriyet*, May 2, 2003.
24. *Hürriyet*, November 19, 2003.
25. *Sabah*, December 24, 2003.
26. The statement made by Abdullah Gül (*Sabah*, August 11, 2003).
27. *Milliyet*, June 5, 2003
28. *Hürriyet*, April 19, 2003

Further reading

Arat, Yeşim, "Group Differentiated Rights and the Liberal Democratic State: Rethinking the Headscarf Controversy in Turkey," *New Perspectives on Turkey* (Istanbul), 25, 2001, 31–46.
Boztemur, Recep, "Political Islam in Secular Turkey in 2000: Change in the Rhetoric Towards Westernization, Human Rights, and Democracy," *International Journal of Turkish Studies*, 7, 2001, 125–37.
Göle, Nilüfer, "Authoritarian Secularism and Islamist Politics: The Case of Turkey," in A.R. Norton, ed., *Civil Society in the Middle East* (Leiden: E.J. Brill, 1996).
Gülalp, Haldun, "Political Islam in Turkey: The Rise and the Fall of Refah Party," *Muslim World*, 89, 1999, 22–41.
Hale, William, "Christian Democrats and the AKP: Parallels and Contrasts," *Turkish Studies*, 6, 2005, 293–310.
Heper, Metin, "Islam and Democracy in Turkey: Toward Reconciliation?" *Middle East Journal*, 35, 1997, 32–45.
— "Islam, Modernity, and Democracy in Contemporary Turkey: The Case of Recep Tayyip Erdoğan," *Muslim World*, 93, 2003, 157–85.
— "The Justice and Development Party Government and the Military in Turkey," *Turkish Studies*, 6, 2005, 215–31.

Kadıoğlu, Ayşe, "Republican Epistemology and Islamic Discourses in Turkey," *Middle East Journal*, 48, 1994, 645–60.

Kaplan, Sam, "*Din-u Devlet* All Over Again: The Politics of Military Secularism and Religious Militarism in Turkey Following the 1980 Coup," *International Journal of Middle East Studies*, 34, 2002, 113–27.

Kasaba, Reşat, "Cohabitation? Islamist and Secular Groups in Modern Turkey," in R. Hefner, ed., *Democratic Civility: The History and Cross-Cultural Possibility of a Modern World* (New Brunswick, NJ: Transaction Publishers, 1998).

Öniş, Ziya, "Political Islam at the Crossroads: From Hegemony to Co-Existence," *Contemporary Politics*, 7, 2001, 281–98.

Özbudun, Ergun, "Islam and Politics in Modern Turkey: The Case of the National Salvation Party," in Barbara Freyer Stowesser, ed., *The Islamic Impulse* (London: Croom Helm, 1987).

Sakallıoğlu, Ümit Cizre, "Parameters and Strategies of Islam-State Interaction in Republican Turkey," *International Journal of Middle East Studies*, 28, 1996, 231–51.

Sayarı, Sabri, "Turkey's Islamist Challenge," *Middle East Quarterly*, 3, 1995, 35–43.

Toprak, Binnaz, "The State, Politics, and Religion in Turkey," in Metin Heper and Ahmet Evin, eds., *State, Democracy, and the Military in Turkey* (New York: Walter de Gruyter, 1988).

— "Islam and Democracy in Turkey," *Turkish Studies*, 6, 2005, 167–86.

White, Jenny, "Islam and Democracy: The Turkish Experience," *Current History*, 94, 1995, 7–12.

CHAPTER 21

Secularism and Democracy in Contemporary India: An Islamic Perspective

Syed Shahabuddin

It is a fact that gradual and steady secularization of society has been a global phenomenon in the world recently. In most of the Muslim majority states, with some exceptions, despite Islamist pressure to reinvent the Islamic society, the pace of secularization and modernization is generally faster than the pace of Muslim minorities, which like all minorities anywhere, tend to be more conservative in order to safeguard their religious identity against pressure of majoritarian assimilation.

Most modern states have adopted, at least in theory, the principles of secularism in order to deal with religious plurality. With the exception of Israel and Saudi Arabia, no modern state is theocratic. Yet the majority religion universally becomes an operational factor and exerts a continuing functional influence on the affairs of the nation-state, as it seeps through the political system, the state structure, the cultural environment, and colors many features of governance and civic affairs.

Communist states have adopted an anti-religious ideology and if Islam happens to have a high profile in national life, the state comes into clash and conflict with Islam, particularly if it is not moribund but resurgent.

State Secularism as the Principle of Governance

State secularism implies that the state is not anti-religious (though it may be irreligious). Its basic principles are:

1. Recognition by the state of the fundamental right of religious freedom, i.e. freedom to profess, practice, and propagate a religion of one's choice.
2. Acceptance of a multi-religious model for the society and non-identification of the state with a religious group and deliberate equidistance towards all religious groups.

3. Non-alignment of the state with any religious group and neutrality in any inter-religious conflict.
4. Recognition by the state of the religious identities of individuals and groups and equal respect for all religions.
5. Equality before law and non-discrimination by the state on the basis of religion.
6. Protection of the legitimate human and constitutional rights of the religious groups.
7. Non-interference in the internal affairs of the religious minorities.

All modern states may not, in practice, live up to the ideal because of political and social compulsions. As, in all human affairs, there is always a gap between perception and practice.

At the level of the individual, the antithesis of secularism is communalism. The term has acquired a special connotation. Just as there are secular and theocratic states, a person may have a secular or communal outlook. But religiosity, even orthodoxy, is not communalism. A person may be religiously orthodox, yet secular in human relations and as a citizen, particularly when exercising public authority. The difference between secularism and communalism can be best illustrated by imagining a human situation.

Imagine a river in flood and a child falling in the swirling waters, about to be taken away. A man, who knows how to swim, jumps into the water to save the child. Another person, who also knows how to swim, inquires about the religion of the child. It is easy to say that the first person represents the secular and humanist impulse and the other represents the communal mindset. But there is a third man who throws children of the "other" into the raging river. How shall we designate him? A monstrous depravity? For the lack of a better word, let us define him as "super communal". Already the modern world has a name for such brutalities committed against the "other" on a mass scale; it is called ethnic cleansing. The legal pundits call it genocide and a crime against humanity.

Secularism and Theocracy

Secularism implies basically that while the state recognizes religion as a social institution and treats all religions professed by its people equally, the state itself has no religion.

An Islamic or a Hindu or a Christian or a Jewish state, however generously it may treat the followers of other religions, would be anti-secular in the sense that there is a state religion; the state identifies itself with or patronizes a religion, that it discriminates in favor of a religion, that it uses its resources to propagate it, to glorify it, to project its religious association in a variety of ways. While it protects the "others," it reserves policy-making positions or the highest echelons of state power for the followers of the forward religions. Such a state is a theocracy by definition though it may be a democracy. Thus secularism and theocracy are the antithesis of each other.

A state may be democratic and yet "theocratic," though in conduct, many dimensions are generally secular. There is a clear definitional distinction between the two modes of statecraft. Yet most modern states, which proclaim themselves Islamic or Christian, are largely secular in conduct and practice and many secular states speak in a religious idiom and behave sometimes like a theocratic state.

The president of the United States of America takes the oath of office on the Bible, the sovereign of the United Kingdom is the head of the Anglican Church and bears the title "Defender of the Faith". The King of Saudi Arabia is the Custodian, lately the Servant of the Holy Places. The president of Iran is a Shi'ite divine, a Grand Ayatollah. On the other hand, a state may proclaim itself secular and in practice become the promoter of the majority religion and act in a partisan manner in inter-religious conflicts, take sides in disputes and differences between religious communities, not on the merits of the situation, but by virtue of individual or collective identification of some members of its political or permanent executive, its personnel or employees, with one of the parties. The state may proclaim equality before law and equality of opportunity for all but dispense its services, deploy its resources, extend its patronage, provide assistance and welfare support in a denominational manner, treat a section of its citizens who belong to a religious minority as unwanted or as untrustworthy or as disposable baggage, and practically shut the doors of public offices or services in their face. Perhaps human failure to achieve the ideal is part of the human condition.

In the name of national unity and integration the dominant group in many states, infected with the majoritarian virus, seeks to promote religious, cultural or linguistic assimilation, by force or otherwise. When the society adopts uniformity as its goal, homogenization as the process and coercion as its method, when the society differentiates among its members on any basis whatsoever, the result is division, disunity, discontent and disaffection; and desperation and defiance are not far behind. The dominant group cannot force the "others" through a common mold. This is against the law of nature. Every human being, every group is as different from the other as one leaf of a tree is from another. And every tree has different foliage. Can you make the leaves of a tree the same size? Can you force all trees to have the same leaf design?

Blurred Distinction – A Gray Zone

At the end of centuries of political evolution, instead of a sharp line of division, one thus sees a gray zone when the secular merges into the theocratic and vice versa, leaving only a few modern states, which are clearly theocratic or ideally secular.

Are the people then fighting over the labels, not the content, over form, not the substance, over words, rather than deeds, over proclamations rather than practices? Yes, to a very large extent. But the battle promises to become more and more meaningless, like shadow boxing, as the society moves forward, faces new challenges, and gropes for solutions and answers to contemporary problems. But the battle can also become fierce when the state tries to reinvent or reinforce its nationhood or to impose a cultural or social uniformity.

The real problem lies in that states and nations or peoples are not coterminous and while there is a universal trend towards democracy, secularism, multiculturalism, and human rights – all expressions of the accepted principles of freedom and human dignity – there is also a counter-trend towards political majoritarianism, cultural nationalism, social uniformity, and marginalization of the "other".

The modern state is the highest political formation for a geographical territory. The ideological state has withered away. Race, language, and increasingly religion do not define the contours of a state, just as the main resource base, agriculture or industry or trade or services fail to define it. A modern state is polyeconomic just as it is multi-racial, multilingual and multi-religious. Even a largely homogeneous state is sometimes forced to acquire increasing doses of imported heterogeneity to keep itself economically going.

The ethnic state is likely to be still-born, though we are at the threshold of what has been called the era of ethnicity. To achieve a total reorganization of the political map of the world, to create a set of states of ethnic purity, is an impossible task. Some changes may come about through simultaneous fusion across political borders as also through fission of political territories and the resultant components may be more ethno-specific and homogeneous. The world may appear to be moving under the umbrella of a multi-ethnic regional or world order. But there is increasing mobility in the global village that the world has shrunk into and no political constituent can ever be totally homogeneous, religiously or otherwise. One cannot envisage future states which are racially, religiously, or linguistically uniform or exclusive or monopolistic. The world has to accept and learn to live with multidimensionality and diversity and adopt an inclusive rather an exclusive approach to ensure harmony and progress within and among all states. The alternative is respect for human and minority rights in all plural societies and decentralized states in a multi-ethnic world.

International Norms

For many years the UN system was working on a draft Declaration for the Rights of the Minorities. Finally the UNGA adopted such a Declaration in December 1991 though with some in-built reservations. Yet the problem has been diagnosed and an international consensus has emerged on the subject which would, to a large extent, determine the terms of interaction between the majority group and the minority groups in any civilized state-member of the international community and set the limits of freedoms and rights to be enjoyed by the minority groups.

Tomorrow no state is likely to be absolutely homogeneous; each will harbor within its political boundaries and under its control a multiplicity of religions, languages, and races.

Each state may have a dominant ethnic group (defined by one or more of those variables) which may control the state apparatus but still share power with the minorities.

Global Dispersal

The global phenomenon of dispersal of minorities and their forming inseparable strands of state demography will serve to brake the pressures of religious, linguistic, and racial chauvinism by bringing into play the self-interest of all religious, linguistic, or racial groups. Self-interest can only be served under a regime of mutual benevolence, under a uniform, internationally accepted code of behavior defined by the Universal Charter of Human Rights, the International Covenants of Political and Social and Economic Rights as well as by the International Convention on Minority Rights, which may emerge from the UN Declaration.

Then and then alone will a Hindu India and a Muslim Bangladesh and a Buddhist Sri Lanka and a Christian United Kingdom have a distinct individuality, a national personality, without being in any way oppressive and unjust to the minority groups and depriving them of their role in national life, without easing them into or out of any field of national endeavor or without coercing them into assimilation, without dehumanizing them, without reducing their equal claim to the bounties of their motherland.

Human rights and minorities rights shall hopefully serve to bridge the gulf between theocracy and secularism in the global village, which has become a marketplace for the exchange of raw materials, technology, energy, capital, and labor on mutually beneficial terms.

The essential question tomorrow would be, as it is today: how the state treats its religious, linguistic, and racial minorities:

- Does it treat them as equal before law, as individuals and as collectivities?
- Does it guarantee their security, of life, limb, honor, and property?
- Does it grant them religious freedom and protect their religious institutions?
- Does it give them equality of opportunity, particularly in the field of economic activity, as producers of marketable surplus, as providers of services, public and private?
- Does it promote the development of their mother tongue and their culture and the transmission of their value system to their succeeding generations?
- Does it try to assimilate them, if they wish to retain their identity?
- Does it keep them separate, if they wish to assimilate themselves?

So long as a state treats its citizens equally and protects their rights as defined nationally and internationally, it may have a religious face without becoming a theocracy, a cultural face without becoming monolingual, a racial face without adopting apartheid.

The future state shall be a secular state, a democratic state, a liberal state, a welfare state, primarily because global homogenization is taking place and a world culture is developing and because no ethnic group will be confined to a particular state as the dominant majority but will spread all over the world as a minority group in many states.

Secularism and Islam: Options for Muslim Communities

Islam for a multi–religious world

Islam presumes a multi-religious world in which the bounties of Allah are available to all human beings in equal measure, whether it is sunlight or air or water, without any distinction as to religion. A secular state essentially means the application of the same principle of non-discrimination in the distribution of national resources and services that the state provides for its citizens. Read with the essential principles *'adl* (justice) and *lā ikrāh fī al-dīn* (no compulsion in matters of faith) there is no inherent dichotomy between Islam and secularism.

On another plane, historically there has been no Islamic state beyond the period of the enlightened caliphs. Monarchy – tribal or racial – with inherent authoritarianism, sometimes sanctified by the religious establishment, in the name of peace and stability, or the blessings of religious divines, provides no model for modern Muslims.

The dilemma of Muslim minorities

Religious minorities all over the world face the same dilemma: where does their interest lie? Struggle for equality in every sphere of life for an ideally secular dispensation, or accept a "protected status," or seek a point of balance and a stable level of equilibrium?

Those who argue that in the final analysis a minority group cannot depend for its well-being on constitutional guarantees and legal processes but only on social goodwill, on its acceptance by the religious majority, are in fact arguing for the protected status. Those who argue that the state culture – the forms, the symbols, the rites, the rituals, the ceremonies, the names, the titles – must have, in the very nature of things, close association with the ethos and psyche of the majority group, its cultural traditions, its myths and legends, are also arguing the inevitability of the national culture, including political culture, evolving in accordance with the conscious and unconscious pressures of the majority and its contemporary forms and casting a shadow over the state. Reflecting the majority culture, the state of the future is bound to move towards a degree of homogeneity, it will speak in the idiom of the majority group and it will take upon itself the role of concretizing the ideas and aspirations, the vision, and the worldview of the majority groups. But a reasonable limit has to be set.

The apprehension is that "protected status," may also imply dissociation, non-participation, and passivity and, in effect, inevitably reduce the religious minority groups to the status of second-class citizens, not only in a political but in an economic and social sense. Human beings may be reduced to useful tools for the working of the state economy. They work because they are needed; they earn because they work; they live a life of their own; they do not participate in decision making or in managing the affairs of society or the state. This happens whether they are workers in a plantation or a factory in a developed state or professionals in a rich but underdeveloped state. Such a development can be prevented, but only by affirmative action by the state, based on an international norm and assertion of religious identity by the religious minorities within the framework of the state and its constitution and a conscious movement by both the state and the religious minorities towards balance and accommodation.

At least 40 percent of the world's Muslim population has the status of religious minorities in non-Muslim states. By far the biggest Muslim minority group is the Muslim Indian whose estimated population is of the order of 150 million, constituting about 13 percent of the national population, an equal percentage of the world Muslim population, and 40 percent of the world's Muslim minority population. The other major Muslim minority concentration states are China, Russia, France, Germany, the UK, and the United States.

These Muslim minorities have no option but to seek a *modus vivendi* based on equality and justice. This calls for the state being both democratic and secular. Democracy by itself will subject them to continuous majority pressure resulting in alienation, which may take the form of assimilation or engender separatism, if the religious minority is concentrated in a part of the state where it forms a majority. Religious minorities are generally wary of religious submergence and only a secular state can maintain the balance between religious identity and equitable participation of the religious minority in the political and economic life of the nation-state.

The other options of a Muslim minority are:

1. quest for political dominance;
2. political quietism with physical isolation;
3. acceptance of majority assimilation, religious and cultural: French model/multiculturalism;
4. mass migration;
5. separation, secession and independence.

All of them are more or less suicidal in a democratic world. However, secular coexistence raises many questions at the global level. Anti-Muslim or anti-Islamic ideologs never tire of harping upon the "contradiction" that in countries where Muslims are in a majority, they wish to establish an Islamic state and where they are in a minority, they demand a "secular" state! There is some truth in the charge. But the dichotomy arose primarily because of identification of secularism as anti-religion and, in the Muslim world, as anti-Islam.

The Muslims of the world have to prepare themselves to adjust to this global reality – through liberal and equitable treatment of non-Muslim minority groups in Muslim-majority states and through coming to terms with the legitimate aspirations of the non-Muslim majority group in states where they have a minority status – so long as their rights as human beings, as Muslims and as citizens are recognized, respected and protected, so long as they enjoy equality and dignity.

Muslim minorities make only one basic demand on the Muslims in the Muslim-majority states and their governments. They have to be just and generous to the non-Muslim nationals and citizens; despite the constitutional and traditional constraints that come in the way of equal treatment. It is for Muslims of those states to endeavor to remove the contradiction between the conduct of the modern Islamic state and the norms of international law.

Democratic and secular Muslim states are the best guarantees for the survival in dignity of Muslim minorities in the non-Muslim states.

Conceptual obstacles in Muslim–majority states

The major obstacle in the path of reciprocity is that democracy and secularism in their full meaning are generally lacking in the Muslim-majority states.

Why are Muslim states not secular? There are many reasons.

Firstly, Muslims generally do not clearly distinguish between the secularization of society and the secularism of the state. Secondly, Muslims generally see establishment of Islamic power as the legitimate objective of a Muslim-majority state, i.e. transformation of the Muslim into an Islamic state. Thirdly, an "Islamic state," by definition, reserves real power in the hands of the Islamic community, to be guided by the *ulama*, as the guardian of *sharī'ah*. Fourthly, the Islamic state protects the non-Muslim natives and foreigners, but does not treat them as equal citizens. It denies them the right to aspire to and attain the highest positions of authority, the right to propagate their religion, the right to build new places of worship, and the right to establish educational institutions of their choice.

On the other hand, all Muslim-majority states today form part of the international state system and are subject to international law, based on international covenants and treaties, international conventions and declarations and bilateral agreements. Torn between rival pulls and pressures, almost all Muslim states are facing internal tension on the place of Islam in the polity. But since individually or collectively they do not operate in a vacuum, they are not really free to ignore the internationally accepted and universally applied norms for the conduct of state power and relations, internally or externally.

Separatism of Muslim minorities

The other facet is the phenomenon of separatism perceptible in some Muslim-minority states. Let us take the example of India, China, and Russia, home to the world's biggest Muslim minorities. India is a secular state, China is a communist state and Russia is a Christian state. Each of them has a frontier region with a Muslim majority, Kashmir, Chechnya, and Sinkiang, which shows secessionist tendencies and casts a shadow on the Muslim community as a whole in the country. But it should be noted that none of the three regions account for a majority of the Muslim population of the country. For example, Kashmir has only 5 percent of the total national Muslim population. But in the case of India, unlike in the other two, there is the burden of recent history and the adversarial and hostile involvement of a neighboring state – Pakistan – which claims this adjacent Muslim majority territory. Such factors – internal and more so external – complicate the peaceful existence of the Muslim minority even within a secular state. There are many similar examples of separatism, born out of hostile discrimination and oppressive treatment, which find support in regions of Muslim concentration, e.g. in Myanmar, the Philippines, Thailand, and even in the wider Muslim world. Sometimes Muslim minorities are charged with extraterritorial loyalties or even with serving as the cat's paw or fifth columnist for the Muslim state next door.

Separatism is not incurable. Though political dialogue, adoption of structural decentralization of power, devolution of resources, and the granting of autonomy will eliminate the tendency, repression never will.

The third major problem for Muslim minorities is that even when the state is democratic it is largely controlled by the religious majority; and power and authority of the state, however egalitarian and secular in principle, are exercised by the state functionaries who largely belong to the religious majority. Situations may vary from state to state but in a nation-state in which the Muslim minority is regarded as a historic adversary or seen as a competitor for political power or even as an organized political factor which can tilt the balance of power, it is liable to be subjected to physical repression, cultural assimilation, economic pressure, political under-representation, social demonization, and educational brain washing. While physical liquidation or expulsion may be out of question, the religious minority is sought to be demoralized, silenced, and assimilated. Thus the democratic state, in effect, becomes a majoritarian state and the secular state is reduced to an exercise in tokenism. While occasional pogroms are meant to demoralize the community, organized propaganda against the religious minority, its beliefs, its institutions, its organizations, its way of life, its history, its suspected extraterritorial loyalty are meant to cut off any recourse by the minority to the final court of appeal in a democracy – the people. Suspicion and distrust generate ill will and hatred and dry up the wells of human solidarity.

However, even in such situations of distress, the Muslim minority has no option but to counteract the propaganda as best as it can, take advantage of the political process, seek judicial redress, and educate the public opinion.

A democratic state, in its plunge towards a police state and even the fascist order faces in-built brakes and has the capacity to reverse on its track. This is because the people will definitely realize at some point that the state or its policy-makers and decision-makers are not acting in the public interest but in the interest of a small minority within the majority, to promote and consolidate its hold on the levers of power, to the detriment of the wider national interest.

The religious minority has to play a constructive and positive political role in saving the state from fascism as well as in restoring democracy and secularism. But its role is essentially to supplement the endeavor of the democratic and secular forces. At the same time, it has to defend itself and maintain its presence in the economy. It has to draw upon its spiritual resources, accord forgiveness, act with forbearance and tolerance and abstain from revenge or retaliation. It can never afford to lose faith or hope.

In the final analysis the situation of a religious minority will depend on its will to maintain its identity and, at the same time, its willingness to contribute to national integrity, its development and progress. Above all, the Muslim minority has to evolve a mindset which does not see secularism as anti-religion or anti-Islam or the secular order as a mask for anti-Islamic repression, but as a humane system which may at times fail to deliver and yet which is the only viable course for the peaceful coexistence of many religions within a nation-state and in the world.

The Secular State: The Indian Experiment

The secular state which the Indian Freedom Movement envisaged and which was given a constitutional shape and form on independence is today under threat from the Hindu right which, armed with a fascist ideology, is committed to destroy the secular order and transform the secular state into the Hindu state of its dreams. Fortunately, as the general election in 2004 has shown, its appeal is still limited to fewer than 25 percent of the people, mostly the urban middle and upper classes. Though it has the potential to terrorize the Muslim and the Christian communities and incite Hindus and tribals into violent atrocities. The secular elements are yet to work out a united strategy for the counter-offensive against the anti-secular forces.

Gujarat Genocide

The Gujarat Genocide in 2002 was not only a great human tragedy but a political watershed. It has led to an ideological polarization more intense than at any time since independence. This is a hopeful sign for the shape of things to come.

Hitler had practiced genocide with Teutonic efficiency and up-to-date technology against the Jews and liquidated millions of them in gas chambers. Almost all leaders of the Hindu right, from Savarkar and Golwalkar downwards, have been and are great admirers of Hitler, who claimed to be an Aryan. In Gujarat, during the first half of 2002, their followers took the first step towards repeating the holocaust on Indian soil. The count is not important. What is important is that the replay was attempted in Gandhi's homeland Gujarat. The conscience of the people of India rebelled against the mini-genocide and the organizers lost power two years later even as they felt certain of reaping the harvest of votes from the blood they had shed and the hatred they had sown. The Hindu right, as a consequence, feels bewildered and confused, partly because of its in-built hypocrisy.

Hinduism formally regards all human beings as part of the same family. It speaks of tolerance of all humans carrying the divine spark, of respect for all religions as equally valid paths to the divine! And yet some Hindus incite hatred, train killers and commit atrocities against fellow citizens and neighbors merely because they follow another religion.

Some analysts tried to rationalize the human tragedy by pointing out that the killers, rapists, and arsonists in Gujarat were all hired for the job, from among the unemployed or semi-employed youth and the poverty-stricken dalits and tribals. The question remained: who hired them and paid for their services, and why. Obviously the organizations whose future depended on the success of their orchestration of hate and violence did. And who contributed funds for the diabolical program? The rich Gujaratis abroad, mainly in the United States and the UK, and the educated middle class, even the affluent elite. And when the show was at its peak, they drove out in expensive cars, called friends on mobiles, to share the loot and enjoy the macabre spectacle of burning homes, burnt and half-burnt corpses of bombed children, and raped women. They spread baseless rumors, distributed handbills and leaflets to incite people, to kill, to drive out the "others," to boycott them socially and economically. Calling them communal or denigrating them as the storm troopers of Hindutva will not suffice. We have to coin some new terms to describe such people with such devilish and inventive mindsets.

Such Hindus may think of themselves as patriotic and nationalist. They are neither. They are not even Hindus as the Hindutva they believe in is far, very far, from Hinduism, which is essentially tolerant of religious differences. They divide the nation, polarize it on religious lines, they incite and sometimes arm, train and pay people to kill, to rape, to torch, to intimidate the "other."

What is the purpose? What is the calculation? They know the other cannot be eliminated. Their purpose, therefore, is not to liquidate him but to force him to deny his identity, to surrender his religion, culture, language, way of life, food habits, to fold away his cap and to shave off his beard, to change his dress, even his name. In short, to terrorize him into assimilation and subjection. Earlier they preached to the "other": "you are all Hindus, some of you are Mohammadi Hindus, some are Masihi Hindus, some are Nanaki Hindus! Why don't you, following the lesser religious streams, merge yourself in the mighty Ganga of Hindu Dharma? This is Bharatiyata."

The name of the game, thus, is not liquidation but assimilation! Assimilation has been the running leitmotif of Indian history and forms the undercurrent of the nationalist stream. That is why populist secularism like mutual participation in religious observances, mixed marriages, synthetic faiths, and syncretic mixes are glorified; and performance of Hindu rituals at official ceremonies and the location of Hindu tokens and emblems in official premises are accepted.

But Indians are indeed all one, sons of the same mother, born on the same soil. But all Indians are not all Hindus. India is a multi-religious, multilingual, multicultural, multi-racial country, with many ways of life, of a continental dimension. Notwithstanding differences and diversity, Indians show emotional unity; they all rejoice when their motherland takes a step forward; they all feel sorrow if the country faces a setback. *This is integration.* But emotional integration is put to the test when social violence erupts and many Indians fail to look upon a male victim as their brother, a raped woman as their sister, and a torched house as their own. The grief they feel is not universal, their compassion is not all embracing.

The route to national integration passes through mutual acceptance and abnegation of any superiority complex, respect for all identities, banishment of fear, coercion or intimidation from intergroup relations, removal of the threat of cultural submergence or racial or linguistic or religious absorption, through equality and justice.

The problem is that nationalist euphoria and patriotic fervor often make the people oblivious of the line of demarcation between integration and assimilation, between multichrome harmony and monochrome dullness, between a mosaic and a melting pot. Inadvertently a major political party, which is essentially secular, speaks of the "unique" virtues of a particular religion and thus denigrates other religions of the country. A prime minister, perhaps sincerely, speaks of "Hindu Dharma" as the universal religion or decries another religion. Some leaders go to the extent of equating their religion with nationhood and their culture with national culture, interpreting territorial nationalism as cultural nationalism, reducing the rich living patterns to a common way of life. And they are lauded as builders and not as destroyers of the multi-splendored mansion of Bharatiyata (Indianness).

What has happened is that as a group, the Hindu Indians have been psychologically conditioned over a period of time to accept the identification of the Indian state with Hinduism and Hindu culture. Today, the difference between the secular and the communal Hindu is not so much in the depiction of India as a Hindu Rashtra but in defining the place of the non-Hindus in the Rashtra. The secular Hindu defends his rights and wants the "others" to be protected; the communal Hindu wants to expel him or to liquidate him or terrorize him with trishuls and occasional pogroms and better still to absorb him peacefully into the Hindu Samaj. We are a nice people: Isn't non-violence our creed? How can we stain our hands with blood? But the "other" deserves to be taught a lesson. He must learn to show due respect to those to whom the country belongs and nurse "goodwill" towards them and surrender to all their "nationalist" demands and commands.

To explain why and how even our educated Hindu elite have come to share this Hindu vision, one has to go back into history. Many people have been made to believe that they gained freedom after "a thousand years of slavery." Many became convinced that the Hindus had suffered terribly under the Muslim rule, that the time has come for the Hindus to assert their exclusive dominance over their country and shape it as they wish; even to balance the account of the centuries. Therefore, whatever the constitutional position, India is "Hindu Rashtra," and every facet of governance and authority must reflect Hindu dominance.

The poison that the Hindu right has been injecting into the national bloodstream for 75 years has begun to work, though it is yet to exert a decisive influence and command over the heads and hearts of even 25 percent of the Indian people. The trouble is that due to political reasons, the secular majority is ambivalent about the basic approach and unconscious of the evil design of the chauvinist forces and lost in electoral calculations. And it lacks unity of vision or purpose.

How does the conditioning process work? One is reminded of the fable of a frog which some people wanted to boil, presumably for a meal. So they boiled a pan of water and threw a live frog in the boiling water. The moment the frog touched the boiling water, it jumped out. So the frog-eaters hit upon another approach. They put the frog in normal water, on a burner at low heat. Slowly, the temperature was raised. Eventually the frog lost his consciousness and sank into the pan. Boiling it then was no problem.

The people of India have been for decades treated like the frog in the fable. The water is reaching the boiling point. The frog-eaters are getting ready for the kill! The pan must be taken off the fire; the fire must be extinguished. The frog must be released.

Democratic politics alone will not do, circumscribed as it always is by numerical compulsions of the moment, and the consequent inability of a party seeking power also playing the role of a reformer.

Flawed secularism

Deviations from secularism, even inadvertently over a period, or conscious or unconscious acceptance of small flaws have debilitated the secular order to the point of facilitating the double-speak, "we believe in Hindutva, cultural nationalism, Hindu Rashtra and Hindu Raj but we are secular!" Therefore, secular education and a strictly secular code of public conduct alone can remove the psychological conditioning of the Indian mind by the communal forces which has been going on uninterruptedly, to a large extent unnoticed, but occasionally encouraged by well-meaning counsel, couched in nationalist jargon, for nearly 100 years.

The polity has to reinvent secularism, free it of all its functional flaws, all its folk accretions, all traces of revivalism, all religious obscurantism. Collectively and individually all Indians have to strive for social peace, intergroup harmony and fraternization, ensure justice and equality to all Indians and seek unity in diversity, equality and justice, rule of law and human rights. Plurality and participation are not only the essential elements to build a viable model for all nation-states but for the world-state of tomorrow. That is the pinnacle of glory all Indians should long for, not the possession of nuclear bombs and long-range missiles.

PART III

The Question of *Jihād* and Terrorism in Contemporary Islamic Thought

22 Islam, Terrorism, and Western Misapprehensions   377
    Muhammad Fathi Osman
23 Indonesian Responses to September 11, 2001   387
    Muhammad Sirozi
24 The World Situation After September 11, 2001   408
    Khursid Ahmad

CHAPTER 22

Islam, Terrorism, and Western Misapprehensions

Muhammad Fathi Osman

Whenever any individual or group from Arab or Muslim countries is suspected of an act of violence, especially when the group's name may be related to *jihād* by any etymological or semantic means, a fierce propaganda war is waged in the Western mass media against Islam. Not a single sensible and conscientious human being accepts terrorism, and all mankind ought to cooperate to defend itself against its various forms. No one can tolerate the horror that may befall one or one's beloved in a hijacked aircraft or where explosives are planted. Fighting a disease or any epidemic, however, requires accuracy in tracing the symptoms and analyzing the possible causes, because a correct diagnosis is a prerequisite for a cure.

A few years ago, a university in a country antagonistic to Arabs organized a conference on "Islam and Terrorism." A selection of the papers submitted has been published. One scholar asked why Islam alone, and not other religions, is associated with terrorism, as even the title of the conference implies. His reply is that since Islam has been both a faith and a state and has included *jihād* in its teaching it becomes legitimate to discuss its relation to terrorism. He has ignored the historical relation between Christianity and the Crusades, the wars between the European kings and the Popes, the bloodshed between Catholics and Protestants in the past and the recent events in Bosnia, as well as the colonial aggression which claimed Christianization as a main purpose, supported and blessed by the missionary organizations. Although the ethnic and social grounds for the differences between the Catholics and Protestants in Northern Ireland are obvious, the religious factor cannot be ignored, and several leaders of the loyal unionists with Britain are Protestant ministers.

Even those unsympathetic to the violence in Ulster do not characterize it as "Christian terrorism." Liberation theology is dominant in the social and political struggle in Latin America, and many of the Catholic clergy support the militants by word and action, including the use of weapons. When a high-ranking figure in the Vatican said that he could not imagine Jesus with a gun, others responded that Jesus also could not be imagined standing passive toward social and political tyranny. He could not stand by while the "House of God" was turned into a "den of thieves. And (he) cast out all them that sold and bought in the temple and overthrew the tables of money-changers . . ." (Mat. 21:12–13).

As for Judaism, the scriptures and Jewish history recorded successive military struggles. If Zionism has its roots in Judaism itself – as most Zionists believe – a modern relation to militancy, and violence, has been added to the historical precedents. I do not now criticize any religion for legitimizing a struggle for justice and human rights including the freedom of belief and expression by force when all other peaceful ways are blocked, since Islam, as no one can deny, takes the same stand. A line can be drawn, however, between legitimate use and the abuse of any principle. A just cause may be stained by the malpractice of those who claim to fight for it.

Such an abuse is human and universal, and if we trace mankind's experience in the past and the present, such an abuse cannot be limited to Arabs or Muslims.

Terrorism has become a universal phenomenon or epidemic. Historians, social scientists, lawyers, criminologists, security specialists, and politicians are showing an increasing awareness of the need for more multidisciplinary approaches toward "the growing international incidents of acts of terrorism perpetrated by extremist groups of almost every ideological hue and in every continent," as Yonah Alexander, David Carlton, and Paul Wilkinson, the editors of *Terrorism: Theory and Practice*, have stated (Boulder, CO: Westview Press, 1978).

Exactly what does the word "terrorism" mean? According to the *Encyclopaedia Britannica*, it is "the systematic use of terror or unpredictable violence, against governments, peoples or individuals to attain a political objective. Terrorism has been used by political organizations with both rightist and leftist objectives, by nationalistic and ethnic groups, by revolutionaries and by armies and secret police of governments themselves."

Terrorism, then, can be connected with human nature itself, not with a special group or belief. *State terrorism*, practiced by government employees, should be labeled as terrorism, whatever the excuses may be. A government cannot use the public power and the public revenues, provided by the people to defend their rights and maintain justice, in order to violate those rights and undermine justice, particularly as state terrorism is likely to be more systematic and enduring than individual terrorism. The *Encyclopaedia Britannica* indicates: "Terrorism was adopted as virtually a state policy, though an unacknowledged one, by such totalitarian regimes as those of Nazi Germany and the Soviet Union under Stalin. In these states, arrest, imprisonment, torture and execution were applied without legal guidance or restraints to create a climate of fear and to encourage adherence to the national ideology and the declared economic, social, and political goals of the state."

Such policies of spreading fear are adopted also by many oppressive regimes in Latin America, the Arab world, South Asia and South East Asia, and other regions of the world.

Under United States law, an "act of terrorism" means any activity that involves a violent act or an act dangerous to human life that is a violation of criminal laws, and appears to be intended to intimidate or coerce a civilian population, to influence the policy of a government by intimidation or coercion, to affect the conduct of a government by assassination or kidnapping.

The physical power that has been granted to the human being to defend himself may be abused and thus lead to aggression and violence (Qur'an 2:30). One should try throughout one's life to use the divine gifts, including physical power, according to divine guidance. The earliest violence was practiced when selfishness dominated and the divine guidance for justice and the gift of human intellect were ignored, and thus Cain, the son of Adam, killed his brother Abel (Qur'an 5:27–31).

The *Britannica* continues:

> Terrorism has been practiced throughout history and throughout the world, according to the ancient Greek historian Xenophon (430–349 BC), against enemy populations . . . The Spanish Inquisition used arbitrary arrest, torture, and execution to punish what it viewed as religious heresy. The use of terror was openly advocated by Robespierre as a means of encouraging revolutionary virtue during the French Revolution, leading to the period of his political dominance called the Reign of Terror (1793–4). After the U.S. Civil War (1861–5), defiant Southerners formed a terrorist organization called the Ku Klux Klan to intimidate supporters of Reconstruction. In the latter half of the 19th century, terrorism was adopted by adherents of anarchism in Western Europe, Russia and the United States. They believed that the best way to effect revolutionary political and social change was to assassinate persons in positions of power . . . The 20th century witnessed great changes in the use and practice of terrorism. Terrorism became the hallmark of a number of political movements extending from the extreme right to the extreme left of the political spectrum . . . Terrorism has most commonly become identified, however, with individuals or groups attempting to destabilize or overthrow existing political institutions. It has been used by one or both sides in anti-colonial conflicts (Ireland and the UK, Algeria and France, Vietnam and France/US), in disputes between different national groups over possession of a contested homeland (Palestinians and Israel), in conflicts between different religious denominations (Catholics and Protestants in Northern Ireland), and in internal conflicts between revolutionary forces and established governments (Malaysia, Indonesia, the Philippines, Iran, Nicaragua, El-Salvador, Argentina).

This is an accurate worldwide picture of terrorism and those who are involved in it. Several factors all over the world have contributed to it, at the top of which we may find the social and political tyranny that in many cases initiates state terrorism. Arabs and Muslims are no exceptions in this regard, but Islam opposes such actions. Wilfred Cantwell Smith was fair enough in *Islam in Modern History* to clarify the general climate of suppression and frustration under which Arabs and Muslims suffer: "The society has deteriorated to a point where violence is almost inevitable. . . . It is the expression of the hatred, frustration, vanity and destructive frenzy of a people who long have been the prey of poverty, impotence and fear."[1]

State violence and the masses' frustration because of internal or external factors have led to public violence all over the world. One can list mere examples: the Red Brigades in Italy, the Bader Meinhof gang in West Germany, ETA (the Basques) in Spain, the Direct Action in France, the Red Army in Japan, the Armenians, the Tamil in Sri

Lanka, the Sikhs in India, and others elsewhere. Under a significant title "Keeping Count of Terror," the special correspondent of *The Economist* reported in the issue of July 26, 1986:

> Three months after the bombing of Libya, the temptation is to call it a success. Was it? The Middle East anyway is not the worst part of the world for Americans. The number of Latin American related acts of terrorism in which Americans have been killed over the past five years is on average 40 percent higher than the number of Middle East related acts. In 1985, there were some 86 terrorist acts in Latin America involving U.S. citizens compared to 16 similar incidents in the Middle East. *Contrary to popular American belief, relatively little Middle East terrorism is directed against Americans.* Terrorism in Europe, according to American statistics, accounted for a fifth of all terrorist deaths in 1985. Europe's own groups (IRA, ETA, etc.) – being credited with the highest scores – killed 118 people. Middle Easterners working in Western Europe killed 65.

State terrorism represents a formidable brand of terrorism which should be considered seriously whether it is conducted against internal or external enemies. In 1957, France intercepted an airplane in which leaders of the Algerian Liberation Front were flying from Morocco to Tunisia, and forced it to France, where these leaders were arrested. In 1986, the United States followed this precedent and intercepted an Egyptian airplane which was taking some Palestinians to Tunisia and forced it to land in Sicily. In the mid-1980s, the United States openly allocated large sums to support the Contras, who aimed to overthrow the government in Nicaragua.

Israel practices state terrorism regularly by bombing Palestinian refugee camps in Lebanon and kidnapping from time to time any citizen from any country who allegedly has harmed Israelis in order to try them in Israeli courts and punish them. Since the last Palestinian Intifada, the entire Palestinian lands, which have been administered by the Palestinian authorities according to the Oslo agreement, have come under full crushing Israeli occupation, which carries on daily killings, demolishing of homes, and erosion of farms.

The former white minority government of South Africa conducts formidable state terrorism against the majority, including the torture of detainees. A child has been shown on an American TV channel with a deformed skull as a result of torture, and some detainees died under torture, as in the case of a white doctor who supported that national struggle. State terrorism has been practiced under totalitarian and despotic regimes in the former communist bloc and in many countries of the Third World, where human rights are mere rhetoric and often just a political and legal decoration.

The modern state, by having an arsenal of oppressive arms through advanced technology supported by continuously increasing political and legal restraining power, forces frustrated dissidents to use violence in order to call public and international attention to their grievances. Advanced technology provides the modern state, as constitutional jurists and political scientists have constantly observed, with developed spying devices and crowd-dispersing equipment that undermines the rights of expression and assembly even if such rights are acknowledged in the first place. Besides, the interference of the state and its authorities, supported by its legal and police forces, engenders bitter feelings of helplessness and frustration among the public. Labor unions, political parties, parliament, and the mass media may be directed and controlled by small interest groups, if not by state agents openly, who do not allow the ordinary citizen any channel for expressing his views and demands. The courts should represent an essential safeguard for the public, but the costs of litigation are often too high for the average citizen, and impossible for the poor. Until some effective way can be found for ordinary citizens to voice their complaints and for the state to respond justly to them, they will be tempted to look to other dissidents to make their feelings heard through extraordinary action. "Technological advances" – says *Encyclopaedia Britannica* – "such as automatic weapons and compact, electronically detonated explosives give terrorists (on the other hand) a new mobility – and lethality. Terrorism's public impact has been greatly magnified by the use of modern communications media."

Italian anarchists called the acts of violence and terrorism "the propaganda of the deed." Even those who may be sympathetic to the cause of any terrorist group, however, as the same source states, "may be alienated by an indiscriminate use of terrorism."

Besides, socio-psychological factors have contributed to the violent attitude of younger generations. Deterioration in family and school discipline for youngsters in addition to social and economic deprivation may lead them to take revenge for such negligence without concern for others. Some television programs, as has been amply proven by recent research, may encourage violence and clarify some of its practices and techniques. Certain games reflect and encourage violent attitudes. The remarkable increase of crimes against the elderly, women, and children, of the use of drugs, and of sexual assaults connected with violence and murder, indicate that television cannot be separated from the general psychopathic phenomena. One can see in Erich Fromm's book, *The Anatomy of Human Destructiveness*, how widely and deeply the roots of aggression and violence are spreading in contemporary society. Like any other community, Arab and Muslim groups will include some psychopathic elements. Many politicians and mass media professionals can always remember scattered incidents of violence attributed to Arabs or Muslims, while forgetting the Muslim world's long history of peaceful and legitimate political performance, including the patient negotiation in the United Nations and other international organizations!

Moorehead Kennedy, who was in the US foreign service for 23 years and was the second in command in the Tehran Embassy when he and 52 other American officials were seized as hostages for 444 days revealed to *The Times* on January 20, 1986, how his captivity led him to an enlightenment about the suffering of those who are labeled as terrorists from his country's unjust and aggressive policies:

> I was suddenly free from having to think like a foreign service officer, free from state department smugness and assumptions – attitudes I had been a part of. I went through a form of mental hygiene. I began to see more clearly that *if we are to confront terrorism we have to change our old-fashioned assumptions*. The crisis held important lessons for Americans, but we didn't learn. The whole thing was treated by the American people as an aberration and the Iranians were dismissed as mad. The Reagan administration makes the old mistakes and is making them in Libya. It makes an effort not to hear. The only way out of this is for

us to *start listening to the Middle East.* We have to *reconsider our attitudes of superiority.* We think and act as if we are God's chosen instrument. We have been brought up to assume that the rest of the world thinks – or should think – as we do. . . . I am not condoning or caving in to terrorism, but we must know the other side. *Terrorism challenges our thinking, not our military might.* I can say these things because my record is good. No one can question my patriotism or my service to my country. . . . When we were captured, we were seeing the end of the American moment. *I could see myself as having a part in an historic evolution.* When I was tied and blindfolded, my captor hissed "Vietnam" in my ear. These people *both admire and envy us.* "We like the Americans, but we hate the United States," they said. We have disappointed them. In the Middle East and elsewhere, *people take the Declaration of Independence more seriously than we do.* We have talked of freedom and human rights, but our conduct in the world has caused disillusionment and bitterness and made us hypocrites. As a victim of terrorism, I abominate it, but it holds up *a mirror* to us. As I say: *we should start listening.*

When Moorehead Kennedy came home to a hero's welcome after his release, he turned down a good position and resigned from the foreign service, since he believed that "you can't be a part of an organization and go around criticizing it in public." Instead, he devoted himself to spreading the lessons of "America's traumatic experience with the Iranian revolution." What he says about it made him a controversial figure among Americans who heard his lectures on terrorism and saw him on television. Through the "Council of International Understanding," which he established in New York, he lectured and wrote tirelessly on terrorism and its challenges to the American mind: "I talk to parents and church groups and schools, wherever people are committed to serious listening and discussion." Similarly, the Italian actress Sandra Milo witnessed the moment of truth and enlightenment during the attack on Rome airport, in which she and her daughter miraculously escaped death. In an interview which was published on December 31, 1985, she stressed that a *miserable life leads one to plant misery in other's lives,* and she gave as an example the situation of Napoli and southern Italy.

As Moorehead Kennedy said, some "make efforts not to hear and try instead to blame terrorism on the victims or their beliefs." Islam teaches believers how to cure egotism and remove hostility and aggression, through both faith and ethics on one side and law and authority on the other. Justice in all fields, social and economic, political and legal, internal and universal, should be maintained. The protection of the human soul, body, property, mind, dignity, family, and freedom of belief and expression represent the main goals of *sharī'ah,* as Muslim jurists have concluded. The divine teachings indicate how grave is the taking of human life. If anyone slays a human being – unless it be (in punishment) for murder or for spreading mischief on earth – it shall be as "*though he had slain all mankind; whereas, if anyone saves a life, it shall be as though he had saved all the lives of mankind*" (Qur'an 5:32).

Those who spread mischief and destruction are condemned and punished severely – whatever their arguments may be: "There is a man whose speech may please you greatly in this world, and who cites God as witness to what is in his heart, and is moreover exceedingly skillful in argument. But when he turns his back, his aim everywhere is to spread mischief through the earth and destroy crops and progeny, and God does not love mischief. And whenever one says to him 'fear God' his fake pride (and arrogance) drives him into sin, wherefore hell will be his allotted portion – and how vile a resting place" (2:204–6). "It is but a just recompense for those who wage war against God and His apostle and endeavor to spread mischief on earth that they are being slain . . . or are being (entirely) banished from (the face of) the earth; such is their ignominy in this world, but in the life to come (yet more) awesome suffering awaits them" (5:33).

Universal cooperation is required to banish terror "from the face of the earth" by securing justice either through reconciliation or fighting the transgressors: "Hence, if two groups of believers fall to fighting, make peace between them; but then, if one of the two (groups) aggresses against the other, fight against the one that commits the aggression until it reverts to God's commandment; and if they revert make peace between them with justice" (49:91). The party that initiates aggression should be treated in the end with justice as soon as it reverts to God's commandments, because only justice can cut the vicious circle or reciprocal violence.

War is allowed in Islam against those who attack the faithful. "And fight in God's cause *against those who are waging war against you*, and do not transgress limits, for God does not love transgressors" (2:190). Translating "*jihād*" as "holy war" is misleading, since Islam has never justified war to impose its faith on others by force. War fought as *jihād* aims to prevent intimidation (2:193), not to spread it. Different races are equal members of one humanity and they have to develop their relations and cooperation (49:12); and justice and fairness should dominate the relations and cooperation (60:8). No collective accusations or punishments can be accepted by Islamic justice, and every individual has to be accountable only for his own deeds and should never bear another's burden (53:38–9). War should be declared openly (8:58), and conducted against the combatants only; therefore the women and children, the elderly, the clergy, and the monks, as well as the peasants and all who have not been involved in fighting Muslims directly, should not be hurt by them. A distinction should be made between a legitimate struggle or revolutionary activity on one side and common criminality on the other, although drawing such a line may be extremely difficult. All houses of worship have to be defended, whatever the belief of the worshippers may be: "For had God not enabled people to defend themselves against one another, (all) monasteries and churches and mosques, in which God's name is abundantly extolled, surely would have been destroyed. And God will most certainly succor Him who succors His cause" (22:400). Even the life of plants and animals should be preserved by the army except in pressing need. A martyrdom is quite distinctive from a meaningless and fruitless suicide: "And let not your own hands throw you unto destruction, and persevere in doing good" (2:195). The goal of legitimate war is to prevent mischief and aggression (2:251), and to replace them with righteousness and justice (11:41). Facts about any matter of war or peace should be presented honestly and objectively, and the concerned authorities are responsible for providing accurate information to the public through the available media: "And if any matter pertaining to (public) safety or fear come within their knowledge, they spread it abroad – whereas, if they would but refer it to the Apostle and to those from among the believers who have been entrusted with authority, such of them who investigate should indeed know (directly the truth of) the matter" (4:83).

Can we expect, in the near future, more fairness in dealing with Islam, and more seriousness in discussing such a widespread epidemic as terrorism, at least among deep thinkers and responsible writers, instead of *a priori* judgments on Islam or Muslims?

Can we hope for less indifference – sometimes deliberate – to state terrorism, and to social and political injustice? Islam has restricted legitimate war with numerous rules and conditions, which match and often exceed modern international regulations. The *jihād* of Islam is no more or less than any legitimate struggle for justice, which many contemporary political powers and intellectuals insist on ignoring whenever they discuss terrorism and Islam.

However, the thousands of victims of the terrorist attacks in New York and Washington on September 11, 2001, the Muslims who carried out the suicide attacks, and the way through which these attacks were executed, have brought again the issue of "Islam and Terrorism" to the fore. On May 26, 2003, a little less than two years after the horrible attack, and following other shocking attacks in Riyadh and Casablanca, *Time* published a lengthy story by Michael Elliot under a significant title, "Why War on Terror Will Never End." The author meaningfully indicates,

> After the latest blasts, no one is talking about turning any tide. Instead, the world is focused again on mourning, on soul-searching, on how to deliver an effective response. Make no mistake about it: Islamic extremists are still angry enough, and organized enough to cause considerable damage to the US and its allies . . . interrogations quickly established that the terrorists were 'indoctrinated, trained, and organized and put into motion by foreign members of the international *jihād* movement . . . in the past 18 months, terrorists have struck from the Philippines to Tunisia, and suspected attackers have been detained from Rome to Chicago. Determining whether the West is gaining in the fight against terrorism requires interpreting shadowy, shapeless data. Yet this much can be said: international terrorism existed long before 9–11 and will continue long after it. . . . It's an apt and frightening image: the emergence of a raw, repulsive killer, when the environmental conditions are on the rise. Al-Qaeda rose to prominence by showing its deadly mantle over various Islamic terrorist groups – in places like the Philippines, Uzbekistan, Algeria – whose principal mission has been directed against local governments. Bin Laden provided an ideological justification, rooted in a super-fundamentalist Islamic doctrine, for internationalizing those conflicts.

Now the relation of such terrorist attacks to Islam in its faith, ethics, and law can always be strongly argued. Their relation to Muslims and their religious views cannot be argued and we have to see how such views have developed. It is obvious that the technological advancement has provided many horrible tools of killing and destruction for individual or group terrorists, and Muslims are not immune from such a trend to which several material and socio-psychological factors contribute, even if Islam as a faith is not by itself responsible for it. Religions and ideologies can always be misused or abused to support certain thoughts or actions when other objective circumstances may provide the effective causes for them. In the same way, such a technological advancement provides the state also with smashing tools for oppression and state terrorism. In such circumstances of terror, material, devastation, and human loss, the morality, or to put it more sharply the immorality of such an evil giant which has been emitted, whether it may be manipulated by individuals or by the state authorities has to be essentially considered far from any fantasy or illusion. Religious directions cannot be formed through coercion and intimidation, for they have to come out of free thinking and genuine conviction, as the Qur'an repeatedly emphasizes: "No coercion can ever be made in matters of faith" (2:256); "And had your Lord so willed, all those who live on earth would surely have attained to faith, all of them; do you, then, think that you could compel people to believe? (10:99); "And had your Lord so willed, He could surely have made all mankind one single community, but [He willed it otherwise, and so] they continue to hold divergent views, [all of them] save those upon whom your Lord has bestowed his grace [through using God's gift of the human mind and God's guidance as a criteria for settling differences]; and to this end He has created them [all to test them through their dealing with one another through and to requite them accordingly for what they freely choose to do]" [11:118–19].

A legacy of *jihād* in modern times was initially developed through a historical era of Muslim expansion and has been invested on through the struggle against colonialism and imperialism in the last two centuries, and has provided the conceptual and mobilizing note for those who may be inclined to terrorism in their given material and sociopsychological circumstances. The "terrorist" trend may be supported sometimes by an admiration of the past and a fervor to restore its glories intellectually and virtually – a tendency which may be called Salafiyyah or Salafism – in its wider sense, which is not merely limited to faith and theology and may involve militancy and violence. The hostile tendency against colonialism and imperialism has developed into hostility for Western domination in general, and for Westernization with regard to those who have felt a vigorous bond with the Islamic past and its restoration. Such a trend may target through its hostilities and struggle the local rulers as Western cultural–political products and agents, and this target – in its turn – may be developed into anti-secularism and a call for the establishment of an Islamic state.

In different degrees a sharp polarization developed and accelerated between Salafism and the establishment of an Islamic state on one side, comprising sometimes militancy and violence, modernism, Westernization, and secularism on the other side. In accommodation of contradictions and the past, coexistence between the two opposite trends has become gradually unattainable. Besides, Islamic political activism has not been allowed by the governments concerned to work openly with various justifications. Whether violence was the cause for the governmental restrictions or the result, the lack of democratic fundamentals – especially the freedom of belief and opinion, expression and assembly, which are within the essentials of Islam and which enable the opposite concepts to argue and challenge each other peacefully – contributed to the rise of militancy and violence.

As for the struggle against Western domination and specifically against the United States, violence has become the only weapon. Globalism has supported the US in claiming a need for confronting militarily the Muslim aggressors in its different bases, and has provided such militants or terrorists with world publicity and communications.

However, no chance for a constructive dialogue has existed. The efforts of official *ulama*, who are merely state employees, have never impressed such militants nor the

Muslim public. On the other hand the horrors and human loss of contemporary terrorism should touch the religious conscience of those who claim a commitment to Islam among the Muslim militants or the oppressive governments. A serious thinking of the realities of time and a genuine practice of *ijtihād* are essential to weigh and plan for concurrent Muslim activism instead of the stagnated repetition of juristic texts, which represented a merely human understanding that developed under particular historical circumstances and did not represent the permanent indication of the Islamic principles of the Qur'an and Sunnah.

In addition to the effect of *jihād* literature and practice and the contemporary juristic stagnation with regard to considering the contemporary changing circumstances, the emerging Muslim militancy and violence has been influenced by certain factors in the present world, which have contributed to a crystallization intellectually and practically. The Maoist views about hijacking airplanes and the practice of violence against civilians as a necessity for the struggle against Western imperialism have provided a basis for a Muslim militant argument, using some Islamic terms to turn the struggle into an Islamic *jihād* against the foreign occupation and domination and for establishing an Islamic state, of which the picture and the main features and distinguishing constituents have been vague. On the Muslim side, the Islamic revolution in Iran and the Islamic *jihād* against the Soviet occupation of Afghanistan, which was supported by the US, have provided an enormous ideological and practical assistance for the Muslim militants. The Iranian and Afghani experiences have revived the traditional conceptual and practical juristic knowledge of *jihād*. It is essential, then, on the Muslim side, to rethink *jihād* and re-read its texts in the Qur'an and Sunnah in the light of contemporary world circumstances, especially the technological development which has made the use of force enormously damaging, whether on the individual or governmental side. Our contemporary world strongly urges Muslims to practice *ijtihād* in understanding and implementing the Islamic legal sources, and to secure human rights in general and freedom of opinion and expression and assembly in particular, to allow an open, peaceful and constructive coexistence of an interaction between divergent views instead of underground hostilities and plans for destructive confrontations.

Note

1. W.C. Smith, *Islam in Modern History* (New York: The New American Library, 1957), 163.

CHAPTER 23

Indonesian Responses to September 11, 2001

Muhammad Sirozi

The events of September 11, 2001 made the world aware of the existence, danger, and scale of international terrorism. They also raised concerns about the relationship between religion and politics, terrorism and American foreign policy, and the United States as "superpower," and the Muslim world. These concerns have motivated people from around the world belonging to all social, political, and religious backgrounds to respond. This chapter argues that Indonesians have been sympathetic to the people of the United States and discusses Indonesian responses to September 11 in light of their deep implications for American–Indonesian relations.

In this chapter, I discuss the responses of two of Indonesia's top leaders, Megawati Soekarno Putri, President of the Republic of Indonesia, and Amien Rais, Chairman of *Majelis Permusyawaratan Rakyat* (MPR) or the People's Consultative Assembly, the highest state institution in Indonesia. These two leaders' responses may not represent the responses of the Indonesian people, but may represent those of the formal leadership. This chapter assumes that Megawati and Amien Rais's responses to September 11 have been shaped by their understanding of the possible implications of the tragedy on both domestic and international politics in Indonesia. In this regard, the most important subsequent events seem to have been US President George Bush's attitude and language in responding to terrorism, US Deputy Defense Secretary Paul Wolfowitz's accusation that Indonesia is a hideout for terrorists, and Bush's military campaign in Afghanistan.

"Deepest Condolences and Sympathy"

The events of September 11 were horrendous. In less than two hours on the morning of the attacks, almost 3000 innocent civilians were murdered in New York, Washington, DC, and Pennsylvania. Ralph Boyce, Ambassador of the United States to Indonesia, notes that more people died in those attacks than on any other single day in American history since one of the worst battles of the American Civil War in 1862.[1] The casualties were citizens from more than 80 different nations. The nature of the terrorist attacks, according to Boyce, "was something unprecedented and up until the time they occurred, completely unexpected. The terrorists hijacked passenger planes and intentionally crashed them into buildings."[2] People all around the world witnessed the attacks, particularly those on the World Trade Center. They were "evil, despicable acts of terror," said George Bush; it is "the new evil in our world today," said the UK Prime Minister Tony Blair; and "it's unbelievable," said Palestinian leader Yasser Arafat.[3] "This was vast, vast, destruction," said Simmons, describing what he saw after the tragedy.[4] "The terrorist attacks of September 11," Gehman compares, "have shaken the U.S. more than any event since the bombing of Pearl Harbor."[5]

President Bush initially responded to the attacks with incredulity. He was particularly curious about the motives of the attackers. "Americans are asking," he said, "why do they [the terrorists] hate us?" He went on to answer his own question and said that the attacks not only aimed to destroy the World Trade Center and Pentagon buildings, but also aimed to destroy American values and systems, such as democracy, freedom, and way of life. In his words:

> They hate what we see right here in this chamber – a democratically elected government. Their leaders are self-appointed. They hate our freedoms – our freedom of religion, our freedom of speech, our freedom to vote and assemble and disagree with each other. They want to overthrow existing governments in many Muslim countries . . . They want to drive Christians and Jews out of vast regions of Asia and Africa . . . These terrorists kill not merely to end lives, but to disrupt and end a way of life. With every atrocity, they hope that America grows fearful, retreating from the world and forsaking our friends. They stand against us, because we stand in their way. We are not deceived by their pretences to piety. We have seen their kind before. They are the heirs of all murderous ideologies of the twentieth century.[6]

Former US Secretary of State George P. Shultz shared Bush's views and heatedly said, "We're not going to allow these terrible people to change our way of life."[7]

September 11 not only prompted the curiosity of President Bush, but also of many others around the world. The tragedy raised theological, cultural, moral, and political questions. Markham and Abu-Rabi' observe, "Many have asked where God was as the airplanes were flown into the World Trade Center and the Pentagon. Many have wondered about 'true Islam' and how those who committed these acts could claim to be acting in the name of Allah."[8] The tragedy also raises ethical questions: "Is the war just? How do we balance human rights and the need for security?"[9] "Why did this happen?"; "Will life ever be the same again?"; Whose agenda matters"; "What's going on?"; "What have I left?"; and "Is there a balm in Giled?" These are some questions raised by pastors all around the United States in sermons after September 11.[10]

Although occurring in the United States, sane humans considered these attacks as directed not just at America, but also at the whole of world humanity. The devastation from these attacks touched the hearts of people around the world and became the concern of all world leaders, many of whom expressed their sympathy and solidarity soon afterward. "We are all New Yorkers," said a leading French scholar.[11] Cuba, China, Iran, and Libya expressed their solidarity. Some, however, were not touched by the tragedy and expressed depressing contrary reactions. In Iraq, for example, state television claimed that the US deserved what it got.[12]

There has been much speculation on the causes of the attacks. Markham identifies four general interpretations. The first interpretation is that of mainstream Americans as represented by President Bush, which assumes that the attacks were triggered by hatred of American values. The second interpretation is the pro-Israel position, which assumes that the attacks were part of a continuing antagonism towards Israel. The third interpretation is pro-Arab and assumes that the attacks were the result of a wrong-headed American policy in the Middle East. The fourth interpretation is that of Christian fundamentalism, as represented by Pat Robertson and Jerry Falwell. Although apologizing for their position, fundamentalist Christian leaders claimed that the United States deserved such a tragedy because of the pressures of "abortionists, feminists, gays, and the American Civil Liberties Union (ACLU), among others."[13] Clearly, there has been a mixture of the cultural, religious, and political in the interpretations of the causes of September 11.

In Indonesia, the most populous Muslim country in the world,[14] the events of September 11 were cause for sorrow and deep regret. Amien Rais, Chairman of Indonesian People's Consultative Assembly, reflected the national mood by saying that 99 percent of Muslims in Indonesia were "shocked and stunned" when they heard about September 11 and its casualties.[15] For Rais, the attacks challenge Islamic teachings on how human beings treat one another. "All Muslims have to respect the sanctity of human beings."[16] Quoting from the Qur'an, he explained that killing innocent people is like killing all humanity; while saving one soul is like saving all humanity.[17] This sense of "shock" also inspired President Megawati to respond to September 11. Douglas Ramage, representative to Indonesia from the Asia Foundation, describes the reaction as "immediate," "sympathetic," "swift," and "spontaneous."[18] A statement released by State Secretariat of the Republic of Indonesia on September 11, 2001 says:

> The Government of the Republic of Indonesia learned with great shock of the tragic incidents that occurred today simultaneously in New York and Washington, D.C. The Government of Indonesia condemned those barbaric and indiscriminate attacks that have resulted in great numbers of innocent people losing their lives and sustaining wounds as well as material damage caused by these attacks. The Government of Indonesia expressed its deepest condolences and sympathy to the Government and people of the United States of America, especially to the bereaved families who lost their loved ones in this tragedy. The Government of Indonesia has instructed its missions in New York and Washington, D.C. to take all necessary measures to assist any Indonesian citizen who might be among the victims in those incidents.

Megawati Soekarno Putri was the first Muslim leader to visit the United States after the attacks. At a meeting with President Bush on September 19, 2001, only one week after the tragedy, she expressed sympathy and pledged Indonesia's cooperation in combating international terrorism.[20] The meeting ended with a joint statement condemning terrorism and asserting a commitment to combat it.[21]

Megawati and her advisers expected that their visit would have a positive impact on US images of Indonesia's national and international politics. Indeed, President Bush himself was very appreciative. However, Megawati received no such appreciation from her own people upon returning to Indonesia. She faced strong criticism from many political groups in the country. She was shocked by attacks from the right on her Islamic credentials, for expressing support of the United States, and from the left from nationalists, who criticized her speech in Houston, Texas, inviting American business to come to Indonesia. Both groups considered her a "lackey of the Americans."[22] Sukma, director of studies at the Center for Strategic and International Studies and a member of Muhammadiyah, one of the largest Islamic movements in Indonesia, was right when he said, "September 11 is a test for the Megawati government: Will it stand the test of not being co-opted by the United States?"[23]

Despite the criticism, Megawati was able to handle the domestic protests calmly and keep her promise to Bush to support the fight against international terrorism. However, when Bush ordered American troops to invade Afghanistan on October 7, 2001, to capture Osama bin Laden and his group, Megawati's critics put even more pressure on her. The critics were successful in shaking the commitment that she had made with Bush. Indonesian groups, particularly hard-line Islamic groups, demonstrated in Jakarta and other big cities in the country to reject Bush's military action in Afghanistan and urged Megawati to condemn it also. Since she was reluctant to do so, protesters accused her of being a servant of the United States. The presidential palace in central Jakarta became a favorite spot for the protesters. Since the collapse of the Suharto regime in 1998, Indonesia has had weak governments, including the current one. Taking this into account, Megawati had to thread between the nationalist left and the Islamic right.[24] She tried to calm domestic criticism by criticizing the US campaign in Afghanistan. She described it as "the spilling of blood to avenge the spilling of blood."[25] On October 8, 2001, the Department of Foreign Affairs released a statement containing six points that expressed deep reservations about the military action undertaken by Washington in Afghanistan.[26]

Domestic reaction to the speech and statement was remarkable. Protesters changed their theme from anti-Megawati to anti-America and, of course, their favorite spot moved from the presidential palace to the US embassy, home of the US Ambassador and the location of US related offices and businesses, such as McDonald's in Jakarta and other big cities, such as Ujung Pandang, Surabaya, Yogyakarta, and Bandung. Most of the protesters were members of hard-liner Islamic organizations, such as *Front Pembela Islam* (FPI) or Islamic Defense Group, *Laskar Jihad*, *Majelis Mujahidin Indonesia* (MMI) or Indonesian Council of Jihad Fighters, JAMI (*Jamaah al-Ikhwan al-Muslimin Indonesia*), *Hizb al-Tahrir* (Party of Liberation), and *Jamaah Islamiyyah*. Members of *Kesatuan Aksi Mahasiswa Muslim Indonesia* (KAMMI) and supporters of *Partai Keadilan* (PK) or the Justice Party were also on the streets of Jakarta and other big cities throughout the country protesting against Bush's military actions in Afghanistan. "America, genuine terrorist" was one of the most popular banners displayed by the protesters. Small radical Islamic groups demonstrated at the US embassy and threatened "sweeps" of American tourists from hotels.[27]

In response, the Megawati government deployed security forces to protect the US embassy and American assets throughout the country. Mainstream moderate Muslim leaders, including the head of Muhammadiyah, Ahmad Syafi'I Ma'arif, who was shocked by the earlier vitriol, began to speak out, to calm the protesters. But since the daily media reported the viciousness of US troops in Afghanistan, anti-American sentiment has never really gone from the minds of the Indonesian public. Indonesian objections to the US Middle East policy and military actions in Afghanistan remained firm and neither the government nor religious leaders could do much about it. No anti-America rally was banned and no protesters were caught or punished. Ramage is curious about this situation and says, "Maybe there is latent sympathy with the views articulated by radicals, or fear of further domestic consequences."[28] Well, maybe. But Megawati may find facing the growing Islamic politics in the country very difficult, because the protesters often have close connections with powerful opportunist politicians who are not hesitant to use religious issues as political commodities in order to spread anti-Megawati sentiment. These politicians would not hesitate to use religious issues to overthrow Megawati from her presidential office. In addition to this political difficulty, the existing legal system under Megawati's weak government does not seem to have sufficient confidence and capability to handle such massive protests. Above all, Megawati's sloppy leadership seems to be insufficient to direct various social and political forces in the country in one policy direction.

Although very quick, warm, sympathetic, and appreciated by President Bush, the Indonesian response to September 11 as represented by President Megawati was not appreciated at home. It even triggered direct political conflict between Megawati and radical Islamic groups in the country. Moreover, it has created a plethora of inconveniences in American–Indonesian relations. Megawati's experience tells us that there seems to be a very big gap between what she was doing and what her people wanted her to do. It also demonstrates that relations between Megawati and radical Islamic groups in the country are very sensitive. Radical Islamic groups seem to have been a significant domestic factor affecting the way Megawati responded to September 11. They make it hard for the President to establish consistent home and foreign policies. Indeed, there has been a growing belief in Indonesian society that an Islamic government is urgently needed in order to save the country from economic, political, and moral collapse. Indeed, a survey conducted in November, 2002, by *Pusat Pengkajian Islam dan Masyarakat* (PPIM) or the Center for the Study of Islam and Society based at the State Islamic University in Jakarta shows that 71 percent of respondents were in favor of the application of Islamic (*shari'ah*) law by the state and 54 percent said that some radical Islamic groups that suggest the implementation of the *shari'ah*, such as *Front Pembela Islam* (FPI) or Islamic Defenders Front and *Laskar Jihad* must be supported. Despite the accuracy and viability of such a survey, this result strongly indicates the potential growth of Islamic radical groups in Indonesia.[29]

If appropriate measures are not taken, radical groups will be a huge problem for Megawati in national and international politics, particularly in managing American–Indonesian relations. It will be very difficult for her to respond to their demands for better representation of Islamic values in state policies and react to their anti-American sentiments.

"With Us or with the Terrorists":"We Don't Love a Bowing Mentality"

On the evening of September 11, President Bush delivered a public speech and stated that the United States would make no distinction between the terrorists who committed the atrocious acts and those who harbored them. He also stated that he would go forward to defend freedom and all that is good and just in this world.[30] On September 20, nine days after the attacks, Bush delivered a speech in a joint session of Congress and to the American people explaining his concrete plans to retaliate and said that "every nation, in every region, now has a decision to make. Either you are with us, or you are with the terrorists."[31] Clearly, Bush expects cooperation from his allies to combat the terrorists and feels entitled to command other nations to participate in the combat. To justify his actions and commands, Bush claims that his plan is "a battle of good against evil."[32] The details of the Bush government's plans were explained by Ralph Boyce, US Ambassador in Jakarta, when he delivered a speech at Paramadina Mulya University on February 25, 2002. "We are committed to the fight against terrorism," said Boyce, "because terrorism threatens the very democracy, human rights, peace and prosperity that people all over the world cherish and to which we believe all people are entitled." "Terrorist actions," he adds, "destroy a sense of security."[34] "The United States," he further adds, "has quickly worked with individual nations and multilaterally to put together an international coalition of more than 180 nations, including Indonesia, that are committed to the fight against terrorism."[35] Boyce believes that al-Qaeda has terrorist cells all over the world – in the United States, Europe, and Southeast Asia – and that they must be prevented from carrying out further terrorist attacks. He explained that the fight against terrorism is not a fight on the battlefield only, but a fight on many fronts, including the diplomatic, financial, and educational.[36] Boyce further explained that nations and individuals must work through their legal and educational systems and religious communities to promote justice, tolerance, respect for the rights of others, and democratic ideals in order to prevent extremism from taking root and growing.[37]

The Indonesian response to the content of Bush's message was very positive, but the response to his commanding attitude was very negative. There has been a strong commitment among Indonesian leaders with regard to international joint efforts to fight terrorism. This commitment was made by President Megawati when she met President Bush in Washington six days after the terrorist attacks. She was one of the first foreign leaders who expressed deep condolences to President Bush and the American people for the tragedy and a commitment to fight terrorism. By the end of the meeting, Megawati and Bush issued a Joint Statement on Terrorism and Religious Tolerance.[38] "Since that time [the meeting]," said Boyce who was present at the meeting, "Indonesia has cooperated with the United States and with the international community in the fight against terrorism."[39] Indeed, he observes, Indonesia has broadened its cooperation with regional and international organizations, including ASEAN, the Organization of the Islamic Conference, and other countries in the Asia-Pacific region. Boyce also observes that Indonesia is involved in countering terrorism efforts with the Philippines, Singapore and Malaysia, including information and intelligence sharing.

Indonesia has signed a Memorandum of Understanding with the Australian government on counter-terrorist efforts. Indonesia has engaged in a regional dialogue on terrorism through APEC. In response to the request from the UN Security Council for all nations to freeze the assets of suspected terrorists and terrorist organizations, Indonesia conducted an investigation and reported to the UN that it had found no assets of groups or individuals with suspected links to al-Qaeda in Indonesia. Boyce gives a very positive response to what he has observed and said in his speech: "We appreciate Indonesia's support in the war against terrorism and look forward to continued, even closer cooperation in what promises to be a long and arduous, but also extremely critical, effort."[40] So, despite the domestic difficulties that she has to face with regard to America–Indonesia relations, Megawati seems to have been able to maintain her positive image in the eyes of the Bush administration.

Along with Megawati, Amien Rais too has used all opportunities to explain Indonesian commitment to fight terrorism. Rais states what he claims to be the position of Indonesian people:

> Let's be a smart nation. We must find the terrorists wherever they are. Whether they are al-Qaeda or not, whether they are Muslim, Christians, Buddhists, or Hinduists, communist, Confucians, or whomever; whether they are from ethnic A, B, or C, they must be given equal punishment. Principally, they are not human beings. They are evils with human face. They are the Satan who appears as the children of Adam.[41]

Clearly, this is the strongest condemnation issued by a top leader of a Muslim country with regard to terrorism. In a 45-minute meeting with Australian Prime Minister John Howard during his short visit to Bali on October 17 and 18, 2002, Rais expressed what he described as the "Indonesian commitment to fight terrorism without further delay."[42] He told Howard, "We will not hesitate to put to justice the perpetrators of this violent act [in Bali], regardless of their religion, institutional, ideological background or the mass support they enjoy in this country or elsewhere."[43] Prime Minister Howard appreciated Rais's gesture and openness to conducting a joint effort between national and international police forces in resolving the tragic incident as soon as possible. Before ending the meeting, Rais reaffirmed his commitment. As he said to Howard: "I will put my weight for Indonesia to work hand in hand with the international community to combat terrorism on the basis of mutual respect."[44] Indeed, it was reported that the two leaders parted on a friendly and warm note, as both understood the importance of cooperation and the mutual importance of fighting terrorism in all its forms.

On Friday, January 18, 2002, when he visited Thai Prime Minister Thaksin Shinawatra, Rais again discussed Indonesia's commitment to combat terrorism. The two Asian leaders agreed to intensify efforts. Rais reemphasized his commitment to fight terrorism when he was questioned by Channel *NewAsia* in Bangkok. "Where they are, the terrorists," he said, "we [Indonesian leaders] are more than willing to crack down on them."[45] Rais also told Channel *NewAsia* that he supports the recent arrests of al-Qaeda agents in Malaysia and Singapore. "Any Indonesians involved," he adds, "should also be brought to justice, with proof."[46]

Amien Rais also articulated Indonesia's commitment to fight terrorism during his visit to the University of Leiden, Netherlands, on Wednesday, March 20, 2002, in a speech that Radio Netherlands described as a "nationalistic performance."[47] This time, Rais not only expressed Indonesian commitment, but also voiced his concerns about the attitude taken by the Bush government. He responded to Bush's "either with us or with the terrorists" remark very critically and, to some extent, very angrily. In Rais's view, Bush was trying to dictate to the whole world. Rais asserted that Indonesia did not want to be so treated, though it remains committed to fighting terrorism. As he said in his speech: "Indonesia will continue to assist the United States of America in fighting terrorism, . . . but [Indonesia] does not want to be dictated to."[48] Bush's words, said Rais, "made us feel rather uneasy."[49] He added that those words were "a rather excessive and unintelligent way to speak."[50] "Being so eager to fight terrorism," Rais criticizes, "has made George Bush lose his [reason?] rationale." Such a remark, Rais further criticized, reflects a "simplistic way of thinking" and is "dangerous."[51] Rais explained to his audience that terrorism was being used by bigger nations in order to discredit weaker nations and impose upon them their own interests. In his words:

> I want to tell you that there is a big nation who lost her sparring partner after the collapse of Soviet Union. This big nation will find itself fine if it has an enemy, and now the Muslim world has been targeted as its enemy. This means that after the Cold War against communism, there is now a Cold War against Islam. And because Indonesia is the largest Muslim country, we are being disturbed and, unfortunately, because of our weak national leadership, the big nation seems to be successful in disturbing us.[52]

This quotation clearly evidences Rais's deep concern about the character of US foreign policy as a single superpower, the policies' inherent threat to Islam, and the inability of the Megawati government's leadership to handle the new challenges presented.

Rais argued in his speech that every nation, including Indonesia, must be left free to choose its own way to fight terrorism without being under the command of the Americans. "I want to tell you," he said, "let us together develop a consciousness that everything that occurs within this country [Indonesia], must be solved by us, without bowing to the foreigners, because the foreigners need to control us and the interests of our nation."[53] Nevertheless, Rais seems to doubt Megawati's ability to handle the situation. He said, "From my reading of international papers, I find that our national leadership is on the brink of collapse."[54] He stressed that "national leadership seems to be a very determinant factor for the future of our nation [Indonesia]." He predicts that if Indonesian leaders fail to do their jobs, Indonesia will be a nation of pariah or a *pariah state*, an *untouchable* nation, isolated from the rest of the world. At present, he adds, other nations no longer see us as a big and civilized nation. "In order to be able to fight terrorism with our own way and will," Rais continued, "we need strong national leadership."[55] The major challenge for Indonesia, Rais believes, is for it to mitigate the negative effects and optimize the positive effects that September 11 had on domestic politics. In this regard, he stressed that Indonesia needs a visionary leader. "If our national leader failed to understand *what's going on in this world*, with no vision," Rais said, "he or she will not have self-esteem, and people will only be the victims of his or her lack of leadership."[56] For Rais, Indonesian leaders must have the capability to create jobs, decide direction, and make policies in order to solve national and international problems.[57]

Clearly, despite sharing Megawati's positive reaction to the content of Bush's message about fighting terrorism, Amien Rais has been very disturbed by the way Bush positioned himself *vis-à-vis* other nations. He also seems to be disappointed with the way Megawati handled the larger national and international implications of the events of September 11. Besides exposing the limitations of Megawati's government, Rais's assessment of the performance of Indonesian national leadership also shows the difficulty Indonesian leaders have with "the superpower." More importantly, Rais's comments show the disunity of Indonesian leaders when dealing with an important problem. Since Megawati represents top executive power and Rais represents top legislative power in the country, his critical assessment of the shortcomings of Megawati's government is evidence of a huge gap between the two Indonesian power holders. Proponents of democracy may see such a gap as good and as conducive to better social control of the Megawati government. In dealing with sensitive and complicated national and international issues like September 11 and the subsequent events, however, such a gap does not seem to be helpful at all. It puts the government in the very weak and difficult situation of simultaneously dealing with domestic and international challenges. As an ordinary citizen, I suppose there is a point where our leaders need to be critical of one another, but not to the point where the national and international reputation of my country is under threat.

"Indonesia the Nest of Terrorists": "Unacceptable, Dangerous, and Baseless Accusation"

The Indonesian response to September 11 was also affected by some premature accusations made by Bush's staff and allies. Right after the tragedy, Wolfowitz identified Indonesia as a place where terrorists could hide out. Senior Prime Minister of Singapore Lee Kuan Yew concurred, saying "Indonesia is the nest of terrorists." He may have been referring to a series of bombings on random targets throughout Jakarta and other big cities in Indonesia.

There has been widespread concern with regard to this accusation in Jakarta. A survey conducted by a leading weekly magazine, *Tempo*, in collaboration with Insight from October 15–18, 2002, reports that 69.38 percent of respondents believe that "the bombing is part of a conspiracy to paint Indonesia as a nest of terrorists." More than 45 percent of respondents believed that "local terrorists could not have been able to assemble such a powerful bomb as was exploded in Bali." More than 53 percent of respondents believed that "Indonesia has been targeted by foreigners determined to brand it a nest of terrorists."[58] What is more, there is suspicion that the bombings were directed by the CIA.[59]

For her own reasons, thus far not disclosed to the public, Megawati did not comment on this accusation. However, other Indonesian leaders and intellectuals have expressed their deep concern. One of the most vocal critics of this accusation is Amien Rais. Rais extensively explained his reaction to the accusation in a speech entitled *Cara Kita*

Memandang Terorisme (The Way We See Terrorism), which he delivered on the graduation day of Jakarta University of Muhammadiyah (UMJ) and the inauguration of his professorship in political science on November 3, 2002. He denied the accusation and described it as being "unacceptable" and "dangerous" to the future of Indonesia in the dynamics of world politics, and thus needed to be responded to. "As a nation," he emphasized, "we must respond to such an accusation."[60]

Rais repeated his regret and rejection of the accusation on Friday, January 18, 2002, when he visited Thai Prime Minister Thaksin Shinawatra. He told Thaksin, "I'm very sorry when I heard that Paul Wolfowitz in Washington said that most probably there are many pockets of Al-Qaeda agents in Indonesia. I think this kind of accusation is not accepted in Indonesia."[61] In particular, Rais expressed his rejection of the US State Department's remarks on the potential for Al-Qaeda-type terror cells to operate in Indonesia. For him, "this is a baseless accusation, with no hard evidence."[62] He went on to challenge the US government to provide sufficient evidence before making such an accusation. He said, "But if Mr. Wolfowitz, or for that matter anybody, has hard evidence, pinpoint the names."[63]

There have been a series of terrorist attacks in Jakarta and other Indonesian cities in the last two decades, and it is necessary to know whether Amien Rais's responses to the accusation made by Wolfowitz and Lee Kuan Yew were substantive or simply political rhetoric. As a professor of political science, chairman of a political party, and chairman of MPR, the highest state institution, Rais must be in the know regarding the series of terrorist attacks in Indonesia during the last two decades. However, I am also sure that Rais did not expect other nations to make such an accusation during such a difficult time in Indonesia. Maybe Rais's concern was not with the evidence *per se*, but with the lack of sensitivity and respect evidenced by Wolfowitz and Lee Kuan Yew and with the potential implications of such an accusation on the future of Indonesian international politics.

Troops in Afghanistan: "Killing Innocent People?"

Based on what has been claimed as intelligent information, Osama bin Laden and Al-Qaeda have been accused as the groups most responsible for the September 11 attacks. For Bush, they are "terrorists, . . . the heirs of all the murderous ideologies of the twentieth century."[64] To Joseph Alphers, a former Mossad official and former Director of the Jaffee Center for Strategic Studies, they are "militant Islam"[65] and for Jerry Falwell, a leading Christian fundamentalist in America, Osama bin Laden and his group are "Islamic fundamentalists," "radical terrorists," "Middle Eastern monsters," and "barbarians" no different from Hitler.[66] When it was believed that Osama bin Laden and his group were hiding in Afghanistan under the protection of the Taliban regime, Bush demanded they be handed over, but was refused. With broad international support and strong protest from some Muslim countries, including Indonesia, Bush started his military campaign in Afghanistan on October 7, 2001. As a result, the fragile infrastructures of an already destitute Afghanistan have been destroyed, many poor civilian Afghans killed and starved, the Taliban regime replaced, and many suspects assumed to be the followers of Osama bin Laden or to have had contact with him detained. Until recently, some leading figures of Al-Qaeda have also been detained, but the whereabouts of the prime suspect, Osama bin Laden, remains a mystery.

Since Osama bin Laden and the supporters of the Taliban regime are Muslims and hold Islamic beliefs, September 11 and Bush's aggressive stance has raised some questions about US policies on Islam and the Muslim world. Despite the documentary, audio, and visual evidence provided by Bush's government, Muslims around the world remain doubtful about whether or not their fellow Muslims were the terrorists. They tend to be suspicious that what was done by Bush's government in Afghanistan was not fighting terrorism, but was rather the beginning of a serial plan to attack Muslims and discredit Islam. The suspicion was further bolstered by random attacks on Muslim women and vandalism of Islamic institutions, such as mosques in big cities around the United States and other countries, such as England and Australia.

President Bush is aware of this suspicion and its potential impact on the home security of the United States and on America's relationship with the Muslim world. With the support of his staff, Bush has made some serious efforts to persuade Muslims within and outside America that the United States is not fighting Islam, but is fighting terrorism. On September 17, 2001, Bush visited the National Islamic Center in Washington and met with Muslim leaders. He welcomed the leaders to the White House for an *Iftaar* (breaking the fast) dinner during Ramadan and described the September 11 attacks as "acts of violence against innocents (that) violate the fundamental tenets of the Islamic faith," that need to be understood by the American people. Bush explained to Muslim leaders that America is "a great country," because its people share the same values of respect and dignity and human worth. He stressed in the meeting that "the face of terror is not the true faith of Islam. That's not what Islam is all about. Islam is peace. These terrorists don't represent peace. They represent evil and war." Bush also called for tolerance towards American Muslims: "America counts millions of Muslims among our citizens, and Muslims make an incredibly valuable contribution to our country. Muslims are doctors, lawyers, law professors, members of the military, entrepreneurs, shopkeepers, moms and dads. And they need to be treated with respect. In our anger and emotion, our fellow Americans must treat each other with respect."[67] Indeed, Bagby, Perl, and Froehle estimated in 2001 that there are 6–7 million Muslims in America and 1209 mosques located in the South (26 percent), East/New England (30 percent), Midwest (29 percent), and Mountain/West (15 percent) of America.[68]

For the most part, the American people have responded positively to Bush's advice. Random street attacks on Muslim women and vandalism of Islamic sites, such as mosques, have drastically reduced in number. Moreover, there seems to be a growing sympathy for the Islamic religion in general and American Muslims in particular. The Qur'an and books on Islam have quickly sold out. Bookstores throughout America have had to restock their shelves to meet the high demand.

Bush, who has done his best to persuade a billion Muslims that the fight is not against Islam or Muslims, also expressed this two days later when he met Megawati on September 19, 2001, one week after the tragedy. As he told Megawati, "We [the American government] don't view this [fighting terrorism] as a war of religion in any way, shape or form." He also told Megawati about the importance of her visit with regard to US relations with Muslim countries: "You represent the nation with the most Muslim people in the world."[69] When he delivered a speech at Paramadina Mulya University in Jakarta, Ralph Boyce confirmed Bush's policy and stressed in his speech that "we [Americans] are fighting a war against terrorism, not against Islam." Referring to Nurcholish Madjid, rector of the university, Boyce said: "Muslim leaders have emphasized, Islam is a religion of peace." He adds, "Muslim leaders in America and in Indonesia have noted that like other great religious traditions, Islam is completely opposed to terrorism – the intentional killing of innocent civilians."[70]

Despite Bush's sympathetic comments, Indonesian leaders tend to be very suspicious of him. Bush's military campaign in Afghanistan has been seen as the result of arrogant and unjust policies with respect to Muslim countries. "The Americans were arrogant,"[71] said Sukma, when referring to the military campaign. "The people of Indonesia are getting angry," said Rais, "because of the arrogances of the United States of America, not because they support the terrorist conduct of Usamah bin Laden."[72] "Killing innocence people," Rais adds, "means destroying all human beings."[73] He went on to argue that using military force to combat terrorism is inappropriate and ineffective and, thus, must not be supported. "If Washington would ask Jakarta to send troops to Afghanistan," he said, "we would say no, thank you. We won't assume a bowing mentality to satisfy the American wishes. We don't want to be trampled upon."[74]

Rais is also cautious about the fact that the targets of the military campaigns have been Muslim countries. "Bush seems to very strongly believe," said Rais, "that America is world police. Whoever needs to be beaten, must be beaten. But we cannot ignore the fact that Muslim countries seem to be the focus of Bush's fight against terrorism."[75]

Rais's rejection of the use of military action in fighting terrorism is shared by Abdillah Toha, a deputy chairman of *Partai Amanat Nasional* (PAN) or the National Mandate Party. For Toha, the use of military force has proven ineffective and thus must be abandoned. Toha observes that there are no clear signs of a drastic reduction of the threat of terrorism after the US government took military action to fight it. "One year after September 11," he writes, "people are now much more apprehensive about terrorist attacks."[76] "If we accept the above observation," he continues, "the first step the world should take is to be brave enough to admit that the American way of fighting terrorism has so far been a failure."[77] "The world, under the collective leadership of the United Nations," Toha suggests, "should now sincerely reverse its mindset and look for more effective short-term and long-term ways of eradicating terrorism."[78] "Instead of using military force," he further suggests, "America should still be in the forefront in the fight against global terrorism using its abundant resources."[79] "President Bush," he said, "should lead the world against corrupt dictators and tyrants who oppress whole societies, against unilateralism, against international financial speculators and greedy transnational corporations responsible for ecological damage."[80] Toha, however, agrees with Bush that "fighting terrorism cannot be done only by one nation and needs the support of the majority of the world population, especially those who feel marginalized."[81]

Clearly, Indonesian responses to Bush's invitation to fight terrorism can be divided into two categories. A very positive response was given to the message of the invitation. Indonesian national leaders and intellectuals have no objection to the idea of fighting terrorists with joint international forces. Nevertheless, a very negative response has been given to the way Bush implemented the idea. Indonesians strongly reject the use of military force in fighting the terrorists. In other words, Indonesian leaders agree with "what" Bush meant, but disagree with "how" he implements it.

Epilogue

Overall, most believe the Indonesian response to September 11 was "good." It seems to have been effective in avoiding misunderstandings and suspicion between the Indonesian government and the government of the United States with regard to the event. Since Indonesia is the largest Muslim country in the world, President Megawati's quick visit to Washington may have reduced some tension and suspicion. The two governments seem to agree that September 11 was a totally unacceptable method of resistance in the name of Islam. Nevertheless, they do not seem to have a clear and definite understanding of such a tragedy, how to respond to it, and how to prevent further incidents. Their responses tend to be reactive in character and contain a mixture of anger, caution, and frustration. The rational, moral, cultural, and religious reasoning and implications of the responses do not seem to have been carefully prepared. There seems to have been very limited reflection, understanding, and dialogue within and between the two sides with regard to September 11 and the subsequent events. Instead of examining "What is going on?" which Gehman suggests is the "most pertinent issue"[82] of September 11, both sides have focused on retaliation and criticism. Instead of trying to understand why the terrorists attacked, they rushed to draw conclusions and fight. Instead of providing the Indonesian government with some ideas about how to prevent and anticipate terrorism, some senior officials of the US government prematurely accused Indonesia of involvement with terrorism. Instead of providing Bush with a better policy, some Indonesian leaders reacted emotionally to his policies in a way that provoked anti-American sentiment in the streets of Jakarta and other big cities in the country. As a result, a very limited understanding and positive impact has been made for the motives of the terrorists and for American–Indonesian relations in the aftermath of September 11. Although not directly related to September 11 and the subsequent events, the relations have so far been fragile and are surrounded by some hostility.

The burning of Liberty Statue, the American flag, and Bush's picture has become typical in anti-American rallies in Indonesia. In response, travel warnings about visiting Indonesia have repeatedly been given to American citizens. Strict regulations have been applied to Indonesian citizens who visit the United States and Indonesia has been categorized as one of the nine most dangerous countries with regard to international terrorism. This clearly shows the failure of diplomacy between the "superpower" and the largest Muslim country in the world. This failure has not only resulted from a lack of sensitivity and reflection on the part of Indonesians, but also from the American side. Both seem to have failed to understand religious and political cultures in the two countries. In order to develop a better atmosphere for positive relations, leaders of the two countries need to take some measures.

"To fully understand what is going on here [in the United States]," Gehman suggests, "a better appreciation of the relationship between the Islamic world and the West is necessary."[83] "Many Muslims," she explains, "feel that their own governments are controlled or at least influenced by US foreign policy in a way that is unfriendly to their freedom to practice their religion."[84] A good start would be if the government of the United States mitigates its use of the language of war, more carefully employs its military forces, and avoids simplistic moral language of good and evil in an attempt to command the whole world. At the same time, the use of the language of humility and responsibility needs to be intensified. "The language of good versus evil," according to Gehman, "may be appropriate, but it is too easy and too irresponsible to answer the question [of September 11]."[85] Referring to the military campaign as a "crusade" and calling it "infinite justice," Gehman criticizes, demonstrates both a lack of religious understanding and moral humility on the part of the Bush government. Instead, Gehman suggests, moral judgment must be made in condemning and responding to the events themselves.[86] Donald Emmerson, senior fellow at Stanford University's Asia/Pacific Research Center, notes some provocative ambiguities and ironies in American policy that need to be reconsidered in order to minimize the negative impact of September 11. He observes that the upsurge in American patriotism after September 11 and the explicit pride the United States takes in establishing global democratic projects are not much different than what devout Muslims practice, in terms of loyal fervor and proselytization. What is needed is time, Emmerson suggests, and long-term solutions, but "American impatience will be a problem."[87]

It is also crucial for Americans to understand the psychology of Indonesian Muslims. Being a large, majority religious group (87 percent of the Indonesian population),[88] Indonesian Muslims are certainly going to be very sensitive to their leaders' cooperation with other powers in disregard of Indonesian interests or when the matter involves fighting against their Muslim brothers. This sensitivity is not only due to the myriad economic and political challenges Indonesians currently face at both national and international levels, but is also due to their previous experiences with colonial powers and authoritarian leadership. It is also crucial to understand the important differences between Islam in Indonesia and Islam in other parts of the world, particularly the Arab world. Azyumardi Azra,[89] rector of Jakarta State Islamic University, says "it is 'simplistic' to think of Indonesian Islam as the same as Islam in the Middle East. . . . Because of its slow, peaceful penetration over centuries, accommodating to and integrating with local beliefs and customs, and because of the less rigid structure of Indonesian traditional society (including the active role of women in public life)," he explains, "the conventional wisdom of Indonesian Islam as tolerant, inclusive and inherently compatible with democracy is valid." Azra further explains that Indonesia is among the "least Arabicized" and the most democratizing of Muslim countries, along with Bangladesh, Nigeria, and Iran, as listed by Freedom House in New York. The way we understand Islam in Indonesia cannot be the same as the way we understand Islam in the Arab world. This is to say that applying the same policies, approaches, and strategies in dealing with the entire Muslim world will not be effective.

At the same time and for the same reasons, it seems to be critical for Indonesian leaders to really understand the strategic value and position of Indonesia as the largest Muslim country on the map of world politics, religion, and culture when they are dealing with national and international issues. The way the US government and other parts of the world understand the Indonesian response to September 11 cannot be the same as the way they understand the responses of other Muslim countries. The political aspects that need to be considered by Indonesian leaders in dealing with the US government cannot be the same as the political aspects that need to be considered by leaders of other Muslim countries. When this value and position is understood, proper responses and policies with regard to American–Indonesian relations can be developed. In this way, Indonesian leaders can cultivate their own style of diplomacy and political rhetoric, without mimicking leaders of other Muslim countries. Labeling the US government as "anti-Islam," "great Satan" or "evil" may be appropriate from the mouths of Iranian or Iraqi leaders, but may not be appropriate from Indonesian leaders.

The concept of "freedom" in American society also needs to be examined in order for others to understand the American people and their political leaders. The concept of "freedom of expression" has made every American feel free to express their opinions, although they may not really understand what they are saying. This may be the reason why there were so many ridiculous misunderstandings about the Islamic faith and *jihād* when the American people responded to Muslim terrorists. Referring to an article written by Andrew Sullivan (2001), "This is a Religious War," published in *New York Times Magazine*, October 7, Abu-Rabi' observes that "the tragic events of September 11, 2001, have raised in the minds of many in the West a number of questions about the connection between the sacred and violence in Islam, and some Western commentators have gone as far as to claim that violence is built into the Qur'an."[90] For sure, there will always be this type of misunderstanding in non-Muslim countries like America, where most people's knowledge of Islam is very much shaped by the media and by their political ideologies and interests, rather than a systematic Islamic education. However, it is a mistake to assume that such an understanding does not exist in Muslim countries. They are many Muslims who claim to represent Islam and fight for Islamic interests, but who may not really understand what they are saying either, and never consider the possible political and religious implications of their words and actions.

In order to have a genuine understanding of September 11 and take the momentum as a starting point for building a more positive and constructive relationship between the United States and the Muslim world in general and Indonesia in particular, much needs to be done by both parties, especially in the area of the roles of religion in political and international affairs, the relationship between faith and politics, the issue of religious freedom, and the possibility for inter-religious dialogue. National and religious leaders in both America and Indonesia need to assist their constituents in reflecting on the more theological aspects of September 11, such as the existence of evil and the role as well as the will of God.[91]

Instead of criticizing one another and focusing on disagreement, world leaders need to develop mutual understanding and focus more on sharing views and developing agreement. "Understanding the complexity surrounding September 11," Markham and Abu-Rabi' suggest, requires an understanding of "the views of the other."[92] Instead of blaming one another, sharing responsibility may be far more productive. Gehman may be right when she said that "the US is not responsible for September 11, but may be responsible for some of the conditions that provided the context for it and we should try to identify and correct those conditions."[93] "There are other parties," she adds, "who have allowed the conditions for terrorism to flourish, and they, too, should carry out this same kind of analysis."[94] These parties can be individuals, groups, organizations or countries anywhere in the world.

Certainly, there is no quick and easy way for anybody to understand September 11 and the subsequent events. This is the point when dialogue is so crucial for future American–Indonesian relations. Leaders of the two countries need to make a greater effort and spend more time and energy designing a continuous and constructive dialogue in order to develop their understanding, sensitivities, and reasoning with regard to the cultural, political, economic, and religious dimensions of September 11 and the future of American–Indonesian relations.

Dialogue, Markham suggests, is not the management of competing demands by the exercise of power as in the "ruthless secular" dialogue of the Nietzschian.[95] Neither is it a conversation on a common subject between two or more persons with differing views in order to learn from one another, as in Leonard Swidler's model.[96] Swidler's model of dialogue, Markham criticizes, operates in a world of sentimentality and ignores the real cultural, social, economic, and gender issues. Thus, it becomes "surface" and "fails to reach down to the underlying dynamics that are really shaping our views."[97] What is needed, Markham suggests, is "the science of dialogue," "a call to locate the conversation more firmly in the traditions, narratives, and contexts that make us real."[98] This type of dialogue, said Markham, requires the participants to move beyond the polite exchange of views, attends to the communal narrative underpinning the world perspective, is aware of the internal explanation for disagreement that is operating, and detects and recognizes the significant gender, economic, and ethnic differences."[99]

If the science of dialogue is to be applied with regard to future American–Indonesian relations, both sides need to listen to one another and have equal chances to articulate their respective positions with clarity in order to untangle the complexity of the relationship. When the complexity is unpacked, both sides will be able to start identifying ways forward that could lead to better American–Indonesian relations.

Acknowledgments

I would like to acknowledge Professor Ibrahim Abu Rabi' at The Duncan Black Macdonald Center for the Study of Islam and Christian–Muslim Relations, Hartford Seminary, for his support and encouragement in the preparation of this article. His comments on my first draft inspired me with some ideas in finalizing this article. I also thank Ian Markham and Jane Smith at Hartford Seminary for their warm, motivating, and inspiring collegial friendship during my six-month visit to Hartford Seminary. My thanks also to Abdurrazak Adesina, Tahir Uluç, Ferry Nahusona, and Tony Tampake for their warm friendship and partnership in Hartford Seminary collegial forum.

Notes

1. See Ralph Boyce, 2002. "*U.S.–Indonesian Relations in the Post-September 11 World,*" http://www.usembassyjakarta.org/press_rel/boyce_paramadina.html, 2002.

2. Ibid.
3. Ian Markham and Ibrahim Abu-Rabi', *September 11: Religious Perspectives on the Causes and Consequences* (Oxford: Oneworld, 2002), 1.
4. Martha Simmons and Frank A. Thomas, eds., *9.11.01: African American Leaders Respond to an American Tragedy* (Valley Forge: Judson Press, 2001), ix.
5. Heidi Gehman, "September 11: The Terrorist Attack on America", in Ian Markham and Ibrahim Abu Rabi', eds., *September 11: Religious Perspectives on the Causes and Consequences* (Oxford: Oneworld, 2002), 18.
6. See "Address to a Joint Session of Congress and the American People," 20 September. See http://www.whitehouse.gov.
7. See "Abroad at Home; A different World," *New York Times*, September 12, 2001.
8. Ian Markham and Ibrahim Abu-Rabi', 2002, 3.
9. Ibid.
10. See William H. Willimon, ed., *The Sunday after Tuesday: College Pulpits Respond to 9/11* (Nashville: Abingdon Press, 2002). See also Martha Simmons and Thomas A. Thomas, eds., *9.11.01: African American Leaders Respond to an American Tragedy* (Valley Forge: Judson Press, 2001).
11. Quoted in Heidi Gehman, 2002, 12.
12. Ibid.
13. Ian Markham, "9.11: Contrasting Reactions and the Challenge of Dialogue," in Ian Markham and Ibrahim Abu Rabi', eds., *September 11: Religious Perspectives on the Causes and Consequences*, (Oxford: Oneworld, 2002), 206–28. See also discussion in Heidi Gehman, 2002, 12–13.
14. Indonesia is the most populous Muslim country in the world. The total population of this country is 234,893,453 consisting of 87 percent Muslim, 9 percent Christians, 2 percent Hindu, and 2 percent followers of other beliefs, such as Buddhism, Confucian, and Javanese Mysticism (see infoplease.com). Historical records of the Chinese Tang Dynasty (AD 618–907) tell that Islam was first brought by Arab traders to Indonesian ports along their way to Guangzhou and other southern Chinese ports. For further discussion, see M.C. Ricklefs, *A History of Modern Indonesia: c. 1300 to the Present* (Bloomington, 1981).
15. The *New York Times* records that the total death toll from the attacks on September 11, including those still missing and presumed dead, was 3117 as of January 9, 2002, and this does not include the 19 hijackers. At the World Trade Center, original estimates hovered between 5000–6000 a few days after the attack, but that figure has dropped steadily, and on January 9 the *New York Times* reported the total to be 2893, including 147 in the two airplanes. The total number includes victims from 62 countries. New York fire fighters suffered a devastating loss of 343 of their comrades who had rushed into the buildings and up the flights of stairs to rescue survivors on the burning floors of the towers. At the Pentagon, the death toll stands at 184, 59 of them on Flight 77. Forty people were on the flight that crashed in Pennsylvania (quoted in Heidi Gehman, 2002, 9–10).
16. Ibid.
17. The quote is taken from Chapter 5 (Al-Ma'idah) verse 32: "For that reason, We decreed for the children of Israel that whoever kills a soul, not in retaliation for a soul or corruption in the land, is like one who has killed the whole of mankind; and whoever saves a life is like one who saves the lives of all mankind. Our Messengers came to them with the clear proofs; but afterwards many of them continued to commit excesses in the land" (Translation by Majid Fakhry, *An Interpretation of the Qur'an English Translation of the Meanings a Bilingual Edition* (New York: New York University Press, 2002).
18. See Douglas Ramage, http://islamlib.com/DISKUSI/islam%20modern.html, 2002.

19. See State Secretariat Republic of Indonesia, http://www.deplu.go.id/policy/releases/pr-as110901eng.htm, 2001.

20. In exchange, Bush promised Megawati a C$833 million trade-and-aid package (see State Secretariat 2001).

21. The joint statement says: "President George W. Bush and President Megawati Soekarnop-utri today condemned the September 11, 2001 attacks on the United States and pledged to strengthen existing cooperation in the global effort to combat international terrorism. On behalf of the 210 million people of Indonesia, President Megawati expressed her deepest sympathies to the American people and pledged solidarity with the United States in this hour of grief. Noting that the victims included innocent civilians of many nationalities, including an Indonesian citizen, the two leaders agreed that these indiscriminate attacks have no place in a civilized world. The two presidents reaffirmed their commitment to the principles of religious freedom and tolerance in relations within and among nations. As leader of the world's largest Muslim population and third largest democracy, President Megawati joined President Bush in underlining the importance of differentiating between the religion of Islam and the acts of violent extremists. Emphasizing that Islam is a religion of peace that neither teaches hatred nor condones violence, President Megawati encour-aged President Bush in his stated purpose of building a broad coalition across religious lines and cultures to deal with these new and dangerous threats. She further emphasized the importance of taking into account the views of the Muslim world as the United States leads an appropriate response to the events of September 11. Noting that Islam is the fastest growing religion in the United States, President Bush assured President Megawati that the American people respect Islam as one of the world's great religions and that the United States would join hands with freedom-loving people of all religions to combat transnational terror (see http://www.yale.edu/lawweb/avalon/sept_11/president_019.htm.)

22. See discussion in Islamlib, http://islamlib.com/DISKUSI/islam%20modern.html, 2002.

23. See Sukma, http://islamlib.com/DISKUSI/islam%20modern.html. 2002.

24. In the midst of power struggles that led up to the selection of a new president by the MPR after the 1999 General Election, Islamic parties in the Poros Tengah (Middle Axis) claimed 34.2 percent of the seats in the DPR, slightly more than PDI-P, the party of Megawati, which had won a plurality of 33.76 percent seats in the election. The Poros Tengah suc-ceeded in electing Abdurrahman Wahid (Gus Dur) to the presidency. It was also the Poros Tengah, except the *Partai Kebangkitan Bangsa* (PKB) that was the main power that caused Gusdur to surrender his Presidential seat in 2000 and hand it over to Megawati. See discussion in Said Ali Damanik, *Fenomena Partai keadilan: Transformasi 20 Tahun Gerakan Tarbiyah di Indonesia*, 2002, 291.

25. See Douglas Ramage, 2002.

26. The points include: "(i) The Government of Indonesia follows with deep concern that military action has been taken in Afghanistan following the terrorists attacks on 11 September 2001 in New York and Washington DC. (ii) The Government of Indonesia takes note of the statement made by the US Government that the military action is specifically targeted towards terrorist training camps and military installations in Afghanistan and that the operation would try to avoid civilian casualties and that it is not directed against the Afghanistan people and the Islamic *ummah*, and will be coupled with the delivery of humanitarian assistance to the Afghanistan people in the form of food and medicine. (iii) The Government of Indonesia urges that the operation which has taken place shall be truly very limited in terms of force deployment, its target and duration and therefore reducing or minimizing casualties of innocent people. (iv) The Government of Indonesia reiterates

its demand to the United Nations Security Council, consistent with its authority and responsibility to maintain international peace and security, to restore the situation and to take charge of the humanitarian aspects resulting from the conflict situation in Afghanistan. (v) The Government of Indonesia calls for the Indonesian people not to overreact in expressing their reaction and sympathy towards the suffering of the Afghanistan people and not to engage in activities that are violating the laws and may disturb security and public order. (vi) The Government of Indonesia has decided to provide and generate humanitarian assistance in the form of food and medicine and encourages the participation of the Indonesian people as a demonstration of sympathy to alleviate the sufferings of the Afghanistan people that have lasted for 25 years" (Department of Foreign Affairs, 2001).

27. See Douglas Ramage, 2002.
28. Ibid.
29. See "Laporan Khusus Agama," *Tempo*, December 24–30, 2002, 32–43.
30. See "After the Attacks: News Analysis," in *New York Times*, September 14, 2001.
31. See "Address to a Joint Session of Congress and the American People," http://www.whitehouse.gov, September 20.
32. See "After the Attacks: News Analysis," in *New York Times*, September 14, 2001.
33. See Ralph Boyce, 2002. "*U.S.–Indonesian Relations in the Post-September 11 World*," http://www.usembassyjakarta.org/press_rel/boyce_paramadina.html, 2002.
34. Ibid.
35. Ibid.
36. Ibid.
37. Ibid.
38. See note 19.
39. Ibid.
40. Ibid.
41. See "*Cara Kita Memandang Terorisme*," a speech delivered on the graduation day of Jakarta University of Muhammadiyah, 2002. See also Biografi Amien Rais, http://www.tokohindonesia.com/alfabet/a/amien%20rais/amien_rais_biografi.html.
42. See full report of the meeting in amienrasi.com.
43. Ibid.
44. Ibid.
45. For an extended report on Amien Rais's visit and remarks in Thailand, see Haseenah Koyakutty, *Amien rejects US remarks about terrorist cells in Indonesia*, http://www.channelnewsasia.com/cna/sept11/news/1801amien.htm, 2002.
46. Ibid.
47. See Radio Netherland, *Amien Rais Tampil Nasionalistis, di Negeri Belanda*, http://www.rnw.nl/ranesi/html/amien_nasionalistis.html, 2003.
48. Ibid.
49. Ibid.
50. Rais compares Bush's words with the words of John Foster Dulles when he said to Asian countries during the old Cold War: "You have only two choices: either Washington or Moscow. The third alternative is immoral." Moreover, said Rais, Bush made Indonesians uneasy when he accused North Korea, Iran, and Iraq of being an "axis of evil." Such an accusation, according to him, "is too harsh and too excessive." See ibid.
51. Rais also criticizes Bush of being "loose in his rationale," when he said there is an *existence of evil* in this world, namely Iran, Iraq, and North Korea. He went on by quoting a German minister of justice who said that there are similarities between George W. Bush and Adolf Hitler. Such an accusation, said Rais, does not mean anything if it was made by

a Palestinian or communist leader, the enemy of the USA. But the accusation is so significant, because it was made by a leader of a big European country. See ibid.

52. Ibid.

53. Ibid.

54. Ibid.

55. Ibid.

56. Ibid.

57. Ibid.

58. See "A Different Class of Terror," *Tempo*, October 22–9, 2002, 9.

59. See Raymond Bonner, "Indonesians see CIA behind terror talk," *International Herald Tribune*, September 25, 2002, 5.

60. See "*Cara Kita Memandang Terorisme*," a speech delivered on the graduation day of Jakarta University of Muhammadiyah, 2002. See also Biografi Amien Rais, http://www.tokohindonesia.com/alfabet/a/amien%20rais/amien_rais_biografi.html.

61. See Haseenah Koyakutty, *Amien rejects US remarks about terrorist cells in Indonesia*, http://www.channelnewsasia.com/cna/sept11/news/1801amien.htm, 2002.

62. Ibid.

63. Ibid.

64. See "Address to a Joint Session of Congress and the American People," September 20, http://www.whitehouse.gov.

65. Joseph Alpher, "Stronger Alliance, Limited Option," *The Jerusalem Report Magazine*, http://www.jrep.com/Israel/Article.

66. Quoted Ian Markham, 2002, 217–18.

67. See US Department of State, International Information Programs, September 17, 2001. Bush remarks at Islamic Center of Washington, DC says "face of terror not true faith of Islam", http://usinfo.state.gov/topical/pol/terror/01091722.htm.

68. Ihsan Bagby, Paul M. Perl, and Bryan T. Froehle, *The Mosque in America: A National Portrait: A Report from the Mosque Study Project* (Washington, DC: Council on American–Islamic Relations, April 26, 2001).

69. See report in Bill Guerin, 2001. "The fear factor weighs heavy in Indonesia," *Asia Times Online Southeast Asia*, atimes.com, http://www.atimes.com/se-asia/CI26Ae01.html.

70. See Ralph Boyce, 2002. "*U.S.–Indonesian Relations in the Post-September 11 World*," http://www.usembassyjakarta.org/press_rel/boyce_paramadina.html, 2002.

71. See Sukma, http://islamlib.com/DISKUSI/islam%20modern.html. 2002.

72. See professorship in political science on http://www.m-amienrais.com/news/one_news.asp?IDNews=602.

73. Ibid.

74. Ibid. "Indonesia: a Nation State in Search of Identity and Structure," *Bijdragen tot de Taal-, Land-, en Volkenkunde*, 157.4, 2001, 881–901; especially on Amien Rais, 886–7.

75. Ibid.

76. Abdillah Toha 2002. *After Bali: Has Bush Succeeded in War Obsession Against Terrorism?* http://www.m-amienrais.com/english/news/one_news.asp?IDNews=542.

77. Ibid.

78. Ibid.

79. Ibid.

80. Ibid.

81. Ibid.

82. Ibid.

83. Ibid.

84. Ibid.
85. Ibid.
86. Ibid.
87. See Emmerson, http://islamlib.com/DISKUSI/islam%20modern.html, 2002.
88. See note 14.
89. See discussion on http://islamlib.com/DISKUSI/islam%20modern.html.
90. Ibrahim Abu Rabi', "A post-September 11 critical assessment of modern Islamic history," in Ian Markham and Ibrahim Abu-Rabi', eds., *September 11 Religious Perspectives on the Causes and Consequences* (Oxford: Oneworld, 2002).
91. See discussion in Gehman, 2002, 16–17.
92. Ian Markham and Ibrahim Abu Rabi', 2.
93. Gehman, 2002, 14.
94. Ibid.
95. See Ian Markham, 2002, 224–6.
96. Ibid.
97. Ibid.
98. Ibid.
99. Ibid.

CHAPTER 24

The World Situation After September 11, 2001

Khursid Ahmad

The events of September 11 and October 7, 2001 have qualitatively changed the global scenario for the Muslim *ummah*. It is not as if these changes have come as a bolt from the blue. Things have been moving in this direction ever since the end of the Cold War, the demise of the socialist bloc, and the fall of the Berlin Wall (1989). The Western world needed a new enemy to keep its guns in good repair. An imaginary green specter was meticulously woven into global politics. Now the specter has blown up into a Frankenstein's monster: the name of the game is "terrorism"! Yet the Muslims must not react with rage or fury. It is our duty to face this challenge with faith, composure, and dignity. Every challenge is also an opportunity. We must seize the moment and use it to open up a meaningful dialogue.

I think we should try to make it clear that Islam and terrorism are worlds apart. We should spell out clearly and forcefully what terrorism is. We have to differentiate between the role of force in society, personal, domestic, national, and global. Every use of force is not terrorism. The use of force and the *illegitimate* use of force, a disproportionate use of force, and a use of force for unjust causes are not the same things. Had it been so, there would have been no legal system, or criminal law in civilized society. And the whole concept of a just war would have to be thrown out of the window. So we have to differentiate between the two. The legitimate use of coercive power in a civilized society and a just war are universally accepted as elements of any legal system and international law. We must not then be overwhelmed by the media war on alleged and real terrorisms. The world is being subjected to a gruesome and multidimensional psychological indictment. It is high time that saner counsels were allowed to prevail, and it is important that the world realizes what is at stake. Terrorism must be checked but not by means that contribute to terrorism, nor should we confuse terrorism with genuine movements for liberation against foreign/alien occupation or the struggle of the oppressed against injustice.

Terrorism stands for the *illegitimate use of force* for *political purposes*, whether by individuals or groups and states. In particular it involves the *indiscriminate use* of *violence* against *innocent civilians*. There are many other elements or nuances such as surprise attack, political mileage etc. that characterize terrorism but these are not the focus here. Nonetheless, we must make it very clear what terrorism is and we must condemn it unequivocally. What happened on September 11, 2001 in New York and Washington was terrorism and has rightly been condemned as such by all, including the Islamic *ummah*.

Islam stands for peace and justice. It can never condone terrorism, which is a human aberration. It has no religion. It has no color. It is monstrous in any context. As against this *jihād* is a comprehensive and positive concept, one that is basically a moral concept. It means to struggle for a just cause. First and foremost, it is a struggle against one's own evil self. Then it means striving at all levels towards promoting good, virtue, and justice. This is done by word of mouth and by one's own good example. It is done by pen and all other means of communication. It also means to struggle against injustice and tyranny. Essentially it covers the whole span of individual and collective effort and it is reformative in its nature and purport. However, in certain situations it can become confrontational. As such armed conflict can also be a part of it but it can never be a war of aggression. It is always a just struggle. Even in war there is a strict code of ethics. The use of force is permitted only for certain purposes, which are subject to certain legal and ethical conditions. We must not shy away from stating the truth and it should always be the whole truth. *Jihād* is a part of an overall framework for human life and endeavor. It is a process of reform with its own discipline and strong moral foundations. As such *jihād* and terrorism are poles apart.

As to what happened on September 11, we have condemned it and must continue to condemn it honestly and forcefully. It was an act of terrorism against civilian people. Such senseless destruction of life and property is totally unjustified in Islam, just as it is by all civilized behavioral norms. While it is correct that through these acts a super-power was humiliated, its invincibility exposed, and its symbols of military, economic, and financial power attacked and humbled, there can *never* be a justification for such acts of terrorism and wanton destruction. Such acts are crimes against humanity and Islam and the Muslim people condemn them unreservedly. It is a global fact that the Muslims, among others, are the victims of American highhandedness, and hegemonic policies. We are at the suffering end. Yet there are moral limits within which efforts to redress grievances should take place. Human responses must always be informed, rational, and moral. We must not be swept away on waves of emotion. It must be clearly stated that the indiscriminate use of force leading to the destruction and assassination of innocent human beings, wherever they are and whatever their faith may be, is against Islam's principled position. The Qur'an makes every human being sacrosanct. Allah says: *laqad karramna bani Adam* (al-Isrā', 17:70), i.e. "We have honored all progeny of Adam, that then, refers to all human beings, not just to Muslims." The Qur'anic injunction prohibits taking the life of any human being, without a just right in law (al-Ma'idah, 5:35). This too is for all human beings and not just for Muslims.

We are obliged to enforce *'adil* – justice for all, which means commitment to the rule of law. Even retribution is allowed only according to law, in keeping with Islamic values and principles. No one can take the law into his own hands and inflict death or injury upon others arbitrarily. This is so for all Muslims and non-Muslims, for friends and foes alike. Islam lays down rules and regulations for different areas of human behavior and spells out values and principles to deal fairly with all, including our enemies. These laws are applicable in peace and in war. So this is the Islamic framework. As such whatever happened on September 11 was not correct. The Islamic view is that if anyone kills a human being, an innocent person, without just cause, then that is like killing the whole human race. And if one saves one life, it is like saving the whole of humanity (al-Ma'idah, 5:35).

Let me also make it clear that any encouragement or promotion of terrorism in any society and particularly in the context of Islam and Muslims is going to generate extremism and violence. If it fails it is a loss of human beings, if it succeeds it is against the whole methodology of Islam and the *modus operandi* of the Islamic movement. Any encouragement of such methodologies would move the *ummah* away from the *manhaj* of *da'wah*; the prophetic way. Islam neither adopted nor condoned the *manhaj* of terrorism. So it is not merely from Islam's principled position, but also from the perspective of strategy that Islamic movements should be careful and deeply concerned about it. This should be clear in our minds and we should also make it very clear to others. Islam aims at repelling evil by good and does not want to replace one evil by another evil. The Qur'an lays down the principle that "good and evil are not equal. Replace evil with what is good and better (*ahsan*). If you pursue this path then one who may have enmity for you may become your friend" (al-Fussilat, 41:34).

We condemn terrorism in *all its forms*. We condemn terrorism against *all people*. The equality of human beings is a cardinal principle and a universal value. There must be one standard for us all. We abhor and condemn duplicity, double talk, and double standards. To condemn terrorism against one country or people and condone or even patronize it, if those who are at the suffering end belong to a different nation, country, or faith, is the height of hypocrisy. Terrorism by individuals or groups is as abominable as terrorism by states or government agencies. If it is atrocious and abominable in America it is equally atrocious and abominable in Palestine and Kashmir, in Rwanda and Bosnia, in Sri Lanka and Chechnya. To condemn terrorism in one place and protect, finance, or condone it in others is outrageous. We must have the same standard for all. Human life and honor are precious and inviolable in the East as in the West. Humans must be treated as humans wherever they are. Rights must be sacrosanct in the Arab world, in Africa, in Kashmir and Central Asia as in Europe and America. This then is the time to convey this message.

The condemnation of terrorism is one thing, but the elimination of terrorism is another. Terrorism cannot be fought by terror. A "war against terrorism" is a misnomer. By use of brute force it may be suppressed for a while but there can never be a military solution to real social, political, ethical, economic, and cultural problems. Terrorism has been described even by people like Huntington as "the weapon of the weak against the strong."[1] The cruel logic of political retaliation has to be understood bluntly. If the strong are not ready to accept the supremacy of law and refuse to follow the rules of the game, if they try to impose their will through brute force, if they exploit the weak beyond endurance, then many an untoward reaction, even violent ones, are bound to appear. If injustice persists, revolts are bound to occur. If you close all avenues for peaceful change and reform, then untoward aberrations are bound to take place. If the doors of dialogue are closed, then violent outbursts are the result. So terrorism cannot be eliminated through counter-terrorism. Violence cannot be stopped by greater violence. It is only through the removal of the causes of violence and terrorism that peace and justice can come to society. Moreover, even acts of terrorism must be dealt with through the power of law and judicial processes. Whether it is individuals or groups, resorting to unabashed terrorism to suppress terrorism, real or alleged, cannot but be counter-productive and futile. We must also make it very clear that the political, ideological, and economic grievances of a people suffering from the unjust policies of the powerful must be addressed and resolved. It is only when the causes of violence and terrorism in society are removed that terrorism can be eliminated. So, in our dialogue we should also make this very clear.

It should be clearly stated that efforts at branding and stereotyping terrorisms along religious or ethnic lines are an offence against humanity. Terrorism is terrorism. It has no religion. Violence in Ireland cannot be presented as Catholic and Protestant ter-rorisms: nor can violence and blood baths in Sri Lanka be projected as Hindu and Buddhist terrorisms. If any act of terrorism is committed by any Muslim, there is no justification for presenting it as "Islamic terrorism." If Timothy McVeigh's act of ter-rorism in Oklahoma was not terrorism of the Christian right, why are other acts of ter-rorism given a religious color? It is significant that when Muslims resisted such media outrage, President Bush and Prime Minister Blair had to come out with an explanation that the so-called war against terrorism was not a war against Islam or Muslims. I am not going into their intentions or actual consequences on the ground, but at least in response to the Muslim protest they had to change their tone and language, even though not their targets!

I am also informed that in the United States, a convention of writers, i.e. the Reli-gious Writers' Association (RWA) was held on September 21, 2001, which adopted a resolution saying that, "we must stop the expression of Islamic terrorism and Islamic terrorists in news coverage of events covering the recent bombing." So if we resist, it *will* have its influence.

We should say very frankly and boldly, that while we are condemning the September 11 terrorism, the Western reaction, particularly the current and outrageous American bombing of the innocent peoples of Afghanistan, is also not condonable. This war against Afghanistan is unjust and unjustifiable. No country, powerful or otherwise, has the right to take the law into its own hands and terrorize nations, kill innocent people, destroy societies, their institutions, and infrastructures. It is all the more out-rageous that the target is a poor country already devastated by 23 years of superpower aggression and internal strife. International law does not allow this. The UN Charter does not allow this. The UN Charter's definition of "self-defense" cannot be extended to these brazen acts of state terrorism.[2] The UN Charter makes it very clear that if there has to be an action on behalf of the world community against any aggressor, it has to be under a Security Council resolution and also under the UN Military Staff Commit-tee (Articles 44, 46, and 47). The United States has thus violated the UN. This has been its attitude all along. In Korea despite a UN Resolution, the United States insisted on American command. American leadership has made it very clear that US forces cannot fight or participate in any war or peace process unless it is under US command. There has also been a violation of Article 33 of the UN Charter, which lays down a clear framework for negotiation, mediation, arbitration, and adjudication for resolving inter-state disputes. The United States has refused to follow this procedure and has arbitrar-ily imposed a war on a poor country, merely on the basis of suspicion. It has no right to do this. So we have to make it very clear and with arguments that have weight that this war is totally unjust and unjustifiable.

We should also try to make it very clear that even the guilt of those alleged to be responsible for the crimes of September 11, is yet to be established through the due process of law. What to say of Afghanistan or of the Taliban, even the guilt of Al-Qaeda and of Osama bin Laden has not been established so far. The use of indiscriminate force and the perpetration of violence on an innocent people on the basis of suspicion only is a heinous crime and a sordid act of terrorism. As for the so-called evidence, the docu-ment that Mr. Blair has released to the Parliament, you will find that the first sentence states that whatever information is being given cannot lead to any conviction in a court of law. Out of the 70 odd items that are listed in the document 61 are totally irrelevant and the remaining nine only give fourth-degree circumstantial evidence, which cannot stand careful scrutiny in any court of law.[3] On this basis nobody could be convicted, and even less executed! The fact is that the US President has acted as prosecutor, judge, and executioner. This is a travesty of justice. We must ask the world to face facts, ask for concrete evidence and the establishment of guilt through the proper judicial process and not mere suspicion.

Whatever be their other failings, no case has been established against Bin Laden and Al-Qaeda. The entire story seems to be inspired. Within half an hour of the collapse of the Twin Towers CNN was using Bin Laden's name. On what basis? Nobody cares to examine the evidence. Claims are heaped over claims and the world is asked to accept this! Thus far they have arrested over 1100 people and interrogated all of them in depth, but so far only one has been charged, not convicted, and that too on violation of immigration laws. Even after seven weeks the American authorities have not been able to provide any worthwhile evidence or even a proper confession from any collab-orator. While they accept that this could not have been done without the collaboration and active participation of at least 50–60 people in the United States and must have taken two to three years in its planning, training, and command over sophisticated technology, no linkage has been established. Indeed the type of evidence that is being paraded is laughable.

Someone who has undertaken training at an aviation school, in a light aircraft, would not have sufficient knowledge to operate computerized jet airplane systems, replace pilots without incident, change the direction of the plane without notice on radars, or pilot it with such precision that it strikes a premeditated point so as to cause the greatest harm to the building. Yet not just one plane, but four planes are hijacked all within a span of an hour, routes diverted, and the planes crashed at their targets to wreak the utmost havoc. Yet nothing was done to avert the tragedy. No one raised the alarm when the planes changed their course, made U-turns, lost contact with their control towers. There is no reaction to this at national level. Hence there are so many question marks. The entire tragedy is shrouded in mystery. The guilty are not being identified. Indeed there seems to be something of a cover-up. Evidence is not only lacking, but no serious effort is being made to investigate and find out the causes, to explain what happened and how and who were responsible. No national or international commission has been formed to find out how such a disaster took place and who were responsible for that catastrophe. No effort is being made to arrive at some worthwhile understanding of the whole scandal. It is a failure of the intelligence system of the only superpower. One that is spending annually some $260 billion on its defense budget, some $30 billion on its budget for the CIA, around $3 billion every year on the FBI budget, $6.5 billion on its National Security Authority, and another $11 billion on nine intelligence agencies attached to different departments of the federal government. This intelligence budget comes to over $50 billion every year. And another $27 billion goes to the budget of non-intelligence information agencies. It is hard to believe that these $77 billion spent a year on intelligence and information agencies do not even afford the United States a whiff of what was happening, over a period of years, that culminated in the events of September 11.[4] Even after the events have occurred, the United States seems unable to investigate and establish a complete picture of what went wrong and how. Can there be any doubt then that the United States is covering up the failure of its own security system, its intelligence network? No head has rolled. The CIA's chief has not been dismissed. The FBI's chief has not been dismissed. No inquiry has been initiated about the whole intelligence system and yet they have found Osama bin Laden. They have found the Taliban. They have found Al-Qaeda. And now the United States is bombarding them and killing them without establishing their guilt. Need I remind readers that even after all the atrocities committed by the Nazi warlords, it was the US President who insisted in 1945 that those responsible could not be executed without the establishment of guilt through judicial process? So the Nuremberg Trials were held and the Nazi leadership was executed after a fair trial.[5] Where have all these principles gone? It seems as if the whole so-called civilized world has stooped to gangsterism and terrorism. Innocent people in Afghanistan are being killed. Even "Daisy Cutter" bombs are now being dropped (*The Guardian*, November 7, 2001), which are described as being the equivalent of tactical nuclear weapons. Each bomb carries 15,000 pounds of slurry explosives in a steel casing that when exploded produces a nuclear mushroom cloud of aluminum powder, which burns at 5500 degrees Celsius (10,000 degrees Fahrenheit) and destroys everything covering a mile wide area. After all this the United States remains civilized, humanitarian and the protector of human rights while the poor Afghans are reduced to "terrorists." The irony is that there are no military installations worth the name in Afghanistan. They had no air defense system or military infrastructure. The United States is destroying a devastated country. It is hitting its villages, hospitals, mosques, and even Red Cross warehouses. This is a tragic situation, nay it is a scandalous situation and it has to be challenged. But the United States is openly refusing any judicial process. President Bush has said "No question of evidence. No question of any judicial investigation. We know he is guilty. You hand him over or we will destroy you." Even Attorney General Ashcroft has stated openly on CNN that "it is not a question of justice. It is a question of punishment." These are his words. And what is America's own record with regards to norms of justice? In the case of Nicaragua in 1985, the International Court of Justice, the Hague, gave a judgment against the United States for financing and supporting terrorist activity in that country. But the

United States simply refused to accept the judgment of the International Court of Justice. Not only that, but because of US resistance, there was a Resolution passed in the Security Council which said that all member states of the United Nations must accept all decisions of the International Court of Justice. Needless to say, the United States vetoed that resolution.[6]

And now there is a treaty signed by some 140 countries of the world to establish an International Criminal Court. Forty-three countries including the UK, Russia, and France have ratified the Treaty but the United States thus far has refused to do so. So this is America's attitude towards the international judicial process. The United States wants to be the accuser, the prosecutor, the judge, and the executioner. This is not an acceptable position.

There are some very critical questions that remain unanswered. A number of retired senior officers formerly attached to the US Army and Air Force have stated openly that the type of hijackers that are being accused could not have accomplished this sophisticated act of terrorism. Indeed it is difficult to believe that amateur pilots could have taken control of planes in such a smooth manner and piloted them through the jungle of New York skyscrapers to hit their targets with such precision. This remains a riddle, one shrouded in mystery. Similarly, the lifestyle of the so-called hijackers, if they belonged to the mujahid group of Al-Qaeda, as is alleged, does not fit into the culture of the suspected group. Even Karen Armstrong has expressed her astonishment at this anomaly.[7] On the one hand, they are being presented as mujahids, and on the other they are drinking, womanizing, and spending nights in clubs. How do we reconcile these extremes?

The whole question of the hijackers' identity and the matter of forging passports remains problematic. It is also intriguing that apart from one case, they have so far not been able to find the black boxes of the destroyed airplanes. After seven weeks there was still no clue. But what they have found intact is a passport belonging to one of the hijackers! To establish how this happened, one has to decipher the miracle!

One can go on commenting on the unending series of mysteries that envelop this case. The fact is that there is no concrete and consistent evidence, nor is there any intention of recourse to the judicial process. The United States is not prepared to respect any law. No one knows who the real terrorists were. But who supported them on US territory? Who is covering for them still? We condemn the happenings of September 11, but we equally condemn whatever is being done in the name of that tragedy. It seems that September 11 is being used to achieve certain pre-set objectives. There is much suspicion and indication that Afghanistan is being used as a scapegoat. Indeed vendetta and not justice is the hallmark of the US reaction; a wounded ego inflicting wounds on others and a show of force masking humiliation. Instead of opting for the bold step of self-examination and searching for their own failures, the United States is trying to find scapegoats and easy targets. Instead of pursuing the path of justice, terrorism has been the choice. This tragedy is as colossal as that of September 11, if not more.

Furthermore, there is some very eye-opening information about stock-exchange dealings prior to September 11. From September 6–10 the shares and stocks of some 32 companies including both major airlines involved and a number of financial companies that collapsed with the World Trade Center were sold and the amount of these sales is mind boggling. One airline sale, for example, was over 250 times the average movement, whereas for the other over 100 times. So was the case of other companies. One investment house defaulted to the tune of $100 million and after the collapse of the towers it has declared itself bankrupt. Many other stories are in circulation. All these things are being bypassed. No thorough investigation in respect of all the clues to the disaster is being undertaken. Why? All attention is only on one target, a poor country, 10,000 miles away, lacking all access to the world, particularly the United States. All blame is on a group, which was already under investigation and which had been monitored for four years, and yet there is still no evidence against them to prove their guilt.

There is also evidence that before September 11, America was planning, in collaboration with Uzbekistan, action against Afghanistan. The *New York Times* has published reports in this respect. Similarly some diplomats have stated publicly that several months before this event there were discussions and deliberations about a planned action against Afghanistan in the near future. All this information is not from any secret source, it is all published information from American and the world press. So the questions arise: Why is the United States ignoring all other leads and pursuing, exclusively, only one suspicion? Why is the United States not investigating the whole colossal phenomena properly?

There could be many forces and factors responsible for this disaster even from within the United States itself. There are dozens of terrorist groups in the United States. The Oklahoma case is a classic example. Originally it was also attributed to the Arabs and then Timothy McVeigh was found out. McVeigh targeted a government establishment and wanted to inflict the largest amount of injury and damage on the United States and its people. He took the lives of 268 people and injured another 1000. He saved two other people who were accused of being in his group and during that investigation, it was found that between 50 and 500 people could have belonged to that Christian Right terrorist group. There are dozens of similar terrorist and separatist groups operating in the United States.[8] So why are all these leads not being followed?

During the last 10 years, some 167 incidents of terrorism have taken place on American soil of which only three have been attributed to Muslims. Why, then, have other terrorist groups now been ignored? Outside the United States, the country where the largest number of terrorist acts against America and Americans has been committed is Greece. And yet no action has ever been taken against Greece, a NATO member. The September 17 Movement openly claimed responsibility for some of the acts of terrorism against the United States. Why has no action been taken against them? Why has their Al-Qaeda equivalent not been destroyed? Israel's state terror is beyond any shadow of a doubt. It is the last occupying power in the Middle East. Why is there no word against Israel's crimes against humanity, its genocide of the Palestinians? Similar is the record of the Indian government in Kashmir. Why then this discrimination? These facts need to be kept in mind and presented to the people in a cool, calculated, and informed manner. We should address the central issues and not get bogged down with fringe matters or react violently in a confrontational manner. This is not the Islamic way.

Now, I would like to submit that in all fairness we should also be self-critical. The role of the Muslim countries and particularly of Muslim political leaderships and of the

Organization of Islamic Conference (OIC) deserves to be condemned. They are guilty of acquiescence, complicity, and surrender. It was a shame to read the proceedings of the Qatar Muslim Foreign Ministers Conference (October 10, 2001). It seems they had no conscience, no vision, no courage, no understanding of Islam as well as of the global issues and the grand game of which they are the target. They were only saying, "please, please don't bomb us. Please, please do not go after any Arab country after destroying Afghanistan." It was a pitiable spectacle. Furthermore, the way Pakistan's military junta has surrendered to US pressure is shameful and outrageous. So is the role of Uzbekistan and Tajikistan. They all deserve to be condemned. However, there is a message in this, a very bold message: *that the political leadership in the Muslim countries and the political conscience of the ummah are at variance.* This leadership does not represent the Muslim people and their aspirations. There is a vast gulf between the two. The Muslim people look upon their rulers as stooges of the West and as collaborators in a superpower's war against a weak and poor Muslim country. These rulers, by and large, are imposed leaders, not freely chosen by the people. They rule by fiat and force. They are a major obstacle in the *ummah*'s search for its destiny.

A critical question then confronts us. Why has the United States chosen to attack Afghanistan and establish a foothold in Uzbekistan and Pakistan? I have thought about it and analyzed it as carefully as I can. The first and foremost reason appears to be an effort to camouflage their own failures, both in intelligence and politically. Secondly they are using it to achieve certain geo-strategic objectives in Central Asia. The United States had been planning for its presence in this area for the last 10 years. It made many political and economic overtures. Even the Taliban were offered a finger in the pie. A leading Texas oil company offered a $5 billion bait. But this did not work. The Bush Administration with its strong links with America's energy industry has definite plans for an energy-rich Central Asia. Access to these resources seems to be a major target, and Afghanistan and Pakistan provide the natural access vehicles. Any pipeline that is economic can come through this route only. There is much at stake, not only the barren mountains and caves of Afghanistan.[9] Thirdly, Israel and India have their own game plans in this context. They want to use this hyperbole about terrorism to promote their own terrorist activities in lands under their occupation. The Russian game is no different for Chechnya. Each of these wants to crush the struggle against their occupation in Palestine, Kashmir, and Chechnya, respectively. They want to change the context of the liberation movements and equate them with terrorism. Their countries have their own agenda. All this fits into the mosaic of the game plan of *Pax Americana*. The so-called first war of the twenty-first century is a war to further US hegemonistic objectives, targets, and strategies. And again there are no secrets. Zbigniew Brzezinski's recent book, *The Grand Chessboard*, is very explicit when it says that America is the only superpower and a major objective of US military and foreign policy should be that no rival power emerges at least for the next 25 years. As those rival powers could be Europe, China, Japan, and the Muslim world, the United States is trying to ensure that no challenger will emerge from these directions.

So these seem to be the four major objectives. But in my view, there are also three side objectives, or byproducts of this crusade. These may not necessarily be the direct targets of the government involved, although that too cannot be ruled out, but definitely these are what the vested interests and specific groups including certain people in government circles are seeking to achieve, viz.:

1. containing Islamic resurgence;
2. driving the world towards some sort of "clash of civilizations" scenario; and
3. financial control, not only of the world, but particularly of financial institutions in a manner that Islamic organizations and movements are dried of financial resources and as such put into a weak and defensive position.

These then appear to be the three side objectives. So what should be the response of Muslims in general and of Islamic movements in particular to this challenge? The major elements of that strategy, in my view, should be as follows:

1. There is no room for a strategy of retreat and withdrawal. Our strategy must be based on *engagement* and *dialogue*. We have to face the challenge. There should be no emotional confrontation. There should be no simplistic retaliation. There should not be any encouragement or condoning of violence, as meeting violence with violence is a trap and a recipe for disaster.
2. We should be firm. We should be clear and uncompromising as to our *objectives*. But we should also be polite, balanced, rational, cool, and considerate in all our responses. Our identity is to be the mid-most nation, a people who adopt a balanced approach (*ummat-e- wasat*). This should be the basis of our strategy.
3. The way that Islam and the Muslims have been targeted provides us with a very important opportunity for the articulation and projection of the Islamic position on major issues including *jihād* and terrorism. I emphasize though that we should not merely address *jihād* and terrorism, bur rather that we should address *all* issues and human concerns. This opportunity must be used to inform the people of Islam and others what Islam stands for. Islam is for the good of all human beings, not merely Muslims. So the Islamic concept of peace, justice, humanity, and the idea of a better life for all human beings should be brought into sharp focus. The need for rediscovering God, of man's linkage with the transcendent and of the rethronement of the moral criterion in human affairs is to be explained. This is the time to present Islam's message to humanity. Here I want to remind you of an instance from history. Let us recall the thirteenth and fourteenth centuries when the Muslims were totally shattered by the onslaught of the Mongols and Tartars. Things had degenerated to an extent unknown to our history. The Muslims were so weak and desperate that they had lost all hope. If the Tartars wanted to line up 100 Muslims to be killed they would simply wait for their turn to be crucified. This was the situation then but there were still those who had vision and faith, who faced the challenge coolly and boldly. Such was the behavior of a great scholar Sheikh Jamaluddin of Bukhara when involved in an incident with Prince Taimur Khan, the grandson of Halaku Khan. The period was the beginning of the second quarter of the fourteenth century. Taimur was

Prince of Kashghar. Tartar terror was at its zenith. This great *'ālim* Sheikh Jamaluddin had walked into Taimur's game reserve and was sitting there with a disciple. Taimur learned of this. He was furious. He asked his guards to bring the Sheikh to him handcuffed. When he was brought before the prince he was abused, beaten, and humiliated. But the Sheikh kept calm. Amazed by the Sheikh's fortitude and serenity, Taimur asked him in utter humiliation, "Tell me are you better or is my dog better than you?" The Sheikh answered "If I am true to my *Imān* and live according to the *dīn* and die in *Imān* then I am better, otherwise this dog is definitely better." This one sentence so moved Taimur that he released the Sheikh and asked his staff to bring the Sheikh for an audience after the hunt. When the Sheikh was brought before the Prince, he treated the Sheikh with respect and showed keen interest in Islam. He asked: "What is this *Imān*? And what does it have to do with my dog?" So the Sheikh explained that "this dog is your pet and is loyal to you. But as human beings we have all been created by God. *Imān* means belief in Allah and His prophets. Islam is a religion of peace and justice. There are rights which belong to Allah and rights which belong to human beings. As a Muslim, if I live by this *Imān* and remain loyal to my Creator till I breathe my last, then I am better because I would have succeeded through my loyalty to my Creator, otherwise as this dog is loyal to its master, it would win over me." T.W. Arnold writes in *The Preaching of Islam*, that that dialogue was so effective that the Prince whose heart was like stone then became like wax and after that a very interesting thing took place. Thereafter the Prince said to the Sheikh that he was moved by his message. "What you have said appeals to me but I cannot accept it now. So you can go, I free you but if I inherit power and become king then you come to me and I promise I will accept your *Imān*." This opportunity did not come in the Sheikh's life-time. But before his death he told his son, Sheikh Arshaduddin, about the whole incident. He asked that when Taimur became king the son should go to him and remind him of his commitment and promise to Sheikh Jamaluddin. And it happened that in 1347 AD that Taimur became king. When hearing this, Sheikh Arshaduddin went to Kashghar and made every effort to meet him. For several months he tried many avenues but could not gain access to him. So he established in what part of the palace Taimur slept. He erected a small hut in the jungle outside the palace and started giving the *Adhan* for *fajr* every morning. After a few days Taimur became aware of this and asked what was going on. So he sent his guards to the Sheikh to inquire and the Sheikh said "Yes I make *Adhan* and please tell Taimur that there is someone who wants to remind him of something. I could not get access to the king, so that is why I am doing this." When this message was relayed to Taimur, he agreed to see him. Sheikh Arshaduddin met him and reminded him of his encounter with his father so many years back. He recited the dia-logue that that had taken place between the two. The king acknowledged that he recalled the event and confirmed that he had been waiting for the Sheikh. Sheikh Arshaduddin then told him of his father's death and his *wasiyyah*. He repeated the invitation to Islam to the king and the latter fulfilled his promise. This is how he came to Islam and this is how history changed its course. Of the episode Iqbal beautifully states, "It is clear from the terrible episode of the Tartars, that those who were the worshippers of idols became the protectors of the Ka'bah." Not just central Asia but the whole Ottoman era owes itself to this new wave. Although I apologize for the detail of this story, the psychology behind it is no different than the situation we now find ourselves in. I am inviting you to give a similar response.

4.   The next element of our strategy should be personal contact, one to one and particularly reaching out to our neighbors. My definition of neighbor is not just the one who lives next door, but whoever is in contact with you. And in the age of the Internet the neighborhood has stretched far and wide. I want then a strategy for our neighbors, so that we reach them all.

5.   The media, the Internet, and communications technology are the next elements of our strategy. All these are extremely important. For the last 30 years I have been in the United States on and off and after September 11 I have noted a sea change in people's interest and inquisitiveness about Islam. So too the participation of Muslims on media networks. The Muslim community, particularly our youth, have tried to appear on different radio and TV programs. I must say that our ISB and MCB colleagues have done very well. I commend them and pray for them but we need to do much more. The media channels are very important and today they can make or break a war. *Al-Jazeerah* is an important medium and is doing a wonderful job. May Allah protect that. But we must reach all platforms. So the media, the Internet, and all forms of information communication technologies have to be harnessed in the service of Islamic *da'wah*. If we can establish an effective presence in these channels and convey correct information about Islam in a sober and calculated manner with proper argumentation I am sure we can achieve a breakthrough.

6.   Some Muslims in America have come up with a very good suggestion that I liked very much: the idea of an *open house* program. This is a golden opportunity for every mosque, Muslim school and home to invite non-Muslims to find out about Islam and Muslims. Give them an opportunity to open up, listen to them, even if they criticize you. Welcome them and also give them your viewpoint, the viewpoint of Islam. So through these open house programs we can reach the community in which we live.

7.   Islamic literature, conferences, and get-togethers are also important instruments for communication and outreach to the community. I understand the demand for Islamic literature in general and for the Qur'an in particular has increased manifold. Let us seize this opportunity.

8.   My next submission relates to the use of political platforms. I think this is very important. I am one of those who believe that when any of your brothers, colleagues, and organizations does a good job it must be appreciated. We are mostly critical of each other but we should also encourage, strengthen, and support each other. The Muslim participation in the political process is

a need of the hour. We must become active at all levels – local, national, international. We are living in the midst of all these people. Our future is tied to the future of all these societies. We cannot remain aloof. The ghetto approach has no future. We must actively participate in all spheres of social and political activity and present our viewpoint boldly, firmly, and politically. We must carve out a place for ourselves. This is important for the sake of *da'wah* and the future role of the Muslim community.

9. Finally, I would suggest that we must reach out to all those individuals, organizations, platforms, Muslim or non-Muslim, where we can share some common ideas and concerns. Whoever is against injustice, against capitalist exploitation, against war, against terrorism, against discrimination, we should try to join hands and make a common cause with them. We should reach every people of the left and right, Muslims and non-Muslims, organized or non-organized. I seek a better way of life for all human beings together.

My main goal behind offering these thoughts is to reflect on the state of Islam and Muslims in the twenty-first century and find ways to develop a comprehensive and multidimensional strategy for the Islamic movements and Muslim communities in Europe and North America.

Notes

1. See Samuel P. Huntington, *The Clash of Civilizations and the Remaking of World Order* (New York: Simon and Schuster, 1996), 187.
2. Geoffrey Robertson QC, the author of an important work, *Crimes Against Humanity: The Struggle for Global Justice*, writes in a recent article in *The Times* (November 7, 2001): "The US relied on its right to self-defence (Article 51 of the UN Charter) as a warrant for bombing, initially (and justifiably) to destroy the terrorist training camps. But self-defence is a primitive doctrine, severely limited by its basis in a necessity which is 'instant and overwhelming'. It cannot sensibly be asserted that invading Afghanistan is necessary, in this sense, to protect America."
3. "This document does not purport to provide a prosecutable case against Osama bin Laden in a court of law. Intelligence often cannot be used evidentially, due to the strict rules of admissibility and for the need to protect the safety of sources. As regards the British Government document presented to Parliament," *The Independent*, London, October 5, 2001. "The Americans are finding it hard to sell in the Middle East the British Government's document 'proving' Osama bin Laden's responsibility for the 11th September atrocities and is unlikely to rally the Arab world to the West's 'war on terrorism'. Only nine of the 70 points in the document relate to the attack on the World Trade Center and the Pentagon, and they often rely on conjectures rather than evidence". Robert Fisk, "This Loose Conjecture is Unlikely to Cut Much Ice with the Arab World," *The Independent*, London, October 5, 2001.
4. After seven weeks of silence *The New York Times* raises a meek voice in its editorial entitled "The CIA Needs Fixing." "The need for radical change was evident on Sept. 11. The failure of the CIA and other spy agencies to anticipate the attacks on New York and Washington was not the fault of a single institution. It was the failure of the government's entire $30

billion, 30-year intelligence apparatus," (editorial of *New York Times* "The CIA Needs Fixing," *International Herald Tribune*, November 6, 2001).

5. Geoffrey Robertson QC raises this issue in his article in *The Times*, November 7, 2001, "But justice as others understand that word, is not America's objective. Its leaders talk of 'justice' when what is really meant is summary execution: bin Laden's head is wanted 'on a plate' and there is deep regret at the missed opportunity to wipe out Mullah Omar by a rocket attack as his car sped from Kabul. Quite apart from the short-sightedness of the CIA's assassination plans, which will only create martyrs and lose the intelligence benefits of interrogation, the murder of enemy leaders cannot be a legitimate objective of any modern war. . . . Truman insisted on their trial at Nuremberg because 'undiscriminating executions or punishments without definite findings of guilt, fairly arrived at, would not sit easily on the American conscience or be remembered by our children with pride.'"

6. See Noam Chomsky, *Rogue States: The Rise of Force in World Affairs* (London: Pluto Press, 2000), 3–4.

7. "This is by far the most wicked and vicious act ever undertaken by fundamentalists of any faith. I must confess, however, that I am puzzled by the terrorist of September 11, because they are like no other fundamentalist that I have studied. It appears that Muhammad Atta was drinking vodka before boarding the airplane. Alcohol is, of course, forbidden by the Koran, and it seems incredible that an avowed martyr of Islam would attempt to enter paradise with vodka on his breath. Again, Ziad Jarrahi, the alleged Lebanese hijacker of the plane that crashed in Pennsylvania, seems to have frequented nightclubs in Hamburg. Muslim fundamentalists lead highly disciplined orthodox lives, and would regard drinking and clubbing as elements of the *jahili*, Godless society that they are fighting to overcome. I have no theory to offer, but would just like to note that these seem to be very unusual fundamentalists indeed." Karen Armstrong, "September Apocalypse," *The Guardian*, October 13, 2001. Karen Armstrong is author of several works on fundamentalism in major world faiths.

8. See Christopher Hewitt and Tom Cheetham, *Encyclopaedia of Modern Separatist Movements* (Oxford: ABC-CLIO, 2000).

9. John Pilger, an award-winning journalist and author of *Hidden Agendas* (Vintage, 1999), in an article in *The Mirror*, October 29, 2001 writes: "The war against terrorism is a fraud. After three weeks of bombing, not a single terrorist implicated in the attacks on America has been caught or killed in Afghanistan. Instead, one of the poorest, most stricken nation has been terrorised by the most powerful – the point where American pilots have run out of dubious 'milliary' targets and are now destroying mud houses, a hospital, Red Cross warehouses, lorries carrying refugees. None of those directly involved in the September 11 atrocity was Afghani. Most were Saudis, who apparently did their planning and training in Germany and the United States. The camps which the Taliban allowed bin Laden to use were emptied weeks ago. Moreover, the Taliban itself is a creation of the Americans and the British. In the 1980s the tribal army that produced them was funded by the CIA and trained by the BAB to fight the Russians. The hypocrisy does not stop there. When the Taliban took Kabul in 1996, Washington said nothing. Why? Because Taliban leaders were soon on their way to Houston, Texas, to be entertained by executives of the oil company Unocal. With secret US government approval, the company offered them a generous cut of the profits of the oil and gas pumped through a pipeline that the Americans wanted to build from Soviet central Asia through Afghanistan. A US diplomat said: 'The Taliban will probably develop like the Saudis did'. He explained that Afghanistan would become an American oil colony, there would be huge profits for the West, no democracy and the legal persecution of women. 'We can live with that,' he said. Although the deal fell through it remains an urgent priority of the

administration of George W. Bush, which is steeped in the oil industry. Bush's concealed agenda is to exploit the oil and gas reserves in the Caspian Basin, the greatest source of untapped fossil fuel on earth and enough according to one estimate to meet America's voracious energy needs for a generation. Only if the pipeline runs through Afghanistan can the Americans hope to control it." George Monbiot in an article published in *The Guardian*, October 23, 2001, points out a similar game plan: "'Is there any man, is there any woman, let me say any child here,' Woodrow Wilson asked a year after the First World War ended, 'that does not know that the seed of war in the modern world is industrial and commercial rivalry?' . . . The invasion of Afghanistan is certainly a campaign against terrorism, but it may also be a late colonial adventure. Afghanistan is as indispensable to the regional control and transport of oil in central Asia as Egypt was in the Middle East . . . In 1998, Dick Cheney, US Vice President, remarked 'I cannot think of a time when we have had a region emerge as suddenly to become as strategically significant as the Caspian Sea' . . . Piping (the oil) through Iran would enrich a regime which the US has been seeking to isolate . . . Through China . . . would be prohibitively expensive. But pipelines through Afghanistan would allow the US to both pursue its aim of 'diversifying energy supply' and to penetrate the world's most lucrative markets."

PART IV

Islamism, Sufism, and Pluralism in Contemporary Islamic Thought

25 *Sirāt al-mustaqīm* – One or Many? Religious Pluralism among Muslim
    Intellectuals in Iran   425
    Ashk Dahlén
26 Contemporary Islamic Movements in Southeast Asia: Challenges and
    Opportunities   449
    Ahmad F. Yousif
27 Transformation of Political Islam in Post-Suharto Indonesia   466
    Mun'im A. Sirry
28 The Pilgrimage to Tembayat: Tradition and Revival in Islamic
    Mysticism in Contemporary Indonesia   482
    Nelly Van Doorn-Harder and Kees De Jong

Sirāt al-mustaqīm – One or Many? Religious Pluralism among Muslim Intellectuals in Iran

Ashk Dahlén

Religious diversity is a *de facto* feature of modern societies, but recognizing this diversity entails more than just taking social and cultural facts into consideration. It requires some form of philosophical and theological orientation as well. It is widely acknowledged that the processes of globalization have heightened our general awareness about the scope and limitation of religious traditions. As a consequence of international communication and mobility, religious believers belonging to various traditions are now more aware of religious diversity and are responding to its challenges in different ways. Even if there have been important theological discussions among premodern Muslim theologians, mystics, and philosophers on the diversity of faiths, the subject of religious pluralism as conceived within the discipline of philosophy of religion is something of a post-nineteenth-century phenomenon.

Contemporary Muslims in Iran, as elsewhere, have been increasingly grappling with the issue of religious pluralism. While some Iranian intellectuals have espoused a form of religious exclusivism based on the assumption that their own faith possesses the only true and final revelation from God, others, disenchanted with such an absolutist position, have responded by proposing various inclusivist models of religious diversity, models which affirm the presence of divine guidance (*huda*) in other faiths as well. Moreover some Muslim thinkers opt for an even more universal approach by arguing that the normative truth claims of Islam do not by any means deny the metaphysical validity of other authentic religious traditions. In Iran, there has been during the last decade a growing interest in the study of comparative religion, as evidenced by the large number of books and journals currently available on the subject. The publication of a Persian translation of the British theologian John Hick's *Philosophy of Religion* as well as 'Abd al-Karim Surush's *Sirāthā-yi mustaqīm* (Straight Paths) in the mid-1990s generated a ground-breaking debate among Iranian intellectuals on religious pluralism, a debate which is still developing in various contexts.[1]

The aim of this chapter is to analyze Surush's notion of religious pluralism and explore its various theological, epistemological, and hermeneutical ramifications.

Focusing on positions in the Iranian debate, my study will also examine the opposing philosophical stance to religious pluralism, namely the exclusivism of 'Abdullah Jawadi-Amuli, a senior traditional scholar and perhaps the most distinguished Iranian traditionalist in terms of philosophical erudition. Jawadi-Amuli's refutation of religious pluralism is primarily based on the metaphysics of Mulla Sadra (d. 1640), and of specific interest to my study are the arguments he employs to support his positions that the validation of conflicting religious truth claims is, epistemologically speaking, not feasible.

'Abd al-Karim Surush – The John Hick of Iran?

A major spokesman of the post-revolutionary intellectual establishment, 'Abd al-Karim Surush (1945–) became well known to the Iranian public for his articles on the philosophy of science and religious epistemology, which were published in the monthly conservative journal *Kaihan-i farhangi* (*Cultural World*) during the years 1988–91.[2] In these articles, Surush analyzes the mechanism behind the alternating moments of epistemic openness and closure of human knowledge with the purpose of substantiating the concepts of the plurality of reasons and the contingency of knowledge with an epistemological basis and creating possibilities for a pluralistic democracy that is an outgrowth of the community of believers. Surush called his cognitive theory "the contraction and expansion of religious knowledge" (*qabz wa bast-i ma'rifat-i dīnī*) and claims that it explains the growth of knowledge as proceeding through the elimination of error, i.e. through the refutation of hypotheses that are either logically inconsistent or entail empirically refuted consequences.[3] The theory of contraction and expansion is unmistakably inspired by Karl Popper's (d. 1994) evolutionary epistemology and his theory of falsification as a critique of "verification" as well as Kantian notions of second-order (*a posteriori*) cognitive theory.

In 1997, the debate on religious epistemology continued in the daily Iranian newspaper *Salam*, which took the initiative for a dialogue between Surush and the traditional scholar Muhsin Kadivar (1959–) on the issue of religious pluralism. Their conversation appeared in five parts in *Salam* in February 1998, and was reprinted under the title *Munāzarah darbārah-yi plurālīsm-i dīnī* (Debate on Religious Pluralism). While Kadivar took the stance of religious inclusivism by claiming, similar to the German theologian Karl Rahner (d. 1984), that all human beings are potential receivers of divine guidance since divine truth is partially reflected in other traditions, Surush principally advocated a form of religious pluralism inspired by John Hick.[4] In the ending of the debate on religious pluralism with Kadivar, Surush wrote an essay in which he substantiated his criticism of religious exclusivism from a pluralistic perspective. This essay, which was polemically called *Sirāthā-yi mustaqīm* (Straight Paths) as against the Qur'anic (1:5) phrase *al-sirāt al-mustaqīm* (the straight path),[5] was published in the bimonthly reformist journal *Kiyān* (*Source*) and reprinted in a book with the same title.[6]

Surush draws on John Hick's (1922–) three labels of religious understanding (exclusivist, inclusivist, and pluralist) to explain various possible human answers to the question of multiple religious phenomena.[7] In depicting a new map of the universe of faiths, he emphasizes that religious pluralism is an epistemological theory belonging to the discipline of philosophy of religion, which gives reason for the validity (*haqqāniyat*) of all religious traditions and religious experiences. Surush argues that philosophy of religion includes an elaboration where religion is seen as a definite enough object to become the object of a systematic investigation that is not aimed at deciding on the truth of a particular religion. He distinguishes philosophy of religion proper from philosophical theology and suggests that reflection on religion is philosophically respectable only if it confines itself to mere theism and is abstracted from all particular religions (anything else is taken to be theology, not philosophy). In Surush's view, religious pluralism is distinct from social pluralism but the two are, however, related as there can be no pluralistic society in practical terms without a theoretical view that justifies social diversity and difference: "A pluralistic society is a society with no official religious interpretations and interpreters; it is established on pluralistic reason and not the sentiments of sacred unity."[8] Considering pluralism a cornerstone of democratic nation building, he asserts that religious pluralism must be officially recognized by Muslims.

Second-order Epistemology of *Construction*: Religions as Cognitive Responses

The principal epistemological premise of Surush's pluralist hypothesis is that it is beyond human cognition to justify the validity of religion. He has no faith in the ability of rational argument to settle differences in religious truth claims. As he argues, we cannot rationally demonstrate if a religion is true or false. By endorsing a form of critical realism, Surush suggests that knowledge is one thing and reality another and that there is no guarantee that our knowledge truthfully represents reality, since reality exists independent of our cognition.[9] Following the complex philosophical architectonic made by Kant in the field of epistemology, Surush accepts the notion of "systematic conjecture" in the sphere of human knowledge and adopts a second-order cognitive theory to substantiate his concept of religious pluralism. Initially, he divides human knowledge into two broad categories, *a priori* and *a posteriori*, to develop a wider epistemological foundation in the realm of religion than Kant originally intended. While *a priori* knowledge consists of natural judgments that take place before the "context of justification," Surush claims that *a posteriori* knowledge takes place after the "context of discovery" and corresponds to the "context of justification," where the production of knowledge takes place. His division of *a priori* and *a posteriori* is therefore not according to logical form but according to their warrant, that is, if the truth claim of a certain sentence is in need of empirical backing or not. Similar to Popper, Surush rejects the claim of a necessary *a priori* validity for Kantian categories of thought and intuition and provides a perspective under which these categories can be seen as highly edited, much tested presumptions, validated only as provisional scientific truth is validated.[11]

A major concern of Surush's pluralist hypothesis is his emphasis on the objectivity of religious truth claims and his confidence in intersubjective justification, which denotes a deontological model of rendering account. With respect to other persons, he believes that we have an unconditional duty to justify our beliefs. By also arguing that science and history have implications for religious truth claims, Surush thinks that religious propositions are subject to falsification just as any other truth claim, even if religion is not a theory in the scientific sense as its basic tenets cannot be proved rationally.[12] While religion differs from science in the sense that trans-historical religious beliefs are not concerned with objectivity in the true sense of the word, he believes that scientific data lends plausibility to some religious doctrines, while falsifying others. Following the dominant Western tradition of thought on the nature of faith from the time of St. Thomas Aquinas, Surush interprets faith as a propositional attitude that comes very close to the notion of faith as unevidenced or inadequately evidenced belief. He considers religion as beyond our rational comprehension, even if he believes that religion is compatible with the concept of freedom that forms the basis of Kant's practical philosophy.[13]

In light of its postpositivist epistemological foundation, Surush's pluralist hypothesis is distinct from the pluralism advocated by mystics in various religions, which emphasizes some kind of esoteric, transcendent unity. The epistemological position of the mystics undercuts, in his view, the particularity of any claims that are made by specific religious traditions. Referring to the British philosopher Walter T. Stace's (d. 1967) argument that all religions share the same mystical experience, he argues that mystics actually lack an ultimate perspective and interpret religious experience according to their differing historical, cultural, or philosophical biases. While Stace believes that mystical experience is unmediated and ineffable and then understood according to culturally conditioned interpretations, Surush claims that mystics do not have context-free experiences but that the nature of mystical experience is socially constructed according to the culture, beliefs, and expectations of the mystics having the experiences.[14] In Surush's view, the exclusive claims of religions cannot be combined with an esoteric or metaphysical perspective on religious diversity, since pluralism is not an attribute of unity. In contrast to the metaphysical principle of transcendent unity, his pluralism is an epistemological, external discourse on factual pluralism at the level of empirical corroboration and explanation of causes:

> Those who witness unity behind diversity in universal terms consistent with their own views (i.e. the mystical view on pluralism), have not at all posed any question or grasped the factual nature of the issue. The debate on pluralism is a discourse on empirical pluralism at the level of empirical corroboration and explanation of causes, not exoteric diversity through esoteric unity or reduction of imaginative pluralism to "true unity".[15]

Religious pluralism, in Surush's view, is the philosophical theory that the great world religions constitute varying responses to the one ultimate, mysterious divine reality, but his focus is not on unity but on matters of fact derived from experience.[16] By considering religious experience as the basis for religious belief, his pluralist hypothesis is empirical and descriptive in its denigration of any significance of *a priori* knowledge and in considering all *a priori* beliefs as *literally* false. It is arrived at inductively, from ground level, using a thoroughly modern epistemology. With reference to Hick's de-absolutized notion of truth, Surush applies the Kantian noumenon/phenomenon distinction to religion, and defines religious experience as a human, "cognitive response" to the ineffable real (*al-haqq*), which we call God. As a *human* response there is always an inescapably *human* element within religion and no revelation can stand apart from humanity.[17] Since the key features of empirical cognition, including the spatial form of intuition and other features of representation, must be traced to our cognitive constitution, Surush formulates a dual classification of God according to which the divine is understood on "the level of namelessness" and "the level of relation." He suggests that there exists a range of changing human images of God at the second level which determine our religious experience:

> [Hick] makes use of Kant's distinction between noumenon and phenomenon, or the real-as-it-is-in-itself and the real-as-perceived. He distinguishes between God at the level of namelessness (*maqām-i lā-ism*) and God at the level of relation (*maqām-i nisbat*). Hick considers the expression of truth in multiple forms as the clue for understanding differences between the religions as well as the proof for the validity of all religions. From this perspective, he reflects on factual pluralism in the sphere of religion.[18]

The Kantian distinction between the noumenon and phenomenon illustrates that Surush essentially adopts a "constructivist" view of truth according to which noumenal realities are experienced through the phenomenal realm. He rejects the idea that man has direct access to the thing in-itself and argues that we think through "interpretative filters" that shape our perceptions of reality. Surush's view that knowledge depends on the structure of the mind and not the world results easily in knowledge having no connection to the world and being no true representation. By arguing that God is ultimately beyond our cognition, he is confronted by the "egocentric dilemma," the suggestion that we are ourselves "creators" of our religious systems. Instead of addressing the question of whether Islam's truth claims can be reconciled with those of other religions, Surush refers to the Kantian principle "equality of proofs" to claim that the ultimate structure of reality, or any metaphysical subject for that matter, is not provable *a priori*:

> When the intellect enters the circle of metaphysics it crosses the threshold of a sphere to which it is uninvited. The intellect cannot categorically validate its propositions. Every opinion [on metaphysical matters] is therefore equal and equivalent to its rival opinions. In other words, equality of proofs occurs.[19]

While Surush's pluralist hypothesis essentially is based on postpositivist readings of Kant's epistemology and John Hick's notion of truth in the discipline of philosophy of religion, it is surprisingly not Kant's *Kritik der reinen Vernunft* or John Hick's systematic, scholarly *oeuvre*, but Jalal al-din Rumi's poetry which is the most frequently and approvingly cited reference in his pluralism discourse. Surush is in particular influenced by Rumi's metaphysical explanations of concepts such as *manzar* (point of view) and *zidd* (opposition) and his differentiation of *surat* (form) and *ma'nā* (meaning).[20] In Surush's view, the Sufi poet adopts these terms to communicate the idea that human knowledge is contextual, contingent, and experienced through the phenomenal religious realm. The famous story of the Indian elephant in the dark house is among the many passages from Rumi's work that Surush consults so as to demonstrate that religious knowledge is formed by external, non-religious contingencies: "The essence of Rumi's words is that we humans are located in a dark house and that none of us can grasp reality in itself. Everyone observes, comprehends, and knows according to his or her own point of view."[21]

Hermeneutics of Suspicion: Religious Truth Claims as Relational

Seeing that the human intellect fails to provide final, sufficient "proof" in the sphere of metaphysics, Surush takes recourse to the "inference of the best explanation" in the understanding of reality. His pluralist hypothesis is intrinsically related to "hermeneutics of suspicion" and the problem of probability given that reality, hermeneutically speaking, possesses "a wide range of probable meanings." Aware of the fact that it is difficult to combine conflicting truth claims of various religions, Surush argues that diversity of faiths "ultimately is attributable to the two fundamental hermeneutic differentiations of *truth* and *understanding of truth*."[22] He compares religions to indexical schemes, consisting of a number of individual hypotheses that are valid in the sense that they are relative to individual persons. In addition to transcendent, metaphysical truth, which is timeless and absolute, Surush puts forward the notion of indexical truth which corresponds to a specific human experience which suggests that two facts of human experience can be held together: "The truth and authenticity of indexical hypotheses are relative in the sense that they consist of an aspect of *for me* and *for you*".[23]

By arguing that most metaphysical (trans-historical) truth claims are irresolvable, Surush avoids the question of whether conflicting theistic and nontheistic truth claims render his pluralistic hypothesis implausible. He argues instead that the distinction noumenon/phenomenon releases the inherent tension between contradictory expressions of religious awareness. In his view, the pluralist hypothesis is not concerned with contradiction or unity, but variation, since he believes that diversity of faiths does not, empirically speaking, reveal contradictions but a variety of human experience.[24] By holding a realist view of religious phenomena in the presence of conflicting truth claims, he faces, however, the risk of internal inconsistency. For instance, most Christians believe that Jesus was God incarnate and part of the Trinity, while both Muslims and Jews hold that it is impossible for any human to be God incarnate, and that no Trinity exists. Christians believe that Jesus died on the cross, while Muslims believe that Jesus was not crucified. Claiming that both Christianity and Islam are absolutely true gives rise to a logical contradiction, and by affirming two mutually exclusive things about reality the pluralist hypothesis would end up being rationally incoherent and violating the "law of identity."[25] While Surush claims that disagreements regarding matters of historical fact, in principle, can be resolved by application of the historical method (such as the Muslim claim that Jesus was not crucified), he never takes this method into logical account. Other scholars, such as Harold Netland, would disagree with Surush's claim that there are no other tradition-independent criteria by which religious traditions can be evaluated. Netland believes that there are at least six such criteria, including the basic principles of logic, recognizing self-defeating statements, coherence, ability to adequately explain all the data, consistency with other fields of knowledge like history and science, and moral considerations.[26] These criteria are used regularly in science, history, and philosophy to evaluate various theories and worldviews.

Since there exist no given facts in the phenomenal world or in the sphere of hermeneutics, Surush argues that the epistemic validity of a religious tradition can in the end only be a matter of hermeneutical meaning, relative to individual believers. Considering the difference between situations as the one and only starting point for understanding, his hermeneutics represents an anti-Kantian perspective that is non-conceptual and non-representational. In the quest for new paradigms, Surush actually attempts to extricate himself from the mode of representational thinking so character-istic for Enlightenment thought and seems to believe in historical condition as a con-stitutive element of meaning where past meaning only can be reconstructed in regard to historical, subjective conditions: "Validity is a matter of relational meaning and understanding, which cannot be proved by means of rational justification."[27] The valid-ity of religious traditions is, however, much more complicated since religion is not limited to some individual assumptions but interconnected to a multifaceted collection of theological doctrines. As Surush argues, it is virtually impossible to empirically attest to the falsification or misrepresentation of a certain religion due to the complex struc-ture of religious phenomena itself:

> First of all we have to acknowledge that each religion is a scheme, a substantial collection of hypotheses, in the sense that every hypothesis is interrelated to a large number of other hypotheses. It is not possible to compare two different hypotheses, but only to compare two separate schemes or systems. As each scheme include a large range of hypotheses, it is extremely difficult to refute a religion as contradictory or false. Each of these systems has its own capacities and incapacities in the interpretation of facts, experiences, explanation of complexities, etc. From this perspective, the claim of one religion over another becomes much more complicated than what first appears to be the case. The exact identification of the nature of contradiction as well as the identification of criteria for discerning truth and false is exceptionally difficult.[28]

On Grading Religions as Cultural Paradigms of Salvation

Since it is difficult to identify the core of truth claims belonging to religions variegated as, for instance, Hinduism, Christianity or Islam, Surush concludes that we must remain agnostic with regards to the differing metaphysical truth claims of religions. The validity of one religion does not, in other words, automatically indicate that others are false but on the contrary, it points to the equal "validity" of all religions. Supposing the possibility to some extent grade religious phenomena, he claims that there is no means to realistically access religions as totalities or systems of salvation. Similar to Hick, Surush compares the great world faiths to the diversity of human cultures and languages and interprets religions as culturally conditioned responses to the ineffable divine reality. He considers religious truth as human experience within a cultural paradigm and defines culture as the primary determinant in religious commitments. As far as religions are embodiments of different conceptions of the divine from within different cultural contexts of being human, Surush believes that the majority of people practice the faith which they are born into and only a few people sincerely explore other religions to scrutinize their own tradition. In his view, most believers are imitators as far as their faith is concerned:

> It is not the case, for instance, that all Christians by exploring all religious traditions and teachings come to the conclusion that Christianity is valid on the basis of definite proof. The faith of the majority of believers is inherited, a kind of emulation. This rule also generally applies to Zoroastrians, Muslims, Jews, and so forth. If a Christian was born into a Muslim society, he or she would be a Muslim, and if a Muslim was born into a Christian society, he or she would be a Christian. The condition of the majority of believers, not only the majority of people but also the majority of religious scholars, is this: "We found Our fathers following a certain religion, and we do guide ourselves by their footsteps" (Qur'an 43:22).[29]

Surush's pluralist hypothesis is developed by his acceptance of the cultural relativity of religious truth claims which suggest that religious presuppositions primarily are set according to "accidents of birth." Referring to Wittgenstein's "family resemblance" concept to compare religions, he asserts that no religion has any fixed and static doctrines or main beliefs, but that the nature of the relationship between different interpretations of a specific religion can be regarded as registers of human believers. In the case of Islam, Surush claims that the traditional concept *Uṣūl al-Dīn* (principles of belief) consists of historical ideas subjected to change in their development, proliferation, and variation. As an alternative to its accidental characteristics, every religion is contingent on its essential "substances" (*zātiyāt*) for its articulation and sustenance. Among the substances, Surush mentions prophecy (*nubuwwat*) and the objectives of revealed law (*maqāsid al-sharī'at*), such as the sacredness of life, dignity, descent, property, and freedom of religion.[30] Inspired by Hick, he concludes that the boundary between true and false does not run between Islam and other religions but within each of the religions. In other words, it is legitimate to grade aspects of religions and to place them in some order of merit. This can be done, he argues, by employing a range of criteria such as the theological coherence of their specific doctrines and the moral integrity of their teachings. With specific reference to Judaism, Christianity, and Islam, Surush distinguishes the higher aspects within every religious tradition from the lower aspects:

> The truth is that incommensurability as well as historical, religious and cultural complexities do not allow us to value these three religions [Judaism, Christianity and Islam] on the basis of culture and history with the purpose of estimating one of them as higher than or as lower than the others. All religions have higher and lower aspects and the revealed texts and teachings of the religions all endorse the prophetic saying: "No man is a true believer unless he desires for his brother that which he desires for himself."[31]

In Surush's view, all religious traditions display contradictory trends within them-selves. While Islam, for instance, bestowed upon humanity artistic and literary rich-ness in the cultural domain (the higher aspect), its jurisprudence came to establish "barbarous" punishments in the legal domain (the lower aspect).[32] There is thus no dis-tinguishable difference between various religions inasmuch as one cannot honestly proclaim the moral superiority or salvific effectiveness of one tradition over others. By relating salvation, guidance (*huda*) in the Islamic parlance, and to the concept of higher and lower aspects of religions, he argues that no human being is outside the realm of God's mercy and that pluralism is indispensable for peaceful coexistence between reli-gious believers of different traditions. By emphasizing that "the Guide" (*al-hādī*) is one of God's attributes according to the Qur'an, Surush suggests that it would be theolog-ically absurd to assume that only Shi'ite Muslims are granted divine guidance.[33] In his view, the salvation of humanity, through its various religious traditions, is morally acceptable and rationally compelling since an all-loving God cannot condemn the vast majority of humans to eternal hell simply because they are born at a certain place and at a certain time. By considering salvation as something truly universal, he does not present Islam, in the sense of the historical Muslim community, as a religious tradition with a universal mission.

Surush's assertion that followers of other religions might be closer to the divine reality than one is oneself, as well as his tolerance concerning theological disagree-ments, is very close to Hick's idea that no religion can claim to teach the only or absolute truth. While Surush accepts Hick's idea that religion is not literally the word of God but mankind's attempt to describe the divine, he does more justice to the fact that world religions hold mutually incompatible beliefs by recognizing their irreducible differences. In contrast to Hick's reductionism, Surush is more attentive to the danger of reducing religious traditions to some common, unintelligible foundation by arguing that every religion has "some unique, exclusive features," which constitute its *raison d'être* and "set it apart from other traditions."[34] The fact that Surush is both a realist and a pluralist about religions exposes him as a "descriptive polytheist" (as opposed to a "cultic poly-theist"). He recognizes the reality of several gods but makes clear that he intends his own religious commitments to find their place within the Islamic tradition. This is, of course, not Kant's own account of religious experience or divine being, but he takes Kant's terminology of our sensory experience of the world and adapts it to serve as a way of understanding religious experience and its objects. Surush also defines plural-ism as a mode of "humanizing" religion where spiritual realization also becomes an individual affair. He comprehends religion as essentially reaching the deepest level of man's solitude, that is, as an attitude of the individual towards the universe aiming at the transformation of man.

'Abdullah Jawadi-Amuli – Religious Exclusivist and Traditionalist

Following the publication of Surush's articles on religious pluralism in 1998, a number of Iranian traditionalist intellectuals went into strong polemics with him on questions such as definitions of pluralism, divine grace, the universal mission of Islam, and the transcendent unity of religions. In the forefront of the Islamic exclusivist position were traditional scholars, such as Sayyid Mahmud Nabawiyan and 'Ali Rabbani-Gulpaigani, who advocate that Shi'ite Islam is the one unique and divinely ordained religion.[35] Surush's most prominent critic is, however, Ayatullah 'Abdullah Jawadi-Amuli (1933–), a senior traditional scholar and perhaps the most distinguished traditionalist in contemporary Iran in terms of philosophical erudition and public influence.[36] Following in the footsteps of his teacher, Muhammad Husain Tabataba'i (d. 1981), Jawadi-Amuli is also regarded as the second highest authority on "transcendental wisdom" (hikmat-i mut'ālīyah) in Iran. Certainly, all his works are distinguished by a clearly recognizable gnostic viewpoint. In his Dīnshināsī (Studies on Religion), Jawadi-Amuli approaches the subject of religious diversity from an exclusivist perspective grounded in the perennial teachings of Islamic metaphysics. This work, containing a number of articles dealing with the philosophy of religion, treats the subject of religious pluralism in two lengthy expositions.

Metaphysical Realism: Religion as a Divine Self-disclosure

The point of departure of Jawadi-Amuli's discussion on religious pluralism is that religion is what constitutes the most innate or primordial (fitrī) in the human being. Referring to the conclusions made by modern sociology of religion, he claims that there has never existed a human society without one form or another of religion. He argues that despite secularization of modern societies, the ideology of secularism has not been successful in eradicating religious traditions and beliefs from collective and individual human conscience.[37] Due to its attribute of being innate in the human being, Jawadi-Amuli does not describe religion as something constructed but as a divine and revealed entity which has its heart of origin in the higher worlds of the divine: "Man does not construct religion but he is the receiver of a divine communication. Man is required to have faith in religion, expose himself to it and model his individual and collective path on its teachings."[38] In this respect, he seeks to provide a traditional framework for an interpretation of religion in which the combination of action and thought is of central importance.

In acknowledging the diversity of religious phenomena, Jawadi-Amuli distinguishes between true religion and false religion on the basis of Qur'anic terminology, and argues that the former is a divine manifestation (tanzīl), which makes itself known in revelation, the natural world, and human nature. Since true religion is manifested in the phenomenal world and the human soul, it corresponds to reality which is metaphysically transparent symbolizing divine archetypes.[39] In contrast to false religion, which is generated by human, separative and dividing elements belonging to man's negative, lower passions, true religion has a divine creative source (mabda'-yi fi'lī) and objective (hadaf). With reference to the Qur'an (4:60 and 29:17), Jawadi-Amuli claims that true religion is the religion of the prophets (anbiyā) as distinguished from the religion of the idol worshipers (tāghūtiyān).[40] God is the objective of true religion in the sense that He has bestowed intellect ('aql) on human beings and guides them from darkness to His light. The intellect is considered in its traditional sense as a source of metaphysics and as such functions self-sufficiently as "an epistemic criterion of corroboration or falsification [operating] beyond empirical, sense perception."[41] Intellection, as he speaks of it, is similar to revelation, a form of God's self-manifestation, and it is not in the category of mere opinion. Insofar as it is directed to God, human reasoning is lifted out of the realm of private judgment to constitute the objective factor that saves the believer from falling into subjectivism. True metaphysical belief counts, in other words, as genuine knowledge, since while God can be known through discursive reasoning, He is only known in His totality through Himself.

In epistemological terms, Jawadi-Amuli's religious exclusivism is based on a precritical form of realism, which considers cognitive matters in the light of a basic sacred cosmology. By claiming that the traditional conception of reality is not to be changed, but rather that modernity must adjust to the truths of religion, his epistemology is premodern and wants to preserve a position anterior to modernity, which is, philosophically speaking, anti-modern. His notion of religious exclusivism is developed on the basis of the idea of an objective knowledge of the cosmic and natural order, and is thus rooted in a correspondence theory asserting that knowledge is true if it corresponds to external reality.[42] Knowledge and reality are, in other words, not two things, but identical, and questions about criterion of knowledge depend upon questions of reality and their capacity to bring forth certain knowledge. Any epistemic belief that contradicts the intrinsic nature of reality is, in Jawadi-Amuli's view, unwarranted and false: "Human knowledge is warranted if it corresponds to reality and unwarranted if it does not correspond to reality, since its data is dependent of reality and cannot alter its [intrinsic] structure."[43]

The starting point for the discussion on religious diversity is, in Jawadi-Amuli's view, that we inhabit a world of differences. Following John Hick's terminology, he positions religious pluralism as diametrically opposite to the theory of religious exclusivism that relates salvation and guidance exclusively to one particular religious tradition. While exclusivism takes many forms, such as in the Catholic dogma of *Extra ecclesiam nulla salus* (there is no salvation outside the church), the neo-orthodoxy of the German theologian Karl Barth (d. 1968), or the thought of Alvin Plantinga, Jawadi-Amuli claims that exclusivism is characterized by the belief that the tenets of one religion are in fact true and that any proposition (other religious beliefs) that is incompatible with those tenets are false. Similar to Plantinga and others who propose that exclusivism is not irrational or unjustified but has epistemic warrant for its beliefs, Jawadi-Amuli argues that exclusivism is not "morally suspect," since it reserves to the Christian the right to believe in propositions that are not believed, for instance, by Muslims and leaves it to the Muslims to decide which propositions are and which are not essential to Islam. His interpretation of exclusivism is thus largely consistent with the connotation the term has acquired in the context of contemporary Christian debates in philosophical theology.[44]

By arguing that religious pluralism is a rational question that belongs to the discipline philosophy of religion, he claims that one can only get to the bottom of different religious truth claims by the use of revelation, intellect, or definite transmitted proof (*naql-i qat'i*).[45] In the latter case, epistemic certainty is deemed to be achieved through God's knowledge as revealed to and transmitted through the Prophet and the Shi'ite

Imāms. In contrast to Surush's notion of indexical system, Jawadi-Amuli considers knowledge of religion as consisting of theoretical doctrines and practical ordinances which are true and valid in the sense that they correspond to reality. He approaches multiplicity from a metaphysical viewpoint and believes that empirical methods are of no use in justifying the validity of religious truth claims, since they cannot grasp the essential aspects of religious diversity which are of metaphysical, ontological nature:

> In an attempt to justify the validity or invalidity of religious truth claims by means of experience and sensation we would have to practice each one of the world's religions for understanding what is true and what is false. The world's religions are many. Before we could fully practice a few of them, our life would have to come to an end and humanity would encounter a growing skepticism concerning the truth claims of different religions.[46]

Suggesting that Surush's pluralist hypothesis is the product of philosophical skepticism in its denigration of metaphysics, Jawadi-Amuli argues that religious pluralism is an epistemological position which has its origin in a philosophical "worldview that regards truth as well as human perception as relativistic."[47] Acknowledging that relativism is associated with an abandonment of an infallible standpoint, he suggests that Surush's skepticism about the ontology of knowledge makes every universal predication of ontology ambiguous by casting doubt on ideas of representation and ultimately relativizing the Absolute. While Surush's position need not be construed as a claim that all conflicting or contradictory claims about God are true, Jawadi-Amuli asserts that Surush misinterprets Rumi's poetry to corroborate his pluralist hypothesis, such as is the case with his reading of the latter's elephant analogy.[48] In his view, Rumi does not allude to the relativity of understanding but rather draws attention to the fact that human reason, in contrast to intellectual intuition and revelation, is an insufficient epistemic device for grasping metaphysical matters. While Surush's reference to Rumi attempts to validate the truth of all religions, it succeeds rather in showing that all religions fail to adequately identify and comprehend God. By demonstrating not that all religions are true but that all religions are largely false, Surush's elephant analogy implies, in Jawadi-Amuli's view, a radical skepticism concerning our knowledge of God by projecting the prophets as blind men rather than as men of illumination.[49]

For Jawadi-Amuli, epistemology is never divorced from the religious ontology. The main premise of his religious exclusivism is that religion addresses that which is most universal and primordial in man. Human beings are perennially driven to seek ways that lead to the sacred and the true, and to love the sacred and the true, the ultimate of which is the Absolute. Since religion is directed towards man's primordial being, which corresponds to God's infinite Oneness and Essence, he starts from the fact that the oneness of truth necessitates one true religion (dīn) at the microcosmic level: "The measure for man's spiritual instruction can only be one since religion is intrinsically connected to man's primordial being, which is common to all human beings."[50] Depicting the cosmological state of man as something constant from which there only are insignificant deviations at certain moments of history, Jawadi-Amuli claims that human nature is a theomorphic being in the sense of constituting a theophany of the divine names. Since God explained the reality of the names to man and not to the angels, man has a high spiritual potential, which is reflected in that all essential knowledge is ultimately based on the identity of the knower and the known. The unity of subject and object means that man's most immediate experience is that of his own intuitive awareness, which can achieve a direct apprehension of ultimate reality that reveals it to be spiritual. Since the knower and the known are ultimately one, the true religion can in the end only be one. This is, according to Jawadi-Amuli, the deeper meaning of the universality of the Islamic doctrine of divine unity (tawḥīd).[51]

The Universality of Revelation and the Plurality of Prophets

With reference to traditional Muslim scholars, such as Mulla 'Abdullah Lahiji, Jawadi-Amuli contemplates on revelation and prophecy in the context of the theological principle of "necessity" (zarūrat). God is the wise (al-hakīm) and has, accordingly, in His wisdom sent prophets with guidance to every nation and community. According to the Prophet Muhammad, God has raised 124,000 prophets among all peoples along the past history of mankind, and 315 of them were messengers. For Jawadi-Amuli, the universality of religion and the oneness of humanity lay the foundation for the necessity of believing in all authentic revelations, which is symbolized in Islam's acceptance of all prophets and holy books. In his view, the mission of the Prophet is not unique, as he is only one of God's messengers to man, but also the last of them.[52] The idea of the universality of revelation brings about the belief that the religion of Muhammad is the culmination and perfection of the whole series of God's revelation to humankind as declared in the Qur'an.[53] By accepting the essential distinction between the universal religion (dīn), on the one hand, and the religion of the last Prophet on the other, Jawadi-Amuli claims that all the prophets of God essentially preached the same religion. While Islam in the first sense refers to religion as such, that is, the principle of universal submission, it signifies the religion of Muhammad in the second sense, that is, the Islam par excellence.[54] Although Jawadi-Amuli acknowledges the universality of prophecy, he does refute the idea that all religions are equally valid as ontologically unwarranted and self-contradictory. As he argues, the various doctrines of religious traditions cannot, metaphysically speaking, be divinely sanctioned since multiple true religions would entail an "association" or partnership" in being:

> The prophets are all unified in their universal teachings even if each of them has a specific method and a particular course of action, which is related to national distinctions and human corporal needs. Religious pluralism in the sense that people during one or various historical epochs would possess one primordial nature and be granted different religions which contradict each other in their principles of belief and basic ethical and legal teachings, is an unwarranted explanation.[55]

As a philosopher in the tradition of Mulla Sadra, Jawadi-Amuli endorses the idea of a hierarchical cosmic order by dividing existence into several ontological degrees and reflects on diversity as a difference (tashkīk) in ontological levels. In his view, religion corresponds to permanent, metaphysical reality on the basis that reality is composed of multiple states of existence (*marātib al-wujūd*), which move substantially towards higher forms. All religious faiths are essentially divine manifestations and participate in God's knowledge, not according to the measure of man, but according to the variations in the divine measure. In the function of manifestations, they correspond in different degrees to the divine source, which they all reflect and symbolize.[56] Since all authentic religions ontologically have elements of truth in them by virtue of the divine self-disclosure, Jawadi-Amuli argues that every religion is true at higher or lower levels within its own ontological potential and possibility:

> The study of religions confirms that religious diversity involves a difference (*tashkīk*) in ontological levels. The divine religions have many doctrinal, ethical, legal and juristic points in common, because they consist of multiple states and levels. Some divine religions are perfect and some are more perfect. The reason for this is that external realities as well as human knowledge implicate such a difference in ontological levels.[57]

"Religions" in its plural form thus indicates the development of religion at the level of its manifestation or descent. Since religions are of different nature as ontological potentialities in contrast to the infinite divine being, some religions have attained higher levels of completion than others which remain immature or not fully formed. Jawadi-Amuli emphasizes, however, that "it is not religion itself but its manifestations which reach perfection and are completed."[58] While all revelations manifest a divine archetype or aspect in the process of God's self-disclosure, some of these revelations are largely imperfect in relation to the divine norm. As a religious exclusivist, Jawadi-Amuli claims that Islam is the one complete religion and that there cannot exist two equally valid religions, which also are substantially different:

> The essence of religion is the same for all peoples since there is only one religion (i.e. Islam), which is accepted by God, the Most High. Man's true reality is one since man is created as the image of God. God is responsible for the fostering of this true reality. God is certainly not subject to ignorance and forgetfulness. He knows all realities from pre-existence to eternity. God does not have two religions or commands as testified in the Qur'an (3:19 and 85).[59]

In Jawadi-Amuli's view, the universal religion is essentially perennial as far as its belief in divine unity and prophecy is concerned, it is only the teachings of its prophets that have differed during the course of history. By considering non-Islamic religions as relative rivals to the one true religion, he argues that the exoteric laws and teachings which pertain to the branches of religion (*furū' al-dīn*) show a formal discrepancy but that the principles of religion (*Uṣūl al-Dīn*) are one (*wāhid*).[60] In this respect, he criticizes Surush's concept of substances/accidentals of religion for being incoherent and for undermining the normativity of traditional Shi'ite principles of belief. In Jawadi-Amuli's view, Surush does not use any religious criterion for determining this distinction, which thus is exposed to a certain theoretical ambivalence: "The distinction between substances and accidentals is in need of a criterion which is either religious or non-religious. In the former case, the criterion is inevitably contingent on individual presuppositions since the determination of substances and accidentals becomes a matter of individual taste."[61] Jawadi-Amuli argues that this, for instance, is the case with Surush's interpretation of jurisprudence (*fiqh*) as both an accidental and substance of religion, and he claims that the latter fails to consider the difference between religious substance and its "intrinsic purpose" (*maqsūd bā lizāt*).

Epistemologically speaking, Jawadi-Amuli's argument against the pluralist hypothesis is essentially that man has the capacity to know the phenomenal world, which in contrast to the infinite divine essence, is ontologically imperfect and thus within the boundaries of human intellection. While we cannot know God's essence, we do have the capacity to know the real nature and intrinsic structure of His creation. By adopting a distinctly traditional and spiritual hermeneutics, Jawadi-Amuli suggests that different human contexts in the understanding of religion does not indicate that religion is multiple but on the contrary that understanding is unified and emerges in the human spirit: "[Epistemic] difference is not between knowers but between hermeneutic and cognitive means and methods. Understanding emerges in the spirit (*rūh*) which is one and universal [to all human beings]."[62] Jawadi-Amuli's hermeneutic is one of appropriation of divine mysteries, that is, to meditatively apply the divine symbols to oneself. He connects to the Islamic philosophical tradition for contemplative purposes, that is, as a means for spiritual progress to divine unity rather than for only having a rational picture of the realm of existence. He calls not simply for the theological affirmation of the divine oneness but also for the spiritual realization of its unity. Human subjectivity is divinely mediated in a total and immediate sense: the immanent subject that transpires to itself the absolute subject. For Jawadi-Amuli, the ideal man is a sage philosopher, a man who fully lives up to the demands of the tradition of theoretical as well as practical knowledge, someone he describes as "the locus of the Supreme Name."[63]

Correct Faith as the Foundation of Salvation

In addition to accusing Surush of imposing alien hermeneutical assumptions on the Islamic tradition through the use of some formal notion of "ultimate reality," Jawadi-Amuli believes that Surush's pluralist hypothesis bypasses the fundamental differences that exist between cultures and their respective languages and worldviews. He suggests that differences do not pertain only to culture and language but also involve concepts and ways of thinking.[64] By arguing that the subject matter of religious diversity is of metaphysical nature rather than historical, sociological, or psychological, he also asserts that the validity of conflicting truth claims cannot be justified on the basis of cultural diversity since the existence of separate cultures is an observable fact (which is not in need of empirical or rational corroboration). In Jawadi-Amuli's view, the validity of religious traditions is not a matter of custom or convention but belief and infidelity (*imān wa kufr*) and there can be no salvation without correct faith.[65] He claims that the criterion of correct belief, or spiritual discernment, is perennially embodied in the primordial, transcendent truths of Islam, which has been manifested in a chain of authentic religions, each one equally valid in its own epoch. With reference to the Qur'anic (2:97) account of succession in prophecy, Jawadi-Amuli believes that every

prophet before Muhammad was superseded by a successor which reinforced the preceding revelations: "All religions, including their exoteric laws and principles, were valid
in their own time, i.e. the epoch of their prophet."[66] The reinforcement of a new revelation indicates, in his view, that the preceding revelations have become subject to
"abrogation" (naskh) in those areas where there is a need for new divine directives.[67]

By claiming the abrogation of other religions by Islam, Jawadi-Amuli's concept of
salvation holds that Islam is alone fully salvific while other religions are either wholly
misleading or inferior approximations to the one true religion. He asserts that other
faiths are correct in so far as they correspond to Islam, the true religion par excellence,
and restricts salvation and supreme happiness to Muslims who believe in Islamic principles of belief and act according to the ethical legal instructions of the Qur'an.[68] Since
man's primordial being is universal, all human beings have, however, the potential for
finding the truth which leads them to salvation, which is not a matter of an arbitrary
decision by God but the natural result of one's life. In contrast to Christian exclusivism
which holds that revelation and salvation are offered only in Christ, Jawadi-Amuli
accepts that all world religions can offer something of spiritual significance, since they
are not outside the circle of God's revelation to humanity.[69] Islam is the true faith but
this superiority is not due to any inherent virtue of Muslims but attributable to Muslims
having received God's revelation in Scripture. While Jawadi-Amuli upholds the idea that
his own religion alone holds out the prospect of salvation, he does not confine final salvation to Muslims but suggests that individuals in other religions ultimately can be for-
given by God due to their ignorance about Islam:

> It is possible that one person is right and the other is wrong but that the latter has not gone
> astray in his discernment of truth. It may be the case that he or she has made a sincere
> effort and attempt in finding the truth but has not succeeded in reaching the destination.
> Even if such a person's beliefs are false, he or she will not be punished but forgiven [by God]
> according to the Qur'an (9:106).[70]

Finally, Jawadi-Amuli does not accept Surush's opinion that acceptance of religious
pluralism is a necessary attribute of a dynamic multi-religious society or the only way
to promote social justice. He believes that pluralism does not automatically generate
peaceful relations between followers of different faiths in the same sense that religious
exclusivism does not give reason for a religiously antagonistic society. The possibility of
creating a peaceful modus vivendi between followers of different faiths is, in his view, not
a question of tolerance or political pragmatism but human sympathy and mercy.[71] The
Qur'an (2:256) categorically inhibits the compulsion of faith upon anybody and no one
is authoritative enough to coerce his faith upon people, so much that even the Prophet
Muhammad was strongly admonished by God not to compel people to follow the truth
of the revelation. The principle of the freedom of conscience is, in Jawadi-Amuli's
view, firmly established in the Qur'an. He argues that there is no necessary logical
connection between religious pluralism and religious freedom, and accentuates that
members of minority religious groups are entirely free to worship and observe their
own convictions in contemporary Iran while Shi'ite Islam is dominant and officially
established.

Conclusion

Modernity has brought forth unparalleled challenges to the Islamic faith by question-ing the relevance and ultimate validity of its metaphysical truth claims. Although there has always been a diversity of religious beliefs, modern technological advances have resulted in a global situation with a growing climate of religious pluralism where close interaction between people of different faiths is more commonly experienced than for-merly. While Muslims are dominant and constitute the religious majority in many con-temporary societies, other faith communities are substantial and together comprise the vast majority of believers. In the view of religious pluralists, the new global condition calls for theological revision, a kind of "global theology" suitable for the world com-munity. As Surush and others argue, it is no longer valid to divide humanity into "we" and "they". No longer should Muslims regard themselves as supreme and others as inferior. By applying the idea of democracy to ultimate truth, Surush takes equal toleration of religion to mean that each religion is equally valid and that all religions ultimately lead to the same soteriological goal. While accepting that Islam is true and valid, he suggests that it is not universally the sole truth. Islam cannot thus claim an absolutist stance.

Surush's notion of philosophy of religion is a second-order activity, standing at one remove from its subject matter. He does not write as a Muslim theologian wanting to understand the place of Islam in the universe of faiths but as a philosopher who wants to understand the general relations between religions and their postulated grounds. As such, he finds it impossible to confine his philosophical thinking within a self-authenticating circle of faith. Surush works with a conceptuality alien to religion that was introduced by Kant and he puts this conceptuality to a purpose fundamentally at odds with Kant's own practice. Surush differs from Kant in that he uses the noumenon/phenomenon distinction not only in the analysis of sensory experience but also of reli-gious experience. By attempting to subordinate the construction of religious experience to the same constraints as those imposed by Kant upon sensible intuition, he implies that religious experience has to do only with human-constructed concepts of the noumenon. In denying the possibility of intellectual intuition of noumenon, he holds that we can be aware of the noumenal reality but we can never know it or experience it. Surush's hypothesis has its dilemmas given that most religious believers are pre-Kantian in the sense that they believe their own beliefs to correspond to noumenal reality. Since religious pluralism is not a claim to know as much as it is a theoretical explanation of religious phenomenon, religious exclusivists consider it as religiously unjustifiable. Jawadi-Amuli argues that the categories of human understanding which structure the phenomenal are divinely structured so as to provide for a genuine, though perhaps finite knowledge of the noumenal. In his view, Surush not only denies an aspect of Muslim self-understanding but he also cancels the cognitive claims of religion by transforming religious belief into a mere phenomenal apprehension of an unknown noumenal, which is an indefinite factor in the generation of religious experience.

The epistemological basis for Surush's pluralist hypothesis is that "the mode of knower" is differently formed within different religious traditions, producing a corresponding range of ways in which the divine is humanly perceived. By accepting the historicist thesis that varying cultural contexts preclude religious truth claims, Surush abandons the traditional view of religious claims as entailing assertions which are true or false and suggests that the world religions are more or less equally effective in the context of salvation. With reference to Kant's principle of "equality of proofs" in the sphere of metaphysics, he claims that it is impossible for human judgment to weigh up religions and compare their merits as systems of salvation. Since all religious traditions are on equal footing, offering more or less adequate responses to the divine noumenon, they cannot be thought of as making truth claims as traditionally understood nor can a doctrine be said to be true or false. Since the Kantian appeal suggests a move to an account of religious traditions that stresses the human and cultural origins, religious exclusivists claim that it represents an agnosticism about the ultimate validity of the religious drive, a move in the direction of religious relativism rather than religious pluralism.

By arguing that philosophy of religion is part of the religious realm and comprises a science of metaphysics, Jawadi-Amuli justifies the privileging of Islam with reference to traditional Islamic philosophy. His point of departure is that religious reality is ontologically accountable since there exists a correspondence between the several modes of knowing within the knower and the several levels of existence within being. He bases epistemology on the sacred function of knowledge and its illumination by the intellect, which is related to a higher and abiding realm in contrast to the world of sense. While Jawadi-Amuli believes that Islam alone is fully true, authentic, and valid (since the Qur'an is the final revelation), he endorses the idea of universal provenience of God's grace by claiming that divine grace is operative in every culture, place, and time in relation to individuals. In contrast to religious inclusivists, who suggest that Islam's recognition of other religious traditions implies a recognition of their claim to conduce salvation, Jawadi-Amuli's exclusivism is not a theory about religions as alternative, though partial and imperfect, mediators or contexts of salvation. It is rather a theory about the salvation of individuals in other religions. By establishing a metaphysical perspective on religious diversity, he is thus a "weak" exclusivist since he does not reject as false those doctrines of other religions that are compatible with Islam. While Jawadi-Amuli acknowledges the Qur'anic doctrine of the universality of revelation and the plurality of prophets, Surush regards his position as an elaborate maneuver for preserving belief in Islam's unique superiority that fails to acknowledge the distinctive religious lives of non-Muslims. In his view, Jawadi-Amuli also disregards the complexity of the conceptual and interpretative element in sense perception which determines all human experience.

Calling for a transformation of traditional Islamic thought, Surush believes that religious pluralism is the only viable spiritual alternative appropriate to the pluralistic vision of a global, democratic society which supports freedom and equal rights for all people. Indisputably inspired by the ethos of political liberalism, he claims that our modern, pluralistic societies are in need of a theoretical view that justifies social difference. While Surush's theory of religious pluralism draws heavily on Western theology, primarily Hick's pluralist hypothesis, its conclusions do not emerge directly out of liberal Protestantism but are articulated in the context of the theoretical debate on religious epistemology and hermeneutics in contemporary Iran. Surush's approach is less culture-specific than Hick's, but the question remains as to whether he is successful in imposing the norms and values of modernity on the long-established Islamic tradition. The struggle with modernity in contemporary Iran is after all not simply a question of creating conditions for a dynamic pluralist society but what matters as well is the cultivation of tradition.

Notes

1. Two other books by John Hick, *The Fifth Dimension* and *Problems of Religious Pluralism*, have recently been published in Persian. The very term "pluralism" has several meanings, depending on the respective discourse to which it refers. In contemporary philosophy, the concept of pluralism refers to the standpoint that the world is interpreted in several ways or to the evaluation that science is enhanced by competition between several interpretations. While religious pluralism is a term with several meanings, and accordingly there are many forms of pluralism, these forms generally refer to theological attempts to overcome religious differences between different religions.

2. These articles were later collected and published under the title *Qabz wa bast-i ti'ūrīk-i sharī'at: Nazariyah-yi takāmul-i ma'rifat-i dīnī*. Surush was born in southern Tehran into a pious lower middle class family. After completing his degree in pharmaceuticals from Tehran University, he went to England in 1973 to study chemistry at the University of London. He received a master's degree in chemistry and then prepared a doctoral thesis in the philosophy of science at Chelsea College. In 1979, the revolutionary events draw Surush back to Iran, and he was elected into the High Council of Cultural Revolution by Ruhullah Khumaini. Until 1997, Surush was teaching philosophy at Tehran University but he was forced to abandon his classes due to his criticism of the religious authorities. He is today a member of the Iranian Academy of Sciences but lives temporarily abroad.

3. 'Abd al-Karim Surush, *Qabz wa bast-i ti'ūrīk-i sharī'at: Nazariyah-yi takāmul-i ma'rifat-i dīnī* (Tehran: Mu'assasah-yi farhangī-yi sirāt, 1996), 32–4.

4. Hick, a minister in the Reformed Church, is commonly regarded as the chief proponent of religious pluralism. He was born in Yorkshire and took a doctorate in philosophy of religion at Oxford University. He has held professorships in the United States and England, and he is currently a fellow of the Institute for Advanced Research in Arts and Social Sciences at the University of Birmingham.

5. While Surush accentuates that the Qur'an (16:121 and 48:2) uses the words *sirāt al-mustaqīm* in indefinite form (which indicates the existence of many "straight paths"), the title of the book is indisputably selected as against verse 1:5, which adopts the term *sirāt* (path) in definite form denoting "the straight path." All Qur'anic references are to *The Holy Quran*. Text, translation, and commentary by Abdullah Yusuf Ali (Lahore, 1937).

6. The book *Sirāthā-yi mustaqīm* contains several articles on the issue of religious pluralism as well as Surush's translation of four essays by John Hick, Alvin Plantinga, and David Basinger.

7. Cf. John Hick, "On Conflicting Religious Truth-claims," *Religious Studies*, 19, 1983, 485–91.

8. 'Abd al-Karim Surush, *Sirāthā-yi mustaqīm* (Tehran: Mu'assasah-yi farhangī-yi sirāt, 1998), 49.

9. Surush, *Sirāthā*, 42. By acknowledging that the complex conflict between realism and anti-realism in philosophy should be sustained, Surush follows the later postpositivism of Popper, who disavowed the early positivist empiricist insistence upon verifiability and induction. In his general epistemology, Popper criticizes rationalism as well as empiricism for looking for certain foundations for knowledge and defines knowledge as hypotheses that have passed critical tests and correspond to reality, a process that he calls falsification.

10. Kant introduced the human mind as an active and autonomic originator of experience, where the self in a sense creates the world, rather than perceives it as a passive recipient by reference to the *a priori* conditions of our empirical knowledge. He turned originally from physical and metaphysical science to ethics to find the grounds of faith. For him, God is not a reality encountered in religious experience, but an object postulated by reason on the basis of its own practical functioning in man's moral agency. The particular choice of Kant as principal model of his exposition on religious pluralism is largely due to Kant's analysis of finiteness, which contributed to the age of anthropological thought, as well as his belief in immortality and the existence of God. Cf. Immanuel Kant, *Prolegomena: To any Future of Metaphysics that will be able to come forward as a Science* (New York: Cambridge University Press, 1997).

11. Cf. Karl R. Popper, *The Poverty of Historicism* (London: Routledge & Kegan Paul, 1963), 47–8.

12. *Sirāthā*, 27. Cf. 'Abd al-Karim Surush, *Rahā'ī az yaqīn wa yaqīn az rahā'ī*, *Kiyān*, No. 48 (Tehran: Mu'assasah-yi farhangī-yi sirāt, 1999), 2–9.

13. 'Abd al-Karim Surush, *Farbihtar az īdi'ūlūzhī* (Tehran: Mu'assasah-yi farhangī-yi sirāt, 1996), 206. Surush does not discuss the topic of the nature of religious faith as a central problem in the epistemology of religion, including the subject of religious faith and its relation to his definition of falsifiability. To my knowledge, he neither defines any criterion of verifiability (where the theological statements of religious mode of experience are either verifiable or illusory) nor explains the nature of the relation between verification and falsification in the manner of, for instance, Hick, which would address some ambiguities regarding his concept of the religious claim of truth. Cf. John Hick, *Faith and Knowledge* (Basingstoke: Macmillan, 1988), 175–6.

14. Cf. *Sirāthā*, 166–7. Stace is most known for his book on *Mysticism and Philosophy* (Philadelphia: Lippincott, 1960), in which he puts forward the argument that mystical experience constitutes the mystical core of all religions. By arguing that the distinctions made are merely doctrinal differences, whereas the experience itself is introvertive, utterly without content, he is not concerned with preservation of religious tradition but only with delineating the "common core" of the various mystical traditions. In Stace's view, all mystical experiences are the same and doctrine is later interpreted into the experience, since what man knows about mystical experience is from the interpretations from the mystics themselves.

15. *Sirāthā*, 63.

16. *Sirāthā*, 64 and 71.

17. *Sirāthā*, 7. The distinction phenomenon/noumenon plays a major part in Kant's distinction of the *a priori* and *a posteriori*. By demanding a critical evaluation of pure reason, its boundaries and possibilities, Kant's most original contribution to philosophy was that it is representation that makes the object possible rather than the object that makes representation possible.

18. *Sirāthā*, 22. Acknowledging the fact that all the world religions bear more or less equal testimony to God's transcendent reality and salvific power, Hick holds that the various world faiths are embodiments of "different perceptions and conceptions of, and correspondingly

different responses to, the Real from within the major variant ways of being human; and that within each of them the transformation of human existence from self-centredness to Reality-centredness is taking place." John, Hick, *An Interpretation of Religion: Human Responses to the Transcendent* (Basingstoke: Macmillan, 1989), 240.

19. *Sirāthā*, 87–8.

20. Referring to the Persian poet Suhrab Sipihri, Surush argues that "point of view " is an analytical term which denotes "nothing and no-one except man himself". Cf. *Sirāthā*, 13–15.

21. The fact that Surush largely justifies the epistemological foundation of his pluralist hypothesis by reference to the epistemic scheme of traditional mysticism has its dilemmas. Cf. Ashk P. Dahlén, *Islamic Law, Epistemology and Modernity. Legal Philosophy in Contemporary Iran* (New York: Routledge, 2003), 301–6.

22. *Sirāthā*, preface.

23. *Sirāthā*, 160. Surush calls to attention the contextual nature of interpretation that renders meaning relative due to its entanglement in formative contexts that are relational. Interpretation in this broad sense is a process by which we use all the available contextual determinants to grasp the actual meaning of a given message in a given situation: "The world of meaning is by definition pluralistic. It is only rarely that one single meaning appears in interpretation. The most important norm of interpretation is plurality," *Sirāthā*, 192.

24. *Sirāthā*, 74.

25. One of most basic notions of logic is the principle of non-contradiction (If a given proposition (P) is true, then its opposite, not (P), cannot be true at the same time). From the principle of excluded middle, any truth claim must either be true or false, which means that if two religions make contradictory truth claims, they cannot both be correct. It is interesting to note that Hick expresses the significance and importance of the man Jesus for Christians and regards the doctrine of the divinity of Christ as a "myth." In Hick's view, the notion of the Son of God as the deification of Jesus is a historical construct, which developed in complexity as Christians came to draw heavily on Greek philosophical concepts. By arguing that the images of the Son of God were ontologized into absolute categories, he suggests that one cannot come to terms with a world of religious pluralism without compromising one's own central beliefs. Cf. John Hick, *The Rainbow of Faiths. Critical Dialogues on Religious Pluralism* (London: SCM, 1995), 52–6.

26. Harold Netland, Dissonant Voices (Grand Rapids: Eerdmans, 1991), 151–95.

27. *Sirāthā*, 116.

28. *Sirāthā*, 157–8.

29. *Sirāthā*, 45. Cf. John Hick, On Grading Religions, *Contemporary Classics in Philosophy of Religion*, eds. Ann Loades and Loyal D. Rue (La Salle, II: Open Court, 1991), 449–70.

30. 'Abd al-Karim Surush, *Bast-i tajrubah-yi nabawī* (Tehran: Mu'assasah-yi farhangī-yi sirāt, 1999), 80–2, 87.

31. *Sirāthā*, 20.

32. *Sirāthā*, 21–3. Cf. *Sirāthā*, 61–6.

33. *Sirāthā*, 33.

34. *Sirāthā*, 28.

35. The American convert Muhammad Legenhausen (1953–) should be included to the exclusivist position. He was born in New York and received his Ph.D. in philosophy from Rice University, Houston, in 1983. He is presently teaching Western philosophy at the Imam Khumaini Education and Research Institute in Qum. Legenhausen substantiates his criticism of Surush, Hick, and Seyyed Hossein Nasr in his *Islam and Religious Pluralism* (London: al-Hoda, 1999), which has been translated into Farsi and Arabic.

36. 'Abdullah Jawadi-Amuli was born in Amul into a family of eminent religious scholars. At the age of 14, he entered a religious seminary in his home town. After finishing the primary level of religious education, he went to Tehran in 1952 to study jurisprudence and theology under the auspices of Muhammad Taqi-Amuli. Jawadi-Amuli completed the mediate level of religious education in Tehran and then went to Qum to study jurisprudence with some of the most renowned Shi'ite scholars of that time. He participated in the philosophy classes of Muhammad Husain Tabataba'i as well, and his 25 years of study under the latter included the highest level of "transcendental wisdom," a subject on which he is recognized as the second highest authority in contemporary Iran.

37. Cf. 'Abdullah Jawadi-Amuli, *Dīnshināsī* (Qum: Markaz-i nashr-i isrā, 2001), preface. Jawadi-Amuli mentions, for instance, the conclusions made by the American sociologist Peter L. Bergson in his book *The Desecularization of the World* (Grand Rapids: Eerdmans, 1999) about the new force of religious movements in our time. It is, however, somewhat surprising that he refers to Bergson who in his numerous books on sociological theory describes reality as "a social construct," which is the very anti-thesis to Jawadi-Amuli's metaphysical realism.

38. Jawadi-Amuli, *Dīnshināsī*, 26.

39. *Dīnshināsī*, 28–34.

40. Inspired by the terminology of Islamic mysticism, Jawadi-Amuli asserts that the kernel of religion is a light which is manifested and diversified through its exoteric dimension. He refers to the Qur'anic (24:35) description of God as "the light of the heavens and the earth" to illustrate that the esoteric as well as the exoteric dimensions of true religion is permeated by divine light in the complete sense. Jawadi-Amuli also mentions Rumi's illustration of revealed law (*sharī'at*) as a light of divine guidance to point out that the spiritual dimensions of Islam will be undermined without an appreciation of its formal dimensions. Cf. *Dīnshināsī*, 64–8, and 70–1.

41. *Dīnshināsī*, 111. Jawadi-Amuli differentiates between theoretical and practical intellect, and argues that the former operates intuitively as a form of metaphysical discernment in contrast to the latter, which is non-syllogistic and receptive to error. In the sense that theoretical intellect is self-subsisting and does not possess any matter, it cannot be corrupted or disintegrated. It yields a necessary knowledge (*'ilm zarūrī*) which is established in the mind through no effort on the subject's part. Jawadi-Amuli is not opposed to the exercise of reason, but only to its modern secular employment. Cf. *Dīnshināsī*, 32 and 132–8.

42. Jawadi-Amuli's notion that knowledge (*'ilm*) must correspond directly to the known (*ma'lūm*) is consistent with the metaphysical realism of his teacher Tabataba'i. Metaphysical realism holds a correspondence theory of truth, according to which knowledge is true and justified only if it corresponds to reality, which is considered to be hierarchically constituted. Implied in the hierarchy of knowing is an ontological analysis of the knowing process in order to get an acquaintance with the things in themselves. In contrast to critical realism, metaphysical realism is primarily concerned with the transparency of the cosmos, which consists of creation as a whole being viewed as symbolic in the sense of being a manifestation of the metacosmic reality, which is realized through man's innermost reality. Cf. Jawadi-Amuli, *Wilāyat dar qur'ān* (Qum: Markaz-i nashr-i isrā, 1998), 9.

43. *Dīnshināsī*, 205.

44. Plantinga's so-called "reformed epistemology" claims that there are "properly basic beliefs," including belief in God, which are foundational and thus in no need of external justification. The problem for his position is, similar to that of Jawadi-Amuli, that if only one of many belief systems is true, it follows that religious experience generally produces false beliefs. Cf. Alvin C. Plantinga, *Warranted Christian Belief* (New York: Oxford University Press, 2000).

45. Cf. 'Abdullah Jawadi-Amuli, *Sharī'at dar ā'īnah-yi ma'rifat* (Qum: Markaz-i nashr-i isrā, 1998), 99.
46. *Dīnshināsī*, 216. Jawadi-Amuli believes that empirical corroboration is of no help in the sphere of metaphysics since its hypotheses are limited to discursive considerations. He argues that positivism by rejecting metaphysics as unwarranted epistemic belief results in a form of agnosticism or skepticism concerning worldviews and religion. Since far from all epistemic corroborations are of empirical or logical nature, Jawadi-Amuli claims that the positivists stumble upon internal inconsistencies in the sphere of ontology and epistemology by excluding revelation and intuitive intellection (*shuhūd*) from the sphere of human knowledge. He claims that Surush's interpretation of religion ultimately is a form of "materialism" in philosophical terms by restricting the significance of religion to some transient, historical and empirical conditions. Cf. *Dīnshināsī*, 47, 113, 187 and 217.
47. *Dīnshināsī*, 207.
48. *Dīnshināsī*, 221–2.
49. According to Sayyid Mahmud Nabawiyan, it is not justified to use poems in scientific discourse since poetry is not a kind of logical demonstration. In his view, the diversity of religious faiths does not in itself corroborate Surush's hypothesis that all religions are equally valid. Sayyid Mahmud Nabawiyan, *Plurālīzm-i dīnī* (Tehran: Mu'assasah-yi farhangī-yi dānish wa andishah-yi mu'āsir, 2002), 50–5, 64–6. 'Ali Rabbani-Gulpaigani argues that Surush does not fully recognize the hierarchical difference between direct intuitive knowledge and empirical understanding and is selective in his reading of Rumi's poetry by ignoring verses where the poet contrasts infallible spiritual knowledge (*nūr*) from analytical "point of view" (*manzar*). 'Ali Rabbani-Gulpaigani, *Tahlīl wa naqd-i plurālīsm-i dīnī* (Tehran: Mu'assasah-yi farhangī-yi dānish wa andishah-yi mu'āsir, 1999), 72–84. Jawadi-Amuli also claims that Surush's pluralist hypothesis reduces the epistemic significance of the Qur'an by considering revelation as a form of religious experience, equivalent to other forms of experience. In Jawadi-Amuli's view, revelation is a purely direct knowledge, which is based on absolute certainty (*yaqīn*) on behalf of its receiver. In contrast to religious experience, which may contain elements of doubt, it constitutes a supra-individual knowledge which is imposed on a few selected people. *Dīnshināsī*, 239–42.
50. *Dīnshināsī*, 169.
51. Cf. Jawadi-Amuli, *Sharī'at*, 136.
52. *Dīnshināsī*, 40–1.
53. In this respect, Jawadi-Amuli refers to a number of Qur'anic verses, such as 42:13: "The same religion (*al-dīn*) has He established for you as that of which He enjoined on Noah – the which He has sent by inspiration to thee [Muhammad] – and that which He enjoined on Abraham and Moses, and Jesus: namely that you should remain steadfast in the religion, and make no divisions therein." Cf. Qur'an 2:136, 2:213, 2:285, 3:84, etc.
54. It is essential that the Qur'an describes all prophets, from Adam to Jesus and Muhammad, and their followers, as "Muslims" in the universal sense of complete submission to the commands of God. The God of the Qur'an is not only the God of Muslims but also the God of all humanity and this is the reason why the first man, Adam, is also the first prophet. The Qur'an (10:47) says: "To every people (was sent) an Apostle."
55. *Dīnshināsī*, 192. Nabawiyan argues that even if resolution of conflicting truth claims were a plausible suggestion, this would not resolve the conflict of practice-claims, since religion is not confined to a particular system of belief, but also contains rituals, ethical ideals and laws. In his view, it is illogical to assume that two contradicting religious laws (such as the prohibition vs. the permission to drink wine) will produce an identical result. Nabawiyan, *Plurālīzm*, 39–45.

56. The ontological foundation of Jawadi-Amuli's account on religious diversity is that *tashkīk* principally consists of four cosmological aspects: true multiplicity, true unity, multiplicity returning to unity, and finally, unity being "diversified" via true multiplicity. By acknowledging the existence of a hierarchy in the nature of reality as well as in human cognition, he agrees to the traditional philosophical mode of perceiving knowledge to be related to the sacred in a hierarchy extending from an empirical and rational mode of knowing to the highest form of intuitive intellection. The concept of divine self-disclosure lies at the very heart of the metaphysics of the school of Ibn 'Arabi, which was largely adopted by the Persian philosopher Mulla Sadra. Cf. *Dīnshināsī* 207–8, and Rabbani-Gulpaigani, *Tahlīl*, 86–90.

57. *Dīnshināsī*, 205.

58. *Dīnshināsī*, 73.

59. *Dīnshināsī*, 73. The Qur'an (3:85) says: "If anyone desires a religion other than Islam (submission to God), never will it be accepted of him, and in the Hereafter, he will be in the ranks of those who have lost (all spiritual good)."

60. *Dīnshināsī*, 229. Jawadi-Amuli refers to the Qur'an (41:43): "Nothing is said unto thee [Muhammad] that was not said to the Apostles before thee", to demonstrate that all religions are the same in beliefs while differing in provisions of works.

61. *Dīnshināsī*, 66.

62. *Dīnshināsī*, 211.

63. *Dīnshināsī*, 212.

64. *Dīnshināsī*, 195–6.

65. For Jawadi-Amuli, infidelity is not a passive condition applying to all those who lack correct belief in Islam but it is an active inward opposition which prevents a person from accepting divine guidance.

66. *Dīnshināsī*, 228.

67. Jawadi-Amuli claims that while the Qur'an (2:62, 4:124, 16:97, 22:67, etc.) speaks positively about diversity of faiths, it insists on the recognition of Muhammad as "the seal of the prophets" as a condition for salvation. The correctness of faith consists, in his view, of belief in divine unity, prophecy, and the hereafter as divinely ordained in the religion of Islam. Cf. *Dīnshināsī*, 223.

68. *Dīnshināsī*, 226.

69. While religious pluralism emerged in Christianity as a reaction against the traditional teaching that there is no way to salvation aside from the redemption offered by Christ, Jawadi-Amuli believes that Islam is in no need of theological adjustments, since it endorses the collective social and political rights of other religious denominations. In his view, religious pluralism is only operative in a Christian context.

70. *Dīnshināsī*, 195.

71. *Dīnshināsī*, 195. In Jawadi-Amuli's view, the Qur'an gives emphasis to meaningful dialogue and peaceful coexistence between the adherents of different religious traditions. He points to the fact that the Qur'an (22:40, 60:8) commands Muslims to act peacefully towards the "People of the Book" (*ahl al-kitāb*), i.e. Christians and Jews, and to defend their cloisters, churches, and oratories. By acknowledging that Islam is the true religion *par excellence*, he declares that non-Muslims living in a Muslim society must either pay a poll tax (*jiziya*) to the Islamic rulers or convert to Islam. Cf. *Dīnshināsī*, 198.

CHAPTER 26

Contemporary Islamic Movements in Southeast Asia: Challenges and Opportunities[1]

Ahmad F. Yousif

Introduction

There are more than 230 million Muslims living in Southeast Asia, the majority of whom live in Indonesia (the largest Muslim country in the world) Malaysia, and Brunei (http://www.factbook.net/muslim_pop.php). In addition, there are sizeable minorities who reside in Singapore, Thailand, the Philippines, Cambodia, Myanmar, Laos, and Vietnam. While historically Islam has existed relatively peacefully with other religious communities in Southeast Asia, in recent years a number of Islamic movements such as *Abu Sayyaf* (Philippines) and *Jemaah Islamiah* (Malaysia–Indonesia) have employed violent means to express their concerns and achieve their goals. Are such groups representative of the majority of contemporary Islamic movements (CIMs) in Southeast Asia or are they just a marginal fringe?

This chapter seeks to classify CIMs in Southeast Asia in order to determine whether the majority are primarily advocates of peace or more revolutionary oriented. Towards this end, a brief history of Islamic expansion in Southeast Asia will be surveyed. Secondly, selected CIMs in six Southeast Asian countries (Indonesia, Malaysia, Brunei, Singapore, Thailand, and the Philippines) will be classified according to their primary objectives and methodologies. Finally, the extent to which CIMs in Southeast Asia can be classified as advocates of peaceful change or revolutionary change will be assessed.

Historical Development of Islam in Southeast Asia

Historical records have indicated that Islam arrived in Southeast Asia or the Malay archipelago as early as the beginning of the eleventh century CE,[2] via Arab traders at selected ports, including Aceh (Indonesia), Melaka (Malaysia), and Pattani (southern

Thailand). Instead of encountering strong opposition from local inhabitants, it was welcomed into the area. According to Abdul Ghani Yakob, a professor of Islamic civilization at the International Islamic University Malaysia, some of the Arab-Muslim traders decided to stay in the area, marry local women, adopt Malay culture, and assimilate into the society.[3]

The Mogul invasion of Baghdad in the middle of the twelfth century CE was another contributing factor to the growth of Islam in the area, since many Muslim scholars and intellectuals migrated to the Malay world, carrying with them the message of Islam. Ironically, this trend also holds true today, whereby a number of Muslims, particularly of Middle Eastern background, have migrated to Southeast Asia, due to political unrest in their homeland.

In the thirteenth century, Sufi (mystical) scholars and traders with a Sufi orientation entered Java, Sumatra, and the Malay Peninsula from the Arab world via India. According to Wan Hussain Azmi, a Malaysian religious historian, Sufi preachers, known as *al-Makhdom* (the servant) or *al-Seyyed* (the master) in Filipino language, brought Islam to the Philippines between the end of the thirteenth century and the middle of the fifteenth century CE. Manila became part of the Islamic empire during the sixteenth century, when it was governed by Sultan Raja Muslim from Brunei.[4]

Sufism was readily embraced by the local population in Southeast Asia, because it coincided with the existing way of thought and tradition. Moreover, the Sufis conveyed the message of Islam in a peaceful manner, which had a positive impact on both the Malays and the indigenous people (*Orang Asli*). As a result, Sufi orders (*tariqats*), including *Naqshabandiyya*, *Qadiriyya*, *Rifayya*, and *Shattariyya* were formed and spread. Today, there are many forms and kinds of "Islamic" mystical orders that have been established and integrated into Southeast Asian culture and societies.

Problem of Definition

Since there is a wide variety of Islamic movements in Southeast Asia with different goals, objectives, and methodologies, Muslim and non-Muslim scholars, intellectuals, government authorities, media personnel, and members of Islamic movements have been unable to reach a consensus on a common definition which would encompass all CIMs. In fact, even the term CIM is not universally utilized, since such movements are also referred to as "Islamic resurgence," "Islamic revival," or "Islamic renewal."

Jeffrey F. Hadden asserts that religious movements in general may be understood as a subcategory of social movements, that is, "organized efforts to cause or prevent changes." Accordingly he arranges religious movements into three distinct types: "endogenous religious movements," which constitute efforts to change the internal character of the religion; "exogenous religious movements," which alter the environment in which the religion resides; and "generative religious movements" that "seek to introduce new religions into the culture or environment."[5]

The term CIM can be divided into three subcomponents: "contemporary", defined by the *Oxford English Dictionary* as "occurring at the same moment of time, or during the same period"; "Islamic," which means pertaining to the religion of Islam; and "movement," defined as "a course or series of actions and endeavors on the part of a group of people working towards a shared goal." Consequently, a CIM can be defined as any group of people who profess the religion of Islam, belong to the present era, and share the goal of promoting and/or implementing Islamic values in society. Based on such an understanding, CIMs in Southeast Asia are not necessarily oppositional. Instead they can encompass governments, semi-government agencies, non-governmental organizations (NGOs), as well as oppositional groups.

Pakistani thinker Anis Ahmad defines a CIM as any movement which calls "for a total Islamic change in the life of the individual, family, society and social, economic, political, legal, educational, and cultural system of a people."[6]

Quintan Wiktorowicz, editor of the monograph *Islamic Activism: A Social Movement Theory Approach*, prefers the term "Islamic activism" to CIM, which he defines as "the mobilization of contention to support Muslim causes."[7] Wiktorowicz further argues that "Islamic activism is rooted in the symbolism, language, and cultural history of Muslim society and as a result has successfully resonated with increasingly disillusioned populations suffering from political exclusion, economic deprivation, and a sense of growing impotence at the expense of outside powers and the faceless process of globalization."[8]

Challenges Facing the Classification of CIMs

A challenge facing scholars of Southeast Asia is how to classify CIMs in a scientific and objective manner. What kind of measurements and tools should be utilized to understand their goals, objectives, and methodologies?

Studying CIMs from the perspective of "objective" outsider poses a number of difficulties, since any classification of the group will be colored by the scholar's personal, historical, political, religious affiliation, and group membership. Data collection is further hindered by the fact that many Islamic activists are driven underground by authoritarian states. While non-Muslim research on CIMs might be more "objective," at times such scholarship lacks the in-depth knowledge of Islamic sources, language, and culture to fully understand the movement that is being studied. In addition, religious sensitivities can also put the non-Muslim "outsider" at a disadvantage. Moreover, both "objective" and "subjective" participant/observer approaches face obstructions due to a lack of security.

Often the classification of CIMs has to be understood within the socio-political environment at the time of study, taking into consideration the history, religious and political orientation, approach and methodology of such movements. The wide variety of motivations, purposes, objectives, and methodologies adopted by scholars studying CIMs is one of the primary factors why no consensus has been reached on one specific classification scheme. Some of the different approaches that have been used to study Islamic groups – both classical and contemporary, Muslim and non-Muslim – will now be highlighted.

Classification of Muslim Groups

Contemporary Muslim perspectives

Legal scholar Taha Jabir al-Alwani organizes Islamic movements into those that are supportive or against the political philosophies in the Muslim world.[9] This classification is particularly relevant to the Malaysian scenario, where Parti Islam Semalaysia (PAS), an Islamic political party, opposes the ruling United Malays National Organization (UMNO).

AbdulHamid A. AbuSulayman, president of the International Institute of Islamic Thought and former rector of the International Islamic University Malaysia, classifies Muslim intellectuals into the *muqalideen* (the imitators) and the *mujadideen* (the reformists).[10]

According to Indonesian thinker Goenawan Mohamad, Indonesian "modernists" who refer to themselves as advocates of "liberal Islam" are essentially young Muslim intellectuals, "who began their studies of religion in Indonesian-style boarding schools, known as '*pesantrens*'" (http://islamlib.com/en/page.php?page=article&id=232).

Bahtiar Effendi, author of *Islam and the State in Indonesia*, classifies Islamic intellectualism and activism in Indonesia into three categories: theological and religious renewal; political and bureaucratic reform; and social transformation. He argues that while theological renewal is essentially a call for desacralization and indigenization, political reform is intended to bridge the gap between "political Islam" and the state, and social transformation has the goal of "diversifying the political meaning of Islam." Each of these categories has been combined in order to generate a "new articulation of Islamic political ideas and practices."[11]

Non–Muslim scholarship

A large amount of literature on CIMs in Southeast Asia has been written from non-Islamic viewpoints. According to Samuel K. Tan, a well-known scholar on the conflict in Mindanao, colonial sources have remained the most substantial and comprehensive material on Muslim history and culture in the region, though "their interpretation of Muslim perceptions is highly questionable."[12]

B.J. Boland, author of *The Struggle of Islam in Modern Indonesia*, asserts that three terms are commonly used to classify CIMs in Indonesia: *reformasi*; *liberalisasi*; and *modernisasi*. One of the shortcomings of these terms, however, is that they are often used indiscriminately, without a precise definition of what each of them means. Boland further states that "*reformasi*" is actually a continuation of the Islamic renewal movement initiated by Muhammad 'Abduh of Egypt at the beginning of the twentieth century. Both reformation and liberalization can be considered as paving the way for modernization, which is essentially "a change in established patterns of life in order to meet the demands of modern times."[13]

Barry Desker, director of the Institute of Defense and Strategic Studies, Singapore, classifies Muslim intellectuals in Southeast Asia (and CIMs by analogy) into moderate Islamic scholars or "liberal Islam" and the *Wahhabi* type or "literal Islam" (http://www.ntu.edu.sg/idss/Perspective/research_050217.htm). In this regard "liberal Islam" refers to CIMs that prefer to separate Islam from the state, while "literal Islam" refers to those groups that prefer to see the practical implementation of Islamic law in society.

In addition to "liberal" Islam, "fundamentalist" and "traditionalist" have also been used to refer to Islamic movements, associations, and organizations in Southeast Asia. For example, Anak Agung Banyu Perwita, a lecturer at the Parahyangan Catholic University, Bandung, Indonesia, groups Islamic revivalist movements in Southeast Asia into four broad categories: fundamentalists; traditionalists; modernists; and pragmatists.[14] M.B. Hooker argues that the terms "fundamentalist" and "liberal" are basically an extension of "traditionalist" and "modernist," but are even more Eurocentric, since respectively they mean "bad" and "good".[15]

In fact the term "fundamentalism" was originally a Christian Protestant term which developed in the early part of the twentieth century. It was used to refer to Christian groups that believed in the inerrancy of the scripture, as opposed to those who sought to make scriptural changes to accommodate the modern world.[16] In the Islamic context, the term is somewhat redundant, since the vast majority of Muslims believe that the Qu'ran remains unchanged from its initial revelation.

William Shepard, a retired professor of religious studies at the University of Canterbury in New Zealand, contrasts the term "Islamic radicalism" with "secularism," "Islamism," and "traditionalism". In his view, a "secular" CIM means that the group is open to ideologies other than Islam, while "Islamism" emphasizes the flexibility of Islam as a social system with "the ideal form of some Western system." "Traditionalists," on the other hand, are "identified with local expressions of Islam and traditional cultural elites such as the *ulama* and the Sufi orders and [are] not interested in major reform of Islamic thought and practice," while "Islamic radicals" do not desire to go back to original Islam, but "along a different path from that of the West or of Western style modernization."[17]

Other popular terms that have been employed by Western scholarship and the global media to describe CIMs and/or their adherents, particularly in the post September 11, 2001 period, have been *jihād*, "fanatic," and "terrorist". Nonetheless, even prior to September 11, some Western scholars tried to focus on the connection between CIMs in Southeast Asia and the current political situation in the Arab world.[18]

The problem Muslim scholars and activists have with many of the above terms is that such terms do not have any roots in Islamic history and civilization. Instead they are foreign terms imposed on a group of people with different social and religious norms and values. Wiktorowicz argues that because the study of Islamic movements is written from a Western standpoint, CIMs only "count" as "studies of Islamic movements if they have the trappings of Western academic discourse, which includes a commitment to the Western project of understanding social movements."[19]

Classification of CIMs According to their Primary Goal

Given the above differences and subjective application of many of the above terms, this work has chosen to circumvent such terminology and classify CIMs in Southeast Asia based upon their goals and methodology. Even such an approach is not without its challenges given the fact that some groups have multiple goals and objectives, which change according to the socio-political circumstances of these movements. Accordingly some groups can be found under more that one category.

Islamic propagation and education

Many CIMs in Southeast Asia are driven by the need to purify and renew Islam in their society through da'wah techniques. Accordingly da'wah organizations in Southeast Asia have often focused on establishing religious schools (madrasahs), community centers, and medical clinics. In addition to producing basic religious publications, many hold public lectures (ceramahs) featuring well-known Muslims scholars/speakers, offer classes which teach basic Islamic tenants (fardu-ain), and use other socio-religious activities, i.e. marriages, funerals, new-births, and Eid ceremonies to increase the faith and understanding of believers.

Because these groups can have a significant influence on an individual's and society's understanding and application of Islamic religious texts, they play a critical role in either enhancing tolerance, respect, and a peaceful coexistence with "other" religious communities or conversely encouraging a lack of tolerance, respect, and an uneasy existence with other religious groups.

The Nahdatul Ulama (NU) (Arabic for "revival of Muslim scholars") is the largest CIM not only in Indonesia, but in the world. This organization, founded in 1926, has a membership of 30 million, the majority of whom are rural and peasant-based (http://philtar.ucsm.ac.uk/encyclopedia/indon/nahdat.html). One of the focuses of the NU is religious education, which includes the scrutiny of textbooks and the establishment of madrasahs for the training of future generations of ulama (religious scholars).

The Muhammadiyah, the oldest and most respected Islamic educational organization in Indonesia, has adopted a rational approach to Islam. The objectives of the Muhammadiyah are to purify Islamic beliefs and teachings from the practices of animistic values in the Indonesian villages. According to Fred R. Von Der Mehden, author of Religion and Nationalism in Southeast Asia: Burma, Indonesia the Philippines, "it was in the field of education that the Muhammadiyah had a powerful influence on the nationalist movement."[20]

In addition to the NU and Muhammadiyah, Dewan Dakwah Islamiyah (DDII – Indonesian Council for Propagation of the Islamic Faith) also plays an important role in disseminating Islamic information among people, and "turning them into better Muslims."[21]

In Malaysia, there are numerous government departments and institutions, NGOs, and Islamic associations that are devoted to Islamic propagation and education. At the government level, the Department of Islamic Development Malaysia (JAKIM) is devoted to "the creation of a progressive and morally upright *ummah* based on Islamic principles in line with the national vision." Towards this end, JAKIM acts as a compiler and disseminator of information on Islamic affairs, via both the Internet and publishing of Islamic literature for the public (http://www.islam.gov.my/english).

The Institute of Islamic Understanding Malaysia (IKIM), a government "think tank," plays an important role in organizing national and international conferences and seminars on contemporary Islamic issues including human rights, non-Muslim minorities, Islam and the media, science and technology, and business and economy based on Islamic perspectives. The government-funded International Islamic University Malaysia (IIUM), on the other hand, provides both graduate and postgraduate degrees in almost all fields of knowledge including Islamic revealed knowledge and heritage, management, law, sciences, engineering, architecture, and medicine, both in English and Arabic languages. Since 2004, the Malaysian government has been propagating the concept of *Islam Hadhari* (civilizational Islam), which Abdullah Ahmad Badawi, the current prime minister, believes "promotes tolerance and understanding, moderation and peace (at the same time), it is the perfect antidote to extremism and militancy" (http://www.atimes.com/ atimes/Southeast_Asia/GA29Ae07.html).

Angkatan Belia Islam Malaysia (Muslim Youth Movements of Malaysia), also known as ABIM, focuses on Islamic study groups, talks, seminars, spiritual training, intellectual discourses, and others. Other Malaysian NGOs catering to Islamic propagation and/or Islamic education for Muslim converts, include *Persatuan Ulama* Malaysia (PUM), *Jemaah Islah* Malaysia (JIM), *Persatuan Darul Fitrah*, *Persatuan Al-Hunaffa*, the Malaysian Chinese Muslim Association (MACMA), and *Belia Perkim*.

In Brunei Darussalam, the smallest country in Southeast Asia, the vast majority of departments and organizations involved in Islamic propagation and education are government sponsored. Towards this end, the government of Brunei has established the Ministry of Religious Affairs. The *Da'wah* Center under the Ministry of Religious Affairs was established for the advancement and expansion of Islam in Brunei Darussalam, as well as promoting the understanding of Islam among non-Muslims in the state. Some of its activities include research on Islamic affairs, publications, exhibitions, and an archive section on Islamic civilization. In addition to producing *fatwas* (Islamic legal rulings), the Brunei State Mufti's Office provides Muslims with *irshad* (guidance) on Islamic legal matters, and is a reference center for Islamic knowledge (http://www.mufti.gov.bn).

For some Muslims, especially those living as minorities, Islamic education is the key to the future of their community. Dr. Surin Pitsuwan, a former Thai minister of foreign affairs (1997–2001) who is also a Muslim, confirms this idea by arguing that "education in Thailand is probably the most central issue not only for the Malay-Muslim emancipation, but also for their sense of recognition of their distinct identity."[22] Accordingly, Thailand has a number of Islamic groups involved in Islamic propagation and education, such as the Central Islamic Committee of Thailand and The College of Islamic Studies, Prince Songkla University, Pattani Campus and The Thai Islamic Global Net (http://www.thaiislamic.com), which propagates Islam via the Internet, in addition to catering to the business interests of the Thai-Muslim community.

Singapore, too, has a number of registered Islamic associations and organizations that provide religious and educational services, as well as looking after the welfare of the Muslim community in the country. The *Majlis Ugama Islam Singapura* (Islamic Religious Council of Singapore), known as MUIS (http://www.muis.gov.sg), is the umbrella organization for Muslim groups in the country. MUIS is involved in a wide range of Islamic religious, social, educational, economic, and cultural activities. In addition to Islamic propagation and education, it administers the affairs of pilgrims going to *Hajj*, issues *ḥalāl* (permissible) certificates, manages mosques and *madrasah*, as well as issues *fatwas*.

Another NGO in Singapore involved in Islamic propagation and education is the Muslim Converts' Association or *Darul Arqam* which represents the interests of converts residing in Singapore. The Association regularly organizes Islamic educational discourses, workshops, and seminars on issues such as family affairs, basic tenets of the religion, and cross-cultural *da'wah* conferences.[23] In addition to religious education, the Islamic Center *Jamiyah* (http://www.jamiyah.org.sg) organizes computer courses to learn about the Internet, design web pages and other IT technicalities, to equip Muslims with the challenge of the digital world.

In the Philippines, a number of Islamic *da'wah* and educational institutions are recognized and registered by the government. The Islamic *Da'wah* Council of the Philippines is an Islamic NGO accredited by the Philippines Department of Social Welfare and Development, which represents 95 Muslim organizations throughout the Philippines (http://www.jannah.org/mamalist/Natl-Intl-Orgs). The Wisdom Enrichment Foundation in Manila disseminates Islamic information via Electronic Books (a free e-book service) and the online WISDOM International Learning program, which focuses on Islamic studies and personality development (http://www.wefound.org/index.htm). Even political organizations such as the Moro Islamic Liberation Front (MILF) stress the need for Islamic education and identification. The MILF movement "deliberately made Islam their rallying point by underscoring 'Islamic' in their group's name . . ."[24]

Social welfare

The majority of Islamic movements in Southeast Asia such as Indonesian's Muhammadiyah and the NU, the Department of Islamic Development in Malaysia, the *Da'wah* Center in Brunei, and the MUIS of Singapore are involved in social welfare activities to varying degrees. These activities include looking after the running of mosques, caring for orphans and the poor.

Economic

Although a small number of Muslims living in Southeast Asia are economically well off, the vast majority live in poor economic conditions. Muslims, who often have a large family size and a meager income frequently turn to Islamic organizations and institutions to assist them financially. As a result, some CIMs focus primarily on meeting the economic challenges faced by their adherents. Islamic banking has been growing in popularity in recent years, to the extent that many well-known conventional banks in Southeast Asia have started to offer Islamic banking services.

Brunei has established a number of financial institutions to serve the economic needs of its Muslims. These include the Insurance Islam (TAIB), the Islamic Bank of Brunei (IBB), and the Islamic Development Bank of Brunei (IDBB). In 2001 the latter launched an Islamic Internet banking system called *Eze-Net Islamic Banking*, to facilitate online banking (www.idbb-bank.com).

Malaysia has recently become an international Islamic banking center. Bank *Muamalat* Malaysia *Berhad* and Bank Islam Malaysia *Berhad* (BIMB) provide comprehensive Islamic financial services in the country. In addition there is the Association of Islamic Banking Institutions Malaysia (AIBIM) (http://www.aibim.com.my/aibim/index.cfm), which aims to "promote the establishment of sound Islamic banking systems and practices in Malaysia."

Bank Muamalat Indonesia and Bank Syariah Mandiri of Indonesia offer Islamic banking based on shari'ah law. Furthermore, the NU has established a number of bodies to promote trade, industry, and agriculture which run along Islamic lines in accordance with shari'ah.

In Singapore, Majlis Ugama Islam Singapore (MUIS) is involved in the administration of *zakat* (alms giving) and *wakaf* (endowment). Through its online e-service, MUIS members can undertake financial transactions such as eNETS credit and eNETS debit banking. Furthermore, members can calculate and make *zakat* payments, register and pay *Hajj* fees, as well as give charitable donations online.

Political – participatory

CIMs that are founded on religio-political grounds can be divided into two subgroups: participatory and separatist. The former prefer to operate within the existing political framework, while the latter favor working outside the existing political order, either by creating their own separate political entity or by overthrowing the political order. Attention will now be focussed on the participatory type of CIM.

One of the primary goals of the NU in Indonesia is "democratic reform." The organization's current chairman Hasyim Muzadi opposes the establishment of Indonesia as an Islamic state and calls for greater cooperation and understanding between all the religious groups in Indonesia (http://en.wikipedia.org/wiki/Nahdlatul_Ulama). Since 1984, the NU has been led by Wahid who in 1991 founded the Democratic Forum, which is dedicated to promoting greater democracy in Indonesia, including freedom of expression. Towards this end, the NU organizes discourses of young *kyai* or *ulama* at the Center for the Development of *Pesantren* and Society. One of the Center's more recent activities, supported by the Ford Foundation, was a forum for women *kyai* to discuss feminist issues from a scholarly Islamic perspective (http://www.insideindonesia.org/edit52/djohan.htm).

The Muhammadiyah, the second largest Islamic organization in Indonesia, is composed primarily of millions of urban and middle class members. M. Din Syamsuddin, a lecturer at the Universitas Muhammadiyah Jakarta, stated that although the Muhammadiyah's political activities are inseparable from religious life, it has never been a political organization nor directly engaged in practical politics. Nevertheless, the organization has been required to deal with political issues, by at times taking on the role of political lobbyist, or public policy think tank, as well as contributing to the discussion of long-term political goals."[25]

The Muhammadiyah, which tries its best to remain neutral and independent, has recently started educating its members on how they can participate in the elections, stopping short, however, of telling voters who to vote for. Although some members of the Muhammadiyah gave significant support to Amien Rais, a former head of the organization and current chairman of the National Mandate Party (NMP founded in 1998), who was contesting the presidential seat during the 2004 national election, Sjafii Maarif, the present chairman of Muhammadiyah, "has denied that the organization had intentionally involved itself in politics."[26]

In addition to the above, there are also a number of smaller Islamic political groups in Indonesia, including *Laskar Jihād*, *Front Pembela* Islam (Islamic Defenders Front), *Partai Keadilan* (Justice Party), and others.

In the Malaysian political scene, *Parti Islam Se Malaysia* (PAS), founded in 1951, seeks to establish an Islamic state in Malaysia "based on the principles of *sharī'ah* and guided by the dictates of the Almighty Allah." The PAS accepts "democracy as the best methodology through which it should realize the ambition, vision and mission of its political struggle (http://www.parti-pas.org)." In fact in 1999, the PAS succeeded in partially realizing its aim, when it came to political power in the two northeastern Malaysian states of Kelantan and Terengganu. In 2004, however, it has seen its position somewhat eroded.

Omar Farouk Bajunid, a professor of comparative politics at Hiroshima City University, Japan, asserts that Muslim NGOs such as the Thai Muslim Students Association (TMSA) help prepare Muslims for national political leadership. In addition, there is close coordination between the Ministry of Interior and the Central Islamic Committee of Thailand to "ensure the appointment of *ulama* loyal to the Bangkok line."[27] Currently, there are a number of Thai Muslims working in senior governmental positions in Bangkok. Despite that, confrontations are taking place in the southern part of the country. Tensions have risen to such an extent that in April 2005, the Thai government advised the residents of Bangkok "to be on the alert for signs of militant attacks following the bombing by suspected Muslim extremists of an airport in the commercial center of the south."[28]

Political – separatist

The majority of CIMs, within this category, reject the current political order and threaten to create their own political system outside of the current order or overthrow the existing order "by any means necessary". As a result, most of the groups in this category are not afraid of employing violent means to resolve their problems and gain public attention. A number of these groups receive theological support for their actions from some Muslim scholars who call for a revolution against any leadership which has rebelled against God and His guidance and is responsible for the suffering of mankind. In the view of such scholars, secular governments are "to be replaced by a leadership that is God-conscious, righteous, and committed to following divine guidance."[29] Rizal Sukma, the director of the Indonesian Center for Strategic and International Studies, argues that many of these groups are motivated by "moral frustration, ideological fear of globalization and Western domination, a desire for a *Pax Islamica* in Indonesia, simple political opportunism, and economic and social resentments" (http://www.usindo.org/miscellaneous/indo-us_conf.pdf).

One example of a CIM with a separatist political agenda is *Jamaah Islamiyah* (JI), which is an Arabic term for "Muslim group", based in Indonesia. Kumar Ramakrishna asserts that the JI is a "radical terrorist Islamic organization (which) has emerged as the biggest threat to Southeast Asia security". He claims that the JI is part of the "Global *Salafi Jihād*" ideology or "*Al-Qaedaism*," which was brought to Southeast Asia by Arab migrants from Yemen. Moreover, the organization "seeks to establish *Daulah Islamiyah Nusantara*, or an Islamic state incorporating Indonesia, Malaysia, the southern Philippines, Brunei, and Singapore."[30] The JI perceives attacks on Western targets as part of a fully justified and legitimate defensive *jihād*, and has openly expressed the fact that they are willing to use force to achieve their goals. A statement issued by the organization immediately after the September 2004 bomb attack in Jakarta stated the following:

> We (in the JI) have sent many messages to the Christian government in Australia regarding its participation in the war against our brothers in Iraq. Therefore, we have decided to punish it as we considered it the fiercest enemy of Allah and the Islamic religion . . . the hands that attacked them in Bali are the same hands that carried out the attack in Jakarta . . .

In a similar manner JI members from Singapore who took part in Muslim–Christian fighting (1999–2000) in the Maluku archipelago in eastern Indonesia saw themselves as defending "fellow Ambonese Muslims from being killed by Christians."[31]

A second political separatist group in Indonesia is the GAM (Acehnese Independent Movement) movement that has been fighting for an independent Islamic state in Aceh since the 1970s. In 1996, the Indonesian government claimed that the Free Aceh or Aceh Merdeka movement had been eliminated, although Aceh was still officially listed as one of Indonesia's three "trouble spots" (along with East Timor and Irian Jaya). Two years later, several caches of foreign arms were discovered in Aceh, resulting in the arrest of suspected rebels who were imprisoned and threatened with torture. In the post September 11 period, Aceh Merdeka has been under increased pressure to come to a settlement with the Indonesian government (http://islamlib.com/en/page.php?page=article&id=257).

In Thailand there are two main CIMs of a political separatist orientation: Liberation Front of Pattani and *Barisan Revolusi Nasional*, both of whom emerged in the 1960s. In March 1968, the more militant Pattani United Liberation Organization (PULO) entered the scene. While initially the organization dealt primarily with the concerns of

ethnic Malay minorities, "during the 1990s, the movements became increasingly associated with radical Islam." Although Pattani continues to be regarded as one of the
centers of Islamic learning in the Malay–Indonesian world, violence in the southern
Thai region has been a serious issue of concern. A wave of revenge started from the
attacks on the *Tak Bai* (Narathiwat) on October 25, 2004, which killed at least 84
Muslims (who were suffocated to death) by the Thai security forces. Moderate leaders
in the Muslim community of Pattani, Yala, and Narathiwat "have appealed to the government to seek a political solution to the problem, warning that further repression will
breed more terrorism" (http://yaleglobal.yale.edu/display.article?id=4922).

Another example of a CIM with a separatist political orientation is the Moro National
Liberation Front (MNLF), which has historically functioned as the main focus of the
Islamic armed resistance to Manila in the southern Philippines. The MNLF, founded by
Nur Misuari in 1971, argued that the Moro people constitute a distinct Islamic historical and cultural identity, and have a legitimate right to determine their own future. In
1980, the Moro Islamic Liberation Front (MILF) was formed as a splinter movement of
the MNLF. This group was critical of the more leftist orientation of the MNLF, and is far
more religious in its orientation than its parent movement, emphasizing the promotion
of Islamic ideals, rather than the broad-based pursuit of nationalist Moro objectives
(http://www.islamonline.net/English/Views/2002/11/article11.shtml).

In 1991, a radical group, which disagreed with the peace process between the
Muslims and the state, left the MNLF and formed the Abu Sayyaf (Bearer of the Sword)
Group. The main goal of Abu Sayyaf is to establish an Islamic state, based on the Islamic
law (sharī'ah) in the southern Philippines. From 2000 until the present day, the group
has been engaged in a series of kidnappings of Filipinos and foreign nationals, in order
to obtain ransom money (http://www.ict.org.il/articles/articledet.cfm?articleid=116).

Kareem M. Kamel, who works at the American University in Cairo, argues that the
persistence of these separatist movements, "demonstrates the failure of the Philippines
in achieving legitimacy for its post-independence political structure, the failure to
address the grievances of Muslims in the Philippines, and the historical role that intru-
sive foreign powers have played in the marginalization and alienation of Muslims." He
supports this idea with the fact that "fifteen of the Philippines' poorest provinces are
located in the south, which additionally has the country's lowest literacy rate (75%)
and life expectancy (57 years)" (http://www.islamonline.net/English/Views/2002/11/
article11.shtml).

Al-Arqam and *al-Ma'unah* groups in Malaysia and Brunei were originally mystical
educational movements, that turned political and violent. Due to deviant elements in
their teachings and the use of violence (in *al-Ma'unah* case), they were banned by the
authorities in the region. Members of these groups, in both Malaysia and Brunei, were
arrested and detained under the Internal Security Act (ISA), which enables it to detain,
without trial, individuals deemed threatening to national security.

Syncretic

Some CIMs are not completely rooted in Islamic teachings and doctrines, but rather
have syncretized indigenous beliefs with Hindu, Buddhist, and Islamic doctrines. One

example of such a movement is *Kebatinan*, which is popular in Indonesia and is an amalgam of animism, Hindu–Buddhist, and Islamic, especially Sufi beliefs. According to Michael Rogge, a Dutch psychologist, "the Javanese mystical tradition is known for its syncretism. In the course of its history, it absorbed all the religious traditions that reached Java and gave it its own interpretation." Rogge further asserts that among the techniques to achieve "unity with God" is *dihkr* (repetitive prayer), fasting, sleep deprivation, and withdrawal from the world (http://www.xs4all.nl/~wichm/javmys1. htm1).

One syncretic group in Indonesia, which has its origins in Qadian, India, is the *Jemaat Ahmadiyah Indonesia* (http://www.ahmadiyya.or.id/pengantar/). The *Jemaat Ahmadiyah* was established in 1889 and is centered around the teachings of Hazrat Mirza Ghulam Ahmad (1835–1908), whom followers believe to be the *mujadid* (reformist) as well as the *mahdi dan al-masih* (messiah). The movement's approach is "to convince the human mind, intellect, conscience and heart, of the truth of Islam." In order to achieve this objective, it presents "reasoned arguments, showing the inherent beauty of Islamic principles and their appeal to true human nature." The movement also believes that the truth and beauty of Islam must be shown through one's practical life and example such as that of its founder Hazrat Mirza Ghulam Ahmad (http://www.muslim.org/ intro/intro.htm).

Conclusion

This chapter has shown that CIMs in Southeast Asia are extremely diverse, since they incorporate any group that is working towards the establishment and strengthening of Islamic values in society. It has been argued that contrary to popular perception, not all CIMs are anti-government, since many "Islamization" policies and programs are initiated by government or semi-government bodies. Such groups generally have tolerant views and are willing to coexist with other religious groups and secular institutions. However, CIMs in Southeast Asia also include NGOs, as well as groups with a more separatist orientation. It is the latter that get most of the publicity, but in reality their membership comprises a small minority of the Muslims in Southeast Asia. While some such as Barry Desker insist that "Islam is the cause of regional terrorism, especially in states where Muslims are minorities such as in Singapore, the Philippines and Thailand" (http://www.ntu.edu.sg/idss/Perspective/ research_050217.htm), in reality such a statement is overly simplified. Many separatist CIMs have historical grievances against central governments which have been unresolved over the years.

This lack of a clear connection between CIMs and terrorism has been summarized aptly by Azyumardi Azra, rector of the State Institute for Islamic Studies (IAIN), Indonesia, who states that,

All radical groups have some connections with theological or organizational groups elsewhere, including the Middle East, but it is difficult to establish a connection with al-Qaeda, and the leaders of the FPI, Laskar Jihād and JAMI have criticized Osama bin Laden.

During the "Islam in Modern Indonesia" conference, held in Washington DC, in 2002, the speakers (including Azyumardi Azra) agreed that although "Islamic piety has increased in recent years there has been no increase in the number of radical Muslims . . . [and] the presence of al-Qaeda in Indonesia has not been proven" (http://www.usindo.org/miscellaneous/indo-us_conf.pdf).

Nevertheless in an attempt to discourage CIMs from utilizing violent means to resolve their problems and gain public attention, in recent years some Muslim author-ities in Southeast Asia have started formulating certain policies, establishing special forces, increasing regional and international coordination against terrorism and organizing intellectual discourses to control the situation. For example, in 2003 dur-ing a conference on tackling religious extremism, participants called on powerful countries to be fair in resolving international conflicts and stressed the need for mutual respect among different religions and cultures (http://www.aljazeerah.info/News%20archives).

In conclusion, the majority of CIMs in Southeast Asia can be classified as advocates of peaceful change in their societies. Like other world religions, the essence of Islam is to provide and promote peaceful solutions to human challenges. In spite of this, some Muslims adopting their own interpretations of Islamic texts prefer to use indiscriminate violence to achieve their political ends. The extent to which such violence is justified often depends upon one's ideological orientation. One point that most religious groups can agree upon, however, is that no religion, Islam included, justifies the killing of innocent people. It is here that religious leaders play a critical role in educating Muslims and directing them towards the good. To paraphrase Tarmizi Taher, former Indonesian minister of religious affairs, religious leaders have a critical role to play in reducing inter-religious conflicts and positively changing society, through their attitudes towards other religious communities (http://www.icipglobal.org/doc).

Notes

1. This article is a revised version of a paper presented at the 19th World Congress of the Inter-national Association for History of Religions (IAHR), University of Tokyo, Japan, March 24–30, 2005.
2. Alijah Gordon, ed., *The Propagation of Islam in the Indonesian–Malay Archipelago* (Kuala Lumpur: Malaysian Sociological Research Institute, 2001), 26.
3. Abdul Ghani Yakob, "Theories on the Arrival of Islam in the Malay Archipelago," *Proceed-ing for the International Seminar on Islamic Studies in Southeast Asia*, Vol. 11 (University of Brunei Darussalam, 1995), 512.
4. Wan Hussain Azmi bin Wan Abdul Kadir, "*Al-Da'wah al-Islamiyyah fi Janub Sharqi Aisyah Mundu Duhuriha ila al-Asr al-Hadir*" (*Islamic Da'wah in Southeast Asia: From the Beginning to Modern Era*). Ph.D. thesis submitted to Usuluddin Department, Al-Azhar University, Cairo, 1974, 503, 513.
5. Jeffery K. Hadden, "Religious Movements", in Edger F. Borgatta, ed., *Encyclopedia of Sociol-ogy* (New York: Macmillan, 1992), 1642.

6. Anis Ahmad, "Islamic Movements as Agents of Social Change: Framework for Analysis," in Muhammad Mumtaz Ali, ed., *Modern Islamic Movements: Models, Problems and Prospects* (Kuala Lumpur: A.S. Noordeen, 2000), 137.

7. Quintan Wiktorowicz, *Islamic Activism: A Social Movement Theory Approach* (Indianapolis: Indiana University Press, 2004), 2.

8. Quintan Wiktorowicz, 25.

9. Taha Jabir al-Alwani, "Missing Dimensions in Contemporary Islamic Movements," in Muhammad Mumtaz Ali, ed., *Modern Islamic Movements: Models, Problems and Prospects* (Kuala Lumpur: A.S. Noordeen, 2000), 170.

10. AbdulHamid A. AbuSulayman, *Crisis in the Muslim Mind*, 2nd edn., trans. Yusuf Talal DeLorenzo (Herndon, VA: International Institute of Islamic Thought, 1994), 40.

11. Bahtiar Effendi, *Islam and the State in Indonesia* (Singapore: Institute of Southeast Asian Studies, 2003), 66 and 86.

12. Samuel K. Tan, *Filipino Muslim Perceptions of their History and Culture as Seen though Indigenous Written Sources* (Philippines: University of the Philippines Press, 2003), 1.

13. B.J. Boland, *The Struggle of Islam in Modern Indonesia* (The Hague: Martinus Nijhoff, 1982), 211–12.

14. Anak Agung Banyu Perwita, "Indonesia: Islam, Globalization and 'Religious' Conflict," *The SEACSN Bulletin* (Southeast Asian Conflict Studies Network), January–June, 2004, 2.

15. M.B. Hooker, *Indonesian Islam: Social Change Through Contemporary Fatwa* (Honolulu: University of Hawaii Press, 2003), 233.

16. Jeffrey K. Hadden, "Religious Fundamentalism," in Edger F. Borgatta, ed., *Encyclopedia of Sociology* (New York: Macmillan, 1992), 1637.

17. William Shepard, "What is 'Islamic Fundamentalism'?", *Studies in Religion*, 17(1), 1988, 7–17.

18. Robert Day McAmis, *Malay Muslims: The History and Challenge of Resurgent Islam in Southeast Asia* (Cambridge: Eerdmans, 2002), 73.

19. Quintan Wiktorowicz, 296.

20. Fred Von Der Mehden, *Religion and Nationalism in Southeast Asia: Burma, Indonesia, the Philippines* (Madison: University of Wisconsin Press, 1963), 197.

21. Martin Van Bruinessen, "'Traditionalist' and 'Islamist' *Pesantren* in Contemporary Indonesia," paper presented at the ISIM workshop on "The Madrasa in Asia," May 23–4, 2004, ISIM, Netherlands, 9.

22. Carool Kersten, "The Predicament of Thailand's Southern Muslims," *American Journal of Islamic Social Science*, 21(4), 2004, 19.

23. Ridzuan Wu, ed., *Readings in Cross-Cultural Da'wah* (Singapore: The Muslim Converts' Association of Singapore, 2001), vii.

24. Arskal Salim, "'*Shari'a* from Below' in Aceh (1930s–1960s): Islamic Identity and the Right to Self-Determination with Comparative Reference to the Moro Islamic Liberation Front (MILF)," *Indonesian and the Malay World*, 32(92), 2004, 94.

25. M. Din Syamsuddin, "The Muhammadiyah *Da'wah* and Allocative Politics in the New Order Indonesia," *Studia Islamika*, 2(2), 1995, 41–2, 65.

26. Tiarma Siboro and Ainur R. Sophiaan, "Muhammadiyah Youth Groups Oppose Amien's Candidacy," *The Jakarta Post*. February 14, 2004.

27. Omar Farouk Bajunid, "Islam and Civil Society in Southeast Asia: A Review," in Makamura Mitsuo, Sharon Siddique, and Omar Farouk Bajunid, eds., *Islam and Civil Society in Southeast Asia* (Singapore: Institute of Southeast Asian Studies, 2001), 192; Carool Kersten, 15.

28. Report (Reuters), "Vigilance in Bangkok after Blasts," *Borneo Bulletin* (Brunei Newspaper), 6(4), 2005, 16.

29. Sayyid Abul A‘la Mawdūdī, *The Islamic Movement: Dynamics of Values, Power and Change*, ed. Khurram Murad (London: Islamic Foundation, 1984), 71.

30. Kumar Ramakrishna, "Constructing the *Jemaah Islamiyah* Terrorist: A Preliminary Inquiry," Paper series, No.71 (Singapore: Institute of Defense and Strategic Studies, 2004), 1.

31. Kumar Ramakrishna, 19 and 44.

Internet references

Ahmadiyya Association for the Propagation of Islam. Accessed 18/3/2005 from http://www.muslim.org/intro/intro.htm.

Asia Times Online. Accessed 10/4/2005 from http://www.atimes.com/atimes/Southeast_Asia/GA29Ae07.html.

Bertil Lintner, "A New Battlefield in Thailand," *Yaleglobal Online*. Yale Center for the Study of Globalization. Accessed 13/3/2005 from http://yaleglobal.yale.edu/display.article?id=4922.

Christos Lacovou, "From MNLF to Abu Sayyaf: The Radicalization of Islam in the Philippines." Accessed 18/3/2005 from http://www.ict.org.il/articles/articledet.cfm?articleid=116.

Darry Desker, "Islam and Society in Southeast Asia after 9/11." Accessed 12/3/2005 from http://www.ntu.edu.sg/idss/Perspective/research_050217.htm.

Goenawan Mohamad, "Liberal Islam in Indonesia: A Beginning." Accessed 26/12/2004 from http://islamlib.com/en/page.php?page=article&id=232.

Insideindonesia.org. Accessed 14/3/2005 from http://www.insideindonesia.org/edit52/djohan.htm.

Islamic Development Bank of Brunei. Accessed 7/4/2005 from http://www.idbb-bank.com.

Islamic Party of Malaysia (PAS). Accessed 17/3/2005 from http://www.parti-pas.org/Islamic-StateDocument.php.

Islamic Religious Council of Singapore. Accessed 13/3/2005 from http://www.muis.gov.sg/english/corporate_info/background_role/Background_Index.aspx?pMenu=2.

Jamiyah Singapore. Accessed 10/4/2005 from http://www.jamiyah.org.sg.

Jemaat Ahmadiyah Indonesia. Accessed 18/3/2005 from http://www.ahmadiyya.or.id/pengantar.

Kareem M. Kamel, "Islam under Siege in Southeast Asia: Conflict in the Philippines." Accessed 16/4/2005 from http://www.islamonline.net/English/Views/2002/11/article11.shtml.

Liberal Islam Network. Accessed 11/4/2005 from http://islamlib.com/en/page.php?page=article&id=257.

MamaList Database. *Jannah.org*. Accessed 14/3/2005 from http://www.jannah.org/mamalist/Natl-Intl-Orgs.

Michael Rogge, "Javanese Mystical Movements." Accessed 26/12/2004 from http://www.xs4all.nl/~wichm/javmysl.html.

Overview of World Religions. "*Nahdatul Ulama*". Accessed 1/1/2005 from http://philtar.ucsm.ac.uk/encyclopedia/indon/nahdat.html.

Oxford English Dictionary Online. Accessed 5/4/2005 from http://www.oed.com.

Parliament of Australia, Parliamentary Library. "Terrorism in Southeast Asia". Accessed 7/4/2005 from http://www.aph.gov.au/library/intguide/FAD/sea.htm.

Report, AFP. "Muslim Scholars Call for Fair Play in Resolving Conflicts," Jakarta, October 16, 2003. Accessed 11/4/2005 from http://www.aljazeerah.info/News%20archives/

2003%20News%20archives/October/16%20n/Muslim%20Scholars%20Call%20for%20
Fairplay%20in%20Resolving%20Conflicts.htm.

Rizal Sukma, Speech Delivered at the Conference on "Islam in Modern Indonesia." Washington
DC, USA, 7/2/2002. Accessed 7/4/2005 from http://www.usindo.org/miscellaneous/indo-
us_conf.pdf.

Romanian Fact Book 2005. "An Analysis of the World Muslim Population by Country/Region."
Accessed 23/2/2005 from http://www.factbook.net/muslim_pop.php.

State Mufti's Office, Brunei Darussalam. Accessed 19/3/2005 from http://www.brunet.bn/
gov/mufti/p_ingsrc.htm.

Tarmizi Taher, "Role of Religious Leaders in Reducing Possible Conflicts." Paper presented at the
Regional Workshop on "Pluralism and Multiculturalism in the Southeast Asia: Formulating
Educational Agendas and Programs". Organized by The International Center for Islam and
Pluralism (ICIP), Jakarta, November 25–8, 2004. Accessed 9/6/2005 from http://
www.icipglobal.org/doc/Vol%202%20No%201/ARTICLES%20ABSTRACT/Tarmizi-Taher%
20-%20article%203.pdf.

The Association of Islamic Banking Institutions Malaysia. Accessed 6/4/2005 from
http://www.aibim.com.my/aibim/dsp_page.cfm?pageid=232.

The Muslim Converts' Association of Singapore. Accessed 10/4/2005 from http://www.
darularqam.org.sg/darul-arqam/web.

US Library of Congress. Accessed 11/4/2005 from http://countrystudies.us/indonesia/37.htm.

Wikipedia, The Free Encyclopedia. Accessed 1/1/2005 from http://en.wikipedia.org/wiki/
Nahdlatul_Ulama.

Wisdom Enrichment Foundation. Accessed 14/3/2004 from http://www.wefound.org/
EnlighteningEbooks.htm.

CHAPTER 27

Transformation of Political Islam in Post-Suharto Indonesia

Mun'im A. Sirry

Following the collapse of the authoritarian Suharto regime on May 21, 1998, there has been enthusiasm for democracy in Indonesia.[1] The era of openness not only encourages the emergence of a large number of political parties, but also diverse religious expressions, including radical understanding of Islam, commonly called Islamism or political Islam. The questions are: How strong is Islamism in Indonesia, the world's largest Muslim-majority country? And what are the trends and tendencies of Islamism *vis-à-vis* public enthusiasm for political participation in this newly restored and fragile democracy?

So far, there are only a few statistical data on the subject, making it not easy to answer the above questions. Journalistic observers often seem tentative or even puzzled in their assessment.[2] In September 2003, for instance, a *New York Times* article relayed that "some have begun to ask whether the Islamists who want to create a caliphate across the Muslim areas of Southeast Asia will at least eventually succeed in Indonesia."[3] Yet just a month earlier, the *Times* had dismissively portrayed a meeting of Islamic militants, intended as a show of strength. The gathering, according to the report, was sparsely attended.[4]

Despite the current uncertainty, there is a long-held near-consensus among specialists that the vast majority of Indonesian Muslims are steadily moderate in their political views. Beginning with the American anthropologist Clifford Geertz in the 1950s through the contemporary political scientists such as R. William Liddle and Robert W. Hefner, all have emphasized the pluralistic nature of Indonesian Islam, which is conducive for furthering the moderation process of political Islam in Indonesia.

This chapter examines the dynamics of political Islam, specifically with regard to the pluralistic nature of Indonesian Islam. As in other Muslim-majority countries, the discourse of Indonesian Muslims on politics and state is not monolithic. There has been a wide range of views about the role Islam should play in the national life. At one end of this spectrum, Muslims have used Islamic principles to justify armed rebellion and the establishment of a breakaway Islamic state. At the other end, they have drawn on the precepts of their faith to support pluralist or even secular positions regarding the role of Islam in the state. But, in contrast to other Muslim countries where the Islamic credentials of Islamist groups tend to strengthen, in Indonesia the trend goes to the opposite side. I tend to argue that there has been tendency toward a political moderation of Indonesian Islam, which is manifested clearly in the last two general elections since Suharto's downfall.[5]

As part of the discussion of Islamic contribution to the democratic transitional phase in Indonesia, this chapter looks at the main variants within Indonesian Islam and the ways in which these have been played out in politics, before discussing the relationship between Islam and the state and the role of Islamic parties during the Sukarno and Suharto eras. To conclude, this chapter will survey the developments in the post-Suharto period.

Characterizing Indonesian Islam

With about 200 million Muslims (88 percent of a total population of more than 230 million), Indonesia has a larger Muslim population than any other country in the world. However, there are several grounds for regarding these figures with caution. To begin with, all Indonesian citizens must profess adherence to one of five officially recognized faiths: that is, Islam, Catholicism, Protestantism, Hinduism, and Buddhism. A significant number of those who describe themselves as Muslim are nominally so, or may not be Muslim at all. Many "unrecognized" religious minorities find it less troublesome to be regarded as Muslims rather than as adherents of an official minority faith.

The picture becomes more complex if one looks at the major subcultures within Indonesian Islam. Historically, scholars have drawn a distinction between the devout and less pious Muslims. The most widely accepted typology is that of *abangan* and *santri*, popularized by the American anthropologist, Clifford Geertz, in his classic *Religion of Java*[6] to describe Javanese Islam.[7] The term *abangan* (literally means the red ones), used by the Javanese to categorize Muslims whose real religious beliefs and practices are a historical layer cake of indigenous animism; Hinduism (brought to the archipelago by Indian traders early in the Common Era); and Islam (also brought, from the thirteenth century, by Indian traders). Of the three layers, the Islamic is the newest and thinnest, the least determinative of personal, social, and political behavior. The *abangan* are also commonly referred to as syncretists.

Pious or orthodox Muslims, called *santri* (literally means students in the traditional Muslim boarding schools called *pesantren*), are further categorized into traditionalists and modernists or reformists.[8] All *santri* believe that they should pray five times a day, fast during Ramadan, prepare to make the pilgrimage to Mecca, and give alms as stipulated in the Qur'an. Traditionalist *santri* adhere to the school of legal interpretation (*madhhab*) within Sunni Islam begun by Imam Shafi'i. They respect and rely upon the knowledge and wisdom of *ulama* or, in Indonesian, *kyai* (religious teacher and scholar).[9]

The most prominent traditionalist social and educational organization, in fact a dense network of *kyai*, is the Nahdlatul Ulama (The Awakening of Scholars, abbreviated as NU). The NU, which claims to have about 40 million members, is based primarily on Java, though it has branches throughout the country.[10] There are many similar organizations, like Al Washliyah in Sumatra, which are less well known, in part because their leaders are less politically active.

Modernists, inspired at the end of the nineteenth century by Muḥammad 'Abduh and other Middle Eastern reformers, renounce all of the classical schools in favor of direct interpretation of the Qur'an and other religious texts by believers. They therefore have less respect for the *ulama*, often viewed as out of touch with modern life and its particular challenges. Sociologically, modernists have tended to be more urban and Western-educated than traditionalists, although this distinction has been breaking down in the last half century with the spread of Western education and modern life styles more generally. The largest modernist organization, which claims more than 20 million members, is the Muhammadiyah.[11]

Some modernists have become liberals, reading the Qur'an in a more open or new way to allow incorporation of borrowed practices and institutions such as banks and parliaments. Liberals tend to accept Christians and other non-Muslims as equal members of Indonesian society. Other modernists have become conservatives, even fundamentalists. Conservatives read the Qur'an and other texts literally and are highly suspicious of the intentions of non-Muslims. Conservatives urge the formation of Islamic banks, the wearing by women of the *jilbab* or Islamic headscarf, the separation of the sexes in state schools, and in broad terms the implementation of Islamic law.

Among modernists, there appears to be no correlation between level of education and tendency toward liberalism or conservatism. Adherents to both tendencies are found throughout the higher education system, especially in the state secular universities like the famed University of Indonesia in Jakarta and Gadjah Mada University (UGM) in Yogyakarta, Central Java. There is, however, probably a positive correlation between conservatism and modernism. That is, most conservatives and fundamentalists are to be found within the modernist, not the traditionalist, camp. The implication is not that most modernists are conservatives, but rather that most conservatives are modernists.

There has been a commonly held view that the great religious divide in Indonesian national politics was (and is still) variously labeled Muslims versus non-Muslims and Muslims versus nationalists. However, I would argue that both of these oppositions are misleading if not misnomers. The actual great divide is between non-Muslims, *abangan* Muslims, traditionalist, and liberal modernist Muslims on one side and conservative modernist Muslims on the other. Conservative modernist politicians typically claim to speak for all of political Islam, as many conservative modernist religious leaders typically claim that their reformed back-to-the Qur'an version is the only true Islam. Many other Muslims, however, dispute both the political and theological claims.

Political Islam in Indonesia

I use the terms "political Islam" or "Islamism" synonymously. I tend to agree with Graham E. Fuller who defines "political Islam" in its broadest sense. In his view, an Islamist is "one who believes that Islam as a body of faith has something important to say about how politics and society should be ordered in the contemporary Muslim world and who seeks to implement this idea in some fashion."[12] I prefer this definition because it is broad enough to capture the full spectrum of Islamist expression that runs the entire range from radical to moderate, violent to peaceful, democratic to authoritarian, traditionalist to modernist.

One of the most essential characteristics of political Islam is its effort to promote "Muslim"[13] aspiration and bring Islamic agenda into the laws and government policy through the electoral process and representative institutions (legislature). As there is no consensus on what constitute "Muslim" aspirations and Islamic agenda, this chapter defines these as political aspirations and agenda ranging from the state's moral foundation to policies produced by the state. These encompass the effort to achieve formal inclusion of sharī'ah into the constitution as well as the effort to promote government policies that are particularly supportive toward the progress and empowerment of "Muslim" society.

Since the early days of independence in 1945, Muslim leaders and Islamic political parties have struggled for the adoption of sharī'ah into the Indonesian constitution. The issue of the formal role of Islam in the state has been one of the most divisive issues in Indonesia's political and constitutional history. In fact, this issue created complex fissures in the political elite. Most non-Muslims and *abangan* were staunchly opposed and *santri* politicians were also divided. While the majority backed constitutional recognition of sharī'ah, some prominent *santri* favored a religiously neutral state. Much of this debate focussed on the so-called Jakarta Charter, particularly the famous seven-word clause which states "Belief in Almighty God with the obligation for Muslims to carry out shari'ah" (*dengan kewajiban menjalankan syari'at Islam bagi pemeluk-pemeluknya*).[14]

However, their efforts have been met with persistent failure. At a meeting on August 18, 1945, the day after independence was proclaimed, pro-Charter Muslim leaders came under strong pressure from *abangan* Muslims, nationalist, and religious minorities to drop the seven words. The main argument was that the predominant non-Muslim regions in Indonesia's east might break away from the republic if an Islamically inclined state was created. Reluctantly, Muslim leaders agreed to exclude the Charter in the interest of national unity. They also dropped the clause requiring the president to be Muslim.

When the Jakarta Charter re-emerged in the late 1950s, once again they failed. The Charter was effectively buried as a serious political issue for almost 40 years. Sukarno discouraged further debate on the matter, and the New Order Suharto regime stigmatized efforts to implement sharī'ah as contrary to Pancasila and inimical to national stability. But the aspiration has not yet died. The latest attempt to adopt sharī'ah occurred during the 2002 Annual Session of the People Consultative Assembly (MPR). Once again it failed.[15]

Today, even the views of Islamic organizations such as the NU and Muhammadiyah have become pluralistic. They have departed from their position in the 1950s, as they no longer share the agenda of formally adopting sharī'ah into the constitution. This does not mean that the NU or Muhammadiyah are no longer Islamic or are no longer articulating "Muslim" aspirations. In a recent development, the NU and Muhammadiyah clearly oppose the Jakarta Charter to be incorporated in the amendment of the 1945 constitution.[16] Their views simply reflect the realization among many Muslims and their leaders that even without formal adoption of sharī'ah in the constitution and formal Islamic political parties, Muslim aspirations can be fulfilled by the state. The focus is no longer on how to bring Islam into the foundation of the state, but how to bring Islamic coloration into policies produced by the state. By adhering to Pancasila and not focusing on the incorporation of sharī'ah into the constitution, Muslims have been able to promote an Islamic agenda like the Basic Law of Religious Justice in 1989 (Law No. 7, 1989) and the Compilation of Islamic Law in 1991 (Presidential Instruction No. 1, 1991).[17] Both are based on sharī'ah. This success changed the status of sharī'ah in the Indonesian legal system. As M.B. Hooker observed, until the early 1990s, "the status of sharī'ah in the Indonesian legal system was as much as the Dutch had left it."[18]

This departure shows that Islamists have become more pragmatic in their politics by focussing more on the policies level than on the state's philosophical foundation. In light of these developments, any analysis of political Islam and political parties should not overlook these dynamics, nor should one assume that political Islam has been static and united in focus on sharī'ah and the ideological basis of the state. Instead, in the post-Suharto era there is an interesting spectrum of political Islam in Indonesia. Political Islam is now represented by parties that are more diverse in platform. It comprises those who still support the formalization of the relationship between the state and Islam and those who support a non-religious-based state but welcome the incorporation of Islamic values and "Muslim" aspirations into government policy.

The results of the 1999 and 2004 parliamentary elections clearly indicate the transformation of political Islam in Indonesia. In the 1999 election, seven political parties passed the electoral threshold requirement, that is, 2.5 percent of total votes. Most observers divide the seven parties into three categories. First is the secular and nationalist parties. The Indonesian Democracy Party of Struggle (PDIP, Partai Demokrasi Indonesia Perjuangan), the Golongan Karya Party (Golkar), and the Democrat Party (PD) are to be included in this category. The PDIP, chaired by Megawati Sukarnoputri, the daughter of Sukarno, won a plurality of votes (34 percent) in the 1999 election. In the general Session of Consultative Assembly, Megawati was appointed as a vice president, and in 2001 she succeeded Abdurrahman Wahid as the president of the Republic of Indonesia. Meanwhile, the Golkar Party took the second position. The Golkar Party, founded in 1964, was the political machine of the Suharto New Order regime. In the 2004 parliamentary election the Democrat Party (PD) surprised many observers of its attractiveness to Indonesian voters although it is newly born party, and was even successful in installing its founder Susilo Bambang Yudhoyono as the current president of Indonesia.

The second category is the exclusivist Islamist parties. The United Development Party (PPP, Partai Persatuan Pembangunan), the Moon and Star Party (PBB, Partai Bulan Bintang), and the Justice Party (PK, Partai Keadilan) fall into this category, since they clearly adhere to Islam as their ideology. The PPP was founded in 1973 through a forced merger of the four Islamic parties: the NU, the Indonesian Muslims' Party (Parmusi, Partai Muslimin Indonesia), the Indonesian Islamic United Party (PSII, Partai Syarikat Islam Indonesia), and the Islamic Education Movement Party (Perti, Partai Pergerakan

Tarbiyah Islam). In 2001, Hamzah Haz, the chairman of the PPP, was elected vice president of the Republic of Indonesia. The PBB and PK were founded in 1998, soon after the collapse of the Suharto regime. The PPP and PBB pursue somewhat similar platforms as Islamic parties did in the 1950s. The PK does not elevate the Islamic state and sharī'ah in its current political agenda.

The third category is inclusivist or pluralist Islamist parties. The National Awakening Party (PKB, Partai Kebangkitan Bangsa) and the National Mandate Party (PAN, Partai Amanat Nasional) represent this trend. The PKB was founded in July 1998 by the NU leadership. As there were four parties affiliated with the NU, the role of Abdurrahman Wahid (chairman of the NU, 1984–99 and the president of Indonesia, 1999–2001) was vital in making the PKB the "official" party of the NU. In August 1998, the PAN came into existence, founded by activists involved in opposing the Suharto regime and led by Amien Rais (chairman of the Muhammadiyah, 1995–8 and leader of the 1998 reform movement to overthrow Suharto). The PAN has been closely associated with the Muhammadiyah. Initially it espoused ideological pluralism but shortly after the 1999 election its Islamic coloration strengthened.[19]

In the 2004 election, the PBB did not pass the electoral threshold requirement, therefore Islamist parties lost their strength in the Indonesian political arena. The PPP and PK (now PKS, Partai Keadilan Sejahtera) explicitly refer to Islam as their platform. The other two parties (PKB and PAN) implicitly refer to Islam and appear inclusive.

Tendency toward a Political Moderation

In the 1950s political Islam was identical with Islamic parties. They pursued the establishment of an Islamic state with the formal adoption of sharī'ah, although they varied in their level of commitment, e.g. the Islamic party, Masyumi, was more committed than the NU on those Islamist agendas. However, dynamic interactions between "Muslim" aspirations and the politics of secular Pancasila during the 1950s and Suharto's tenure have resulted in the pluralism of political Islam, not only in the electorates but in the parties' official platforms as well.

In 1955, during the run up to Indonesia's first parliamentary elections (after 10 years of independence), it was widely expected that the country's large majority of Muslim voters would return an Islamic government. Two major parties, the Masyumi and the NU, campaigned on platforms that included the call for the Jakarta Charter to be incorporated into the constitution of the country, that is, the declaration of belief in God by adding the phrase "with the obligation for Muslims to carry out sharī'ah."

Masyumi was originally an umbrella association of all major Muslim social and educational organizations. By 1955, its national leadership was dominated by the Muhammadiyah, then and now Indonesia's largest association of Islamic modernists. Masyumi and the NU failed to meet the expectations of observers in the 1955 election. The two parties received only 21 percent and 19 percent of the vote, respectively, and so were unable to advance their Islamic state agenda during the rest of the first democratic period (which ended in 1959). They were matched by two secular parties, the Indonesian National Party (PNI, created in the 1920s by Indonesia's charismatic founding father, Sukarno), with 22 percent of the vote, and the Indonesian Communist Party (PKI), with 17 percent.

In 1959, a coalition led by Sukarno and the leaders of the army overthrew the fledgling democracy, ushering in four decades of autocratic rule. In 1966, Major General Suharto replaced Sukarno, retaining the presidency for 32 years until he resigned in 1998. Democratic parliamentary elections took place the following year, and in October 1999 – under Indonesia's unique hybrid political system – parliament elected NU leader Abdurrahman Wahid as president. In July 2001, the same body dismissed Wahid, replacing him with the vice-president (and eldest daughter of Sukarno), Megawati Sukarnoputri.

One important indicator of the political moderation of Indonesian Muslims today is the decline in popular support for pro-sharī'ah parties since 1955. In the 1999 election, seven parties won significant percentages of the vote. Only three of the seven are based on Islam: Hamzah Haz's PPP, with 11 percent; the Crescent Moon and Star Party (PBB), with 2 percent; and the Justice Party (PK), with just 1 percent. It is also worth noting that the result of the 2004 election indicated that the two Islamic political parties (PPP and PBB), which were involved in the coalition government led by Megawati, lost significant votes. The PPP's popular vote declined from 11 percent in 1999 to only 8 percent in 2004. At the same time, the PBB did not pass the electorate threshold requirement.

The remaining four, which together took a resounding 76 percent of the vote, are all committed to the secular state. They include PDI-P with 34 percent; Golkar with 22 percent; PKB with 13 percent; and PAN, with 7 percent. Golkar was the military-backed state party that regularly won well over half the vote in the tightly controlled elections of the Suharto period, but it now competes on equal terms with the other parties. The PKB, headed by former president Abdurrahman Wahid, is the party of the NU but opposes implementation of sharī'ah. The PAN was founded by Amien Rais, national chair of the Muhammadiyah for much of the 1990s, and seems to have received much of its 1999 vote from Muhammadiyah members. Its national board includes several non-Muslims, and it also opposes implementation of sharī'ah.[20]

What accounts for the already modest levels of support for pro-sharī'ah parties in 1955 (40 percent in a population that was 87 percent Muslim) and the substantial drop in 1999 (to a total of 14 percent for the PPP, PBB, and PK)? The most widely accepted answer to the first part of this question was provided by the anthropologist Clifford Geertz in his 1960 classic *Religion of Java*. Among the ethnic Javanese who make up about half of Indonesia's population, Geertz argued, the main line of cleavage is between *orthodox* Muslims (including both the traditionalist and the modernist camps outlined above) and *syncretic* Muslims. (For comparison between the 1955 election and the 1999 and 2004 elections, see Table 27.1.)

Among syncretic Muslim Javanese, indigenous animism and Hinduism – which came to the archipelago long before Islam – powerfully influence contemporary religious beliefs and practices. PNI and PKI voters were disproportionately Javanese and (at least ostensibly) syncretic Muslims. Though no independent figures were available, many observers in the 1950s believed that up to two-thirds of Javanese Muslims were syncretists. Since orthodox Muslims were deemed unlikely to vote for secular parties,

Table 27.1   Political moderation of Indonesian Islam

	1955 election	1999 election	2004 election
Islamist parties			
Masyumi	21%	–	–
NU	19%	–	–
PPP	–	12%	8%
PBB	–	2%	2%
PK	–	1%	8%
Nationalist parties			
PNI	22%	–	–
PKI	17%	–	–
PDI-P	–	34%	19%
Golkar	–	22%	22%
PD	–	–	8%
Pluralist parties			
PKB	–	13%	13%
PAN	–	7%	6%

the Javanese vote for the PNI and PKI was often taken as evidence of the existence of a large group of syncretists.[21]

Two explanations are typically offered for the decline in the pro-sharī'ah vote between 1955 and 1999. First, the pro-sharī'ah forces were never as strong as they appeared to be, principally on account of the traditional political quietism of Indonesian Muslims. In the 1930s, NU leaders famously issued a *fatwa* accepting the legitimacy of Dutch rule. In the 1950s, they joined in the call for sharī'ah mainly to avoid being outflanked by the larger and more assertive Masyumi. Moreover, very few Masyumi leaders were in fact religious ideologs. Most were Western-educated, wanted to create a modern state and society, and were willing to join coalitions with secular parties. Their calls for an Islamic state were a device meant to attract unsophisticated village Muslims whom they assumed would vote automatically for a Muslim party.

The second explanation claims that Sukarno's and Suharto's repression of political Islam between 1955 and 1999 – and the response of Muslim politicians and intellectuals to that repression – produced a sea change in Muslim political culture. A few turned to violence, but the government crushed them. Many more, notably the Masyumi ideolog Mohammad Natsir and his followers, maintained their pro-sharī'ah position but retreated into the world of education while awaiting a more favorable political climate. After the fall of Suharto, this group reemerged as the PBB, winning only 2 percent of the 1999 vote.

The largest group, however, consisted of young Muslims leaving the schools and universities from the 1970s onward who wanted to make their peace with the secular state.

They were led on the modernist side by the religious thinker Nurcholish Madjid and on the traditionalist side by the activist Abdurrahman Wahid.[22] They and their descendants today hold many key positions in government and civil society. They control Golkar, PKB, and PAN, and are responsible for those parties' opposition to state enforcement of sharī'ah.

Cultural and Political Explanation

What explains this moderation, in contrast to the explosive growth of militancy in so many Muslim-majority countries? In addition to the previous two explanations, there are probably several other parts to a complete answer. First, there was a long history of moderation both among the traditionalists and the modernists. The NU had in the 1930s issued a *fatwa* declaring Dutch rule legitimate.[23] The early leaders of the Muhammadiyah and indeed to some extent of Masyumi focussed more on internal reform (*tajdīd*), making better Muslims one by one, as opposed to capturing the state in the name of Islam.

The second explanation is the success that the process of modernization has played in enlightening Indonesian people. Today, more and more Indonesian Muslims have become convinced that sharī'ah is not the solution to the sociopolitical and economic problems faced by modern Indonesia. The latest example of this tendency is the application of Islamic law in Aceh, which has not solved the Acehnese problems. Although Acehnese people have expressed their grievances by demanding the implementation of Islamic law, the real issues prevalent among them are economic, political, and social discontent. In other words, Islamic law is no longer considered as a divine solution to the worldly affairs of human beings.

Third, some government policies were directed at and welcomed by most *santri*, and indeed by many *abangan*. For example, beauty contests were prohibited and films were censored. A private Suharto foundation built thousands of mosques across the country, each with a distinctive pentagonal Pancasila logo at the top of its dome. Most importantly, compulsory religious education in state primary and secondary schools was introduced in Sukarto's time. The long-term result was a much commented-on process known as *santrinization*, the transformation from the 1960s onward of a significant proportion of *abangan* children into pious *santri*.[24]

Finally and yet importantly, much credit must be given to a remarkably creative and dedicated group of young religious and social thinkers and activists who chose early in the New Order to reject the Islamic state approach. Their intellectual and political influence has been enormous. In the 1960s and 1970s they were primarily modernists, perhaps because Western-style education was more accessible to city-dwelling, relatively affluent modernist youth in the 1950s. The outstanding religious thinker was Nurcholish Madjid, chair of the HMI, the association of Muslim university students, in the late 1960s.[25]

He delivered a controversial speech on January 3, 1970, in front of a large gathering of Muslim students and other young activists. This may be a usual pattern in the battles of ideas among Muslims in Indonesia: deadly serious, often profound, intellectual arguments take the platform of organizational politics. The speech was entitled *Keharusan Pembaharuan Pemikiran Islam and Masalah Integrasi Umat* (The Necessity of Renewing Islamic Thought and the Problem of the Integration of the *Umma*) in which he called on Muslims to embrace secularization.[26] By secularization, he meant (he said) not the secularism of the West, which was itself an ideology, but rather a rethinking of the relationship between religion and society, a reassessment of how Islam required its adherents to act in the world. By "to secularize" what he actually meant was "to desacralize" things profane but made sacral – like the idea of an Islamic state. In other words, Muslims should "secularize" the political while preserving what is truly sacred in Islam.[27]

It is hard to overstate the impact of Nurcholish's speech, then and now.[28] Delivered in the early years of the New Order, it was interpreted by some as a sell-out to Suharto. This reaction was particularly strong at the old Masyumi headquarters, which had become the office of the conservative Indonesian Islamic Proselytizing Council, headed by the grand old man of modernist politics, Mohammad Natsir. Once regarded as the young Natsir, Nurcholish now became the apostate, the traitor to the cause of an Islamic state. But he also began to develop a following of his own, particularly among young modernists who shared his values and goals but had not yet been able to formulate them so clearly and convincingly.[29]

By the 1980s, young traditionalists had become a vital part of the new theological and social mix. The outstanding traditionalist figure was, and still is, Abdurrahman Wahid.[30] Grandson of a founder of the NU, son of a prominent NU politician who had been minister of religion during parliamentary democracy, Abdurrahman is a legendary figure before his time. After desultory study at the University of Baghdad and Al Azhar University in Cairo and extensive travel in Europe, he settled down in Jakarta in the 1970s and rejoined young modernist and socialist activists at LP3ES (Lembaga Penelitian, Pendidikan dan Penerangan Ekonomi dan Sosial, Institute for Economic and Social Research, Education and Information), a development studies think tank and publisher of *Prisma*, the most imaginative applied social science periodical of its time.

While at LP3ES, Abdurrahman participated in an innovative program to introduce vocational and other non-religious subjects, including English, to the curriculum of the traditional *pesantren*.[31] He wrote an extraordinary series of columns in *Tempo* extolling the virtues of *kyai* who solve contemporary problems, that is, help to create a modern society, with traditional wisdom.[32] Abdurrahman was a member of the Jakarta Arts Council, served on film juries, including the Indonesian equivalent of the Academy Awards competition, and performed to acclaim as a commentator for European soccer games broadcast on Indonesian television. He also founded his own *pesantren*. In 1984, he was elected head of the NU, a position he held until he became president of Indonesia in 1999.

As in the case of Nurcholish, it is hard to overstate Abdurrahman's impact on his times. A social thinker and activist rather than a theologian, he inspired and shaped a new generation of Muslim liberals from within the traditionalist camp.[33] Equally important, he reached out to embrace non-Muslims and became by the early 1990s the first Muslim leader in Indonesian history to be fully trusted by non-Muslim political and social activists, including ex-communists. His 20-month presidency, from October

1999 to July 2001, was a disaster, but it is likely that history will remember him kindly for his earlier accomplishments.[34]

Critical to Abdurrahman's success was the role played by the 14 IAINs (State Institute for Islamic Studies) in spreading a more moderate understanding of Islamic politics throughout the archipelago. For most of the past half century, few *santri* village youth have had the credentials to enter the prestigious secular state universities. Educated at primary and secondary levels in the traditional *pesantren* and the more modernized but still basically Islamic madrasah, they have been able to continue to the tertiary level only through the IAINs, originally established to provide Islamic teachers for the secondary schools.

From the early 1970s, IAIN educational philosophy was heavily influenced by two remarkable men, Harun Nasution and Mukti Ali, who created for their students a kind of inter-civilizational dialogue. Nasution was educated in Islamic studies at Al-Azhar and Cairo universities and earned a Ph.D. at McGill University in Montreal. He taught that there are many *madhahib*, in philosophy, theology, *fiqh*, and mysticism, all of which should be recognized as legitimate parts of Islamic history and tradition. He emphasized liberal thought, including the Mu'tazilah and Muḥammad 'Abduh. His two-volume text, *Islam Ditinjau dari Berbagai Aspeknya* (*Islam Seen from its Various Aspects*) was required reading in all IAINs in the 1970s and 1980s. Mukti Ali, also a McGill graduate, served as minister of religion in the 1970s. He stressed the importance of understanding other religions from within their own systems of belief, and also of studying modern secular thought.[35]

The impact of IAINs on liberal Muslim movements was multiplied many times over by its social and cultural context, in particular its roots in the NU and Muhammadiyah communities. At present, throughout Indonesia there are 14 IAINs and 33 STAINs (State Higher Education for Islamic Studies). All the IAINs are located in the capital cities of provinces: IAIN ar-Raniry, Banda Aceh (Nanggroe Aceh Darussalam Special Province); IAIN Sumatera Utara, Medan (North Sumatra Province); IAIN Sultan Syarif Qasim, Pekanbaru (Riau Province); IAIN Imam Bonjol, Padang (West Sumatra Province); IAIN Sultan Taha Saifuddin, Jambi (Jambi Province); IAIN Raden Patah Palembang (South Sumatra Province); IAIN Raden Patah Palembang (South Sumatra Province), IAIN Raden Intan, Bandar Lampung (Lampung Province); IAIN Syarif Hidayatullah (Jakarta); IAIN Sunan Gunung Jati, Bandung (West Java Province); IAIN Walisongo, Semarang (Central Java Province); IAIN Sunan Kalijaga, Yogyakarta (Yogyakarta Special Province); IAIN Sunan Ampel, Surabaya (East Java Province); IAIN Antasari, Banjarmasin (South Kalimantan Province); and IAIN Alauddin, Makasar (South Sulawesi Province).[36] Between 1979–91 the academic staffs of these institutes more than doubled to 2200. The total number of students almost quadrupled, from 28,000 to 100,000. Today student enrollment in Indonesia's 14 IAINs comprises 18 percent of the student population in higher education.[37]

In the 1950s, as we have seen, NU *ulama* and politicians tended to go along with Masyumi's insistence that Indonesia become an Islamic state by restoring to the constitution the seven words obliging Muslims to carry out sharī'ah, however, few NU *ulama* or PKB politicians are in the conservative camp. Instead, they serve as a primary bastion against Islamic state activists from within the *ummah* itself. This change occurred to a large extent because of the role played within the NU and PKB of NU-affiliated graduates of the IAINs. Many of these graduates now sit in parliament and the assembly or serve as opinion makers in society. At the top of the NU hierarchy, the most important opinion makers are of course the *ulama*, led for the last two decades by Abdurrahman Wahid. NU *ulama* are today among the most effective delegitimizers of the idea of an Islamic state.

As far as political explanation is concerned, I think the current political moderation of Indonesian Muslims has something to do with the complex relationship between Islam and political regimes throughout the history of Indonesia, especially during the New Order Suharto regime.[38] As I noted above, at the height of the New Order's political repression of Islam during the late 1970s and early 1980s, a new pattern of thinking emerged in the *ummah*, particularly among younger intellectuals, which would have a major impact on the nature of political articulation of Islam. This phenomenon, which was initially called the "reform movement (*gerakan pembaharuan*)" is perhaps best summed up in Nurcholish Madjid's 1972 dictum: "Islam yes, Islamic parties no." This new generation is, to some extent, successful in desacralizing and delegitimizing the notion of Islamic parties.

At the same time, the New Order's own stance toward Islam began to change from the late 1980s. A series of legislative and institutional concessions to Islamic sentiment provided tangible evidence of this. Prominent among them were the promulgation of Islamic family law in 1989, the establishment of the ICMI (Indonesian Muslim Intellectuals Association) in 1990, the lifting of a ban on female state school students wearing *jilbab* in 1991, the founding of an Islamic bank (Bank Muamalat) in 1992, and the abolition of the state lottery (Porkas, SDSB). The ICMI proved especially significant. Led by Suharto favorite and then his vice president, B.J. Habibie, it became a major vehicle for patronage and rapid career advancement for senior Muslim bureaucrats, intellectuals, and professionals. In contrast to the preceding two decades, Suharto now appeared set on pursuing a "proportionality" policy whereby the number of Muslims in cabinet and senior military and bureaucratic positions would roughly reflect the percentage of Muslims in society. In his own personal behavior, Suharto appeared also to embrace a more *santri* form of Islam. He took the pilgrimage to Mecca in 1991 and began appearing regularly thereafter at events to mark major Islamic celebrations. The media also began carrying accounts of the president's interest in and knowledge of the Qur'an and prominent *ulama* became increasingly frequent visitors to the palace.

The reasons for this change of heart are open to some dispute. Many of the Muslims who benefited from this rapprochement asserted that Suharto had realized the error of his previous repression of Islam. Some also believed it reflected a genuine awakening of interest in Islam for the aging president. Political analysts such as R. William Liddle believed that Suharto's relations with the armed forces were under growing strain and that he was cultivating Islamic support in order to counterbalance the declining loyalty of the military.[39]

Conclusion

The central questions underlying this discussion have been: First, to what extent has Islam contributed to the moderation process of Indonesian politics, and second, why is the transformation of political Islam in Indonesia possible? The answer to the first question is that Islam has been a contributory factor in shaping the state but hardly a decisive one. It is important to note that under the governments of President Sukarno and, especially, President Suharto, political Islam was usually seen as a threat, which enable them to develop a cultural approach, rather than a political approach, to promote their cultural and religious aspirations. Today, in the democratic climate following the fall of Suharto's New Order regime, the mainstream of Indonesian Islamic movements tend to refuse the call for expanded Muslim influence in the government and the introduction of sharī'ah in the constitution, and instead, are in favor of maintaining secular Indonesian politics.

The transformation of political Islam or Islamism in Indonesia is possible, because Islam is not totally divorced from the political arena. Islam is allowed to play its political role, and the incapability of the Islamist elite to perform and attract the constituents leads them to the inevitable decline. I think the vast majority of Indonesian Muslims have now become convinced that the so-called "Islamists" or "political Islam" are not ready, or even that they have no clear and applicable political concept and agenda. If this transformation yields fruitful results to foster democratization, then it not only reverses Huntington's thesis that democracy may not be viable beyond Western shores, but also will lead Indonesia to become the third largest democracy in the world.

Notes

1. For a discussion on the dramatic event of Suharto's downfall, see Geoff Forrester and R.J. May, eds., *The Fall of Soeharto* (Singapore: Select Books, 1999); Geoff Forrester (ed.), *Post-Soeharto Indonesia: Renewal or Chaos* (Singapore: Institute of Southeast Asia Studies, 1999); Adam Schwarz and Jonathan Paris, eds., *The Politics of Post-Suharto Indonesia* (New York: Council on Foreign Relations Press, 1999); Bilveer Singh, *Succession Politics in Indonesia* (New York: St. Martin's Press, 2000); Stefan Eklof, *Indonesian Politics in Crisis: The Long Fall of Suharto, 1996–98* (Copenhagen: Nordic Institute of Asian Studies, 1999).
2. Saiful Mujani and R. William Liddle, "Politics, Islam, and Public Opinion," *Journal of Democracy*, 15(1), 2003.
3. Jane Perlez, "Islam Lite [?] in Indonesia is Looking More Scary," *New York Times*, September 3, 2003, A6.
4. Jane Perlez, "Militant Islamic Congress is Sparsely Attended in Indonesia," *New York Times*, August 11, 2003.
5. For discussion on the emergence of diverse political Islam after the collapse of the Suharto regime, see Peter G. Riddel, "The Diverse Voices of Political Islam in Post-Suharto Indonesia," *Islam and Christian-Muslim Relations*, 13(1), 2002.
6. Clifford Geertz, *Religion of Java* (New York: Free Press, 1960).
7. Some scholars have argued that the recent Indonesian Muslim dynamics have made these distinctions less apparent than when first formulated by Clifford Geertz five decades ago; they are no longer accurate in describing the religious pattern of Indonesian society, as all Muslims have become increasingly pious. However, I would argue that, while these distinctions might have melted down in everyday Indonesian life, they are still operating in Indonesian politics. This categorization is still useful for understanding the polarization of the political elite and for analyzing political Islam in Indonesia.

8. The term "modernism" is commonly used in the literature on Indonesian Islam to mean both "reformism" (that is, the movement to internally reform Islam as a faith by, among other things, purging it of impure practices) and modernism, the process of making Islam relevant to the modern world.

9. In Indonesian, the term *ulama* is both singular and plural.

10. For a discussion about the relationship between the NU and state, see, for instance, Andree Feillard, "Traditionalist Islam and the State in Indonesia," in Robert W. Hefner and Patricia Horvatich (eds.), *Islam in an Era of Nation-States* (Honolulu: University of Hawaii Press, 1997), 129–53; Muhammad Fajrul Falah, "Nahdlatul Ulama and Civil Society in Indonesia," in Nakamura Mitsuo, Sharon Siddique, and Omar Farouk Majunid (eds.), *Islam and Civil Society in Southeast Asia* (Singapore: Institute of Southeast Asian Studies, 2001), 33–42.

11. On the Muhammadiyah, see M. Sirajuddin Syamsuddin, *Religion and Politics in Islam: The Case of Muhammadiyah in Indonesia's New Order* (unpublished Ph.D. dissertation at UCLA, 1991); M. Amien Abdullah, "Muhammadiyah's Experience in Promoting Civil Society on the Eve of the 21st Century," in Nakamura Mitsuo, op. cit., 43–54. For comparison, see Donald J. Porter, *Managing Politics and Islam in Indonesia* (London: Routledge, 2002), 40.

12. Graham E. Fuller, *The Future of Political Islam* (New York: Palgrave Macmillan, 2003), xi

13. The term "Muslim" (with quotation marks) refers only to the devout/practicing Muslim. The term Muslim (without quotation marks) refers to all Muslim (the devout/practicing and the nominal/non-practicing).

14. For a detailed discussion on the Jakarta Charter, see Robert W. Hefner, *Civil Islam: Muslims and Democratization in Indonesia* (New Jersey: Princeton University Press, 2000), 41–4.

15. No vote was taken on the issue at the annual MPR session but in the deliberations on the Jakarta Charter, seemingly fewer than 20 percent of members were in favor of its reinsertion.

16. Greg Fealy is absolutely right when he says that "the proposed re-inclusion of the 'seven words' in the constitution attracted support from only a small minority and were emphatically rejected by mainstream Muslim organizations such as NU and Muhammadiyah." See Greg Fealy, "Divided Majority: Limits of Indonesian Political Islam," in Shahran Akbarzadeh and Abdullah Saeed, eds., *Islam and Political Legitimacy* (New York: Routledge, 2003), 150–68.

17. The compilation consists of three books: (1) marriage law; (2) inheritance; and (3) *wakaf* (charitable trust). It is a guide for judges in the religious court in solving the cases submitted to them.

18. M.B. Hooker, *Indonesian Islam: Social Change Through Contemporary Fatwa* (Honolulu: University of Hawaii Press, 2003), 20.

19. Zainal Abidin Amir, *Peta Islam Politik pasca-Soeharto* (Jakarta: LP3ES, 2003), 59–187. See also Anies Rasyid Baswedan, "Political Islam in Indonesia: Present and Future Trajectory," paper presented at the conference on "Political Islam in Southeast Asia" at the Paul H. Nitze School of Advanced International Studies, Johns Hopkins University, March 25, 2003.

20. Saiful Mujani and R. William Liddle, "Politics, Islam, and Public Opinion," *Journal of Democracy*, 15(1), 2004.

21. Fealy, "Divided Majority," 152.

22. See Fachry Ali, *Merambah Jalan Baru Islam: Rekonstruksi Pemikiran Islam Indonesia Masa Orde Baru* (Bandung: Mizan, 1996).

23. Harry J. Benda, *The Crescent and the Rising Sun: Indonesian Islam under the Japanese Occupation, 1942–45* (The Hague: W. van Hoeve, 1958).

24. This phenomenon was first pointed out by the anthropologist Robert Hemer, "Islamizing Java? Religion and Politics in Rural East Java," *Journal of Asian Studies*, 46(3), 1987, 533–54. It was confirmed in survey research by Liddle and Mujani, "The Triumph of Leadership." In terms of their answers to a series of questions about religious belief, only 3 percent of our respondents were classifiable as *abangan*. The apparent smallness of the *abangan* group in 1999 raises a further question as to how large they were in the 1950s, when first identified by anthropologists.

25. The best known collection of Nurcholish's voluminous writings is *Islam: Doktrin dan Peradaban* (Jakarta: Paramadina, 1992).

26. Nurcholish Madjid, "The Necessity of Renewing Islamic Thought and Reinvigorating Religious Understanding," in Charles Kurzman, ed., *Liberal Islam: A Sourcebook*, 284–94.

27. For discussion on Nurcholish's thought, see Robert Hefner, *Civil Islam*, 115–19.

28. Nurcholish's secularization speech is an excellent example of what the sociologist Robert Wuthnow calls figural action, a preferred solution to a social problem that is rooted in but imaginatively transcends ongoing discourse, making cultural change possible. Wuthnow's most striking example is also religious: a speech by Martin Luther that constituted a turning point in the history of protestantism. Robert Wuthnow, *Communities of Discourse: Ideology and Social Structure in the Reformation, the Enlightenment, and European Socialism* (Cambridge, MA: Harvard University Press, 1989).

29. For a detailed discussion on the impact of Madjid's idea on Indonesian younger generations, see Fachry Ali and Bahtiar Effendy, *Merambah Jalan Baru Islam: Rekonstruksi Pemikiran Islam Indonesia Masa Orde Baru* (Bandung: Mizan, 1986).

30. Valuable collections of articles about Abdurrahman in English are Harry Bhaskara, ed., *Understanding Gus Dur* (Jakarta: Jakarta Post, 2000); and Harry Bhaskara, ed., *Questioning Gus Dur* (Jakarta: Jakarta Post, 2000).

31. M. Dawam Rahardjo, ed., *Pergulatan Dunia Pesantren: Membangun Dari Bawah* (Jakarta: P3M, 1985).

32. Abdurrahman's approach was mocked by the rationalist V.S. Naipaul in *Among the Believers: An Islamic Journey* (New York: Knopf, 1981).

33. For example, Ulil Abshar-Abdalla, *Membakar Rumah Tuhan: Pergulatan Agama Privat dan Publik* (Bandung: Remaja Rosdakarya, 1999).

34. On Abdurrahman's failed presidency, see R. William Liddle, "Indonesia in 2000: A Shaky Start for Democracy," *Asian Survey*, XLI(2), 2001.

35. On Harun Nasution, see Saiful Mujani, "Mu'tazilah Theology and the Modernization of the Indonesian Muslim Community: Intellectual Portrait of Harun Nasution," *Studia Islamika*, I(I), 1994. On Mukti Ali, see Ali Munhanif, "Islam and the Struggle for Religious Pluralism in Indonesia: A Political Reading of the Religious Thought of Mukti Ali," *Studia Islamika*, III(I), 1995.

36. Azyumardi Azra, "Islamic Legal Education in Indonesia," paper presented at Harvard Law Conference on Islamic Law in Current Indonesia, April 17–18, 2004.

37. These statistics are from Nakamura Mitsuo, "The Emergence of an Islamizing Middle Class and the Dialectics of Political Islam in the New Order of Indonesia: Prelude to the Formation of the ICMI," paper presented at the conference "Islam and the Social Construction of Identities: Comparative Perspectives on Southeast Asia Muslims," Center for Southeast Asian Studies, University of Hawaii-Manoa, Honolulu, Hawaii, August 4–6, 1993.

38. A good explanation about the complex relationship between Islam and state during the Suharto era is provided by M. Syafi'i Anwar. He divides the complex relationship into three phases. First, from the early period of New Order through the 1970s in which the pattern of relationship between Islam and state is marked with the repressive policy of the Suharto

government. That is to say, both the New Order and Muslims show politics of distrust. The second phase is the period of the 1980s in which a reciprocal relationship between Islam and state develops. Both develop mutual understanding. The state realizes that Islam cannot be marginalized. The third phase is an accommodative relation between Islam and state. Many observers label this period as the era of honeymoon between the two. See M. Syafi'i Anwar, *Pemikiran dan Aksi Islam Indonesia: Sebuah Kajian Politik tentang Cendekiawan Muslim Orde Baru* (Jakarta: Paramadina, 1995).

39.   R. William Liddle, "The Islamic Turn in Indonesia: A Political Explanation," *Journal of Asian Studies*, 55(3), 1996, 613–34.

CHAPTER 28

The Pilgrimage to Tembayat: Tradition and Revival in Islamic Mysticism in Contemporary Indonesia

Nelly Van Doorn-Harder and Kees De Jong

Visiting a holy grave or another spiritually potent site, especially at night, is a favorite practice for many Javanese. Yogyakarta is surrounded by some of the preeminent spiritual pilgrimage sites of Central Java. To the south is the coast area of Parangtritis, the location of the mythical spirit Queen of the South (*Ratu Kidul*). Close to that is the mausoleum of Imogiri with the grave of Sultan Agung (1613–46), the third and greatest king of the Muslim empire of Mataram. To the north is the active volcano Merapi, while to the northeast is the grave of one of the founders of Islam in Central Java: Sunan Bayat. This landscape still invites pilgrims and it is thought that cosmic forces and legendary characters are constantly present.[1]

Pilgrimage to a holy place in Indonesia is called *ziarah*. Basically, sites for *ziarah* on Java are the graves of Muslim saints or Muslim kings and nobles. For example, the graves of the *wali sanga*, the founders of Islam on Java, draw visitors from all over the archipelago, while many graves of Muslim leaders, mystics, or initiators of *pesantren* (Islamic boarding schools), the *kyai*, are of local importance. Pilgrimages are also made to sites situated in impressive natural landscapes, for example, mountaintops and caverns often considered to be holy places, loci of spiritual and magical forces. Popular belief holds that a grave on top of a mountain considerably adds to the atmosphere of holiness. Thus, several graves of Muslim saints are situated on tops of mountains. The Javanese people – Muslims, Christians, Hindus, and Buddhists – like to spend the night in such places while holding vigils of fasting and meditating, or to give a *selamatan*, a meal of blessing.[2]

Ziarah in Java

Undertaking a pilgrimage to a grave or an otherwise potent holy site is popular in Java. According to Franz Magnis-Suseno, "Faced with important events of life or in need, the Javanese will perform prayers, and possibly undertake a pilgrimage to a magically potent site."[3] Although, in a way, most of the sites on Java are considered Islamic (due to the fact that 87 percent of the Indonesian population is Muslim), at many sites Islamic rituals are combined with Javanese syncretistic rituals. Similarly, at Christian sites elements of both Christian and non-Christian beliefs and rituals are found in happy coexistence. This reality makes it a challenge to categorize Javanese pilgrimage sites along well-defined theological lines. Broadly speaking, *ziarah* takes place in three types of sites: Javanese syncretistic sites; Muslim, Christian, Hindu, or Buddhist sites; and sites that are officially considered Muslim, but in reality are Javanese-syncretistic.

Javanese syncretistic sites are considered holy because they are situated in impressive landscapes. These can be found on mountaintops, in caves or trees, and in or near the ocean. For example, pilgrims come to a Javanese syncretistic site in nature such as Mount Lawu (east of Solo) to practice various techniques of Javanese meditation (*semedi* and *tapa*), such as standing up to one's neck in a sacred pool. The goals of this type of *ziarah* range from seeking esoteric knowledge (*ngelmu*) to obtaining magical powers *(kasekten)*, to seeking unity with God.[4] Many hope that their newly acquired spiritual powers will eventually be translated into tangible material gains. Muslim sites are the graves of Muslim saints, especially those of the *wali sanga*, and famous mystics and teachers of *pesantren* (*kyai*). Many Muslims recite the Qur'an over these graves and participate in chanting *tahlilan* (praise). The grave at Tembayat belongs to this category. In spite of the Islamic character of such sites, many pilgrims still pursue practices and rituals that would be considered non-Islamic by orthodox Islamic teaching. Some consider the graves of Muslim kings, princes, and nobles to be holy, such as the grave of Sultan Agung. The Sultan embodies Javenese Islam and Javanese culture. His grave is frequented by all sorts of Muslims who desire to recite the Qur'an or simply choose to visit the place for the sake of deriving inspiration from being close to the Sultan's burial place.

The custom of *ziarah* in Java is also related to that of visiting the graves of deceased ancestors (*nyekar*). This is done mostly in the week prior to the beginning of Ramadan. At that time, the graves are cleaned and prayers said for the deceased. Some people ask the deceased to bless, for example, their wedding plans. Most Javanese believe that the ancestors display pleasure at the prayers of children and grandchildren. "It is the same as bringing them choice food while they are still alive," a preacher once explained, "it makes them happy."[5] The living are also expected to facilitate the journey of the dead in the afterlife by giving *selamatan* at specific moments after death (up to the thousandth-day commemoration). This practice is believed to help the souls advance upward to heaven.[6] Both *ziarah* and *nyekar* are based on the belief that after death, the soul, at least temporarily, resides in the grave. Saints are thought to have the ability to commute between heaven and their tombs.[7]

There is a wide range of reasons why pilgrims visit certain sites. It is almost impossible to categorize these neatly. Most Javanese Muslims would identify themselves as believers in the one and only God, even if they practice *Kejawen*, the indigenous Javanese religion. The difference between an orthodox Muslim and a *Kejawen* is often explained in terms of religious duties. The *Kejawen* Muslim performs prayers, but not five times a day; he or she fasts, but not necessarily during Ramadan, and honors certain objects such as daggers and swords (*kris*) that are thought to hold intrinsic powers. Apart from magical knowledge or powers, *ziarah* always has a religious or spiritual connotation. Rituals and spiritual practices of pilgrims at all types of sites can overlap depending on the pilgrim's intentions and religious affiliation. Pilgrims visiting graves offer requests and prayers, ask for the deceased's blessing, or come to fulfill a vow. Motivations range from seeking true spiritual experiences, to wishing to honor the dead, to blatantly seeking worldly gains.

The Time

Correct timing is considered crucial for a successful *ziarah*. The correct day is decided by a system of time calculation based on combining the Javanese and the Islamic calendars. When certain days of the Javanese week (that has five days) coincide with the Islamic seven-day week, it will be considered a good time for *ziarah*. In cycles of 35 days, certain favorable combinations appear. Furthermore, *ziarah* takes place during the night since, in Javanese calculation, the new day begins at dusk. The nights preceding Tuesday and Friday (*Malam Selasa* and *Malam Jumaat*) are considered especially beneficial times. Also, the pilgrim should not leave the gravesite before midnight.[8] A preeminent time for pilgrimage according to the Javanese calendar is the eve of the first of the month of *Sura*, the Javanese New Year.

Modifications in Pilgrimage

Since the 1980s, observers of *ziarah* have noticed three modifications in its practice. First, some places have become more popular while others declined. Second, pilgrims try to avoid syncretistic rituals, focussing more on those that are in agreement with normative Islam. Third, pilgrims spend less energy on strenuous journeys to holy sites, instead choosing places that are nearby and easy to reach. Often, *ziarah* is simply a pleasant excursion to a place full of blessings. As a result of this, trips to remote mountaintops or caves that require a high degree of endurance and asceticism seem to be in decline, while pilgrims prefer to visit the graves and mausoleums that can be reached via smoothly paved asphalt roads. As John Pemberton observed, "the powers that the Central Javanese landscape once presented are now, it would seem, in sharp decline, . . . the spiritual attentions of most contemporary Javanese are focused on grave sites and the possible blessings they contain."[9]

Several factors may explain the shift from valuing potent landscapes to preferring graves of Muslim saints: the efforts of the Suharto regime (1966–98), a revival of

Indonesian Islam, and the demands of modern life that prevent pilgrims from making long and time-consuming trips.

The so-called New Order (*Orde Baru*) government of President Suharto avidly promoted interest in human-made monuments such as graves and mausoleums. Grand projects such as the restoration of the Buddhist Borobudur and Hindu Prambanan temples were undertaken to promote local and foreign tourism. Restoration of Muslim monuments, combined with the building of roads and convenient staircases leading to the sites, encouraged Indonesians to visit graves and other holy places in droves. Along the way, a new place could be added in the hope that somehow one day a religious cult would spring up around it. An example of such a place is the grave of Suharto's wife, Mrs. Tien Suharto. Before the fall of the regime in 1998, members of Dharma Want, the (then obligatory) organization for civil servants' wives, would make bus trips to the grave in Solo in order to pay "respect" to Ibu Tien. A Java packed with monuments of supernatural holiness became the religious ideal and was considered the fundament on which the authority and power of the worldly government could rest.[10] Furthermore, having Indonesians congregate at gravesites to pursue religious goals provided a substitute for political gatherings, practically forbidden at the time. To the Orde Baru government, *ziarah* was an outlet for religious energies that could have turned political, thus serving as a tool of control. By definition, *ziarah* is practiced by Muslims open to cultural influences on their faith. Hence, the Orde Baru regime promotion of *ziarah* can also be interpreted as a tool to keep Indonesian Muslims from becoming affiliated with more unwanted interpretations of Islam.

Partly due to this government repression, Indonesian Islam has experienced a strong renaissance since the 1980s. Fearing a spillover of the revolution in Iran and a call for an Islamic state, the Suharto regime tried to curb and streamline Muslim activities. According to Van Bruinessen, the result of this was that "many former political activists have devoted their passions and energies to the awakening and developing of an Islamic awareness among their compatriots."[11] Former political activists turned into religious activists, following the slogan "Up to now we used politics for mission, now we will use mission for politics."[12] Their teachings, discussions, and writings about Islam created a religious renaissance leading to improvements in Islamic education. When awareness about the non-Islamic rituals and beliefs connected with *ziarah* grew, it became contested activity within Muslim circles that had tolerated it up to then.

The discussion concerning *ziarah* in Indonesia also serves as an indicator of the differences between the two largest Muslim organizations: the Muhammadiyah and the Nahdatul Ulama (NU). *Ziarah* is frowned upon by followers of the Muhammadiyah movement, founded in 1912. As a reformist movement, the Muhammadiyah has asked Muslims to stay away from Javanese (and other local) beliefs and practices. On the other hand, the Nahdatul Ulama, founded in 1926, has encouraged visiting the graves of their influential leaders (*kyai*) and of the *wali sanga*. This is connected with the belief that NU teachers are considered links in a chain of Muslim scholars beginning in the sixth century. In NU circles, students of Islam, when confronted with important decisions in their lives, or when preparing to be teachers of Islam themselves, will seek the blessing of their deceased masters. Three days after being elected president of Indonesia on October 20, 1999, the former head of the NU, Abdurahman Wahid, made his first trip to the grave of his teacher and ancestor, K.H. Hasyim Ashari, in order to seek blessings on his new calling. The NU traditionally is tolerant of Javanese practices that are not explicitly forbidden by Islam, such as holding a *selamatan* (meal of blessing). However, since the 1980s, there has been a movement within the NU to emphasize the Islamic rituals and heritage and expel customs and rituals that are considered syncretistic. Hence, Islamic professionals watch over Islamic rituals such as reciting the Qur'an that take place near the tombs.

Because the Muhammadiyah and NU have expressed different opinions about visiting the graves, the position of *ziarah* has become ambiguous. Indonesian publications on pilgrimage are about the *Hajj* to Mecca and little material about *ziarah* by Indonesian authors exists. Also, many pilgrims feel uncomfortable to admit that they are visiting holy graves at night.

Recently, large mosques and Muslim centers began to organize pilgrimages to the Muslim holy places in order to Islamize what is syncretistic and "nationalize" what used to be local. Hence, one runs into tour buses with pilgrims from Sumatra who in less than one week cover an average of 20 pilgrimage sites in Java. Invariably, the imam of the mosque or another Muslim authority will guide the pilgrims in reciting texts of the Qur'an, and in performing the rituals at the grave. While moving from grave to grave, the pilgrims eat in the bus, sleep on the graves, and use the taps as their sanitary equipment for the ritual washing.

In Central Java, the so-called Kraton culture has also influenced pilgrimage. As descendants of the former Hindu and the early Muslim rulers, the sultans of Solo and Yogyakarta embody both Islamic and Javanese culture. In the Javanese worldview, society in all its layers is centered on the sultan's power. He himself is thought to represent the divine on earth, expressing God's norm of earthly existence via perfection of the arts, architecture, and etiquette in the Kraton culture.[13] The sultans' heritage endows them with spiritual powers that are still feared and respected by many Javanese. Yet, especially in Yogyakarta, the Kraton culture seeks to be compatible with official Islam. It considers the NU interpretation of Islam as the most congruous with Javanese culture.[14] The Kraton encourages the practice of Islamic rituals at graves of former kings and sultans, yet it does not yield control of the pilgrimages to those graves to Muslim clerics.

The final reason for a shift in the landscape of pilgrimage is that religious or ascetic endeavors that are time consuming are in decline not only in Java but also in many other regions of the world. Fewer people wish or are able to make time for a pilgrimage or spiritual exercise that takes months. Although there are still people who spend time in caves and trees and on mountaintops to acquire wisdom or inspiration, the demands and requirements of a fast-paced contemporary life are also taking their toll there. Contemporary pilgrims consider visiting a nearby grave a more efficient use of time, with no decrease in the great power of blessing it yields.

The Landscape of Tembayat

The *ziarah* site at Tembayat is of particular interest in relation to the development of Islam in Java. The grave has strong links with Islam in Java resulting from the support given by Sunan to the powerful king of Mataram, Sultan Agung, whose kingdom replaced the great Hindu–Buddhist power of Majapahit (around 1294–1527). Although the site at Tembayat is squarely placed in the history of Java, it has remained a local place of pilgrimage. Being situated between the two centers of Javanese culture and history, the Kratons of Yogyakarta and Surakarta, the grave is managed differently from the graves of the other *wali sanga*. Sunan Bayat's grave competes with the powerful mausoleum where Sultan Agung, once Sunan's protege, is buried in Imogiri. Seeking to increase or preserve their worldly power, politicians from Jakarta usually prefer the Imogiri mausoleum to the grave of Tembayat.

More often than not, *ziarah* is an expression of popular religion tied to a locality; that is, the Javanese system of beliefs differs from that of Indonesians in other parts of the country. In *ziarah*, religion becomes an articulated ideology based on the local symbols and local understandings.[15] Beliefs surrounding a place of pilgrimage are constructed by its myths, its history, and by the efforts of those who were and are in charge of the place. Pilgrimages have to be kept "alive"; thus, guardians inform the pilgrims of the stories surrounding the saint, so that they will not lose interest in coming regularly. This constellation of features can be called the "landscape" of any pilgrimage. The term "landscape" here forms a "powerful organizing metaphor" that "consists not only of a physical terrain and architecture, but also of all the myths, traditions and narratives associated with natural and man-made features. In progressing through the physical geography, a pilgrim travels and lives through a terrain of culturally constructed symbols."[16]

Tembayat

Situated in Central Java, Tembayat is a one-hour drive east of Yogyakarta. Legends about this saint inform us that he started his career as the rich governor of the city of Semarang. He is thought to have died in 1512 CE, a period in Javanese history coinciding with the replacement of the Hindu–Buddhist empire of Majapahit with the Muslim kingdom of Mataram. Furthermore, this time of important political change witnessed an intensive process of Islamic missionary activity aimed at converting the Javanese to Islam. At that time, Sunan Bayat's name was Adipati Pandan Arang. After being called to embrace Islam repeatedly, the Adipati left his riches and power behind and devoted himself to prayer, meditation, and the preaching of Islam.[17] Already during his lifetime, Sunan Bayat became a famous religious teacher who regularly performed miracles. He gathered a great following of students around him, who immediately after his death built him a grand tomb, after which Sunan Bayat's fame grew even more.

What started out as a single tomb has now grown into a mausoleum where Sunan's grave, situated on top of a mountain called Jabalkat, crowns a landscape filled with the saint's family members, local Muslim leaders (*kyai*), and dignitaries, and people from the village of Bayat. It is a typical Javanese phenomenon to observe that although a Muslim saint is the center of the mausoleum in Bayat, there are also several Christian graves to be found in the burial complex.

The Historic Background of Tembayat as a Center of Pilgrimage

Although Sunan Bayat's grave is visited with great enthusiasm, there is some confusion about exactly whose body is buried at Bayat. Some say it is the governor and founder of Semarang, Ki Gede Pandan Arang, who at the end of his life moved to the south of the island of Java. Others say it is his son who is resting in the grave. This son, Adipati Mangkubumi, became the second governor (*bupati*) of Semarang, but passed on his worldly duties to his younger brother in order to devote himself entirely to meditation and the spreading of Islam. Other versions of the myth surrounding this Adipati tell that he was the last ruler of the Hindu–Buddhist kingdom of Majapahit, Brawijaja, who had fled to Semarang after being defeated by the rulers of the new Mataram empire.[18] In Semarang, he became the governor, converted from Hinduism to Islam and later on became the famous Sunan Bayat. This myth, of course, is meant to import the power of the Hindu–Buddhist Majapahit dynasty into the succeeding Muslim Mataram dynasty (starting ca. 1584).[19] Other versions say that Sunan Bayat was the son of Sunan Pandan Arang I, who came from the Middle East, and that his real name was Abdullah. His son, who later would become Sunan Bayat, was born from the marriage with a princess from the Islamic empire of Demak, situated close to Semarang.

Whoever Sunan Bayat really was, and whoever is buried in the grave that bears his name, for the Javanese believers, Tembayat is regularly mentioned in old Javanese manuscripts, and mythical tales that surround the place.[20] The gist of those tales is that Sunan Bayat converted the inhabitants of Central Java to Islam, thus he is considered to be the tenth *wali*, or one of the saints who brought Islam to Java. According to the Javanese myths, the *walis* would regularly meet at Demak. When their number was reduced to eight because *wali* number nine, Siti Jenar, was accused of heretical teachings, it was decided to choose a replacement for him. The great *wali* Sunan Kalijaga was in charge of this process. In spite of the fact that Sunan Bayat had not become a religious leader yet and was still the governor of Semarang, he was already predestined for this high position. As the tenth *wali*, Sunan Bayat plays an important role in the Javanese–Islamic myths. Also, the place Tembayat is sometimes mentioned in connection with political developments in the Mataram empire.

The Story of Sunan Bayat

A common story is still reported in Java about how Sunan Bayat converted to Islam, after which he left his hometown Semarang and became a religious leader outside the area where he was known. Interestingly enough, the story is very similar to the one about how Sunan Kalijaga himself went from riches to rags and became a Muslim saint.[21] It goes as follows.

The governor of Semarang, who was then called Ki Gede Pandan Arang, or Mangkubumi, was well known for his lavish lifestyle. In order to maintain his way of living, he used to buy goods below their price and sell them at exorbitant prices. One day, Sunan Kalijaga visited him disguised as a poor seller of grass (*alang-alang*). As usual, the governor bought the grass for the minimum price. Opening the bag, to his great surprise he found a golden sword holder hidden in the grass (*kandelan*). The governor did not understand that this golden object contained a message that was relayed to him via a typical Javanese word play. The message was: "do have trust and turn to me." Here is how he was supposed to read this message: "to resist, to obstruct." By giving the governor the grass, Sunan Kalijaga asked him why he was constantly resisting the call to become a religious man. In the word for sword holder, *kandelan*, is found the word "*andel*," which means "to trust, to believe." Had the governor understood the message, he would have seen the exhortation "have trust and turn to me." But since the time had not yet come for him to understand, the governor turned his attention to building a lavish house that was richly decorated with gold. When it was ready, he organized a huge party and invited many guests. Sunan Kalijaga was not invited but appeared nevertheless, dressed in a simple outfit. Because of this outfit, his presence went unnoticed. Then, Sunan Kalijaga went outside and changed into a gorgeous robe. He now was invited to take a seat of honor at the table. While leaving the house, Sunan Kalijaga changed back to the simple outfit. The governor thought that this was a practical joke and failed to understand that this action had a deeper spiritual meaning.

Now Sunan Kalijaga understood that he had to take stronger action to bring the governor to his senses. He started to visit the governor in disguise as a beggar. Several times the governor threw some coins to him but when the beggar refused to leave, the governor became angry. Sunan Kalijaga then told him that he had not come to receive coins, but that he was waiting for the sound of the *bedug*, the drum that is used for the call to prayer in Javanese mosques. After this he threw a fistful of clay to the governor; when the governor caught it the clay immediately changed into gold. This was the moment of enlightenment for the governor and he finally understood that all earthly goods are temporary. Now the governor wanted to become the spiritual student of Sunan Kalijaga. But before the master would accept him, he had to fulfill four requirements. The first requirement was that the governor had to pray continuously and preach Islam, converting all the inhabitants under his power in Semarang to Islam. The second was that he had to feed the students (*santri*) and teachers of Islam (*ulama*), craft the drums for the call to prayer and build prayer houses (*langgar*). The third requirement was to give to charity with a sincere heart and to donate his riches to the poor in the form of *zakat*. The final requirement to become a student was to follow the master into his house and light the lamps for him there. At that time, Sunan Kalijaga lived in Jabalkat, near the present-day Tembayat. The governor accepted these requirements and joined the master, leaving behind everything he owned. His first wife joined him since she did not want to leave him. Because, however, she was not yet ready and able to let go of her possessions, she filled a bamboo stick with gold and jewelry.

The trip to Tembayat on foot (around 100 miles) was full of adventures which foretold that the governor was on his way to become a Muslim holy man. Legends tell us that on the road an incident with three robbers took place. The governor's wife could not move as fast as the rest of the party since she was carrying her child on her back. Halfway through the journey, three robbers jumped in front of the governor and demanded his money. He referred them to his wife and advised them to take her bamboo stick so that they would have enough money for the rest of their lives. After grabbing the stick, the robbers started to harass the woman, thinking that she might be hiding more gold. Her husband came to her rescue when she started to call for help. That is how the town now situated on the spot where this incident took place was given its name: Salatiga. The governor cried out "*oleh ketiga*" "by those three," "*mereka telah berbuat salah*," "they were doing something wrong." Salah and tiga thus became Salatiga.

The robbers, however, were not impressed by being called wrongdoers and continued to strip the wife in search of valuables. That is when the governor, with the help of God, changed two of them into creatures with animal heads: one with the head of a sheep and one with the head of a snake. This led the robbers to immediate contrition and conversion to Islam, and they vowed to be in the service of the governor. Thus, they became his first disciples and were called Seh Domba (sheep head) and Seh Kewel (the biter). After long and faithful service, they slowly regained their original forms.

At a hamlet called Wedi, in the neighborhood near Tembayat, the governor, now called Sunan Bayat, settled down and started to work for a rice merchant called Gus Slamet. Seh Domba and Seh Kewel were instructed to withdraw to the mountains and live a life of meditation. Due to Sunan Bayat's involvement in the rice business, it flourished like never before. Not all miracles, however, were positive. It is told that one day Sunan Bayat was looking for rice to buy. He stopped a rice seller who was on his way to the market. The man did not feel like selling his goods and lied, saying that he was just carrying sand (*wedi*). Upon his arrival at the marketplace, the contents of his bag turned out to be sand. In another incident, Sunan Bayat joined the wife of his boss at the market where she sold cooked food. When the wife realized that he had forgotten to bring the wood for burning, she became angry and started to call him names. This induced him to offer his hands as fuel for the fire. He put them on the fireplace, where they immediately started to glow. Of course, such incidents made Sunan very famous. Another miracle took place when Sunan exercised his function as the one who fills the water basin for the ritual washing before the Islamic prayer. One day he filled a bamboo basket with water instead. Everyone was amazed when the water did not run out of the basket and could be used for the ritual washing.

After a while, Sunan Bayat felt that the time had come for him to move on to Jabalkat in order to receive the right directions from his master. On his way there, he picked up Seh Domba and Seh Kewel from their isolated places. Halfway through the journey, his child became thirsty and started to cry. According to Sunan there was no need for crying because all he had to do to find water was to press his staff into the ground. Indeed, a well with fresh water emerged. This well exists to this day and still yields drinking water. Finally, the party arrived at Mount Jabalkat where nowadays the village of Bayat is situated.

Upon his arrival in Tembayat, Sunan Bayat immediately proceeded to build a mosque on top of Mount Jabalkat. This mosque also functioned as a religious school and soon he gathered a following of future teachers of Islam. This center was in fact the first *pesantren*, or Islamic boarding school, in Central Java. His first assistants were the erstwhile robber Seh Domba and his future second wife, a girl called Nji Endang. At first, the new teacher met with fierce resistance from the leaders of the mystical Javanese religion. They questioned Sunan Bayat's powers of *ngelmu*, knowledge or wisdom, which is a form of mystical, even magical knowledge that one derives from "higher beings" such as spirits or God. Without solid proof of possessing *ngelmu*, Sunan could never become an acceptable leader of religion in Java.

As a result, a meeting was held with the powerful Javanese mystic Prawira Sakti to test Sunan's wisdom. In the first test, he had to catch a high-flying pigeon that was released by Prawira. Sunan took his wooden slipper and threw it in the air, thus killing the pigeon. After that, Prawira threw his hat so high that it became almost invisible. Yet, Sunan's slipper could easily reach it and bring it back to earth. Finally, it is told that Prawira hid under an enormous rock and was easily found. Prawira, however, failed to find Sunan's hiding place, between Prawira's eyebrows!

As a result of Sunan's spiritual power, many joined him in his mosque. Finally, on the Kliwon Friday of the Javanese month of Ruwah, God granted Sunan enlightenment. After that, whenever Sunan performed the *Adhan* (call to prayer), he would be heard in Demak, more than 100 miles northeast of Bayat. One of the nine *walis*, who lived in Demak, became so annoyed with Sunan's call to prayer that he asked him to tone it down. In order to be less audible, Sunan decided to use his power to drag the mosque downhill and place it in the village of Tembayat, where it can be found to this day. After spreading Islam for 25 years, Sunan died on a Kliwon Friday, also in the month of Ruwah, and was buried on the top of Mount Jabalkat.

This story of Sunan's conversion and his life as a Muslim teacher, however, is just one version. According to another oral source provided by the current descendants of Sunan, his death took place on the 21st of the Muslim month of Mulud. Since 1973, they have a *Mawlid* at Tembayat on this day.

Meeting of Worldly and Spiritual Powers

Tembayat also played a role of some importance in Javanese history. The greatest ruler of Mataram, Sultan Agung (1613–46 AD), made a special pilgrimage to Tembayat and redecorated the grave. In his capacity as the worldly ruler of a Javanese kingdom, the king is the one upon whom "the whole system pivots, for he stands at the juncture of the divine and the human, with, so to speak, a foot in each camp."[22] In the Javanese hierarchy of powers, a religious leader is closer to God than a worldly leader. Hence, the king always has to seek the guidance of a saint. Sultan Agung himself would later also be regarded as a man of significant spiritual powers, and today pilgrims still visit his grave on the south side of Yogyakarta to meditate and seek advice. Yet, when alive, the sultan was obliged to pay his respects to the saint of his area, Sunan Bayat. From the notes of Batavia (which is the current Jakarta), the diary of the Dutch colonial rulers written between 1631–4, we know that "the ruler of Mataram personally set out for a place called Tembaijat to make a sacrifice there, and that on leaving he gave the order to assemble 50,000 men: 40,000 to be sent to Batavia and 10,000 to Balimbaon with the command to wait for his return from Tambaijat and then for each army to leave its destination . . ."[23]

Two legends are told about this visit. According to the first one, Sultan Agung was lost in the woods surrounding his palace and was getting desperate because he could not find his faithful assistant Juru Taman. To find his way out, the sultan decided to meditate in order to reach a state of perfect wisdom but failed in his attempt. All of a sudden, a nobleman (*priai*) appeared to him, offering his help. After discussing the sultan's problems, the nobleman suggested that the sultan could become a student of mysticism (*ilmu gaib*). After the sultan completed his learning, the nobleman finally introduced himself as "Sunan who lives in Bayat." Sunan helped the sultan miraculously return to his palace by transporting him in his sleeve. In the palace, the sultan's assistant Juru Taman was found as well. He turned out to be residing in the quarters of the sultan's wives. Of course, Juru Taman had a strong excuse for his presence there, claiming "he was looking for the sultan." All the ministers, courtiers, servants, and wives of the Sultan were relieved to see him back, and it was decided that in thanks for his return, he should build a new mausoleum for the grave of Sunan Bayat. Since Sunan was considered a very holy man, it was deemed appropriate that the mausoleum be constructed in an extraordinary way. Hence, it was forbidden to use horses, regular masons, or workers. The people building the mausoleum were carefully selected on the basis of their impeccable spirituality and outstanding behavior. Over 300,000 men were chosen. They lined the street from the stone quarry all the way to the grave. Sitting in the reverent *sila* position of kneeling on their ankles with bent toes, they would pass on the stones by hand. It is believed that, due to this special sacrifice, the mausoleum became one of the most beautiful in the whole of Java.

Other stories surrounding the relationship between Sultan Agung and Sunan Bayat mention the sultan visiting a classical Javanese shadow puppet show (*wayang*) that was presented in a place far away from his palace. During the show he learned that the empires of Balambangan and Bali were conspiring against him. Even worse, it was also said that the aforementioned assistant Juru Taman was courting the sultan's main wife, which meant that he was trying to become the sultan himself. When the sultan was overcome by desperation, he prostrated on the floor to ask God forgiveness for his many sins that had led to this ordeal. At that moment, Sunan Bayat appeared to him in the disguise of an old man. Sunan Bayat helped the sultan get back to his palace as soon as possible by holding out his walking stick and catapulting the sultan to his palace with the stick. According to this story, in order to express his gratefulness, the sultan decided to renovate the grave of Sunan Bayat in extraordinary fashion.

Today, the results of the sultan's building activities can still be witnessed in Tembayat. For example, on the gate leading up to the grave the Javanese year 1555 is engraved. This corresponds with the year 1633 CE, the year in which Sultan Agung introduced the Javanese calendar. Until that time, the Javanese had used the Hindu–Saka system based on the solar months, but the new Javanese year combines this system and the Muslim lunar calendar. All the gates at Tembayat and some of the graves are built in a distinct style reminiscent of the Hindu temples of the Hindu Majapahit empire. What distinguishes the gates from a regular Hindu temple gate, however, is the fact that there are no longer engravings of animals, as is usual in Hindu gates. While monuments in Hindu style surround Sunan's grave, the grave itself is purely Islamic, as it represents the Ka'bah in Mecca.

When considering Tembayat's architecture and all the stories surrounding the "owner of its grave," it is clear that this location reflects the gradual change from the

Hindu–Javanese culture to a Muslim–Javanese culture in Central Java. The ensuing Muslim culture is dominated by a mystical form of Islam filled with holy saints who are capable of appearing to people in need and of performing miracles. Sunan Bayat's biography harkens back to the life of Sunan Kalijaga, and several universal themes of miracles performed by saints run through the stories, such as Sunan's staff finding water. According to the Javanese tradition, Sunan Kalijaga also performed a similar miracle.[24] Sunan Bayat's senior wife wanted to share her husband's fate; that is, she believed in his new calling and was willing to give up everything "not heeding the children or wealth left behind."[25] Her commitment reminds one of the wives of the Prophet Muhammad: his first wife Khadijah was the Prophet's first convert, while his later wives all had absolute trust in his mission. Sunan Bayat's wife, however, was not fully obedient in that she did not heed Sunan's wish not to take any of their riches with her. She stuffed some jewelry in her staff for "just in case." The emphasis of the story, however, is not her disobedience. The jewels' function is to introduce the robbers and the ensuing miracles and conversions. The stories stress Sunan's praiseworthy behavior in the face of adversity, such as performing a miracle instead of showing anger when being scolded by one of his bosses, a woman. This kind of information places Sunan firmly in the company of valid saints and missionaries of Islam. Furthermore, the stories stress the struggle between the Islamic saint and the Javanese holy men. Their power is considerable, yet they lose against the saint, because his *ngelmu* is stronger than theirs. Along with his Islamic sanctity, however, he does possess the mystical knowledge that is indispensable for being accepted by the Javanese as a powerful holy person.

The stories about Sunan Bayat's conversion are mostly recorded in Javanese historic sources, which are considered biased by leading scholars of Javanese history because they favor the Islamic Mataram dynasty.[26] In a way, they do acknowledge the power and strength of the former Javanese religion and empire, yet Islam always comes out victorious. Formerly powerful men become Muslims, but do not let go of their Javanese heritage and knowledge. The Javanese heritage is also guarded by the Kratons, the palaces of the sultans of Surakarta and Yogyakarta that still embody the expression of true Islamic and true Javanese culture. The tradition thus built is kept alive even today by the guards of the graves and the pilgrims. Although few people have actually read the existing manuscripts, the stories continue to be transmitted orally. So, just as they were created in the beginning to "construct an Islamic saint," they can now be used to recreate and revive the Islamic identity of the saint and eliminate any contradictory Javanese elements that lingered in the pilgrimage to Tembayat.

The Contemporary Pilgrimage to Tembayat

Nowadays, there is a wide paved road going up to Tembayat, built at the end of the 1970s. Most present-day pilgrims arrive by tour buses, cars, or motorbikes. The parking lot holds everything they need for a successful pilgrimage: toilets and washbasins for the ritual washing, in case the pilgrim wishes to perform the Islamic prayers during the visit, and endless rows of stalls where mostly women sell flowers and frankincense. The colorful arrangements of flowers consist of white and red roses, jasmine, and a flower that has not opened yet called "*kantil*." These flowers, brought as a gift to Sunan, are considered to be a source of blessing. The pilgrims believe that their fragrance will help to "carry the petitions to God" and thus facilitate the process of asking for something.

In order to reach the grave, the pilgrim has to climb the winding stairs that go up the mountain. To enter the burial complex, one must buy a ticket at a booth that is situated at the foot of the stairs. The first building the pilgrim finds is an Islamic prayer house, a *musholla*. The prayer house was built in 1990 as a result of reformist Islamic influences and serves the pilgrims who, concurring with reformist Islamic beliefs, say that it is forbidden to pray in the neighborhood of a grave. Praying there allows the pilgrim to avoid the grave sin of *shirk*, honoring other gods than the One and True God. Halfway up the stairs, the pilgrim takes off his/her shoes and climbs to the top barefoot. Taking off one's shoes is an act of politeness in regular Javanese houses, and when entering a mosque or other holy space, the worshipper takes off his/her shoes as a sign of reverence for the holiness of the place. The stairs leading up to the grave are lined with little booths that sell snacks, drinks, and souvenirs such as water jars and plates with Qur'anic texts. Most of them were opened during the early 1990s. Right behind the booths are the old and new graves where the villagers and several members from Sunan Bayat's family are buried.

At the top of the stairs the pilgrim has to register and pay more fees. This is euphemistically called "donating money." The pilgrims who wish to sleep on the graves have to pay more for this privilege. This income pays the guards, the "*juru kunci*," holders of the key, whose function is not only to ensure peace and quiet, but also to guide the pilgrims through the process of making the pilgrimage. Opposite the registration point stands the mosque where pilgrims pray who do not object to praying in front of a grave and who, on the contrary, consider the vicinity of the grave to hold an extra blessing. After entering the first of the five Hindu-style gates, the pilgrim steps into the main cemetery in which the saint's grave is situated. Between the second and the third gate a special pavilion is built where women can spend the night. Between the third and fourth is the pavilion for the men. Most people, however, avoid these special constructions and prefer to stay right next to the grave.

The door to the antechamber of the saint's grave is so low that the pilgrim has to bend over. In the middle of the antechamber is an open fire; in front of it sits a *juru doa*, a guard who offers prayers on behalf of the pilgrims. He also receives the flowers and frankincense pilgrims buy in the parking lot. The pilgrim lets the guard know what the subject of the prayer is. The length of the prayer depends on how serious the problem is, and also on the amount of the tip that is discreetly put in his hand. After this, the guard spreads the flowers and frankincense out on a large tray and starts praying the *Fatihah*, the first sura of the Qur'an in Arabic. The *Fatihah* is followed by the mentioning of the requests and uttering prayers and praises in formal High Javanese (*kromo*). The prayers are closed by again reciting the *Fatihah* in Arabic.

The Javanese part of the prayers starts with mentioning the name of those who offer the petition, saying that they have especially brought flowers as a gift to the saint. The guard then proceeds with asking forgiveness in advance for mistakes and breaches that might be made in the protocol while visiting the grave. After "honoring the spirit of

Sunan Bayat," the prayer asks God to bless the saint. Only then follows the actual request: it always starts with a supplication for general wellness, then mentions the problem at hand, and ends with a "please grant that the faith and belief of these pilgrims will be strengthened." Then the guard starts a new prayer in which he asks God to grant the pilgrims their wishes "through the mediation of the Sunan, . . . of his family, his grandchildren and all those who were his followers." All for whom the prayers were said answer "amen" and are then allowed to climb the steep steps that lead into the actual burial chamber.

In the chamber, the tomb is built on a platform surrounded by a square construction in the shape of the Ka'bah, the focal point for every Muslim's life. Five times a day the devout Muslim turns to Mecca, to the direction of the graves of Sunan's two spouses: Nyai Ageng Kaliwungu and Nyai Ageng Krakitan. The pilgrim enters the platform while kneeling, as if visiting a royal Javanese person. The Ka'bah-like structure around the grave is pitch dark and can only hold 10 persons at a time. It is considered a dangerous taboo to put light in this chamber "since in the Ka'bah there is no light either." According to the guards, it is not necessary to add prayers while in the grave itself, except for "in the heart." In fact, it is preferable to be silent here as, according to the guards, "it is the place where one confronts the most high." Those who cannot control the urge to pray are requested to limit their uttering to *wird* or *zikr*, a repetitive prayer or recitation of just one sentence of praise, yet one can hear furious recitation of the *Fatihah*, followed by prayers in Javanese. Hardly ever are prayers pronounced in the Indonesian language. In addition to praying, the pilgrims throw the blessed flowers on top of the tomb and mix them up by hand, but keep some flowers for the graves of Sunan's spouses and helpers. The pilgrims then begin to examine the flowers for *kantils*, or blessing buds. According to Javanese belief, the pilgrim now will know if the prayers will be heard, depending on the number of *kantils* he or she finds. These *kantils* should be different from the ones brought, however. Hence, in the pitch-dark chamber there is intense activity as pilgrims try "spontaneously" to find the blessing buds. When the guard outside deems that enough blessing has been found, he urges the pilgrims to come out in order to make space for another 10 of the many hundreds that are still waiting in line for their turn to harvest their blessings. The leftover flowers are first brought to the graves of the spouses and spread out, while a short prayer is recited.

All the tombs are covered with a white cotton cloth. According to the guards, this is to protect the marble. The deeper Javanese meaning of the color white, however, is that it symbolizes death and tranquility. A death in the neighborhood on Java, for instance, is announced by hanging out a white flag. Islamic influence also could have inspired the choice of the color white, since it is an Islamic symbol of holiness.[27] Once a year, on the 27th of the month of Ruwah, the material is replaced. The old cloth is cut up into tiny pieces, which are given to the pilgrims as amulets believed to be filled with power of blessing from the tomb.

Performing a Successful Pilgrimage

Visiting the mausoleum and touching the tomb are the highlights of the pilgrims' trip. Carefully planning the day and time of entering the tomb is important to ensure the success of the pilgrimage. Most people try to enter the grave around midnight, because it seems impolite to rush. Lingering around for half a night, however, is seen to be more proper pilgrimage behavior. The lingering also has a self-serving aspect in that the Javanese believe midnight to be the prime time for encounters with the supernatural. The point of spending considerable time near the grave, according to John Pemberton, is "to put oneself in the right place, at the right time, and then wait."[28] It is important to stay awake; when one is asleep at the moment that "boons are bestowed," what is asked for will not be given.[29] In case a revelation should come in the form of a dream, however, dream explainers are at hand to help the pilgrims.

Not only Muslims, but also many Christian or Confucian Indonesians of Chinese ancestry will come to Sunan's grave. After that they head for two graves outside the mausoleum that contain the remains of a merchant from Semarang and of Sunan's accountant, Kwi Pawilangan. These graves are important to those who seek success in business. One of the main methods to ensure success is "counting stones." The decorative stones on the accountant's grave are so worn down that it is hard to see how many exactly there are. Pilgrims try to count them three times in a row on their knees. If this exercise results in a higher number the third time, this can be taken as a sure proof of success in business, but a lower number means the reverse. The other grave, the merchant's, is rather long. For Indonesians, who are generally not tall in stature, it is nearly impossible to reach both the foot and the head of the grave at the same time. The one who succeeds in touching both ends is applauded enthusiastically while members of his or her family try to touch the lucky one in order to derive a part of this blessing. Needless to say, tall visitors gain deep respect when they effortlessly manage to embrace the grave. After having visited all the important graves, most people return home. Others stay for a nightly picnic or for a nap on the grave, hoping that their reward will be an interesting dream or perhaps even a vision of some sort.

Many pilgrims come from Middle Java, especially from Semarang, Sunan's home-town. There is little difference either in number between men and women or in the way they view or perform the pilgrimage. All go through the same routine, say the same prayers and sleep on the graves, mixed or segregated. Until 1985, the pilgrims used the mosque on top of the mountain as a lodging place where men and women slept together. Still today, this mixing of the sexes is a source of great anxiety for the guards, who fear "irregularities" that could harm their reputation.[30]

Tembayat is getting more national attention since it has become a stop on tours to the graves of the *wali sanga* and is now visited by large groups of religious tourists. Civil servants and merchants seeking blessings on their businesses especially like to go there. This is not a new phenomenon, as writers from the beginning of this century mention the same types of visitors.[31] Also, there are many batik sellers from Solo who compete with each other to be the one who will provide the cloth that covers the graves. Occasionally, high dignitaries visit Bayat, such as the mayor of Klaten and Semarang, the governor of Boyolali, or a general. After Sultan Agung had his famous connection with Tembayat, it was no longer considered a place where one can find both spiritual and political power. One seldom sees a black Mercedes filled with ministers or generals who fly in from Jakarta visiting Tembayat in order to seek esoteric wisdom or to support their political legitimation. Those officials go to Imogiri and consult the grave of Sultan

Agung, who is buried there on top of a mountain and who is still considered powerful as the "guardian of the world."[32]

The best times to visit Sunan Bayat's grave are Thursday nights before Friday Kliwon or Friday Legi of the Javanese calendar. Although Friday Kliwon is the day of preference for visiting graves in Java, in Tembayat, Legi was added because it is believed that Sunan was born on that day and died on Kliwon. His descendants highlighted this date and managed to increase interest in the site. When the day of birth was added as a worthy time for a visit, the number of visitors grew. Pilgrims who prefer to visit another grave on Kliwon can now visit Sunan on Legi.

On an average night of Kliwon or Legi, some 6000 pilgrims come to the grave. There is a great variety of reasons for pilgrims to come. Muslims say that graves are locations where one can find *tentrem*, tranquility and inner peace. Many pilgrims agree that graves serve as a source of power that the pilgrims can draw from, provided they come at the right time, with the correct attitude, and follow the proper rituals of offering flowers, frankincense, and prayers. That is how one can obtain a part of blessing (*berkah*); if the pilgrim is lucky, he or she can even acquire "a piece of the saint's power" (*kesakten*).[33] In order to facilitate this process of deriving blessing and power, Muslims honor the saint by reciting the Qur'an and chanting *tahlilan*, or praises, continuously repeating the words *La ilaha illa Allah* (There is no god but God). This *tahlilan* can take from one hour to a whole night. Noteworthy as pilgrims are the students of traditional Qur'an schools (*santri*). In these Qur'an schools, it is customary to visit the founders' grave every Thursday evening. If the founder is still alive, the *santri* might frequent the grave of a saint who is somehow related to their school. *Santris* are the experts of *tahlilan* and often will chant all through the night. Students like to do their homework in the vicinity of a saint's grave. This, according to our informants, guarantees a higher level of concentration. Most of the pilgrims who visit Tembayat hope for tangible, that is, material results. Business people, especially those of Chinese background, are convinced that somehow traces are left of Sunan's former riches. It is believed those former riches put him in a preeminent position to serve as intercessor when asking for financial gains. Pilgrims ask for help with exams, infertility, finding a spouse, a job or promotion.

When asked why they made the pilgrimage to Tembayat, pilgrims do not volunteer information easily. They tend to mumble vague reasons for their visit, such as "I come here every week. You see I own a business. Yes, I do feel that in the long run Sunan will bless my business," or "I come to pray for good health." This reluctance to discuss the *ziarah* is remarkable since Indonesians usually generously volunteer information about their religion and beliefs. It can perhaps best be explained as a symptom of the ambiguous feelings of pilgrims concerning the "orthodoxy" of the rituals and beliefs involved in the visits.

The true motives behind the visits are most evident when listening to the prayers said by the *juru doa*. For example, the prayer for Mr. Suratno, a civil servant who has been trying for a long time to find a better job, went as follows: ". . . may Mr. Suratno while doing his work as a civil servant, gain more respect, may his colleagues be satisfied with his work, and may he be popular with his superiors. May he reach his promotion with ease and may, by the intercession of the saint and his grandchildren, his income be blessed." Like the income of most civil servants, Mr. Suratno's is not enough to live on, so he also runs a modest business of selling cookies. Hence the prayer continues with: "And may Mr. Suratno's business activities prosper and not be hindered by problems."

At the graves of the merchant Dampu Awang and the accountant, Ki Pawilangan, a special *juru doa* sits in front of an open fire to ask their intercession. For example, for Mrs. Darsih, who runs a small kiosk, he prayed: "God most High, by the intercession of . . . Dampu Awang and . . . Ki Pawilangan, Mrs. Darsih . . . has brought rice and flowers as a gift, and she will also donate a plate with food to Dampu Awang and Ki Pawilangan . . . [We also pray] that her kiosk will prosper and that she will be able to sell her goods easy and fast. May all these requests be heard. [We also pray] that she can find her goods for cheap prices and sell them quick with a lot of profit. We hope that the blessing of . . . Dampu Awang and . . . Ki Pawilangan will be on her so that all Mrs. Darsih asks for will be accepted."

Of course, many come to improve their health or to pray for their family's health. An elderly widow stated that she has come every week since the beginning of the 1980s. Before that she used to go to the grave of Prince Mangkunagara I (1757–95), which is situated closer to Salatiga, the town in which she lives. Now she comes to Tembayat, but always on a Sunday, and never at night because she cannot stand the crowds. She always brings flowers from home to put on the grave and takes a few handfuls back to put in her bath water. Since she has started doing this, she feels rejuvenated and does not even experience pain or problems when climbing the steep stairs that lead up to the grave. The week we met her, she had a special request for the saint concerning her son's career.

Juru Kunci or the Guardians of the Keys

Although during the prime visiting nights thousands of pilgrims are present at the gravesite, the traffic of all these people seems to be arranged smoothly. Farmers from the village come up to serve as "soldiers" and see that peace and quiet is maintained. They help with the *juru kunci* who are in charge of the grave and make the rules for visiting. The power of the *juru kunci* is considerable, since the tombs can only be approached with their cooperation and through their mediation. At a large complex such as in Tembayat, there are several *juru kunci* on duty according to rotating schedules. They guard the mausoleum while at the same time being the bearers of its traditions. They know the stories about Sunan Bayat, which high officials came to visit, what the requests were, and whose pleas were heard. They are also keenly aware of rejected requests. The *juru kunci* at Imogiri like to tell the story of a visit made by some ministers and high military officials from Jakarta in 1997. However, these visitors never made it to the mausoleum since sudden heavy rain prevented their plane from landing. Of course, to the *juru kunci*, this was a sure sign that the spirit of Sultan Agung rejected their worldly authority. From then on, the *juru kunci* expected that the Suharto regime would not last for much longer.[34] The religious knowledge of the *juru kunci*, however, is not rooted in Islamic education. They are more familiar with Javanese traditions and religious formulas. In Tembayat, they also safeguard the traditions of the Kraton. The position is exclusive and hereditary and sons join their fathers at a young age.[35]

While some do farming on the side, the guards earn their income mostly from the fees and gifts of the pilgrims. Although the sultans do not control their salaries, at Temabayat the guards feel an obligation to respect the rules for visitation customary for the Kratons at Solo and Yogyakarta. For example, Sunan's grave is closed during the Muslim fasting month of Ramadan, while in east Java this is the most preferred month for visiting the graves of Muslim saints.[36] As mentioned before, a popular tradition is to recite the Qur'an, or chant *tahlilan* near a grave. This is considered a gift to the saint and a worthy activity that will yield the saint's blessing. Also it is popular to have a meal near a grave, especially when the meal is a *selamatan*, a religious meal offered to express gratefulness for granted prayers. All these practices, popular near other graves, especially those of the *wali sanga*, are forbidden in Tembayat. There are few booklets available with the hagiography of Sunan, while near the graves of other Muslim saints stacks of books about their exemplary lives are available. The *juru kunci* in Tembayat fear that "mistakes might be made and incorrect data given" if too many books were to circulate. Their fear is based on the fact that "only the Sultan's palace (according to them, the Kraton at Yogyakarta) has access to the original manuscripts with Sunan Bayat's real biography." According to one of the *juru kunci*, forbidding them is mandatory. If he were to allow *tahlilan* near the grave, for example, it might result in "punishment from a higher power." "I am afraid that the ancestors will start to accuse me. If a governor is angry with me, I don't mind. The worst that can happen to me in such a case is that they lock me up for three months. But if Sunan gets angry with me, I will get paralyzed. Then I will not be able to walk, I will be confined to my chair all day long, and not a doctor will be able to help me."[37] Because of this fear, *tahlilan* in Bayat is held in a pavilion down the hill close to the entrance. While the chanting of *tahlilan* near other graves draws hundreds of visitors who join in or just listen, the distance from the grave in Tembayat causes pilgrims to lose interest in attending these otherwise meaningful sessions. At best, a few dozen come on a crowded night. In order to increase the attraction, the Muslim clerics who lead the chanting have started to diverge from its original goal of honoring the saint, and add: "that it may help to grant the requests made today."

Most probably the reason for the different rules found in Tembayat is that it is situated in Central Java, which means it falls under the jurisdiction of the local sultanate. Instead of allowing the customs practiced at the graves of the *wali sanga*, the supervisors at Tembayat seem to follow what is practiced at the royal graves in Imogiri. The Sultan of Yogyakarta decreed that the royal graves should be closed during Ramadan and that eating or chanting near the graves is forbidden. This underscores the historic relation between the grave and the worldly rulers.

The management of the gravesite of Sunan Bayat and its pilgrimage are considered part of the royal territory of the Kraton. The architectural design of the cemetery, following the shape of the Kraton, also expresses its royal connections. In fact, each component of the gravesite has a name that corresponds to a room found in the Kraton. According to Hindu–Javanese architectural ideology, the Kraton, and thus the grave of

Sunan Bayat, is a reflection of society and the universe. Moreover, the location of the grave on top of Mount Jabalkat invites comparisons with the Javanese cosmic mountain, a place where worldly and supernatural powers meet, and one that contains a concentration of otherworldly powers.

According to the *juru kunci*, the grave is such a holy place that a visit to it can replace the *Hajj* to Mecca. Since the distance between Indonesia and Saudi Arabia is considerable, we can assume that the majority of Indonesian Muslims will never be able to make the *Hajj*. That is why several Indonesian locations are considered to be cosmic centers that possess the same degree of spiritual power as can be encountered in Mecca. For example, Javanese Muslims believe that climbing up and down Mount Ciremai in Kuningan three times contains spiritual strength equal to performing the *Hajj*.[38] In Java, as is also true in Morocco, poor Muslims can substitute the "*Hajj* for the poor," which consists of making a pilgrimage to the graves of certain saints, or participating in festivals in honor of saints.[39]

The Nahdatul Ulama (NU) and Visiting the Graves

As mentioned earlier, opinions vary as to whether or not Islam allows visits to the graves of holy persons. Reformist Muslims condemn every pilgrimage that does not lead to Mecca and teach that going to the graves is equal to polytheism (*shirk*). Traditional Muslims (represented by the Nahdatul Ulama, NU) in Indonesia, however, not only allow pilgrimages to graves, but also encourage them, provided the *ziarah* avoids rituals incompatible with Islam.[40] This stance is based on their belief that prophets (*nabis*), holy persons (*walis*), and Qur'anic scholars (*ulama*) are nearer to God than ordinary believers and that such proximity allows them to intercede for the believers.[41] Traditional Muslim students believe that the teacher who has passed away can always be considered as a source of spiritual guidance and intercession. That is why within NU circles the students (*santri*) of *pesantren* regularly visit the grave of the scholar who founded their school, or of those of other famous scholars. Prayers and Qur'anic verses recited near the grave are considered to be gifts to the teacher, as was the case with reciting near the grave of a saint. Once a year, on the death-day of the founder of a Qur'an school, a special ceremony (*khaul*) is held near the grave. This ceremony, similar to the *Mawlid* in the Middle East, consists of Qur'anic recitations, *tahlilan*, and a communal meal next to the grave. Celebration of a *khaul* is not limited to pilgrimage sites. For example, graduation ceremonies are celebrated according to the same pattern.

Pesantren Sunan Pandan Aran and Islamic Revival

According to the tradition, Sunan Bayat did open a *pesantren* during his life, yet until the 1970s, there was never a *khaul* organized near his grave. His direct male descendants lived in the Tembayat area but held no significant religious positions, most being farmers. But the fourteenth descendant, Mufid Mas'ud, was acknowledged for his brightness, first as a student at the prestigious *pesantren* of Krapyak in Yogyakarta. He was so successful in his studies that his teacher offered Mufid one of his daughters in marriage. After a long period of study, Mufid Mas'ud became a religious teacher himself. On December 20, 1975, after many years of teaching in Krapyak, Mufid Mas'ud ful-filled the goal of every *kyai*, opening his own boarding school in a village north of Yogyakarta. The school was named after Sunan Bayat: "Sunan Pandan Aran." The remote location of the school harkened back to the days when *pesantren* were situated in isolated spots in the countryside, on the theory that isolation would help the students to focus on their religious education so that a "cadre of devout religious specialists" could be built.[42] The school's curriculum comprises pre-school to high school and many students come for its specialty of memorizing the Qur'an. It is especially famous because it helps the students to do this within two years. Currently, the number of female stu-dents far outnumber the male students (600 girls and 300 boys).

The choice of the name "Sunan Pandan Aran" might seem illogical since the grave is far from the school. The name of a saint closer by could have been chosen. Kyai Mufid Mas'ud explained that the name symbolizes the school's goal: "to bring Islam to all the villages and hamlets." This reflects the original mission of Sunan Bayat to spread Islam in Central Java. By reviving an almost forgotten tradition, Mufid Mas'ud contributed to the general revival of Indonesian Islam and Islamic mission (*dakwah*) that started some-time during the 1980s.

Being the descendant of Sunan Bayat, Kyai Mufid started to spread Islam by first forging a relationship between the *pesantren* and the gravesite in Tembayat. Once a year, a *khaul* was organized to commemorate Sunan Bayat's passing away. When the fame of the *pesantren* spread, the reason to hold the *khaul* shifted to commemorating the founding of the *pesantren*. That meant a freedom of choice whether to hold the *khaul* at the *pesantren* or in Tembayat. Groups of Qur'an students were regularly sent to the gravesite in order to recite the Qur'an and chant *tahlilan*. In the long run, the *pesantren* opened a branch in Tembayat, right on the slopes of Jabalkat. Now students who mem-orized the Qur'an stay there in order to recite continuously. Consequently, according to Javanese Muslim beliefs, the environment of the grave is not sanctified by unceasing Qur'anic recital.

Kyai Mufid also tried to purify the pilgrimage from non-Islamic elements. According to the Kyai, "prayers can only be directed to Allah. That is what Islam means by *tawhid* (God's oneness). We are not allowed to change this. Practices such as burning and offer-ing frankincense are un-Islamic. Pilgrims to Tembayat follow these practices based on their own desire, not because Islam instructs them to do this. There are no rules for the contents of the prayers as long as they are directed to God. It is, however, not good when pilgrims misuse (*salah mengunakan*) the *ziarah*. Asking to get rich or to win the lottery is a disgraceful thing to do."[43] Part of Kyai Mufid's mission is also to "convert" the vil-lagers of the village of Tembayat to Islam. Most of them are nominal Muslims and, according to Kyai Mufid, "people in Tembayat have a very limited Islamic mind."[44] By this he refers to the fact that the village of Tembayat is famous for the performance of un-Islamic rituals in order to satisfy the village spirits, as well as for its Javanese rituals and ghostly creatures, *thuyul*, that appear in the form of children and steal from the rich.[45]

The trend towards Islamization in Indonesia coincided with initiatives of the government to preserve popular sites of pilgrimage because of their archeological value. Before the government allocated funds for restoration, the sultan from Solo paid for the maintenance of the gravesite. At that time the mausoleum fell under the jurisdiction of the Kraton Surakarta. After his wealth diminished, the costs were divided among the sultan, the government, and the local community. During the 1970s, Indonesia started to produce some *nouveau riche*. Since the wealth of most of them came from commerce, they were interested in investing in places that were heavy on blessings. Thus, Tembayat became accessible by a paved road because a group of businessmen from Jakarta financed the project. Concurrent with the revival of Indonesian Islam, the gravesite was renovated and modernized in the 1980s. As recently as 1985, the gravesite on top of the mountain did not have electricity or running water, so water for the Muslim ritual washing had to be carried up the mountain. This condition limited Tembayat's capacity to receive pilgrims. Nowadays there is running water near the gravesite.

The number of pilgrims has been growing steadily since the renovations. This increase, of course, is also the result of improved means of transportation in Indonesia. "Doing a pilgrimage" has become a favorite way to spend a holiday of the Thursday night before the weekend. A continuous stream of groups, clubs, and students on outings come to the graves. On Thursday evenings, students like to come on their motorbikes and spend a night of pleasure and blessing. Also, mosques organize pilgrimages. As was mentioned earlier, bus tours have become increasingly popular. These are led by a *kyai*, and carry pilgrims from site to site. This creates the phenomenon of "*wisata ziarah*," the tourist pilgrimage. The tourist pilgrim comes not only for blessing, but also for entertainment and some souvenirs. As a result of this trend, during the 1990s, Tembayat had to build an extra prayer house and more souvenir shops, thus reflecting the dual need of the spiritual and the material.

As thanks for prayers are granted, pilgrims donate goods to embellish the gravesite, another sign of increased wealth. Until the 1980s, it was customary to bring food that was distributed among the guards and the pilgrims. Food is a token of gratefulness. They bring gifts that vary from material to cover the graves, to expensive watches and clocks and even elaborate chandeliers. When I asked one of the *juru kunci* if he ever received a gift as an expression of thanks for prayers heard, he muttered, "My house is packed with hundreds of clocks and watches."

In the old days, pilgrims would seek peace and quiet at the holy sites. They preferred to come alone, or in small groups of like-minded people. Now the preference has shifted to doing the pilgrimage *en masse*. This trend was actively encouraged by the Suharto regime, which also widened the pool of pilgrim sites and tried to convince the pilgrims to pay their respects at what were basically secular sites as well. An example of such a place is the grave of Mrs. Tien Suharto, as mentioned earlier. In general, however, holy places such as caves, mountaintops, and lakes where pilgrims used to come for meditation and prayer are losing their attraction. Interest has shifted to sites with beautifully renovated monuments, such as the site of Sunan Bayat. Having pilgrims come to certain sites also means that it is more convenient to control them and to keep track of them. Also, religious authorities such as Kyai Mufid can gently move the pilgrims into the Islamic mainstream, which means eliminating indigenous, non-Islamic customs and beliefs. Yet, we can observe that as Indonesia is more strongly Islamic than ever before, a new type of pilgrim is slowly emerging: the pilgrim who, rather than spiritual gain, seeks material rewards and entertainment. This type of pilgrim is clearly more focussed on the present world.

At the same time, the site remains part of the sacred credentials of the Kraton and firmly forges the relationships between the Javanese version of Islam of the Kraton and orthodox Islam. At the graves of the *wali sanga*, part of the Islamic mission (*dakwah*) is the dissemination of the histories and hagiographies of these saints written by students of *pesantren* that have a special relationship with the grave.[46] We do not yet find these pamphlets at the grave of Sunan Bayat. Kyai Mufid has not yet managed to take control of this aspect of the grave's mission.

Conclusion

The pilgrimage to a site such as Tembayat provides a vivid example of how Islam, Javanese mysticism, and folk religion happily coexist while being modified by modernization and secularization. Following the earliest traditions, the prime dates for going on a pilgrimage are based on the Islamic–Javanese calendar. The Kraton and the mystical Javanese ideas and beliefs of the guards, the *juru kunci*, continue to dictate the rules and directions concerning the rituals surrounding the pilgrimage. Even the stronger Islamic influence has failed to change these rules. Islam has, however, influenced the attitude of the pilgrims. Many of them consider themselves to be practicing Muslims and are no longer sure that all the rituals and prayers they perform during the pilgrimage are correct. That is why they prefer not to talk about the goal of their visit, or their relationship with the saint. Muslim leaders increase this sense of guilt by stressing the Islamic character of the site, by frequently reciting the Qur'an and assigning religious leaders to tour groups. All this is directed at eroding the Javanese-mystical elements of the pilgrimage. Yet Sunan is addressed mostly in the Javanese language and many pilgrims cannot resist the temptation to visit the graves of his accountant and the merchant from Semarang. The Islamic ritual comes first, yet it seems acceptable to pilgrims to combine it with an expression of what is considered harmless Javanese folk belief.

The physical and religious landscapes of Tembayat seem confusing. Hindu monuments surround the tomb inspired by one of the prime symbols of Islam, the Ka'bah. To the mix of mystical Javanese Islam, Javanese syncretistic belief, and orthodox Islam have been added the ingredients of contemporary times, increased materialism, and a greater desire for worldly pleasures. All the traditions about the saint testify to his being a true Muslim who lived according to the five pillars of Islam and used his considerable spiritual powers to convert people to his religion. Yet, many today come to seek material wealth, basing their supplications on the time the saint was still a rich man.

In spite of all these competing influences and of the many revolutionary changes in communication, transportation and technology, at the heart of the mausoleum in

Tembayat is an ancient Islamic–Javanese tradition that continues to attract visitors. Each of them is free to adapt a reading of the tomb's landscape to his/her own background, education, culture, hopes, and beliefs.

Notes

1. John Pemberton, *On the Subject of "Java"* (Ithaca: Cornell University Press, 1994), 270.
2. A *selamatan* is a religious meal held at time-of-life passages such as birth, marriage, and death. *Selamat* comes from the Arabic and means "blessing." To hold such a meal of blessing at a holy place is very popular as it increases the atmosphere of blessing and thus the beneficial result of the meal. See Clifford Geertz, *The Religion of Java* (Chicago: University of Chicago Press, 1976), 11–120.
3. S.J. Franz Magnis-Suseno, *Javanese Ethics and World-view* (Jakarta: Balai Pustaka, 1984), 339, 340.
4. Koentjaraningrat, *Javanese Culture* (New York: Oxford University Press, 1990), 374, 375.
5. Sermon of *Kyai* Azari at Krapyak *pesantren*, December 12, 1997.
6. Mark Woodward, *Islam in Java. Normative Piety and Mysticism in the Sultanate of Yogyakarta* (Tucson: The University of Arizona Press, 1989), 174.
7. Jane Smith and Yvonne Haddad, *The Islamic Understanding of Death and Resurrection* (Albany: State University of New York Press, 1981), 52–3.
8. James J. Fox, "Ziarah Visits to the Tombs of the *Walis*, the Founders of Islam on Java," in M.C. Ricklefs, ed., *Islam in the Indonesian Social Context* (Clayton: Monash University, 1991), 21.
9. Pemberton, *Java*, 274, 276.
10. Ibid., chapter 7.
11. Martin van Bruinessen, "New Perspectives on Southeast Asian Islam?" Review article in *Bijdragen tot de Tall – Land – en Volkendunde*, Leiden: KITLV, Volume 143 (1987), 531.
12. *"Selama ini kita berdakwa dengan politik, sekarang ini kits berpolitik dengan dakwah."*
13. M.P. van Bruggen and R.S. Wassing, *Djokja, Solo. Beeld van de vorstensteden* (Purmerend: Asia Minor, 1998), 101.
14. The current Sultan Hamengkubuwana X expressed this opinion during a meeting about inter–religious relations held at the Kraton palace in July, 1998.
15. See Dale F. Eickelman, *Moroccan Islam, Tradition and Society in a Pilgrimage Center* (Austin: University of Texas Press, 1976).
16. Simon Coleman and John Elsner, *Pilgrimage. Past and Present in the World Religions* (Cambridge, MA: Harvard University Press, 1995), 212.
17. In spite of the many tales about his life, it is not certain who the historical Sunan Bayat was exactly.
18. Pemberton in *Java*, 279 assumes that it is Adipati Pandan Arang who is buried in Bayat. After having been the *bupati* (local governor) or Semarang, he lived in Tembayat between 1498 and 1512.
19. See Amen Budiman, *Semarang Riwayatmu Dulu* (*Semarang, Your History*) (Tanjung Sari: Semarang, 1978), 103. This book is the first of a projected series of four. The fourth volume will contain the footnotes. Unfortunately, at the time of this writing, we only have the first volume and thus cannot check the author's sources.
20. D.A. Rinkes in *Nine Saints of Java* (Kuala Lumpur: Malaysian Sociological Research Institute, 1996, originally 1910, 1911) in chapter IV "Ki Panda Arang at Tembayat," mentions

the sources as *Sajarah-dalem* (a comprehensive list of the Mataram dynasty royal family by Ki Padma Susastra), *Serat Kanda* and *Babad Tanah Djawi* (Central Javanese historical traditions written during the Mataram period), two *Babad Nitik Dagh-Register gehouden int Casteel Batavia* (the daily record kept at the Batavia Castle, 1631–34 AD, published in The Hague, 1898).

21. Clifford Geertz, *Islam Observed* (Chicago: University of Chicago Press, 1968), 28.
22. Ibid., 87.
23. Rinkes, *Nine Saints,* 112, quotes from the *DaDagh-Register,* 185.
24. Ibid., 88, note 62.
25. Ibid., 87.
26. Koentjaraningrat, *Javanese Culture,* 49–50.
27. See Denys Lombard, *Le Carrefour Javanais* (Paris: Ecole des Hautes Etudes et Sciences Sociales, 1990) Part III, 93 and Huub de Jonge, "Heiligen, middelen en doel. Ontwikkelingen en betekenis van twee Islamitische bedevaartsoorden op Java," in *Islamitische Pelgrimstochten,* eds. Willy Jansen and Huub de Jonge (Muiderberg: Dick Coutinho, 1991), 87. Islam adopted the color white for holiness from pre-Islamic culture.
28. Pemberton, *Java,* 285.
29. Ibid.
30. In Indonesia, it is not unusual for men and women to freely socialize with each other. Muslims, mainly reformists, see this as a grave problem, especially when both men and women are preparing for important rituals such as going on the *Hajj.* See Kees van Dijk, "Indonesische hadji's op reis," in Willy Jansen and Huub de Jonge, eds., *Islamimtische Pelgrimstochten,* 49.
31. H.J. de Graaf, *Geschiedenis van Indonesies'* (Gravenhage/Bandung: N.V. Uitgeverij W. van Hoeve, 1949), 201.
32. In "The Idea of Power in Javanese Culture," *Language and Power. Exploring Political Cultures in Indonesia* (Ithaca: Cornell University Press, 1990), 45; Benedict R. Anderson observed that Javanese rulers often used the words "world" or "universe" in their titles.
33. Also see James J. Fox, "Ziarah Visits to the Tombs of the Walis, the Founders of Islam on Java," in *Islam in the Indonesian Social Context,* op. cit.
34. Rejection by the saint as a sign of waning power also occurred in Tembayat. When Sultan Panjang tried to remove the Mataram dynasty, he found the door to the grave firmly locked and the key could not open it. Before that, he and his army had been caught in an eruption of volcano Merapi. The *juru kunci* stems from a time when Islamic knowledge was mastered only by a few who were socially and spiritually qualified.
35. The *juru kunci* described by Robert Hefner in *Hindu Javanese. Tengger Tradition and Islam* (Princeton: Princeton University Press, 1985) pronounced "a long prayer of invocation to village ancestors and guardian spirits" (108). According to Hefner, the specific role of *juru kunci* stems from a time when Islamic knowledge was mastered only by a few who were socially and spiritually qualified. He credits the growth of *pesantren* in rural Java with the increase of Islamic learning and the demise of the number of *juru kunci,* 109.
36. James Fox, "Ziarah visits," 21.
37. Interview with *Juru Kunci* Kertosono, September 28, 1997.
38. Martin van Bruinessen, *Kitab Kuning. Pesantren dan Tarekat* (Bandung: Mizan, 1995), 44.
39. Henk Driesen, "Pelgrimage, etnografie en theorie. Een overzicht uit de culturele antropologie," in Jansen and de Jonge, 18. Herman Beck writes that Moroccan Muslims believe that attending the festival of Saint Moulay Idris seven times can replace the *Hajj.* "De Moessem van Idris I. Een Islamitisch bedevaartsfeest in Moulay Idris, Marokko," in J. Pieper, P. Post,

and M. van Uden, eds., *Bedevaart en pelgrimage. Tussen traditie en moderniteit* (Baarn: Gooi & Sticht, 1994), 147.

40. Van Brusnessen, op. cit., 179.
41. Interview with Kyai Mufid Mas'ud, May 28, 1997.
42. Booklet published by the *pesantren* called: Dwi Windi Pondok *Pesantren* Sunan Panda Aran 1975–1991 (Yogyakarta, 1991), 3–4.
43. Interview May 28, 1976.
44. Interview July 17, 1997.
45. Koentjaraningrat, *Javanese Culture*, 342.
46. Fox, in "Ziarah visits" gives an example of literature about the *wali* Sunan Giri produced by the *pesantren* Luhur Islam "on the basis of collective research," 27.

PART V

Justice, Dependency, and International Relations in Contemporary Islamic Thought

29 Hindu Fundamentalism in Contemporary India: A Muslim Perspective   509
    Zafarul-Islam Khan
30 Political Discourse of the Organization of the Islamic Conference   527
    Abdullah al-Ahsan
31 Culture of Mistrust: A Sociological Analysis of Iranian Political Culture   544
    Mehrdad Mashayekhi
32 What Do We Mean By Islamic Futures?   562
    Ziauddin Sardar
33 Islam and the Science of Economics   587
    Syed Farid Alatas

CHAPTER 29

Hindu Fundamentalism in Contemporary India: A Muslim Perspective

Zafarul-Islam Khan

"Hinduism is in danger!" is the war cry of a plethora of Indian mass organizations that believe in Hindu *jagaran* (awakening), which, in effect, seeks to secure total Hindu hegemony. This movement is called "Hindutva" or Hinduness. Mass propaganda for decades has led a section of India's Hindu majority to develop a minority complex. They are made to believe that their religion, culture, and even their very existence is in danger, supposedly from Muslims (about 140 million compared to over 800 million Hindus), who, according to official figures, have been relegated to a marginal existence in India after Independence in 1947.

The hapless Muslim minority stands nowhere compared to Hindus who control every aspect of the life and activity in India.[1] Hindus, who form a majority of about 6:1 *vis-à-vis* Muslims, are made to believe that a conspiracy of sociology and demography will soon render them a minority in their own land! This is asserted while Hindus totally monopolize every aspect of power in the country.

This hate-mongering resulted in the so-called "Hindu backlash," a term coined during the 1984 elections when the ruling Congress (I) Party openly courted Hindu voters while the Muslim vote, hitherto a deciding factor in the Congress electoral strategy since Independence, was announced to be redundant. The Hindu "backlash" was largely a result of the media hype over the conversion of 181 Dalit families (the so-called "untouchables" or the outcastes under the Hindu caste system) to Islam in the South Indian state of Tamil Nadu's Meenakshipuram village in 1981.[2]

The conversion, caused by the social alienation of the Dalits, led to impassioned cries about a "resurgent Islam" riding in on the strength of Arab petrol dollars. Dalits have been converting to Buddhism in search of emancipation and a respectful place in society. A renowned Dalit leader, Dr. B.R. Ambedkar, converted to Buddhism with thousands of his so-called "untouchable" followers on October 14, 1956 in a public ceremony at Nagpur. Dalits do not lose their special benefits if they convert to Buddhism, which is considered an "Indian" religion. But conversion to Islam was different.

Hindu leaders met the then prime minister, Indira Gandhi, demanding a ban on conversions. She agreed with their demand and advised them to create a peaceful atmosphere to facilitate the task of the government.[3] The Bharatiya Janata Party (BJP) president, Atal Bihari Vajpayee, was so pleased with Indira Gandhi that he likened her to the goddess "Chandi Devi" who spills the blood of enemies. The erstwhile maharaja of Kashmir, Karan Singh, a Congress leader and a former central minister, established Vrat Hindu Samaj in September 1981, to protect Hinduism, with the cooperation of Rashtriya Swayamsevak Sangh (RSS) and BJP leaders who later hijacked the movement.

In the following general elections (November 1989) the Hindu "backlash" relegated the Congress Party to opposition benches and the National Front came to power with BJP help. It was only after this that the Congress and other secular parties started to make a hue and cry about "communalism," while the Hindutva political front, the BJP, slowly rose as a major power in the political arena.

The second source of danger to "Hindu" India is seen in Christian missionaries who are portrayed as misusing their Western-backed monetary clout and social, healthcare, and educational institutions to lure outcaste and low-caste Hindus into the fold of Christianity. In recent years communists too have been added to the Hindutva's list of India's "enemies." The then BJP president, L.K. Advani, had identified in 1986 three challenges to Hinduism: Islam, communism. and Western consumerism.

Hindu "revival" has been an old dream in India although there is no proven golden past which may be "revived." To the early "Hindu" leaders of the late nineteenth and early twentieth century, like Bankim Chandra Chatterjee, Dayanand Saraswati, Vivekananda, and Bal Gangadhar Tilak, anti-colonialism was synonymous with resurgent Hinduism. Some of these leaders were friends of the British raj, which they saw as a useful tool to crush Muslim power in India. B.C. Chatterjee was a great fan of the British rule, and declared that with British rule there was no need to have Hindu rule.

Incidentally, it was Chatterjee who invented the idea of *Bharat Mata* (Mother India, i.e., India the goddess), which today forms an article of faith for believers in Hindutva. The pre-Gandhi nationalist movement had a marked Hindu content, like the movement of *shuddhi* ("purification," i.e., reconversion of Muslims to Hinduism), demand for a ban on cow slaughter, creation of a Shivaji cult, and celebration of the Ganapati festival which Tilak (d. 1920) had innovated. Congress leader M.K. Gandhi used religious symbolism liberally in his political struggle.

The official history and common belief in India holds Muslims responsible for the partition of the country in 1947, but the fact is that the concept of Hindu *Rashtra* (state) and the Aryan theory of a superior race were being propagated decades before the Muslim League's "Pakistan" resolution of March 23, 1940.[4] The RSS people did not take part in the Independence struggle. Instead, they used to ridicule it. Their top ideolog Veer Savarkar wrote a mercy petition a few months after his incarceration in Cellular Jail at Andaman promising to be the "staunchest advocate of constitutional progress and loyalty to the British government."[5] And former prime minister, A.B. Vajpayee, BJP's leader, has been accused of betraying freedom fighters.[6]

The Hindu supremacy movement was articulated by the Hindu Sangathan (HS) in the early years of the last century. Lala Hardayal (1884–1939), founder of the HS, had said in his book, *Mere Vichar* (*My Views*), "I declare that the future of Hindu race of Hindustan and of Punjab rests on these four pillars: (1) Hindu *Sangathan* [unity]; (2) Hindu *raj* [rule]; (3) *shuddhi of Muslims*; (4) conquest and *shuddhi* of Afghanistan and frontiers. So long as the Hindu nation does not accomplish these four things the safety of the Hindu race will be impossible." These still remain the aims of the present-day Hindutva forces.

This movement has continued in various shapes and forms: Arya Samaj (Aryan Society – established in 1875); Hindu Mahasabha (established in 1915); Rashtriya Swayamsevak Sangh (RSS (National Volunteers Corps) – established in 1925); Jana Sangh (JS – a political party established in 1951 with the slogans of "Hindi, Hindu, Hindustan," which did not prove popular at the hustings); Virat Hindu Sammelan; Hindu Samajotsav, Jana Sangh's current incarnation, the Bharatiya Janata Party (BJP); Vishwa Hindu Parishad (VHP) and its youth wings Bajrang Dal and Durga Vahini; Youth Volunteer Corps; Shiv Sena; Hindu Shiv Sena; Hindu Manch; Hindu Surakhsha Samiti; Hindu Shiv Shakti Dal; and Rashtriya Hindu Sangathan etc. Scions of big business families, like Dalmias, Birlas, Singhanias, Ambanis and Modis, patronize many of these organizations.

According to its self-image, this movement goes back two centuries. Movements like Arya Samaj and Hindu Mahasabha aimed basically to organize the *shuddhi* movement, cow protection, and demand for "Hindi" language in Devnagri script (as against Hindustani or Urdu in Persian script) as a way to galvanize Hindu unity. The movement took a firm institutional shape when the RSS was established at Nagpur by Dr. Hedgewar, a Maharshtrian Brahmin. Vinayak Damodar Savarkar, one of its ideologs, coined the word "Hindutva" in his book *Hindutva* (Nagpur, 1923), which sought to claim that Hindus are a separate "nation" and that all Indians are Hindus with the exception of Muslims and Christians because these two communities believe in "foreign" religions. This idea was articulated by the RSS's second chief M.S. Golwalkar in his books, *We or Our Nationhood Defined* (1939) and *Bunch of Thoughts* (1966).[7]

Since Hindus are divided in innumerable castes and belief systems spanning from idol worship to atheism, the RSS based itself on three main pillars: (i) geographical unity; (ii) shared racial roots; and (iii) common culture. To unite Hindus, the RSS focused on inculcating discipline. To achieve this aim it started organizing early morning weekly ideological and physical training meetings. These are called *shakhas* in which participants listen to lectures by senior members, learn how to use *lathis* (batons) and practice martial arts. In 1927 the RSS adopted for itself a saffron flag and continues to hold it as the real flag of the country. It is commonly believed that the RSS was inspired by the German Nazi and Italian fascist ideologies. Its senior leaders visited both Germany and Italy to study these movements in their heyday. The only other similar surviving outfit formed on the German Nazi party lines is the Phalange of the Lebanon.

The RSS is an emulation of the idea of a *single* Muslim community, the *ummah*. The aim is to galvanize Hindus into a single *qaum*, or community, out of the umpteen castes, sub-castes and religious groups. But thanks to in-built casteism and the sacrosanct Hindu *varna* system, it is impossible to evolve a single community out of Hindus. With its emphasis on physical training and the philosophy of *advaita* ("non-dualism"), the

RSS has tried to bring into reality Vivekananda's dream of "an Islamic body and a Vedantic heart."[8]

The RSS received its first big jolt in 1948 when it was banned temporarily from February 1948 to July 1949 for the role of some of its members and ideolog Savarkar in the assassination of the father of the nation, Mahatma Gandhi, for his alleged pro-Muslim and pro-Pakistan policies. By this time the RSS was claiming to run 5000 *shakhas* around the country.

As a precondition for lifting the ban, the RSS for the first time in its history laid down a constitution and started claiming that it was a "cultural" organization. After the ban was lifted in July 1949, the RSS began establishing specialized autonomous organizations, which are controlled through *parcharaks* (preachers) loaned by the parent organization. The purpose was that the RSS work should continue if and when another ban is clamped in future, which has since taken place twice: during the Emergency (1975–8), when the RSS claimed to be running 10,000 *shakhas* around the country; and again for two years after the demolition of the Babari Mosque in December 1992.[9] In 1994 the RSS made unsubstantiated claims to have more than 30,000 *shakhas* and over 2.5 million members around the country.

The ideological framework of Hindutva aims at striving to establish a Hindu *Rashtra*, or state, based on a way of life led by religious and cultural factors of a people commonly called Hindus, who live within a given geographical area and share distinct ethnic, linguistic, and social traditions. In such a state the people of Semitic religions, Muslims and Christians, are considered the "other," whose loyalty to the land is suspect. Hindutva's ideolog M.S. Golwalkar in the creed's bible, *Bunch of Thoughts*, identifies three "internal threats": Muslims, Christians, and communists, in that order.[10]

It is said that unless and until these people forget their "foreign" roots and merge themselves completely in the culture of the country they will not be accepted as "Indians" and will be treated as "guests" who have no rights whatsoever. In its English-language publications, the RSS may not appear as extremist and fascist, but in its Indian languages publications, like Hindi and Gujarati, it minces no words. Muslims here have been described as "foreign snakes" (*yawan saanp*).[11] Now liberal, secular, and Westernized Hindus too have been added to this list in Sangh Parivar's literature. They are routinely dubbed as "pseudo-secularists."

Muslims are accused by Hindutva groups of growing faster than Hindus as a result of polygamy and non-compliance of family planning. This myth is parroted *ad nauseum* although both counts have been authoritatively refuted and Hindus have been shown in official data to be more polygamous than Muslims.[12]

Hindu communalists use any opportunity to hurt and insult Muslims. They were in the forefront of the Shah Bano campaign for extra-sharī'ah rights for divorced Muslim women and when the Indian government conceded in 1986 to a united Muslim demand for the restoration of the Muslim personal laws in this respect, it turned its wrath against the government. To spite Muslims, these groups go out of their way to support the likes of Salman Rushdie, Taslima Nasrin, and now V.S. Naipaul who openly justify their crimes to "correct historical injustices" and endorse the Hindutva cultural program and demolition of the Babari Mosque.

Indeed, as of rule they will oppose anything Muslims support and will support anything Muslims oppose. One of them even went to a Calcutta court in 1986 to get the Qur'an banned! While demanding a ban on the conversion of Hindus to Islam and Christianity, they actively work to "reconvert" Muslims and Christians to Hinduism. In recent years, the BJP has been most vocal about declaring war on Pakistan. It kept the country on tenterhooks throughout 2002 threatening to unleash a "fight-to-the-finish" (*aar paar*) war against Pakistan for its role in encouraging secessionist violence in Kashmir.

The Hindu revivalist movement benefits a few groups and individuals who have realized their political ambitions and amassed incredible funds as donations[13] for various activities like the Rama temple and the reconversion drive (which is afoot in all backward and tribal areas). It preoccupies the majority with superficial and emotional issues, sapping its energies and robbing it of its mental peace, which is necessary for progress and innovation. At the same time it drives the minorities to the wall forcing them to take militant postures, which in turn are used to justify violence against minorities.

Urdu, one of the world's most beautiful and melodious languages which grew around the northern Indian centers of Delhi and Lucknow, was effectively killed overnight after Independence as a result of this myopic view. Urdu was the subcontinent's lingua franca and the official language of courts and education in north India but this was abruptly abolished after Independence, and Hindi, in Devnagri script, was made the official language although it had defeated Urdu by only one vote in the Constituent Assembly and that casting vote, ironically, belonged to a Muslim lady (Begum Azaz Rasool). Before Independence, Muslims were assured that independent India's official language would be "Hindustani" written in both Persian and Devnagri scripts.

There have been many promises to give Urdu its due but nothing has materialized. Recommendations of the Gujral Committee (1975) and Ali Sardar Jafari Committee (1990), both on Urdu, gather dust. Urdu-speaking children are forced to study in Hindi schools despite declared government policies. Urdu today exists only in some Muslim homes and *madrasah* as well as in Bollywood film productions, which are passed off as "Hindi films."

India's secular march received a jolt after Nehru's death in 1964. Nehru believed that Hindu communalism posed the greatest danger to India. Since then Hindu communalism has raised its head again after it remained discredited as a result of Mahatma Gandhi's murder by some of its proponents. Morarji Desai gave it acceptability by coopting Jana Sangh into his Janata Party government in 1977. Atal Behari Vajpayee was made foreign minister and L.K. Advani information minister.

According to historian Rajni Kothari, the privileged among the Hindus seem to feel insecure in the face of what they consider to be growing demands of the minorities as well as the already achieved upward mobility by some sections of the minorities. According to Kothari, "India is a people and a land made up of a series of minorities, for Hindu society itself is intrinsically highly structural and diverse and pluralistic. There are castes and sub-castes and clans and all manners of groupings and sub-groupings . . . It is really a set of minorities. It is thus wrong to think of Hindus as a 'majority' . . ." Kothari adds that for the last 15 years or so the relationship between the Hindu "majority" and the various minorities is at a point of crisis.[14]

In its early years, the RSS remained obsessively committed to the Hindi language, which limited its influence to north India. This has been toned down during the last two decades, allowing the organization to penetrate into the non-Hindi speaking states of Kerala, Karnataka, Andhra Pradesh, and Tamil Nadu in south India. Working through various fronts, the RSS has found popular emotive causes in recent years to arouse Hindus. It observed in its annual report for 1990 that "substantial progress has been made towards the creation of the Hindu State."[15]

The Emergency in 1975 got the better of the outfit. Its leadership was shaken. In his letters to Prime Minister Indira Gandhi from Yeravada Jail, the then RSS chief, Balasaheb Deoras, promised that his organization would be at the disposal of the government "for national uplift" if the ban on the RSS were lifted and its members freed from jails.[16] After the Emergency, the Jana Sangh (JS) merged with the Janata Party (JP). But soon in 1980 it had to leave the JP on the question of its members' retaining dual membership (of the RSS, which they were reluctant to renounce). The JS now re-emerged as the BJP and started preaching "Gandhian socialism" instead of its old line of supporting an American-style economy.

Indira Gandhi exhibited a marked tilt toward Hindu communalists after losing the general elections in 1977 in the wake of Emergency. She started courting communal elements and introduced "cow and calf" as the symbol of the party she led. Mrs. Gandhi adopted political expediency and soft Hindutva in lieu of secularism, which alone is suited to the diverse Indian society. Mrs. Gandhi broke conventions by inaugurating the VHP's Bharat Mata Temple at Hardwar on May 15, 1983. Rajiv Gandhi followed the same line. During the 1989 general elections he started his poll campaign from Ayodhya, a Hindu holy town, declaring that his aim was to establish *Ramrajya* (rule of Rama, the mythological god king).

During the 1980s the state television network aired religious serials during prime time on themes like *Ramrajya* and *Mahabharata*, creating a misplaced pride in a mythological past. This process was described by K.R. Narayanan, who later became president of India in 1997, as "a slow injection of communalism." These serials stoked the fires of Hindutva and made it respectable as never before even among the middle classes. The Rajiv government went far ahead of previous regimes in observing Hindu rituals at ceremonies, like offering *puja*, *arti*, etc. Previous governments had sufficed with candle lighting and coconut breaking at such ceremonies. A *hawan* (religious worship) for 40 days (in May–June 1987) was observed when the Nehru family's *National Herald* newspaper reappeared after a year-long strike.

During Rajiv Gandhi's reign, the RSS, through the VHP, started for the first time a movement for building "Rama Temple" at the site of the Babari Mosque in Ayodhya which had remained under locks since some local Hindus had placed idols inside it in December 1949. The Rama Temple movement was perceived as a sure prescription to arouse passions and thereby grab political power, which had eluded these extremist elements since Independence. In July 1984 Sri Rama Janamabhoomi Mukti Yagna Samiti was formed to "liberate" the Babari site. *Shila Poojan* ("worship of bricks" to be used for the construction of the proposed temple) was organized all over the country and each village was asked to send in bricks for the proposed temple. *Yatras* (rallies) were undertaken all over the country to mobilize the Hindu masses.

Under an official conspiracy hatched by the Rajiv government, Babari Mosque locks were suddenly broken in 1986 on the strength of a fraudulently acquired judicial order by a local court which had no *locus standi* in the case. State television was ready in that remote town to capture and relay the great event to all corners of the country. (Years later BJP leader L.K. Advani said that his party reaped the benefits of the mistake committed by Rajiv Gandhi.) The Rajiv government also allowed the VHP to observe *shilanyas* (foundation stone-laying ceremony) of the temple on November 9–10, 1987 in the land adjacent to the Babari Mosque (a Muslim graveyard).

The BJP

The BJP believes in "positive secularism" and "integral humanism" and denounces other parties' policies towards Muslims and Christians as "minorityism." It calls for a uniform civil code to be applicable to all, especially Muslims who enjoy their own personal laws (like *all* other religious communities in the country *including Hindus*). Hindutva to it is synonymous with nationalism and everything lying outside it is alien.

For a decade after its emergence, the BJP remained a marginal party. Its fortunes brightened only after it hijacked the Rama Temple issue in the mid-1980s. It did surprisingly well in the 1989 elections, winning 86 seats in parliament (earlier it had only two seats). This was matched by winning a majority in the states of Madhya Pradesh and Himachal Pradesh in the state legislature elections of March 1990, which allowed the BJP to form state governments there as well as to enter as ruling coalition partner in Gujarat and Rajasthan.

The National Front government, led by V.P. Singh (1989–90), was dependent on BJP support in parliament. It fell like a pack of cards when the BJP withdrew its support in October 1990 after the government's arrest of L.K. Advani and its tough stand against the BJP's agitation to build the Rama Temple on the Babari Mosque site.

The 1991 elections brought the BJP to power in Uttar Pradesh (which lasted until the central rule was imposed in the wake of the demolition of the Babari Mosque on December 6, 1992). In the 1993 elections the BJP failed to make a comeback in the states it previously ruled but it managed to capture the state of Delhi and emerged as a ruling coalition partner in Rajasthan.

Elections in early 1995 saw the beginning of BJP rule in Gujarat, which has since become its base and "laboratory," where Hindutva's various ideas, theories, and schemes have been tested and perfected including how to deal with Muslims, a glimpse of which was seen during the 2002 pogroms which, in turn have successfully marginalized Muslims in that state. The idea is to push minorities to accept the status of second-class citizens with no rights or demands.

These advances, thanks to unethical coalitions and seat adjustments during the elections, led to a tacit approval by the Indian ruling classes of the Hindutva philosophy which in turn has changed the political and communal face of India. From the untouchable of the Indian polity since Independence, Hindutva is a major political force today. Until the early 1990s it lacked this acceptability and legitimacy.

In 1998 the BJP managed to form a minority government at the Center, which lasted for only 13 days. Soon thereafter it bounced back to power for one year as a result of broadening its coalition base. In the next general elections in 1999 it managed to secure 182 seats in the Indian parliament and ruled the Center for the next four and a half years at the head of the National Democratic Alliance (NDA), a shaky coalition of 23 parties. However, it lost in the May 2004 elections when the combined seats of all the NDA partners failed to cross even the simple majority mark in the national parliament.

Temple Politics

Sometime in the mid-1980s the BJP realized that the Rama Temple issue had the emotional potential to get it votes of certain classes of Hindus. Hitherto the movement had been non-partisan and supporters came from various rightist and centrist groups. Soon it became an exclusive BJP plank, which was whipped hard for the next 15 years. The party position somewhat mellowed only once it formed its own government at the Center and partners of different hues had to be satisfied.

During September–October 1990, L.K. Advani took out *Rath yatra* (symbolic chariot journey), which crisscrossed the country igniting dozens of communal riots in its trail causing the massacre of over 3000 Muslims and looting and burning properties worth trillions of rupees. This momentum soon led to the demolition of the Babari Mosque, which again set in motion a series of riots including the infamous Bombay riots of late 1992 and early 1993 in which the police openly sided with the criminals on the rampage led by Shiv Sena, a staunch BJP ally. Reaction to the Babari demolition and the blatantly open police collusion with the rioters led a few Muslim youths with underworld support to cause the Bombay blasts in March 1993. While the rioters, including the accused policemen and Shiv Sena leaders, have been let off one after another, those accused of the blasts, many innocents, are still languishing in jails under the draconian TADA law and the Indian state is still busy hunting potential bombers all over the world.

The Congress Party's long-standing pro-Temple policy was brought to its logical conclusion when the Rao government allowed the demolition of the Babari on December 6, 1992 and chose to intervene only after a makeshift temple had already been erected on the site, 40 hours after the demolition. But in public Rao shed crocodile tears and said what has been demolished will be rebuilt. A few months later his home minister claimed that Rao had never said that the mosque would be rebuilt "at the same spot." The Supreme Court of India frustrated the Rao government's attempts in 1994 to obtain a judicial sanction to build the proposed grand temple at the site of the demolished mosque.

The VHP has also launched a campaign to capture the Gyanvapi and Idgah mosques at Varanasi and Mathura, respectively. These (with the Babari) are the first three on its list of 3000 mosques that the outfit claims had been built on the sites of demolished temples.

The BJP uses the VHP and other RSS affiliates to arouse Hindus since under Indian electoral law it will be banned should it openly raise communal, religious, and divisive issues. This is why the VHP has been in the forefront of the Rama Temple campaign, while the BJP reaps the political dividends. It is a neat division of labor. Whenever the BJP is in trouble or elections approach, the VHP raises the pitch over the Temple issue.

The Hindutva plank steadily raised the political fortunes of the BJP whose electoral share by 1991 rose to 21 percent. In the 1998 elections the BJP managed to capture 179 seats of the Lok Sabha, the elected house of the Indian parliament. Its strength in parliament rose to 182 in the next year's general elections. This allowed it to form a broad coalition which ruled at the Center, under the name of the National Democratic Alliance (NDA), from 1999 to 2004. The NDA was voted out in the elections held in May 2004 when the BJP on its own could win only 138 seats out of parliament's 543 elected seats. Scandals, pro-rich policies, Gujarat riots of 2002, and insulting slogans like "India Shining" and "Feel Good" ruined the BJP. It had tried badly during the elections to woo Muslims but after the defeat it has gone back to reaffirm its belief in Hindutva, saying that distancing from the Hindutva plank drove away its traditional supporters. To its traditional supporters, the BJP while in government failed in all its sentimental promises to the Hindu masses: it could not build the Rama Temple on the Babari Mosque site; it failed to introduce a uniform civil code; and it could not abolish the Indian Constitution's Article 370 which guarantees autonomy to the Indian part of Kashmir.

The Congress Party, for all its secular pretensions, always followed a soft Hindutva line, especially since Indira Gandhi's second coming in 1979. But with the advent of the BJP's real or hard Hindutva, the Congress Party's "soft" Hindutva was doomed. Muslims had forsaken the Congress en masse after the Babari demolition in 1992. As a result, the Congress lost power at the Center as well as in many states traditionally ruled by it. It is only during the last few years that the Congress has started to regain momentum. Muslims have come to forgive the Congress and now treat it as the lesser evil compared to the BJP. The Congress had perfected an electoral formula of using Muslims, Dalits, tribals, and rural communities as its vote bank. Muslims voted for the Congress in many constituencies during the May 2004 polls as a result of their real-ization that they must play an active role in preventing the onward march of the BJP which did a lot of harm during its rule, especially by introducing school textbooks which were "saffronized", i.e., given a Hindu color. The new government is reversing this process.

Although a creation of the RSS, the BJP's relations with the parent body during the 1980–88 period were frosty as it was found wanting in its enthusiasm for Hindu causes and interests. The RSS preferred to support the Congress instead in the elections of 1984 (when the BJP came a cropper with only two seats in parliament). The BJP–RSS relationship is undergoing a similar strain at present. RSS and VHP leaders on a number of occasions have hinted at the possibility of supporting the Congress for better and surer results. The BJP's policy of wooing Muslim voters (that very same "minorityism" and "appeasement" it blamed others of all these years) during the May 2004 elections did not go down well in RSS and VHP circles. Both have blamed the BJP's policy of neglecting Hindu interests as the main reason for its debacle in these elections while most BJP leaders as well as all its NDA allies have said that the Gujarat riots did not help its cause. After the May 2004 elections the VHP threatened to float a new political party which would be faithful to Hindu interests.

Growth of Communal Politics since Independence

The post-Independence era witnessed a steady growth of the Hindu communal ideology taking the form of numerous Hindu hard-line organizations using various political and cultural masks. The RSS floated the political party, Jan Sangh (or Bharatiya Jan Sangh), in October 1951. The RSS found it necessary to have a political platform to carry out its agenda in the political field.

On August 29, 1964, the RSS chief M.S. Golwalkar set up the Vishwa Hindu Parishad (VHP) in Mumbai. On May 1, 1977, the Jan Sangh dissolved itself to merge with the Janata Party. On April 5, 1980, the Jan Sangh was revived as "Bharatiya Janata Party" (Indian People's Party – BJP). In April 1984, the VHP passed a resolution calling for the liberation of the Babari Mosque site at Ayodhya. As a result, Sri Rama Janamabhoomi Mukti Yagna Samiti was founded on July 24, 1984. On September 25 of the same year this Samiti set out on a *yatra* from Sitamarhi (the birthplace of Lord Rama's wife Sita) in Bihar and reached Ayodhya on October 6, 1984. In 1989, Bajrang Dal held a *Bajrang Bhakti Diksha Samaroh*, a training program, for 6000 volunteers to prepare them for a fight that lay ahead. During the Advani-led *Rath yatra* to Ayodhya to "liberate" Rama's birthplace in September–October 1990, Bajrang Dal activists accompanied the *Rath yatra*. It was Bajrang Dal that was in the forefront of the attack on the Babari Mosque on October 30, 1990 and again during its demolition on December 6, 1992.

In 2001, Bajrang Dal organized open camps for arms training, including firearms, to its cadres in Lucknow and other areas of Uttar Pradesh. No restrictions were imposed on such training by the state's BJP-led government. The organizers of these training camps claimed that it is for the "defense of *Bharat Mata*" against the "Muslim threat." These arms training camps became more active and open during the BJP-led government at the Center and are still continuing in the states of Uttar Pradesh, Madhya Pradesh, and Gujarat even after the downfall of the BJP-led government at the Center in May 2004.

Hindutva outfits, known as the Sangh Parivar (the RSS family), function in a loose affiliation with the mother organization. They sprouted from the RSS for specialized work in various fields, like students (Akhil Bharatiya Vidhyarti Parishad (ABVP – est. 1949), farmers (Bharatiya Kisen Sangh, est. 1979), tribals (Vanvasi Kalyan Ashram, est. 1952), labor (Bharatiya Mazdoor Sangh, est. 1955), politics (Bharatiya Janata Party, est. April 1980 in the place of the erstwhile Jana Sangh which was established for the same purpose in October 1951 and still survives as an extremist fringe outfit), Vishwa Hindu Parishad (World Hindu Council, est. 1964 to unite Hindus culturally all over the world), Bajrang Dal and Durga Vahini (est. 1984, the former as the VHP's male youth militia and the latter as its women's wing), Dharam Sansad (religious parliament – a *sadhus* wing – est. 1984, in place of Sadhu Sansad), ex-servicemen (Yurosainik Sewa Parishad, est. 1992), history writing (Bharatiya Itihas Sanghtan, est. 1973 – Vidya

Bharati to run schools and prepare textbooks, and so on).[17] See Figure 29.1 for RSS family map.

On the cultural and religious fronts the flag of Hindutva is carried by the VHP which came into the limelight in 1982 after the Meenakshipuram conversions of Dalits to Islam. In recent years it has made exaggerated claims to have reconverted hundreds of thousands of Muslims to Hinduism in Rajasthan state.

One of the Hindu revivalist movement's significant feats was the creation of the Dharam Sansad (religious parliament) in 1984 at Udupi in Karnataka, to guide the VHP and in effect usurp the religious leadership of Hindus. It consists of about 900 representatives of just about every Hindu sect and order including Sikhs. There is considerable opposition to these efforts by the established Hindu clergy. Sadhu Samaj, for instance, is openly opposed to the VHP. Religious leaders in Ayodhya itself are now sharply opposed to the VHP. In addition to this there are a number of militias, or self-defense groups, particularly in Uttar Pradesh and Gujarat, consisting mainly of unemployed youth and small-time shopkeepers. *Trishul*, or Shiva's trident, is the symbol of these militant groups which participate in muscle-flexing events and communal riots, which occur routinely wherever the VHP is active, killing Muslims and destroying their properties, especially since the issue of Rama Temple at the site of the Babari Mosque was raised in the early 1980s. A hot favorite with the VHP has been the following slogan: "*Musalmanon kay do hi asthan, Pakistan ya qabristan*" (there are only two abodes for Muslims: Pakistan or a graveyard). The authorities have yet to take any action against these venomous and murderous slogans, which constitute a clear offence under section 153 of the Indian penal code.

While the majority of Hindus (like their Muslim neighbors) are illiterate, live below the poverty line, and suffer from centuries-old meaningless social customs and rituals, Hindutva organizations do not fight for real issues like poverty, untouchability, illiteracy, criminalization of politics, rampant crime (especially against Hindu women), corruption, hoarding of essential commodities (by their *Banya* [trader class] backers, in order to raise prices), and black money etc. Instead, they prefer to raise emotional issues and imaginary dangers from a persecuted and demoralized minority. The message hammered home to the illiterate Hindu masses is that for too long the minorities (Muslims and Christians and even Sikhs now) have been appeased and pampered while the majority is restrained from asserting the only basis for unifying the country – Hindu culture and nationalism.

Appeasement

One of the major planks of Hindutva is the issue of "appeasement" of minorities, which in effect means Muslims who according to all available data now stand on the lowest rung of Indian society.[18] Recommendations of the Gopal Singh Commission, appointed by Indira Gandhi in 1981, to probe the plight of the minorities, are gathering dust in the Home Ministry together with umpteen reports of commissions of inquiry on anti-Muslim riots. Similarly, no action has ever been taken on National Commission of Minorities' annual reports. Indira Gandhi's much publicized 15-point

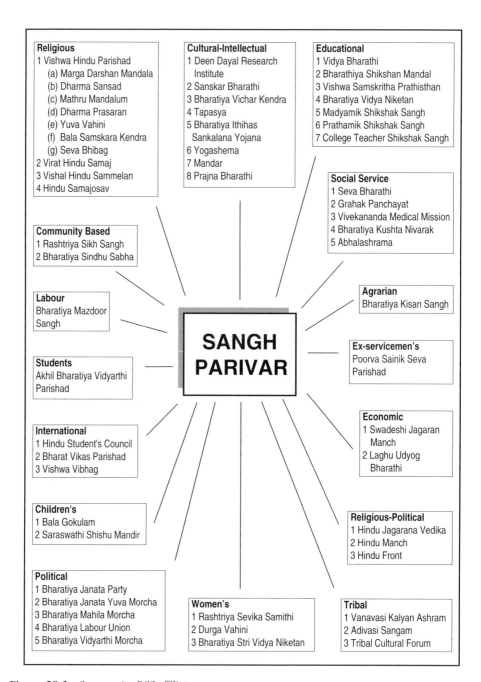

Figure 29.1 Some major RSS affiliates

program for the uplift of the minorities remains on paper. Economically, politically, and educationally, Muslims today are ahead of only the Dalits, according to recent studies, a far cry from their pre-Independence position.

Hindutva forces allege that all successive governments since Independence have "appeased" Muslims and "suppressed" Hindus. The "proof" of appeasement is normally as follows: allowing Muslims to observe their personal laws, special status to Kashmir, travel subsidy for *Hajj* pilgrims, national holiday on Prophet Muhammads birthday and the like.[19] All these are no great concessions. In any case, these "concessions" were offered without any Muslim demand.

Muslims were allowed to observe their personal laws like many other religious and tribal communities, including Hindus, in British India. This tradition was maintained after Independence. Kashmir was given a special status to keep it within India and ward off Pakistani claims but this special status has long been eroded and Kashmir, despite its special status, remains the most interfered with and neglected state in the Union of India. *Hajj* subsidy was introduced around 1974 when, after the first oil crisis, pilgrimage by ships was discontinued. The government undertook to pay the difference in the fare at that time. Muslims have said time and again that the government may stop it. Continuation of the *Hajj* subsidy is not a universal Muslim demand. The national holiday of the Prophet's birthday was not a Muslim demand. It was a unilateral sop announced by Prime Minister V.P. Singh on August 15, 1990.

Nehru had a vision of positive discrimination in favor of minorities. Later rulers, especially the Hindutva brand, reversed this policy. India maintains a policy of positive discrimination in favor of (Hindu) Dalits, and other classes including tribals, for political reasons: to keep them within the Hindu fold and to mitigate its own sense of guilt for treating these people as sub-humans for thousands of years. But the special benefits offered to keep the Dalits within the Hindu fold, like reservation in jobs and education, are withdrawn the moment one of them converts to Islam or Christianity. Needless to say, these religion-based benefits fly in the face of the spirit of secularism, human rights, and equality.

Hindus enjoy special income tax laws where the earning member(s) income is spread over all the family members under what is known as "Hindu Undivided Family" (HUF), which effectively lowers the tax liability and in effect deprives the exchequer of trillions of rupees every year. Non-Hindus are assessed individually. Hindu communities and tribals in various areas are governed by their own customary personal laws.

Fanatic groups, which benefit from Hindu–Muslim discord, keep finding non-issues in order to alienate Muslims and create their own Hindu vote bank. Cow-slaughter, Aligarh Muslim University's "minority character" (abolished in 1965 and restored in 1981 after sustained Muslim agitation), Shah Bano and "common civil code," Babari and other mosques alleged to have been built on temple sites, the status of Kashmir, Triple Ṭalāq, polygamy, terms like *kāfir* and *jihād*, and out-of-context quotations from the Qur'an have been exploited for this purpose. The aim is to keep Muslims forever on the defensive, in order to blackmail them and to divert their attention from their real problems.

Hard-line communal groups also constantly raise the issues of "conversions," "assault on Hindu religion and culture," "foreign conspiracy to destabilize India," that

Christian and Muslims are "invaders," "looters," "foreigners," "anti-India," "pro-Pakistani," and "unpatriotic." Muslims marrying Hindu women are accused of "kidnapping" them. According to the communalists such people should not remain in India, and if they did they must constantly prove their patriotism and adopt and follow the Hindu way of life.[20]

Communal Riots

Communal conflict is a daily affair in India. Demoralization and economic ruin of Muslims and the polarization of Hindu voters in favor of certain forces are the main aims of this ongoing saga in which even the police and state machinery sometimes play a role. Alleged cow slaughter, offensive passage of Hindu religious processions through Muslim localities, playing music before a mosque during prayers, desecration and burning of Muslim religious texts, defamation of Muslim personalities, marriage of a Muslim with a Hindu woman and the like are often the causes for riots which are engineered on purpose by political beneficiaries.[21] Venomous rumors are floated, which are liberally reproduced in the non-English media, and soon an area burns. The media, especially the non-English press, plays a key role in disseminating false or exaggerated reports and keeping the communal passions alive. This is crucial since Muslims are seriously under-represented in the national media.

There has been a history of Hindu–Muslim riots since the beginning of the twentieth century under the British rule, which perfected divide-and-rule techniques and at times even caused communal riots. In 1947 millions perished on both sides of the India–Pakistan borders during the Partition riots. Communal riots again became a fact of daily life since 1961. Some landmarks are Nellie (1983), Bhagalpur (1989), Hashimpura and Maliana (1989), Bombay (1992–3), and Gujarat (2002).

The Rama Temple agitation led to the eruption of many communal riots all over India in 1990 and again after the Mosque's demolition in December 1992. Gujarat riots of 2002 were instigated and abetted by the BJP government of the state after the burning of a railway coach at Godhra on February 27, 2002. This incident, which still remains an enigma, was blamed on Muslims and immediately pogroms were ignited in many parts of the western state of Gujarat for close to two months. According to various estimates between 2000–5000 Muslims were brutally killed, often burnt alive, women raped, their abdomens slit, children thrown into burning fire, and over 200,000 people were made refugees in their own homeland. State chief minister Modi received the support of the BJP's central leadership and remains in power without any sign of remorse. Some victims of Gujarat pogroms still live in temporary shelters, unable to return to their homes in villages which have been declared "Muslim-free" and sport signboards of "Hindu *Rashtra*."[22]

Christians and their institutions have been increasingly attacked since the rise in the early 1990s of the political fortunes of the BJP. During the last decade, attacks on churches, Christian institutions, homes, and nuns have been reported from various parts of India, especially in Gujarat and Madhya Pradesh. Among the most gruesome attacks was the brutal killing of the Australian missionary Graham Stuart Staines and his two young children, Philip and Timothy, in Manoharpur, Baripada, Orissa on January 23, 1999 by VHP elements. On September 22, 2003, Dara Singh, a VHP leader, was sentenced to death while 12 of his accomplices were awarded life imprisonment by a court in Orissa. No such sentence, however, has ever been awarded in anti-Muslim riot cases.

Terrorism

Like elsewhere since September 11, Hindu organizations in India, led by the BJP and VHP, lapped up the "terrorism" plank and tried hard to insinuate that Muslims in India are involved in terrorism, that *madrasahs* and mosques are dens of terrorists and storehouses of arms, that Muslim areas shelter terrorists and Pakistan military intelligence (ISI) agents and the like. But to date these people, despite ruling at the Center for more than five and a half years, have failed to substantiate their vague claims or to pinpoint which particular *madrasah* and Muslim locality is a "den of terrorism." They have failed to discover arms or arms training in any of India's ca. 35,000 *madrasahs*.[23]

There is no proof whatsoever that any Indian Muslim ever went to fight in Bosnia or Chechnya or even in Kashmir within India where one does not require a passport or visa. Top police officials in India have time and again refuted these allegations but somehow the Hindutva people and their sympathizers in the media keep repeating them, always using carefully crafted vague language. Former Deputy Prime Minister Advani, who was also the home minister, failed to publish his much-promised white paper on *madrasahs* and terrorism in India. Senior US State Department official Richard Haas came to India late in October 2002. On his return he said that there is no proof that Indian Muslims are involved in terrorism.[24]

Islam's problem with Hindutva is basic, going to the core as Islam refused to bend and adapt to Hinduism. According to Professor Ashok Rudra of Mumbai University, "Hinduism has been tolerant only of such other ways of life and systems of thought and values which consented to let themselves be Hinduized" and "Sanskritised" in their fundamentals. Rudra adds that the reason for the hatred of Muslims is precisely because Islam has not consented to be Hinduized in its fundamentals. According to him,

> The underlying reason for this 700 years of history of hatred and intolerance lies in the failure of Brahminism to swallow up Islam in India. If Islam would have accepted, Brahminism would have gladly extended to it the honor of being one more Hindu sect.[25]

Indian Muslims' attachment to their faith is very strong but their attachment to their homeland is strong too. They helped create a beautiful and distinct "Ganga–Jamuni" civilization which is distinctly Indian and shares little with the Arab or Persian cultures. They have innovated many arts and crafts over the centuries and these are now part and parcel of the Indian civilization and culture. Indian Muslims have even invented a mythology to prove their ancient roots in India. But all this is not enough for Hindutva zealots who continue raising the stakes and finding new non-issues to keep Muslims away from the national mainstream.

Acknowledgments

The author would like to thank Professor Shamsul Islam of Satyawati College, Delhi University, who went through the manuscript and offered valuable suggestions. Figure 29.1 is adapted from "RSS tree" in Parvathy Appaiah, *Hindutva – Ideology and Politics* (Delhi: Deep & Deep, 2003), 108.

Notes

1. Vinod Mehta, one of India's prominent journalists, wrote at the height of the VHP propaganda: "Make no mistake, despite all the propaganda purveyed through audio cassettes, Hindu rule in India is total and absolute. They are the unchallenged masters of the nation's political, economic and military might . . . Hindus dominate not only because they constitute over 80 percent of the population, but because they have securely in their grasp all the instruments that help rule a sovereign state. So who is oppressed and who the oppressor . . . Muslims of India have been reduced to second-class citizens . . . they are never going to be a threat to those who have the commanding heights of the state firmly in their hands. . . . Hindus have nothing to fear but the myths fostered by Hindus about themselves" (*Sunday* Magazine, Calcutta, December 16, 1990 – reproduced in *Muslim and Arab Perspectives*, 2(4–7), 1995, 136f).

2. See for an account: Mumtaz Ali Khan, *Mass Conversion of Meenakshipuram: A Sociological Enquiry* (Madras: Christian Literature Society, 1983).

3. During its rule at the Center (1999–2004), the BJP tried and failed to muster enough support to pass a federal law to ban conversions, but the AIDMK government (a BJP ally at the time) in Tamil Nadu passed a law in October 2002 banning conversions, the BJP government in Gujarat followed suit in March 2003 (see the text of the Tamil Nadu law in *Muslim India*, 21(11), 2003, 1038f.). After the poll debacle the AIDMK government in Tamil Nadu hastily abrogated this controversial law in May 2004.

4. See H.M. Seervai, *Partition of India: Legend and Reality* (Mumbai: N.M. Tripathi, 1994). New Hindutva line negates the Aryan theory in view of the recent political upsurge of Dalits and backward classes who claim to be the true sons of soil and regard Aryans as invaders. R.C. Majumdar, who is regarded as the only true Hindu historian by the RSS, admitted that the nineteenth-century Hindu leaders from Bengal, like Nabha Gopal Mitra, "forstalled Jinnah's theory of two nations by more than half a century," R.C. Majumdar, *Three Phases of India's Struggle for Freedom* (Mumbai: Bhartiya Vidya Bhavan, 1961), 8.

5. See http://pd.cpim.org/2003/0302/03022003_savarkar.htm

6. See http://pd.cpim.org/2004/0411/04112004_Vajpayee-1.htm / http://pd.cpim.org/2004/0411/04112004_Vajpayee-2.htm

7. *We Or Our Nationhood Defined*, published by Bharat Publications (Nagpur, 1939) is not available in its original form, as subsequent editions have been altered to suit the changing political needs of the RSS. The original will shortly be reprinted by Pharos Media, New Delhi.

8. Vivekananda said this in a letter to a Muslim from Nainital. But he also said, which is often quoted by Hindutva people, in a lecture in April, 1899: "every man going out of the Hindu pale is not only a man less, but an enemy the more" (http://www.ramakrishnavivekananda.info/vivekananda/volume_5/interviews/on_the_bounds_of_hinduism.htm).

9. For more information on this aspect, see Haris Basheer, *Aar Ess Ess- ek mutala'ah* (RSS – A Study, in Urdu) (Delhi: Cosmos, 2003), 171f. Also banned with the RSS were two of its off-shoots, VHP and Bajrang Dal along with two Muslim organizations, Jamaat-e Islami Hind and Islamic Sewak Sangh of Kerala. The two Muslim organizations had nothing to do with the demolition of the Babari Mosque, stoking communalism or instigating riots but they were banned nonetheless in order to strike a "balance" in treatment of "communalists" of both communities. The ban on VHP was renewed for another two years in December 1994 but this remained on paper only while the outfit carried out its normal activities.
10. (Bangalore: Sahitya Sindhu Prakashan, 2000), 177–201.
11. See Haris Basheer, op. cit., 70.
12. During the state elections in 2003, Gujarat chief minister Narendra Modi was repeating in his election speeches that Muslims believe in *"hum paanch, hamarey pachchees"* (we are five [husband plus four wives] and we have 25 [sons and daughters]) but, according to a study of an area in the capital city of Modi's own state, "A recent survey in eight blocks of a Muslim majority area in Ahmedabad revealed that only two people had four wives, two other people had three wives and 279 people had two wives. As opposed to this there were 20,950 cases of 'Maitri Karar' (friendship agreement) registered by Hindus with the collector in this single district. This is a term specific to Gujarat and is essentially a method to bypass the stringent provisions of the Hindu Marriage Act and enter into an "undeclared second marriage" (Anil Chamadia and Subhash Gatade, "Poison Myths," *The Indian Express*, New Delhi, November 5, 2003). According to the findings of the government census of 1961, a survey of polygamous marriages shows the following: polygamous marriages were highest among adivasis, Buddhists, Jains, and Hindus, in that order. Muslims figured last on the list. The National Survey Commission on the Status of Women in India (1975) found that incidence of bigamy and polygamy is higher among Hindus than Muslims. During 1951–61 Hindu polygamous families were 5.06 percent (0.65 percent more than Muslims) while Muslim polygamous families were only 4.31 percent (http://geocities.com/indianfascism/fascism/population_of_minorities.htm).
13. This includes large-scale foreign donations from Hindus settled in the United States and the UK as well as other organizations ostensibly for good purposes but such donations were utilized to further RSS's communal agenda. For some documented reports see: www.stopfundinghate.org / A Foreign Exchange of Hate: www.ektaonline.org/cac/about/.
14. Rajni Kothari in Iqbal A Ansari, ed., *Readings on Minorities* (Delhi: Institute of Objective Studies, 1996), I/36f.
15. *The Statesman*, Delhi, April 3, 1990.
16. Arvind Rajagopal, "The Emergency and the Sangh," *The Hindu*, June 13, 2003.
17. There are many more such outfits designed to take care of and benefit from any possible activity, like teachers, community service, promotion of local industry, research, lawyers, literature, intellectuals, scientists etc. (see Figure 29.1).
18. See Zafarul-Islam Khan, "Muslims in post-independence India," *Muslim India*, 22(2), 2004, 131–40.
19. Even the BJP at times takes "pride" in such appeasement, e.g., BJP president M. Venkaiah Naidu's speech at Rampur (U.P.), included the following:
    – the party favored the construction of a mosque alongside the Rama Temple at Ayodhya;
    – he promised more ministerial berths to the community in lieu of electoral support;
    – he listed the Rs. 120 crore (1200 million) Hajj subsidy and the recently launched Lucknow–Jeddah flight among the achievements of the BJP-led NDA government;
    – the proposed commission on reservation for the economically backward in government jobs, would also benefit the Muslims;

– he had on several occasions visited a *dargah* (tomb of a Muslim saint) and offered prayers. "I myself go to the *dargah* in my native place," he told the rally (Press Trust of India, May 31, 2003). BJP leaders, especially Vajpayee, made many such statements during the election campaigning in 2004.

20. Sebastian Vempney, *Minorities in Contemporary India* (Delhi: Kanishka, 2003), 303.

21. See Paul R Brass, *The Production of Hindu–Muslim violence in Contemporary India* (Delhi: Oxford University Press, 2003); Vibhuti Narain Rai, *Combating Communal Conflicts: Perception of Police Neutrality during Hindu–Muslim Riots in India* (New Delhi: Renaissance, 1998). According to a "White Paper" published by the All India Milli Council and other organizations on the eve of the May 2004 elections, 731 "major" communal riots took place in India during the first five years of the BJP-led National Democratic Alliance rule during 1998–2002, in which 1570 persons were killed and 4908 persons were injured (full text in *Muslim India*, 2(4–5), 2004, 411–17).

22. Some books on the Gujarat pogroms of 2002 include: "Gujarat", in *The Making of a Tragedy*, ed., Siddharth Varadarajan (New Delhi: Penguin, 2002); M.L. Sondhi *et al.*, eds., *The Black Book of Gujarat* (New Delhi: Manak Publications, 2002); John Dayal (ed.), *Gujarat 2000: Untold and Re-told stories of Hindutva Lab* (Delhi: Justice & Peace Commission and All India Christian Council, 2002); Concerned Citizens Tribunal, *Gujarat 2002: An Inquiry into the Carnage in Gujarat Report: Crime against Humanity* (Mumbai: Citizens for Justice & Peace, 2002); PUCL, *"Maaro! kaapo! baalo!": State, Society, and Communalism in Gujarat* (Delhi: People's Union for Democratic Rights, 2002); CPIM, *State Sponsored Genocide: Factsheet Gujarat 2002: Official Reports* (New Delhi: Communist Party of India (Marxist), 2002); Ram Nath Sharma, *Gujarat Holocaust: Communalism in the Land of Gandhi* (New Delhi: Shubhi Publications, 2002); Rafiq Zakaria, *Communal Rage in Secular India* (Mumbai: Popular Prakashan, 2002).

23. For details, see Zafarul-Islam Khan, "Madrasahs: Seats of Learning or Dens of Terrorism," *Muslim India*, 22(1), 2004, 6–10.

24. When Haas visited India, he made it a point to meet a cross-section of Indian Muslim leaders, because Indian Muslims are the second largest Muslim population in the world. He said later that none of them is a member of Al-Qaeda or its affiliates. "I asked the leaders why this was so," Haas said, "and they said we live in a secular democracy. When we have problems we have alternatives to terrorism" (*Hindustan Times*, January 1, 2003, http://www.hindustantimes.com/news/181_129067,0030.htm).

25. Vempeny, op. cit., 305.

CHAPTER 30

Political Discourse of the Organization of the Islamic Conference

Abdullah al-Ahsan

The Organization of the Islamic Conference (OIC) is an international organization and serves as a political platform incorporating most Muslims in the world today. One unique characteristic of the OIC is that it is based on a religious identity while other international governmental organizations are based on regional, ethnic, or ideological identities. This unique characteristic places the Muslim society in general and the OIC in particular in a very critical situation. This identity crisis has occurred because of the conflict between the traditional Muslim identity and the newly emerged nation-state identity in the modern world. The main goal of this chapter is to analyze the OIC's political ideas and how they have impacted on the contemporary political discourse.

The decision to establish the OIC was made at a summit conference of Muslim-majority nation-states in September 1969 when an arson attack on al-Aqsa mosque in Jerusalem by a Zionist activist caused angry reaction among Muslims throughout the world. These leaders were also aware of the emotional attachment of their people to the idea of Muslim unity and the huge potential of their cooperative achievements. As a result they extended the scope and objectives of OIC activities to economic, cultural, and legal developments in their countries. This chapter investigates the cooperative achievements of the OIC since its inception more than three decades ago.

Since the OIC was established in connection with an event in Palestine, it has always considered the Palestinian issue as one of its fundamental objectives to resolve. However, the OIC has also adopted numerous other resolutions on cooperation among its member states. These resolutions reflect the general intellectual trend, popular demands, and the political dynamics of these countries. That is why we shall briefly evaluate those resolutions to understand the current state of affairs in Muslim countries. However, we shall first briefly describe the political situation in the Muslim world in the latter half of the twentieth century in order to understand the historical context of this political institution.

The Muslim World in the Latter Half of the Twentieth Century

To a great extent European colonial penetrations have shaped the history and geography of the Muslim world today. In response to early colonial invasions Muslims fought *jihād* against Europeans, but by the middle of the nineteenth century many Muslim statesmen realized that the Muslim community or the *ummah* was much weaker than the Europeans. They became convinced that the Muslim civilization had not only declined, but that it wouldn't survive without gaining substantial knowledge from Europe. Muslim leaders encouraged their co-religionists to join European educational institutions by identifying positive values of Islamic civilization with those of the European civilization.[1] Gradually Muslims adopted the European idea of nationalism, and by the middle of the twentieth century many independent and sovereign Muslim nation-states emerged in the world map. In the process Muslims developed an identity crisis.[2] Traditionally Muslims have recognized the existence of different nationalities within the *ummah*, but only as a secondary identity. After gaining independence, however, they realized that they were legally separated from their fellow Muslims. Although political division existed within the Muslim *ummah* before European penetration, those divisions had little effect in the life of individual common Muslims. They generally could travel and work, conduct business, and pursue education in any part of the Muslim world without restriction. Most important of all, they generally followed Islamic law wherever they lived. All these aspects of the Muslim life were now affected under the new nation-state system.

Independent and sovereign Muslim nation-states in the latter half of the twentieth century soon developed conflict between Islamic and European ideas. One Turkish historian describes this conflict as:

> It is in the field of constitutional law that the major problems have arisen. Where is the foundation of legitimacy in a Muslim state? The Qur'an? Or the people? Who is the sovereign? The people or God? And who is to interpret this sovereign? Legislative assemblies somehow elected? Or the *ulama* who have traditionally interpreted the body of Islamic teachings?[3]

In the context of Pakistan one Orientalist observed:

> What is Islam? If Islam were but a religion, the Hindus and Christians of Pakistan would simply be religious minorities. But if Islam is not only a religious or political unity, but an ideology, a religious or a political ideology or both in one, the position of a religious minority must be different. . . . How can a Hindu accept an Islamic ideology? If he cannot subscribe to it what will be his position as citizen?[4]

But who would answer to these questions? The political elite were confused about the role of Islamic ideas in politics.[5] The political elite were not interested in any discussion with the intellectuals and community members about the future directions of their countries. In Turkey the Islamic ideas were constitutionally banned; in Pakistan President Iskandar Ali Khan Mirza warned the "*ulama* to keep out of politics."[6] As a result a wide gap was created between the nationalist oriented elite and the religious oriented people in most Muslim countries. A wide gap was also created between the newly educated Muslim youth and the Muslim nationalist foundations of the state in most countries. A veteran Pakistani educationalist observed:

> It was the Pakistan Movement that weaned most [Muslim youth] from Indian nationalism and some from Marxist materialism. The enthusiasm for Pakistan created the feeling that all was well with the Muslim youth. Even earlier that was the general sentiment. A generation that had pursued the aim of economic welfare through the acquisition of the new education and had remained Muslim in sentiment because of tradition and the influence of its parents and homes thought that what had happened to it would happen to its children as well, forgetting that the Islamic influence grew more and more diluted because of the ever increasing impact of new influences percolating through literature and amoral and religiously neutral education. The nature of the education was such that the potentially positive influence that could have been exerted in favor of the Islamic code of morals and beliefs was eliminated and the subtle European suggestions conveyed through literature and text-books were permitted to play their role unhindered.[7]

This is not to suggest that all Muslim nation-states had similar orientation following their independence in the second half of the twentieth century, but they generally lacked the culture of public discussion on the relationship between Islamic and Western ideas. Although prior to independence Islamic ideas played a very significant role in the formation of the idea of nationalism, the nationalist elite refused to accommodate Islamic ideas in the growth of new independent and sovereign Muslim nations.

To complicate the growth of the newly established nation-states the armed forces began to intervene in politics. Egypt witnessed a military coup in 1952, and began to influence the neighboring countries against the traditional monarchs, mostly installed earlier by the colonial administrations. In response to Egyptian attempts to forge Arab unity the Saudis began to advocate for Islamic unity to face the realities of the increasing number of military coups in the Arab world. It is in this context that the OIC was established. The increasing aggression by Israel – first its establishment in 1948 against the will of the local population, then the wars of 1956 and 1967 – convinced more and more Muslims that the only alternative to counter Israeli threat was to achieve Muslim unity, and the OIC was expected to attain this goal.

Origin of the OIC

One may trace the ideas related to the origin of the OIC in the early 1920s when the Turkish Grand National Assembly abolished the institution of the *khilāfah*, and a number of conferences were held in different parts of the Muslim world to discuss the future direction of the *ummah*.[8] But because of the fact that most parts of the Muslim world were still under European colonial occupation, the idea of Muslim political unity of Muslims remained only in the minds of Muslim thinkers, scholars, and activists. The idea was renewed when a number of Muslim countries emerged as sovereign states following the Second World War with an initiative by Pakistan. Conferences were held but with little success in establishing a political platform incorporating Muslims all over the world. Then in the 1950s, faced with the challenge of Arab nationalism led by Egypt, some traditional monarchies in the Arab world such as Saudi Arabia, Jordan, and Morocco, attempted to establish an institution based on the Islamic idea of the *ummah*. But it was not until 1969 that the idea of establishing a political institution combining Muslims all over the world succeeded.

On August 21, 1969 an arson attack on al-Aqsa mosque in Jerusalem under Israeli occupation angered Muslims all over the world. By then because of the defeat by Israel in 1967 the idea of Arab nationalism became weak. On the invitation of the Moroccan king an Islamic summit conference was held in Rabat which declared that, "Muslim governments would consult with a view to promoting between themselves close cooperation and mutual assistance in the economic, scientific, cultural and spiritual fields, inspired by the immortal teachings of Islam."[9] A formal institution, the Organization of the Islamic Conference (OIC) combining most Muslim-majority nation-states, was established. Leaders also declared that:

> Strict adherence to Islam and to Islamic principles and values as a way of life constitutes the highest protection for Muslims against the dangers which confront them. Islam is the only path which can lead them to strength, dignity and prosperity and a better future. It is the pledge and guarantee of the authenticity of the Ummah safeguarding it from the tyrannical onrush of materialism. It is the powerful stimulant for both leaders and peoples in their struggle to liberate their Holy Places and to regain their rightful place in the world so that they may, in concert with other nations, strive for the establishment of equality, peace and prosperity for the whole [of] mankind. . . . It is our conviction that the Ummah of 1000 million people, composed of various races, spread over vast areas of the globe and possessing enormous resources, fortified by its spiritual power and utilizing to the full its human and material potential, can achieve an outstanding position in the world and ensure for itself the means of prosperity in order to bring about a better equilibrium for the benefit of all mankind.[10]

In the Preamble of its Charter the OIC stated that, "Their [member states] common belief constitutes a strong factor for rapprochement and solidarity between Muslim people." In the emblem of the OIC appears the Qur'anic verse "Hold fast the bond of Allah and don't divide" (3:103). These references to common belief raise a fundamental question about the foundation of the OIC: What is the status of a non-Muslim citizen of a member country? The complementary question may also be cited: What is the status of a Muslim citizen of a non-member country in the view of the OIC? It does not appear from its declarations and resolutions that the OIC has taken any definite position on this issue. This has created practical problems for the OIC; a few instances may be mentioned here. At the Third Islamic Summit Conference (1981), the inaugural session was held inside the Ka'bah in Mecca where no non-Muslim is allowed to enter. The Lebanese president, who according to Lebanese National Pact must be a Christian, therefore could not attend the function. In contrast, the Islamic Foundation for Science, Technology and Development (IFSTAD), one of the many subsidiary organs of the OIC, defines Muslim talent, in its study of brain drain from member countries, as "the Muslim and non-Muslim citizens of member states as well as the Muslims of the minority Muslim communities in non-member developing countries."[11] As for employment within the OIC system, the OIC maintains an unwritten understanding that only

Muslim citizens from member countries are eligible for its jobs. The Islamic Development Bank (IDB), an affiliated organ of the OIC, on the other hand, employs Muslims from non-member countries also.

The primary members of the OIC are nation-states, not individuals. The question arises as to what is the primary basis of the *ummah*. In the classical Islamic context the formation of the question would be whether individuals or tribes formed the primary basis of the Muslim community. Obviously when the Islamic *ummah* was first established, individuals constituted the primary basis of the community, although the individual retained his tribal identity. But his/her life now was guided by Qur'anic teachings and values, rather than tribal customs. In the context of the OIC the member states are as sovereign as were the tribes during the early days of Islam.

According to Article Eight of the Charter, every Muslim state is eligible to join the Islamic Conference upon submission of an application expressing its desire and preparedness to adopt this Charter. The Charter does not define what it means by "Muslim state," but it appears from OIC publications and lectures delivered at OIC meetings that the term means "a nation-state where Muslims constitute a majority of the population." In practice, however, the OIC has not followed any consistent policy concerning what it calls a Muslim state. In 1969, during the preparations for the First Islamic Summit Conference in Rabat, for example, India, a nation-state with a Hindu majority, filed an application to become a member of the new organization. India argued that it had a sizable number of Muslims, and that population should be represented in the forum. This argument was rejected by the preparatory committee of the Summit Conference. But an Indian appeal requesting representation of Indian Muslims was later accepted by the Summit Conference itself; the meeting was obviously under way when the decision was made. India decided to send a delegation headed by a Muslim minister at the federal government. The Indian government also instructed its ambassador to Morocco, a Sikh, to represent India at the Summit Conference during the time that the delegation needed to arrive from New Delhi. When the president of Pakistan, leading the Pakistani delegation, noted a non-Muslim was supposedly representing Indian Muslims, he declined to participate at the Summit. The Pakistani president argued that, at a time when Indian Muslims were being massacred in India by the Hindu majority (an anti-Muslim communal riot was going on in the Indian city Ahmadabad at that time,) he could not participate at the Summit with a representative of the Indian government. Moreover, membership was granted to Indian Muslims not to the Indian government, he argued. In order to accommodate Pakistan's protest India's brief membership in the organization was cancelled.

On the other hand, the OIC has accepted the membership of Uganda, although the majority of its population is not Muslim. Uganda applied and was admitted to the Organization in 1974, during the Second Summit Conference, apparently because Uganda at that time had a Muslim president. But Uganda is still a regular member of the OIC although its president is no longer a Muslim. In the 1990s the South American country Suriname and the African country Togo became regular members of the OIC even though these countries do not have Muslim-majority population. Muslim-majority Tanzania, on the other hand, never applied to be a member of the OIC, although its island partner Zanzibar tried membership of the Organization independently.

The Charter mentions in the Preamble that its member states "reaffirm their commitment to the UN Charter and fundamental human rights, the purposes and principles of which provide the basis for fruitful cooperation amongst all people." It also declares that the participating states resolve "to preserve Islamic spiritual, ethical, social and economic values, which will remain one of the important factors for achieving progress for mankind." Again it may be asked whether or not the UN Declaration of Human Rights and the Islamic value system are congruent. The UN Declaration advocates absolute freedom of choice – will Muslim nations enact laws challenging the Qur'anic values? To be more specific, will Muslim nations legalize sexual relations outside the institution of marriage or will they approve homosexual relations?

In a statement of objectives, the Charter declares the OIC's commitment to "strengthen the struggle of all Muslim peoples with a view to safeguarding their dignity, independence, and national rights." This led to a problem of OIC's relations with countries having Muslim minorities. How could the OIC strengthen the struggle for independence of Muslims in Thailand, the Philippines, Russia, China, or India? Soon the OIC realized this problem and in a resolution it decided to proceed "very carefully to avoid having the Organization of the Islamic Conference accused of interference in the affairs of non-Islamic states, which may have Muslim minorities, and yet be valuable allies in the fight against Zionism and in the pursuance of the other aims of the organization."[12] The statement is somewhat unclear. Does it mean that the OIC could trade off the fate of one group of Muslims for another? For surely a nation-state could adopt an anti-Zionist policy but at the same time persecute its own Muslim minority.

The Charter of the OIC has apparently attempted to reconcile Islamic ideals with late twentieth-century realities. The OIC claims to revive the ideal *ummah* of Islamic history, but it faces the reality of the Muslim world being divided into nation-states, many of whom have adopted and incorporated many ideas from Europe. Such attempts reflect a crisis of the Muslim society. The society has accepted the domination of European ideas but has not abandoned its Islamic ideals. The OIC Charter stands a challenge to constitutions of a number of member countries. Formally declared Islamic states such as Revolutionary Iran, Mauritania, the Comoros, Pakistan, and Saudi Arabia justified the conflicts on the grounds that they have no control on international affairs, and they have submitted to certain secular ideas for the sake of international relations. But the Islamic ideas of the OIC have more seriously challenged constitutionally declared secular republics such as Bangladesh, Indonesia, Lebanon, Turkey, and Tunisia. Bangladesh is committed to secularism as one of its state policies; the Lebanese National Pact demands a Christian serves as president; Indonesia is committed to its *Panjtsila* program, which is based on secularism; and Islamic ideas are constitutionally banned in Turkey and Indonesia from playing any role in politics. These are some of many conceptual problems with strong implications to contemporary Muslim politics and society. In spite of all these problems, however, the OIC has grown. Its membership has grown from an initial 24 to 57 in 2002. Let us now examine achievements of the OIC.

Achievements of the OIC

The OIC has not been able to achieve much in real terms. Its failure is mainly reflected in the current situation in Palestine. Even though the OIC was established in connection with a problem related to the Palestinian crisis, and devoted most of its efforts to supporting the people of Palestine, the condition of the Palestinians has deteriorated to a very alarming level. This in turn has created a dilemma in the Muslim world: A sense of uneasy powerlessness prevails in Muslim society today. However, if one adopts a highly pragmatic view about this situation because of the military weakness of most Muslim countries, and considering the difficulties related to the question of Palestine and highly organized worldwide Zionist lobby supporting Israel, one must agree that achieving any substantial positive result on the issue wouldn't be easy. But has the OIC made any breakthrough in achieving its economic objectives? No. In spite of its awareness of the potential for high comparative advantages, the OIC has barely been able to mobilize its resources to stop further economic deterioration of its member countries. The external debt problem has become one of the fundamental difficulties of economic growth for most OIC countries during the last quarter of the twentieth century. According to the director of statistics and information of the OIC affiliated organ SESRTCIC:

> The external debt of the Islamic countries accumulated rapidly simply because they needed increasing amounts of foreign exchange to pay their ever-growing imports while their earnings from exports of goods and services continuously lagged behind. This created a growing foreign exchange gap, which had to be closed by borrowing larger amounts from abroad. Yet soon the debts thus accumulated created an additional need for foreign resources besides those needed for the growing imports: debt-service payments. With lagging export earnings and substantially exhausted international reserves, the foreign exchange gap grew larger every year and, thus, more had to be borrowed than before.[13]

One way that the OIC countries could avoid being victims of the cycle of increased debt is to attract investment from foreign countries. But why have they failed to attract such investment? According to the same author:

> The impediments to foreign investment in the OIC countries are well known: the small size of the domestic markets and low world market share; inefficiency, lack of transparency and stability of investment policies and regulations; financial and monetary obstacles; lack of infrastructure and the high cost of certain factors of production; economic and political instability; and lack of promotional activities and information on investment opportunities.[14]

Of course these are only some well-known problems of OIC countries; similar observations may be made on many other aspects of OIC activities. What is the solution then? In order for survival most of these countries went begging for assistance to the World Bank and the International Monetary Fund (IMF). The same author further observed:

Faced with the recent downward trends in the inflow of official development assistance, most of the Islamic countries increased their borrowings from private sources, namely commercial banks, on shorter terms and higher costs. Since these funds were borrowed to finance longer-term development projects, debt accumulation accelerated. Their dependence on foreign trade and external borrowing, on the one hand, and their concomitant susceptibility to external developments and disturbances emanating from the developed industrialized counties, on the other, thus grew.[15]

The author thus recommended:

More fundamental action, rather than ad hoc arrangements with a limited optique that aim to buy time, would be needed to turn the side on the debt crisis and bring it to an eventual and lasting solution. There is even a considerable risk that the present policies and arrangements involving rescheduling, with their stringent conditions, might eventually prove counter-productive for the debtor countries, since the original structural defects and other fundamental issues would not only remain untouched, but may even be exacerbated on account of the piecemeal and ad hoc arrangements being applied.[16]

In fact, OIC members do not need to seek assistance from outside sources; they are themselves equipped with adequate resources to improve their economic conditions. According to a leading Pakistani economist:

A firm commitment should be made by the OIC members to enter into some suitable form of economic integration – by eliminating the intra-tariff and non-tariff barriers on the free movement of goods, capital, labour and services and by undertaking joint projects at the regional level – as a means to a faster rate of economic progress. . . . It is only through such a systematic, all-embracing effort that we can meet the grave economic social and political challenges – external and internal – of modern times. The good part is that doing so will simultaneously raise the region's welfare as well as the world's welfare.[17]

This, however, is not the first time that such recommendations have been made to the OIC in order to overcome the problems of ineffectiveness and powerlessness. For a long time the OIC has been discussing problems of economic growth of its member countries. It has discussed the possibility of economic integration, the establishment of an Islamic common market and increased trade among its member countries, created funds to support such activities, established research institutions, and has laid down foundation of numerous organizations to facilitate its activities. Many such recommendations have been noted on various OIC resolutions and papers. Yet its affiliated organ, the Islamic Development Bank (IDB), has reported that intra-OIC trade has not gone beyond 10 percent of individual member counties during the past 10 years. One main reason for the failure of the OIC in achieving substantial progress in economic cooperation among member countries is the lack of commitment in achieving such growth on the part of the capital-rich member countries. They seem to be interested only in cheap slogans for unity of the *ummah* for consumption of common Muslims.

The failure of the OIC is even more clearly manifested in its role in the current political developments, particularly in connection with Iraq. In the 1980s, during the

Iran–Iraq war, the OIC generally adopted a pro-Iraq stand, apparently because of the influence of oil-rich Arab member countries. In 1990 the OIC clearly took an anti-Iraq stand when the latter attacked Kuwait. The OIC, however, was officially opposed to an attack on Iraq in 2003 by the US/UK-led forces. And yet a number of neighboring countries provided unconditional support to the US-led forces in Iraq. This was done in spite of a number of resolutions that the OIC had adopted on the subject of "Security and Solidarity of Islamic States." In these resolutions the OIC expressed its "deep concern at the threats to security of member states," determined "to vigorously oppose foreign domination, hegemonism (sic.) and spheres of influence, which result in the limitation of the freedom of member states to determine their own political systems and pursue economic, social and cultural development without any coercion, intimidation and pressure from outside," and reaffirmed "the permanent and full sovereignty of the Islamic countries and peoples and all other countries and peoples over their natural resources and economic activities."[18] The OIC leaders seem to adopt such resolutions to express their support for Islam and Muslims all over the world; but in reality they only harm their own legitimacy. This raises the fundamental question whether or not the OIC or any other institution in the Muslim countries could play a significant role in the international political system in the twenty-first century with such a state of affairs.

The OIC and the Current International Political System

Samuel Huntington's thesis of the clash of civilizations has received so much publicity that one can't really afford to ignore him while discussing any issue related to the current international system. Huntington observed about the situation in Muslim countries:

> Beginning in the 1970s, Islamic symbols, beliefs, practices, institutions, policies, and organizations won increasing commitment and support throughout the world of 1 billion Muslims stretching from Morocco to Indonesia and from Nigeria to Kazakhstan. . . . In 1995 every country with predominantly Muslim population, . . . was more Islamic and Islamist culturally, socially and politically than it was fifteen years ago.[19]

In response, "political leaders rushed to identify their regimes and themselves with Islam," observed Huntington. He says:

> King Hussein of Jordan, convinced that secular governments had little future in the Arab world, spoke of the need to create "Islamic democracy" and a "modernizing Islam." King Hassan of Morocco emphasized his descent from the Prophet and his role as "Commander of the faithful." The Sultan of Brunei, not previously noted for Islamic practices, became "increasingly devout" and defined his regime as a "Malay Muslim monarchy." Ben Ali of Tunisia began regularly to invoke Allah in his speeches and "wrapped himself in the mantle of Islam" to check the growing appeal of Islamic groups. In the early 1990s Suharto explicitly adopted a policy of becoming "more Muslim." In Bangladesh the principle of "secularism" was dropped from the constitution in the mid-1970s, and by early

1990s the secular, Kemalist identity of Turkey was, for the first time, coming under serious challenge. To underline their Islamic commitment, governmental leaders – Ozal, Suharto, Karimov – hastened to their *hajh*.[20]

It is interesting to note that Huntington fails to record Saddam Hussain's introduction of the inscription "*Allāhu Akbar*" in Iraq's national flag. He also failed to note that the late Saudi King Fahd ibn Abdul Aziz had adopted the title *Khādim al-Ḥaramain* (custodian of the two sacred mosques) to demonstrate his Islamic commitments.

Huntington seems to approve these superficial and Machiavellian manifestations of "Islamic commitments" by governmental leaders in the Muslim world. For, he doesn't analyze the roles of these leaders for their failures in achieving their stated national goals. He also fails to note that most of the Muslim governments under discussion were considered "moderate" by the US administration and the Western press. It is also interesting to note that Huntington acknowledges the fact that most of these governments failed to address many genuine problems of the common people in their countries. He also recognizes that on many occasions Islamic organizations, banned from participating in politics, filled the vacuum left by the government, and provided health, welfare, educational, and other services to the common people.[21] And yet Huntington concludes that as a result of their (Muslim government's) failures, "conceivably even more intensely anti-Western nationalisms could emerge, blaming the West for the failures of Islam."[22] Huntington does not seem to realize that many Muslim activists believe that most of these Muslim governments wouldn't have survived without the support either of their former colonial masters or of the United States.

The events of September 11, 2001 seem to come in support of Huntington's thesis of the clash of civilizations. He furthered his argument reiterating in an article entitled "The Age of Muslim Wars," that "throughout the Muslim world, . . . there exists a great sense of grievance, resentment, envy and hostility toward the West and its wealth, power and culture."[23] Are the Muslims really envious of the West because the West is wealthier, more powerful and has a superior culture? Muslims would hardly agree with such remarks. This, however, demands some references to the relationship between Islam and the West. This discussion is also related to any future role of the OIC in the international political system in the twenty-first century.

Introducing the discussion on "Islam and West" during the Clinton administration, Huntington suggested that:

Some Westerners, including President Bill Clinton, have argued that the West does not have problems with Islam but only with violent Islamist extremists. Fourteen hundred years of history demonstrate otherwise. The relations between Islam and Christianity, both Orthodox and Western, have often been stormy. Each has been the other's Other.[24]

Huntington's knowledge of history of both Islamic and Western civilization seems very shallow. Anybody with the simple knowledge of the Qur'an and Islamic history knows that the Qur'an does not single out Christians as enemies of Muslims. In fact the Qur'an encouraged friendly relations with Christians, and early Muslims sought refuge with the Christian king of Ethiopia. They also favored the Byzantine Christians in their conflict against the Persians. It is also a well-known fact that the earliest enemies of Islam were the Prophet's own ethnic and linguistic fellow tribesmen – the Qureish. This is not to suggest that Muslim rulers never considered Christians their enemies; rather to suggest that there has not been any specific "other" for Islam. Also it is not true that Muslims were always the "other" either for Orthodox or Western Christians. One should note that the Jews and Christians considered each other enemies before the birth of the Prophet Muhammad. Following the conversion of the Romans to Christianity the Christians persecuted the Jews many times in history. Also at times Orthodox Christians were the "other" of Western Christians who fought Crusades against them. Huntington also suggests that, the "twentieth-century conflict between liberal democracy and Marxist-Leninism is only a fleeting and superficial historical phenomenon compared to the continuing and deeply conflictual relation between Islam and Christianity."[25] But haven't the Western Christians fought among themselves for several centuries in the name of religion, racism, and nationalism? Who fought the Hundred Years War (1337–1453), and the Thirty Years War (1618–48)? Which were the main participating forces in the two devastating world wars of the twentieth century? This is not to suggest that there hasn't been conflict between Muslims and Christians during the last 1400 years of history; rather, this is to argue that Muslims and Christians have not been each other's "Other" as has been suggested by Huntington.

Huntington clearly advocates a perpetual conflict between Islam and Christianity. The Bush administration's policy toward the Muslim world seems to suggest that Huntington has succeeded in his mission to create a clash of civilization scenario in international politics. Commenting on the events of September 11, the late Edward Said rightly pointed out in an article published in the Cairo-based *Al-Ahrām* that, "the carefully planned and horrendous, pathologically motivated suicide attack and mass slaughter by a small group of deranged militants has turned into proof of Huntington's thesis."[26] Politically motivated academicians and journalists are currently pursuing the agenda of the clash of civilizations. Now the question is whether or not the idea of the clash of civilizations is going to dominate international politics in the twenty-first century. One needs to cast a view in history in order to address this question.

What were the general characteristics of conflict between Islam and Western Christendom in history? An in-depth analysis will definitely find mistakes committed by both sides. But many centuries later Catholicism itself has admitted that the Crusaders had not only made mistakes; they also committed major crimes in their wars against Muslims. As for the relationship during the European colonial penetration into the Muslim world, most European historians now acknowledge the inhuman and savage penetration of the European colonizers into Asia and Africa. Huntington's reference to the Muslim "sense of grievance, resentment, envy and hostility toward the West and its wealth" should be viewed in the proper historical context. In fact, if there is any resentment against the West, it is found among all Muslim and non-Muslim victims of European colonization. They are aware of the colonial plunder of their wealth by the colonizers. Describing the British plunder of wealth after the occupation of Muslim Bengal in 1757 one British historian noted that, "men made fortunes, returned to England, lost them and returned to India for more."[27] One should highlight the point here that the conflict between European colonizers and Muslims of Asia and Africa originated during the latter's struggle for freedom and self-determination, and not because of the "wealth, power, and culture" of the former. Therefore, a historian must always examine the nature of the conflict before passing judgments.

The main weakness of Huntington's hypothesis lies in his *Weltanschauung*. Quoting a novelist, whom he calls a Venetian nationalist demagog, he says, "Unless we hate what we are not, we cannot love what we are," Huntington expresses his belief that, "the unfortunate truth in these old truths cannot be ignored by statesmen and scholars."[28] That is why Huntington tries to create a new identity for Western civilization by attempting to identify enemies for, "enemies are essential" for "people seeking identity." Throughout his work, therefore, Huntington identifies mainly Islamic and occasionally Chinese civilization as enemies of Western civilization. But Huntington barely realizes that such attempts can hardly be called civilized behavior. In other words he himself resorts to an uncivilized behavior in order to create a clash of civilizations.

Huntington would like to see the United States identify itself with the Christian tradition of Europe and maintain its domination in world affairs. He at the same time would like Western civilization to subscribe to the fundamental values of the Enlightenment such as freedom, equality, human rights, and human dignity. However, he does not seem to realize that his prescription of the domination of the European races in the US not only contradicts these values; it also contradicts the very principles of the US Constitution. In fact Huntington's interest "to preserve Western civilization in the face of declining Western power" is closer to the social Darwinist view of late nineteenth-century Europe rather than the views of the Enlightenment philosophers, and of the founding fathers of the United States of America. But the current political situation seems to suggest that Huntington has become successful in manipulating the policies of the Bush administration. What will happen to the Muslim world in the political system of the twenty-first century under such circumstances? What will be the fate of the OIC in the twenty-first century? Let us discuss these questions in the concluding segment of this chapter.

Prospects for Muslims in the Twenty-First Century

The Huntingtonian thesis and the events of September 11 have already brought the Muslim world to the center of international politics. But are Muslims ready to play a significant role in the political system of the twenty-first century? Muslim countries would definitely love to have some say in international affairs but are they capable of securing any meaningful position in the international arena? Will the current power brokers allow Muslims a role? Huntington asks his readers to imagine a possible scenario of a "global civilizational war" in which "the United States, Europe, Russia and India . . . become engaged in a truly global struggle against China, Japan, and most of Islam" in the year 2010. Such a conflict may spark and escalate "if aspiring Muslim core states compete to provide assistance to their co-religionists."[29] It is interesting to note that although Huntington conceives China and Japan along with the Muslim world in the opposite camp, he perceives the Muslim world to play the key role in a potential global conflict. In fact in his whole work only Western civilization and

Islamic civilization seem to be at the center, and the rest on the periphery. Now the question is whether Muslims of "core states" will keep quiet in the face of the sufferings of their co-religionists in Palestine, Chechnya, Southern Philippines, or Kashmir? We have already indicated that Muslim governments are already losing legitimacy in the eyes of common Muslims because of their failure to act in support of innocent Muslim victims all over the world. The Iraq war of 2003 is another factor that alienates common Muslims from the ruling elite in the Muslim world for their failure to take a supporting stand for Iraqi Muslims.

Under such circumstances the first question that arises is whether or not it would be at all possible to ensure world peace in the twenty-first century with a hostile relationship between the two major civilizations in the world today? Will the United States decide to serve the interests of historical Christianity of Europe? Will the US Constitution and the American people allow such a policy on the part of the US government? Is it possible to enslave the whole Muslim community? Or is it possible to eradicate them like the Aborigines and the so-called American Indians? Will the United States or any other coalition of states be able to establish world peace without the participation of almost a quarter of the world population? Consider the geographical distribution of Muslims in the world today. On top of the world's known fuel deposits, most important trade routes – the Mediterranean, the Red Sea, the Bosporus, the Black Sea, the Straits of Malacca – are all heavily populated by Muslims. Even if one ignores humanitarian arguments, i.e., the Muslim right to self-determination, how could the rest of the world establish a peaceful atmosphere by ignoring such a diverse community? What is the alternative then? To create a privileged elite among Muslims who would abandon the interests of the common people and would be loyal to the privileged elite in the West? No. Such Machiavellian efforts have already failed. And any continuation of such efforts will only encourage desperate Muslims to subscribe to terrorism.[30] In our opinion the only way that would ensure international peace and stability is the recognition and implementation of human rights and dignity *universally*. But the question is how can this be achieved and ensure civilizational coexistence in the twenty-first century? Under the present context we shall confine our discussion to the relationship between Islamic and Western civilizations.

First of all, one must recognize the fact that there is a problem of understanding of one by the other. In order to develop a relationship of peaceful coexistence, therefore, one needs to identify common values between the two civilizations. As many Christians today find common values between the Enlightenment and Judeo-Christian traditions, one would also find those values common in Islamic civilization. Both civilizations then would need to cultivate those values in their practical life; both will need to admit that they have made mistakes in history, and there is a need to make a determined and concerted effort to correct those mistakes. Any potential conflict between the values of these two civilizations must be resolved rationally to the satisfaction of both groups. Nations belonging to both civilizations will need to place these values above their national, ethnic, linguistic, and racial interests. To translate the values under the current situation, international observers under the banner of the UN may be immediately deployed in the zone of conflict in Palestine. And this will be possible only through dialogue and discussion, as has been pointed out by Immanuel Wallerstein.[31]

Secondly people belonging to both civilizations will need to give up the social Darwinist superiority complex. The idea that Third-World nations are destined to suffer from poverty, malnutrition, disease, and other calamities because they lack the intellectual ability to overcome those problems must be abandoned. One must recognize that colonialism played a significant role in the growth of the current relationship of dependency between the developed and developing nations of the world today. Universal human rights and human dignity must be recognized *universally*; not just on paper, but also in practice. People in the Muslim world also must give up the belief that Muslims are the only people who deserve divine salvation. They should rather let God decide who should receive His mercy. Many Muslims identify double standards by many Western governments in their treatment of Israel as opposed to Iraq. Even though both countries violated UN resolutions, only the latter has been punished by the international body. In order to comprehend the situation better Muslims should develop a deeper understanding of the political systems in those Western countries: even though these countries claim to be democratic, pressure groups play a decisive role in their policy-making system. Policies toward Israel are not always supported by public opinion in those countries. Muslims must also appreciate the fact that there are millions of people in the West who might not be Muslim, but care for justice and human rights. In the recent Iraqi crisis, for example, as compared to Muslims many more Westerners have come out to demonstrate their opposition to aggression against Iraq.

Democracy has been claimed to be one of the fundamental values of Western civilization. But when in 1991 the military in Algeria, with the support of its colonial master France, brought down the democratically elected government, neither the Algerian military nor the government of France was severely criticized by other Western countries. On the other hand, Iran – which has been holding elections regularly since the Islamic revolution in 1979 – is still blacklisted as belonging to the "axis of evil." Any observer of political events in the Muslim world will notice that there is no fundamental difference between "the democratic elections" that have been conducted in Egypt and Iraq. Yet it seems that the process was acceptable only in the case of Egypt, but not for Iraq. Therefore, one must admit that there have been gaps between words and deeds on the part of many Western governments.

The problem of double standards and the gap between words and deeds exist not only among some Western governments, but also among some Muslims. Muslims are generally very vocal against Israeli aggression, but do they react in the same manner when Muslim countries behave aggressively? Many Muslim countries sided with Iraq in the Iran–Iraq conflict of the 1980s. They never protested against Iraq's aggressive behavior and its use of chemical weapons against Iran. Did any Muslim government protest when in 1982 the Syrian government killed thousands of innocent people in Hama? Muslims protested severely when an Israeli reservist killed many Muslims engaged in prayers in the Ibrahimi mosque (named after the Prophet Abraham) in Hebron or Al-Khalīl. However, similar killings have become a common phenomenon between Shi'ite and Sunni Muslims in Pakistan for more than a decade, and hardly any effective action has been taken against such attacks. Interestingly these killings have not been criticized as severely as have been the killings by Israelis. Also many Muslims do not seem to appreciate the fact that many of their co-religionists have found refuge in many Western countries after being persecuted by their own governments. These clear cases of double standards must be resolved in order to develop any better understanding between the two civilizations.

After developing a better understanding about each other, people belonging to both civilizations will need to minimize the gap between the elite and the common people in their respective countries. The elite–mass gap in many Muslim countries has dipped to a very low ebb. For a long time public opinion in Saudi Arabia, for example, has been against allowing the US a base to initiate aggression against Afghanistan and Iraq or any other Muslim country. But the ruling elite has not been able to follow this up. As a result the legitimacy of the elite suffers, and the Unites States hardly wants to understand this dilemma of the Muslim ruling elite. Pakistan, for example, is heavily indebted to the World Bank, the IMF, and to a number of other international private banks; the United States has been exploiting this weakness of Pakistan to gather Pakistan's support against what it calls terrorist establishments in Pakistan and Afghanistan or for Pakistan's support in the Security Council on Iraq. The US may call these activities diplomatic maneuvers, but in the eyes of common Pakistanis they might just be considered as undue pressure.

The elite–mass gap exists not only in the Muslim world; it also exists in the US. The government seems to be totally ignoring public sentiment on the Iraq issue, although demonstrations against the war in Iraq have been compared with those of the war in Vietnam. In response the US administration has imposed censorship on the coverage from Iraq. Similarly on the issue of environment, the US government has broken its commitment made in Kyoto. The US government seems to have made this decision to protect the interests of large industries. Any genuine democratic government would have put such critical issues to a national referendum. But the current US administration doesn't seem to have any such motive. Such a role of the leading nation in the contemporary world could only lead to disaster for human civilization in the twenty-first century. What effective measures can the Muslims take to save themselves and the world civilization? And what can the OIC do in this?

Huntington wants at least one Muslim country to be present in the United Nations Security Council, and he wants the OIC to make the selection of that country.[32] But will this ensure Muslim participation in world affairs? How many times has the world body failed to conduct investigations in the occupied territories in Palestine? The power of manipulation by stronger countries of smaller and economically weaker countries in the Security Council is well known. Then there is the question of veto power; this only reminds a Muslim how many times legitimate issues such as Palestine and Kashmir have been vetoed by one or other permanent members of the Security Council. In the recent Iraq crisis, the US and the UK have gone to war without the approval of the Security Council. Therefore, Huntington's recommendation is definitely doomed to fail.

Since the OIC has not been able achieve any substantial progress so far, should it be abandoned? But then the question arises as to who would represent the *ummah* if the OIC is abolished? Currently the OIC is the only institution that may claim to legitimately represent all Muslims. And also the OIC is powerless because its member states have made it so. Can the member states assert themselves? All international organizations are always dependent on the attitude of their member states. The war in Iraq has severely curtailed the role even of the UN. The situation will change only if there is a determined will on the part of the Muslim leadership. Failure to do so will only increase the frustration of the victims, which may lead to a further sharp increase in terrorism. It must also be pointed out that in the current global village it is not the Muslim world that is looking for a more just and dignified world, rather the whole of humanity is looking for a positive change in the twenty-first century.

There is a general consensus in the Muslim world that Malaysia could play a major role in leading the *ummah* in the twenty-first century. The country has already set an example in serving the *ummah* through the office of its first prime minister Tengku Abdul Rahman, who served as the first secretary general of the OIC. Today Malaysia is highly appreciated throughout the Muslim world as a model for economic development and has set an example as a democracy where representative governments have ruled since independence almost half a century ago. Malaysia, perhaps, may play the same role of a catalyst in uniting the *ummah* as Cavour's Piedmont-Sardinia did in the Italian unification in nineteenth-century Europe. Most important of all Malaysia doesn't suffer from the acute problem of financial debt to institutions such as the World Bank or the IMF, and therefore, it has the courage to stand against injustices committed against Muslims. This has been demonstrated well during the recent Afghanistan and Iraq crises. Malaysia has also taken the initiative to introduce alternative financial institutions for "reshaping the international financial architecture for balanced and stable growth."[33]

Turkey also has gained a reputation for effectively maintaining a balance between its Islamic background and its desire to be part of Western civilization. Recently with the election of the new secretary general of the OIC, Muslim countries have expressed their acceptance of Turkish leadership. A dual leadership of Turkey and Malaysia, with the secretary general from one country and the chairman from another, might be able to save the OIC and the Muslim world from a complete disaster. So far the OIC has let itself be exploited by vested interests, but there is still time to save the community from a catastrophic disaster of anarchy and terrorism. For this Muslims must act, and act swiftly and decisively, in order to avert a complete disaster. This will also make a decisive impact on humanity at large in the twenty-first century.

Notes

1. Most important among these leaders were Sayyid Ahmad Khan (1817–98), Sayyid Amir Ali (1849–1928) in South Asia and Muḥammad 'Abduh (1849–1905) in the Arab world.
2. On this subject, see Abdullah al-Ahsan, *Ummah or Nation: Identity Crisis in Contemporary Muslim Society* (Leicester; The Islamic Foundation, 1992).
3. Nur Yalman, "Some Observations of Secularism in Islam: The Cultural Revolution in Turkey," *Daedalus* 102, 1973, 147.
4. E.I.J. Rosenthal, *Islam in the Modern Nation State* (Cambridge: Cambridge University Press, 1965), 70.
5. On the formation of this elite, see Abdullah al-Ahsan, "Elite-Formation under Colonial Rule: Capable Administrators or Loyal Servants? A General Survey of Colonial Rule in Muslim Countries," *Islamic Studies*, 37(1), 1998.

6. See G.W. Choudhury, *Constitutional Development in Pakistan* (London: Longman, 1959), 174–5.

7. Ishtiaq H. Qureshi, *Education in Pakistan: An Inquiry into Objectives and Achievements* (Karachi: Ma'aref, 1975), 7–71.

8. On the overall situation of Muslims following the abolition of the institution, see Sylvia Haim's concluding chapter in T.W. Arnold, ed., *The Caliphate* (New York: Barnes and Noble, 1966), and D.S. Margoliouth, "The Latest Developments of the Caliphate Question," *The Muslim World*, 14, 1924, 334–41.

9. OIC General Secretariat, "Declaration of the First Islamic Summit Conference," *Organization of the Islamic Conference: Declarations and Resolutions of Heads of State and Ministers of Foreign Affairs 1389–1401 H. 1969–1981*, n.d., 18.

10. Ibid., 23–4.

11. OIC document IS/3–81/CS/D.2. Also see Ziauddin Sardar, *Science and Technology in the Middle East: A Guide to Issues, Organizations and Institutions* (London: Longman, 1982), 113–14.

12. Resolution 1/8-AF.

13. Ilhan Ugurel, "External Debt of the Islamic Countries: The Present Situation and Future Prospects," *Journal of Economic Cooperation*, 20(4), 1999, 73–106 and 81.

14. Ibid., 89.

15. Ibid., 91.

16. Ibid.

17. Syed Nawab Haider Naqvi, "Globalization, Regionalism, and the OIC," *Journal of Economic Cooperation among Islamic Countries*, 19(1–2), 1998, 285–308.

18. See, for example, OIC resolution 20/19-P.

19. Samuel P. Huntington, *The Clash of Civilizations and the Remaking of World Order* (New York: Simon & Schuster, 1996), 111.

20. Ibid., 115.

21. This has happened in Egypt and Turkey following earthquakes in the 1990s.

22. Ibid., 121.

23. Samuel P. Huntington, *Special Davos Edition Newsweek* (December 2001–February 2002), 9.

24. Huntington, *The Clash*, 209.

25. Ibid.

26. Edward W. Said, "The Clash of Ignorance," http://www.zmag.org/saidclash.htm.

27. Percival Spear, *The Oxford History of India*, 4th edn. (Delhi: Oxford University Press, 1958), 474.

28. Huntington, *The Clash*, 20.

29. Ibid., 312–18.

30. See the statement of Ayman az-Zawahiri in *As-Sharq al-Awsat*, September 7, 2001. The author explains the position of their group in a number of articles published in the paper.

31. Immanuel Wallerstein, "Islam, the West, and the World," *Journal of Islamic Studies*, 10(2), 1999, 125.

32. Huntington, *The Clash*, 317.

33. See the inaugural speech by the Malaysian prime minister at www.IFSB.org.

CHAPTER 31

Culture of Mistrust: A Sociological Analysis of Iranian Political Culture

Mehrdad Mashayekhi

The political culture of modern Iran, one in which myths about the power and motives of foreign states have a vivid life, is in part a product of these earlier, and by no means imagined, external interventions. This supposedly paranoid streak in Iranian nationalism has its historical national roots, just as the anxiety and illusions of individuals can have roots in their own earlier traumatic experiences.

Fred Halliday, *The Iranian Revolution and Great-Power Politics*[1]

The 1972 publication of Iraj Pezeshkzad's comic novel *My [Dear] Uncle Napoleon* in Iran and the subsequent television series based on the book, truly captured the nation's imagination.[2] As a social satire exaggerating the widely held Iranian obsession with the hidden hand of the British, this novel soon became an all-time bestseller in Iran. Dick Davis, the book's translator, relates the book's immediate success and its cultural popularity to the author's portrayal of a "paranoid patriarch," a relatively common persona in Iranian political culture. Accordingly, the novel's success was responsible for "a Persian equivalent of the term 'Dear Uncle Napolean-itis' (*Dayee Jan Napoleonism*) being adopted as a name for such readiness to see conspiracy theories and the hidden hand of the West behind any and every local Iranian event."[3]

The aforementioned socio-psychological streak has indeed attracted the attention of many observers of Iranian politics and culture. These observers have variably referred to this relatively high degree of mistrust as "paranoid style," "conspiracy-mindedness," "xenophobia," "cynicism," and "suspiciousness." This observation, while emphasized more frequently during the twentieth century, has been cited in earlier times. A fourth-century Roman historian, Ammianus Marcellinus, in his description of Persians noted, that they are "extremely cautious and suspicious."[4] Likewise Lord Curzon, the British statesman and writer, since his *Persia and the Persian Question*, similarly comments that the "natives are a suspicious people."[5]

For most of the twentieth century, Britain was the central target of Iranian "Anglophobia." Richard Cottam, commenting on the Iranian press during the Mossadeq premiership in the early 1950s writes: "Nowhere in the world is British cleverness so wildly exaggerated as in Iran, and nowhere are the British more hated for it." According to this press, "all Iran's politicians, without exception, were British agents."[6] Nothing is more expressive of this political attitude than the Iranian approach toward *power*. As Andrew Westwood has aptly put it, Iranians "distrust the possession and exercise of power."[7] Their historical experience and collective memory have somehow convinced them that "powerful foreigners in league with the powerful Iranians lie behind unpleasant events."[8]

Iranian journalists and social scientists have raised similar comments. A 1966 editorial in the Iranian journal *Sahar* stated:

> The people are not indifferent they are distrustful. If you want the truth, the people have lost confidence in everybody and everything . . . This distrust in oneself, gained through actual experience, extends, naturally, to others too. They no longer trust anyone.[9]

Ahmad Ashraf, an Iranian sociologist, maintains that "the appeal of conspiracy theories" among Persians "is more widespread . . . than in other societies" and is a form of a "collective defense mechanism, particularly during periods of powerlessness, defeat, and political turmoil."[10] Another Iranian scholar, in focussing on the nexus between foreign powers and the dependent domestic political elite, refers to the latter as a "xenocracy, with various sets of pro-British, pro-Russian, and later pro-American politicians vying to exercise power."[11]

A cautionary remark is in order here. Some of the characterizations, particularly those raised by Western diplomats, may have come from an orientalistic discourse, one that tried to read a distrustful and paranoid essence in Iran's "national character." Realistically speaking, in the course of history, Iranian political culture has changed as a result of both internal and external contradictions, state policies, Western penetration, intellectual innovations, globalization, religious reactions, and socioeconomic development. Even the "culture of mistrust" itself has adapted to broader political and ideological changes taking place in the country.

In terms of its cultural role, I agree with Ervand Abrahamian that "political paranoia" in Iran is only "a political style and mode of expression, not a clinical and deep-seated psychological disorder." Similarly, Marvin Zonis calls mistrust a "characteristic mode of interpersonal relations in Iran".[13] Accordingly, such an attitude, common to both the political elite and the opponents of the regime, is essentially a mass psychological defense mechanism to protect Iranians from uncertain and uncontrollable forces.

The purpose of this chapter is fourfold: (i) to provide a historical background to the rise of the culture of mistrust; (ii) to explore major orientations toward understanding the culture of mistrust; (iii) to offer a detailed description of this culture and its decline/metamorphosis in the post-revolutionary Iran; and (iv) to evaluate the role of mistrust, and by implication, *trust*, in the emergence and the future of civil society in Iran.

Historical Background: Reproduction of "Certainty of Uncertainty"

Some scholars of Iranian culture and society have identified three major value orientations or cultural legacies contributing to Iran's contemporary macro-cultural configuration.[14] They consist of what has been variably referred to as: (i) *Pre-Islamic-national* or *historical* culture; (ii) *Islamic* (Shi'ite) culture; and (iii) *Western* culture. An incessant and dynamic process of interaction among these three value systems has largely shaped contemporary Iranian culture, in general, and its political culture, in particular. Despite profound cultural changes taking place in Iran since the mid-nineteenth century, certain belief systems and value orientations in the political culture such as authoritarianism, factionalism, patriarchism, and, indeed, mistrust, have demonstrated considerable resilience. Since they have survived over several millennia, a review of the basic historical, economic, geographic, ecological, political, and social factors that gave rise to such cultural patterns, and later reproduced them, is in order.

Iranian territory has historically suffered from a lack of precipitation, and even today, less than 10 percent of the land is cultivated. The average annual rainfall in Iran is estimated to be 25–30 centimeters, and for the central and southern areas, the average figure is less than 20 centimeters per year. Most of the country consists of sparsely inhabited arid and semi-arid lands. The obstacles to agriculture become clear when one considers that the majority of precipitation falls outside the growing season in Iran and that the areas in the north and west receiving enough rain are generally too mountainous to cultivate.[15]

These environmental conditions have shaped all aspects of life: ecological, cultural, and political. Sadeq Ziba Kalam, an Iranian political scientist, has focussed on three such influences: *community dispersion*; *nomadic and tribal lifestyles*; and *autocratic states*.[16] For thousands of years, three lifestyles – rural (village), tribal, and urban – have coexisted in Iran. The rural and urban communities have remained isolated and extremely scattered due to climatic conditions, particularly, scarcity of water. This has had a dampening effect on the development of productive forces, the formation of economic surplus, and trade with other communities. Instead, self-sufficiency and economic stagnation have prevailed.

The nomadic and tribal groups lived extremely unstable lives. Their total reliance on nature required a constant movement in search of water, pasture, and, occasionally, wealth, and led to raids and wars with other tribes, villages, and even cities. Indeed it was this peculiarly hard life in a harsh and insecure environment which Reza Behnam dubs "the certainty of uncertainty," that necessitated militancy, chivalry, hospitality, and tribal cohesion, in order for *survival*.[17] The history of Iran is replete with rivalries among tribal groups or between tribes and urbanites over pastures and fertile areas. On numerous occasions nomads destroyed cities, overthrew governments, and subsequently replaced them. With the exception of the Pahlavis, all dynasties assuming power in Iran after 1000 AD have been of tribal origin.[18] The continual struggle for resources generated cycles of violence, insecurity, and destruction in Iran. Since the eleventh century, tribes from central Asia (Seljuk Turks, Turkmans, Uzbeks, Tatars, Tajiks, Mongols) have invaded Iran. The outcome has been more instability, anarchy, pillaging of towns; destruction of civilization, culture, and economies; constant move of the capital city; and certainly a mentality of hopelessness, fear, and mistrust against the "other," domestic or foreign invader. The next major factor shedding light on the historical background pertains to the despotic structure of the state.

Oriental Despotism in Iran

Throughout history, extreme concentration of power has been one of the fundamental socio-political features of Iran. There are many indications that "oriental despotism" as Karl Wittfogel described it, or at least many of its known features, were indeed in place at various periods in Iranian political history.[19] The primary characteristic of this political structure is its absolute and highly monopolistic nature. According to Homa Katouzian, "The distinctive characteristic of the Iranian state is that it monopolized not just power, but *arbitrary power* – not the absolute power of laying down the law, but the absolute power of exercising lawlessness."[20] As Marx and Engels, in their concept of the Asiatic mode of production, and Wittfogel, in his theory of hydraulic society have argued, the general aridity of these societies was the point of departure for the emergence of highly centralized and bureaucratic state structures. In dry areas, the distribution of limited water resources was a life and death issue requiring the management of dam construction, digging of canals, and other forms of artificial irrigation. "Hence an economical function devolved upon all Asiatic governments, the function of providing public works."[21] The administrative system under the Achaemenian dynasty, and later the Sassanid rule, developed a vast infrastructure to manage the vital task of water distribution. Government's omnipresence extended into the ownership of the key means of production, particularly land. Most scholars maintain that state ownership of land in Iran has been quite extensive, whereas other forms of private or public ownership have been mostly tentative without much security.[22]

Ann Lambton provides extensive information regarding the Iranian state's vital role during the medieval period.[23] The state's economic and administrative functions led to an absolutist type of government controlling most aspects of life which necessitated religious legitimization such as calling the king "shadow of God on earth." Katouzian, commenting on the state's structures notes: "The system of state administration was rigidly hierarchical: the *shartradar* (*satrap*), and the *marzaban* were, respectively, the civilian and military governors appointed by the king-emperor to each and every province; they were each directly responsible to the king-emperor himself; and they usually were watched by undercover agents from within or outside their departments."[24] Indications are that oriental despotic state structures reproduced themselves over time. Javad Tabatabai, discussing Safavid Iran under Shah Abbas (1581–1628), confirms this analysis and refers to Shah Abbas as "the nation's sole institution." To rule the country, the king was so autocratic and distrustful of others that he even ordered his own children killed or blinded. This was also the fate of many grand *vazirs* (prime ministers). Furthermore, the Shah employed many informers and relied on them to provide firsthand information from both inside and outside the country.[25]

One social impact of such political structures has been the lack of formation of almost any *independent* associations, unions, or organizations outside of religion. Thus, cooperation and teamwork have greatly suffered in Iranian culture.

According to another analyst, in addition to the Asian/oriental nature of the state in Iran, there has been a second independent influence on the absolutist style of political rule. The tribal character of governments, particularly after the eleventh century, introduced a patriarchal subculture, attributing absolute authority to the leader (*ilkhan*).[26] This type of government did not typically last long enough to develop more sophisticated institutions and norms of ruling. Soon, another tribe challenged and eventually replaced the extant government. Anticipating invasions, each government attempted to gain control of all potential sources of conflict by reverting to force and centralization. This succession of tribal governments continued well into the early twentieth century.

Iran's historical and geopolitical position at the crossroad of Asian, African, and European trade routes also contributed to a centralized state by placing additional responsibilities on the administration to construct roads and communication networks, and to ensure protection against bandits and invaders. Several cities in Iranian territory were actively involved in trade with Chinese and Indian merchants on the one hand, and Greek and Roman merchants on the other.

In the nineteenth century, under the Qajar dynasty, many characteristics of oriental despotism continued.[27] Reflecting upon the arbitrary nature of power under the Qajar kings, British emissary Sir John Malcolm recalls the Shah's response to checks and balances in Britain: "Your king then appears to be no more than the first magistrate of the state! . . . I can elevate and degrade all the high nobles and officers you see around me!"[28] During this century, European powers, particularly Russia and Britain, played increasingly greater roles in controlling Iranian politics and economy. Incapable of warding off these threats, Qajar governments simply pressured the populace. Many observers of Iranian politics consider the state to be the main factor of insecurity in this period.[29] In the meantime, "factional strife" and "communal conflicts" continued, rendering life more insecure.

The Role of Foreign Invasions

Foreign invasions undoubtedly have had a fundamental impact on Iranian political culture and mass psychology. Considering the fact that most of these attacks resulted in mass destruction of productive forces and culture one can view Iran's history as a series of victory–construction and defeat–contraction cycles, a factor that may explain the resilience of certain cultural values until very recent times. These especially persistent values include hopelessness, individualism, xenophobia, fatalism, dualistic views of life, messianism, nationalism-nativism, mysticism, and mistrust.[30]

The following foreign invasions have been pivotal events in Iranian history: the Achaemenian Empire (500–331 BC) was conquered by Alexander of Macedonia; the Parthians (129–224 AD) repeatedly fought Roman incursions; and the Sassanid dynasty (224–641 AD) was defeated by Muslim Arabs, resulting in the domination of Iranian territory by the Islamic Empire (the Ummayads and the Abbasids) until the thirteenth-century Mongol invasion led by Genghis Khan.

Under the Islamic Empire a succession of Iranian dynasties, including the *Buyids*, *Tabarids*, and *Samanids*, established brief local control. However, by the eleventh century, the Turkish *Seljuk* tribe disrupted this semi-autonomous trend. The most destructive invasion of Mongols followed, plundering and destroying civilization and material culture throughout the region. The decline of *ilkhanis* by the mid-fourteenth century brought another round of semi-autonomous local governments, such as the *Chupanids* in Azerbaijan, *Es haqis* in Gilan, and *Atabaks* in western Iran, all of whom competed with each other for supremacy. Teimur the Lame, a central Asian Turk, led another destructive invasion lasting until his death in 1405. The fifteenth century was witness to more internal instability and conflict between different governments. According to one study, just before the Safavids took power, more than 20 local governments were at war.[31] Historians have pointed out that Iran has experienced around 1200 major wars throughout history.

For the first time in eight centuries, the Safavids (1500–1736) unified Iran, mainly due to the ideological role of Shi'ite Islam and the use of brutal force against dissidents. While the Ottoman Empire was the main foreign threat against the Safavids, it was, in fact, the Afghan invasion of 1722 that put an end to the Safavids' rule and initiated another period of decline, chaos, and instability in Iran. Due to internal and external tribal strife, many Iranian cities were partially destroyed and lost significant numbers of their population. Isfahan's population, for example, was reduced from approximately 600,000 to 10,000 during this time.[32] Except for a brief period of relative calm during Karim Khan's rule (1750–79), the country experienced chaos until Agha Mohammad Khan united the Turkish Qajar tribes in 1794 and took over the central government. Their rule (1794–1925) is associated with a new element of instability and domination – this time by European powers such as Russia, Britain, and France.

Foreign Domination in the Modern Era

During the Qajar dynasty in the nineteenth century, increasing contact with the West matched by the state's politico-economic underdevelopment, and military weakness introduced an era of foreign domination, machination, and political struggle.

In 1812, after Napoleon's failed attempt to win concessions with the Qajars, Russia seized several northern provinces, giving rise to the humiliating treaties of Golestan (1813) and Torkomanchay (1828). This drove Qajar Iran into the arms of Great Britain who, at the time, was competing to maintain access to the Persian Gulf and protect its colonial interests in India. In 1814, a defensive alliance was signed with Britain, angering the Russians and intensifying Anglo–Russian competition in Iran. In order to finance their extravagances, Qajar monarchs attempted to pit the foreign powers against each other; however, their attempts often had unintended consequences. In the second half of the nineteenth century, as the court's coffers were increasingly depleted, the British and, to a lesser extent, the Russians, gained unparalleled influence in the country; so much so that "the Qajar Shahs could not even designate their successors without the explicit approval of the two imperial representatives."[33] Among the major events involving foreign powers, one can list: the 1879 formation of a Cossack brigade under the Russian influence; the tobacco concession of 1890 granted to the British; and the oil concession of 1901 to a British syndicate, that eventually resulted in the formation of the Anglo–Iranian Oil Company in 1908. After the Constitutional Revolution of 1906 and the ascendancy of nationalist forces, Russia and Britain became alarmed by the new role of the *Majlis* (parliament). The foreign powers' apprehension became the backdrop for the so-called Anglo–Russian Convention signed in 1907 which divided Iran into three "spheres of influence." Eventually, Anglo–Russian joint action in favor of the deposed Shah, Mohammad Ali, in 1911, undermined the Constitutionalists' power: northern Iran under Russian control, southern Iran under British control, and central Iran under the Qajar government.

While the Russian influence and intervention in Iran declined due to the October Revolution, the British role became more visible. Their intervention in Iranian affairs is symbolically demonstrated by the fact that, in May 1918, "the British began paying a monthly subsidy of fifteen thousand toumans to the Shah as long as he retained Vossugh od-Dowleh as prime minister. [He], it is not difficult to imagine, was known as the most pro-British politician in Iran."[34]

Special emphasis needs to be placed on two major coups. First, the 1921 pro-British coup by Reza Khan and his Cossack brigade that put an end to the Qajar dynasty and, shortly thereafter, founded the Pahlavi monarchy. The Allied Forces of World War Two, however, occupied Iran in 1941 and forced Reza Shah to abdicate power to his son Mohammad Reza Pahlavi. Reza Shah's neutral stance toward the First World War and the presence of some Germans in the country provided the necessary pretext for the Allies' decision. Another recent example of foreign intervention in Iran deals with the role of the Soviet Union at the end of the Second World War. The Soviets refused to withdraw their troops from northwestern Iran and helped set up autonomy-seeking movements in Azerbaijan and Kurdistan. Finally, after challenges from the Shah's government and the Americans, the Soviets agreed to pull out their forces in 1946.

The second and far more pivotal event is the August 1953 coup overthrowing liberal-nationalist prime minister, Dr. Mohammad Mossadeq. The coup was engineered by the United States CIA and executed by Royalist army officers headed by General Fazlollah Zahedi. James Bill thus concludes his analysis of the 1953 coup, known as "Operation Ajax".

> 14. The intervention damaged the image of the United States in the eyes of the nationalists who swept to power in the Middle East . . .

> 15. The 1953 intervention aborted the birth of revolutionary nationalism in Iran that would burst forth twenty-five years later in a deeply xenophobic and extremist form.[35]

American intervention in the post-1953 era went beyond political support for the Shah. It included cooperation on internal security, military, socio-political reforms, as well as appointment of sensitive government positions including prime ministers, ministers, and the like.

Twenty-six years of unrelenting support for the Shah and his authoritarian policies only added to the dominant distrustful attitude among Iranians toward foreign power intervention, in general, and US policies, in particular. During the 1970s, almost all opposing political and intellectual circles in Iran – Islamist, liberal-nationalist, Marxist – couched their ideas in a radical, Third-Worldist, anti-Western, and nationalistic discourse. From Ali Shariati's notion of a "return to Islamic self" to confront Western cultural imperialism, to Jalal Al-e Ahmad's concept of "west-toxication," and Bijan Jazani's "dependent capitalism," all took opposition to the West as their point of departure.[36]

The above reactions by political intellectuals, as well as popular conspiratorial mindsets against the CIA, the British, Zionists, the KGB, Freemasons, Bahais, and the like, indeed are all imbedded in a broader political-cultural paradigm defined by mistrust toward the "other."

Political Culture of Mistrust: Major Orientations

By "culture of mistrust" we understand a historically formed set of values, norms, symbols, beliefs, and discourses, organized around a dichotomous view of the world which is transmitted from generation to generation. This cultural orientation tends to be most common in the Middle East and less-developed societies; although it may also be detected in other societies. The Manichean worldview, inherent in this culture, divides society into a category of the innocent, well-intentioned, sincere, friendly "self" versus the malicious, ill-intentioned, Janus-faced, conspiratorial, enemy: "other." Accordingly, the world becomes a dangerous and insecure place in which the "good" forces are constantly on the alert to contain the forces of "evil." In keeping with such constructions of reality, all those who are not one of "us" are not trustworthy. This "self" in Iran has historically been defined variously as one's family, clan, tribe, town, religion, and more recently, political circles and the nation. Conversely, the "other" must be defined as a potential enemy in the guise of a non-kin, non-tribe, non-Shi'ite (Muslim), non-Iranian, whose declared objectives and plans, in all likelihood, may inflict harm and pain on the "self."

The *political* culture of mistrust constitutes a subset of this broader culture. Its sphere of judgment is limited to issues such as power and economic inequality, government's role, imperialism, social change, etc. In Iranian political culture during the twentieth century, the following dichotomies of good/evil were most frequently utilized: progressive/reactionary, people/anti-people, nation/imperialism, independent/dependent, and insider/outsider.

As Ruth Benedict asserts, cultures usually develop around one or a few dominant concerns and, furthermore, cultural practices serve adaptive functions.[37] As was previously discussed, the problem of survival has historically dominated the everyday concerns of the majority in Iran. In addition to climatic-ecological uncertainties, I described the impact of absolutist states, as well as internal and external invasions and interventions, on the formation of the culture of mistrust. Consequently, mistrust and xenophobia should be viewed as forms of adaptation to the social and physical environment. Since both common people and the elite have been periodically victimized by invasion, conspiracy, and manipulation, there is no notable difference in their respective political cultures. Indeed, one may be struck by similarities between the late Shah's views on the British, Ayatollah Khomeini's skeptical attitudes on the Americans and the popular conspiratorial beliefs circulating among the Iranian masses.[38]

While the political culture of mistrust is strongly associated with ideas and beliefs regarding conspiracy, cynicism, suspiciousness, and xenophobia, there are also a range of *secondary* values and beliefs that are closely associated and correlated with mistrust. They include:

1. Hopelessness and pessimism: This refers to the tendency to lower expectations about socio-economic and/or political progress. Several millennia of relatively fruitless challenges against the natural environment, absolutist governments, and tribal invaders have dampened high hopes regarding the people's survival. Two Persian proverbs best capture this mentality: *in niz bogzarad* (this will also pass) and *har cheh pish ayad, khosh ayad* (whatever happens, is well taken).[39]

2. Fatalism: Closely associated with hopelessness, fatalism represents a resigned attitude in coping with the world; a mentality that does not believe in the possibility of human control over either the forces of nature or perpetual autocratic governments. The Persian expressions *qesmat nabood* (it wasn't meant), and *Insha' allah* (God willing) are representatives of this outlook among Iranians and can be viewed as a cultural defense mechanism against suffering.

3. Factionalism and fragmentation: In a culture dominated by attitudes of cynicism and apprehension toward "others," trust can mainly be expressed through more reliable primordial lines such as kinship, ethnicity, and religion. The geographical isolation of communities, and the limited social and commercial relations between them, has created a highly diverse social structure whose major constitutive elements are in periodic conflict. In the absence of a modern social contract and norms of trust integrating various fragments, factionalism, particularly in politics, has been the order of the day.[40] There is an effective process of political socialization into conflict and mistrust that keeps the old lines of rivalry alive. This fragmented political culture has been evident among and within all major political currents in Iran: the left, Islamists, liberal-nationalists, and most recently, the monarchists.

James Bill has argued that in the Middle East in general, and Iran in particular, patrimonial leadership promotes division and rivalry among the subordinates in order to reinforce their power. He labels this as "balanced conflict."[41] In Iran after the revolution, he continues, Ayatollah Khomeini tried to stay above the political fray by periodical attempts at balancing the conflicting factions (radical leftists vs. the conservatives on the right) within the Islamic Republic.[42]

4. Iranian individualism: This orientation needs to be disassociated from the notion of individualism in the West that originated during the Enlightenment. One researcher prefers to call it "Iranian self-centeredness" (*Khodmadari*).[43] The latter basically refers to a lack of systematic and institutionalized group-oriented activity. Lack of personal security, and defined social and political rights as well as the arbitrary nature of government decision making have driven the average Iranian to take refuge in a private or family level of domain. Marvin Zonis's observation of Iranian politics in the late 1960s still holds true today: "Iranian political parties are primarily collections of individuals gathered about a prominent political activist or activists and effected for office-seeking purposes . . . They play no role as a group in the policy process itself."[44] Thirty years later, a similar judgment is presented about one of Iran's major political parties (*Kargozaran-e Sazandegi*) headed by the ex-president, Hashemi Rafsanjani:

    > Rafsanjani's family is a symbolic representation of power relations in a society in which hidden diplomacy is still the established tool of its politicians and the state's legitimacy is shaped in the back chambers of authoritative families and not through the ballot box. [This is why] the state's organizational cell is still power families rather than political parties.[45]

5. Opportunism, dissimulation, hypocrisy: Living under "certainty of uncertainty," Iranians have learned to establish a contradictory relationship with all sources of power. They have criticized it in private, while praising it in public. The centuries-old practice of *taqiyeh* or dissimulation, popular among the Shi'ites, represents another angle of this hypocritical attitude toward power. During the early Islamic era, when Shi'ites were a small minority threatened by the Sunnis, they learned to engage in *taqiyeh* to disguise their beliefs. Over time, the practice lost its religious character and became an integral element of the Iranian socialization process. *Ta'arof* (a formal, elaborate, and exaggerated expression of hospitality or courtesy in everyday life) is another cultural practice that when exercised toward authority figures *could* be viewed as excessive and, at times, hypocritical.

No doubt the list may continue: there are other value orientations such as messianism, authoritarianism, and lack of cooperation/teamwork that could also fit here.

The Islamic Revolution and the Culture of Mistrust

The 1978–9 Islamic Revolution was the culmination of a fairly long period of politico-cultural challenges against the Shah's dictatorship, armed and supported by the United States. In the early years of the Revolution, there was an unprecedented level of cooperation and a great sense of trust, both among the participants, as well as between the latter and the government. However, this did not last. The higher level of trust was more a product of the unusual revolutionary situation than a profound change in the political culture. The guiding ideology of this movement – "political Islam" – was firmly rooted in what I have characterized elsewhere as a radical, "Third-Worldist discourse."[46] Hamid Dabashi, alternatively, terms it "the postcolonial Islamic political culture."[47] Dabashi, in his brilliant analysis, deconstructs the Islamic movement's ideological obsession with the West:

> The postcolonial culture has thus robbed the Muslim intellectuals of any possibility of coming to terms with their own history on their own terms, with the power and profusion of their own fantasies and facts, their own intelligence and stupidities. This "Other-centered" culture of defining everything . . . in terms of "The West" has denied the successive generations of Muslims unmitigated access to terms of their own enchantments.[48]

This analysis of Muslim thinkers and politicians cannot be separated from the broader political culture of mistrust prevalent in the Middle East.[49] In one sense, the Islamic Revolution only solidified mistrust and cynicism towards the West in general, and especially the United States. The first decade of the Revolution is a vivid demonstration of the practical implications of this collective mind-frame. The seizure of the American Embassy in Tehran in November 1979 is a symbolic point of reference. Generally speaking, the post-revolutionary regime perpetuated mistrust on two levels:

1. Foreign relations: Extreme suspiciousness applied to both superpowers and is reflected in the strategic slogan "Neither East, Nor West." The United States came to be recognized as the major threat to the revolution and, thus nicknamed "The Great Satan." This attitude affected both diplomatic and cultural relations with the United States.
2. Domestic relations: The ruling Islamists split the society into binaries of Muslim/non-Muslim, religious/secular, pro-revolution/anti-revolution, *mostaz'af* (downtrodden)/*mostakbar* (the arrogant rich), pro-West/anti-West, and the like. In essence, an apartheid-like system of "insiders" versus "outsiders" was established that denied the latter the opportunities, rights, and resources available to the former. While this may apply to any revolutionary transformation, in Iran it was infused with a stronger dose of mistrust leveled against the "others." In the post revolutionary years, for example, relatives and neighbors were encouraged by the ruling clergy to report on "anti-revolutionary" dissidents. The practice was also in place in educational institutions, where pro-government students spied on their classmates. To root out the "non-committed" in institutions of higher education, a complex Inquisition-like system of application selection was designed after the Islamic "cultural revolution" of the early 1980s. Accordingly, having passed the entrance exams, prospective students had to go through a religious "ideological exam." In addition, hundreds of college professors and staff, as well as thousands of students, were purged on the grounds of lacking political or religious credentials. Similar exams were imposed on prospective job-seekers in the public sector. Cinema, art, and other cultural expressions were simi-

larly under fire, and attempts to purify them from Western influence were institutionalized in the revolution's first decade. Particular mistrust was evident toward secular intellectuals who were viewed as the carriers of corrupt and alienating values. In a blunt 1980 New Year's message, Ayatollah Khomeini provided the green light for the coming purges:

> All of our backwardness has been due to the failure of most university-educated intellectuals to acquire correct knowledge of Iranian Islamic society, and unfortunately, this is still the case . . . Committed, responsible intellectuals! Abandon your factionalism and separation and show some concern for the people . . . Rid yourselves of the "isms" of the East and the West; stand on your own feet and stop relying on foreigners . . . They must abandon the slogans of deviant groups and replace all incorrect forms of thought with the true Islam that we cherish.[50]

All in all, the first decade of the revolution constructed a discourse of what can effectively be termed "Muslims and the Rest." The "Rest" included seculars, non-Shi'ites, liberals, Marxists, nationalists, monarchists, feminists, ethnic minorities, intellectuals, and army officers. A partial list of terms used to characterize the above is a testimony to the highly conspiratorial and mistrustful political culture prevalent during the 1980s: *taghooti* (one disobeying the rule of God); anti-revolutionary; mercenary; treacherous; *monafeq* (hypocrite); fifth column; *vabastegan-e estekbar-e jahani* (those dependent on "world arrogance"); enemies of Islam; *mofsed-e fi al-arz* (corrupt on the earth); co-opted intellectuals; and *gharb-zadeh* ("West-intoxicated"). Shadows of mistrust were cast all over the country, separating the religious believers from non-believers.

While the Islamic Revolution accentuated the pre-existing political culture of mistrust on both domestic and international dimensions, paradoxically, it also set the stage for its decline and metamorphosis in the years to come.

The end of the Iran–Iraq War in1988, and the death of the Ayatollah Khomeini, the Revolution's charismatic leader, in June 1989, marked a new era in which limited economic and cultural reforms were introduced by the new administration, headed by Hashemi-Rafsanjani. By the second half of the 1990s, a shift toward new political value orientations and practices, especially "reform," was quite visible in Iran. This politico-cultural transformation was a product of a myriad economic and cultural policies, post-war rising expectations, generational and intellectual paradigm shifts,[51] acceleration of globalization, the collapse of "really existing socialism," and most importantly, the people's direct experience with the theocracy. The emerging political culture should be regarded as a fundamental and historically significant type of social change; one in which the radical, religious, and authoritarian culture of the 1980s' generation started to give way to a more moderate, secular, reformist, democratic, pluralistic, pragmatic, and less mistrustful political culture among vast sectors of urbanite Iranians. There are also growing evidences such as impressionistic accounts, interviews with activists, and content analysis of Iranian reformist media, clearly demonstrating a decline in the level of mistrust and a more cooperative attitude. Additionally, a partial replacement of one form of mistrust with another has also been evident. The most explicit example of the latter is a shift away from the United States and the British (the old sources of conspiracy) in the public's imagery and more focus on the Islamic regime as the ultimate conspirator; a metamorphosis that could be referred to as a shift from Conspiracy Theory Type I to Conspiracy Theory Type II. This implication of the regime as the main source of every dreadful event is best captured by the common expression "*kar-e khodeshan ast*" (it is their doing). Despite some continuity with the past, there are many indications that a cultural break is about to take place among the younger generation. While they have no illusions about the conservative Islamists in power, the new generation avoids blaming *all* the country's problems on imperialism, America, Zionists, or even the regime. They simply refuse to submit to the dominant dualistic, and Manichaeanistic worldviews. The younger generation, along with reform-minded intellectuals, whether secular or reformist Islamist, have embraced a new paradigm to explain Iran's major socio-economic and political ills; one that focuses on the historical and *internal* sources of underdevelopment.[52] This shift is significant for paving the way toward a civic culture and a more trustful mode of interpersonal relations.

The major reasons responsible for the (partial) decline of mistrust in the post-revolutionary Iranian culture can be summarized as follows:

1. The Islamic Revolution temporarily bridged the immense historic gap separating the populace and the state. This mainly affected the more religious and traditional segments and facilitated their participation in the affairs of society, particularly the domains associated with religious traditions and institutions.

2. The decline of radical and revolutionary political ideologies, such as Third Worldism, communism, and political Islam, since the 1980s, has shifted the dominant reference point of post-revolutionary Iranian intellectuals (the West/the United States). As a result, the US image among the younger generation is becoming more positive. The summer of 1998 meeting, in Paris, between Abass Abdi, a leader of the 1979 American Embassy takeover, and Barry Rosen, an ex-hostage, was symbolic of this politico-cultural shift.

3. Several decades of direct experience with a religious state has provided Iranians with a rich understanding of the requisites of a theocracy, including its strategies to divide the opposition and preserve political power. In fact, most methods of promoting hopelessness, fear, and mistrust – for instance, fabricating crises to block reform, falsely attributing rumors and confessions to opposition figures, the application of brutal force, and associating intellectuals to Western agencies have mostly backfired.

4. An improvement in the circulation of information and news has undermined the main foundation of rumors, wild guesses, and conspiratorial "explanations." A proliferation of alternative, reformist, and increasingly secular press since the mid-1990s, as well as growing availability of foreign-based sources of information, have brought about much of this progress. In addition, access to advanced technologies associated with video machines, facsimiles, the

Internet, satellite television, and radio broadcasting has revolutionized the circulation and content of information. Despite their shortcomings, most of these sources are a significant improvement over the limited, state-controlled, and, at best, semi-open media available in the country. Today, more reliable information about domestic and global events has discouraged the formation, reproduction, and acceptance of conspiratorial views among a growing portion of the populace.

5. The Revolution's "second generation" coming of age today has developed a distinct view about Iranian politics and the world that is significantly different from the previous generation of the Islamic Revolution. For the most part, it represents a new *Weltanschauung* that is simply more open, pragmatic, goal-oriented, less ideological, and relatively speaking, more trustful. An Iranian social scientist has described this new (sub)culture as "a growing movement for joy, a movement against the state's cultural project . . . A movement embedded in the experiences of everyday life and shaped by ordinary people's deviance and their embracing of the scorned and the unacceptable . . . a movement shaped by the desire to 'sin.' "[53] Their new value system is the harbinger of a civil society in the making. Trust is a major prerequisite of the civic, open, and cooperative culture possibly emerging in Iran.

6. The Islamist reformist movement, since 1997, also contributed to this cultural metamorphosis. By challenging the authoritarian-conservative faction of the state it managed to further expose the latter's public image, plans and conspiracies. While reforms were never institutionalized, the reformists were more successful in changing the dominant political discourse by circulating novel concepts such as reform, civil society, rule of law and *shaffafiyat* (transparency).

Politics of Trust, Civil Society, and the Future

Since the early 1990s, the political culture of mistrust in Iran has been undergoing a slow transformation, the causes of which were briefly discussed earlier. The change is less evident in the populace's attitudes toward the ruling clerical regime, than it is in the more trustful forms of engagement practiced in Iran's embryonic "civil community." Despite the fact that common explanations blame the feebleness of civil society and the politics of mistrust only on authoritarian *political* systems, the role of the political *culture* of mistrust should not be underestimated. These old value orientations are gradually giving way to a new political culture and the emergence of a "politics of trust" could, in fact, be within the reach of younger Iranians.

Despite the fact that *modern* Iran has been less successful with cultivating norms of trust, ironically, traditional institutions and networks in Iran have harbored a few communities of trust within the broader culture of mistrust. In the context of traditional relations and culture, some areas of Iranian life have operated chiefly on the basis of trust. The Islamic Community Charity Funds (loan associations) (*Qarz ol-hassaneh*), and charity organizations (both popular today), and the tradition of *bazaari* merchants borrowing without offering collateral, constitute prime examples.[54] Another example is *javanmardi*, a code of ethics centered around justice, courage, humility, and trustworthiness.[55] In most Middle Eastern societies, however, the prime arena in which trust has become institutionalized and extensive forms of cooperation occur, is still the family. Francis Fukuyama refers to such kinship societies, where unrelated people find it very hard to trust one another, as "low-trust" societies.[56]

In advanced democracies, however, social trust is an integral part of civil society. Sociologist James Coleman popularized the term "social capital" referring to the social resources that members of a community possess and can employ in the process of decision making. Social capital includes knowledge, social networks, and norms of trust that enable people to work collectively together.[57]

Political scientist Robert Putnam and his colleagues applied the concept of social capital to Italy's regional governments. The researchers examined the link between institutional effectiveness and the strength of civic engagement, taking into account the role of civic trust and traditions. Their study revealed a strong correlation between institutional effectiveness and the role of civic trust.[58] Also, Fukuyama has devoted an entire volume to the relationship between trust as the "art of association" and economic prosperity in different cultures. He convincingly demonstrates that in "high-trust" societies, such as Japan and Germany, where social capital is abundant, both the economy and the polity perform better.[59]

Present-day Iranian society, politics and culture can best be conceptualized as *transitional*; they are taking the first steps from authoritarian to democratic, from statist to civic (civil society), from religious to secular, and from a culture of mistrust to a culture of trust. How long this transitional phase will last is open to debate, but the signs of metamorphosis are already evident. In the absence of empirical studies on the degree of mistrust (or trust) in post-revolutionary Iran, we must rely on secondary evidences such as analytical reports on new behavior patterns likely associated with trust. Such patterns are most evident in the public's increasing participation in elections, attentiveness to print media, younger generations' interest in weblogs, participation in protest movements, and the formation of independent non-governmental organizations (NGOs). A recent study conducted by the Iranian Civil Society Organizations Resource Center (ICSORC), which surveyed over 400 NGOs, based in Tehran, found that over 50 percent of these organizations have been established since the year 1997, with only 6.4 percent predating the Islamic Revolution.[60] On the rise since the mid-1990s, these activities could be collectively interpreted as a sign of growing civic involvement, rather than a manifestation of trust in the government.

The relationship between trust and engagement in political activism and cooperation is not causal; both could activate and reinforce the other variable. In the spring of 1997, during the course of the seventh presidential elections, millions of students and other youth engaged in a spontaneous movement of activism. Based on pre-existing neighborhood or school networks, as well as ordinary friendship and kinship circles (network of trust), they shocked the system and secured the victory of Mohammad Khatami. Over 20 million Iranians participated in that election. The political and cultural momentum created as a result continued into early 2000. From March 1997 to March 2000 Iranian society witnessed some of the most intense and collective forms of activism, including the formation of diverse student organizations,[61] women's associations, environmental organizations, Islamic political parties, artistic groups, counter-culture gangs, the publication of reformist and pro-democracy literature, and at least two mass football celebrations. Though political activism has suffered some-what since early 2000, modern social and cultural associations have continued to expand. And higher levels of civic cooperation will, in turn, enhance trust.

However, the democratic state and the rule of law, two fundamental structural pre-requisites, are still lacking in Iran; a circumstance which prevents institutionalization of trust on a more permanent basis. As a society in transition, Iran can only look ahead. But the future cannot be constructed with the sterile and archaic tools of the past, with a political culture based on currents of pessimism, fatalism, factionalism, messianism, and mistrust. For trust to flourish, Iranians cannot expect the state to take the lead. They must take the first steps and transcend the vicious cycles fostered by millennia of mistrust. Otherwise, as Diego Gambetta has aptly stated: "Deep distrust . . . [may lead] them to behavior which bolsters the validity of distrust itself . . ."[62]

Notes

1. Fred Halliday, "The Iranian Revolution and Great-Power Politics," in Nikki Keddi and Mark Gasiorowski, eds., *Neither East Nor West* (New Haven: Yale University Press, 1990), 248.
2. Iraj Pezeshkzad, *My Uncle Napoleon* (Washington, DC: Mage Publishers, 2000).
3. Ibid., 12.
4. Mohammad-Ali Jamalzadeh, *Kholqiyat-e Ma Iranian* (Germany: Navid Publishers, 1992), 68.
5. George Curzon, "Persia and the Persian Question," in Ervand Abrahamian, ed., *Khomein-ism* (New York: I.B. Tauris, 1993), 113.
6. Richard W. Cottam, *Nationalism in Iran* (Pittsburg: University of Pittsburg Press, 1979), 217–19.
7. Andrew F. Westwood, "Politics of Distrust in Iran," *The Annals of the American Academy of Political and Social Sciences*, 358, 1965, 124.
8. Ibid., 125.
9. "Not Indifferent but Distrustful," *Sahar* (Tehran), July 30, 1966, in Marvin Zonis, ed., *The Political Elite of Iran* (Princeton: Princeton University Press, 1971), 13.
10. Ahmad Ashraf, "The Appeal of Conspiracy Theories to Persians," *Princeton Papers*, 1997, 1.
11. Houchang E. Chehabi, *Iranian Politics and Religious Modernism* (Ithaca: Cornell University Press), 12.
12. Ervand Abrahamian, op. cit., 115–16.
13. Marvin Zonis, op. cit., 272.
14. Abdolkarim Soroush, *"Seh Farhang," Ayineh-e Andisheh* (February–March 1991).
15. Sadeq Zibakalam, *Ma Chegooneh Ma Shodim* (Tehran: Rowzaneh, 1998), Chapter 2.
16. Ibid., 80.
17. Reza Behnam, *Cultural Foundations of Iranian Politics* (Salt Lake City: University of Utah Press, 1986), 98.
18. Sadeq Zibakalam, op. cit., 86.

19. For a detailed discussion of "oriental despotism" in ancient Iran see the following: Homa Katouzian, *The Political Economy of Modern Iran* (New York: New York University Press, 1981); Mohammad-Ali Khonji, *Naqd-e Tarikh-e Maad* (Tehran: Tahura, 1979).

20. Homa Katouzian, ibid., 21.

21. Fredrick Engels and Karl Marx, "British Rule in India," quoted in "Oriental Despotism: The Case of Qajar Iran," *International Journal of Middle East Studies*, 5, 1974, 6.

22. Abdol Ghafoor Mirzai, "Reesheh-Yabi-e Vizhegi-hay-e Estebdad," *The Future Held Captive by the Past* (Costa Mesa: Mazda, 1998), 307–53.

23. Ann Lambton, *Islamic Society in Persia* (Oxford: Oxford University Press, 1954).

24. Homa Katouzian, op. cit., 14.

25. Sayyed Javad Tabatabai, *Dibachehi bar Nazariyeh-e Enhetat-e Iran* (Tehran: Negah-e Mo'aser, 2002), 66–8.

26. Hassan Qazi-Moradi, *Dar Peeramoon-e Khodmadari-e Iranian* (Tehran: Armaghan, 2000), 60–1.

27. For an excellent article regarding "orientalistic" features of the state under the Qajars see Ervand Abrahamian, (1974) op. cit.

28. Ibid., 10.

29. Mohammad Salar Kasrai, *The Conflict of Tradition and Modernity in Iran* (Tehran: Nashr-e Markaz, 2001), 1215.

30. For detailed accounts of these cultural characteristics see Seyyed-Aliasghar Kazemi, *The Crisis of Modernity and Political Culture in Contemporary Iran* (Tehran: Ghoomes, 1997); Hassan Qazi-Moradi, op. cit.

31. Zibakalam, op. cit., 92.

32. Mohammad Salar Kasrai, op. cit., 193.

33. Ervand Abrahamian (1993), op. cit., 116.

34. Marvin Zonis, *Majestic Failure* (Chicago: University of Chicago Press, 1991), 181.

35. James A. Bill, *The Eagle and the Lion* (New Haven: Yale University Press, 1988), 94.

36. For a detailed and elaborate analysis of these concepts see Samih Farsoun and Mehrdad Mashayekhi, eds., *Iran: Political Culture in the Islamic Republic* (New York: Routledge, 1992).

37. Ruth Benedict, *Patterns of Culture* (New York: Mentor, 1934), 42.

38. Mohammed Reza Shah's mistrustful views on foreign governments, particularly the British, are found in the following: Ehsan Naraghi, *From Palace to Prison* (Chicago: Ivan R. Dee, 1994).

39. On the subject of "hopelessness and pessimism" in Iran's history see Qazi-Moradi, op. cit., 178–84.

40. On the subject of the social basis of political and cultural fragmentation see Hossein Bashiriyeh, *Obstacles to Political Development in Iran* (Tehran: Gam-e No, 2001) and Ervand Abrahamian, "Factionalism in Iran," *Middle Eastern Studies*, 14(9), 1978.

41. James A. Bill, *Politics in the Middle East* (New York: Addison Wesley Longman, 2000), 123–5.

42. Ibid., 124.

43. Qazi Moradi, op. cit.

44. Marvin Zonis (1971), op. cit., 215.

45. Mohammad Qoochani, *Pedarkhaandeh va Chap-hay-e Javan* (Tehran: Nashr e Nay, 2000), 35.

46. Mehrdad Mashayekhi, "The Politics of Nationalism and Political Culture," in Samih Farsoun and Mehrdad Mashayekhi, eds., op. cit., 82–115.

47. Hamid Dabashi, *Theology of Discontent* (New York: New York University Press, 1993).

48. Ibid., 510.

49. For two interesting analyses of historical and sociological conditions shaping culture of mistrust in the Middle East and the Arab world, respectively, see James A. Bill (2000), op. cit., and Halim Barakat, *The Arab World: Society, Culture and State* (Berkeley: University of California Press, 1993).

50. Ruh Allah Khomeini, "March 21, 1980 – New Year's Message," in *Islam and Revolution*, trans., Hamid Algar (Berkeley: Mizan Press, 1981), 291–2.

51. On the subject of Islamist reformists and their political viewpoints see Ahmad Sadri, "The Varieties of Religious Reform: Public Intelligentsia in Iran," *International Journal of Politics, Culture and Society*, 15(2), 2001, 271–82.

52. This intellectual shift toward internal roots of Iran's major socioeconomic problems are most evident in: Sadeq Sibakalam, *op. cit.*; Kazem Alamdari, *Why Iran Lagged Behind and the West Moved Forward* (Tehran: Gam-e No, 2000); and Abdol Ghafoor Mirzai, (1998), op. cit.

53. BehzadYaghmaian, *Social Change in Iran* (Albany: State University of New York Press, 2002), 48.

54. For a more comprehensive account of trust-based networks in pre-modern (Safavid) Iran, see John Foran, *Fragile Resistance* (Boulder: Westview Press, 1993), 48–9.

55. Fariba Adelkhah, *Being Modern in Iran* (New York: Columbia University Press, 2000), 33–35.

56. Francis Fukuyama, *Trust* (New York: The Free Press, 1995), Part II.

57. James Coleman, *Foundations of Social Theory* (Cambridge, MA: Harvard University Press, 1990).

58. Robert Putnam, *Making Democracy Work* (Princeton: Princeton University Press, 1993).

59. Francis Fukuyama, *op. cit.*, Part III.

60. This information was obtained through a personal interview with Sussan Tahmasebi, researcher. It is based on the ISCORC research "Situation Analysis of Tehran-based NGO's" (forthcoming).

61. For detailed information on student activism, see Mehrdad Mashayekhi, "The Revival of Student Movement in Post-Revolutionary Iran," *International Journal of Politics, Culture and Society*, 15(2), 2001, 283–314.

62. Diego Gambetta, "Can We Trust Trust?" in Diego Gambetta, ed., *Trust: Making and Breaking Cooperative Relations* (Oxford: Blackwell, 1988), 234.

CHAPTER 32

What Do We Mean By Islamic Futures?

Ziauddin Sardar

At the dawn of the twenty-first century, the Muslim world finds itself in a state of total helplessness and uncertainty, marginalized, suppressed, angry, and frustrated. While a great deal has changed in the last hundred years, little has changed in terms of power politics. At the beginning of the twentieth century, when Jamāl al-Dīn al-Afghānī was calling for the revival of *ijtihād* and a global pan-Islamic alliance, most of the Muslim world was under colonial rule, but a fledgling caliphate was still in existence. The condition of the Muslim people – the *ummah* – its subjugation by the West, poverty and dependence, engendered a mood of despondency. Within two decades the caliphate had ended. A decade later a renewed struggle for independence began as calls for *ijtihād* and *jihād* reverberated throughout the Muslim world. Halfway through the twentieth century, most Muslim countries had gained their independence only to discover, after a couple of decades of development and Westernization, that economically and politically they were still the subjects of the West. In the 1970s and the 1980s, there was a brief period of euphoria about "Islamic resurgence" before, in the beginning of the 1990s, the rediscovery of their utter helplessness in a rapidly changing world brought the Muslims back to the cycle that began the century: as the French proverb has it, *plus ça change, plus c'est la même chose* – the more things change the more they stay the same.

During the twentieth century the Muslims stumbled from one crisis to another. Even the hard-won successes, like the creation of Pakistan as "the first Islamic state," the liberation of Algeria after a bitter and savage struggle against the French, and the strenuously gained independence of so many Muslim countries, have not improved the overall conditions of the Muslim people. In many parts of the Muslim world, particularly in Africa and Asian states like Bangladesh and Iran, the daily lives of ordinary folks are harsher and more poverty-stricken then during the colonial period. Large-scale famine is a constant presence in sub-Saharan Muslim Africa. Seven out of 10 of all refugees – running away from war, oppression and famine – in the world today are Muslims. The impotence of the Muslim states was revealed, in the glaring presence of global television networks, by their inability to prevent "ethnic cleansing" and the genocide of Muslims in Bosnia. The "war against terror" as well as internal feuds and strife have turned Afghanistan and Iraq into wastelands.

As things stand, this state of affairs is set to continue. In a world where the rate of change is itself rapidly changing, the structures that oppress and suppress the Muslim people will become even more entrenched. Under globalization, change is characterized not just by its global nature but also by instant, rapid feedback, complexity, chaos, and irreversibility. What this means is that the globe is constantly being transformed by swift scientific, technological, cultural, and political developments. The power of those who are managing and enhancing these changes – North America, Western Europe, and multinational corporations – is increasing in equal proportions. In the Muslim world, rapid and perpetual change will bring newer and deeper crisis to the fore, generate further confusion and bewilderment, and make the Muslim societies even more volatile and unstable and thus more amenable to manipulation, subjugation, and domination.

Consider how rapidly the Muslim world has itself been transformed in the last three decades. The early 1970s saw unbound enthusiasm and hope in the Muslim world. The Muslim countries and communities were said to be going through a cultural revival. Everywhere there was talk of "Islamic resurgence" and the dawn of a new glorious age for the Muslim people. Islam, it was said, was fast becoming a force in international politics. The Organization for the Petroleum Exporting Countries (OPEC) had come of age and was beginning to flex its muscles; there was an infinite pool of financial resources for development and modernization. The Sudan was going to be transformed into the "bread basket" of the Middle East. A new kind of Muslim unity, hitherto unimagined, was in the air as the Organization of the Islamic Conference (OIC) held one "Islamic Summit" after another. There were "Islamic conferences" on every conceivable subject, held in almost every major location in the Muslim world. Apparently, Islamic thought was being dragged from the Middle Ages to contemporary times. The "Islamic revolution" in Iran added extra fuel to this euphoria. Islam, it was announced, finally had a modern success story. And "Islamic revolution" had produced the first "Islamic state" in history; and where Iran led, other Muslim states were bound to follow. Suddenly, revolutions were supposed to break out everywhere in the Muslim world. Muslims everywhere demanded the implementation of *sharī'ah* and Islamic movements in Pakistan, the Sudan, and Egypt began their struggle to transform their respective countries into Islamic states. Pakistan and the Sudan even succeeded in implementing some form of *sharī'ah* and declared themselves to be "Islamic states." In the 1980s, "Islamization" became the norm throughout the Muslim world. Meanwhile the mujahidin in Afghanistan took on the might of a superpower. With over $5 billion in aid from Saudi Arabia alone, and ultra-advanced American weapons, they began to push the Russian bear out of Afghanistan and eventually, after a decade-long bloody struggle, succeeded in driving the Soviet armies from their lands.

But then things began to go sour; or, perhaps, the real world intervened to bring the Muslim *ummah* down to earth. The political, administrative, and organizational incompetence of various governments in Afghanistan, including the Taliban, produced a fractured and fragmented state. The mujahidin may have brought about the disintegration of the Soviet Union, as Ali Mazuri has argued,[1] but replacing the government of President Najibullah was another story. It proved beyond their capabilities to transform themselves from a band of undisciplined but fearless mountain warriors into disciplined, united party politicians capable of forming and leading a government. And the revolution in Iran, despite its Islamic credentials, turned out to be no different from any other revolution in history. The petro-dollars on which so much hope was pinned have been swallowed up by American and European banks and the bottomless purses of arms merchants. The "Arab money" which found its way as aid to various Muslim countries has produced little or no dividends in terms of development or modernization. On the contrary, absolute poverty increased manifold as certain Muslim countries, most notably the Sudan, Pakistan, and Bangladesh went into a downward spiral of poverty and degradation. The experiment with Islamization and implementation of *sharī'ah* turned out to be a superannuated farce which succeeded only in subverting social justice and increasing communal strife. The Islamic movements, which only two decades ago were so buoyant and full of promise, revealed themselves not just to be totally out of touch with reality but intellectually bankrupt and dangerously incompetent.

So, what went wrong? Why did the promises and hopes of the 1970s turn so quickly into the nightmares and bitter haplessness of the 1990s? Why has terrorism suddenly become the dominant theme in Muslim societies during the last decade?

Where did "Islamic resurgence" take a wrong turn? Whatever happened to the Muslim reassertion of "cultural identity"? The failures of the last two decades, indeed the shortcomings of the past century, has been the inability of Muslims to appreciate their own strengths, comprehend the reality of the contemporary world, and adjust to rapid change. The Muslims have been forced to react to one challenge after another, moving from one *cul de sac* to another: reacting, reacting, reacting. The way forward, and it seems to me to be the only rational way ahead, is for Muslims to become proactive: shape the future with foresight and a genuine appreciation of their present predicament, truthful assessment of their historic shortcomings, and a deep understanding of contemporary, global reality.

The purpose of Islamic futures is to chart out a path from the present impasse, develop insights into managing and anticipating change, and map out desirable alternative futures for the Muslim people. The enterprise of Islamic futures demands a sharp break from conventional Muslim thought – based as it is on ossified traditionalism and a one-dimensional understanding of modern and postmodern worlds – and a bold and imaginative grasp of the challenges that confront the Muslim people. It requires a fresh, deeper, futuristic understanding of Islam and a conscious, collective will to overcome the present impasse. And it needs intellectual boldness and imagination: to imagine what has hitherto been impossible to imagine, to develop ideas that have existed only on the margins, and envision what may appear to be unrealizable dreams. Let us then move to the future.

Where is the Future?

It is not easy to think about the future; the very idea of working out what things might look like 20, 50, 100 years from today is daunting. The difficulty is compounded by the fact that the future does not really exist: it is always a time that has yet to be reached.

Moreover, the future will not exist even in the future for the future exists only when it becomes the present at which point it ceases to be the future. As the future does not actually exist, it has to be invented; to put it another way, ideas about the future must be generated and studied. Ideas about the future are important because our thoughts and actions are influenced not just by our notions of what happened in the past but also by our images of what may yet happen in the future. Thus, while the future is elusive and uncertain, it is also a domain over which we can exercise some power. We cannot change the past; we can only interpret and reinterpret history; but we can't actually change it. We cannot change the present either: that requires instantaneous change, which is impossible. But our inability to have definite knowledge about the future is balanced by our ability to mold it. It is within the capabilities of individuals and societies to shape their own future.

How can we shape the future? Imagine a devout Muslim whose only desire is to visit Mecca to perform the pilgrimage. He knows how the pilgrimage is performed but he has never been to Mecca and he is not in Mecca now. There is no room for this image in the past or the present; but there is room for this cherished image to perform the pilgrimage in the future. Future time is the only domain where he is able to receive as "possible" an image that is "false" in the present. And the future in which he now places his cherished image reaches out to him to make the image a reality. To transform this future image into reality, the devout Muslim begins to save; and saves for a number of years before he has enough financial resources to undertake the journey to Mecca. But his plans are concerned not just with financial resources. He also plans to make arrangements for his family and business to be looked after while he is away, perhaps as long as two months. And he also plans for certain contingencies. What if, due to unforeseen circumstances, he cannot perform the *Hajj* on the actual year he had planned? What if he is taken ill in Mecca; or, given his age, dies! Thus, the realization of a simple future image requires serious planning which includes asking a number of "what if?" questions.

What is true of individuals is also largely true of societies. To shape a viable future, a society needs an image, a vision, of its future. It then has to map out a path toward the realization of that future: How is it going to move from "here" to "there"? Incorporated in that map must be a host of "what if?" questions: the variables that could go wrong; the hurdles that could appear almost as though from nowhere; the different paths that are available; and the alternatives and options that will generate choices that will have to be made. What we are then presented with is not just one future but a whole array of alternative *futures*.

In futures studies we always think of "the future" in terms of the plural: *futures*. The objective is not so much to predict the future (a highly hazardous exercise) but to anticipate possible futures and work toward shaping the most desirable ones. Consciously and rationally thinking and acting toward desirable futures implies developing a sense of direction: behaving in anticipation. A society with a sense of direction moves toward a planned future of desired goals and realizable visions and anticipates all the possible alternatives, including undesirable futures that it may encounter in its journey. In contrast, an aimless society drifts from one undesirable future to another. A society that is continuously reacting to one change after another will move from crisis to crisis until it reaches one from which there can be no escape.

An aimless society considers the future as a mighty river. The great force of history flows inexorably along, carrying everyone with it. Attempts to change its course amount to little more than throwing pebbles in the river: they cause a few ripples but have no real effect on the mighty river. The river's course can change but only by natural disasters such as earthquakes and landslides: by the will of God. This is fatalism in action. On the other hand, a society with a sense of direction sees the future as a great ocean. There are many possible destinations and many alternative paths to these destinations. A good navigator takes advantage of the main current of change and adjusts his course accordingly, keeping a sharp lookout for possible typhoons or changes in weather conditions, and moving carefully through fog or through uncharted waters thus getting safely to the intended destinations.

When thinking of alternative futures, we tend to think in terms of five basic time horizons:

1. The *immediate* future: the one-year time horizon. As a planning horizon it presents rather limited choice for it is largely dictated by the past. Present decisions or actions have little or no effect over this time-horizon frame; only major events cause perturbations in this range.

2. *Near* future: from one to five years. This is the time frame chosen for the conventional development plans of most Third-World countries. Decisions and policy choices made now can cause certain shifts in this time frame; however, it is not really possible to bring about revolutionary change in this time horizon. The near future works well for evolutionary advances; development plans have succeeded only when success has been accumulated from one plan to the next. However, the history of development planning teaches us that, in most developing countries, each five-year plan has marked a departure from the previous and the next five-year plan. The end result has been a sort of drunk random walk! After successive development plans many Third-World countries have ended up exactly where they started.

3. *One-generation* future: 20 years from now. This is the time required for one generation to grow and mature. The decisions taken today will not change the world we will experience in the next five years, but they could dramatically change the world we experience 20 years from now; the next generation would be maturing with those experiences. Almost anything can be done in this time frame. This sounds astonishing but consider the fact that it took the Prophet Muhammad just 23 years to totally change the tribal society of Arabia and evolve a civilization virtually from nothing; in more recent times, once the decisions had been made, it took just four years to build the atom bomb and just eight years to put a man on the moon! One generation is basically all it takes to realize any realistic vision of the future.

4. *Multi-generational* or *long-range* future: from one to several generations, extending up to 50 or 60 years. Although it is a largely uncontrollable (i.e. from today) open future, it is possible to see/trigger the opportunities/crisis ahead.

Figure 32.1   The extended present – a family chain

5. The *far* future: from 50 years and beyond. The domain of science fiction: it is possible only to speculate in this time frame. However, this time frame is not as far out as one may think. Consider yourself, your parents, your grandparents – that's at least 100 years of your personal history. Consider yourself, your children, your grandchildren – that's 100 years of your personal future. An individual walks around wrapped in 200 years of the extended present: the family chain (see Figure 32.1).[2]

Which time horizon is most suited for futures studies? Well, the faster the car, the further the headlights must go if we are to avoid dangers and pitfalls. The faster the pace of change the further into the future we must look. Given the extremely rapid rate of change, and its interrelated nature, we need to work with at least one-generation, if not multi-generational, time frames. Most futures planning and visionary work is thus carried out between 20 to 50 years' horizons.

The future is, of course, a product of both the past and present. And both our history and our present circumstances have to be taken into account in futuristic planning. That is to say futures thinking requires *prospective*: the inclusion of knowledge from the past and the present. History is the domain of identity; and a future without one's identity is no future at all. But not all history plays a part in the future; if it did then we would simply be living in history. All societies have living histories, often described as tradition, which molds their historic identity. It is tradition, in its living, life-enhancing form, and not its ossified, suffocating form (which truly belongs to the dim and distant past), that we must take into account when thinking about shaping viable futures. When considering contemporary reality, we have to ensure that we do not start from an impossible or untenable position. The modern world has to be appreciated in all its complexities and contradictions.

There are certain central features of contemporary reality that have to be taken into account in all futures-oriented work. In the globalized world, everything is connected to everything else. *Interconnection* and *interdependence* are the dominant global norms. That means problems do not exist in isolation; neither can they be resolved in isolation. A "simple" health problem, for example, does not only have a medical bearing but also scientific, educational, lifestyle, environmental, social, and economic components. A viable solution would therefore require inputs from all these areas. Thus even apparently "simple" problems turn out to be complex: *complexity* is the essence of contemporary problems[3] most of which seem to be interlinked to each other forming a web of problems – or *problematique*. The situation is made worse by the rapid pace of change. To appreciate the pace of change consider the fact that the evolution of the modern ship took over a 1000 years but the airplane evolved in fewer then 60; the evolution of the personal computer has followed a path similar to that of the printed book, but in 40 years instead of 600; most high technology becomes obsolete and is replaced in fewer then five years; the power of the microchip doubles every two years! The complexity of modern problems is thus being continuously enhanced by the changes ushered in by scientific and technological development. The truly mindboggling intricacy of our problems often generates a paralysis of decision-making processes characterized by perpetual postponement and avoidance of decisions – the so-called "disappearing decision" syndrome.[4] The time for easy solutions is history.

The interconnection and interdependence of the world also means that isolation is now untenable. Developments in communication and information technology, global television networks, and the evolution of the Internet, the network of all networks of computers around the globe, means that the globe is shrinking rapidly. All cultures, big or small, are obliged to interact with each other, generating synthesis and countersynthesis. Notions of cultural purity and monolithic institutions of all types are doomed. What has always been true in agriculture – a single crop, if repeatedly planted on the same field, exhausts the land and gives rapidly diminishing yields – is now also true of human cultures: large structures dominated by single modes of thought or straightjacketed by a single, all-embracing ideology cannot sustain themselves. The rapid collapse of the Soviet Union was as much due to the vacuous nature of Soviet communism as the monolithic nature of the Soviet state. *Plurality* and *diversity* are not only the essence of sustainability in nature but also the bedrock of stable societies and dynamic cultures. Monocultures have no place in the future.

Given the nature of contemporary reality, it is not possible for futures studies to be a unified, single subject discipline. By the very nature of what it sets out to tackle, futures studies is a *transdisciplinary* and *multidimensional* activity. It tackles both the *complexity* as well as the *contradictions* inherent in the world; considers both the *global* as well as the *local* dimensions of planning; emphasizes both *interdependence* as well as *interconnections*; and incorporates *plurality* as well as *participation* across all levels of societies and cultures. In so far as futures studies involves systematic and disciplined, empirical and rational exploration of future possibilities, futures studies is a science. But experimentation is not a possibility in futures studies; so, in that sense, futures studies is not a science. In so far as future studies involves foresight, prospective analysis, creation of visions and images, future studies is an art. It is the art of anticipation based on the science of exploration.

So how do we shape a desirable future, say, 20 or 40 years from hence?

First we need certain basic tools. We need pictures of what the future could look like. Essentially, we need two varieties of pictures. The first variety tells us what the future would look like if things continue as they are. We can get an idea of how the future is shaping up, given the present trends, by *projections* or *trend extrapolations*. Projections are linear analyses of current trends which go from the past to the present and into the future. Demographic developments are often predicted on the basis of this kind of projection. Trend extrapolations can be simple, involving one variable, or highly complex and sophisticated involving a whole array of variables as well as the probabilities of their interdependence and occurrence – in the latter case it is normally referred to as *morphological analysis*. We can also get an idea of what the future will be like by asking a selection of experts: if this is done in a systematic manner, the experts are polled a number of times, allowed to challenge each others' opinion and rethink their opinions, a consensus emerges giving us a general idea of what the future has in store. This is known as the *Delphi method*. When the Delphi method is used to identify future trends and then linked with possible future events, and the impact of trends on trends and of events on trends and events is analyzed in a systematic manner a more sophisticated picture of the future emerges – this is known as the cross-impact matrix method. An even more sophisticated method is to develop a simulation model of a system – say the world, or a city, or an economy – and then study what happens when various variables are changed.

The first major study of the future in recent times, *The Limits to Growth*, sponsored by the Club of Rome, was based on computer simulation models. These, and other methods, of studying the future generate *predictions* and *forecasts*. A prediction is a reasonably confident statement about a future state of affairs. A forecast is a more guarded statement of possible future outcomes based on "what if?" type of analysis: if a certain trend continues, and certain conditions are fulfilled, then we can expect a certain outcome with a certain level of confidence. Pictures of the future generated by these methods can be turned into *scenarios*. A scenario is defined as "the description of future situations together with the progression of events leading from the base situation to the future situation."[6]

Pictures of the futures generated in this way warn us of the potential threats and dangers ahead. They provide us with early warning signals so that we may change course, develop contingency plans, prepare ourselves to confront the emerging challenge. But this variety of futures images has a serious limitation: they contain only three types of basic information: (i) there will be continued growth and business as usual; (ii) things will retard and there will be a backward slide; or (iii) there will be total collapse or catastrophe. Since change is inevitable, and we cannot stand still, there can only be three options: things go up, or down, or break apart. This type of futures analysis is too dependent on historical momentum and present complexities. Such images of the future do not have transformational potential.

The second archetypal variety of images of the future is concerned with what we would like the future to be. It is our individual or collective picture of the future. Here, we could be really imaginative, really bold: instead of predicting the future, we try to invent it, to envision it. Our images of the future, at both individual and societal level, play an important role in actually determining the future. An enumerated image of the future, with most of the contours and details worked out, is a *vision*; and visions have transformational power. It is through well-articulated visions that societies break out of their cocoons, surpass their limitations, and transform, like a butterfly, into higher levels of existence.

How do visions help us shape the future? To transform visions into realizable futures we start with a vision and then plan backwards to present time. Consider, for example, a vision of a city like Karachi 40 years, some two generations, from today. What is my vision of Karachi in the year 2045? I envision Karachi free from ethnic and communal strife and pollution and traffic congestion, most of its inhabitants are in gainful employment and have adequate housing with clean water and electricity and a good network of public transport, business is booming thanks to the port which has become a focus for shipping in South Asia, there is law and order and a responsible and accountable local government. Now, while this is a pretty realistic vision of Karachi it is far removed from Karachi of today. To make this vision into a workable proposition we ask a series of questions working backwards from the year 2045: what conditions must be fulfilled in the year 2043 for my vision of Karachi to be in place by 2045? Well, for most of the inhabitants to be in gainful employment some sort of employment policy must be in full swing, the basic infrastructure of the city, including the public transport system, should be in position, an adequate number of low-cost housing units directed toward the urban poor must have been built. So, for these things to have occurred by 2043, what should have happened by 2041? And 2039, 2037, 2035 . . . and so on to the present time. We also have to explore negative possibilities: what can happen to undermine the successful implementation of certain targets? What could possibly go wrong? At the completion of the exercise, we have two products: a vision of Karachi in 2045 and a detailed plan, worked out backwards from 2045, with yearly goals and targets, of how that particular vision could be realized. This kind of planning is known as *backcasting* (as oppose to forecasting) and is a highly empowering tool. It brings what appear to be unachievable, distant goals, into the realms of realizable, possible alternatives. The more detailed and realistic the vision, the more thorough the backcasting, the more amenable the future! Of course, my individual vision and backcasting exercise is neither adequate, nor by itself, able to shape a viable future for Karachi. To be really meaningful both envisioning and backcasting must be a collective, social endeavor: shaping the future is a participatory endeavor!

Visions provide a society with a sense of direction, a future destination. Backcasting furnishes it with paths, ways, and means to get "there" from "here and now." This kind of future studies is thus a highly empowering as well as action-oriented process. It invites participation in both the formulation, as well as developing routes toward, desirable futures; and, by making what appears to be "impossible" accessible to systematic action, it makes belief in the genuine transformation of society possible. By its very nature, future studies is optimism writ large!

The purpose of generating images of the future, both by conventional methodologies of futures studies and by vision analysis and backcasting, is to improve our decision-making processes. Futures studies is a highly practical and pragmatic undertaking. When the visions and images, ideas and empirical work about alternative futures are distilled, we are left with choices and options that have to be made now:

> The fact is that problems of today did not appear suddenly out of thin air; they have been building up, often for many years, and might have been dealt with fairly easily if they had been tackled earlier. The crisis that we face today is generally the minor problem we

neglected yesterday. . . . The whole point of studying future possibilities . . . is to improve the quality of decisions that are *being made* right now. Today's decisions are shaping tomorrow's world, yet only too often we make decisions with little concern about their impact on the longer-term future.[7]

So, how does futures studies relate to Islam?

Islam and Future Awareness

Islam is perforce a future-oriented worldview. The Qur'an specifically asks believers to be conscious of their history as well as their future: "Beware of what lies before and behind you, so that you may be given mercy" (36:45). The idea of the future and the notion of accountability in Islam are tied up in two fundamental concepts: *ākhirah* (the Hereafter) and *khilāfah* (trusteeship of human beings). The concept of *ākhirah* is related to the Islamic notion of time. In rationalist and materialistic philosophies time is a linear progression: it ends with an individual's life. Beyond his/her life there is no time, at least as far as his/her own individual identity is concerned. In contrast, Islam sees time as a tapestry in which earthly time and eternal heavenly time are woven together. This life is life in earthly time, while the Hereafter is the life in eternity, where we are able to pass beyond the limits of space, time, and causality. One's life, thus, does not end with one's death and one's deeds on earth continue to have an impact on one's life in the Hereafter. Future time, that is time both in this world and the Hereafter, is the time of accountability: a believer will produce results for his/her deeds both in this world and *ākhirah*, the Hereafter. The concept of *khilāfah* adds another dimension to the synthesis of accountability and future. As trustees of God's creation, the believers are required to manage the trust (*amānah*) in an ethically and socially responsible way: it must be delivered to future generations in at least as good, if not much better, conditions than they found it. Certain Islamic social institutions inherently display the future orientation contained in the fundamental concepts of *ākhirah* and *khilāfah*. For example, throughout history, Muslims have been keen to establish *waqfs* (pious foundations) for both social and individual purposes: by looking after the needs of the future generations the *waqfs* generate blessings in perpetuity for the individuals who established them, enriching their afterlife. The same future-oriented logic is evident in the establishment of *ḥarām*, inviolate zones in which development is prohibited by Islamic law, and *ḥimā*, reserves for the conservation of wildlife and forests. Concern for the future is thus intrinsic to Islam.

We can see a demonstration of future awareness in the life of the Prophet Muhammad. The Prophet constantly anticipated future possibilities before taking action. The *Hijrah*, the migration from Mecca to Medina, was made on the anticipation of a more viable future for the then small Muslim community, was planned to the minutest degree, and the path for the migration was systematically cleared over several months. The Prophet anticipated the Quraysh tribe rebelling against him, prepared in advance, and met the advancing Quraysh army outside Medina, at a point he knew would give the small Muslim army a strategic advantage – the well of Badr. The Prophet realized that the future of the Muslim community depended on a negotiated comprehensive peace and a constitution for the pluralistic community of Medina where Muslims, Christians, and Jews lived together. Despite complaints from his companions that he was giving too much away, the Prophet concluded the Ḥudaybiyyah Agreement and used it as a basis to establish the first constitution in the world. Months before the battle the Prophet anticipated the coming conflict and prepared to defend Medina by digging a trench around the city thus actually preventing a major conflict. These are just a few examples from a life so full of anticipation, planning, and one of the most profound reshaping of the future: that where there was virtually nothing, within a generation, the foundations of a global civilization were laid!

And after the Prophet, the rightly guided caliphs continued the tradition of future-oriented thinking and actions. Abu Bakr, the first caliph, foresaw the expansion of Muslim lands and realized that future needs could not be fulfilled with the existing system of administration. He therefore developed a new, and profoundly flexible, system of administration and management, which could adjust to future needs. Umar, the second caliph, realized that the future survival of the Muslim *ummah* was dependent on available resources, and that all resources could not be consumed by one generation. Against the explicit wishes of his companions and even at the risk of a conflict, he refused to distribute the conquered lands of Syria, Iraq, Iran, and Egypt among the conquerors. Declaring that they were for "succeeding generations," he set them aside as future resources for the rapidly expanding Muslim community.

Islam does not only emphasize that Muslims be aware of their future, it insists that the believers should actively shape their future. By the very nature of their faith, Muslims are required both to engage with the world and change it. The Qur'an repeatedly asks Muslims both to change themselves and to constantly strive to change the world so that it could become a more just, equitable, and peaceful abode for humanity: "Man will only have what he has worked towards, that his labor will be seen and in the end he will be paid in full for it" (53:39–41). This is why at the core of *sharī'ah*, we find the principle of *ijtihād* (sustained and reasoned struggle) which is concerned primarily with change and with shaping and reshaping the future.

However, Muslim societies have not just abandoned *ijtihād*, whose "gates" were allegedly "closed" some centuries ago, but they have also ignored the future-oriented message of their faith – the very source of dynamism of the classic Muslim civilization. As a result, Muslim understanding of the worldview of Islam was frozen in history. During its long decline and eventual colonization, the Muslim civilization lost its capability for developing fresh insights, appreciations and interpretations of the fundamental sources of Islam: the Qur'an and the Sunnah of the Prophet Muhammad. Colonization produced further ossification where obscurantist traditionalism came to be seen as the sole protection from the encroachment of the West. Finally, development and accompanied Westernization has systematically stripped the holistic ethical layers from Muslim societies leaving them with the fragmented shell of what the late Fazlur Rahman called "minimal Islam" – rituals, pieties and a list of do's and don'ts. In the contemporary world, Islam manifests itself in a number of fractured, fragmented, and reductive ways. Contemporary Muslim societies prefer to look back, wallow in nostalgia for their "golden past" rather than plan and work toward a vibrant future.

Principles of Islamic Futures

The process of shaping desirable futures for the Muslim world must begin with an awareness of contemporary reality and the world of *real politick*. From the perspective of future studies, we know that there are no simple, one-dimensional answers to contemporary problems, let alone the increasingly complex web of problems that will confront us in the future. Thus the classical atomistic, jurisprudence (*fiqh*) oriented methodology of solving problems, which requires looking for guidance, arguments, and positions (by quoting single verses of the Qur'an or one or two traditions of the Prophet Muhammad or the opinion of the classical jurists) and produces a single answer, is totally inadequate for tackling modern problems. Simplistic legal rulings cannot engage the increasingly complex and rapidly changing world where problems are interconnected and interdependent. To transform the world proactively, the driving forces of the contemporary world, science, technology, modernity and postmodernism, must be engaged at fundamental levels: at the level of axioms, values, and ethical concerns. Thus, Islam must be seen not just as a faith and religion, but an integrated, holistic *worldview*. As a worldview, Islam interacts with contemporary reality through an integrated matrix of such concepts and values as *tawhīd* (unity of God, humanity, and humanity and nature), *khilāfah* (humanity's trusteeship of God's creation), *ākhirah* (accountability in the Hereafter), *'ilm* (distributive knowledge), *'adl* (distributive justice), *'ibādah* (worship), *istislah* (public interest), and other concepts found in the Qur'an and *sharī'ah*. Contemporary problems and challenges are analyzed from the perspective of this matrix – that is, each problem is analyzed with all the relevant fundamental concepts individually as well as collectively – to generate a host of possible Islamic choices from which each Muslim society chooses those which are most appropriate to its needs. When contemporary problems are examined and analyzed with ethical and value concepts, *sharī'ah* is transformed, from a historic body of rules and injunctions that must be "imposed" on Muslim societies, into a multidimensional problem-solving methodology. This, then, is the first principle of Islamic futures: *Islam engages with the contemporary world as a worldview whose conceptual matrix serves as a methodology for tackling problems and generating future choices and possibilities for Muslim societies.*

The fragmentation of the Muslim world means that Muslims appear to be nothing more than a collection of nation-states each with limited resources and a myriad of insoluble problems. In a globalized world, the nation-state is coming under pressure from two contradictory forces. It is leaking power downward to dissenting, and often suppressed and marginalized, ethnic groups and minorities. And it is diffusing power upward by being forced into regional economic and political alliances. Global politics is now too complex either to be divided into three portions (first, second, and third world) or analyzed by pre-cold war logic. The emerging political divisions are increasingly being based on what Samuel Huntington has called the "civilizational paradigm."[8] Global politics will thus increasingly become civilizational politics. Thus, it is imperative for Muslims to see themselves not in terms of nation-states and national interests, but as a civilization and in terms of civilizational interests. As a global civilization,

Muslims possess vast resources and enormous potentials, which would enable them to
solve most of their problems.

This is the second principle of Islamic futures: *Only when molded into a civilization,
which involves pooling of resources and sharing of potentials of Muslim countries to tackle
common problems and goals, would Muslims be able to move beyond parochial concerns of
fragmenting nation-state and acute global marginalization toward shaping a vibrant and
dynamic future for themselves.*

One of the main strengths of Islam is its diversity: a diversity that exhibits itself in
numerous historic ways of expressing Islam: a diversity that is enveloped by a unity:
a unity that manifests itself as a matrix of concepts and values that all Muslims
accept without qualification. Those who see Islam simply as a private faith; those
who are committed to various traditions within the religion – the historic trend of
literal interpretation of the Qur'an and the Sunnah; those who subscribe to the equally
old and established trend of mystical interpretations, the Sufis; those who emphasize
juristic traditions; those who are committed to the political differences arising from
various interpretations, the Shi'ites: each group contributes to the richness and diversity of Islam and each group has an important contribution to make in shaping
the future civilization of Islam in a collective, cooperative framework. When this religious diversity is combined with an ethnic plurality, the bewildering number of eth-
nicities within the world of Islam, the true multicultural nature of Islam comes to the
fore. Here then we have the third principle of Islamic futures: *the plurality and diversity
of Islam are the cornerstones for shaping a dynamic, thriving Muslim civilization of the
future.*

This principle has profound consequences for certain exclusivist and isolationist,
more commonly known as the fundamentalist, perspectives on Islam. The Qur'anic
directive to "change things," to work toward shaping a future, writes Anwar Ibrahim,

> emphasize collectivity and cooperation, self-development and self-adjustment. From the
> Islamic perspective, it is not man but God who created values. For Islam, values are *a priori*,
> given. Moreover, values do not change; they are eternal. There are no new values out there
> waiting to be discovered. There is complete consensus of the *ummah* on this issue; in
> fact, the definition of a Muslim is one who accepts the values and norms laid down in the
> Qur'an and the Sunnah of the Prophet Muhammad. The *ummah* (international Muslim
> community) tries to "change things" with a consensus of values; consensus rather than
> conflict and competition become the operating parameter. Moreover, as things are being
> changed with a cooperative endeavor, there is no place for domination and control in this
> framework.[9]

Shaping Islamic futures is thus a participatory exercise based on exploration of alternatives and possibilities and making choices. A puritan and dominating interpretation
of Islam cannot engage in such an exercise for in its framework there are no alternatives, no choices to be made: there can be only one future, the inevitable extension of
the perpetual and brutal struggle of the present.

Islam is pre-eminently a doctrine of truth. But believing in Islam does not amount
to *possessing* the truth. Those who claim that only their version of Islam is the absolute

truth, not only deny the manifest diversity and plurality of Islam, but also arrogate divine powers to themselves. What distinguishes fundamentalism from traditional Islam, as Parvez Manzoor has argued so convincingly, is that "the cognitive theory of "state" is "fundamental" to its vision of Islam and represents a paramount fact of its consciousness." Thus, from a "totalistic theocentric worldview, a God-centered way of life and thought, of knowledge and action," Islam is transformed into a "totalitarian theocratic world order that submits every human situation to the arbitration of the state."[10] When society and state become one, politics disappears, cultural and social spaces are totally homogenized, and the end product mirrors fascism. When Islam is transformed into an exclusivist ideology, the sacred is politicized and politics becomes sacred and everything is bulldozed into uniformity. The fundamentalist interpretation of Islam not only does violence to its tradition, history, and pluralistic outlook, but also has no appreciation of either the complexity and interdependence of contemporary reality or of the ecological laws of nature. Fundamentalism is "all cause and no program" and thus superfluous and irrelevant to contemporary times. As a homogenized, mentally monocultural, monolithic outlook on state and society, it is an unnatural phenomenon: it cannot survive; therefore it has no future; and, as such, it has no place in the purview of Islamic futures.

Pluralism and diversity lead by necessity to participation and hence to the fourth principle of Islamic futures: *shaping viable and desirable futures for Muslim civilization involves active participation of communities and conscious effort at consultation (shūra) at all levels of society with the aim of achieving a broad consensus (ijmā').* Both ijmā' and shūra are the basic and essential values of governance in any Muslim community. The process of consultation and consensual politics not only strengthens the civic institutions of Muslim societies but also legitimizes pluralistic identities and interests within a Muslim community. While a liberal polity allows the loudest, most powerful voices to win out, participatory structures of governance based on ijmā' and shūra ensure equality and justice by making consultation mandatory with all segments of society – thus giving voice and power to all minorities. The direct articulation of interests, needs, and preferences peculiar to different groups in society enables more appropriate and just policies to be formulated. New agents of social and economic change are produced moving society toward healthier and positive directions. Conflict is reduced if not eliminated and a cohesive society generated. In contrast, the fundamentalist agenda, as Anwar Ibrahim notes, "sets a false agenda of peripheral issues as the only topics that get serious and sustained attention" and thus "violates the necessary moral meaning of the concept of *ummah*" because it "causes division and engenders unnecessary conflict" and "enables some expressions to become Muslim imperialism writ large or writ small." Classical Muslim discourse, on the other hand, emphasized ideals of ijmā' and shūra as well as the notion of a pluralistic community bounded by faith, the *ummah*. Ibrahim sees the *ummah*, which is "not a cultural entity patterned upon the norms of any one dominant group" but "exists within and is expressed through diverse cultural groups," as the basis for a viable future for the Muslim civilization. The Muslim identity, he argues, is not only rooted in Islamic history and tradition, it is also intrinsically connected to the notion of the *ummah*. The idea of the *ummah* is not simply that Muslims are a community, but how Muslims should *become* a community in relation to each other, other communities and the natural world. It is manifesting in thought, action and openness a distinctive moral vision that is the *raison d'être* of the *ummah*. It is enduring commitment to the dynamism of a constant set of moral concepts and precepts that creates the contours and ultimate configuration of the *ummah*.[11]

Pluralistic participation and consultative and consensual politics, at the level of society, nation, and civilization, provide the circumference within which Muslims become a community in relation to each other.

The interconnected and interdependent nature of the modern world makes isolation a thing of the past. Even when it is desired, it is not possible for a society or a state to exist in splendid cultural, economic, or political isolation. Moreover, the complexity and contradictory nature of modern times means that it is not possible to consider, or label, a single institution, idea, or group of people as all bad or all good, all black or all white. The world consists not of dichotomies and bipolar choices but of complexities that have reduced everything to shades of gray. This is why the ethical concepts of Islam are of such paramount importance in analytical and methodological explorations. *To shape desirable alternative futures Muslims must engage constructively with the contemporary world in all its dimensions.* This is the fifth – and last – principle of Islamic futures. There is, for example, no escaping the West: there is nowhere on this globe that one can hide to get away from Western civilization! However, constructive engagement with the West could not only produce dividends for Muslim societies but also has the potential of actually transforming the West to the benefit of the entire planet! This principle also contrasts sharply with clannish approaches to Islam (evident even in the names of certain groups: "The Muslim Brotherhood," "Jamaat-e-Islami," "Hizbullah," "Hizb-al-Tahrir"), which encircle a minority to the exclusion of the majority. The very nature of these insular movements, based as they are on the retrieval of imagined "pristine" beginnings, leads them to engage with the world in terms of dichotomies: Dār al-Islām versus Dar al-Ḥarb, fundamentalism versus modernism, normativism versus accultur-ationism, revivalism versus re-entrenchment, Islam versus the West. Thus everything must be rejected; and the rejection begins by cutting off ties with the West and all its ills and ends with intolerance of all interpretations of Islam which differ from those of the clan. Similar ideas lead to a total rejection of democracy. But democracy, or indeed any notion, Western or non-Western, clashes with Islam only when it conceives itself as a doctrine of truth or violates one of the fundamental notions of Islam. Only when democracy becomes wedded to atheistic humanism and lays claims to being a dogma of truth, or when secularism interprets itself as an epistemology, does it clash with the faith of Islam. As a mechanism for representative government, devoid of its ideological pretensions and trappings, democracy hardly clashes with Islam. Similarly, a total rejection of modernity is insane. In a world dominated by technological development, one cannot create a non-technological society. What is needed is a detailed analysis of modernity and rejection of its core values such as instrumental rationality, alienating modes of production, artificial and conflict-ridden nation-states etc. But, in the end, Muslims will have to engage with modernity by producing their own ways of being (traditionally?) modern. Rejectionist ideologies produce one-dimensional answers far removed from contemporary reality. Once Islam is isolated from the real world and framed into a cardboard ideology, it ceases to be an actor shaping individuals and societies but becomes a simple point of reference. Islam therefore becomes an instrument in attempts to create a totalitarian state based on intolerance and martyrdom. This type of reductionism and bipolarization is the product of intellectual capriciousness and exaggeration, wavering and anemia, and pretension and intolerance, none of which were dominant in pre-modern Islamic history.

Constructive engagement involves reducing conflict both within Muslim societies and between Islam and the West. Conflicts within Muslim societies can be tackled by successfully managing competing interests and loyalties on the basis of *shūra* and consensual politics. Imparting humility to the West involves a great deal more. Muslim understanding of Western civilization, tempered by centuries of conflict and the experience of colonialism, is extremely skewed. On the whole, Muslims have developed stereotype images of the West as pernicious and immoral ("the Great Satan") just as the West has developed orientalist images of Islam and Muslims. The myopic understanding of the West means that Muslims are unable to see the contradictions within Western societies nor are they able to martial their natural allies within the West who are often alienated by extreme and one-dimensional rhetoric. There are essentially two points of conflict between Islam and the West. The first point is that economically and technologically, the world is structured as though the developing countries were the colonies of the industrialized states of the West. About 90 percent of scientists live in developed countries and technology is one of their main exports. Banks and insurance companies, airlines and shipping companies, and multinational corporations of the West all tie the world together. The World Bank, the International Monetary Fund (IMF), and the World Trade Organization (WTO) ensure that the oppressive and the unjust nature of the system is maintained. Muslims have to change the global system by managing the conflict through alliances with other civilizations – China, India, Latin America – and taking advantage of the contradictions and fractures within the Western alliance. To some extent this process has already begun with the industrialization of Southeast Asia and re-emergence of China as an economic superpower of the future. The second point relates to the West's insistence on demonizing Islam and Muslims and flaming the fires of conflict. That a bloodthirsty Muslim civilization is ready to pounce on the West is one of the main assertions of Huntington's "clash of civilizations" thesis; and it is an intrinsic assumption of such notions as "axis of evil" and the "war on terror." Demonization of Islam in Western thought has a history going back even before the crusades.[12] It is, in fact, very much part of the Western psyche and consciousness. At this juncture of history, we should not be too surprised by it. Far from being hurt by this type of stereotyping, Muslims must engage with the West and demonstrate the false nature of these historic images. Instead of being alarmed by Western saber rattling, the Muslims have to manage this variety of perceived conflicts by creative tension where resolution is achieved by the qualitative transformation of the opponent – in the well-known Hegelian sense!

It is quite evident that the principles of Islamic futures are as much about the future as they are a critique of existing Muslim thought. When the concerns of the future are brought to bear on contemporary situations a critique is always generated and the critique *per se* becomes a program of action. The function of the principles of Islamic futures is to enable Muslim societies to creatively manage the four global features of our time: change, complexity, contradictions, and conflicts. The process of managing the 4Cs – that is improving the present – is related to operationalizing the principles that will shape desirable and possible futures for the Muslim people. The future is a function of the present. And the present demands a set of pragmatic first steps. A fresh, contemporary understanding of Islam, that transforms Islam from a mere faith, to which it has been reduced, into an integrative worldview with an analytical ethical and conceptual matrix, has to be developed. Muslim states have to reconstruct and transform themselves, almost brick by brick, into a dynamic, contemporary, global civilization. Isolationist, puritanical, and monolithic tendencies have to be checked. Plurality and participation, on the basis of consultation and consensual politics, have to be instituted. And Muslims have to avoid being cast as a new demon or become entangled, like the Ottoman caliphate at the beginning of this century, with the hegemonic rivalries of old adversaries. Formidable though these challenges are, they are, nevertheless, not as daunting as they first appear. Already, there are considerable intellectual and scholarly resources to draw upon; and the momentum of history is on the side of the Muslims!

Future Paths Already Taken

The euphoria and upheaval, the swings of the pendulum, over the last two decades has generated an important side-effect: Muslims everywhere have realized the acute need for Islamic reform, a realization that has acquired urgency after the tragic events of 9/11 and its aftermath. Numerous calls for internal reforms in Islam and to shape a new, "progressive" Islam have been made. The American group "Progressive Muslims" have presented an agenda for change, including ideas on justice, gender relations, sexual orientation, and pluralism.[13] While wishing to engage seriously with Islamic thought, tradition, and practice, Progressive Muslims want to "translate" the social ideals of the Qur'an into contemporary idiom, seek full "human and religious rights" for Muslim women, and aim at restoring "compassionate humaneness" into contemporary Islam. In contrast, Malaysian Prime Minister, Abdullah Badawi, has proposed another model of progressive Islam he calls "Islam *ḥadhārī*."[14] The term "*ḥadhārī*" is taken from Ibn Khaldun and signifies urban civilization; and Islam *ḥadhārī* places considerable emphasis on economic development, civic life, and cultural progress. It gives equal emphasis to the present and the future, encourages moderation and pragmatism, emphasizes the central role of knowledge in Islam, preaches hard work and honesty, and appeals to Muslims to be "inclusive," tolerant and outward-looking toward other faiths and ideologies. Both the work of the "Progressive Muslims" and Islam *ḥadhārī* are contemporary efforts at all round *ijtihād*.

Elsewhere, the emphasis has been on what I have called the three "metaphysical catastrophes"[15] that have undermined our ability to undertake *ijtihād*: the elevation of *sharī'ah* to the level of the divine; the equation of Islam with the state; and the removal of agency from the believers. Muslims throughout the world now realize that much of

Islamic law and jurisprudence is socially constructed and has little relevance for contemporary society. We need to reconstruct Islam law and ethics from first principles – from the matrix of concepts and values embedded in the Qur'an, that define the spirit of Islam. Moreover, the spectacular failure of contemporary "Islamic states" – in Iran, the Sudan, Saudi Arabia, Afghanistan, Pakistan, and elsewhere – has led to the questioning of the conventional "Islamic movement" formulation of the relationship between Islam and the state. The idea that Islam should be the basis of the state, *sharī'ah* should be adopted as state constitution, political sovereignty should rest in the hands of the divine (by which is meant the *ulama*), and the principles of *shūra* (consultation) are inimical to the notion of democracy, has now been totally discredited. While certain segments of the "Islamic movement" – most notably Jamaat-e-Islami of Pakistan and Muslim Brotherhood of Egypt – still hang on desperately to these ideas, the vast majority of Muslims know from wide-ranging experience that this is a recipe for totalitarianism.

Similarly, many thinking Muslims have begun to question the traditional wisdom that all interpretative authority in Islam should belong to a particular class of people – the *ulama* – and the vast majority of believers can be nothing but empty vessels who have to follow the dictates of a select few.

Efforts to reframe Islamic law, both theoretically and practically, have already begun. In works such as Mawil Izzi Dien's *Islamic Law*,[16] *sharī'ah* is being historicized in an attempt to rethink its current purpose. In Britain, attempts are being made to develop a "minority *fiqh*." Taha Jabir Al-Alwani, for example, has suggested that minority *fiqh* can be formulated by a "combined reading" of the "Revelation for an understanding of the physical world and its laws and principles, and a reading of the physical world to appreciate and recognize the value of Revelation."[17] Al-Alwani also calls for a review of the relationship between the Qur'an and the Sunnah and insist that the questions we ask of *sharī'ah* are contextual. Each minority has to consider the political system it is living under, the kind of majority it is living with, what kinds of rights and protections it enjoys, what kind of common ground it shares with other cultures, and so on. The end product is thus not some "universal" legal framework but law that is specific to the minority that undertakes the exercise to reformulate *sharī'ah* according to its own needs and circumstances.

By far the most radical and practical changes to Islamic law have been undertaken in Morocco. Over a decade of agitation by women's rights groups as well as reform-minded organizations has produced a radically new Islamic family law. Introduced in February 2004, it sweeps away centuries of bigotry and blatant bias against women. Morocco retained much of the legal system France left behind, but followed conventional Islamic family law, known locally as *Mudawana*, which regulated marriage, divorce, inheritance, polygamy, and child custody. *Mudawana* encouraged a long list of abuses against women, including domestic violence and sexual harassment, polygamy, biased divorce rights, inequality at work and in education, and denial of inheritance. The new law totally reformulates the conventional notions of *sharī'ah*. Thus, the traditional idea that husband is the head of the family has gone, placing the family under the joint responsibility of both spouses. The debasing language previously used in reference to women has been replaced with gender-sensitive terminology. So, women become men's partners in rights and obligation rather than their underlings in need of guidance and protection. Women's marriageable age has been raised from 15 to 18 bringing it on a par with men. Women and men now have the right to contract their own marriage without the legal approval of a guardian. Women have the right to divorce; and men's right to unilateral divorce has been ditched. Men now require prior authorization from a court before they can obtain a divorce. Verbal divorce has been outlawed. Moreover, husbands are required to pay all monies owed to the wife and children in full, before divorce can be duly registered. Polygamy has been all but abolished. Men can take second wives only with the full consent of the first wife and only if they can prove, in a court of law, that they can treat them both with absolute justice – an impossible condition. Women can now claim alimony and can be granted custody of their children even if they remarry. Indeed, a woman can even regain custody of her children if the courts initially ruled in favor of the husband but the husband failed to fulfill his responsibilities. There is also provision for the child to get suitable accommodation consistent with his or her living conditions prior to the parents' divorce. This requirement is separate from the other alimony obligations, which conventionally consisted of a paltry lump sum. The new law also protects the child's right to acknowledgement of paternity in case the marriage has not been officially registered or the child was born outside wedlock. Moreover, the new law requires that husbands and wives share the property acquired during marriage. Husbands and wives can have separate estates but the law makes it possible for the couple to agree, in a document other than the marriage contract, on how to manage and develop assets acquired during marriage. The traditional tribal custom of favoring male heirs in the sharing of inherited land has also been dropped making it possible for the grandchildren on the daughter's side to inherit from their grandfather, just like the grandchildren on the son's side. The new family law also assigns a key role to the judiciary. Public prosecutors must now be involved in every legal action involving family affairs. New family courts have been set up and a family mutual assistance fund has been established to ensure that the new code is effectively enforced. The new law also enshrines the principle that minorities should be allowed to follow their own laws. So Moroccan Jews will now be governed by the provisions of the Hebraic Moroccan family law. Its radical nature notwithstanding, every change in the law is justified – chapter and verse – from the Qur'an; and the examples and traditions of the Prophet Muhammad. What the new Moroccan Islamic family law demonstrates most vividly is that *sharī'ah* is not a prior given; it can be changed, reinterpreted, and reformulated according to contemporary needs.

Similar radical transformations are taking place in the relationship between Islam and the state. Here, Indonesia is providing a lead. The new Islamic intellectualism in Indonesia, which has evolved over the last two decades, is based on a three-point agenda: (i) to re-examine the theological and philosophical underpinnings of political Islam; (ii) to redefine the political objectives of Islam; and (iii) to reassess the ways in which these political objectives can be effectively realized.[18] Through an intense debate and lengthy discussions, Islamic organizations such as the Muhammadiyah and Nahdatul Ulama, which have a combined following of over 80 million, have used this agenda to reassert several important propositions and packaged these propositions into a new Islamic perspective on the relationship between Islam and the state. Thus,

Indonesian intellectuals, like Amin Rais and Nurcholish Madjid, reject the notion that the Qur'an and Sunnah provide a clear-cut directive for Muslims to establish an "Islamic state." Moreover, they recognize that Islam does not contain a set of political principles and cannot be viewed as an ideology. Therefore, there is no such thing as an "Islamic ideology." Furthermore, they believe that absolute truth is possessed by Allah alone. As such, our comprehension of Islam's religious doctrine is essentially relative and subject to change and multiple interpretations. When we combine this realization with the fact that Islam does not recognize priesthood, we cannot but reach the conclusion that no individual has the authority to claim that his interpretation is truer or more authoritative than those of others – so the *ulama* have no real authority over the masses. Using these fundamental premises, the new Islamic intellectual movement in Indonesia has campaigned for substantial, rather than symbolic, change in the political system, focusing their attention, for example, on corruption and more accountable and transparent forms of governance. They have also fought to separate *sharī'ah* from the political realms, arguing that Islamic law cannot be imposed from above and has to evolve from below.

All these developments – various agenda-setting attempts to reform Islam, efforts to reformulate *sharī'ah*, and articulations of a new relationship between Islam and the state – are trends that one way or another will have an impact on the future of Islam. When thinking about Islamic futures, we need to be aware of trends already set in motion that could act as a catalyst for ushering in more desirable futures for the Muslim *ummah*.

Foresights for the Coming Decades

In today's globalized world, what may appear to be a small, insignificant trend can actually contain seeds of radical shifts. So while changes in law in Morocco, or politics in Indonesia, or ideas buried in obscure scholarly journals or learned books, may appear to be rather inconsequential, they can, under certain circumstances, lead to transformative change. To understand how this can happen, we need to appreciate the true nature of globalization.

Whatever the pros and cons of globalization itself, we need to grasp the fact that it has connected and interconnected the world in numerous ways. Everything is now connected, as I noted earlier, to everything else; and everyone is connected to some sort of network. So potential for feedback, for things to multiply, for ideas to spread rapidly, is enormous. And these are ideal conditions for chaos: The theory that tells us that apparently insignificant changes can trigger major perturbations, that order can emerge from apparent disorder, and social and political systems can spontaneously self-organize. This insight has a particular significance for Muslim people.

At present, the Muslim world looks very fragmented, disordered, driven by internal strife, being torn apart by sectarian and political violence. The absence of an overall charismatic, dominant leader – or, as some would call him, a caliph – means that no one has overall authority; and Muslim societies, like the clouds, look the same from all perspectives – disordered, confused, panic ridden. Yet, at the same time the Muslim world is totally connected – thanks to telephones, the Internet, satellite television, 24-

hour news channels – and behaves like a network. Moreover, the *ummah* is a complex system – a network of numerous cultures, truly astonishing diversity and plurality, spread across the globe, incorporating around 1.3 billion people. And, all kinds of feedback loops are being established in this complex network. In other words, the Muslim world is at the "edge of chaos": the entire system is in a kind of suspended animation between stability and total dissolution into anarchy.[19]

So the Muslim world is at a point where any factor, however small, can push it toward one or other direction. Further acts of terrorism, undertaken in the name of Islam, can lead to total collapse. But positive trends and ideas can equally transform it: Like any complex system, the *ummah* has the ability to spontaneously self-organize itself and "evolves" impulsively into a new mode of existence. Think of a flock of birds taking off in a haphazard manner: They adjust and adapt to their neighbors and unconsciously organize themselves into a patterned flock. So order emerges from disorder. Similarly, changes in Islamic law or political organization in one or two Muslim countries can lead to major transformations throughout the *ummah*.

However, for such transformations to occur, it is necessary for us to understand the chaotic nature of the globalized world. So we have to seek actively to be connected to all sorts of networks, Muslim and non-Muslim alike, to learn to think of ourselves as connected to numerous networks, and behave as a truly globalized community with a global system. We have to appreciate that apparent insignificant individual actions can make all the difference in the world. To actively transform chaotic life to our advantage, we have to understand that our problems are interconnected and have to learn to recognize joined-up problems. Thinking chaotically means seeing the connections and searching for joined-up answers. That's the moral of chaos. It requires new thinking, but old Islamic morals and virtues remain intact.

The coming decades will witness minor as well as profound changes both within the Muslim world and at global levels – and any, or a combination, of them can lead to transformative chaotic shifts. Muslim societies would do well to anticipate these changes and to prepare for them.

The first change we can anticipate will be ushered in when Turkey joins the European Union (EU). Turkey is part of Europe even though conventionally both Europeans and Muslims have seen it as part of the Muslim world. While we can expect considerable resistance and opposition from the European citizenry to Turkey's membership of the EU – particularly from France and Germany – eventually Turkey will be accepted as a full member. It may not happen for at least a decade or two, but it will happen. Europeans know that Turkey cannot be kept out of the EU indefinitely; and, in the end, it is to the advantage of the EU that Turkey is included.

Turkey's inclusion will change both the Muslim perception of Europe and European perceptions of Islam. Muslims will begin to see that European values are not alien to Islam; indeed, many cherished European values – its liberal humanism, its concern for accountable governance, its emphasis on research and development – have their origins in Islam, especially Islamic philosophy and *adab* literature that Europe acquired through Ottoman Turkey. Europe will notice that Islam is not inimical to European concerns; and a Muslim republic can be just as European as any other European nation. The newly enlarged European Union, with a quarter of its population now Muslim, may align itself increasingly with its thriving Muslim neighbors, than with America. New checks and balances may emerge in a world solely dominated by America.

But we should not take American domination of the globe for granted. American pre-eminence and its staying power are both greatly exaggerated. The power of American rests largely in its advanced technology, which is increasingly available to the rest of the world. Economically, America is a crippled power kept afloat largely by Japanese and German credit. Soon, it will face incurable balance-of-payments problems, made worse by permanent loss of manufacturing and difficulties in maintaining oil imports. Meanwhile, both China and India are emerging as major, global economic powers – the economies of both China and India are likely to overtake the US economy in size in the next few decades.[20] It is likely, as Paul Kennedy predicts, that the US will go the way of the British Empire in the next few decades and we will return to a multi-polar world.[21] The emergence of China will undoubtedly usher in serious changes in international relations; and if India joins the Security Council of the United Nations a new era of international relations will emerge. Thus, within the next two decades, no major power, or centers of power, will be able to establish its hegemony over the whole world, not even over large parts of it. We will, instead, see a world of competing civilizations.

At the same time, authoritarian structures within Muslim societies will begin to crumble. States such as Saudi Arabia and theocracies like Iran cannot survive the future. The breakdown of such states will undoubtedly cause a great deal of havoc; and the pendulum may swing from one extreme to another in the initial stages. But in the long run, models of accountable and participatory governance will emerge. Nothing succeeds like success; and successful democracies such as Turkey and Indonesia may become the prototype for the rest of the Muslim world to follow.

Thus, both locally and globally the world is set to change. How the Muslims meet the coming challenges depends largely on what steps they take – as individuals, communities and states – now; what note they take of the early warning signals and how they inform their present decision making with the anticipation of things to come. The future is always shaped in the present!

Moving On

The ideas embedded in Islamic futures, and its basic principles, serve to empower the Muslim people and to encourage them – as states, communities, and individuals – to engage with their problems on a broad front. This engagement must begin with an unreserved confidence in their own ability to determine a pragmatic, sustainable path toward desirable change and empowerment. Without empowerment Muslims can only react to initiatives derived from elsewhere – as they have been doing for the past few centuries. A reacting civilization is a civilization whose future has been colonized and systematically confined to the contours of dependency and utter helplessness. An empowered civilization, on the other hand, is in control of its own destiny.

The essential *problematique* set out here is not that Muslims should engage in concerted future studies. From the analysis of contemporary problems that beset Muslims everywhere it is clear that commitment to effective futures planning is the only path to empowerment, the only true self-determined trajectory open to them. The real problem we face is how, given the current imbalance of resources with and between nations and the lack of genuinely effective organization and cooperation at the level of the *ummah*, the appropriate infrastructure and resources to undertake futures thought and planning can be amassed and set to work. Here, the first and most enduring challenge is creating the political and civilizational will to take responsibility for changing things. Such commitment cannot be rhetorical, it must be based on the allocation of real resources and the patient building of resilient mechanisms, that have the support and confidence of national authorities as well as ordinary citizens, for undertaking study and dissemination of futures ideas and action.

The utility of futures studies, of envisioning and shaping futures, as I have argued, is how it informs present actions and creates the sense of empowerment to choose between various responses to contemporary problems. But no responsible choice can be made without a strong sense of civilizational identity. A prerequisite of taking responsibility for the continuity of Muslim identity is reforging our own understanding of what it means to be a Muslim. Simple piety and diligent observance of rituals is not enough. We need to activate the concepts and values that define the Muslim personality and use them to shape viable and desirable futures by engaging not just with our own problems but the problems of the whole world. There are no isolated problems and no isolated answers that can be confined to a special reserve set aside for Muslims. The Muslim ethical sense is the prime ingredient in constructing the link between individual piety and civilizational action, the main elements in creating alternative futures where Muslims can be at home with their identity and sanity intact, and the main feature for operating as contributory members of the global community that strives for human betterment.

The basic concepts and principles of the Qur'an are the building blocks of Islamic futures. However, the Islamic worldview cannot be a creative tool through approximation, we can no longer afford to allow imported patterns of modernity, or relativism of postmodernism, to set the agenda of understanding or interpretation of our worldview. Islamic concepts and principles are enduring yet dynamic, their meaning has to be unfolded through intellectual effort and practical endeavor. Our concepts have to be articulated and disseminated through education and our media; there must be widespread discussion and debate that enables contemporary implications to be defined and refined so that the precepts of our most personal and deeply rooted identity become handholds on solutions to the problems we face. Just as we need to devise a language for Islamic futures so we have to incorporate this into a new language of discourse on Islam and an Islamic worldview in the contemporary world. This search for an Islamic discourse cannot be seen as a battle for authority or authoritative interpretations, unless Muslims everywhere participate and unless they seek to regain the open mindedness, tolerance and participatory spirit of the early Muslim community, they will foreclose on their future prospects and resign themselves to being the unwilling instruments of change they neither desire nor choose in perpetuity.

The future will always remain an undiscovered country where none of us can exist. Yet creating confidence in the future potential of Muslim states, communities, and peoples – integrated into a dynamic, thriving civilization – is the only viable means to exert a refined Islamic influence on present circumstances. To be responsible Muslims today means balancing the reverence for the enduring importance of the prophetic model, the guiding example set in the defining moments of Islamic history, with commitment to envisioning futures where the central concepts and principles of the model find new ways to shape possibilities, choices, and actions. The essential link between our past and our future is to take a responsibility for informed changes in the present.

Notes

1. Ali Mazuri, "The Resurgence of Islam and the Decline of Communism," *Futures*, 23(3), 1991, 273–88.
2. I am grateful to Richard Slaughter for this insight. The diagram is, in fact, part of his email signature!
3. For a wide-ranging discussion of complexity see Roger Lewin, *Complexity: Life at the Edge of Chaos*, (New York: Macmillan, 1992) and Mitchell Waldrop, *Complexity: The Emerging Science at the Edge of Order and Chaos* (New York: Simon and Schuster, 1992). For an analysis of complexity from the futures perspective see the special issue of *Futures*, 26(6), 1994, "Complexity: Fad or Future" eds., Ziauddin Sardar and Jerome R Ravetz.
4. For a discussion of "disappearing decisions" see G.D. Kay and K.E. Solem, "Decision Making for Global Problems," *Futures*, 24(1), 1992, 54–64.
5. D. Meadows *et al.*, *The Limits to Growth* (New York: Potomac Associates, 1972). The Club of Rome was also responsible for other reports on the future of the world, based on different methodologies, such as M. Mesarovic and E. Pestel, *Mankind at the Turning Point* (London: Hutchinson, 1974) and J. Tinbergen, *RIO: Reshaping the International Order* (London: Hutchinson, 1976).
6. Michel Godet, *Scenarios and Strategic Management* (London: Butterworth, 1987), 21. Quoted by Elenora Masini, *Why Future Studies?* (London: Grey Seal, 1994), 91. Masini provides an excellent introduction to various methodologies of future studies. See also Richard Slaughter, ed., "Futures of Futures Studies," *Futures*, 34(3), 2002 (special issue) and Sohail Inayatullah, ed., "Layered methodologies," *Futures*, 34(5), 2002 (special issue).
7. Edward Cornish, *The Study of the Future* (Washington DC: World Future Society, 1977), 99.
8. Samuel P. Huntington, *The Clash of Civilizations and Remaking of the World Order* (New York: Simon and Schuster, 1997).
9. Anwar Ibrahim, "From 'Things Change' to 'Changing Things'," in Ziauddin Sardar, ed., *An Early Crescent: The Future of Knowledge and Environment in Islam* (London: Mansell, 1989), 19.
10. S. Parvez Manzoor, "The Future of Muslim Politics: Critique of the 'Fundamentalist' Theory of the Islamic State," *Futures*, 23(3), 1991, 289–301.
11. Anwar Ibrahim, "The Ummah and Tomorrow," *Futures*, 23(3), 1991, 302–10.
12. For a history of Western antagonism towards Islam see Ziauddin Sardar and Merryl Wyn Davies, *Distorted Imagination: Lessons from the Rushdie Affair* (London: Grey Seal, 1990); and Ziauddin Sardar, *Orientalism*, (Buckingham: Open University Press, 1999).
13. See their manifesto edited by Omid Safi, *Progressive Muslims* (Oxford: One World, 2003).
14. Ziauddin Sardar, "Can Islam Change?" *New Statesman*, September 13, 2004, 24–7.
15. "Rethinking Islam" in Sohail Inayatullah and Gail Boxwell, eds., *Islam, Postmodernism and Other Futures: A Ziauddin Sardar Reader* (London: Pluto Press, 2003).

16. Mawil Izzi Dien, *Islamic Law: From Historical Foundations to Contemporary Practice* (Edinburgh: Edinburgh University Press, 2004).

17. Taha Jabir al-Alwani, *Towards a Fiqh for Minorities* (London: IIIT, 2003), 15.

18. For a detailed analysis of the new Islamic intellectualism in Indonesia, see Bahtiar Effendy, *Islam and the State in Indonesia* (Singapore: Institute of Southeast Asian Studies, 2003).

19. For a more analytical explanation of what happens at the "edge of chaos," see Ziauddin Sardar, *Introducing Chaos* (Cambridge: Icon Books, 1998).

20. Jeffrey D Sachs, "Welcome to the Asian Century: by 2050, China and Maybe India Will Overtake the US Economy in Size," *Fortune*, January 12, 2004, 53–4.

21. Paul Kennedy, *The Rise and Fall of the Great Powers* (New York: Random House, 1989).

CHAPTER 33

Islam and the Science of Economics

Syed Farid Alatas

Economists have generally maintained a rigorous separation between positive and normative economics. In the Muslim world, however, concerted attempts have been made to relate moral conduct to economic institutions and practices. Demands for an alternative theory and practice of development to both modernization and Marxist theories had led to the rise of Islamic economics. But while Islamic economic thinking presents an ideal of development that is based on an Islamic philosophy of life, it is beset by a number of problems which make it difficult to be considered as an alternative to modernist discourse as far as empirical theory is concerned. As such, so-called Islamic economics cannot be considered as presenting a counter-modernist and alternative development theory. As an ethical theory of development Islam offers an alternative to modernization, dependency, and neo-Marxist theories. However, as an empirical theory, so-called Islamic economic theory remains within the fold of Western modernist discourse in terms of its theoretical concerns and methodology. This chapter provides a theoretical critique and suggests an exemplar for a political economy approach for the Muslim world.

This chapter begins with a brief introduction to development studies as a modernist discourse. This is followed by a concise overview of the Islamic ideal of development which is juxtaposed with the economic realities of Muslim societies. I then proceed in the next three sections to outline and theoretically assess attempts in Muslim countries such as Malaysia, Pakistan, and Saudi Arabia to create an alternative discourse on development that draws on Islamic law and an Islamic philosophical anthropology. The first of these sections presents Islamic economics as a response to modernization. The second makes a distinction between ethical and empirical dimensions of Islamic economics and suggests that it is Islamic economics as empirical theory that is theoretically problematic. The third of these sections critiques Islamic economics as a component of ideology in the context of the role of the state in development. The chapter then takes a prescriptive turn, suggesting that an exemplar for a political economy approach for the Muslim world can be found in the work of 'Abd al-Rahman Ibn

Khaldun. I conclude this essay with some general remarks on the problem of "Islamic economics".

Development Studies as Modernist Discourse

The vast majority of Muslims around the world live in economically underdeveloped countries, with high rates of inflation, low rates of economic growth, low life expectancy, and a high level of adult illiteracy. There are also severe problems in the health and nutritional status of Muslims worldwide, which have serious implications for the quality of human resources. Muslim countries also lag behind industrialized nations in educational attainment, especially where access to tertiary education is concerned.[1]

Such is the relative economic state of affairs of the Muslim world. It is also a fair description of the Muslim world in the 1930s, 40s, and 50s, when economists and social scientists in the West first began to give their attention to the economic problems of the Third World. It was also during this period that development theory started to be uncritically adopted in a wholesale manner throughout the Third World. The type of scholarship along these lines later came to be known by reference to the phenomenon of the captive mind, as conceptualized by Syed Hussein Alatas.[2] Mental captivity connotes a mode of thinking that is characterized by the uncritical imitation of external ideas and techniques. There is a lack of capacity to be creative and raise original problems, to forge original methods. There is also a general alienation from the main issues of the local society, and the unquestioning imitation of the Occident.[3]

The structural context of mental captivity can be understood in terms of the idea of academic dependency. The structure of academic dependency links social scientists in advanced industrialized nations to their counterparts in the Third World. The nature of these links is such that scholars in the Third World are dependent on colleagues and contacts in the industrialized West and, to some extent, Japan for research funds and opportunities, gaining recognition and other types of rewards from such relationships.[4]

In addition to the problems of mental captivity and academic dependency is the state of development theory itself.[5] It was primarily the disciplines of sociology, economics, and political science that dealt with the modernization of Asia, Africa, and Latin America in the 1950s and 1960s. Modernization theory can be understood in terms of its structural and psychological components.

The structural version of modernization theory is founded on an evolutionary vision of social, political, and economic development. It derives its inspiration from classical theory, that is, the belief in progress and increasing complexities in the social, economic, and political spheres.[6] It was perhaps Rostow who gave modernization theory its best known form,[7] suggesting that there are five stages which all societies would go through in order to industrialize. Despite the fact that these five stages were derived from the experience of industrialized nations and are, therefore, questionable in this light, Rostow's stages of economic growth were applied to underdeveloped countries as well.

The psychological version of modernization theory views Western society as possessing those psychological traits, such as a high need for achievement and economic rationality, that are prerequisites for economic success.[8]

By now it is well understood that the trajectory of development experienced by advanced industrialized nations in both its structural or psychological terms, is not necessarily an experience that is available to underdeveloped countries. According to Marxist and neo-Marxist theories underdeveloped countries would never be able to catch up with developed countries because of the historical evolution of a highly unequal capitalist system of relations between rich and poor countries. Unequal power relationships between advanced industrialized and underdeveloped countries do not enable the latter to experience independent and sustainable development. To a great extent, underdevelopment is attributed to the policies of industrialized countries and their extensions in the form of elite groups on the periphery. World-system theory sees the world as constituting a single division of labor, this division of labor being hierarchical. These approaches are correct to criticize modernization theory for its lack of attention to the structure of the world economy and its hierarchical relationships. Nevertheless, their inadequacies are not to be denied, particularly those they share with modernization theory. Both modernization and Marxist-inspired theories can be said to fall within the orbit of a modernist discourse which is informed by the principles of nineteenth-century liberal philosophy and which confines its understanding of development to Westernization,[9] democratization, economic growth, and other technical aspects of economic development.[10]

Development in the Muslim World: Between Ideals and Reality

The Islamic ideal of development can be adequately captured by referring to the Arabic term, *iqtisād*, which is conventionally translated as economy. The term *iqtisād* is derived from the root, *qasada*, which together with the derivation, *iqtasāda*, convey the notion of economizing and being moderate, frugal, thrifty, and provident. However, this is only one of the meanings. The verb *iqtasada* also connotes adopting a middle course or a mediatory position. We could understand *iqtisād*, therefore, not simply as economy in the technical sense of the term, but as economy in the context of thrift, frugality, and providence and, above all, moderation. Indeed, the Qur'an stresses moderation in economic affairs: "Make not thy hand tied to thy neck, nor stretch it forth to its utmost reach, so that thou become blameworthy and destitute" (17:29).

Here Muslims are exorted to be neither niggardly nor extravagant. Such moderation in economic as well as other behavior defines Muslims as constituting a median community (*ummatan wasatan*, Qur'an, 2:143). The median path is, therefore, the right path (*al-sirāt al-mustaqīm*), that is, the path that leads to God (Qur'an, 11:56). The ideal of the economy in Islam, therefore, is not divorced from the notion of human beings as moral creatures with obligations to God as well as to each other.

At the philosophical level, the foundations of development from an Islamic point of view can be understood in terms of four concepts.[11] *Tawhid* or the principle of the unity of God establishes the nature of the relationship between God and man as well as that between men. *Rububiyyah* refers to the belief that it is God who determines the sustenance and nourishment of man and it is He who will guide believers to success. It follows that successful development is a result of man's work as well as the workings of the divine order. *Khilāfah* is the concept of man as God's vicegerent on earth. This defines man as a trustee of God's resources on earth. *Tazkiyyah* refers to the growth and purification of man in terms of his relationship with God, his fellow men, and with the natural environment. The putting into practice of these principles results in *falah*, that is, prosperity in this world as well as the hereafter.[12] The Islamic concept of development is, therefore, *tazkiyyah* or purification combined with growth.[13] This concept encompasses the spiritual, moral, and material aspects of development and the ultimate aim is to maximize welfare both in this life and in the hereafter.

At the more practical level, the organization and functioning of the economy, apart from being based on the above philosophy of development, are also guided by three economic principles.[14] In the principle of double ownership neither private nor public or state ownership are fundamental principles of the economy. Both forms of ownership are acceptable in Islam, but only in their respective areas of the economy. In the principle of limited economic freedom economic activities must take place within the boundaries of a both self-imposed and socially enforced normative order, which is, of course, defined by Islam. Finally, the principle of social justice refers to the Islamic theory of distribution of produced as well as natural wealth, and is based on the notion of mutual responsibility and equity.

Arising from this philosophy of development are a number of policy goals:[15]

1. Human resource development should be concentrated on the development of the right attitudes, aspirations, character, personality, physical and moral well-being, and efficiency,[16] and would call for the Islamization of education.[17]
2. Production and consumption would be restricted to those goods and services which are deemed useful for man in light of the value constellations of Islam. This refers to the adoption of a middle way between crass materialism and other-worldly asceticism.[18]
3. Efforts to improve the quality of life include employment creation, the institutionalization of *zakat* (poor tax), and the equitable distribution of income and wealth through tax policies, charity, inheritance laws, the prohibition of usury, speculation, and so on.[19]
4. Development should be along the lines of regional and sectoral equality to achieve balanced development for the Muslim world.[20]
5. Technology must be indigenized to suit the conditions of Muslim society and must, therefore, be in harmony with the goals and aspirations of the community without, at the same time, causing serious social disruption.[21]
6. Economic dependency on the non-Muslim world must be reduced and integration within the Muslim world must be brought about.[22]

The Muslim Response to Modernization: The Case of Economics

The Islamic ideal of development, as described above, has far from been realized in the empirical world. Muslim responses to the problems of modernization have taken the form of the articulation of broad ideological orientations such as modernism, neo-modernism, and traditionalism. But some Muslims have attempted to respond to the problems of modernization and underdevelopment by developing a new discipline, that of Islamic economics. This is in line with other calls within specific disciplines to revamp theoretical perspectives and create visions of a new Islamic order along social, economic, and political lines. Hence, the notions of Islamic sociology, Islamic political science, and Islamic economics. Here, I focus on the economic.

Due to the problems associated with modernist discourse as well as the state of development in Muslim countries, there were demands for alternative discourses to both modernization and Marxist theories.[23] The perceived crisis in development studies had resulted in efforts in the Muslim world to ground development theory in Islamic law and philosophical anthropology, resulting in what is referred to as Islamic economics.[24] The question of whether Islamic social science in general is possible on philosophical and epistemological grounds has been dealt with elsewhere.[25] In this and the next section, I lay out in broad outline and assess the fundamental premises of what is presented as Islamic economics.[26]

The notion of Islamic economics did not arise from within the classical tradition in Islamic thought. In the classical Islamic tradition, there were discussions and works on economic thought, institutions and practices in the Muslim world,[27] but the notion of an Islamic science of economics and a specifically Islamic economy did not exist.[28] Islamic economics, therefore, is a modern creation. It emerged as a result of dissatisfaction with capitalist and socialist models and theories of development in the 1950s.[29] It is mainly in Pakistan and Saudi Arabia that Islamic economic research is being carried out, although there has also been a great deal of interest in this field in Egypt, India, Iran, Malaysia, and Sudan. Interest in Islamic economics predates the rise of the modern Islamic states of Iran, Libya, Pakistan, Saudi Arabia, and Sudan. Islamic economics rejects the ideology of "catching up" with the West and is committed to discerning the nature and ethos of economic development from an Islamic point of view. The need is, therefore, to identify the Islamic ideal of economic development.[30]

Islamic economics rejects various ethnocentric misconceptions to be found in modernization theory with regard to Muslim society such as its alleged fatalism and the lack of the achievement motive.[31] They maintain that the prerequisites of development are to be found in Islam but that development within an Islamic framework is based on the constellation of values that are found in the Qur'an and the Sunnah (the traditions of the Prophet of Islam).[32] Western development theory and policy, on the other hand, are based on the peculiar characteristics, problems, and value constellations that are found in Western society.

The Islamic economic critique of development studies is not directed only at modernization theory but more generally at the entire body of modernist development thought encompassing perspectives from the left to the right. The modernist call is to promote development by recasting Islam in a modern light, by tempering its traditionalist tendencies, by accepting Western notions of economic and political development, in short, by recasting itself in a Western mold.[33] Islam, on the other hand, has a different outlook on life and the nature of social change, and implies a unique set of policy options for the solution of the problems of development. Muslim scholars have attempted to articulate an alternative concept of development, refusing to evaluate the backwardness and progress of Muslim societies in terms of Western theoretical per-spectives and values. In this way it is counter-modernist in tone and can be added to the list of those other critiques of developmentalism such as liberation theology and feminist ecology.[34] Nevertheless, Islamic economics suffers from a number of problems, some of which have been dealt with by others.[35] The following remarks on Islamic eco-nomics, however, are centered around the distinction between ethical and empirical forms of theory.

Islamic Economics as Ethical and Empirical Theory

Ethical theories express preference or distaste about reality in accordance with certain standards of evaluation. In addition to this, they specify the ideal goal toward which changes should be made. In contrast, empirical theories are generalizations about observable reality and require the process of abstraction and conceptualization.[36]

Islamic economics presents an ideal of development that is based on an Islamic philosophy of life. Arising from this alternative vision of development, various policy options have been suggested such as the introduction of interest-free banking and *zakat* (poor tax).[37] What is presented as Islamic economics are in fact ethical theories of pro-duction, distribution, price, and so on.[38] The exception to this are works on Islamic banking and *zakat*, regarding which I shall make some comments shortly. Generally, when Islamic economists discuss the traditional categories of economics such as income, consumption, government expenditure, investment, and savings they do so in terms of ethical statements and prescriptions and not in terms of analyses and empir-ical theory.[39] In his comprehensive discussion of the various approaches in Islamic economics, Behdad[40] lists the following, all of which are ethical theories:

1. radical approach;
2. populist approach;
3. populist-statist approach;
4. conservative, laissez faire approach.

Despite what appears to be important substantive differences among these approaches, they share a number of problems as far as normative prescriptions in Islamic economics go.

One has to do with the reality of assumptions. The Islamic ideal of development as understood by Islamic economists, seems to be founded on the notion of what Kuran calls "generalized altruism."[41] Kuran is correct in saying that it is not safe to assume that "rational processes would not displace moral motives" in a Muslim society.[42] It is reasonable to say that thought and action in a modern society with millions of people, as Kuran puts it, may not always be consistent with the norms specified by the ideal. He suggests that altruism is more likely to be displayed within smaller groups in which people have close ties on the basis of kinship, locality, tradition, and occupation.[43] This is something that should be apparent to anyone but seems to have escaped the Islamic economists.[44]

Islamic economists generally assume that profit and loss sharing (*mudarabah*) is a viable alternative to interest.[45] In *mudarabah* the bank enters into an arrangement or partnership with the suppliers or users of capital and the profit or loss is shared between the two parties.[46] Islamic economists assume that in an Islamic economy profit and loss sharing would be the basis of all productive activities even if it meant that people would not have the right to allocate risk among themselves in a way that was consistent with their willingness to bear it.[47] Furthermore, for people in profit and loss sharing ventures there would be more incentive to act opportunistically, as in the under-reporting of profit.[48] The idea that Islamic ethical norms, as understood and presented by Islamic economists are clear and unambiguous and that the attainment of economic justice is simply a procedural matter has been critiqued by others[49] and it is not necessary to repeat them here. It should be pointed out, however, that when assumptions concerning the putting into practice of ethical norms are unrealistic, it follows that the economic models founded on such norms will be equally unrealistic. Apart from that, the preoccupation with Islamic ethical theories rather than empirical economic theories had led proponents of Islamic economics to make erroneous comparisons between the Islamic theory of development as an ideal with Marxist and liberal theories of actually existing development.[50] It would be more appropriate to make comparisons between theories within the same genre, that is, ethical or empirical.

If what is meant by Islamic economics is empirical theories, that is, generalizations about observable economic reality founded on the process of abstraction and conceptualization, it would be difficult to refer to an Islamic science of economics, although we do have the scientific study of economies in Muslim countries, as well as the study of Muslim economic institutions and commercial techniques. Here, it is important to introduce the distinction made by Muhammad Bāqir al-Sadr between economics as a science (*'ilm*) and economics as a school of thought (*madhhab*). Economic science deals with the interpretation of economic life, with both its outward forms as well as its underlying reasons, while an economic school of thought refers to the economic path that a society wishes to embark upon.[51]

This distinction is extremely important. As al-Sadr says, the science of economics refers to facts and describes their causes and does not offer prescriptions as to what should and should not be. The function of science is discovery and that of the school of thought is evaluation.[52] The implication of this distinction is important. What al-Sadr understands by the term "Islamic economy" (*al-iqtisād al-islami*) is an approach to the organization of economic life and not a science of economics. As he puts it, the goal of Islam is not to discover the phenomenon of economic life and state its laws. It has nothing to do with the scientific discovery of existing economic phenomena.[53]

In contrast, Choudhury's definition (of Islamic economic theory) as "the sum total of the historical, empirical and theoretical studies that analyse the human and societal needs in the light of an integrated Islamic value system"[54] is much too broad to be helpful as it encompasses both what al-Sadr calls economic science and schools of economics without making a distinction between the two.

When Islamic economists *are* doing empirical theory, what is presented as Islamic economics turns out not to be an alternative to modernist discourse as far as empirical theory is concerned. The foci and method that have been selected by Muslim economists for economic analysis is essentially that of neo-classical, Keynesian or monetarist economics. The foci are the traditional questions that come under the purview of theories of price, production, distribution, trade cycle, growth, and welfare economics with Islamic themes and topics involved such as *zakat*, interest-free banking, and profit-sharing. There are at least three problems associated with this.

First of all, the techniques of analysis that have been selected, that is, the building up of abstract models of the economic system, have not been translated by Islamic economists into empirical work. For example, works on interest tend to construct models of how an interest-free economy would work. For example, according to Mahdi "alternative economic models have successfully eliminated interest and using either Keynesian IS-LM framework or portfolio asset management approach have demonstrated that interest-free Islamic economy is feasible and desirable not only for Muslim countries, but for all countries."[55]

There is no empirical work on existing economic systems and on the nature, functions, and effects of interest in these systems, in a manner that could be regarded in theoretical and methodological terms as a departure from mainstream economics.[56] In general, Islamic economists are very much attached to the deductive methodological approach so characteristic of neo-classical economics.[57]

Secondly, these attempts at Islamic economics have sought to ground the discourse in a theory of wealth and distribution in very much the manner that Western economic science does, as a glance at some of their works will reveal.[58] When it is engaged in the sort of discourse that one could understand as constituting empirical theory, it is not doing so from a specifically Islamic economic approach, and despite their frequent references to numerous fundamental Islamic concepts, "Islamic economics is little more than one huge attempt to cast Islamic institutions and dictates, like *zakat* and prohibition of interest into a Western economic mould."[59] What "Islamic economics" amounts to is neo-classical, Keynesian or monetarist economics dressed and made up in Islamic terminology. Islamic economics is very much embedded in the tradition of British and American economics in terms of its near exclusive concern with technical factors such as growth, interest, tax, profits, and so on. According to Sardar,[60] over 80 percent of the Islamic economic literature is on monetarism.

Even where there is the use of empirical data, as in the case of studies of *zakat* collection and distribution,[61] it is difficult to see what makes such economics Islamic other than the fact the subject matter concerns Islam and Muslims. Neither the theoretical nor empirical literature that is known as Islamic economics and that would come under the heading of what al-Sadr calls economic science, has generated new theories, concepts and methods from the tradition of Muslim thought or the experience of Muslim countries in a way that can justify our referring to this literature as Islamic economics or a new science of economics.

Furthermore, there is a host of conceptual issues that have not been seriously dealt with. For example, M. Nejathullah Siddiqi raised the interesting issue of the non-applicability of the concept of economic rationality in the analysis of behavior of Muslims. He suggests that the concept of economic rationality is unsuitable for analysis because it is unrealistic. This is a valid criticism that holds for the study of behavior in general, not just Muslim behavior. Islamic economists have suggested the concept of

Islamic rationality in place of economic rationality.[62] This, however, is a normative concept in the sense that it refers to conformity with Islamic norms. As such, it belongs to ethical and not empirical theories. So far, Islamic economists have not advanced an alternative concept of rationality that can serve as a cornerstone of an empirical economic theory, that is, a concept of rationality that specifies the attributes of economic agents as they exist and not as they should be.

The State and Development in Muslim Societies: Islamic Economics as Ideology

We have seen from the discussion above that Islamic economics, in attempting to ground itself in a theory of rational man and a hypothetical-deductive methodology, has merely substituted Islamic terms for neo-classical ones, retaining the latter's assumptions, procedures, and modes of analysis.[63] As such, it has failed to engage in the analysis and critique of a highly unequal world economic order in which the gaps are ever widening. That this supposedly anti-Western economics was co-opted and made to serve those very trends that it outwardly opposes must be considered. The main problem with this state of affairs is that under the guise of "Islamic economics" the policies generated in industrialized capitalist centers are implemented in the Muslim world and are legitimated, thereby undermining the very project that Islamic economics is committed to. For example, *mudharabah* is "reinterpreted and projected as a sacred religious principle to justify the maximization of profits under capitalism."[64] A host of issues relating to political economy such as uneven development, unequal exchange, bureaucratic capitalism, corruption, and the role of the state that have been addressed by structuralist, neo-Marxist, dependency, and new institutional economic theorists, are not dealt with at the theoretical and empirical levels by Islamic economists.

This suggests that Islamic economics plays an important role as ideology. Ideology refers to thought that is so interest-bound to a situation that the real conditions of society are concealed or obscured by the collective unconscious of a given group. This functions to support or stabilize the given order.[65]

The problems that beset Islamic economics in terms of its theoretical perspectives, methodology, and practical results are not disconnected from the political contexts of Muslim societies. As noted above, Islamic economics has generally neglected those areas of interest that have become the trademarks of neo-Marxism, dependency, and world-systems theories. Islamic economics, therefore, has been rather innocent of political economy, which is ironic considering the ominous role that the state plays in the Muslim world. Indeed, the neglect of the state in Islamic economics is in stark contrast to the all-encompassing presence of the state in Muslim societies. This neglect, however, is not ironic if we understand Islamic economics in terms of its ideological role. Islamic economics in its neo-classical guise, by this reading, can be considered as an academic argument for a form of state-led or state-dominated capitalist development that is prevalent in many Muslim countries.

The political economy of most Muslim countries is such that the state intervenes directly in the relations of production making surplus extraction and capital accumulation a major political issue. Rather than the market or social classes it is the state that is the main driving force in the political economy of these countries. This is due to the autonomy of the state from the dominant classes. But what is important is the manner in which this autonomy in manifested. The notion of the autonomy of the state from dominant class interests implies that the state has interests of its own.

In Malaysia and Indonesia we have the ersatz form of capitalism, due to the peculiar nature of state involvement in development.[66] Ersatz capitalism is capitalism that is based on state patronage, and the investment of transnational corporations and their technology. Muslim countries outside Southeast Asia are not even blessed with this less than dynamic form of capitalism for a variety of geopolitical reasons. The focus on ersatz capitalism leads to a consideration of patronage and related phenomena such as rent seeking and corruption. Capitalists are dependent on the state for assistance in order to be successful. Kleptocrats[67] or corruptors extend various forms of favors to private capitalists, that encompass incentives, licensing, protectionism, low-interest loans from state banks, concessions, and joint ventures. The relationship between kleptocrat and capitalist is one of patron and client. This is a special relation between a politically powerful patron and a client who needs his/her protection due to the inadequacies of formal economic institutions. Therefore, the role that state officials play in advancing their private material interests takes its toll on economic development. Here we are referring to the activities of corrupt state officials. Their presence in various Muslim countries is sufficiently felt and has generated some research.[68]

The kleptocratic state is one that is dominated by state officials who subordinate the interests of the public to their private interests. But the kleptocratic state refers to more than just a state in which corruption is present.[69] It refers to a state in which the dominant means of capital accumulation is via corruption. Much of the debate in Asia on democracy and authoritarianism tends to overlook the fact that corruption is what Syed Hussein Alatas calls transystemic.[70]

At best, under the guise of "Islamic economics" the neglect of issues that usually come under the purview of political economy such as the relationship between the state and the economy, and corruption, are tantamount to the legitimation of the status quo, the very state of affairs that Islamic economics claims it wishes to eradicate. At worst, Islamic economics in its neo-classical versions actively promotes the type of economic system that it claims to criticize.

Ibn Khaldun as an Exemplar for a Political Economy Approach

Political economy, that is, the study of the interactions of the state and economy, is virtually non-existent among Islamic development scholars. Whenever the subject of the state is broached, it is done so in terms of ethical statements and not in terms of analyses and empirical theory. While it is necessary to understand the political ideals of Islam, it is equally important to examine the realities. Statements to the effect that the Islamic state is an instrument of Allah and a symbol of divine power on earth[71] are true and generally acceptable to Muslims. The problem lies elsewhere, that is, in the nature and functioning of contemporary states in Muslim countries. For this reason, the study of economic development in the Muslim world must lie within the field of political economy. Given the distinction made by al-Sadr between economic science and schools of economics, Muslim economists should dispense with the idea of developing an "Islamic" science of economics and instead concentrate on developing political economy perspectives founded on those traditional ideas that continue to be relevant. This must be done without neglecting the important contributions of existing modern perspectives in economics and political economy.

Islamic economists in search of an alternative approach to the study of development and the economy, that is, for an alternative science of economics that is original and has roots in the tradition of Muslim thought might do well to consider the work of Ibn Khaldun.

Writing 600 years ago, Ibn Khaldun initiated a new field of inquiry consisting of, among other things, the study of the state (al-dawla), royal (mulk) and caliphate authority, and the crafts, ways of making a living, and occupations.[72] In the language of modern economic science, what Ibn Khaldun concerned himself with was political economy.

Consider Ibn Khaldun on the transition from khilāfah (caliphate) to mulk (royal) authority. The khilāfah was a political institution, the exercise of which means

> To cause the masses to act as required by religious insight into their interests into the other world. (The worldly interests) have bearing upon (the interests in the other world), since according to the Lawgiver (Muhammad), all worldly conditions are to be considered in their relation to their value for the other world. Thus, (the Caliphate) in reality substitutes for the Lawgiver (Muhammad), in as much as it serves, like him, to protect the religion and to exercise (political) leadership of the world.[73]

The head of the Muslim state during the khilāfah period was, therefore, the keeper of sharī'ah, there to ensure that it was enforced. From the khilāfah period we have a transition to what Ibn Khaldun refers to as mulk.

> By dint of their nature, human beings need someone to act as a restricting influence and mediator in every social organization, in order to keep the members from (fighting) with each other. That person must, by necessity, have superiority over the others in matters of group feeling. If not, his power to (exercise a restraining influence) could not materialize. It is more than leadership. Leadership means being a chieftain, and the leader is obeyed, but he has no power to force others to accept his rulings. Royal authority means superiority and the power to rule by force.[74]

Mulk is distinguished from khilāfah by the ability of the ruler to rule by force. Although the rulers of the dynasties following the khilāfah period continued to use the title of khilāfah (caliph) many of them were not khulafa' (sing. khilāfah) in the true sense of the term as they ruled by force and not by allegiance to the divine order. Thus, in the mulk periods of Arab history, the merchant classes were in constant danger of having their property confiscated due to the jealousy of their rulers. This injustice is to be understood in a more general sense then as the confiscation of property and money. It includes forced labor, the imposition of duties not required by Islamic law, the collection of unjustified taxes and so on.

Ibn Khaldun's account of the decline of the dynasty elaborates, as pointed out by Gellner, "a Keynesian theory of economics, clearly containing the concept of the multiplier."[75] The difference is that Keynes blamed the middle class for inadequate aggregate demand while Ibn Khaldun blames the governmental propensity to save at a time when private investment is weak.[76]

> Curtailment of allowances given by the ruler implies curtailment of the tax revenue . . . Now, if the ruler holds on to property and revenue . . . then the property in the possession of the ruler's entourage will be small. . . . (When they stop spending), business slumps and commercial profits decline because of the shortage of capital. Revenues from the land tax decrease, because the land tax and taxation depend on cultural activity, commercial transactions, business prosperity, and the people's demand for gain and profit . . . The dynasty is the greatest market, the mother and base of all trade, the substance of income and expenditure. If government business slumps and the volume of trade is small, the dependent markets will naturally show the same symptoms, and to a greater degree.[77]

The political down cycle of a dynasty is correlated with the economic down cycle.

> It should be known that at the beginning of a dynasty, taxation yields a large revenue from large assessments.
> The reason for this is that when the dynasty follows the ways of Islam, it imposes only such taxes as are stipulated by the religious law, such as charity taxes, the land tax, and the poll tax. These have fixed limits that cannot be exceeded . . .
> When the dynasty continues in power and their rulers follow each other in succession, they become sophisticated. The Bedouin attitude and simplicity lose their significance, and the Bedouin qualities of moderation and restraint disappear . . . Every individual impost and assessment is greatly increased, in order to obtain a higher tax revenue . . .
> The assessments increase beyond the limits of equity. The result is that the interest of the subjects in cultural enterprises disappears, since when they compare expenditures and taxes with their income and gain and see the little profit they make, they lose all hope. Therefore, many of them refrain from all cultural activity. The result is that the total tax revenue goes down, as individual assessments go down. Often, when the decrease is noticed, the amounts of individual imposts are increased. This is considered a means of compensating for the decrease. Finally, individual imposts and assessments reach their limit . . . Finally, civilization is destroyed because the incentive for cultural activity is gone.[78]

The result is a downturn in the production, fiscal, and political cycles of the dynasty.

The purpose of this brief discussion of Ibn Khaldun is not to present his political economy framework in any detail but merely to suggest that there is a mode of thinking in his work that is properly speaking political economic. Beyond that, there is a number of tasks that need to be taken seriously:

1.   To include Ibn Khaldun in the history of economic thought by assessing his contributions to the study of the economy. There are already some works that

do this.[79] Nevertheless, the task of reconstructing a Khaldunian political economy framework of analysis based on his theoretical contributions has yet to be attempted.

2. To develop a tradition of political economy based on his work. This would require the elaboration of a Khaldunian political economy framework that is then systematically applied in empirical studies. An example is my own work.[80] I attempt to integrate a modes of production framework into Ibn Khaldun's theory of state formation, the field of application being Iranian and Ottoman history. While the economic system of Safavi Iran is couched in terms of Marxist concepts, their dynamics is explained in terms of Ibn Khaldun's theory of state formation. Ibn Khaldun's work provides us with a theoretical framework with which to understand the rise and dynamics of the Safavi and Ottoman polities.

3. A Khaldunian or any other approach can only be constructed and developed if there is serious attention given to the study of actually existing Muslim economic institutions and systems of the past as well as the present. This would imply going beyond merely specifying an Islamic ideal of development to the systematic investigation of the practice of Islamic economic institutions in history. While there are such studies,[81] these tend to be done by non-economists who are not concerned with the development of economic theory. On the other hand, proponents of Islamic economics have generally not taken such works into account.

Conclusion

This brief assessment of the response of Islamic economists to the general issue of modernization yields a number of conclusions about this discourse that can be itemized as follows.

1. While economists have generally maintained the rigorous separation between positive and normative economics, in the Muslim world, however, concerted attempts have been made to relate moral conduct to economic institutions and practices. This is a result of dissatisfaction with both modernization and Marxist-inspired theories that are understood by Islamic economists as being located within the orbit of ideological orientations that are at odds with Islam. Demands for an alternative theory and practice of development to both modernization and Marxist theories had led to the rise of Islamic economics.

    But while Islamic economic thinking presents an ideal of development that is based on an Islamic philosophy of life, it is beset by a number of problems which make it difficult to be considered as an alternative to modernist discourse as far as empirical theory is concerned. As such, so-called Islamic economics cannot be considered as presenting an indigenous and alternative development theory. As an ethical theory of development Islam offers an alternative to modernization, dependency, and neo-Marxist theories. However, as an empirical theory, so-called Islamic economic theory remains within the fold of Western modernist discourse in terms of its theoretical concerns and methodology.

2. Islamic economics is innocent of political economy. It generally neglects the role of the state as far as empirical theorizing is concerned. Problems to do with corrupt leadership, a weak civil society, and the lack of will to implement good laws and to build sound executive, legislative, and legal institutions that lie at the heart of the economic problems of a good many Muslim countries are not priorities in the research agenda of Islamic economists.

3. That any theory of development must take into account the role of the state as well as civil society is obvious. Islamic economics, however, tend to shun a political economy approach. This is despite the fact that there is a tradition akin to the political economy approach in Islam.

4. A more creative approach among Muslim economists would result neither in the uncritical adoption of Western models and theories of development with the customary terminological adornments, nor in the wholesale rejection of the Western contribution to economic thought, but in a system that is cognizant of the realities of economic life in the Muslim world and that is not innocent of political economy. An exemplar for this approach would be Ibn Khaldun.

5. Such an approach must be accompanied by historical and empirical studies of existing Muslim economic institutions and practices to aid in the process of concept formation and theory building as well as to provide lessons for contemporary applications.

Notes

1. Riaz Hassan, "The Muslim World in the International Economic System – An Overview," *Journal of the Institute of Muslim Minority Affairs*, 1992.

2. Syed Hussein Alatas, "The Captive Mind in Development Studies," *International Social Science Journal*, 34(1), 1972, 9–25; Syed Hussein Alatas, "The Captive Mind and Creative Development," *International Social Science Journal*, 36(4), 1974, 691–9.

3. Alatas, "The Captive Mind in Development Studies"; Alatas "The Captive Mind and Creative Development"; S.C. Dube, "Social Sciences for the 1980s: From Rhetoric to Reality," *International Social Science Journal*, 34(3), 1982, 497–500; Ziauddin Sardar, *The Future of Muslim Civilization* (London: Mansell Publishing, 1987), 56.

4. Dube, "Social Sciences for the 1980s," 499. Various aspects of academic dependency have been discussed elsewhere. See C. Ake, *Social Science as Imperialism: The Theory of Political Development*. (Ibadan: University of Ibadan Press, 1979); Philip G. Altbach, "Servitude of the Mind? Education, Dependency, and Neocolonialism," *Teachers' College Record*, 79(2), 1977, 187–204; Frederick H. Garreau, "Another Type of Third World Dependency: The Social Sciences," *International Sociology*, 3(2), 1988, 171–8; Edward Said, *Culture and Imperialism* (London: Chatus & Windus, 1993); Priscilla Weeks, "Post-colonial Challenges to Grand Theory," *Human Organization*, 49(3), 1990, 236–44; Syed Farid Alatas, "Academic

Dependency in the Social Sciences: Reflections on India and Malaysia," *American Studies International*, 38(2), 2000, 80–96.

5. David Booth, "Marxism and Development Sociology: Interpreting the Impasse," *World Development*, 13(7), 1985, 761–87; Michael Edwards, "The Irrelevance of Development Studies," *Third World Quarterly*, 11(1), 1989, 116–35; Kate Manzo, "Modernist Discourse and the Crisis of Development Theory," *Studies in Comparative International Development*, 26(2), 1991, 3–36; D.L. Sheth, "Alternative Development as Political Practice," *Alternatives*, 12, 1987, 155–71; T. Smith, "Requiem or New Agenda for Third World Studies," *World Politics*, 37(4), 1985, 532–61; P. Vandergeest and F.H. Buttel, "Marx, Weber and Development Sociology: Beyond the Impasse," *World Development*, 16(6), 1988, 683–95; H. Wiarda, "Rethinking Political Development: A Look Back over Thirty Years, and a Look Ahead," *Studies in Comparative International Development*, 24(4), 1989, 65–82.

6. A. Portes, "On the Sociology of National Development," *American Journal of Sociology*, 82(1), 1976, 55–85.

7. W.W. Rostow, *The Stages of Economic Growth: A Non-Communist Manifesto* (Cambridge: Cambridge University Press, 1960).

8. E.E. Hagen, *On the Theory of Social Change: How Economic Growth Begins* (Homewood, IL: Dorsey, 1962); D.C. McClelland, *The Achieving Society* (New York: Free Press, 1967); A. Inkeles and D. Smith, *Becoming Modern: Individual Change in Six Developing Countries* (Cambridge, MA: Harvard University Press, 1974).

9. Syed Hussein Alatas, *Modernization and Social Change: Studies in Modernization, Religion, Social Change and Development in South-East Asia* (Sydney: Angus and Robertson, 1972), chapter 2.

10. Manzo, "Modernist Discourse and the Crisis of Development Theory," 6.

11. Kurshid Ahmad, "Economic Development in an Islamic Framework," In Kurshid Ahmad, ed., *Studies in Islamic Development* (Jeddah: International Centre for Research in Islamic Economics, King Abdul Aziz University, 1980), 178–9; Ghazali Aidit, *Development: An Islamic Perspective* (Petaling Jaya: Pelanduk Publications, 1990), 22–3. The following account draws from previous sketches of the Islamic view of development: Syed Farid Alatas, "The Sacralization of the Social Sciences: A Critique of an Emerging Theme in Academic Discourse," *Archives de Sciences Sociales des Religions*, 91, 1995, 93; Syed Farid Alatas, "Islam and Counter Modernism: Towards Alternative Development Paradigms," in Masudul Alam Choudhury, M.Z. Abdad, and Muhammad Syukri Salleh, eds., *Islamic Political Economy in Capitalist-Globalization: An Agenda for Change* (Kuala Lumpur: Utusan, 1997), 71–2.

12. Khurshid Ahmad, "Economic Development in an Islamic Framework," 179.

13. Ibid.

14. Muhammad Baqir Sadr, "General Edifice of the Islamic Economy," in Muhammad Baqer Sadr and Ayatullah Sayyid Mahmud, eds., Taleghani *Islamic Economics: Contemporary Ulama Perspectives* (Kuala Lumpur: Iqra, 1991).

15. Kurshid, "Economic Development," 180–4.

16. Afzal-ur-Rahman, *Economic Doctrines of Islam*, Vol. 1 (Lahore: Islamic Publications, 1980), 189–99.

17. Syed Muhammad Al-Naquib Al-Attas, *The Concept of Education in Islam: A Framework for an Islamic Philosophy of Education* (Kuala Lumpur: ABIM, 1980).

18. Afzal-ur-Rahman. *Economic Doctrines of Islam*, Vol. 2 (Lahore: Islamic Publications, 1980), 11.

19. Ibid., 55–105, 268–72.

20. Sardar, *The Future of Muslim Civilization*, 107–12.

21. Ibid., 146.

22. Syed Farid Alatas, "An Islamic Common Market and Economic Development," *Islamic Culture*, 61(1), 1987, 28–38.

23. Md. Anisur Rahman, "Towards an Alternative Development Paradigm," *IFDA Dossier*, 81, 1991, 18–27.

24. Muhammad Nejatullah Siddiqi, "Muslim Economic Thinking: A Survey of Contemporary Literature," in Kurshid Ahmad, ed., *Studies in Islamic Economics* (Jeddah: International Centre for Research in Islamic Economics, King Abdul Aziz University and London: The Islamic Foundation, 1980), 191–315; Mahmoud Abu Saud, "Toward Islamic Economics," in *Toward Islamization of Disciplines* (Herndon, Virginia: International Institute of Islamic Thought, 1989).

25. Fazlur Rahman, "Islamization of Knowledge: A Response," *American Journal of Islamic and Social Science*, 5(1), 1988; Syed Farid Alatas, "Reflections on the Idea of Islamic Social Science," *Comparative Civilizations Review*, 17, 1987, 60–86; Syed Farid Alatas, "Agama dan Ilmu Kemasyarakatan: Masalah Teoretis" (Religion and Social Science: Theoretical Problems), *Journal Antropologi dan Sosiologi*, 21, 1993; Alatas, "The Sacralization of the Social Science," 89–111.

26. Afzal-ur-Rahman. *Economic Doctrines of Islam*, Vol. 1; Masudul Alam Choudhury, "Principles of Islamic Economics," *Middle Eastern Studies*, 19(1), 1983, 93–103; Ijas Shafi Gilani, "The Political Context of Islamic Economics," in Kurshid Ahmad, ed., *Studies in Islamic Development* (Jeddah: International Centre for Research in Islamic Economics, King Abdul Aziz University, 1980); Muhammad Akram Khan, "Islamic Economics: The State of the Art," in *Toward Islamization of Disciplines* (Herndon, Virginia: International Institute of Islamic Thought, 1989); Thomas Phillipp, "The Idea of Islamic Economics," *Die Welt des Islams*, 30, 1990, 117–39; Frederic L. Pryor, "The Islamic Economic System," *Journal of Comparative Economics*, 9, 1985, 197–223; Muhammad Baqir as-Sadr, *Iqtisaduna: Our Economy*. (Tehran: World Organization for Islamic Services, 1982–84); Sayyid Muhammad Baqar Sadr, *Toward an Islamic Economy* (Tehran: Bonyad Be'that, 1984); Muhammad Baqir al-Sadr, *Iqtisaduna: Our Economy* (Paris: Islamic Book Foundation, 1983, Arabic); Muhammad Nejatullah Siddiqi, *Some Aspects of the Islamic Economy* (Delhi: Markazi Maktaba Islami, 1981); Seyyed Mahmood Taleqani, *Islam and Ownership* (Lexington, Kentucky: Mazda Publishers, 1983).

27. For discussions on early economic thought in the Muslim world see Harro Bernardelli, "The Origins of Modern Economic Theory," *Economic Record*, 37, 1961, 320–38; S.M. Ghazanfar and A. Azim Islahi, "Economic Thought of an Arab Scholastic: Abu Hamid al-Ghazali (A.H.450–505/A.D.1058–1111)," *History of Political Economy*, 22(2), 1990, 381–403; S.M. Ghazanfar and A. Azim Islahi, "Explorations in Medieval Arab-Islamic Economic Thought: Some Aspects of Ibn Taimiyah's Economics," in S. Todd Lowry, ed., *Perspectives on the History of Economic Thought*. Vol. 7 (Brookfield: Edward Elgar, 1992), 45–63; S.M. Ghazanfar, "The Economic Thought of Abu Hamid Al-Ghazali and St. Thomas Aquinas: Some Comparative Parallels and Links," *History of Political Economy*, 32, 2000, 857–88.

28. On Muslim economic institutions of the past see Abdullah Alwi bin Haji Hassan, "Al-Mudarabah (Dormant Partnership) and its Identical Islamic Partnerships in Early Islam," *Hamdard Islamicus*, 12(2), 1989, 11–38; Bruce Masters, *The Origins of World Economic Dominance* (New York: New York University Press, 1988); A.L. Udovitch, *Partnership and Profit in Medieval Islam* (Princeton: Princeton University Press, 1970a); A.L. Udovitch, "Commercial Techniques in Early Medieval Islamic Trade," *Journal of the American Oriental Society*, 87, 1967, 260–4.

29. Abdul Rauf, *A Muslim's Reflections on Democratic Capitalism* (Washington, DC: American Enterprise Institute, 1984); Seyyed Vali Reza Nasr, "Religious Modernism in the Arab

World, India and Iran: The Perils and Prospects of Discourse," *Muslim World*, 83(1), 1993, 20–47; Sayyid Muhammad Baqar Sadr, *Towards an Islamic Economy* (Tehran: Bonyad Be'that, 1984); Ali Shari'ati, *Marxism and Other Western Fallacies: An Islamic Critique* (Berkeley: Mizan Press, 1980); Timur Kuran, "On the Notion of Economic Justice in Contemporary Islamic Thought," *International Journal of Middle East Studies*, 21(2), 1989, 171–91.

30.   Ahmad, "Economic Development in an Islamic Framework," 171.

31.   Ibid., 173.

32.   Syed Othman Alhabshi, "Peranan Akhlak dalam Pengurusan Ekonomi dan Kewangan" (The Role of Morality in Economic and Financial Management), in Shafie Hj. Mohd. Salleh and Mohd. Affandi Hassan, eds., *Kecemerlangan Pentadbiran: Dasar dan Amalan dalam Islam* (Administrative Excellence: Policy and Practice in Islam) (Kuala Lumpur: INTAN, 1990).

33.   Bassam Tibi, *The Crisis of Modern Islam: A Preindustrial Culture in a Scientific-Technological Age* (Salt Lake City: University of Utah Press, 1988); Nasr, "Religious Modernism in the Arab World, India and Iran," 20–47.

34.   Manzo, "Modernist Discourse and the Crisis of Development Theory," 3–36.

35.   Timur Kuran, "Behavioral Norms in the Islamic Doctrine of Economics: A Critique," *Journal of Economic Behavior and Organization*, 4, 1983, 353–79; Kuran, "On the Notion of Economic Justice in Contemporary Islamic Thought," 171–91; Fazlur Rahman, "Riba and Interest," *Islamic Studies*, 3, 1964, 1–43; Fazlur Rahman, "Islam and the Problem of Economic Justice," *Pakistan Economist*, 14, 1974, 14–39.

36.   The discussion here, founded on the distinction between ethical and empirical theories, draws from Alatas "The Sacralization of the Social Sciences," 93–5; Alatas, "Islam and Counter Modernism," 72–4.

37.   Ziauddin Ahmad, "Interest-Free Banking in Pakistan," *Journal of Islamic Banking and Finance*, 4, 1987, 8–30; Mohammad Ariff, ed., *Money and Banking in Islam* (Jeddah: ICRIE, 1982); F.R. Faridi, "Zakat and Fiscal Policy," in Kurshid Ahmad, ed., *Studies in Islamic Development* (Jeddah: International Centre for Research in Islamic Economics, King Abdul Aziz University, 1980); Zubair Iqbal and Abbas Mirakhor, *Islamic Banking*. Occasional Paper no. 49 (Washington, DC: International Monetary Fund, 1987); Ingo Karsten, "Islam and Financial Intermediation," *IMF Staff Papers*, 29(1), 1982, 108–42; Mohsin S. Khan, "Islamic Interest-Free Banking: A Theoretical Analysis," *IMF Staff Papers*, 33(1), 1986, 1–27; Mohsin S. Khan and Abbas Mirakhor (eds.), *Theoretical Studies in Islamic Banking and Finance* (Houston: Institute for Research and Islamic Studies, 1987); Mohsin S. Khan and Abbas Mirakhor, "Islamic Banking: Experiences in the Islamic Republic of Iran and in Pakistan," *Economic Development and Cultural Change*, 38(2), 1990, 353–75; Sayyid Muhammad Baqir Sadr, *An Introduction to Principles of Islamic Banking* (Tehran: Bonyad Be'that, 1982); Muhammad Uzair, "Some Conceptual and Practical Aspects of Interest-Free Banking," in Kurshid Ahmad, ed., *Studies in Islamic Development* (Jeddah: International Centre for Research in Islamic Economics, King Abdul Aziz University, 1980), 37–57.

38.   For an excellent survey of Islamic economics as ethical theory see Siddiqi, "Muslim Economic Thinking," 194–235.

39.   See, for example, as-Sadr, *Iqtisādunā;* Taleqani, *Islam and Ownership;* Syed Nawab Haider Naqvi, H.U. Beg, Rafiq Ahmed and Mian M. Nazeer, "Principles of Islamic Economic Reform," in K.S. Jomo, ed., *Islamic Economic Alternatives: Critical Perspectives and New Directions* (Basingstoke: Macmillan, 1992), 153–87; M. Umer Chapra, "The Need for a New Economic System," *Review of Islamic Economics*, 1(1), 1991, 9–47; Khalid bin Sayeed, "Roles of Public and Private Sectors in an Islamic Economy," in *Proceedings of the 2nd Seminar on Islamic Economics* (Herndon, Virginia: International Institute of Islamic Thought, November 18–20, 1988).

40. Sohrab Behdad, "Property Rights and Islamic Economic Approaches," in K.S. Jomo, ed., *Islamic Economic Alternatives* (Basingstoke: Macmillan, 1992), 77–103; Sohrab Behdad, "A Disputed Utopia: Islamic Economics in Revolutionary Iran," *Comparative Studies in Society and History*, 36(4), 1994, 775–813.

41. Timur Kuran, "The Economic System in Contemporary Islamic Thought," in K.S. Jomo, ed., *Islamic Economic Alternatives* (Basingstoke: Macmillan, 1992), 13.

42. Ibid., 13.

43. Ibid.

44. For more on the problematic nature of assumptions regarding economic justice in Islamic economic discourse see Kuran, "On the Notion of Economic Justice in Contemporary Islamic Thought," 171–91.

45. See Muhammad Uzair, "Some Conceptual and Practical Aspects of Interest-Free Banking," 44–8. For critical discussions of the rationale for the prohibition of interest see Rahman "Riba and Interest," 1–43; and Ashghar Ali Engineer, "Islam and the Question of Riba (Interest)," *Progressive Perspective*, 1(4) (Bombay: Institute of Islamic Studies, 1995).

46. Muhammad Uzair, "Some Conceptual and Practical Aspects of Interest-Free Banking," 46.

47. Timur Kuran, "The Economic System in Contemporary Islamic Thought," 32.

48. Ibid., 29.

49. Kuran, "On the Notion of Economic Justice in Contemporary Islamic Thought," 171–91.

50. For example, Sulayman S. Nyang, "The Islamic State and Economic Development: A Theoretical Analysis," *Islamic Culture*, 50(2), 1976, 1–23.

51. Al-Sadr, *Iqtisādunā* (*Our Economy*), [Arabic], 6–7. See Al-Sadr (1982–4) for the English translation.

52. Sayyid Muhammad Baqar Sadr, *Towards an Islamic Economy* (Tehran: Bonyad Be'that, 1984), 117.

53. Ibid., 131.

54. Masudul Alam Choudhury, "Towards an Definition of Islamic Economic Theory and Development," *Contemporary Review*, 239(1387), 1981, 78.

55. Syed Iqbal Mahdi, "Methodological Issues in Islamic Economics," in *Proceedings of the 2nd Seminar on Islamic Economics* (Herndon, Virginia: International Institute of Islamic Thought, November 18–20, 1988), 8–9.

56. See also S.A. Siddiqui, "Savings, Investment and Output in an Islamic Economic System I," In *Proceedings of the 2nd Seminar on Islamic Economics* (Herndon, Virginia: International Institute of Islamic Thought, November 18–20, 1988).

57. For an example of this approach see Masudul Alam Choudhury, *The Principles of Islamic Political Economy* (New York: St. Martin's Press, 1992). See also Salim Rashid, "An Agenda for Muslim Economists: A Historico-Inductive Approach," *JKAU: Islamic Economics*, 3, 1991, 45–55, for a plea to adopt an inductive approach.

58. Monzer Kahf, "Savings and Investment Functions in a Two- Sector Islamic Economy," in Mohammad Ariff, ed., *Monetary and Fiscal Economics of Islam* (Jeddah: ICRIE, 1982); Khan, "A Macro Consumption Function in an Islamic Framework," 1–24; Khan, "Islamic Interest-Free Banking: A Theoretical Analysis," 1–27; Muhammad Abdul Mannan, "Allocative Efficiency, Decision and Welfare Criteria in an Interest-Free Islamic Economy: A Comparative Policy Approach," in Mohammad Ariff, ed., *Monetary and Fiscal Economics of Islam* (Jeddah: ICRIE, 1982); Shamim Ahmad Siddiqui and Asad Zaman, "Investment and Income Distribution Pattern under Musharka Finance: A Certainty Case," *Pakistan Journal of Applied Economics*, 8(1), 1989a, 1–30; Shamim Ahmad Siddiqui and Asad Zaman, "Investment and Income Distribution Pattern under Musharka Finance: The Uncertainty Case," *Pakistan Journal of Applied Economics*, 8(1), 1989b, 31–71; Mohammed Anas Zarqa,

"Stability in an Interest-Free Islamic Economy: A Note," *Pakistan Journal of Applied Economics*, 2, 1983, 181–8.

59. Ziauddin Sardar, "Islamic Economics: Breaking Free From the Dominant Paradigm," *Afkar Inquiry*, 2(4), 1985, 42–3.

60. Ibid., 43.

61. See for example Ismail Muhd Salleh and Rogayah Ngah, "Distribution of the *Zakat* Burden on Padi Producers in Malaysia," in M. Raqibuz Zaman, ed., *Some Aspects of the Economics of Zakah* (Gary, Indiana: Association of Muslim Social Scientists, 1981), 80–153; Abdin Ahmed Salama, "Fiscal Analysis of Zakah with Special Reference to Saudi Arabia's Experience in Zakah," in M. Ariff, ed., *Monetary and Fiscal Economics of Islam* (Jeddah: International Centre for Research in Islamic Economics, 1982).

62. M. Nejathullah Siddiqi, "Teaching of Economics at the University Level in Muslim Countries," in Mohamed Taher, ed., *Encyclopaedic Survey of Islamic Culture, vol. 8 Studies in Islamic Economics* (New Delhi: Anmol Publications, 1997), 32.

63. For an account of an Islamic neo-classical Keynesian university curriculum, see Sohrab Behdad, "Islamization of Economics in Iranian Universities," *International Journal of Middle East Studies*, 27, 1995, 204–10.

64. Ziaul Haque, "Islamic Perpsectives and Class Interests," in K.S. Jomo, ed., *Islamic Economic Alternatives* (Basingstoke: Macmillan, 1992), 112.

65. Karl Mannheim, *Ideology and Utopia: An Introduction to the Sociology of Knowledge* (London: Routledge & Kegan Paul, 1936), 36–7.

66. Yoshihara Kunio, *The Rise of Ersatz Capitalism in Southeast Asia* (Singapore: Oxford University Press, 1988).

67. Stanislav Andreski, "Kleptocracy or Corruption as a System of Government," in *The African Predicament* (New York: Atherton, 1968).

68. Syed Hussein Alatas. *Corruption: Its Nature, Causes and Functions* (Aldershot: Avebury, 1990); El-Wathig Kameir and Ibrahim Kursany, "Corruption as the 'Fifth' Factor of Production in the Sudan," Research Report no 72 (Uppsala: Scandinavian Institute of African Studies, 1985); John Waterbury, "Corruption, Political Stability and Development: Comparative Evidence from Egypt and Morocco," *Government and Opposition*, 2, 1976.

69. On the need for a theory of the kleptocratic state see Alatas, "Agama dan Ilmu Kemasyarakatan: Masalah Teoretis," 382–3; Syed Farid Alatas, "The Post-Colonial State: Dual Functions in the Public Sphere," *Humboldt Journal of Social Relations*, 23(1–2), 1997, 285–307.

70. Syed Hussein Alatas, *Corruption*.

71. Sulayman S. Nyang, "The Islamic State and Economic Development," 22.

72. Ibn Khaldun, *Muqaddimat Ibn Khaldun* (Bayrut: Dar al-Kalam, 1981), 154, 380.

73. Ibid., 190–1 (Arabic). For the English translation, see Ibn Khaldun, *The Muqaddimah*, 3 vols., trans. Franz Rosenthal (New York: Pantheon Books, 1958), 155.

74. Ibid., 139 (Arabic). For the English translation, see Ibn Khaldun, *The Muqaddimah*, 3 vols., trans. Franz Rosenthal (New York: Pantheon Books, 1958), 107–8.

75. Ernest Gellner, *Muslim Society* (Cambridge: Cambridge University Press, 1981), 34.

76. Ibid.

77. Ibn Khaldun., op.cit., 237–8.

78. Ibn Khaldun., op.cit., 279–80.

79. For example, Joseph Desomogyi, "Economic Theory in Classical Arabic Literature," in Mohamed Taher, ed., *Encyclopaedic Survey of Islamic Culture, vol. 8 Studies in Islamic Economics* (New Delhi: Anmol Publications, 1997), 3–6; Dieter Weiss, "Ibn Khaldun on Economic Transformation," *International Journal of Middle East Studies*, 27, 1995; Sule Ahmed

Gusau, "Economic Thoughts of Ibn Khaldun," *Journal of Islamic Economics*, 3(1), 1993; Syed Farid Alatas, "Introduction to the Political Economy of Ibn Khaldun," *Islamic Quarterly*, 45, 2001, 307–24.

80.   Syed Farid Alatas, "Ibn Khaldun and the Ottoman Modes of Production," *Arab Historical Review for Ottoman Studies*, January, 1990, 45–64; Syed Farid Alatas, "A Khaldunian Perspective on the Dynamics of Asiatic Societies," *Comparative Civilizations Review*, 29, 1993a, 29–51.

81.   For example, A.L. Udovitch, "At the Origins of the Western Commenda: Islam, Israel, Byzantium?" *Speculum*, 37, 1962, 198–207; A.L. Udovitch, "Credit as a Means of Investment in Medieval Islamic Trade," *Journal of the American Oriental Society*, 87, 1967, 260–4; Udovitch, *Partnership and Profit in Medieval Islam*; Udovitch, "Commercial Techniques in Early Medieval Islamic Trade"; Udovitch, "Reflections on the Institutions of Credit and Banking in the Medieval Islamic Near East," *Studia Islamica*, 41, 1975, 5–21; Bruce Masters, *The Origins of Western Economic Dominance: Mercantilism and the Islamic Economy in Aleppo, 1600–1700* (New York: New York University Press, 1988); Abdullah Alwi Haji Hassan, "The Arabian Commercial Background in Pre-Islamic Times," *Islamic Culture*, 61(2), 1987, 70–83; Abdullah Alwi, "Al-Mudarabah (Dormant Partnership) and its Identical Islamic Partnerships in Early Islam," 11–38; Sabri Orman, "Sources of the History of Islamic Economic Thought," *Al-Shajarah*, 2(1), 1997, 21–62; Sabri Orman, "Sources of the History of Islamic Economic Thought II," *Al-Shajarah*, 3(1), 1998, 1–17; Ahmad Oran and Salim Rashid, "Fiscal Policy in Early Islam," *Public Finance*, 44(1), 1989, 75–101; Muhammad Al-Faruque, "Jizyah in Early Islam," in Mohamed Taher, ed., *Encyclopaedic Survey of Islamic Culture, vol. 8 Studies in Islamic Economics* (New Delhi: Anmol Publications, 1997), 107–19; S. Khuda Bukhsh, "Fiscal Matters in Islam," in Mohamed Taher, ed., *Encyclopaedic Survey of Islamic Culture, vol. 8 Studies in Islamic Economics* (New Delhi: Anmol Publications, 1997), 158–213.

PART VI

Women in Contemporary Islamic Thought

34 Muslim Feminist Debates on the Question of Headscarf in
    Contemporary Turkey   609
    Ayşe Kadıoğlu
35 "Islamic Feminism": Negotiating Patriarchy and Modernity in Iran   624
    Nayereh Tohidi
36 An Islamic Critique of Patriarchy: Mawlana Sayyed Kalbe Sadiq's
    Approach to Gender Relations   644
    Yoginder Sikand

CHAPTER 34

Muslim Feminist Debates on the Question of Headscarf in Contemporary Turkey

Ayşe Kadıoğlu

On November 6, 2003, a female citizen of Turkey, Hatice Hasdemir Şahin was expelled from the courtroom by the judge who is the head of the Fourth Criminal Department of the Court of Cassation for refusing to take off her headscarf. The judge claimed that he knew that Hatice Hasdemir Şahin was also a lawyer and since she was within the boundaries of the "public realm" he asked her to either take off her headscarf or leave. She chose to leave. A day later, the chief judge of the Court, Eraslan Özkaya, declared that it is against the law to enter the courtrooms wearing the headscarf.

The headscarf debate or the question of *ḥijāb* is usually referred to as the "question of *türban*" in Turkey. Türban refers to a particular style of headscarf tied at the back. It was considered more modern by the president of the Higher Education Council in Turkey in 1984. Hence, it was suggested that the students could wear it in place of the more religious styles of headscarf if they had to cover their heads at the university campuses. The women in the frontline of the struggle against the ban of the headscarf in the university campuses use the expression "headscarf" instead of "türban". The women who are active in the struggle against the ban are sometimes referred as "Islamic women" or "Muslim women". In the Seminar on Muslim Women in Western Societies held in Istanbul on June 11, 2004, the women speakers maintained that they prefer to be referred to as "religious women".[1]

The controversy surrounding the headscarf in Turkey acquired a political momentum during the course of the 1990s. This was partly due to the imposition of a ban on headscarves at the university campuses.[2] The initial ban came after the military coup of September 12, 1980. In 1981, the Council of Ministers approved a statute banning the headscarf for public employees and students in institutions attached to the Ministry of Education. The ban came to the universities in 1982. It was met with protests by Islamic groups. In 1984, the Higher Education Council allowed the "türban" in place of the "headscarf" since the former was considered to be more modern. This was met with protests by secularist groups. In 1987, the Higher Education Council withdrew the article that allowed "türban".

In 1987, Prime Minister Turgut Özal tried to manage the issue by relaxing the dress codes in the university campuses. Accordingly, in 1988, a new article was adopted in the Regulations of the Higher Education Council. It stated that the students were allowed to cover their heads and necks in accordance with their religious beliefs. When the president of the Republic, Kenan Evren, objected to this, a legislative process began that paved the way to the annulment of the article in 1989. Nevertheless, a new article was added to the Higher Education Council legislation in 1990 (Article 17) which indicates that "provided that they abide by the prevailing laws, all types of costumes are free in higher education institutions." When this article was objected by a legal suit, the Constitutional Court rejected its annulment. Yet in its explanation of the rejection, it stated that "this article does not apply to the students with the headscarf".[3]

The decision of the Constitutional Court, which became the basis of the ban at university campuses, was backed by a decision taken by the European Human Rights Commission in 1993. This decision was taken in response to the complaints of two students who could not get their diplomas since they had submitted photographs of themselves with the headscarf. The Commission declared that when a student chooses to have her education in a secular institution, she should comply with the requirements pertaining to secularism in that institution.[4]

The headscarf issue has been studied and debated extensively in Turkey. The existing literature approaches the question of the headscarf from the angle of backwardness and progress. Headscarf is usually taken as the emblem of tradition and backwardness whereas its removal is usually associated with modernization and progress. In sum, the question of headscarf has so far been studied and debated from the angle of modernization. The case of Hatice Hasdemir Şahin's removal from a courtroom portrays the need to approach the issue from the angle of modernity and citizenship. The headscarf issue has increasingly become an issue of citizenship. It has more to do with women's rights over their bodies than the modernization of the national society. It portrays the relationship between rights and democracy. Hence, the issue is increasingly being removed from the realm of modernization, secularization, and progress to the realm of modernity and citizenship. The resolution of the question is based very much on the changing meaning of citizenship as well as setting the boundaries of the public realm.

In what follows, I will, first of all, refer to the Republican modernization project that paved the way to the association of the headscarf with backwardness. In reviewing the parameters of the literature, I will also refer to the literature that associates the issue of the headscarf with democratization. Secondly, I will refer to the accounts of the women with the headscarf portrayed either in the literature authored by themselves or some studies that contain interviews with them.

Headscarf: A Symbol of Backwardness?[5]

Women's public visibility acquired renewed importance during the early Republican era when the Kemalists promoted Turkish nationalism and Westernization at the expense of Islam and traditional culture. The manufactured Western image of the

Muslim world epitomized the secluded, veiled, and hence oppressed women of the Muslim world. The founder of the Turkish Republic, Mustafa Kemal, who unleashed a series of fundamental Westernizing reforms in the 1920s, referred to the incivility of veiling and expressed an uneasy feeling of embarrassment at being ridiculed by the civilized world.[6]

The early Republican Westernization reforms in Turkey never went so far as banning the veil at the national level. At a Congress of the People's Republican Party in 1935, a proposal regarding the abolition of the veil was discussed, yet no national action was taken except in some municipalities where the practice of veiling was outlawed. Interestingly, the religious headgear of men, the fez, was abolished and all men were compelled legally to wear hats.[7] Nevertheless, the instigation from above of policies regarding women were extensive enough to warrant their later characterization as "state feminism."[8] In the aftermath of the proclamation of the Republic in 1923, many steps, including the abolition of the caliphate and the closure of *sharī'ah* courts, represented the Republic's "clear distaste for religion."[9] The ensuing secularization brought dramatic changes to the Turkish social and political structure. In the course of the 1920s and early 1930s, a series of fundamental reforms were launched including the prohibition of the fez, the dissolution of the dervish orders, the reform of the calendar, the adoption of the Latin alphabet, and the use of Turkish instead of Arabic in the Islamic call to prayer.

The reforms regarding women were included in the Turkish Civil Code that was adopted in 1926 to replace *sharī'ah*. The new law declared polygyny and marriage by proxy illegal, and granted women equal rights with men regarding divorce, custody of children, and inheritance.[10] Women were given the right to vote in local elections in 1934 and national elections in 1935. Despite the existence of a women's movement from below which was led by a woman activist, Nezihe Muhiddin (1889–1958), women's political activities were thwarted by pressures from above.[11] Hence all the major rights conferred on Turkish women during these years were the result of the efforts of a male revolutionary elite, who had the goal of bringing Turkey to the level of contemporary Western civilization.

Even though the early Republican reforms encouraged women to participate in the public realm, women's primary responsibility remained within the private domain. This was also encouraged by the founders of the Republic. In 1923, Mustafa Kemal said:

> History shows the great virtues shown by our mothers and grandmothers. One of these has been to raise sons of whom the race can be proud. Those whose glory spread over Asia and as far as the limits of the world had been trained by highly virtuous mothers who taught them courage and truthfulness. I will not cease to repeat it, *woman's most important duty, apart from her social responsibilities, is to be a good mother.* As one progresses in time, as civilization advances with giant steps, it is imperative that mothers be enabled to raise their children according to the needs of the century.[12]

The early Republican reforms constituted an onslaught on existing cultural practices. They created an image of a modern Turkish woman who was honorable, chaste, enlightened, and modest. These virtues suppressed her sexuality while highlighting her modern outlook. The women who became products of the early Republican reforms were similar to the *noblesse de robe* (nobility by virtue of dress) of pre-Revolutionary France who joined the ranks of the nobility by purchasing offices and putting on aristocratic clothes. These women of twentieth-century Turkish history became *modernes de robe*, who wore modern clothes and adopted Western codes of conduct, but nevertheless remained traditional, especially regarding relations with men and their self-perceptions within the confines of the family. They became simulated images of modernity.[13] Their clothes symbolized the political ends of the male Republican elite.[14] Hence, a state feminism instigated from above inhibited the evolution of a feminist consciousness on the part of these women.

The evolution of women's movements in Turkey after the early Republican era carried in it the initial limitations of a state feminism which was instigated from above. It was not possible to refer to a feminist movement "of women, by women and for women" until the 1980s. There were two constant themes in the expression of women's issues in Turkey until the 1980s. First of all, women's issues were always viewed as part of "greater" social projects such as Kemalism, socialism, and political Islam. Their pleas were absorbed within the larger goals of these social movements. Secondly, all of these movements had a view of women not as individuals who are in need of a "room of their own" but as members of the family unit.[15]

In the early years of the Republic, women were viewed as the motor of modernization in Turkey. Their appearance was taken as the symbol of modernization. This emphasis laid on appearance became a significant aspect of the views of the Kemalists on women in the later years of the Republic as well. In short, the Kemalists had a view of women as an emblem of modernity who at the same time were primarily responsible for the well-being of the unit of the family in the society. In spite of the fact that they advocated women's rights and encouraged female participation in social life, the Republican white males had envisaged domestic, nurturing images of women.

Women writers were also absorbed in this Republican rhetoric. Halide Edip Adıvar (1883–1964), the most prominent female writer of the early Republican period as well as an eloquent speaker and an advisor to Mustafa Kemal, became the proponent of a nationalist feminist discourse that had anti-Western tones regarding femininity and sexuality.[16] She extolled the modest, self-sacrificing, and maternal virtues of women and encouraged men to have a view of women as asexual comrades who selflessly accompany their men in their endeavors. The new Republican woman was a martyr enduring the double burden of jobs (mostly as teachers) and family. She was critical of the sexual promiscuity of Western women. She was an honorable, asexual sister-in-arms. She was first and foremost a devout wife and a mother. She was self-sacrificing, nurturing, humble. She was the comrade and companion of her husband, his partner in social gatherings. She was the invisible monument of chastity and endurance behind each successful man.

In the aftermath of the military coup of September 12, 1980, all political movements came to a halt and all political parties were closed. Ironically, it was during those years that an independent feminist movement was able to find room for itself since all the other "greater" social movements were penalized. Hence, woman as an individual with her daily problems became the subject matter of novels and feature films.[17] Her problems in the private realm, her femininity and sexuality became legitimate topics of investigation. This was accelerated by a rising liberal tide during the years when Turgut Özal became the prime minister after the elections that ended the military regime in 1983. Hence, women's issues paved the way to the problematization of the private realm in Turkey. Women who were viewed as appendages of the greater Republican project had found a room for voicing their more private grievances.

The headscarf issue began to appear on the agenda of Turkish politics in the course of these years when women's issues were being divorced from greater social projects such as Kemalism and socialism. This was also an indicator of the arrival of new political cleavages to the Turkish political scene that were not limited with divisions of modern politics between the left and right. The 1980s and 1990s symbolized the end of modern politics based on a division between the left and the right. With the end of modern politics that has relegated religious, ethnic, racial, and gender-related identities into the private realm, these identities began to make their debut in the public realm. Women did not just want to practice religion at home; they now began to ask for approval for their religious appearances in the public realm. Kurds did not want to speak Kurdish only at home but began to ask for official recognition of their native language. The identities that were relegated to the private realm were now demanding recognition in the public realm.

This novelty in the political realm is not specific to Turkey. It is a process that was unleashed by globalization processes in the world. These processes paved the way to an increasing scrutiny of the modern category of citizenship that suppressed and homogenized such identities under the rubric of national identity. Globalization processes paved the way to their revival and presence in the public realm.

The issue of women's headscarf appeared on the agenda of Turkish politics in the course of such major changes that challenged the modern notion of citizenship. Today, the modern notion of citizenship is in the process of getting a divorce from the unit of the nation-state. It is in the process of becoming less enchanted, less holy. It is being demystified. In the Turkish context, the question around the headscarf of religious women appeared in such a context. Hence, it contained in it an element of democratization of modern categories. Yet, whether the decision to cover their heads is a decision taken by women out of their individual convictions or whether it is being imposed on them by various Islamic communities is still vague. On the one hand, Kemalists are convinced that the headscarf is imposed on these gullible, deceived women. Some of these women, on the other hand, are convinced that the headscarf issue is related to their "rights" over their own bodies. The resulting conflict is quite akin to the divisions between the pro-life and pro-choice activists on the abortion issue in the United States.

The most important analysis of the headscarf issue in Turkey from the perspective of citizenship debates was undertaken by Yeşim Arat.[18] Arat evaluates the headscarf controversy in Turkey from the angle of group-differentiated rights and how they reconcile with the dictates of liberal democratic states. In this context, she asks a critical question:

> Should Islamist women be granted this special "privilege" to protect them from the difference-blind rules of the state? Or do these women belong to an illiberal community, one undeserving of special protection from difference-blind rules?[19]

Arat bases her analysis on the existing literature that criticizes the seemingly universal, homogeneous notions of citizenship and laws that are oblivious to special problems and discrimination of women.[20] She refers to Will Kymlicka's distinction between the notions of "external protections" and "internal restrictions," the former referring to protections of minority groups from the overbearing power of dominant groups; and the latter referring to rights exercised by minorities against their own members to restrict individual choice in the name of cultural tradition or integrity.[21] In sum, it is via external protections that group-differentiated rights can be sought *vis-à-vis* neutral definitions of citizenship while it is via internal restrictions that communities can curb individual rights of their members. Against this background, Arat formulates the most critical question surrounding the headscarf controversy in Turkey as follows:

> The ban on headscarves stipulates that dress codes of the secular universities apply equally to all. Under these conditions, are the Islamist women exposed to the overbearing power of the majority, and are they justified in seeking "external protection" to practice their religion free from the constraints imposed by the latter? Or are the Islamist groups imposing "internal restrictions" on their members, particularly their women, not only to wear headscarves, but also to abide by certain traditional roles, which they claim Islam prescribes? Are the women in the Islamist groups thoroughly socialized if not indoctrinated to accept these internal restrictions rather than to rebel individually against them?[22]

In other words, are the women who are covering their heads freely carrying their right to be believers in the dictates of religion into the public realm or are they being forced to adopt this practice by the elder, male members of their groups? In the former case, the headscarf debate contains an element of democratization since it opens up the neutral public realm into differences that were relegated into the private realm by the dictates of modernity. In the latter case, it becomes an imposition of group identity on individual members. This brings the headscarf controversy into line with the abortion controversy since it elevates the factor of "choice" to the forefront. Are these women covering their heads out of free choice, or are they simply abiding by the dictates of their group? The answer is affirmative on both accounts with different groups of women. While some women behind the headscarf movement in Turkey have become believers due to their own convictions, others were pressured by family and peers into wearing the headscarf. Hence, the controversy surrounding the issues of citizenship, group-differentiated rights, democracy and the headscarf is not an easy one.

Accounts of Women

There are various studies in the literature on the headscarf issue that portray the experiences of women themselves. An evaluation of this literature makes it quite evident that it is not possible to refer to a single set of reasons that prompt the adoption of the headscarf as well as an Islamic lifestyle. Some women are forced by their family members to adopt these practices against their will whereas others have clearly chosen the headscarf and an Islamic lifestyle as an instrument for protesting the decadent modern lifestyles that subdue women in general. Most of the women in the frontline of the struggle to acquire the right to wear the headscarf, especially in the university campuses, claim that they have made a conscious decision to adopt Islamic clothing as a result of a religious awakening in their lives. Others claim that they cover their heads since that has always been the custom with the women in their family. In what follows, I will refer to some of the descriptions of the women of their own experiences *vis-à-vis* the issue of the headscarf.

In one of the early works on Muslim women, Nilüfer Göle refers to how women have chosen to wear the headscarf in order to hide their sexuality and portray their personality.[23] Seclusion, then, has become a way of denouncing sexuality outside the confines of a marital arrangement. Similarly, motherhood and the reproduction of future generations have become the sole purpose of sex. Feride Acar, who conducted fieldwork with secluded university students, presents a psycho-sociological explanation in accounting for these women's attraction to the political Islamic discourse.[24] She maintains that a sudden exposure to the medium at the universities signifying male–female dynamics is a crucial impetus in paving the way to their reception of Islam. Acar argues that these women have always experienced a fundamental contradiction between the conservative, Islamic values conveyed to them by their families and the ones that they are taught at the secular institutions of education in Turkey. Islamic discourse seems to offer them a means for justifying their primary roles within the household as wives and mothers.

Aynur İlyasoğlu's work is particularly important within the literature on the headscarf issue since she evaluates the women with the headscarf, first and foremost as women.[25] İlyasoğlu argues that the women do not necessarily use the headscarf as a denial of femininity but rather as an effort to relegate femininity into the private realm. In other words, they oppose the utilization of the woman's body as a sexual symbol in modern societies. Theirs is an attempt to desexualize the public realm. İlyasoğlu refers to how some of the women that she interviewed said that they had tried to look nice by wearing soft clothes and putting on religiously approved perfumes in the evenings before their husbands got back home from work. İlyasoğlu evaluates this as a sign of a different kind of femininity, one that is limited within the confines of the private realm of the household. Hence, she argues that seclusion is not necessarily a denial of femininity. It rather symbolizes its relegation into the private realm. İlyasoğlu's work is also important in introducing the readers to some of the literature authored by secluded women themselves. Various revelations pertaining to the decision to use the headscarf as well as expectations and frustrations of these women in marital relationships are portrayed in this literature. Two of these accounts are especially interesting and hence will be reviewed here at length. The first one is a novel titled *Müslüman Kadının Adı Var* (*Muslim Woman Has A Name*) authored by Şerife Katırcı.[26]

The title of Katırcı's novel brings to mind one of the epoch-making books in Turkish women's literature by Duygu Asena which was published two years earlier and titled *Kadının Adı Yok* (*Woman Has No Name*).[27] Asena's book was one of the first of its kind that viewed women as individuals and that delved into their problems of independence in the private realm. It voiced the misgivings of a woman who felt trapped in the household and with the roles that were given to her by the men around her. The novel symbolized the emergence of a view of women outside the confines of the family.

Şerife Katırcı's novel is about a woman named Dilara. Dilara is the daughter of a professor of biology. Her mother died and she was raised by her father with the help of a nanny. In the novel, she is portrayed as the top student of the school of medicine in Ankara. She feels isolated from her classmates and does not feel comfortable observing what seems to her like degenerate relations between men and women. She feels at home in her father's small hometown environment. One day, a couple with a child have an accident near their house. The woman dies. Dilara and her father host the survivors, the man and the baby, in their house until they get better. This man introduces Dilara to the Qur'an and Islamic teachings. She develops a liking for this man but is unable to express it.

One day, when she is praying, she has a vision of an apple. A voice tells her that every fruit has an outer cover, a shell, and that a woman's outer cover or shell is her veil. Hence, she decides to go into seclusion at that moment.

After her decision to go into seclusion, Dilara begins to face many difficulties. When she goes back to school in Ankara, she is expelled from the dormitory. The university administration feels awkward about giving her the prize for highest achievement in the commencement ceremony. She hears the professors talk about how they think that she has been deceived and is being used by Islamic orders and organizations. Soon, she rents her own apartment. She has no furniture in her place. All she has is a carpet, some pillows and a bookcase as well as a small cupboard for her clothes. She does not want to be the prisoner of furniture. She feels sorry for the women who spend their days dusting their furniture. She wants to be free from such domestic chores. The hospital that she works for sends her to Mekke in order to serve those who are on pilgrimage. There she meets once again this man who earlier introduced her to Islam. They get married. Their reunion is portrayed as a gift to her for her belief in Allah.

Katırcı's novel is symbolic of the literature that maintains that women, once they are believers in Allah, do not only have a "name" but also a "voice." The Qur'an and Islamic teachings are viewed as instruments in the liberation of women as well as their discovery of their femininity within the confines of the private realm.

Another book that İlyasoğlu analyzes is by one of the most outspoken authors about Muslim women, Cihan Aktaş.[28] Cihan Aktaş's book contains stories about women who find a "voice" via Islamic teachings. After getting married, these women are portrayed as being trapped with domestic chores and the societal expectations about wives. Hence, they lose their "voice." In one of the stories, the woman lives independently as a university student. After getting married, her husband, with whom she shared a belief in Allah, begins to change and give in to some societal expectations. He begins to lead a life attached to his job and that excludes his wife. Her life is limited to the household. She has to perform domestic chores and look after their child. The people around her demand submission and passivity from her. She is expected to wear expensive things and show them off in women's gatherings. Aktaş portrays how women whose existence is limited to the household are also expected to compete in terms of their belongings such as jewelry, carpets, furniture, their children's test scores, their husband's income, their cars, and even their driver's licenses. Since they lack any other form of protest, these women go back to the days when they were able to find a "voice" in their religious beliefs. Finding a "voice" via seclusion and Islamic teachings seems to be the experience of some of these women. The women portrayed in Aktaş's stories feel disillusioned with their marriages and find comfort and strength in what once made them feel like individuals: their belief in Islam.

Aktaş's portrayal of the misgivings of these women are akin to universal feminist claims:

> These domestic chores and days that are always the same . . . I will cease to exist like this. Like it has happened to so many people. I cannot stand this feeling. I am filled with an enormous feeling of failure. But what could have I done, I was unable to find a job with my headscarf after school.[29]

The women who voiced these misgivings had chosen to marry without a bridal dress. They had rejected the Western imposition of a white bridal costume on women with all its pacifist connotations. They had found a feminist voice in Islam. Yet, they had lost this voice after getting married and leading lives that are confined to the household. In what seemed somewhat like a paradox, their religious convictions which gave them their voice had also kept them away from the public realm. Their distance from the public realm contained a criticism of the societal mores that discriminated against women with the headscarf within the job market in Turkey. Hence, what gave them voice was used as the pretext for silencing them.

The literature about the women with the headscarf points to their search for an independent realm between non-political, traditional Islamic practices that are encouraged by their families and political Islamic practices that are sometimes emboldened by various Islamic communities. One can distinguish a quest for individualism on the part of these women by adopting styles of headgear that are neither encouraged by their non-political families nor the political Islamic communities. Some women even resorted to the practice of wearing a wig on top of their headscarves in order to be allowed into university campuses.

The ban on the headscarf in the universities has sometimes paved the way to strife between these women and their families. In some cases, while their families wanted them to abide by the legal codes and urged them to take off their headscarves while walking through the gates of the university, their friends had placed pressure on them to keep their headscarves and join the demonstrations at the gates of the university. Taking off the headscarf would allow them into campuses and classes whereas resisting it would jeopardize their education. Most of the women who later became radical protestors of the headscarf ban in university campuses were the ones who were unable to complete their university education for insisting on wearing the headscarf.[30]

In one of the cases, which is described in detail by Elizabeth Özdalga, the woman who wears the headscarf finds herself in a position to make a judgment pertaining to her university education.[31] In spite of the fact that her family members were devout Muslims, they encouraged her to take off her headscarf so that she could continue her education. They told her that for the time being she should abide by the legal codes, and in the future, after graduating from the university, she can make a decision about her headscarf. They were, in other words, suggesting that she postponed the headscarf issue until after her graduation from the university. Her uncle tried to convince her to say the following to herself, in order to have a clear conscience: "My Allah, I am not responsible for all that is happening. I have to uncover in order to attend my classes." Yet, at the peak moment of the clash between the police and the demonstrators, she found herself in a position to make a decision. She decided to take off her headscarf and walk through the gates of the university. She described her riddle as follows:

> It was Tuesday morning at 9.10 a.m. We took off our headscarves (with a friend) and ran from the gate of entrance (of the university) to the small mosque. You feel like you are naked. It was really very difficult to do it. Still, when I think about it now, I feel like laughing at the whole thing . . . We were a group of girls who did not want to miss classes. We thought of this as a responsibility. We clung to each other during these difficult days.[32]

She maintains that things had become a bit more polarized by the time of the exams. Some of the girls who took off their headscarves and attended the classes were now refusing to take the exams:

> Those who decided to take the exams were only a few girls. I went there with a friend. The second day, two of the girls who decided to unveil like us were in front of us. There was a huge crowd of demonstrating students at the gates. The demonstrators began to clap their hands and whistle when they saw these two girls. We could not comprehend what was going on. Then, when it was time for us to go through the gates, we realized that they were protesting us. I was embarrassed. I blushed. I was so hurt that, after going through the gates and leaving the university, I walked all the way to Ulus (a neighborhood) without a pause . . . It was a good thing that I was with a friend. It would have been a lot more difficult if I was alone. If I knew about the protests, I would have waited all day until dark (before leaving the university) . . . Anyways, we both walked all the way to Ulus for about an hour. We were angry. It was as if we had taken off our headscarf due to our own wishes! Others did not comprehend that you were lonely, and you had responsibilities to your family![33]

This woman finally arrived at the conviction that wearing the headscarf is not the only way to fulfill one's religious responsibilities. In fact, she argued that she had known women who were secluded yet were not good human beings. Hence, she finally made peace with her decision that seclusion was not a measurement of good religious conduct and under the circumstances the more utilitarian thing to do was to postpone the practice.

In another study, seclusion appears as a reaction to pressures against it. One female medical student said:

> The minute a woman responsible for the operating room entered into our classroom, she crossed her eyes on the two students with the headscarf. And then she said "I do not allow students with the headscarf into my classroom. Leave. I will not consider you absent." I was so troubled with this situation that as they were leaving, I got up and left with them. There were others who left with them too. I was considering wearing the headscarf but

waiting for the lift of the ban. Yet, with the impact of this incident, I went into seclusion soon.[34]

A secluded woman describes the pressures placed on them at the university campuses as follows:

> We tried to listen to the lectures in faculty halls with a continuous anxiety of being thrown out of the classroom. We were allowed in and out of lectures, exams according to the consciences of the professors. We were exiled from classrooms, laboratories, even corridors via measures that were not even applied to those who were cheating in exams and resorting to sexual promiscuity. We were thrown out of the universities by janitors who could not even read and write. As we waited in front of the university gates in order to be allowed in we have got acquainted with police sticks . . . Those who finally unveiled due to their inability to cope with these difficulties became permanent patients at psychiatry clinics since they were unable to match their beliefs with their life styles.[35]

In another study, Ruşen Çakır locates the traces of individualism in the worldviews of women who had made a conscious decision to go into seclusion. Çakır has conducted a long interview with one of the prominent figures in the struggle against the ban, Hidayet Şefkatli Tuksal, who articulated the headscarf with universal feminist claims and individualism. When asked about secluded women who divorce their husbands, Tuksal said:

> I heard of one case (a secluded woman divorcing her husband in order to marry someone else) and I know she was shamed and criticized. I criticized those who criticized her. Because, men always do this and nobody criticizes them. They go to their weddings all together, all the gentlemen and ladies, yet when a woman does it she is excluded from the society.[36]

Tuksal implies that she is able to see a common ground of resistance among secluded women and homosexuals, transsexuals, and other people who are excluded from society. She has expressed the misgivings of secluded women as part of a larger dilemma of women or even other excluded groups in the society. She says:

> Pain, to be lost, exclusion is not specific to us. I share the pain of every blow of a police stick on a leftist or a transvestite. We have acquired such a common ground.[37]

Conclusion

The experiences of the women described above portray that the headscarf is not viewed as a symbol of backwardness by them. On the contrary, the decision to go into seclusion is part of the struggle to find their own voice, a room of their own in a male-centered society. In an interview in June 2003, Nilüfer Göle maintains that:

> The Kemalist women are not aware of the change in the symbolic meaning of the headscarf . . . About twenty years ago, headscarf was a symbol of backwardness, illiteracy,

inequality of men and women and the confinement of women in the household. Today, it is the women who want to go to school and have a career as well as an upper hand in modern spaces who want to go into seclusion.[38]

In another interview in December 2003, Tülin Bumin refers to the headscarf not as a religious symbol but rather an individual symbol.[39] She considers the headscarf as a step in the direction of individualization:

> Today, the individual defines herself through her sense of belonging. If she is turning to religion (in this process), she is doing this out of an individual choice . . . She does not use her mother's style of headscarf since she thinks, contrary to her mother, she was not born into that religion. Rather, she is trying to convey to us that she has *chosen* that religion. This is a sign of becoming an individual because she is saying "I do not belong to religion. Religion belongs to me." The Republican model is unable to read this. They think this (the headscarf issue) is the return of religion. It is not.[40]

It is obvious that the debate on the headscarf boils down to the presence and absence of a "choice" made by these women to cover their heads. Whether these women have made independent choices toward seclusion or whether they were forced into it by the communities that they find themselves in seems to be the critical issue. The headscarf debate is being articulated with the new debate on the notion of citizenship. The latter debate is paving the way to the divorce of the notion of citizenship from the nation-state as well as its redefinition in less holy and less celebrated forms.[41]

Hence, an evaluation of the headscarf issue from the angle of backwardness and progress is inadequate. It should rather be viewed in terms of the rights of these women over their own bodies. In order for women to "freely make their own choices" over their bodies, their struggle should not be in the shadow of a larger Muslim project. For that to happen, there should be "women as individuals" in the society prior to the absorption of their claims in other political projects. This requires the establishment of formal equality between men and women in legal, institutional, and practical terms. It is only after the establishment of this equality that the group-differentiated rights of these women can be viewed as part of the process of democratization. Otherwise, there is always the potential that they may hamper it.

The debate on the headscarf inevitably requires a clear definition of the "public realm" in Turkey. For some, the public realm extends to the parliament, university campuses, and the courtroom. Public realm refers to the boundaries in which the state defines the codes of conduct. Yet, the definition of the space is laden with potential problems. Perhaps, another dimension of the definition of the public realm should involve the functions of the individuals in that space. The members of parliament, for instance, are the elected representatives of the national elite. Their vocation is to represent the people. They are not civil servants. They do not define the parameters of their activities with the idea of *raison d'état*. Similarly, university students are not civil servants. They do not serve the state but rather receive service from it. Public realm as the realm of the state has been defined rather widely in Republican Turkey. In line with a civic Republican tradition, Turkish citizens were burdened with duties *vis-à-vis* the state.

Returning to the courtroom example at the beginning of this article, perhaps what is needed is the redefinition of the boundaries of the public realm by taking into account the differences between the accused and the judge in a courtroom. The tension over the headscarf issue can only be lifted through such adjustments pertaining to the boundaries of the public realm by taking into account the differences between the civil servants who serve the state and lay citizens who receive service from them.

Notes

1. Seminar on Muslim Women in Western Societies organized by TESEV (Turkish Economic and Social Studies Foundation) and the Consulate of Netherlands, June 11, 2004, Istanbul.
2. See Elizabeth Özdalga, *The Veiling Issue, Official Secularism and Popular Islam in Modern Turkey* (Surrey, UK: Curzon Press, 1998) on the history of the ban on the headscarf in Turkey.
3. The secularist groups are banning entry of the students with the headscarf to the universities on the basis of this "exception" indicated in the Constitutional Court's explanation. The Islamic groups are suggesting that the Constitutional Court is contradicting itself by not annulling free style of dress for everyone at the university campuses and bringing an exception for the headscarf in its explanation of the rejection of annulment. They argue that it is the decision and not the rationale in the explanation that is binding and such contradictory legislation is against the Article 153/2 of the Constitution.
4. The Islamic groups ridicule this decision by arguing that no one can "freely" choose to attend a secular institution in Turkey since all institutions are secular by law. In sum, the Turkish secularist educational institutions have no alternatives. This makes the "choice" of secular institutions a far outcry.
5. In this section, I have benefited from an earlier article, Ayşe Kadıoğlu, "Women's Subordination in Turkey: Is Islam Really the Villain?", *Middle East Journal*, 48(4), 1994, 645–61.
6. Leila Ahmed, *Women and Gender in Islam: Historical Roots of a Modern Debate* (New Haven, CT: Yale University Press, 1992), 164.
7. The fact that legislation pertaining to dress codes was first passed for men can be viewed as a sign of men setting the pace of modernization. See Nükhet Sirman, "Feminism in Turkey: A Short History," *New Perspectives on Turkey*, 3(1), 1989, 1–34.
8. For the expression "state feminism," see Şirin Tekeli, "Emergence of the New Feminist Women in Turkey," in D. Dahlerup, ed., *The New Women's Movement* (London: Sage, 1986), 179–99.
9. Şerif Mardin, "European Culture and the Development of Modern Turkey," in Ahmet Evin and Geoffrey Denton, eds., *Turkey and the European Community* (Opladen, Germany: Leske and Budrich, 1990), 21.
10. Nermin Abadan-Unat, "Social Change and Turkish Women," in Nermin Abadan-Unat, ed., *Women in Turkish Society* (Leiden: E.J. Brill, 1981), 13–14.
11. See Zafer Toprak, "Halk Fırkası'ndan Once Kurulan Parti: Kadınlar Halk Fırkası" (The Party Founded Before the Republican People's Party: People's Party of Women), *Tarih ve Toplum*, 9(51), 1988, 30–1. On Nezihe Muhiddin, see Yaprak Zihnioğlu, *Kadınsız İnkilap: Nezihe Muhiddin, Kadınlar Halk Fırkası, Kadın Birliği* (Revolution Without Women: Nezihe Muhiddin, People's Party of Women, Women's Unity), (Istanbul: Metis, 2003).
12. Cited in Kumari Jayawardena, *Feminism and Nationalism in the Third World* (London: Zed Books, 1986), 36 (italics mine).

13. I believe an exaggeration of such simulated images of modernity is reminiscent of an art current of the 1960s to mid-1970s called hyper-realism and/or photo realism, which generated realist paintings with a photographic vision of reality. These paintings were similar to the modern images of women that were created in the early Republican years in the sense that they looked natural, but, in fact, were manufactured.

14. Interestingly, men's ties in Turkey are popularly called "the reins of civilization." It is also interesting to note that the most conspicuous items displayed in the museum located at Atatürk's mausoleum in Ankara are his clothes, all of which are tailored in modern European fashions.

15. I have argued these limitations of the feminist movement in Turkey in an earlier article. See, Ayşe Kadıoğlu, "Cinselliğin İnkarı: Büyük Toplumsal Projelerin Nesnesi Olarak Türk Kadınları"(Denial of Sexuality: Turkish Women as Objects of Grand Societal Projects), 75 Yılda Kadınlar ve Erkekler (Women and Men in 75 Years), Türkiye Ekonomik ve Toplumsal Tarih Vakfı, Bilanço 98 dizisi (Istanbul: Tarih Vakfı Yayınları,1998).

16. Ayşe Durakbaşı, "Cumhuriyet Döneminde Kemalist Kadın Kimliğinin Oluşumu" (The Formation of the Kemalist Women's Identity in the Republican Era), Tarih ve Toplum, 9(51), 1988, 167–71.

17. One of the epoch-making novels that appeared at this time was by Duygu Asena, Kadının Adı Yok (Woman Has No Name), (Istanbul: Afa Yayınları, 1987) which became a best seller. Some of the pioneer movies directed by Atıf Yılmaz also focused on woman as an individual.

18. Yeşim Arat, "Group Differentiated Rights and the Liberal Democratic State: Rethinking the Headscarf Controversy in Turkey," New Perspectives on Turkey, 25, 2001, 31–46.

19. Ibid., 32.

20. See for instance, Iris Marion Young, Justice and the Politics of Difference (Princeton, NJ: Princeton University Press, 1990).

21. Yeşim Arat, "Group Differentiated Rights and the Liberal Democratic State: Rethinking the Headscarf Controversy in Turkey," 34. See also Will Kymlicka, "Liberal Complacencies," in J. Cohen et al., eds., Is Multiculturalism: Bad for Women? (Princeton, NJ: Princeton University Press, 1999) and Will Kymlicka, Multicultural Citizenship (Oxford: Oxford University Press, 1995).

22. Yeşim Arat, "Group Differentiated Rights and the Liberal Democratic State: Rethinking the Headscarf Controversy in Turkey," 35.

23. Nilüfer Göle, Modern Mahrem: Medeniyet ve Örtünme (The Forbidden Modern), (Istanbul: Metis, 1991), 125.

24. Feride Acar, "Türkiye'de İslamcı Hareket ve Kadın: Kadın Dergileri ve Bir Grup Üniversite Öğrencisi Üzerinde Bir İnceleme" (Women and Islamic Movements in Turkey: A Survey on Women's Journals and a Group of University Students), in Şirin Tekeli, ed., Kadın Bakış Açısından 1980'ler Türkiye'sinde Kadınlar (An Account of Women By Women in the 1980s), (Istanbul: İletişim Yayınları, 1990).

25. Aynur İlyasoğlu, Örtülü Kimlik (Secluded Identity), (Istanbul: Metis, 1994).

26. Şerife Katırcı, Müslüman Kadının Adı Var (Muslim Woman Has A Name), (Istanbul: Seha Yayınları, 1989).

27. Duygu Asena, Kadının Adı Yok (Woman Has No Name), (Istanbul: Afa Yayınları, 1987).

28. Cihan Aktaş, Üç İhtilal Çocuğu (Three Children of Revolution), (Istanbul: Nehir Yayınları, 1991). Other books by Cihan Aktaş are Sistem İçinde Kadın (Woman in the System), (Istanbul: Beyan Yayınları, 1988); Tesettür ve Toplum (Seclusion and Society), (Istanbul: Nehir Yayınları, 1992); Son Büyülü Günler (The Last Magical Days), (Istanbul: Nehir Yayınları, 1995); Bacıdan Bayana (From Sister to Miss), (Istanbul: Pınar Yayınları, 2001).

29. Cited in Aynur İlyasoğlu, *Örtülü Kimlik*, 82.
30. All the women that I interviewed in a study of Islamic civil societal organization had joined these organizations since they were unable to complete their university education due to their headscarf. Hence, wearing the headscarf had become the main aspect of their political identity. See my account of these women in "Civil Society, Islam and Democracy in Turkey: A Study of Three Islamic Non Governmental Organizations," *Muslim World*, 95(1), 2005, 23–43.
31. Elizabeth Özdalga, "Sivil Toplum ve Düşmanları" (Civil Society and Its Rivals), in Elizabeth Özdalga and Sune Persson, *Sivil Toplum, Demokrasi ve İslam Dünyası* (Civil Society, Democracy and the World of Islam), (Istanbul: Tarih Vakfı Yurt Yayınları, 1998).
32. Ibid., 103–4.
33. Ibid., 104.
34. Cihan Aktaş, *Tesettür ve Toplum*, p. 113. In the interviews that I have conducted with secluded women who had joined civil societal organizations, I had also met a woman who decided to go into seclusion after hearing how modern-looking women referred to the secluded women as the "other" by resorting to the expression "them." She claimed that this had created a sense of solidarity with these women who were constantly excluded. Hence, she decided to emulate their practices. See, Ayşe Kadıoğlu, "Civil Society, Islam and Democracy in Turkey: A Study of Three Islamic Non Governmental Organizations," *Muslim World*, 95(1), 2005, 23–43.
35. Cited in Ibid., 171–2. See also a book by a woman wearing the headscarf who described in detail the difficulties she has endured in one of the state universities, Zekiye Oğuzhan, *Bir Başörtüsü Günlüğü*, (A Memo of the Headscarf Issue), (Istanbul: İz Yayıncılık, 1998).
36. Cited in Ruşen Çakır, *Direniş ve İtaat* (Resistance and Submisson), (Istanbul: Metis, 2000), 27. Hidayet Şefkatli Tuksal is also the author of *Kadın Karşıtı Söylemin İslam Geleneğindeki İzdüşümü* (The Representations of Misogyny in the Islamic Tradition), (Istanbul, Kitabiyat Yayınları, 2000).
37. Cited in Ruşen Çakır, *Direniş ve İtaat*, 31.
38. *Milliyet* (Istanbul daily), June 10, 2003, 17.
39. *Radikal* (Istanbul daily), December 29, 2003, 6.
40. Ibid.
41. For an elaboration of the possibility of such a notion of citizenship in Turkey see, Ayşe Kadıoğlu, "Can We Envision Citizenship as Non-Membership in Turkey" in Fuat Keyman and Ahmet İçduygu, eds., *Citizenship and Identity in a Globalizing World: European Questions/Turkish Experiences* (Routledge, 2005), 105–23.

CHAPTER 35

"Islamic Feminism": Negotiating Patriarchy and Modernity in Iran

Nayereh Tohidi

Since the inception of the Islamic Republic in 1979, gender contestation has gained extra saliency and unprecedented intensity in Iranian society and polity. The current gender regime in Iran and the women's movement challenging it have complex, contradictory, and paradoxical characteristics. This chapter is an attempt to explain one aspect of this complexity concerning Iranian women's negotiation with the ruling patriarchy. Its focus is on one of the strategies used by many Muslim reformers, women as well as men, in dealing with the traditional Islamic discourse, particularly the patriarchal construct of *sharīʿah*. As one of the various ways of women's struggle, this strategy – known in the West as "Islamic feminism" – represents a resistance and subversion from within the religious framework and Islamic institutions. It is an attempt by Muslim believers to reconcile their faith with modernity and gender egalitarianism.

Though a very important factor, religion is only one determinant of women's status and rights and its impact is mediated or modified through socio-economic factors, state policy, the educational system, and other sociocultural institutions.[1] However, the recent surge of Islamism and the political instrumentalization of religion have practically increased the significance of the role of Islam, especially *sharīʿah*. Islam, like the other two Abrahamic religions, originated in pre-industrial, pre-modern, and patriarchal social orders. All of the three religions have waged battles in coming to terms with modernity, especially with the egalitarian changes in gender roles and sexual attitudes. In the Islamic world today, including Iran, three main religious groups (trends) have to be distinguished from one another with regard to human/women's rights: conservative traditionalists; liberal reformists (modernists); and radical revolutionary Islamists. We may ask: What is the gender dimension of the current religious revivalism? And: How does each one of the aforementioned three groups (tendencies) view women's/human rights?

- **Traditional/Conservative Islam**: Advocated mainly by traditionalist *ulama*, and the traditional layers of popular classes, especially bazaar merchants, this group insists on preservation of a patriarchal gender regime. They confine women to the private domain and consider wifehood and motherhood to be the sole roles and obligations of women. Veiling is used as the main device for the maintenance of strict sex-based division of labor and segregated spaces.

Human rights, seen as a secular notion based on an individualistic and human-centered universe is incompatible with a God-centered universe that gives primacy to duties (rather than rights) and to the clan/kin/family (rather than the individual). Inequality in male–female rights and duties, as defined in the old *sharī'ah* and *fiqh* (Islamic jurisprudence), is justified on the basis of a divine order and natural sex differences.

- **Liberal/modern or reform Islam**: Advocates of this tendency are modern thinking *ulama*, new Islamic intellectuals, including Islamic feminists, and members of the modern, educated, and urban middle class. The background of this trend goes back to the late nineteenth- and early twentieth-century modernist Muslim thinkers such as Jamāl al-Dīn al-Afghānī [Asadabadi] (1838–97) (from Iran), Muḥammad 'Abduh (1849–1905) (from Egypt) and Namik Kemal (1840–88) (from Turkey) and to the subsequent *jadīd* (modern) movement in Central Asia. Much like the Enlightenment in Europe this trend was generally male-centered. Yet, they advocated modern education for women as well as men and pushed for reform in *sharī'ah* and matters such as polygamy. Influenced by the women's movements and feminist critiques and eager to distance themselves from the conservative traditionalists and militant Islamists, advocates of reform or modernist/liberal Islam have become increasingly open to and receptive toward egalitarian gender relations and feminist ideas.

- **Revolutionary Islamism or radical Islam**: Neo-patriarchy. Islamism has posed itself as an alternative or solution for all of the social ills and gender-related "moral decadence" experienced in both traditional and modern systems. The Islamists' agenda with regard to gender issues, though not always in line with the conservative traditionalists, is in reaction to the gender regimes and sexual mores promoted by secular Westernized modernists, liberals, socialists, and feminists. Unlike the very extreme cases of Islamists such as the Taliban of the extremely underdeveloped and devastated Afghanistan, many Islamists influenced by a more advanced socio-economic milieu (such as Egypt and Iran), have been forced to accommodate themselves to a gender project that is a "mixed bag," entailing some paradoxical implications for women's rights.[2]

Because their goal is to seize state power, Islamists utilize the sense of alienation and the grievances of females as well as male middle classes and the poor. Unlike traditionalists, by mobilizing women and engaging them in social and political activism, Islamists benefit from the support of many women in their bid for political power. To increase their political competitiveness, and aware of the economic exigencies of the modern urban middle and working classes, especially the changing role of women, many Islamists accept women's right to vote, and the right to education and employment in certain fields. Yet, like the traditionalists, they obsessively insist on an "Islamic" dress code (though usually less restrictive than the older traditional code), sex-segregation, control of women's sexuality, and *sharīʿah*-based family law. As a result, many Islamists (as in Iran, Egypt, Turkey, Indonesia, Lebanon, and the like) articulate a neo-patriarchy that may not be as restrictive as the one advocated by the Taliban, but which is still quite male-supremacist and oppressive.[3]

A clear and fascinating example of the distinction between these three trends, especially concerning gender and women's rights can be observed in the current political, theological, and philosophical debates in Iran.[4] Without the triumph of the modernist *ulama* and intellectuals in their attempts to reform *sharīʿah* and *fiqh*, no democracy and certainly no equal rights for women can be achieved in the Muslim world. Such an Islamic reformation is needed in all Muslim majority countries even the ones with secular states. To avoid the essentialization of Islam, let us cast a glance over some global patterns concerning women's rights and religion within both Islamic and non-Islamic societies as they have inevitably interacted with the Islamic politics, gender discourses, and the women's movement in Iran.

Global Patterns of Women's Rights

The twentieth century has been called "the century of women" due to the significant transformations in women's roles and the increased visibility of women's agency in all social, cultural, and political domains. Thanks to women's movements and feminist intellectual and political interventions, the male-normative understanding and practice of civil and human rights underwent significant egalitarian transformation by the end of the twentieth century. Yet, as is revealed by a number of recent studies (for example, the United Nations report in commemoration of the fiftieth anniversary of the Universal Declaration of Human Rights, December 1998; the Human Development Report of 1999 by the UNDP; and the Human Rights Watch World Report, 2000), a majority of women throughout the world (both Muslim and non-Muslim) are still suffering from systemic patterns of violence, inequality, discrimination, abuse and neglect in the home, in the labor market, and in society at large, particularly in situations of international war, civil war, and inter-ethnic conflict. These patterns are also widespread in migration and refugee camps, networks of sexual trafficking, "honor killings," dowry-related violence and murder, genital mutilation, and violence perpetrated or condoned by national states.

Legal changes in favor of equal rights for women and the discourses on women's rights as human rights have yet to be translated into effective policies and practices in many parts of the world, especially in the Muslim world. Many governments in the Muslim world, Islamic and otherwise, refuse to recognize, let alone remedy, discriminatory laws, traditions, and practices that perpetuate the second-class status of women. Sexism is not peculiar to Iran or to the Islamic world; what is peculiar is the current persistence of patriarchal norms and the strength of resistance to equal rights in many Muslim societies in comparison with the Christian West.

For instance, while the majority of the UN member states, including many Muslim states, have ratified the international bill of rights for women, that is, the Convention on the Elimination of All Forms of Discrimination Against Women (CEDAW) adopted by the UN in 1979, many of them have only ratified it with reservations, feeling that it is their right to modify or exclude any of its terms that are not compatible with their domestic-national laws. Actually, more reservations have been attached to CEDAW than to any other convention, some of which are essentially incompatible with the purpose of the treaty, which is the equality of women's rights.[5]

This has resulted in what Ann Elizabeth Mayer (1995) has called "the new world hypocrisy;" rhetorical strategies that proclaim support for women's equality while pursuing policies that are inimical to women's rights.[6] As Mayer (1995) and Bayes and Tohidi (2001) have documented, this hypocrisy and double talk about women's rights is not limited to Muslim states. To evade international responsibility with regard to safeguarding of women's equal rights, the United States invokes its Constitution and the Vatican invokes natural law and Church tradition just as Muslim countries invoke Islamic law (*sharī'ah*) as being incompatible with CEDAW.[7]

Two interesting cases in point are Saudi Arabia and the Islamic Republic of Iran, a brief comparison and contrast of which reveals interesting paradoxes about religious patriarchy in modern times. Because of international pressures, and for the sake of public relations and image mending, the patriarchal government of Saudi Arabia has recently joined CEDAW – albeit formally and hypocritically, as its numerous *sharī'ah*-based reservations indicate. The patriarchal resistance in Iran, however, has succeeded in blocking even a formal and hypocritical ratification of CEDAW. This is clear evidence that Iranian polity – held hostage by traditionalist jurisprudence – is still inflexible about *sharī'ah* whenever it pertains to women's rights and family law, while in reality women in Iran are far more integrated and visible in public and political domains than are women in Saudi Arabia. For example, while Saudi women have been, until very recently, deprived from even the right to possess individual identity cards and are still deprived of many civil and political rights, including the right to drive cars, Iranian women have achieved more social and political rights than their counterparts in Arabia.

Furthermore, Iranian women have been far more politicized due to their active and massive participation in social movements from the Constitutional Revolution of 1905–11 up to the 1979 Revolution. Although the 1979 Revolution resulted in an Islamist state and regressive gender policies, it has ironically brought women's issues to the surface; paradoxically speeding up the process of feminist consciousness. Again thanks, in part, to a history of revolutionary movements, Iran's polity (as well as its society) is more heterogeneous, diverse, and dynamic than the rather homogeneous and centralized political culture of the Saudi state. Therefore, even a diplomatically motivated ratification of CEDAW by the Iranian government can open up a new space for women and reformers both within the parliament and among the opposition to challenge the hypocrisy of the state by pointing to the incompatibility of the present laws, especially family law and the penal code, with the objectives and principles of CEDAW.

Thus, it has, strangely, been harder to ratify CEDAW in Iran than in Saudi Arabia, as its ratification in Iran would have to entail real changes and reforms in the legal system and the gender policies of the Islamic regime while in Saudi Arabia, a hypocritical and formal ratification could be undertaken without much immediate challenge from the society at large. A growing trend toward secularization, a vigorous debate over democratization, the increasing influence of liberal and reform Islam in Iranian society, a higher level of women's social activism, the women's press, and a growing feminist consciousness among Iranian women both inside Iran and abroad (among the Iranian diaspora), including the presence of vocal and active Muslim feminists ("Islamic feminists") in the sixth parliament (*majlis*) have all placed the Iranian patriarchy and its main bastion of power, the conservative Shi'ite *ulama*, in a defensive position.

The Islamic Republic of Iran, therefore, cannot even formally join CEDAW without conceding to significant revisions and reformations in its Islamist outlook and patriarchal interpretation of Islam. This reality has rendered the governing traditionalist jurisprudence and *sharī'ah* a main barrier against political and legal reforms and democratization, especially in the areas concerning women's equal rights. The gender question, thus, has become the blind spot of democratization and secularization in Iran.

To untangle this ideological barrier against democracy and equal rights for women, many modernist reformers and democrats have come to believe that a prerequisite for modernity and democratization in the Muslim world in general and in Iran in particular is an Islamic reformation. One recent case in point that drew international attention is Hashem Aghajari, a university lecturer and Islamic reformer whose call for "Islamic Protestantism" led to his imprisonment and death penalty (the sentence was later reduced to five years in jail, thanks to a national and international outcry).

Several other Muslim reformers, including prominent clerics such as Hojat ol-Islams Yusef Eshkevari, Mohsen Kadivar, Mohammad Mojtahed Shabestari, and Seyyed Muhsen Saeed-zadeh, as well as lay Islamic intellectuals such as Abdolkarim Soroush, Mostafa Malekian, Akbar Ganji and Alireza Alavi-tabar have also called for Islamic reformation and the replacement of "traditionalist jurisprudence" (*fiqh-e sunnati*) with "dynamic jurisprudence" (*fiqh-e pouya*). This new reformist trend among Muslim intellectuals, identified in Iran as the "religious intellectuals" (*rowshanfekran-e dini*) or the "new religious thinkers" (*nov andishan-e dini*), represents modern thinking and behavior that tries to reconcile modernity, democracy, and feminism with the Islamic faith. Some of these Islamic new-thinkers have specifically called for a gender egalitarian interpretation of Islamic texts and have been supportive of Muslim feminists. An important dimension of this Islamic reformation, then, is Muslim feminism ("Islamic feminism").

Historically speaking, the extent and degree of the present challenge in Iran against the patriarchal and patrimonial relations, especially the religious patriarchy in Iran has been unprecedented. One reason for the present strength and hopefully long-term effectiveness of women's challenge to the patriarchal gender regime has been the recent convergence of faith-based Muslim feminism and secular feminism, which exerts pressure against male domination both from within and from outside the religious framework.

A brief reference again to the politics of ratification of CEDAW by Iran's government may illustrate this further. Following a period of campaign by women's groups and the women's press in Iran (religious as well as secular) demanding that the government join CEDAW, including intense negotiations between the reformist Muslim women deputies and some influential *ulama* (Islamic clerics) in Tehran and Qum in order to earn religious sanction for CEDAW, in December 2001, Khatami's government proposed draft legislation to the parliament for its ratification, albeit with some reservations attached by the *ulama*.

After an intense deliberation within the Cultural Commission of the Parliament, the legislation was passed. But before being presented to the parliament for final voting at the general assembly, the legislation was placed on hold by the head of the parliament, Hojat ol-Islam Mehdi Karrobi. Since then, women's groups such as "Women's Cultural Center," and the women's press such as *Zanan* and *Zanan-e Iran*, and reformist women deputies such as Azam Naseripour (representative of Islamabad-gharb) and Shahrbanu Emami (representative of Urumiyyeh) kept protesting this procedural violation and questioned the reasons behind ending discussion about the CEDAW legislation. Yet each time, they were advised to be patient since more urgent matters for deliberation and voting were in order.

In a later parliamentary session (in early May 2003), when women deputies did not give up and demanded a transparent explanation, Karrobi finally admitted that it was because of the intervention and "opposition of the nation's elders (*bozorgan-e qowm*) and the Qum Seminary (*huzeh-ye elmiyyeh Qum*)" that the CEDAW legislation was removed from further discussion. He went on to say that government was supposed, "to consult and resolve some concerns in the minds of our *ulama*" about the incompatibility of CEDAW with *sharī'ah*.[8] As a response from women, the online weekly *Zanan-e Iran* began collecting a petition for a class action against this illegal and procedural violation of parliamentary rules.[9]

The halt in the process of ratification of CEDAW is another indication that the traditionalists along with the radical Islamists are still in control of the law and the legal process with regard to gender issues in Iran. This unfortunate reality has left differing choices for women of different convictions. While many secular women may see replacement of this religious state with a secular democratic one as the only effective path toward achieving equal rights, for many Islamic women the end of the Islamic state does not necessarily mean the end of Islamic patriarchy. To these women, unless Islam itself is understood, practiced, and reconstructed in an egalitarian framework, Muslim women will not feel liberated from sexism and male domination. The project of "Islamic feminism," then, is seen by some Iranian Muslim reformers such as Saeedzadeh[10] and Alavi-tabar,[11] and several non-Iranian Muslim feminists in other Muslim societies, as a historical necessity for modernization of Islam and reconciliation of Muslims with new exigencies of changed and changing gender roles and sexuality in modern times.

Muslim Feminism and Modern Reform in a Global Context

In recent decades many Muslim societies, including the Middle East, have witnessed an unprecedented rise in women's literacy rates (over 65 percent in 2000 compared with less than 50 percent in 1980 among the women population of 15 years or over).[12] The traditional gender gap in the realm of education is closing and in some societies, including Iran, women's enrollment in higher education is becoming equal to or even surpassing men's.

In Iran, only 35.6 percent of women were literate in 1976. By 1999, the literacy rate rose to 80 percent (for rural women the rise has been from 17.4 percent to 62.4 percent). As of 2001, 62 percent of students enrolled in Iran's universities are women. This striking advance in women's education has naturally resulted in women's increasing engagement in cultural and social life outside the private realm. Not only are women influenced by modernity, but also, as a highly educated professional group, they themselves have become significant agents of change and modernization.

But the dramatic increases in literacy rates have not achieved a parallel degree of employment for women in the formal sector of the economy (14.3 percent as of 1999).[13] Changes in the patriarchal and patrimonial structure of the legal system, and the political, religious and economic institutions of Middle Eastern societies in general and Iran in particular, especially in the areas of family law, family structure, gender stereotypes, and sexual mores have lagged far behind the modern changes in the levels of socialization and political awareness of the new middle-class women.

On top of this contradiction in gender dynamics, and in part because of it, women have faced a surge of Islamism and conservatism that has commonly entailed a retrogressive gender agenda. Islamism in the case of Iran, especially during the earlier years of the emergence of the Islamic Republic of Iran, blatantly demonstrated a retrogressive impact on women's rights, yet the nature and intensity of that impact have varied among women of different class, ethnic, and religious backgrounds.[14] Islamism in Iran, as in some other Muslim societies such as Turkey, Egypt, and Malaysia, has brought about many actual or potential setbacks for the individual rights of modernized and privileged urban upper and middle-class women, and has also promoted sex discrimination against working class and rural women, yet paradoxically it has pushed a considerable number of the previously marginalized, recently urbanized middle-class traditional women into social, political, and religious activism.

Islamization of public as well as private life, for instance, the requirement of head-covering by women and girls and the sex segregation have removed some of the excuses used by the traditional male authority against the entrance of young women and girls into public arenas such as high schools, universities, public transportation, car driving, media and the movie industry. This development has ironically opened new areas of intervention for this stratum of women, areas that were earlier inaccessible to Muslim females – whether they were physical spaces, including the mosques, or intellectual forums, such as learned theological debates.

It is with this background and at this juncture in the history of encountering and negotiating with modernity in the Muslim world that during the past two decades a reform-oriented modernist religious feminism – known in the West as "Islamic feminism" or "Muslim feminism" – has grown up among women in societies that are faced with a serious Islamist challenge. As mentioned earlier, intellectually this is the gender-related component of a broader reform movement within Islamic thought and institutions in particular and the larger societies of Muslim majority in general.

Muslim feminism emerges primarily in urban centers among the highly educated, middle-class professional Muslim women who, unlike many earlier pioneers of women's rights and feminism in the Muslim world who were of secular liberal, or socialist ("Western") orientation, are unwilling to break away from their religious orientation and thus hold Islam as a significant component of their ethnic, cultural, or even national identity. An active and illuminating example of this trend is "Sisters in Islam" in Malaysia whose motto is "Justice, Democracy, and Equality."[15]

A growing body of literature and discussion on "Islamic feminism" has emerged in the field of Middle East women's studies, stimulating useful and at times divisive debates among scholars and activists concerned with women's issues in the Middle East and other Muslim societies, including Iran (e.g., Abu-Lughod 1998; Afshar 1998; Ahmed 1992; Al-Hibri 1997; Badran 1999; Barlas 2002; Cooke 2001; Fernea 1998; Friedl 1997; Hassan 1995; Hatem 1998; Hoodfar 1996; Kamalkhani 1998; Kian-Thiebaut 1997; Kar 2001; Karam 1998; Keddie 2000; Mernissi 1991; Mir-Hosseini 1996 and 1999; Moghadam 2000; Moghissi 1998; Najmabadi 1998; Nakanishi 1998; Paidar 1982 and 2001; Roald 1998; Smith, 1985; Stowasser 1994; Tohidi, 1996,1998, and 2001; Torab 2002; and Wadud 1999).[16]

The confusion and controversy begin with the very name "Islamic feminism" and its definition. In the context of Iran, for example, two ideologically and politically opposite groups have expressed the strongest objection to this term and to any mixture of Islam and feminism. On the one hand are the right-wing conservative traditionalists and radical Islamists ("fundamentalists") inside Iran who adamantly oppose Islamic feminism because of their strong anti-feminist views and feelings. On the other hand are some expatriate, leftist secularist feminists outside Iran who hold strong anti-Islamic views and feelings. Both groups essentialize Islam and feminism and see the two mutually exclusive, and hence the term "Islamic feminism" as an oxymoron. In the press run by the right-wing hardliners, feminism or feminist tendencies ("*gerayeshha-ye femenisti*") among "Muslim sisters" has become a subject of attack. Even Ayatollah Khamenei – the *rahbar* or *vali-ye faqih* (the Supreme leader of Jurisprudence) – has publicly denounced feminist tendencies during a number of his meetings with women's groups. For example, during a meeting with women deputies of *majlis* (October 6, 2001), Khamenei insisted that women should hold only those social positions "that are not contradictory to their innate characteristics and nature." While rejecting any hostility toward women, he warned the deputies against "any feminist tendencies."[17] On the very same day, however, during a panel on "Women Reformers and the Future of the Reform," one of the most outspoken women deputies, Fatima Haqiqatjou, implicitly cautioned Islamic authorities about an emerging "dangerous social movement" [feminism] should they fail to respond to women's demands.[18]

What is in the Name?

Aside from the two aforementioned hostile objections to "Islamic feminism" in the Iranian context, in other communities as well some feelings of unease and concern have arisen among Muslim women activists and also among some scholars and professionals about the confusing and divisive implications that this new categorization – coined mainly by secular, Western-based feminist scholars – may entail. For example, in an article in the *Middle East Women's Studies Review* (Winter/Spring, 2001, 1–3), Omaima Abou-Bakr raised a number of interesting points about the notion of "Islamic feminism." While not opposing the name as such, she drew attention to the confusion and political abuses of the term and offered some useful definitional features from the point of view of a Muslim believer. One main reservation discussed by Abou-Bakr concerns the dynamics of naming and formulating this concept that "says a lot more about the observer, the person who coins, than about the object itself." She warns us about the possible divisive nature of this categorization of Muslim women as it may imply that if one is not dealing directly with Islamic teaching, the Qur'an, hadith, and the like, then one is outside the circle of Islamic/Muslim feminists.

It should also be borne in mind that in most parts of the world (Muslim and non-Muslim), including Iran, many women rights advocates, whether religious or secular, do not care for or may actually refuse to be categorized under any sort of feminist label. Most women activists, secular or religious, try to do all they can to empower themselves and improve women's rights using a pragmatic approach and an eclectic theoretical framework.

Another broader concern is that the recent overemphasis upon and fascination with Islamic feminism by some Western feminists and journalists may result in two unwanted negative repercussions, one political in nature and the other theoretical or conceptual. Politically, this may alarm and further threaten the anti-feminist Islamist patriarchy and cause further opposition to and repression of Muslim feminist reformers. Consequently, it may result in more reluctance on the part of Muslim women activists to associate themselves with feminist discourse in general and secular feminists in particular.

Theoretically or conceptually, a potential problem is a sort of Islamic determinism, characterized by continually "foregrounding the Islamic spirit or influence as the regularly primary force in Middle Eastern societies, hence disregarding the complexities of social/political and economic transformations."[19] During an interview, Shirin Ebadi (a prominent feminist lawyer in Iran and the Nobel Laureate for Peace in 2003), referred to the same problematic implication, saying: "If Islamic feminism means that a Muslim woman can also be a feminist and feminism and Islam or Muslimhood do not have to be incompatible, I would agree with it. But if it means that feminism in Muslim societies is somehow peculiar and totally different from feminism in other societies so that it has to be always Islamic, I do not agree with such a concept."[20]

I would also add that, to view Islamic feminism as the *only* or the most *authentic* path for emancipation of Muslim women may also imply a sort of orientalistic or essentialistic Islamic determinism usually manifested in the views of those who see Islam either as the primary cause of women's subordination or as the only path for women's emancipation. All history up to now, including the case of the Islamic Republic of Iran, has proved both of these approaches wrong. Historically, the interplay of many factors, including geopolitical, socio-economic, and developmental factors, colonialism, and state policies, patriarchal religion and culture, and local customs and traditions have shaped women's status in any given country.

I would also like to draw attention to some practical and conceptual problems associated with the way we, as scholars and activists based in the West, name, categorize, and treat the struggles of Muslim women for their human rights, civil rights, and empowerment. In the spirit of dialogue, coalition-building, inclusiveness, pluralism, and diversity, I would suggest we avoid polarizing or dichotomizing a "faith position" and a "secular position" with regard to commitment to women's rights. To set secular and Islamic feminism in a conflict can only benefit the reactionary patriarchal forces, be it of traditional or new Islamist patriarchy or secular modern patriarchy. To equate secular or modern with equality and feminism is as naive and misinformed as equating faith and religion with anti-modernity and anti-feminism. Not all Muslims are against equal rights for women, and not all secular people are pro-feminism or in favor of women's equal rights.

Definition and Characteristics

So, let us make it clear what we mean by Islamic feminism and how we would define it. When it is used as an identity, I personally find the term "Muslim feminist/m" (a Muslim who is feminist) less troubling and more pertinent to current realties than the term "Islamic feminism." The term "Islamic feminism," on the other hand, seems to be more appropriate for use as an analytical concept in feminist research and feminist theology, or as a term for discourse. The definition of either term, however, is difficult because a Muslim feminist (believer) would probably define it differently from a laic social scientist like myself. While Christian and Jewish feminism have a longer and more established place within feminist movements, Muslim feminism as such is a relatively new, still fluid, undefined, and more contested and politically charged trend. I see Muslim feminism as one of the ways or discourses created or adopted by certain strata of women (middle-class, urbanized, and educated) in the predominantly Muslim societies or in Muslim diaspora communities in response to three interrelated sets of domestic, national, and global pressures of today's realities:

1. *Responding to traditional patriarchy sanctioned and reinforced by religious authorities*
   While some women activists of the modernized, educated, upper- and middle-classes see religion, including Islam as a pre-modern, oppressive patriarchal institution and maintain a secular or even anti-religious perspective, many others have not broken away from their faith and their religious identities. That is, they have tried to resist and fight patriarchy within a religious framework. A basic claim among various religious feminist reformers, including Muslim and Christian feminists, is that their respective religions, if understood and interpreted correctly, do not support the subordination of women. As a theological as well as political response, these reformers maintain that the norms of society and the norms of God are

presently at odds. An egalitarian revision, therefore, is not only possible but also necessary. In reclaiming the "egalitarian past," reformist feminist scholars note that before these religions became closely associated with state power (in the first through the fourth centuries of Christianity and in the early years of the Islamic tradition in the eighth century), women did hold positions of leadership.

2. *Responding to modernity, modernization, and globalization*
Because of the expanding impact of modernity in Muslim societies (e.g., the growing rates of urbanization, literacy, and employment among women as well as men), Muslim women, like women in any modern society, naturally move forward toward egalitarian ideas and feminist reconstruction of modern life, especially of the family structure, gender roles, and gender relations. Muslim feminism is then a negotiation with modernity, accepting modernity (which emerged first in the West) yet presenting an "alternative" that is to look distinct and different from the West, Western modernism, and Western feminism. This is an attempt to "nativize" or legitimize feminist demands in order to avoid their being cast as Western imports. As Leila Ahmed argues, "reforms pursued in a native idiom and not in terms of the appropriation of the ways of other cultures" are probably more intelligible and persuasive to more traditional classes (i.e., not merely to modern upper and middle classes) and thus they may quite possibly prove more durable.[21]

The language and reasoning of reform-minded Islamic women activists in Iran is a clear example of this. The following quotation from Fatima Haqiqatjou, the aforementioned woman deputy in *majlis*, represents the way they have been bargaining with patriarchy. During a press conference, she talked about their petition to the president in which 34 deputies had recommended five women candidates for the position of governor for Tehran. However, to their disappointment, no woman governor was appointed. Therefore, she goes on by saying:

> The women fraction of the Majlis has reached a bitter conclusion. Due to a masculinist perspective among the top-level directors and managers, there is a disbelief in women's merits and capabilities for holding managerial positions . . . We are after improvement of women's status and rights on the basis of religious thinking and ideas and through Iranian and native forms. The Islamic order (*nezam-e Islami*) ought to be able to respond to our aspirations and demands. But if the society and the political will of the state authorities do not allow actualization of women's demands, there will certainly emerge a very dangerous social movement.[22]

Successful or not, this trend is related to the legacy of Western colonialism, a post-colonial insistence on forging and asserting an independent or "native" national identity, including "native feminism," especially in the face of growing globalization. Another aspect of globalization that contributes to this trend is the growing transnational migration (which is not predominantly a male practice any longer) or the diasporization or deterritorialization of cultural identities. This has facilitated a wider exposure to global and modern discourses of feminism, human rights, and democracy that have been directly or indirectly changing women's consciousness and expectations in countries like Iran. The impact of such factors has been intensified through an increasing access to the Internet, satellite TV, and other communications technology.

3. *Responding to the recent surge of patriarchal Islamism*
    Due to the growing Islamist environment since the 1970s, which involves imposition of a retrogressive gender project, many Muslim women feel compelled to change and improve women's roles and rights within an Islamic framework. For the educated women who want to reconcile the religious dimension of their identities with an empowered social status based on egalitarian gender relationships and freedom of choice in their personal, family, and socio-political life, Muslim feminism offers a mechanism for resisting and challenging the sexist nature of the existing identity politics, particularly Islamism. Some scholars too, religious or laic (e.g., Leila Ahmed, Riffat Hassan, Fatima Mernissi, and Ziba Mir-Hosseini) see a modern liberal and gender egalitarian reformation of Islam as a requirement for the success of a broader societal and political reform movement toward democracy, pluralism and civil rights, including women's rights. Such an approach, therefore, would stress the urgent need for equipping women with the tools (for instance, knowledge of Arabic, the Qur'an and the *fiqh* as well as feminist knowledge) that will enable them to redefine, reinterpret, and reform Islam into a more women-friendly and gender-egalitarian religion. The goal is to enable women to "turn the table" on Islamist authorities, to take Islamist men to task about what they preach and practice in the name of Islam. During a seminar at Radcliff College, a Muslim feminist put it this way: "The mullahs are trying to use the Qur'an against us, but we have a surprise for them, we're going to beat them at their own game."

In short, I see Muslim feminism or "Islamic feminism" as a faith-based response of a certain stratum of Muslim women in their negotiation with and struggle against patriarchy (the old traditionalist Islamic patriarchy and the neo-patriarchy of the Islamists) on the one hand and the new (modern and post-modern) realities on the other. Its limits and potentials for women's empowerment, however, like those of other ideology-based feminisms, have to be accounted for in its deeds and practices more so than in its theological or theoretical strengths or inconsistencies.

A Few Comparative Observations

I would also like to suggest a few comparative and historical observations that may help us achieve a better feminist strategy with regard to diversity within the global women's movement as well as the women's movement in Iran *vis-à-vis* Muslim feminism.

We tend to forget that Islam, like all other religions, is a human or social construct, and hence it is neither ahistoric nor monolithic, reified, and static. This becomes more evident when compared with the experience of women in the Christian context, as elaborated in Bayes and Tohidi (2001).[23] The struggle to adjust or reconstruct religion to the new realities of the modern, egalitarian, and democratic gender regime has taken place both from within and from without the religious institutions, and it has been an ongoing process in the Christian (Protestant and Catholic) contexts (Schuster-Fiorenza 1992; and Radford Ruther, 1993).[24] Thanks to the emergence of a stronger middle class, the advent of modernity, and the vigorous bourgeois liberal fight for individual rights and humanism, the reformation of religion, secularization, and the democratization of society have been achieved much more successfully in the more advanced and industrialized Christian West. In the Muslim context, however, the interplay of geographic and geopolitical disadvantages, colonialism and underdevelopment has hindered the progress of similar processes, thus further complicating the attainment of civil rights, especially women's rights.

As noted in previous pages, modernist rational and liberal attempts to reinterpret or reform Islam were initiated almost a century ago by theologians and jurists such as the Egyptian Muḥammad 'Abduh (d. 1905). By the turn of the twentieth century, some Muslim women thinkers and writers as well had gradually begun framing their gender conscious and women-friendly writings within the Islamic ethics (for example, Tahira Qurratulein; Bibi Khanum Astarabadi; Zeinab Fawwaz; and Ayesha Taymuriya). Yet, it is only in retrospect that one may or may not consider them to be Muslim feminists because such categorization has been formulated very recently and – for the most part – by Western or Western-based feminists rather than by Muslim feminists themselves. For instance, when Elizabeth Cady Stanton and her female friends wrote *The Woman's Bible* in 1895, nobody called her a Christian feminist, but today because of the currency of feminist discourse, Amina Wadud's work in the United States[25] is naturally seen as an example of Islamic/Muslim feminism. Such a naming in the present context can be harmless if it does not imply a deliberate or unwitting "otherizing" or essentializing of Muslim women. It can be harmless if it does not limit the diverse spectrum of the women's movement in Muslim societies to the Muslim women only and to a primarily religious feminism at the expense of ignoring, excluding, or silencing women of non-Muslim religious minorities or women of secular, laic, or atheist orientation.

Like other components of the modern (and arguably post-modern) reform movements within Islam, Muslim feminism is a Qur'an-centered discourse. The Qur'an, seen as the "eternal and inimitable" text, provides for Muslims both the foundational basis and the point of convergence of many different human interpretations in the light of specific socio-economic and political situations (Stowasser 1998).[26] Feminist Muslims like Azizah al-Hibri see flexibility and evolution as "an essential part of Qur'anic philosophy, because Islam was revealed for all people and for all times. Consequently, its jurisprudence must be capable of responding to widely diverse needs and problems"(al-Hibri 1997, 2).[27] Muslims rely on *ijtihād*, which is the ability to analyze a Qur'anic text or a problematic situation within the relevant cultural and historic context and then devise an appropriate interpretation or solution based on a thorough understanding of Qur'anic principles and the Sunnah.[28]

However, an important challenge for Muslim feminists, some writers such as Anne Sofie Roald argue, is that the Qur'an is seen as the "word of God" and consequently immutable.[29] In response, Muslim modernists (such as Mohammad Mojtahed Shabestari and Abdolkarim Soroush) and feminists have pointed out that the symbolic wording of the Qur'an is not critical (Mir-Hosseini, 1999). Indeed the *interpretation* of the Qur'an by men currently forms the basis of Islamic law, application, and practice. This male (*ulama*) monopoly of authority to interpret the Qur'an or engage in *ijtihād* is what Muslim feminists are challenging now. Friedl (1997) explains this quite clearly in the context of Iran:

> Theoretically these texts are beyond negotiation because they are claimed to emanate from divine or divinely inspired authority. Practically, however, the Holy Writ has to be translated, taught, and made understandable to the faithful, especially to illiterate and semiliterate people who cannot read original Arabic texts. . . . This means it has to be interpreted. Interpretation is a political process: the selection of texts from among a great many that potentially give widely divergent messages, and their exegesis are unavoidably influenced, if not outrightly motivated, by the political programs and interests of those who control the formulation and dissemination of ideologies (p. 146).[30]

The text is read and understood based on our presuppositions, and these presuppositions vary across time and across cultures, the new Islamic reformers argue. It is with such an approach to religion that the women's press in Iran has embarked on both political and theological debates on gender issues taking on the Islamic reformers (cleric as well as lay) in face-to-face encounters, interviews, and panel discussions.

For example, after numerous books and contributions to the journal *Zanan* (*Women*) of radical and feminist writings based on *ijtihād* in Islamic foundations, Hojat ol-Islam Seyyed Mohsen Saeedzadeh (a young cleric) was imprisoned and after release was defrocked and banned from publishing.[31] Hojat ol-Islam Yusef Eshkevari is another reformist liberal cleric who is still in jail, in part due to his declaration that *ḥijāb* is not an Islamic mandate. In line with them, Alireza Alavi-tabar, although a lay scholar, has openly defended feminism, including Islamic feminism, on the basis of clear sociological as well as theological definitions. His progressive ideas and bold and non-sectarian advocacy of women's rights have made him one of the popular Muslim reformers among Iranian women and men.

Alavi-tabar identifies three mechanisms that have been used for reform and reinterpretation of Islamic conjunctions: suspending the primary conjunctions and legislating instead on the basis of the secondary conjunctions and governmental rules; dynamic jurisprudence (*fiqh-e pouya*) of the secondary conjunctions; and *ijtihād* in the Islamic foundations. He argues that although the first two mechanisms are necessary for the articulation of equal rights for women and men, they are not sufficient. As a real solution for the present problem of the incompatibility of Islamic *fiqh* with women's equal rights and human rights, and in order to reach truly new and modern perspectives, "advocates of the new religious thinking (*nov andishan-e dini*) have to eventually seek *ijtihād* in the Islamic foundations only."[32] Based on such a radical *ijtihād*, the Islamic jurisprudence (*fiqh*) is seen, in its entirety, as a secondary (not essential or primary) component of Islam; a human (rather than divine) revelation and a history- and time-bound construct, and thus subject to change, revision, and reconstruction.

When asked what he thinks about the existence or viability of Islamic feminism, Alavi-tabar says:

> It depends on what we mean and how we use this concept. If it means that one can advocate equal social and legal rights for women and men while remaining loyal to religious ethics and values, it is certainly present here and viable too. Islamic feminism is a call for re-reading of our interpretations of the Islamic texts and history of religious life. By putting aside the patriarchally-inspired values and tendencies, and upholding a new perspective, many of what have been taken for granted as "obvious" ought to be questioned and proved that they are not obvious elements of Sharī'ah, but products of our worldly way of livings and traditions . . . Islamic feminism, in this sense, is very close to the project of modern religious intellectualism (p. 41).[33]

Like other modernist reform movements within religion, Muslim feminism emphasizes individual agency and insists upon women's right to a direct relationship with God with no human (clerical) mediators. Based on the idea of "intersubjectivity," this places the woman/man and God as the subjects of interaction rather than seeing the interaction as being between the male clerics and the woman/man believer. This was a basic principle of reformation within Christianity raised in 1551 by Martin Luther, leading to the Protestant Reformation. This principle, if applied seriously among Muslims, can challenge the (male) clerical monopoly over religion, transforming women's understanding of religion from a male cleric-centered authoritarian institution to a non-hierarchical spiritual one that involves both individual and group-based processes in women's daily lives.

Policy Implications: Perils and Promises

Feminist believers from the three Abrahamic religions have much to learn from one another's experience in "reclaiming" their faith and spirituality from the clergy-centered patriarchal monopoly of religious authorities. Achievement of women's rights in Iran or any other Muslim society cannot depend solely or even primarily on women's reinterpretation of Islamic texts. Because a literal reading of the Qur'an, like other ancient scriptures, is male supremacist, and because most Muslims and non-Muslims are still more inclined to accept the male authority, more should be done about the need to have men re-educated at home and in school.

But spiritual feminism and faith-based feminists, including Islamic feminists, will not be much different from religious fundamentalists if they do not respect freedom of choice and diversity but instead try to impose their version of feminism on secular, laic, and atheist feminists. What can be troubling in regard to religious feminism, be it Islamic or Christian, is the tendency toward sectarianism or totalitarianism. The real danger is when a single brand of ideological feminism, be it secular Marxist or religious Islamic (in this case it becomes Islamist) presents itself as the only legitimate or authentic voice for *all* women or the "true path for liberation," negating, excluding, and silencing other voices and ideas among women in any given society. Appreciation for ideological, cultural, racial, sexual, and class diversity is critical for local and global feminist movements.

For effective feminist strategizing, the importance of dialogue, conversation, and coalition building among women activists of various ideological inclinations cannot be overemphasized. The feminist movement is not one movement but many. What unites feminists is a belief in human dignity, human rights, freedom of choice, and the further empowerment of women rather than any ideological, spiritual, or religious stance. Secularity works better for all when secularism means impartiality toward religion, not anti-religionism.

Some secularist and Marxist feminists have treated Muslim or Christian feminists as rivals or foes of secular feminism and have been preoccupied with academic concerns over their philosophical and ideological inconsistencies and post-modern limits (as if the various brands of secular feminism are free from such limits). We may see religious and spiritual feminism, including Muslim feminism, as a welcome addition to the wide spectrum of feminist discourse, as long as these religious feminists contribute to the empowerment of women, tolerance, and cultural pluralism. However, when their discourse and actions impose their religious strictures on all, when they co-opt the meaning of feminism to fight against equal rights for women or women's empowerment, or when they cooperate with and serve as arms of repressive and anti-democratic Islamist states, Muslim feminists are not helpful. Muslim feminism has served the women's cause when it complements, diversifies, and strengthens both the material and spiritual force of the women's movements in any given Muslim society.

Observations on the recent Islamist and other religious fundamentalist movements indicate that theocratic states are not able to empower women nor are they able to provide an inclusive democracy for their citizens. Religion is important but should be separated from state power. Muslim feminists seem to be an inevitable and positive component of the ongoing change, reform, and development of Muslim societies as they face modernity. In the short term, Muslim feminists may serve as a sort of Islamization of feminism for some. In the long term, in a society that allows for and protects open debate and discussion, Muslim feminism (as did Christian feminism) can facilitate the modernization and secularization of Islamic societies and states. Negotiating modernity takes many forms. Although feminism and the women's movement have become more global than ever before, as a Jewish feminist colleague (Simona Sharoni) once noted, sisterhood is not global nor is it local; women's solidarity has to be negotiated within each specific context.

Women's experiences in many Muslim and non-Muslim societies show that women's rights and empowerment, and democratization in general, cannot be left wholly in the hands of the elites (female or male) and their theological and intellectual debates, but rather have to be pushed and supervised by elements from broader civil society, including women's grassroots movements and organizations. Though important, Muslim/Islamic reformism and feminism are only one necessary component of social transformation toward women's equal human rights. Economic changes that provide equal opportunities for women to achieve gainful employment, changes in the gender-based division of labor, integration of women into political processes and decision making, and an egalitarian shift in cultural stereotypes about gender roles and relations and double standards in sexual mores are all necessary processes for improvement in women's status in Iran and other parts of the Muslim world.

Conclusion

Historically speaking, sexism has not been peculiar to the Islamic world nor to the Islamic religion. What is peculiar is that a visible gap has emerged in modern times between the Islamic world and the Christian West with regard to the degree of egalitarian improvement in women's rights. This gap has been due to the legacy of colonialism, underdevelopment, defective modernization, the weakness of a modern middle class, democratic deficit, the persistence of cultural and religious patriarchal constructs such as sharī'ah stemming from the failure of reform and secularization within Islam, and the weakness of civil society organizations – especially women's organizations – in the Muslim world.

The recent surge in identity politics, Islamism, and religio-nationalist movements is in part due to socio-economic and cultural dislocation, polarization, and alienation caused by modernization, Westernization, and globalization, and in part it is a "patriarchal protest movement" in reaction to the challenges that the emergence of modern middle-class women poses to traditional patriarchal gender relations. The main premise of this chapter is that processes of democratization, civil society building, and the consolidation of civil rights and universal human/women's rights are intertwined with reformation in Islam, feminist discourse, and women's movements.

Gender has become the blind spot of democratization in the Islamic world. In terms of national and international policy implications, it should be recognized that women and youth have become the main forces of modernization and democratization in the Islamic world, especially in Iran. Democracy cannot be established without a new generation of Muslim leaders and state elite who are more aware of the new realities of a globalized world and more committed to universal women's/human rights.

To win the war against terrorism and patriarchal Islamism, we need more than military might. In the short and medium term, a just resolution of the Israeli–Palestinian conflict can alter the present socio-psychological milieu that has allowed the growth of extremism and male-biased identity politics; in the long term, democratization and comprehensive gender-sensitive development seems to be the only effective strategy. A significant component of this strategy has to be Islamic reformation, which requires international dialogue with and support for secular as well as religious egalitarian and democratic voices in the Muslim world.

Acknowledgments

I would like to acknowledge Jennifer Olmsted, Nikki Keddie, and Mahmood Monshipouri for their helpful comments on an earlier and shorter version of this article.

Notes

1. For studies on the interplay between Islam and other social institutions, see, for example, Yvonne Yazbcek Haddad and John L. Esposito, eds., *Islam, Gender, and Social Change* (Oxford: Oxford University Press, 1998); Deniz Kandiyoti, ed., *Women, Islam and the State* (Temple University Press, 1991).

2. See Mervat Hatem, "Secularist and Islamist Discourses on Modernity in Egypt and the Evolution of the Post-Colonial Nation-State" and also Afsaneh Najmabadi, "Feminism in an Islamic Republic: Years of Hardship, Years of Growth" both articles in Y.Y. Haddad and J.L. Esposito, eds., *Islam, Gender and Social Change* (1998).

3. For such similarities and differences between Islamists of Iran and Afghanistan (Taliban), see MehrangizKar, "Women's Strategies in Iran from the 1979 Revolution to 1999" in Jane Bayes and Nayereh Tohidi, eds., *Globalization, Gender and Religion* (2001).

4. For a fascinating narration of such debates, see Ziba Mir-Hosseini, *Islam and Gender: The Religious Debate in Contemporary Iran* (Princeton University Press, 1999).

5. Belinda Clark, "The Vienna Convention Reservations Regime and the Convention on Discrimination Against Women," *American Journal of International Law*, 85, 1991, 317.

6. Ann Elizabeth Mayer, "Rhetorical Strategies and Official Policies on Women's Rights" in Mahnaz Afkhami, ed., *Faith and Freedom: Women's Human Rights in the Muslim World* (New York: I.B. Tauris, 1995), 104.

7. See Jane Bayes and Nayereh Tohidi, eds., *Gender, Globalization, and Religion: The Politics of Women's Rights in Catholic and Muslim Contexts* (New York: Palgrave, 2001), 2–6. Also see Colum Lynch "Islamic Bloc, Christian Right Team Up to Lobby UN," in *Washington Post*, June 17, 2002, A01.

8. See, *Rouydad*, 19 Urdibehesht, 1382 or *Iran-Emrooz*, May 7, 2003 (www.iran-emrooz.de).

9. See www.zananiniran.com, Urdibehest 14, 1382/May 4, 2003.

10. See Mir-Hosseini, 1999.

11. See "Mas'ale-ye zanan: Nov-andishi-ye dini ve feminism" (The Women Question: New Religious Thinking and Feminism), interview with Alireza Alavi-tabar, in the monthly *Aftab*, No. 24, Farvardin 1382/March 2003, 38–41.

12. Rough estimates based on three regions in Asia as reported in *The World's Women 2000: Trends and Statistics* (New York: United Nations Publications, 2000), 89, chart 4.5.

13. In the government offices, this rate is higher – 31 percent – and in the informal sector, much higher than the formal, see Poya Maryam, *Women, Work and Islamism: Ideology and Resistance in Iran* (London: Zed Books, 1999), 77–87.

14. Elsewhere, several scholars, including myself, have explained the reasons for the surge of Islamism and the significance of its gender dimension and the historical, geographic, economic, political, and cultural reasons for the extra strength and resistant nature of patriarchy in Iran and several other Muslim societies. See, for instance, Keddie 2002; Kandiyoti 1988; Moghadam 1993; Tohidi and Bayes 2001.

15. For information on this active Muslim feminist group, see www.muslimtents.com/sistersinislam/.

16. Lila Abu-Lughod, ed., *Remaking Women: Feminism and Modernity in the Middle East* (Princeton, NJ: Princeton University Press, 1998); Haleh Afshar, *Islam and Feminisms: An Iranian Case Study* (London: Macmillan, 1998); Leila Ahmed, *Women and Gender in Islam* (New Haven: Yale University Press, 1992); Aziza Al-Hibri, "Islam, Law and Custom: Redefining Muslim Women's Rights," *American University Journal of International Law and Policy*, 12, 1997, 1–44; Margot Badran, "Toward Islamic Feminisms: A Look at the Middle East," in

Asma Afsaruddin, ed., *Hermeneutics and Honor: Negotiating Female Public Space in Islamicate Societies* (Cambridge, MA: Harvard University Press, 1999), 159–88; Asma Barlas, *"Believing Women" in Islam: Understanding Patriarchal Interpretations of the Quran* (Austin: Texas University Press, 2002); Miriam Cooke, *Women Claiming Islam: Creating Islamic Feminism Through Literature* (London: Routledge, 2000); Elizabeth W. Fernea, *In Search of Islamic Feminism* (New York: Doubleday, 1998); Erika Friedl, "Ideal Womanhood in Postrevolutionary Iran," in Judy Brink and Joan Mencher, eds., *Mixed Blessings: Gender and Religious Fundamentalism Cross-Culturally* (New York: Routledge, 1997); Riffat Hassan, "Women's Rights and Islam: From the I.C.P.D. to Beijing," papers written for a Ford Foundation project in Cairo in 1994, for an International Planned Parenthood Federation Conference held in Tunis in July 1995, and for the Family Planning Association of Pakistan in April, 1995; Mervat Hatem, "Secularist and Islamist Discourses on Modernity in Egypt and the Evolution of the Postcolonial Nation-State," in Y.Y. Haddad and J.L. Esposito, eds., *Islam, Gender and Social Change* (Oxford: Oxford University Press, 1998); Zahra Kamalkhani, *Women's Islam: Religious Practice among Women in Today's Iran* (London: Kegan Paul, 1998); Mehrangiz Kar, "Women' Strategies in Iran from the 1979 Revolution to 1999," in Jane Bayes and Nayereh Tohidi, eds., *Globalization, Religion and Gender: The Politics of Women's Rights in Catholic and Muslim Contexts* (New York: Palgrave, 2001), 177–203; Azza Karam, *Women, Islamism, and State: Contemporary Feminism in Egypt* (London: Macmillan, 1998); Nikki Keddie, "Women in Iran since 1979," *Social Research*, 67, 2000, 407–38; Azadeh Kian-Thiebaut, "Women and Politics in Post-Islamist Iran," *British Journal of Middle Eastern Studies*, 24, 1997, 75–96; Fatema Mernissi, *The Veil and the Male Elite: A Feminist Interpretation of Women's Rights in Islam* (Reading, MA: Addison-Wesley, 1991); Ziba Mir-Hosseini, "Stretching the Limits: A Feminist Reading of Shari'a in Iran Today," in M. Yamani, ed., *Feminism and Islam: Legal and Literary Perspectives* (London: Ithaca Press, 1996) and *Islam and Gender: The Religious Debate in Contemporary Iran* (New Jersey: Princeton University Press, 1999); Valentine Moghadam, "Islamic Feminism and Its Discontents: Notes on a Debate," *Iran Bulletin* (www.iran-bulletin.org/islamic_feminism.htm), 2000; Afsaneh Najmabadi, "Feminism in an Islamic Republic: Years of Hardship, Years of Growth," in Y.Y. Haddad and J.L. Esposito, eds., *Islam, Gender, and Social Change* (Oxford: Oxford University Press, 1998); Hisae Nakanishi, "Power, Ideology, and Women's Consciousness in Postrevolutionary Iran," in H. Bodman and N. Tohidi, eds., *Women in Muslim Societies: Diversity within Unity* (Boulder: Lynne Rienner, 1998); Parvin Paidar (Nahid Yeganeh), "Women's Struggles in the Islamic Republic of Iran," in Azar Tabari and Nahid Yeganeh, eds., *In the Shadow of Islam* (London: Zed Books, 1982), 26–74; Parvin Paidar, *Women and the Political Process in Twentieth-Century Iran.* (Cambridge: Cambridge University Press, 1995); and "Gender of Democracy: The Encounter between Feminism and Reformism in Contemporary Iran," *Democracy, Governance and Human Rights Program*, Paper Number 6, United Nations Research Institute for Social Development, October 2001; Anne Sofie Roald, "Feminist Reinterpretation of Islamic Sources: Muslim Feminist Theology in the Light of the Christian Tradition of Feminist Thought," in Karin Ask and Marit Tjomsland, eds., *Women and Islamization: Contemporary Dimensions of Discourse on Gender Relations* (Oxford: Berg, 1998); Jane Smith, "Women, Religion and Social Change in Early Islam," in Y.Y. Haddad and Elison Banks Findly, eds., *Women, Religion and Social Change* (Albany: State University of New York Press, 1985); Barbara F. Stowasser, *Women in The Quran, Traditions and Interpretation* (New York: Oxford University Press, 1994); Nayereh Tohidi, *Feminizm, Demokrasi ve Eslam-geraì* (Feminism, Democracy, and Islamism in Iran) (Los Angeles: Ketabsara, 1996); Nayereh Tohidi, "Conclusion: The Issues At Hand," in Herbert Bodman, and Nayereh Tohidi, eds., *Women in Muslim Societies: Diversity within Unity* (Boulder: Lynne

Rienner, 1998); Nayereh Tohidi and Jane Bayes, "Women Redefining Modernity and Religion in the Globalized Context," in Jane Bayes and Nayereh Tohidi, eds., *Globalization, Gender, and Religion: The Politics of Women's Rights in Catholic and Muslim Contexts* (New York: Palgrave, 2001); Azam Torab, "The Politicization of Women's Religious Circles in Post-Revolutionary Iran," in Sarah Ansari and Vanessa Martin, eds., *Women, Religion, and Culture in Iran* (London: Curzon, 2002); Amina Wadud, *Quran and Woman: Rereading Sacred Text from a Woman's Perspective* (Oxford: Oxford University Press, 1999).

17. See www.bbc.co.uk/persian/news/011006_vleader.shtml, October 6, 2001.

18. Ibid.

19. Quoted from Hoda El-Sadda by Abou-Bakr in her article in *Middle East Women's Studies Review*, Winter/Spring 2001.

20. Author's interview with Shirin Ebadi, December 1999.

21. Leila Ahmed, *Women and Gender in Islam* (New Haven: Yale University Press, 1992), 168.

22. See www.bbc.co.uk/persian/news/011006_vleader.shtml, October 6, 2001.

23. Jane Bayes and Nayereh Tohidi, eds., *Globalization, Gender, and Religion: The Politics of Women's Rights in Catholic and Muslim Contexts* (New York: Palgrave, 2001).

24. See, for instance, Elizabeth Schuster-Fiorenza, *But She Said: Feminist Practices of Biblical Interpretation* (Boston: Beacon Press, 1992) and Rosemary Radford Ruther, "Christianity and Women in the Modern World," in Arvind Sharma, ed., *Today's Woman in World Religions* (Albany: State University of New York Press, 1993).

25. Amina Wadud, *Quran and Women: Rereading Sacred Text from a Woman's Perspective* (Oxford: Oxford University Press, 1999).

26. See Barbara F. Stowasser, "Gender Issues and Contemporary Quran Interpretation" in Y.Y. Haddad and J. Esposito, eds., *Islam, Gender and Social Change* (Oxford: Oxford University Press, 1998).

27. Azizah Al-Hibri, "Islam, Law, and Custom: Redefining Muslim Women's Rights," *American University Journal of International Law and Policy*, 12, 1997, 1–44.

28. Ibid.

29. Anne SofieRoald, "Feminist Reinterpretation of Islamic Sources: Muslim Feminist Theology in the Light of the Christian Tradition of Feminist Thought" in Karin Ask and Marit Tjomsland, eds., *Women and Islamization: Contemporary Dimensions on Gender Relations* (Oxford: Berg, 1998), 41.

30. Erika Friedl, "Ideal Womanhood in Post-Revolutionary Iran," in Judy Brink and Joan Mencher, eds., *Mixed Blessings: Gender and Religious Fundamentalism Cross-Culturally* (New York: Routledge, 1997), 146.

31. For the significant contributions of Saeedzadeh (some of which appeared under female pseudonyms), see Mir-Hosseini 1999 and Kar 2001.

32. See "Mas'ale-ye zanan: Nov andishi-ye dini ve feminism" (The Women Question: New Religious Thinking and Feminism), interview with Alireza Alavi-tabar, in the monthly *Aftab*, No. 24, Farvardin 1382/March 2003, 39.

33. Ibid., 41.

CHAPTER 36

An Islamic Critique of Patriarchy: Mawlana Sayyed Kalbe Sadiq's Approach to Gender Relations

Yoginder Sikand

Perhaps because they form only a small minority, relatively little has been written about India's Ithna Ashari or "Twelver" Shi'ite community. While some works on the history of the Indian Shi'ites are available, Shi'ite voices are almost completely absent in writings on Muslims in present-day India. This is particularly unfortunate, given the rich scholarly tradition of the Indian Shi'ites.[1] Being a minority within a larger minority, Indian Shi'ite voices often reflect concerns and articulate perspectives that are missing or else marginal in dominant Sunni discourses. The Lucknow-based Mawlana Sayyed Kalbe Sadiq is one of the leading and best-known present-day Indian Shi'ite scholars. This chapter looks at his approach to the issue of gender in Islam, examining how he interprets the Islamic tradition in order to promote gender justice. It is based on an analysis of some of his *majālis* (sing. *majlis*) or sermons that are hosted on various sites on the Internet.[2]

Kalbe Sadiq: A Mawlana With a Difference

Kalbe Sadiq is regarded as one of the most prominent "liberal" and "progressive" Islamic scholars in India today. Although he is commonly referred to as a Mawlana, the honorific title generally used in South Asia for a learned Muslim scholar, he challenges the stereotypical image of a Mawlana as a diehard conservative. He hails from a Lucknow-based family that claims descent from the Prophet and which has produced numerous illustrious Shi'ite scholars over several generations. Born in 1939, he received a traditional Islamic education from the Sultan ul-Madaris, at that time a leading center of Shi'ite learning in Lucknow, alongside a modern education. He went on to do a doctoral thesis, based on an early medieval Arabic poet, at the Aligarh Muslim University. Thereafter, he immersed himself in a range of social activities, first in Lucknow and then elsewhere in India. Over the years he has set up a number of major institutions, including the Unity College, the Era Medical College, the Hazrat Imam Zainul Abideen Hospital, and the Tauhid ul-Muslimin Welfare Trust in Lucknow, and the Madinat ul-'Ulum College in Aligarh. In recognition of his stature as the leading Indian Shi'ite scholar, he was appointed as the vice-president of the Sunni-dominated All-India Muslim Personal Law Board, a position that he still holds.[3]

Despite his various preoccupations, Sadiq continues in his family's tradition of addressing *majālis* in gatherings in India and abroad. The *majlis* is a major institution of Shi'ite mass education. *Majālis* are generally delivered in *imāmbaras*, mosques, and people's homes, and are open to the general public. No special occasion is needed for a *majlis*. Pious or rich Shi'ites invite *ulama* to organize *majālis* on a range of occasions, such as a birth, marriage, or death in the family, or to commemorate one of the 12 Ithna Ashari imams. Numerous *majālis* are held in the month of Muharram, when the story of the martyrdom of Imam Husain is recounted over a period of several days, accompanied by public expressions of grief. The *ulama* who deliver the *majālis* are normally paid by the organizers, who consider the holding of a *majlis* as a meritorious act.

Sadiq's *majālis* are extremely popular among many Shi'ites as well as some Sunnis, and he is regularly invited by Shi'ite groups in India, Pakistan, Europe, and North America to speak. Like traditional *majālis*, Sadiq's *majālis* begin with an invocation to God and praises of the Prophet and the imams. This is followed by quotations from the Qur'an, carefully selected according to the topic that the particular *majlis* is devoted to, which is normally decided beforehand by Sadiq in consultation with the organizers. Unlike traditional *majālis*, however, Sadiq's *majālis* are not simply about recounting the deeds of the Prophet and the imams. Rather, they are a class apart, and explicitly seek to relate religious injunctions and beliefs to issues of contemporary social concern. Among the favorite issues that Sadiq deals with in his *majālis* are the need for modern education, inter-community dialogue and understanding, better relations between Shi'ites and Sunnis, and the promotion of women's rights.[4] In this way, Sadiq's *majālis* serve an important pedagogical purpose and provide innovative and creative approaches from within a broadly defined Islamic tradition to engage with questions that are crucial for Muslims today.

Sadiq on the "Women's Question"

Some of Sadiq's *majālis* hosted on various sites on the Internet deal exclusively with women, focussing particularly on the question of women's rights. Several others of his *majālis* deal with women only in passing, being centered on other related issues. Sadiq's basic purpose in addressing the question of gender in Islam is twofold: to counter the claim that Islam is inherently misogynist, and, at the same time, to critique misogynist interpretations of Islam. This is not a simple apologetic defense of Islam as might be imagined, for Sadiq forcefully critiques widely held patriarchal assumptions and beliefs among many of his fellow *ulama*. Further, since his primary audience in the *majālis* are

Muslims, particularly Shi'ites, and not non-Muslim critics, his main concern in his *majālis* is not so much to defend Islam from its detractors as to provide a reformist, and what he sees as the "correct," understanding of Islam, including on the "women's question."

Sadiq's innovative approach to women's rights must be seen in the broader context of his understanding of justice as a central pillar of Islam. He argues that God's purpose in sending a succession of prophets, heavenly books, and laws was simply one: to eliminate injustice and ensure the rights of all creatures of God. The purpose of religion is not simply to instruct people to worship God, he says, but, equally importantly, to inspire them to promote love and justice in society. Islam, he says, teaches that the "rights of God's creatures" (*ḥuqūq ul-'ibād*) are as important as the "rights of God" (*ḥuqūq allah*). He goes so far as to say that if one is confronted with the choice between the two, one should choose the former, for "creatures of God need to have their rights respected," while God is in need of nothing. God will not forgive one's sins, he says, if one violates the *ḥuqūq ul-'ibād*, and these include the rights of women as well. On the Day of Judgment, one's prayers and ritual worship will not be of any help to a person who tramples on the rights of others, he warns.

The concept of *ḥuqūq ul-'ibād*, Sadiq explains, is a comprehensive one that includes the rights of all of God's creatures, animate and well as inanimate. Even the earth has its rights that need to be respected. Misuse of the earth's resources is also a sin. Likewise, animals, too, have their rights, and so do trees and plants. All human beings, irrespective of religion and gender, also have their basic human rights to dignity, equality, and freedom, and one cannot be a Muslim in God's eyes unless one respects these rights as well. Respecting the *ḥuqūq ul-'ibād*, as Sadiq sees it, is not a passive acceptance of the rights of others, and nor is it an individualistic affair. Rather, it is a task incumbent on all Muslims to actively struggle against injustice and to work for a socially just world where there shall be no poverty, illiteracy, hunger, and want, and where all people, irrespective of sect, religion, ethnicity, and gender, will live in prosperity and harmony. A true Muslim must dedicate his or her life to working toward the establishment of such a society. The ideal society that the "Imam of the Age," the twelfth imam whom most Shi'ites believe is presently in occultation, will usher in, would, Sadiq claims, be one where everyone is contented, and where peace and justice prevail. But, in the meanwhile, every Muslim must struggle for social justice for all. God, Sadiq says, has taken an "oath" (*ahad*) from the true *ulama* (*sahih 'ulama*) that "they shall not rest for even a moment till they eliminate every injustice from the world."[5] This includes injustices meted out to women as well.

Sadiq's Qur'anic Hermeneutics

Sadiq's basic starting point in dealing with the issue of women and women's rights is that Islam is God's chosen religion for all humankind and is valid for all times, and that no other way to salvation is possible. Hence, he believes, Islam provides women with a position far superior to that in other religions. This claim he asserts both by discussing Islam's teachings on gender relations and by comparing these with the teachings of other religions. Sadiq's understanding of gender equality and gender relations in Islam follows from what he sees as the basic underlying message of the Qur'an, and, indeed, of the mission of all the prophets that God has sent to humankind. He repeatedly quotes the Qur'an to suggest that God's purpose in sending a long chain of messengers, with scriptures and revealed laws, was to establish a just social order and to eliminate injustice and tyranny. Hence, he argues, any interpretation of Islam that goes against justice is itself un-Islamic. From this it follows that understandings of Islam that promote injustice toward women cannot be said to faithfully represent God's intentions, and hence must be revised or else rejected.

Following from this, Sadiq makes a critical distinction between God's word, in the form of the Qur'an, on the one hand, and our diverse human understandings of it, on the other. He argues that human efforts to understand the true import of God's revelation are always limited by the fact of us being human. God, the "Limitless" (*lā-maḥdūd*), he says, can hardly be fully understood by "limited" (*maḥdūd*) beings. The fact that humans (other than the prophets and the "innocent" imams) are limited beings forms an insurmountable barrier to our gaining a complete understanding of God's will as contained in the Qur'an. This does not mean, however, that we cannot move in that direction, although Sadiq is quite clear that a perfect and total comprehension of God's will is impossible for ordinary humans. This is said to be clear proof that the Qur'an is God's word, for, Sadiq says, while books written by ordinary mortals can be properly translated into other languages, the Qur'an cannot be faithfully represented in any other language because it is of divine origin. There can be, he says, no final translation of the Qur'an, because translators, being humans after all, are limited by their humanness and their limited knowledge of the world through which they interpret the Qur'an. As he puts it, translation is static (*jāmid*) while the Qur'an "moves along with time." Hence, new meanings of the Qur'an can be uncovered over time as the stock of human knowledge expands. This, of course, has vital implications for how Sadiq looks at the centuries-old Islamic traditions as developed by the *ulama*. Sadiq seems to suggest that although Muslims must respect the scholars of the past and learn or be inspired by them, they need not be bound by their opinions, including those on notions of the normative Muslim woman and on relations between the sexes, which were influenced by their own historical location.

Sadiq's case for a dynamic interpretation of the Qur'an, from which his own formulations on the gender question derive, rests on his willing acknowledgment that human knowledge is always in a state of development and progress. This, in turn, reflects on how we read and understand the Qur'an and the conclusions that we draw from it. The interpretation of the text is heavily influenced by the location and personal biography of the interpreter, Sadiq stresses. Although one must respect the "elders" for their knowledge and their dedication to Islamic scholarship, he says, one must also recognize that their understanding of the Qur'an was indelibly influenced by the available human knowledge of their own times. None of the classical Qur'anic commentators (*mufassirūn*), other than the 12 imams, claimed infallibility (*'isma*), he says, and this explains why and how the Qur'an has been understood and interpreted in diverse ways by different scholars at different times. As time progresses and the corpus of human knowledge, both of the natural and the human sciences, expands, our understanding and interpretation of the holy text must also correspondingly widen, uncovering new meanings that were not accessible to past interpreters. Far from suggesting any inadequacy in the Qur'an, Sadiq argues that this itself provides conclusive proof of the Qur'an being God's word, for in this way it proves its continuing relevance in every age. As regards the question of gender, therefore, this dynamic reading of the Qur'an allows for the possibility of new meanings to be read into the text with the passage of time, which, in turn, makes for new gender-just understandings of the divine mandate.

Sadiq's advocacy of a dynamic hermeneutics of the Qur'an naturally brings to the fore the twin questions of *taqlīd*, blind following of past jurisprudential precedent, and *ijtihād*, creative exercise of reason in understanding the sources of Islamic jurisprudence. This has a vital bearing on issues of jurisprudence involving women. Ithna Ashari Shii'tism has kept open the "doors of *ijtihād*" (*bāb ul-ijtihād*), but insists on the need for *taqlīd* on the part of "ordinary" believers of a living *mujtahid*. Sadiq confesses that he is himself a *muqallid*, of Ayatollah Sayyed 'Ali Sistani of Iraq, but argues that being a *muqallid* is far from being the same as a "blind follower." He refuses, he says, to surrender his right to think for himself, and while he acknowledges that he would act, in any particular matter, in accordance with the *ijtihād* of Ayatollah Sistani, he argues that he has the right to put into practice the *ijtihād* of his *mujtahid* in the manner that he himself deems most appropriate, in accordance with the exigencies of particular social contexts.

Critique of Misogynist so-called *Ahadith*

Sadiq's gender-just understanding of Islam is based on an approach to the Qur'an and the hadith (pl. ahadith) that differs significantly from that generally associated with traditional *ulama*. Of particular concern here is the way in which Sadiq deals with the corpus of hadith that is regularly invoked to justify the marginalization and oppression of women. Sadiq suggests that while the Qur'an advocates gender justice, the corpus of hadith contains many statements that are clearly misogynist. In part because of this, he repeatedly stresses that he rests his arguments only on the Qur'an, and that it is the Qur'an alone from which he seeks to develop his understanding of women's rights. God, he says, has Himself announced in the Qur'an that He has taken on Himself the responsibility of preserving the book free from any error or change (*tahrīf*). On the other hand, he says, God has made no such undertaking in the case of the hadith. Sadiq recognizes that it is largely from selective quotations from the corpus of hadith that upholders of patriarchy have sought to develop "Islamic" arguments to oppress and subordinate women. Hence, he devotes considerable attention to critically interrogating several misogynist so-called ahadith. This he does by pointing out that many so-called ahadith are pure fabrications, concocted well after the death of the Prophet and then wrongly attributed to him. This was done for a variety of reasons, such as to promote certain political factions or to bolster patriarchy. A major source of misogyny in the corpus of hadith is what is commonly known as *isra'iliyat* or *isra'ili rivayat*. These are stories that trace their origins to early Jewish converts to Islam, who brought with them their own inherited misogynist attitudes, which some of them either attributed to the Prophet as so-called ahadith, or else disseminated as tales that later became an integral part of popular lore among many Muslim communities. Given this, Sadiq says, extreme caution is necessary when using the hadith for advancing certain positions, and here he refers to both the Sunni and the Shi'ite hadith collections. Only those ahadith must be accepted that are in accordance with the Qur'an, he says. If they contradict the Qur'an they are to be discarded, and Sadiq argues that this is precisely what the Prophet and the imams had themselves insisted on.

In his critique of patriarchal ahadith, Sadiq focuses particularly on the Sunni collection of hadith, which differs in many respects from its Shi'ite counterpart, although this does not mean that he uncritically accepts the corpus of Shi'ite hadith as fully authentic. In this way he appears to fulfill two purposes: firstly, to critique patriarchal interpretations of Islam by showing them to be based on concocted ahadith wrongly attributed to the Prophet; and secondly, to implicitly critique the Sunni tradition and offer the Shi'ite understanding of Islam as both more "authentic" and somehow more gender friendly. The latter he does in a subtle way while insisting that he has "full respect" for Sunni scholars and the companions of the Prophet, stressing that he considers Sunnis to be his "brothers" in their capacity of being fellow Muslims.

In his treatment of what he regards as concocted ahadith, Sadiq is at pains to point out that such traditions are in conflict with Qur'anic ethical commandments and so cannot be said to have any authoritative value and nor can they be considered as genuine sayings of the Prophet. One widely-known so-called hadith often quoted by Sunni *ulama* which Sadiq critically examines has it that the Prophet declared that a husband must seek the advice of his wife in any matter in which he has a doubt, but must do precisely the opposite of what his wife suggests. This so-called hadith has been widely used to denigrate women as intellectually deficient to men, and as unable to make sensible decisions. Sadiq insists that this story is fabricated and has no merit at all. To back his claim he refers to another hadith, according to which, during the battle of Hudaibiyyah, when some of his companions differed with him on his peace proposal, the Prophet sought his wife Umm Salama and did precisely what she advised him to do. The Prophet is shown here as doing precisely the reverse of what he is alleged to have advised his companions in the first so-called hadith. Because the Prophet could not possibly have acted against his own advice, Sadiq stresses, the first statement attributed is clearly concocted.

Sadiq employs the same method of hadith criticism in dealing with another so-called hadith regarded as authoritative by many Sunnis, according to which, while on his nightly heavenly ascension (*mi'rāj*), the Prophet passed by hell and saw that it was full of women. This story has been taken by many Muslim scholars to suggest that women are somehow more prone to evil than men. Sadiq argues that it was impossible for the Prophet ever to make such a claim. As evidence, he cites a hadith according to which the Prophet said that if a man gives his daughter a good education and if she is virtuous and pious, she can stop the angels from dragging him to hell, with God's leave. In other words, instead of being congenitally disposed to evil or evil in themselves, women, if pious, can actually save men from hell-fire. A second hadith that Sadiq uses to counter the above misogynist one has it that the Prophet declared that heaven lies at the feet of mothers. Sadiq further critiques the first so-called hadith by reminding his listeners that in their supplications (*duru'*) they beseech God for welfare (*hasana*) in this world and in the next, adding that a great source of *hasana* in this world is a pious wife (*nek bivi*). Hence, he says, the story of hell being full of women, which has been routinely used to subordinate women, cannot be said to be authentic.

Sadiq is particularly critical of certain grossly misogynist so-called ahadith that are found in the *Ṣaḥīḥ* of al-Bukhari, which many Sunnis consider to be the most reliable and authentic collection of Prophetic traditions. While questioning these so-called ahadith he is careful not to appear to hurt Sunni sentiments, adding that although the narrators of these traditions, like other companions of the Prophet, were not infallible, they ought to be respected. Sadiq critically interrogates some so-called ahadith narrated by Abu Hurayrah, and contained in al-Bukhari's *Ṣaḥīḥ*, to illustrate his argument that many false stories have been wrongly attributed to the Prophet in order to bolster patriarchy and subordinate women. Sadiq's critique of Abu Hurayrah rests on the argument that although Abu Hurayrah had spent relatively very little time with the Prophet, he later narrated an enormous number of traditions that he attributed to the Prophet. Many of these so-called ahadith were definitely fabricated. These include certain plainly misogynist traditions, which Sadiq explains as a result of Abu Hurayrah's alleged "psychological allergy" to women. Thus, he cites a story narrated by Abu Hurayrah claiming that the Prophet once said that if a dog, a donkey, or a woman crosses in front of a man while he is praying, his prayer gets nullified. This is taken to suggest that a woman's worth was the same as a donkey's or a dog's. Sadiq counters Abu Hurayrah's story by arguing that when some Muslims complained to 'A'ishah, youngest wife of the Prophet, about Abu Hurayrah's statement, she said that the Prophet could never have uttered these words since she herself sometimes lay down in front of the Prophet while he prayed and she would not move from that position for fear of disturbing him.

Sadiq critiques another so-called hadith narrated by Abu Hurayrah, according to which the Prophet told his followers that three things were bad omens: a house, a horse, and women. When 'A'ishah heard that Abu Hurayrah had circulated this story she remarked that he was not a good listener. She said that she was present when the Prophet was giving the discourse when he mentioned this, but added that the Prophet had actually said that the Jews, who think that the home, the horse, and women are accursed, are wrong. However, she said, Abu Hurayrah entered the room when the Prophet was midway in this sentence, and so misunderstood what he had meant.

A third so-called hadith found in al-Bukhari's collection which Sadiq critically interrogates and then dismisses as false relates to the story of the creation of Adam and Eve. According to this story, God created Adam from mud, and then fashioned Eve from out of Adam's rib. This is why, this so-called hadith alleges the Prophet said, women will always remain "bent." Hence, it is claimed, the Prophet declared that one should never try to "straighten" a woman, for, being like a bent rib, she would inevitably "break." This so-called hadith is widely used to justify the argument that women are derived from, and hence biologically inferior to, men, and that they are also inherently "crooked." Sadiq dismisses this story as a pure fabrication, asking how, if women are the "molds" (*sancha*) of their children, and if they are congenitally "bent" or "crooked," they can produce "proper" male offspring. That this story has no Qur'anic sanction, Sadiq argues, is clearly evident from the fact that the word "rib" is not used even once in the Qur'an. In this regard Sadiq refers to another popular story, according to which God first created Adam, and when Adam felt lonely He created Eve to keep him company. Sadiq says that this story, too, completely contradicts the Qur'anic account of creation, where Adam and Eve are described as being produced simultaneously, and that too from the same substance and hence sharing the same essence. Similarly, Sadiq dismisses the theory, held by many Muslims, that Eve succumbed to Satan's temptation and so was the cause of Adam's expulsion from heaven. He says that this story is not found in the Qur'an, and is probably the result of a later influence of Christians with whom Muslims came into contact as Islam spread outside the Arabian Peninsula following the death of the Prophet.

By subjecting these and other so-called ahadith to a critical examination, Sadiq concludes that such misogynist stories and statements must not be accepted blindly, and nor should they be used to justify women's subjugation in the name of Islam. Indeed, he seems to suggest, since they directly violate the Qur'an's clear dictum of the fundamental equality of men and women, they must be treated as fabrications, and, therefore, should be firmly rejected.

A Gender-Just Qur'anic Exegesis

Sadiq's critique of misogyny in an "Islamic" garb goes along with an advocacy of an Islamic theology of gender equality. Islam, or, more properly, the Ithna Ashari Shi'ite interpretation of Islam, offers ideal models of womanhood, Sadiq claims. The ideal Muslim woman, as expressed through these models, is far from being a passive creature confined to her home. Sadiq cites the instance of many women of the *ahl ul-ba'it*, the family of the Prophet whom the Shi'ites hold in great reverence, who were great scholars themselves and also actively struggled against oppression and worked for the cause of Islam. Such, for instance, was Sayyeda Zainab, daughter of Imam 'Ali, who participated in the battle of Karbala against the army of the tyrant Yazid, son of Mu'awiyah. Another ideal woman was Hazrat Fatima, daughter of the Prophet, wife of Imam 'Ali and mother of Sayyeda Zainab and the Imams Hasan and Husain. Hazrat Fatima, Sadiq remarks, was so honorable in the eyes of the Prophet that he would stand up whenever she entered his presence; this being a privilege that she alone enjoyed. Sadiq also cites the examples of Mary, mother of Jesus, and Asiya, wife of the Pharaoh, whom the Qur'an upholds for all Muslims, not just Muslim women alone, to emulate. Another sign of the great respect in which pious women are held in Islam, Sadiq says, is the annual *Hajj* pilgrimage, when the pilgrims run between the hills of Safa and Marwah to relive the plight of Hagar (Hajra) searching for water for her thirsty son Isma'il.

Citing these examples, Sadiq sees the Qur'an as clearly and unambiguously mandating gender justice. The project that Sadiq seeks to promote involves both highlighting the positive Qur'anic teachings in this regard as well as critically examining and dealing with those verses of the Qur'an that some commentators have used to uphold and bolster patriarchy. In developing a gender-just Qur'anic perspective, Sadiq points out that the Qur'an constantly refers to men and women as equal partners (*zauj*) of each other. It speaks of men and women being born of the same substance, and as fellow creatures of the one God, hence suggesting that, ontologically, they are not just equal but, in a very fundamental sense, identical, despite their physical differences. Sadiq argues that what most distinguishes humans from animals is the soul or spirit (*ruh*). The soul is the "basic reality" of human beings, while the body is simply a "garment" for it. The soul, he says, is neither male nor female. Hence, he argues, despite their biological differences, men and women have the same status (*martaba*). The Qur'an points to this, in, for instance, its story of the creation of humankind and its separate references to believing men and women where it relates the similar spiritual rewards they would receive in the afterlife. From this it follows, Sadiq asserts, that it is not one's biology, but, rather, one's character, piety, knowledge, and deeds, that determine one's status (*fazilat*) and make one inferior or superior to others. Neither of the genders can claim to be superior to the other as a whole. A man may be considered superior to a particular woman, not because of his gender, but, instead, because of his piety or knowledge. On the other hand, if a certain woman is more pious and knowledgable than a particular man, she is clearly superior to him. In fact, Sadiq says, arguing against those who believe women to be intellectually inferior than men, God has given the capacity to reason (*'aql*) equally to men and women. If girls are provided equal opportunities to study, he says with approval, they could even excel boys.

Sadiq's advocacy of gender equality is not a call for gender identity in terms of roles, for he argues that although men and women are equal, and in an ontological sense, the same, they are biologically prepared to engage in different tasks for the sake of a more harmonious family and society. There is nothing in the Qur'an, Sadiq says, that prohibits women from going out of the house or even working outside, under certain conditions. Yet, their most essential task, he says, is to maintain the home and look after the children. On them rests the onerous responsibility of rearing the new generation, for a mother is the "first school" of her children. It is a mark of the great respect that Islam accords women, he says, that it has given her this responsibility on which depends the future of the entire community. A woman who is herself well educated, both in Islamic as well as modern disciplines, can perform this task in the most effective way. Hence the need for women's religious and secular education that Sadiq repeatedly stresses.

In his discussion of the Qur'an, Sadiq directly addresses certain issues of jurisprudential import mentioned in the text that relate to women and that have often been used either to deny Muslim women their Islamic rights or else to argue that Islam is itself a misogynist religion. His discussion of these issues is geared both to critiquing misogynist interpretations of the Qur'an as well as to rebutting the claims of the critics of Islam. One such issue is that of inheritance rights. Sadiq takes on critics of Islam who claim that the Qur'an legally sanctions women's subordination by giving them inheritance rights half that of men. This claim, Sadiq says, is not true at all. For one thing, the Qur'an nowhere makes such a specification, and does not deal with men and women as two monolithic categories for matters of inheritance. While daughters do get half the share of their brothers in their deceased father's property, this rule does not apply for other categories of heirs in all cases. Thus a deceased son's parents inherit equally, a deceased man's daughter's son gets half the share of his son's daughter, and his mother's brother and sister get the same share. Arguing for the inherent justness of the Qur'anic rules of inheritance, Sadiq points out that while a woman would inherit half the share of her brother in the event of the death of their father, she would also receive a sum of money as *mehr* on marriage from her husband, the amount of which she can specify in the marriage contract. All gifts, other than articles meant solely for men's use, given to the couple at the time of marriage also belong legally to the wife. The wife is not obliged to spend anything on running the household, even if she has an independent source of income. All that she earns is hers, and the husband may not demand that she contribute to meeting the family's expenses. The reason why a daughter inherits less than a son has nothing to do with any presumed inferiority of woman. Rather, Sadiq says, it is entirely just, given the fact that a woman's financial needs must be provided for by males – by her father, or, in his absence, her elder brother, until her marriage, and, after that, by her husband. "A woman's income is a hundred per cent saving, while a husband's income is a hundred per cent expense," Sadiq says, rounding off a discussion of what he regards as the Quran's women-friendly rules of inheritance.

Another contentious issue relates to women's testimony (*shahadat*). Some Islamic scholars consider a woman's testimony as half that of a man, based on a selective reading of a certain Qur'anic verse. Sadiq offers an alternative reading, suggesting that this verse must be seen in the particular historical context in which it was revealed, and stressing that it must not be arbitrarily transposed onto a different context to argue the case that women are somehow congenitally less intelligent than men, as some Muslim scholars indeed insist. That this provision was intended for only a particular context, and was not to be generalized for all women and for all times, is evident, Sadiq says, from the fact that any true Muslim would readily accept the evidence of a single woman, Hazrat Fatima, daughter of the Prophet, even if the entire population of the world were arraigned against her. With the help of this argument of contextuality, Sadiq is able to willingly approve of the current practice in Iran, for instance, where, he says, a third of the members of the country's parliament are women, whose vote has the same value as that of male members.

A third vexed issue is that of divorce (*ṭalāq*). Sadiq's discussion of divorce is geared to several purposes: to contrast the Shi'ite position on the matter with the general Sunni position and thereby implicitly assert the superiority of the former over the latter; to critique and condemn widespread misuse of Sunni *fiqh* provisions related to *ṭalāq*; and to counter the argument that draws on *ṭalāq*-related provisions in Sunni *fiqh* to claim that Islam is inherently misogynist. He points out that the practice of "triple *ṭalāq*," according to which if a man pronounces the word "*ṭalāq*" three times in one sitting, even if in jest, anger, or in a state of inebriety, his marriage is nullified, has led to widespread abuse and oppression of women. It has resulted in numerous hapless women being arbitrarily divorced by their husbands. In case the husband repents and wishes to regain his wife, his wife would have to marry someone else, consummate the marriage, obtain a divorce and then remarry her first husband. This practice is known as *halala*. This form of *ṭalāq* is widely accepted by most Sunni *ulama* in India. Sadiq argues that "triple *ṭalāq*" actually has no Qur'anic basis. He also declares that it is forbidden in the Ja'fari *mazhab*, the school of law that the Ithna Ashari Shi'ites follow, where even if the word *ṭalāq* is uttered thrice in one sitting it is considered as constituting a single *ṭalāq*, not three. Sadiq offers to allow divorced Sunni couples who wish to save themselves the embarrassment of *halala* and desire to be reunited to resort to the Ja'fari school while still remaining Sunnis. In this way, he holds out the prospect of a more gender-just law on divorce, works out a practical means for Sunni–Shi'ite dialogue and, at the same time, presents an argument to indirectly put forward the claim of the Shi'ite *fiqh* being more gender-just than the Sunni.

Another question that Sadiq addresses is the Qur'anic verse, in *Sūrah al-Baqarah*, which refers to God having given men an "edge" over women. This verse has been used by many commentators to claim unrestricted male superiority over women in every matter or sphere. Sadiq vehemently disagrees with this claim, pointing out that this Qur'anic reference is clearly made in the context of divorce, and is not meant to apply in general terms. The "edge" here is said to refer to the fact that a man can divorce his wife whenever he wants to, but in the absence of any conditions written into the marriage contract, a woman can have the marriage dissolved only by approaching the *qazi*, who, after being convinced that the husband has failed in his marital duties, can announce the marriage to be dissolved.

Yet another vexed issue that Sadiq deals with in the course of his elaboration of the Qur'anic vision of gender relations is a verse in *Sūrah al-Nisa* that suggests that if a wife is disobedient, her husband can admonish her. If that does not work he can send her to her bed, and, finally, if this does not change her attitude, he can beat her. This does not mean, Sadiq says, that Islam gives husbands the unrestricted right to beat their wives, as some scholars claim. A husband cannot beat his wife if she refuses to cook for him or clean the house, for instance, for she is not duty bound to do so. Sadiq says that the actual import of the word "beating" (*ḍarb*) in this Qur'anic verse has been greatly debated and fiercely contested by various Islamic scholars. He relates that Imam Tabari, in his commentary on the Qur'an, devotes 27 pages to discussing the word, and says that over 200 meanings have been offered to explain it. Sadiq opines that it is wrong to equate *ḍarb* with beating, and adds that several *ulama* who have done so have also laid down that a husband can beat a wife only with a toothbrush. This implies, he says, that there must be no seriousness in this sort of "beating." Rather, it suggests a form of "love" and "joking," further stressing the fact that one is forbidden to actually beat one's wife in a harmful way. In this regard, he reminds his listeners that the Prophet is the model for all Muslims to follow. The Prophet is not known to have ever beaten his wives, even if he was sometimes troubled by some of them. Likewise, none of the imams of the Shi'ites are said to have beaten their wives, although some of their wives even plotted against them. Hence, Sadiq says, Muslim men must follow their example, refrain from beating their wives, and, instead, treat them with love and compassion.

The Ideal Islamic Family

An interesting feature of Sadiq's gender discourse is its framing in terms of the rights of women, particularly in their capacity as wives. Sadiq remarks that while it is true that women, like men, have their duties as well, unfortunately traditionalist scholars generally ignore women's Islamic rights and focus, instead, on their responsibilities alone. This must, however, change, Sadiq stresses. In order to help people to take their commitment to Islam seriously, he says, focus must first be given to their rights, after which one must stress their duties. To violate the natural rights that God has granted every human being, he argues, is a grave sin, an act of oppression that God will not forgive unless the person whose rights have been trampled upon forgives the culprit. Women, like other creatures of God, have their own rights, and Sadiq insists that men must respect and uphold these if their commitment to Islam is to be acceptable to God.

Bitterly critiquing patriarchal custom, Sadiq says that treating women as virtual servants of their husbands has no sanction whatsoever in Islam. This constitutes a fundamental violation of their God-given rights. A man cannot force a woman to meet his personal needs. He cannot insist that she wash his clothes or cook food for him. She is not legally obliged to do so, and can refuse if she wants to. On the other hand, Sadiq says, a man, through his sincere love and respect for and loyalty to his wife, can cement such a close spiritual bond with her that they both willingly look after the personal needs of each other. However, this is not the fundamental objective of marriage in Islam, which, instead is, Sadiq says, to produce a future generation that would be, in spiritual, moral, and intellectual terms, superior to the preceding one. For this, he stresses, both husband and wife have equally crucial roles to play.

Being, to use a Qur'anic term, the *zauj* of each other, husband and wife are equals. Sadiq likens them to the two wheels of a vehicle that can only work if they are of the same size. "If one wheel is bigger than the other," he says, "the vehicle cannot move." Hence, for the "vehicle of life" to be able to function, "both husband and wife must be considered to be equal." Marriage, in Sadiq's words, is a "major form of worship." While the ritual prayers, fasting during the month of Ramadan, and the pilgrimage to Mecca are time-bound, marriage, Sadiq says, is a life-long form of worship, and so, in a certain sense, superior to ritual worship. Hence, he says, marriage should be treated with all the sanctity that it deserves. Relations between husband and wife must be that between two equals brought together through bonds of love and affection and respect for each other.

Conclusion

Sadiq's explorations of the Qur'anic vision of gender relations provide new avenues both to critique patriarchal traditions that are sought to be given an "Islamic" gloss, and to press the claim for a gender-just understanding of the faith. This, in turn, has practical relevance in terms both of scriptural exegesis (*tafsir*) and jurisprudence (*fiqh*). Not surprisingly, Sadiq is an ardent advocate of women's education, both religious and secular, seeing this as a fundamental duty as well a means to promote a gender-just understanding of Islam. He suggests that one of the major reasons why the patriarchal tradition that many Muslim scholars continue to uphold has not been effectively challenged is because there have been so few women Islamic scholars. To address this he points to the need for more Muslim women to study Islam seriously.

Sadiq's gender-sensitive understanding of Islam marks a major shift from the approach of many traditional Islamic scholars, but he does not go as far as some would like him to in his espousal of women's rights, for one can discern a distinctly apologetic and defensive tone underlying some of his claims. Critics could also point to his perhaps deliberate glossing over of certain patently patriarchal aspects of the Shi'ite tradition, as, for instance, the practice of *mut'ah* or temporary marriage. Likewise, in his fulsome praise of post-Revolution Iran he ignores the very real problems that many Iranian women have to face precisely because of a certain narrow understanding of Shi'ite Islam. Yet, on the whole, despite these obvious limitations, Sadiq's elaborate reworking of the Islamic tradition does appear to offer new and refreshing perspectives through which to view the question of gender relations in Islam.

As the leading contemporary Indian Ithna Ashari scholar, Sadiq's views on women carry particular prestige among South Asian Shi'ites. His efforts to promote women's rights have not remained confined to his *majālis*. Rather, he has also sought to put them into action, such as by providing modern education to Muslim girls in the educational institutions that he runs in Lucknow and by supporting numerous other such initiatives by Shi'ites in other parts of India. Sadiq has had to face the ire of numerous conservative *ulama* for some of his outspoken views on women. Thus, in September 2004, when he issued a statement that family planning was permissible in Islam, numerous Sunni *ulama*, including several leaders of the All-India Muslim Personal Law Board, of which he himself is the vice-president, came out in vehement protest, declaring that family planning was *ḥarām* and alleging that Sadiq's claim was opposed to *sharī'ah*.[6] Yet, undeterred, Sadiq continues his mission, offering new ways of creatively understanding Islam and what it means to be an ideal Muslim woman in today's world.

Notes

1. The most authoritative work on the Indian Shi'ites is Saiyid Athar Abbas Rizvi, *A Socio-Intellectual History of the Ithna Ashari Shi'ites in India* (2 vols.) (New Delhi: Munshiram Manoharlal, 1986). See also John Norman Hollister, The Shia of India. 2nd edn. (New Delhi: Oriental Books Reprint, 1979).
2. These include www.victorynewsmagazine.com, www. al-murtaza.org, www.ezsoftech.com/giknowledge/majālis.asp,   www.ezsoftech.com/giknowledge/majālis.asp,   http://www.yahusain.com, www.islamicentre.org, and www.winislam.com/web/maj.htm.
3. Interview with Kalbe Sadiq, New Delhi, October 4, 2004.
4. Yoginder Sikand, *Shi'a–Sunni Dialogue: Mawlana Kalbe Sadiq's Theology of Islamic Ecumenism* (http://www.islaminterfaith.org/may2004/article-05-04-c.htm).
5. Ibid.
6. "Family Planning Divides Muslim Clerics," *Mid-Day*, September 16, 2004. See also, Yoginder Sikand, *Furore over Family Planning* (http://www.islaminterfaith.org/oct2004/article3.htm).

Index

Note

The index is in word-by-word alphabetical order. Arabic names beginning with al- are filed under the following part of the name, eg; al-Mahdi is filed under M, al-Qaeda under Q. Titles such as Mawlana, Sultan, appear after the name. As far as possible names that are transliterated in different styles in the text have been gathered under one heading with cross-references from alternative forms.

Aaron, 200
abangan, 467, 474
Abbas, Shah, 547
Abd al-Aziz, Umar, 197
Abdallah, Abdalla Fadallah, 148
'Abduh, Muḥammad, 7, 9, 190, 288, 341, 342, 452, 468, 476, 542, 625, 636
Abdul Ghani Yakob, 450
AbdulHamid A. AbuSulayman, 452
Abdulhamid II, *Sultan*, 322
Abdurrahim, Imaduddin, 205
Abou-Bakr, Omaima, 632
Abraham, 222
Abrahamian, Ervand, 545
abrogation, 163
Abu al-A'la al-Mawdūdī, *see* Mawdūdī
Abu Bakr, 308, 572
Abu Daud/Dawud, 162, 197
Abu Hurayrah, 197, 650
Abu Sayyaf, 449, 460
Abu'l Ala Maududi *see* Mawdūdī
Abu'l al-Mawdūdī *see* Mawdūdī
Abu-Rabi', Ibrahim M., 298, 388, 401, 402
Abu-Zahra, Muhammad, *Shaykh*, 147
academic dependency, 588
Acar, Feride, 615
accountability, 166
acculturationism, 576
Acehnese Independent Movement, 459
Achaemenian Empire, 549

adab, 582
Adam and Eve, 650
Adivar, Halide Edip, 30, 125, 612
'*adl* (distributive justice), 573
administration, 572
adulterers, 147
adultery, 168
Advani, L.K., 516
al-Afghānī, Jamāl al-Din, 7, 9, 259, 288, 341, 562, 625
Afghanistan, 15, 112, 117, 165, 202, 343, 386, 390, 411, 412
Africa, 258, 318, 410, 562, 588
Afyon, Nursi trials at, 68
Aghajari, Hashem, 628
agnosticism, 442
agriculture, 91
Agung, *Sultan*, 482, 483, 487, 491, 492, 496, 498
Ahl al-Sunnah, 257
Ahl-e Hadith, 107, 113
Ahmad Khan, Syed, 7, 9, 13, 19, 190, 542
Ahmad Syafi'I Ma'arif, 391
Ahmad, Anis, 451
Ahmad, Hazrat Mirza Ghulam, 461
Ahmad, Israr, 180
Ahmad, Khurshid, 9, 14, 178, 193, 601
Ahmadi community, 182
Ahmed I, 329
Ahmed, Ishtiaq, 155

Ahmed, Leila, 634, 635
Akbarabadi, Sa'id Ahmad, 83
Akdeniz University, 134
ākhirah (the Hereafter), 571, 573
Akif, Mehmet, 42
Aktaş, Cihan, 616
Al Washliyah, 468
'Ala, Sayyed 'Abdul, 89
Alatas, Syed Hussein, 588, 596
Alavi-tabar, Alireza, 628, 629
'Alawī, 331
Alexander of Macedonia, 549
Alexander, Yonah, 378
Algeria, 258, 302, 562
Algerian Liberation Front, 380
Algerian National Liberation Front, 215
'Ali, Ahmad, *Mawlana*, 89
Ali Aybar, Mehmet, 27
'Ali ibn Abi Ùalib, 162
Ali Miyan, *see* Nadwi, Sayyed Abul
     Hasan 'Ali
Ali, Mohammad, 550
Ali, Mukti, 476
Ali Sardar Jafari Committee, 513
alienation, 368
Aligarh Muslim University, 645
Aligarh school, 107
Alighrah movement, 9, 13
'Allāl al-Fāsī, 9
All-India Muslim League, 179
Al-Risāla movement, 75, 78
amānah (trust), 230
'*amal* (action), 264
Ambedkar, B.R., 97, 509
America, 203, 293, 410
American Civil Liberties Union, 389
American Civil War, 388
American University, 460
Ammianus Marcellinus, 544
Amos, 222
Anadolu University, 141
analogy, 163
anarchy, 66
Anderson, Benedict, 314, 316
angels, 263
Angkatan Belia Islam Malaysia, 455
   Ankara University, 130
   Faculty of Ilahiyat, 123, 133
Ankara, 25, 69

An-Na'im, Abdullahi, 154
al-Ansārī, Abū Ayyūb, 202
antiheroism, 296
anti-Semitism, 305
Antun, Farah, 258
apostasy, 147, 168
Appadurai, Arjun, 318, 319
'*aql* (reason), 264
al-Aqsa mosque, 530
Aquinas, Thomas, *St.*, 428
Arab Renaissance, 258
Arabia, 206
Arabic, 25, 127
Arafat, Yasser, 388
Arat, Yeşim, 613
archetype, 245
architecture, 91
ard (land), 264
arid, 242
Arinç, Bülent, 355
aristocracy, 346
Aristotle, 258, 333, 335
Arkoun, Muhammad, 156
Armagan, Mustafa, 298
armed robbery, 168
Armenians, 322, 379
Armstrong, Karen, 414
Arnold, T.W., 418
Arshaduddin, *Sheikh*, 418
art, 91, 246
Arvas, Ibrahim, 128
Arya Samaj, 511
asbāb al-nuzūl, 260
Asena, Duygu, 615
Ashaari Muhammad, *see* Ashaari, Ustaz
Ashaari, Ustaz, 5, 21, 195, 196, 199, 200,
     201, 202, 203, 204, 205, 206, 207,
     208, 210, 211, 212
Ashari, Ithna, 656
Ashari, K.H. Hasyim, 486
Ash'arism, 257
Ash'arite conception, 272
Ashcroft, John, *Attorney General*, 413
Ashok Rudra, 523
Ashraf, Ahmad, 545
Asia, 258, 318, 588
asoib, 203
Assam, 109
assimilation, 368, 372

Association of Independent Industrialists and Businessmen, 354
Astarabadi, Bibi Khanum, 636
Al-Suhaimi, Muhammad Abdullah, *Shaykh*, 199
Atabaks, 549
Atatürk University, 132
Atatürk, Kemal, 11, 24, 156, 164, 346; *see also* Kemalism
Ateş, Süleyman, 140
Athenagoras, *Patriarch*, 69
al-'Attār, Ḥassan, 9
Aurad Muhammadiah, 198
authenticity, 257
authoritarianism, 596
Avcioğlu, Doğan, 31
'Awdah, 'Abd al-Qādir, 9
Ayatollah Khomeini, 10, 164, 205, 552, 631
aydin, 26
Aydin, Mehmed S., 140
Aydin, Mehmet, 355
Azad, Abul Kalam, 78
Azamgarh, 90
Azerbaijan, 549, 550
al-Azhar, 108, 175, 190
Azmi, Wan Hussain, 450
Azra, Azyumardi, 400, 461

Babacan, Ali, 355
Babacan, Zeynep, 355
Baban, Cihat, 129
Babari Mosque, 512
Babri Masjid Action Committee, 96
backcasting, 570
Bacon, *Sir* Francis, 335
Badawi, Abdullah Ahmad, 205, 455, 578
Bader Meinhof, 379
Badr, well of, 571
Baghdad Pact, 69
Baghdad, 106, 171, 450
Bahais, 169, 551
Bajrang Dal, 518
Bajunid, Omar Farouk, 458
Balambangan, 492
Bali, 393, 492
Balqis, (queen of the kindom of Saba'), 169
Baltacioğlu, İsmail Hakki, 31
Baluchistan, 113

Bandung Conference, 215
Bangkok, 393
Bangladesh, 13, 96, 109, 120, 176, 305, 366, 400, 532, 535, 562, 564
Banguoğlu, Tahsin, 129
Bani Tamim, 200–1
Bank Muamalat Indonesia, 457
Bank Syariah Mandiri of Indonesia, 457
al-Banna, Hassan, 288
Barelwi Tanzim, 111
Barelwi, Sayyed Ahmad, 89
Barelwis, 107
Barisan Revolusi Nasional, 459
Barth, Karl, 435
al-Basri, al-Hasan, 279
al-Bashir, 'Umar, 165, 166
Batini, 331
Bayar, Celal, 69
Bayat, Sunan, 482, 487, 488, 490, 491, 492, 493, 494, 495, 497, 498, 499, 500, 501, 502, 503, 504
Bayes, Jane, 627, 636
Bayezid II, 329
Bayraklı, Bayraktar, 133
Behdad, Sohrab, 592
Behnam, Reza, 546
Bektāshī order, 331
belief, 61–2
Belli, Mihri, 27
Ben Bella, Ahmad, President, 215
Benedict, Ruth, 248, 551
  Bengal, 108
  nationalism, 13
Bennabi, Malik, 213, 245
Berkes, Niyazi, 24, 29
Bey, Ali Sedat, 124
Bey, Sadrettin Celal, 126
Bey, Vasif, 124
Bharat Mata, 510
Bharatiya Janata Party (BJP), 510, 511, 518
Bharatiyata, 372, 373
Bhiwandi, 101
Bihar, 108
Bill, James, 550, 552
bin 'Abd al-Wahhab, Muhammad, 14, 261, 309, 332
bin Laden movement, 15
bin Laden, Osama, 164, 313, 384, 390, 396, 412, 461

Bin-Bāz, 'Abdul-Azīz, *Shaykh*, 147
BJP, *see* Bharatiya Janata Party (BJP)
Black Sea, 539
Blair, Tony, 388, 411
Boland, B.J., 452
Boratav, Pertev Naili, 29
Borobudur temple, 485
Bosnia, 293, 377, 410, 563
Bosporus, 539
bourgeoisie, 346
Boyce, Ralph, 387, 392, 398
Boyle, Robert, 335
Britain, 548
British Empire, 583
British Raj, 179
Bronowski, Jacab, 335
Brubaker, Rogers, 315
Bruce Lawrence, 321
Brunei, 204
Brunei Darussalam, 455
Brzezinski, Zbigniew, 416
Buddhism, 509
Buddhist, 97, 411
al-Bukhari, 145–6, 162, 650
Bukhara, 203
    Sheikh Jamaluddin, 417
Bulaç, Ali, 292
Bumin, Tülin, 620
Bush, George, 387, 411, 413

Çakir, Ruşen, 619
Çakmak, Ibrahim, 357
Cairo, 108, 215, 460
Calcutta, 107
Calhoun, Craig, 316
caliphate, *see khilāfah*
caliphs, 146, 572, 581
Cantwell Smith, Wilfred, 379
capitalism, 185, 314, 595
capitalist system, 589
captive mind, 588
Carlton, David, 378
Cartesian rationalism, 295
Cartesianism, 290
Casablanca, 384
Castells, Manuel, 322
Catholic Church, 152, 286
Catholics and Protestants, 377, 411
Çelik, Hilmi, 355

Çelik, Ömer, 352
Central Asia, 204, 206, 410
Central Intelligence Agency (CIA), 322, 413
Çerman, Osman Nuri, 28
Cevdet, Abdullah, 23
Cevdet, Ahmet, 125
Chatterjee, Partha, 12
Chechnya, 293, 369, 410, 416
Chelghoum Laid, 214
child custody, 579
China, 202, 204, 324, 368, 369, 577, 583
choseisme, 249
Choudhury, Masudul Alam, 593
Christianity, 147, 221, 377
Chupanids, 549
CIA, *see* Central Intelligence Agency (CIA)
citizenship, 610
civilization, 228, 249
cleanliness, 63
Cold War, 408
Coleman, James, 558
collectivity, 65
colonial domination, 187
colonialism, 2, 6, 9, 12, 17, 107, 164, 179,
    254, 259, 261, 266, 318, 321, 322,
    323, 385, 510, 540, 577, 632, 634,
    636, 640
colonizability, 233, 249
Comaroff, John, 315
communalism, 363
communism, 52, 90, 185, 257
compassion, 66
comprehensive secularism, 292, 295
consensus, 163
conservatism, 37, 153, 468
conservative traditionalists, 624
Constantine, 214
Constantinople, 202
constitutionalism, 69
constructivist, 41
consultation, 575
consumerism, 218, 240
contemporaneity, 258
contextualist, 41
Copernicus, 286, 335
Cottam, Richard, 545
coup d'état, 166
Crusades, 328, 377, 577
Çukurova University, 134

culture, 235, 238, 243, 249
culture crisis, 249, 250
Cumhuriyet University, 134, 141
Custodian (Saudi Arabia), 364

Dağ, Mehmed, 140
Dahlan, Muhammad, 8
Dajjal, 197
Dalit Voice, 97
Damascus, 90
Dar al-Ḥarb, 576
Dār al-Islām, 576
Dar al-Ulum, 13, 108
al-Dari, Tamim, 199
Darul Arqam, 195, 196, 198
Darulfünun Faculty of Ịlahiyat, 126
Darwinism, 293
Delhi, 107, 176
Delphi method, 569
democracy, 44, 53, 94, 101, 151, 153, 157,
    165, 267, 324, 349, 365, 388, 392,
    441, 576, 626
democracy reconciliation, 52
Democrat Party (DP) (Turkey), 70, 346
Democratic Party (Indonesia), 470
Democratic Party *see* Democrat Party (DP)
    (Turkey)
democratization, 589, 636
Denizli, Nursi trials at, 69
Deoband, 13, 90
Deobandi Wifaq, 111
Deobandis, 107
Deoras, Balasaheb, 514
Descartes, René, 216, 217, 289, 295, 335
Desker, Barry, 453, 461
despotism, 249
deterritorialization, 318
Deutsch, Karl, 315
Dewan Dakwah Islamiyah (DDII), 454
dhikr (invocation), 332
dialogue, 170, 248, 264
Dicle University, 134
dictatorship, 150
Dilipak, Abdurrahman, 46
Dini Ta'limi Council, 90
Direct Action, 379
diversity, 568
divine, 578
Divine Unity, 91

divorce, 579
Diyarbakir, 70
dogmatism, 165, 189
double ownership, 590
dress, 91
dualism, 257
Dubos, René, 218
Dutch Java, 198

Ebadi, Shirin, 632
economic development, 589
economic growth, 588, 589
economists, 587–606
ecumenical humanism, 236
Efendi, Emrullah, 123
Efendi, Hoca Tahsin, 124
Effendi, Bahtiar, 452
egocentrism, 249
egotism, 65
Egypt, 9, 25, 258, 302, 563, 572
Eichmann, Otto Adolf, 293
Elliot, Michael, 384
Elmessiri, Abdelwahab, 292–4
Emami, Shahrbanu, 629
Emmerson, Donald, 400
empire, 313–14, 322–5
empirical theories, 592
empiricism, 286
Encyclopaedia Britannica, 378, 381
Engels, Friedrich, 547
Enlightenment, 17, 23, 286, 295
enmity, 263
epistemology, 243, 286, 427
Erbakan, Necmettin, 47, 347
Erdoğan, Recep Tayyip, 26, 348
Erlangen University, 142
escapism, 240
eschatology, 162
Eshkevari, Yusef, 628
Esposito, John, 291, 303
esthetics, 242
ETA (the Basques), 379
ethical theories, 592
ethico–esthetic plasma, 243
ethics, 61, 62, 286
ethos, 230, 243
Europe, 1–20, 16, 66, 90, 163, 169, 204,
    216, 250, 286, 304, 392, 410, 475,
    538

European Union, 37, 142, 353, 582
Evren, Kenan, 610
exclusivism, 425, 426, 435, 574
existentialism, 293
extremism, 165
Eyyüboğlu, Sabahattin, 28

factionalism, 552
Faculty of Divinity, 130
Faculty of Islamic Sciences, Erzurum, 132
Faḍlallah, Muḥammad, 9
Faḍlallah, Muḥammad Ḥussain, 9, 10
Fahd ibn Abdul Aziz, (King of Saudi Arabia),
    536
Faisalabad, 110
faith, 61, 258, 342
falah, 590
Falwell, Jerry, 389
Far East, 201
al-Farabi, 162
Farangi Mahalli, 'Abd al-Bari, 108
Faruqi, Ziya-ul Hasan, 82
al-Faruqi, Ismail Raji, 190
fascism, 370, 575
fasiqūn (vicious), 267
fatalism, 552
al-Fatih, Muhammad, 202
Fatima, 162
fatwa, 163
Fawwaz, Zeinab, 636
Fazl al-Rahman, *Mawlana, see* Fazlur Rahman
Fazlur Rahman, 114, 572
Federal Bureau of Investigation (FBI), 413
Felicity Party, 347
feminism, Islamic, 624–43
feminist movement, 612
feminist theology, 633
Fergan, Eşref Edip, 42
Fiğlali, Etem Ruhi, 140
fiqh, 579
Firat University, 134
flat-earthism, 290
flexibility, 154
Fodio, Osman dan, 309
folk Islam, 25
Fontenelle, Bernand le Bovierde, 336
formalism, 236
Foucault, Michel, 218
fragmentation, 552

France, 204, 215, 345, 368, 414, 582
free will, 167
freedom, 153, 286, 349, 382
French Revolution, 379
Freud, Sigmund, 315
Friedl, Erika, 637
Fromm, Erich, 187, 381
Front Pembela Islam, 390, 391
frugality, 63
Fukuyama, Francis, 218, 558
Fuller, Graham E., 468
fundamentalism, 153, 289, 302, 349, 453,
    574, 575, 576
future studies, 568, 583

Gadjah Mada University, 468
Galileo, 286, 335
Gambetta, Diego, 559
Gandhi, Indira, 510, 514, 517
Gandhi, Mahatma, 512
Ganji, Akbar, 628
gas chamber, 371
Gaza, 302
Gazı University, 134
Geerts, Clifford, 235, 306, 466
Gellner, Ernest, 306, 598
gender equality, 647
generalized altruism, 592
Geneva, 90
Geneva Convention, 322
Genghis Khan, (1162–1227), 549
genital mutilation, 626
Germany, 142, 214, 345, 368, 378, 511,
    558, 582
Ghafur, Abdul, *Shaykh*, 205
Ghannoushi, Rāshid, 9
al-Ghazālī, Abu Hamid, 286, 331
Giddens, Anthony, 289
Gilan, Eshaqis in, 549
Gilbert, William, 286
global television networks, 568
globalization, 16, 318, 350, 545, 581, 634
Gog (tribe), 197
Gökberk, Macit, 28
Gökmen, Fatin, 128
Göle, Nilüfer, 615, 619
Golestan, treaty of, 549
Golkar Party, 470
Golongan Karya Party, 470

Golwalkar, M.S., 371, 512
Gorbachev, Mikhail, 26
Görüş, Millî, 48
governmentality, 316
Gramsci, Antonio, 5
Grand Ayatollah, 364
grand narrative, 296
Great Britain, 176, 549
Greece, 415
Gujarat Genocide, 371
Gül, Abdullah, 348, 350
Gülen, Fethullah, 5, 12, 19
Gulf states, 1–20
Günaltay, Şemseddin, 130
Güngör, Erol, 25, 26, 35
Gürüz, Kemal, 356
Gus Slamet, 490
Gush Emunim, 306

Haas, Richard, 523
Habermas, Jürgen, 289
Habibie, B.J., 477
Hadar, Leon, 303
Hadden, Jeffrey F., 450
Hadith, 135, 155, 257
Haghia Sofia, 347
Hague, 413
Hakki, İzmirli İsmail, 124
Hakki, Kiliçzade, 23
Hale-Bopp, (comet), 197
Halley, Edmund, 335
   Halley's comet, 197
Hamid Dabashi, 554
Hanania, 222
Haq, General Ziyaul, 181
Haqiqatjou, Fatima, 631, 634
haqis, 549
ḥarām, 571
Haramayn, 203
al-Harith Harrath, 202
Harland, Richard, 289
Harran University, 134
Harras, Abdussalam, 205
Hartford Seminary, 402
Hasani, Sayyed 'Abdul Hai, 89
Hasdemir Şahin, Hatice, 609
Hassan Hanafi, 257, 276
Hassan, Riffat, 635
Hassan, Sa'd Muhammad, Shaykh, 161

Hatipzade, 336
Hayderbad, 100, 108
Haz, Hamzah, 471
headscarf, 607–23
Hedgewar, Dr., 511
Hefner, Robert W., 466
hellfire, 263
Helmstad University, 337
al-Hibri, Azizah, 636
Hick, John, 425, 435
ḥijāb, 607–23, 637
Hijrah, 571
Hilmy Bakar Almascaty, 206
ḥimā, 571
Hindu Dharma, 372
Hindu Mahasabha, 511
Hindu Raj, 374
Hindu Rashtra, 373, 374
Hindu Samajotsav, 511
Hinduism, 371, 372
Hindutva, 372, 374, 511
Hiroshima City University, 458
Hitler, Adolph, 293, 371
Hizb-al-Tahrir, 390, 576
Hizbullah, 576
Hobbes, Thomas, 335
Hocazade, 336
Holocaust, 293, 318
holy war, 383
homo religiosus, 232
honor killing, 626
Hooker, M.B., 453, 470
horizontalization, 260
Horstius, 337
Howard, John, 393
Ḥudaybiyyah Agreement, 572
human arrogance, 176
human ego, 176
human rationality, 217
human resources, 588
human rights, 155, 365, 382, 392
humanism, 236, 316
humanity, 417
Huntington, Samuel, 303, 311, 410, 478,
   535, 573, 577
Husain, Sayyid Abdul, 171
Hussain, Abid, 82
Hussain, Saddam, 171, 536
Hussain, Taha, 164

Hussain, Zakir, 82
Huwaydi, Fahmi, 170
Huygens, Christiaan, 335
Hyderabad, 100, 108

'ibādah (worship), 573
Ibn 'Arabi, 200
Ibn Bādis, 'Abd al-Hamid, Shaykh, 214
Ibn Hanbal, 279
Ibn Ishaqe, 339
Ibn Khaldun, 'Abd al-Rahman, 161, 230,
    277, 578, 587–8, 596
  khilāfah (caliphate), 597
  mulk (royal), 597
Ibn Maja, 162
Ibn Malik, 148
Ibn Taymiyya, 332
Ibrahim, Anwar, 574
ideological polarization, 371
ideology, 183
idolatry, 91, 249
Ihsan, Mehmet Oğlu, 126
ijmā', 575
ijtihād, 264, 562, 572, 578, 648
İlahiyat, Faculty of, 123
İlhan, Attila, 26, 29
'ilm (science), 264, 573
Ilyas, Muhammad, Mawlana, 90
İlyasoğlu, Aynur, 615
Imam-Hatip schools, 126
imamate (politics), 272
imitation, 163
immanentization, 292
imperialism, 240, 293, 385
inclusivism, 426, 578
Independence, 6, 8, 20, 27, 353, 360, 382,
    509, 510, 513, 514, 516, 518, 521
indexical truth, 430
India, 25, 75, 90, 105, 108, 165, 175,
    176, 179, 302, 309, 369, 372, 577,
    583
  modern nation state, 2
Indian Freedom Movement, 371
Indian National Congress, 179, 344
individualism, 286
Indonesia, 1–20, 204, 459, 596
  intellectual history, 3
  nation state, 2
Indonesian Council of Jihad Fighters, 390

Indonesian Democracy Party of Struggle,
    470
Indonesian Islamic United Party, 470
inductive method, 261
industry, 91
inequality, 183
inflation, 588
information technology, 568
inheritance, 579
injustice, 263
İnönü University, 134
İnönü, İsmet, 125
Institute of Islamic Understanding Malaysia,
    455
integration, 372
interconnection, 567
interdependence, 567
interest-free banking, 594
Internal Security Act, 195
International Court of Justice, 413
International Islamic University Malaysia,
    191, 206, 455
international law, 155
International Monetary Fund, 354, 577
Internet, 419, 568
Iqbal, 'Allamah Muhammad, 90, 179, 419
iqtisād, 589
Iraq, 9, 353, 540, 572
al-Iraqi, Hasan, Shaykh, 200
Iran, 10, 165, 202, 205, 302, 318, 425,
    562, 572, 591
Ireland, 411
irrationalism, 290, 296
Işik, Hüseyin Hilmi, 44
Islam, 178, 221, 576
  economy, 185
  modernity, 15–18
Islamabad, 191, 203
Islamic approach, 177
Islamic banking, 186, 192, 457, 592
  Insurance Islam, 457
  Islamic Bank of Brunei, 457
  Islamic Development Bank of Brunei, 457
Islamic civilization, 195, 207, 334
Islamic Constitution, 192
Islamic Defenders Front, 391
Islamic Defense Group, 390
Islamic economics, 186, 587, 591, 599
Islamic Education Movement Party, 470

Islamic eschatology, 206
Islamic ethics, 636
Islamic feminism, 624–43
Islamic heritage, 156
Islamic ideology, 180, 581
Islamic idiom, 182
Islamic intellectualism, 171
Islamic intellectuals, 5, 625, 628
Islamic judicial, 182
Islamic law, 148, 165, 166, 171, 182, 264,
    474, 581, 582, 587
Islamic leadership, 191
Islamic lines, 190
Islamic Mataram dynasty, 493
Islamic modernism, 7–8, 140; see also
    'Abduh, Muḥammad; al-Afghānī;
    Ahmad Khan, Syed; Azad, Abul Kalam;
    Nursi, Bediuzzaman Said; Riḍa, Rashīd
Islamic movement, 257
Islamic patriarchy, 629
Islamic philosophy of knowledge, 191
Islamic political theory, 182
Islamic Protestantism, 628
Islamic reassertion, 192
Islamic redistribution system, 186
Islamic reformism, 158
Islamic republic, 182
Islamic resurgence, 206, 562
Islamic revivalism, 2, 14, 15, 78, 154, 328,
    576
Islamic revolution, 189, 557, 563
Islamic Salvation Front, 302, 305
Islamic scheme, 183
Islamic sciences, 175
Islamic society, 177
Islamic state, 13, 14, 41, 43, 49, 55, 78, 81,
    82, 90, 92, 93, 94, 148, 149, 152, 154,
    165, 179, 181, 182, 184, 185, 192,
    193, 195, 200, 201, 308, 338, 339,
    340, 367, 368, 369, 385, 386, 457,
    458, 459, 460, 466, 471, 473, 474,
    475, 476, 485, 562, 563, 581, 596,
    629
Islamic Summit, 563
Islamic system, 183, 193
Islamic values, 189, 191
Islamic way of life, 182, 191
Islamism, 2, 9, 18, 25, 26, 27, 35, 36, 37,
    38, 39, 40, 41, 42, 43, 44, 45, 47, 49,

50, 51, 52, 53, 151, 153, 158, 257,
    298, 300, 313, 321, 423, 453, 466,
    468, 478, 624, 625, 630, 635, 640,
    641, 642
Islamization, 116, 165, 166, 182, 191, 563
Islamized sciences, 290
isomorphism, 318
Israel, 7, 305, 318, 362, 389, 415, 540
Istanbul, 25, 66, 128, 358
Istanbul University, 134
istislah (public interest), 573
Italy, 345, 511
Izmir Ïzmir, 25, 135

Jabalkat, Mount, 489
Jabir al-Alwani, Taha, 452, 579
al-Jabiri, Muhammad 'Abid, 277
Jakarta, 390, 468
Jakarta University of Muhammadiyah, 396
Jalal Al-e Ahmad, 551
Jama'ah al-Islamiyya, 9, 257
Jamaah Islamiyyah, 390
Jamaat-e-Islami, 13, 14, 25, 92, 176, 338,
    576, 579
Jamāl al-Dīn al-Afghānī, see al-Afghānī
Jamaluddin, Sheikh, of Bukhara, 417
Jamia Millia Islamia, 108
Jami'ah Nizamiyya, 108
Jami'at al-Ulama, 343
Jana Sangh, 511
Japan, 16, 379, 558
Jawadi-Amuli, 'Abdullah, 26, 433–40
al-Jazā'irī, 'Abd al-Qādir, 8
Jazani, Bijan, 551
Jemaah Islamiah, 449
Jeremiah, 221
Jerusalem, 530
Jesus, 197, 223, 377
Jews, 140, 371
jihād, 9, 15, 66, 178, 187, 193, 194, 264,
    377, 383, 390, 459, 521, 562
jinn, 263
Jinnah, Muhammad 'Ali, 12, 179
Jordan, 9, 171, 204, 530
Judaism, 147, 221, 306, 378
Jung, Carl G., 221, 245
Jungian analytic psychology, 245
jurisprudence, 42, 439
juristic preference, 163

Juru Taman, 492
Justice and Development Party, 26, 50, 52, 345–61
Justice Party, 5, 347, 390, 458, 470, 472
justice, 63, 68, 100, 263, 417

kadd (pain, labor, examination), 264
Kadivar, Mohsen, 628
Kadivar, Muhsin, 426
kāfir, 521
kafirūn (infidel), 267
Kalam, Sadeq Ziba, 546
Kalijaga, Sunan, 476, 488, 489, 493
Kaliwungu, Nyai Ageng, 495
Kamel, Kareem M., 460
Kant, Immanuel, 289, 427, 441
    noumenon, 429
    phenomenon, 429
Kaplan, Rasih, 127
Karadeniz Tecnical University, 134
Karrobi, Mehdi, 629
Kashmir, 88, 117, 369, 410
Katirci, Şerife, 615, 616
Katouzian, Homa, 547
Kazamias, Andreas M., 124
Kebatinan, 461
Kebenaran, 204
kelam, 124
Kelang, 199
Kemal, Mustafa, *see* Atatürk, Kemal
Kemal, Yaşar, 30
Kemalism, 3, 5, 12, 24, 25, 27, 29, 31, 32, 36, 42, 43, 44, 46, 49, 50, 52, 128, 345, 352, 353, 536, 610, 611, 619, 622
Kennedy, Moorehead, 381–2
Kennedy, Paul, 583
Kepler, Johannes, 286, 335
Kerala, 109
Khalid, Mansour, 150
Al-Khalīl, 540
Khan, Agha Mohammad, 549
Khan, Ayub, 110, 182
Khan, Halaku, 417
Khan, Karim, 549
Khan, *Prince* Taimur, 417
Khan, Wahiduddin, *Mawlana*, 75–87
khanqahs, 330
Kharijism, 257

Khartoum, 151
khawd (reservoir, lake), 263
khilāfah (trusteeship of human beings/caliphate), 164, 230, 571, 573, 589, 597
al-Khilafat movement, 13
Khurasan, 202
King, Martin Luther, 351
Kisakürek, Necip Fazil, 44
Kivilcimli, Hikmet, 27
kleptocratic state, 596
knowledge, 191
Köprülü, Fuad, 24, 34
Korea, 411
Kothari, Rajni, 513
Krakitan, Nyai Ageng, 495
Kraton culture, 486
Krauthammer, Charles, 323
Ku Klux Klan, 379
Kuala Lumpur, 195
Küçükömer, Idris, 29
Kurdistan, 550
Kurds, 613
Kuwait, 10
Kwi Pawilangan, 496
Kymlicka, Will, 614

Labuan, island, Borneo, 196
Lacan, Jacques, 315
Lahiji, Mulla, 'Abdullah, 437
Lahore, 89, 110, 179
laicism, 126
    laic, 638
    laicity, 40
Lambton, Ann, 547
landlordism, 186
language, 91
Laskar Jihad, 391
Latin America, 258, 377, 378, 577, 588
Lavoisier, Antoine-Laurent de, 244
Lebanon, 171
Lee Kuan Yew, 395
Leviathan, 321
Lewis, Bernard, 302, 306
liberal Islam, 453
liberal reformists, 624
liberalism, 37, 257, 468
Liberation Front of Pattani, 459
Libya, 198, 591

Liddle, R. William, 466, 477
literal Islam, 453
literature, 91
Locke, John, 335
London University, 145
Lord Curzon, *Lord* George, 544
love, 100
Lovejoy, O., 3
Lucknow, 108, 513, 518, 645, 656
Luxembourg, 90
Lyotard, Jean François, 218

Maarif, Sjafii, 458
al-Madani, 'Abdel Harith, 304
madāris, 105–21
madrasah, 330
Madrasah Aliyah Arabiyyah Fatehpuri, 176
Madrasah 'Aliyah Calcutta, 108
Madrasah 'Aliyah Rampur, 108
Madrasah Nizamiyya, 108
Madrasah Shams al-Huda Patna, 108
Magnis-Suseno, Franz, 483
Magog (tribe), 197
al-Mahdhī, Aḥmad, 8
al-Mahdi, 'Abd al-Rahman, 161
al-Mahdi, Imām (messiah), 197–204
Mahdi, Syed Iqbal, 594
Mahdism, 161
Mahdiyyah, 161
Mahmoud Muhammad Taha, 154, 166, 169
Mahmud, Mufti, 114
Mahmud, Zaki Najib, 258, 276
majālis, 645
Majapahit, (Buddhist empire), 487
Majelis Mujahidin Indonesia, 390
Majelis Permusyawaratan Rakyat, 387
Majlis Ugama Islam Singapore, 457
Majlis-e Muttahida-ye Amal, 114
Majlis-i Mushawarat, 95
majoritarianism, 365
al-Makhdom (the servant), 450
Malaysia, 186, 191, 195, 392, 459, 596
Malaysian Chinese Muslim Association, 455
Malcolm, John, 548
Malekian, Mostafa, 628
Malthus, Thomas, 317
al-Ma'munn, 279
management, 572
Mangkubumi, *adipati*, 488

Manila, 450
Maoist, 386
Mardin, Şerif, 32
Markham, Ian, 388, 401, 402
Marrakesh, 90
marriage, 227, 579
Mars, 197
Marseille, 214
Marx, Karl, 227, 547
    Marxism, 244
    Marxist theories, 589
Masyumi, 471
materialism, 90, 99, 221, 240, 258
materialist, 218
Mawdūdī, Sayyid Abul A'la, *Mawlana*, 9, 13,
    14, 45, 92, 149, 153, 175, 260, 322,
    328
Mawil Izzi Dien, 579
Mayer, Ann Elizabeth, 627
Mazhar, Ismail, 258
Mazuri, Ali, 563
McCarthyism, 305
McVeigh, Timothy, 411, 415
Mecca, 80, 90, 203, 565
Medina, 90, 149, 151, 203
Medina arrangement, 149
Medina University, 108
Mediterranean, 539
Medreseci, 124
Megawati Soekarno Putri, 387, 389, 470
Mehmet, *the Conqueror*, 202
mekteb, 124
melting pot, 372
Menderes, Adnan, 24, 69
Mernissi, Fatima, 635
messianism, 197, 205
meta-narrative, 296
metaphysical truth, 430
metapsychism, 223
methodological pluralism, 262
methodology, 154, 275
Middle East, 1–20, 8, 66, 115, 202, 204,
    305, 415, 461, 563
military coup, 25, 49, 166, 612
military, 346
millenarianism, 197
Miller, Judith, 303
Milo, Sandra, 382
mimesis, 240

mimetic, 318
Mindanao, 452
Ministry of Education, 124, 140
Mir-Hosseini, Ziba, 635
Mirza, Iskandar Ali Khan, 528
Misuari, Nur, 460
mizān (scale), 263
modernism, 298, 576, 590
   subjectivism, 27
   temporalism, 27
modernity, 15–18, 53, 217, 258, 285, 293,
   573, 584
   capitalism, 15–18
modernization, 153, 292, 318, 341, 362,
   564, 587, 589, 610, 634
modernization theory, 588
Mohamad, Goenawan, 452
monasticism, 333
monetarism, 594
Mongol invasion, 328, 334, 549
monotheism, 221
Moon and Star Party, 470
moral, 63
moral ideal, 230
morality, 167, 186, 339, 351
Moro Islamic Liberation Front, 456
Moro National Liberation Front, 460
Morocco, 205, 380, 530, 579
mosaic, 372
Moses, 200, 223
Mossadeq, Mohammad, 550
Motherland Party, 27
Mount Lawu, 483
Mu'awiyah Abu Sufyan, *Caliph*, 202
Mudawana, 579
mudharabah, 595
Mughal Empire, 13, 309
Muhammad, *prophet*, 77, 177, 566, 571,
   573, 580
Muhammadiyah, 8, 390, 454, 468, 485, 580
Muhiddin, Nezihe, 611
mujaddid, 197, 205
mujahidin, 117, 563
Mujeeb, Mohammad, 82
Multan, 110
multiculturalism, 365, 368
Mumbai University, 523
münevver, 26
murāqabah (contemplation), 332

Murad IV, 329
Murruwa, Hussain, 276
Musa, Hashim, 206
Musa, Salama, 164, 258
Musharraf, Parvez, General, 105
Mushir-ul Haq, 83
Muslim Brotherhood, The, 14, 25, 145, 146,
   257, 576, 579
Muslim feminism, 628
Muslim League, 13, 92
Muslim Personal Law Board, 96
Muslim Students Association, 214
Muslim world
   liberalism, 10
   Marxism, 10
   nationalism, 10
al-Mu'tasim, 279
al-Mutawakkil, 279
Mu'tazilah, 106
Mu'tazilism, 257
Mu'tazilites, 273
Müteferrika, Ibrāhīm, 337
Myanmar, 370
mysticism, 240, 492

Nabawiyan, Sayyid Mahmud, 434
Nadi, Nadir, 129
Nadwat ul-'Ulama madrasah, 89
Nadwi, Sayyed Abul Hasan 'Ali, 13, 88
Nadwi, Sayyed Sulamian, 89
Nagpur, 99
Nahdatul Ulama (NU), 14, 206, 454, 467,
   485, 580
Nahusona, Ferry, 402
Najibullah, 564
Nakhsibandi Order, 347
Namik Kemal, 69, 625
Napoleon, 549
Napoli, 382
narcissism, 294
Nasr, Seyyed Hossein, 15–18
al-Nasser, Jamal 'Abd, President, 12, 190
Nasr, Seyyed Hossein, 295
Nasserism, 257
Nasution, Harun, 476
nation, 66, 314–19, 321–2
National Awakening Party, 471
National Fatwa Council, 198
National Front, 145

National Islamic Center, 397
National Islamic Front, 165
National Liberation Army, 215
National Mandate Party, 471
National Order Party, 347
national prejudice, 187
National Salvation Party, 27, 45, 347
nationalism, 2, 8, 9, 11, 12, 13, 17, 19, 23,
    25, 26, 27, 28, 29, 30, 31, 32, 34, 37,
    40, 42, 44, 47, 48, 49, 58, 90, 103,
    175, 179, 257, 267, 268, 314, 315,
    317, 320, 321, 322, 323, 343, 346,
    365, 373, 374, 515, 519, 528, 529,
    530, 537, 544, 548, 550, 610
   Third-World nationalism, 12–15
Nationalist Movement Party, 27
nation–state, 317
Natsir, Mohammad, 473
naturalism, 59
naturalization, 292
   Nazi, 187, 378, 413
   Nazism, 293
neo-Marxist, 589
neo-modernism, 591
neo-Salafis, 146
Netherlands, The, 393
Netland, Harold, 430
New York, 382, 387, 409, 414
New Zealand, 453
Newton, *Sir* Isaac, 216, 335
Nicaragua, 380, 413
Nietzsche, Friedrich, 219
Nietzcheanism, 293
Nigeria, 165
nihilism, 218, 266, 297
normative, 318
normativism, 576
North Africa, 1–20, 206, 214
North America, 1–20, 16, 176, 563
Northern Ireland, 377
Northwestern University, 357
Numairi, Ja'far, 145, 147, 150, 165
Nu'mani, Shibli, *Mawlana*, 89
Nur community, 12, 56, 64, 66, 67, 70
Nurcholish Madjid, 398, 474, 581
Nuremberg Trials, 413
Nuri, Celal, 23
Nursi, Bediuzzaman Said, 7, 12, 19, 21, 42,
   44, 54, 55–71, 319, 320–1

Objectives Resolution, 181
objectivity, 153
Occident, 588
Ogbern, William, 248
Oklahoma, 411
Onsekiz Mart University, 134
ontological, 243
oppression, 183
Orabi Movement, 268
Oran, 214
Organization for the Petroleum Exporting
   Countries, 563
Organization of the Islamic Conference, 416,
   527, 563
Orthodox Islam, 330
orthodox Muslims, 338
Orwell, George, 2
Oslo agreement, 380
Osman Gazi University, 134
otherization, 320
Ottoman caliphate, 9
Ottoman Empire, 23, 287, 334, 345, 549
Özal, Turgut, 26, 27, 46, 610, 613
Özdalga, Elizabeth, 617
Özel, İsmet, 46
Özkan, Ercümend, 47
Özkaya, Eraslan, 609
Öztürk, Yaşar Nuri, 51

Pahlavi monarchy, 550
Pakistan, 8, 25, 88, 91, 105, 117, 165, 175,
   176, 202, 338, 528, 562, 563, 591
Palestine, 7, 118, 410
Palestinians, 294
pan-Arabism, 90
Pandan Arang, Ki Gede, *see* Bayat, Sunan
paradise, 263
Parahyangan Catholic University, 453
Paramadina Mulya University, 392, 362–74
Parangtritis, 482
Parekh, 'Abdul Karim, *Mawlana*, 99
Paris, 214
Partai Amanat Nasional (PAN), 398
Partai Keadilan (PK), 390
Parthians, 549
Parti Islam Se Malaysia, 458
participation, 166
Parvez Manzoor, S., 289, 291, 295, 575
Pasha, Said Halim, 42

Pasqua, Charles, 304
Pattani United Liberation Organization, 459
peace, 100, 392, 417
Pearl Harbor, 388
Pektaş, Mesut, 357
Pemberton, John, 484, 496
penalty, 147
Pennsylvania, 387
Pentagon, 105, 205
People's Consultative Assembly, 387
Perestroika, 26
Perinçek, Doğu, 27
Persatuan Ulama Malaysia, 455
Persian, 127, 139
Persian Gulf, 176
personification, 249
Perwita, Anak Agung Banyu, 453
pessimism, 552
phenomenology, 293
Philippines, 204, 370, 392, 459
philosophy, 59, 62, 246
pilgrimage, 482, 493, 565
Pitsuwan, Surin, 455
Plantinga, Alvin, 435
pluralism, 84, 425, 442
    pluralist, 426
    plurality, 568
Poland, 293
polarization, 249
political Islam, 466, 468, 612
political radicalism, 187
politics, 183
polity, 339
polygamy, 579
polytheism, 91, 221
ponderousness, 240
Pope, the, 69, 377
Popper, Karl, 426
population, 316
positivism, 59, 221, 293
post-communist, 318
postmodernism, 45, 293, 298, 573, 584
postmodernity, 217, 218, 285
power, 316
practical logic, 240
pragmatism, 293
    pragmatists, 453
Prambanan temple, 485
pre-destination, 167

prejudice, 98
priesthood, 91
print capitalism, 314
profit-sharing, 594
progressive, 29
prophetic traditions, 162
prosperity, 392
Protestant Reformation, 17
Protestant, *see* Catholics and Protestants
Ptolemy, 258
public order, 67
Punjab, 89, 112
Putnam, Robert, 558

Qaddianes, 169
al-Qaeda, 318, 321, 384, 392, 393, 396,
    412
Qatar Muslim Foreign Ministers Conference,
    416
qawm (people), 264
Qum, 629
Qur'an, 43, 64, 155, 178, 232, 261, 572,
    580
    wa'd (promise), 232
    wa'id (warning), 232
Qur'anic exegesis, 149, 156
Qur'anic revelation, 221, 228
Qur'anic wisdom, 320
Quraysh, 80
Qurratulein, Tahira, 636
Quṭb, Muḥammad, 9
Quṭb, Sayyid, 9, 44, 45, 153, 164, 260, 288,
    322

Rabbani-Gulpaigani, 'Ali, 434
racism, 293
radical revolutionary Islamists, 624
Rafsanjani, Hashemi, 553, 555
Rahner, Karl, 426
Rais, Amien, 387, 389, 393–5, 581
Raja Muslim, *Sultan*, 450
Rama Temple, 519
Ramage, Douglas, 389
Ramakrishna, Kumar, 459
Rashtriya Swayamsevak Sangh (RSS), 100,
    511
rationalism, 286, 342
rationality, 153, 351
Ratu Adil, 204

Rawang, 196, 204
reactionary, 29
reactionism, 27
reason, 58, 167, 189, 216, 258
Red Army, 379
Red Brigades, 379
Red Indians, 294
Red Sea, 539
reductionism, 217
reductionist, 218
re-entrenchment, 576
Refah party, 12
reform, 154, 157, 271
rejectionist, 167
relativism, 217, 260, 442, 584
religion, 129, 219, 231, 246, 257, 342
religious intellectuals, 5
Religious Writers' Association, 411
Renaissance, 293
Republican Brothers, 169
republicanism, 69
respect, 66
revelation, 58, 63, 167, 219, 223
revivalism, 576
revolution, 187–9
   prophetic revolution, 188
Reza Shah, 550
Riḍa, Rashīd, 7, 9
Rifki, Falih, 125
Risale-i Nur, 44, 52, 55, 57, 65
   'aqā'id, 60
   faith, 61
   tafsīr, 60
ritualism, 259
Riyadh, 384
Roald, Anne Sofie, 636
Robertson, Pat, 389
Robespierre, Maximilien, 379
Rodinson, Maxime, 10
Rogge, Michael, 461
Roman Empire, 286
Romanticism, 293
Rorty, Richard, 18
Rosen, Barry, 556
Rostow, 588
RSS, *see* Rashtriga Swayamsevak Sangh (RSS)
Rububiyyah, 589
Rufaqa' Corporation, 198
Rule of Law, 166

Rumi, Jalal al-din, 429
Rushdie, Salman, 303, 512
Russia, 203, 318, 368, 369, 414, 548, 563
Russian revolution, 187
Rustow, Dankwart A., 352
Rwanda, 410

Saba, kingdom of, 169
sacredness, 244
al-Sadiq al Mahdi, 161–74
Sadiq, Sayyed Kalbe, *Mawlana*, 99, 644–56
al-Ṣadr, Muḥammad Bāqir, 9, 10, 593
Sadra, Mulla, 426, 437
Saeedzadeh, Seyyed Muhsen, 628, 629, 637
Safavid Iran, 547
Saharanpur, 108
Said, Edward, 537
al-Saffār, 9
Sakarya University, 134
Salafi movement, 164
Salafis, 146
Salafism, 257–70, 385
Salafiyyah, 8–10
salvation, 165, 435
Samarqand, 203
Samsun Ondokuz Mayis University, 133
sanctity, 244
santri, 467, 474
al-Sanūsī, 8
Sanūsī, 332
Sarai Mir, 75
Sardar, Ziauddin, 16, 594
Sassanid dynasty, 549
Saudi Arabia, 108, 147, 309, 338, 362, 530, 591, 627
Savarkar, 371
sa'y (effort), 264
scholasticism, 333
Science of Dogma, 272
science, 189, 216, 238, 246, 258
Second Isaiah, 222
sectarianism, 249
secular fundamentalist, 342
secular, 24, 126, 638
secularism, 52, 53, 56, 82, 84, 94, 101, 129, 154, 257, 286, 293, 338, 342, 532
secularization, 57, 153, 158, 292, 362–74, 475, 610, 636
Seh Domba, 490

Seh Kewel, 490
Selangor, 196
Selçuk, Ziya, 352
Selim III, 329
Sena, Cemil, 28
separatism, 99, 368, 370
sex segregation, 626
al-Seyyed (the master), 450
Sezer, Ahmet Necdet, 355
Sezer, Baykan, 26, 32
sha'b (nation), 264
Shabestari, Mohammad Mojtahed, 628
Shaikh Said Revolt, 57
Shamsul Islam, 524
sharī'ah, 10, 154, 181, 332, 391, 458, 563, 572, 579, 611, 624
Shari'ati, 'Ali, 170
Shariati, Ali, 10, 45, 551
Shaykh, 171
Shepard, William, 453
Shinawatra, Thaksin, 393, 396
shirk, 176
Shi'ism, 257
Shi'ite, 10, 106, 110, 162, 164, 198, 273, 331, 364, 649
Shukri, Ghali, 9
Shultz, George P., 388
Shumayl, Shibli, 258
shūra, 575, 579
al-Sibā'ī, Yūsuf, 9
Siddiqi, Muhammad Nejatullah, 207, 594
Sikh, 89, 97, 380, 519
Simmons, Martha, 388
sincerity, 63
Sindh, 112
Singapore, 392, 459
Singh, Karan, 510
Sinkiang, 369
ṣirāt (bridge), 263
Sistani, Sayyed 'Ali, Ayatollah, 648
Siti Jenar, 488
slavery, 167
Smith, Adam, 185
Smith, Jane, 402
social closure, 314
social life, 226
social obscurantism, 187
social phenomena, 250
social security, 185

socialism, 612
socialist, 36
Soekarno Putri, Megawati, *see* Megawati
Son Telgraf, 126
Sorokin, Pitirim, 248
Soroush, Abdolkarim, *see* Surush, 'Abd al-Karim
South Asia, 2, 3, 1–20, 7, 8, 9, 13, 21, 106, 107, 110, 118, 119, 175, 378, 542, 570, 644
Southeast Asia, 1–20, 195, 378, 392, 449–65
Soviet Union, 26, 66, 378
Spain, 206
Spanish Inquisition, 379
spirit, 65
spiritual, 183
Sri Lanka, 176, 366, 410
Stace, Walter T., 428
Stalin, Joseph, 378
Stanford University, 400
Stanton, Elizabeth Cady, 636
state, 351
state feminism, 612
state ideology, 2, 37
State Institute for Islamic Studies, 461
state ownership, 590
static, 189
statist, 36
stock exchange, 414
Straits of Malacca, 539
struggle, 263
subjugation, 263
Sudan, 146, 148, 157, 158, 165, 198, 563
Sudanese Socialist Union, 145
Sufi, 89, 162, 198, 461, 574
Sufi Islam, 330
Sufi orders, 450
Sufism, 60, 205
Suharto, (President of Indonesia), 204, 466
Sukarno, Ahmed, 12, 467
Sukarnoputri, Megawati, *see* Megawati
Sukma, Rizal, 390, 459
Süleyman Demirel University, 134
Süleyman, *the Magnificent*, 336
Sullivan, Andrew, 401
Sunnah, 572, 581

sunnatization, 117
Sunni, 649
Sunni Islam, 146, 197
Sunni Muslims, 145
Sunnite, 10, 162
Surush, 'Abd al-Karim, 425–33, 434, 441–3, 628
Sütçüiman University, 134
al-Suyuti, Jalal al-din, 199
Swidler, Leonard, 402
Switzerland, 76, 345
Syam, 203
Syamsuddin, M. Din, 457
synagogue, 358
Syria, 9, 258, 572

Tabari, Imam, 654
Tabataba'i, Muhammad Husain, 434
Tabatabai, Javad, 547
Tablighi Jamaat, 94
Tafsir, 135
Taha Suhaimi, Mohd., 199
Tahāfut (incoherence), 336
Taher, Tarmizi, 462
Tahir, Kemal, 30
al-Tahtawi, 259
Tajikistan, 416
Takiya Kalan, 89
Taliban, 15, 117, 165, 343, 396, 412, 416, 563, 626
Tamil, 379
Tampake, Tony, 402
Tan, Samuel K., 452
Tanzimat, 11, 57, 124
Tartar, 418
Taşer, Dündar, 26
Taslima, Nasreen, 303
Taslima, Nasrin, 303–4, 512
tawḥīd, 573, 589
Taylor, Charles, 294
Taymuriya, Ayesha, 636
tazkiyyah, 590
technique, 240
technology, 573
tefekkür, 58
Tehran, 629
Tembayat, 486, 496
temporal, 183
Termez, 203

terror, 263
terrorism, 378, 387, 411, 564
Thai Muslim Students Association, 458
Thailand, 204, 370
Thanawi, Ashraf 'Ali, *Mawlana*, 91
theft, 168
theocracy, 267
Third World nationalism, 12
Third World, 1–20, 588
Tibi, Bassam, 288
Tien, *Ibu*, 485
Tien Suharto, 485
al-Tirmidhi, 162
Tizini, Tayyib, 276
Toha, Abdillah, 398
Tohidi, Nayoreh, 627, 636
tolerance, 286, 306
Torkomanchay, treaty of, 549
totalitarianism, 579
totemism, 221, 315
Toynbee, Arnold, 227
trade, 91
traditional Islam, 575
traditionalism, 591
traditionalist, 157, 453
traditionalization, 116
transcendence, 248
transformation, 233
transparency, 166
Tribals, 97
trust, 62
truth, 216
Tuksal, Hidayet Şefkatli, 619
Tunahan, Süleyman Hilmi, 44
Tunaya, Tarik Zafir, 32, 128
Tunisia, 380
al-Tunisi, Khayr al-Din, 259
Turabi, Hassan, 145–58
türban, 609
Turhan, Mümtaz, 26, 34
Türkdoğan, Orhan, 26
Turkey, 23, 156, 204, 206, 318, 330, 350, 528, 582, 609
Turkish Labor Party, 28
Turkish Qajar tribes, 549
Turkish Republic, 3, 5, 24, 26, 122, 124, 128, 140, 322, 611
Turkish Republican party, 345
Turkist, 36

Uganda, 531
ulama, 336, 385, 454, 581
Ülken, Hilmi Ziya, 24, 34
Ulster, 377
Uluç, Tahir, 402
Uludağ University, 135
'Umar ibn al-Khattab, *Caliph*, 163, 168, 572
Umma Party, 161
ummah, 314, 319–25, 408, 572, 575, 581, 582
Ummayads, 164
UN Charter, 412
UN Military Staff Committee, 411
Unakitan, Ahsen, 355
Unakitan, Kemal, 355
United Development Party, 470
United Kingdom, 204, 364, 366, 368, 372, 414
United Malays National Organization, 452
United Nations, 166
United States, 1–20, 66, 90, 155, 169, 302, 364, 368, 372, 613
Universal Declaration of Human Rights, 166
universalism, 286
University of Canterbury, 453
University of Leiden, 393
University of Malaya, 206
Uran, Hilmi, 69
Urdu, 25, 177
Ustaz Ashaari *see* Ashaari, Ustaz
utilitarianism, 293, 314, 316
Uttar Pradesh, 90, 108
Uzbekistan, 202, 204, 415, 416

vagueness, 240
Vajpayee, Atal Behari, 510, 513
Vatican, 152, 377
Vatikiotis, P.J., 303
Vattimo, Gianni, 18
verticalization, 260
VHP *see* Vishwa Hindu Parishad (VHP)
viceregency, 231
Vietnam, 293, 379, 541
violence, 187
Virat Hindu Sammelan, 511
Virtue Party, 347
Vishwa Hindu Parishad (VHP), 511, 514, 516, 517, 518, 519, 523
Von Der Mehden, Fred R., 454

Wadud, Amina, 636
Wahabiyyah, 8
Wahid, Abdurrahman, 204, 457, 470
Wali Ullah, Shah, 107, 309
Wallerstein, Immanuel, 539
waqfs (pious foundations), 571
Washington, 384, 387, 409
Wasil ibn "Ata", 279
Watt, 306
Weber, Max, 314
Welfare Party, 49, 347
West Africa, 309
West Bank, 302
Western capitalism, 186
Western civilization, 192, 538, 577
Western Europe, 563
Western imperialism, 313
Western philosophy, 124
Westernist, 36
Westernization, 2, 9, 11, 19, 23, 26, 30, 32, 33, 34, 35, 36, 37, 38, 51, 55, 57, 65, 122, 124, 164, 259, 290, 291, 299, 322, 345, 360, 385, 562, 572, 589, 610, 611, 640
Westernized sciences, 290
Westwood, Andrew, 545
Wiktorowicz, Quintan, 451, 453
Wilkinson, Paul, 378
Will of God, 167
Wittfogel, Karl, 547
Wittgenstein, Ludwig, 432
Wolfowitz, Paul, 387, 395
women, 169
    divorce, 170
    marriage, 170
    narrator, 169
    polygamy, 170
    representation, 170
women's movement, 624
women's rights, 626, 645
    divorce (*t.alāq*), 653
    testimony (*shahadat*), 653
Woolsey, James, 322
World Bank, 577
World Trade Center, 105, 205, 388
World Trade Organization, 577
worship, 168

Xenophon, 379

yaqazah, 199
Yazicioğlu, Mustafa S., 134, 135
Yazir, Muhammed Hamdi, 42
Yön movement, 28
Young Turks, 322
Yücel, Hasan Ali, 29
Yudhoyono, Susilo Bambang, 470
Yugoslavia, 318
Yunnan, 202
Yüreğir, Ahmed Remzi, 130
Yüzüncü Yil University, 134

Zahedi, Fazlollah, 550
Zaidi, 171
Zait Kotku, Mehmet, 347
Zakariyya, Fouad, 258
zakat, 112, 185, 590, 592
zalimūn (injust), 267
Zengin, Bahri, 46
Zionism, 293, 378
Zionists, 551
Ziya Gökalp, 33
Ziyaul Haq, 338
Zonis, Marvin, 545
Zoroastrian, 332

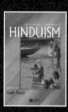